D0102588

GO!

with Microsoft®

Excel 2010
Comprehensive

Shelley Gaskin, Alicia Vargas, and Suzanne Marks

Prentice Hall

Boston   Columbus   Indianapolis   New York   San Francisco   Upper Saddle River
Amsterdam   Cape Town   Dubai   London   Madrid   Milan   Munich   Paris   Montreal   Toronto
Delhi   Mexico City   São Paulo   Sydney   Hong Kong   Seoul   Singapore   Taipei   Tokyo

Associate VP/Executive Acquisitions Editor, Print:
Stephanie Wall
Editorial Project Manager: Laura Burgess
Editor in Chief: Michael Payne
Product Development Manager: Eileen Bien Calabro
Development Editor: Ginny Munroe
Editorial Assistant: Nicole Sam
Director of Marketing: Kate Valentine
Marketing Manager: Tori Olson Alves
Marketing Coordinator: Susan Osterlitz
Marketing Assistant: Darshika Vyas
Senior Managing Editor: Cynthia Zonneveld
Associate Managing Editor: Camille Trentacoste
Production Project Manager: Mike Lackey
Operations Director: Alexis Heydt
Operations Specialist: Natacha Moore

Senior Art Director: Jonathan Boylan
Cover Photo: © Ben Durrant
Text and Cover Designer: Blair Brown
Manager, Cover Visual Research & Permissions:
Karen Sanatar
Manager, Rights and Permissions: Zina Arabia
AVP/Director of Online Programs, Media: Richard Keaveny
AVP/Director of Product Development, Media: Lisa Strite
Media Project Manager, Editorial: Alana Coles
Media Project Manager, Production: John Cassar
Full-Service Project Management: PreMediaGlobal
Composition: PreMediaGlobal
Printer/Binder: Quebecor World Book Services
Cover Printer: Lehigh-Phoenix Color
Text Font: Bookman Light

Credits and acknowledgments borrowed from other sources and reproduced, with permission, in this textbook appear on appropriate page within text.

Microsoft® and Windows® are registered trademarks of the Microsoft Corporation in the U.S.A. and other countries. Screen shots and icons reprinted with permission from the Microsoft Corporation. This book is not sponsored or endorsed by or affiliated with the Microsoft Corporation.

Copyright © 2011 Pearson Education, Inc., publishing as Prentice Hall, One Lake Street, Upper Saddle River, New Jersey, 07458. All rights reserved. Manufactured in the United States of America. This publication is protected by Copyright, and permission should be obtained from the publisher prior to any prohibited reproduction, storage in a retrieval system, or transmission in any form or by any means, electronic, mechanical, photocopying, recording, or likewise. To obtain permission(s) to use material from this work, please submit a written request to Pearson Education, Inc., Permissions Department, One Lake Street, Upper Saddle River, New Jersey, 07458.

Many of the designations by manufacturers and seller to distinguish their products are claimed as trademarks. Where those designations appear in this book, and the publisher was aware of a trademark claim, the designations have been printed in initial caps or all caps.

Library of Congress Cataloging-in-Publication Data
Go! with Microsoft Excel 2010 / Shelley Gaskin ... [et al.].
p. cm.
Includes index.
ISBN-13: 978-0-13-509821-9
ISBN-10: 0-13-509821-1
1. Microsoft Office.   2. Business—Computer programs.   I. Gaskin, Shelley.
HF5548.4.M525G6254 2011
005.5—dc22

2010019576

10 9 8 7 6 5 4 3 2 1

Prentice Hall
is an imprint of

www.pearsonhighered.com

ISBN 10: 0-13-509821-1
ISBN 13: 978-0-13-509821-9

Brief Contents

Contents

Excel

Chapter 1   Creating a Worksheet and Charting Data 49

Chapter 3   Analyzing Data with Pie Charts, Line Charts, and What-If Analysis Tools 177

Chapter 5 Managing Large Workbooks and Using Advanced Sorting and Filtering

GO! System Contributors

We thank the following people for their hard work and support in making the *GO!* System all that it is!

Instructor Resource Authors

Adickes, Erich	Parkland College	Holland, Susan	Southeast Community College-Nebraska
Baray, Carrie	Ivy Tech Community College	Jacob, Sherry	Kentucky Community and Technical College
Bornstein, Abigail	City College of San Francisco		
Bowman, Valeria	National College		
Callahan, Michael	Lone Star College	Leinbach, Andrea	Harrisburg Area Community College
Cleary, Kevin	University at Buffalo		
Clausen, Jane	Western Iowa Tech Community College	Lutz, Mary	Southwestern Illinois College
		Miller, Abigail	Gateway Community and Technical College
Colucci, William	Montclair State University		
Crossley, Connie	Cincinnati State Technical and Community College	Monson, Shari	Black Hawk College
		Landenberger, Toni	Southeast Community College-Nebraska
Damanti, Lori			
Edington, Barbara	St. Francis College	McMahon, Richard	University of Houston—Downtown
Emrich, Stefanie	Metropolitan Community College of Omaha, Nebraska	Miller, Sandra	Wenatchee Valley College
		Neal, Ruth	Navarro College
Faix, Dennis	Harrisburg Area Community College	Niebur, Katherine	Dakota County Technical College
		Nowakowski, Anthony	Buffalo State
Hadden, Karen	Western Iowa Tech Community College	Pierce, Tonya	Ivy Tech Community College
		Reynolds, Mark	Lone Star College
Hammerle, Patricia	Indiana University/Purdue University at Indianapolis	Roselli, Diane	Harrisburg Area Community College
		Shing, Chen-Chi	Radford University
Hines, James	Tidewater Community College	St. John, Steve	Tulsa Community College
Hicks, Janette	Binghamton University / State University of New York	Sterr, Jody	Blackhawk Technical College
		Thompson, Joyce	Lehigh Carbon Community College
Hollingsworth, Mary Carole	Georgia Perimeter College	Tucker, William	Austin Community College
		Volker, Bonita	Tidewater Community College
Holly, Terri	Indian River State College	Walters, Kari	Louisiana State University

Technical Editors

Matthew Bisi	Sarah Evans	Joyce Nielsen	Jan Snyder
Mary Corcoran	Adam Layne	Janet Pickard	Sam Stamport
Lori Damanti	Elizabeth Lockley	Sean Portnoy	Mara Zebest
Barbara Edington			

Student Reviewers

Albinda, Sarah Evangeline	Phoenix College	Frye, Alicia	Phoenix College
Allen, John	Asheville-Buncombe Tech Community College	Gadomski, Amanda	Northern Michigan University
		Gassert, Jennifer	Harrisburg Area Community College
Alexander, Steven	St. Johns River Community College		
Alexander, Melissa	Tulsa Community College	Gross, Mary Jo	Kirkwood Community College
Bolz, Stephanie	Northern Michigan University	Gyselinck, Craig	Central Washington University
Berner, Ashley	Central Washington University	Harrison, Margo	Central Washington University
Boomer, Michelle	Northern Michigan University	Hatt, Patrick	Harrisburg Area Community College
Busse, Brennan	Northern Michigan University	Heacox, Kate	Central Washington University
Butkey, Maura	Central Washington University	Hedgman, Shaina	Tidewater College
Cates, Concita	Phoenix College	Hill, Cheretta	Northwestern State University
Charles, Marvin	Harrisburg Area Community College	Hochstedler, Bethany	Harrisburg Area Community College Lancaster
Christensen, Kaylie	Northern Michigan University	Homer, Jean	Greenville Technical College
Clark, Glen D. III	Harrisburg Area Community College	Innis, Tim	Tulsa Community College
		Jarboe, Aaron	Central Washington University
Cobble, Jan N.	Greenville Technical College	Key, Penny	Greenville Technical College
Connally, Brianna	Central Washington University	Klein, Colleen	Northern Michigan University
Davis, Brandon	Northern Michigan University	Lloyd, Kasey	Ivy Tech Bloomington
Davis, Christen	Central Washington University	Moeller, Jeffrey	Northern Michigan University
De Jesus Garcia, Maria	Phoenix College	Mullen, Sharita	Tidewater Community College
Den Boer, Lance	Central Washington University	Nelson, Cody	Texas Tech University
Dix, Jessica	Central Washington University	Nicholson, Regina	Athens Tech College
Downs, Elizabeth	Central Washington University	Niehaus, Kristina	Northern Michigan University
Eiser, Julie	Harrisburg Area Community College	Nisa, Zaibun	Santa Rosa Community College
		Nunez, Nohelia	Santa Rosa Community College
Erickson, Mike	Ball State University	Oak, Samantha	Central Washington University

Oberly, Sara	Harrisburg Area Community College Lancaster
Oertii, Monica	Central Washington University
Palenshus, Juliet	Central Washington University
Pohl, Amanda	Northern Michigan University
Presnell, Randy	Central Washington University
Reed, Kailee	Texas Tech University
Ritner, April	Northern Michigan University
Roberts, Corey	Tulsa Community College
Rodgers, Spencer	Texas Tech University
Rodriguez, Flavia	Northwestern State University
Rogers, A.	Tidewater Community College
Rossi, Jessica Ann	Central Washington University
Rothbauer, Taylor	Trident Technical College
Rozelle, Lauren	Texas Tech University
Schmadeke, Kimberly	Kirkwood Community College
Shafapay, Natasha	Central Washington University
Shanahan, Megan	Northern Michigan University
Sullivan, Alexandra Nicole	Greenville Technical College
Teska, Erika	Hawaii Pacific University
Torrenti, Natalie	Harrisburg Area Community College
Traub, Amy	Northern Michigan University
Underwood, Katie	Central Washington University
Walters, Kim	Central Washington University
Warren, Jennifer L.	Greenville Technical College
Wilson, Kelsie	Central Washington University
Wilson, Amanda	Green River Community College
Wylie, Jimmy	Texas Tech University

Series Reviewers

Abraham, Reni	Houston Community College
Addison, Paul	Ivy Tech Community College
Agatston, Ann	Agatston Consulting Technical College
Akuna, Valeria, Ph.D.	Estrella Mountain Community College
Alexander, Melody	Ball Sate University
Alejandro, Manuel	Southwest Texas Junior College
Alger, David	Tidewater Community College Chesapeake Campus
Allen, Jackie	Rowan-Cabarrus Community College
Ali, Farha	Lander University
Amici, Penny	Harrisburg Area Community College
Anderson, Patty A.	Lake City Community College
Andrews, Wilma	Virginia Commonwealth College, Nebraska University
Anik, Mazhar	Tiffin University
Armstrong, Gary	Shippensburg University
Arnold, Linda L.	Harrisburg Area Community College
Ashby, Tom	Oklahoma City Community College
Atkins, Bonnie	Delaware Technical Community College
Aukland, Cherie	Thomas Nelson Community College
Bachand, LaDonna	Santa Rosa Community College
Bagui, Sikha	University of West Florida
Beecroft, Anita	Kwantlen University College
Bell, Paula	Lock Haven College
Belton, Linda	Springfield Tech. Community College
Bennett, Judith	Sam Houston State University
Bhatia, Sai	Riverside Community College
Bishop, Frances	DeVry Institute—Alpharetta (ATL)
Blaszkiewicz, Holly	Ivy Tech Community College/Region 1
Boito, Nancy	HACC Central Pennsylvania's Community College
Borger-Boglin, Grietje L.	San Antonio College/Northeast Lakeview College
Branigan, Dave	DeVry University
Bray, Patricia	Allegany College of Maryland
Britt, Brenda K.	Fayetteville Technical Community College
Brotherton, Cathy	Riverside Community College
Brown, Judy	Western Illinois University
Buehler, Lesley	Ohlone College
Buell, C	Central Oregon Community College
Burns, Christine	Central New Mexico Community College
Byars, Pat	Brookhaven College
Byrd, Julie	Ivy Tech Community College
Byrd, Lynn	Delta State University, Cleveland, Mississippi
Cacace, Richard N.	Pensacola Junior College
Cadenhead, Charles	Brookhaven College
Calhoun, Ric	Gordon College
Cameron, Eric	Passaic Community College
Canine, Jill	Ivy Tech Community College of Indiana
Cannamore, Madie	Kennedy King
Cannon, Kim	Greenville Technical College
Carreon, Cleda	Indiana University—Purdue University, Indianapolis
Carriker, Sandra	North Shore Community College
Casey, Patricia	Trident Technical College
Cates, Wally	Central New Mexico Community College
Chaffin, Catherine	Shawnee State University
Chauvin, Marg	Palm Beach Community College, Boca Raton
Challa, Chandrashekar	Virginia State University
Chamlou, Afsaneh	NOVA Alexandria
Chapman, Pam	Wabaunsee Community College
Christensen, Dan	Iowa Western Community College
Clay, Betty	Southeastern Oklahoma State University
Collins, Linda D.	Mesa Community College
Cone, Bill	Northern Arizona University
Conroy-Link, Janet	Holy Family College
Conway, Ronald	Bowling Green State University
Cornforth, Carol G.	WVNCC
Cosgrove, Janet	Northwestern CT Community
Courtney, Kevin	Hillsborough Community College
Coverdale, John	Riverside Community College
Cox, Rollie	Madison Area Technical College
Crawford, Hiram	Olive Harvey College
Crawford, Sonia	Central New Mexico Community College
Crawford, Thomasina	Miami-Dade College, Kendall Campus
Credico, Grace	Lethbridge Community College
Crenshaw, Richard	Miami Dade Community College, North
Crespo, Beverly	Mt. San Antonio College
Crooks, Steven	Texas Tech University
Crossley, Connie	Cincinnati State Technical Community College

Contributors continued

Curik, Mary	Central New Mexico Community College	Haley-Hunter, Deb	Bluefield State College
De Arazoza, Ralph	Miami Dade Community College	Hall, Linnea	Northwest Mississippi Community College
Danno, John	DeVry University/Keller Graduate School	Hammerschlag, Dr. Bill	Brookhaven College
Davis, Phillip	Del Mar College	Hansen, Michelle	Davenport University
Davis, Richard	Trinity Valley Community College	Hayden, Nancy	Indiana University—Purdue University, Indianapolis
Davis, Sandra	Baker College of Allen Park	Hayes, Theresa	Broward Community College
Dees, Stephanie D.	Wharton County Junior College	Headrick, Betsy	Chattanooga State
DeHerrera, Laurie	Pikes Peak Community College	Helfand, Terri	Chaffey College
Delk, Dr. K. Kay	Seminole Community College	Helms, Liz	Columbus State Community College
Denton, Bree	Texas Tech University		
Dix, Jeanette	Ivy Tech Community College	Hernandez, Leticia	TCI College of Technology
Dooly, Veronica P.	Asheville-Buncombe Technical Community College	Hibbert, Marilyn	Salt Lake Community College
		Hinds, Cheryl	Norfolk State University
Doroshow, Mike	Eastfield College	Hines, James	Tidewater Community College
Douglas, Gretchen	SUNYCortland	Hoffman, Joan	Milwaukee Area Technical College
Dove, Carol	Community College of Allegheny	Hogan, Pat	Cape Fear Community College
Dozier, Susan	Tidewater Community College, Virginia Beach Campus	Holland, Susan	Southeast Community College
		Holliday, Mardi	Community College of Philadelphia
Driskel, Loretta	Niagara Community College		
Duckwiler, Carol	Wabaunsee Community College	Hollingsworth, Mary Carole	Georgia Perimeter College
Duhon, David	Baker College		
Duncan, Mimi	University of Missouri-St. Louis	Hopson, Bonnie	Athens Technical College
Duthie, Judy	Green River Community College	Horvath, Carrie	Albertus Magnus College
Duvall, Annette	Central New Mexico Community College	Horwitz, Steve	Community College of Philadelphia
Ecklund, Paula	Duke University	Hotta, Barbara	Leeward Community College
Eilers, Albert	Cincinnati State Technical and Community College	Howard, Bunny	St. Johns River Community
		Howard, Chris	DeVry University
Eng, Bernice	Brookdale Community College	Huckabay, Jamie	Austin Community College
Epperson, Arlin	Columbia College	Hudgins, Susan	East Central University
Evans, Billie	Vance-Granville Community College	Hulett, Michelle J.	Missouri State University
		Humphrey, John	Asheville Buncombe Technical Community College
Evans, Jean	Brevard Community College		
Feuerbach, Lisa	Ivy Tech East Chicago	Hunt, Darla A.	Morehead State University, Morehead, Kentucky
Finley, Jean	ABTCC		
Fisher, Fred	Florida State University	Hunt, Laura	Tulsa Community College
Foster, Nancy	Baker College	Ivey, Joan M.	Lanier Technical College
Foster-Shriver, Penny L.	Anne Arundel Community College	Jacob, Sherry	Jefferson Community College
		Jacobs, Duane	Salt Lake Community College
Foster-Turpen, Linda	CNM	Jauken, Barb	Southeastern Community
Foszcz, Russ	McHenry County College	Jerry, Gina	Santa Monica College
Fry, Susan	Boise State University	Johnson, Deborah S.	Edison State College
Fustos, Janos	Metro State	Johnson, Kathy	Wright College
Gallup, Jeanette	Blinn College	Johnson, Mary	Kingwood College
Gelb, Janet	Grossmont College	Johnson, Mary	Mt. San Antonio College
Gentry, Barb	Parkland College	Jones, Stacey	Benedict College
Gerace, Karin	St. Angela Merici School	Jones, Warren	University of Alabama, Birmingham
Gerace, Tom	Tulane University	Jordan, Cheryl	San Juan College
Ghajar, Homa	Oklahoma State University	Kapoor, Bhushan	California State University, Fullerton
Gifford, Steve	Northwest Iowa Community College		
		Kasai, Susumu	Salt Lake Community College
Glazer, Ellen	Broward Community College	Kates, Hazel	Miami Dade Community College, Kendall
Gordon, Robert	Hofstra University		
Gramlich, Steven	Pasco-Hernando Community College	Keen, Debby	University of Kentucky
		Keeter, Sandy	Seminole Community College
Graviett, Nancy M.	St. Charles Community College, St. Peters, Missouri	Kern-Blystone, Dorothy Jean	Bowling Green State
Greene, Rich	Community College of Allegheny County	Kerwin, Annette	College of DuPage
		Keskin, Ilknur	The University of South Dakota
Gregoryk, Kerry	Virginia Commonwealth State	Kinney, Mark B.	Baker College
Griggs, Debra	Bellevue Community College	Kirk, Colleen	Mercy College
Grimm, Carol	Palm Beach Community College	Kisling, Eric	East Carolina University
Guthrie, Rose	Fox Valley Technical College	Kleckner, Michelle	Elon University
Hahn, Norm	Thomas Nelson Community College	Kliston, Linda	Broward Community College, North Campus

Knuth, Toni	Baker College of Auburn Hills	Martin, Paul C.	Harrisburg Area Community College
Kochis, Dennis	Suffolk County Community College	Martyn, Margie	Baldwin-Wallace College
Kominek, Kurt	Northeast State Technical Community College	Marucco, Toni	Lincoln Land Community College
		Mason, Lynn	Lubbock Christian University
Kramer, Ed	Northern Virginia Community College	Matutis, Audrone	Houston Community College
		Matkin, Marie	University of Lethbridge
Kretz, Daniel	Fox Valley Technical College	Maurel, Trina	Odessa College
Laird, Jeff	Northeast State Community College	May, Karen	Blinn College
		McCain, Evelynn	Boise State University
Lamoureaux, Jackie	Central New Mexico Community College	McCannon, Melinda	Gordon College
		McCarthy, Marguerite	Northwestern Business College
Lange, David	Grand Valley State	McCaskill, Matt L.	Brevard Community College
LaPointe, Deb	Central New Mexico Community College	McClellan, Carolyn	Tidewater Community College
		McClure, Darlean	College of Sequoias
Larsen, Jacqueline Anne	A-B Tech	McCrory, Sue A.	Missouri State University
Larson, Donna	Louisville Technical Institute	McCue, Stacy	Harrisburg Area Community College
Laspina, Kathy	Vance-Granville Community College		
		McEntire-Orbach, Teresa	Middlesex County College
Le Grand, Dr. Kate	Broward Community College	McKinley, Lee	Georgia Perimeter College
Lenhart, Sheryl	Terra Community College	McLeod, Todd	Fresno City College
Leonard, Yvonne	Coastal Carolina Community College	McManus, Illyana	Grossmont College
		McPherson, Dori	Schoolcraft College
Letavec, Chris	University of Cincinnati	Meck, Kari	HACC
Lewis, Daphne L, Ed.D.	Wayland Baptist University	Meiklejohn, Nancy	Pikes Peak Community College
Lewis, Julie	Baker College-Allen Park	Menking, Rick	Hardin-Simmons University
Liefert, Jane	Everett Community College	Meredith, Mary	University of Louisiana at Lafayette
Lindaman, Linda	Black Hawk Community College		
Lindberg, Martha	Minnesota State University	Mermelstein, Lisa	Baruch College
Lightner, Renee	Broward Community College	Metos, Linda	Salt Lake Community College
Lindberg, Martha	Minnesota State University	Meurer, Daniel	University of Cincinnati
Linge, Richard	Arizona Western College	Meyer, Colleen	Cincinnati State Technical and Community College
Logan, Mary G.	Delgado Community College		
Loizeaux, Barbara	Westchester Community College	Meyer, Marian	Central New Mexico Community College
Lombardi, John	South University		
Lopez, Don	Clovis-State Center Community College District	Miller, Cindy	Ivy Tech Community College, Lafayette, Indiana
Lopez, Lisa	Spartanburg Community College	Mills, Robert E.	Tidewater Community College, Portsmouth Campus
Lord, Alexandria	Asheville Buncombe Tech		
Lovering, LeAnne	Augusta Technical College	Mitchell, Susan	Davenport University
Lowe, Rita	Harold Washington College	Mohle, Dennis	Fresno Community College
Low, Willy Hui	Joliet Junior College	Molki, Saeed	South Texas College
Lucas, Vickie	Broward Community College	Monk, Ellen	University of Delaware
Luna, Debbie	El Paso Community College	Moore, Rodney	Holland College
Luoma, Jean	Davenport University	Morris, Mike	Southeastern Oklahoma State University
Luse, Steven P.	Horry Georgetown Technical College		
		Morris, Nancy	Hudson Valley Community College
Lynam, Linda	Central Missouri State University		
Lyon, Lynne	Durham College	Moseler, Dan	Harrisburg Area Community College
Lyon, Pat Rajski	Tomball College		
Macarty, Matthew	University of New Hampshire	Nabors, Brent	Reedley College, Clovis Center
MacKinnon, Ruth	Georgia Southern University	Nadas, Erika	Wright College
Macon, Lisa	Valencia Community College, West Campus	Nadelman, Cindi	New England College
		Nademlynsky, Lisa	Johnson & Wales University
Machuca, Wayne	College of the Sequoias	Nagengast, Joseph	Florida Career College
Mack, Sherri	Butler County Community College	Nason, Scott	Rowan Cabarrus Community College
Madison, Dana	Clarion University		
Maguire, Trish	Eastern New Mexico University	Ncube, Cathy	University of West Florida
Malkan, Rajiv	Montgomery College	Newsome, Eloise	Northern Virginia Community College Woodbridge
Manning, David	Northern Kentucky University		
Marcus, Jacquie	Niagara Community College	Nicholls, Doreen	Mohawk Valley Community College
Marghitu, Daniela	Auburn University		
Marks, Suzanne	Bellevue Community College	Nicholson, John R.	Johnson County Community College
Marquez, Juanita	El Centro College		
Marquez, Juan	Mesa Community College	Nielson, Phil	Salt Lake Community College
Martin, Carol	Harrisburg Area Community College	Nunan, Karen L.	Northeast State Technical Community College

Contributors continued

O'Neal, Lois Ann	Rogers State University	Sinha, Atin	Albany State University
Odegard, Teri	Edmonds Community College	Skolnick, Martin	Florida Atlantic University
Ogle, Gregory	North Community College	Smith, Kristi	Allegany College of Maryland
Orr, Dr. Claudia	Northern Michigan University South	Smith, Patrick	Marshall Community and Technical College
Orsburn, Glen	Fox Valley Technical College	Smith, Stella A.	Georgia Gwinnett College
Otieno, Derek	DeVry University	Smith, T. Michael	Austin Community College
Otton, Diana Hill	Chesapeake College	Smith, Tammy	Tompkins Cortland Community Collge
Oxendale, Lucia	West Virginia Institute of Technology	Smolenski, Bob	Delaware County Community College
Paiano, Frank	Southwestern College	Smolenski, Robert	Delaware Community College
Pannell, Dr. Elizabeth	Collin College	Southwell, Donald	Delta College
Patrick, Tanya	Clackamas Community College	Spangler, Candice	Columbus State
Paul, Anindya	Daytona State College	Spangler, Candice	Columbus State Community College
Peairs, Deb	Clark State Community College	Stark, Diane	Phoenix College
Perez, Kimberly	Tidewater Community College	Stedham, Vicki	St. Petersburg College, Clearwater
Porter, Joyce	Weber State University	Stefanelli, Greg	Carroll Community College
Prince, Lisa	Missouri State University-Springfield Campus	Steiner, Ester	New Mexico State University
Proietti, Kathleen	Northern Essex Community College	Stenlund, Neal	Northern Virginia Community College, Alexandria
Puopolo, Mike	Bunker Hill Community College	St. John, Steve	Tulsa Community College
Pusins, Delores	HCCC	Sterling, Janet	Houston Community College
Putnam, Darlene	Thomas Nelson Community College	Stoughton, Catherine	Laramie County Community College
Raghuraman, Ram	Joliet Junior College	Sullivan, Angela	Joliet Junior College
Rani, Chigurupati	BMCC/CUNY	Sullivan, Denise	Westchester Community College
Reasoner, Ted Allen	Indiana University—Purdue	Sullivan, Joseph	Joliet Junior College
Reeves, Karen	High Point University	Swart, John	Louisiana Tech University
Remillard, Debbie	New Hampshire Technical Institute	Szurek, Joseph	University of Pittsburgh at Greensburg
Rhue, Shelly	DeVry University	Taff, Ann	Tulsa Community College
Richards, Karen	Maplewoods Community College	Taggart, James	Atlantic Cape Community College
Richardson, Mary	Albany Technical College	Tarver, Mary Beth	Northwestern State University
Rodgers, Gwen	Southern Nazarene University	Taylor, Michael	Seattle Central Community College
Rodie, Karla	Pikes Peak Community College	Terrell, Robert L.	Carson-Newman College
Roselli, Diane Maie	Harrisburg Area Community College	Terry, Dariel	Northern Virginia Community College
Ross, Dianne	University of Louisiana in Lafayette	Thangiah, Sam	Slippery Rock University
Rousseau, Mary	Broward Community College, South	Thayer, Paul	Austin Community College
Rovetto, Ann	Horry-Georgetown Technical College	Thompson, Joyce	Lehigh Carbon Community College
Rusin, Iwona	Baker College	Thompson-Sellers, Ingrid	Georgia Perimeter College
Sahabi, Ahmad	Baker College of Clinton Township	Tomasi, Erik	Baruch College
Samson, Dolly	Hawaii Pacific University	Toreson, Karen	Shoreline Community College
Sams, Todd	University of Cincinnati	Townsend, Cynthia	Baker College
Sandoval, Everett	Reedley College	Trifiletti, John J.	Florida Community College at Jacksonville
Santiago, Diana	Central New Mexico Community College	Trivedi, Charulata	Quinsigamond Community College, Woodbridge
Sardone, Nancy	Seton Hall University	Tucker, William	Austin Community College
Scafide, Jean	Mississippi Gulf Coast Community College	Turgeon, Cheryl	Asnuntuck Community College
Scheeren, Judy	Westmoreland County Community College	Turpen, Linda	Central New Mexico Community College
Scheiwe, Adolph	Joliet Junior College	Upshaw, Susan	Del Mar College
Schneider, Sol	Sam Houston State University	Unruh, Angela	Central Washington University
Schweitzer, John	Central New Mexico Community College	Vanderhoof, Dr. Glenna	Missouri State University-Springfield Campus
Scroggins, Michael	Southwest Missouri State University	Vargas, Tony	El Paso Community College
Sedlacek, Brenda	Tidewater Community College	Vicars, Mitzi	Hampton University
Sell, Kelly	Anne Arundel Community College	Villarreal, Kathleen	Fresno
Sever, Suzanne	Northwest Arkansas Community College	Vitrano, Mary Ellen	Palm Beach Community College
		Vlaich-Lee, Michelle	Greenville Technical College
Sewell, John	Florida Career College	Volker, Bonita	Tidewater Community College
Sheridan, Rick	California State University-Chico	Waddell, Karen	Butler Community College
Silvers, Pamela	Asheville Buncombe Tech	Wahila, Lori (Mindy)	Tompkins Cortland Community College
Sindt, Robert G.	Johnson County Community College		
Singer, Noah	Tulsa Community College	Wallace, Melissa	Lanier Technical College
Singer, Steven A.	University of Hawai'i, Kapi'olani Community College	Walters, Gary B.	Central New Mexico Community College

Contributors continued

Waswick, Kim	Southeast Community College, Nebraska	Wilms, Dr. G. Jan	Union University
Wavle, Sharon M.	Tompkins Cortland Community College	Wilson, Kit	Red River College
		Wilson, MaryLou	Piedmont Technical College
Webb, Nancy	City College of San Francisco	Wilson, Roger	Fairmont State University
Webb, Rebecca	Northwest Arkansas Community College	Wimberly, Leanne	International Academy of Design and Technology
Weber, Sandy	Gateway Technical College	Winters, Floyd	Manatee Community College
Weissman, Jonathan	Finger Lakes Community College	Worthington, Paula	Northern Virginia Community College
Wells, Barbara E.	Central Carolina Technical College	Wright, Darrell	Shelton State Community College
Wells, Lorna	Salt Lake Community College	Wright, Julie	Baker College
Welsh, Jean	Lansing Community College Nebraska	Yauney, Annette	Herkimer County Community College
		Yip, Thomas	Passaic Community College
White, Bruce	Quinnipiac University	Zavala, Ben	Webster Tech
Willer, Ann	Solano Community College	Zaboski, Maureen	University of Scranton
Williams, Mark	Lane Community College	Zlotow, Mary Ann	College of DuPage
Williams, Ronald D.	Central Piedmont Community College	Zudeck, Steve	Broward Community College, North
		Zullo, Matthew D.	Wake Technical Community College

About the Authors

Shelley Gaskin, Series Editor, is a professor in the Business and Computer Technology Division at Pasadena City College in Pasadena, California. She holds a bachelor's degree in Business Administration from Robert Morris College (Pennsylvania), a master's degree in Business from Northern Illinois University, and a doctorate in Adult and Community Education from Ball State University. Before joining Pasadena City College, she spent 12 years in the computer industry where she was a systems analyst, sales representative, and Director of Customer Education with Unisys Corporation. She also worked for Ernst & Young on the development of large systems applications for their clients. She has written and developed training materials for custom systems applications in both the public and private sector, and has written and edited numerous computer application textbooks.

This book is dedicated to my students, who inspire me every day.

Alicia Vargas is a faculty member in Business Information Technology at Pasadena City College. She holds a master's and a bachelor's degree in business education from California State University, Los Angeles, and has authored several textbooks and training manuals on Microsoft Word, Microsoft Excel, and Microsoft PowerPoint.

This book is dedicated with all my love to my husband Vic, who makes everything possible; and to my children Victor, Phil, and Emmy, who are an unending source of inspiration and who make everything worthwhile.

Suzanne Marks is a faculty member in Business Technology Systems at Bellevue Community College, Bellevue, Washington. She holds a bachelor's degree in business education from Washington State University, and was project manager for the first IT Skills Standards in the United States.

This book is dedicated to my son, Jeff, and to my sisters, Janet Curtis and Joan Wissmann, for their brilliance, wisdom, and encouragement.

Teach the Course You Want in Less Time

A Microsoft® Office textbook designed for student success!

- **Project-Based** – Students learn by creating projects that they will use in the real world.

- **Microsoft Procedural Syntax** – Steps are written to put students in the right place at the right time.

- **Teachable Moment** – Expository text is woven into the steps—at the moment students need to know it—not chunked together in a block of text that will go unread.

- **Sequential Pagination** – Students have actual page numbers instead of confusing letters and abbreviations.

Student Outcomes and Learning Objectives – Objectives are clustered around projects that result in student outcomes.

Project Activities – A project summary stated clearly and quickly.

Project Files – Clearly shows students which files are needed for the project and the names they will use to save their documents.

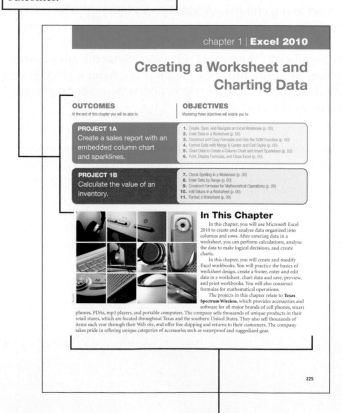

Scenario – Each chapter opens with a story that sets the stage for the projects the student will create.

Project Results – Shows students how their final outcome will appear.

Microsoft Procedural Syntax – Steps are written to put the student in the right place at the right time.

Color Coding – Color variations between the two projects in each chapter make it easy to identify which project students are working on.

Sequential Pagination – Students are given actual page numbers to navigate through the textbook instead of confusing letters and abbreviations.

Teachable Moment – Expository text is woven into the steps—at the moment students need to know it—not chunked together in a block of text that will go unread.

End-of-Chapter

Content-Based Assessments – Assessments with defined solutions.

Objective List - Every project includes a listing of covered objectives from Projects A and B.

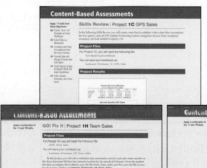

End-of-Chapter

Outcomes-Based Assessments – Assessments with open-ended solutions.

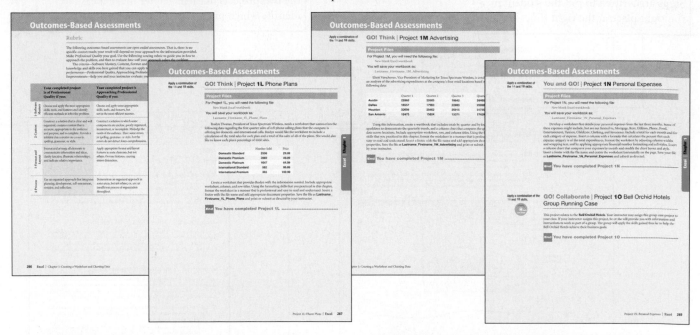

Task-Specific Rubric – A matrix specific to the **GO! Solve It** projects that states the criteria and standards for grading these defined-solution projects.

Outcomes Rubric – A matrix specific to the **GO! Think** projects that states the criteria and standards for grading these open-ended assessments.

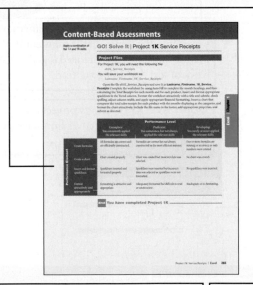

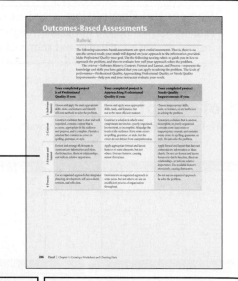

Student CD – All student data files readily available on a CD that comes with the book.

Podcasts – Videos that teach some of the more difficult topics when working with Microsoft applications.

Student Videos – A visual and audio walk-through of every A and B project in the book (see sample images on following page).

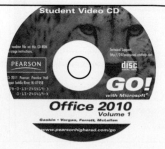

 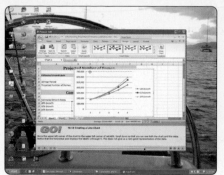 

Student Videos! – Each chapter comes with two videos that include audio, demonstrating the objectives and activities taught in the chapter.

 **All Instructor materials available on the IRCD**

Instructor Materials

Annotated Instructor Edition - An instructor tool includes a full copy of the student textbook annotated with teaching tips, discussion topics, and other useful pieces for teaching each chapter.

Assignment Sheets – Lists all the assignments for the chapter. Just add in the course information, due dates, and points. Providing these to students ensures they will know what is due and when.

Scripted Lectures – Classroom lectures prepared for you.

Annotated Solution Files – Coupled with the assignment tags, these create a grading and scoring system that makes grading so much easier for you.

PowerPoint Lectures – PowerPoint presentations for each chapter.

Scoring Rubrics – Can be used either by students to check their work or by you as a quick check-off for the items that need to be corrected.

Syllabus Templates - For 8-week, 12-week, and 16-week courses.

Test Bank – Includes a variety of test questions for each chapter.

Companion Website – Online content such as the Online Study Guide, Glossary, and Student Data Files are all at **www.pearsonhighered.com/go**.

Using the Common Features of Microsoft Office 2010

OUTCOMES

At the end of this chapter you will be able to:

OBJECTIVES

Mastering these objectives will enable you to:

PROJECT 1A
Create, save, and print a Microsoft Office 2010 file.

1. Use Windows Explorer to Locate Files and Folders (p. 3)
2. Locate and Start a Microsoft Office 2010 Program (p. 6)
3. Enter and Edit Text in an Office 2010 Program (p. 9)
4. Perform Commands from a Dialog Box (p. 11)
5. Create a Folder, Save a File, and Close a Program (p. 13)
6. Add Document Properties and Print a File (p. 18)

PROJECT 1B
Use the Ribbon and dialog boxes to perform common commands in a Microsoft Office 2010 file.

7. Open an Existing File and Save It with a New Name (p. 22)
8. Explore Options for an Application (p. 25)
9. Perform Commands from the Ribbon (p. 26)
10. Apply Formatting in Office Programs (p. 32)
11. Use the Microsoft Office 2010 Help System (p. 43)
12. Compress Files (p. 44)

o.ly/Shutterstock

In This Chapter

In this chapter, you will use Windows Explorer to navigate the Windows folder structure, create a folder, and save files in Microsoft Office 2010 programs. You will also practice using the features of Microsoft Office 2010 that are common across the major programs that comprise the Microsoft Office 2010 suite. These common features include creating, saving, and printing files.

Common features also include the new Paste Preview and Microsoft Office Backstage view. You will apply formatting, perform commands, and compress files. You will see that creating professional-quality documents is easy and quick in Microsoft Office 2010, and that finding your way around is fast and efficient.

The projects in this chapter relate to **Oceana Palm Grill**, which is a chain of 25 casual, full-service restaurants based in Austin, Texas. The Oceana Palm Grill owners plan an aggressive expansion program. To expand by 15 additional restaurants in North Carolina and Florida by 2018, the company must attract new investors, develop new menus, and recruit new employees, all while adhering to the company's quality guidelines and maintaining its reputation for excellent service. To succeed, the company plans to build on its past success and maintain its quality elements.

Project 1A PowerPoint File

myitlab Project 1A Training

Project Activities

In Activities 1.01 through 1.06, you will create a PowerPoint file, save it in a folder that you create by using Windows Explorer, and then print the file or submit it electronically as directed by your instructor. Your completed PowerPoint slide will look similar to Figure 1.1.

Project Files

For Project 1A, you will need the following file:

New blank PowerPoint presentation

You will save your file as:

Lastname_Firstname_1A_Menu_Plan

Project Results

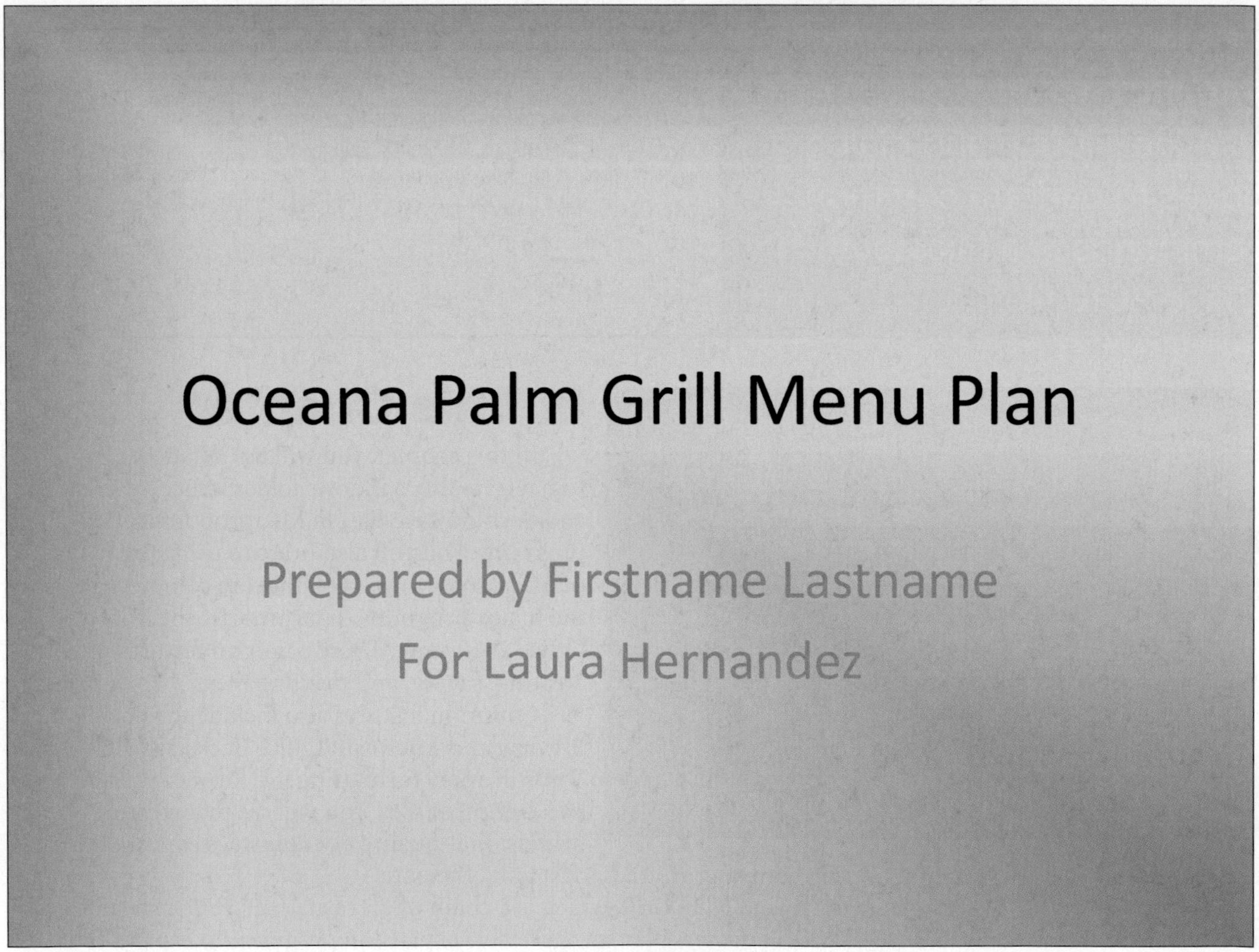

Oceana Palm Grill Menu Plan
Prepared by Firstname Lastname
For Laura Hernandez

Figure 1.1
Project 1A Menu Plan

Objective 1 | Use Windows Explorer to Locate Files and Folders

A *file* is a collection of information stored on a computer under a single name, for example, a Word document or a PowerPoint presentation. Every file is stored in a *folder*—a container in which you store files—or a *subfolder*, which is a folder within a folder. Your Windows operating system stores and organizes your files and folders, which is a primary task of an operating system.

You *navigate*—explore within the organizing structure of Windows—to create, save, and find your files and folders by using the ***Windows Explorer*** program. Windows Explorer displays the files and folders on your computer, and is at work anytime you are viewing the contents of files and folders in a *window*. A window is a rectangular area on a computer screen in which programs and content appear; a window can be moved, resized, minimized, or closed.

Activity 1.01 | Using Windows Explorer to Locate Files and Folders

1 Turn on your computer and display the Windows ***desktop***—the opening screen in Windows that simulates your work area.

> **Note** | Comparing Your Screen with the Figures in This Textbook
>
> Your screen will match the figures shown in this textbook if you set your screen resolution to 1024 × 768. At other resolutions, your screen will closely resemble, but not match, the figures shown. To view your screen's resolution, on the Windows 7 desktop, right-click in a blank area, and then click Screen resolution. In Windows Vista, right-click a blank area, click Personalize, and then click Display Settings. In Windows XP, right-click the desktop, click Properties, and then click the Settings tab.

2 In your CD/DVD tray, insert the **Student CD** that accompanies this textbook. Wait a few moments for an **AutoPlay** window to display. Compare your screen with Figure 1.2.

> *AutoPlay* is a Windows feature that lets you choose which program to use to start different kinds of media, such as music CDs, or CDs and DVDs containing photos; it displays when you plug in or insert media or storage devices.

> **Note** | If You Do Not Have the Student CD
>
> If you do not have the Student CD, consult the inside back flap of this textbook for instructions on how to download the files from the Pearson Web site.

Figure 1.2

AutoPlay window

Close button

Windows desktop (yours may vary in color and arrangement)

3 In the upper right corner of the **AutoPlay** window, move your mouse over—*point to*—the **Close** button ![Close button], and then *click*—press the left button on your mouse pointing device one time.

4 On the left side of the **Windows taskbar**, click the **Start** button ![Start] to display the **Start menu**. Compare your screen with Figure 1.3.

The *Windows taskbar* is the area along the lower edge of the desktop that contains the *Start button* and an area to display buttons for open programs. The Start button displays the *Start menu*, which provides a list of choices and is the main gateway to your computer's programs, folders, and settings.

Figure 1.3

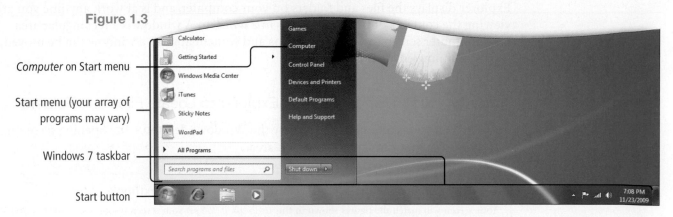

Computer on Start menu

Start menu (your array of programs may vary)

Windows 7 taskbar

Start button

5 On the right side of the **Start menu**, click **Computer** to see the disk drives and other hardware connected to your computer. Compare your screen with Figure 1.4, and then take a moment to study the table in Figure 1.5.

The *folder window* for *Computer* displays. A folder window displays the contents of the current folder, *library*, or device, and contains helpful parts so that you can navigate within Windows.

In Windows 7, a library is a collection of items, such as files and folders, assembled from *various locations*; the locations might be on your computer, an external hard drive, removable media, or someone else's computer.

The difference between a folder and a library is that a library can include files stored in *different locations*—any disk drive, folder, or other place that you can store files and folders.

Figure 1.4

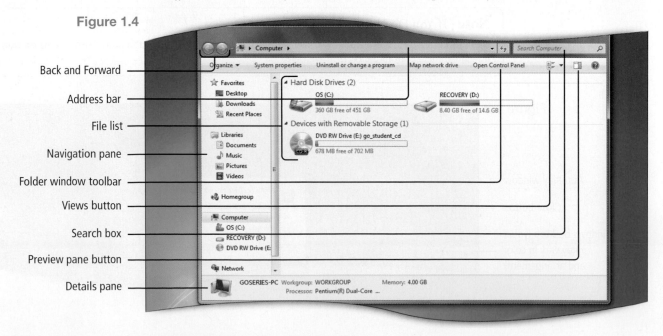

Back and Forward

Address bar

File list

Navigation pane

Folder window toolbar

Views button

Search box

Preview pane button

Details pane

Window Part	Use to:
Address bar	Navigate to a different folder or library, or go back to a previous one.
Back and Forward buttons	Navigate to other folders or libraries you have already opened without closing the current window. These buttons work in conjunction with the address bar; that is, after you use the address bar to change folders, you can use the Back button to return to the previous folder.
Details pane	Display the most common file properties—information about a file, such as the author, the date you last changed the file, and any descriptive *tags*, which are custom file properties that you create to help find and organize your files.
File list	Display the contents of the current folder or library. In Computer, the file list displays the disk drives.
Folder window for *Computer*	Display the contents of the current folder, library, or device. The Folder window contains helpful features so that you can navigate within Windows.
Folder window toolbar	Perform common tasks, such as changing the view of your files and folders or burning files to a CD. The buttons available change to display only relevant tasks.
Navigation pane	Navigate to, open, and display favorites, libraries, folders, saved searches, and an expandable list of drives.
Preview pane button	Display (if you have chosen to open this pane) the contents of most files without opening them in a program. To open the preview pane, click the Preview pane button on the toolbar to turn it on and off.
Search box	Look for an item in the current folder or library by typing a word or phrase in the search box.
Views button	Choose how to view the contents of the current location.

Figure 1.5

6 On the toolbar of the **Computer** folder window, click the **Views button arrow** ⊞▾ — the small arrow to the right of the Views button—to display a list of views that you can apply to the file list. If necessary, on the list, click **Tiles**.

> The Views button is a *split button*; clicking the main part of the button performs a *command* and clicking the arrow opens a menu or list. A command is an instruction to a computer program that causes an action to be carried out.

> When you open a folder or a library, you can change how the files display in the file list. For example, you might prefer to see large or small *icons*—pictures that represent a program, a file, a folder, or some other object—or an arrangement that lets you see various types of information about each file. Each time you click the Views button, the window changes, cycling through several views—additional view options are available by clicking the Views button arrow.

Another Way

Point to the CD/DVD drive, right-click, and then click Open.

7 In the **file list**, under **Devices with Removable Storage**, point to your **CD/DVD Drive**, and then *double-click*—click the left mouse button two times in rapid succession—to display the list of folders on the CD. Compare your screen with Figure 1.6.

> When double-clicking, keep your hand steady between clicks; this is more important than the speed of the two clicks.

Figure 1.6

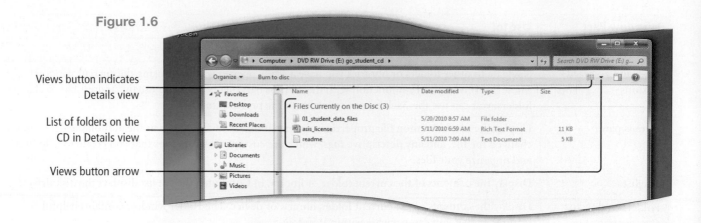

Views button indicates Details view

List of folders on the CD in Details view

Views button arrow

8 In the **file list**, point to the folder **01_student_data_files** and double-click to display the list of subfolders in the folder. Double-click to open the folder **01_common_features**. Compare your screen with Figure 1.7.

The Student Resource CD includes files that you will use to complete the projects in this textbook. If you prefer, you can also copy the **01_student_data_files** folder to a location on your computer's hard drive or to a removable device such as a *USB flash drive*, which is a small storage device that plugs into a computer USB port. Your instructor might direct you to other locations where these files are located; for example, on your learning management system.

Figure 1.7

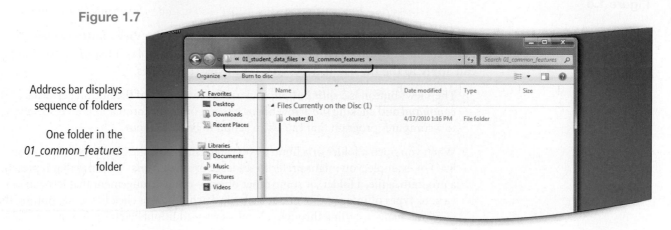

Address bar displays sequence of folders

One folder in the *01_common_features* folder

9 In the upper right corner of the **Computer** window, click the **Close** button to redisplay your desktop.

Objective 2 | Locate and Start a Microsoft Office 2010 Program

Microsoft Office 2010 includes programs, servers, and services for individuals, small organizations, and large enterprises. A *program*, also referred to as an *application*, is a set of instructions used by a computer to perform a task, such as word processing or accounting.

Activity 1.02 | Locating and Starting a Microsoft Office 2010 Program

1 On the **Windows taskbar**, click the **Start** button to display the **Start** menu.

2 From the displayed **Start** menu, locate the group of **Microsoft Office 2010** programs on your computer—the Office program icons from which you can start the program may be located on your Start menu, in a Microsoft Office folder on the **All Programs** list, on your desktop, or any combination of these locations; the location will vary depending on how your computer is configured.

> *All Programs* is an area of the Start menu that displays all the available programs on your computer system.

3 Examine Figure 1.8, and notice the programs that are included in the Microsoft Office Professional Plus 2010 group of programs. (Your group of programs may vary.)

> *Microsoft Word* is a word processing program, with which you create and share documents by using its writing tools.

> *Microsoft Excel* is a spreadsheet program, with which you calculate and analyze numbers and create charts.

> *Microsoft Access* is a database program, with which you can collect, track, and report data.

> *Microsoft PowerPoint* is a presentation program, with which you can communicate information with high-impact graphics and video.

> Additional popular Office programs include *Microsoft Outlook* to manage e-mail and organizational activities, *Microsoft Publisher* to create desktop publishing documents such as brochures, and *Microsoft OneNote* to manage notes that you make at meetings or in classes and to share notes with others on the Web.

> The Professional Plus version of Office 2010 also includes *Microsoft SharePoint Workspace* to share information with others in a team environment and *Microsoft InfoPath Designer and Filler* to create forms and gather data.

Figure 1.8

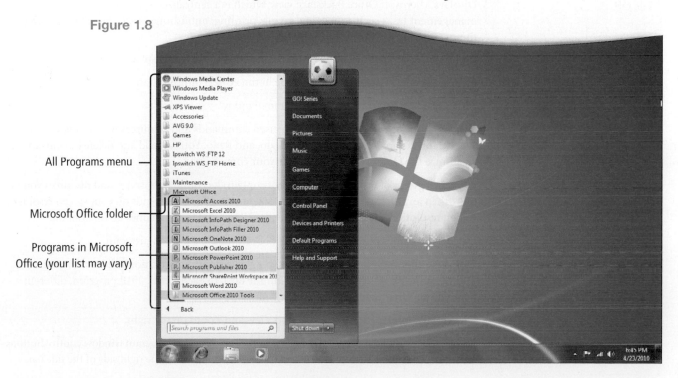

All Programs menu

Microsoft Office folder

Programs in Microsoft Office (your list may vary)

4 Click to open the program **Microsoft PowerPoint 2010**. Compare your screen with Figure 1.9, and then take a moment to study the description of these screen elements in the table in Figure 1.10.

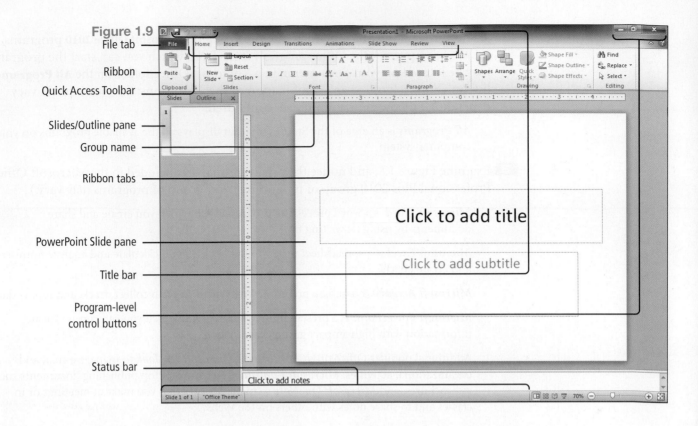

Figure 1.9

File tab
Ribbon
Quick Access Toolbar
Slides/Outline pane
Group name
Ribbon tabs
PowerPoint Slide pane
Title bar
Program-level control buttons
Status bar

Screen Element	Description
File tab	Displays Microsoft Office Backstage view, which is a centralized space for all of your file management tasks such as opening, saving, printing, publishing, or sharing a file—all the things you can do *with* a file.
Group names	Indicate the name of the groups of related commands on the displayed tab.
PowerPoint Slide pane	Displays a large image of the active slide in the PowerPoint program.
Program-level control buttons	Minimizes, restores, or closes the program window.
Quick Access Toolbar	Displays buttons to perform frequently used commands and resources with a single click. The default commands include Save, Undo, and Redo. You can add and delete buttons to customize the Quick Access Toolbar for your convenience.
Ribbon	Displays a group of task-oriented tabs that contain the commands, styles, and resources you need to work in an Office 2010 program. The look of your Ribbon depends on your screen resolution. A high resolution will display more individual items and button names on the Ribbon.
Ribbon tabs	Display the names of the task-oriented tabs relevant to the open program.
Slides/Outline pane	Displays either thumbnails of the slides in a PowerPoint presentation (Slides tab) or the outline of the presentation's content (Outline tab). In each Office 2010 program, different panes display in different ways to assist you.
Status bar	Displays file information on the left and View and Zoom on the right.
Title bar	Displays the name of the file and the name of the program. The program window control buttons—Minimize, Maximize/Restore Down, and Close—are grouped on the right side of the title bar.

Figure 1.10

Objective 3 | Enter and Edit Text in an Office 2010 Program

All of the programs in Office 2010 require some typed text. Your keyboard is still the primary method of entering information into your computer. Techniques to *edit*—make changes to—text are similar among all of the Office 2010 programs.

Activity 1.03 | Entering and Editing Text in an Office 2010 Program

1 In the middle of the PowerPoint Slide pane, point to the text *Click to add title* to display the ⬚I⬚ pointer, and then click one time.

The ***insertion point***—a blinking vertical line that indicates where text or graphics will be inserted—displays.

In Office 2010 programs, the mouse ***pointer***—any symbol that displays on your screen in response to moving your mouse device—displays in different shapes depending on the task you are performing and the area of the screen to which you are pointing.

2 Type **Oceana Grille Info** and notice how the insertion point moves to the right as you type. Point slightly to the right of the letter *e* in *Grille* and click to place the insertion point there. Compare your screen with Figure 1.11.

Figure 1.11

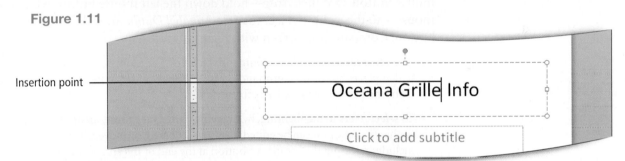

Insertion point ——————

3 On your keyboard, locate and press the ⬚Backspace⬚ key to delete the letter *e*.

Pressing ⬚Backspace⬚ removes a character to the left of the insertion point.

4 Point slightly to the left of the *I* in *Info* and click one time to place the insertion point there. Type **Menu** and then press ⬚Spacebar⬚ one time. Compare your screen with Figure 1.12.

By ***default***, when you type text in an Office program, existing text moves to the right to make space for new typing. Default refers to the current selection or setting that is automatically used by a program unless you specify otherwise.

Figure 1.12

Menu inserted ——————

5 Press [Del] four times to delete *Info* and then type **Plan**

> Pressing [Del] removes—deletes—a character to the right of the insertion point.

6 With your insertion point blinking after the word *Plan*, on your keyboard, hold down the [Ctrl] key. While holding down [Ctrl], press [←] three times to move the insertion point to the beginning of the word *Grill*.

> This is a **keyboard shortcut**—a key or combination of keys that performs a task that would otherwise require a mouse. This keyboard shortcut moves the insertion point to the beginning of the previous word.

> A keyboard shortcut is commonly indicated as [Ctrl] + [←] (or some other combination of keys) to indicate that you hold down the first key while pressing the second key. A keyboard shortcut can also include three keys, in which case you hold down the first two and then press the third. For example, [Ctrl] + [Shift] + [←] selects one word to the left.

7 With the insertion point blinking at the beginning of the word *Grill*, type **Palm** and press [Spacebar].

8 Click anywhere in the text *Click to add subtitle*. With the insertion point blinking, type the following and include the spelling error: **Prepered by Annabel Dunham**

9 With your mouse, point slightly to the left of the *A* in *Annabel*, hold down the left mouse button, and then **drag**—hold down the left mouse button while moving your mouse—to the right to select the text *Annabel Dunham*, and then release the mouse button. Compare your screen with Figure 1.13.

> The **Mini toolbar** displays commands that are commonly used with the selected object, which places common commands close to your pointer. When you move the pointer away from the Mini toolbar, it fades from view.

> To **select** refers to highlighting, by dragging with your mouse, areas of text or data or graphics so that the selection can be edited, formatted, copied, or moved. The action of dragging includes releasing the left mouse button at the end of the area you want to select. The Office programs recognize a selected area as one unit, to which you can make changes. Selecting text may require some practice. If you are not satisfied with your result, click anywhere outside of the selection, and then begin again.

Figure 1.13

Mini toolbar displays

Annabel Dunham selected

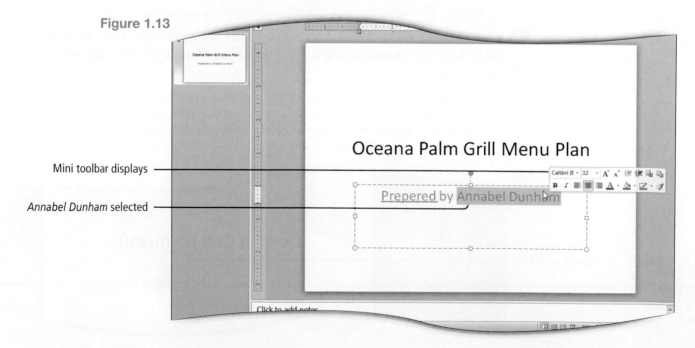

Oceana Palm Grill Menu Plan

Prepered by Annabel Dunham

Click to add notes

10 With the text *Annabel Dunham* selected, type your own firstname and lastname.

> In any Windows-based program, such as the Microsoft Office 2010 programs, selected text is deleted and then replaced when you begin to type new text. You will save time by developing good techniques to select and then edit or replace selected text, which is easier than pressing the `Del` key numerous times to delete text that you do not want.

11 Notice that the misspelled word *Prepered* displays with a wavy red underline; additionally, all or part of your name might display with a wavy red underline.

> Office 2010 has a dictionary of words against which all entered text is checked. In Word and PowerPoint, words that are *not* in the dictionary display a wavy red line, indicating a possible misspelled word or a proper name or an unusual word—none of which are in the Office 2010 dictionary.

> In Excel and Access, you can initiate a check of the spelling, but wavy red underlines do not display.

12 Point to *Prepered* and then ***right-click***—click your right mouse button one time.

> The Mini toolbar and a ***shortcut menu*** display. A shortcut menu displays commands and options relevant to the selected text or object—known as ***context-sensitive commands*** because they relate to the item you right-clicked.

> Here, the shortcut menu displays commands related to the misspelled word. You can click the suggested correct spelling *Prepared*, click Ignore All to ignore the misspelling, add the word to the Office dictionary, or click Spelling to display a ***dialog box***. A dialog box is a small window that contains options for completing a task. Whenever you see a command followed by an ***ellipsis*** (…), which is a set of three dots indicating incompleteness, clicking the command will always display a dialog box.

13 On the displayed shortcut menu, click **Prepared** to correct the misspelled word. If necessary, point to any parts of your name that display a wavy red underline, right-click, and then on the shortcut menu, click Ignore All so that Office will no longer mark your name with a wavy underline in this file.

More Knowledge | Adding to the Office Dictionary

The main dictionary contains the most common words, but does not include all proper names, technical terms, or acronyms. You can add words, acronyms, and proper names to the Office dictionary by clicking Add to Dictionary when they are flagged, and you might want to do so for your own name and other proper names and terms that you type often.

Objective 4 | Perform Commands from a Dialog Box

In a dialog box, you make decisions about an individual object or topic. A dialog box also offers a way to adjust a number of settings at one time.

Activity 1.04 | Performing Commands from a Dialog Box

1 Point anywhere in the blank area above the title *Oceana Palm Grill Menu Plan* to display the ⬦ pointer.

2 Right-click to display a shortcut menu. Notice the command *Format Background* followed by an ellipsis (…). Compare your screen with Figure 1.14.

> Recall that a command followed by an ellipsis indicates that a dialog box will display if you click the command.

Figure 1.14

Shortcut menu

Ellipsis following command

3 Click **Format Background** to display the **Format Background** dialog box, and then compare your screen with Figure 1.15.

Figure 1.15

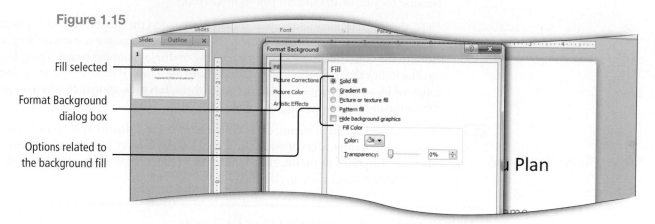

Fill selected

Format Background dialog box

Options related to the background fill

4 On the left, if necessary, click **Fill** to display the **Fill** options.

> *Fill* is the inside color of an object. Here, the dialog box displays the option group names on the left; some dialog boxes provide a set of tabs across the top from which you can display different sets of options.

5 On the right, under **Fill**, click the **Gradient fill** option button.

> The dialog box displays additional settings related to the gradient fill option. An ***option button*** is a round button that enables you to make one choice among two or more options. In a gradient fill, one color fades into another.

6 Click the **Preset colors arrow**—the arrow in the box to the right of the text *Preset colors*—and then in the gallery, in the second row, point to the fifth fill color to display the ScreenTip *Fog*.

> A ***gallery*** is an Office feature that displays a list of potential results. A ***ScreenTip*** displays useful information about mouse actions, such as pointing to screen elements or dragging.

7 Click **Fog**, and then notice that the fill color is applied to your slide. Click the **Type arrow**, and then click **Rectangular** to change the pattern of the fill color. Compare your screen with Figure 1.16.

Figure 1.16

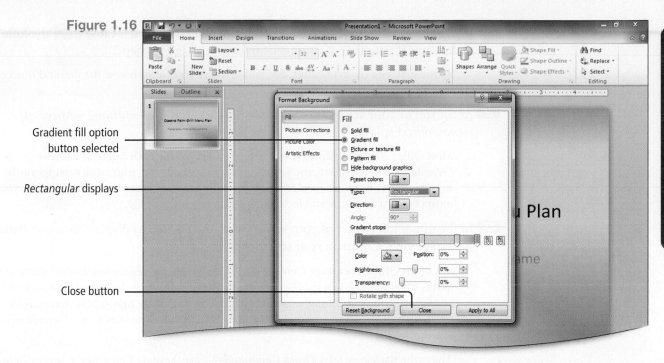

Gradient fill option button selected

Rectangular displays

Close button

8 At the bottom of the dialog box, click **Close**.

As you progress in your study of Microsoft Office, you will practice using many dialog boxes and applying dramatic effects such as this to your Word documents, Excel spreadsheets, Access databases, and PowerPoint slides.

Objective 5 | Create a Folder, Save a File, and Close a Program

A *location* is any disk drive, folder, or other place in which you can store files and folders. Where you store your files depends on how and where you use your data. For example, for your classes, you might decide to store primarily on a removable USB flash drive so that you can carry your files to different locations and access your files on different computers.

If you do most of your work on a single computer, for example your home desktop system or your laptop computer that you take with you to school or work, store your files in one of the Libraries—Documents, Music, Pictures, or Videos—provided by your Windows operating system.

Although the Windows operating system helps you to create and maintain a logical folder structure, take the time to name your files and folders in a consistent manner.

Activity 1.05 | Creating a Folder, Saving a File, and Closing a Program

A PowerPoint presentation is an example of a file. Office 2010 programs use a common dialog box provided by the Windows operating system to assist you in saving files. In this activity, you will create a folder on a USB flash drive in which to store files. If you prefer to store on your hard drive, you can use similar steps to store files in your My Documents folder in your Documents library.

1 Insert a USB flash drive into your computer, and if necessary, **Close** [×] the **AutoPlay** dialog box. If you are not using a USB flash drive, go to Step 2.

> As the first step in saving a file, determine where you want to save the file, and if necessary, insert a storage device.

2 At the top of your screen, in the title bar, notice that *Presentation1 – Microsoft PowerPoint* displays.

> Most Office 2010 programs open with a new unsaved file with a default name—*Presentation1*, *Document1*, and so on. As you create your file, your work is temporarily stored in the computer's memory until you initiate a Save command, at which time you must choose a file name and location in which to save your file.

3 In the upper left corner of your screen, click the **File tab** to display **Microsoft Office Backstage** view. Compare your screen with Figure 1.17.

> Microsoft Office **Backstage view** is a centralized space for tasks related to *file* management; that is why the tab is labeled *File*. File management tasks include, for example, opening, saving, printing, publishing, or sharing a file. The **Backstage tabs**—*Info*, *Recent*, *New*, *Print*, *Save & Send*, and *Help*—display along the left side. The tabs group file-related tasks together.

> Above the Backstage tabs, **Quick Commands**—*Save*, *Save As*, *Open*, and *Close*—display for quick access to these commands. When you click any of these commands, Backstage view closes and either a dialog box displays or the active file closes.

> Here, the **Info tab** displays information—*info*—about the current file. In the center panel, various file management tasks are available in groups. For example, if you click the Protect Presentation button, a list of options that you can set for this file that relate to who can open or edit the presentation displays.

> On the Info tab, in the right panel, you can also examine the **document properties**. Document properties, also known as **metadata**, are details about a file that describe or identify it, such as the title, author name, subject, and keywords that identify the document's topic or contents. On the Info page, a thumbnail image of the current file displays in the upper right corner, which you can click to close Backstage view and return to the document.

More Knowledge | Deciding Where to Store Your Files

Where should you store your files? In the libraries created by Windows 7 (Documents, Pictures, and so on)? On a removable device like a flash drive or external hard drive? In Windows 7, it is easy to find your files, especially if you use the libraries. Regardless of where you save a file, Windows 7 will make it easy to find the file again, even if you are not certain where it might be.

In Windows 7, storing all of your files within a library makes sense. If you perform most of your work on your desktop system or your laptop that travels with you, you can store your files in the libraries created by Windows 7 for your user account—Documents, Pictures, Music, and so on. Within these libraries, you can create folders and subfolders to organize your data. These libraries are a good choice for storing your files because:

- From the Windows Explorer button on the taskbar, your libraries are always just one click away.
- The libraries are designed for their contents; for example, the Pictures folder displays small images of your digital photos.
- You can add new locations to a library; for example, an external hard drive, or a network drive. Locations added to a library behave just like they are on your hard drive.
- Other users of your computer cannot access your libraries.
- The libraries are the default location for opening and saving files within an application, so you will find that you can open and save files with fewer navigation clicks.

Figure 1.17

Save command

Information about the
file you are working on

Info tab selected

Backstage tabs,
Info tab active

Groups

Indicates unsaved file
with default name

Document Properties

Screen thumbnail

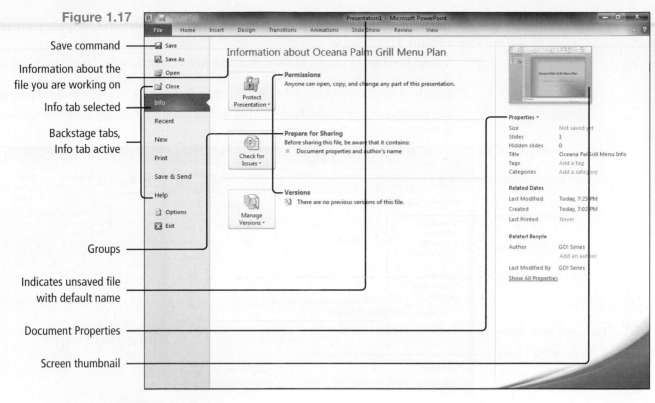

4 Above the **Backstage tabs**, click **Save** to display the **Save As** dialog box.

Backstage view closes and the Save As dialog box, which includes a folder window and an area at the bottom to name the file and set the file type, displays.

When you are saving something for the first time, for example a new PowerPoint presentation, the Save and Save As commands are identical. That is, the Save As dialog box will display if you click Save or if you click Save As.

Note | Saving Your File

After you have named a file and saved it in your desired location, the Save command saves any changes you make to the file without displaying any dialog box. The Save As command will display the Save As dialog box and let you name and save a new file based on the current one—in a location that you choose. After you name and save the new document, the original document closes, and the new document—based on the original one—displays.

---

5 In the **Save As** dialog box, on the left, locate the **navigation pane**; compare your screen with Figure 1.18.

By default, the Save command opens the Documents library unless your default file location has been changed.

Figure 1.18

Save As dialog box
Address bar

Default save location
Navigation pane

File list (yours will vary)

File name box
Save as type defaults to
PowerPoint Presentation

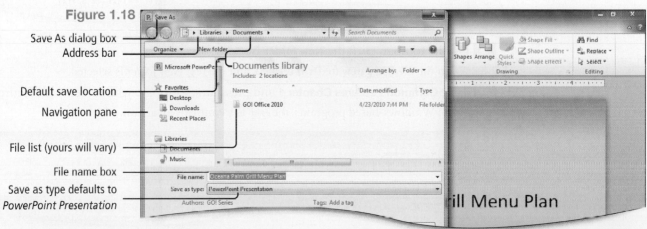

6 On the right side of the **navigation pane**, point to the **scroll bar**. Compare your screen with Figure 1.19.

> A *scroll bar* displays when a window, or a pane within a window, has information that is not in view. You can click the up or down scroll arrows—or the left and right scroll arrows in a horizontal scroll bar—to scroll the contents up or down or left and right in small increments.
>
> You can also drag the *scroll box*—the box within the scroll bar—to scroll the window in either direction.

Figure 1.19

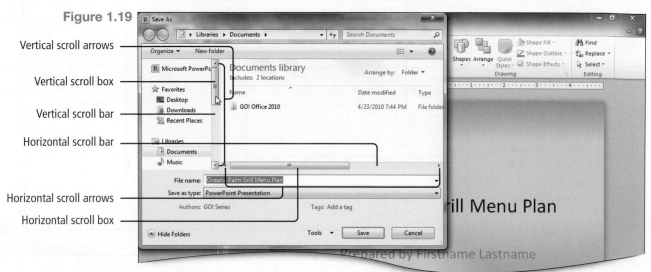

Vertical scroll arrows
Vertical scroll box
Vertical scroll bar
Horizontal scroll bar
Horizontal scroll arrows
Horizontal scroll box

7 Click the **down scroll arrow** as necessary so that you can view the lower portion of the **navigation pane**, and then click the icon for your USB flash drive. Compare your screen with Figure 1.20. (If you prefer to store on your computer's hard drive instead of a USB flash drive, in the navigation pane, click Documents.)

Figure 1.20

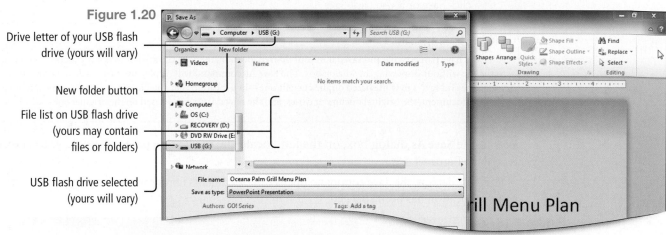

Drive letter of your USB flash drive (yours will vary)
New folder button
File list on USB flash drive (yours may contain files or folders)
USB flash drive selected (yours will vary)

8 On the toolbar, click the **New folder** button.

> In the file list, a new folder is created, and the text *New folder* is selected.

9 Type **Common Features Chapter 1** and press Enter. Compare your screen with Figure 1.21.

> In Windows-based programs, the Enter key confirms an action.

Figure 1.21

New folder

10 In the **file list**, double-click the name of your new folder to open it and display its name in the **address bar**.

11 In the lower portion of the dialog box, click in the **File name** box to select the existing text. Notice that Office inserts the text at the beginning of the presentation as a suggested file name.

12 On your keyboard, locate the ⊡ key. Notice that the Shift of this key produces the underscore character. With the text still selected, type **Lastname_Firstname_1A_Menu_Plan** Compare your screen with Figure 1.22.

> You can use spaces in file names, however some individuals prefer not to use spaces. Some programs, especially when transferring files over the Internet, may not work well with spaces in file names. In general, however, unless you encounter a problem, it is OK to use spaces. In this textbook, underscores are used instead of spaces in file names.

Figure 1.22

File name box indicates your file name

Save as type box indicates *PowerPoint Presentation*

Save button

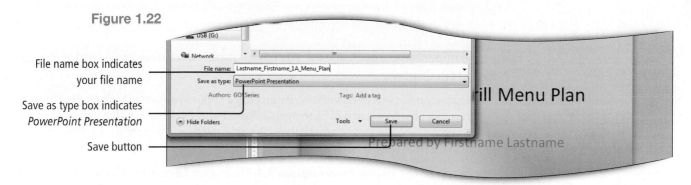

13 In the lower right corner, click **Save**; or press Enter. See Figure 1.23.

> Your new file name displays in the title bar, indicating that the file has been saved to a location that you have specified.

Figure 1.23

File name in title bar

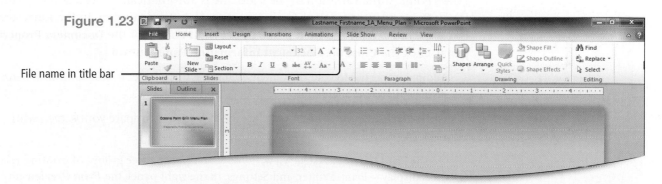

14 In the text that begins *Prepared by*, click to position the insertion point at the end of your name, and then press Enter to move to a new line. Type **For Laura Hernandez**

15 Click the **File tab** to display **Backstage** view. At the top of the center panel, notice that the path where your file is stored displays. Above the Backstage tabs, click **Close** to close the file. In the message box, click **Save** to save the changes you made and close the file. Leave PowerPoint open.

> PowerPoint displays a message asking if you want to save the changes you have made. Because you have made additional changes to the file since your last Save operation, an Office program will always prompt you to save so that you do not lose any new data.

Objective 6 | Add Document Properties and Print a File

The process of printing a file is similar in all of the Office applications. There are differences in the types of options you can select. For example, in PowerPoint, you have the option of printing the full slide, with each slide printing on a full sheet of paper, or of printing handouts with small pictures of slides on a page.

Activity 1.06 | Adding Document Properties and Printing a File

> **Alert!** | **Are You Printing or Submitting Your Files Electronically?**
>
> If you are submitting your files electronically only, or have no printer attached, you can still complete this activity. Complete Steps 1-9, and then submit your file electronically as directed by your instructor.

1 In the upper left corner, click the **File tab** to display **Backstage** view. Notice that the **Recent tab** displays.

> Because no file was open in PowerPoint, Office applies predictive logic to determine that your most likely action will be to open a PowerPoint presentation that you worked on recently. Thus, the Recent tab displays a list of PowerPoint presentations that were recently open on your system.

2 At the top of the **Recent Presentations** list, click your **Lastname_Firstname_1A_Menu_Plan** file to open it.

3 Click the **File tab** to redisplay **Backstage** view. On the right, under the screen thumbnail, click **Properties**, and then click **Show Document Panel**. In the **Author** box, delete the existing text, and then type your firstname and lastname. Notice that in PowerPoint, some variation of the slide title is automatically inserted in the Title box. In the **Subject** box, type your Course name and section number. In the **Keywords** box, type **menu plan** and then in the upper right corner of the **Document Properties** panel, click the **Close the Document Information Panel** button [×].

> Adding properties to your documents will make them easier to search for in systems such as Microsoft SharePoint.

Another Way

Press Ctrl + P or Ctrl + F2 to display the Print tab in Backstage view.

4 Redisplay **Backstage** view, and then click the **Print tab**. Compare your screen with Figure 1.24.

> On the Print tab in Backstage view, in the center panel, three groups of printing-related tasks display—Print, Printer, and Settings. In the right panel, the *Print Preview* displays, which is a view of a document as it will appear on the paper when you print it.

> At the bottom of the Print Preview area, on the left, the number of pages and arrows with which you can move among the pages in Print Preview display. On the right, *Zoom* settings enable you to shrink or enlarge the Print Preview. Zoom is the action of increasing or decreasing the viewing area of the screen.

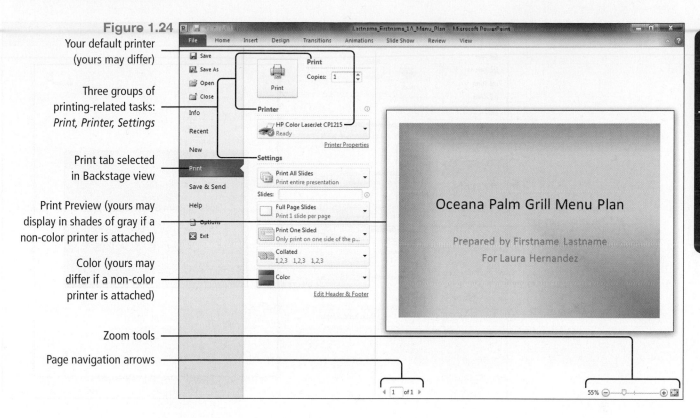

Figure 1.24

Your default printer (yours may differ)

Three groups of printing-related tasks: *Print, Printer, Settings*

Print tab selected in Backstage view

Print Preview (yours may display in shades of gray if a non-color printer is attached)

Color (yours may differ if a non-color printer is attached)

Zoom tools

Page navigation arrows

---

5 Locate the **Settings group**, and notice that the default setting is to **Print All Slides** and to print **Full Page Slides**—each slide on a full sheet of paper.

6 Point to **Full Page Slides**, notice that the button glows orange, and then click the button to display a gallery of print arrangements. Compare your screen with Figure 1.25.

Figure 1.25

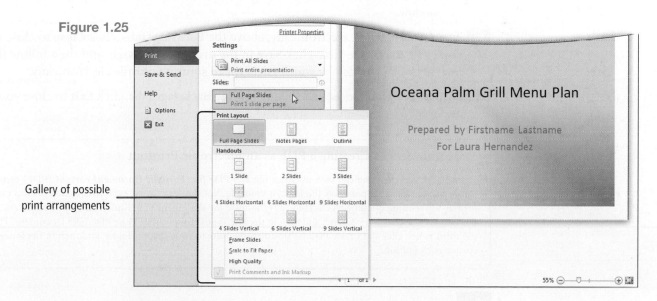

Gallery of possible print arrangements

---

7 In the displayed gallery, under **Handouts**, click **1 Slide**, and then compare your screen with Figure 1.26.

The Print Preview changes to show how your slide will print on the paper in this arrangement.

Figure 1.26

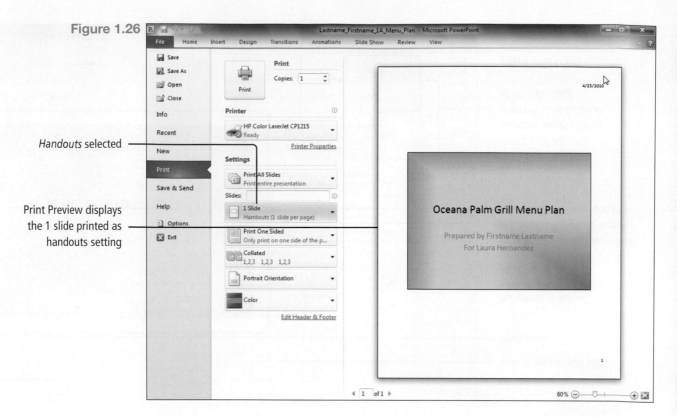

Handouts selected

Print Preview displays
the 1 slide printed as
handouts setting

8 To submit your file electronically, skip this step and move to Step 9. To print your slide, be sure your system is connected to a printer, and then in the **Print group**, click the **Print** button. On the Quick Access Toolbar, click **Save** [icon], and then move to Step 10.

> The handout will print on your default printer—on a black and white printer, the colors will print in shades of gray. Backstage view closes and your file redisplays in the PowerPoint window.

9 To submit your file electronically, above the **Backstage tabs**, click **Close** to close the file and close **Backstage** view, click **Save** in the displayed message, and then follow the instructions provided by your instructor to submit your file electronically.

Another Way

In the upper right corner of your PowerPoint window, click the red Close button.

10 Display **Backstage** view, and then below the **Backstage tabs**, click **Exit** to close your file and close PowerPoint.

More Knowledge | **Creating a PDF as an Electronic Printout**

From Backstage view, you can save an Office file as a *PDF file*. *Portable Document Format* (PDF) creates an image of your file that preserves the look of your file, but that cannot be easily changed. This is a popular format for sending documents electronically, because the document will display on most computers. From Backstage view, click Save & Send, and then in the File Types group, click Create PDF/XPS Document. Then in the third panel, click the Create PDF/XPS button, navigate to your chapter folder, and then in the lower right corner, click Publish.

End **You have completed Project 1A** ————————————————

Project 1B Word File

myitlab
Project 1B Training

Project Activities

In Activities 1.07 through 1.16, you will open, edit, save, and then compress a Word file. Your completed document will look similar to Figure 1.27.

Project Files

For Project 1B, you will need the following file:

cf01B_Cheese_Promotion

You will save your Word document as:

Lastname_Firstname_1B_Cheese_Promotion

Project Results

Memo

TO:	Laura Mabry Hernandez, General Manager
FROM:	Donna Jackson, Executive Chef
DATE:	December 17, 2014
SUBJECT:	Cheese Specials on Tuesdays

To increase restaurant traffic between 4:00 p.m. and 6:00 p.m., I am proposing a trial cheese event in one of the restaurants, probably Orlando. I would like to try a weekly event on Tuesday evenings where the focus is on a good selection of cheese.

I envision two possibilities: a selection of cheese plates or a cheese bar—or both. The cheeses would have to be matched with compatible fruit and bread or crackers. They could be used as appetizers, or for desserts, as is common in Europe. The cheese plates should be varied and diverse, using a mixture of hard and soft, sharp and mild, unusual and familiar.

I am excited about this new promotion. If done properly, I think it could increase restaurant traffic in the hours when individuals want to relax with a small snack instead of a heavy dinner.

The promotion will require that our employees become familiar with the types and characteristics of both foreign and domestic cheeses. Let's meet to discuss the details and the training requirements, and to create a flyer that begins something like this:

Oceana Palm Grill Tuesday Cheese Tastings

Lastname_Firstname_1B_Cheese_Promotion

Figure 1.27
Project 1B Cheese Promotion

Objective 7 | Open an Existing File and Save It with a New Name

In any Office program, use the Open command to display the *Open dialog box*, from which you can navigate to and then open an existing file that was created in that same program.

The Open dialog box, along with the Save and Save As dialog boxes, are referred to as *common dialog boxes*. These dialog boxes, which are provided by the Windows programming interface, display in all of the Office programs in the same manner. Thus, the Open, Save, and Save As dialog boxes will all look and perform the same in each Office program.

Activity 1.07 | Opening an Existing File and Saving it with a New Name

In this activity, you will display the Open dialog box, open an existing Word document, and then save it in your storage location with a new name.

1 Determine the location of the student data files that accompany this textbook, and be sure you can access these files.

> For example:
>
> If you are accessing the files from the Student CD that came with this textbook, insert the CD now.
>
> If you copied the files from the Student CD or from the Pearson Web site to a USB flash drive that you are using for this course, insert the flash drive in your computer now.
>
> If you copied the files to the hard drive of your computer, for example in your Documents library, be sure you can locate the files on the hard drive.

2 Determine the location of your **Common Features Chapter 1** folder you created in Activity 1.05, in which you will store your work from this chapter, and then be sure you can access that folder.

> For example:
>
> If you created your chapter folder on a USB flash drive, insert the flash drive in your computer now. This can be the same flash drive where you have stored the student data files; just be sure to use the chapter folder you created.
>
> If you created your chapter folder in the Documents library on your computer, be sure you can locate the folder. Otherwise, create a new folder at the computer at which you are working, or on a USB flash drive.

3 Using the technique you practiced in Activity 1.02, locate and then start the **Microsoft Word 2010** program on your system.

> **Another Way**
>
> In the Word (or other program) window, press Ctrl + F12 to display the Open dialog box.

4 On the Ribbon, click the **File tab** to display **Backstage** view, and then click **Open** to display the **Open** dialog box.

5 In the **navigation pane** on the left, use the scroll bar to scroll as necessary, and then click the location of your student data files to display the location's contents in the **file list**. Compare your screen with Figure 1.28.

> For example:
>
> If you are accessing the files from the Student CD that came with your book, under Computer, click the CD/DVD.
>
> If you are accessing the files from a USB flash drive, under Computer, click the flash drive name.
>
> If you are accessing the files from the Documents library of your computer, under Libraries, click Documents.

Figure 1.28

Open dialog box

Scroll bar in navigation pane

Navigation pane

CD/DVD selected (or location of your student files)

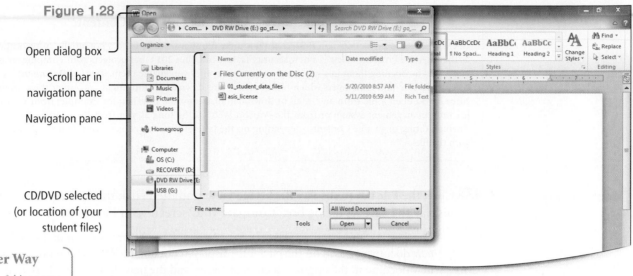

Another Way

Point to a folder name, right-click, and then from the shortcut menu, click Open.

6 Point to the folder **01_student_data_files** and double-click to open the folder. Point to the subfolder **01_common_features**, double-click, and then compare your screen with Figure 1.29.

Figure 1.29

File list displays the contents of the *01_common_features* folder

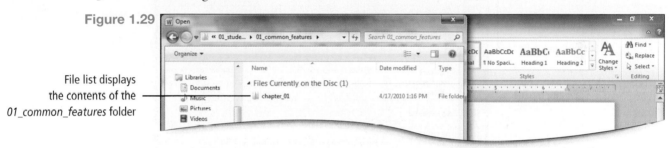

Another Way

Click one time to select the file, and then press Enter or click the Open button in the lower right corner of the dialog box.

7 In the **file list**, point to the **chapter_01** subfolder and double-click to open it. In the **file list**, point to Word file **cf01B_Cheese_Promotion** and then double-click to open and display the file in the Word window. On the Ribbon, on the **Home tab**, in the **Paragraph group**, if necessary, click the **Show/Hide** button ¶ so that it is active—glowing orange. Compare your screen with Figure 1.30.

On the title bar at the top of the screen, the file name displays. If you opened the document from the Student CD, (*Read-Only*) will display. If you opened the document from another source to which the files were copied, (*Read-Only*) might not display. ***Read-Only*** is a property assigned to a file that prevents the file from being modified or deleted; it indicates that you cannot save any changes to the displayed document unless you first save it with a new name.

Figure 1.30

File name displays in the title bar (*Read-only* will display if opened from the CD)

Show/Hide button active

Word document displays in the Word window

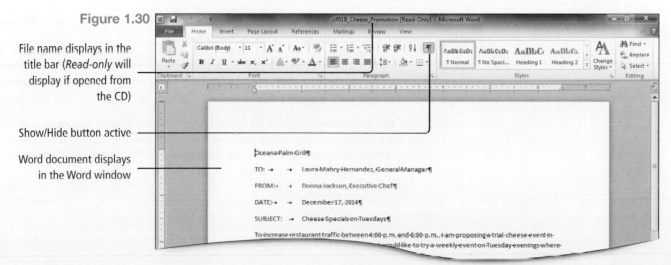

Alert! | Do You See a Message to Enable Editing or Enable Content?

In Office 2010, some files open in *Protected View* if the file appears to be from a potentially risky location, such as the Internet. Protected View is a new security feature in Office 2010 that protects your computer from malicious files by opening them in a restricted environment until you enable them. *Trusted Documents* is another security feature that remembers which files you have already enabled. You might encounter these security features if you open a file from an e-mail or download files from the Internet; for example, from your college's learning management system or from the Pearson Web site. So long as you trust the source of the file, click Enable Editing or Enable Content—depending on the type of file you receive—and then go ahead and work with the file.

Another Way

Press F12 to display the Save As dialog box.

8 Click the **File tab** to display **Backstage** view, and then click the **Save As** command to display the **Save As** dialog box. Compare your screen with Figure 1.31.

> The Save As command displays the Save As dialog box where you can name and save a *new* document based on the currently displayed document. After you name and save the new document, the original document closes, and the new document—based on the original one—displays.

Figure 1.31

Save As dialog box

Navigation pane

Current file name selected

Default type is *Word Document*

9 In the **navigation pane**, click the location in which you are storing your projects for this chapter—the location where you created your **Common Features Chapter 1** folder; for example, your USB flash drive or the Documents library.

10 In the **file list**, double-click the necessary folders and subfolders until your **Common Features Chapter 1** folder displays in the **address bar**.

11 Click in the **File name** box to select the existing file name, or drag to select the existing text, and then using your own name, type **Lastname_Firstname_1B_Cheese_Promotion** Compare your screen with Figure 1.32.

> As you type, the file name from your 1A project might display briefly. Because your 1A project file is stored in this location and you began the new file name with the same text, Office predicts that you might want the same or similar file name. As you type new characters, the suggestion is removed.

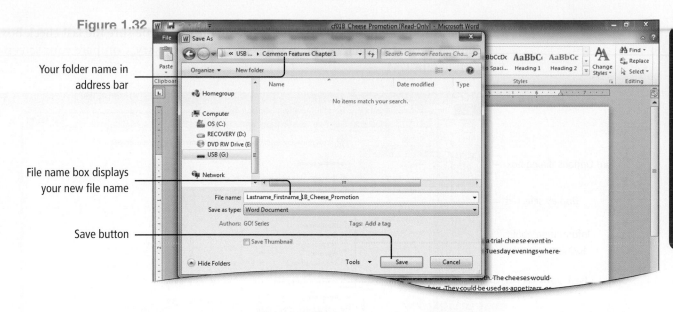

Figure 1.32

Your folder name in address bar

File name box displays your new file name

Save button

12 In the lower right corner of the **Save As** dialog box, click **Save**; or press Enter. Compare your screen with Figure 1.33.

The original document closes, and your new document, based on the original, displays with the name in the title bar.

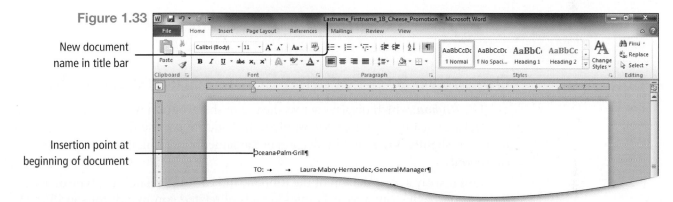

Figure 1.33

New document name in title bar

Insertion point at beginning of document

Objective 8 | Explore Options for an Application

Within each Office application, you can open an *Options dialog box* where you can select program settings and other options and preferences. For example, you can set preferences for viewing and editing files.

Activity 1.08 | Viewing Application Options

1 Click the **File tab** to display **Backstage** view. Under the **Help tab**, click **Options**.

2 In the displayed **Word Options** dialog box, on the left, click **Display**, and then on the right, locate the information under **Always show these formatting marks on the screen**.

When you press Enter, Spacebar, or Tab on your keyboard, characters display to represent these keystrokes. These screen characters do not print, and are referred to as *formatting marks* or *nonprinting characters*.

3 Under **Always show these formatting marks on the screen**, be sure the last check box, **Show all formatting marks**, is selected—select it if necessary. Compare your screen with Figure 1.34.

Figure 1.34

Word Options dialog box

Display selected

Information about formatting marks

Check box selected

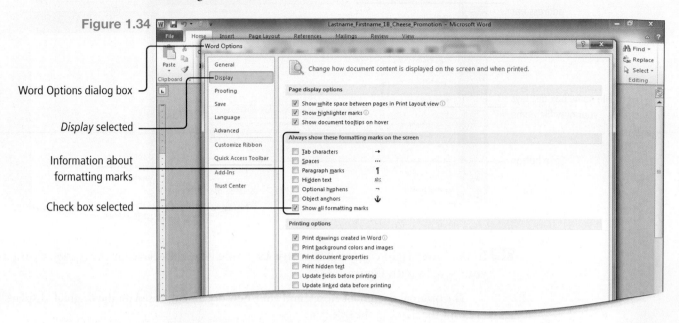

4 In the lower right corner of the dialog box, click **OK**.

Objective 9 | Perform Commands from the Ribbon

The ***Ribbon***, which displays across the top of the program window, groups commands and features in a manner that you would most logically use them. Each Office program's Ribbon is slightly different, but all contain the same three elements: ***tabs***, ***groups***, and ***commands***.

Tabs display across the top of the Ribbon, and each tab relates to a type of activity; for example, laying out a page. Groups are sets of related commands for specific tasks. Commands—instructions to computer programs—are arranged in groups, and might display as a button, a menu, or a box in which you type information.

You can also minimize the Ribbon so only the tab names display. In the minimized Ribbon view, when you click a tab the Ribbon expands to show the groups and commands, and then when you click a command, the Ribbon returns to its minimized view. Most Office users, however, prefer to leave the complete Ribbon in view at all times.

Activity 1.09 | Performing Commands from the Ribbon

1 Take a moment to examine the document on your screen.

This document is a memo from the Executive Chef to the General Manager regarding a new restaurant promotion.

2 On the Ribbon, click the **View tab**. In the **Show group**, if necessary, click to place a check mark in the **Ruler** check box, and then compare your screen with Figure 1.35.

> When working in Word, display the rulers so that you can see how margin settings affect your document and how text aligns. Additionally, if you set a tab stop or an indent, its location is visible on the ruler.

Figure 1.35

Quick Access Toolbar ⎯

Ruler selected ⎯

Button to minimize Ribbon ⎯

Rulers ⎯

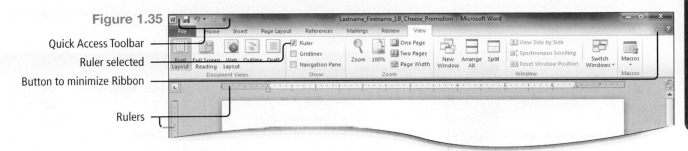

3 On the Ribbon, click the **Home tab**. In the **Paragraph group**, if necessary, click the **Show/Hide** button ¶ so that it glows orange and formatting marks display in your document. Point to the button to display information about the button, and then compare your screen with Figure 1.36.

> When the Show/Hide button is active—glowing orange—formatting marks display. Because formatting marks guide your eye in a document—like a map and road signs guide you along a highway—these marks will display throughout this instruction. Many expert Word users keep these marks displayed while creating documents.

Figure 1.36

Show/Hide button glows orange

Paragraph group

ScreenTip for Show/Hide button

Paragraph mark

Tab mark

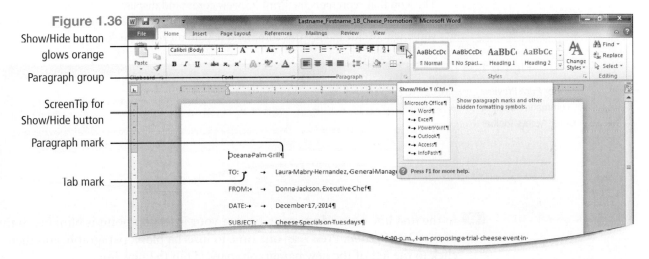

4 In the upper left corner of your screen, above the Ribbon, locate the **Quick Access Toolbar.**

> The *Quick Access Toolbar* contains commands that you use frequently. By default, only the commands Save, Undo, and Redo display, but you can add and delete commands to suit your needs. Possibly the computer at which you are working already has additional commands added to the Quick Access Toolbar.

5 At the end of the Quick Access Toolbar, click the **Customize Quick Access Toolbar** button.

6 Compare your screen with Figure 1.37.

> A list of commands that Office users commonly add to their Quick Access Toolbar displays, including *Open*, *E-mail*, and *Print Preview and Print*. Commands already on the Quick Access Toolbar display a check mark. Commands that you add to the Quick Access Toolbar are always just one click away.
>
> Here you can also display the More Commands dialog box, from which you can select any command from any tab to add to the Quick Access Toolbar.

Figure 1.37

Customize Quick
Access Toolbar

Popular commands to add

Existing commands
checked

Displays *More
Commands* dialog box

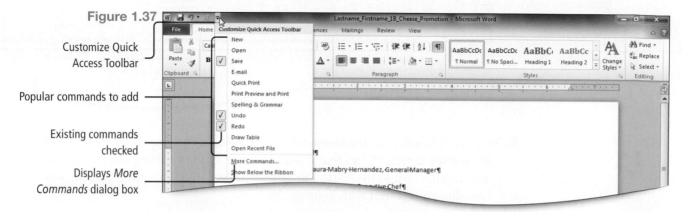

Another Way

Right-click any command on the Ribbon, and then on the shortcut menu, click Add to Quick Access Toolbar.

7 On the displayed list, click **Print Preview and Print**, and then notice that the icon is added to the **Quick Access Toolbar**. Compare your screen with Figure 1.38.

> The icon that represents the Print Preview command displays on the Quick Access Toolbar. Because this is a command that you will use frequently while building Office documents, you might decide to have this command remain on your Quick Access Toolbar.

Figure 1.38

Icon for Print Preview
command added to
Quick Access Toolbar

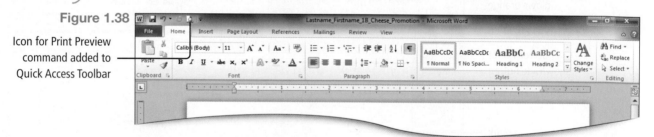

8 In the first line of the document, be sure your insertion point is blinking to the left of the *O* in *Oceana*. Press [Enter] one time to insert a blank paragraph, and then click to the left of the new paragraph mark (¶) in the new line.

> The ***paragraph symbol*** is a formatting mark that displays each time you press [Enter].

9 On the Ribbon, click the **Insert tab**. In the **Illustrations group**, point to the **Clip Art** button to display its ScreenTip.

> Many buttons on the Ribbon have this type of ***enhanced ScreenTip***, which displays more descriptive text than a normal ScreenTip.

10 Click the **Clip Art** button.

> The Clip Art ***task pane*** displays. A task pane is a window within a Microsoft Office application that enables you to enter options for completing a command.

28   **Office** | Chapter 1: Using the Common Features of Microsoft Office 2010

11 In the **Clip Art** task pane, click in the **Search for** box, delete any existing text, and then type **cheese grapes** Under **Results should be:**, click the arrow at the right, if necessary click to *clear* the check mark for **All media types** so that no check boxes are selected, and then click the check box for **Illustrations**. Compare your screen with Figure 1.39.

Figure 1.39

Search term

Blank paragraph

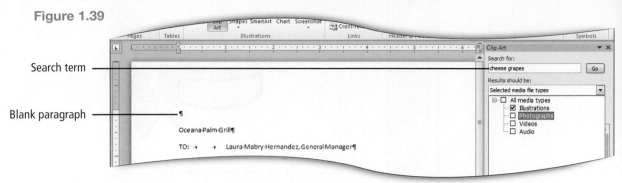

12 Click the **Results should be arrow** again to close the list, and then if necessary, click to place a check mark in the **Include Office.com content** check box.

By selecting this check box, the search for clip art images will include those from Microsoft's online collections of clip art at www.office.com.

13 At the top of the **Clip Art** task pane, click **Go**. Wait a moment for clips to display, and then locate the clip indicated in Figure 1.40.

Figure 1.40

Check box selected

Locate this image

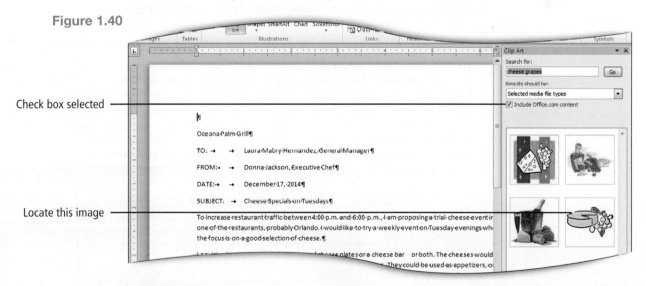

14 Click the image indicated in Figure 1.40 one time to insert it at the insertion point, and then in the upper right corner of the **Clip Art** task pane, click the **Close** ☒ button.

Alert! | If You Cannot Locate the Image

If the image shown in Figure 1.40 is unavailable, select a different cheese image that is appropriate.

---

15 With the image selected—surrounded by a border—on the Ribbon, click the **Home tab**, and then in the **Paragraph group**, click the **Center** button ☰. Click anywhere outside of the bordered picture to *deselect*—cancel the selection. Compare your screen with Figure 1.41.

Figure 1.41

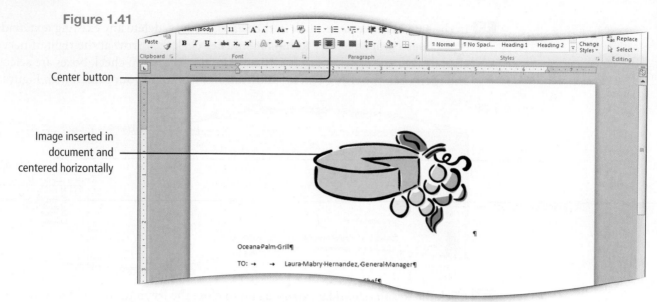

Center button

Image inserted in document and centered horizontally

16 Point to the inserted clip art image, and then watch the last tab of the Ribbon as you click the image one time to select it.

The *Picture Tools* display and an additional tab—the *Format* tab—is added to the Ribbon. The Ribbon adapts to your work and will display additional tabs—referred to as **contextual tabs**—when you need them.

17 On the Ribbon, under **Picture Tools**, click the **Format tab**.

Alert! | **The Size of Groups on the Ribbon Varies with Screen Resolution**

Your monitor's screen resolution might be set higher than the resolution used to capture the figures in this book. In Figure 1.42 below, the resolution is set to 1024 × 768, which is used for all of the figures in this book. Compare that with Figure 1.43 below, where the screen resolution is set to 1280 × 1024.

At a higher resolution, the Ribbon expands some groups to show more commands than are available with a single click, such as those in the Picture Styles group. Or, the group expands to add descriptive text to some buttons, such as those in the Arrange group. Regardless of your screen resolution, all Office commands are available to you. In higher resolutions, you will have a more robust view of the commands.

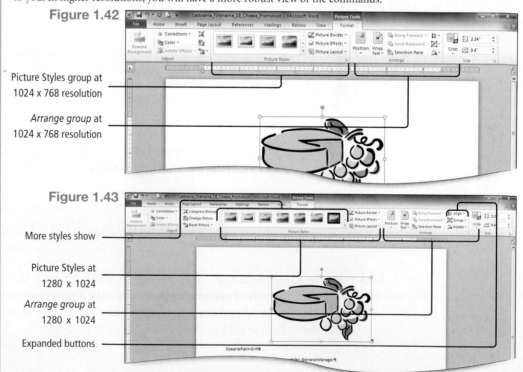

Figure 1.42

Picture Styles group at 1024 x 768 resolution

Arrange group at 1024 x 768 resolution

Figure 1.43

More styles show

Picture Styles at 1280 x 1024

Arrange group at 1280 x 1024

Expanded buttons

---

18 In the **Picture Styles group**, point to the first style to display the ScreenTip *Simple Frame, White*, and notice that the image displays with a white frame.

19 Watch the image as you point to the second picture style, and then to the third, and then to the fourth.

This is *Live Preview*, a technology that shows the result of applying an editing or formatting change as you point to possible results—*before* you actually apply it.

20 In the **Picture Styles group**, click the fourth style—**Drop Shadow Rectangle**—and then click anywhere outside of the image to deselect it. Notice that the Picture Tools no longer display on the Ribbon. Compare your screen with Figure 1.44.

Contextual tabs display only when you need them.

Figure 1.44

Picture Tools no longer display on the Ribbon

Drop Shadow Rectangle picture style applied to image

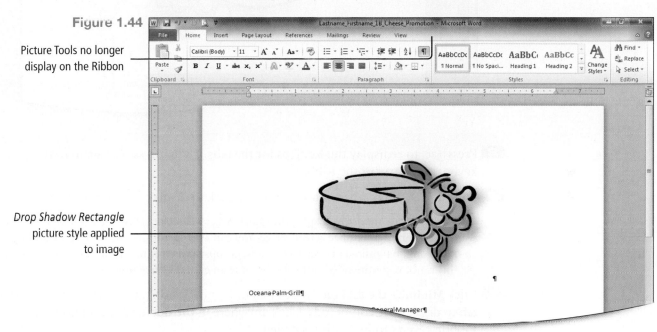

21 In the upper left corner of your screen, on the Quick Access Toolbar, click the **Save** button to save the changes you have made.

Activity 1.10 | Minimizing and Using the Keyboard to Control the Ribbon

Instead of a mouse, some individuals prefer to navigate the Ribbon by using keys on the keyboard. You can activate keyboard control of the Ribbon by pressing the Alt key. You can also minimize the Ribbon to maximize your available screen space.

1 On your keyboard, press the Alt key, and then on the Ribbon, notice that small labels display. Press N to activate the commands on the **Insert tab**, and then compare your screen with Figure 1.45.

Each label represents a *KeyTip*—an indication of the key that you can press to activate the command. For example, on the Insert tab, you can press F to activate the Clip Art task pane.

Figure 1.45

KeyTips indicate that
keyboard control
of the Ribbon is active

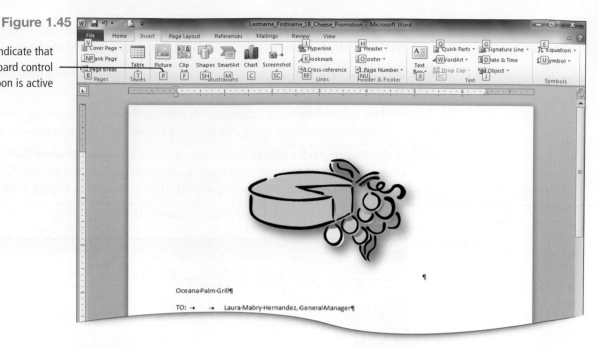

2 Press Esc to redisplay the KeyTips for the tabs. Then, press Alt again to turn off keyboard control of the Ribbon.

3 Point to any tab on the Ribbon and right-click to display a shortcut menu.

Here you can choose to display the Quick Access Toolbar below the Ribbon or minimize the Ribbon to maximize screen space. You can also customize the Ribbon by adding, removing, renaming, or reordering tabs, groups, and commands on the Ribbon, although this is not recommended until you become an expert Office user.

Another Way

Double-click the active tab; or, click the Minimize the Ribbon button at the right end of the Ribbon.

4 Click **Minimize the Ribbon**. Notice that only the Ribbon tabs display. Click the **Home tab** to display the commands. Click anywhere in the document, and notice that the Ribbon reverts to its minimized view.

Another Way

Double-click any tab to redisplay the full Ribbon.

5 Right-click any Ribbon tab, and then click **Minimize the Ribbon** again to turn the minimize feature off.

Most expert Office users prefer to have the full Ribbon display at all times.

6 Point to any tab on the Ribbon, and then on your mouse device, roll the mouse wheel. Notice that different tabs become active as your roll the mouse wheel.

You can make a tab active by using this technique, instead of clicking the tab.

Objective 10 | Apply Formatting in Office Programs

Formatting is the process of establishing the overall appearance of text, graphics, and pages in an Office file—for example, in a Word document.

Activity 1.11 | Formatting and Viewing Pages

In this activity, you will practice common formatting techniques used in Office applications.

1 On the Ribbon, click the **Insert tab**, and then in the **Header & Footer group**, click the **Footer** button.

Another Way

On the Design tab, in the Insert group, click Quick Parts, click Field, and then under Field names, click FileName.

2 At the top of the displayed gallery, under **Built-In**, click **Blank**. At the bottom of your document, with *Type text* highlighted in blue, using your own name type the file name of this document **Lastname_Firstname_1B_Cheese_Promotion** and then compare your screen with Figure 1.46.

> Header & Footer Tools are added to the Ribbon. A **footer** is a reserved area for text or graphics that displays at the bottom of each page in a document. Likewise, a **header** is a reserved area for text or graphics that displays at the top of each page in a document. When the footer (or header) area is active, the document area is inactive (dimmed).

Figure 1.46

Design tab added

Header & Footer Tools active

Document area inactive (dimmed) when footer area is active

Close Header and Footer button

Your file name

Footer area displays

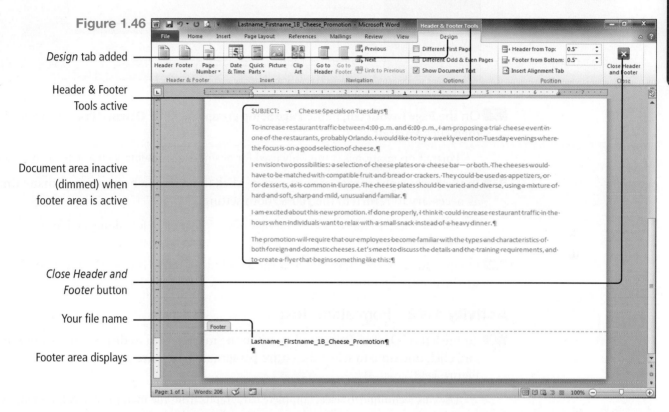

3 On the Ribbon, on the **Design tab**, in the **Close group**, click the **Close Header and Footer** button.

4 On the Ribbon, click the **Page Layout tab**. In the **Page Setup group**, click the **Orientation** button, and notice that two orientations display—*Portrait* and *Landscape*. Click **Landscape**.

> In **portrait orientation**, the paper is taller than it is wide. In **landscape orientation**, the paper is wider than it is tall.

5 In the lower right corner of the screen, locate the **Zoom control** buttons.

> To **zoom** means to increase or decrease the viewing area. You can zoom in to look closely at a section of a document, and then zoom out to see an entire page on the screen. You can also zoom to view multiple pages on the screen.

6 Drag the **Zoom slider** to the left until you have zoomed to approximately *60%*. Compare your screen with Figure 1.47.

Figure 1.47

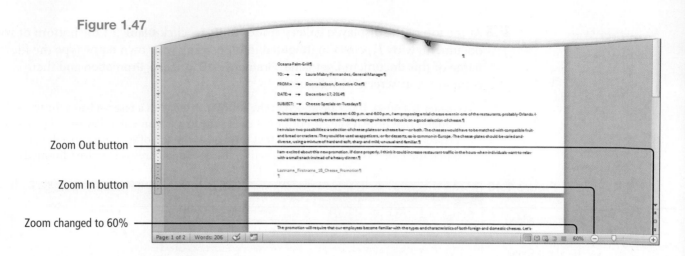

Zoom Out button

Zoom In button

Zoom changed to 60%

7 On the **Page Layout tab**, in the **Page Setup group**, click the **Orientation** button, and then click **Portrait**.

Portrait orientation is commonly used for business documents such as letters and memos.

8 In the lower right corner of your screen, click the **Zoom In** button ⊕ as many times as necessary to return to the **100%** zoom setting.

Use the zoom feature to adjust the view of your document for editing and for your viewing comfort.

9 On the Quick Access Toolbar, click the **Save** button 🖫 to save the changes you have made to your document.

Activity 1.12 | Formatting Text

1 To the left of *Oceana Palm Grill*, point in the margin area to display the 🖈 pointer and click one time to select the entire paragraph. Compare your screen with Figure 1.48.

Use this technique to select complete paragraphs from the margin area. Additionally, with this technique you can drag downward to select multiple-line paragraphs—which is faster and more efficient than dragging through text.

Figure 1.48

Paragraph selected

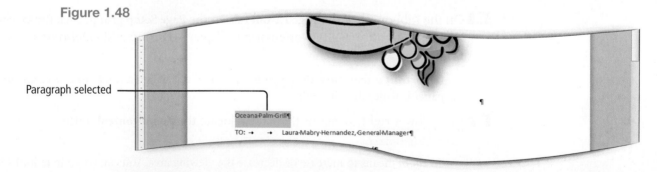

2 On the Ribbon, click the **Home tab**, and then in the **Paragraph group**, click the **Center** button ≡ to center the paragraph.

Alignment refers to the placement of paragraph text relative to the left and right margins. *Center alignment* refers to text that is centered horizontally between the left and right margins. You can also align text at the left margin, which is the default alignment for text in Word, or at the right margin.

3 On the **Home tab**, in the **Font group**, click the **Font button arrow** [Calibri (Body) ▾]. At the top of the list, point to **Cambria**, and as you do so, notice that the selected text previews in the Cambria font.

> A *font* is a set of characters with the same design and shape. The default font in a Word document is Calibri, which is a *sans serif* font—a font design with no lines or extensions on the ends of characters.
>
> The Cambria font is a *serif* font—a font design that includes small line extensions on the ends of the letters to guide the eye in reading from left to right.
>
> The list of fonts displays as a gallery showing potential results. For example, in the Font gallery, you can see the actual design and format of each font as it would look if applied to text.

4 Point to several other fonts and observe the effect on the selected text. Then, at the top of the **Font** gallery, under **Theme Fonts**, click **Cambria**.

> A *theme* is a predesigned set of colors, fonts, lines, and fill effects that look good together and that can be applied to your entire document or to specific items.
>
> A theme combines two sets of fonts—one for text and one for headings. In the default Office theme, Cambria is the suggested font for headings.

5 With the paragraph *Oceana Palm Grill* still selected, on the **Home tab**, in the **Font group**, click the **Font Size button arrow** [11 ▾], point to **36**, and then notice how Live Preview displays the text in the font size to which you are pointing. Compare your screen with Figure 1.49.

Figure 1.49

Font Size button

Font button

Font Size list

Pointing to 36 pt font size

Oceana Palm Grill centered,
Cambria font applied

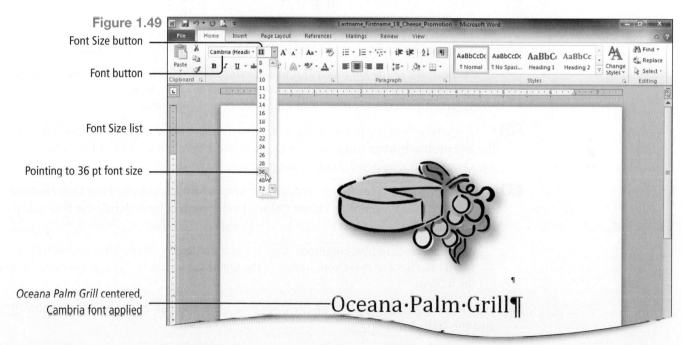

6 On the displayed list of font sizes, click **20**.

> Fonts are measured in *points*, with one point equal to 1/72 of an inch. A higher point size indicates a larger font size. Headings and titles are often formatted by using a larger font size. The word *point* is abbreviated as *pt*.

7 With *Oceana Palm Grill* still selected, on the **Home tab**, in the **Font group**, click the **Font Color button arrow** [A ▾]. Under **Theme Colors**, in the seventh column, click the last color—**Olive Green, Accent 3, Darker 50%**. Click anywhere to deselect the text.

8 To the left of *TO:*, point in the left margin area to display the ⬧ pointer, hold down the left mouse button, and then drag down to select the four memo headings. Compare your screen with Figure 1.50.

Use this technique to select complete paragraphs from the margin area—dragging downward to select multiple-line paragraphs—which is faster and more efficient than dragging through text.

Figure 1.50

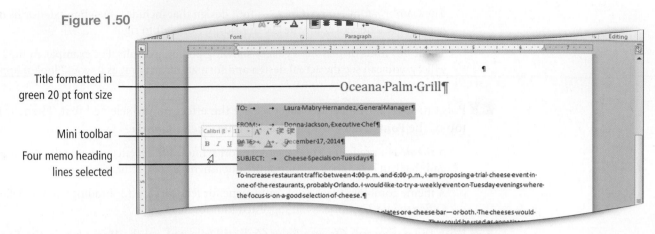

Title formatted in green 20 pt font size

Mini toolbar

Four memo heading lines selected

9 With the four paragraphs selected, on the Mini toolbar, click the **Font Color** button ◢A⧫◣, which now displays a dark green bar instead of a red bar.

The font color button retains its most recently used color—Olive Green, Accent 3, Darker 50%. As you progress in your study of Microsoft Office, you will use other buttons that behave in this manner; that is, they retain their most recently used format.

The purpose of the Mini toolbar is to place commonly used commands close to text or objects that you select. By selecting a command on the Mini toolbar, you reduce the distance that you must move your mouse to access a command.

10 Click anywhere in the paragraph that begins *To increase*, and then ***triple-click***—click the left mouse button three times—to select the entire paragraph. If the entire paragraph is not selected, click in the paragraph and begin again.

11 With the entire paragraph selected, on the Mini toolbar, click the **Font Color button arrow** ◢A⧫◣, and then under **Theme Colors**, in the sixth column, click the first color—**Red, Accent 2**.

It is convenient to have commonly used commands display on the Mini toolbar so that you do not have to move your mouse to the top of the screen to access the command from the Ribbon.

12 Select the text *TO:* and then on the displayed Mini toolbar, click the **Bold** button ◢B◣ and the **Italic** button ◢I◣.

Font styles include bold, italic, and underline. Font styles emphasize text and are a visual cue to draw the reader's eye to important text.

13 On the displayed Mini toolbar, click the **Italic** button ◢I◣ again to turn off the Italic formatting. Notice that the Italic button no longer glows orange.

A button that behaves in this manner is referred to as a ***toggle button***, which means it can be turned on by clicking it once, and then turned off by clicking it again.

14 With *TO:* still selected, on the Mini toolbar, click the **Format Painter** button ◈. Then, move your mouse under the word *Laura*, and notice the ▣Ⅰ mouse pointer. Compare your screen with Figure 1.51.

> You can use the ***Format Painter*** to copy the formatting of specific text or of a paragraph and then apply it in other locations in your document.
>
> The pointer takes the shape of a paintbrush, and contains the formatting information from the paragraph where the insertion point is positioned. Information about the Format Painter and how to turn it off displays in the status bar.

Figure 1.51

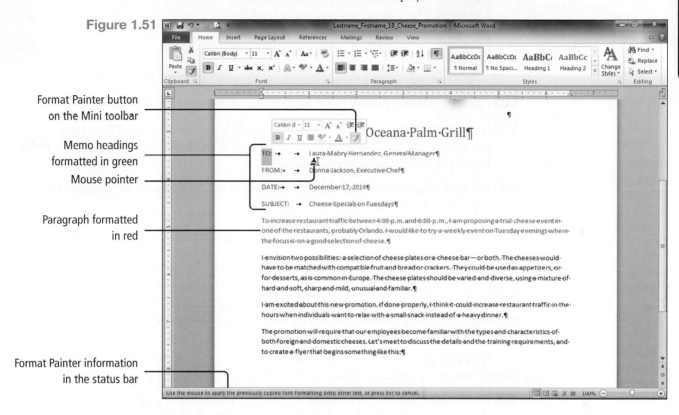

Format Painter button on the Mini toolbar

Memo headings formatted in green

Mouse pointer

Paragraph formatted in red

Format Painter information in the status bar

15 With the ▣Ⅰ pointer, drag to select the text *FROM:* and notice that the Bold formatting is applied. Then, point to the selected text *FROM:* and on the Mini toolbar, *double-click* the **Format Painter** button ◈.

16 Select the text *DATE:* to copy the Bold formatting, and notice that the pointer retains the ▣Ⅰ shape.

> When you *double-click* the Format Painter button, the Format Painter feature remains active until you either click the Format Painter button again, or press [Esc] to cancel it—as indicated on the status bar.

17 With Format Painter still active, select the text *SUBJECT:*, and then on the Ribbon, on the **Home tab**, in the **Clipboard group**, notice that the **Format Painter** button ◈ is glowing orange, indicating that it is active. Compare your screen with Figure 1.52.

Figure 1.52

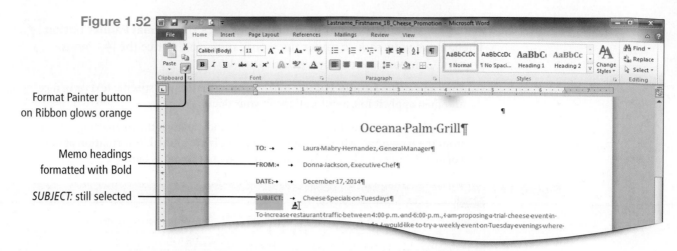

Format Painter button on Ribbon glows orange

Memo headings formatted with Bold

SUBJECT: still selected

18 Click the **Format Painter** button on the Ribbon to turn the command off.

19 In the paragraph that begins *To increase*, triple-click again to select the entire paragraph. On the displayed Mini toolbar, click the **Bold** button and the **Italic** button . Click anywhere to deselect.

20 On the Quick Access Toolbar, click the **Save** button to save the changes you have made to your document.

Activity 1.13 | Using the Office Clipboard to Cut, Copy, and Paste

The *Office Clipboard* is a temporary storage area that holds text or graphics that you select and then cut or copy. When you *copy* text or graphics, a copy is placed on the Office Clipboard and the original text or graphic remains in place. When you *cut* text or graphics, a copy is placed on the Office Clipboard, and the original text or graphic is removed—cut—from the document.

After cutting or copying, the contents of the Office Clipboard are available for you to *paste*—insert—in a new location in the current document, or into another Office file.

1 Hold down Ctrl and press Home to move to the beginning of your document, and then take a moment to study the table in Figure 1.53, which describes similar keyboard shortcuts with which you can navigate quickly in a document.

To Move	Press
To the beginning of a document	Ctrl + Home
To the end of a document	Ctrl + End
To the beginning of a line	Home
To the end of a line	End
To the beginning of the previous word	Ctrl + ←
To the beginning of the next word	Ctrl + →
To the beginning of the current word (if insertion point is in the middle of a word)	Ctrl + ←
To the beginning of a paragraph	Ctrl + ↑
To the beginning of the next paragraph	Ctrl + ↓
To the beginning of the current paragraph (if insertion point is in the middle of a paragraph)	Ctrl + ↑
Up one screen	PgUp
Down one screen	PageDown

Figure 1.53

Another Way

Right-click the selection, and then click Copy on the shortcut menu; or, use the keyboard shortcut Ctrl + C.

2 To the left of *Oceana Palm Grill*, point in the left margin area to display the 🔄 pointer, and then click one time to select the entire paragraph. On the **Home tab**, in the **Clipboard group**, click the **Copy** button 📋.

> Because anything that you select and then copy—or cut—is placed on the Office Clipboard, the Copy command and the Cut command display in the Clipboard group of commands on the Ribbon.

> There is no visible indication that your copied selection has been placed on the Office Clipboard.

3 On the **Home tab**, in the **Clipboard group**, to the right of the group name *Clipboard*, click the **Dialog Box Launcher** button 🔲, and then compare your screen with Figure 1.54.

> The Clipboard task pane displays with your copied text. In any Ribbon group, the ***Dialog Box Launcher*** displays either a dialog box or a task pane related to the group of commands.

> It is not necessary to display the Office Clipboard in this manner, although sometimes it is useful to do so. The Office Clipboard can hold 24 items.

Figure 1.54

Copy button

Dialog Box Launcher in Clipboard group

Clipboard task pane displays

Selected text on the Office Clipboard

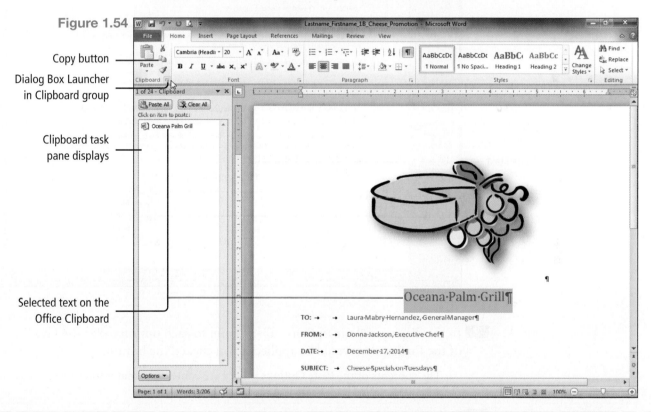

4 In the upper right corner of the **Clipboard** task pane, click the **Close** button ❌.

Another Way

Right-click, on the shortcut menu under Paste Options, click the desired option button.

5 Press Ctrl + End to move to the end of your document. Press Enter one time to create a new blank paragraph. On the **Home tab**, in the **Clipboard group**, point to the **Paste** button, and then click the *upper* portion of this split button.

> The Paste command pastes the most recently copied item on the Office Clipboard at the insertion point location. If you click the lower portion of the Paste button, a gallery of Paste Options displays.

6 Click the **Paste Options** button 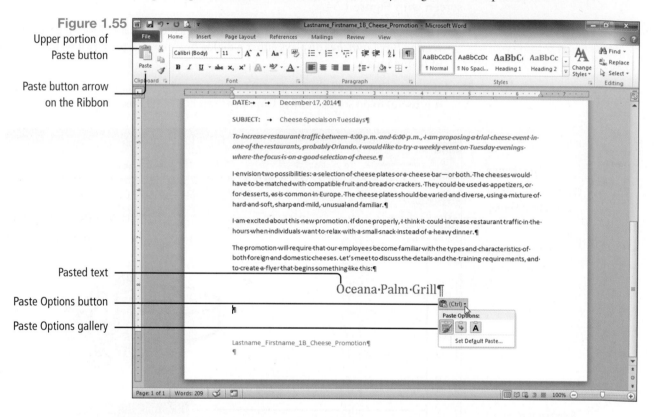 that displays below the pasted text as shown in Figure 1.55.

> Here you can view and apply various formatting options for pasting your copied or cut text. Typically you will click Paste on the Ribbon and paste the item in its original format. If you want some other format for the pasted item, you can do so from the *Paste Options gallery*.
>
> The Paste Options gallery provides a Live Preview of the various options for changing the format of the pasted item with a single click. The Paste Options gallery is available in three places: on the Ribbon by clicking the lower portion of the Paste button—the Paste button arrow; from the Paste Options button that displays below the pasted item following the paste operation; or, on the shortcut menu if you right-click the pasted item.

Figure 1.55

Upper portion of Paste button

Paste button arrow on the Ribbon

Pasted text

Paste Options button

Paste Options gallery

7 In the displayed **Paste Options** gallery, *point* to each option to see the Live Preview of the format that would be applied if you clicked the button.

> The contents of the Paste Options gallery are contextual; that is, they change based on what you copied and where you are pasting.

8 Press [Esc] to close the gallery; the button will remain displayed until you take some other screen action.

Another Way

On the Home tab, in the Clipboard group, click the Cut button; or, use the keyboard shortcut [Ctrl] + [X].

9 Press [Ctrl] + [Home] to move to the top of the document, and then click the **cheese image** one time to select it. While pointing to the selected image, right-click, and then on the shortcut menu, click **Cut**.

> Recall that the Cut command cuts—removes—the selection from the document and places it on the Office Clipboard.

10 Press [Del] one time to remove the blank paragraph from the top of the document, and then press [Ctrl] + [End] to move to the end of the document.

11 With the insertion point blinking in the blank paragraph at the end of the document, right-click, and notice that the **Paste Options** gallery displays on the shortcut menu. Compare your screen with Figure 1.56.

Figure 1.56

Paste Options on shortcut menu

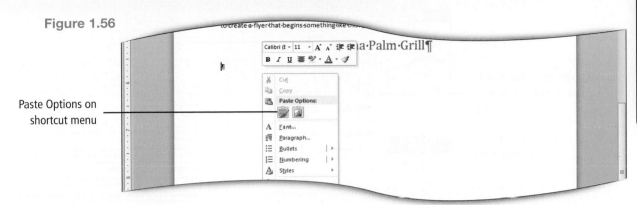

12 On the shortcut menu, under **Paste Options**, click the first button—**Keep Source Formatting** .

13 Click the picture to select it. On the **Home tab**, in the **Paragraph group**, click the **Center** button .

14 Above the cheese picture, click to position the insertion point at the end of the word *Grill*, press [Spacebar] one time, and then type **Tuesday Cheese Tastings** Compare your screen with Figure 1.57.

Figure 1.57

Heading

Picture inserted and centered

Activity 1.14 | Viewing Print Preview and Printing a Word Document

1 Press [Ctrl] + [Home] to move to the top of your document. Select the text *Oceana Palm Grill*, and then replace the selected text by typing **Memo**

2 Display **Backstage** view, on the right, click **Properties**, and then click **Show Document Panel**. Replace the existing author name with your first and last name. In the **Subject** box, type your course name and section number, and then in the **Keywords** box, type **cheese promotion** and then **Close** the **Document Information Panel**.

Another Way

Press ⌃ Ctrl + F2 to
display Print Preview.

3 On the Quick Access Toolbar, click **Save** 🖫 to save the changes you have made to your document.

4 On the Quick Access Toolbar, click the **Print Preview** button 🔍 that you added. Compare your screen with Figure 1.58.

Figure 1.58

Memo typed

If no printer is attached to your system, OneNote is the default printer

Print tab active in Backstage view

Print Preview (if you have a non-color printer as your default printer, the preview may display in shades of gray)

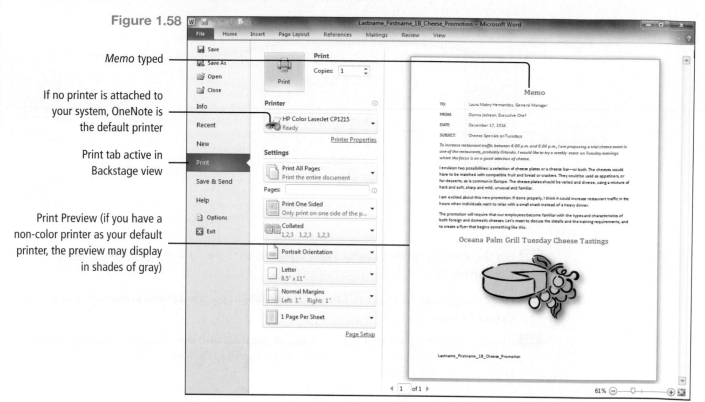

5 Examine the **Print Preview**. Under **Settings**, notice that in **Backstage** view, several of the same commands that are available on the Page Layout tab of the Ribbon also display.

For convenience, common adjustments to Page Layout display here, so that you can make last-minute adjustments without closing Backstage view.

6 If you need to make any corrections, click the Home tab to return to the document and make any necessary changes.

It is good practice to examine the Print Preview before printing or submitting your work electronically. Then, make any necessary corrections, re-save, and redisplay Print Preview.

7 If you are directed to do so, click Print to print the document; or, above the Info tab, click Close, and then submit your file electronically according to the directions provided by your instructor.

If you click the Print button, Backstage view closes and the Word window redisplays.

8 On the Quick Access Toolbar, point to the **Print Preview icon** 🔍 you placed there, right-click, and then click **Remove from Quick Access Toolbar**.

If you are working on your own computer and you want to do so, you can leave the icon on the toolbar; in a lab setting, you should return the software to its original settings.

9 At the right end of the title bar, click the program **Close** button ⊠.

10 If a message displays asking if you want the text on the Clipboard to be available after you quit Word, click **No**.

> This message most often displays if you have copied some type of image to the Clipboard. If you click Yes, the items on the Clipboard will remain for you to use.

Objective 11 | Use the Microsoft Office 2010 Help System

Within each Office program, the Help feature provides information about all of the program's features and displays step-by-step instructions for performing many tasks.

Activity 1.15 | Using the Microsoft Office 2010 Help System in Excel

In this activity, you will use the Microsoft Help feature to find information about formatting numbers in Excel.

Another Way

Press F1 to display Help.

1 **Start** the **Microsoft Excel 2010** program. In the upper right corner of your screen, click the **Microsoft Excel Help** button 🔘.

2 In the **Excel Help** window, click in the white box in upper left corner, type **formatting numbers** and then click **Search** or press Enter.

3 On the list of results, click **Display numbers as currency**. Compare your screen with Figure 1.59.

Figure 1.59

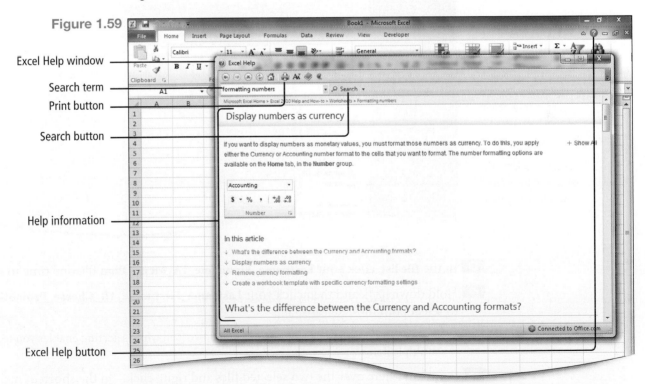

Excel Help window
Search term
Print button
Search button
Help information
Excel Help button

4 If you want to do so, on the toolbar at the top of the **Excel Help** window, click the Print 🖶 button to print a copy of this information for your reference.

5 On the title bar of the Excel Help window, click the **Close** button ![x]. On the right side of the Microsoft Excel title bar, click the **Close** button ![x] to close Excel.

Objective 12 | Compress Files

A *compressed file* is a file that has been reduced in size. Compressed files take up less storage space and can be transferred to other computers faster than uncompressed files. You can also combine a group of files into one compressed folder, which makes it easier to share a group of files.

Activity 1.16 | Compressing Files

In this activity, you will combine the two files you created in this chapter into one compressed file.

1 On the Windows taskbar, click the **Start** button ![icon], and then on the right, click **Computer**.

2 On the left, in the **navigation pane**, click the location of your two files from this chapter—your USB flash drive or other location—and display the folder window for your **Common Features Chapter 1** folder. Compare your screen with Figure 1.60.

Figure 1.60

Address bar displays path —

Your chapter files in file list (your name displays) —

Folder window for your chapter folder —

Location selected in navigation pane (your location may vary) —

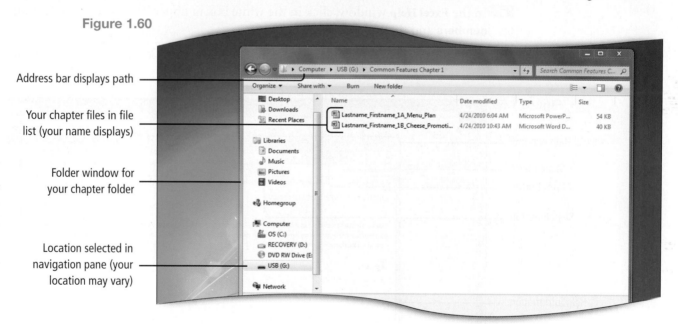

3 In the **file list**, click your **Lastname_Firstname_1A_Menu_Plan** file one time to select it.

4 Hold down (Ctrl), and then click your **Lastname_Firstname_1B_Cheese_Promotion** file to select both files. Release (Ctrl).

In any Windows-based program, holding down (Ctrl) while selecting enables you to select multiple items.

5 Point anywhere over the two selected files and right-click. On the shortcut menu, point to **Send to**, and then compare your screen with Figure 1.61.

Figure 1.61

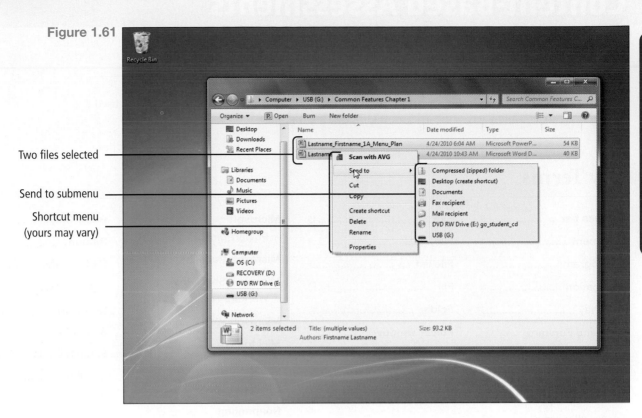

Two files selected

Send to submenu

Shortcut menu
(yours may vary)

6 On the shortcut submenu, click **Compressed (zipped) folder**.

Windows creates a compressed folder containing a *copy* of each of the selected files. The folder name is the name of the file or folder to which you were pointing, and is selected—highlighted in blue—so that you can rename it.

7 Using your own name, type **Lastname_Firstname_Common_Features_Ch1** and press Enter.

The compressed folder is now ready to attach to an e-mail or share in some other electronic format.

8 **Close** ✕ the folder window. If directed to do so by your instructor, submit your compressed folder electronically.

More Knowledge | Extracting Compressed Files

Extract means to decompress, or pull out, files from a compressed form. When you extract a file, an uncompressed copy is placed in the folder that you specify. The original file remains in the compressed folder.

End **You have completed Project 1B** ——————————

Content-Based Assessments

Summary

In this chapter, you used Windows Explorer to navigate the Windows file structure. You also used features that are common across the Microsoft Office 2010 programs.

Key Terms

Content-Based Assessments

Matching

Match each term in the second column with its correct definition in the first column by writing the letter of the term on the blank line in front of the correct definition.

_____ 1. A collection of information stored on a computer under a single name.

_____ 2. A container in which you store files.

_____ 3. A folder within a folder.

_____ 4. The program that displays the files and folders on your computer.

_____ 5. The Windows menu that is the main gateway to your computer.

_____ 6. In Windows 7, a window that displays the contents of the current folder, library, or device, and contains helpful parts so that you can navigate.

_____ 7. In Windows, a collection of items, such as files and folders, assembled from various locations that might be on your computer.

_____ 8. The bar at the top of a folder window with which you can navigate to a different folder or library, or go back to a previous one.

_____ 9. An instruction to a computer program that carries out an action.

_____ 10. Small pictures that represent a program, a file, a folder, or an object.

_____ 11. A set of instructions that a computer uses to perform a specific task.

_____ 12. A spreadsheet program used to calculate numbers and create charts.

_____ 13. The user interface that groups commands on tabs at the top of the program window.

_____ 14. A bar at the top of the program window displaying the current file and program name.

_____ 15. One or more keys pressed to perform a task that would otherwise require a mouse.

A Address bar
B Command
C File
D Folder
E Folder window
F Icons
G Keyboard shortcut
H Library
I Microsoft Excel
J Program
K Ribbon
L Start menu
M Subfolder
N Title bar
O Windows Explorer

Multiple Choice

Circle the correct answer.

1. A small toolbar with frequently used commands that displays when selecting text or objects is the:
   A. Quick Access Toolbar
   B. Mini toolbar
   C. Document toolbar

2. In Office 2010, a centralized space for file management tasks is:
   A. a task pane
   B. a dialog box
   C. Backstage view

3. The commands Save, Save As, Open, and Close in Backstage view are located:
   A. above the Backstage tabs
   B. below the Backstage tabs
   C. under the screen thumbnail

4. The tab in Backstage view that displays information about the current file is the:
   A. Recent tab
   B. Info tab
   C. Options tab

5. Details about a file, including the title, author name, subject, and keywords are known as:
   A. document properties
   B. formatting marks
   C. KeyTips

6. An Office feature that displays a list of potential results is:
   A. Live Preview
   B. a contextual tab
   C. a gallery

7. A type of formatting emphasis applied to text such as bold, italic, and underline, is called:
   A. a font style **B.** a KeyTip **C.** a tag

8. A technology showing the result of applying formatting as you point to possible results is called:
   A. Live Preview **B.** Backstage view **C.** gallery view

9. A temporary storage area that holds text or graphics that you select and then cut or copy is the:
   A. paste options gallery **B.** ribbon **C.** Office clipboard

10. A file that has been reduced in size is:
   A. a compressed file **B.** an extracted file **C.** a PDF file

Creating a Worksheet and Charting Data

Kwest/Shutterstock

In This Chapter

In this chapter, you will use Microsoft Excel 2010 to create and analyze data organized into columns and rows. After entering data in a worksheet, you can perform calculations, analyze the data to make logical decisions, and create charts.

In this chapter, you will create and modify Excel workbooks. You will practice the basics of worksheet design, create a footer, enter and edit data in a worksheet, chart data, and then save, preview, and print workbooks. You will also construct formulas for mathematical operations.

The projects in this chapter relate to **Texas Spectrum Wireless**, which provides accessories and software for all major brands of cell phones, smart phones, PDAs, mp3 players, and portable computers. The company sells thousands of unique products in their retail stores, which are located throughout Texas and the southern United States. They also sell thousands of items each year through their Web site, and offer free shipping and returns to their customers. The company takes pride in offering unique categories of accessories such as waterproof and ruggedized gear.

Project 1A Sales Report with Embedded Column Chart and Sparklines

my i tlab
Project 1A Training

Project Activities

In Activities 1.01 through 1.16, you will create an Excel worksheet for Roslyn Thomas, the President of Texas Spectrum Wireless. The worksheet displays the first quarter sales of wireless accessories for the current year, and includes a chart to visually represent the data. Your completed worksheet will look similar to Figure 1.1.

Project Files

For Project 1A, you will need the following file:

New blank Excel workbook

You will save your workbook as:

Lastname_Firstname_1A_Quarterly_Sales

Project Results

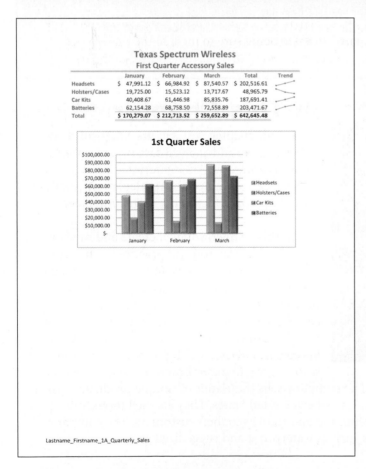

Figure 1.1
Project 1A Quarterly Sales

Objective 1 | Create, Save, and Navigate an Excel Workbook

On startup, Excel displays a new blank ***workbook***—the Excel document that stores your data—which contains one or more pages called a ***worksheet***. A worksheet—or ***spreadsheet***—is stored in a workbook, and is formatted as a pattern of uniformly spaced horizontal rows and vertical columns. The intersection of a column and a row forms a box referred to as a ***cell***.

Activity 1.01 | Starting Excel and Naming and Saving a Workbook

1 **Start** Excel. In the lower right corner of the window, if necessary, click the Normal button 🔲, and then to the right, locate the zoom—magnification—level.

> Your zoom level should be 100%, although some figures in this textbook may be shown at a higher zoom level.

Another Way

Use the keyboard shortcut F12 to display the Save As dialog box.

2 In the upper left corner of your screen, click the **File tab** to display **Backstage** view, click **Save As**, and then in the **Save As** dialog box, navigate to the location where you will store your workbooks for this chapter.

3 In your storage location, create a new folder named **Excel Chapter 1** Open the new folder to display its folder window, and then in the **File name** box, notice that *Book1* displays as the default file name.

4 In the **File name** box, click *Book1* to select it, and then using your own name, type **Lastname_Firstname_1A_Quarterly_Sales** being sure to include the underscore (Shift + -) instead of spaces between words. Compare your screen with Figure 1.2.

Figure 1.2

Path to your new *Excel Chapter 1* folder in address bar (yours may vary)

File name with your name and underscores between words

Save button

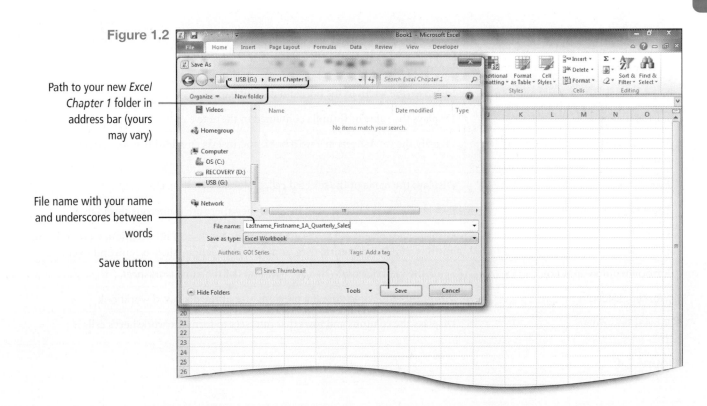

5 Click **Save**. Compare your screen with Figure 1.3, and then take a moment to study the Excel window parts in the table in Figure 1.4.

Figure 1.3

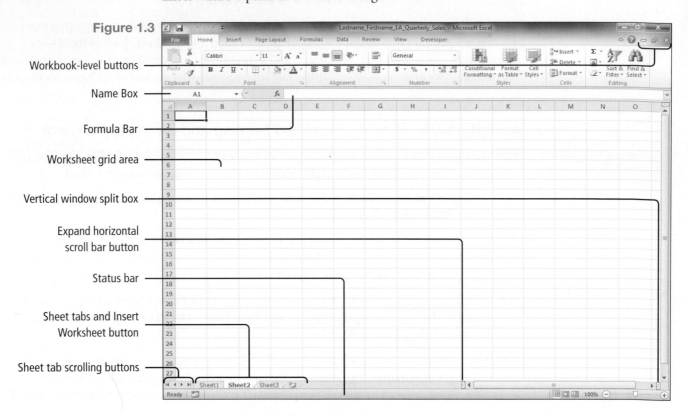

Workbook-level buttons
Name Box
Formula Bar
Worksheet grid area
Vertical window split box
Expand horizontal scroll bar button
Status bar
Sheet tabs and Insert Worksheet button
Sheet tab scrolling buttons

Parts of the Excel Window

Screen Part	Description
Expand horizontal scroll bar button	Increases the width of the horizontal scroll bar.
Formula Bar	Displays the value or formula contained in the active cell; also permits entry or editing.
Sheet tabs and Insert Worksheet button	Identify the worksheets in a workbook and inserts an additional worksheet.
Name Box	Displays the name of the selected cell, table, chart, or object.
Sheet tab scrolling buttons	Display sheet tabs that are not in view when there are numerous sheet tabs.
Status bar	Displays the current cell mode, page number, worksheet information, view and zoom buttons, and for numerical data, common calculations such as Sum and Average.
Vertical window split box	Splits the worksheet into two vertical views of the same worksheet.
Workbook-level buttons	Minimize, close, or restore the previous size of the displayed workbook.
Worksheet grid area	Displays the columns and rows that intersect to form the worksheet's cells.

Figure 1.4

Activity 1.02 | Navigating a Worksheet and a Workbook

1 Take a moment to study Figure 1.5 and the table in Figure 1.6 to become familiar with the Excel workbook window.

Figure 1.5

Expand Formula Bar button
Lettered column headings
Select All box
Numbered row headings
Excel pointer
Horizontal window split box

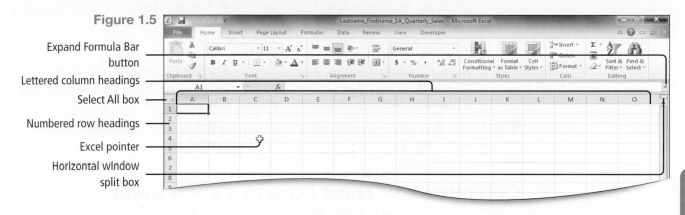

Excel Workbook Window Elements

Workbook Window Element	Description
Excel pointer	Displays the pointer in Excel.
Expand Formula Bar button	Increases the height of the Formula Bar to display lengthy cell content.
Horizontal window split box	Splits the worksheet into two horizontal views of the same worksheet.
Lettered column headings	Indicate the column letter.
Numbered row headings	Indicate the row number.
Select All box	Selects all the cells in a worksheet.

Figure 1.6

2 In the lower right corner of the screen, in the horizontal scroll bar, click the **right scroll arrow** one time to shift **column A** out of view.

A *column* is a vertical group of cells in a worksheet. Beginning with the first letter of the alphabet, *A*, a unique letter identifies each column—this is called the *column heading*. Clicking one of the horizontal scroll bar arrows shifts the window either left or right one column at a time.

3 Point to the **right scroll arrow**, and then hold down the left mouse button until the columns begin to scroll rapidly to the right; release the mouse button when you begin to see pairs of letters as the column headings.

4 Slowly drag the horizontal scroll box to the left, and notice that just above the scroll box, ScreenTips with the column letters display as you drag. Drag the horizontal scroll box left or right—or click the left or right scroll arrow—as necessary to position **column Z** near the center of your screen.

Column headings after column Z use two letters starting with AA, AB, and so on through ZZ. After that, columns begin with three letters beginning with AAA. This pattern provides 16,384 columns. The last column is XFD.

5 In the lower left portion of your screen, click the **Sheet2 tab**.

The second worksheet displays and is the active sheet. Column A displays at the left.

6 In the vertical scroll bar, click the **down scroll arrow** one time to move **Row 1** out of view.

> A *row* is a horizontal group of cells. Beginning with number 1, a unique number identifies each row—this is the *row heading*, located at the left side of the worksheet. A single worksheet has 1,048,576 rows.

7 In the lower left corner, click the **Sheet1 tab**.

> The first worksheet in the workbook becomes the active worksheet. By default, new workbooks contain three worksheets. When you save a workbook, the worksheets are contained within it and do not have separate file names.

8 Use the skills you just practiced to scroll horizontally to display **column A**, and if necessary, **row 1**.

Objective 2 | Enter Data in a Worksheet

Cell content, which is anything you type in a cell, can be one of two things: either a *constant value*—referred to simply as a *value*—or a *formula*. A formula is an equation that performs mathematical calculations on values in your worksheet. The most commonly used values are *text values* and *number values*, but a value can also include a date or a time of day.

Activity 1.03 | Entering Text and Using AutoComplete

A text value, also referred to as a *label*, usually provides information about number values in other worksheet cells. For example, a title such as First Quarter Accessory Sales gives the reader an indication that the data in the worksheet relates to information about sales of accessories during the three-month period January through March.

1 Click the **Sheet1 tab** to make it the active sheet. Point to and then click the cell at the intersection of **column A** and **row 1** to make it the *active cell*—the cell is outlined in black and ready to accept data.

> The intersecting column letter and row number form the *cell reference*—also called the *cell address*. When a cell is active, its column letter and row number are highlighted. The cell reference of the selected cell, *A1*, displays in the Name Box.

2 With cell **A1** as the active cell, type the worksheet title **Texas Spectrum Wireless** and then press Enter. Compare your screen with Figure 1.7.

> Text or numbers in a cell are referred to as *data*. You must confirm the data you type in a cell by pressing Enter or by some other keyboard movement, such as pressing Tab or an arrow key. Pressing Enter moves the selection to the cell below.

Figure 1.7

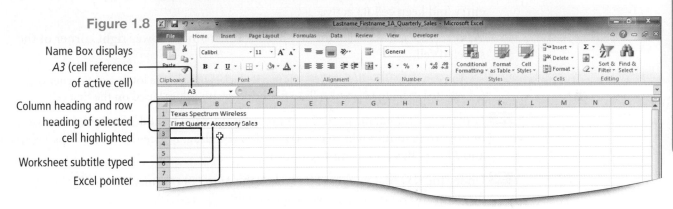

Name Box displays
active cell—A2

Column heading and row
heading of the active
cell highlighted

Worksheet title entered

3 In cell **A1**, notice that the text does not fit; the text spills over and displays in cells **B1** and **C1** to the right.

> If text is too long for a cell and cells to the right are empty, the text will display. If the cells to the right contain other data, only the text that will fit in the cell displays.

4 In cell **A2**, type the worksheet subtitle **First Quarter Accessory Sales** and then press Enter. Compare your screen with Figure 1.8.

Figure 1.8

Name Box displays
A3 (cell reference
of active cell)

Column heading and row
heading of selected
cell highlighted

Worksheet subtitle typed

Excel pointer

5 Press Enter again to make cell **A4** the active cell. In cell **A4**, type **Headsets** which will form the first row title, and then press Enter.

> The text characters that you typed align at the left edge of the cell—referred to as *left alignment*—and cell A5 becomes the active cell. Left alignment is the default for text values.

6 In cell **A5**, type **H** and notice the text from the previous cell displays.

> If the first characters you type in a cell match an existing entry in the column, Excel fills in the remaining characters for you. This feature, called *AutoComplete*, assists only with alphabetic values.

Another Way

Use the keyboard shortcut Ctrl + S to Save changes to your workbook.

7 Continue typing the remainder of the row title **olsters/Cases** and press Enter.

> The AutoComplete suggestion is removed when the entry you are typing differs from the previous value.

8 In cell **A6**, type **Car Kits** and press Enter. In cell **A7**, type **Batteries** and press Enter. In cell **A8**, type **Total** and press Enter. On the Quick Access Toolbar, click **Save**.

Excel | Chapter 1

Activity 1.04 | Using Auto Fill and Keyboard Shortcuts

1 Click cell **B3**. Type **J** and notice that when you begin to type in a cell, on the **Formula Bar**, the **Cancel** and **Enter** buttons become active, as shown in Figure 1.9.

Figure 1.9

Cancel and Enter buttons

Row titles entered

Excel pointer when entering text in a cell

2 Continue to type **anuary** On the **Formula Bar**, notice that values you type in a cell also display there. Then, on the **Formula Bar**, click the **Enter** button ✔ to confirm the entry and keep cell **B3** active.

3 With cell **B3** active, locate the small black square in the lower right corner of the selected cell.

> You can drag this *fill handle*—the small black square in the lower right corner of a selected cell—to adjacent cells to fill the cells with values based on the first cell.

4 Point to the **fill handle** until the ➕ pointer displays, hold down the left mouse button, drag to the right to cell **D3**, and as you drag, notice the ScreenTips *February* and *March*. Release the mouse button.

5 Under the text that you just filled, click the **Auto Fill Options** button ⧉▾ that displays, and then compare your screen with Figure 1.10.

> *Auto Fill* generates and extends a *series* of values into adjacent cells based on the value of other cells. A series is a group of things that come one after another in succession; for example, *January, February, March*.

> The Auto Fill Options button displays options to fill the data; options vary depending on the content and program from which you are filling, and the format of the data you are filling.

> *Fill Series* is selected, indicating the action that was taken. Because the options are related to the current task, the button is referred to as being *context sensitive*.

Figure 1.10

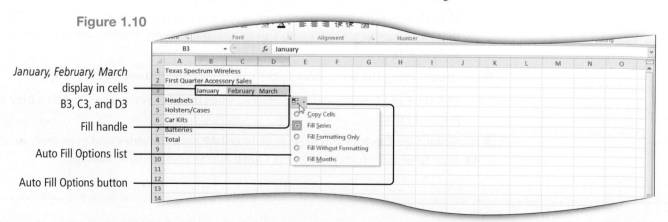

January, February, March display in cells B3, C3, and D3

Fill handle

Auto Fill Options list

Auto Fill Options button

6 Click in any cell to cancel the display of the Auto Fill Options list.

> The list no longer displays; the button will display until you perform some other screen action.

7 Press Ctrl + Home, which is the keyboard shortcut to make cell **A1** active.

8 On the Quick Access Toolbar, click **Save** 🖫 to save the changes you have made to your workbook, and then take a moment to study the table in Figure 1.11 to become familiar with additional keyboard shortcuts with which you can navigate the Excel worksheet.

Keyboard Shortcuts to Navigate the Excel Window

To Move the Location of the Active Cell:	Press:
Up, down, right, or left one cell	↑, ↓, →, ←
Down one cell	Enter
Up one cell	Shift + Enter
Up one full screen	Page Up
Down one full screen	PageDown
To column A of the current row	Home
To the last cell in the last column of the active area (the rectangle formed by all the rows and columns in a worksheet that contain entries)	Ctrl + End
To cell A1	Ctrl + Home
Right one cell	Tab
Left one cell	Shift + Tab

Figure 1.11

Activity 1.05 │ Aligning Text and Adjusting the Size of Columns

1 In the **column heading area**, point to the vertical line between **column A** and **column B** to display the ➕ pointer, press and hold down the left mouse button, and then compare your screen with Figure 1.12.

A ScreenTip displays information about the width of the column. The default width of a column is 64 *pixels*. A pixel, short for *picture element*, is a point of light measured in dots per square inch. Sixty-four pixels equal 8.43 characters, which is the average number of digits that will fit in a cell using the default font. The default font in Excel is Calibri and the default font size is 11.

Figure 1.12

Column heading area

Mouse pointer

ScreenTip

2 Drag to the right, and when the number of pixels indicated in the ScreenTip reaches **100 pixels**, release the mouse button. If you are not satisfied with your result, click Undo ⟲ on the Quick Access Toolbar and begin again.

This width accommodates the longest row title in cells A4 through A8—*Holsters/Cases*. The worksheet title and subtitle in cells A1 and A2 span more than one column and still do not fit in column A.

3 Point to cell **B3** and then drag across to select cells **B3**, **C3**, and **D3**. Compare your screen with Figure 1.13; if you are not satisfied with your result, click anywhere and begin again.

The three cells, B3 through D3, are selected and form a ***range***—two or more cells on a worksheet that are adjacent (next to each other) or nonadjacent (not next to each other). This range of cells is referred to as *B3:D3*. When you see a colon (:) between two cell references, the range includes all the cells between the two cell references.

A range of cells that is selected in this manner is indicated by a dark border, and Excel treats the range as a single unit so you can make the same changes to more than one cell at a time. The selected cells in the range are highlighted except for the first cell in the range, which displays in the Name Box.

Figure 1.13

First cell in selected range—B3—displays in Name Box

Column A widened to 100 pixels

Range B3:D3 selected

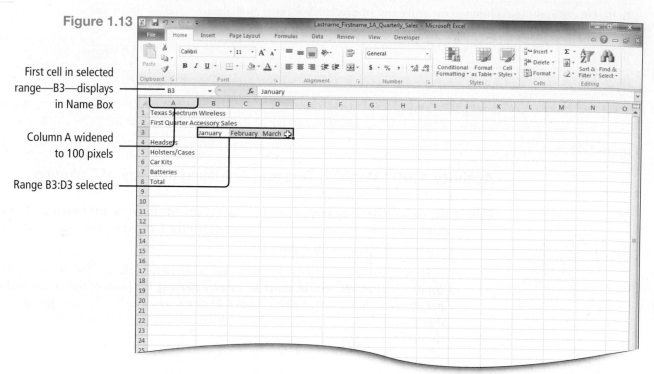

4 With the range **B3:D3** selected, point anywhere over the selected range, right-click, and then on the Mini toolbar, click the **Center** button ▤. On the Quick Access Toolbar, click **Save** 🖫.

The column titles *January*, *February*, *March* align in the center of each cell.

Activity 1.06 | Entering Numbers

To type number values, use either the number keys across the top of your keyboard or the numeric keypad if you have one—laptop computers may not have a numeric keypad.

1 Under *January*, click cell **B4**, type **47991.12** and then on the **Formula Bar**, click the **Enter** button ☑ to maintain cell **B4** as the active cell. Compare your screen with Figure 1.14.

By default, *number* values align at the right edge of the cell. The default **number format**—a specific way in which Excel displays numbers—is the **general format**. In the default general format, whatever you type in the cell will display, with the exception of trailing zeros to the right of a decimal point. For example, in the number 237.50 the *0* following the *5* is a trailing zero.

Data that displays in a cell is the **displayed value**. Data that displays in the Formula Bar is the **underlying value**. The number of digits or characters that display in a cell—the displayed value—depends on the width of the column. Calculations on numbers will always be based on the underlying value, not the displayed value.

Figure 1.14

Underlying value in the Formula Bar

Displayed value in the cell

General indicated as the Number format

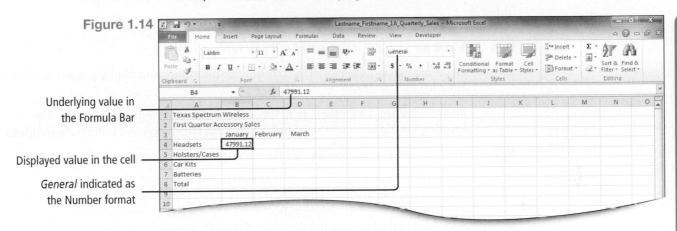

2 Press [Tab] to make cell **C4** active. Then, enter the remaining sales numbers as shown by using the following technique: Press [Tab] to confirm your entry and move across the row, and then press [Enter] at the end of a row to move to the next row.

	January	February	March
Headsets	47991.12	66984.92	87540.57
Holsters/Cases	19725	15523.12	13717.67
Car Kits	40408.67	61446.98	85835.76
Batteries	62154.28	68758.50	72558.89

3 Compare the numbers you entered with Figure 1.15 and then **Save** 🖫 your workbook.

In the default general format, trailing zeros to the right of a decimal point will not display. For example, when you type *68758.50*, the cell displays 68758.5 instead.

Figure 1.15

Values entered for each category in each month

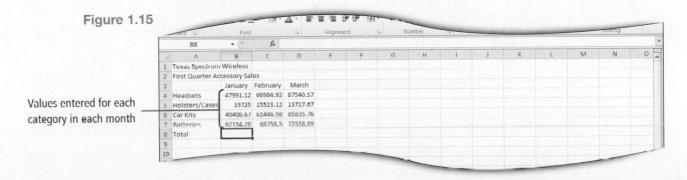

Objective 3 | Construct and Copy Formulas and Use the SUM Function

A cell contains either a constant value (text or numbers) or a formula. A formula is an equation that performs mathematical calculations on values in other cells, and then places the result in the cell containing the formula. You can create formulas or use a *function*—a prewritten formula that looks at one or more values, performs an operation, and then returns a value.

Activity 1.07 | Constructing a Formula and Using the SUM Function

In this activity, you will practice three different ways to sum a group of numbers in Excel.

1 Click cell **B8** to make it the active cell and type **=**

The equal sign (=) displays in the cell with the insertion point blinking, ready to accept more data.

All formulas begin with the = sign, which signals Excel to begin a calculation. The Formula Bar displays the = sign, and the Formula Bar Cancel and Enter buttons display.

2 At the insertion point, type **b4** and then compare your screen with Figure 1.16.

A list of Excel functions that begin with the letter *B* may briefly display—as you progress in your study of Excel, you will use functions of this type. A blue border with small corner boxes surrounds cell B4, which indicates that the cell is part of an active formula. The color used in the box matches the color of the cell reference in the formula.

Figure 1.16

Cell B4 outlined in blue to show it is part of an active formula

Cell B8 displays the beginning of the formula, with *b4* in blue to match outlined cell

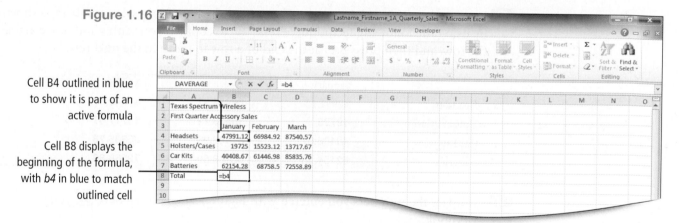

3 At the insertion point, type **+** and then type **b5**

A border of another color surrounds cell B5, and the color matches the color of the cell reference in the active formula. When typing cell references, it is not necessary to use uppercase letters.

4 At the insertion point, type **+b6+b7** and then press Enter.

The result of the formula calculation—*170279.1*—displays in the cell. Recall that in the default General format, trailing zeros do not display.

5 Click cell **B8** again, look at the **Formula Bar**, and then compare your screen with Figure 1.17.

> The formula adds the values in cells B4 through B7, and the result displays in cell B8. In this manner, you can construct a formula by typing. Although cell B8 displays the *result* of the formula, the formula itself displays in the Formula Bar. This is referred to as the *underlying formula*.
>
> Always view the Formula Bar to be sure of the exact content of a cell—*a displayed number may actually be a formula*.

Figure 1.17

Formula displays in Formula Bar

Total of values in cells B4:B7 displays in cell B8

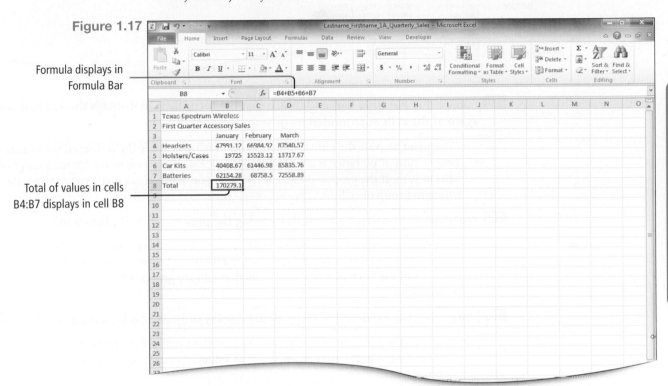

6 Click cell **C8** and type = to signal the beginning of a formula. Then, point to cell **C4** and click one time.

> The reference to the cell C4 is added to the active formula. A moving border surrounds the referenced cell, and the border color and the color of the cell reference in the formula are color coded to match.

7 At the insertion point, type + and then click cell **C5**. Repeat this process to complete the formula to add cells **C4** through **C7**, and then press Enter.

> The result of the formula calculation—*212713.5*—displays in the cell. This method of constructing a formula is the *point and click method*.

Another Way

Use the keyboard short-cut Alt + =; or, on the Formulas tab, in the Function Library group, click the AutoSum button.

8 Click cell **D8**. On the **Home tab**, in the **Editing group**, click the **Sum** button Σ, and then compare your screen with Figure 1.18.

> *SUM* is an Excel function—a prewritten formula. A moving border surrounds the range D4:D7 and =*SUM(D4:D7)* displays in cell D8.
>
> The = sign signals the beginning of a formula, *SUM* indicates the type of calculation that will take place (addition), and *(D4:D7)* indicates the range of cells on which the sum calculation will be performed. A ScreenTip provides additional information about the action.

Figure 1.18

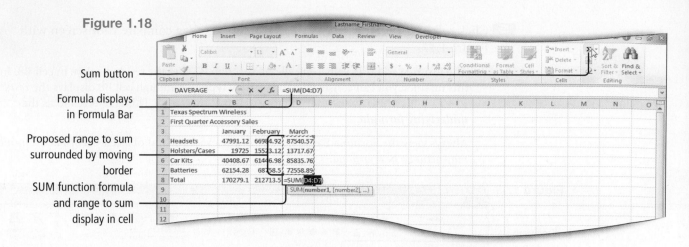

Sum button

Formula displays
in Formula Bar

Proposed range to sum
surrounded by moving
border

SUM function formula
and range to sum
display in cell

9 Look at the **Formula Bar**, and notice that the formula also displays there. Then, look again at the cells surrounded by the moving border.

When you activate the Sum function, Excel first looks *above* the active cell for a range of cells to sum. If no range is above the active cell, Excel will look to the *left* for a range of cells to sum. If the proposed range is not what you want to calculate, you can select a different group of cells.

10 Press Enter to construct a formula by using the prewritten SUM function.

Your total is *259652.9*. Because the Sum function is frequently used, it has its own button in the Editing group on the Home tab of the Ribbon. A larger version of the button also displays on the Formulas tab in the Function Library group. This button is also referred to as *AutoSum*.

11 Notice that the totals in the range **B8:D8** display only *one* decimal place. Click **Save** 🖫.

Number values that are too long to fit in the cell do *not* spill over into the unoccupied cell to the right in the same manner as text values. Rather, Excel rounds the number to fit the space.

Rounding is a procedure that determines which digit at the right of the number will be the last digit displayed and then increases it by one if the next digit to its right is 5, 6, 7, 8, or 9.

Activity 1.08 | Copying a Formula by Using the Fill Handle

You have practiced three ways to create a formula—by typing, by using the point-and-click technique, and by using a Function button from the Ribbon. You can also copy formulas. When you copy a formula from one cell to another, Excel adjusts the cell references to fit the new location of the formula.

1 Click cell **E3**, type **Total** and then press Enter.

The text in cell E3 is centered because the centered format continues from the adjacent cell.

2 With cell **E4** as the active cell, hold down Alt, and then press =. Compare your screen with Figure 1.19.

Alt + = is the keyboard shortcut for the Sum function. Recall that Excel first looks above the selected cell for a proposed range of cells to sum, and if no data is detected, Excel looks to the left and proposes a range of cells to sum.

Figure 1.19

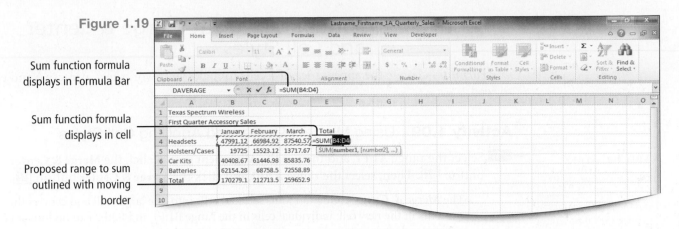

Sum function formula displays in Formula Bar

Sum function formula displays in cell

Proposed range to sum outlined with moving border

3 On the **Formula Bar**, click the **Enter** button ☑ to display the result and keep cell **E4** active.

> The total dollar amount of *Headsets* sold in the quarter is *202516.6*. In cells E5:E8, you can see that you need a formula similar to the one in E4, but formulas that refer to the cells in row 5, row 6, and so on.

4 With cell **E4** active, point to the fill handle in the lower right corner of the cell until the ➕ pointer displays. Then, drag down through cell **E8**; if you are not satisfied with your result, on the Quick Access Toolbar, click Undo ↺ and begin again. Compare your screen with Figure 1.20.

Figure 1.20

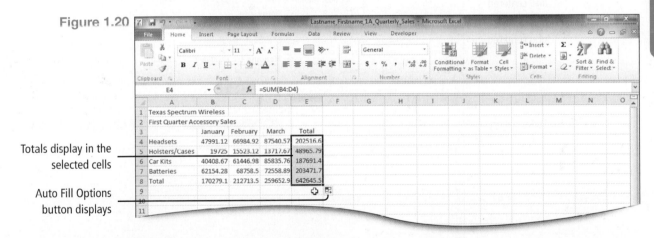

Totals display in the selected cells

Auto Fill Options button displays

5 Click cell **E5**, look at the **Formula Bar**, and notice the formula *=SUM(B5:D5)*. Click cell **E6**, look at the **Formula Bar**, and then notice the formula *=SUM(B6:D6)*.

> In each row, Excel copied the formula but adjusted the cell references *relative to* the row number. This is called a ***relative cell reference***—a cell reference based on the relative position of the cell that contains the formula and the cells referred to.

> The calculation is the same, but it is performed on the cells in that particular row. Use this method to insert numerous formulas into spreadsheets quickly.

6 Click cell **F3**, type **Trend** and then press Enter. **Save** 💾 your workbook.

Excel | Chapter 1

Objective 4 | Format Cells with Merge & Center and Cell Styles

Format—change the appearance of—cells to make your worksheet attractive and easy to read.

Activity 1.09 | Using Merge & Center and Applying Cell Styles

Another Way

Select the range, right-click over the selection, and then on the Mini toolbar, click the Merge & Center button.

1 Select the range **A1:F1**, and then in the **Alignment group**, click the **Merge & Center** button 🔳. Then, select the range **A2:F2** and click the **Merge & Center** button 🔳.

The *Merge & Center* command joins selected cells into one larger cell and centers the contents in the new cell; individual cells in the range B1:F1 and B2:F2 can no longer be selected—they are merged into cell A1 and A2 respectively.

2 Click cell **A1**. In the **Styles group**, click the **Cell Styles** button, and then compare your screen with Figure 1.21.

A *cell style* is a defined set of formatting characteristics, such as font, font size, font color, cell borders, and cell shading.

Figure 1.21

Cell Styles button

Cell A1 merged and centered

Cell A2 merged and centered

Cell Styles gallery

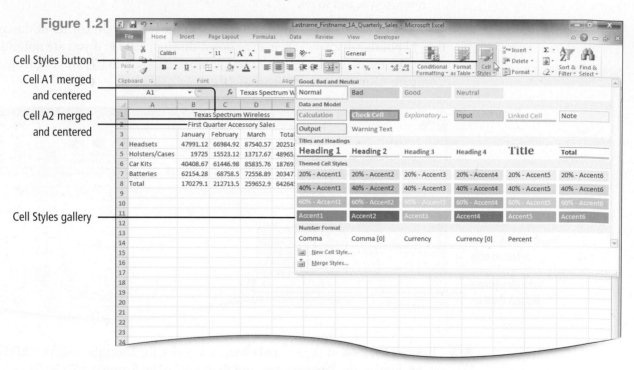

3 In the displayed gallery, under **Titles and Headings**, click **Title** and notice that the row height adjusts to accommodate this larger font size.

4 Click cell **A2**, display the **Cell Styles** gallery, and then under **Titles and Headings**, click **Heading 1**.

Use cell styles to maintain a consistent look in a worksheet and across worksheets in a workbook.

5 Select the range **B3:F3**, hold down Ctrl, and then select the range **A4:A8** to select the column titles and the row titles.

Use this technique to select two or more ranges that are nonadjacent—not next to each other.

6 Display the **Cell Styles** gallery, click **Heading 4** to apply this cell style to the column titles and row titles, and then **Save** 🖫 your workbook.

Another Way

In the Name Box type b4:e4,b8:e8 and then press Enter.

Activity 1.10 | Formatting Financial Numbers

1 Select the range **B4:E4**, hold down Ctrl, and then select the range **B8:E8**.

This range is referred to as *b4:e4,b8:e8* with a comma separating the references to the two nonadjacent ranges.

Another Way

Display the Cell Styles gallery, and under Number Format, click Currency.

2 On the **Home tab**, in the **Number group**, click the **Accounting Number Format** button $ ▾ . Compare your screen with Figure 1.22.

The *Accounting Number Format* applies a thousand comma separator where appropriate, inserts a fixed U.S. dollar sign aligned at the left edge of the cell, applies two decimal places, and leaves a small amount of space at the right edge of the cell to accommodate a parenthesis when negative numbers are present. Excel widens the columns to accommodate the formatted numbers.

Figure 1.22

Accounting Number Format button

Nonadjacent ranges selected with Accounting Number Format applied

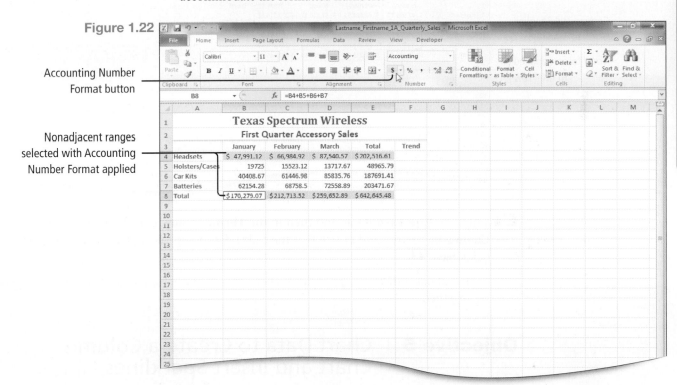

3 Select the range **B5:E7**, and then in the **Number group**, click the **Comma Style** button ' .

The *Comma Style* inserts thousand comma separators where appropriate and applies two decimal places. Comma Style also leaves space at the right to accommodate a parenthesis when negative numbers are present.

When preparing worksheets with financial information, the first row of dollar amounts and the total row of dollar amounts are formatted in the Accounting Number Format; that is, with thousand comma separators, dollar signs, two decimal places, and space at the right to accommodate a parenthesis for negative numbers, if any. Rows that are *not* the first row or the total row should be formatted with the Comma Style.

Excel | Chapter 1

4 Select the range **B8:E8**. From the **Styles group**, display the **Cell Styles** gallery, and then under **Titles and Headings**, click **Total**. Click any blank cell to cancel the selection, and then compare your screen with Figure 1.23.

> This is a common way to apply borders to financial information. The single border indicates that calculations were performed on the numbers above, and the double border indicates that the information is complete. Sometimes financial documents do not display values with cents; rather, the values are rounded up. You can do this by selecting the cells, and then clicking the Decrease Decimal button two times.

Figure 1.23

Comma style applied to range B5:E7

Total format applied to total row

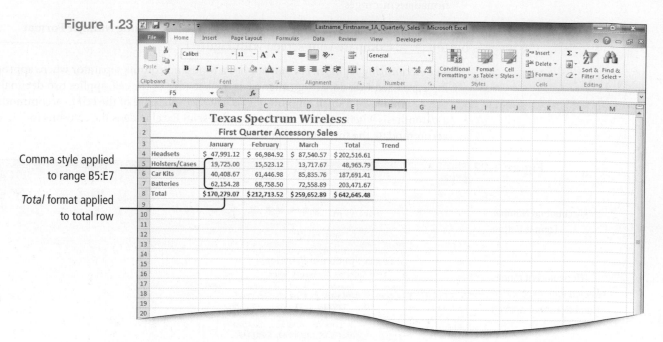

5 Click the **Page Layout tab**, and then in the **Themes group**, click **Themes**. Click the **Composite** theme, and notice that the cell styles change to match the new theme. Click **Save**.

> Recall that a theme is a predefined set of colors, fonts, lines, and fill effects that look good together.

Objective 5 | Chart Data to Create a Column Chart and Insert Sparklines

A **chart** is a graphic representation of data in a worksheet. Data presented as a chart is easier to understand than a table of numbers. **Sparklines** are tiny charts embedded in a cell and give a visual trend summary alongside your data. A sparkline makes a pattern more obvious to the eye.

Activity 1.11 | Charting Data in a Column Chart

In this activity, you will create a **column chart** showing the monthly sales of accessories by category during the first quarter. A column chart is useful for illustrating comparisons among related numbers. The chart will enable the company president, Rosalyn Thomas, to see a pattern of overall monthly sales.

1 Select the range **A3:D7**. Click the **Insert tab**, and then in the **Charts group**, click **Column** to display a gallery of Column chart types.

When charting data, typically you should *not* include totals—include only the data you want to compare. By using different *chart types*, you can display data in a way that is meaningful to the reader—common examples are column charts, pie charts, and line charts.

2 On the gallery of column chart types, under **2-D Column**, point to the first chart to display the ScreenTip *Clustered Column*, and then click to select it. Compare your screen with Figure 1.24.

A column chart displays in the worksheet, and the charted data is bordered by colored lines. Because the chart object is selected—surrounded by a border and displaying sizing handles—contextual tools named *Chart Tools* display and add contextual tabs next to the standard tabs on the Ribbon.

Figure 1.24

Chart Tools display three additional tabs—*Design, Layout, Format*

Border and sizing handles indicate chart is selected

Charted data range bordered by colored lines (green = legend, blue = columns, purple = category labels)

Clustered column chart displays in worksheet

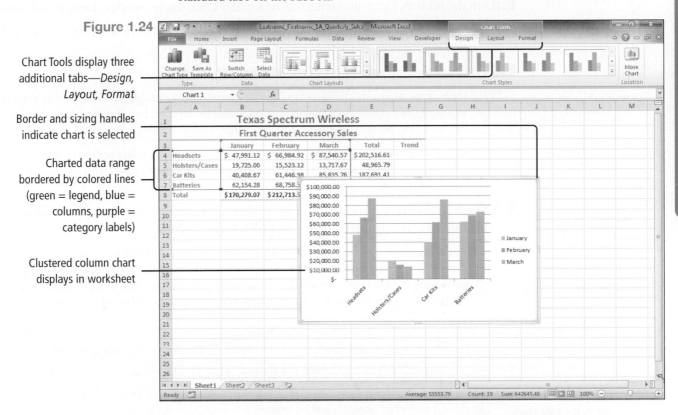

3 Point to the top border of the chart to display the ⟦⟧ pointer, and then drag the upper left corner of the chart just inside the upper left corner of cell **A10**, approximately as shown in Figure 1.25.

Based on the data you selected in your worksheet, Excel constructs a column chart and adds *category labels*—the labels that display along the bottom of the chart to identify the category of data. This area is referred to as the *category axis* or the *x-axis*. Excel uses the row titles as the category names.

On the left, Excel includes a numerical scale on which the charted data is based; this is the *value axis* or the *y-axis*. On the right, a *legend*, which identifies the patterns or colors that are assigned to the categories in the chart, displays.

Figure 1.25

New chart location

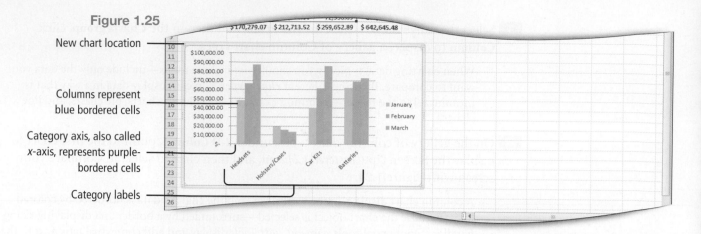

Columns represent
blue bordered cells

Category axis, also called
x-axis, represents purple-
bordered cells

Category labels

4 On the Ribbon, locate the contextual tabs under **Chart Tools—Design**, **Layout**, and **Format**.

When a chart is selected, Chart Tools become available and three tabs provide commands for working with the chart.

5 Locate the group of cells bordered in blue.

Each of the twelve cells bordered in blue is referred to as a *data point*—a value that originates in a worksheet cell. Each data point is represented in the chart by a *data marker*—a column, bar, area, dot, pie slice, or other symbol in a chart that represents a single data point.

Related data points form a *data series*; for example, there is a data series for *January*, for *February*, and for *March*. Each data series has a unique color or pattern represented in the chart legend.

6 On the **Design tab** of the Ribbon, in the **Data group**, click the **Switch Row/Column** button, and then compare your chart with Figure 1.26.

In this manner, you can easily change the categories of data from the row titles, which is the default, to the column titles. Whether you use row or column titles as your category names depends on how you want to view your charted data. Here, the president wants to see monthly sales and the breakdown of product categories within each month.

Figure 1.26

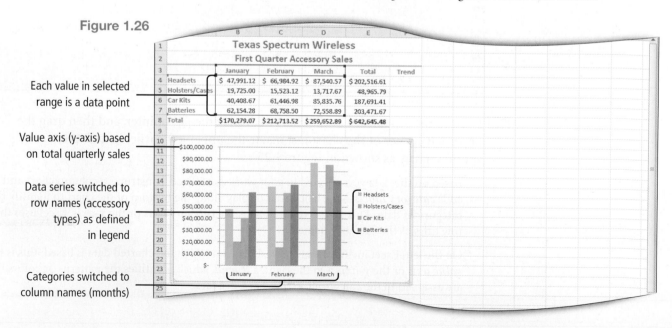

Each value in selected
range is a data point

Value axis (y-axis) based
on total quarterly sales

Data series switched to
row names (accessory
types) as defined
in legend

Categories switched to
column names (months)

7 On the **Design tab**, in the **Chart Layouts group**, locate and click the **More** button ⊡. Compare your screen with Figure 1.27.

> In the *Chart Layouts gallery*, you can select a predesigned *chart layout*—a combination of chart elements, which can include a title, legend, labels for the columns, and the table of charted cells.

Figure 1.27

Chart Layouts gallery

More buttons in Chart Styles group

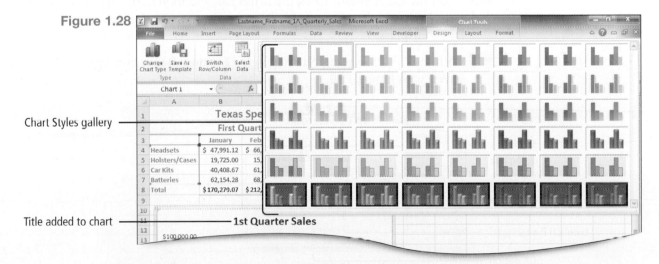

8 Click several different layouts to see the effect on your chart, and then using the ScreenTips as your guide, locate and click **Layout 1**.

9 In the chart, click anywhere in the text *Chart Title* to select the title box, watch the **Formula Bar** as you type **1st Quarter Sales** and then press [Enter] to display the new chart title.

10 Click in a white area just slightly *inside* the chart border to deselect the chart title. On the **Design tab**, in the **Chart Styles group**, click the **More** button ⊡. Compare your screen with Figure 1.28.

> The *Chart Styles gallery* displays an array of pre-defined *chart styles*—the overall visual look of the chart in terms of its colors, backgrounds, and graphic effects such as flat or beveled columns.

Figure 1.28

Chart Styles gallery

Title added to chart — 1st Quarter Sales

11 Using the ScreenTips as your guide, locate and click **Style 26**.

> This style uses a white background, formats the columns with theme colors, and applies a beveled effect. With this clear visual representation of the data, the president can see the sales of all product categories in each month, and can see that the sale of headsets and car kits has risen quite markedly during the quarter.

Excel | Chapter 1

12 Click any cell to deselect the chart, and notice that the *Chart Tools* no longer display in the Ribbon. Click **Save** 💾, and then compare your screen with Figure 1.29.

Contextual tabs display when an object is selected, and then are removed from view when the object is deselected.

Figure 1.29

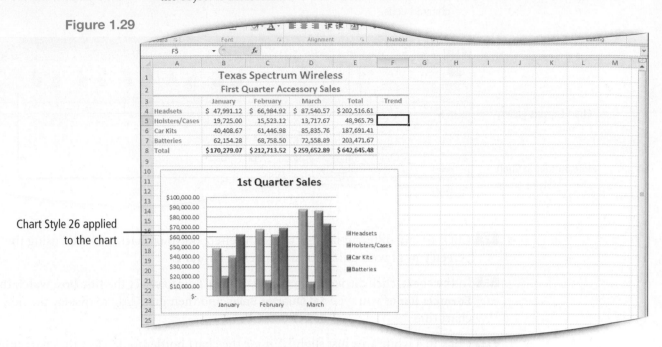

Chart Style 26 applied to the chart

Activity 1.12 | Creating and Formatting Sparklines

By creating sparklines, you provide a context for your numbers. Your readers will be able to see the relationship between a sparkline and its underlying data quickly.

Another Way

In the worksheet, select the range F4:F7 to insert it into the Location Range box.

1 Select the range **B4:D7**. Click the **Insert tab**, and then in the **Sparklines group**, click **Line**. In the displayed **Create Sparklines** dialog box, notice that the selected range *B4:D7* displays.

2 With the insertion point blinking in the **Location Range** box, type **f4:f7** Compare your screen with Figure 1.30.

Figure 1.30

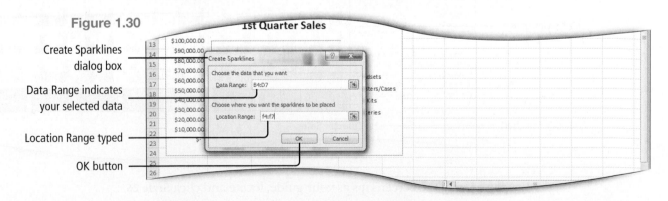

Create Sparklines dialog box

Data Range indicates your selected data

Location Range typed

OK button

3 Click **OK** to insert the trend lines in the range F4:F7, and then on the **Design tab**, in the **Show group**, click the **Markers** check box to select it.

Alongside each row of data, the sparkline provides a quick visual trend summary for sales of each accessory item over the three-month period. For example, you can see instantly that of the four items, only Holsters/Cases had declining sales for the period.

4 In the **Style group**, click the **More** button ⊡. In the second row, click the fourth style—**Sparkline Style Accent 4, Darker 25%**. Click cell **A1** to deselect the range. Click **Save** 💾. Compare your screen with Figure 1.31.

Use markers, colors, and styles in this manner to further enhance your sparklines.

Figure 1.31

Sparklines inserted and formatted

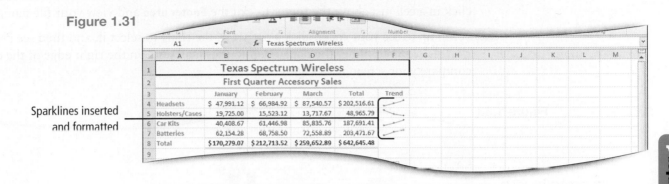

Objective 6 | Print, Display Formulas, and Close Excel

Use *Page Layout view* and the commands on the Page Layout tab to prepare for printing.

Activity 1.13 | Changing Views, Creating a Footer, and Using Print Preview

For each Excel project in this textbook, you will create a footer containing your name and the project name.

1 Be sure the chart is *not* selected. Click the **Insert tab**, and then in the **Text group**, click the **Header & Footer** button to switch to Page Layout view and open the **Header area**. Compare your screen with Figure 1.32.

In Page Layout view, you can see the edges of the paper of multiple pages, the margins, and the rulers. You can also insert a header or footer by typing in the areas indicated and use the Header & Footer Tools.

Figure 1.32

Go to Footer button

Rulers

Header area with three sections open; center section selected

Margin

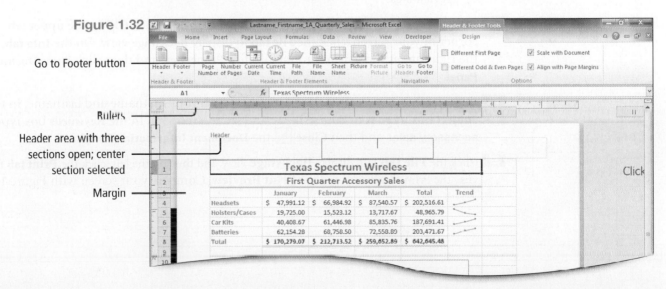

2 On the **Design tab**, in the **Navigation group**, click **Go to Footer** to open the **Footer area**, and then click just above the word *Footer* to place the insertion point in the **left section** of the **Footer area**.

3 In the **Header & Footer Elements group**, click the **File Name** button to add the name of your file to the footer—&*[File]* displays in the left section of the **Footer area**. Then, click in a cell just above the footer to exit the **Footer area** and view your file name.

4 Scroll up to see your chart, click a corner of the chart to select it, and then see if the chart is centered under the data. *Point* to the small dots on the right edge of the chart; compare your screen with Figure 1.33.

Figure 1.33

Horizontal resize pointer

Border indicates chart is selected

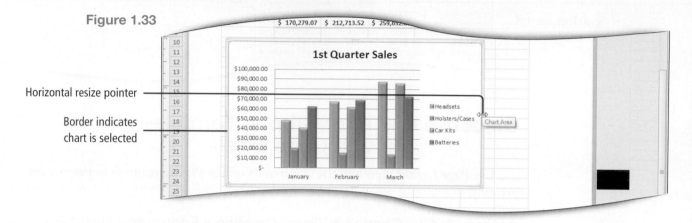

5 Drag the ↔ pointer to the right so that the right border of the chart is just inside the right border of **column F**. Be sure the left and right borders of the chart are just slightly **inside** the left border of **column A** and the right border of **column F**—adjust as necessary.

6 Click any cell to deselect the chart. Click the **Page Layout tab**, in the **Page Setup group**, click the **Margins** button, and then at the bottom of the **Margins** gallery, click **Custom Margins**. In the **Page Setup** dialog box, under **Center on page**, select the **Horizontally** check box.

This action will center the data and chart horizontally on the page, as shown in the Preview area.

7 In the lower right corner of the **Page Setup** dialog box, click **OK**. In the upper left corner of your screen, click the **File tab** to display **Backstage** view. On the **Info tab**, on the right under the screen thumbnail, click **Properties**, and then click **Show Document Panel**.

8 In the **Author** box, replace the existing text with your firstname and lastname. In the **Subject** box, type your course name and section number. In the **Keywords** box type **accessory sales** and then **Close** ⊠ the **Document Information Panel**.

Another Way

Press Ctrl + F2 to view the Print Preview.

9 Click the **File tab** to redisplay **Backstage** view, and then on the left, click the **Print tab** to view the Print commands and the **Print Preview**. Compare your screen with Figure 1.34.

Figure 1.34

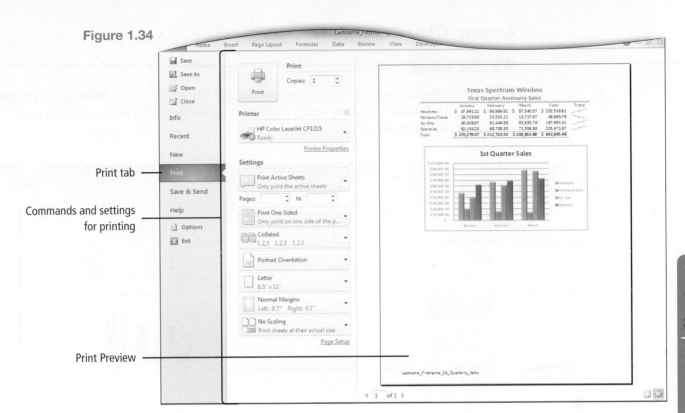

Print tab

Commands and settings for printing

Print Preview

10 Note any adjustments that need to be made, and then on the Ribbon, click the **Home tab** to close Backstage view and return to the worksheet. In the lower right corner of your screen, click the **Normal** button 🏢 to return to the Normal view, and then press Ctrl + Home to return to cell **A1**.

> The *Normal view* maximizes the number of cells visible on your screen and keeps the column letters and row numbers closer. The vertical dotted line between columns indicates that as currently arranged, only the columns to the left of the dotted line will print on the first page. The exact position of the vertical line may depend on your default printer setting.

11 Make any necessary adjustments, and then **Save** 🖫 your workbook.

Activity 1.14 | Deleting Unused Sheets in a Workbook

A new Excel workbook contains three blank worksheets. It is not necessary to delete unused sheets, but doing so saves storage space and removes any doubt that additional information is in the workbook.

1 At the bottom of your worksheet, click the **Sheet2 tab** to display the second worksheet in the workbook and make it active.

Another Way

On the Home tab, in the Cells group, click the Delete button arrow, and then click Delete Sheet.

2 Hold down Ctrl, and then click the **Sheet3 tab**. Release Ctrl, and then with both sheets selected (the tab background is white), point to either of the selected sheet tabs, right-click, and then on the shortcut menu, click **Delete**.

> Excel deletes the two unused sheets from your workbook. If you attempt to delete a worksheet with data, Excel will display a warning and permit you to cancel the deletion. *Sheet tabs* are labels along the lower border of the Excel window that identify each worksheet.

Activity 1.15 | Printing a Worksheet

1 Click **Save** 🖫.

2 Display **Backstage** view and on the left click the Print tab. Under **Print**, be sure **Copies** indicates *1*. Under **Settings**, verify that *Print Active Sheets* displays. Compare your screen with Figure 1.35.

Figure 1.35

Copies indicates *1*

Print Active Sheets

Print Preview

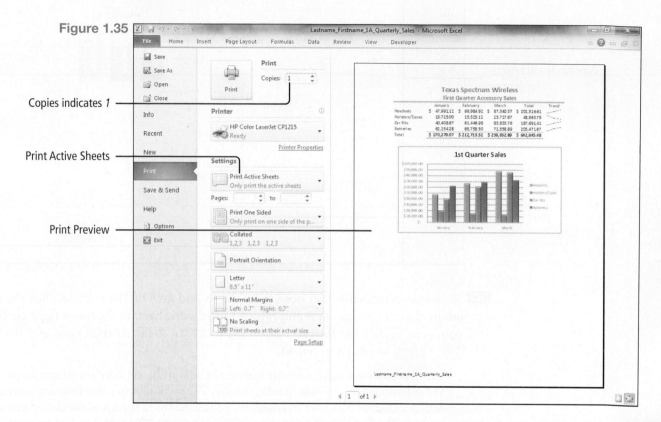

3 To print on paper, be sure that a printer is available to your system, and then in the **Print group**, click the **Print** button. To create an electronic printout, on the Backstage tabs, click the **Save & Send tab**, under **File Types** click **Create PDF/XPS Document**, and then on the right, click **Create PDF/XPS**. In the **Publish as PDF or XPS** dialog box, navigate to your storage location, and then click the **Publish** button to create the PDF file. Close the Adobe window.

Activity 1.16 | Displaying, Printing, and Hiding Formulas

When you type a formula in a cell, the cell displays the *results* of the formula calculation. Recall that this value is called the displayed value. You can view and print the underlying formulas in the cells. When you do so, a formula often takes more horizontal space to display than the result of the calculation.

1 If necessary, redisplay your worksheet. Because you will make some temporary changes to your workbook, on the Quick Access Toolbar, click **Save** 🖫 to be sure your work is saved up to this point.

> **Another Way**
>
> Hold down Ctrl, and then press \` (usually located below Esc).

2 On the **Formulas tab**, in the **Formula Auditing group**, click the **Show Formulas** button. Then, in the **column heading area**, point to the **column A** heading to display the ↓ pointer, hold down the left mouse button, and then drag to the right to select columns **A:F**. Compare your screen with Figure 1.36.

Figure 1.36

Dotted line shows page break

Underlying formulas displayed

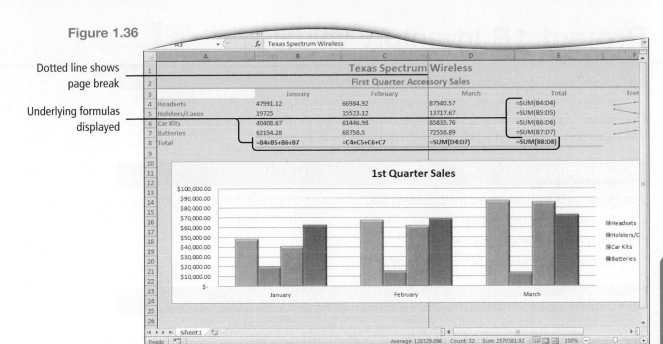

Note | Turning the Display of Formulas On and Off

The Show Formulas button is a toggle button. Clicking it once turns the display of formulas on—the button will glow orange. Clicking the button again turns the display of formulas off.

3 Point to the column heading boundary between any two of the selected columns to display the ⊞ pointer, and then double-click to AutoFit the selected columns.

AutoFit adjusts the width of a column to fit the cell content of the *widest* cell in the column.

Another Way

In the Scale to Fit group, click the Dialog Box Launcher button to display the Page tab of the Page Setup dialog box. Then, under Scaling, click the Fit to option button.

4 On the **Page Layout tab**, in the **Page Setup group**, click **Orientation**, and then click **Landscape**. In the **Scale to Fit** group, click the **Width arrow**, and then click **1 page** to scale the data to fit onto one page.

Scaling shrinks the width (or height) of the printed worksheet to fit a maximum number of pages, and is convenient for printing formulas. Although it is not always the case, formulas frequently take up more space than the actual data.

Another Way

In the Page Setup group, click the Dialog Box Launcher button to display the Page tab of the Page Setup dialog box. Then, under Orientation, click the Landscape option button.

5 In the **Page Setup group**, click the **Dialog Box Launcher** button 🖾. In the **Page Setup** dialog box, click the **Margins tab**, and then under **Center on page**, if necessary, click to select the **Horizontally** check box.

6 Click **OK** to close the dialog box. Check to be sure your chart is centered below the data and the left and right edges are slightly inside column A and column F—drag a chart edge and then deselect the chart if necessary. Display the **Print Preview**, and then submit your worksheet with formulas displayed, either printed or electronically, as directed by your instructor.

7 Click the **File tab** to display **Backstage** view, click **Close**, and when prompted, click **Don't Save** so that you do *not* save the changes you made—displaying formulas, changing column widths and orientation, and scaling—to print your formulas.

8 In the upper right corner of your screen, click the **Close** button 🗙 to exit Excel.

End You have completed Project 1A ————————

Project 1B Inventory Valuation

myitlab
Project 1B Training

Project Activities

In Activities 1.17 through 1.24, you will create a workbook for Josette Lovrick, Operations Manager, which calculates the retail value of an inventory of car convenience products. Your completed worksheet will look similar to Figure 1.37.

Project Files

For Project 1B, you will need the following file:

> New blank Excel workbook

You will save your workbook as:

> Lastname_Firstname_1B_Car_Products

Project Results

Texas Spectrum Wireless
Car Products Inventory Valuation
As of December 31

	Warehouse Location	Quantity In Stock	Retail Price	Total Retail Value	Percent of Total Retail Value
Antenna Signal Booster	Dallas	1,126	$ 19.99	$ 22,508.74	8.27%
Car Power Port Adapter	Dallas	3,546	19.49	69,111.54	25.39%
Repeater Antenna	Houston	1,035	39.99	41,389.65	15.21%
SIM Card Reader and Writer	Houston	2,875	16.90	48,587.50	17.85%
Sticky Dash Pad	Houston	3,254	11.99	39,015.46	14.33%
Window Mount GPS Holder	Dallas	2,458	20.99	51,593.42	18.95%
Total Retail Value for All Products				$ 272,206.31	

Lastname_Firstname_1B_Car_Products

Figure 1.37
Project 1B Car Products

Objective 7 | Check Spelling in a Worksheet

In Excel, the spelling checker performs similarly to the other Microsoft Office programs.

Activity 1.17 | Checking Spelling in a Worksheet

1 **Start** Excel and display a new blank workbook. In cell **A1**, type **Texas Spectrum Wireless** and press Enter. In cell **A2**, type **Car Products Inventory** and press Enter.

2 On the Ribbon, click the **File tab** to display **Backstage** view, click **Save As**, and then in the **Save As** dialog box, navigate to your **Excel Chapter 1** folder. As the **File name**, type **Lastname_Firstname_1B_Car_Products** and then click **Save**.

3 Press Tab to move to cell **B3**, type **Quantity** and press Tab. In cell **C3**, type **Average Cost** and press Tab. In cell **D3**, type **Retail Price** and press Tab.

4 Click cell **C3**, and then look at the **Formula Bar**. Notice that in the cell, the displayed value is cut off; however, in the **Formula Bar**, the entire text value—the underlying value—displays. Compare your screen with Figure 1.38.

> Text that is too long to fit in a cell spills over to cells on the right only if they are empty. If the cell to the right contains data, the text in the cell to the left is truncated. The entire value continues to exist, but is not completely visible.

Figure 1.38

Entire contents of C3
display in Formula Bar

Cell C3 active, text cut off

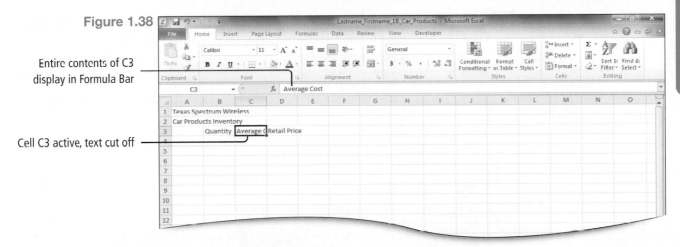

5 Click cell **E3**, type **Total Retail Value** and press Tab. In cell **F3**, type **Percent of Total Retail Value** and press Enter.

6 Click cell **A4**. *Without* correcting the spelling error, type **Antena Signal Booster** Press Enter. In the range **A5:A10**, type the remaining row titles shown below. Then compare your screen with Figure 1.39.

> **Car Power Port Adapter**
>
> **Repeater Antenna**
>
> **SIM Card Reader and Writer**
>
> **Sticky Dash Pad**
>
> **Window Mount GPS Holder**
>
> **Total Retail Value for All Products**

Figure 1.39

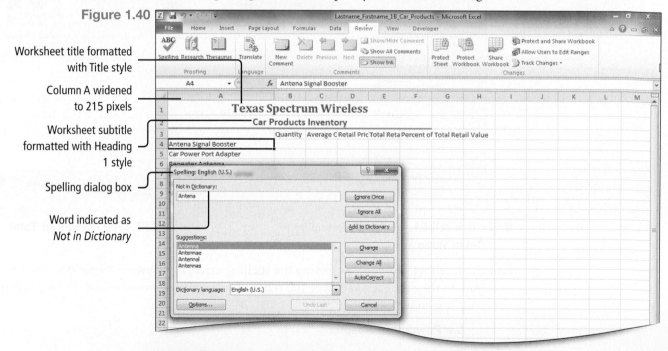

Column titles

Row titles

7 In the **column heading area**, point to the right boundary of **column A** to display the ↔ pointer, and then drag to the right to widen **column A** to **215** pixels.

8 Select the range **A1:F1**, **Merge & Center** 🔄 the text, and then from the **Cell Styles** gallery, apply the **Title** style.

9 Select the range **A2:F2**, **Merge & Center** 🔄 the text, and then from the **Cell Styles** gallery, apply the **Heading 1** style. Press Ctrl + Home to move to the top of your worksheet.

> **Another Way**
>
> Press F7, which is the keyboard shortcut for the Spelling command.

10 With cell **A1** as the active cell, click the **Review tab**, and then in the **Proofing group**, click the **Spelling** button. Compare your screen with Figure 1.40.

Figure 1.40

Worksheet title formatted with Title style

Column A widened to 215 pixels

Worksheet subtitle formatted with Heading 1 style

Spelling dialog box

Word indicated as *Not in Dictionary*

> **Alert! | Does a Message Display Asking if You Want to Continue Checking at the Beginning of the Sheet?**
>
> If a message displays asking if you want to continue checking at the beginning of the sheet, click Yes. The Spelling command begins its checking process with the currently selected cell and moves to the right and down. Thus, if your active cell was a cell after A4, this message may display.

11 In the **Spelling** dialog box, under **Not in Dictionary**, notice the word *Antena*.

The spelling tool does not have this word in its dictionary. Under *Suggestions*, Excel provides a list of suggested spellings.

12 Under **Suggestions**, click **Antenna**, and then click the **Change** button.

> *Antena*, a typing error, is changed to *Antenna*. A message box displays *The spelling check is complete for the entire sheet*—unless you have additional unrecognized words. Because the spelling check begins its checking process starting with the currently selected cell, it is good practice to return to cell A1 before starting the Spelling command.

13 Correct any other errors you may have made. When the message displays, *The spelling check is complete for the entire sheet*, click **OK**. Save 💾 your workbook.

Objective 8 | Enter Data by Range

You can enter data by first selecting a range of cells. This is a time-saving technique, especially if you use the numeric keypad to enter the numbers.

Activity 1.18 | Entering Data by Range

1 Select the range **B4:D9**, type **1126** and then press Enter.

> The value displays in cell B4, and cell B5 becomes the active cell.

2 With cell **B5** active in the range, and pressing Enter after each entry, type the following, and then compare your screen with Figure 1.41:

> 4226
> 1035
> 2875
> 3254
> 2458

> After you enter the last value and press Enter, the active cell moves to the top of the next column within the selected range. Although it is not required to enter data in this manner, you can see that selecting the range before you enter data saves time because it confines the movement of the active cell to the selected range.

Figure 1.41

Cell C4 active

Range B4:D9 selected

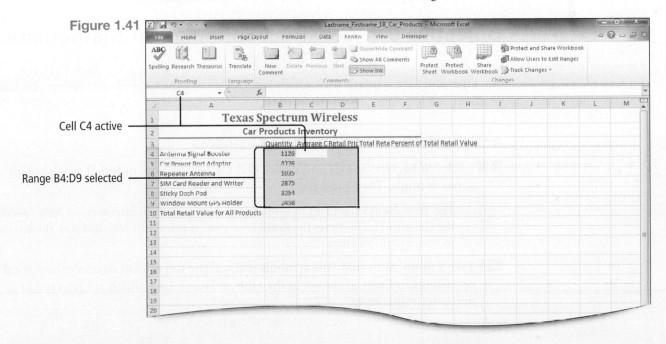

3 With the selected range still active, from the following table, beginning in cell **C4** and pressing Enter after each entry, enter the data for the **Average Cost** column and then the **Retail Price** column. If you prefer, deselect the range to enter the values—typing in a selected range is optional.

Average Cost	Retail Price
9.75	19.99
9.25	19.49
16.90	39.99
9.55	16.90
4.20	12.99
10.45	20.99

Recall that the default number format for cells is the *General* number format, in which numbers display exactly as you type them and trailing zeros do not display, even if you type them.

4 Click any blank cell, and then compare your screen with Figure 1.42. Correct any errors you may have made while entering data, and then click **Save** 🔲.

Figure 1.42

Data entered

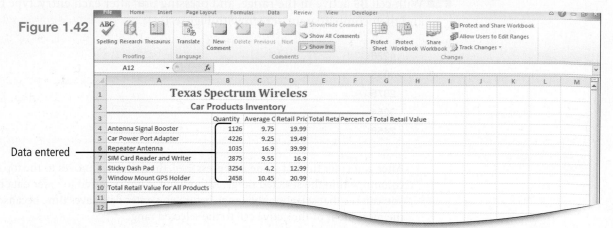

Objective 9 | Construct Formulas for Mathematical Operations

Operators are symbols with which you can specify the type of calculation you want to perform in a formula.

Activity 1.19 | Using Arithmetic Operators

1 Click cell **E4**, type **=b4*d4** and notice that the two cells are outlined as part of an active formula. Then press Enter.

The *Total Retail Value* of all *Antenna Signal Booster* items in inventory—*22508.74*—equals the *Quantity* (1,126) times the *Retail Price* (selling price) of 19.99. In Excel, the asterisk (*) indicates multiplication.

2 Take a moment to study the symbols you will use to perform basic mathematical operations in Excel, as shown in the table in Figure 1.43, which are referred to as *arithmetic operators*.

Symbols Used in Excel for Arithmetic Operators	
Operator Symbol	**Operation**
+	Addition
-	Subtraction (also negation)
*	Multiplication
/	Division
%	Percent
^	Exponentiation

Figure 1.43

3 Click cell **E4**.

> You can see that in cells E5:E9, you need a formula similar to the one in E4, but one that refers to the cells in row 5, row 6, and so forth. Recall that you can copy formulas and the cell references will change *relative to* the row number.

4 With cell **E4** selected, position your pointer over the fill handle in the lower right corner of the cell until the + pointer displays. Then, drag down through cell **E9** to copy the formula.

Another Way

Select the range, display the Cell Styles gallery, and then under Number Format, click Comma [0].

5 Select the range **B4:B9**, and then on the **Home tab**, in the **Number group**, click the **Comma Style** button . Then, in the **Number group**, click the **Decrease Decimal** button two times to remove the decimal places from these values.

> Comma Style formats a number with two decimal places; because these are whole numbers referring to quantities, no decimal places are necessary.

6 Select the range **E4:E9**, and then at the bottom of your screen, in the status bar, notice the displayed values for **Average**, **Count**, and **Sum**—*48118.91833, 6* and *288713.51*.

> When you select numerical data, three calculations display in the status bar by default—Average, Count, and Sum. Here, Excel indicates that if you averaged the selected values, the result would be *48118.91833*, there are 6 cells in the selection that contain values, and that if you added the values the result would be 288713.51.

7 Click cell **E10**, in the **Editing group**, click the **Sum** button Σ, notice that Excel selects a range to sum, and then press Enter to display the total *288713.5*.

8 Select the range **C5:E9** and apply the **Comma Style** ; notice that Excel widens **column E**.

9 Select the range **C4:E4**, hold down Ctrl, and then click cell **E10**. Release Ctrl and then apply the **Accounting Number Format** $ ▾. Notice that Excel widens the columns as necessary.

10 Click cell **E10**, and then from the **Cell Styles** gallery, apply the **Total** style. Click any blank cell, and then compare your screen with Figure 1.44.

Figure 1.44

Accounting Number Format applied to C4:E4, E10

Comma Style applied to C5:E9

Total style applied to E10

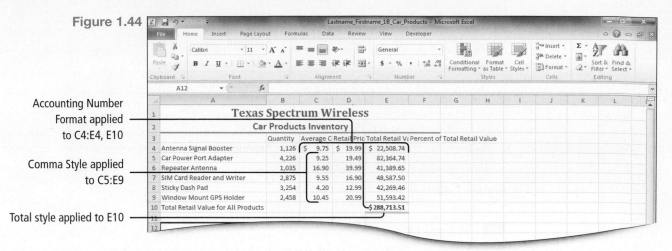

11 Save your workbook.

More Knowledge | Multiple Status Bar Calculations

You can display a total of six calculations on the status bar. To add additional calculations—Minimum, Maximum, and Numerical Count (the number of selected cells that contain a number value)—right-click on the status bar, and then click the additional calculations that you want to display.

Activity 1.20 | Copying Formulas Containing Absolute Cell References

In a formula, a relative cell reference refers to a cell by its position *in relation to* the cell that contains the formula. An *absolute cell reference*, on the other hand, refers to a cell by its *fixed* position in the worksheet, for example, the total in cell E10.

A relative cell reference automatically adjusts when a formula is copied. In some calculations, you do *not* want the cell reference to adjust; rather, you want the cell reference to remain the same when the formula is copied.

1 Click cell **F4**, type = and then click cell **E4**. Type / and then click cell **E10**.

The formula =*E4/E10* indicates that the value in cell E4 will be *divided* by the value in cell E10. Why? Because Ms. Lovrick wants to know the percentage by which each product's Total Retail Value makes up the Total Retail Value for All Products.

Arithmetically, the percentage is computed by dividing the *Total Retail Value* for each product by the *Total Retail Value for All Products*. The result will be a percentage expressed as a decimal.

2 Press Enter. Click cell **F4** and notice that the formula displays in the **Formula Bar**. Then, point to cell **F4** and double-click.

The formula, with the two referenced cells displayed in color and bordered with the same color, displays in the cell. This feature, called the *range finder*, is useful for verifying formulas because it visually indicates which workbook cells are included in a formula calculation.

3 Press [Enter] to redisplay the result of the calculation in the cell, and notice that approximately 8% of the total retail value of the inventory is made up of Antenna Signal Boosters.

4 Click cell **F4** again, and then drag the fill handle down through cell **F9**. Compare your screen with Figure 1.45.

> Each cell displays an error message—*#DIV/0!* and a green triangle in the upper left corner of each cell indicates that Excel detects an error.
>
> Like a grammar checker, Excel uses rules to check for formula errors and flags errors in this manner. Additionally, the Auto Fill Options button displays, from which you can select formatting options for the copied cells.

Figure 1.45

Auto Fill Options button

Cells F5:F9 display error message and green triangles

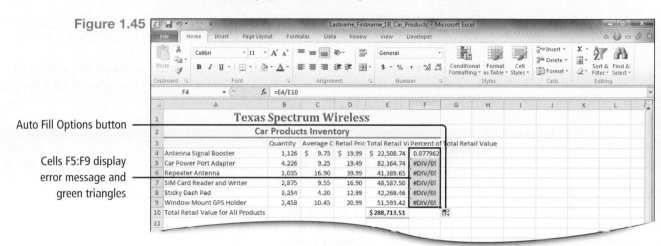

5 Click cell **F5**, and to the left of the cell, point to the **Error Checking** button ◈ to display its ScreenTip—*The formula or function used is dividing by zero or empty cells.*

> In this manner, Excel suggests the cause of an error.

6 Look at the **Formula Bar** and examine the formula.

> The formula is *=E5/E11*. The cell reference to *E5* is correct, but the cell reference following the division operator (/) is *E11*, and E11 is an *empty* cell.

7 Click cell **F6**, point to the **Error Checking** button ◈, and in the **Formula Bar** examine the formula.

> Because the cell references are relative, Excel builds the formulas by increasing the row number for each equation. But in this calculation, the divisor must always be the value in cell E10—the *Total Retail Value for All Products*.

8 Point to cell **F4**, and then double-click to place the insertion point within the cell.

> **Another Way**
> Edit the formula so that it indicates *=E4/$E$10*

9 Within the cell, use the arrow keys as necessary to position the insertion point to the left of *E10*, and then press [F4]. Compare your screen with Figure 1.46.

> Dollar signs ($) display, which changes the reference to cell E10 to an absolute cell reference. The use of the dollar sign to denote an absolute reference is not related in any way to whether or not the values you are working with are currency values. It is simply the symbol that Excel uses to denote an absolute cell reference.

Figure 1.46

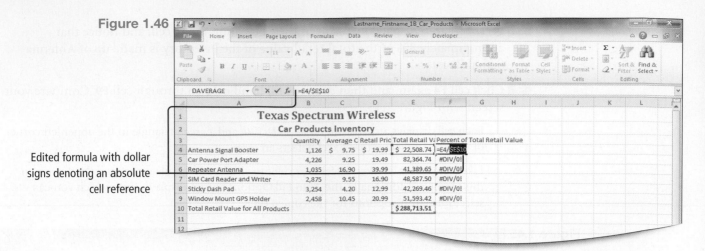

Edited formula with dollar signs denoting an absolute cell reference

10 On the **Formula Bar**, click the **Enter** button ✓ so that **F4** remains the active cell. Then, drag the fill handle to copy the new formula down through cell **F9**. Compare your screen with Figure 1.47.

Figure 1.47

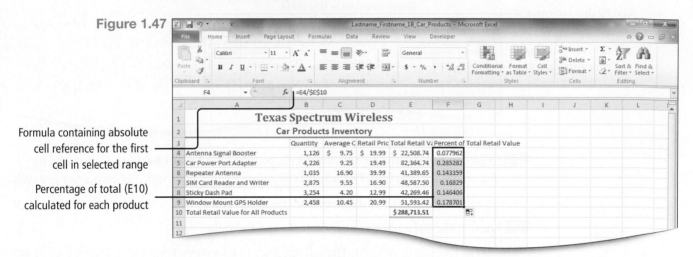

Formula containing absolute cell reference for the first cell in selected range

Percentage of total (E10) calculated for each product

11 Click cell **F5**, examine the formula in the **Formula Bar**, and then examine the formulas for cells **F6**, **F7**, **F8**, and **F9**.

> For each formula, the cell reference for the *Total Retail Value* of each product changed relative to its row; however, the value used as the divisor—*Total Retail Value for All Products* in cell F10—remained absolute. Thus, using either relative or absolute cell references, it is easy to duplicate formulas without typing them.

12 Save 🔲 your workbook.

More Knowledge | **Calculate a Percentage if You Know the Total and the Amount**

Using the equation *amount/total = percentage*, you can calculate the percentage by which a part makes up a total—with the percentage formatted as a decimal. For example, if on a test you score 42 points correctly out of 50, your percentage of correct answers is 42/50 = 0.84 or 84%.

Objective 10 | Edit Values in a Worksheet

Excel performs calculations on numbers; that is why you use Excel. If you make changes to the numbers, Excel automatically *re*-calculates. This is one of the most powerful and valuable features of Excel.

Activity 1.21 | Editing Values in a Worksheet

You can edit text and number values directly within a cell or on the Formula Bar.

1 In cell **E10**, notice the column total *$288,713.51*. Then, click cell **B5**, and to change its value type **3546** Watch cell **E5** and press [Enter].

> Excel formulas *re-calculate* if you change the value in a cell that is referenced in a formula. It is not necessary to delete the old value in a cell; selecting the cell and typing a new value replaces the old value with your new typing.

> The *Total Retail Value* of all *Car Power Port Adapters* items recalculates to *69,111.54* and the total in cell E10 recalculates to *$275,460.31*. Additionally, all of the percentages in column F recalculate.

2 Point to cell **D8**, and then double-click to place the insertion point within the cell. Use the arrow keys to move the insertion point to left or right of *2*, and use either [Del] or [Backspace] to delete *2* and then type **1** so that the new Retail Price is *11.99*.

3 Watch cell **E8** and **E10** as you press [Enter], and then notice the recalculation of the formulas in those two cells.

> Excel recalculates the value in cell E8 to *39,015.46* and the value in cell E10 to *$272,206.31*. Additionally, all of the percentages in column F recalculate because the *Total Retail Value for All Products* recalculated.

4 Point to cell **A2** so that the [✛] pointer is positioned slightly to the right of the word *Inventory*, and then double-click to place the insertion point in the cell. Edit the text to add the word **Valuation** pressing [Spacebar] as necessary, and then press [Enter].

5 Click cell **B3**, and then in the **Formula Bar**, click to place the insertion point after the letter *y*. Press [Spacebar] one time, type **In Stock** and then on the **Formula Bar**, click the **Enter** button [✓]. Click **Save** [💾], and then compare your screen with Figure 1.48.

> Recall that if text is too long to fit in the cell and the cell to the right contains data, the text is truncated—cut off—but the entire value still exists as the underlying value.

Figure 1.48

In Stock added to column title

Valuation added to subtitle

New value in cell B5

New value in cell D8

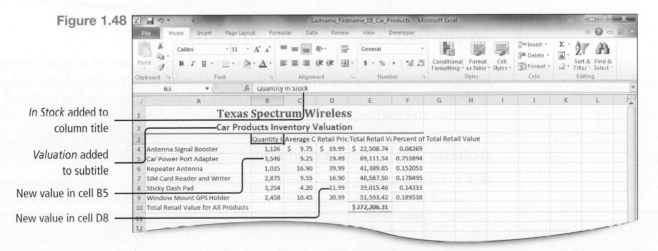

Excel | Chapter 1

Activity 1.22 │ Formatting Cells with the Percent Style

A percentage is part of a whole expressed in hundredths. For example, 75 cents is the same as 75 percent of one dollar. The Percent Style button formats the selected cell as a percentage rounded to the nearest hundredth.

1 Click cell **F4**, and then in the **Number group**, click the **Percent Style** button %.

> Your result is 8%, which is *0.08269* rounded to the nearest hundredth and expressed as a percentage. Percent Style displays the value of a cell as a percentage.

2 Select the range **F4:F9**, right-click over the selection, and then on the Mini toolbar, click the **Percent Style** button %, click the **Increase Decimal** button two times, and then click the **Center** button.

> Percent Style may not offer a percentage precise enough to analyze important financial information—adding additional decimal places to a percentage makes data more precise.

3 Click any cell to cancel the selection, **Save** your workbook, and then compare your screen with Figure 1.49.

Figure 1.49

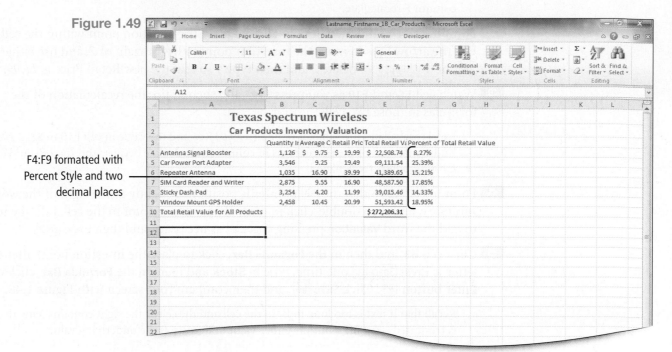

F4:F9 formatted with
Percent Style and two
decimal places

Objective 11 │ Format a Worksheet

Formatting refers to the process of specifying the appearance of cells and the overall layout of your worksheet. Formatting is accomplished through various commands on the Ribbon, for example, applying Cell Styles, and also from shortcut menus, keyboard shortcuts, and the Format Cells dialog box.

Activity 1.23 │ Inserting and Deleting Rows and Columns

1 In the **row heading area** on the left side of your screen, point to the row heading for **row 3** to display the ➡ pointer, and then right-click to simultaneously select the row and display a shortcut menu.

Another Way

Select the row, on the
Home tab, in the Cells
group, click the Insert
button arrow, and then
click Insert Sheet Rows.
Or, select the row and
click the Insert button—
the default setting of the
button inserts a new
sheet row above the
selected row.

2 On the displayed shortcut menu, click **Insert** to insert a new **row 3**.

The rows below the new row 3 move down one row, and the Insert Options button
displays. By default, the new row uses the formatting of the row *above*.

3 Click cell **E11**. On the **Formula Bar**, notice that the range changed to sum the new
range **E5:E10**. Compare your screen with Figure 1.50.

If you move formulas by inserting additional rows or columns in your worksheet, Excel
automatically adjusts the formulas. Excel adjusted all of the formulas in the worksheet
that were affected by inserting this new row.

Figure 1.50

Formula Bar displays
the formula in E11

New row 3 inserted

Insert Options button

Cell E11 selected

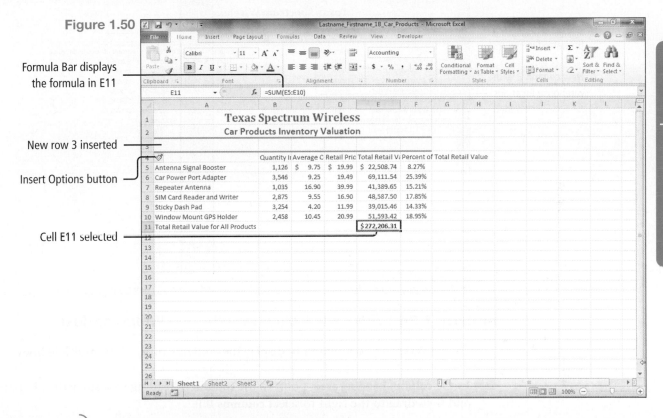

Another Way

Select the column, on
the Home tab, in the
Cells group, click the
Insert button arrow, and
then click Insert Sheet
Columns. Or, select the
column and click the
Insert button—the
default setting of the
button inserts a new
sheet column to the
right of the selected
column.

4 Click cell **A3**, type **As of December 31** and then on the **Formula Bar**, click the **Enter**
button ✓ to maintain **A3** as the active cell. **Merge & Center** 🔲 the text across the
range **A3:F3**, and then apply the **Heading 2** cell style.

5 In the **column heading area**, point to **column B** to display the ⬇ pointer, right-click,
and then click **Insert**.

By default, the new column uses the formatting of the column to the *left*.

6 Click cell **B4**, type **Warehouse Location** and then press Enter.

7 In cell **B5**, type **Dallas** and then type **Dallas** again in cells **B6** and **B10**. Use
AutoComplete to speed your typing by pressing Enter as soon as the AutoComplete
suggestion displays. In cells **B7**, **B8**, and **B9**, type **Houston**

8 In the **column heading area**, point to **column D**, right-click, and then click **Delete**.

The remaining columns shift to the left, and Excel adjusts all the formulas in the worksheet accordingly. You can use a similar technique to delete a row in a worksheet.

9 Compare your screen with Figure 1.51, and then **Save** 🖫 your workbook.

Figure 1.51

Text entered and formatted in cell A3

New column B with warehouse locations added

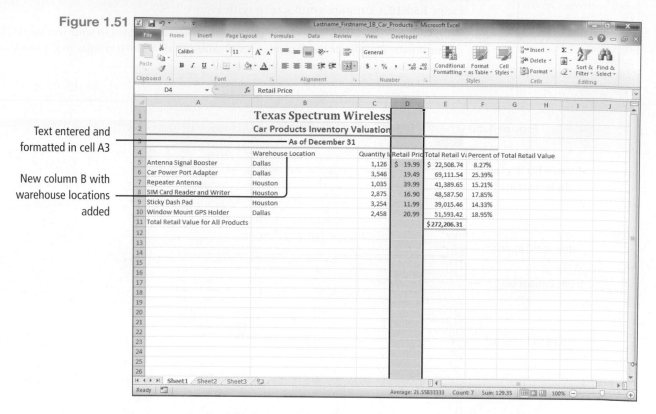

Activity 1.24 | Adjusting Column Widths and Wrapping Text

Use the Wrap Text command to display the contents of a cell on multiple lines.

1 In the **column heading area**, point to the **column B** heading to display the ⬇ pointer, and then drag to the right to select **columns B:F**.

2 With the columns selected, in the **column heading area**, point to the right boundary of any of the selected columns to display the ✛ pointer, and then drag to set the width to **90 pixels**.

Use this technique to format multiple columns or rows simultaneously.

3 Select the range **B4:F4** that comprises the column headings, and then on the **Home tab**, in the **Alignment group**, click the **Wrap Text** button 📑. Notice that the row height adjusts.

4 With the range **B4:F4** still selected, in the **Alignment group**, click the **Center** button ≡ and the **Middle Align** button ≡. With the range **B4:F4** still selected, apply the **Heading 4** cell style.

The Middle Align command aligns text so that it is centered between the top and bottom of the cell.

5 Select the range **B5:B10**, right-click, and then on the shortcut menu, click the **Center** button ☰. Click cell **A11**, and then from the **Cell Styles** gallery, under **Themed Cell Styles**, click **40% - Accent1**. Click any blank cell, and then compare your screen with Figure 1.52.

Figure 1.52

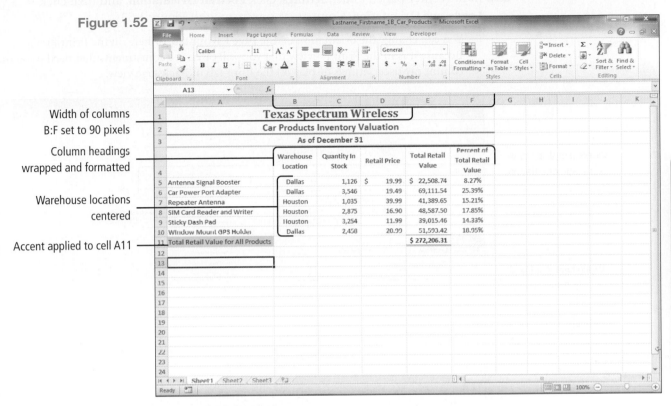

Width of columns B:F set to 90 pixels

Column headings wrapped and formatted

Warehouse locations centered

Accent applied to cell A11

6 Click the **Insert tab**, and then in the **Text group**, click **Header & Footer** to switch to Page Layout view and open the **Header area**.

7 In the **Navigation group**, click the **Go to Footer** button to move to the bottom of the page and open the **Footer area**, and then click just above the word *Footer* to place the insertion point in the **left section** of the **Footer area**.

8 In the **Header & Footer Elements group**, click the **File Name** button to add the name of your file to the footer—&*[File]* displays in the left section of the **Footer area**. Then, click in a cell above the footer to exit the **Footer area** and view your file name.

9 Click the **Page Layout tab**, in the **Page Setup group**, click the **Margins** button, and then at the bottom of the **Margins gallery**, click **Custom Margins**. In the **Page Setup** dialog box, under **Center on page**, select the **Horizontally** check box; click **OK**.

10 In the upper left corner of your screen, click **File** to display **Backstage** view. On the **Info tab**, on the right under the screen thumbnail, click **Properties**, and then click **Show Document Panel**.

11 In the **Author** box, replace the existing text with your firstname and lastname. In the **Subject** box, type your course name and section number. In the **Keywords** box, type **car products, inventory** and then **Close** ⊠ the **Document Information Panel**.

12 Press [Ctrl] + [F2] to view the **Print Preview**. At the bottom of the **Print Preview**, click the **Next Page** button ▶, and notice that as currently formatted, the worksheet occupies two pages.

13 In the center panel, under **Settings**, click **Portrait Orientation**, and then click **Landscape Orientation**. Compare your screen with Figure 1.53.

You can change the orientation on the Page Layout tab, or here, in the Print Preview. Because it is in the Print Preview that you will often see adjustments that need to be made, commonly used settings display on the Print tab in Backstage view.

Figure 1.53

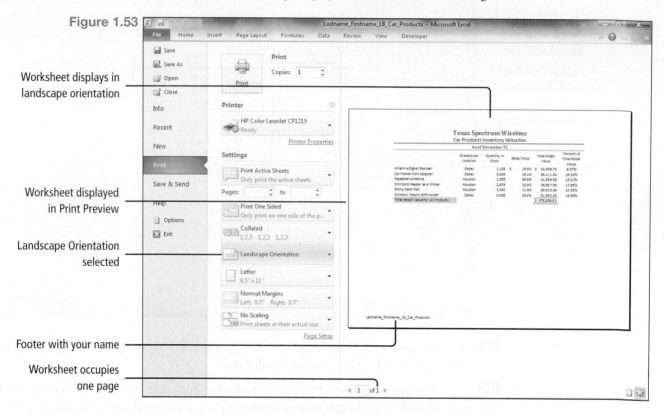

Worksheet displays in landscape orientation

Worksheet displayed in Print Preview

Landscape Orientation selected

Footer with your name

Worksheet occupies one page

14 Note any additional adjustments or corrections that need to be made, and then on the Ribbon, click **Home** to redisplay your worksheet. In the lower right corner of your screen, on the right side of the status bar, click the **Normal** button 🖿 to return to the Normal view, and then press [Ctrl] + [Home] to return to cell **A1**.

15 Make any necessary corrections. Then, at the bottom of your worksheet, click the **Sheet2 tab** to make it the active worksheet. Hold down [Ctrl], and then click the **Sheet3 tab**. Release [Ctrl], and then with both sheets selected (tab background is white), point to either of the selected sheet tabs, right-click, and click **Delete** to delete the unused sheets in the workbook.

16 Save 🔲 your workbook.

17 Print or submit your worksheet electronically as directed by your instructor. If required by your instructor, print or create an electronic version of your worksheet with formulas displayed using the instructions in Activity 1.16 in Project 1A.

18 Close your workbook and close Excel.

End **You have completed Project 1B** _____

Content-Based Assessments

Summary

In this chapter, you used Microsoft Excel 2010 to create and analyze data organized into columns and rows and to chart and perform calculations on the data. By organizing your data with Excel, you will be able to make calculations and create visual representations of your data in the form of charts.

Key Terms

Matching

Match each term in the second column with its correct definition in the first column by writing the letter of the term on the blank line in front of the correct definition.

_____ 1. An Excel file that contains one or more worksheets.

_____ 2. Another name for a worksheet.

_____ 3. The intersection of a column and a row.

A Cell

B Cell address

C Cell content

Content-Based Assessments

_____ 4. The labels along the lower border of the Excel window that identify each worksheet.

_____ 5. A vertical group of cells in a worksheet.

_____ 6. A horizontal group of cells in a worksheet.

_____ 7. Anything typed into a cell.

_____ 8. Information such as numbers, text, dates, or times of day that you type into a cell.

_____ 9. Text or numbers in a cell that are not a formula.

_____ 10. An equation that performs mathematical calculations on values in a worksheet.

_____ 11. A constant value consisting of only numbers.

_____ 12. Another name for a cell reference.

_____ 13. Another name for a constant value.

_____ 14. The small black square in the lower right corner of a selected cell.

_____ 15. The graphic representation of data in a worksheet.

D Chart
E Column
F Constant value
G Data
H Fill handle
I Formula
J Number value
K Row
L Sheet tabs
M Spreadsheet
N Value
O Workbook

Multiple Choice

Circle the correct answer.

1. On startup, Excel displays a new blank:
   A. document   **B.** workbook   **C.** grid

2. An Excel window element that displays the value or formula contained in the active cell is the:
   A. name box   **B.** status bar   **C.** formula bar

3. An Excel window element that displays the name of the selected cell, table, chart, or object is the:
   A. name box   **B.** status bar   **C.** formula bar

4. A box in the upper left corner of the worksheet grid that selects all the cells in a worksheet is the:
   A. name box   **B.** select all box   **C.** split box

5. A cell surrounded by a black border and ready to receive data is the:
   A. active cell   **B.** address cell   **C.** reference cell

6. The feature that generates and extends values into adjacent cells based on the values of selected cells is:
   A. AutoComplete   **B.** Auto Fill   **C.** fill handle

7. The default format that Excel applies to numbers is the:
   A. comma format   **B.** accounting format   **C.** general format

8. The data that displays in the Formula Bar is referred to as the:
   A. constant value   **B.** formula   **C.** underlying value

9. The type of cell reference that refers to cells by their fixed position in a worksheet is:
   A. absolute   **B.** relative   **C.** exponentiation

10. Tiny charts embedded in a cell that give a visual trend summary alongside your data are:
    A. embedded charts   **B.** sparklines   **C.** chart styles

Content-Based Assessments

Apply 1A skills from these Objectives:

◼1 Create, Save, and Navigate an Excel Workbook

◼2 Enter Data in a Worksheet

◼3 Construct and Copy Formulas and Use the Sum Function

◼4 Format Cells with Merge & Center and Cell Styles

◼5 Chart Data to Create a Column Chart and Insert Sparklines

◼6 Print, Display Formulas, and Close Excel

Skills Review | Project **1C** GPS Sales

In the following Skills Review, you will create a new Excel worksheet with a chart that summarizes the first quarter sales of GPS (Global Positioning System) navigation devices. Your completed worksheet will look similar to Figure 1.54.

Project Files

For Project 1C, you will need the following file:

> New blank Excel workbook

You will save your workbook as:

> Lastname_Firstname_1C_GPS_Sales

Project Results

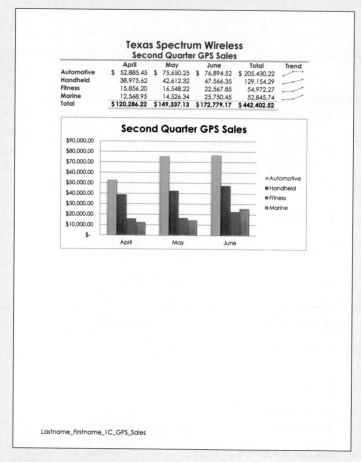

Figure 1.54

(Project 1C GPS Sales continues on the next page)

Content-Based Assessments

1 **Start** Excel. Click the **File tab** to display **Backstage** view, click **Save As**, and then in the **Save As** dialog box, navigate to your **Excel Chapter 1** folder. In the **File name** box, using your own name, type **Lastname_Firstname_ 1C_GPS_Sales** and then press Enter.

a. With cell **A1** as the active cell, type the worksheet title **Texas Spectrum Wireless** and then press Enter. In cell **A2**, type the worksheet subtitle **Second Quarter GPS Sales** and then press Enter.

b. Click in cell **A4**, type **Automotive** and then press Enter. In cell **A5**, type **Handheld** and then press Enter. In cell **A6**, type **Fitness** and then press Enter. In cell **A7**, type **Marine** and then press Enter. In cell **A8**, type **Total** and then press Enter.

c. Click cell **B3**. Type **April** and then in the **Formula Bar**, click the **Enter** button to keep cell **B3** the active cell. With **B3** as the active cell, point to the fill handle in the lower right corner of the selected cell, drag to the right to cell **D3**, and then release the mouse button to enter the text *May* and *June*.

d. Press Ctrl + Home, to make cell **A1** the active cell. In the **column heading area**, point to the vertical line between **column A** and **column B** to display the ⊞ pointer, hold down the left mouse button and drag to the right to increase the column width to **100 pixels**.

e. Point to cell **B3**, and then drag across to select cells **B3** and **C3** and **D3**. With the range **B3:D3** selected, point anywhere over the selected range, right-click, and then on the Mini toolbar, click the **Center** button.

f. Click cell **B4**, type **52885.45** and press Tab to make cell **C4** active. Enter the remaining values, as shown in **Table 1**, pressing Tab to move across the rows and Enter to move down the columns.

2 Click cell **B8** to make it the active cell and type =

a. At the insertion point, type **b4** and then type + Type **b5** and then type **+b6+b7** Press Enter. Your result is *120286.2*.

b. Click in cell **C8**. Type = and then click cell **C4**. Type + and then click cell **C5**. Repeat this process to complete the formula to add cells **C4** through **C7**, and then press Enter. Your result is *149337.1*.

c. Click cell **D8**. On the **Home tab**, in the **Editing group**, click the **Sum** button, and then press Enter to construct a formula by using the SUM function. Your result is *172779.2*. You can use any of these methods to add values; the Sum button is the most efficient.

d. In cell **E3** type **Total** and press Enter. With cell **E4** as the active cell, hold down Alt, and then press =. On the **Formula Bar**, click the **Enter** button to display the result and keep cell **E4** active.

e. With cell **E4** active, point to the fill handle in the lower right corner of the cell. Drag down through cell **E8**, and then release the mouse button to copy the formula with relative cell references down to sum each row.

3 Click cell **F3**. Type **Trend** and then press Enter.

a. Select the range **A1:F1**, and then on the **Home tab**, in the **Alignment group**, click the **Merge & Center** button. Select the range **A2:F2**, and then click the **Merge & Center** button.

b. Click cell **A1**. In the **Styles group**, click the **Cell Styles** button. Under **Titles and Headings**, click **Title**. Click cell **A2**, display the **Cell Styles** gallery, and then click **Heading 1**.

c. Select the range **B3:F3**, hold down Ctrl, and then select the range **A4:A8**. From the **Cell Styles** gallery, click **Heading 4** to apply this cell style to the column and row titles.

d. Select the range **B4:E4**, hold down Ctrl, and then select the range **B8:E8**. On the **Home tab**, in the **Number group**, click the **Accounting Number Format** button. Select the range **B5:E7**, and then in the **Number group**, click the **Comma Style** button. Select the range **B8:E8**. From the **Styles group**, display the **Cell Styles** gallery, and then under **Titles and Headings**, click **Total**.

Table 1

	April	May	June
Automotive	52885.45	75650.25	76894.52
Handheld	38975.62	42612.32	47566.35
Fitness	15856.20	16548.22	22567.85
Marine	12568.95	14526.34	25750.45

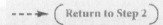 - - - ➤ (Return to Step 2)

(Project 1C GPS Sales continues on the next page)

Content-Based Assessments

e. On the Ribbon, click the **Page Layout tab**, and then from the **Themes group**, click the **Themes** button to display the **Themes** gallery. Click the **Austin** theme.

4 Select the range **A3:D7**. Click the **Insert tab**, and then in the **Charts group**, click **Column**. From the gallery of column chart types, under **2-D Column**, click the first chart—**Clustered Column**.

a. On the Quick Access Toolbar, click the **Save** button to be sure that you have saved your work up to this point. Point to the top border of the chart to display the ⌖ pointer, and then drag to position the chart inside the upper left corner of cell **A10**.

b. On the **Design tab**, in the **Data group**, click the **Switch Row/Column** button so that the months display on the Horizontal (Category) axis and the types of GPS equipment display in the legend.

c. On the **Design tab**, in the **Chart Layouts group**, click the first layout—**Layout 1**.

d. In the chart, click anywhere in the text *Chart Title* to select the text box. Type **Second Quarter GPS Sales** and then press Enter.

e. Click anywhere in the chart so that the chart title text box is not selected. On the **Design tab**, in the **Chart Styles group**, click the **More** button. Using the ScreenTips as your guide, locate and click **Style 18**.

f. Point to the lower right corner of the chart to display the ⬊ pointer, and then drag down and to the right so that the lower right border of the chart is positioned just inside the lower right corner of cell **F26**.

5 Select the range **B4:D7**. Click the **Insert tab**, and then in the **Sparklines group**, click **Line**. In the **Create Sparklines** dialog box, in the **Location Range** box, type **f4:f7** and then click **OK** to insert the sparklines.

a. On the **Design tab**, in the **Show group**, select the **Markers** check box to display markers in the sparklines.

b. On the **Design tab**, in the **Style group**, click the **More** button, and then in the second row, click the fourth style—**Sparkline Style Accent 4, Darker 25%**.

6 On the **Insert tab**, in the **Text group**, click **Header & Footer** to switch to **Page Layout** view and open the **Header** area.

a. In the **Navigation group**, click the **Go to Footer** button to open the Footer area. Click just above the word *Footer* to place the insertion point in the **left section** of the Footer.

b. In the **Header & Footer Elements group**, click the **File Name** button, and then click in a cell just above the footer to exit the Footer area.

7 On the right side of the status bar, click the **Normal** button to return to Normal view, and then press Ctrl + Home to make cell **A1** active.

a. Click the **File tab**, and then on the right, click **Properties**. Click **Show Document Panel**, and then in the **Author** box, delete any text and type your firstname and lastname. In the **Subject** box, type your course name and section number, and in the **Keywords** box, type **GPS sales Close** the Document Information Panel.

b. At the bottom of your worksheet, click the **Sheet2** tab. Hold down Ctrl, and then click the **Sheet3** tab. With both sheets selected, point to either of the selected sheet tabs, right-click, and then click **Delete** to delete the sheets.

c. Click the **Page Layout tab**. In the **Page Setup group**, click the **Margins** button, and then at the bottom of the **Margins** gallery, click **Custom Margins**. In the **Page Setup** dialog box, under **Center on page**, select the **Horizontally** check box.

d. In the lower right corner of the **Page Setup** dialog box, click **OK**. On the **File tab**, click **Print** to view the **Print Preview**. Click the **Home tab** to return to Normal view and if necessary, make any necessary corrections and resize and move your chart so that it is centered under the worksheet.

e. On the Quick Access Toolbar, click the **Save** button to be sure that you have saved your work up to this point.

f. Print or submit your workbook electronically as directed by your instructor. If required by your instructor, print or create an electronic version of your worksheets with formulas displayed by using the instructions in Activity 1.16. **Exit** Excel without saving so that you do not save the changes you made to print formulas.

End **You have completed Project 1C**

Content-Based Assessments

Apply 1B skills from these Objectives:

7 Check Spelling in a Worksheet

8 Enter Data by Range

9 Construct Formulas for Mathematical Operations

10 Edit Values in a Worksheet

11 Format a Worksheet

Skills Review | Project **1D** Charger Inventory

In the following Skills Review, you will create a worksheet that summarizes the inventory of cell phone chargers. Your completed worksheet will look similar to Figure 1.55.

Project Files

For Project 1D, you will need the following file:

New blank Excel workbook

You will save your workbook as:

Lastname_Firstname_1D_Charger_Inventory

Project Results

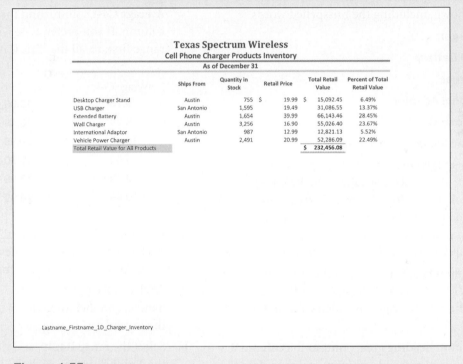

Figure 1.55

(Project 1D Charger Inventory continues on the next page)

Content-Based Assessments

1 **Start** Excel and display a new blank workbook. **Save** the workbook in your **Excel Chapter 1** folder, as Lastname_Firstname_1D_Charger_Inventory In cell **A1** type **Texas Spectrum Wireless** and in cell **A2** type **Cell Phone Charger Products Inventory**

a. Click cell **B3**, type **Quantity in Stock** and press [Tab]. In cell **C3** type **Average Cost** and press [Tab]. In cell **D3**, type **Retail Price** and press [Tab]. In cell **E3**, type **Total Retail Value** and press [Tab]. In cell **F3** type **Percent of Total Retail Value** and press [Enter].

b. Click cell **A4**, type **Desktop Charger Stand** and press [Enter]. In the range **A5:A10**, type the remaining row titles as shown, including the misspelled words.

   USB Charger

   Extended Battery

   Wall Charger

   International Adaptor

   Vehicle Powr Charger

   Total Retail Value for All Products

c. Press [Ctrl] + [Home] to move to the top of your worksheet. On the **Review tab**, in the **Proofing group**, click the **Spelling** button. Correct *Powr* to **Power** and any other spelling errors you may have made, and then when the message displays, *The spelling check is complete for the entire sheet*, click **OK**.

d. In the **column heading area**, point to the right boundary of **column A** to display the ⊞ pointer, and then drag to the right to widen **column A** to **225** pixels.

e. In the **column heading area**, point to the **column B** heading to display the ⬇ pointer, and then drag to the right to select **columns B:F**. With the columns selected, in the **column heading area**, point to the right boundary of any of the selected columns, and then drag to the right to set the width to **100 pixels**.

f. Select the range **A1:F1**. On the **Home tab**, in the **Alignment group**, click the **Merge & Center** button, and then from the **Cell Styles** gallery, apply the **Title** style. Select the range **A2:F2**. **Merge & Center** the text across the selection, and then from the **Cell Styles** gallery, apply the **Heading 1** style.

2 Select the empty range **B4:D9**. With cell B4 active in the range, type **755** and then press [Enter].

a. With cell **B5** active in the range, and pressing [Enter] after each entry, type the following data in the *Quantity in Stock* column:

   1595

   2654

   3256

   987

   2491

b. With the selected range still active, from the following table, beginning in cell **C4** and pressing [Enter] after each entry, enter the following data for the **Average Cost** column and then the **Retail Price** column. If you prefer, type without selecting the range first; recall that this is optional.

Average Cost	Retail Price
9.75	19.99
9.25	19.49
16.90	39.99
9.55	16.90
14.20	12.99
10.45	20.99

3 In cell **E4**, type **=b4*d4** and then press [Enter] to construct a formula that calculates the *Total Retail Value* of the *Desktop Charger Stands* (Quantity × Retail Price).

a. Click cell **E4**, position your pointer over the fill handle, and then drag down through cell **E9** to copy the formula.

b. Select the range **B4:B9**, and then on the **Home tab**, in the **Number group**, click the **Comma Style** button. Then, in the **Number group**, click the **Decrease Decimal** button two times to remove the decimal places from these non-currency values.

c. Click cell **E10**, in the **Editing group**, click the **Sum** button, and then press [Enter] to calculate the *Total Retail Value for All Products*. Your result is *272446.1*.

d. Select the range **C5:E9** and apply the **Comma Style**. Select the range **C4:E4**, hold down [Ctrl], and then click cell **E10**. With the nonadjacent cells selected, apply the **Accounting Number Format**. Click cell **E10**, and then from the **Cell Styles** gallery, apply the **Total** style.

(Project 1D Charger Inventory continues on the next page)

e. Click cell **F4**, type **=** and then click cell **E4**. Type **/** and then click cell **E10**. Press F4 to make the reference to cell *E10* absolute, and then on the **Formula Bar**, click the **Enter** button so that **F4** remains the active cell. Drag the fill handle to copy the formula down through cell **F9**.

f. Point to cell **B6**, and then double-click to place the insertion point within the cell. Use the arrow keys to move the insertion point to left or right of *2*, and use either Del or Backspace to delete 2, and then type **1** and press Enter so that the new *Quantity in Stock* is *1654*. Notice the recalculations in the worksheet.

4 Select the range **F4:F9**, right-click over the selection, and then on the Mini toolbar, click the **Percent Style** button. Click the **Increase Decimal** button two times, and then **Center** the selection.

a. In the **row heading area** on the left side of your screen, point to **row 3** to display the ➡ pointer, and then right-click to simultaneously select the row and display a shortcut menu. On the displayed shortcut menu, click **Insert** to insert a new **row 3**.

b. Click cell **A3**, type **As of December 31** and then on the **Formula Bar**, click the **Enter** button to keep cell **A3** as the active cell. **Merge & Center** the text across the range **A3:F3**, and then apply the **Heading 2** cell style.

5 In the **column heading area**, point to **column B**. When the ⬇ pointer displays, right-click, and then click **Insert** to insert a new column.

a. Click cell **B4**, and type **Ships From** and press Enter. In cell **B5**, type **Austin** and then press Enter. In cell **B6**, type **San Antonio** and then press Enter

b. Using AutoComplete to speed your typing by pressing Enter as soon as the AutoComplete suggestion displays, in cells **B7**, **B8**, and **B10** type **Austin** and in cell **B9** type **San Antonio**

c. In the **column heading area**, point to the right boundary of **column B**, and then drag to the left and set the width to **90 pixels**. From the **column heading area**, point to **column D**, right-click, and then click **Delete**.

d. Select the range **B4:F4**, and then on the **Home tab**, in the **Alignment group**, click the **Wrap Text** button, the **Center** button, and the **Middle Align** button. With the range still selected, apply the **Heading 4** cell style.

e. Select the range **B5:B10**, right-click, and then click the **Center** button. Click cell **A11**, and then from the **Cell Styles** gallery, under **Themed Cell Styles**, click **40% - Accent1**.

6 On the **Insert tab**, in the **Text group**, click **Header & Footer**. In the **Navigation group**, click the **Go To Footer** button, and then click just above the word *Footer*. In the **Header & Footer Elements group**, click the **File Name** button to add the name of your file to the footer. Click in a cell just above the footer to exit the **Footer area**, and then return the worksheet to **Normal** view.

a. Press Ctrl + Home to move the insertion point to cell **A1**. On the **Page Layout tab**, in the **Page Setup group**, click **Orientation**, and then click **Landscape**.

b. In the **Page Setup group**, click the **Margins** button, and then at the bottom of the **Margins gallery**, click **Custom Margins**. In the **Page Setup** dialog box, under **Center on page**, select the **Horizontally** check box, and then click **OK**.

c. Click the **File tab** to display **Backstage** view, and then on the right, click **Properties**. Click **Show Document Panel**, and then in the **Author** box, delete any text and type your firstname and lastname. In the **Subject** box type your course name and section number, in the **Keywords** box type **cell phone chargers** and then **Close** the **Document Information Panel**.

d. Select **Sheet2** and **Sheet3**, and then **Delete** both sheets.

e. **Save** your file and then print or submit your workbook electronically as directed by your instructor. If required by your instructor, print or create an electronic version of your worksheet with formulas displayed by using the instructions in Activity 1.16. **Exit** Excel without saving so that you do not save the changes you made to print formulas.

End **You have completed Project 1D** ——

Content-Based Assessments

Apply **1A** skills from these Objectives:

1. Create, Save, and Navigate an Excel Workbook
2. Enter Data in a Worksheet
3. Construct and Copy Formulas and Use the SUM Function
4. Format Cells with Merge & Center and Cell Styles
5. Chart Data to Create a Column Chart and Insert Sparklines
6. Print, Display Formulas, and Close Excel

Mastering Excel | Project **1E** Hard Drives

In the following Mastering Excel project, you will create a worksheet comparing the sales of different types of external hard drives sold in the second quarter. Your completed worksheet will look similar to Figure 1.56.

Project Files

For Project 1E, you will need the following file:

New blank Excel workbook

You will save your workbook as:

Lastname_Firstname_1E_Hard_Drives

Project Results

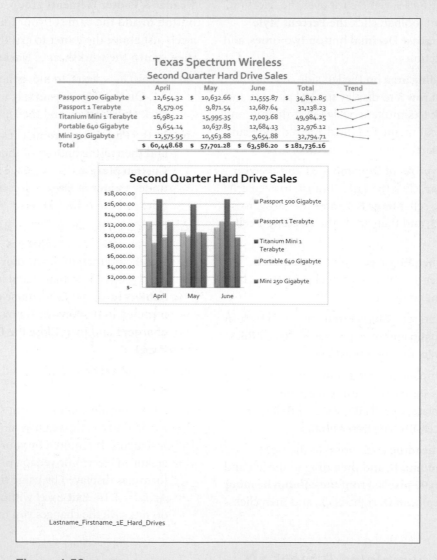

Figure 1.56

(Project 1E Hard Drives continues on the next page)

Content-Based Assessments

Mastering Excel | Project **1E** Hard Drives (continued)

1 **Start** Excel. In cell **A1**, type **Texas Spectrum Wireless** and in cell **A2**, type **Second Quarter Hard Drive Sales** Change the **Theme** to **Module**, and then **Save** the workbook in your **Excel Chapter 1** folder as **Lastname_Firstname_1E_Hard_Drives**

2 In cell **B3**, type **April** and then use the fill handle to enter the months *May* and *June* in the range **C3:D3**. In cell **E3**, type **Total** and in cell **F3**, type **Trend**

3 **Center** the column titles in the range **B3:F3**. **Merge & Center** the title across the range **A1:F1**, and apply the **Title** cell style. **Merge & Center** the subtitle across the range **A2:F2**, and apply the **Heading 1** cell style.

4 Widen **column A** to **170 pixels**, and then in the range **A4:A9**, type the following row titles:

Passport 500 Gigabyte

Passport 1 Terabyte

Titanium Mini 1 Terabyte

Portable 640 Gigabyte

Mini 250 Gigabyte

Total

5 Widen columns **B:F** to **100 pixels**, and then in the range **B4:D8**, enter the monthly sales figures for each type of hard drive, as shown in **Table 1** at the bottom of the page.

6 In cell **B9**, **Sum** the *April* hard drive sales, and then copy the formula across to cells **C9:D9**. In cell **E4**, **Sum** the *Passport 500 Gigabyte sales*, and then copy the formula down to cells **E5:E9**.

7 Apply the **Heading 4** cell style to the row titles and the column titles. Apply the **Total** cell style to the totals in the range **B9:E9**. Apply the **Accounting Number Format**

to the first row of sales figures and to the total row. Apply the **Comma Style** to the remaining sales figures.

8 To compare the monthly sales of each product visually, select the range that represents the sales figures for the three months, including the month names, and for each product name—do not include any totals in the range. With this data selected, **Insert** a **2-D Clustered Column** chart. Switch the Row/Column data so that the months display on the category axis and the types of hard drives display in the legend.

9 Position the upper left corner of the chart in the approximate center of cell **A11** so that the chart is visually centered below the worksheet, as shown in Figure 1.56. Apply **Chart Style 26**, and then modify the **Chart Layout** by applying **Layout 1**. Change the **Chart Title** to **Second Quarter Hard Drive Sales**

10 In the range **F4:F8**, insert **Line** sparklines that compare the monthly data. Do not include the totals. Show the sparkline **Markers** and apply **Sparkline Style Accent 2, Darker 50%**—in the first row, the second style.

11 Insert a **Footer** with the **File Name** in the **left section**, and then return the worksheet to **Normal** view. Display the **Document Panel**, add your name, your course name and section, and the keywords **hard drives, sales** Delete the unused sheets, and then center the worksheet **Horizontally** on the page. Check your worksheet by previewing it in **Print Preview**, and then make any necessary corrections.

12 **Save** your workbook, and then print or submit electronically as directed. If required by your instructor, print or create an electronic version of your worksheets with formulas displayed by using the instructions in Activity 1.16. **Exit** Excel without saving so that you do not save the changes you made to print formulas.

Table 1

	April	May	June
Passport 500 Gigabyte	12654.32	10632.66	11555.87
Passport 1 Terabyte	8579.05	9871.54	12887.84
Titanium Mini 1 Terabyte	16985.22	15995.35	17003.68
Portable 640 Gigabyte	9654.14	10637.85	12684.13
Mini 250 Gigabyte	12575.95	10563.88	9654.88

(Return to Step 6)

End **You have completed Project 1E**

Excel | Chapter 1

Project 1E: Hard Drives | Excel 101

Apply **1B** skills from these Objectives:

7   Check Spelling in a Worksheet

8   Enter Data by Range

9   Construct Formulas for Mathematical Operations

10   Edit Values in a Worksheet

11   Format a Worksheet

Mastering Excel | Project **1F** Camera Accessories

In the following Mastering Excel project, you will create a worksheet that summarizes the sale of digital camera accessories. Your completed worksheet will look similar to Figure 1.57.

Project Files

For Project 1F, you will need the following file:

New blank Excel workbook

You will save your workbook as:

Lastname_Firstname_1F_Camera_Accessories

Project Results

Texas Spectrum Wireless
Digital Camera Accessories Sales

	Month Ending August 31			
	Quantity Sold	Retail Price	Total Sales	Percent of Total Sales
Small Cloth Gear Bag	254	$ 19.99	$ 5,077.46	10.69%
Large Cloth Gear Bag	182	24.99	4,548.18	9.58%
Lens Cap	351	6.99	2,453.49	5.17%
Lens Hood	125	5.49	686.25	1.44%
Remote Switch	750	22.50	16,875.00	35.53%
Mini Tripod	554	24.99	13,844.46	29.15%
Cleaning Kit	365	10.99	4,011.35	8.45%
Total Sales for All Products			$ 47,496.19	

Lastname_Firstname_1F_Camera_Accessories

Figure 1.57

(Project 1F Camera Accessories continues on the next page)

Content-Based Assessments

1 **Start** Excel and display a new blank workbook. **Save** the workbook in your **Excel Chapter 1** folder as **Lastname_Firstname_1F_Camera_Accessories** In cell **A1**, type **Texas Spectrum Wireless** In cell **A2**, type **Digital Camera Accessories Sales** and then **Merge & Center** the title and the subtitle across **columns A:F**. Apply the **Title** and **Heading 1** cell styles respectively.

2 Beginning in cell **B3**, type the following column titles: **Product Number** and **Quantity Sold** and **Retail Price** and **Total Sales** and **Percent of Total Sales**

3 Beginning in cell **A4**, type the following row titles, including misspelled words:

> Small Cloth Gear Bag
>
> Large Cloth Gear Bag
>
> Lens Cap
>
> Lens Hood
>
> Remote Switch
>
> Mini Tripod
>
> Cleening Kit
>
> Total Sales for All Products

4 Make cell **A1** the active cell, and then check spelling in your worksheet. Correct *Cleening* to **Cleaning**, and make any other necessary corrections. Widen **column A** to **180 pixels** and **columns B:F** to **90 pixels**.

5 In the range **B4:D10**, type the data shown in **Table 1** at the bottom of the page.

6 In cell **E4**, construct a formula to calculate the *Total Sales* of the *Small Cloth Gear Bags* by multiplying the *Quantity Sold* times the *Retail Price*. Copy the formula down for the remaining products. In cell **E11**, use the **SUM** function to calculate the *Total Sales for All Products*, and then apply the **Total** cell style to the cell.

7 Using absolute cell references as necessary so that you can copy the formula, in cell **F4**, construct a formula to calculate the *Percent of Total Sales* for the first product by dividing the *Total Sales* of the *Small Cloth Gear Bags* by the *Total Sales for All Products*. Copy the formula down for the remaining products. To the computed percentages, apply **Percent Style** with two decimal places, and then **Center** the percentages.

8 Apply the **Comma Style** with no decimal places to the *Quantity Sold* figures. To cells **D4**, **E4**, and **E11** apply the **Accounting Number Format**. To the range **D5:E10**, apply the **Comma Style**.

9 Change the *Retail Price* of the *Mini Tripod* to **24.99** and the *Quantity Sold* of the *Remote Switch* to **750** Delete **column B**, and then **Insert** a new **row 3**. In cell **A3**, type **Month Ending August 31** and then **Merge & Center** the text across the range **A3:E3**. Apply the **Heading 2** cell style. To cell **A12**, apply the **Accent1** cell style. Select the four column titles, apply **Wrap Text**, **Middle Align**, and **Center** formatting, and then apply the **Heading 3** cell style.

10 Insert a **Footer** with the **File Name** in the **left section**, and then return to **Normal** view. Display the **Document Panel**, add your name, your course name and section, and the keywords **digital camera accessories, sales**

11 Delete the unused sheets, and then center the worksheet **Horizontally** on the page. Preview the worksheet in **Print Preview**, and make any necessary corrections.

12 **Save** your workbook, and then print or submit electronically as directed. If required by your instructor, print or create an electronic version of your worksheets with formulas displayed by using the instructions in Activity 1.16. **Exit** Excel without saving so that you do not save the changes you made to print formulas.

Table 1

	Product Number	Quantity Sold	Retail Price
Small Cloth Gear Bag	CGB-3	254	19.99
Large Cloth Gear Bag	CGB-8	182	24.99
Lens Cap	LC-2	351	6.99
Lens Hood	LH-4	125	5.49
Remote Switch	RS-5	677	22.50
Mini Tripod	MTP-6	554	29.99
Cleaning Kit	CK-8	365	10.99

- - - → (Return to Step 6)

End **You have completed Project 1F**

Content-Based Assessments

1 Create, Save, and Navigate an Excel Workbook

2 Enter Data in a Worksheet

3 Construct and Copy Formulas and Use the SUM Function

4 Format Cells with Merge & Center and Cell Styles

5 Chart Data to Create a Column Chart and Insert Sparklines

6 Print, Display Formulas, and Close Excel

7 Check Spelling in a Worksheet

8 Enter Data by Range

9 Construct Formulas for Mathematical Operations

10 Edit Values in a Worksheet

11 Format a Worksheet

Mastering Excel | Project **1G** Sales Comparison

In the following Mastering Excel project, you will create a new worksheet that compares annual laptop sales by store location. Your completed worksheet will look similar to Figure 1.58.

Project Files

For Project 1G, you will need the following file:

New blank Excel workbook

You will save your workbook as:

Lastname_Firstname_1G_Sales_Comparison

Project Results

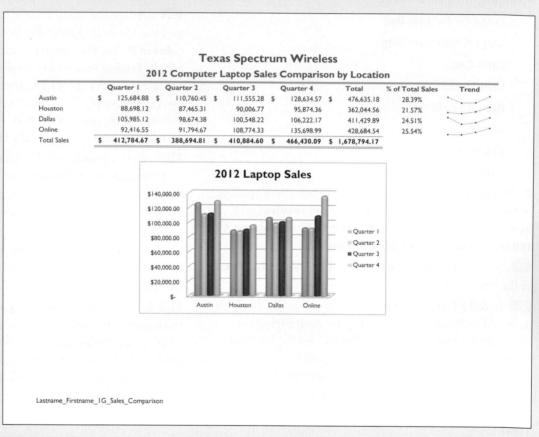

Figure 1.58

(Project 1G Sales Comparison continues on the next page)

Content-Based Assessments

Mastering Excel | Project 1G Sales Comparison (continued)

1 **Start** Excel. In a new blank workbook, as the worksheet title, in cell **A1**, type **Texas Spectrum Wireless** As the worksheet subtitle, in cell **A2**, type **2012 Computer Laptop Sales Comparison by Location** and then **Save** the workbook in your **Excel Chapter 1** folder as **Lastname_Firstname_1G_Sales_Comparison**

2 In cell **B3**, type **Quarter 1** and then use the fill handle to enter *Quarter 2*, *Quarter 3*, and *Quarter 4* in the range **C3:E3**. In cell **F3**, type **Total** In cell **G3**, type **% of Total Sales** In cell **H3**, type **Trend**

3 In the range **A4:A7**, type the following row titles: **Austin** and **Houston** and **Online** and **Total Sales**

4 Widen columns **A:H** to **115 pixels**. **Merge & Center** the title across the range **A1:H1**, and then apply the **Title** cell style. **Merge & Center** the subtitle across the range **A2:H2**, and then apply the **Heading 1** cell style. Select the seven column titles, apply **Center** formatting, and then apply the **Heading 4** cell style.

5 In the range **B4:E6**, enter the sales values for each Quarter as shown in **Table 1** at the bottom of the page.

6 **Sum** the *Quarter 1* sales, and then copy the formula across for the remaining Quarters. **Sum** the sales for the *Austin* location, and then copy the formula down through cell **F7**. Apply the **Accounting Number Format** to the first row of sales figures and to the total row, and the **Comma Style** to the remaining sales figures. Format the totals in **row 7** with the **Total** cell style.

7 **Insert** a new **row 6** with the row title **Dallas** and the following sales figures for each quarter: **105985.12** and **98674.38** and **100548.22** and **106222.17** Copy the formula in cell **F5** down to cell **F6** to sum the new row.

8 Using absolute cell references as necessary so that you can copy the formula, in cell **G4** construct a formula to calculate the *Percent of Total Sales* for the first location by dividing the *Total* for the *Austin* location by the *Total Sales* for all Quarters. Copy the formula down for the remaining locations. To the computed percentages, apply

Percent Style with two decimal places, and then **Center** the percentages.

9 Insert **Line** sparklines in the range **H4:H7** that compare the quarterly data. Do not include the totals. Show the sparkline **Markers** and apply the second style in the second row—**Sparkline Style Accent 2, Darker 25%**.

10 **Save** your workbook. To compare the quarterly sales of each location visually, select the range that represents the sales figures for the four quarters, including the quarter names and each location—do not include any totals in the range. With this data selected, **Insert** a **Column, Clustered Cylinder** chart.

11 Switch the row/column data so that the locations display on the category axis. Position the top edge of the chart in **row 10** and visually center it below the worksheet data. Apply **Chart Style 26**, and then modify the **Chart Layout** by applying **Layout 1**. Change the **Chart Title** to **2012 Laptop Sales**

12 Deselect the chart. Change the **Orientation** to **Landscape**, center the worksheet **Horizontally** on the page, and then change the **Theme** to **Solstice**. Scale the worksheet so that the **Width** fits to **1 page**. Insert a **Footer** with the **File Name** in the **left section**. Return the worksheet to **Normal** view and make **A1** the active cell so that you can view the top of your worksheet.

13 Display the **Document Panel**, add your name, your course name and section, and the keywords **laptops, sales** Delete the unused sheets, preview your worksheet in **Print Preview**, and then make any necessary corrections.

14 **Save** your workbook, and then print or submit electronically as directed. If required by your instructor, print or create an electronic version of your worksheets with formulas displayed by using the instructions in Activity 1.16. **Exit** Excel without saving so that you do not save the changes you made to print formulas.

Table 1

	Quarter 1	Quarter 2	Quarter 3	Quarter 4
Austin	125684.88	110760.45	111555.28	128634.57
Houston	88698.12	87465.31	90006.77	95874.36
Online	92416.55	91794.67	108774.33	135698.99

- - - → (Return to Step 6)

End **You have completed Project 1G**

Content-Based Assessments

Apply a combination of
the **1A** and **1B** skills.

GO! Fix It | Project **1H** Team Sales

Project Files

For Project 1H, you will need the following file:

　e01H_Team_Sales

You will save your workbook as:

　Lastname_Firstname_1H_Team_Sales

In this project, you will edit a worksheet that summarizes sales by each sales team member at the Texas Spectrum Wireless San Antonio location for the month of February. From the student files that accompany this textbook, open the file e01H_Team_Sales, and then save the file in your Excel Chapter 1 folder as **Lastname_Firstname_1H_Team_Sales**

To complete the project, you must find and correct errors in formulas and formatting. View each formula in the Formula Bar and edit as necessary. In addition to errors that you find, you should know:

- There are two spelling errors.
- Worksheet titles should be merged and centered and appropriate cell styles should be applied.
- Appropriate number and accounting format with zero decimals should be applied to the data and text should be wrapped where necessary. Percent style formatting should be applied appropriately where necessary.
- Column headings should be formatted with the Heading 4 style.
- In the chart, the team member names should display on the Horizontal (Category) axis and the week names should display in the legend.
- The chart should include the title **February Team Member Sales**
- The worksheet should be centered horizontally on one page in Landscape orientation. Remove unused sheets.
- A footer should be inserted that includes the file name, and document properties should include the keywords **team sales, San Antonio**

Save your workbook, and then print or submit electronically as directed. If required by your instructor, print or create an electronic version of your worksheets with formulas displayed by using the instructions in Activity 1.16. Exit Excel without saving so that you do not save the changes you made to print formulas.

End You have completed Project 1H ————————————————

Content-Based Assessments

GO! Make It | Project 1I Printer Sales

Project Files

For Project 1I, you will need the following file:

New blank Excel workbook

You will save your workbook as:

Lastname_Firstname_1I_Printer_Sales

Create the worksheet shown in Figure 1.59. Use the Pushpin theme and change the Orientation to Landscape. Construct formulas in the Total Sold, Total Sales, and Percent of Total Sales columns, and in the Total row. Apply cell styles and number formatting as shown. Use Style 26 for the chart. Insert sparklines for the monthly data using the first style in the second row— Sparkline Style Accent 1, Darker 25%. Add your name, your course name and section, and the keywords **inkjet, printer, sales** to the document properties. Save the file in your Excel Chapter 1 folder as **Lastname_Firstname_1I_Printer_Sales**

Project Results

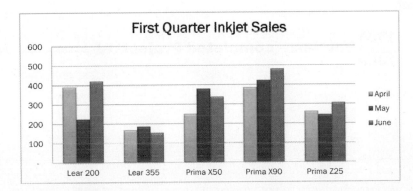

Texas Spectrum Wireless
First Quarter Inkjet Printer Sales

Model	April	May	June	Total Sold	Retail Price	Total Sales	Percent of Total Sales	Trend
Lear 200	390	224	421	1,035	$ 79.99	$ 82,789.65	8.50%	
Lear 355	168	186	153	507	169.99	86,184.93	8.85%	
Prima X50	250	379	339	968	199.99	193,590.32	19.88%	
Prima X90	386	423	482	1,291	249.99	322,737.09	33.15%	
Prima Z25	261	244	307	812	354.99	288,251.88	29.61%	
Total	1,455	1,456	1,702	4,613		$ 973,553.87		

First Quarter Inkjet Sales

Lastname_Firstname_1I_Printer_Sales

Figure 1.59

End You have completed Project 1I

Content-Based Assessments

Apply a combination of the **1A** and **1B** skills.

GO! Solve It | Project **1J** Warranty Sales

Project Files

For Project 1J, you will need the following file:

  e01J_Warranty_Sales

You will save your workbook as:

  Lastname_Firstname_1J_Warranty_Sales

Open the file e01J_Warranty_Sales and save it as **Lastname_Firstname_1J_Warranty_Sales**
Complete the worksheet by using Auto Fill to enter the Quarter headings, and then calculating
Total Sold, *Total Sales*, *Total For All Products*, and *Percent of Total Sales*. Format the worksheet
attractively, and apply appropriate financial formatting. Insert a chart that compares the total
number of warranties sold for each item across Quarters, and format the chart to display the
information appropriately. Include the file name in the footer, add appropriate document
properties, and submit as directed.

		Performance Level		
		Exemplary: You consistently applied the relevant skills	**Proficient:** You sometimes, but not always, applied the relevant skills	**Developing:** You rarely or never applied the relevant skills
Performance Element	Create formulas	All formulas are correct and are efficiently constructed.	Formulas are correct but not always constructed in the most efficient manner.	One or more formulas are missing or incorrect; or only numbers were entered.
	Create a chart	Chart created properly.	Chart was created but incorrect data was selected.	No chart was created.
	Format attractively and appropriately	Formatting is attractive and appropriate.	Adequately formatted but difficult to read or unattractive.	Inadequate or no formatting.

End You have completed Project 1J

Content-Based Assessments

Apply a combination of the **1A** and **1B** skills.

GO! Solve It | Project **1K** Service Receipts

Project Files

For Project 1K, you will need the following file:

e01K_Service_Receipts

You will save your workbook as:

Lastname_Firstname_1K_Service_Receipts

Open the file e01K_Service_Receipts and save it as **Lastname_Firstname_1K_Service_Receipts** Complete the worksheet by using Auto Fill to complete the month headings, and then calculating the Total Receipts for each month and for each product. Insert and format appropriate sparklines in the Trend column. Format the worksheet attractively with a title and subtitle, check spelling, adjust column width, and apply appropriate financial formatting. Insert a chart that compares the total sales receipts for each product with the months displaying as the categories, and format the chart attractively. Include the file name in the footer, add appropriate properties, and submit as directed.

		Performance Level		
		Exemplary: You consistently applied the relevant skills	**Proficient:** You sometimes, but not always, applied the relevant skills	**Developing:** You rarely or never applied the relevant skills
Performance Element	Create formulas	All formulas are correct and are efficiently constructed.	Formulas are correct but not always constructed in the most efficient manner.	One or more formulas are missing or incorrect; or only numbers were entered.
	Create a chart	Chart created properly.	Chart was created but incorrect data was selected.	No chart was created.
	Insert and format sparklines	Sparklines inserted and formatted properly.	Sparklines were inserted but incorrect data was selected or sparklines were not formatted.	No sparklines were inserted.
	Format attractively and appropriately	Formatting is attractive and appropriate.	Adequately formatted but difficult to read or unattractive.	Inadequate or no formatting.

End You have completed Project 1K

Outcomes-Based Assessments

Rubric

The following outcomes-based assessments are *open-ended assessments*. That is, there is no specific correct result; your result will depend on your approach to the information provided. Make *Professional Quality* your goal. Use the following scoring rubric to guide you in *how* to approach the problem, and then to evaluate *how well* your approach solves the problem.

The *criteria*—Software Mastery, Content, Format and Layout, and Process—represent the knowledge and skills you have gained that you can apply to solving the problem. The *levels of performance*—Professional Quality, Approaching Professional Quality, or Needs Quality Improvements—help you and your instructor evaluate your result.

	Your completed project is of Professional Quality if you:	Your completed project is Approaching Professional Quality if you:	Your completed project Needs Quality Improvements if you:
1-Software Mastery	Choose and apply the most appropriate skills, tools, and features and identify efficient methods to solve the problem.	Choose and apply some appropriate skills, tools, and features, but not in the most efficient manner.	Choose inappropriate skills, tools, or features, or are inefficient in solving the problem.
2-Content	Construct a solution that is clear and well organized, contains content that is accurate, appropriate to the audience and purpose, and is complete. Provide a solution that contains no errors in spelling, grammar, or style.	Construct a solution in which some components are unclear, poorly organized, inconsistent, or incomplete. Misjudge the needs of the audience. Have some errors in spelling, grammar, or style, but the errors do not detract from comprehension.	Construct a solution that is unclear, incomplete, or poorly organized; contains some inaccurate or inappropriate content; and contains many errors in spelling, grammar, or style. Do not solve the problem.
3-Format and Layout	Format and arrange all elements to communicate information and ideas, clarify function, illustrate relationships, and indicate relative importance.	Apply appropriate format and layout features to some elements, but not others. Overuse features, causing minor distraction.	Apply format and layout that does not communicate information or ideas clearly. Do not use format and layout features to clarify function, illustrate relationships, or indicate relative importance. Use available features excessively, causing distraction.
4-Process	Use an organized approach that integrates planning, development, self-assessment, revision, and reflection.	Demonstrate an organized approach in some areas, but not others; or, use an insufficient process of organization throughout.	Do not use an organized approach to solve the problem.

Outcomes-Based Assessments

Apply a combination of the 1A and 1B skills.

GO! Think | Project **1L** Phone Plans

Project Files

For Project 1L, you will need the following file:

New blank Excel workbook

You will save your workbook as:

Lastname_Firstname_1L_Phone_Plans

Roslyn Thomas, President of Texas Spectrum Wireless, needs a worksheet that summarizes the following data regarding the first quarter sales of cell phone calling plans that the company is offering for domestic and international calls. Roslyn would like the worksheet to include a calculation of the total sales for each plan and a total of the sales of all of the plans. She would also like to know each plan's percentage of total sales.

	Number Sold	Price
Domestic Standard	2556	29.99
Domestic Premium	3982	49.99
Domestic Platinum	1647	64.99
International Standard	582	85.99
International Premium	365	102.99

Create a worksheet that provides Roslyn with the information needed. Include appropriate worksheet, column, and row titles. Using the formatting skills that you practiced in this chapter, format the worksheet in a manner that is professional and easy to read and understand. Insert a footer with the file name and add appropriate document properties. Save the file as **Lastname_Firstname_1L_Phone_Plans** and print or submit as directed by your instructor.

End **You have completed Project 1L** ————————————————

Outcomes-Based Assessments

GO! Think | Project **1M** Advertising

Project Files

For Project 1M, you will need the following file:

New blank Excel workbook

You will save your workbook as:

Lastname_Firstname_1M_Advertising

Eliott Verschoren, Vice President of Marketing for Texas Spectrum Wireless, is conducting an analysis of the advertising expenditures at the company's four retail locations based on the following data:

	Quarter 1	Quarter 2	Quarter 3	Quarter 4
Austin	22860	25905	18642	28405
Dallas	18557	17963	22883	25998
Houston	32609	28462	25915	31755
San Antonio	12475	15624	13371	17429

Using this information, create a workbook that includes totals by quarter and by location, sparklines to demonstrate the quarterly trends, and a column chart that compares the quarterly data across locations. Include appropriate worksheet, row, and column titles. Using the formatting skills that you practiced in this chapter, format the worksheet in a manner that is professional and easy to read and understand. Insert a footer with the file name and add appropriate document properties. Save the file as **Lastname_Firstname_1M_Advertising** and print or submit as directed by your instructor.

End **You have completed Project 1M** ————————————

Outcomes-Based Assessments

You and GO! | Project **1N** Personal Expenses

Project Files

For Project 1N, you will need the following file:

New blank Excel workbook

You will save your workbook as:

Lastname_Firstname_1N_Personal_Expenses

Develop a worksheet that details your personal expenses from the last three months. Some of these expenses might include, but are not limited to, Mortgage, Rent, Utilities, Phone, Food, Entertainment, Tuition, Childcare, Clothing, and Insurance. Include a total for each month and for each category of expense. Insert a column with a formula that calculates the percent that each expense category is of the total expenditures. Format the worksheet by adjusting column widths and wrapping text, and by applying appropriate financial number formatting and cell styles. Insert a column chart that compares your expenses by month and modify the chart layout and style. Insert a footer with the file name and center the worksheet horizontally on the page. Save your file as **Lastname_Firstname_1N_Personal_Expenses** and submit as directed.

End You have completed Project 1N ————————————————

Using Functions, Creating Tables, and Managing Large Workbooks

OUTCOMES

At the end of this chapter you will be able to:

OBJECTIVES

Mastering these objectives will enable you to:

PROJECT 2A

Analyze inventory by applying statistical and logical calculations to data and by sorting and filtering data.

1. Use the SUM, AVERAGE, MEDIAN, MIN, and MAX Functions (p. 117)
2. Move Data, Resolve Error Messages, and Rotate Text (p. 121)
3. Use COUNTIF and IF Functions and Apply Conditional Formatting (p. 123)
4. Use Date & Time Functions and Freeze Panes (p. 128)
5. Create, Sort, and Filter an Excel Table (p. 130)
6. Format and Print a Large Worksheet (p. 133)

PROJECT 2B

Summarize the data on multiple worksheets.

7. Navigate a Workbook and Rename Worksheets (p. 138)
8. Enter Dates, Clear Contents, and Clear Formats (p. 139)
9. Copy and Paste by Using the Paste Options Gallery (p. 143)
10. Edit and Format Multiple Worksheets at the Same Time (p. 144)
11. Create a Summary Sheet with Column Sparklines (p. 150)
12. Format and Print Multiple Worksheets in a Workbook (p. 154)

grafica/Shutterstock

In This Chapter

In this chapter, you will use the Statistical functions to calculate the average of a group of numbers, and use other Logical and Date & Time functions. You will use the counting functions and apply conditional formatting to make data easy to visualize. In this chapter, you will also create a table and analyze the table's data by sorting and filtering the data. You will summarize a workbook that contains multiple worksheets.

The projects in this chapter relate to **Laurales Herbs and Spices**. After ten years as an Executive Chef, Laura Morales started her own business, which offers quality products for cooking, eating, and entertaining in retail stores and online. In addition to herbs and spices, there is a wide variety of condiments, confections, jams, sauces, oils, and vinegars. Later this year, Laura will add a line of tools, cookbooks, and gift baskets. The company name is a combination of Laura's first and last names, and also the name of an order of plants related to cinnamon.

Project 2A Inventory Status Report

Project Activities

In Activities 2.01 through 2.15, you will edit a worksheet for Laura Morales, President, detailing the current inventory of flavor products at the Oakland production facility. Your completed worksheet will look similar to Figure 2.1.

Project Files

For Project 2A, you will need the following file:

e02A_Flavor_Inventory

You will save your workbook as:

Lastname_Firstname_2A_Flavor_Inventory

Project Results

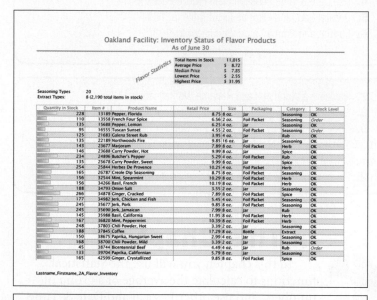

Figure 2.1
Project 2A Flavor Inventory

Objective 1 | Use the SUM, AVERAGE, MEDIAN, MIN, and MAX Functions

A *function* is a predefined formula—a formula that Excel has already built for you—that performs calculations by using specific values in a particular order or structure. *Statistical functions*, which include the AVERAGE, MEDIAN, MIN, and MAX functions, are useful to analyze a group of measurements.

Activity 2.01 | Using the SUM and AVERAGE Functions

Laura has a worksheet with information about the inventory of flavor product types currently in stock at the Oakland facility. In this activity, you will use the SUM and AVERAGE functions to gather information about the product inventory.

1 **Start** Excel. From **Backstage** view, display the **Open** dialog box, and then from the student files that accompany this textbook, locate and open **e02A_Flavor_Inventory**. Click the **File tab** to redisplay **Backstage** view, and then click **Save As**. In the **Save As** dialog box, navigate to the location where you are storing your projects for this chapter.

2 Create a new folder named **Excel Chapter 2** open the new folder, and then in the **File name** box, type **Lastname_Firstname_2A_Flavor_Inventory** Click **Save** or press Enter.

3 Scroll down. Notice that the worksheet contains data related to types of flavor products in inventory, including information about the *Quantity in Stock*, *Item #*, *Product Name*, *Retail Price*, *Size*, *Packaging*, and *Category*.

4 Leave row 3 blank, and then in cell **A4**, type **Total Items in Stock** In cell **A5**, type **Average Price** In cell **A6**, type **Median Price**

5 Click cell **B4**. Click the **Formulas tab**, and then in the **Function Library group**, click the **AutoSum** button. Compare your screen with Figure 2.2.

The *SUM function* that you have used is a predefined formula that adds all the numbers in a selected range of cells. Because it is frequently used, there are several ways to insert the function.

For example, you can insert the function from the Home tab's Editing group, by using the keyboard shortcut Alt + =, from the Function Library group on the Formulas tab, and also from the Math & Trig button in that group.

Excel | Chapter 2

Figure 2.2

AutoSum button

Formulas tab

Function Library group

Row 3 blank

Row titles entered

SUM function in cell B4

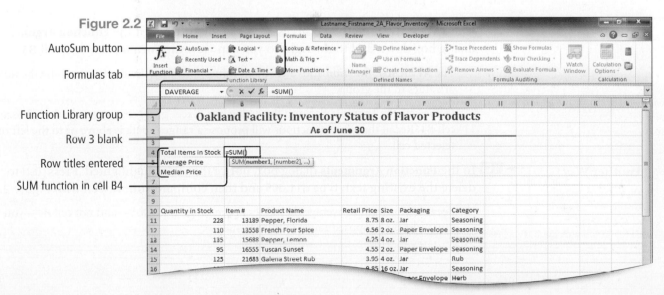

6 With the insertion point blinking in the function, select the range **A11:A65**, dragging down as necessary, and then press Enter. Scroll up to view the top of your worksheet, and notice your result in cell **B4**, *11015*.

7 Click cell **B4** and look at the **Formula Bar**: Compare your screen with Figure 2.3.

> *SUM* is the name of the function. The values in parentheses are the ***arguments***—the values that an Excel function uses to perform calculations or operations. In this instance, the argument consists of the values in the range A11:A65.

Figure 2.3

Function and arguments display in Formula Bar

Result of SUM function displays in B4

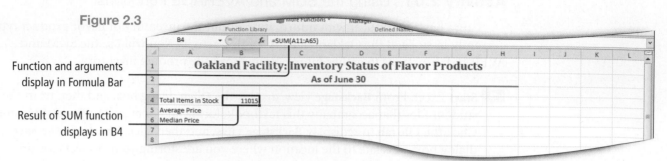

8 Click cell **B5**. In the **Function Library group**, click the **More Functions** button, point to **Statistical**, point to **AVERAGE**, and notice the ScreenTip. Compare your screen with Figure 2.4.

> The ScreenTip describes how the AVERAGE function will compute the calculation.

Figure 2.4

More Functions button

Statistical functions

ScreenTip describes function

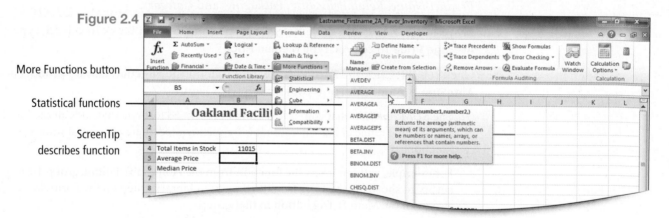

9 Click **AVERAGE**, and then if necessary, drag the title bar of the **Function Arguments** dialog box down and to the right so you can view the **Formula Bar** and cell **B5**.

> The ***AVERAGE function*** adds a group of values, and then divides the result by the number of values in the group.

> In the cell, the Formula Bar, and the dialog box, Excel proposes to average the value in cell B4. Recall that Excel functions will propose a range if data is above or to the left of a selected cell.

Another Way

Alternatively, with the existing text selected, select the range D11:D65 and press Enter.

10 In the **Function Arguments** dialog box, notice that *B4* is highlighted. Press Del to delete the existing text, type **d11:d65** and then compare your screen with Figure 2.5.

> Because you want to average the values in the range D11:D65—and not cell B4—you must edit the proposed range in this manner.

Figure 2.5

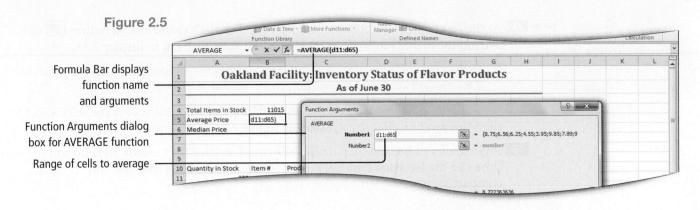

Formula Bar displays
function name
and arguments

Function Arguments dialog
box for AVERAGE function

Range of cells to average

11 In the **Function Arguments** dialog box, click **OK**, and then **Save** 🖫.

The result indicates that the average Retail Price of all products is *8.72*.

Activity 2.02 | Using the MEDIAN Function

The *MEDIAN function* is a statistical function that describes a group of data—you may have seen it used to describe the price of houses in a particular geographical area. The MEDIAN function finds the middle value that has as many values above it in the group as are below it. It differs from AVERAGE in that the result is not affected as much by a single value that is greatly different from the others.

1 Click cell **B6**. In the **Function Library group**, click the **More Functions** button, display the list of **Statistical** functions, scroll down as necessary, and then click **MEDIAN**.

2 In the **Function Arguments** dialog box, to the right of the **Number 1** box, click the **Collapse Dialog** button 🔢.

The dialog box collapses to a small size with space only for the first argument so you can see more of your data.

3 Select the range **D11:D65**, and then compare your screen with Figure 2.6.

When indicating which cells you want to use in the function's calculation—known as *defining the arguments*—you can either select the values with your mouse or type the range of values, whichever you prefer.

Figure 2.6

Formula Bar displays
function and argument

Collapsed dialog box
displays selected range

Selected range surrounded
by moving border

40	95	43625 Orange Peel	8.19	4 oz.	Tin	Seasoning					
41	211	43633 Peppermint	5.65	4 oz.	Bottle	Extract					
42	244	43813 Marjoram	4.45	4 oz.	Jar	Herb					
43	168	44482 Garlic Powder	5.89	6 oz.	Jar	Seasoning					
44	75	44587 Tand									
45	235	44589 Garli									
46	160	44879 Ging									
47	165	45265 Pickling Spice	6.19	2 oz.	Jar	Spice					
48	100	45688 Nutmeg	7.85	8 oz.	Jar	Spice					
49	265	46532 Oregano	10.19	8 oz.	Jar	Herb					
50	73	49652 Rojo Taco	5.29	4 oz.	Paper Envelope	Seasoning					
51	185	52164 Cloves, Whole	18.70	8 oz.	Jar	Spice					
52	165	53634 Vanilla, Double Strength	16.75	8 oz.	Bottle	Extract					
53	325	54635 Dill Weed	2.65	4 oz.	Paper Envelope	Herb					
54	195	55255 Sea Salt, Pacific	2.55	8 oz.	Tin	Seasoning					
55	312	56853 Peppercorns, Indian	4.59	2 oz.	Jar	Spice					
56	152	64525 Onion Powder	4.85	4 oz.	Jar	Seasoning					
57	215	78655 Garlic Salt	2.58	6 oz.	Jar	Seasoning					
58	540	85655 Peppercorns, Red	3.69	2 oz.	Tin	Spice					
59	225	92258 Vanilla	15.95	4 oz.	Bottle	Extract					
60	368	93157 Almond	7.33	4 oz.	Bottle	Extract					
61	285	93553 Lemon	24.90	6 oz.	Bottle	Extract					
62	126	94236 Cumin	3.55	4 oz.	Paper Envelope	Spice					
63	423	96854 Vanilla	31.95	6 oz.	Bottle	Extract					
64	325	98225 Orange	24.19	6 oz.	Bottle	Extract					
65	211	98655 Cloves, Ground	4.55	6 oz.	Jar	Spice					
66											

Excel | Chapter 2

Another Way

Press Enter to expand the dialog box.

4 At the right end of the collapsed dialog box, click the **Expand Dialog** button to expand the dialog box to its original size, and then click **OK** to display *7.85*.

In the range of prices, 7.85 is the middle value. Half of all flavor products are priced *above* 7.85 and half are priced *below* 7.85.

5 Scroll up to view **row 1**. Select the range **B5:B6** and right-click over the selection. On the Mini toolbar, click the **Accounting Number Format** button $.

6 Right-click cell **B4**, and then on the Mini toolbar, click the **Comma Style** button one time and the **Decrease Decimal** button two times. Click **Save** and compare your screen with Figure 2.7.

Figure 2.7

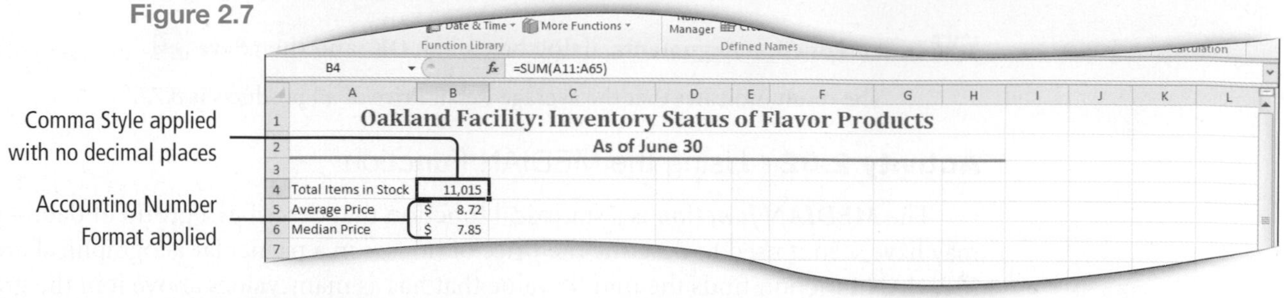

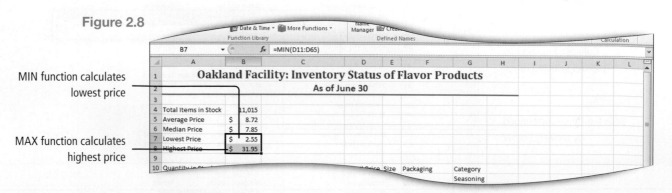

Comma Style applied with no decimal places

Accounting Number Format applied

Activity 2.03 | Using the MIN and MAX Functions

The statistical *MIN function* determines the smallest value in a selected range of values. The statistical *MAX function* determines the largest value in a selected range of values.

1 In cell **A7**, type **Lowest Price** and then in cell **A8**, type **Highest Price**

2 Click cell **B7**. On the **Formulas tab**, in the **Function Library group**, click the **More Functions** button, display the list of **Statistical** functions, scroll as necessary, and then click **MIN**.

3 At the right end of the **Number1** box, click the **Collapse Dialog** button , select the range **D11:D65**, and then click the **Expand Dialog** button . Click **OK**.

The lowest Retail Price is *2.55*.

4 Click cell **B8**, and then by using a similar technique, insert the **MAX** function to determine the highest **Retail Price**—*31.95*.

5 Select the range **B7:B8** and apply the **Accounting Number Format** $, click **Save** , and then compare your screen with Figure 2.8.

Figure 2.8

MIN function calculates lowest price

MAX function calculates highest price

Objective 2 | Move Data, Resolve Error Messages, and Rotate Text

When you move a formula, the cell references within the formula do not change, no matter what type of cell reference you use.

If you move cells into a column that is not wide enough to display number values, Excel will display a message so that you can adjust as necessary.

You can reposition data within a cell at an angle by rotating the text.

Activity 2.04 | Moving Data and Resolving a # # # # # Error Message

1 Select the range **A4:B8**. Point to the right edge of the selected range to display the pointer, and then compare your screen with Figure 2.9.

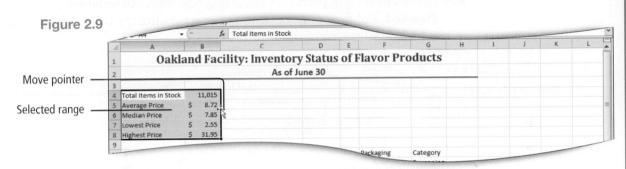

Figure 2.9

Move pointer

Selected range

2 Drag the selected range to the right until the ScreenTip displays *D4:E8*, release the mouse button, and then notice that a series of # symbols displays in **column E**. Point to any of the cells that display # symbols, and then compare your screen with Figure 2.10.

Using this technique, cell contents can be moved from one location to another; this is referred to as ***drag and drop***.

If a cell width is too narrow to display the entire number, Excel displays the ##### error, because displaying only a portion of a number would be misleading. The underlying values remain unchanged and are displayed in the Formula Bar for the selected cell. An underlying value also displays in the ScreenTip if you point to a cell containing # symbols.

Figure 2.10

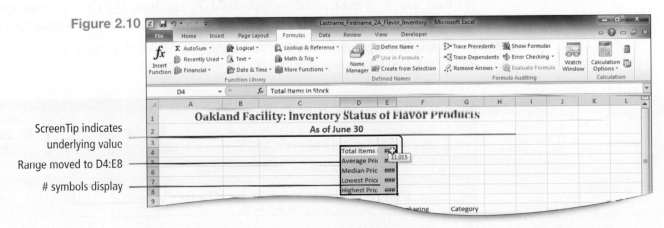

ScreenTip indicates underlying value

Range moved to D4:E8

symbols display

3 Select **column E** and widen it to **50** pixels, and notice that two cells are still not wide enough to display the cell contents.

4 In the **column heading area**, point to the right boundary of **column E** to display the ⊞ pointer. Double-click to AutoFit the column to accommodate the widest entry.

5 Using the same technique, AutoFit **column D** to accommodate the widest text entry.

6 Select the range **D4:E8**. On the **Home tab**, in the **Styles group**, display the **Cell Styles** gallery. Under **Themed Cell Styles**, click **20%-Accent1**. Click **Save** 🖫.

Activity 2.05 │ Rotating Text

Rotated text is useful to draw attention to data on your worksheet.

Another Way

Type the number of degrees directly into the Degrees box or use the spin box arrows to set the number.

1 In cell **C6**, type **Flavor Statistics** Select the range **C4:C8**, right-click over the selection, and then on the shortcut menu, click **Format Cells**. In the **Format Cells** dialog box, click the **Alignment tab**. Under **Text control**, select the **Merge cells** check box.

2 In the upper right portion of the dialog box, under **Orientation**, point to the **red diamond**, and then drag the diamond upward until the **Degrees** box indicates **30**. Compare your screen with Figure 2.11.

Figure 2.11

Range of cells moved and formatted

Format Cells dialog box

Orientation set to 30 degrees

Merge cells selected

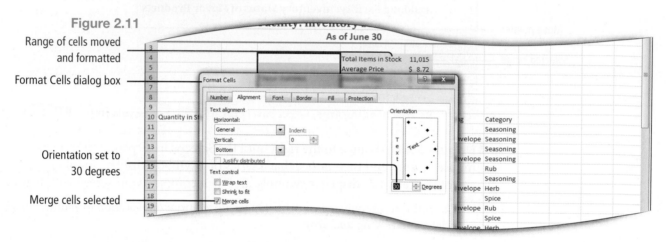

3 In the lower right corner of the **Format Cells** dialog box, click **OK**.

4 With the merged cell still selected, on the **Home tab**, in the **Font group**, change the **Font Size** 11 ▾ to **14**, and then apply **Bold** 🅱 and **Italic** 𝐼. Click the **Font Color arrow** 🅰▾, and then in the fourth column, click the first color—**Dark Blue, Text 2**.

5 In the **Alignment group**, apply **Align Text Right** 🖹. Click cell **A1**, **Save** 🖫 your workbook, and then compare your screen with Figure 2.12.

Figure 2.12

Text rotated and formatted

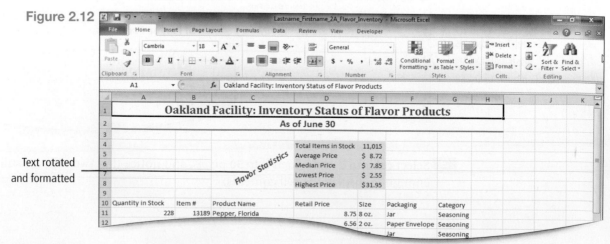

Objective 3 | Use COUNTIF and IF Functions and Apply Conditional Formatting

Recall that statistical functions analyze a group of measurements. Another group of Excel functions, referred to as *logical functions*, test for specific conditions. Logical functions typically use conditional tests to determine whether specified conditions—called *criteria*—are true or false.

Activity 2.06 | Using the COUNTIF Function

The *COUNTIF function* is a statistical function that counts the number of cells within a range that meet the given condition—the criteria that you provide. The COUNTIF function has two arguments—the range of cells to check and the criteria.

The seasonings of Laurales Herbs and Spices will be featured on an upcoming segment of a TV shopping channel. In this activity, you will use the COUNTIF function to determine the number of *seasoning* products currently available in inventory.

1 In the **row heading area**, point to **row 9** and right-click to select the row and display the shortcut menu. Click **Insert**, and then press F4 two times to repeat the last action and thus insert three blank rows.

> F4 is useful to repeat commands in Microsoft Office programs. Most commands can be repeated in this manner.

2 From the **row heading area**, select **rows 9:11**. On the **Home tab**, in the **Editing group**, click the **Clear** button, and then click **Clear Formats** to remove the blue accent color in columns D and E from the new rows.

> When you insert rows or columns, formatting from adjacent rows or columns repeats in the new cells.

3 Click cell **E4**, look at the **Formula Bar**, and then notice that the arguments of the **SUM** function adjusted and refer to the appropriate cells in rows 14:68.

> The referenced range updates to *A14:A68* after you insert the three new rows. In this manner, Excel adjusts the cell references in a formula relative to their new locations.

4 In cell **A10**, type **Seasoning Types:** and then press Tab.

5 With cell **B10** as the active cell, on the **Formulas tab**, in the **Function Library group**, click the **More Functions** button, and then display the list of **Statistical** functions. Click **COUNTIF**.

> Recall that the COUNTIF function counts the number of cells within a range that meet the given condition.

6 In the **Range** box, click the **Collapse Dialog** button ![icon], select the range **G14:G68**, and then at the right end of the collapsed dialog box, click the **Expand Dialog** button ![icon]. Click in the **Criteria** box, type **Seasoning** and then compare your screen with Figure 2.13.

Figure 2.13

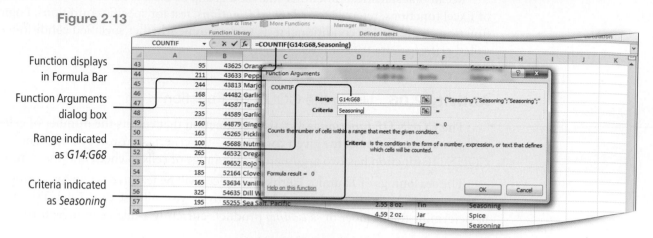

Function displays in Formula Bar

Function Arguments dialog box

Range indicated as *G14:G68*

Criteria indicated as *Seasoning*

7 In the lower right corner of the **Function Arguments** dialog box, click **OK**.

There are *20* different *Seasoning* products available to feature on the TV show.

8 On the **Home tab**, in the **Alignment group**, click **Align Text Left** ![icon] to place the result closer to the row title. **Save** ![icon] your workbook.

Activity 2.07 | Using the IF Function

A ***logical test*** is any value or expression that you can evaluate as being true or false. The ***IF function*** uses a logical test to check whether a condition is met, and then returns one value if true, and another value if false.

For example, *C14=228* is an expression that can be evaluated as true or false. If the value in cell C14 is equal to 228, the expression is true. If the value in cell C14 is not 228, the expression is false.

In this activity, you will use the IF function to determine the inventory levels and determine if more products should be ordered.

1 Click cell **H13**, type **Stock Level** and then press Enter.

2 In cell **H14**, on the **Formulas tab**, in the **Function Library group**, click the **Logical** button, and then in the list, click **IF**. Drag the title bar of the **Function Arguments** dialog box up or down to view **row 14** on your screen.

3 With the insertion point in the **Logical_test** box, click cell **A14**, and then type **<125**

This logical test will look at the value in cell A14, which is *228*, and then determine if the number is less than 125. The expression *<125* includes the < ***comparison operator***, which means *less than*. Comparison operators compare values.

4 Examine the table in Figure 2.14 for a list of comparison operator symbols and their definitions.

Comparison Operators

Comparison Operator	Symbol Definition
=	Equal to
>	Greater than
<	Less than
>=	Greater than or equal to
<=	Less than or equal to
<>	Not equal to

Figure 2.14

5 Press [Tab] to move the insertion point to the **Value_if_true** box, and then type **Order**

> If the result of the logical test is true—the Quantity in Stock is less than 125—cell H14 will display the text *Order* indicating that additional product must be ordered.

6 Click in the **Value_if_false** box, type **OK** and then compare your dialog box with Figure 2.15.

> If the result of the logical test is false—the Quantity in Stock is *not* less than 125—then Excel will display *OK* in the cell.

Figure 2.15

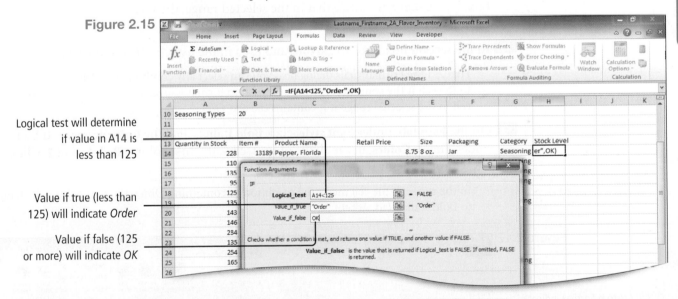

Logical test will determine if value in A14 is less than 125

Value if true (less than 125) will indicate *Order*

Value if false (125 or more) will indicate *OK*

7 Click **OK** to display the result *OK* in cell **H14**.

8 Using the fill handle, copy the function in cell **H14** down through cell **H68**. Then scroll as necessary to view cell **A18**, which indicates *125*. Look at cell **H18** and notice that the **Stock Level** is indicated as *OK*. **Save** your workbook. Compare your screen with Figure 2.16.

> The comparison operator indicated <125 (less than 125) and thus a value of *exactly* 125 is indicated as *OK*.

Figure 2.16

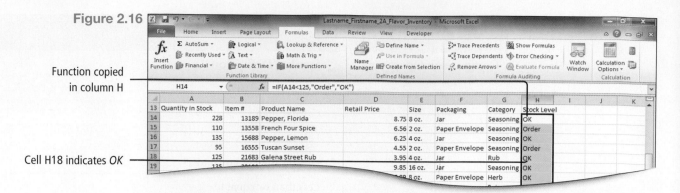

Function copied in column H

Cell H18 indicates *OK*

Activity 2.08 | Applying Conditional Formatting by Using Highlight Cells Rules and Data Bars

A ***conditional format*** changes the appearance of a cell based on a condition—a criteria. If the condition is true, the cell is formatted based on that condition; if the condition is false, the cell is *not* formatted. In this activity, you will use conditional formatting as another way to draw attention to the Stock Level of products.

1 Be sure the range **H14:H68** is selected. On the **Home tab**, in the **Styles group**, click the **Conditional Formatting** button. In the list, point to **Highlight Cells Rules**, and then click **Text that Contains**.

2 In the **Text That Contains** dialog box, with the insertion point blinking in the first box, type **Order** and notice that in the selected range, the text *Order* displays with the default format—Light Red Fill with Dark Red Text.

3 In the second box, click the **arrow**, and then in the list, click **Custom Format**.

Here, in the Format Cells dialog box, you can select any combination of formats to apply to the cell if the condition is true. The custom format you specify will be applied to any cell in the selected range if it contains the text *Order*.

4 On the **Font tab**, under **Font style**, click **Bold Italic**. Click the **Color arrow**, and then under **Theme Colors**, in the sixth column, click the first color—**Red, Accent 2**. Click **OK**. Compare your screen with Figure 2.17.

In the range, if the cell meets the condition of containing *Order*, the font color will change to Bold Italic, Red, Accent 2.

Figure 2.17

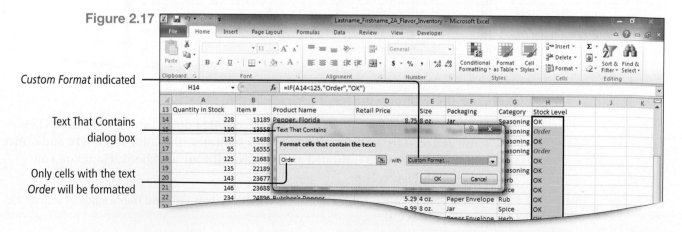

Custom Format indicated

Text That Contains dialog box

Only cells with the text *Order* will be formatted

5 In the **Text That Contains** dialog box, click **OK**.

6 Select the range **A14:A68**. In the **Styles group**, click the **Conditional Formatting** button. Point to **Data Bars**, and then under **Gradient Fill**, click **Orange Data Bar**. Click anywhere to cancel the selection; click [image]. Compare your screen with Figure 2.18.

A *data bar* provides a visual cue to the reader about the value of a cell relative to other cells. The length of the data bar represents the value in the cell. A longer bar represents a higher value and a shorter bar represents a lower value. Data bars are useful for identifying higher and lower numbers quickly within a large group of data, such as very high or very low levels of inventory.

Figure 2.18

Orange Data Bars applied to stock quantities

Conditional font formatting applied to *Order*

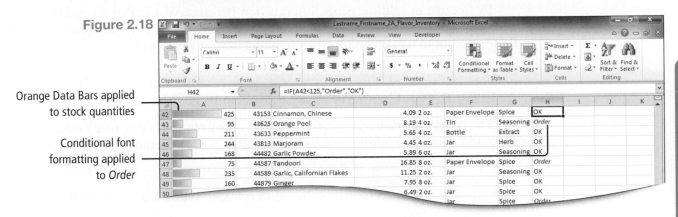

Activity 2.09 | Using Find and Replace

The *Find and Replace* feature searches the cells in a worksheet—or in a selected range—for matches, and then replaces each match with a replacement value of your choice.

Comments from customers on the company's blog indicate that, for dried herbs and seasonings, customers prefer a sealable foil packet rather than a paper envelope. Thus, all products of this type have been repackaged. In this activity, you will replace all occurrences of *Paper Envelope* with *Foil Packet*.

1 Select the range **F14:F68**.

Restrict the find and replace operation to a specific range in this manner, especially if there is a possibility that the name occurs elsewhere.

2 On the **Home tab**, in the **Editing group**, click the **Find & Select** button, and then click **Replace**.

3 Type **Paper Envelope** to fill in the **Find what** box. In the **Replace with** box, type **Foil Packet** and then compare your screen with Figure 2.19.

Figure 2.19

Find & Select button in Editing group

Find *Paper Envelope*

Replace with *Foil Packet*

Replace All button

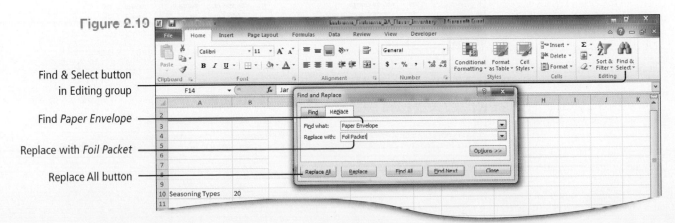

4 Click the **Replace All** button. In the message box, notice that 19 replacements were made, and then click **OK**. In the lower right corner of the **Find and Replace** dialog box, click the **Close** button. Click **Save** 🖫.

Objective 4 | Use Date & Time Functions and Freeze Panes

Excel can obtain the date and time from your computer's calendar and clock and display this information on your worksheet.

By freezing or splitting panes, you can view two areas of a worksheet and lock rows and columns in one area. When you freeze panes, you select the specific rows or columns that you want to remain visible when scrolling in your worksheet.

Activity 2.10 | Using the NOW Function to Display a System Date

The *NOW function* retrieves the date and time from your computer's calendar and clock and inserts the information into the selected cell. The result is formatted as a date and time.

1 Scroll down as necessary, and then click cell **A70**. Type **Edited by Frank Barnes** and then press [Enter].

2 With cell **A71** as the active cell, on the **Formulas tab**, in the **Function Library group**, click the **Date & Time** button. In the list of functions, click **NOW**. Compare your screen with Figure 2.20.

Figure 2.20

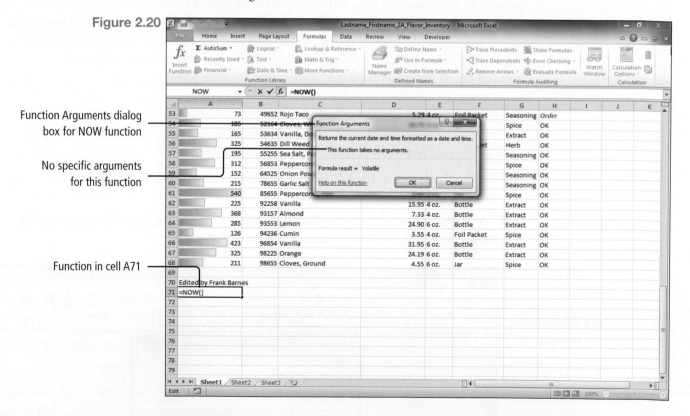

Function Arguments dialog box for NOW function

No specific arguments for this function

Function in cell A71

3 Read the description in the **Function Arguments** dialog box, and notice that this result is *Volatile*.

> The Function Arguments dialog box displays a message indicating that this function does not require an argument. It also states that this function is **volatile**, meaning the date and time will not remain as entered, but rather the date and time will automatically update each time you open this workbook.

4 In the **Function Arguments** dialog box, click **OK** to close the dialog box to display the current date and time in cell **A71**. **Save** 🔲 your workbook.

More Knowledge | NOW Function Recalculates Each Time a Workbook Opens

The NOW function updates each time the workbook is opened. With the workbook open, you can force the NOW function to update by pressing F9 , for example, to update the time.

Activity 2.11 | Freezing and Unfreezing Panes

In a large worksheet, if you scroll down more than 25 rows or scroll beyond column O (the exact row number and column letter varies, depending on your screen resolution), you will no longer see the top rows or first column of your worksheet where identifying information about the data is usually placed. You will find it easier to work with your data if you can always view the identifying row or column titles.

The **Freeze Panes** command enables you to select one or more rows or columns and then freeze (lock) them into place. The locked rows and columns become separate panes. A **pane** is a portion of a worksheet window bounded by and separated from other portions by vertical or horizontal bars.

1 Press Ctrl + Home to make cell **A1** the active cell. Scroll down until **row 40** displays at the top of your Excel window, and notice that all of the identifying information in the column titles is out of view.

2 Press Ctrl + Home again, and then from the **row heading area**, select **row 14**. Click the **View tab**, and then in the **Window group**, click the **Freeze Panes** button. In the list, click **Freeze Panes**. Click any cell to deselect the row, and then notice that a line displays along the upper border of **row 14**.

> By selecting row 14, the rows above—rows 1 - 13—are frozen in place and will not move as you scroll down.

3 Watch the row numbers below **row 13**, and then begin to scroll down to bring **row 40** into view again. Notice that rows 1:13 are frozen in place. Compare your screen with Figure 2.21.

> The remaining rows of data continue to scroll. Use this feature when you have long or wide worksheets.

Figure 2.21

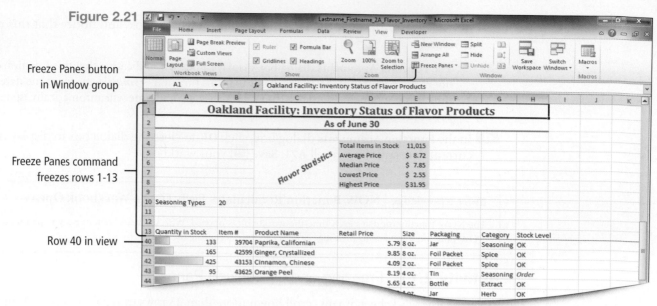

Freeze Panes button in Window group

Freeze Panes command freezes rows 1-13

Row 40 in view

4 In the **Window group**, click the **Freeze Panes** button, and then click **Unfreeze Panes** to unlock all rows and columns. **Save** 🔲 your workbook.

> **More Knowledge** | Freeze Columns or Freeze both Rows and Columns
>
> You can freeze columns that you want to remain in view on the left. Select the column to the right of the column(s) that you want to remain in view while scrolling to the right, and then click the Freeze Panes command. You can also use the command to freeze both rows and columns; click a *cell* to freeze the rows *above* the cell and the columns to the *left* of the cell.

Objective 5 | Create, Sort, and Filter an Excel Table

To analyze a group of related data, you can convert a range of cells to an *Excel table*. An Excel table is a series of rows and columns that contains related data that is managed independently from the data in other rows and columns in the worksheet.

Activity 2.12 | Creating an Excel Table

1 Be sure that you have applied the Unfreeze Panes command—no rows on your worksheet are locked. Then, click any cell in the data below row 13.

Another Way

Select the range of cells that make up the table, including the header row, and then click the Table button.

2 Click the **Insert tab**. In the **Tables group**, click the **Table** button. In the **Create Table** dialog box, if necessary, click to select the **My table has headers** check box, and then compare your screen with Figure 2.22.

The column titles in row 13 will form the table headers. By clicking in a range of contiguous data, Excel will suggest the range as the data for the table. You can adjust the range if necessary.

Figure 2.22

Moving border surrounds range

Column titles will form table headers

Create Table dialog box

Range of data selected

Check box selected

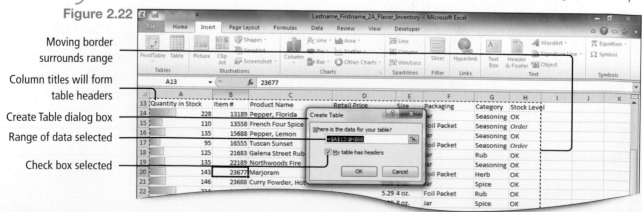

3 Click **OK**. With the range still selected, on the Ribbon notice that the **Table Tools** are active.

4 On the **Design tab**, in the **Table Styles group**, click the **More** button ⬝, and then under **Light**, locate and click **Table Style Light 16**.

5 Press [Ctrl] + [Home]. Click **Save** 🖫, and then compare your screen with Figure 2.23.

Sorting and filtering arrows display in the table's header row.

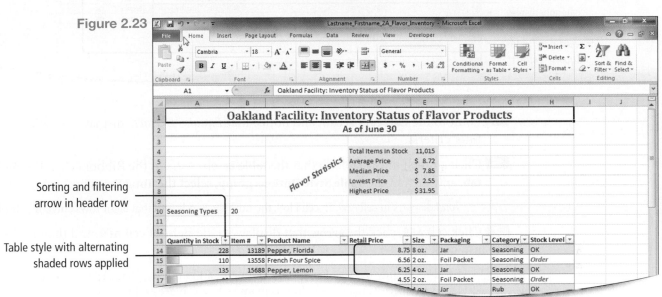

Figure 2.23

Sorting and filtering arrow in header row

Table style with alternating shaded rows applied

Activity 2.13 | Sorting and Filtering an Excel Table

You can *sort* tables—arrange all the data in a specific order—in ascending or descending order. You can *filter* tables—display only a portion of the data based on matching a specific value—to show only the data that meets the criteria that you specify.

1 In the header row of the table, click the **Retail Price arrow**, and then on the menu, click **Sort Smallest to Largest**. Next to the arrow, notice the small **up arrow** indicating an ascending (smallest to largest) sort.

The rows in the table are sorted from the lowest retail price to highest retail price.

2 In the table's header row, click the **Category arrow**. On the menu, click **Sort A to Z**. Next to the arrow, notice the small **up arrow** indicating an ascending (A to Z) sort.

The rows in the table are sorted alphabetically by Category.

3 Click the **Category arrow** again, and then sort from **Z to A**.

The rows in the table are sorted in reverse alphabetic order by Category name, and the small arrow points downward, indicating a descending (Z to A) sort.

4 Click the **Category arrow** again. On the menu, click the **(Select All)** check box to clear all the check boxes. Click to select only the **Extract** check box, and then click **OK**. Compare your screen with Figure 2.24.

Only the rows containing *Extract* in the Category column display—the remaining rows are hidden from view. A small funnel—the filter icon—indicates that a filter is applied to the data in the table. Additionally, the row numbers display in blue to indicate that some rows are hidden from view. A filter hides entire rows in the worksheet.

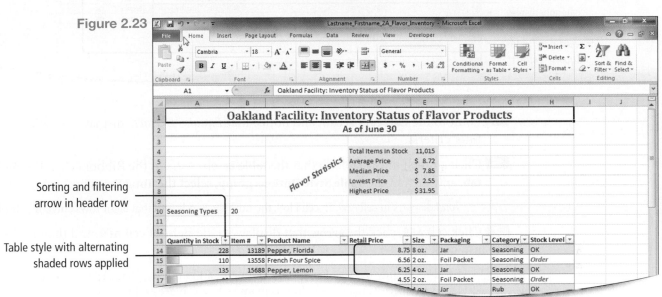

Figure 2.24

Funnel indicates filter applied

Blue row numbers indicate some rows hidden

Only products in *Extract* category display

ScreenTip indicates *Equals "Extract"*

9						Lowest Price Highest Price	
10	Seasoning Types	20					
11							
12							
13	**Quantity in Stock** ▼	**Item #** ▼	**Product Name** ▼	**Retail Price** ▼	**Size** ▼	**Packaging** ▼	**Category** ᴛ▼	**Stock Level** ▼
61	211	43633	Peppermint	5.65	4 oz.	Bottle	Extract	
62	368	93157	Almond	7.33	4 oz.	Bottle	Extract	Category: Equals "Extract"
63	225	92258	Vanilla	15.95	4 oz.	Bottle	Extract	OK
64	165	53634	Vanilla, Double Strength	16.75	8 oz.	Bottle	Extract	OK
65	188	37845	Coffee	17.29	8 oz.	Bottle	Extract	OK
66	325	98225	Orange	24.19	6 oz.	Bottle	Extract	OK
67	285	93553	Lemon	24.90	6 oz.	Bottle	Extract	OK
68	423	96854	Vanilla	31.95	6 oz.	Bottle	Extract	OK
69								
70	Edited by Frank Barnes							
71	5/2/2010 10:07							
72								
73								

5 Point to the **Category arrow**, and notice that *Equals "Extract"* displays to indicate the filter criteria.

6 Click any cell in the table so that the table is selected. On the Ribbon, click the **Design tab**, and then in the **Table Style Options group**, select the **Total Row** check box.

> *Total* displays in cell A69. In cell H69, the number *8* indicates that eight rows currently display.

7 Click cell **A69**, click the **arrow** that displays to the right of cell **A69**, and then in the list, click **Sum**.

> Excel sums only the visible rows in Column A, and indicates that 2190 products in the Extract category are in stock. In this manner, you can use an Excel table to quickly find information about a group of data.

8 Click cell **A11**, type **Extract Types:** and press Tab. In cell **B11**, type **8 (2,190 total items in stock)** and then press Enter.

9 In the table header row, click the **Category arrow**, and then on the menu, click **Clear Filter From "Category"**.

> All the rows in the table redisplay. The Z to A sort on Category remains in effect.

10 Click the **Packaging arrow**, click the **(Select All)** check box to clear all the check boxes, and then click to select the **Foil Packet** check box. Click **OK**.

11 Click the **Category arrow**, click the **(Select All)** check box to clear all the check boxes, and then click the **Herb** check box. Click **OK**, and then compare your screen with Figure 2.25.

> By applying multiple filters, Laura can quickly determine that seven items in the Herb category are packaged in foil packets with a total of 1,346 such items in stock.

Figure 2.25

Seven items in *Herb* category are packaged in *Foil Packets*

10	Seasoning Types	20			Highest Price		
11	Extract Types:	8 (2,190 total items in stock)					
12							
13	**Quantity in Stock** ▼	**Item #** ▼	**Product Name** ▼	**Retail Price** ▼	**Size** ▼	**Packaging** ᴛ▼	**Category** ᴛ▼	**Stock Level** ▼
52	325	54635	Dill Weed	2.65	4 oz.	Foil Packet	Herb	OK
54	143	23677	Marjoram	7.89	8 oz.	Foil Packet	Herb	OK
55	156	34266	Basil, French	10.19	8 oz.	Foil Packet	Herb	OK
57	254	25844	Herbes De Provence	10.25	4 oz.	Foil Packet	Herb	OK
58	156	32544	Mint, Spearmint	10.29	8 oz.	Foil Packet	Herb	OK
59	167	36820	Mint, Peppermint	10.39	8 oz.	Foil Packet	Herb	OK
60	145	35988	Basil, California	11.95	8 oz.	Foil Packet	Herb	OK
69	1346							7
70	Edited by Frank Barnes							
71	5/2/2010 10:12							
72								
73								

12 Click the **Category arrow**, and then click **Clear Filter From "Category"**. Use the same technique to remove the filter from the **Packaging** column.

13 In the table header row, click the **Item# arrow**, and then click **Sort Smallest to Largest**, which will apply an ascending sort to the data using the *Item#* column. **Save** 💾 your workbook.

Activity 2.14 | Converting a Table to a Range of Data

When you are finished answering questions about the data in a table by sorting, filtering, and totaling, you can convert the table into a normal range. Doing so is useful if you want to use the feature only to apply an attractive Table Style to a range of cells. For example, you can insert a table, apply a Table Style, and then convert the table to a normal range of data but keep the formatting.

> **Another Way**
>
> With any table cell selected, right click, point to Table, and then click Convert to Range.

1 Click anywhere in the table to activate the table and display the **Table Tools** on the Ribbon. On the **Design tab**, in the **Table Style Options group**, click the **Total Row** check box to clear the check mark and remove the Total row from the table.

2 On the **Design tab**, in the **Tools group**, click the **Convert to Range** button. In the message box, click **Yes**. Click **Save** 💾, and then compare your screen with Figure 2.26.

Figure 2.26

Table converted to a normal range, color and shading formats remain

	Quantity in Stock	Item #	Product Name	Retail Price	Size	Packaging	Category	Stock Level
12								
13	Quantity in Stock	Item #	Product Name	Retail Price	Size	Packaging	Category	Stock Level
14	228	13189	Pepper, Florida	8.75	8 oz.	Jar	Seasoning	OK
15	110	13558	French Four Spice	6.56	2 oz.	Foil Packet	Seasoning	*Order*
16	135	15688	Pepper, Lemon	6.25	4 oz.	Jar	Seasoning	OK
17	95	16555	Tuscan Sunset	4.55	2 oz.	Foil Packet	Seasoning	*Order*
18	125	21683	Galena Street Rub	3.95	4 oz.	Jar	Rub	OK
19	135	22189	Northwoods Fire	9.85	16 oz.	Jar	Seasoning	OK
20	143	23677	Marjoram	7.89	8 oz.	Foil Packet	Herb	OK
21	146	23688	Curry Powder, Hot	9.99	8 oz.	Jar	Spice	OK
22	224	24896	Butcher's Pepper	5.29	4 oz.	Foil Packet	Rub	OK
23				9.99	8 oz.	Jar	Spice	OK
					4 oz.	Foil Packet	Herb	OK

(header rows also show: tract Types: 8 (2,190 total items in stock))

Objective 6 | Format and Print a Large Worksheet

A worksheet might be too wide, too long—or both—to print on a single page. Use Excel's ***Print Titles*** and ***Scale to Fit*** commands to create pages that are attractive and easy to read.

The Print Titles command enables you to specify rows and columns to repeat on each printed page. Scale to Fit commands enable you to stretch or shrink the width, height, or both, of printed output to fit a maximum number of pages.

Activity 2.15 | Printing Titles and Scaling to Fit

1 Press Ctrl + Home to display the top of your worksheet. Select the range **A13:H13**. On the **Home tab**, from the **Styles group**, apply the **Heading 4** cell style, and then apply **Center** ▤.

2 On the **Insert tab**, in the **Text group**, click **Header & Footer**. In the **Navigation group**, click the **Go to Footer** button, and then click just above the word *Footer*.

3 In the **Header & Footer Elements group**, click the **File Name** button to add the name of your file to the footer—*&[File]* displays. Then, click in a cell just above the footer to exit the Footer and view your file name.

4 Delete the unused sheets **Sheet2** and **Sheet3**. On the right edge of the status bar, click the **Normal** button 🔲, and then press ⌈Ctrl⌉ + ⌈Home⌉ to display the top of your worksheet.

> Dotted lines indicate where the pages would break if printed as currently formatted; these dotted lines display when you switch from Page Layout view to Normal view.

5 On the **Page Layout tab**, in the **Themes group**, click the **Themes** button, and then click **Concourse**.

6 In the **Page Setup group**, click **Margins**, and then at the bottom, click **Custom Margins**. In the **Page Setup** dialog box, under **Center on page**, select the **Horizontally** check box, and then click **OK**.

7 In the **Page Setup group**, click **Orientation**, and then click **Landscape**. Press ⌈Ctrl⌉ + ⌈F2⌉ to display the **Print Preview**. At the bottom of the **Print Preview**, click the **Next Page** button ▶. Compare your screen with Figure 2.27.

> As currently formatted, the worksheet will print on five pages, and the columns will span multiple pages. Additionally, after Page 1, no column titles are visible to identify the data in the columns.

Figure 2.27

No identifying column titles at top of page

Additional columns not visible on this page

Page 2 indicated

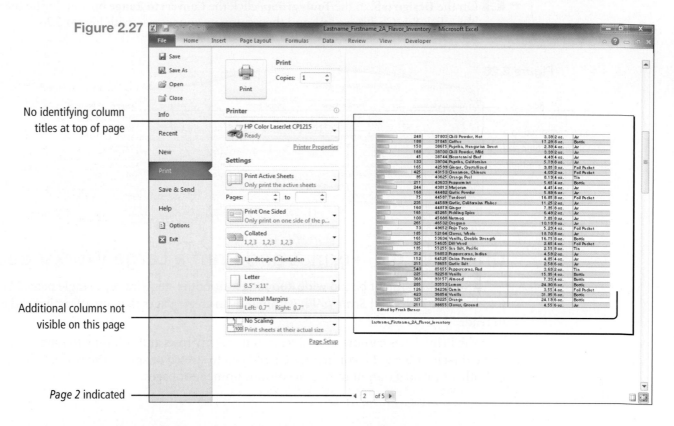

8 Click **Next Page** ▶ two times to display **Page 4**, and notice that two columns move to an additional page.

9 On the Ribbon, click **Page Layout** to redisplay the worksheet. In the **Page Setup group**, click the **Print Titles** button. Under **Print titles**, click in the **Rows to repeat at top** box, and then at the right, click the **Collapse Dialog** button 🔳.

10 From the **row heading area**, select **row 13**, and then click the **Expand Dialog** button 🔳. Click **OK** to print the column titles in row 13 at the top of every page.

Adding the titles on each page increases the number of pages to 6.

Another Way

With the worksheet displayed, on the Page Layout tab, in the Scale to Fit group, click the Width button arrow, and then click 1 page.

- ▶ 11 Press ⌃Ctrl + F2 to display the **Print Preview**. In the center panel, at the bottom of the **Settings group**, click the **Scaling** button, and then on the displayed list, point to **Fit All Columns on One Page**. Compare your screen with Figure 2.28.

This action will shrink the width of the printed output to fit all the columns on one page. You can make adjustments like this on the Page Layout tab, or here, in the Print Preview.

Figure 2.28

Settings group

Fit All Columns on One Page command

Scaling button

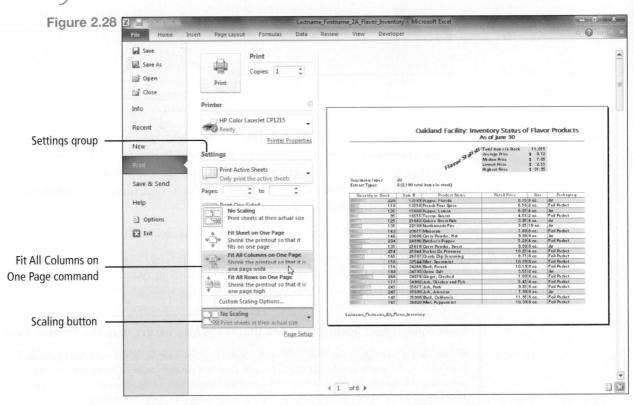

12 Click **Fit All Columns on One Page**. Notice in the **Print Preview** that all the columns display on one page.

13 At the bottom of the **Print Preview**, click the **Next Page** button ▶ one time. Notice that the output will now print on two pages and that the column titles display at the top of **Page 2**. Compare your screen with Figure 2.29.

Figure 2.29

Column titles display
on Page 2

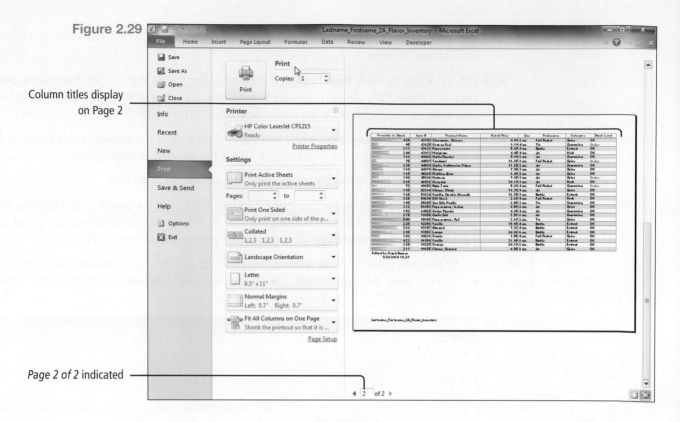

Page 2 of 2 indicated

14 In **Backstage** view, click the **Info tab**. On the right, under the document thumbnail, click **Properties**, and then click **Show Document Panel**. In the **Author** box, replace the existing text with your firstname and lastname. In the **Subject** box, type your course name and section number. In the **Keywords** box, type **inventory, Oakland** and then **Close** ✕ the **Document Information Panel**.

15 **Save** your workbook, and then print or submit electronically as directed.

16 If required by your instructor, print or create an electronic version of your worksheets with formulas displayed by using the instructions in Activity 1.16, and then **Close** ✕ Excel without saving so that you do not save the changes you made to print formulas.

More Knowledge | Scaling for Data that is Slightly Larger than the Printed Page

If your data is just a little too large to fit on a printed page, you can scale the worksheet to make it fit. Scaling reduces both the width and height of the printed data to a percentage of its original size or by the number of pages that you specify. To adjust the printed output to a percentage of its actual size, for example to 80%, on the Page Layout tab, in the Scale to Fit group, click the Scale arrows to select a percentage.

End You have completed Project 2A

Project 2B Weekly Sales Summary

myitlab
Project 2B Training

Project Activities

In Activities 2.16 through 2.26, you will edit an existing workbook for Laura Morales. The workbook summarizes the online and in-store sales of products during a one-week period in July. The worksheets of your completed workbook will look similar to Figure 2.30.

Project Files

For Project 2B, you will need the following file:
e02B_Weekly_Sales

You will save your workbook as:
Lastname_Firstname_2B_Weekly_Sales

Project Results

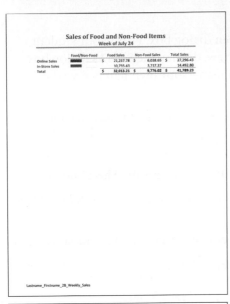

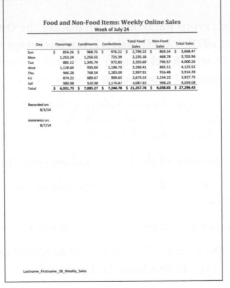

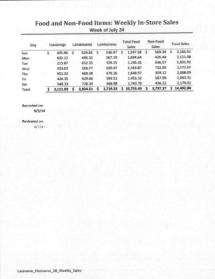

Figure 2.30
Project 2B Weekly Sales

Excel | Chapter 2

Objective 7 | Navigate a Workbook and Rename Worksheets

Use multiple worksheets in a workbook to organize data in a logical arrangement. When you have more than one worksheet in a workbook, you can *navigate* (move) among worksheets by clicking the *sheet tabs*. Sheet tabs identify each worksheet in a workbook and are located along the lower left edge of the workbook window. When you have more worksheets in the workbook than can be displayed in the sheet tab area, use the four sheet tab scrolling buttons to move sheet tabs into and out of view.

Activity 2.16 | Navigating Among Worksheets, Renaming Worksheets, and Changing the Tab Color of Worksheets

Excel names the first worksheet in a workbook *Sheet1* and each additional worksheet in order—*Sheet2*, *Sheet3*, and so on. Most Excel users rename the worksheets with meaningful names. In this activity, you will navigate among worksheets, rename worksheets, and change the tab color of sheet tabs.

> **Another Way**
>
> Press Ctrl + F12 to display the Open dialog box. Press F12 to display the Save As dialog box.

1 **Start** Excel. From **Backstage** view, display the **Open** dialog box. From your student files, open **e02B_Weekly_Sales**. From **Backstage** view, display the **Save As** dialog box, navigate to your **Excel Chapter 2** folder, and then using your own name, save the file as **Lastname_Firstname_2B_Weekly_Sales**

In the displayed workbook, there are two worksheets into which some data has already been entered. For example, on the first worksheet, the days of the week and sales data for the one-week period displays.

2 Along the bottom of the Excel window, point to and then click the **Sheet2 tab**.

The second worksheet in the workbook displays and becomes the active worksheet. *Sheet2* displays in bold.

3 In cell **A1**, notice the text *In-Store*—this worksheet will contain data for in-store sales.

4 Click the **Sheet1 tab**. Then, point to the **Sheet1 tab**, and double-click to select the sheet tab name. Type **Online Sales** and press Enter.

The first worksheet becomes the active worksheet, and the sheet tab displays *Online Sales*.

5 Point to the **Sheet2 tab**, right-click, and then from the shortcut menu, click **Rename**. Type **In-Store Sales** and press Enter. Compare your screen with Figure 2.31.

You can use either of these methods to rename a sheet tab.

Figure 2.31

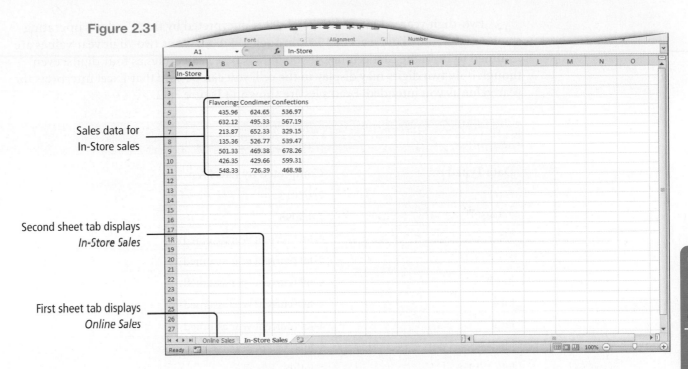

Sales data for
In-Store sales

Second sheet tab displays
In-Store Sales

First sheet tab displays
Online Sales

Another Way

Alternatively, on the
Home tab, in the Cells
group, click the Format
button, and then on the
displayed list, point to
Tab Color.

6 Point to the **In-Store Sales sheet tab** and right-click. On the shortcut menu, point to **Tab Color**, and then in the last column, click the first color—**Orange, Accent 6**.

7 Using the technique you just practiced, change the tab color of the **Online Sales sheet tab** to **Aqua, Accent 5**—in the next to last column, the first color. **Save** 🖫 your workbook.

Objective 8 | Enter Dates, Clear Contents, and Clear Formats

Dates represent a type of value that you can enter in a cell. When you enter a date, Excel assigns a serial value—a number—to the date. This makes it possible to treat dates like other numbers. For example, if two cells contain dates, you can find the number of days between the two dates by subtracting the older date from the more recent date.

Activity 2.17 | Entering and Formatting Dates

In this activity, you will examine the various ways that Excel can format dates in a cell. Date values entered in any of the following formats will be recognized by Excel as a date:

Format	Example
m/d/yy	7/4/12
d-mmm	4-Jul
d-mmm-yy	4-Jul-12
mmm-yy	Jul-12

On your keyboard, - (the hyphen key) and / (the forward slash key) function identically in any of these formats and can be used interchangeably. You can abbreviate the month name to three characters or spell it out. You can enter the year as two digits, four digits, or even leave it off. When left off, the current year is assumed but does not display in the cell.

A two-digit year value of 30 through 99 is interpreted by the Windows operating system as the four-digit years of 1930 through 1999. All other two-digit year values are assumed to be in the 21st century. If you always type year values as four digits, even though only two digits may display in the cell, you can be sure that Excel interprets the year value as you intended. Examples are shown in Figure 2.32.

How Excel Interprets Dates

Date Typed As:	Completed by Excel As:
7/4/12	7/4/2012
7-4-98	7/4/1998
7/4	4-Jul (current year assumed)
7-4	4-Jul (current year assumed)
July 4	4-Jul (current year assumed)
Jul 4	4-Jul (current year assumed)
Jul/4	4-Jul (current year assumed)
Jul-4	4-Jul (current year assumed)
July 4, 1998	4-Jul-98
July 2012	Jul-12 (first day of month assumed)
July 1998	Jul-98 (first day of month assumed)

Figure 2.32

1 On the **Online Sales** sheet, click cell **A16** and notice that the cell indicates *8/3* (August 3). In the **Formula Bar**, notice that the full date of August 3, 2014 displays in the format *8/3/2014*.

2 With cell **A16** selected, on the **Home tab**, in the **Number group**, click the **Number Format arrow**. At the bottom of the menu, click **More Number Formats** to display the **Number tab** of the **Format Cells** dialog box.

Under Category, *Date* is selected, and under Type, *3/14* is selected. Cell A16 uses this format type; that is, only the month and day display in the cell.

3 In the displayed dialog box, under **Type**, click several other date types and watch the **Sample** area to see how applying the selected date format would format your cell. When you are finished, click the **3/14/01** type, and then compare your screen with Figure 2.33.

Figure 2.33

Format Cells dialog box

Number tab active

8/3/14 displays in
Sample box

Date category selected

3/14/01 indicated as Type

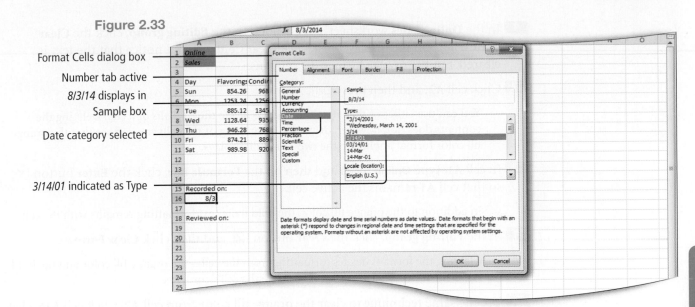

4 At the bottom of the dialog box, click **OK**. Click cell **A19**, type **8-7-14** and then press Enter.

Cell A19 has no special date formatting applied, and thus displays in the default date format *8/7/2014*.

> **Alert! | The Date Does Not Display as 8/7/2014?**
>
> Settings in your Windows operating system determine the default format for dates. If your result is different, it is likely that the formatting of the default date was adjusted on the computer at which you are working.

5 Click cell **A19** again. Hold down Ctrl and press ; (semicolon) on your keyboard. Press Enter to confirm the entry.

Excel enters the current date, obtained from your computer's internal calendar, in the selected cell using the default date format. Ctrl + ; is a quick method to enter the current date.

6 Click cell **A19** again, type **8/7/14** and then press Enter.

Because the year *14* is less than 30, Excel assumes a 21st century date and changes *14* to *2014* to complete the four-digit year. Typing *98* would result in *1998*. For two-digit years that you type that are between 30 and 99, Excel assumes a 20th century date.

7 Click cell **A16**, and then on the **Home tab**, in the **Clipboard group**, click the **Format Painter** button. Click cell **A19**, and notice that the date format from cell **A16** is copied to cell **A19**. **Save** your workbook.

Activity 2.18 | Clearing Cell Contents and Formats

A cell has *contents*—a value or a formula—and a cell may also have one or more *formats* applied, for example bold and italic font styles, fill color, font color, and so on. You can choose to clear—delete—the *contents* of a cell, the *formatting* of a cell, or both.

Clearing the contents of a cell deletes the value or formula typed there, but it does *not* clear formatting applied to a cell. In this activity, you will clear the contents of a cell and then clear the formatting of a cell that contains a date to see its underlying content.

1 In the **Online Sales** worksheet, click cell **A1**. In the **Editing group**, click the **Clear** button 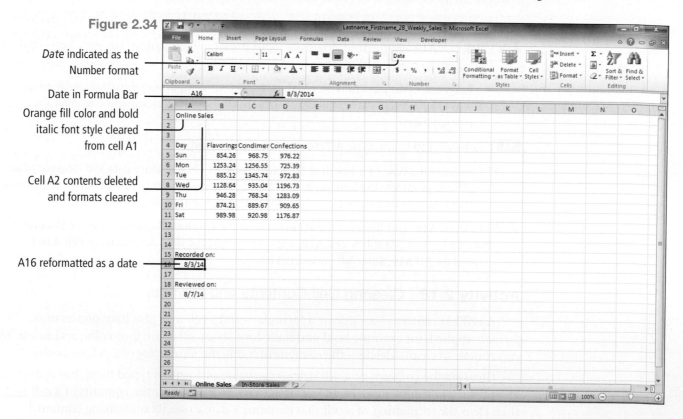. On the displayed list, click **Clear Contents** and notice that the text is cleared, but the orange formatting remains.

2 Click cell **A2**, and then press Del.

> You can use either of these two methods to delete the *contents* of a cell. Deleting the contents does not, however, delete the formatting of the cell; you can see that the orange fill color format applied to the two cells still displays.

3 In cell **A1**, type **Online Sales** and then on the **Formula Bar**, click the **Enter** button ✓ so that cell **A1** remains the active cell.

> In addition to the orange fill color, the bold italic text formatting remains with the cell.

4 In the **Editing group**, click the **Clear** button, and then click **Clear Formats**.

> Clearing the formats deletes formatting from the cell—the orange fill color and the bold and italic font styles—but does not delete the cell's contents.

5 Use the same technique to clear the orange fill color from cell **A2**. Click cell **A16**, click the **Clear** button, and then click **Clear Formats**. In the **Number group**, notice that *General* displays as the number format of the cell.

> The box in the Number group indicates the current Number format of the selected cell. Clearing the date formatting from the cell displays the date's serial number. The date, August 3, 2014, is stored as a serial number that indicates the number of days since January 1, 1900. This date is the 41,854th day since the reference date of January 1, 1900.

6 On the Quick Access Toolbar, click the **Undo** button to restore the date format. **Save** your workbook, and then compare your screen with Figure 2.34.

Figure 2.34

Date indicated as the Number format

Date in Formula Bar

Orange fill color and bold italic font style cleared from cell A1

Cell A2 contents deleted and formats cleared

A16 reformatted as a date

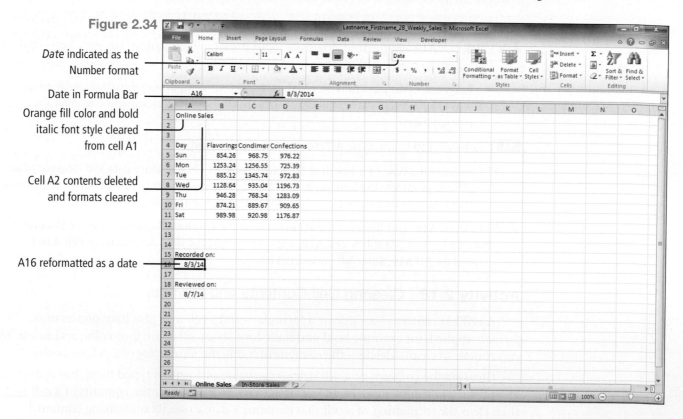

Objective 9 | Copy and Paste by Using the Paste Options Gallery

Data in cells can be copied to other cells in the same worksheet, to other sheets in the same workbook, or to sheets in another workbook. The action of placing cell contents that have been copied or moved to the Office Clipboard into another location is called *paste*.

Activity 2.19 | Copying and Pasting by Using the Paste Options Gallery

Recall that the Office Clipboard is a temporary storage area maintained by your Windows operating system. When you select one or more cells, and then perform the Copy command or the Cut command, the selected data is placed on the Office Clipboard. From the Office Clipboard storage area, the data is available for pasting into other cells, other worksheets, other workbooks, and even into other Office programs. When you paste, the *Paste Options gallery* displays, which includes Live Preview to preview the Paste formatting that you want.

1 With the **Online Sales** worksheet active, select the range **A4:A19**.

A range of cells identical to this one is required for the *In-Store Sales* worksheet.

Another Way

Use the keyboard short-cut for Copy, which is Ctrl + C; or click the Copy button in the Clipboard group on the Home tab

2 Right-click over the selection, and then click **Copy** to place a copy of the cells on the Office Clipboard. Notice that the copied cells display a moving border.

3 At the bottom of the workbook window, click the **In-Store Sales sheet tab** to make it the active worksheet. Point to cell **A4**, right-click, and then on the shortcut menu, under **Paste Options**, *point* to the first button—**Paste**. Compare your screen with Figure 2.35.

Live Preview displays how the copied cells will be placed in the worksheet if you click the Paste button. In this manner, you can experiment with different paste options, and then be sure you are selecting the paste operation that you want. When pasting a range of cells, you need only point to or select the cell in the upper left corner of the *paste area*—the target destination for data that has been cut or copied using the Office Clipboard.

Figure 2.35

Paste Options (6 option buttons)

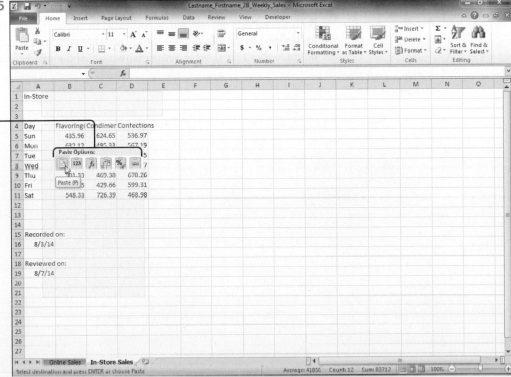

Excel | Chapter 2

Another Way

Use the keyboard short-cut for Paste, which is Ctrl + V; or click the Paste button in the Clipboard group on the Home tab.

4 Click the first button, **Paste**. In the status bar, notice that the message still displays, indicating that your selected range remains available on the Office Clipboard.

5 Display the **Online Sales** worksheet. Press Esc to cancel the moving border. **Save** 💾 your workbook.

The status bar no longer displays the message.

Note | Pressing Enter to Complete a Paste Action

If you want to paste the same text more than one time, click the Paste button so that the copied text remains available on the Office Clipboard. Otherwise, you can press Enter to complete the Paste command.

Objective 10 | Edit and Format Multiple Worksheets at the Same Time

You can enter or edit data on several worksheets at the same time by selecting and grouping multiple worksheets. Data that you enter or edit on the active sheet is reflected in all selected sheets. If you apply color to the sheet tabs, the name of the sheet tab will be underlined in the color you selected. If the sheet tab displays with a background color, you know the sheet is not selected.

Activity 2.20 | Grouping Worksheets for Editing

In this activity, you will group the two worksheets, and then format both worksheets at the same time.

1 With the **Online Sales** sheet active, press Ctrl + Home to make cell **A1** the active cell. Point to the **Online Sales sheet tab**, right-click, and then from the shortcut menu, click **Select All Sheets**.

2 At the top of your screen, notice that *[Group]* displays in the title bar. Compare your screen with Figure 2.36.

Both worksheets are selected, as indicated by *[Group]* in the title bar and the sheet tab names underlined in the selected tab color. Data that you enter or edit on the active sheet will also be entered or edited in the same manner on all the selected sheets in the same cells.

Figure 2.36

[Group] displays in title bar

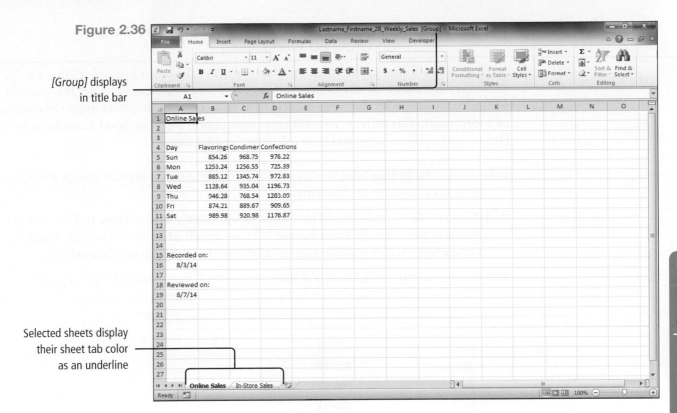

Selected sheets display their sheet tab color as an underline

3 Select **columns A:G**, and then set their width to **85 pixels**.

4 Click cell **A2**, type **Week of July 24** and then on the **Formula Bar**, click the **Enter** button ✓ to keep cell **A2** as the active cell. **Merge & Center** 🔳 the text across the range **A2:G2**, and then apply the **Heading 1** cell style.

5 Click cell **E4**, type **Total Food Sales** and then press Tab. In cell **F4**, type **Non-Food Sales** and then press Tab. In cell **G4**, type **Total Sales** and then press Enter.

6 Select the range **A4:G4**, and then apply the **Heading 3** cell style. In the **Alignment group**, click the **Center** ≡, **Middle Align** ≡, and **Wrap Text** 🔳 buttons. **Save** 🖫 your workbook.

Another Way

Right-click any sheet tab, and then click Ungroup Sheets.

7 Display the **In-Store Sales** worksheet to cancel the grouping, and then compare your screen with Figure 2.37.

> As soon as you select a single sheet, the grouping of the sheets is canceled and [Group] no longer displays in the title bar. Because the sheets were grouped, the same new text and formatting was applied to both sheets. In this manner, you can make the same changes to all the sheets in a workbook at one time.

Figure 2.37

[Group] no longer displays in title bar

In-Store Sales sheet active

Subtitle entered

Formatting applied to column widths and column titles

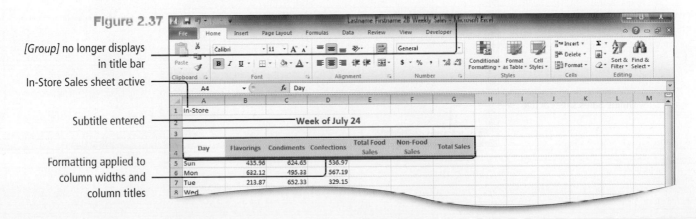

Activity 2.21 | Formatting and Constructing Formulas on Grouped Worksheets

Recall that formulas are equations that perform calculations on values in your worksheet and that a formula starts with an equal sign (=). Operators are the symbols with which you specify the type of calculation that you want to perform on the elements of a formula. In this activity, you will enter sales figures for Non-Food items from both Online and In-Store sales, and then calculate the total sales.

1 Display the **Online Sales** worksheet. Verify that the sheets are not grouped—*[Group]* does *not* display in the title bar.

2 Click cell **A1**, type **Food and Non-Food Items: Weekly Online Sales** and then on the **Formula Bar**, click the **Enter** button ✓ to keep cell **A1** as the active cell. **Merge & Center** 🔳 the text across the range **A1:G1**, and then apply the **Title** cell style.

3 In the column titled *Non-Food Sales*, click cell **F5**, in the range **F5:F11**, type the following data for Non-Food Sales, and then compare your screen with Figure 2.38.

	Non-Food Sales
Sun	869.24
Mon	468.78
Tue	796.57
Wed	865.11
Thu	916.48
Fri	1154.22
Sat	968.25

Figure 2.38

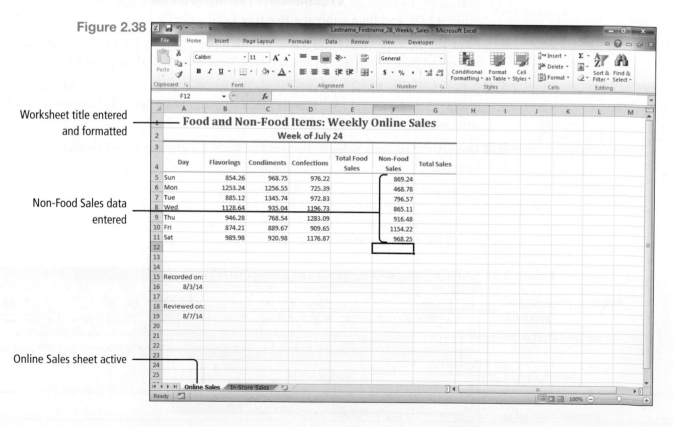

Worksheet title entered and formatted

Non-Food Sales data entered

Online Sales sheet active

4 Display the **In-Store Sales** sheet. In cell **A1**, replace *In-Store* by typing **Food and Non-Food Items: Weekly In-Store Sales** and then on the **Formula Bar**, click the **Enter** button ☑ to keep cell **A1** as the active cell. **Merge & Center** 🔳 the text across the range **A1:G1**, and then apply the **Title** cell style.

5 In the column titled *Non-Food Sales*, click cell **F5**, in the range **F5:F11**, type the following data for Non-Food Sales, and then compare your screen with Figure 2.39.

	Non-Food Sales
Sun	569.34
Mon	426.44
Tue	636.57
Wed	721.69
Thu	359.12
Fri	587.99
Sat	436.22

Figure 2.39

Worksheet title entered and formatted for In-Store Sales sheet

Non-Food Sales data entered

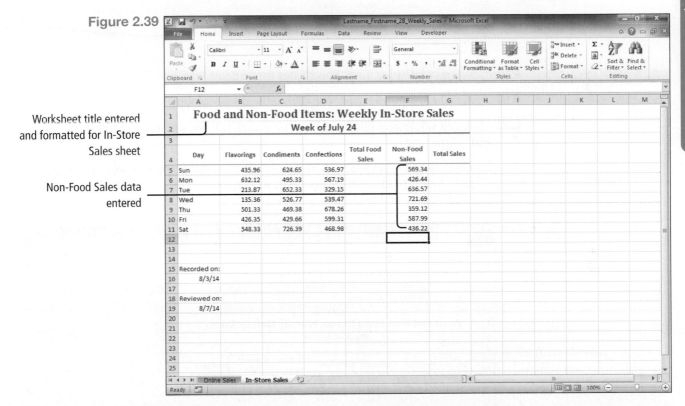

6 **Save** 🔲 your workbook. Right-click the **Online Sales sheet tab**, and then from the shortcut menu, click **Select All Sheets**.

> The first worksheet becomes the active sheet, and the worksheets are grouped. *[Group]* displays in the title bar, and the sheet tabs are underlined in the tab color to indicate they are selected as part of the group. Recall that when grouped, any action that you perform on the active worksheet is *also* performed on any other selected worksheets.

7 With the sheets *grouped* and the **Online Sales** sheet active, click cell **E5**. On the **Home tab**, in the **Editing group**, click the **Sum** button Σ. Compare your screen with Figure 2.40.

> Recall that when you enter the SUM function, Excel looks first above and then left for a proposed range of cells to sum.

Figure 2.40

[Group] indicates the worksheets are grouped

SUM function in cell

Proposed range of cells to sum surrounded by moving border

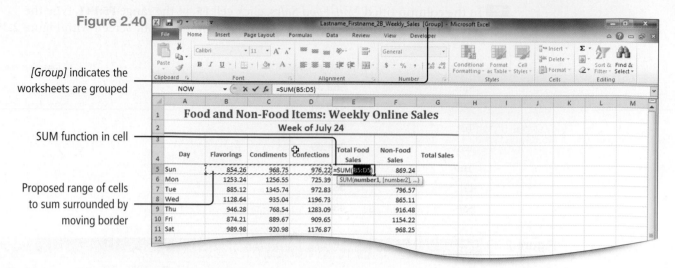

8 Press Enter to display Total Food Sales for Sunday, which is *2799.23*.

9 Click cell **E5**, and then drag the fill handle down to copy the formula through cell **E11**.

10 Click cell **G5**, type = click cell **E5**, type + click cell **F5**, and then compare your screen with Figure 2.41.

> Using the point-and-click technique to construct this formula is only one of several techniques you can use. Alternatively, you could use any other method to enter the SUM function to add the values in these two cells.

Figure 2.41

Formula in cell G5

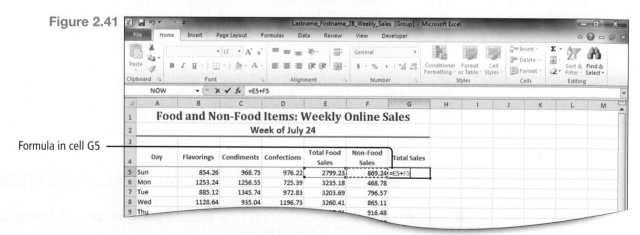

11 Press Enter to display the result *3668.47*, and then copy the formula down through cell **G11**.

12 In cell **A12**, type **Total** and then select the range **B5:G12**, which is all of the sales data and the empty cells at the bottom of each column of sales data.

13 With the range **B5:G12** selected, hold down Alt and press = to enter the **SUM** function in each empty cell.

> Selecting a range in this manner will place the Sum function in the empty cells at the bottom of each column.

14 Select the range **A5:A12**, and then apply the **Heading 4** cell style.

15 To apply financial formatting to the worksheets, select the range **B5:G5**, hold down Ctrl, and then select the range **B12:G12**. With the nonadjacent ranges selected, apply the **Accounting Number Format** $ ▾.

16 Select the range **B6:G11** and apply **Comma Style** ▾. Select the range **B12:G12** and apply the **Total** cell style.

17 Press Ctrl + Home to move to the top of the worksheet; compare your screen with Figure 2.42.

Figure 2.42

Total sales for each day

Row titles formatted

Columns totaled; financial formatting applied

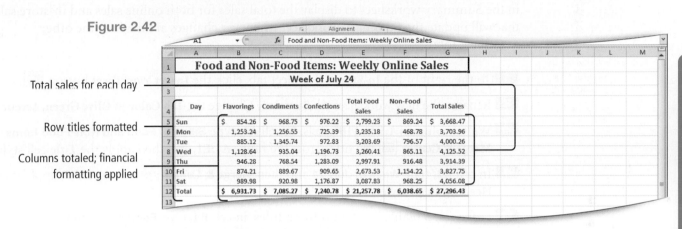

18 Click the **In-Store Sales sheet tab** to cancel the grouping and display the second worksheet. Click **Save** ▤, and then compare your screen with Figure 2.43.

> With your worksheets grouped, the calculations on the first worksheet were also performed on the second worksheet.

Figure 2.43

Total sales for each day

Row titles formatted

Columns totaled; financial formatting applied

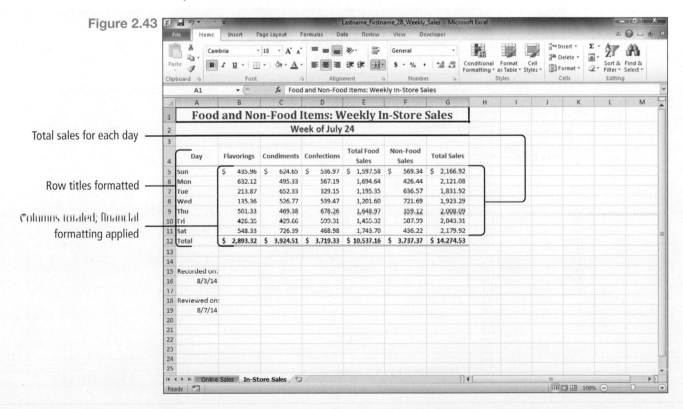

Objective 11 | Create a Summary Sheet with Column Sparklines

A *summary sheet* is a worksheet where totals from other worksheets are displayed and summarized. Recall that sparklines are tiny charts within a single cell that show a data trend.

Activity 2.22 | Constructing Formulas that Refer to Cells in Another Worksheet

In this activity, you will insert a new worksheet in which you will place the totals from the Online Sales worksheet and the In-Store Sales worksheet. You will construct formulas in the Summary worksheet to display the total sales for both online sales and in-store sales that will update the Summary worksheet whenever changes are made to the other worksheet totals.

1 To the right of the **In-Store Sales** sheet tab, click the **Insert Worksheet** button.

2 Rename the new worksheet tab **Summary** Change the **Tab Color** to **Olive Green, Accent 3**.

3 Widen **columns A:E** to **110** pixels. In cell **A1**, type **Sales of Food and Non-Food Items** **Merge & Center** the title across the range **A1:E1**, and then apply the **Title** cell style.

4 In cell **A2**, type **Week of July 24** and then **Merge & Center** across **A2:E2**; apply the **Heading 1** cell style.

5 Leave **row 3** blank. To form column titles, in cell **B4**, type **Food/Non-Food** and press Tab. In cell **C4**, type **Food Sales** and press Tab. In cell **D4**, type **Non-Food Sales** and press Tab. In cell **E5**, type **Total Sales** Press Enter. Select the range **B4:E4**. Apply the **Heading 3** cell style and **Center**.

6 To form row titles, in cell **A5**, type **Online Sales** In cell **A6**, type **In-Store Sales** and then compare your screen with Figure 2.44.

Figure 2.44

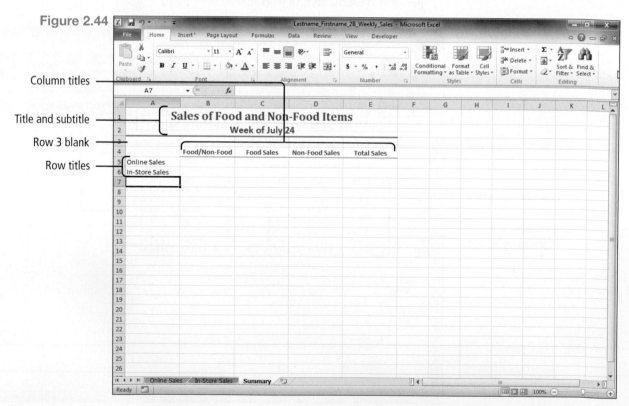

7 Click cell **C5**. Type = Click the **Online Sales sheet tab**. On the **Online Sales** worksheet, click cell **E12**, and then press Enter to redisplay the **Summary** worksheet and insert the total **Food Sales** amount of *$21,257.78*.

8 Click cell **C5** to select it again. Look at the **Formula Bar**, and notice that instead of a value, the cell contains a formula that is equal to the value in another cell in another worksheet. Compare your screen with Figure 2.45.

> The value in this cell is equal to the value in cell E12 of the *Online Sales* worksheet. The Accounting Number Format applied to the referenced cell is carried over. By using a formula of this type, changes in cell E12 on the *Online Sales* worksheet will be automatically updated in this *Summary* worksheet.

Figure 2.45

Formula Bar indicates formula referring to cell in another worksheet

Total Food Sales from Online Sales worksheet

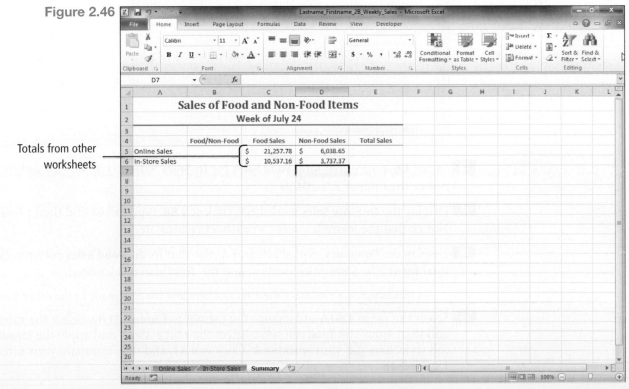

9 Click cell **D5**. Type = and then click the **Online Sales sheet tab**. Click cell **F12**, and then press Enter to redisplay the **Summary** worksheet and insert the total **Non-Food Sales** amount of *$6,038.65*.

10 By using the techniques you just practiced, in cells **C6** and **D6** insert the total **Food Sales** and **Non-Food Sales** data from the **In-Store Sales** worksheet. Click **Save**, and then compare your screen with Figure 2.46.

Figure 2.46

Totals from other worksheets

Activity 2.23 | Changing Values in a Detail Worksheet to Update a Summary Worksheet

The formulas in cells C5:D6 display the totals from the other two worksheets. Changes made to any of the other two worksheets—sometimes referred to as *detail sheets* because the details of the information are contained there—that affect their totals will display on this Summary worksheet. In this manner, the Summary worksheet accurately displays the current totals from the other worksheets.

1 In cell **A7**, type **Total** Select the range **C5:E6**, and then click the **Sum** button Σ to total the two rows.

> This technique is similar to selecting the empty cells at the bottom of columns and then inserting the SUM function for each column. Alternatively, you could use any other method to sum the rows. Recall that cell formatting carries over to adjacent cells unless two cells are left blank.

2 Select the range **C5:E7**, and then click the **Sum** button Σ to total the three columns. Compare your screen with Figure 2.47.

Figure 2.47

Rows and columns totaled

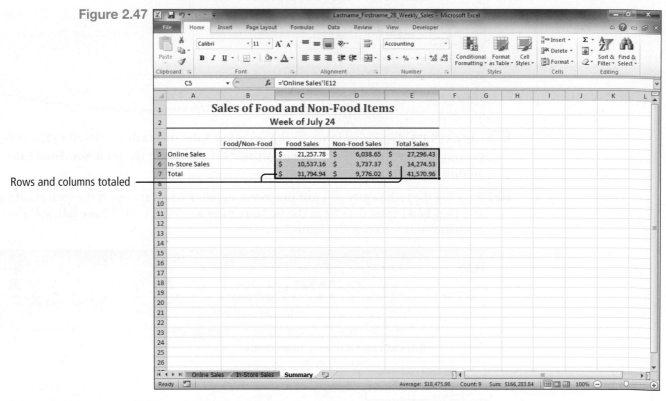

3 In cell **C6**, notice that total **Food Sales** for **In-Store** Sales is *$10,537.16*, and in cell **C7**, notice the total of *$31,794.94*.

4 Display the **In-Store Sales** worksheet, click cell **B8**, type **353.63** and then press Enter. Notice that the formulas in the worksheet recalculate.

5 Display the **Summary** worksheet, and notice that in the **Food Sales** column, both the total for the *In-Store Sales* location and the *Total* also recalculated.

> In this manner, a Summary sheet recalculates any changes made in the other worksheets.

6 Select the range **C6:E6** and change the format to **Comma Style**. Select the range **C7:E7**, and then apply the **Total** cell style. Select the range **A5:A7** and apply the **Heading 4** cell style. **Save** 💾 your workbook. Click cell **A1**, and then compare your screen with Figure 2.48.

Figure 2.48

Total style applied to C7:E7

Comma Style applied to C6:E6

Heading 4 cell style applied to row titles

Food sales recalculates to $32,013.21

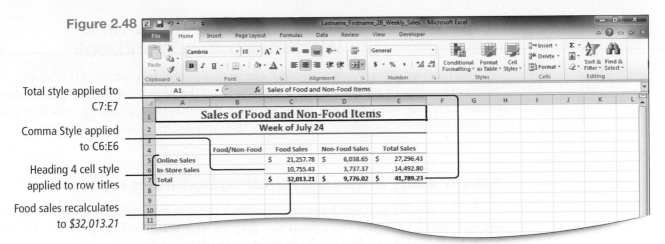

Activity 2.24 | Inserting Sparklines

In this activity, you will insert column sparklines to visualize the ratio of Food to Non-Food sales for both Online and In-Store.

1 Click cell **B5**. On the **Insert tab**, in the **Sparklines group**, click **Column**. In the **Create Sparklines** dialog box, with the insertion point blinking in the **Data Range** box, select the range **C5:D5**. Compare your screen with Figure 2.49.

Figure 2.49

Range C5:D5 selected

Create Sparklines dialog box

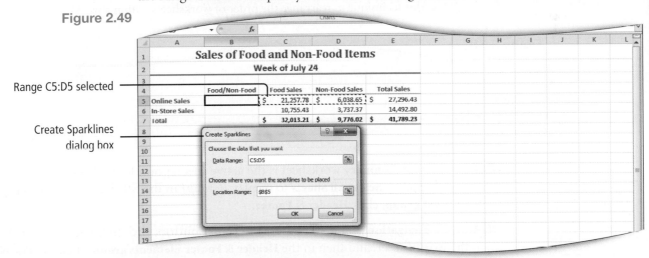

2 Click **OK**. Click cell **B6**, and then **Insert** a **Column Sparkline** for the range **C6:D6**. In the **Style group**, apply **Sparkline Style Accent 2, Darker 25%**—in the second row, the second style. Press Ctrl + Home, click **Save** 🖫, and then compare your screen with Figure 2.50.

You can see, at a glance, that for both Online and In-Store sales, Food sales are much greater than Non-Food sales.

Figure 2.50

Column sparklines compare sales of Food to Non-Food in both Online and In-Store

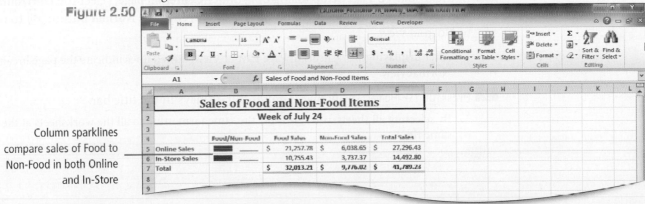

Objective 12 | Format and Print Multiple Worksheets in a Workbook

Each worksheet within a workbook can have different formatting, for example different headers or footers. If all the worksheets in the workbook will have the same header or footer, you can select all the worksheets and apply formatting common to all of the worksheets; for example, you can set the same footer in all of the worksheets.

Activity 2.25 | Moving and Formatting Worksheets in a Workbook

In this activity, you will move the Summary sheet to become the first worksheet in the workbook. Then you will format and prepare your workbook for printing. The three worksheets containing data can be formatted simultaneously.

1 Point to the **Summary sheet tab**, hold down the left mouse button to display a small black triangle—a caret—and then notice that a small paper icon attaches to the mouse pointer.

2 Drag to the left until the caret and mouse pointer are to the left of the **Online Sales sheet tab**, as shown in Figure 2.51, and then release the left mouse button.

Use this technique to rearrange the order of worksheets within a workbook.

Figure 2.51

Caret moved to the left; mouse pointer with paper icon attached

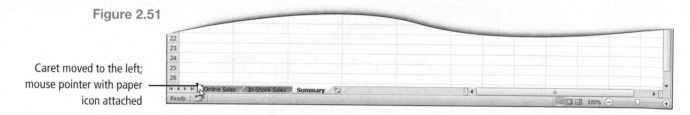

3 Be sure the **Summary** worksheet is the active sheet, point to its sheet tab, right-click, and then click **Select All Sheets** to display *[Group]* in the title bar. On the **Insert tab**, in the **Text group**, click **Header & Footer**.

4 In the **Navigation group**, click the **Go to Footer** button, click in the **left section** above the word *Footer*, and then in the **Header & Footer Elements group**, click the **File Name** button.

5 Click in a cell above the footer to deselect the **Footer area**. On the **Page Layout tab**, in the **Page Setup group**, click the **Margins** button, and then at the bottom of the **Margins** gallery, click **Custom Margins**.

6 In the displayed **Page Setup** dialog box, under **Center on page**, select the **Horizontally** check box. Click **OK**, and then on the status bar, click the **Normal** button 🔲 to return to Normal view.

After displaying worksheets in Page Layout View, dotted lines indicate the page breaks in Normal view.

7 Press Ctrl + Home; verify that *[Group]* still displays in the title bar.

By selecting all sheets, you can apply the same formatting to all the worksheets at the same time.

8 Display **Backstage** view, show the **Document Panel**, type your firstname and lastname in the Author box, and then type your course name and section number in the **Subject** box. As the **Keywords** type **weekly sales, online, in-store** and then **Close** ☒ the **Document Information Panel**.

9 Press ⌃Ctrl + F2 ; compare your screen with Figure 2.52.

> By grouping, you can view all sheets in Print Preview. If you do not see *1 of 3* at the bottom of the Preview, click the Home tab, select all the sheets again, and then redisplay Print Preview.

Figure 2.52

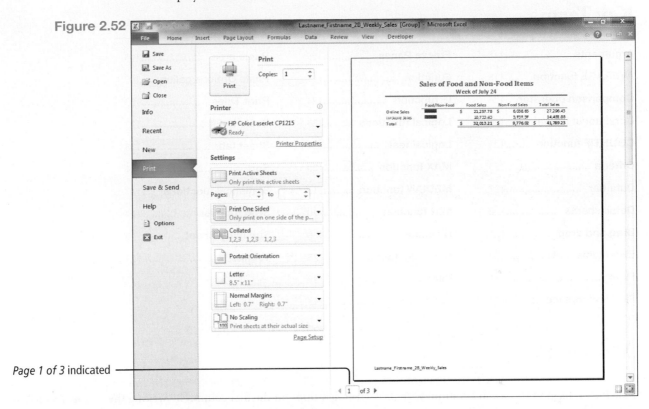

Page 1 of 3 indicated

10 At the bottom of the **Print Preview**, click the **Next Page** ▶ button as necessary and take a moment to view each page of your workbook.

Activity 2.26 | Printing All the Worksheets in a Workbook

1 In **Backstage** view, click the **Save** button to save your workbook before printing. To submit your workbook electronically, follow the instructions provided by your instructor. To print your workbook, continue to Step 2.

2 Display **Backstage** view, click the **Print tab**, verify that the worksheets in your workbook are still grouped—*[Group]* displays in the title bar—and then in the center panel, in the **Print group**, click the **Print** button.

3 If required, print or create an electronic version of your worksheets with formulas displayed by using the instructions in Activity 1.16, and then **Close** ☒ Excel without saving so that you do not save the changes you made to print formulas.

End **You have completed Project 2B** ——————————————————

Content-Based Assessments

Summary

In this chapter, you used the Statistical, Logical, and Date & Time functions from the Function Library. You created a table and analyzed the table's data by sorting and filtering. You also created a workbook with multiple worksheets, and then summarized all the worksheets on a summary worksheet.

Key Terms

Arguments 118
AVERAGE function 118
Comparison operator ..124
Conditional format 126
COUNTIF function 123
Criteria 123
Data bar 127
Detail sheets 152
Drag and drop 121
Excel table 130
Filter 131
Find and replace 127

Freeze Panes 129
Function 117
IF function 124
Logical functions 123
Logical test 124
MAX function 120
MEDIAN function 119
MIN function 120
Navigate 138
NOW function 128
Pane................................129
Paste 143

Paste area 143
Paste Options gallery 143
Print Titles 133
Scale to Fit 133
Sheet tab 138
Sort 131
Statistical functions 117
SUM function 117
Summary Sheet 150
Volatile 129

Matching

Match each term in the second column with its correct definition in the first column by writing the letter of the term on the blank line in front of the correct definition.

_____ 1. A predefined formula that performs calculations by using specific values in a particular order or structure.

_____ 2. Excel functions such as AVERAGE that are useful to analyze a group of measurements.

_____ 3. A predefined formula that adds all the numbers in a selected range.

_____ 4. A function that adds a group of values, and then divides the result by the number of values in the group.

_____ 5. A function that finds the middle value that has as many values above it in the group as are below it.

_____ 6. A function that determines the smallest value in a range.

_____ 7. A function that determines the largest value in a range.

_____ 8. The action of moving a selection by dragging it to a new location.

_____ 9. A group of functions that tests for specific conditions, and which typically use conditional tests to determine whether specified conditions are true or false.

_____ 10. Conditions that you specify in a logical function.

_____ 11. A statistical function that counts the number of cells within a range that meet the given condition and which has two arguments—the range of cells to check and the criteria.

_____ 12. Any value or expression that can be evaluated as being true or false.

A AVERAGE function

B Comparison operators

C Conditional format

D COUNTIF function

E Criteria

F Drag and drop

G Function

H IF function

I Logical functions

J Logical test

K MAX function

L MEDIAN function

M MIN function

N Statistical functions

O SUM function

_____ 13. A function that uses a logical test to check whether a condition is met, and then returns one value if true, and another value if false.

_____ 14. Symbols that evaluate each value to determine if it is the same (=), greater than (>), less than (<), or in between a range of values as specified by the criteria.

_____ 15. A format that changes the appearance of a cell based on a condition.

Multiple Choice

Circle the correct answer.

1. A shaded bar that provides a visual cue about the value of a cell relative to other cells is a:
   A. data bar   B. detail bar   C. filter

2. The function that retrieves and then displays the date and time from your computer is the:
   A. DATE function   B. NOW function   C. CALENDAR function

3. The command that enables you to select one or more rows or columns and lock them into place is:
   A. drag and drop   B. scale to fit   C. freeze panes

4. A series of rows and columns with related data that is managed independently from other data is a:
   A. table   B. pane   C. detail sheet

5. The process of arranging data in a specific order based on the value in each field is called:
   A. filtering   B. sorting   C. scaling

6. The process of displaying only a portion of the data based on matching a specific value to show only the data that meets the criteria that you specify is called:
   A. filtering   B. sorting   C. scaling

7. The Excel command that enables you to specify rows and columns to repeat on each printed page is:
   A. navigate   B. print titles   C. conditional format

8. The labels along the lower border of the workbook window that identify each worksheet are the:
   A. data bars   B. sheet tabs   C. detail sheets

9. A worksheet where totals from other worksheets are displayed and summarized is a:
   A. summary sheet   B. detail sheet   C. table

10. The worksheets that contain the details of the information summarized on a summary sheet are called:
    A. summary sheets   B. detail sheets   C. tables

Content-Based Assessments

Apply **2A** skills from these Objectives:

- ◼ Use the SUM, AVERAGE, MEDIAN, MIN, and MAX Functions
- ◼ Move Data, Resolve Error Messages, and Rotate Text
- ◼ Use COUNTIF and IF Functions and Apply Conditional Formatting
- ◼ Use Date & Time Functions and Freeze Panes
- ◼ Create, Sort, and Filter an Excel Table
- ◼ Format and Print a Large Worksheet

Skills Review | Project **2C** Sauces Inventory

In the following Skills Review, you will edit a worksheet for Laura Morales, President, detailing the current inventory of sauces at the Portland facility. Your completed workbook will look similar to Figure 2.53.

Project Files

For Project 2C, you will need the following file:

e02C_Sauces_Inventory

You will save your workbook as:

Lastname_Firstname_2C_Sauces_Inventory

Project Results

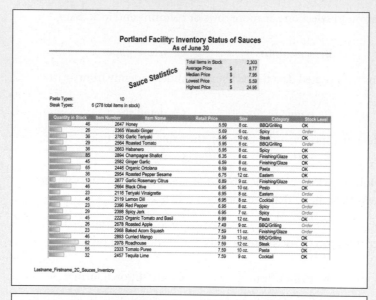

Figure 2.53

(Project 2C Sauces Inventory continues on the next page)

Content-Based Assessments

1 **Start** Excel. From your student files, locate and open **e02C_Sauces_Inventory**. From **Backstage** view, display the **Save As** dialog box, navigate to your **Excel Chapter 2** folder, and then save the workbook as **Lastname_ Firstname_2C_Sauces_Inventory**

a. Click cell **B4**. Click the **Formulas tab**, and then in the **Function Library group**, click the **AutoSum** button. Select the range **A14:A68**, and then press Enter.

b. With cell **B5** active, in the **Function Library group**, click the **More Functions** button. Point to **Statistical**, click **AVERAGE**, and then in the **Number1** box, type **d14:d68** Click **OK**.

c. Click cell **B6**. In the **Function Library group**, click the **More Functions** button, point to **Statistical**, and then click **MEDIAN**. In the **Function Arguments** dialog box, to the right of the **Number1** box, click the **Collapse Dialog** button. Select the range **D14:D68**, click the **Expand Dialog** button, and then click **OK**.

d. Click cell **B7**, and then by using a similar technique to insert a statistical function, insert the **MIN** function to determine the lowest **Retail Price**. Click cell **B8**, and then insert the **MAX** function to determine the highest **Retail Price**.

2 Right-click cell **B4**. On the Mini toolbar, click the **Comma Style** button, and then click the **Decrease Decimal** button two times. Select the range **B5:B8**, and apply the **Accounting Number Format**.

a. Select the range **A4:B8**. Point to the right edge of the selected range to display the ⌖ pointer. Drag the selected range to the right until the ScreenTip displays *D4:E8*, and then release the mouse button.

b. With the range **D4:E8** selected, on the **Home tab**, in the **Styles group**, display the **Cell Styles** gallery, and then under **Themed Cell Styles**, click **20% - Accent1**.

c. In cell **C6**, type **Sauce Statistics** Select the range **C4:C8**, right-click over the selection, and then click **Format Cells**. In the **Format Cells** dialog box, click the **Alignment tab**. Under **Text control**, select the **Merge cells** check box.

d. In the upper right portion of the dialog box, under **Orientation**, point to the **red diamond**, and then drag the diamond upward until the **Degrees** box indicates *20*. Click **OK**.

e. With the merged cell still selected, on the **Home tab**, in the **Font group**, change the **Font Size** to 18, and then apply **Bold** and **Italic**. Click the **Font Color**

button arrow, and then in the fourth column, click the first color—**Dark Blue, Text 2**.

3 Click cell **B10**. On the **Formulas tab**, in the **Function Library group**, click the **More Functions** button, and then display the list of **Statistical** functions. Click **COUNTIF**.

a. At the right edge of the **Range** box, click the **Collapse Dialog** button, select the range **F14:F68**, and then press Enter. Click in the **Criteria** box, type **Pasta** and then click **OK** to calculate the number of *Pasta* types.

b. Click cell **G14**. On the **Formulas tab**, in the **Function Library group**, click the **Logical** button, and then in the list, click **IF**. If necessary, drag the title bar of the **Function Arguments** dialog box up so that you can view **row 14** on your screen.

c. With the insertion point in the **Logical_test** box, click cell **A14**, and then type **<30** Press Tab to move the insertion point to the **Value_if_true** box, and then type **Order** Press Tab to move the insertion point to the **Value_if_false** box, type **OK** and then click **OK**. Using the fill handle, copy the function in cell **G14** down through cell **G68**.

4 With the range **G14:G68** selected, on the **Home tab**, in the **Styles group**, click the **Conditional Formatting** button. In the list, point to **Highlight Cells Rules**, and then click **Text that Contains**.

a. In the **Text That Contains** dialog box, with the insertion point blinking in the first box, type **Order** and then in the second box, click the **arrow**. In the list, click **Custom Format**.

b. In the **Format Cells** dialog box, on the **Font tab**, under **Font style**, click **Bold Italic**. Click the **Color arrow**, and then under **Theme Colors**, in the sixth column, click the first color—**Red, Accent 2**. In the lower right corner of the **Format Cells** dialog box, click **OK**. In the **Text That Contains** dialog box, click **OK** to apply the font color, bold, and italic to the cells that contain the word *Order*.

c. Select the range **A14:A68**. In the **Styles group**, click the **Conditional Formatting** button. In the list, point to **Data Bars**, and then under **Gradient Fill**, click **Orange Data Bar**. Click anywhere to cancel the selection.

d. Select the range **F14:F68**. On the **Home tab**, in the **Editing group**, click the **Find & Select** button, and then click **Replace**. In the **Find and Replace** dialog box, in the **Find what** box, type **Hot** and then in the

(Project 2C Sauces Inventory continues on the next page)

Replace with box type **Spicy** Click the **Replace All** button and then click **OK**. In the lower right corner of the **Find and Replace** dialog box, click the **Close** button.

e. Scroll down as necessary, and then click cell **A70**. Type **Edited by Michelle Albright** and then press [Enter]. With cell **A71** as the active cell, on the **Formulas tab**, in the **Function Library group**, click the **Date & Time** button. In the list of functions, click **NOW**, and then click **OK** to enter the current date and time.

5 Select the range **A13:G68**. Click the **Insert tab**, and then in the **Tables group**, click the **Table** button. In the **Create Table** dialog box, if necessary, select the My table has headers check box, and then click **OK**. On the **Design tab**, in the **Table Styles group**, click the **More** button, and then under **Light**, locate and click **Table Style Light 9**.

a. In the header row of the table, click the **Retail Price arrow**, and then from the menu, click **Sort Smallest to Largest**. Click the **Category arrow**. On the menu, click the **(Select All)** check box to clear all the check boxes. Scroll as necessary and then click to select only the **Steak** check box. Click **OK**.

b. On the **Design tab**, in the **Table Style Options group**, select the **Total Row** check box. Click cell **A69**, click the **arrow** that displays to the right of cell **A69**, and then in the list, click **Sum**. In cell **B11**, type the result **6 (278 total items in stock)** and then press [Enter].

c. In the header row of the table, click the **Category arrow** and then click **Clear Filter From "Category"** to redisplay all of the data. Click anywhere in the table. Click the **Design tab**, in the **Table Style Options group**, clear the **Total Row** check box, and

then in the **Tools group**, click the **Convert to Range** button. Click **Yes**.

d. On the **Page Layout tab**, in the **Themes group**, click the **Themes** button, and then click **Horizon**.

6 On the **Page Layout tab**, click the **Margins** button, and then click **Custom Margins**. On the **Margins tab**, under **Center on page**, select the **Horizontally** check box. Click **OK**. On the **Page Layout tab**, in the **Scale to Fit group**, click the **Width button arrow**, and then click **1 page**.

a. In the **Page Setup group**, click the **Print Titles** button. Under **Print titles**, click in the **Rows to repeat at top** box, and then to the right, click the **Collapse Dialog** button. From the **row heading area**, select **row 13**, and then click the **Expand Dialog** button. Click **OK**.

b. On the **Insert tab**, in the **Text group**, click the **Header & Footer** button. Insert the **File Name** in the **left section** of the footer. Return to **Normal** view, make cell **A1** the active cell, and then delete the unused sheets.

c. Display the **Document Panel**, and then add your name, your course name and section, and the keywords **inventory, Portland** Close the **Document Information Panel**.

d. **Save** your workbook. Print or submit electronically as directed by your instructor. If required by your instructor, print or create an electronic version of your worksheets with formulas displayed by using the instructions in Activity 1.16, and then **Close** Excel without saving so that you do not save the changes you made to print formulas.

End **You have completed Project 2C**

Content-Based Assessments

Apply 2B skills from these Objectives:

- **7** Navigate a Workbook and Rename Worksheets
- **8** Enter Dates, Clear Contents, and Clear Formats
- **9** Copy and Paste by Using the Paste Options Gallery
- **10** Edit and Format Multiple Worksheets at the Same Time
- **11** Create a Summary Sheet with Column Sparklines
- **12** Format and Print Multiple Worksheets in a Workbook

Skills Review | Project 2D February Sales

In the following Skills Review, you will edit a workbook that summarizes in-store and online sales in the California and Oregon retail locations. Your completed workbook will look similar to Figure 2.54.

Project Files

For Project 2D, you will need the following file:

e02D_February_Sales

You will save your workbook as:

Lastname_Firstname_2D_February_Sales

Project Results

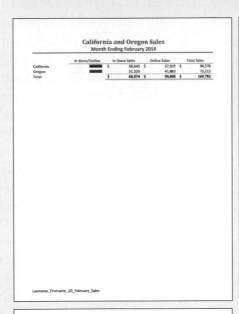

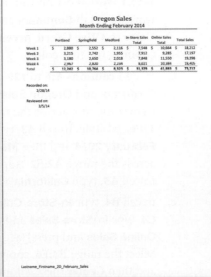

Figure 2.54

(Project 2D February Sales continues on the next page)

Content-Based Assessments

Skills Review | Project **2D** February Sales (continued)

1 **Start** Excel. From your student files, locate and open **e02D_February_Sales**. Click the **File tab**, click **Save As**, navigate to your **Excel Chapter 2** folder, and then using your own name, save the file as **Lastname_Firstname_ 2D_February_Sales**

a. Point to the **Sheet1 tab**, and then double-click to select the sheet tab name. Type **California Sales** and then press Enter.

b. Point to the **Sheet2 tab**, right-click, and then from the shortcut menu, click **Rename**. Type **Oregon Sales** and press Enter.

c. Point to the **California Sales sheet tab** and right-click. On the shortcut menu, point to **Tab Color**, and then in the last column, click the first color—**Orange, Accent 6**.

d. Using the technique you just practiced, change the tab color of the **Oregon Sales sheet tab** to **Aqua, Accent 5**—in the next to last column, the first color.

e. Click the **California Sales sheet tab**, and then click cell **A13**. On the **Home tab**, in the **Number group**, click the **Number Format arrow**. From the bottom of the displayed menu, click **More Number Formats** to display the **Number tab** of the **Format Cells** dialog box. Click the **3/14/01** type, and then at the bottom of the dialog box, click **OK**.

f. Click cell **A16**, type **3/5/14** and then press Enter. Click cell **A13**, and then on the **Home tab**, in the **Clipboard group**, click the **Format Painter** button. Click cell **A16** to copy the date format from cell **A13** to cell **A16**.

g. Click cell **A1**. In the **Editing group**, click the **Clear** button. From the displayed list, click **Clear Formats**.

h. Select the range **A4:A16**. On the **Home tab**, in the **Clipboard group**, click the **Copy** button. At the bottom of the workbook window, click the **Oregon Sales sheet tab** to make it the active worksheet. Right-click cell **A4**, and then under **Paste Options**, click the first button—**Paste**. Display the **California Sales** sheet. Press Esc to cancel the moving border.

2 With the **California Sales** sheet active, press Ctrl + Home to make cell **A1** the active cell. Point to the sheet tab, right-click, and then on the shortcut menu, click **Select All Sheets**. Verify that *[Group]* displays in the title bar.

a. **Merge & Center** the text in cell A1 across the range **A1:G1**, and then apply the **Title** cell style. Select **columns A:G**, and then set their widths to **85 pixels**.

b. Click cell **A2**, type **Month Ending February 2014** and then on the **Formula Bar**, click the **Enter** button to keep cell **A2** as the active cell. **Merge & Center** the text across the range **A2:G2**, and then apply the **Heading 1** cell style.

c. Select the range **B4:G4**, and then apply the **Heading 3** cell style. In the **Alignment group**, click the **Center**, **Middle Align**, and **Wrap Text** buttons.

d. With the sheets still *grouped* and the **California Sales** sheet active, click cell **E5**. On the **Home tab**, in the **Editing group**, click the **Sum** button, and then press Enter. Click cell **E5**, and then drag the fill handle down to copy the formula through cell **E8**.

e. Click cell **G5**, type = click cell **E5**, type + click cell **F5**, and then press Enter. Copy the formula down through cell **G8**. In cell **A9**, type **Total** Select the range **B5:G9**, and then press Alt + = to enter the SUM function for all the columns. Select the range **A5:A9**, and then apply the **Heading 4** cell style.

f. Select the range **B5:G5**, hold down Ctrl, and then select the range **B9:G9**. Apply the **Accounting Number Format** and decrease the decimal places to zero. Select the range **B6:G8**, and then apply **Comma Style** with zero decimal places. Select the range **B9:G9** and apply the **Total** cell style.

3 Click the **Oregon Sales sheet tab** to cancel the grouping and display the second worksheet.

a. To the right of the **Oregon Sales** sheet tab, click the **Insert Worksheet** button. Rename the new worksheet tab **Summary** and then change the **Tab Color** to **Olive Green, Accent 3**—in the seventh column, the first color.

b. Widen **columns A:E** to **125** pixels. In cell **A1**, type **California and Oregon Sales** and then **Merge & Center** the title across the range **A1:E1**. Apply the **Title** cell style. In cell **A2**, type **Month Ending February 2014** and then **Merge & Center** the text across the range **A2:E2**. Apply the **Heading 1** cell style. In cell **A5**, type **California** and in cell **A6**, type **Oregon**

c. In cell **B4**, type **In-Store/Online** and press Tab. In cell **C4**, type **In-Store Sales** and press Tab. In cell **D4**, type **Online Sales** and press Tab. In cell **E4**, type **Total Sales** Select the range **B4:E4**, apply the **Heading 3** cell style, and then **Center** these column titles.

(Project 2D February Sales continues on the next page)

Content-Based Assessments

d. Click cell **C5**. Type = and then click the **California Sales sheet tab**. In the **California Sales** worksheet, click cell **E9**, and then press ⏎. Click cell **D5**. Type = and then click the **California Sales sheet tab**. Click cell **F9**, and then press ⏎.

e. By using the techniques you just practiced, in cells **C6** and **D6**, insert the total **In-Store Sales** and **Online Sales** data from the **Oregon Sales** worksheet.

f. Select the range **C5:E6**, and then click the **Sum** button to total the two rows. In cell **A7**, type **Total** and then select the range **C5:E7**. Click the **Sum** button to total the three columns. Select the nonadjacent ranges **C5:E5** and **C7:E7**, and then apply **Accounting Number Format** with zero decimal places. Select the range **C6:E6**, and then apply **Comma Style** with zero decimal places. Select the range **C7:E7**, and then apply the **Total** cell style. Select the range **A5:A7** and apply the **Heading 4** cell style.

g. Click cell **B5**. On the **Insert tab**, in the **Sparklines group**, click **Column**. In the **Create Sparklines** dialog box, with the insertion point blinking in the **Data Range** box, select the range **C5:D5** and then click **OK**.

h. Click cell **B6**, and then **Insert** a **Column Sparkline** for the range **C6:D6**. In the **Style group**, apply the second style in the second row—**Sparkline Style Accent 2, Darker 25%** to this sparkline.

4 Point to the **Summary sheet tab**, hold down the left mouse button to display a small black triangle, and drag to the left until the triangle and mouse pointer are

to the left of the **California Sales sheet tab**, and then release the left mouse button.

a. Be sure the **Summary** worksheet is the active sheet, point to its sheet tab, right-click, and then click **Select All Sheets** to display *[Group]* in the title bar. On the **Insert tab**, in the **Text group**, click the **Header & Footer** button. Display the **Footer** area, and then in the **left section**, insert the **File Name**. Center the worksheets **Horizontally** on the page, return to **Normal** view, and make cell **A1** active.

b. Display the **Document Panel**, and then add your name, your course name and section, and the keywords **February sales Close** the **Document Information Panel**.

c. **Save** your workbook. To submit your workbook electronically, follow the instructions provided by your instructor. To print your workbook, continue to Step d.

d. Display **Backstage** view, verify that the worksheets in your workbook are still grouped—*[Group]* displays in the title bar—and then on the left click **Print**. Under **Settings**, verify that **Print Active Sheets** displays. At the top of the screen, verify that the **Number of Copies** is **1**. Click the **Print** button.

e. If required by your instructor, print or create an electronic version of your worksheets with formulas displayed by using the instructions in Activity 1.16, and then **Close** Excel without saving so that you do not save the changes you made to print formulas.

End You have completed Project 2D

Content-Based Assessments

Apply **2A** skills from these Objectives:

1. Use the SUM, AVERAGE, MEDIAN, MIN, and MAX Functions
2. Move Data, Resolve Error Messages, and Rotate Text
3. Use COUNTIF and IF Functions and Apply Conditional Formatting
4. Use Date & Time Functions and Freeze Panes
5. Create, Sort, and Filter an Excel Table
6. Format and Print a Large Worksheet

Mastering Excel | Project **2E** Desserts

In the following Mastery project, you will edit a worksheet for Laura Morales, President, detailing the current inventory of desserts produced at the San Diego facility. Your completed worksheet will look similar to Figure 2.55.

Project Files

For Project 2E, you will need the following file:

e02E_Desserts

You will save your workbook as:

Lastname_Firstname_2E_Desserts

Project Results

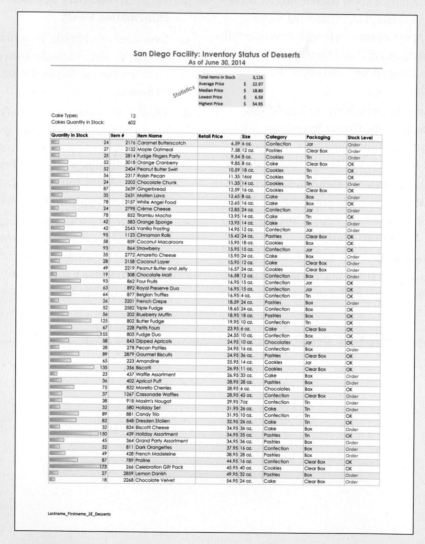

Figure 2.55

(Project 2E Desserts continues on the next page)

Content-Based Assessments

Mastering Excel | Project **2E** Desserts (continued)

1 **Start** Excel, from your student files, locate and open **e02E_Desserts**, and then **Save** the file in your **Excel Chapter 2** folder as **Lastname_Firstname_2E_Desserts**

2 In cell **B4**, calculate the **Total Items in Stock** by summing the **Quantity in Stock** data, and then apply **Comma Style** with zero decimal places to the result. In each cell in the range **B5:B8**, insert formulas to calculate the Average, Median, Lowest, and Highest retail prices, and then apply the **Accounting Number Format** to each result.

3 Move the range **A4:B8** to the range **D4:E8**, and then apply the **20% - Accent1** cell style. Widen **column D** to **130 pixels**. In cell **C6**, type **Statistics** select the range **C4:C8**, and then from the **Format Cells** dialog box, merge the selected cells. Change the text **Orientation** to **25 Degrees**, and then apply **Bold** and **Italic**. Change the **Font Size** to **14** and the **Font Color** to **Pink, Accent 1, Darker 25%**. Apply **Middle Align** and **Align Text Right**.

4 In cell **B10**, use the **COUNTIF** function to count the number of **Cake** items. In the **Packaging** column, **Replace All** occurrences of **Cellophane** with **Clear Box**

5 In cell **H14**, enter an **IF** function to determine the items that must be ordered. If the **Quantity in Stock** is less than **50** the **Value_if_true** is **Order** Otherwise the **Value_if_false** is **OK** Fill the formula down through cell **H65**. Apply **Conditional Formatting** to the **Stock Level** column so that cells that contain the text *Order* are formatted with **Bold Italic** and with a **Color** of **Blue, Accent 5**. Apply conditional formatting

to the **Quantity in Stock** column by applying a **Gradient Fill Orange Data Bar**.

6 Format the range **A13:H65** as a **Table** with headers, and apply the **Table Style Light 16** style. Sort the table from smallest to largest by **Retail Price**, and then filter on the **Category** column to display the **Cake** types. Display a **Total Row** in the table and then in cell **A66**, **Sum** the **Quantity in Stock** for the **Cake** items. Type the result in cell **B11**, and apply appropriate number formatting. Click in the table, and then on the **Design tab**, remove the total row from the table. Clear the **Category** filter and convert the table to a range.

7 Change the theme to **Composite**. Display the footer area, and insert the **File Name** in the **left section**. Center the worksheet **Horizontally**, and then use the **Scale to Fit** option to change the **Width** to **1 page**. Return to **Normal** view and make cell **A1** the active cell. In **Backstage** view, display the **Print Preview**, and then make any necessary corrections.

8 Add your name, your course name and section, and the keywords **desserts inventory, San Diego** to the Document Panel. **Save**, and then print or submit electronically as directed. If required by your instructor, print or create an electronic version of your worksheets with formulas displayed by using the instructions in Activity 1.16, and then **Close** Excel without saving so that you do not save the changes you made to print formulas.

End **You have completed Project 2E**

Content-Based Assessments

7 Navigate a
Workbook and
Rename Worksheets

8 Enter Dates, Clear
Contents, and Clear
Formats

9 Copy and Paste by
Using the Paste
Options Gallery

10 Edit and Format
Multiple Worksheets
at the Same Time

11 Create a Summary
Sheet with Column
Sparklines

12 Format and Print
Multiple Worksheets
in a Workbook

Mastering Excel | Project **2F** Compensation

In the following Mastery project, you will edit a workbook that summarizes the Laurales Herb
and Spices salesperson compensation for the month of November. Your completed worksheet will
look similar to Figure 2.56.

Project Files

For Project 2F, you will need the following file:

e02F_Compensation

You will save your workbook as:

Lastname_Firstname_2F_Compensation

Project Results

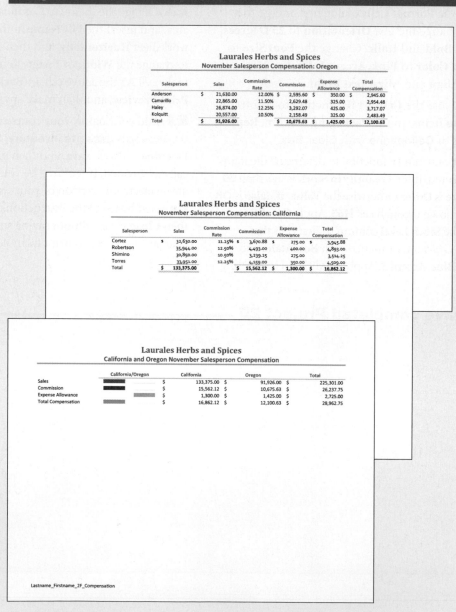

Figure 2.56

(Project 2F Compensation continues on the next page)

Mastering Excel | Project **2F** Compensation (continued)

1 **Start** Excel, from your student files, open **e02F_ Compensation**, and then save the file in your **Excel Chapter 2** folder as **Lastname_Firstname_2F_ Compensation**

2 Rename **Sheet1** as **California** and change the **Tab Color** to **Green, Accent 1**. Rename **Sheet2** as **Oregon** and change the **Tab Color** to **Gold, Accent 3**.

3 Click the **California sheet tab** to make it the active sheet, and then group the worksheets. In cell **A1**, type **Laurales Herbs and Spices** and then **Merge & Center** the text across the range **A1:F1**. Apply the **Title** cell style. **Merge & Center** the text in cell **A2** across the range **A2:F2**, and then apply the **Heading 1** cell style.

4 With the sheets still grouped, in cell **D5** calculate **Commission** for *Cortez* by multiplying the **Sales** by the **Commission Rate**. Copy the formula down through cell **D8**. In cell **F5**, calculate **Total Compensation** by summing the **Commission** and **Expense Allowance** for *Cortez*. Copy the formula down through the cell **F8**.

5 In **row 9**, sum the **Sales, Commission, Expense Allowance**, and **Total Compensation** columns. Apply the **Accounting Number Format** with two decimal places to the appropriate cells in **row 5** and **row 9** (do not include the percentages). Apply the **Comma Style** with two decimal places to the appropriate cells in **rows 6:8** (do not include the percentages). Apply the **Total** cell style to the appropriate cells in the Total row.

6 Insert a new worksheet. Change the sheet name to **Summary** and then change the **Tab Color** to **Periwinkle, Accent 5**. Widen **columns A:E** to **165** pixels, and then move the **Summary** sheet so that it is the first sheet in the workbook. In cell **A1**, type **Laurales Herbs and Spices Merge & Center** the title across the range **A1:E1**, and then apply the **Title** cell style. In cell **A2**, type **California and Oregon November Salesperson Compensation** and then **Merge & Center** the text across the range **A2:E2**. Apply the **Heading 1** cell style.

7 In the range **A5:A8**, type the following row titles and then apply the **Heading 4** cell style:

Sales

Commission

Expense Allowance

Total Compensation

8 In the range **B4:E4**, type the following column titles, and then **Center** and apply the **Heading 3** cell style.

California/Oregon

California

Oregon

Total

9 In cell **C5**, enter a formula that references cell **B9** in the **California** worksheet so that the total sales for California displays in **C5**. Create similar formulas to enter the total **Commission, Expense Allowance** and **Total Compensation** for California in the range **C6:C8**. Using the same technique, enter formulas in the range **D5:D8** so that the **Oregon** totals display.

10 Sum the **Sales, Commission, Expense Allowance**, and **Total Compensation** rows.

11 In cell **B5**, insert a **Column Sparkline** for the range **C5:D5**. In cells **B6, B7**, and **B8**, insert **Column** sparklines for the appropriate ranges to compare California totals with Oregon totals. To the sparkline in **B6**, apply the second style in the third row—**Sparkline Style Accent 2, (no dark or light)**. In **B7** apply the third style in the third row—**Sparkline Style Accent 3, (no dark or light)**. In **B8** apply the fourth style in the third row—**Sparkline Style Accent 4, (no dark or light)**.

12 **Group** the three worksheets, and then insert a footer in the left section with the **File Name**. Center the worksheets **Horizontally** on the page, and then change the **Orientation** to **Landscape**. Return the document to **Normal** view.

13 Display the **Document Panel**. Add your name, your course name and section, and the keywords **November sales Save** your workbook, and then print or submit electronically as directed. If required by your instructor, print or create an electronic version of your worksheets with formulas displayed by using the instructions in Activity 1.16, and then **Close** Excel without saving so that you do not save the changes you made to print formulas.

End You have completed Project 2F —————————

Excel | Chapter 2

Content-Based Assessments

Apply 2A and 2B skills from these Objectives:

1 Use the SUM, AVERAGE, MEDIAN, MIN, and MAX Functions

2 Move Data, Resolve Error Messages, and Rotate Text

3 Use COUNTIF and IF Functions and Apply Conditional Formatting

4 Use Date & Time Functions and Freeze Panes

5 Create, Sort, and Filter an Excel Table

6 Format and Print a Large Worksheet

7 Navigate a Workbook and Rename Worksheets

8 Enter Dates, Clear Contents, and Clear Formats

9 Copy and Paste by Using the Paste Options Gallery

10 Edit and Format Multiple Worksheets at the Same Time

11 Create a Summary Sheet with Column Sparklines

12 Format and Print Multiple Worksheets in a Workbook

Mastering Excel | Project 2G Inventory Summary

In the following Mastery project, you will edit a worksheet that summarizes the inventory status at the Petaluma production facility. Your completed workbook will look similar to Figure 2.57.

Project Files

For Project 2G, you will need the following file:

e02G_Inventory_Summary

You will save your workbook as:

Lastname_Firstname_2G_Inventory_Summary

Project Results

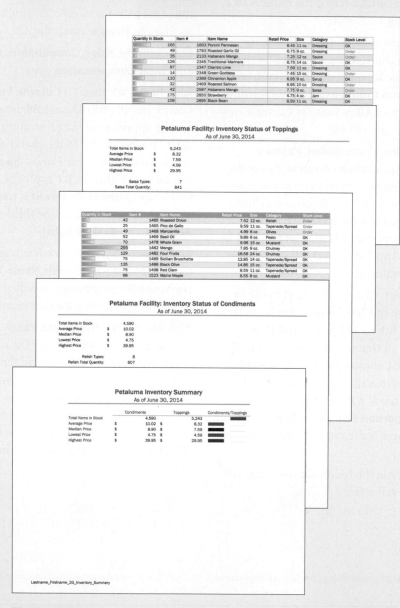

Figure 2.57

(Project 2G Inventory Summary continues on the next page)

168 Excel | Chapter 2: Using Functions, Creating Tables, and Managing Large Workbooks

Mastering Excel | Project **2G** Inventory Summary (continued)

1 **Start** Excel. From your student files, open **e02G_Inventory_Summary**. Save the file in your **Excel Chapter 2** folder as **Lastname_Firstname_2G_Inventory_Summary**

2 Rename **Sheet1** as **Condiments** and **Sheet2** as **Toppings** Make the following calculations in each of the two worksheets *without* grouping the sheets:

- In cell **B4**, enter a formula to sum the **Quantity in Stock** data, and then apply **Comma Style** with zero decimal places to the result.

- In cells **B5:B8**, enter formulas to calculate the Average, Median, Lowest, and Highest retail prices, and then apply the **Accounting Number Format**.

3 In each of the two worksheets, make the following calculations *without* grouping the sheets:

- In cell **B10**, enter a COUNTIF function to determine how many different types of **Relish** products are in stock on the **Condiments** sheet and how many different types of **Salsa** products are in stock on the **Toppings** worksheet.

- In cell **G15**, enter an **IF** function to determine the items that must be ordered. If the **Quantity in Stock** is less than **50** the **Value_if_true** is **Order** Otherwise the **Value_if_false** is **OK** Fill the formula down through all the rows.

- Apply **Conditional Formatting** to the **Stock Level** column so that cells that contain the text *Order* are formatted with **Bold Italic** with a **Font Color** of **Gold, Accent 1, Darker 25%**. Apply **Gradient Fill Green Data Bars** to the **Quantity in Stock** column.

4 In the **Condiments** sheet, format the range **A14:G64** as a table with headers and apply **Table Style Medium 2**. Insert a **Total Row**, filter by **Category** for **Relish**, and then **Sum** the **Quantity in Stock** column. Record the result in cell **B11**.

5 Select the table, clear the filter, **Sort** the table on the **Item #** column from **Smallest to Largest**, remove the **Total Row**, and then convert the table to a range. On the **Page Layout tab**, set **Print Titles** so that **row 14** repeats at the top of each page.

6 In the **Toppings** sheet, format the range **A14:G61** as a table with headers and apply **Table Style Light 16**. Insert a **Total Row**, filter by **Category** for **Salsa**, and then **Sum** the **Quantity in Stock** column. Record the result in cell **B11**.

7 Select the table, clear the filter, **Sort** the table on the **Item #** column from **Smallest to Largest**, remove the **Total Row**, and then convert the table to a range.

8 On the **Page Layout tab**, set **Print Titles** so that **row 14** repeats at the top of each page, and then **Save** your workbook. **Group** the two worksheets. **Center** the worksheets **Horizontally**, and then use the **Scale to Fit** option to change the **Width** to **1 page**.

9 Insert a new worksheet. Change the sheet name to **Summary** and then widen **columns A:D** to **170** pixels. Move the **Summary** sheet so that it is the first sheet in the workbook. In cell **A1**, type **Petaluma Inventory Summary** **Merge & Center** the title across the range **A1:D1**, and then apply the **Title** cell style. In cell **A2**, type **As of June 30, 2014** and then **Merge & Center** the text across the range **A2:D2**. Apply the **Heading 1** cell style.

10 On the **Condiments sheet**, **Copy** the range **A4:A8**. Display the **Summary sheet** and **Paste** the selection to cell **A5**. Apply the **Heading 4** cell style to the selection. In the **Summary sheet**, in cell **B4**, type **Condiments** In cell **C4**, type **Toppings** and in cell **D4**, type **Condiments/Toppings** Center the column titles, and then apply the **Heading 3** cell style.

11 In cell **B5**, enter a formula that references cell **B4** in the **Condiments sheet** so that the **Condiments Total Items in Stock** displays in **B5**. Create similar formulas to enter the **Average Price**, **Median Price**, **Lowest Price**, and **Highest Price** from the **Condiments sheet** into the **Summary** sheet in the range **B6:B9**.

12 Enter formulas in the range **C5:C9** that reference the appropriate cells in the **Toppings** worksheet. To the range **B5:C5**, apply **Comma Style** with zero decimal places. In cells **D5, D6, D7, D8,** and **D9**, insert **Column** sparklines using the values in the *Condiments* and *Toppings* columns. Format each sparkline using the first five Sparkline styles in the first row.

13 Center the **Summary** worksheet **Horizontally** and change the **Orientation** to **Landscape**. **Group** the worksheets and insert a footer in the left section with the **File Name**. In **Normal** view, make cell **A1** the active cell. Display the **Document Panel**. Add your name, your course name and section, and the keywords **Petaluma inventory**

14 **Save** your workbook, and then print or submit electronically as directed. If required by your instructor, print or create an electronic version of your worksheets with formulas displayed by using the instructions in Activity 1.16, and then **Close** Excel without saving so that you do not save the changes you made to print formulas.

End **You have completed Project 2G** ——————

Content-Based Assessments

Apply a combination of the 2A and 2B skills.

GO! Fix It | Project 2H Confections

Project Files

For Project 2H, you will need the following file:

e02H_Confections

You will save your workbook as:

Lastname_Firstname_2H_Confections

In this project, you will correct a worksheet that contains the confection inventory for the month of June at the Laurales Herb and Spices Petaluma production facility. From the student files that accompany this textbook, open the file e02H_Confections, and then save the file in your chapter folder as **Lastname_Firstname_2H_Confections**

To complete the project, you must find and correct errors in formulas and formatting. View each formula in cells B4:B8 and edit as necessary. In addition to errors that you find, you should know:

- The table should be sorted smallest to largest by Item #.
- New stock should be ordered when the Quantity in Stock is less than 50, and the word *Order* should be formatted with bold, italic, in font color Red, Accent 3.
- The table should be converted to a range.
- Gradient fill red data bars should be applied to the Quantity in Stock column.

Insert the file name in the left section of the footer, center the worksheet horizontally, and repeat the table column titles on each page. Edit the document properties with your name, course and section, and the keywords **Petaluma, confections** Save your file, and then print or submit your worksheet electronically as directed by your instructor. If required by your instructor, print or create an electronic version of your worksheets with formulas displayed by using the instructions in Activity 1.16, and then Close Excel without saving so that you do not save the changes you made to print formulas.

End You have completed Project 2H ——————————————

Content-Based Assessments

GO! Make It | Project **2I** Salary Summary

Project Files

For Project 2I, you will need the following file:

e02I_Salary_Summary

You will save your workbook as:

Lastname_Firstname_2I_Salary_Summary

Open e02I_Salary_Summary and save the file in your Excel Chapter 2 folder as **Lastname_Firstname_2I_Salary_Summary** Edit the worksheet as shown in Figure 2.58. To calculate Commission for each salesperson, multiply the Sales by the Commission Rate, using absolute cell references as necessary. To determine the Bonus, construct an IF function where the Logical Test determines if Sales are greater than 21,500, the Value_if_true is 500, and the Value_if_false is 0. Calculate Total Compensation by adding the Commission and the Bonus for each salesperson. Determine the Sales and Compensation totals, averages, medians, and highest and lowest amounts. Insert a table, apply Table Medium Style 16, sort the table as shown in Figure 2.58, apply cell styles and number formatting as indicated, and convert the table to a range. Insert a footer with the file name in the left section, center the worksheet horizontally, and add your name, your course name and section, and the keywords **commission, sales** to the document properties. Print or submit electronically as directed by your instructor.

Project Results

Figure 2.58

End You have completed Project 2I

Content-Based Assessments

GO! Solve It | Project 2J Toppings

Project Files

For Project 2J, you will need the following file:

> e02J_Toppings

You will save your workbook as:

> Lastname_Firstname_2J_Toppings

Open the file e02J_Toppings and save it as **Lastname_Firstname_2J_Toppings** Complete the worksheet by entering appropriate formulas in cells B5 and B6. In the Stock Level column, enter an IF function that determines whether the quantity in stock is greater than 65. If the Quantity in Stock is greater than 65, then the Stock Level should display the text **OK** Otherwise the Stock Level should display the text **Order** Insert a Table with a total row and apply an attractive table style. Sort the table by Item #, calculate the values for B7 and B8, and then clear all filters and remove the total row from the table. Convert the table to a range. Format the worksheet attractively, and apply appropriate Data Bars to the Quantity in Stock column and conditional formatting to the Stock Level column so that items that need to be ordered are easily identified. Include the file name in the footer, add appropriate properties, and submit as directed.

		Performance Level		
		Exemplary: You consistently applied the relevant skills	**Proficient:** You sometimes, but not always, applied the relevant skills	**Developing:** You rarely or never applied the relevant skills
Performance Element	**Create formulas**	All formulas are correct and are efficiently constructed.	Formulas are correct but not always constructed in the most efficient manner.	One or more formulas are missing or incorrect; or only numbers were entered.
	Insert and format a table	Table was created and formatted properly.	Table was created but incorrect data was selected or the table was not formatted.	No table was created.
	Format worksheet data attractively and appropriately	Formatting is attractive and appropriate.	Adequately formatted but difficult to read or unattractive.	Inadequate or no formatting.

End You have completed Project 2J

Content-Based Assessments

Apply a combination of the **2A** and **2B** skills.

GO! Solve It | Project **2K** First Quarter Summary

Project Files

For Project 2K, you will need the following file:

e02K_First_Quarter

You will save your workbook as:

Lastname_Firstname_2K_First_Quarter

Open the file e02K_First_Quarter and save it as **Lastname_Firstname_2K_First_Quarter** This workbook contains two worksheets; one that includes California sales data by product and one that includes Oregon sales data by product. Complete the two worksheets by calculating totals by product and by month. Then calculate the Percent of Total by dividing the Product Total by the Monthly Total, using absolute cell references as necessary. Format the worksheets attractively with a title and subtitle, and apply appropriate financial formatting. Insert a new worksheet that summarizes the monthly totals by state. Enter the months as the column titles and the states as the row titles. Include a Product Total column and a column for sparklines titled **Jan./Feb./March** Format the Summary worksheet attractively with a title and subtitle, insert column sparklines that compare the months, and apply appropriate financial formatting. Include the file name in the footer, add appropriate document properties, and submit as directed.

	Performance Level		
	Exemplary: You consistently applied the relevant skills	**Proficient:** You sometimes, but not always, applied the relevant skills	**Developing:** You rarely or never applied the relevant skills
Create formulas	All formulas are correct and are efficiently constructed.	Formulas are correct but not always constructed in the most efficient manner.	One or more formulas are missing or incorrect; or only numbers were entered.
Create Summary worksheet	Summary worksheet created properly.	Summary worksheet was created but the data, sparklines, or formulas were incorrect.	No Summary worksheet was created.
Format attractively and appropriately	Formatting is attractive and appropriate.	Adequately formatted but difficult to read or unattractive.	Inadequate or no formatting.

Performance Element (vertical label)

End You have completed Project 2K

Outcomes-Based Assessments

Rubric

The following outcomes-based assessments are *open-ended assessments*. That is, there is no specific correct result; your result will depend on your approach to the information provided. Make *Professional Quality* your goal. Use the following scoring rubric to guide you in *how* to approach the problem, and then to evaluate *how well* your approach solves the problem.

The *criteria*—Software Mastery, Content, Format and Layout, and Process—represent the knowledge and skills you have gained that you can apply to solving the problem. The *levels of performance*—Professional Quality, Approaching Professional Quality, or Needs Quality Improvements—help you and your instructor evaluate your result.

	Your completed project is of Professional Quality if you:	Your completed project is Approaching Professional Quality if you:	Your completed project Needs Quality Improvements if you:
1-Software Mastery	Choose and apply the most appropriate skills, tools, and features and identify efficient methods to solve the problem.	Choose and apply some appropriate skills, tools, and features, but not in the most efficient manner.	Choose inappropriate skills, tools, or features, or are inefficient in solving the problem.
2-Content	Construct a solution that is clear and well organized, contains content that is accurate, appropriate to the audience and purpose, and is complete. Provide a solution that contains no errors in spelling, grammar, or style.	Construct a solution in which some components are unclear, poorly organized, inconsistent, or incomplete. Misjudge the needs of the audience. Have some errors in spelling, grammar, or style, but the errors do not detract from comprehension.	Construct a solution that is unclear, incomplete, or poorly organized; contains some inaccurate or inappropriate content; and contains many errors in spelling, grammar, or style. Do not solve the problem.
3-Format and Layout	Format and arrange all elements to communicate information and ideas, clarify function, illustrate relationships, and indicate relative importance.	Apply appropriate format and layout features to some elements, but not others. Overuse features, causing minor distraction.	Apply format and layout that does not communicate information or ideas clearly. Do not use format and layout features to clarify function, illustrate relationships, or indicate relative importance. Use available features excessively, causing distraction.
4-Process	Use an organized approach that integrates planning, development, self-assessment, revision, and reflection.	Demonstrate an organized approach in some areas, but not others; or, use an insufficient process of organization throughout.	Do not use an organized approach to solve the problem.

Outcomes-Based Assessments

Apply a combination of the **2A** and **2B** skills.

GO! Think | Project **2L** Seasonings

Project Files

For Project 2L, you will need the following file:

    e02L_Seasonings

You will save your workbook as:

    Lastname_Firstname_2L_Seasonings

Laura Morales, President of Laurales Herbs and Spices, has requested a worksheet that summarizes the seasonings inventory data for the month of March. Laura would like the worksheet to include the total Quantity in Stock and Number of Items for each category of items and she would like the items to be sorted from lowest to highest retail price.

Edit the workbook to provide Laura with the information requested. Format the worksheet titles and data and include an appropriately formatted table so that the worksheet is professional and easy to read and understand. Insert a footer with the file name and add appropriate document properties. Save the file as **Lastname_Firstname_2L_Seasonings** and print or submit as directed by your instructor.

 End You have completed Project 2L ———————————

Apply a combination of the **2A** and **2B** skills.

GO! Think | Project **2M** Expense Summary

Project Files

For Project 2M, you will need the following file:

    e02M_Expense_Summary

You will save your workbook as:

    Lastname_Firstname_2M_Expense_Summary

Sara Lopez, Director of the San Diego production facility, has requested a summary analysis of the administrative expenses the facility incurred in the last fiscal year. Open e02M_Expense_Summary and then complete the calculation in the four worksheets containing the quarterly data. Summarize the information in a new worksheet that includes formulas referencing the totals for each expense category for each quarter. Sum the expenses to display the yearly expense by quarter and expense category. Format the worksheets in a manner that is professional and easy to read and understand. Insert a footer with the file name and add appropriate document properties. Save the file as **Lastname_Firstname_2M_Expense_Summary** and print or submit as directed by your instructor.

End You have completed Project 2M ———————————

Outcomes-Based Assessments

Apply a combination of the 2A and 2B skills.

You and GO! | Project 2N Annual Expenses

Project Files

For Project 2N, you will need the following file:

New blank Excel workbook

You will save your workbook as:

Lastname_Firstname_2N_Annual_Expenses

Develop a workbook that details the expenses you expect to incur during the current year. Create four worksheets, one for each quarter of the year and enter your expenses by month. For example, the Quarter 1 sheet will contain expense information for January, February, and March. Some of these expenses might include, but are not limited to, Mortgage, Rent, Utilities, Phone, Food, Entertainment, Tuition, Childcare, Clothing, and Insurance. Include monthly and quarterly totals for each category of expense. Insert a worksheet that summarizes the total expenses for each quarter. Format the worksheet by adjusting column width and wrapping text, and by applying appropriate financial number formatting and cell styles. Insert a footer with the file name and center the worksheet horizontally on the page. Save your file as **Lastname_Firstname_2N_Annual_Expenses** and submit as directed.

 You have completed Project 2N —————————

Analyzing Data with Pie Charts, Line Charts, and What-If Analysis Tools

OUTCOMES
At the end of this chapter you will be able to:

OBJECTIVES
Mastering these objectives will enable you to:

PROJECT 3A
Present budget data in a pie chart.

1. Chart Data with a Pie Chart (p. 179)
2. Format a Pie Chart (p. 182)
3. Edit a Workbook and Update a Chart (p. 188)
4. Use Goal Seek to Perform What-If Analysis (p. 189)

PROJECT 3B
Make projections using what-if analysis and present projections in a line chart.

5. Design a Worksheet for What-If Analysis (p. 195)
6. Answer What-If Questions by Changing Values in a Worksheet (p. 202)
7. Chart Data with a Line Chart (p. 205)

iofoto/Shutterstock

In This Chapter

In this chapter, you will work with two different types of commonly used charts that make it easy to visualize data. You will create a pie chart in a separate chart sheet to show how the parts of a budget contribute to a total budget. You will also practice using parentheses in a formula, calculate the percentage rate of an increase, answer what-if questions, and then chart data in a line chart to show the flow of data over time. In this chapter you will also practice formatting the axes in a line chart.

The projects in this chapter relate to **The City of Orange Blossom Beach**, a coastal city located between Fort Lauderdale and Miami. The city's access to major transportation provides both residents and businesses an opportunity to compete in the global marketplace. Each year the city welcomes a large number of tourists who enjoy the warm climate and beautiful beaches, and who embark on cruises from this major cruise port. The city encourages best environmental practices and partners with cities in other countries to promote sound government at the local level.

Project 3A Budget Pie Chart

Project Activities

In Activities 3.01 through 3.11, you will edit a worksheet for Lila Darius, City Manager, that projects expenses from the city's general fund for the next fiscal year, and then present the data in a pie chart. Your completed worksheet will look similar to Figure 3.1.

Project Files

For Project 3A, you will need the following file:

e03A_Fund_Expenses

You will save your workbook as:

Lastname_Firstname_3A_Fund_Expenses

Project Results

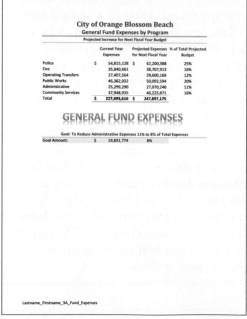

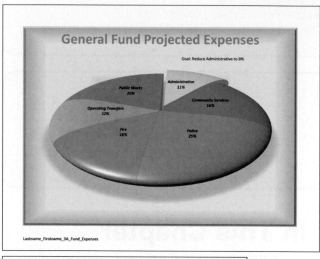

Figure 3.1
Project 3A Fund Expenses

Objective 1 | Chart Data with a Pie Chart

A *pie chart* shows the relationship of each part to a whole. The size of each pie slice is equal to its value compared to the total value of all the slices. The pie chart style charts data that is arranged in a single column or single row, and shows the size of items in a single data series proportional to the sum of the items. Whereas a column or bar chart can have two or more data series in the chart, a pie chart can have only one data series.

Consider using a pie chart when you have only one data series to plot, you do not have more than seven categories, and the categories represent parts of a total value.

Activity 3.01 | Creating a Pie Chart and a Chart Sheet

A *fund* is a sum of money set aside for a specific purpose. In a municipal government like the City of Orange Blossom Beach, the *general fund* is money set aside for the normal operating activities of the city, such as police, fire, and administering the everyday functions of the city.

1 **Start** Excel. From the student files that accompany this textbook, open **e03A_Fund_Expenses**. From **Backstage view**, display the **Save As** dialog box. Navigate to the location where you are storing projects for this chapter.

2 Create a new folder named **Excel Chapter 3** and open the new folder. In the **File name** box, type **Lastname_Firstname_3A_Fund_Expenses** Click **Save** or press Enter.

> The worksheet indicates the expenses for the current year and the projected expenses for the next fiscal year.

3 Click cell **D5**, and then type = to begin a formula.

4 Click cell **C5**, which is the first value that is part of the total Projected Expenses, to insert it into the formula. Type **/** to indicate division, and then click cell **C11**, which is the total Projected Expenses.

> Recall that to determine the percentage by which a value makes up a total, you must divide the value by the total. The result will be a percentage expressed as a decimal.

5 Press F4 to make the reference to the value in cell **C11** absolute, which will enable you to copy the formula. Compare your screen with Figure 3.2.

> Recall that an *absolute cell reference* refers to a cell by its fixed position in the worksheet. The reference to cell C5 is a *relative cell reference*, because when you copy the formula, you want the reference to change *relative* to its row.

> Recall also that dollar signs display to indicate that a cell reference is absolute.

Figure 3.2

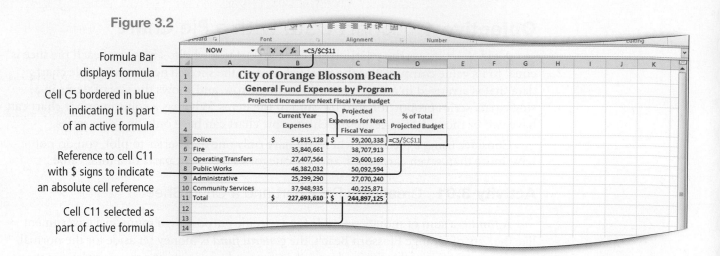

Formula Bar displays formula

Cell C5 bordered in blue indicating it is part of an active formula

Reference to cell C11 with $ signs to indicate an absolute cell reference

Cell C11 selected as part of active formula

6 On the **Formula Bar**, click the **Enter** button ✓ to confirm the entry and to keep cell **D5** the active cell. Copy the formula down through cell **D10**, and then compare your screen with Figure 3.3.

Figure 3.3

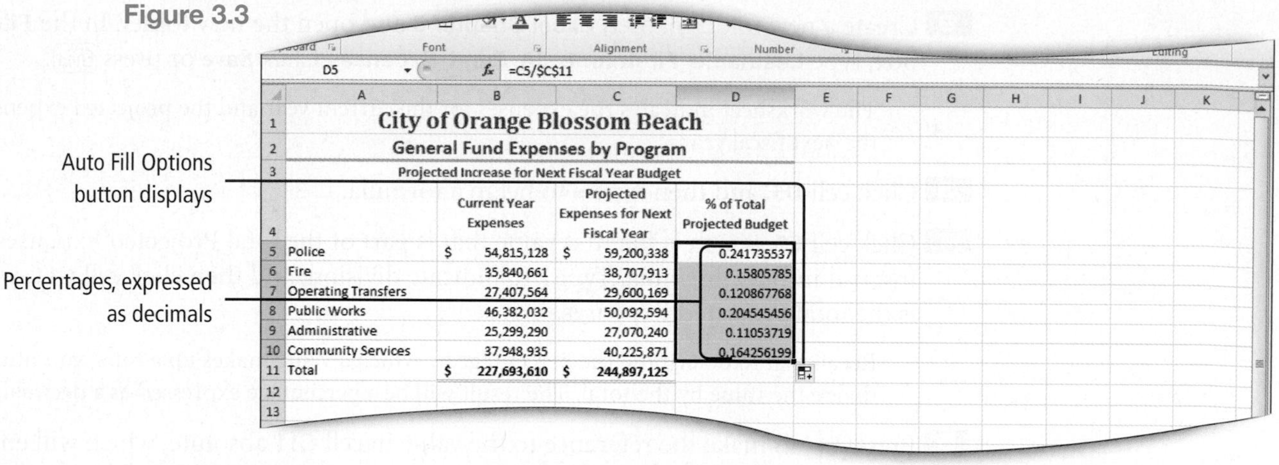

Auto Fill Options button displays

Percentages, expressed as decimals

7 With the range **D5:D10** still selected, right-click over the selection, and then on the Mini toolbar, click the **Percent Style** button % and the **Center** button. Click cell **A1** to cancel the selection, and then **Save** your workbook. Compare your screen with Figure 3.4.

Figure 3.4

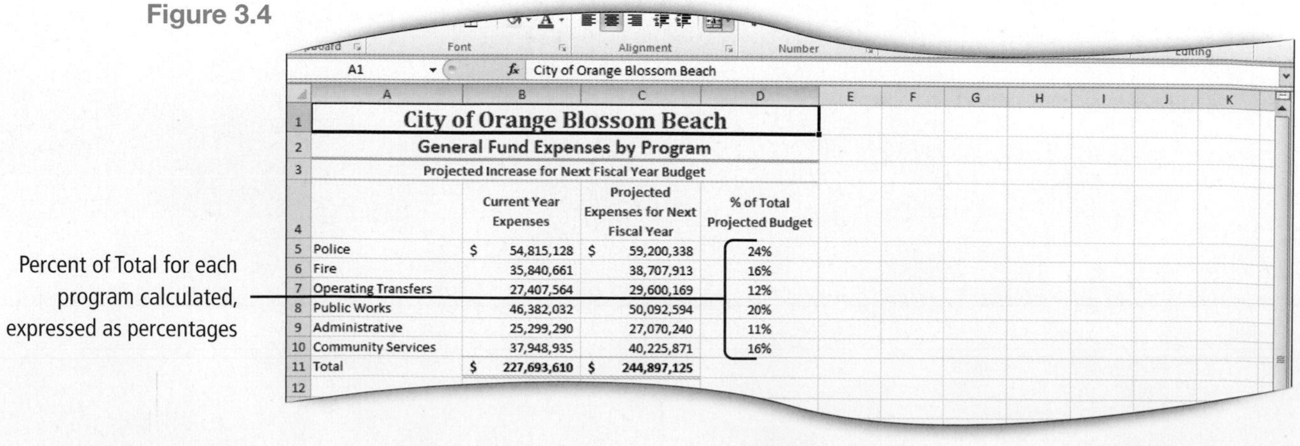

Percent of Total for each program calculated, expressed as percentages

8 Select the range **A5:A10**, hold down [Ctrl], and then select the range **C5:C10** to select the nonadjacent ranges with the program names and the projected expense for each program.

> To create a pie chart, you must select two ranges. One range contains the labels for each slice of the pie chart, and the other range contains the values that add up to a total. The two ranges must have the same number of cells and the range with the values should *not* include the cell with the total.

> The program names (Police, Fire, and so on) are the category names and will identify the slices of the pie chart. Each projected expense is a ***data point***—a value that originates in a worksheet cell and that is represented in a chart by a ***data marker***. In a pie chart, each pie slice is a data marker. Together, the data points form the ***data series***—related data points represented by data markers—and determine the size of each pie slice.

9 With the nonadjacent ranges selected, click the **Insert tab**, and then in the **Charts group**, click **Pie**. Under **3-D Pie**, click the first chart—**Pie in 3-D**—to create the chart on your worksheet.

10 On the **Design tab**, at the right end of the Ribbon in the **Location group**, click the **Move Chart** button. In the **Move Chart** dialog box, click the **New sheet** option button.

11 In the **New sheet** box, replace the highlighted text *Chart1* by typing **Projected Expenses Chart** and then click **OK** to display the chart on a separate worksheet in your workbook. Compare your screen with Figure 3.5.

> The pie chart displays on a separate new sheet in your workbook, and a ***legend*** identifies the pie slices. Recall that a legend is a chart element that identifies the patterns or colors assigned to the categories in the chart.

> A ***chart sheet*** is a workbook sheet that contains only a chart; it is useful when you want to view a chart separately from the worksheet data. The sheet tab indicates *Projected Expenses Chart*.

Figure 3.5

Chart Tools active

Move Chart button on Design tab

Chart displays on a separate new worksheet

Legend identifies pie slices

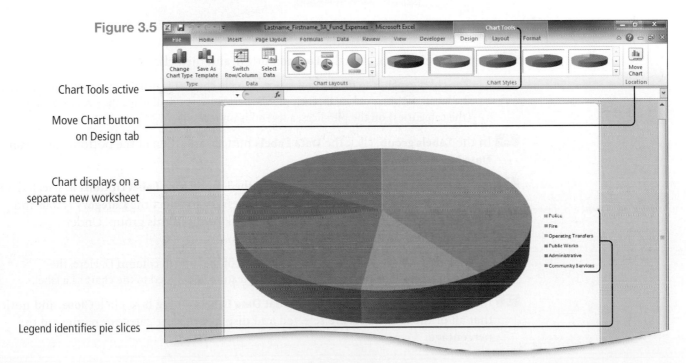

Objective 2 | Format a Pie Chart

Activity 3.02 | Applying Percentages to Labels in a Pie Chart

In your worksheet, for each expense, you calculated the percent of the total in column D. These percentages can also be calculated by the Chart feature and added to the pie slices as labels.

1 On the Ribbon under **Chart Tools**, click the **Layout tab**, and then in the **Labels group**, click the **Chart Title** button. On the displayed list, click **Above Chart**.

2 With the **Chart Title** box selected, watch the **Formula Bar** as you type **General Fund Projected Expenses** and then press [Enter] to create the new chart title in the box.

3 Point to the chart title text, right-click to display the Mini toolbar, and then change the **Font Size** to **36** and change the **Font Color** [A ▾] to **Olive Green, Accent 1, Darker 25%**— in the fifth column, the fifth color. Compare your screen with Figure 3.6.

Figure 3.6

Text displays in Formula Bar as you type

New chart title text entered and formatted

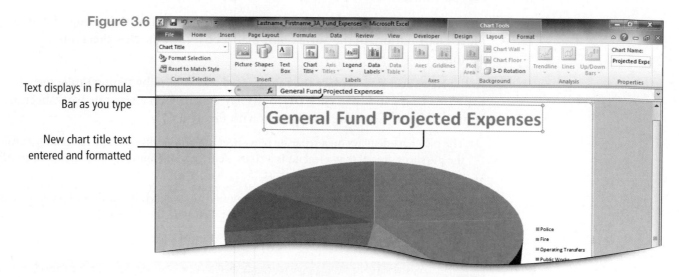

4 In the **Labels group**, click the **Legend** button, and then click **None**.

> The chart expands to fill the new space. In a pie chart, it is usually more effective to place the labels within, or close to, each pie slice. Because you will place the program names (the categories) on the pie slices, a legend is unnecessary.

5 In the **Labels group**, click the **Data Labels** button, and then at the bottom, click **More Data Label Options**.

6 In the **Format Data Labels** dialog box, on the left, be sure **Label Options** is selected. On the right, under **Label Contains**, click as necessary to select the **Category Name** and **Percentage** check boxes. *Clear* any other check boxes in this group. Under **Label Position**, click the **Center** option button.

> In the worksheet, you calculated the percent of the total in column D. Here, the percentage will be calculated by the Chart feature and added to the chart as a label.

7 In the lower right corner of the **Format Data Labels** dialog box, click **Close**, and notice that all of the data labels are selected and display both the category name and the percentage.

8 Point to any of the selected labels, right-click to display the Mini toolbar, and then change the **Font Size** to **11**, apply **Bold** **B**, and apply **Italic** **I**.

9 **Save** **[icon]** your workbook. Press Esc to deselect the labels, and then compare your screen with Figure 3.7.

Figure 3.7

Data labels on pie slices replace legend; labels include category name and percentage; data labels centered in slice, 11 pt font, bold and italic

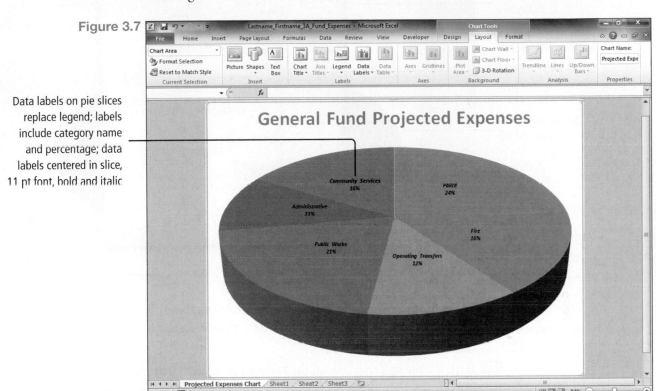

Activity 3.03 | Formatting a Pie Chart with 3-D

3-D, which is short for *three-dimensional*, refers to an image that appears to have all three spatial dimensions—length, width, and depth.

1 Click in any pie slice outside of the label to select the entire pie; notice that selection handles display on the outside corners of each slice.

2 Click the **Format tab**. In the **Shape Styles group**, click the **Shape Effects** button, point to **Bevel**, and then at the bottom of the gallery, click **3-D Options**.

3 In the **Format Data Series** dialog box, on the right, under **Bevel**, click the **Top** button. In the displayed gallery, under **Bevel**, point to the first button to display the ScreenTip *Circle*. Click the **Circle** button. Then click the **Bottom** button, and apply the **Circle** bevel.

> *Bevel* is a shape effect that uses shading and shadows to make the edges of a shape appear to be curved or angled.

4 In the four **Width** and **Height** spin boxes, type **512 pt** and then compare your screen with Figure 3.8.

Figure 3.8

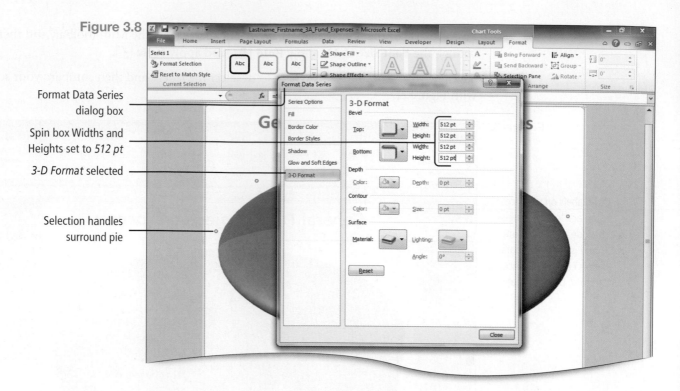

Format Data Series
dialog box

Spin box Widths and
Heights set to *512 pt*

3-D Format selected

Selection handles
surround pie

5 In the lower portion of the dialog box, under **Surface**, click the **Material** button. Under **Standard**, click the third button—**Plastic**. In the lower right corner, click **Close**.

6 With the pie still selected, on the **Format tab**, in the **Shape Styles group**, click **Shape Effects**, and then point to **Shadow**. At the bottom of the displayed gallery, scroll if necessary, and then under **Perspective**, click the third button, which displays the ScreenTip *Below* to display a shadow below the pie chart. Click **Save** 💾.

Activity 3.04 | Rotating a Pie Chart

The order in which the data series in pie charts are plotted in Excel is determined by the order of the data on the worksheet. To gain a different view of the chart, you can rotate the chart within the 360 degrees of the circle of the pie shape to present a different visual perspective of the chart.

1 Notice the position of the **Fire** and **Police** slices in the chart. Then, with the pie chart still selected—sizing handles surround the pie—point anywhere in the pie and right-click. On the displayed shortcut menu, click **Format Data Series**.

(**Another Way**
Drag the slider to 100.)

‣ **2** In the **Format Data Series** dialog box, on the left, be sure **Series Options** is selected. On the right, under **Angle of first slice**, click in the box and type **100** to rotate the chart 100 degrees to the right.

3 Close the **Format Data Series** dialog box. Click **Save** 💾, and then compare your screen with Figure 3.9.

> Rotating the chart can provide a better perspective to the chart. Here, rotating the chart in this manner emphasizes that the Fire and Police programs represent a significant portion of the total expenses.

Figure 3.9

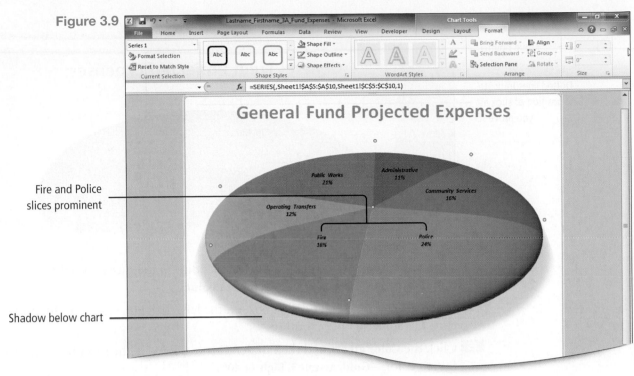

Fire and Police
slices prominent

Shadow below chart

Activity 3.05 | Exploding and Coloring a Pie Slice

You can pull out—*explode*—one or more slices of a pie chart to emphasize a specific slice or slices. Additionally, there is a different chart type you can select if you want *all* the slices to explode and emphasize all the individual slices of a pie chart—the exploded pie or exploded pie in 3-D chart type. The exploded pie chart type displays the contribution of *each* value to the total, while at the same time emphasizing individual values.

1 Press Esc to deselect all chart elements. Click any slice to select the entire pie, and then click the **Administrative** slice to select only that slice. Compare your screen with Figure 3.10.

Figure 3.10

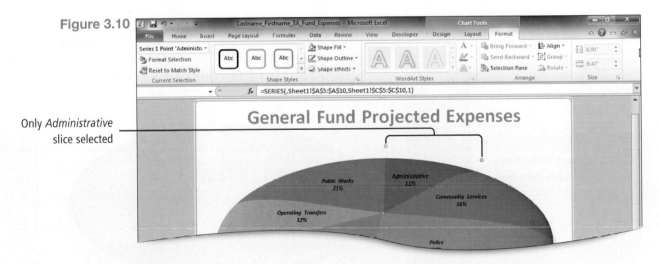

Only *Administrative*
slice selected

2 Point to the **Administrative** slice to display the ⊹ pointer, and then drag the slice slightly upward and away from the center of the pie, as shown in Figure 3.11, and then release the mouse button.

Figure 3.11

Move pointer

Dotted lines indicate
position of slice as
you move it

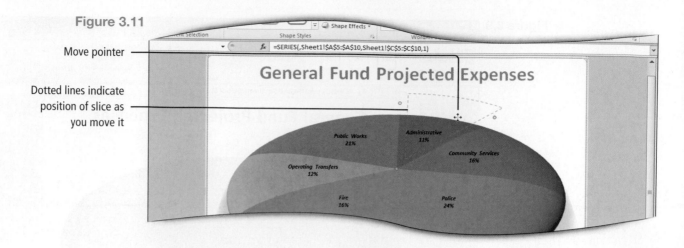

General Fund Projected Expenses

Public Works 21%
Administrative 11%
Community Services 16%
Operating Transfers 12%
Fire 16%
Police 24%

3 With the **Administrative** slice still selected, point to the slice and right-click, and then on the shortcut menu, click **Format Data Point**.

4 In the **Format Data Point** dialog box, on the left, click **Fill**. On the right, under **Fill**, click the **Solid fill** option button.

5 Click the **Color arrow**, and then under **Theme Colors**, in the seventh column, click the fourth color—**Gold, Accent 3, Lighter 40%**.

6 In the lower right corner of the **Format Data Point** dialog box, click the **Close** button.

Activity 3.06 | Formatting the Chart Area

The entire chart and all of its elements comprise the ***chart area***.

1 Point to the white area just inside the border of the chart to display the ScreenTip *Chart Area*. Click one time.

2 On the **Format tab**, in the **Shape Styles group**, click the **Shape Effects** button, point to **Bevel**, and then under **Bevel**, in the second row, click the third bevel—**Convex**.

3 Press Esc to deselect the chart element and view this effect—a convex beveled frame around your entire chart—and then compare your screen with Figure 3.12.

Figure 3.12

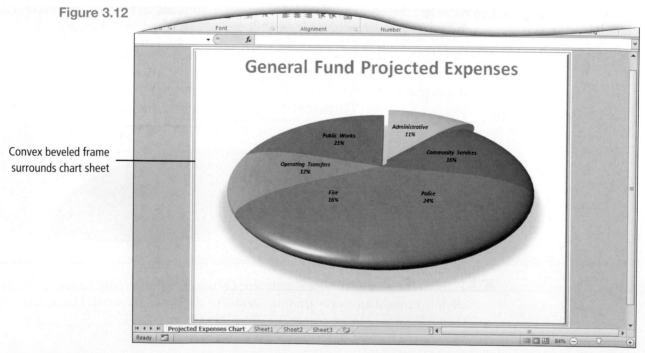

General Fund Projected Expenses

Convex beveled frame
surrounds chart sheet

Public Works 21%
Administrative 11%
Community Services 16%
Operating Transfers 12%
Fire 16%
Police 24%

Projected Expenses Chart Sheet1 Sheet2 Sheet3

4 Point slightly inside the border of the chart to display the ScreenTip *Chart Area*, right-click, and then on the shortcut menu, click **Format Chart Area**.

5 In the **Format Chart Area** dialog box, on the left, be sure that **Fill** is selected. On the right, under **Fill**, click the **Gradient fill** option button.

6 Click the **Preset colors** arrow, and then in the second row, click the last preset, **Fog**. Click the **Type arrow**, and then click **Path**. Click the **Close** button.

7 Compare your screen with Figure 3.13, and then **Save** 🖫 your workbook.

Figure 3.13

Chart area formatted with *Fog* gradient

Bevel effect added to chart area

Border indicates that the chart is selected

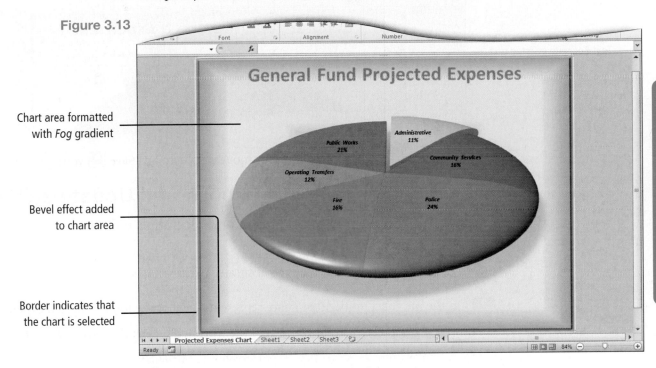

Activity 3.07 | Inserting a Text Box in a Chart

A **text box** is a movable, resizable container for text or graphics.

1 With the Chart Area still selected, click the **Layout tab**, and then in the **Insert group**, click the **Text Box** button, and then move the pointer into the chart area.

2 Position the displayed ↧ pointer under the *c* in *Projected* and about midway between the title and the pie—above the *Administrative* slice. Hold down the left mouse button, and then drag down and to the right approximately as shown in Figure 3.14; your text box need not be precise.

Figure 3.14

Text Box button

Text box drawn

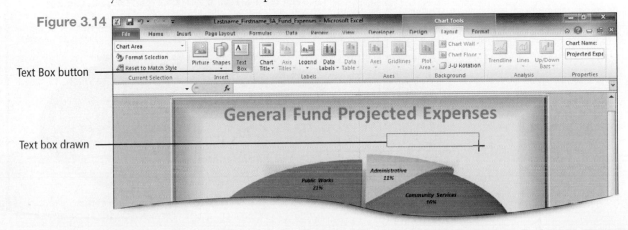

3 With the insertion point blinking inside the text box, type **Goal: Reduce Administrative to 8%** Press (Esc) or click outside the chart area to deselect the chart element, and then compare your screen with Figure 3.15.

Figure 3.15

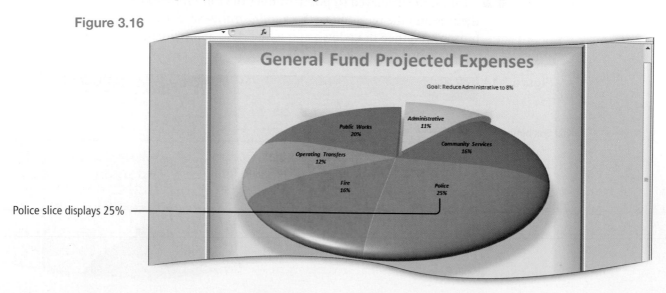

Text Box with inserted text

4 If necessary, select and then adjust or move your text box. **Save** 💾 your workbook.

Objective 3 | Edit a Workbook and Update a Chart

Activity 3.08 | Editing a Workbook and Updating a Chart

If you edit the data in your worksheet, the chart data markers—in this instance the pie slices—will adjust automatically to accurately represent the new values.

1 On the pie chart, notice that *Police* represents 24% of the total projected expenses.

2 In the sheet tab area at the bottom of the workbook, click the **Sheet1 tab** to redisplay the worksheet.

Another Way

Double-click the cell to position the insertion point in the cell and edit.

3 Click cell **C5**, and then in **Formula Bar**, change *59,200,338* to **62,200,388**

4 Press (Enter), and notice that the total in cell **C11** recalculates to *$247,897,175* and the percentages in **column D** also recalculate.

5 Display the **Projected Expenses Chart** sheet. Notice that the pie slices adjust to show the recalculation—*Police* is now *25%* of the projected expenses. Click **Save** 💾, and then compare your screen with Figure 3.16.

Figure 3.16

General Fund Projected Expenses

Goal: Reduce Administrative to 8%

Public Works 20%
Administrative 11%
Operating Transfers 12%
Community Services 16%
Fire 16%
Police 25%

Police slice displays 25%

Activity 3.09 | Inserting WordArt in a Worksheet

WordArt is a gallery of text styles with which you can create decorative effects, such as shadowed or mirrored text. In an Excel worksheet, WordArt can be effective if you plan to display your worksheet in a PowerPoint presentation, or if readers will be viewing the worksheet data online.

1 In the sheet tab area at the bottom of the workbook, click the **Sheet1 tab** to redisplay the worksheet. Click the **Insert tab**, and then in the **Text group**, click the **WordArt** button.

2 In the WordArt gallery, in the last row, click the last style—**Fill – Olive Green, Accent 1, Metal Bevel, Reflection**.

The WordArt indicating *YOUR TEXT HERE* displays in the worksheet.

3 With the WordArt selected, type **general fund expenses** and then point anywhere on the dashed border surrounding the WordArt object. Click the dashed border one time to change it to a solid border, indicating that all of the text is selected.

4 On the **Home tab**, in the **Font group**, change the **Font Size** to **28**.

5 Point to the WordArt border to display the ⟨❖⟩ pointer, and then drag to position the upper left corner of the WordArt approximately as shown in Figure 3.17. If necessary, hold down Ctrl and press any of the arrow keys on your keyboard to move the WordArt object into position in small increments. Click any cell to deselect the WordArt, and then click **Save** 🖫.

Figure 3.17

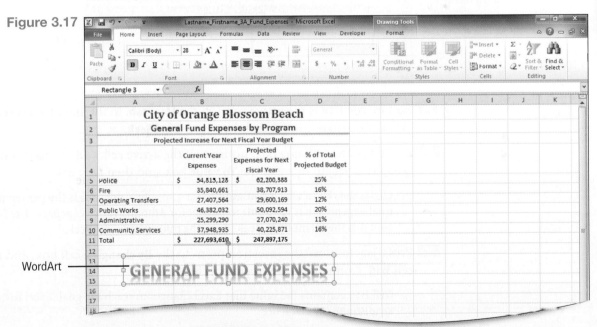

WordArt

Objective 4 | Use Goal Seek to Perform What-If Analysis

Activity 3.10 | Using Goal Seek to Perform What-If Analysis

The process of changing the values in cells to see how those changes affect the outcome of formulas in your worksheet is referred to as *what-if analysis*. A what-if analysis tool that is included with Excel is *Goal Seek*, which finds the input needed in one cell to arrive at the desired result in another cell.

1 In cell **A17**, type **Goal: To Reduce Administrative Expenses from 11% to 8% of Total Expenses** Merge and center the text across the range **A17:D17**, and then apply the **Heading 3** Cell Style.

2 In cell **A18**, type **Goal Amount:** and press [Enter].

3 Select the range **C9:D9**, right-click over the selection, and then click **Copy**. Point to cell **B18**, right-click, and then under **Paste Options**, click the **Paste** button.

4 Press [Esc] to cancel the moving border, click cell **C18**, and then compare your screen with Figure 3.18.

Figure 3.18

Formula Bar indicates formula in C18

Cell C18 active

Heading entered and formatted

Row title entered

Pasted data

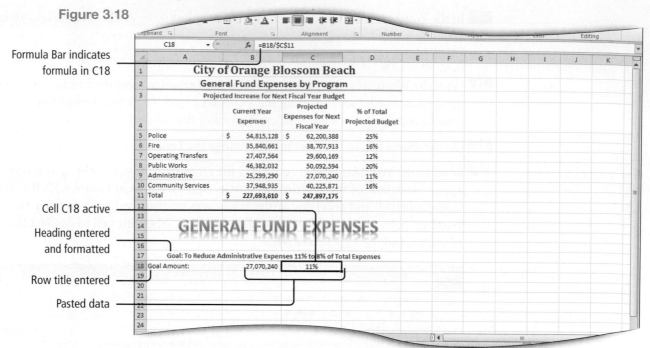

5 Be sure cell **C18** is the active cell. On the **Data tab**, in the **Data Tools group**, click the **What-If Analysis** button, and then click **Goal Seek**.

6 In the **Goal Seek** dialog box, notice that the active cell, **C18**, is indicated in the **Set cell** box. Press [Tab] to move to the **To value** box, and then type **8%**

C18 is the cell in which you want to set a specific value; 8% is the percentage of the total expenses that you want to budget for Administrative expenses. The Set cell box contains the formula that calculates the information you seek.

7 Press [Tab] to move the insertion point to the **By changing cell** box, and then click cell **B18**. Compare your screen with Figure 3.19.

Cell B18 contains the value that Excel changes to reach the goal. Excel formats this cell as an absolute cell reference.

Figure 3.19

Goal Seek dialog box

To value indicates 8%

By changing cell formatted as absolute cell reference

Set cell references a cell with a formula

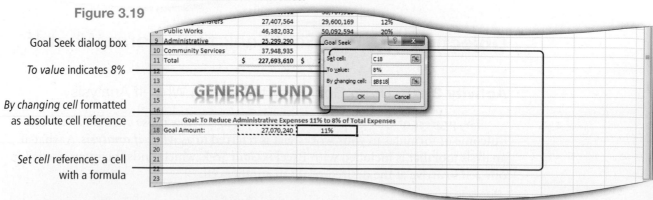

8 Click **OK**. In the displayed **Goal Seek Status** dialog box, click **OK**.

9 Select the range **A18:C18**. From the **Home tab**, display the **Cell Styles** gallery. Under **Themed Cell Styles**, apply **20% - Accent3**. Click cell **B18**, and then from the **Cell Styles** gallery, at the bottom of the gallery under **Number Format**, apply the **Currency [0]** cell style.

10 Press [Ctrl] + [Home], click **Save** 💾, and then compare your screen with Figure 3.20.

> Excel calculates that the City must budget for *$19,831,774* in Administrative expenses in order for this item to become 8% of the total projected budget.

Figure 3.20

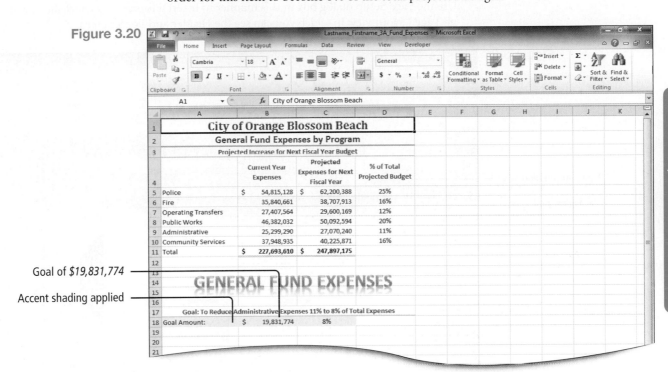

Goal of *$19,831,774*

Accent shading applied

Activity 3.11 | Preparing and Printing a Workbook with a Chart Sheet

Another Way

Right-click the sheet tab, click Rename, type, and press [Enter].

1 With your worksheet displayed, in the sheet tab area, double-click *Sheet1* to select the text, and then type **Projected Expenses Data** and press [Enter].

2 Select **Sheet2** and **Sheet3**, right-click over the selected tabs, and then click **Delete** to delete the unused sheets.

3 On the **Insert tab**, click **Header & Footer**. In the **Navigation group**, click the **Go to Footer** button, click in the **left section** above the word *Footer*, and then in the **Header & Footer Elements group**, click the **File Name** button.

4 Click in a cell above the footer to deselect the **Footer area** and view your file name. On the **Page Layout tab**, in the **Page Setup group**, click the **Margins** button, and then at the bottom click **Custom Margins**.

5 In the displayed **Page Setup** dialog box, under **Center on page**, select the **Horizontally** check box. Click **OK**, and then on the status bar, click the **Normal** button ⊞ to return to Normal view.

> Recall that after displaying worksheets in Page Layout View, dotted lines display to indicate the page breaks when you return to Normal view.

6 Press [Ctrl] + [Home] to move to the top of the worksheet.

7 Click the **Projected Expenses Chart** sheet tab to display the chart sheet. On the **Insert tab**, in the **Text group**, click **Header & Footer** to display the **Header/Footer tab** of the **Page Setup** dialog box.

8 In the center of the **Page Setup** dialog box, click **Custom Footer**. With the insertion point blinking in the **Left section**, in the row of buttons in the middle of the dialog box, locate and click the **Insert File Name** button. Compare your screen with Figure 3.21.

> Use the Page Setup dialog box in this manner to insert a footer on a chart sheet, which has no Page Layout view in which you can see the Header and Footer areas.

Figure 3.21

Page Setup dialog box

Footer dialog box

Insert File Name button

Left section displays *&[File]*

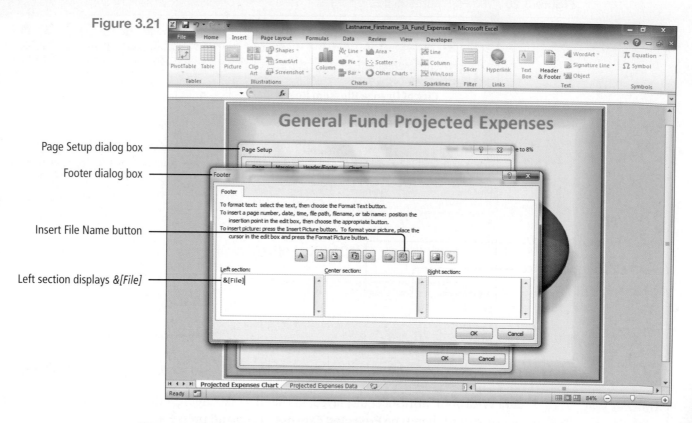

9 Click **OK** two times. Display **Backstage** view, on the right under the thumbnail, click **Properties**, and then click **Show Document Panel**. In the **Author** box, replace the existing text with your firstname and lastname. In the **Subject** box, type your course name and section number. In the **Keywords** box type **general fund, expenses, pie chart** and then **Close** ⊠ the **Document Information Panel**.

10 Right-click either of the sheet tabs, and then click **Select All Sheets**. Verify that *[Group]* displays in the title bar.

> Recall that by selecting all sheets, you can view all of the workbook pages in Print Preview.

11 Press Ctrl + F2 to display the **Print Preview**. Examine the first page, and then at the bottom of the **Print Preview**, click the **Next Page** ▶ button to view the second page of your workbook.

Note | Printing a Chart Sheet Uses More Toner

Printing a chart that displays on a chart sheet will use more toner or ink than a small chart that is part of a worksheet. If you are printing your work, check with your instructor to verify whether or not you should print the chart sheet.

12 Click **Save** to redisplay the workbook. Print or submit electronically as directed by your instructor.

13 If you are directed to submit printed formulas, refer to Activity 1.16 in Project 1A to do so.

14 If you printed your formulas, be sure to redisplay the worksheet by clicking the Show Formulas button to turn it off. **Close** the workbook. If you are prompted to save changes, click **No** so that you do not save the changes to the worksheet that you used for printing formulas. **Close** Excel.

More Knowledge | Setting the Default Number of Sheets in a New Workbook

By default, the number of new worksheets in a new workbook is three, but you can change this default number. From Backstage view, display the Excel Options dialog box, click the General tab, and then under When creating new workbooks, change the number in the Include this many sheets box.

End You have completed Project 3A ————————————

Project 3B Growth Projection with Line Chart

Project Activities

In Activities 3.12 through 3.19, you will assist Lila Darius, City Manager, in creating a worksheet to estimate future population growth based on three possible growth rates. You will also create a line chart to display past population growth. Your resulting worksheet and chart will look similar to Figure 3.22.

Project Files

For Project 3B, you will need the following files:

e03B_Population_Growth
e03B_Beach

You will save your workbook as:

Lastname_Firstname_3B_Population_Growth

Project Results

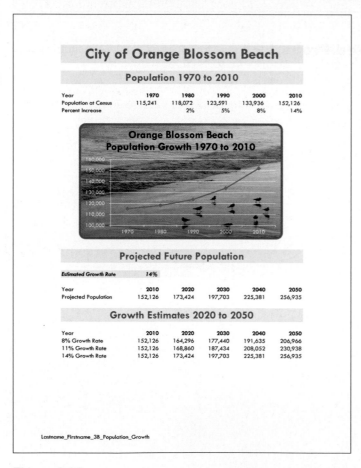

Figure 3.22
Project 3B Population Growth

Objective 5 | Design a Worksheet for What-If Analysis

Excel recalculates; if you change the value in a cell referenced in a formula, Excel automatically recalculates the result of the formula. Thus, you can change cell values to see *what* would happen *if* you tried different values. Recall that this process of changing the values in cells to see how those changes affect the outcome of formulas in your worksheet is referred to as what-if analysis.

Activity 3.12 | Using Parentheses in a Formula to Calculate a Percentage Rate of Increase

Ms. Darius has the city's population figures for the past five 10-year census periods. In each 10-year census period, the population has increased. In this activity, you will construct a formula to calculate the ***percentage rate of increase***—the percent by which one number increases over another number—for each 10-year census period since 1970. From this information, future population growth can be estimated.

1 **Start** Excel. From your student files, open the file **e03B_Population_Growth**. From **Backstage** view, display the **Save As** dialog box. Navigate to your **Excel Chapter 3** folder, in the **File name** box, name the file **Lastname_Firstname_3B_Population_Growth** and then click **Save** or press Enter.

2 Leave **row 4** blank, and then click cell **A5**. Type **Year** and then press Tab. In cell **B5**, type **1970** and then press Tab.

3 In cell **C5**, type **1980** and then press Tab. Select the range **B5:C5**, and then drag the fill handle to the right through cell **F5** to extend the series to 2010.

> By establishing a pattern of 10-year intervals with the first two cells, you can use the fill handle to continue the series. The AutoFill feature will do this for any pattern that you establish with two or more cells.

4 With the range **B5:F5** still selected, right-click over the selection, and then on the Mini toolbar, click **Bold** B. Compare your screen with Figure 3.23.

Figure 3.23

AutoFill used to fill 10-year periods to create column titles

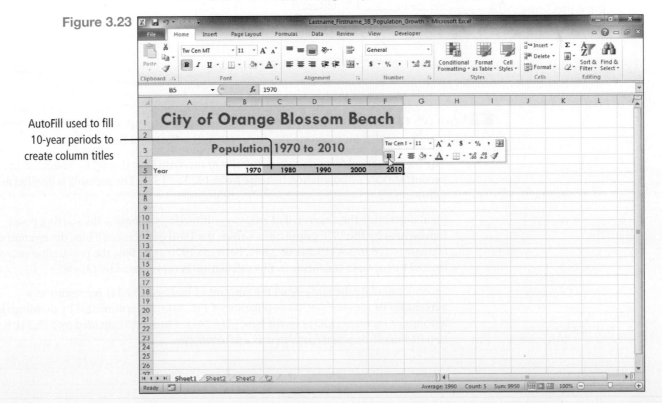

5 In cell **A6**, type **Population at Census** and press `Enter`. In cell **A7**, type **Percent Increase** and press `Enter`.

6 Click cell **B6**, and then beginning in cell **B6**, and pressing `Tab` to move across the row, enter the following values for the population in the years listed:

1970	1980	1990	2000	2010
115241	**118072**	**123591**	**133936**	**152126**

7 Select the range **B6:F6**, right-click, on the Mini toolbar, click **Comma Style** `,`, and then click **Decrease Decimal** `.00` two times.

8 Click cell **C7**. Being sure to include the parentheses, type **=(c6-b6)/b6** and then on the **Formula Bar**, click the **Enter** button `✓` to keep cell **C7** active; your result is *0.02456591* (or *0.02*). Compare your screen with Figure 3.24.

Recall that as you type, a list of Excel functions that begin with the letter *C* and *B* may briefly display. This is *Formula AutoComplete*, an Excel feature which, after typing an = (equal sign) and the beginning letter or letters of a function name, displays a list of function names that match the typed letter(s). In this instance, the letters represent cell references, *not* the beginning of a function name.

Figure 3.24

Formula Bar displays formula

Formula result in cell C7 (yours may display *0.02*)

Values entered for population, Comma Style with no decimals applied

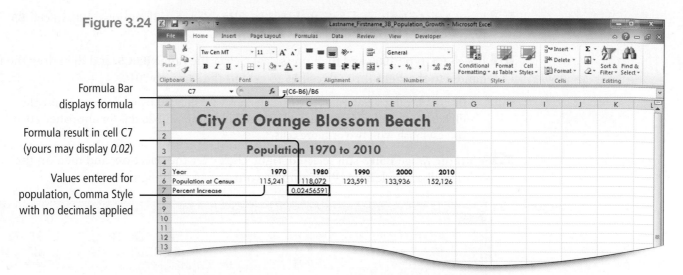

9 With cell **C7** active, on the **Home tab**, in the **Number group**, click the **Percent Style** button `%`, and then examine the formula in the **Formula Bar**.

The mathematical formula *rate = amount of increase/base* is used to calculated the percentage rate of population increase from 1970 to 1980. The formula is applied as follows:

First, determine the *amount of increase* by subtracting the *base*—the starting point represented by the 1970 population—from the 1980 population. Thus, the *amount of increase* = 118,072 – 115,241 or 2,831. Between 1970 and 1980, the population increased by 2,831 people. In the formula, this calculation is represented by *C6-B6*.

Second, calculate the *rate*—what the amount of increase (2,831) represents as a percentage of the base (1970's population of 115,241). Determine this by dividing the amount of increase (2,831) by the base (115,241). Thus, 2,831 divided by 115,241 is equal to 0.02456591 or, when formatted as a percent, 2%.

10 In the **Formula Bar**, locate the parentheses enclosing *C6-B6*.

Excel follows a set of mathematical rules called the ***order of operations***, which has four basic parts:

- Expressions within parentheses are processed first.
- Exponentiation, if present, is performed before multiplication and division.
- Multiplication and division are performed before addition and subtraction.
- Consecutive operators with the same level of precedence are calculated from left to right.

11 Click cell **D7**, type = and then by typing, or using a combination of typing and clicking cells to reference them, construct a formula similar to the one in cell **C7** to calculate the rate of increase in population from 1980 to 1990. Compare your screen with Figure 3.25.

Recall that the first step is to determine the *amount of increase*—1990 population minus 1980 population—and then to write the calculation so that Excel performs this operation first; that is, place it in parentheses.

The second step is to divide the result of the calculation in parentheses by the *base*—the population for 1980.

Figure 3.25

Formula to calculate percent increase from 1980 to 1990

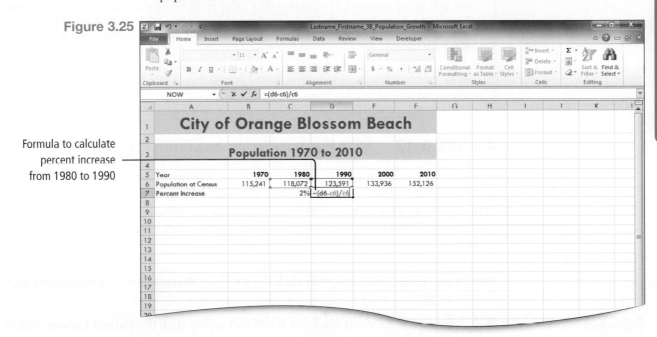

12 Press [Enter]; your result is *0.04674267* (or *0.05*). Format cell **D7** with the **Percent Style** [%].

Your result is *5%*; Excel rounds up or down to format percentages.

13 With cell **D7** selected, drag the fill handle to the right through cell **F7**. Click any empty cell to cancel the selection, **Save** [💾] your workbook, and then compare your screen with Figure 3.26.

Because this formula uses relative cell references—that is, for each year, the formula is the same but the values used are relative to the formula's location—you can copy the formula in this manner. For example, the result for 1990 uses the 1980 population as the base, the result for 2000 uses the 1990 population as the base, and the result for 2010 uses the 2000 population as the base.

The formula results show the percent of increase for each 10-year period between 1970 and 2010. You can see that in each 10-year period, the population has grown as much as 14%—from 2000 to 2010—and as little as 2%—from 1970 to 1980.

Figure 3.26

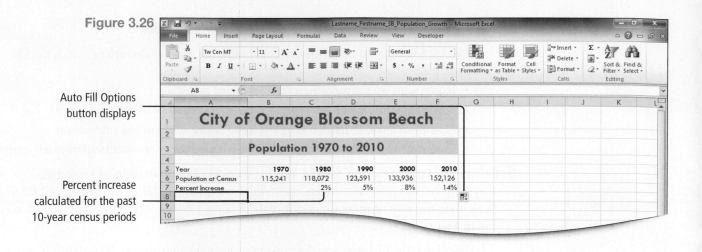

Auto Fill Options button displays

Percent increase calculated for the past 10-year census periods

---

> **More Knowledge | Use of Parentheses in a Formula**
>
> When writing a formula in Excel, use parentheses to communicate the order in which the operations should occur. For example, to average three test scores of 100, 50, and 90 that you scored on three different tests, you would add the test scores and then divide by the number of test scores in the list. If you write this formula as =100+50+90/3, the result would be 180, because Excel would first divide 90 by 3 and then add 100+50+30. Excel would do so because the order of operations states that multiplication and division are calculated *before* addition and subtraction.
>
> The correct way to write this formula is =(100+50+90)/3. Excel will add the three values, and then divide the result by 3, or 240/3 resulting in a correct average of 80. Parentheses play an important role in ensuring that you get the correct result in your formulas.

Activity 3.13 | Using Format Painter and Formatting as You Type

You can format numbers as you type them. When you type numbers in a format that Excel recognizes, Excel automatically applies that format to the cell. Recall that once applied, cell formats remain with the cell, even if the cell contents are deleted. In this activity, you will format cells by typing the numbers with percent signs and use Format Painter to copy text (non-numeric) formats.

1 Leave **row 8** blank, and then click cell **A9**. Type **Projected Future Population** and then press Enter.

> **Another Way**
>
> On the Home tab, in the Clipboard group, click the Format Painter button.

2 Point to cell **A3**, right-click, on the Mini toolbar click the **Format Painter** button, and then click cell **A9**.

The format of cell A3 is *painted*—applied to—cell A9, including the merging and centering of the text across the range A9:F9.

3 Leave **row 10** blank, and then click cell **A11**, type **Estimated Growth Rate** and then press Enter.

4 Leave **row 12** blank, and then click cell **A13**. Type **Year** and then in cell **A14**, type **Projected Population**

5 In cell **B13**, type **2010** and then press Tab. In cell **C13**, type **2020** and then press Tab.

6 Select the range **B13:C13**, and then drag the fill handle through cell **F13** to extend the pattern of years to *2050*. Apply **Bold** to the selected range. Compare your screen with Figure 3.27.

Figure 3.27

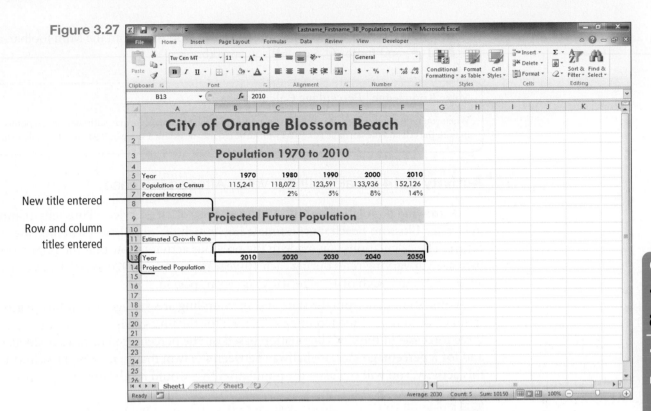

New title entered ────

Row and column
titles entered ────

7 Click cell **B14**, and then on the **Home tab**, in the **Number group**, notice that the **Number Format** box indicates *General*. Then, being sure to type the comma, type **152,126**

8 On the **Formula Bar**, click the **Enter** button ☑ to keep the cell active, and then in the **Number group**, notice that the format changed to *Number*.

9 Press ⌈Del⌋, and then in the **Number group**, notice that the *Number* format is still indicated.

Recall that deleting the contents of a cell does not delete the cell's formatting.

10 *Without* typing a comma, in cell **B14**, type **152126** and then press ⌈Enter⌋.

The comma displays even though you did not type it. When you type a number and include a formatting symbol such as a comma or dollar sign, Excel applies the format to the cell. Thus, if you delete the contents of the cell and type in the cell again, the format you established remains applied to the cell. This is referred to as *format as you type*.

11 Examine the format of the value in cell **B14**, and then compare it to the format in cell **B6** where you used the **Comma Style** button to format the cell. Notice that the number in cell **B14** is flush with the right edge of the cell, but the number in cell **B6** leaves a small amount of space on the right edge.

When you type commas as you enter numbers, Excel applies the *Number* format, which does *not* leave a space at the right of the number for a closing parenthesis in the event of a negative number. This is different from the format that is applied when you use the *Comma Style* button on the Ribbon or Mini toolbar, as you did for the numbers entered in row 6. Recall that the Comma Style format applied from either the Ribbon or the Mini toolbar leaves space on the right for a closing parenthesis in the event of a negative number.

12 In cell **B11**, type **8%** Select the range **A11:B11**, and then from the Mini toolbar, apply **Bold** B and **Italic** I. **Save** 🖫 your workbook.

> **More Knowledge | Percentage Calculations**
>
> When you type a percentage into a cell—for example *8%*—the percentage format, without decimal points, displays in both the cell and the Formula Bar. Excel will, however, use the decimal value of *0.08* for actual calculations.

Activity 3.14 | Calculating a Value After an Increase

A growing population results in increased use of city services. Thus, city planners in Orange Blossom Beach must estimate how much the population will increase in the future. The calculations you made in the previous activity show that the population has increased at varying rates during each 10-year period from 1970 to 2010, ranging from a low of 2% to a high of 14% per 10-year census period.

Population data from the state and surrounding areas suggests that future growth will trend close to that of the recent past. To plan for the future, Ms. Darius wants to prepare three forecasts of the city's population based on the percentage increases in 2000, in 2010, and for a percentage increase halfway between the two; that is, for 8%, 11%, and 14%. In this activity, you will calculate the population that would result from an 8% increase.

1 Click cell **C14**. Type **=b14*(100%+b11)** and then on the **Formula Bar**, click the **Enter** ✓ button to display a result of *164296.08*. Compare your screen with Figure 3.28.

This formula calculates what the population will be in the year 2020 assuming an increase of 8% over 2010's population. Use the mathematical formula *value after increase = base × percent for new value* to calculate a value after an increase as follows:

First, establish the *percent for new value*. The *percent for new value = base percent + percent of increase*. The *base percent* of 100% represents the base population and the *percent of increase* in this instance is 8%. Thus, the population will equal 100% of the base year plus 8% of the base year. This can be expressed as 108% or 1.08. In this formula, you will use 100% + the rate in cell B11, which is 8%, to equal 108%.

Second, enter a reference to the cell that contains the *base*—the population in 2010. The base value resides in cell B14—*152,126*.

Third, calculate the *value after increase*. Because in each future 10-year period the increase will be based on 8%—an absolute value located in cell B11—this cell reference can be formatted as absolute by typing dollar signs.

Figure 3.28

Formula includes absolute reference to cell B11

Formula result

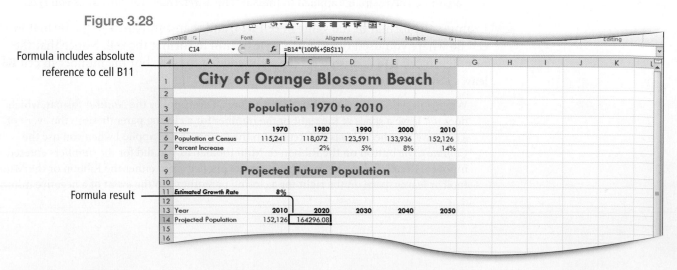

200 **Excel** | Chapter 3: Analyzing Data with Pie Charts, Line Charts, and What-If Analysis Tools

2 With cell **C14** as the active cell, drag the fill handle to copy the formula to the range **D14:F14**.

3 Point to cell **B14**, right-click, click the **Format Painter** ✎ button, and then select the range **C14:F14**. Click an empty cell to cancel the selection, click **Save** 🖫 and then compare your screen with Figure 3.29.

This formula uses a relative cell address—B14—for the *base*; the population in the previous 10-year period is used in each of the formulas in cells D14:F14 as the *base* value. Because the reference to the *percent of increase* in cell B11 is an absolute reference, each *value after increase* is calculated with the value from cell B11.

The population projected for 2020—*164,296*—is an increase of 8% over the population in 2010. The projected population in 2030—*177,440*—is an increase of 8% over the population in 2020 and so on.

Figure 3.29

Each value represents an 8% increase over the previous base year

Projection calculated using an 8% growth rate

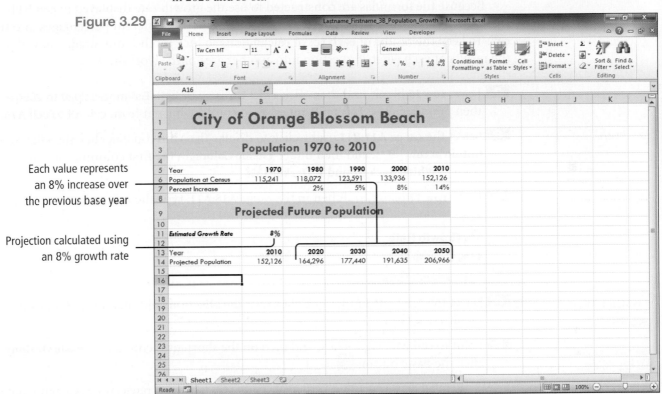

> **More Knowledge | Percent Increase or Decrease**
>
> The basic formula for calculating an increase or decrease can be done in two parts. First determine the percent by which the base value will be increased or decreased, and then add or subtract the results to the base. The formula can be simplified by using (1+amount of increase) or (1–amount of decrease), where 1, rather than 100%, represents the whole. Thus, the formula used in Step 1 of Activity 3.14 could also be written =b14*(1+b11), or =(b14*b11)+b14.

Objective 6 | Answer What-If Questions by Changing Values in a Worksheet

If a formula depends on the value in a cell, you can see what effect it will have if you change the value in that cell. Then, you can copy the value computed by the formula and paste it into another part of the worksheet where you can be compare it to other values.

Activity 3.15 | Answering What-If Questions and Using Paste Special

A growth rate of 8% in each 10-year period will result in a population of almost 207,000 people by 2050. The city planners will likely ask: *What if* the population grows at the highest rate (14%)? *What if* the population grows at a rate that is halfway between the 2000 and 2010 rates (11%)?

Because the formulas are constructed to use the growth rate displayed in cell B11, Ms. Darius can answer these questions quickly by entering different percentages into that cell. To keep the results of each set of calculations so they can be compared, you will paste the results of each what-if question into another area of the worksheet.

1 Leave **row 15** blank, and then click cell **A16**. Type **Growth Estimates 2020 to 2050** and then press Enter. Use **Format Painter** 🖌 to copy the format from cell **A9** to cell **A16**.

2 Select the range **A11:B11**, right-click to display the Mini toolbar, click the **Fill Color button arrow** 🖌▾, and then under **Theme Colors**, in the first column, click the third color—**White, Background 1, Darker 15%**.

3 Leave **row 17** blank, and then in the range **A18:A21**, type the following row titles:

Year

8% Growth Rate

11% Growth Rate

14% Growth Rate

Another Way

Press Ctrl + C; or, on the Home tab, in the Clipboard group, click the Copy button.

4 Select the range **B13:F13**, right-click over the selection, and then on the shortcut menu, click **Copy**.

5 Point to cell **B18**, right-click, and then on the shortcut menu, under **Paste Options**, click the **Paste** button 📋.

Recall that when pasting a group of copied cells to a target range, you need only point to or select the first cell of the range.

6 Select and **Copy** the range **B14:F14**, and then **Paste** it beginning in cell **B19**.

7 Click cell **C19**. On the **Formula Bar**, notice that the *formula* was pasted into the cell, as shown in Figure 3.30.

This is *not* the desired result. The actual *calculated values*—not the formulas—are needed in the range.

Figure 3.30

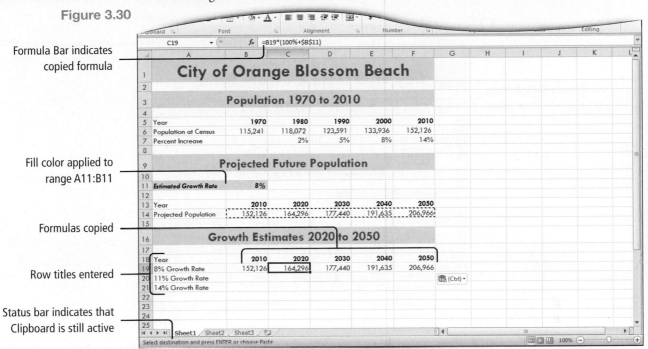

Formula Bar indicates copied formula

Fill color applied to range A11:B11

Formulas copied

Row titles entered

Status bar indicates that Clipboard is still active

8 On the Quick Access Toolbar, click the **Undo** button. With the range **B14:F14** still copied to the Clipboard—as indicated by the message in the status bar and the moving border—point to cell **B19**, and then right-click to display the shortcut menu.

9 Under **Paste Options**, point to **Paste Special** to display another gallery, and then under **Paste Values**, point to the **Values & Number Formatting** button to display the ScreenTip as shown in Figure 3.31.

The ScreenTip *Values & Number Formatting (A)* indicates that you can paste the *calculated values* that result from the calculation of formulas along with the formatting applied to the copied cells. *(A)* is the keyboard shortcut for this command.

Figure 3.31

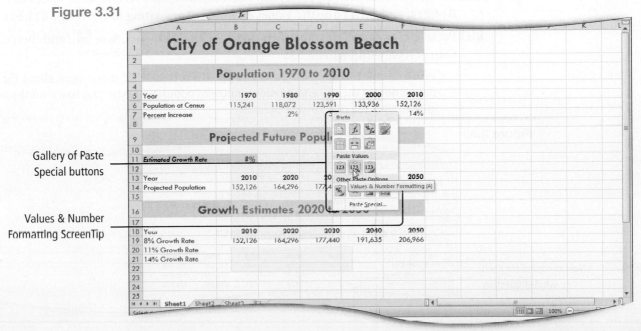

Gallery of Paste Special buttons

Values & Number Formatting ScreenTip

10 Click the **Values & Number Formatting** button 📋, click cell **C19** and notice on the **Formula Bar** that the cell contains a *value*, not a formula. Press Esc to cancel the moving border. Compare your screen with Figure 3.32.

> The calculated estimates based on an 8% growth rate are pasted along with their formatting.

Figure 3.32

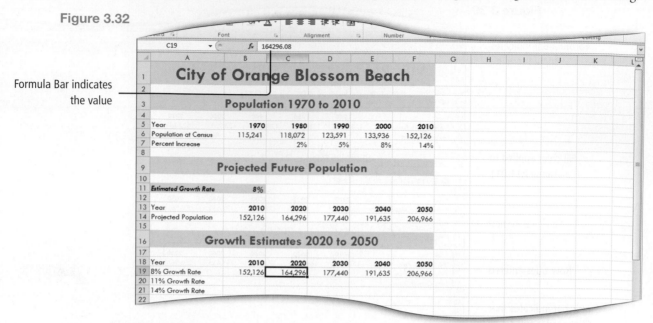

Formula Bar indicates the value

11 Click cell **B11**. Type **11** and then watch the values in **C14:F14** *recalculate* as, on the **Formula Bar**, you click the **Enter** button ✓.

> The value *11%* is halfway between 8% and 14%—the growth rates from the two most recent 10-year periods.

12 Select and **Copy** the new values in the range **B14:F14**. Point to cell **B20**, right-click, and then on the shortcut menu, point to **Paste Special**. Under **Paste Values**, click the **Values & Number Formatting** button 📋.

13 In cell **B11**, change the percentage by typing **14** and then press Enter. Notice that the projected values in **C14:F14** recalculate.

14 Using the skills you just practiced, select and copy the recalculated values in the range **B14:F14**, and then paste the **Values & Number Formatting** to the range **B21:F21**.

15 Press Esc to cancel the moving border, click cell **A1**, click **Save** 💾, and then compare your screen with Figure 3.33.

> With this information, Ms. Darius can answer several what-if questions about the future population of the city and provide a range of population estimates based on the rates of growth over the past 10-year periods.

Figure 3.33

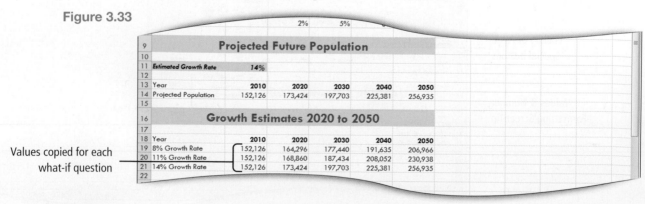

Values copied for each what-if question

Objective 7 | Chart Data with a Line Chart

A *line chart* displays trends over time. Time is displayed along the bottom axis and the data point values connect with a line. The curve and direction of the line makes trends obvious to the reader.

Whereas the columns in a column chart and the pie slices in a pie chart emphasize the distinct values of each data point, the line in a line chart emphasizes the flow from one data point value to the next.

Activity 3.16 | Inserting Multiple Rows and Creating a Line Chart

So that city council members can see how the population has increased over the past five census periods, in this activity, you will chart the actual population figures from 1970 to 2010 in a line chart.

1 In the **row header area**, point to **row 8** to display the ➡ pointer, and then drag down to select **rows 8:24**. Right-click over the selection, and then click **Insert** to insert the same number of blank rows as you selected. Compare your screen with Figure 3.34.

Use this technique to insert multiple rows quickly.

Figure 3.34

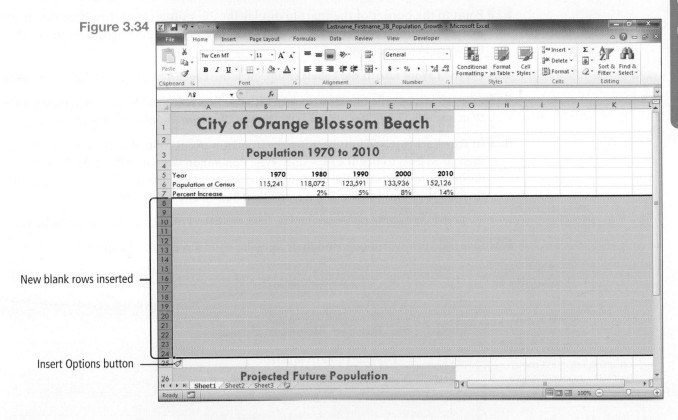

New blank rows inserted

Insert Options button

2 Near **row 25**, click the **Insert Options** button, and then click the **Clear Formatting** option button to clear any formatting from these rows.

You will use this blank area in which to position your line chart.

3 Select the range **A6:F6**. On the **Insert tab**, in the **Charts group**, click the **Line** button.

4 In the displayed gallery of line charts, in the second row, point to the first chart type to display the ScreenTip *Line with Markers*. Compare your screen with Figure 3.35.

Figure 3.35

Line button in Charts group

Line with Markers chart type

Data selected for charting

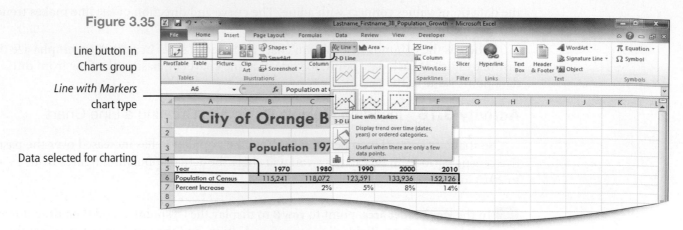

5 Click the **Line with Markers** chart type to create the chart as an embedded chart in the worksheet.

6 Point to the border of the chart to display the ⬚ pointer, and then drag the chart so that its upper left corner is positioned in cell **A9**, aligned approximately under the *t* in the word *Percent* above.

7 On the **Layout tab**, in the **Labels group**, click the **Legend** button, and then click **None**.

8 Click the chart title one time to select it and display a solid border around the title. Watch the **Formula Bar** as you type **Orange Blossom Beach** and then press Enter.

9 In the chart title, click to position the insertion point following the *h* in *Beach*, and then press Enter to begin a new line. Type **Population Growth 1970 to 2010** Click the dashed border around the chart title to change it to a solid border, right-click, and then on the Mini toolbar, change the **Font Size** of the title to **20**.

Recall that a solid border around an object indicates that the entire object is selected.

10 **Save** 💾 your workbook, and then compare your screen with Figure 3.36.

Figure 3.36

Line with Markers chart inserted, upper left corner aligned in cell A9

Chart title on two lines, 20 pt font size

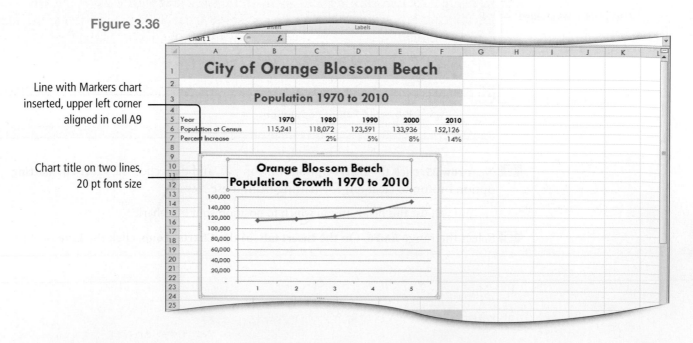

Activity 3.17 | Formatting Axes in a Line Chart

An *axis* is a line that serves as a frame of reference for measurement; it borders the chart *plot area*. The plot area is the area bounded by the axes, including all the data series. Recall that the area along the bottom of a chart that identifies the categories of data is referred to as the *category axis* or the *x-axis*. Recall also that the area along the left side of a chart that shows the range of numbers for the data points is referred to as the *value axis* or the *y-axis*.

In this activity, you will change the category axis to include the names of the 10-year census periods and adjust the numeric scale of the value axis.

Another Way

At the bottom of the chart, point to any of the numbers 1 through 5 to display the ScreenTip *Horizontal (Category) Axis*. Right-click, and then from the shortcut menu, click Select Data.

1 Be sure the chart is still selected—a pale frame surrounds the chart area. Click the **Design tab**, and then in the **Data group**, click the **Select Data** button.

2 On the right side of the displayed **Select Data Source** dialog box, under **Horizontal (Category) Axis Labels**, locate the **Edit** button, as shown in Figure 3.37.

Figure 3.37

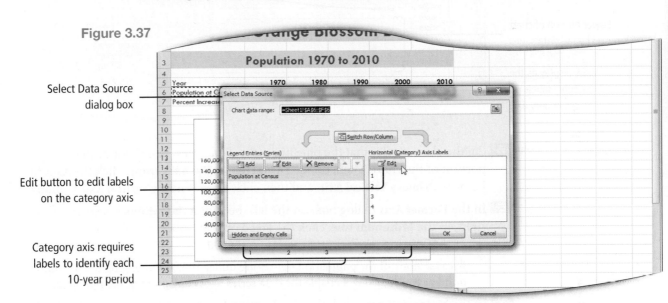

- Select Data Source dialog box
- Edit button to edit labels on the category axis
- Category axis requires labels to identify each 10-year period

3 In the right column, click the **Edit** button. If necessary, drag the title bar of the **Axis Labels** dialog box to the right of the chart so that it is not blocking your view of the data, and then select the years in the range **B5:F5**. Compare your screen with Figure 3.38.

Figure 3.38

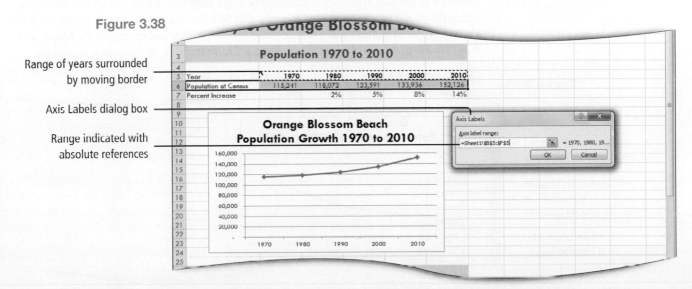

- Range of years surrounded by moving border
- Axis Labels dialog box
- Range indicated with absolute references

4 In the **Axis Labels** dialog box, click **OK**, and notice that in the right column of the **Select Data Source** dialog box, the years display as the category labels. Click **OK** to close the **Select Data Source** dialog box. Compare your screen with Figure 3.39.

Figure 3.39

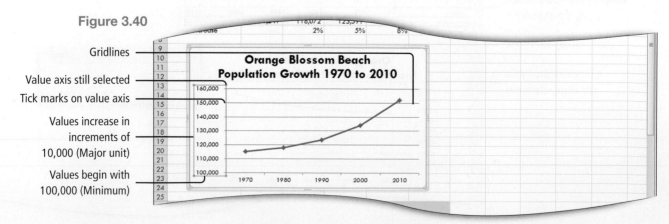

Lower portion of chart unused by the data series

Years display as the category labels on the category axis

Another Way

On the left side of the chart, point to any of the numbers to display the ScreenTip *Vertical (Value) Axis*, and then right-click. From the shortcut menu, click Format Axis.

5 On the chart, notice that the blue line—the data series—does not display in the lower portion of the chart. Then, on the **Layout tab**, in the **Axes group**, click the **Axes** button. Point to **Primary Vertical Axis**, and then click **More Primary Vertical Axis Options**.

6 In the **Format Axis** dialog box, on the left, be sure **Axis Options** is selected. On the right, in the **Minimum** row, click the **Fixed** option button. In the box to the right, select the existing text *0.0*, and then type **100000**

Because none of the population figures are under 100,000, changing the Minimum number to 100,000 will enable the data series to occupy more of the plot area.

7 In the **Major unit** row, click the **Fixed** option button, select the text in the box to the right *20000.0*, and then type **10000** In the lower right corner, click **Close**. Save 💾 your workbook, and then compare your screen with Figure 3.40.

The *Major unit* value determines the spacing between *tick marks* and thus between the gridlines in the plot area. Tick marks are the short lines that display on an axis at regular intervals. By default, Excel started the values at zero and increased in increments of 20,000. By setting the Minimum value on the value axis to 100,000 and changing the Major unit from 20,000 to 10,000, the line chart shows a clearer trend in the population growth.

Figure 3.40

Gridlines

Value axis still selected

Tick marks on value axis

Values increase in increments of 10,000 (Major unit)

Values begin with 100,000 (Minimum)

Activity 3.18 | Formatting the Chart and Plot Areas

An Excel chart has two background elements—the plot area and the chart area—which, by default display a single fill color. To add visual appeal to a chart, you can insert a graphic image as the background.

When formatting chart elements, there are several ways to display the dialog boxes that you need. You can right-click the area you want to format and choose a command on the shortcut menu. In this activity, you will use the Chart Elements box in the Current Selection group on the Format tab of the Ribbon, which is convenient if you are changing the format of a variety of chart elements.

1 Click the **Format tab**, and then in the **Current Selection group**, point to the small arrow to the right of the first item in the group to display the ScreenTip *Chart Elements*. Compare your screen with Figure 3.41.

From the *Chart Elements box*, you can select a chart element so that you can format it.

Figure 3.41

Chart Elements box ————

Chart Elements arrow ————

ScreenTip describing the Chart Elements box ————

Format tab selected ————

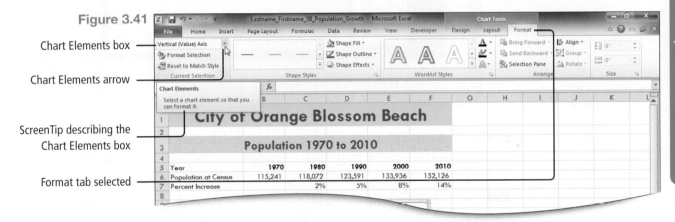

2 Click the **Chart Elements arrow**, and then from the displayed list, click **Chart Area**. Directly below the **Chart Elements** box, click the **Format Selection** button.

The Format Chart Area dialog box displays. Use this technique to select the chart element that you want to format, and then click the Format Selection button to display the appropriate dialog box.

3 In the **Format Chart Area** dialog box, on the left, be sure that **Fill** is selected.

4 On the right, under **Fill**, click the **Picture or texture fill** option button, and then under **Insert from**, click the **File** button. In the **Insert Picture** dialog box, navigate to your student files, and then insert the picture **e03B_Beach**. Leave the dialog box open, and then compare your screen with Figure 3.42.

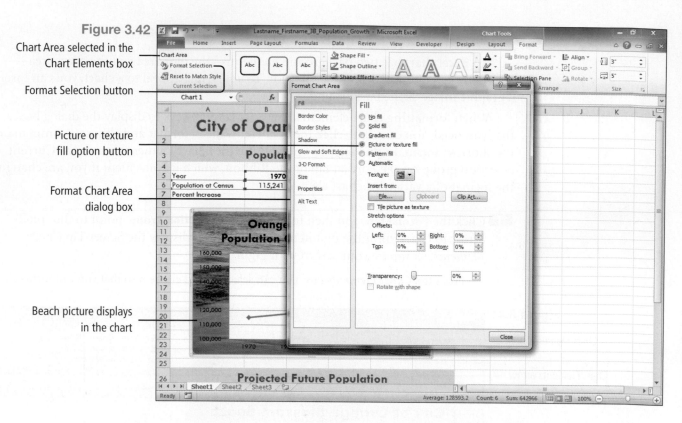

Figure 3.42

Chart Area selected in the Chart Elements box

Format Selection button

Picture or texture fill option button

Format Chart Area dialog box

Beach picture displays in the chart

---

5 In the **Format Chart Area** dialog box, on the left, click **Border Color**, on the right click the **Solid line** option button, click the **Color arrow**, and then under **Theme Colors**, in the fourth column, click the first color—**Dark Teal, Text 2**.

6 On the left, click **Border Styles**. On the right, select the text in the **Width** box and type **4 pt** At the bottom select the **Rounded corners** check box, and then **Close** the dialog box.

A 4 pt teal border with rounded corners frames the chart.

7 In the **Current Selection group**, click the **Chart Elements arrow**, on the list click **Plot Area**, and then click the **Format Selection** button.

8 In the **Format Plot Area** dialog box, on the left, be sure that **Fill** is selected, and then on the right, click the **No fill** option button. **Close** the dialog box.

The fill is removed from the plot area so that the picture is visible as the background.

9 Click the **Chart Elements arrow**, on the list click **Vertical (Value) Axis**, and then click the **Format Selection** button.

10 In the **Format Axis** dialog box, on the left click **Line Color**, on the right click the **Solid line** option button, click the **Color arrow**, and then click the first color—**White, Background 1**. Compare your screen with Figure 3.43.

The vertical line with tick marks displays in white.

Figure 3.43

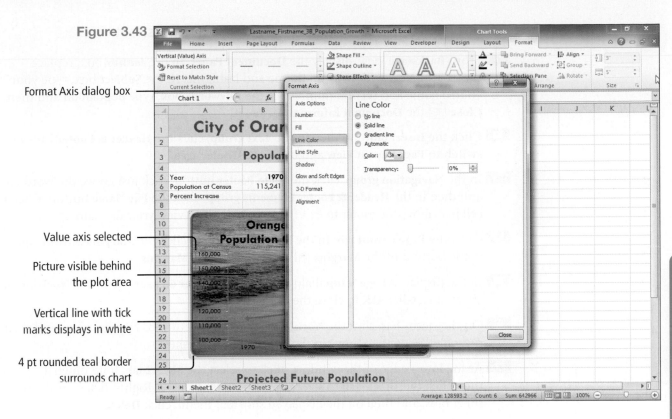

Format Axis dialog box

Value axis selected

Picture visible behind the plot area

Vertical line with tick marks displays in white

4 pt rounded teal border surrounds chart

11 **Close** the dialog box. From the **Chart Elements** box, select the **Vertical (Value) Axis Major Gridlines**, and then click **Format Selection**. Change the **Line Color** to a **Solid line**, and then apply the **White, Background 1** color. **Close** the dialog box.

12 From the **Chart Elements** list, select the **Horizontal (Category) Axis**, and then click **Format Selection**. In the **Format Axis** dialog box, change the **Line Color** to a **Solid line**, and then apply the **White, Background 1** color. **Close** the dialog box.

13 Point to any of the numbers on the vertical value axis, right-click, and then on the Mini toolbar, change the **Font Color** $\boxed{\text{A}}$ to **White, Background 1**. Point to any of the years on the horizontal category axis, right-click, and then change the **Font Color** $\boxed{\text{A}}$ to **White, Background 1**.

> For basic text-formatting changes—for example changing the size, font, style, or font color—you must leave the Chart Tools on the Ribbon and use commands from the Home tab or the Mini toolbar.

14 Click any cell to deselect the chart, press Ctrl + Home to move to the top of your worksheet, click **Save** $\boxed{\blacksquare}$, and then compare your screen with Figure 3.44.

Figure 3.44

Values display in white

Gridlines display in white

Years display in white

Excel | Chapter 3

Activity 3.19 | Preparing and Printing Your Worksheet

1 From **Backstage** view, display the **Document Panel**. In the **Author** box, replace the existing text with your firstname and lastname. In the **Subject** box, type your course name and section number. In the **Keywords** box, type **population** and then **Close** ⊠ the **Document Information Panel**.

2 Click the **Insert tab**, and then in the **Text group**, click the **Header & Footer** button to switch to **Page Layout View** and open the **Header area**.

3 In the **Navigation group**, click the **Go to Footer** button, click just above the word *Footer*, and then in the **Header & Footer Elements group**, click the **File Name** button. Click in a cell just above the footer to exit the **Footer area** and view your file name.

4 Click the **Page Layout tab**. In the **Page Setup group**, click the **Margins** button, and then at the bottom of the **Margins** gallery, click **Custom Margins**.

5 In the displayed **Page Setup** dialog box, under **Center on page**, select the **Horizontally** check box. Click **OK** to close the dialog box.

6 On the status bar, click the **Normal** button 🖿 to return to Normal view, and then press ⌨Ctrl + ⌨Home to move to the top of your worksheet.

7 At the lower edge of the window, click to select the **Sheet2 tab**, hold down ⌨Ctrl, and then click the **Sheet3 tab** to select the two unused sheets. Right-click over the selected sheet tabs, and then on the displayed shortcut menu, click **Delete**.

8 **Save** 🖫 your workbook before printing or submitting. Press ⌨Ctrl + ⌨F2 to display the **Print Preview** to check your worksheet. Compare your screen with Figure 3.45.

Figure 3.45

Completed worksheet in Print Preview

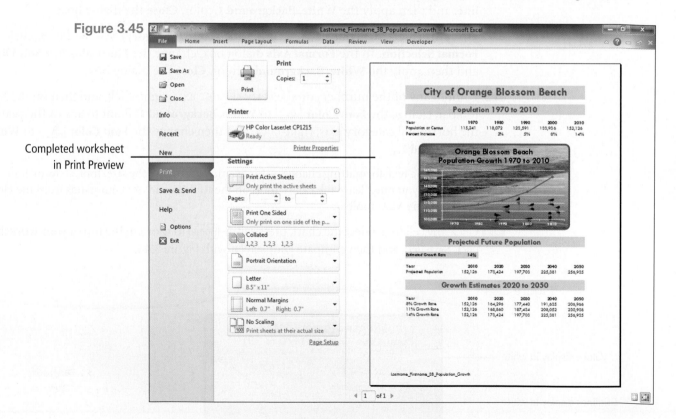

9 If necessary, return to the worksheet to make any necessary adjustments or corrections, and then **Save**.

10 Print or submit electronically as directed. If you are directed to submit printed formulas, refer to Activity 1.16 to do so.

11 If you printed your formulas, be sure to redisplay the worksheet by clicking the Show Formulas button to turn it off. From **Backstage** view, click **Close**. If the dialog box displays asking if you want to save changes, click **No** so that you do *not* save the changes you made for printing formulas. **Close** Excel.

End **You have completed Project 3B** ————————————————————

Content-Based Assessments

Summary

In this chapter, you created a pie chart to show how the parts of a budget contribute to a total budget. Then you formatted the pie chart attractively and used Goal Seek. You also practiced using parentheses in a formula, calculating the percentage rate of an increase, answering what-if questions, and charting data in a line chart to show the flow of data over time.

Key Terms

Matching

Match each term in the second column with its correct definition in the first column by writing the letter of the term on the blank line in front of the correct definition.

_____ 1. A chart that shows the relationship of each part to a whole.

_____ 2. The term used to describe money set aside for the normal operating activities of a government entity such as a city.

_____ 3. In a formula, the address of a cell based on the relative position of the cell that contains the formula and the cell referred to.

_____ 4. A column, bar, area, dot, pie slice, or other symbol in a chart that represents a single data point.

_____ 5. A workbook sheet that contains only a chart.

_____ 6. A shape effect that uses shading and shadows to make the edges of a shape appear to be curved or angled.

_____ 7. The entire chart and all of its elements.

_____ 8. The process of changing the values in cells to see how those changes affect the outcome of formulas in a worksheet.

_____ 9. The mathematical formula to calculate a rate of increase.

A Axis

B Bevel

C Category axis

D Chart area

E Chart sheet

F Data marker

G Format as you type

H General Fund

I Order of operations

J Pie chart

K Rate=amount of increase/base

L Relative cell reference

M Tick marks

N Value axis

O What-if analysis

Content-Based Assessments

_____ 10. The mathematical rules for performing multiple calculations within a formula.

_____ 11. The Excel feature by which a cell takes on the formatting of the number typed into the cell.

_____ 12. A line that serves as a frame of reference for measurement and that borders the chart plot area.

_____ 13. The area along the bottom of a chart that identifies the categories of data; also referred to as the x-axis.

_____ 14. A numerical scale on the left side of a chart that shows the range of numbers for the data points; also referred to as the y-axis.

_____ 15. The short lines that display on an axis at regular intervals.

Multiple Choice

Circle the correct answer.

1. A sum of money set aside for a specific purpose is a:
   A. value axis
   B. fund
   C. rate

2. A cell reference that refers to a cell by its fixed position in a worksheet is referred to as being:
   A. absolute
   B. relative
   C. mixed

3. A value that originates in a worksheet cell and that is represented in a chart by a data marker is a data:
   A. point
   B. cell
   C. axis

4. Related data points represented by data markers are referred to as the data:
   A. slices
   B. set
   C. series

5. The action of pulling out a pie slice from a pie chart is called:
   A. extract
   B. explode
   C. plot

6. A gallery of text styles with which you can create decorative effects, such as shadowed or mirrored text is:
   A. WordArt
   B. shape effects
   C. text fill

7. The percent by which one number increases over another number is the percentage rate of:
   A. decrease
   B. change
   C. increase

8. A chart type that displays trends over time is a:
   A. pie chart
   B. line chart
   C. column chart

9. The area bounded by the axes of a chart, including all the data series, is the:
   A. chart area
   B. plot area
   C. axis area

10. The x-axis is also known as the:
    A. category axis
    B. value axis
    C. data axis

Content-Based Assessments

Apply **3A** skills from these Objectives:

1 Chart Data with a Pie Chart

2 Format a Pie Chart

3 Edit a Workbook and Update a Chart

4 Use Goal Seek to Perform What-If Analysis

Skills Review | Project **3C** Fund Revenue

In the following Skills Review, you will edit a worksheet for Jennifer Carson, City Finance Manager, which details the City general fund revenue. Your completed worksheets will look similar to Figure 3.46.

Project Files

For Project 3C, you will need the following file:

e03C_Fund_Revenue

You will save your workbook as:

Lastname_Firstname_3C_Fund_Revenue

Project Results

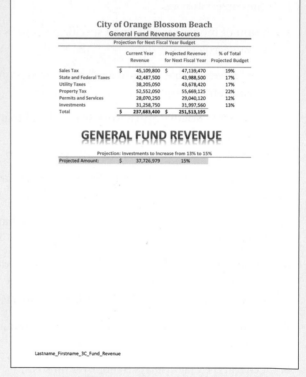

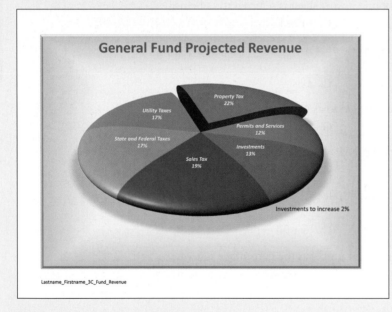

Figure 3.46

(Project 3C Fund Revenue continues on the next page)

Content-Based Assessments

1 **Start** Excel. From your student files, open the file **e03C_Fund_Revenue**. **Save** the file in your **Excel Chapter 3** folder as **Lastname_Firstname_3C_Fund_Revenue**

a. Click cell **D5**, and then type = to begin a formula. Click cell **C5**, type **/** and then click cell **C11**. Press F4 to make the reference to the value in cell **C11** absolute. On the **Formula Bar**, click the **Enter** button, and then fill the formula down through cell **D10**.

b. With the range **D5:D10** selected, right-click over the selection, and then on Mini toolbar, click the **Percent Style** button and the **Center** button.

2 Select the nonadjacent ranges **A5:A10** and **C5:C10** to select the revenue names and the projected revenue. Click the **Insert tab**, and then in the **Charts group**, click **Pie**. Under **3-D Pie**, click the first chart—**Pie in 3-D**.

a. On the **Design tab**, in the **Location group**, click the **Move Chart** button. In the **Move Chart** dialog box, click the **New sheet** option button. In the **New sheet** box, replace the highlighted text *Chart1* by typing **Projected Revenue Chart** and then click **OK**.

b. On the **Layout tab**, in the **Labels group**, click the **Chart Title** button, and then click **Above Chart**. With the **Chart Title** box selected, type **General Fund Projected Revenue** and then press Enter to create the new chart title.

c. Point to the chart title text, and then right-click to display the Mini toolbar. Change the **Font Size** to **32** and change the **Font Color** to **Blue-Gray, Text 2**— in the fourth column, the first color.

d. Click in a white area of the chart to deselect the chart title. On the **Layout tab**, in the **Labels group**, click the **Legend** button, and then click **None**.

e. In the **Labels group**, click the **Data Labels** button, and then click **More Data Label Options**. In the **Format Data Labels** dialog box, on the left, be sure **Label Options** is selected. On the right, under **Label Contains**, click as necessary to select the **Category Name** and **Percentage** check boxes. *Clear* any other check boxes in this group. Under **Label Position**, click the **Center** option button. Click **Close**.

f. Point to any of the selected labels, right-click to display the Mini toolbar, and then change the **Font Size** to **12**, the **Font Color** to **White, Background 1, Darker 5%**, and then apply **Bold** and **Italic**.

3 3. Click in any pie slice outside of the label to select the entire pie. Click the **Format tab**, and then in the **Shape**

(Project 3C Fund Revenue continues on the next page)

Styles group, click the **Shape Effects** button. Point to **Bevel**, and then at the bottom of the gallery, click **3-D Options**.

a. In the **Format Data Series** dialog box, on the right, under **Bevel**, click the **Top** button. In the gallery, under **Bevel**, in the first row, click the first button— **Circle**. Then click the **Bottom** button, and apply the **Circle** bevel. In the four **Width** and **Height** spin boxes, type **512**

b. In the lower portion of the dialog box, under **Surface**, click the **Material** button. Under **Standard**, click the third button—**Plastic**. In the lower right corner, click the **Close** button.

c. On the **Format tab**, in the **Shape Styles group**, click **Shape Effects**, and then point to **Shadow**. Under **Perspective**, click the third button—**Below**.

d. With the pie chart still selected, point anywhere in the pie and right-click. On the displayed shortcut menu, click **Format Data Series**. In the **Format Data Series** dialog box, on the left, be sure **Series Options** is selected. On the right, click in the box under **Angle of first slice**, change *0* to type **150** to move the largest slice—*Property Tax*—to the top of the pie. Click **Close**.

e. Click in the area outside of the chart sheet to deselect all chart elements. Then, on the pie chart, click the outer edge of the **Property Tax** slice one time to select the pie chart, and then click the **Property Tax** slice again to select only that slice.

f. Point to the **Property Tax** slice, and then explode the slice by dragging it slightly away from the center of the pie.

g. With the **Property Tax** slice still selected, point to the slice and right-click. On the shortcut menu, click **Format Data Point**. In the displayed **Format Data Point** dialog box, on the left, click **Fill**. On the right, under **Fill**, click the **Solid fill** option button. Click the **Color arrow**, and then under **Theme Colors**, in the sixth column, click the fifth color—**Dark Yellow, Accent 2, Darker 25%**. Click **Close**.

4 Point to the white area just inside the border of the chart to display the ScreenTip **Chart Area**, and then click one time.

a. On the **Format tab**, in the **Shape Styles group**, click the **Shape Effects** button, point to **Bevel**, and then under **Bevel**, in the second row, click the third bevel—**Convex**.

b. With the chart area still selected, right-click in a white area at the outer edge of the chart, and then on the shortcut menu, click **Format Chart Area**. In the **Format Chart Area** dialog box, on the left, be sure that **Fill** is selected. On the right, under **Fill**, click the **Gradient fill** option button. Click the **Preset colors** arrow, and then in the third row, click the fourth preset, **Parchment**. Click the **Type arrow**, and then click **Path**. Click the **Close** button.

c. Click the **Layout tab**, and then in the **Insert group**, click the **Text Box** button. Position the pointer near the lower corner of the *Investments* slice. Hold down the left mouse button, and then drag down and to the right so that the text box extends to the end of the chart area and is approximately one-half inch high. With the insertion point blinking inside the text box, type **Investments to increase 2%** Select the text and then on the Mini toolbar, change the **Font Size** to **12**. If necessary, use the sizing handles to widen the text box so that the text displays on one line.

5 In the sheet tab area at the bottom of the workbook, click the **Sheet1 tab** to redisplay the worksheet.

a. Click the **Insert tab**, and then in the **Text group**, click the **WordArt** button.

b. In the **WordArt** gallery, in the last row, click the last style—**Fill – Red, Accent 1, Metal Bevel, Reflection**. Type **general fund revenue** and then point anywhere on the dashed border surrounding the WordArt object. Click the dashed border one time to change it to a solid border, indicating that all of the text is selected. Right-click the border to display the Mini toolbar, and then change the **Font Size** to **28**.

c. Drag to position the upper left corner of the WordArt in cell **A13**, centered below the worksheet.

6 In cell **A17**, type **Projection: Investments to Increase from 13% to 15%** and then **Merge & Center** the text across the range **A17:D17**. Apply the **Heading 3** cell style.

a. In cell **A18**, type **Projected Amount:** and press Enter. Select the range **C10:D10**, right-click over the selection, and then click **Copy**. Point to cell **B18**, right-click, and then under **Paste Options**, click the **Paste** button. Press Esc to cancel the moving border.

b. Click cell **C18**. On the **Data tab**, in the **Data Tools group**, click the **What-If Analysis** button, and then click **Goal Seek**. In the **Goal Seek** dialog box, press Tab to move to the **To value** box, and then type **15%**

c. Press Tab to move the insertion point to the **By changing cell** box, and then click cell **B18**. Click

OK. In the displayed **Goal Seek Status** dialog box, click **OK**.

d. Select the range **A18:C18**. From the **Home tab**, display the **Cell Styles** gallery. Under **Themed Cell Styles**, apply **40% - Accent3**. Click cell **B18**, and then from the **Cell Styles** gallery, apply the **Currency [0]** cell style.

7 With your worksheet displayed, in the sheet tab area, double-click *Sheet1* to select the text, and then type **Projected Revenue Data** and press Enter.

a. On the **Insert tab**, in the **Text group**, click **Header & Footer**. In the **Navigation group**, click the **Go to Footer** button, click in the **left section** above the word *Footer*, and then in the **Header & Footer Elements group**, click the **File Name** button. Click in a cell above the footer to deselect the **Footer area** and view your file name.

b. On the **Page Layout tab**, in the **Page Setup group**, click the **Margins** button, and then at the bottom of the **Margins gallery**, click **Custom Margins**. In the **Page Setup** dialog box, under **Center on page**, select the **Horizontally** check box. Click **OK**, and then on the status bar, click the **Normal** button. Press Ctrl + Home to move to the top of your worksheet.

c. Click the **Projected Revenue Chart** sheet tab to display the chart sheet. On the **Insert tab**, click **Header & Footer**. In the center of the **Page Setup** dialog box, click **Custom Footer**. With the insertion point blinking in the **Left section**, in the row of buttons in the middle of the dialog box, locate and click the **Insert File Name** button. Click **OK** two times.

d. Right-click either of the sheet tabs, and then click **Select All Sheets**. From **Backstage** view, show the **Document Panel**. In the **Author** box, replace the existing text with your firstname and lastname. In the **Subject** box, type your course name and section number. In the **Keywords** box type **general fund, projected revenue** **Close** the **Document Information Panel**.

e. With the two sheets still grouped, press Ctrl + F2 to display the **Print Preview**, and then view the two pages of your workbook.

f. **Save** your workbook. Print or submit electronically as directed by your instructor. If required by your instructor, print or create an electronic version of your worksheets with formulas displayed by using the instructions in Activity 1.16, and then **Close** Excel without saving so that you do not save the changes you made to print formulas.

End You have completed Project 3C

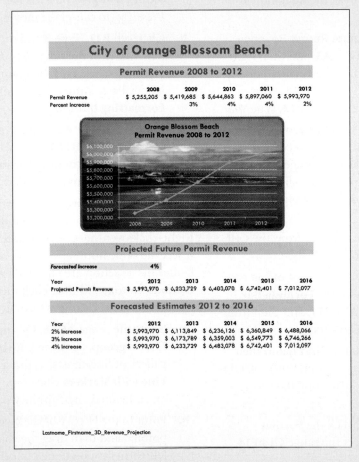

Content-Based Assessments

Apply 3B skills from these Objectives:

5 Design a Worksheet for What-If Analysis

6 Answer What-If Questions by Changing Values in a Worksheet

7 Chart Data with a Line Chart

Skills Review | Project **3D** Revenue Projection

In the following Skills Review, you will edit a worksheet for Jennifer Carson, City Finance Manager, which forecasts the permit revenue that the City of Orange Blossom Beach expects to collect in the next five years. Your completed worksheet will look similar to Figure 3.47.

Project Files

For Project 3D, you will need the following files:

e03D_Revenue_Projection
e03D_Shoreline

You will save your workbook as:

Lastname_Firstname_3D_Revenue_Projection

Project Results

Figure 3.47

(Project 3D Revenue Projection continues on the next page)

Content-Based Assessments

Skills Review | Project **3D** Revenue Projection (continued)

1 **Start** Excel. From your student files, open the file **e03D_Revenue_Projection**. **Save** the file in your **Excel Chapter 3** folder with the file name **Lastname_Firstname_3D_Revenue_Projection**

  a. Click cell **C7**. Being sure to include the parentheses, type **=(c6-b6)/b6** and then on the **Formula Bar**, click the **Enter** button. In the **Number group**, click the **Percent Style** button.

  b. Click cell **D7**, type **=** and then by typing, or using a combination of typing and clicking cells to reference them, construct a formula similar to the one in cell **C7** to calculate the rate of increase in population from 2009 to 2010. Format cell **D7** with the **Percent Style**. With cell **D7** selected, drag the fill handle to the right through cell **F7**.

  c. In cell **A9**, type **Projected Future Permit Revenue** and then press Enter. Point to cell **A3**, and then right-click. On the Mini toolbar, click the **Format Painter** button, and then click cell **A9**. In cell **A11**, type **Forecasted Increase** and then in cell **A13**, type **Year**

  d. In cell **A14**, type **Projected Permit Revenue** and then in cell **B13**, type **2012** and press Tab. In cell **C13**, type **2013** and then press Tab. Select the range **B13:C13**, and then drag the fill handle through cell **F13** to extend the pattern of years to *2016*. Apply **Bold** to the selection.

  e. Click cell **B14**, type **5993970** and then from the **Cell Styles** gallery, apply the **Currency [0]** style.

  f. In cell **B11**, type **2%** which is the percent of increase from 2011 to 2012, and then on the **Formula Bar**, click **Enter**. Select the range **A11:B11**, and then from the Mini toolbar, apply **Bold** and **Italic**.

2 Click cell **C14**. Type **=b14*(100%+b11)** and then on the **Formula Bar**, click the **Enter** button. With cell **C14** as the active cell, drag the fill handle to copy the formula to the range **D14:F14**.

  a. Point to cell **B14**, right-click, click the **Format Painter** button, and then select the range **C14:F14**.

  b. Click cell **A16**. Type **Forecasted Estimates 2012 to 2016** and then press Enter. Use **Format Painter** to copy the format from cell **A9** to cell **A16**.

  c. Select the range **A11:B11**, right-click to display the Mini toolbar, click the **Fill Color button arrow**, and then under **Theme Colors**, in the first column, click the third color—**White, Background 1, Darker 15%**.

  d. In the range **A18:A21**, type the following row titles:

    Year

    2% Increase

    3% Increase

    4% Increase

3 Select the range **B13:F13**, right-click over the selection, and then on the shortcut menu, click **Copy**. **Paste** the selection to the range **B18:F18**.

  a. Select the range **B14:F14**, right-click over the selection, and then on the shortcut menu, click **Copy**. Point to **B19**, right-click, and then from the shortcut menu, point to **Paste Special**. Under **Paste Values**, click the second button—**Values & Number Formatting**. Press Esc to cancel the moving border,

  b. Click cell **B11**. Type **3** and then press Enter. **Copy** the new values in the range **B14:F14**. Point to cell **B20** and right-click, and then point to **Paste Special**. Under **Paste Values**, click the **Values & Number Formatting** button.

  c. In cell **B11**, type **4** and then press Enter. Select and copy the range **B14:F14**, and then paste the values and number formats to the range **B21:F21**. Press Esc to cancel the moving border.

4 In the **row header area**, point to **row 8** to display the ➡ pointer, and then drag down to select **rows 8:24**. Right-click over the selection, and then click **Insert** to insert the same number of blank rows as you selected. Under the selection area near cell **A25**, click the **Insert Options** button, and then click the **Clear Formatting** option button to clear any formatting from these rows.

  a. Select the range **A6:F6**. On the **Insert tab**, in the **Charts group**, click the **Line** button. In the displayed gallery of line charts, in the second row, click the **Line with Markers** chart type to create the chart as an embedded chart in the worksheet.

  b. Point to the border of the chart to display the pointer, and then drag the chart so that its upper left corner is positioned in cell **A9**, aligned approximately under the *r* in the word *Increase* above.

  c. On the **Layout tab**, in the **Labels group**, click the **Legend** button, and then click **None**. Click the chart title one time to select it. Type **Orange Blossom Beach** and then press Enter.

(Project 3D Revenue Projection continues on the next page)

d. In the chart title, click to position the insertion point following the *h* in *Beach*, and then press Enter to begin a new line. Type **Permit Revenue 2008 to 2012** Click the dashed border around the chart title to change it to a solid border, right-click the solid border, and then on the Mini toolbar, change the **Font Size** of the title to **14**.

5 With the chart selected, click the **Design tab**, and then in the **Data group**, click the **Select Data** button. On the right side of the **Select Data Source** dialog box, under **Horizontal (Category) Axis Labels**, in the right column, click the **Edit** button. If necessary, drag the title bar of the Axis Labels dialog box to the right of the chart so that it is not blocking your view of the data, and then select the years in the range **B5:F5**. Click **OK** two times to enter the years as the category labels.

a. On the **Layout tab**, in the **Axes group**, click the **Axes** button. Point to **Primary Vertical Axis**, and then click **More Primary Vertical Axis Options**. In the **Format Axis** dialog box, on the left, be sure **Axis Options** is selected. On the right, in the **Minimum** row, click the **Fixed** option button. In the box to the right, select the existing text, and then type **5200000**

b. In the **Major unit** row, click the **Fixed** option button, select the value *200000.0* in the box to the right, and then type **100000** In the lower right corner, click **Close**.

c. Click the **Format tab**, and then in the **Current Selection group**, click the **Chart Elements arrow**. From the displayed list, click **Chart Area**. Directly below the **Chart Elements** box, click the **Format Selection** button.

d. In the **Format Chart Area** dialog box, on the left, be sure that **Fill** is selected. On the right, under **Fill**, click the **Picture or texture fill** option button, and then under **Insert from**, click the **File** button. In the **Insert Picture** dialog box, navigate to your student files, and then insert the picture **e03D_Shoreline**. In the **Format Chart Area** dialog box, on the left, click **Border Color**. On the right click the **Solid line** option button, and then click the **Color arrow**. Under **Theme Colors**, in the fourth column, click the first color—**Brown, Text 2**.

e. On the left, click **Border Styles**. On the right, select the text in the **Width** box and type **4** Select the **Rounded corners** check box, and then click **Close** the dialog box.

6 In the **Current Selection group**, click the **Chart Elements arrow**, on the list click **Plot Area**, and then click the **Format Selection** button. In the **Format Plot Area** dialog box, on the left, be sure that **Fill** is selected, and then on the right, click the **No fill** option button. **Close** the dialog box.

a. Click the **Chart Elements arrow**, on the list click **Vertical (Value) Axis**, and then click the **Format Selection** button. In the **Format Axis** dialog box, on the left, click **Line Color**. On the right, click the **Solid line** option button, click the **Color arrow**, and then click the first color—**White, Background 1**. **Close** the dialog box.

b. From the **Chart Elements** box, select the **Vertical (Value) Axis Major Gridlines**, and then click **Format Selection**. Change the **Line Color** to a **Solid line**, and then apply the **White, Background 1** color. **Close** the dialog box.

c. From the **Chart Elements** box, select the **Horizontal (Category) Axis**, and then click **Format Selection**. Change the **Line Color** to a **Solid line**, and then apply the **White, Background 1** color. **Close** the dialog box.

d. Point to any of the numbers on the **vertical value axis**, right-click, and then on the Mini toolbar, change the **Font Color** to **White, Background 1**. Point to any of the years on the **horizontal category axis**, right-click, and then change the **Font Color** to **White, Background 1**.

e. Click any cell to deselect the chart. Insert a **Header & Footer** with the **file name** in the **left section** of the footer, and then center the worksheet **Horizontally** on the page. Return to **Normal** view, and press Ctrl + Home. From **Backstage** view, show the **Document Panel**. In the **Author** box, replace the existing text with your firstname and lastname. In the **Subject** box, type your course name and section number. In the **Keywords** box type **permit revenue, forecast Close** the **Document Information Panel**.

f. **Save** your workbook. Print or submit electronically as directed by your instructor. If required by your instructor, print or create an electronic version of your worksheet with formulas displayed by using the instructions in Activity 1.16, and then **Close** Excel without saving so that you do not save the changes you made to print formulas.

End **You have completed Project 3D**

Excel | Chapter 3

Content-Based Assessments

Apply **3A** skills from these Objectives:

1. Chart Data with a Pie Chart
2. Format a Pie Chart
3. Edit a Workbook and Update a Chart
4. Use Goal Seek to Perform What-If Analysis

Mastering Excel | Project **3E** Investments

In the following project, you will you will edit a worksheet for Jennifer Carson, City Finance Manager, that summarizes the investment portfolio of the City of Orange Blossom Beach. Your completed worksheets will look similar to Figure 3.48.

Project Files

For Project 3E, you will need the following file:

e03E_Investments

You will save your workbook as:

Lastname_Firstname_3E_Investments

Project Results

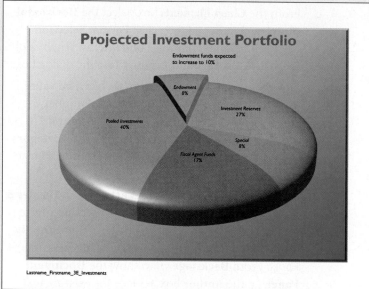

Figure 3.48

(Project 3E Investments continues on the next page)

Content-Based Assessments

1 **Start** Excel. From your student files, locate and open **e03E_Investments**. **Save** the file in your **Excel Chapter 3** folder as **Lastname_Firstname_3E_Investments**

2 In cells **B10** and **C10**, enter formulas to calculate totals for each column. Then, in cell **D5**, enter a formula to calculate the % of Total Projected Investments for Pooled Investments by dividing the **Projected Investments for Next Fiscal Year** for the **Pooled Investments** by the **Total Projected Investments for Next Fiscal Year**. Use absolute cell references as necessary, format the result in **Percent Style**, and **Center** the percentage. Fill the formula down through cell **D9**.

3 Select the nonadjacent ranges **A5:A9** and **C5:C9**, and then insert a **Pie in 3-D** chart. Move the chart to a **New sheet** named **Projected Investment Chart** Insert a **Chart Title** above the chart with the text **Projected Investment Portfolio** Change the chart title **Font Size** to **32** and change the **Font Color** to **Brown, Accent 6**—in the last column, the first color.

4 Remove the **Legend** from the chart, and then add **Data Labels** formatted so that only the **Category Name** and **Percentage** display positioned in the **Center**. Change the data labels **Font Size** to **11**, and then apply **Italic**.

5 Select the entire pie, display the **Shape Effects** gallery, point to **Bevel**, and then at the bottom of the gallery, click **3-D Options**. Change the **Top** and **Bottom** options to the last **Bevel** type—**Art Deco**. Set the **Top Width** and **Height** boxes to **256** and then set the **Bottom Width** and **Height** boxes to **0** Change the **Material** to the third **Standard** type—**Plastic**.

6 With the pie chart selected, display the shortcut menu, and then click **Format Data Series**. Change the **Angle of first slice** to **200** to move the *Endowment* slice to the top of the pie. Select the **Endowment** slice, and then explode the slice slightly.

7 Change the **Fill Color** of the **Pooled Investments** slice to **Gray-50%, Accent 1, Lighter 40%**. Format the **Chart Area** by applying a **Convex Bevel**. To the **Chart Area**, apply the **Moss, Preset Gradient fill**. In the **Angle** box, type **45** and then **Close** the **Format Chart Area** dialog box.

8 **Insert** a **Text Box** positioned approximately halfway between the *Endowment* pie slice and the *v* in the word *Investment* in the title. In the text box, type **Endowment funds expected to increase to 10%** Select the text and then on the Mini toolbar, change the **Font Size** to **12**. Size the text box as necessary so that the text displays on two lines as shown in Figure 3.48.

9 Display **Sheet1** and rename the sheet as **Projected Investment Data** Insert a **WordArt**—in the fifth row, insert the last WordArt style—**Fill – Gray-50%, Accent 1, Plastic Bevel, Reflection**. Type **General Fund Investments** and then change the **Font Size** to **20**. Drag to position the upper left corner of the WordArt in cell **A12**, centered below the worksheet.

10 In cell **A16**, type **Goal: Increase Endowment Fund from 8% to 10%** and then **Merge & Center** the text across the range **A16:D16**. Apply the **Heading 3** cell style. In cell **A17**, type **Goal Amount**

11 **Copy** the range **C6:D6** to cell **B17**. Click cell **C17**, and then use **Goal Seek** to determine the projected amount of endowment funds in cell **B17** if the value in **C17** is **10%**.

12 Select the range **A17:C17**, and then apply the **20% - Accent2** cell style. In **B17**, from the **Cell Styles** gallery, apply the **Currency [0]** cell style.

13 Insert a **Header & Footer** with the file name in the **left section** of the footer. In Page Layout view, check that the WordArt is centered under the worksheet data. Center the worksheet **Horizontally** on the page, and then return to **Normal** view. Display the **Projected Investment Chart** sheet and insert a **Custom Footer** with the file name in the **Left section**.

14 Group the sheets, and then display the **Document Panel**. Add your name, your course name and section, and the keywords **investment portfolio**

15 **Save** your workbook. Print or submit electronically as directed by your instructor. If required by your instructor, print or create an electronic version of your worksheets with formulas displayed by using the instructions in Activity 1.16, and then **Close** Excel without saving so that you do not save the changes you made to print formulas.

End You have completed Project 3E

Content-Based Assessments

Apply **3B** skills from these Objectives:

⑤ Design a Worksheet for What-If Analysis

⑥ Answer What-If Questions by Changing Values in a Worksheet

⑦ Chart Data with a Line Chart

Mastering Excel | Project **3F** Benefit Analysis

In the following project, you will edit a worksheet that Jeffrey Lovins, Human Resources Director, will use to prepare a five-year forecast of the annual cost of city employee benefits per employee. Your completed worksheet will look similar to Figure 3.49.

Project Files

For Project 3F, you will need the following file:

> e03F_Benefit_Analysis

You will save your workbook as:

> Lastname_Firstname_3F_Benefit Analysis

Project Results

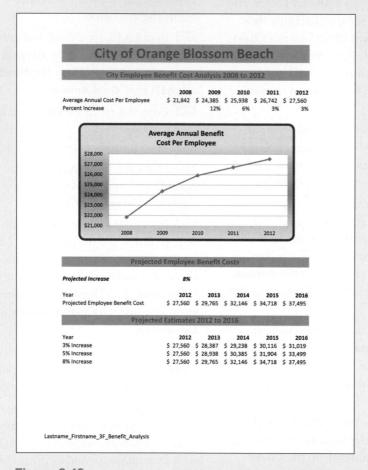

Figure 3.49

(Project 3F Benefit Analysis continues on the next page)

Content-Based Assessments

Mastering Excel | Project **3F** Benefit Analysis (continued)

1 **Start** Excel. From your student files, open the file **e03F_Benefit_Analysis**. **Save** the file in your **Excel Chapter 3** folder as **Firstname_Lastname_3F_Benefit_Analysis**

2 In cell **C7**, construct a formula to calculate the percent of increase in employee annual benefit costs from 2008 to 2009. Format the result with the **Percent Style** and then fill the formula through cell **F7**.

3 In cell **A9**, type **Projected Employee Benefit Costs** and then use **Format Painter** to copy the formatting from cell **A3** to cell **A9**. In cell **A11**, type **Projected Increase** and then in cell **A13**, type **Year** In cell **A14**, type **Projected Employee Benefit Cost** and then in the range **B13:F13**, use the fill handle to enter the years 2012 through 2016. Apply **Bold** to the years. In cell **B14**, type **27560** and then from the **Cell Styles** gallery, apply the **Currency [0]** format. In cell **B11**, type **3%** which is the percent of increase from 2011 to 2012. To the range **A11:B11**, apply **Bold** and **Italic**.

4 In cell **C14**, construct a formula to calculate the annual cost of employee benefits for the year 2013 after the projected increase of 3% is applied. Fill the formula through cell **F14**, and then use **Format Painter** to copy the formatting from cell **B14** to the range **C14:F14**.

5 In cell **A16**, type **Projected Estimates 2012 to 2016** and then use **Format Painter** to copy the format from cell **A9** to cell **A16**. In cells **A18:A21**, type the following row titles:

> Year
> 3% Increase
> 5% Increase
> 8% Increase

6 **Copy** the range **B13:F13**, and then **Paste** the selection to **B18:F18**. Copy the range **B14:F14** and then paste the

Values & Number Formatting to the range **B19:F19**. Complete the Projected Estimates section of the worksheet by changing the *Projected Increase* in **B11** to **5%** and then to **8%** copying and pasting the **Values & Number Formatting** to the appropriate ranges in the worksheet.

7 Select **rows 8:24**, and then **Insert** the same number of blank rows as you selected. **Clear Formatting** from the inserted rows. By using the data in **A5:F6**, insert a **Line with Markers** chart in the worksheet. Move the chart so that its upper left corner is positioned in cell **A9** and centered under the data above. Remove the **Legend**, and then replace the existing chart title with the two-line title **Average Annual Benefit Cost Per Employee** The text *Cost per Employee* should display on the second line. Change the title **Font Size** to **14**.

8 Format the **Primary Vertical Axis** so that the **Minimum** is **21000** and the **Major unit** is **1000** Format the **Chart Area** with a **Gradient fill** by applying the third **Preset color** in the third row—**Wheat**. Change the **Border Color** by applying a **Solid line   Orange, Accent 1, Darker 50%**. Change the **Width** of the border to **4** and apply the **Rounded corners** option.

9 Deselect the chart, and then insert a **Header & Footer** with the file name in the **left section** of the footer; center the worksheet **Horizontally** on the page. In the **Document Panel**, add your name, your course name and section, and the keywords **employee benefits, forecast**

10 **Save** your workbook. Print or submit electronically as directed by your instructor. If required by your instructor, print or create an electronic version of your worksheets with formulas displayed by using the instructions in Activity 1.16, and then **Close** Excel without saving so that you do not save the changes you made to print formulas.

End **You have completed Project 3F** ——————————————————

Content-Based Assessments

Apply **3A** and **3B** skills from these Objectives:

1. Chart Data with a Pie Chart
2. Format a Pie Chart
3. Edit a Workbook and Update a Chart
4. Use Goal Seek to Perform What-If Analysis
5. Design a Worksheet for What-If Analysis
6. Answer What-If Questions by Changing Values in a Worksheet
7. Chart Data with a Line Chart

Mastering Excel | Project **3G** Operations Analysis

In the following project, you will you will edit a workbook for Jennifer Carson, City Finance Manager, that summarizes the operations costs for the Public Works Department. Your completed worksheets will look similar to Figure 3.50.

Project Files

For Project 3G, you will need the following file:

e03G_Operations_Analysis

You will save your workbook as:

Lastname_Firstname_3G_Operations_Analysis

Project Results

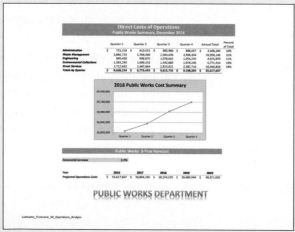

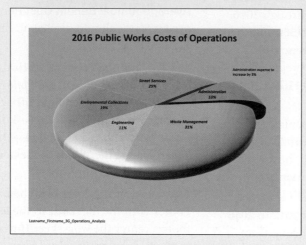

Figure 3.50

(Project 3G Operations Analysis continues on the next page)

226 **Excel** | Chapter 3: Analyzing Data with Pie Charts, Line Charts, and What-If Analysis Tools

Content-Based Assessments

Mastering Excel | Project **3G** Operations Analysis (continued)

1 **Start** Excel. From your student files, open **e03G_Operations_Analysis**. **Save** the file as in your **Excel Chapter 3** folder as **Lastname_Firstname_3G_Operations_ Analysis**

2 In the **Public Works** sheet, calculate totals in the ranges **F5:F9** and **B10:F10**. In cell **G5**, construct a formula to calculate the **Percent of Total** by dividing the **Annual Total** for **Administration** in cell **F5** by the **Annual Total** for all quarters in cell **F10**. Use absolute cell references as necessary, format the result in **Percent Style**, and then **Center**. Fill the formula down through cell **G9**.

3 Select the nonadjacent ranges **A5:A9** and **F5:F9**, and then insert a **Pie in 3-D** chart. Move the chart to a **New sheet** with the name **Public Works Summary Chart** Insert a **Chart Title** above the chart with the text **2016 Public Works Costs of Operations** and then change the **Font Size** to **28**.

4 Remove the **Legend** from the chart and then add **Data Labels** formatted so that only the **Category Name** and **Percentage** displays positioned in the **Center**. Change the data labels **Font Size** to **12**, and apply **Bold** and **Italic**.

5 Select the chart, and then modify the pie chart **Shape Effects** by changing the **Bevel, 3-D Options**. Change the **Top** and **Bottom** options to the first **Bevel** type—**Circle**. Set the **Top Width** and **Height** boxes to **256 pt** and then set the **Bottom Width** and **Height** boxes to **50 pt** Change the **Material** to the fourth **Standard Effect** type—**Metal**.

6 In the displayed **Format Data Series** dialog box, on the left, click **Series Options**, and then change the **Angle of first** slice to **50** Explode the **Administration** slice slightly away from the pie. Format the **Chart Area** with a **Solid fill**—**Aqua, Accent 2**—in the sixth column, the first color.

7 Insert a **Text Box** positioned outside the upper corner of the **Administration** pie slice extending to the edge of the chart area and that is about one-half inch in height. In the text box, type **Administration expense to increase by 3%** Change the **Font Size** to **10.5**. Size the text box so that the text displays on two lines. On this chart sheet, insert a **Custom Footer** with the file name in the **left section**.

8 In the **Public Works** sheet, using the data in the nonadjacent ranges **B4:E4** and **B10:E10**, insert a **Line with Markers** chart in the worksheet. Move the chart so that its upper left corner is positioned in cell **A12**, aligned approximately under the *t* in the word *Collections* above.

Remove the **Legend** and then add a **Chart Title** above the chart with the text **2016 Public Works Cost Summary** Edit the **Primary Vertical Axis** so that the **Minimum** is **Fixed** at **8600000** and the **Major unit** is **Fixed** at **200000** Format the **Chart Area** with a **Solid fill** by applying **Aqua, Accent 2, Lighter 40%**—in the sixth column, the fourth color.

9 In cell **B35**, type **35617667** and then apply the **Currency [0]** cell style. In cell **C35**, construct a formula to calculate the **Projected Operations Costs** after the forecasted increase is applied. Fill the formula through cell **F35**, and then use **Format Painter** to copy the formatting from cell **B35** to the range **C35:F35**.

10 Insert a **WordArt** using the last style—**Fill - Brown, Accent 1, Metal Bevel, Reflection** Type **Public Works Department** and then change the **Font Size** to **32**. Drag to position the WordArt in cell **A38**, centered below the worksheet.

11 Change the **Orientation** to **Landscape**, and then use the **Scale to Fit** options to fit the **Height** to **1 page**. Insert a **Header & Footer** with the **file name** in the left area of the footer. In **Page Layout** view, check and adjust if necessary the visual centering of the chart and the WordArt. Center the worksheet **Horizontally** on the page, and then return to **Normal** view.

12 Display the **Projected Decrease sheet**. In cell **C5**, calculate the **Percent of Total** by dividing the *Administration Annual Total* by the *Totals by Quarter*, using absolute cell references as necessary. Apply **Percent Style** and then fill the formula from **C5:C9**.

13 **Copy** cell **B5**, and then use **Paste Special** to paste the **Values & Number Formatting** to cell **B13**. **Copy** and **Paste** cell **C5** to **C13**. With cell **C13** selected, use **Goal Seek** to determine the goal amount of administration expenses in cell **B13** if the value in **C13** is set to **7%**

14 On the **Projected Decrease** sheet, insert a **Header & Footer** with the file name in the **left section** of the footer, and then center the worksheet **Horizontally** on the page. Show the **Document Panel**. Add your name, your course name and section, and the keywords **public works**

15 **Save** your workbook. Print or submit electronically as directed by your instructor. If required by your instructor, print or create an electronic version of your worksheets with formulas displayed by using the instructions in Activity 1.16, and then **Close** Excel without saving so that you do not save the changes you made to print formulas.

End **You have completed Project 3G** ―――――――――――――

Content-Based Assessments

GO! Fix It | Project **3H** Recreation

Project Files

For Project 3H, you will need the following file:

> e03H_Recreation

You will save your workbook as:

> Lastname_Firstname_3H_Recreation

In this project, you will correct a worksheet that contains the annual enrollment of residents in city-sponsored recreation programs. From the student files that accompany this textbook, open the file e03H_Recreation, and then save the file in your chapter folder as **Lastname_Firstname_3H_Recreation**

To complete the project, you must find and correct errors in formulas and formatting. View each formula in the worksheet and edit as necessary. Review the format and title of the pie chart and make corrections and formatting changes as necessary. In addition to errors that you find, you should know:

- The pie chart data should include the Age Group and the Total columns.
- The Chart Area should include a blue solid fill background and the title font color should be white.
- The pie chart should be in a separate worksheet named **Enrollment Analysis Chart**

Add a footer to both sheets, and add your name, your course name and section, and the keywords **Parks and Recreation, enrollment** to the document properties. Save your file and then print or submit your worksheet electronically as directed by your instructor. If required by your instructor, print or create an electronic version of your worksheets with formulas displayed by using the instructions in Activity 1.16, and then close Excel without saving so that you do not save the changes you made to print formulas.

End **You have completed Project 3H** ————————————————

Content-Based Assessments

GO! Make It | Project 3I Tax Projection

Project Files

For Project 3I, you will need the following file:

New blank Excel workbook

You will save your workbook as:

Lastname_Firstname_3I_Tax_Projection

Start a new blank Excel workbook and create the worksheet shown in Figure 3.51. In the range C7:F7, calculate the rate of increase from the previous year. In the range C31:F31, calculate the projected property tax for each year based on the forecasted increase. Complete the worksheet by entering in the range B36:F38, the projected property tax revenue for each year based on 2%, 3%, and 4% increases. Insert the chart as shown, using the 2010 through 2014 Property Tax Revenue data. Fill the chart area with the Daybreak gradient fill and change the chart title font size to 14. Scale the width to fit to one page, and then add your name, your course name and section, and the keywords **property tax** to the document properties. Save the file in your Excel Chapter 3 folder as **Lastname_Firstname_3I_Tax_Projection** and then print or submit electronically as directed by your instructor.

Project Results

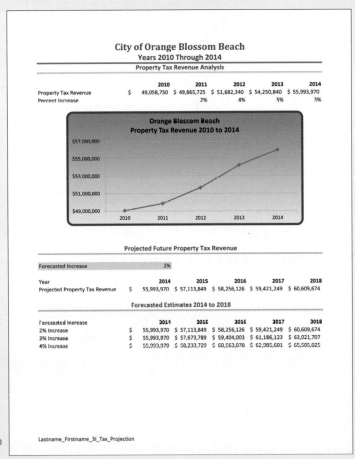

Figure 3.51

End You have completed Project 3I

Apply a combination of the 3A and 3B skills.

GO! Solve It | Project 3J Staffing

Project Files

For Project 3J, you will need the following file:

e03J_Staffing

You will save your workbook as:

Lastname_Firstname_3J_Staffing

Open the file e03J_Staffing and save it as **Lastname_Firstname_3J_Staffing** Complete the worksheet by calculating totals and the % of Total Employees. Format the worksheet attractively including appropriate number formatting. Insert a pie chart in a separate sheet that illustrates the Two-Year Projection staffing levels by department and use the techniques that you practiced in this chapter to format the chart so that it is attractive and easy to understand. Change the angle of the first slice so that the Public Safety slice displays below the title. Then, insert a text box that indicates that the increase in Public Safety staffing is contingent upon City Council approval. Include the file name in the footer, add appropriate properties, save and submit as directed.

Performance Criteria	Performance Level: Exemplary: You consistently applied the relevant skills	Proficient: You sometimes, but not always, applied the relevant skills	Developing: You rarely or never applied the relevant skills
Create formulas	All formulas are correct and are efficiently constructed.	Formulas are correct but not always constructed in the most efficient manner.	One or more formulas are missing or incorrect; or only numbers were entered.
Chart inserted and formatted	Chart was inserted and formatted properly.	Chart was inserted but incorrect data was selected or the chart was not formatted.	No chart was inserted.
Format attractively and appropriately	Formatting is attractive and appropriate.	Adequately formatted but difficult to read or unattractive.	Inadequate or no formatting.

End **You have completed Project 3J**

Content-Based Assessments

Apply a combination of
the 3A and 3B skills.

GO! Solve It | Project 3K Water Usage

Excel | Chapter 3

Project Files

For Project 3K, you will need the following file:

New blank Excel workbook
e03K_Beach

You will save your workbook as:

Lastname_Firstname_3K_Water_Usage

The City of Orange Blossom Beach is a growing community and the City Council has requested an analysis of future resource needs. In this project, you will create a worksheet for the Department of Water and Power that lists residential water usage over the past ten years and that forecasts the amount of water that city residents will use in the next ten years. Create a worksheet with the following data:

	2008	2010	2012	2014	2016
Water Use in Acre Feet	62500	68903	73905	76044	80342

Calculate the percent increase for the years 2010 to 2016. Below the Percent Increase, insert a line chart that illustrates the city's water usage from 2008 to 2016. Below the chart, add a section to the worksheet to calculate the projected water usage for the years 2016 to 2024 in two-year increments based on a 4% annual increase. The 2016 amount is 80,342. Format the chart and worksheet attractively with a title and subtitle, and apply appropriate formatting. If you choose to format the chart area with a picture, you can use e03K_Beach located with your student files. Include the file name in the footer and enter appropriate document properties. Save the workbook as **Lastname_Firstname_3K_Water_Usage** and submit it as directed.

Performance Level

Performance Criteria	Exemplary: You consistently applied the relevant skills	Proficient: You sometimes, but not always, applied the relevant skills	Developing: You rarely or never applied the relevant skills
Create formulas	All formulas are correct and are efficiently constructed.	Formulas are correct but not always constructed in the most efficient manner.	One or more formulas are missing or incorrect or only numbers were entered.
Insert and format line chart	Line chart created correctly and is attractively formatted.	Line chart was created but the data was incorrect or the chart was not appropriately formatted.	No line chart was created.
Format attractively and appropriately	Formatting is attractive and appropriate.	Adequately formatted but difficult to read or unattractive.	Inadequate or no formatting.

End You have completed Project 3K

Project 3K: Water Usage | **Excel** 231

Outcomes-Based Assessments

Rubric

The following outcomes-based assessments are *open-ended assessments*. That is, there is no specific correct result; your result will depend on your approach to the information provided. Make *Professional Quality* your goal. Use the following scoring rubric to guide you in *how* to approach the problem, and then to evaluate *how well* your approach solves the problem.

The *criteria*—Software Mastery, Content, Format and Layout, and Process—represent the knowledge and skills you have gained that you can apply to solving the problem. The *levels of performance*—Professional Quality, Approaching Professional Quality, or Needs Quality Improvements—help you and your instructor evaluate your result.

	Your completed project is of Professional Quality if you:	Your completed project is Approaching Professional Quality if you:	Your completed project Needs Quality Improvements if you:
1-Software Mastery	Choose and apply the most appropriate skills, tools, and features and identify efficient methods to solve the problem.	Choose and apply some appropriate skills, tools, and features, but not in the most efficient manner.	Choose inappropriate skills, tools, or features, or are inefficient in solving the problem.
2-Content	Construct a solution that is clear and well organized, contains content that is accurate, appropriate to the audience and purpose, and is complete. Provide a solution that contains no errors in spelling, grammar, or style.	Construct a solution in which some components are unclear, poorly organized, inconsistent, or incomplete. Misjudge the needs of the audience. Have some errors in spelling, grammar, or style, but the errors do not detract from comprehension.	Construct a solution that is unclear, incomplete, or poorly organized; contains some inaccurate or inappropriate content; and contains many errors in spelling, grammar, or style. Do not solve the problem.
3-Format and Layout	Format and arrange all elements to communicate information and ideas, clarify function, illustrate relationships, and indicate relative importance.	Apply appropriate format and layout features to some elements, but not others. Overuse features, causing minor distraction.	Apply format and layout that does not communicate information or ideas clearly. Do not use format and layout features to clarify function, illustrate relationships, or indicate relative importance. Use available features excessively, causing distraction.
4-Process	Use an organized approach that integrates planning, development, self-assessment, revision, and reflection.	Demonstrate an organized approach in some areas, but not others; or, use an insufficient process of organization throughout.	Do not use an organized approach to solve the problem.

Outcomes-Based Assessments

Apply a combination of the **3A** and **3B** skills.

GO! Think | Project **3L** School Enrollment

Project Files

For Project 3L, you will need the following file:

New blank Excel workbook

You will save your workbook as:

Lastname_Firstname_3L_School_Enrollment

Marcus Chavez, the Superintendent of Schools for the City of Orange Blossom Beach, has requested an enrollment analysis of students in the city public elementary schools in order to plan school boundary modifications resulting in more balanced enrollments. Enrollments in district elementary schools for the past two years are as follows:

School	2014 Enrollment	2015 Enrollment
Orange Blossom	795	824
Kittridge	832	952
Glenmeade	524	480
Hidden Trails	961	953
Beach Side	477	495
Sunnyvale	515	502

Create a workbook to provide Marcus with the enrollment information for each school and the total district enrollment. Insert a column to calculate the percent change from 2014 to 2015. Note that some of the results will be negative numbers. Format the percentages with two decimal places. Insert a pie chart in its own sheet that illustrates the 2015 enrollment figures for each school and format the chart attractively. Format the worksheet so that it is professional and easy to read and understand. Insert a footer with the file name and add appropriate document properties. Save the file as **Lastname_Firstname_3L_School_Enrollment** and print or submit as directed by your instructor.

End You have completed Project 3L ——————————————————

Outcomes-Based Assessments

GO! Think | Project **3M** Park Acreage

Project Files

For Project 3M, you will need the following files:

New blank Excel workbook
e03M_Park

You will save your workbook as:

Lastname_Firstname_3M_Park_Acreage

The City of Orange Blossom Beach wants to maintain a high ratio of parkland to residents and has established a goal of maintaining a minimum of 50 parkland acres per 1,000 residents. The following table contains the park acreage and the population, in thousands, since 1980. Start a new blank Excel workbook and then enter appropriate titles. Then, enter the following data in the worksheet and calculate the *Acres per 1,000 residents* by dividing the Park acreage by the Population in thousands.

	1980	1990	2000	2010
Population in thousands	118.4	123.9	133.5	152.6
Park acreage	5,800	6,340	8,490	9,200
Acres per 1,000 residents				

Create a line chart that displays the Park Acres Per 1,000 Residents for each year. Format the chart professionally and insert the picture e03M_Park from your student files in the chart fill area. Below the chart, create a new section titled **Park Acreage Analysis** and then copy and paste the Years and the Park acreage values to the new section. Calculate the *Percent increase* from the previous ten years for the 1990, 2000, and 2010 years. Below the Park Acreage Analysis section, create a new worksheet section titled **Park Acreage Forecast** and then enter the following values.

	2010	2020	2030	2040
Population in thousands	152.6	173.2	197.7	225.3
Park acreage necessary				
Percent increase				

Calculate the *Park acreage necessary* to reach the city's goal by multiplying the Population in thousands by 50. Then calculate the *Percent increase* from the previous ten years for the 2020, 2030, and 2040 years. Use techniques that you practiced in this chapter to format the worksheet professionally. Insert a footer with the file name and add appropriate document properties. Save the file as **Lastname_Firstname_3M_Park_Acreage** and print or submit as directed by your instructor.

End **You have completed Project 3M** ————————————

Outcomes-Based Assessments

Apply a combination of the **3A** and **3B** skills.

You and GO! | Project **3N** Expense Analysis

Project Files

For Project 3N, you will need the following file:

New blank Excel workbook

You will save your workbook as:

Lastname_Firstname_3N_Expense_Analysis

Develop a worksheet that details the expenses you have incurred during the past two months and list the expenses for each month in separate columns. Calculate totals for each column and then add a column in which you can calculate the percent change from one month to the next. Insert and format a pie chart that illustrates the expenses that you incurred in the most recent month. After reviewing the pie chart, determine a category of expense in which you might be overspending, and then pull that slice out of the pie and insert a text box indicating how you might save money on that expense. Insert a footer with the file name and center the worksheet horizontally on the page. Save your file as **Lastname_Firstname_3N_Expense_Analysis** and submit as directed.

End **You have completed Project 3N** ⸻⸻⸻⸻⸻

Business Running Case

Razvan CHIRNOAGA/Shutterstock

This project relates to **Front Range Action Sports**, which is one of the country's largest retailers of sports gear and outdoor recreation merchandise. The company has large retail stores in Colorado, Washington, Oregon, California, and New Mexico, in addition to a growing online business. Major merchandise categories include fishing, camping, rock climbing, winter sports, action sports, water sports, team sports, racquet sports, fitness, golf, apparel, and footwear.

In this project, you will apply the skills you practiced from the Objectives in Excel Chapters 1 through 3. You will develop a workbook for Frank Osei, the Vice President of Finance, that contains year-end sales and inventory summary information. In the first two worksheets, you will summarize and chart net sales. In the next three worksheets, you will detail the ending inventory of the two largest company-owned production facilities in Seattle and Denver. Mr. Osei is particularly interested in data regarding the new line of ski equipment stocked at these two locations. In the last worksheet, you will summarize and chart annual expenses. Your completed worksheets will look similar to Figure 1.1.

Project Files

For Project BRC1, you will need the following files:

eBRC1_Annual_Report
eBRC1_Skiing

You will save your workbook as:

Lastname_Firstname_BRC1_Annual_Report

Project Results

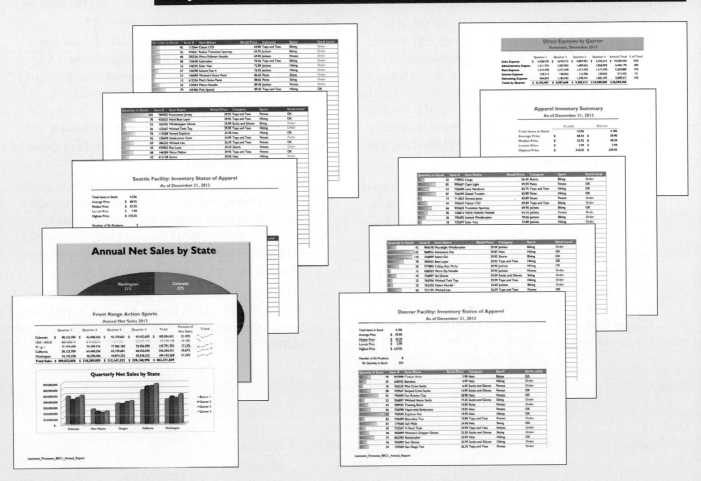

Figure 1.1

Business Running Case 1: Includes Objectives from Excel Chapters 1-3

Business Running Case

Front Range Action Sports

1 **Start** Excel. From the student files that accompany this textbook, locate and open **eBRC1_Annual_Report**. In the location where you are storing your projects, create a new folder named **Front_Range_Action_Sports** or navigate to this folder if you have already created it. **Save** the new workbook as **Lastname_Firstname_BRC1_Annual_Report**

a. Familiarize yourself with the workbook by clicking each sheet tab, and then display the **Net Sales** worksheet. Click cell **B3**, and then use the fill handle to enter *Quarter 2*, *Quarter 3*, and *Quarter 4* in the range **C3:E3**. In the range **C4:E8**, enter the sales data for Quarter 2, Quarter 3, and Quarter 4 shown in **Table 1** at the bottom of the page.

b. Adjust the width of columns **B:F** to **125** pixels. Adjust the width of columns **G:H** to **100** pixels. In cell **F3**, type **Total** and then in the range **F4:F8**, calculate the annual total sales for each state. In the range **B9:F9**, calculate totals. In cell **G3**, type **Percent of Net Sales** and apply **Wrap Text** formatting to this cell. In cell **H3**, type **Trend** Using absolute cell references as necessary, in cell **G4**, construct a formula to calculate the percent that the *Colorado Total* is of the *Total Sales*. Fill the formula down through the range **G5:G8**. **Center** the results and then format the percentages with **Percent Style** and **two decimal places**.

c. Apply **Accounting Number Format** with **no decimal places** to the nonadjacent ranges **B4:F4** and **B9:F9**. Apply **Comma Style** with **no decimal** places to the range **B5:F8**. **Merge & Center** the two worksheet titles across columns **A:H**, and then to cell **A1**, apply the **Title** style and to cell **A2**, apply the **Heading 1** style. Apply the **Total** style to the range **B9:F9** and apply the **Heading 4** style to the range **B3:H3**. **Center** the column headings in **B3:H3** both horizontally and vertically.

d. In the range **H4:H8**, insert **Line** sparklines to represent the trend of each state across the four quarters. Add **Markers** and apply **Sparkline Style Accent 2** (**no dark or light**).

e. Select the range **A3:E8**, and then insert a **3-D Clustered Column** chart. Align the upper left corner of the chart inside the upper left corner of cell **A11**, and then size the chart so that its lower right corner is slightly inside cell **H24**. Apply chart **Style 26** and chart **Layout 1**. Replace the chart title text with **Quarterly Net Sales by State** Insert the file name in the **left section** of the footer, set the orientation to **Landscape**, and center the worksheet horizontally. Return to **Normal** view.

2 To show the percent that each state contributes to the total sales, select the nonadjacent ranges that represent the state names and state totals. Insert a **Pie in 3-D** chart and move the chart to a **New sheet**. Name the sheet **Net Sales by State** and then move the sheet so that it is the second sheet in the workbook.

a. Insert a **Chart Title** above the chart with the text **Annual Net Sales by State** Change the chart title **Font Size** to **36**. Remove the **Legend** from the chart, and then add **Data Labels** that display only the **Category Name** and **Percentage** positioned in the **Center**. Change the data labels **Font Size** to **14**, and then apply **Bold** and **Italic**. Change the **Font Color** to **White, Background 1**.

b. Select the entire pie, display the **Shape Effects** gallery, point to **Bevel**, and then at the bottom of the gallery, click **3-D Options**. Change the **Top** and **Bottom** options to the first **Bevel** type—**Circle**. Set all of the **Width** and **Height** boxes to **512** and then change the **Material** to the third **Standard** type—**Plastic**.

c. Format the **Chart Area** by applying a **Convex Bevel** and a **Solid fill—Dark Green, Accent 4, Lighter 60%**. Insert a **Custom Footer** with the **File Name** in the **left section**, and then **Save** the workbook.

Table 1

	Quarter 1	Quarter 2	Quarter 3	Quarter 4
Colorado	48123789	42468256	45159681	49452695
New Mexico	25783516	21985365	19987269	22252487
Oregon	35658498	34689526	37986369	39456899
California	58123789	64468256	65159681	68452695
Washington	42143258	46598456	44874332	50546222

---▶ (Return to Step 1-b)

(Business Running Case: Front Range Action Sports continues on the next page)

Business Running Case

Front Range Action Sports (continued)

3 Display the **Seattle Inventory** worksheet, and then in cell **B4**, construct a formula to calculate the *Total Items in Stock* by summing the **Quantity in Stock** column. Format the result with **Comma Style** and **no decimal places**.

a. In cell **B5**, construct a formula to calculate the average of the **Retail Price** column. In the range **B6:B8**, construct similar formulas to calculate the median, lowest, and highest retail prices. Format the results in **B5:B8** with **Accounting Number Format**. In cell **B10**, use the **COUNTIF** function to count the number of **Skiing** items that the Seattle location stocks.

b. In cell **G14**, enter an **IF** function to determine the items that must be ordered. If the **Quantity in Stock** is less than **50** then **Value_if_true** is **Order** Otherwise the **Value_if_false** is **OK** Fill the formula down through cell **G87**. Apply **Conditional Formatting** to the **Stock Level** column so that cells that contain the text *Order* are formatted with **Bold Italic** and with a **Font Color** of **Orange, Accent 1**. Apply **Orange Gradient Fill Data Bars** to the **Quantity in Stock** column.

c. Insert a table with headers using the range **A13:G87**. Apply **Table Style Light 11**. **Sort** the table from smallest to largest on the **Retail Price** column, and then filter the table on the **Sport** column to display the **Skiing** types. Display a **Total Row** in the table, and then in cell **A88**, **Sum** the **Quantity in Stock** for the **Skiing** items. Type the result in cell **B11**. Remove the total row from the table, clear the **Sport** filter so that all of the data displays, and then convert the table to a range.

d. Change the **Print Titles** option so that **row 13** prints at the top of each page. Insert the file name in the **left section** of the footer, set the orientation to **Landscape**, and center the worksheet horizontally. Return to **Normal** view.

4 Display the **Denver Inventory** worksheet, and then in cell **B4**, construct a formula to calculate the *Total Items in Stock* by summing the **Quantity in Stock** column. Format the result with **Comma Style** and **no decimal places**.

a. In the range **B5:B8**, use the appropriate statistical functions to calculate the price data. Format the results with **Accounting Number Format**. In cell **B10**, use the **COUNTIF** function to count the number of **Skiing** items that the Denver location stocks.

b. In cell **G14**, enter an **IF** function to determine the items that must be ordered. If the **Quantity in Stock** is less than **50 Value_if_true** is **Order** Otherwise the **Value_if_false** is **OK** Fill the formula down through cell **G87**. Apply **Conditional Formatting** to the **Stock Level** column so that cells that contain the text *Order* are formatted with **Bold Italic** and with a **Font Color** of **Dark Blue, Accent 3**. Apply **Light Blue Gradient Fill Data Bars** to the **Quantity in Stock** column.

c. Create a table with headers using the range **A13:G87**. Apply **Table Style Light 9**. **Sort** the table from smallest to largest on the **Retail Price** column, and then filter the table on the **Sport** column to display the **Skiing** types. Display a **Total Row** in the table and then in cell **A88**, **Sum** the **Quantity in Stock** for the **Skiing** items. Type the result in cell **B11**. Remove the total row from the table, clear the **Sport** filter so that all of the data displays, and then convert the table to a range.

d. Change the **Print Titles** option so that **row 13** prints at the top of each page. Insert the file name in the **left section** of the footer, set the orientation to **Landscape**, and center the worksheet horizontally. Return to **Normal** view.

e. Display the **Inventory Summary** sheet. In cell **B5**, enter a formula that references cell **B4** in the **Seattle Inventory** sheet so that the Seattle *Total Items in Stock* displays in **B5**. Create similar formulas to enter the **Average Price**, **Median Price, Lowest Price,** and **Highest Price** in the range **B6:B9**. Enter similar formulas in the range **C5:C9** so that the **Denver** totals display. Be sure the range **B6:C9** is formatted with **Accounting Number Format**. Insert the file name in the **left section** of the footer, set the orientation to **Portrait**, and center the worksheet horizontally. Return to **Normal** view. **Save** the workbook.

5 Display the **Annual Expenses** worksheet. Construct formulas to calculate the *Totals by Quarter* in the range **B10:E10** and the *Annual Totals* in the range **F5:F10**.

a. Using absolute cell references as necessary, in cell **G5**, construct a formula to calculate the *% of Total* by dividing the **Sales Expense Annual Total** by the **Annual Totals by Quarter**. Apply **Percent Style**, fill the formula down through the range **G6:G9**, and **Center** the percentages.

(Business Running Case: Front Range Action Sports continues on the next page)

Front Range Action Sports (continued)

b. Apply appropriate financial formatting to the data using no decimal places, and apply the **Total** cell style to the *Totals by Quarter*. **Center** the column headings and apply the **Heading 4** cell style.

c. **Merge & Center** the worksheet title and subtitle across columns **A:G**, and then to cell **A1**, apply the **Title** style and to cell **A2**, apply the **Heading 1** style. To the range **A1:A2**, apply a **Fill Color** using **Dark Blue, Accent 3, Lighter 60%**.

d. Using the data in the nonadjacent ranges **B4:E4** and **B10:E10**, insert a **Line with Markers** chart. Position the upper left corner of the chart slightly inside cell **B12** and resize the chart so that the lower right corner is inside cell **F25**. Remove the **Legend** and then add a **Chart Title** above the chart with the text **2012 Direct Expenses**

e. Apply chart **Style 13**, and then format the **Chart Area** with the picture **eBRC1_Skiing** from your student files. Format the **Plot Area** by changing the **Fill** option to **No fill**. Edit the **Vertical (Value) Axis** so that the **Minimum** is **8000000** and the **Major unit** is **1000000**

6 Use **Format Painter** to copy the formatting from cell **A2** to **A27**. In cell **B32**, enter a formula that references the value in cell **F10**.

a. Using absolute cell references as necessary, in cell **C32**, construct a formula to calculate the projected expenses for 2013 after the *Forecasted increase* in cell **B29** is applied. Fill the formula through cell **F32**. If necessary, use Format Painter to copy the format in cell B32 to the remaining cells in the row.

b. On the **Page Layout tab**, in the **Scale to Fit group**, set both the **Width** and **Height** to scale to **1 page**. Insert the file name in the **left section** of the footer, set the orientation to **Landscape**, and center the worksheet horizontally. Return to **Normal** view. Display the **Document Properties**. Add your name, your course name and section, and the keywords **annual report**

c. **Save** your workbook. Select all the sheets, and then display and check the Print Preview. There are a total of 10 pages. Print or submit electronically as directed. If required by your instructor, print or create an electronic version of your worksheets with formulas displayed by using the instructions in Activity 1.16, and then **Close** Excel without saving so that you do not save the changes you made to print formulas.

End **You have completed Business Running Case 1** ————————

Use Financial and Lookup Functions, Define Names, and Validate Data

OUTCOMES

At the end of this chapter you will be able to:

OBJECTIVES

Mastering these objectives will enable you to:

PROJECT 4A
Calculate loan options and create a loan amortization schedule.

1. Use Financial Functions (p. 243)
2. Use Goal Seek (p. 246)
3. Create a Data Table (p. 249)

PROJECT 4B
Automate workbooks to look up information automatically and to validate data.

4. Define Names (p. 257)
5. Use Defined Names in a Formula (p. 265)
6. Use Lookup Functions (p. 267)
7. Validate Data (p. 273)

Natalia Barsukova/Shutterstock

In This Chapter

In this chapter, you will use Financial functions and What-If Analysis tools to make your worksheets more valuable for analyzing data and making financial decisions. In addition, you will define names and use them in a formula. You will use the lookup functions to locate information that is needed in a form and create a validation list to ensure that only accurate data is entered.

The projects in this chapter relate to **Rubanne Specialties**, a Montreal-based retailer of quality leather and fabric accessories for men and women. Products include wallets, belts, handbags, key chains, backpacks, business cases, and travel bags. The company distributes its products to department and specialty stores in the United States and Canada.

Project 4A Amortization Schedule

myitlab
Project 4A Training

Project Activities

In Activities 4.01 through 4.05, you will create a worksheet for Yvonne Dubois, International Sales Director for Rubanne Specialties, that details the loan information to purchase furniture and fixtures for a new store in Chicago. Your completed worksheet will look similar to Figure 4.1.

Project Files

For Project 4A, you will need the following file:

e04A_Store_Loan

You will save your workbook as:

Lastname_Firstname_4A_Store_Loan

Project Results

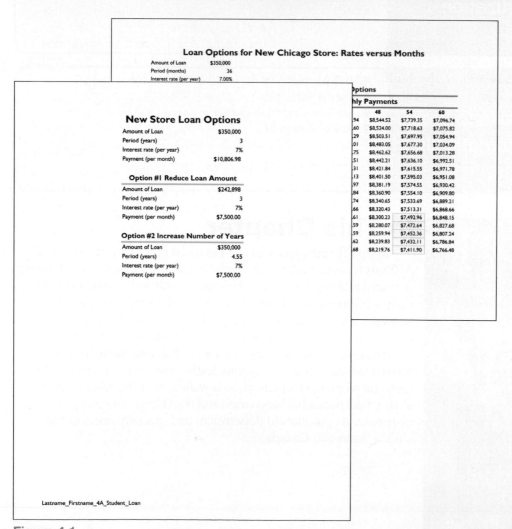

Figure 4.1
Project 4A Amortization Schedule

Objective 1 | Use Financial Functions

Financial functions are prebuilt formulas that make common business calculations such as calculating a loan payment on a vehicle or calculating how much to save each month to buy something. Financial functions commonly involve a period of time such as months or years.

When you borrow money from a bank or other lender, the amount charged to you for your use of the borrowed money is called *interest*. Loans are typically made for a period of years, and the interest that must be paid is a percentage of the loan amount that is still owed. In Excel, this interest percentage is called the *rate*.

The initial amount of the loan is called the *Present value (Pv)*, which is the total amount that a series of future payments is worth now, and is also known as the *principal*. When you borrow money, the loan amount is the present value to the lender. The number of time periods—number of payments—is abbreviated *nper*. The value at the end of the time periods is the *Future value (Fv)*—the cash balance you want to attain after the last payment is made. The future value is usually zero for loans.

Activity 4.01 | Inserting the PMT Financial Function

In this activity, you will calculate the monthly payments that Rubanne Specialties must make to finance the purchase of the furniture and fixtures for the new store in Chicago, the total cost of which is $350,000. You will calculate the monthly payments, including interest, for a three-year loan at an annual interest rate of 4.0%. To stay within Yvonne's budget, the monthly payment must be approximately $7,500.

1 **Start** Excel. From your student files, open **e04A_Store_Loan**. Display the **Save As** dialog box, navigate to the location where you will store your workbooks for this chapter, and then create a new folder named **Excel Chapter 4** Open your new folder, and then **Save** the workbook as **Lastname_Firstname_4A_Store_Loan**

2 In the range **A2:B5**, enter the following row titles and data. Recall that you can format the numbers as you type by typing them with their symbols as shown. Compare your screen with Figure 4.2:

Amount of Loan	$350,000
Period (years)	3
Interest rate (per year)	7%
Payment (per month)	

Figure 4.2

Your name in workbook title

Row titles and data entered in range A2:B5

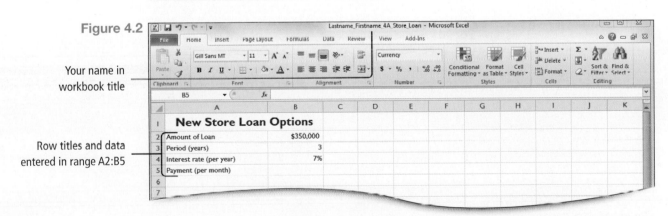

3 Click cell **B5**. On the **Formulas tab**, in the **Function Library group**, click the **Financial** button. In the displayed list, scroll down as necessary, and then click **PMT**.

> The Function Arguments dialog box displays. Recall that *arguments* are the values that an Excel function uses to perform calculations or operations.

4 If necessary, drag the Function Arguments dialog box to the right side of your screen so you can view columns A:B.

> The *PMT function* calculates the payment for a loan based on constant payments and at a constant interest rate. To complete the PMT function, first you must determine the total number of loan payment periods (months), which is 12 months x 3 years, or 36 months.

<table>
<tr><td>Another Way
Click cell B4 and then type /12.</td></tr>
</table>

5 With your insertion point positioned in the **Rate** box, type **b4/12** and then compare your screen with Figure 4.3.

> Excel will divide the annual interest rate of 7%, which is 0.07 in decimal notation, located in cell B4 by 12 (months), which will result in a *monthly* interest rate.

> When borrowing money, the interest rate and number of periods are quoted in years. The payments on a loan, however, are usually made monthly. Therefore, the number of periods, which is stated in years, and the *annual* interest rate, must be changed to a monthly equivalent in order to calculate the monthly payment amount. You can see that calculations like these can be made as part of the argument in a function.

Figure 4.3

Function Arguments dialog box

Cell B4 contains the interest rate

Rate entered

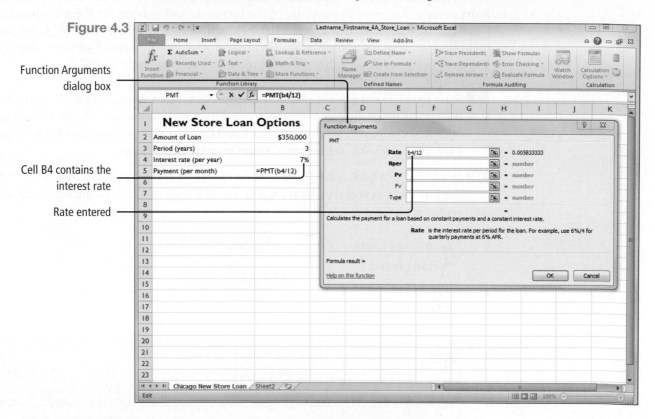

6 Press `Tab` to move the insertion point to the **Nper** box. In the lower portion of the dialog box, notice Excel points out that *Nper is the total number of payments for the loan* (number of periods).

7 Type **b3*12** to have Excel convert the number of years in the loan in cell B3 (3 years) to the total number of months.

> Recall that the PMT function calculates a *monthly* payment. Thus, all values in the function must be expressed in months.

8 Press `Tab` to move to the **Pv** box, and then type **b2** to indicate the cell that contains the amount of the loan.

> Pv represents the present value—the amount of the loan before any payments are made—in this instance $350,000.

9 In cell **B5** and on the **Formula Bar**, notice that the arguments that comprise the PMT function are separated by commas. Notice also, in the **Function Arguments** dialog box, that the value of each argument displays to the right of the argument box. Compare your screen with Figure 4.4.

Figure 4.4

Formula displayed in Formula Bar; arguments separated by commas

Cell references entered for PMT function

Optional arguments

Argument values

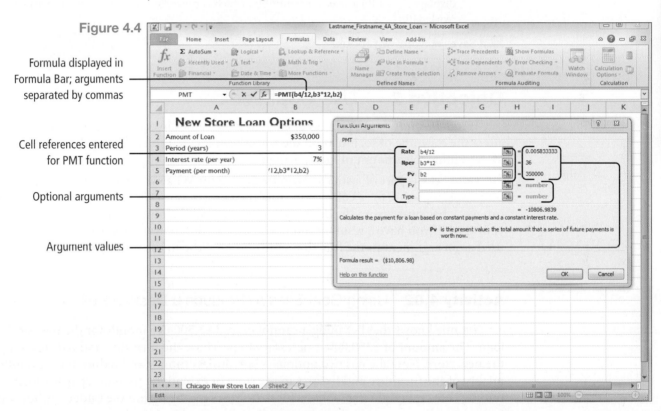

> **Note** | Optional Arguments
>
> The PMT function has two arguments not indicated by bold; these are optional. The Future value (Fv) argument assumes that the unpaid portion of the loan should be zero at the end of the last period. The *Type argument* assumes that the payment will be made at the end of each period. These default values are typical of most loans and may be left blank.

10 In the lower right corner of the **Function Arguments** dialog box, click **OK**.

The monthly payment amount—(*$10,806.98*)—displays in cell B5. The amount displays in red and in parentheses to show that it is a negative number, a number that will be *paid out*. This monthly payment of $10,806.98 is over the budget of $7,500 per month that Yvonne has in mind.

11 Click in the **Formula Bar**, and then by using the arrow keys on the keyboard, position the insertion point between the equal sign and *PMT*. Type **–** (minus sign) to insert a minus sign into the formula, and then press Enter.

By placing a minus sign in the formula, the monthly payment amount, $10,806.98, displays in cell B5 as a *positive* number, which is more familiar and less distracting to work with.

12 Save 💾 your workbook.

Objective 2 | Use Goal Seek

What-If Analysis is a process of changing the values in cells to see how those changes affect the outcome of formulas on the worksheet; for example, varying the interest rate to determine the amount of loan payments.

Goal Seek is part of a suite of data tools used for What-If Analysis. It is a method to find a specific value for a cell by adjusting the value of one other cell. With Goal Seek, you can work backward from the desired outcome to find the number necessary to achieve your goal. If you have a result in mind, you can try different numbers in one of the cells used as an argument in the function until you get close to the result you want.

Activity 4.02 | Using Goal Seek to Produce a Desired Result

Yvonne knows that her budget cannot exceed $7,500 per month for the new store loan. The amount of $350,000 is necessary to purchase the furniture and fixtures to open the new store. Now she has two options—borrow less money and reduce the amount or quality of the furniture and fixtures in the store or extend the time to repay the loan. To find out how much she can borrow for three years to stay within the budget or how much to increase the repayment period, you will use the Goal Seek tool.

1 Click cell **B5**. On the **Data tab**, in the **Data Tools group**, click the **What-If Analysis** button, and then in the displayed list, click **Goal Seek**. In the **Goal Seek** dialog box, in the **Set cell** box, confirm that *B5* displays.

The cell address in this box is the cell that will display the desired result.

2 Press Tab. In the **To value** box, type the payment goal of **7500.00** and press Tab. In the **By changing cell** box, type **b2**, which is the amount of the loan, and then compare your dialog box with Figure 4.5.

Figure 4.5

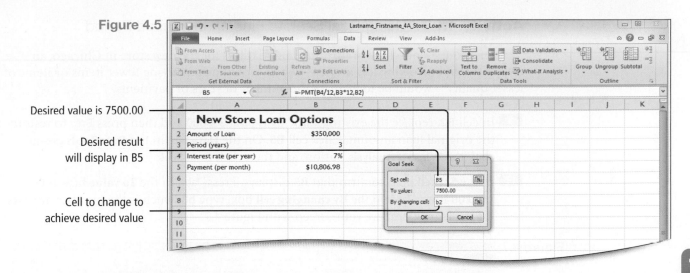

Desired value is 7500.00

Desired result
will display in B5

Cell to change to
achieve desired value

3 Click **OK**, and then in the displayed **Goal Seek Status** dialog box, click **OK**.

Excel's calculations indicate that to achieve a monthly payment of $7,500.00 using a 3-year loan, Yvonne can borrow only *$242,898*—not $350,000.

4 Click cell **A7**. Type **Option #1 Reduce Loan Amount** and then on the **Formula Bar**, click the **Enter** button ☑ to keep the cell active. **Merge and Center** ☒ this heading across the range **A7:B7**, on the **Home tab**, display the **Cell Styles** gallery, and then apply the **Heading 2** cell style.

Another Way

Click cell A8, right-click, and then click Paste Special. In the Paste Special dialog box, under Paste, click the Values and number formats option button, and then click OK.

5 Select the range **A2:B5**, right click, and then click **Copy**. Point to cell **A8**, right-click, point to **Paste Special**, and then under **Paste Values,** click the **second** button—**Values & Number Formatting (A)**. Press [Esc] to cancel the moving border.

→ **6** **Save** 🖫 your workbook, click anywhere to deselect, and then compare your worksheet with Figure 4.6.

Recall that by using the Paste Special command, you can copy the *value* in a cell, rather than the formula, and the cell formats are retained—cell B5 contains the PMT function formula, and here you need only the value that *results* from that formula.

Figure 4.6

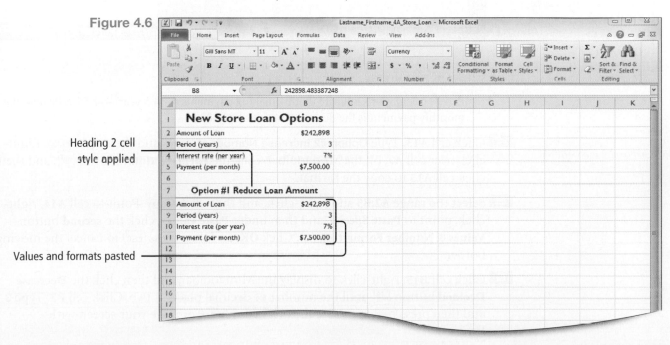

Heading 2 cell
style applied

Values and formats pasted

Activity 4.03 | Using Goal Seek to Find an Increased Period

For Yvonne's purchase of furniture and fixtures for the new store in Chicago, an alternative to borrowing less money—which would mean buying fewer items or items of lesser quality—would be to increase the number of years of payments.

1 In cell **B2**, replace the existing value by typing **350000** and then press Enter to restore the original loan amount. Click cell **B5**. On the **Data tab**, in the **Data Tools group**, click the **What-If Analysis** button, and then click **Goal Seek**.

2 In the **Set cell** box, confirm that **B5** displays. Press Tab. In the **To value** box, type **7500.00** Press Tab. In the **By changing cell** box, type **b3** which is the number of years for the loan. Compare your screen with Figure 4.7.

Figure 4.7

Original loan amount $350,000 restored

Cell with the number of payment periods indicated as the *change* cell

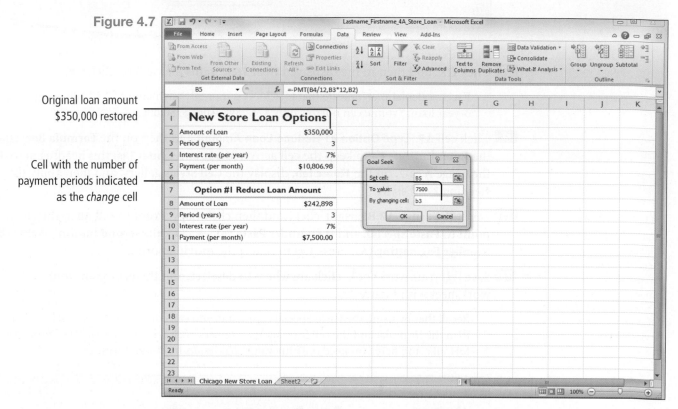

3 Click **OK** two times.

> Excel's calculations indicate that by making payments for 4.5 years—*4.552648969*—the monthly payment is the desired amount of $7,500.00.

4 Click cell **A13**. Type **Option #2 Increase Number of Years** and then press Enter. Right-click over cell **A7**, on the Mini toolbar, click the **Format Painter** button, and then click cell **A13** to copy the format.

5 Select the range **A2:B5** and right-click, and then click **Copy**. Point to cell **A14**, right-click, point to **Paste Special**, and then under **Paste Values**, click the **second** button— **Values & Number Formatting (A)**. Click **OK**, and then press Esc to cancel the moving border.

6 Click cell **B15**, right-click to display the Mini toolbar, and then click the **Decrease Decimal** button until the number of decimal places is two. Click cell **B3**. Type **3** and then press Enter to restore the original value. Compare your screen with Figure 4.8.

Figure 4.8

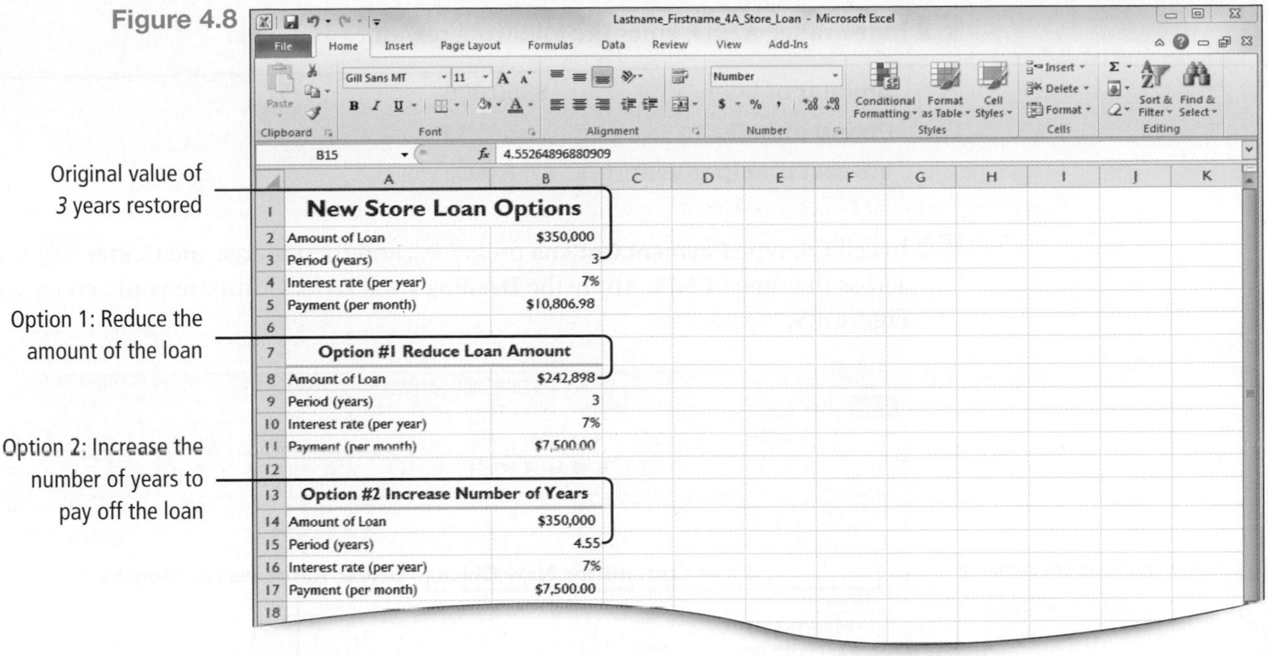

Original value of
3 years restored

Option 1: Reduce the
amount of the loan

Option 2: Increase the
number of years to
pay off the loan

7 Save 🖫 your workbook.

Objective 3 | Create a Data Table

A *data table* is a range of cells that shows how changing certain values in your formulas affects the results of those formulas. Data tables make it easy to calculate multiple versions in one operation, and then to view and compare the results of all the different variations.

For example, banks may offer loans at different rates for different periods of time, which require different payments. By using a data table, you can calculate the possible values for each argument.

A *one-variable data table* changes the value in only one cell. For example, use a one-variable data table if you want to see how different interest rates affect a monthly payment. A *two-variable data table* changes the values in two cells—for example, if you want to see how different interest rates *and* different payment periods will affect a monthly payment.

Activity 4.04 | Designing a Two-Variable Data Table

Recall that the PMT function has three required arguments: Present value (Pv), Rate, and Number of periods (Nper). Because Yvonne would still like to borrow $350,000 and purchase the fixtures and furniture that she has selected for the new store in Chicago, in this data table, the present value will *not* change. The two values that *will* change are the Rate and Number of periods. Possible periods will range from 24 months (2 years) to 60 months (5 years) and the Rate will vary from 8% to 6%.

1 Double-click the **Sheet2 tab**, rename it **Payment Table** and then press Enter.

2 In cell **A1**, type **Loan Options for New Chicago Store: Rates versus Months** and then press Enter. **Merge and Center** 🔲 this title across the range **A1:I1**, and then apply the **Title** cell style.

3 In the range **A2:B4**, enter the following row titles and data:

Amount of Loan	$350,000
Period (months)	36
Interest rate (per year)	7.00%

4 In cell **C5**, type **Payment Options** press Enter, and then **Merge and Center** ⊞ this title across the range **C5:I5**. Apply the **Heading 1** cell style. Compare your screen with Figure 4.9.

Figure 4.9

Payment Options centered across range C5:I5

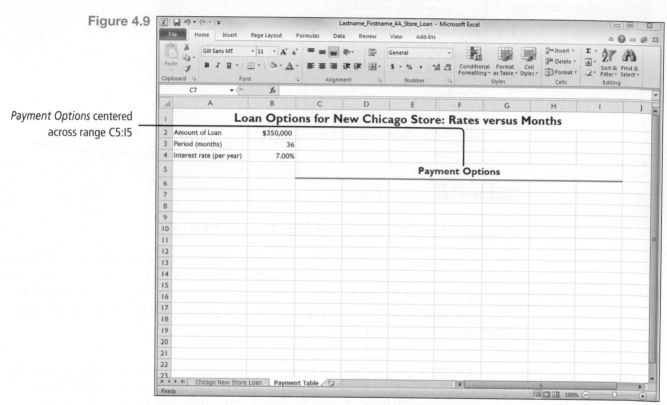

5 In cell **C6**, type **Number of Monthly Payments** press Enter, and then use the **Format Painter** ✅ to apply the format of cell **C5** to cell **C6**.

6 In cell **C7**, type **24** and then press Tab. Type **30** and then press Tab. Select the range **C7:D7**, point to the fill handle, and then drag to the right through cell **I7** to fill in a pattern of months from 24 to 60 in increments of six months.

> Recall that the Auto Fill feature will duplicate a pattern of values that you set in the beginning cells.

7 In cell **B8**, type **8.000%** and then press Enter. In cell **B9**, type **7.875%** and then press Enter.

> Excel rounds both values up to two decimal places.

8 Select the range **B8:B9**. Point to the fill handle, and then drag down through cell **B24** to fill a pattern of interest rates in increments of .125 from 8.00% down to 6.00%.

9 Right-click anywhere over the selected range, and then on the Mini toolbar, click the **Increase Decimal** button ⊞ one time. **Save** ⊞ your workbook. Compare your screen with Figure 4.10.

Row 7 represents the number of monthly payments, and column B represents a range of possible annual interest rates. These two arguments will be used to calculate varying payment arrangements for a loan of $350,000.

Figure 4.10

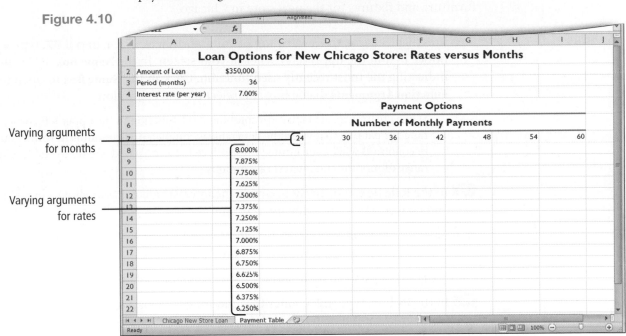

Varying arguments for months

Varying arguments for rates

10 In cell **A8**, type **Rates** and then press ⏎. Select the range **A8:A24**. On the **Home tab**, in the **Alignment group**, click the **Merge and Center** button ⊞, click the **Align Text Right** button ⊞, and then click the **Middle Align** button ⊞. Display the **Cell Styles** gallery, and then under **Data and Model**, apply the **Explanatory Text** style. Compare your screen with Figure 4.11.

Figure 4.11

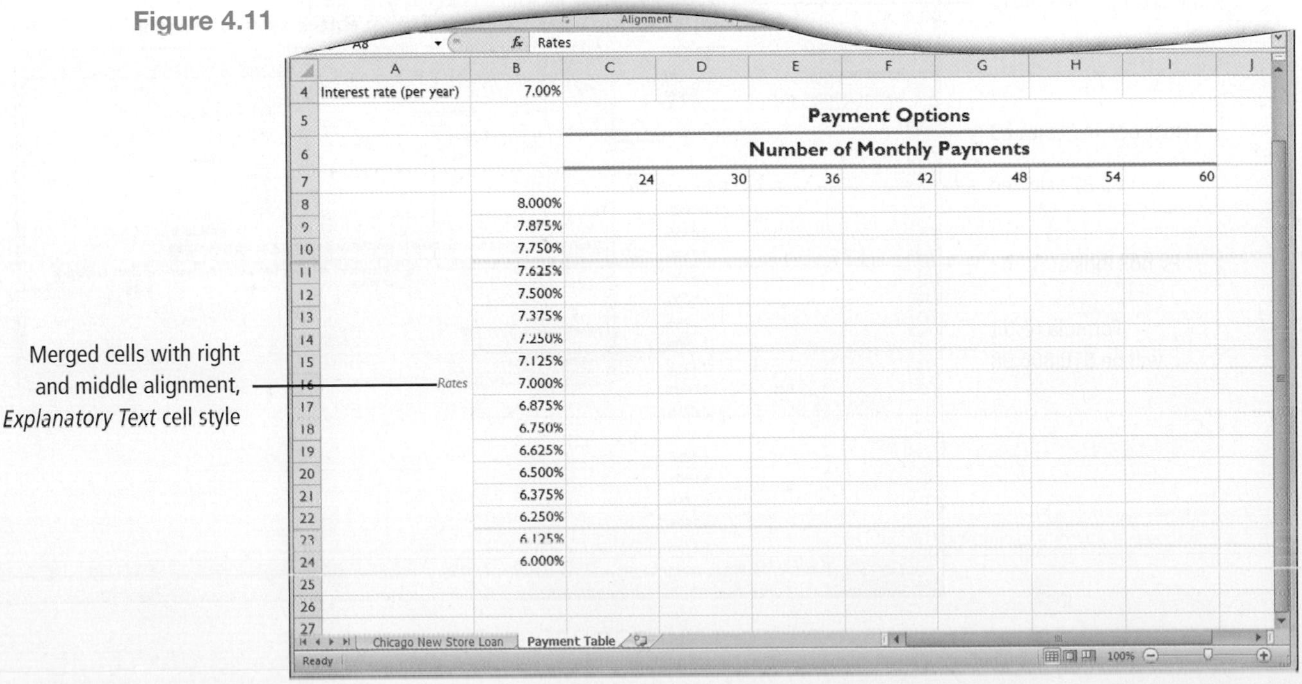

Merged cells with right and middle alignment, *Explanatory Text* cell style

Activity 4.05 | Using a Data Table to Calculate Options

Recall that a data table is a range of cells that shows how changing certain values in your formulas affects the results of those formulas.

In this activity, you will create a table of payments for every combination of payment periods, which are represented by the column titles under *Number of Monthly Payments*, and interest rates, which are represented by the row titles to the right of *Rates*. From the resulting table, Yvonne can find a combination of payment periods and interest rates that will enable her to go forward with her plan to borrow $350,000 to purchase the necessary furniture and fixtures for the new store in Chicago.

Another Way

Use one of the other methods you have practiced to insert the PMT function.

1 Press Ctrl + Home to view the top of your worksheet. Then, in cell **B7**, type **=** and notice that in the upper left corner of your screen, in the **Name Box**, *PMT* displays indicating the most recently used function. Click in the **Name Box** to open the **Function Arguments** dialog box and select the **PMT** function.

When creating a data table, you enter the PMT function in the upper left corner of your range of data, so that when the data table is completed, the months in row 7 and the rates in column B will be substituted into each cell's formula and will fill the table with the range of months and interest rate options.

2 In the **Rate** box, type **b4/12** to divide the interest rate per year shown in cell B4 by 12 and convert it to a monthly interest rate.

3 Press Tab to move the insertion point to the **Nper** box. Type **b3** which is the cell that contains the number of months, and then press Tab.

The periods in cell B3 are already stated in months and do not need to be changed.

4 In the **Pv** box, type **-b2** to enter the amount of the loan as a negative number. Compare your dialog box with Figure 4.12.

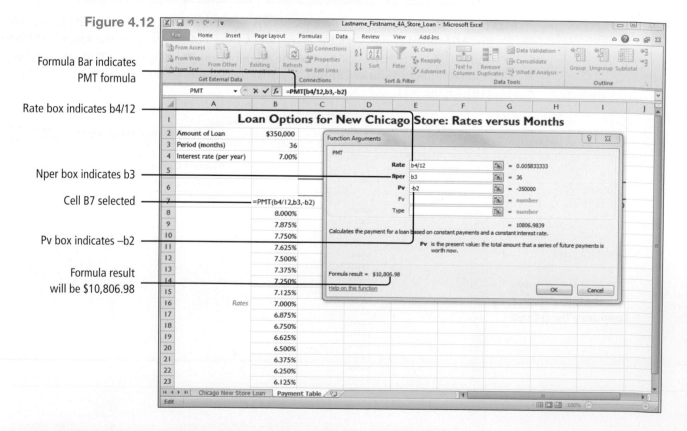

Figure 4.12

Formula Bar indicates PMT formula

Rate box indicates b4/12

Nper box indicates b3

Cell B7 selected

Pv box indicates –b2

Formula result will be $10,806.98

5 Click **OK** to close the **Function Arguments** dialog box and display the result in cell **B7**.

The payment—*10,806.98*—is calculated by using the values in cells B2, B3, and B4. This is the same payment that you calculated on the first worksheet. Now it displays as a positive number because you entered the loan amount in cell B2 as a negative number.

6 Select the range **B7:I24**, which encompasses all of the months and all of the rates. With the range **B7:I24** selected, on the **Data tab**, in the **Data Tools group**, click the **What-If Analysis** button, and then in the displayed list, click **Data Table**.

7 In the **Data Table** dialog box, in the **Row input cell** box, type **b3** and then press [Tab]. In the **Column input cell** box, type **b4** and then compare your screen with Figure 4.13.

The row of months will be substituted for the value in cell B3, and the column of interest rates will be substituted for the value in cell B4.

Figure 4.13

Selected area indicates data table range

Row values substituted for months

Column values substituted for interest rates

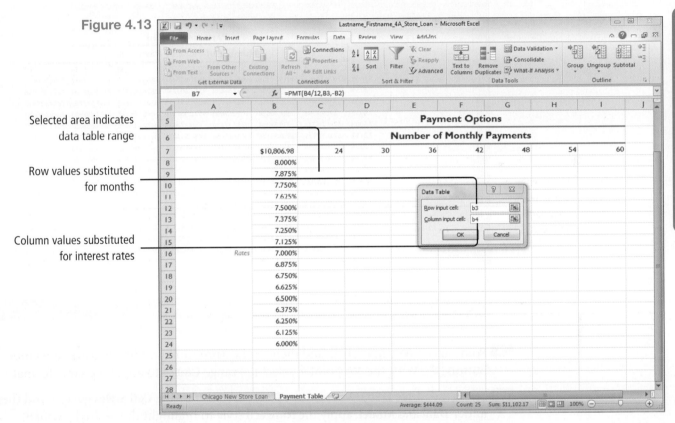

8 Click **OK**. Click cell **H20**, and then examine the formula in the **Formula Bar**. Compare your screen with Figure 4.14.

The table is filled with payment options that use the month and interest rate corresponding to the position in the table. Thus, if Yvonne chooses a combination of 54 months at an interest rate of 6.5%, the monthly payment will be $7,492.96, which is almost the exact monthly payment she wanted. The data table is one of a group of Excel's What-If Analysis tools.

Figure 4.14

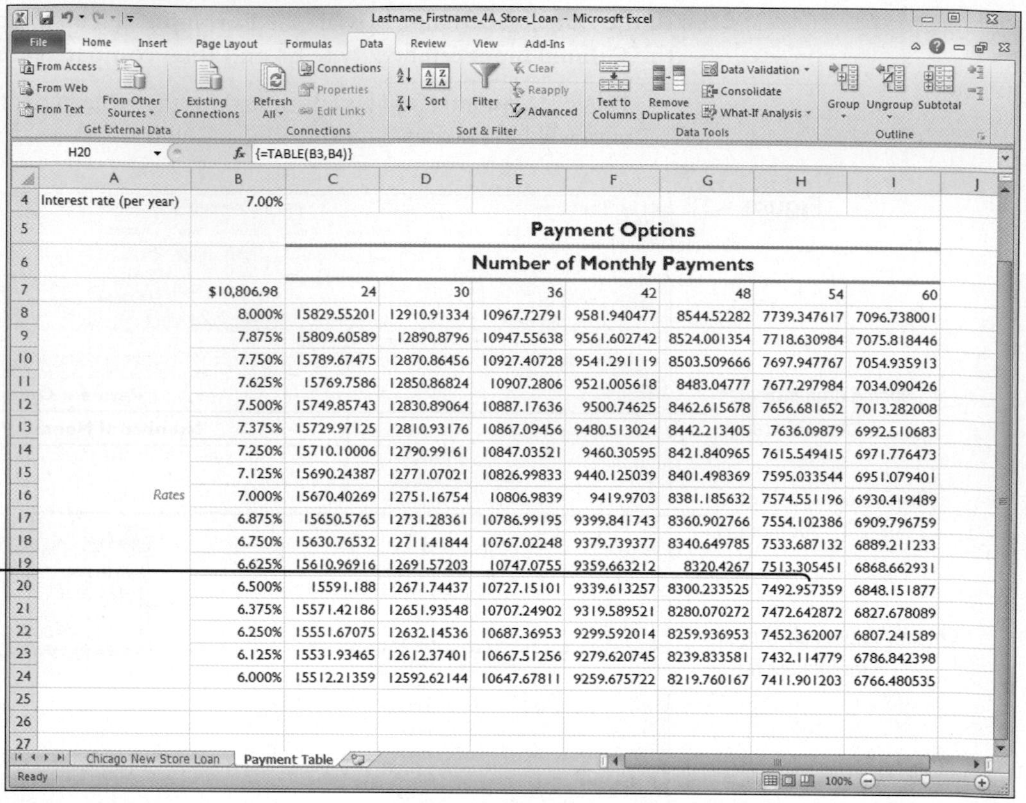

Period of 54 months, at 6.500% interest, results in payment of 7492.957359

Formula bar: {=TABLE(B3,B4)}

	A	B	C	D	E	F	G	H	I
4	Interest rate (per year)	7.00%							
5					**Payment Options**				
6					**Number of Monthly Payments**				
7		$10,806.98	24	30	36	42	48	54	60
8		8.000%	15829.55201	12910.91334	10967.72791	9581.940477	8544.52282	7739.347617	7096.738001
9		7.875%	15809.60589	12890.8796	10947.55638	9561.602742	8524.001354	7718.630984	7075.818446
10		7.750%	15789.67475	12870.86456	10927.40728	9541.291119	8503.509666	7697.947767	7054.935913
11		7.625%	15769.7586	12850.86824	10907.2806	9521.005618	8483.04777	7677.297984	7034.090426
12		7.500%	15749.85743	12830.89064	10887.17636	9500.74625	8462.615678	7656.681652	7013.282008
13		7.375%	15729.97125	12810.93176	10867.09456	9480.513024	8442.213405	7636.09879	6992.510683
14		7.250%	15710.10006	12790.99161	10847.03521	9460.30595	8421.840965	7615.549415	6971.776473
15		7.125%	15690.24387	12771.07021	10826.99833	9440.125039	8401.498369	7595.033544	6951.079401
16	Rates	7.000%	15670.40269	12751.16754	10806.9839	9419.9703	8381.185632	7574.551196	6930.419489
17		6.875%	15650.5765	12731.28361	10786.99195	9399.841743	8360.902766	7554.102386	6909.796759
18		6.750%	15630.76532	12711.41844	10767.02248	9379.739377	8340.649785	7533.687132	6889.211233
19		6.625%	15610.96916	12691.57203	10747.0755	9359.663212	8320.4267	7513.305451	6868.662931
20		6.500%	15591.188	12671.74437	10727.15101	9339.613257	8300.233525	7492.957359	6848.151877
21		6.375%	15571.42186	12651.93548	10707.24902	9319.589521	8280.070272	7472.642872	6827.678089
22		6.250%	15551.67075	12632.14536	10687.36953	9299.592014	8259.936953	7452.362007	6807.241589
23		6.125%	15531.93465	12612.37401	10667.51256	9279.620745	8239.833581	7432.114779	6786.842398
24		6.000%	15512.21359	12592.62144	10647.67811	9259.675722	8219.760167	7411.901203	6766.480535
25									
26									
27									

Sheet tabs: Chicago New Store Loan | Payment Table

9 Point to cell **B7**, right-click, and then on the Mini toolbar, click the **Format Painter** button. With the pointer, select the range **C8:I24** to apply the same format.

10 Select the range **H20:H24**. From the **Home tab**, display the **Cell Styles** gallery, and then under **Data and Model**, apply the **Note** cell style to highlight the desired payment options.

11 Select the range **B8:B24**, hold down Ctrl, and then select the range **C7:I7**. Right-click over the selection, and then from the Mini toolbar, apply **Bold** B and **Center**. Click anywhere to deselect the range, and then compare your worksheet with Figure 4.15.

By using a data table of payment options, you can see that Yvonne must get a loan for at least 54 months (4.5 years) for any of the interest rates between 6.500% and 6.00% in order to purchase the furniture and fixtures she wants and still keep the monthly payment at approximately $7,500.

Figure 4.15

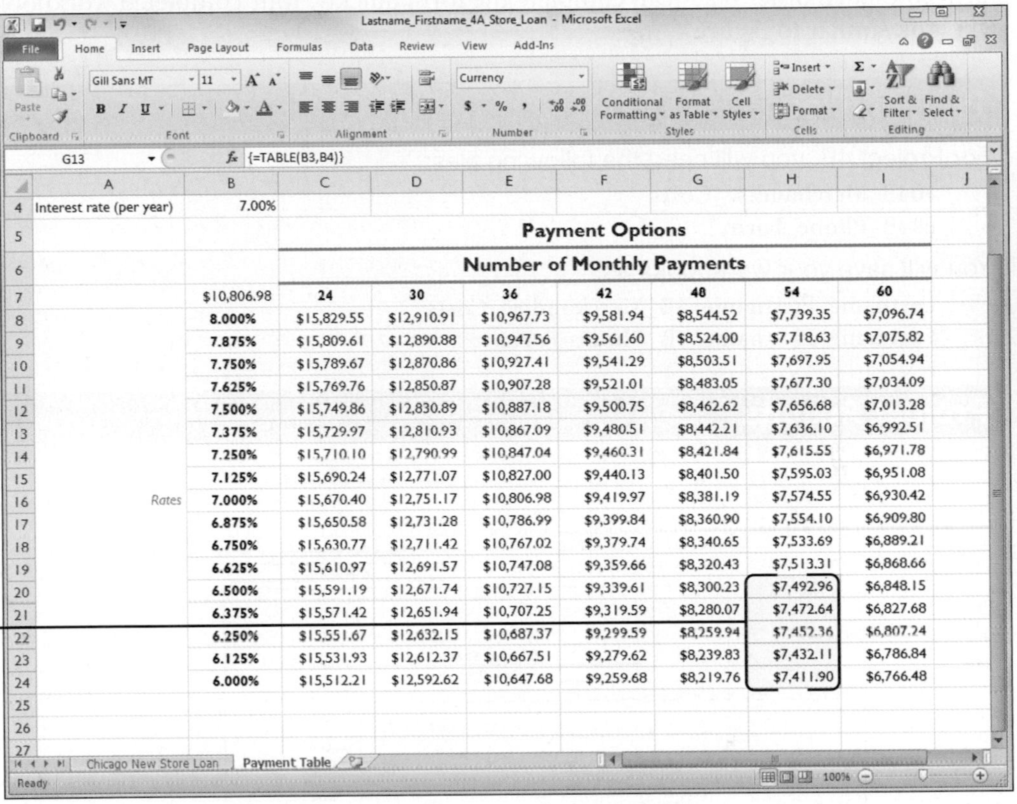

	A	B	C	D	E	F	G	H	I
4	Interest rate (per year)	7.00%							
5			Payment Options						
6			Number of Monthly Payments						
7		$10,806.98	24	30	36	42	48	54	60
8		8.000%	$15,829.55	$12,910.91	$10,967.73	$9,581.94	$8,544.52	$7,739.35	$7,096.74
9		7.875%	$15,809.61	$12,890.88	$10,947.56	$9,561.60	$8,524.00	$7,718.63	$7,075.82
10		7.750%	$15,789.67	$12,870.86	$10,927.41	$9,541.29	$8,503.51	$7,697.95	$7,054.94
11		7.625%	$15,769.76	$12,850.87	$10,907.28	$9,521.01	$8,483.05	$7,677.30	$7,034.09
12		7.500%	$15,749.86	$12,830.89	$10,887.18	$9,500.75	$8,462.62	$7,656.68	$7,013.28
13		7.375%	$15,729.97	$12,810.93	$10,867.09	$9,480.51	$8,442.21	$7,636.10	$6,992.51
14		7.250%	$15,710.10	$12,790.99	$10,847.04	$9,460.31	$8,421.84	$7,615.55	$6,971.78
15		7.125%	$15,690.24	$12,771.07	$10,827.00	$9,440.13	$8,401.50	$7,595.03	$6,951.08
16	Rates	7.000%	$15,670.40	$12,751.17	$10,806.98	$9,419.97	$8,381.19	$7,574.55	$6,930.42
17		6.875%	$15,650.58	$12,731.28	$10,786.99	$9,399.84	$8,360.90	$7,554.10	$6,909.80
18		6.750%	$15,630.77	$12,711.42	$10,767.02	$9,379.74	$8,340.65	$7,533.69	$6,889.21
19		6.625%	$15,610.97	$12,691.57	$10,747.08	$9,359.66	$8,320.43	$7,513.31	$6,868.66
20		6.500%	$15,591.19	$12,671.74	$10,727.15	$9,339.61	$8,300.23	$7,492.96	$6,848.15
21		6.375%	$15,571.42	$12,651.94	$10,707.25	$9,319.59	$8,280.07	$7,472.64	$6,827.68
22		6.250%	$15,551.67	$12,632.15	$10,687.37	$9,299.59	$8,259.94	$7,452.36	$6,807.24
23		6.125%	$15,531.93	$12,612.37	$10,667.51	$9,279.62	$8,239.83	$7,432.11	$6,786.84
24		6.000%	$15,512.21	$12,592.62	$10,647.68	$9,259.68	$8,219.76	$7,411.90	$6,766.48

For a 54-month period, loan options in this range will be within the budget

12 With the two sheets grouped, insert a footer in the **left section** that includes the **file name**. Click outside the footer area, open the **Page Setup** dialog box, click the **Margins tab**, and then center the sheets **Horizontally**. On the status bar, click the **Normal** button. Ungroup the sheets, and click on the **Payment Table sheet**. On the **Page Layout tab**, set the orientation to **Landscape**. Press Ctrl + Home to move to the top of the worksheet.

13 From **Backstage** view, display the **Document Panel**. In the **Author** box, delete any text, and then type your firstname and lastname. In the **Subject** box, type your course name and section number, and in the **Keywords** box, type **amortization schedule, payment table Close** X the **Document Panel**.

14 Press Ctrl + F2, examine the **Print Preview**, make any necessary adjustments, and then **Save** your workbook.

15 Print or submit the two worksheets in this workbook electronically as directed by your instructor. If required, print or create an electronic version of your worksheets with formulas displayed using the instructions in Activity 1.16 in Project 1A.

End **You have completed Project 4A**

Project 4B Quarterly Cost Report and Lookup Form

myitlab
Project 4B Training

Project Activities

In Activities 4.06 through 4.13, you will assist Connor Fereday, the Vice President of Marketing at Rubanne Specialties, by defining names for ranges of cells in a workbook containing quarterly merchandise costs and by adding lookup functions to a phone order form so that an order taker can complete the form quickly. Your completed workbooks will look similar to Figure 4.16.

Project Files

For Project 4B, you will need the following files:

e04B_Merchandise_Costs
e04B_Phone_Form

You will save your workbooks as:

Lastname_Firstname_4B_Merchandise_Costs
Lastname_Firstname_4B_Phone_Form

Project Results

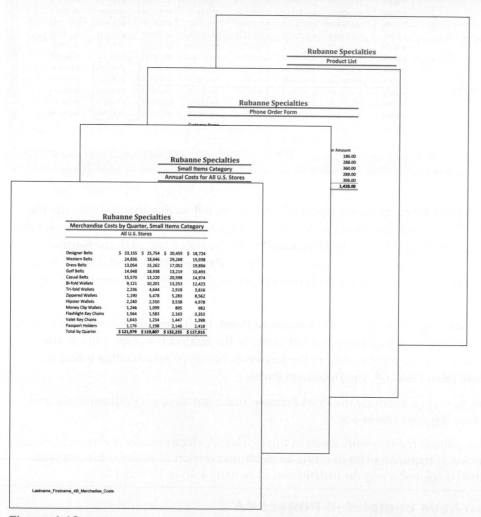

Figure 4.16

Project 4B Quarterly Cost Report and Lookup Form

Objective 4 | Define Names

A *name*, also referred to as a **defined name**, is a word or string of characters in Excel that represents a cell, a range of cells, a formula, or a constant value. A defined name that is distinctive and easy to remember typically defines the *purpose* of the selected cells. When creating a formula, the defined name may be used instead of the cell reference.

All names have a *scope*, which is the location within which the name is recognized without qualification. The scope of a name is usually either to a specific worksheet or to an entire workbook.

Activity 4.06 | Defining a Name

In this activity, you will use three ways to define a name for a cell or group of cells. After defining a name, you can use the name in a formula to refer to the cell or cells. Names make it easier for you and others to understand the meaning of formulas in a worksheet.

1 **Start** Excel. From your student files, open the file **e04B_Merchandise_Costs**, and then S**ave** the file in your **Excel Chapter 4** folder as **Lastname_Firstname_4B_Merchandise_Costs**

Another Way

With the range selected, use the keyboard shortcut [Alt] + [=] for the SUM function.

2 Select the range **B6:E18**, which includes the adjacent empty cells in **row 18**, and then click the **Sum** button [Σ]. Click anywhere to cancel the selection.

Use this technique to sum a group of columns or rows simultaneously.

3 Select the range **B6:E6**, hold down [Ctrl] and select the range **B18:E18**, and then from the **Cell Styles** gallery, under **Number Format**, apply the **Currency [0]** cell style. Select the range **B7:E17**, display the **Cell Styles** gallery, and then under **Number Format**, click **Comma [0]**.

You can use these number formats from the Cell Styles gallery in a manner similar to the Accounting Number Format button and the Comma Style button on the Ribbon. The advantage to using these styles from the Cell Styles gallery is that you can select the option that formats automatically with zero [0] decimal places.

4 Select the range **B18:E18**, and then from the **Cell Styles** gallery, apply the **Total** cell style. Press [Ctrl] + [Home] to move to the top of the worksheet, and then compare your screen with Figure 4.17.

Figure 4.17

Numbers formatted ⎯

Total cell style applied ⎯

Columns summed ⎯

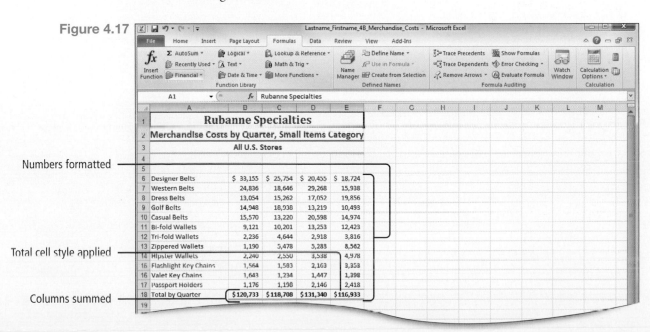

5 Select the range **B6:E9**. On the **Formulas tab**, in the **Defined Names group**, click the **Define Name** button. Compare your screen with Figure 4.18.

> The New Name dialog box displays. In the Name box, Excel suggests *Designer_Belts* as the name for this range of cells, which is the text in the first cell adjacent to the selected range. Excel will attempt to suggest a logical name for the selected cells.

Figure 4.18

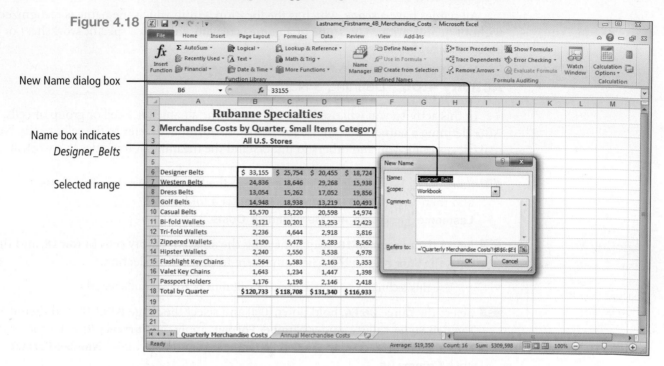

New Name dialog box

Name box indicates *Designer_Belts*

Selected range

6 With *Designer_Belts* highlighted, type **Belt_Costs** as the name.

> Naming cells has no effect on the displayed or underlying values; it simply creates an easy-to-remember name that you can use when creating formulas that refer to this range of cells.

7 At the bottom of the dialog box, at the right edge of the **Refers to** box, point to and click the **Collapse Dialog Box** button [icon]. Compare your screen with Figure 4.19.

> The dialog box collapses (shrinks) so that only the *Refers to* box is visible, and the selected range is surrounded by a moving border.

> When you define a name, the stored definition is an absolute cell reference and includes the worksheet name.

Figure 4.19

Collapsed dialog box

Selected range includes the worksheet name

Dollar signs ($) indicate absolute cell references

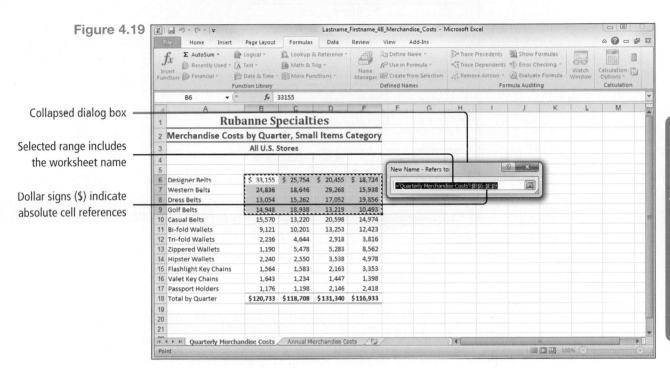

8 If necessary, drag the collapsed dialog box by its title bar to the right of your screen so that it is not blocking the selection. Then, change the range selection by selecting the range **B6:E10**.

> A moving border surrounds the new range. The range, formatted with absolute cell references, displays in the *Refers to* box of the collapsed dialog box. In this manner, it is easy to change the range of cells referred to by the name.

9 Click the **Expand Dialog Box** button [icon] to redisplay the entire **New Name** dialog box, and then click **OK**.

Another Way

Another method to define a name is to select the range, and then type a name in the Name Box.

10 Select the range **B11:E14**. In the upper left corner of the Excel window, to the left of the **Formula Bar**, click in the **Name Box**, and notice that the cell reference *B11* moves to the left edge of the box and is highlighted in blue. Type **Billfold_Costs** as shown in Figure 4.20.

Figure 4.20

Name Box arrow

Name Box indicates
Billfold_Costs

Selected range

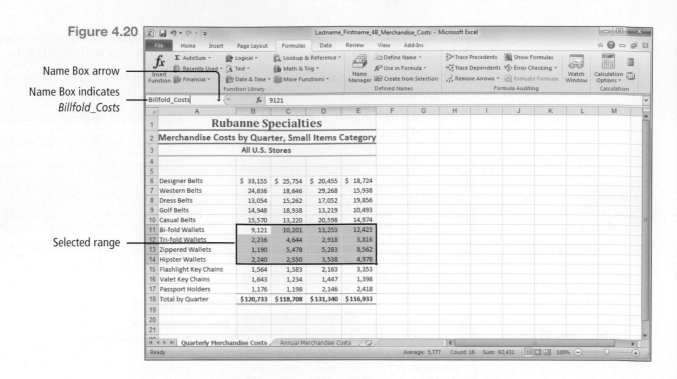

11 Press Enter, and then take a moment to study the rules for defining names, as described in the table in Figure 4.21.

Rules for Defining Names

The first character of the defined name must be a letter, an underscore (_), or a backslash (\).
After the first character, the remaining characters in the defined name can be letters, numbers, periods, and underscore characters.
Spaces are not valid in a defined name; use a period or the underscore character as a word separator, for example *1st.Quarter* or *1st_Qtr*.
The single letter *C* or *R* in either uppercase or lowercase cannot be defined as a name, because these letters are used by Excel for selecting a row or column when you enter them in a Name or a Go To text box.
A defined name can be no longer than 255 characters; short, meaningful names are the most useful.
Defined names cannot be the same as a cell reference, for example M$10.
Defined names can contain uppercase and lowercase letters, however Excel does not distinguish between them. Thus, for example, if you create the name *Sales* and then create another name *SALES* in the same workbook, Excel considers the names to be the same and prompts you for a unique name.

Figure 4.21

12 Click any cell to cancel the selection. Then, click the **Name Box arrow** and compare your screen with Figure 4.22.

> Your two defined names display in alphabetical order.

Figure 4.22

Name Box arrow

List of defined names

13 From the displayed list, click **Belt_Costs** and notice that Excel selects the range of values that comprise the cost of various Belt styles.

14 Click the **Name Box arrow** again, and then from the displayed list, click **Billfold_Costs** to select the range of values that comprise the Billfold costs.

15 Select the range **B15:E16**. On the **Formulas tab**, in the **Defined Names group**, click the **Name Manager** button, and notice that the two names that you have defined display in a list.

16 In the upper left corner of the **Name Manager** dialog box, click the **New** button. With *Flashlight_Key_Chains* highlighted, type **Key_Chain_Costs** and then click **OK**. Compare your screen with Figure 4.23.

> This is another method to define a name—by creating a new name in the Name Manager dialog box. The Name Manager dialog box displays the three range names that you have created, in alphabetical order.

Figure 4.23

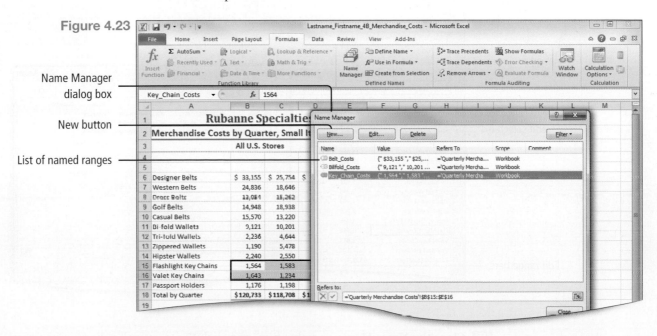

Name Manager dialog box

New button

List of named ranges

17 **Close** the **Name Manager** dialog box and **Save** your workbook.

Activity 4.07 | Inserting New Data into a Named Range

You can insert new data into the range of cells that a name represents. In this activity, you will modify the range named *Billfold_Costs* to include new data.

Another Way

With the row selected, on the Home tab, in the Cells group, click the Insert button arrow, and then click Insert Sheet Rows.

1 On the left side of your window, in the **row heading area**, click the **row 15** heading to select the entire row. Right-click over the selected row, and then click **Insert** to insert a new blank row above.

A new row 15 is inserted, and the remaining rows move down one row. Recall that when new rows are inserted in this manner, Excel adjusts formulas accordingly.

2 Click the **Name Box arrow**, and then click **Key_Chain_Costs**. Notice that Excel highlights the correct range of cells, adjusting for the newly inserted row.

If you insert rows, the defined name adjusts to the new cell addresses to represent the cells that were originally defined. Likewise, if you move the cells, the defined name goes with them to the new location.

3 In cell **A15**, type **Money Clip Wallets** and then press [Tab]. In cell **B15**, type **1246** and press [Tab]. In cell **C15**, type **1099** and press [Tab]. In cell **D15**, type **895** and press [Tab]. In cell **E15**, type **982** and press [Enter].

The cells in the newly inserted row adopt the Currency [0] format from the cells above.

4 On the **Formulas tab**, from the **Defined Names group**, display the **Name Manager** dialog box.

5 In the **Name Manager** dialog box, in the **Name** column, click **Billfold_Costs**. At the bottom of the dialog box, click in the **Refers to** box and edit the reference, changing **$E$14** to **$E$15** as shown in Figure 4.24.

This action will include the Money Clip Wallet values in the named range.

Figure 4.24

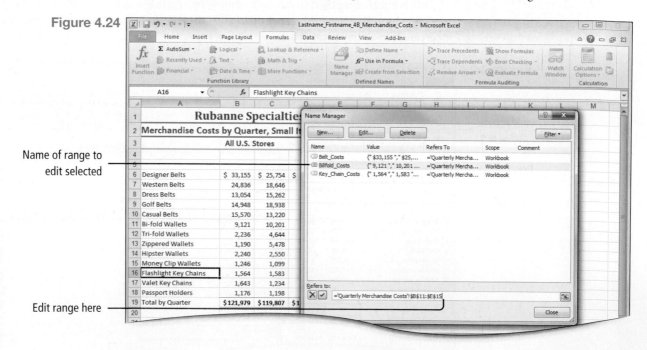

Name of range to edit selected

Edit range here

6 **Close** the **Name Manager** dialog box, and click **Yes** to save the changes you made to the name reference.

7 **Save** 🖫 your workbook.

Activity 4.08 | Changing A Defined Name

You can change a defined name. If the defined name is used in a formula, the new name is automatically changed in any affected formulas. In this activity, you will change the defined name *Billfold_Costs* to *Wallet_Costs*.

1 On the **Formulas tab**, from the **Defined Names group**, display the **Name Manager** dialog box. Click **Billfold_Costs**, and then click the **Edit** button.

2 In the displayed **Edit Name** dialog box, with *Billfold_Costs* highlighted, type **Wallet_Costs** Compare your screen with Figure 4.25.

Figure 4.25

Edit Name dialog box

Type new name in Name box

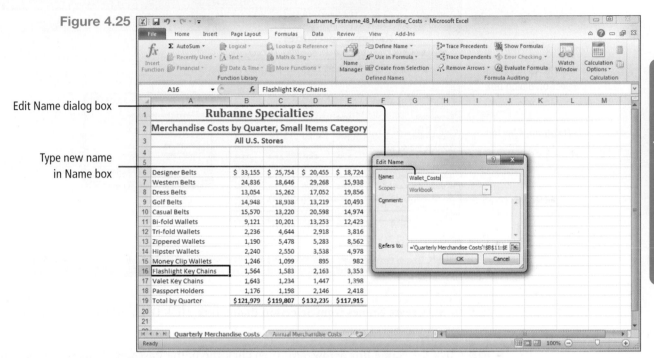

3 Click **OK**, and then **Close** the **Name Manager** dialog box.

4 In the upper left corner of the window, click the **Name Box arrow** and notice the modified range name, *Wallet_Costs*.

5 Click any cell to close the list, and then **Save** your workbook.

Activity 4.09 | Creating a Defined Name by Using Row and Column Titles

You can use the Create from Selection command to use existing row or column titles as the name for a range of cells.

1 Select the range **A18:E18**. On the **Formulas tab**, in the **Defined Names group**, click **Create from Selection**. Compare your screen with Figure 4.26.

> The Create Names from Selection dialog box displays. A check mark displays in the *Left column* check box, which indicates that Excel will use the value of the cell in the leftmost column of the selection as the range name, unless you specify otherwise.

Figure 4.26

Create Names from Selection dialog box

Left column selected

Selected range

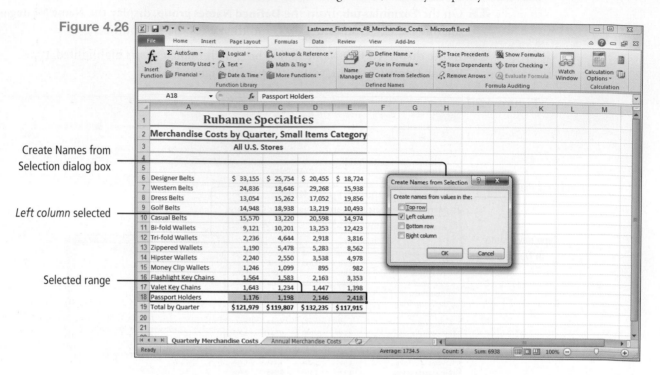

2 In the **Create Names from Selection** dialog box, click **OK**, and then click anywhere to cancel the selection.

3 Click the **Name Box arrow**, and then click the name **Passport_Holders**. Notice that in the new range name, Excel inserted the underscore necessary to fill a blank space in the range name. Also notice that the actual range consists of only the numeric values, as shown in Figure 4.27.

> This method is convenient for naming a range of cells without having to actually type a name—Excel uses the text of the first cell to the left of the selected range as the range name and then formats the name properly.

Figure 4.27

Defined name formatted
properly by Excel

Range consists of
numeric values

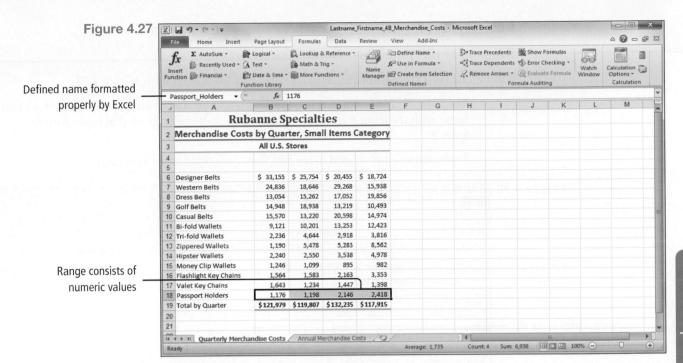

Note | Deleting a Defined Name

If you create a defined name and then decide that you no longer need it, you can delete the name and its accompanying range reference. Display the Name Manager dialog box, select the defined name, and then at the top of the dialog box, click Delete. Deleting a defined name does not modify the cell contents or formatting of the cells. Deleting a defined name does not delete any cells or any values. It deletes only the name that you have applied to a group of cells. However, any formula that contains the range name will display the #NAME? error message, and will have to be adjusted manually.

4 Save 🖫 your workbook.

Objective 5 | Use Defined Names in a Formula

The advantage to naming a range of cells is that you can use the name in a formula in other parts of your workbook. The defined name provides a logical reference to data. For example, referring to data as *Belt_Costs* is easier to understand than referring to data as *B6:E10*.

When you use a defined name in a formula, the result is the same as if you typed the cell references.

Activity 4.10 | Using Defined Names in a Formula

1 Display the Annual Merchandise Costs worksheet.

2 In cell **B5**, type **=sum(B** and then compare your screen with Figure 4.28.

The Formula AutoComplete list displays containing all of Excel's built-in functions that begin with the letter *B* and any defined names in this workbook that begin with the letter B.

To the left of your defined name *Belt_Costs*, a defined name icon displays.

Figure 4.28

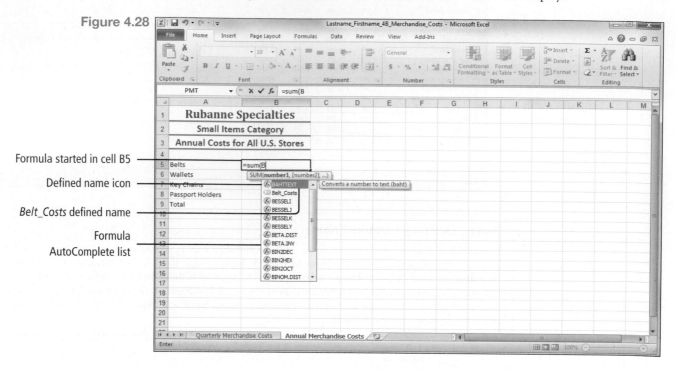

Formula started in cell B5

Defined name icon

Belt_Costs defined name

Formula
AutoComplete list

3 Continue typing **elt_Costs** and then press **Enter**.

Your result is *373960*. Recall that SUM is a function—a formula already built by Excel—that adds all the cells in a selected range. Thus, Excel sums all the cells in the range you defined as Belt_Costs on the first worksheet in the workbook, and then places the result in cell B5 of this worksheet.

4 In cell **B6**, type **=sum(W** and then on the displayed **Formula AutoComplete list**, double-click **Wallet_Costs** to insert the formula. Press **Enter** to display the result *96653*.

5 Click cell **B7**, type **=sum(** and then on the **Formulas tab**, in the **Defined Names group**, click the **Use in Formula** button. From the displayed list, click **Key_Chain_Costs**, and then press **Enter** to display the total *14385*.

6 In cell **B8**, use any of the techniques you just practiced to sum the cells containing the costs for **Passport Holders** and to display a result of *6938*. Sum the column in cell **B9** to display a result of *491936*.

7 Select the nonadjacent cells **B5** and **B9**, and then from the **Home tab**, display the **Cell Styles** gallery. Under **Number Format**, apply the **Currency [0]** cell style. Select the range **B6:B8**, display the **Cell Styles** gallery, and then under **Number Format**, click **Comma [0]**.

8 Click cell **B9** and apply the **Total** cell style. Press [Ctrl] + [Home] to move to the top of the worksheet. Compare your screen with Figure 4.29.

Figure 4.29

Totals derived from formulas using defined names

Cells formatted as currency with no decimal places

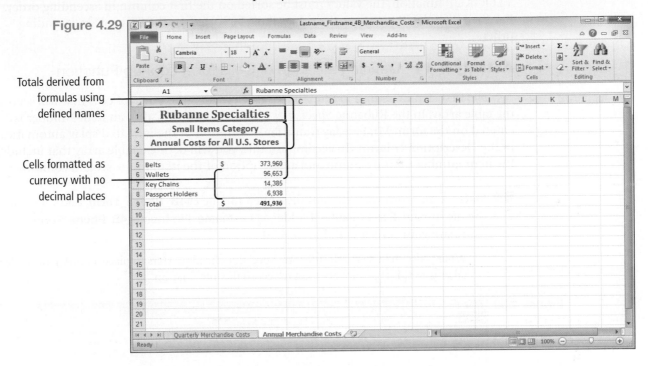

9 Select both worksheets so that *[Group]* displays in the title bar. With the two worksheets grouped, insert a footer in the **left section** that includes the file name. Center the worksheets **Horizontally** on the page.

10 Display the **Document Panel** and in the **Author** box, type your **firstname** and **lastname** In the **Subject** box, type your course name and section number, and in the **Keywords** box, type **Small Items Category, Merchandise Costs** Close ☒ the **Document Panel**. Return to **Normal** view and make cell **A1** active, display the grouped worksheets in **Print Preview**, **Close** the **Print Preview**, and then make any necessary corrections or adjustments.

11 **Save** 🖫 your workbook. Print or submit the two worksheets in this workbook electronically as directed by your instructor. If required, print or create an electronic version of your worksheets with formulas displayed using the instructions in Activity 1.16 in Project 1A. **Close** this workbook.

Objective 6 | Use Lookup Functions

Lookup functions look up a value in a defined range of cells located in another part of the workbook to find a corresponding value. For example, you can define a two-column range of cells containing names and phone numbers. Then, when you type a name in the cell containing the lookup formula, Excel fills in the phone number by looking it up in the defined range. In the lookup formula, the defined range is referred to as the *table array*.

The *VLOOKUP* function looks ups values in a table array arranged as vertical columns. The function searches the first column of the table array for a corresponding value, and then returns a value from any cell on the same row. The *HLOOKUP* function looks up values in a table array arranged in horizontal rows. The function searches the top row of the table array for a corresponding value, and then returns a value from any cell in the same column.

There is one requirement for the lookup functions to work properly: *the data in the table array, which can be numbers or text, must be sorted in ascending order.* For the VLOOKUP function, the values must be sorted on the first column in ascending order. For the HLOOKUP function, the values must be sorted on the first row in ascending order.

Activity 4.11 | Defining a Range of Cells for a Lookup Function

The first step in using a lookup function is to define the range of cells that will serve as the table array. In the Rubanne Specialties Phone Order form, after an Item Number is entered on the form, Mr. Fereday wants the description of the item to display automatically in the Description column. To accomplish this, you will define a table array that includes the item number in one column and a description of the item in the second column.

1 **Start** Excel. From your student files, open the file **e04B_Phone_Form**, and then **Save** the file in your **Excel Chapter 4** folder as **Lastname_Firstname_4B_Phone_Form** Compare your screen with Figure 4.30.

When store managers call Rubanne Specialties headquarters to place an order, the order taker uses this type of worksheet to record the information.

Figure 4.30

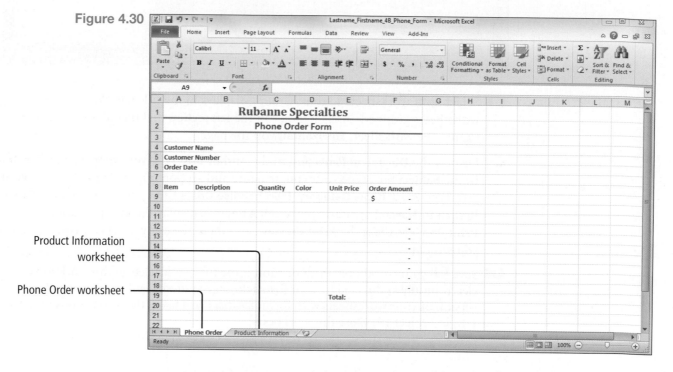

Product Information worksheet

Phone Order worksheet

2 Click the **Product Information sheet tab** to display the second worksheet.

The Product Information worksheet contains the Style Code, Description, and Unit Price of specific wallets and belts.

3 On the displayed **Product Information** worksheet, select the range **A4:C11**. On the **Data tab**, in the **Sort & Filter group**, click the **Sort** button. If necessary, drag the **Sort** dialog box to the right side of your screen so you can view **columns A:C**.

> To use this list to look up information with the Excel VLOOKUP function, you must sort the list in ascending order by Style Code, which is the column that will be used to look up the matching information.

4 In the **Sort** dialog box, under **Column**, click the **Sort by arrow**. Notice that the selected range is now **A5:C11** and that the column titles in the range **A4:C4** display in the **Sort by** list. Compare your screen with Figure 4.31.

> When the selected range includes a header row that should remain in place while the remaining rows are sorted, Excel usually recognizes those column headings, selects the *My data has headers* check box, and then displays the column headings in the Sort by list.

Figure 4.31

My data has headers check box selected

Sort dialog box

Range that will be sorted

Selected range changed to A5:C11

Column headings display in the Sort by list

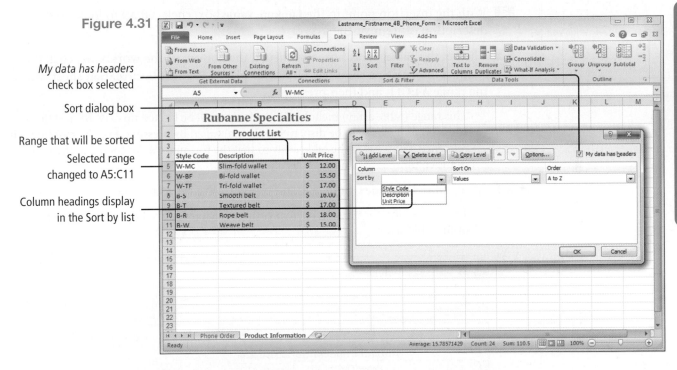

5 From the **Sort by** list, click **Style Code**, which is the first column heading and the column heading that Excel selects by default.

6 Under **Sort On**, verify that *Values* displays, and under **Order**, verify that *A to Z* displays.

> *Values* indicates that the sort will be based on the values in the cells of the first column, rather than cell color or some other cell characteristic. *A to Z* indicates that the cell will be sorted in ascending order.

7 Click **OK** to sort the data by *Style Code* in ascending order.

> Excel sorts the data alphabetically by Style Code; *B-R* is first in the list and *W-TF* is last.

8 **Save** 🖫 your workbook.

Activity 4.12 | Inserting the Vlookup Function

Recall that the VLOOKUP function looks ups values in a range of cells arranged as vertical columns. The arguments for this function include *lookup_value*—the value to search in the first column of the table array, *table_array*—the range that contains the data, and *col_index_num*—the column number (1, 2, 3, 4, and so on) in the table array that contains the result you want to retrieve from the table, which in this instance, is the Description.

Another Way

Click the Insert Function button located to the left of the Formula Bar, select the Lookup & Reference category, and then under Select a function, scroll to locate and then click VLOOKUP.

1 Display the **Phone Order** sheet. In cell **A9**, type **W-BF** and press Tab.

2 With cell **B9** as the active cell, on the **Formulas tab**, in the **Function Library group**, click **Lookup & Reference**, and then click **VLOOKUP**.

The Function Arguments dialog box for VLOOKVUP displays.

3 With the insertion point in the **Lookup_value** box, click cell **A9** to look up the description of Item W-BF.

4 Click in the **Table_array** box, and then at the bottom of the workbook, click the **Product Information sheet tab**. On the displayed **Product Information** sheet, select the range **A4:C11**, and then press F4.

This range (table array) includes the value that will be looked up—*W-BF* and the corresponding value to be displayed—*Bi-fold wallet*. By pressing F4, the absolute cell reference is applied to the table array so that the formula can be copied to the remainder of the column in the Phone Order sheet.

5 Click in the **Col_index_num** box and type **2** Compare your screen with Figure 4.32.

The description for the selected item—the value to be looked up—is located in column 2 of the table array.

Figure 4.32

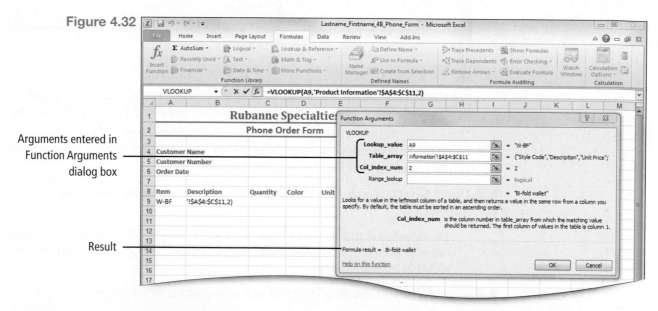

Arguments entered in Function Arguments dialog box

Result

6 Click **OK**.

The description for Item W-BF displays in cell B9.

7 With cell **B9** as the active cell and containing the VLOOKUP formula, point to the fill handle in the lower right corner of the cell, and then drag to fill the VLOOKUP formula down through cell **B18**. Compare your screen with Figure 4.33.

The #N/A error notation displays in the cells where you copied the formula. Excel displays this error when a function or formula exists in a cell but has no value available with which to perform a calculation; values have not yet been entered in column A in those rows.

Figure 4.33

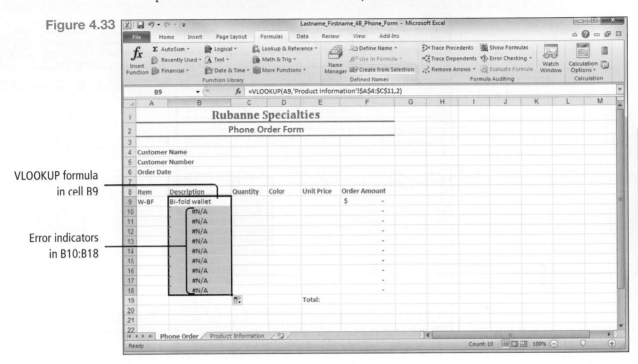

VLOOKUP formula in cell B9

Error indicators in B10:B18

8 Click cell **C9**, type **12** as the quantity ordered and press Tab. In cell **D9**, type **Black** and press Tab.

9 With cell **E9** as the active cell, on the **Formulas tab**, in the **Function Library group**, click **Lookup & Reference**, and then click **VLOOKUP**.

10 With the insertion point in the **Lookup_value** box, click cell **A9** to look up information for Item W-BF. Click in the **Table_array** box, display the **Product Information** sheet, and then select the range **A4:C11**.

11 Press F4 to make the values in the range absolute. In the **Col_index_num** box, type **3** to look up the price in the third column of the range, and then click **OK**.

The Unit Price for the Bi-fold wallet—*$15.50*—displays in cell E9.

12 Click cell **F9**, and notice that a formula to calculate the total for the item, Quantity times Unit Price, has already been entered in the worksheet.

This formula has also been copied to the range F10:F18.

13 Click cell **E9**, and then copy the VLOOKUP formula down through cell **E18**. Compare your screen with Figure 4.34.

> The *#N/A* error notation displays in the cells where you copied the formula, and also in cells F10:F18, because the formulas there have no values yet with which to perform a calculation—values have not yet been entered in column A in those rows.

Figure 4.34

Error notation in columns E and F

Total amount for 12 W-BF items

VLOOKUP formula in cell E9

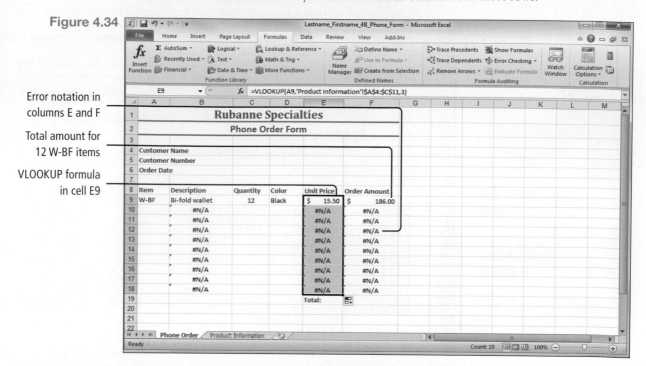

14 Click cell **A10**, type **W-MC** and press Tab two times.

> Excel looks up the product description and the product price in the vertical table array on the Product Information sheet, and then displays the results in cells B10 and E10.

15 In cell **C10**, type **24** and press Tab. Notice that Excel calculates the total for this item in cell **F10**—*288.00*.

16 In cell **D10**, type **Burgundy** and then press `Enter`. Notice that after data is entered in the row, the error notations no longer display. **Save** 🖫 your workbook. Compare your screen with Figure 4.35.

Figure 4.35

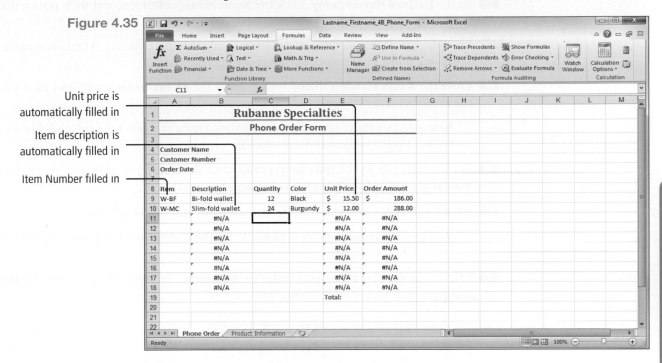

Unit price is automatically filled in

Item description is automatically filled in

Item Number filled in

Objective 7 | Validate Data

Another technique to improve accuracy when completing a worksheet is ***data validation***—a technique in which you control the type of data or the values that are entered into a cell. This technique improves accuracy because it limits and controls the type of data an individual, such as an order taker, can enter into the form.

One way to control the type of data entered is to create a ***validation list***—a list of values that are acceptable for a group of cells. Only values on the list are valid; any value *not* on the list is considered invalid. For example, in the Phone Order sheet, it would be useful if in the Item column, only valid Style Codes could be entered.

Activity 4.13 | Creating a Validation List

A list of valid values must either be on the same worksheet as the destination cell, or if the list is in another worksheet, the cell range must be named. In this activity, you will create a defined name for the Style Codes, and then create a validation list for column A of the Phone Order worksheet.

1 Display the **Product Information sheet**. Select the range **A4:A11**. On the **Formulas tab**, in the **Defined Names group**, click **Create from Selection**.

Recall that by using the Create from Selection command, you can automatically generate a name from the selected cells that uses the text in the top row or the leftmost column of a selection.

2 In the **Create Names from Selection** dialog box, be sure the **Top row** check box is selected, and then click **OK** to use *Style Code* as the range name.

3 In the **Defined Names group**, click the **Name Manager** button, and then notice that the new defined name is listed with the name *Style_Code*.

> *Style_Code* displays as the defined name for the selected cells. Recall that Excel replaces spaces with an underscore when it creates a range name.

4 **Close** the **Name Manager** dialog box. Display the **Phone Order** sheet, and then select the range **A9:A18**.

> Before you set the validation requirement, you must first select the cells that you want to restrict to only valid entries from the list.

5 On the **Data tab**, in the **Data Tools group**, click the **Data Validation** button. In the **Data Validation** dialog box, be sure the **Settings tab** is selected.

6 Under **Validation criteria**, click the **Allow arrow**, and then click **List**.

> A Source box displays as the third box in the Data Validation dialog box. Here you select or type the source data.

7 Click to position the insertion point in the **Source** box, type **=Style_Code** and then compare your screen with Figure 4.36.

Figure 4.36

Data Validation dialog box ——

Values will be looked up in a list ——

Source is the range you named *Style_Code* ——

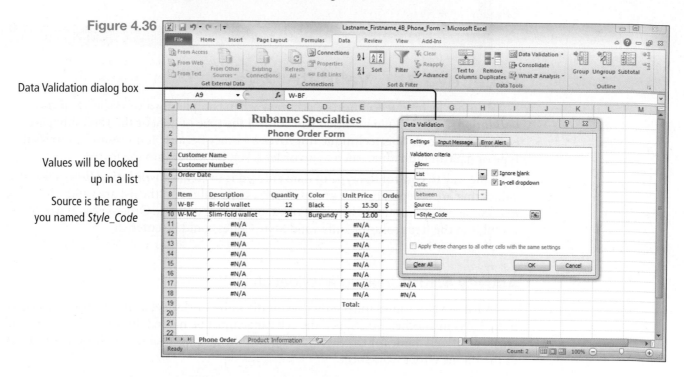

8 Click **OK**. Click cell **A11**, and notice that a list arrow displays at the right edge of the cell.

9 In cell **A11**, click the list arrow to display the list, and then compare your screen with Figure 4.37.

Figure 4.37

List arrow

List of Style Codes

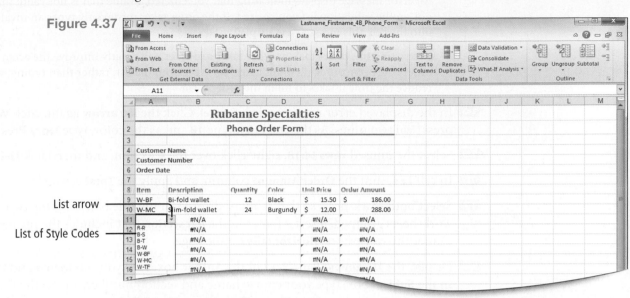

10 From the displayed list, click **B-W**.

> The Style Code is selected from the list and the Item, Description, and Unit Price cells are filled in for row 11.

11 Press Tab two times, type **24** and press Tab, type **Brown** and then press Enter to return to the beginning of the next row. Compare your screen with Figure 4.38.

> You can see that when taking orders by phone, it will speed the process if all of the necessary information can be filled in automatically. Furthermore, accuracy will be improved if item codes are restricted to only valid data.

Figure 4.38

Order completed using a validation list

List arrow displays in selected cell

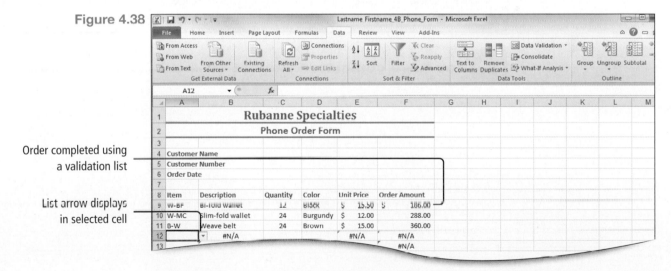

12 With cell **A12** active, click the **list arrow**, and then click **B-S**. As the **Quantity,** type **18** and as the **Color** type, type **Tan** Press Enter.

13 In cell **A13**, type **G-W** and press ⸤Tab⸥.

> An error message displays indicating that you entered a value that is not valid; that is, it is not on the validation list you created. If the order taker mistakenly types an invalid value into the cell, this message will display.

> Restricting the values that an order taker can enter will greatly improve the accuracy of orders. Also, encouraging order takers to select from the list, rather than typing, will reduce the time it takes to fill in the order form.

14 In the displayed error message, click **Cancel**. Click the **list arrow** again, click **W-TF** and press ⸤Tab⸥ two times. As the **Quantity,** type **18** and as the color, type **Ivory** Press ⸤Enter⸥.

15 Select the unused **rows 14:18**, right-click over the selection, and then click **Delete**.

16 In cell **F14**, sum the **Order Amount** column, and apply the **Total** cell style.

17 Select both worksheets so that *[Group]* displays in the title bar. With the two worksheets grouped, insert a footer in the **left section** that includes the file name. Center the worksheets **Horizontally** on the page.

18 Display the **Document Panel** and in the **Author** box, type your **firstname** and **lastname** In the **Subject** box, type your course name and section number, and in the **Keywords** box, type **phone order form Close** ⸤X⸥ the **Document Panel**. Return to **Normal** view and make cell **A1** active, display the grouped worksheets in **Print Preview**, **Close** the **Print Preview**, and then make any necessary corrections or adjustments.

19 **Save** ⸤🖫⸥ your workbook. Print or submit the two worksheets in this workbook electronically as directed by your instructor. If required, print or create an electronic version of your worksheets with formulas displayed using the instructions in Activity 1.16 in Project 1A. **Close** this workbook.

More Knowledge | Creating Validation Messages

In the Data Validation dialog box, you can use the Input Message tab to create a ScreenTip that will display when the cell is selected. The message can be an instruction that tells the user what to do. You can also use the Error Alert tab to create a warning message that displays if invalid data is entered in the cell.

End **You have completed Project 4B** ——————————————

Content-Based Assessments

Summary

In this chapter, you used the Financial function PMT to calculate the payment for a loan. You also used two of Excel's What-If Analysis tools: Goal Seek to get a result that you want and Data Tables to see the results of many different inputs. You defined names for a range of cells and created a table in which one can look up data. Finally, you used data validation to ensure the accuracy of data entry.

Key Terms

Matching

Match each term in the second column with its correct definition in the first column by writing the letter of the term on the blank line in front of the correct definition.

_____ 1. Predefined formulas that perform common business calculations, and which typically involve a period of time such as months or years.

_____ 2. The amount charged for the use of borrowed money.

_____ 3. In the Excel PMT function, the term used to indicate the interest rate for a loan.

_____ 4. The total amount that a series of future payments is worth now.

_____ 5. Another term for present value.

_____ 6. The abbreviation for *number of time periods* in various Excel functions.

_____ 7. The value at the end of the time periods in an Excel function; the cash balance you want to attain after the last payment is made—usually zero for loans.

_____ 8. The values that an Excel function uses to perform calculations or operations.

_____ 9. An Excel function that calculates the payment for a loan based on constant payments and at a constant interest rate.

_____ 10. An optional argument in the PMT function that assumes that the payment will be made at the end of each time period.

_____ 11. The process of changing the values in cells to see how those changes affect the outcome of formulas in the worksheet.

_____ 12. One of Excel's What-If Analysis tools that provides a method to find a specific value for a cell by adjusting the value of one other cell—you can find the right input when you know the result you want.

A Arguments

B Data table

C Financial functions

D Future value (Fv)

E Goal Seek

F Interest

G Nper

H One-variable data table

I PMT function

J Present value (Pv)

K Principal

L Rate

M Two-variable data table

N Type argument

O What-if analysis

_____ 13. A range of cells that shows how changing certain values in your formulas affects the results of those formulas, and which makes it easy to calculate multiple versions in one operation.

_____ 14. A data table that changes the value in only one cell.

_____ 15. A data table that changes the values in two cells.

Multiple Choice

Circle the correct answer.

1. Loans are typically made for a period of:
   A. days   B. months   C. years

2. The future value at the end of a loan is typically:
   A. zero   B. 100%   C. loan balance

3. A word or string of characters that represents a cell, a range of cells, a formula, or a constant value is a defined:
   A. scope   B. name   C. grouping

4. In the Cell Styles gallery, the Currency [0] style and the Comma [0] style format the selected cell with how many decimal places?
   A. 0   B. 1   C. 2

5. When you use a defined name in a formula, the result is the same as if you typed a:
   A. column reference   B. cell reference   C. row reference

6. A group of Excel functions that look up a value in a defined range of cells located in another part of the workbook to find a corresponding value is referred to as:
   A. logical functions   B. lookup functions   C. tab

7. An Excel function that looks up values that are displayed vertically in a column is the:
   A. VLOOKUP function   B. HLOOKUP function   C. Sum function

8. A defined range of cells, arranged in a column or a row, used in a VLOOKUP or HLOOKUP function, is called a table:
   A. defined name   B. list   C. array

9. When creating a VLOOKUP or an HLOOKUP function, the one requirement is that the data in the table array is sorted in:
   A. Ascending order   B. Descending order   C. Lookup order

10. A list of values that are acceptable for a group of cells is a:
    A. data list   B. information list   C. validation list

Content-Based Assessments

Apply **4A** skills from these Objectives:

1. Use Financial Functions
2. Use Goal Seek
3. Create a Data Table

Skills Review | Project **4C** Auto Loan

In the following Skills Review, you will create a worksheet for Lauren Feeney, U.S. Sales Director, that details loan information for purchasing seven automobiles for Rubanne Specialties sales representatives. The monthly payment for the seven automobiles cannot exceed $3,000. Your completed two worksheets will look similar to Figure 4.39.

Project Files

For Project 4C, you will need the following file:

e04C_Auto_Loan

You will save your workbook as:

Lastname_Firstname_4C_Auto_Loan

Project Results

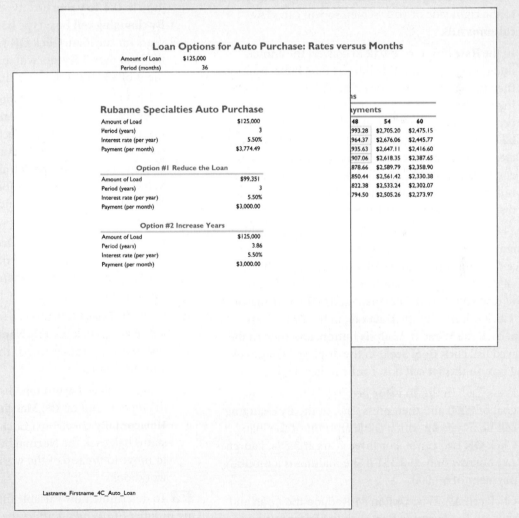

Loan Options for Auto Purchase: Rates versus Months

Amount of Loan	$125,000
Period (months)	36

Rubanne Specialties Auto Purchase

Amount of Load	$125,000
Period (years)	3
Interest rate (per year)	5.50%
Payment (per month)	$3,774.49

Option #1 Reduce the Loan

Amount of Load	$99,351
Period (years)	3
Interest rate (per year)	5.50%
Payment (per month)	$3,000.00

Option #2 Increase Years

Amount of Load	$125,000
Period (years)	3.86
Interest rate (per year)	5.50%
Payment (per month)	$3,000.00

Payments

48	54	60
993.28	$2,705.20	$2,475.15
964.37	$2,676.06	$2,445.77
935.63	$2,647.11	$2,416.60
907.06	$2,618.35	$2,387.65
878.66	$2,589.79	$2,358.90
850.44	$2,561.42	$2,330.38
822.38	$2,533.24	$2,302.07
794.50	$2,505.26	$2,273.97

Lastname_Firstname_4C_Auto_Loan

Figure 4.39

(Project 4C Auto Loan continues on the next page)

Content-Based Assessments

1 **Start** Excel. From your student files, open the file **e04C_Auto_Loan**, and then **Save** the file in your **Excel Chapter 4** folder as **Lastname_Firstname_4C_Auto_Loan**

a. In the range **A2:B5**, enter the following row titles and data.

Amount of Loan	$125,000
Period (years)	3
Interest rate (per year)	5.5%
Payment (per month)	

b. Click cell **B5**. On the **Formulas tab**, in the **Function Library group**, click the **Financial** button, and then click **PMT**. Drag the **Function Arguments** dialog box to the right side of your screen so you can view **columns A:B**.

c. In the **Rate** box, type **b4/12** to convert the annual interest rate to a monthly interest rate. Press Tab, and then in the **Nper** box, type **b3*12** to have Excel convert the number of years in the loan (3) to the total number of months. Press Tab, and then in the **Pv** box, type **b2** to enter the present value of the loan. Click **OK** to create the function. In the **Formula Bar**, between the equal sign and *PMT*, type – (minus sign) to insert a minus sign into the formula, and then press Enter to display the loan payment as a positive number.

2 The result of *$3,774.49* is higher than the monthly payment of $3,000 that Lauren wants. One option is to reduce the amount of money that she is going to borrow; she can determine the maximum amount that she can borrow and still keep the payment at $3,000 by using Goal Seek. Click cell **B5**. On the **Data tab**, in the **Data Tools group**, click the **What-If Analysis** button, and then in the displayed list, click **Goal Seek**. In the displayed **Goal Seek** dialog box, in the **Set cell** box, confirm that *B5* displays.

a. Press Tab. In the **To value** box, type the payment goal of **3000** and then press Tab. In the **By changing cell** box, type **b2** which is the amount of the loan. Click **OK** two times. For three years at 5.5%, Lauren can borrow only $99,351 if she maintains a monthly payment of $3,000.

b. Click cell **A7**. Type **Option #1 Reduce the Loan** and then on the **Formula Bar**, click the **Enter** button to keep the cell active. **Merge and Center** the title across the range **A7:B7**, display the **Cell Styles** gallery, and then apply the **Heading 2** cell style.

c. Select the range **A2:B5**, right-click, and then click **Copy**. Point to cell **A8** right-click, point to **Paste Special**, and then under **Paste Values**, click the second button—**Values & Number Formatting**. Press Esc to cancel the moving border.

d. In cell **B2**, type **125000** and then press Enter to restore the original loan amount. Another option that Lauren can explore with Goal Seek is to increase the number of years over which she finances the automobiles. Click cell **B5**. On the **Data tab**, in the **Data Tools group**, click the **What-If Analysis** button, and then click **Goal Seek**.

e. In the **Set cell** box, confirm that **B5** displays. Press Tab. In the **To value** box, type **3000** Press Tab. In the **By changing cell** box, type **b3** which is the number of years for the loan. Click **OK** two times. Extending the loan over 3.8 years will maintain a monthly payment of $3,000 at the current interest rate.

f. Click **A13**. Type **Option #2 Increase Years** and then press Enter. Use the **Format Painter** to copy the format from cell **A7** to cell **A13**. Select the range **A2:B5**, right-click, and then click **Copy**. Point to cell **A14**, right-click, point to **Paste Special**, and then under **Paste Values**, click the second button—**Values & Number Formatting**. Press Esc to cancel the moving border.

g. Point to cell **B15**, right-click to display the Mini toolbar, and then click the **Decrease Decimal** button until the number of decimal places is two. Click cell **B3**. Type **3** and then press Enter to restore the original value.

h. Click the **Insert tab**, insert a footer, and then in the left section, click the **File Name** button. Click in a cell just above the footer to exit the **Footer area** and view your file name.

i. From the **Page Layout tab**. display the **Page Setup** dialog box, and on the **Margins tab**, select the **Horizontally** check box. Click **OK**, and then on the status bar, click the **Normal** button. Press Ctrl + Home to move to the top of the worksheet. **Save** your workbook.

3 To determine how variable interest rates and a varying number of payments affect the payment amount, Lauren will set up a two-variable data table. Double-click the **Sheet2 tab**, rename it **Payment Table** and then press Enter. In cell **A1**, type **Loan Options for Auto Purchase: Rates versus Months** and then press Enter.

(Project 4C Auto Loan continues on the next page)

Content-Based Assessments

Merge and Center this title across the range **A1:I1**, and then apply the **Title** cell style.

a. In the range **A2:B4**, enter the following row titles and data.

Amount of Loan	$125,000
Period (months)	36
Interest rate (per year)	5.5%

b. Click cell **C8**. Type **24** and then press Tab. Type **30** and then press Tab. Select the range **C8:D8**. Drag the fill handle to the right through cell **I8** to fill a pattern of months from 24 to 60 in increments of six months.

c. In cell **B9**, type **7.0%** and press Enter. Type **6.5%** and press Enter. Select the range **B9:B10**, and then drag the fill handle down through cell **B16** to fill a pattern of interest rates in increments of .5% from 7.00% down to 3.50%.

d. Click cell **C6**. Type **Payment Options** and then press Enter. **Merge and Center** this title across the range **C6:I6**. Apply the **Heading 1** cell style. Click cell **C7**. Type **Number of Monthly Payments** and then use the **Format Painter** to apply the format of cell **C6** to cell **C7**.

e. Click cell **A9**, type **Rates** and then press Enter. Select the range **A9:A16**. On the **Home tab**, in the **Alignment group**, click the **Merge and Center** button, click the **Align Text Right** button, and then click the **Middle Align** button. Apply the Explanatory Text cell style.

f. Click cell **B8**. On the **Formulas tab**, in the **Function Library group**, click the **Financial** button, and then click **PMT**. In the **Rate** box, type **b4/12** to divide the interest rate per year by 12 to convert it to a monthly interest rate. Press Tab, and then in the **Nper** box, type **b3** Press Tab. In the **Pv** box, type **-b2** and then click **OK**.

g. Select the range **B8:I16**. On the **Data tab**, in the **Data Tools group**, click the **What-If Analysis** button, and then in the displayed list, click **Data Table**.

In the **Data Table** dialog box, in the **Row input cell** box, type **b3** and then press Tab. In the **Column input cell** box, type **b4** In the **Data Table** dialog box, click **OK** to create the data table. Click in any cell outside of the table to deselect.

h. Right-click cell **B8**, and then on the Mini toolbar, click the **Format Painter** button. Select the range **C9:I16** to apply the same format. Notice that in cell **G9**, the payment is *$2,993.28*, which is close to Lauren's goal of a monthly payment of $3,000. At any of the interest rates, she will have to extend the loan over at least 48 months to stay within her goal of $3,000 per month.

i. Select the range **G9:G12** and apply the **Note** cell style to highlight the desired payment option. Select the nonadjacent ranges **C8:I8** and **B9:B16**, apply **Bold** and **Center**. On the **Page Layout tab**, set the orientation for this worksheet to **Landscape**.

j. Click the **Insert tab**, insert a footer, and then in the left section, click the **File Name** button. Click in a cell just above the footer to exit the **Footer area** and view your file name. From the **Page Layout tab**, display the **Page Setup** dialog box, and on the **Margins tab**, select the **Horizontally** check box. Click **OK**, and then on the status bar, click the **Normal** button. Press Ctrl + Home to move to the top of the worksheet.

k. Display the **Document Panel** and in the **Author** box, type your **firstname** and **lastname**; in the **Subject** box type, your course name and section number; and in the **Keywords** box, type **amortization schedule, payment table**. Return to **Normal** view and make cell **A1** active. Display each worksheet in **Print Preview**, and then make any necessary corrections or adjustments. Close the print preview.

l. **Save** your workbook. Print or submit the two worksheets in this workbook electronically as directed by your instructor. If required, print or create an electronic version of your worksheets with formulas displayed using the instructions in Activity 1.16 in Project 1A.

End You have completed Project 4C

Content-Based Assessments

Skills Review | Project **4D** Quarterly Cost Report and Lookup Form

In the following Skills Review, you will assist Connor Fereday, the Vice President of Marketing at Rubanne Specialties, by defining names for ranges of cells in a workbook containing quarterly Store Supply costs and by adding lookup functions to a Packing Slip form so that an order taker can complete the form quickly. Your completed workbooks will look similar to Figure 4.40.

Project Files

For Project 4D, you will need the following files:

> e04D_Store_Supplies
> e04D_Packing_Slip

You will save your workbooks as:

> Lastname_Firstname_4D_Store_Supplies
> Lastname_Firstname_4D_Packing_Slip

Project Results

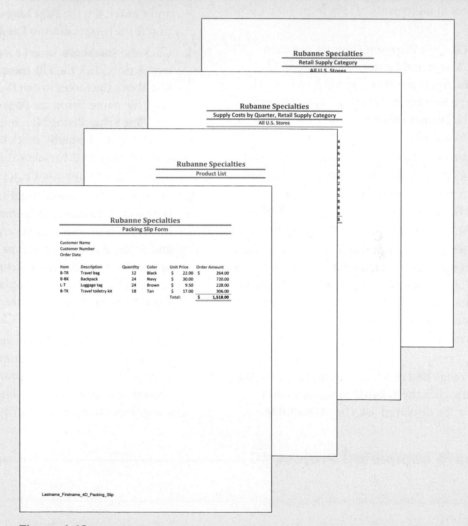

Figure 4.40

(Project 4D Quarterly Cost Report and Lookup Form continues on the next page)

Skills Review | Project 4D Quarterly Cost Report and Lookup Form (continued)

1 **Start** Excel. From your student files, open the file e04D_Store_Supplies, and then **Save** the file in your **Excel Chapter 4** folder as **Lastname_Firstname_4D_Store_Supplies**

a. Select the range **B6:E18**, which includes the empty cells in **row 18**, and then click the **Sum** button. Click anywhere to cancel the selection. Select the range **B6:E6**, hold down Ctrl and select the range **B18:E18**, and then from the **Cell Styles** gallery, under **Number Format**, apply the **Currency [0]** cell style. Select the range **B7:E17**, display the **Cell Styles** gallery, and then under **Number Format**, click **Comma [0]**. Select the range **B18:E18**, and then apply the **Total** cell style.

b. Select the range **B6:E9**. On the **Formulas tab**, in the **Defined Names** group, click the **Define Name** button. With *Revolving_Glass_Towers* selected, type **Showcase_Costs** as the name. At the bottom of the dialog box, at the right edge of the **Refers to** box, point to and click the **Collapse Dialog Box** button. Change the range by selecting the range **B6:E10**.

c. Click the **Expand Dialog Box** button to redisplay the **New Name** dialog box, and then click **OK**. Select the range **B11:E14**. In the upper left corner of the Excel window, to the left of the **Formula Bar**, click in the **Name Box**, and notice that the cell reference *B11* moves to the left edge of the box and is highlighted in blue. Type **Wrapping_Costs** and press Enter.

d. Select the range **B15:E16**. On the **Formulas tab**, in the **Defined Names group**, click the **Name Manager** button. In the upper left corner of the **Name Manager** dialog box, click the **New** button. With *Slant_Back_Counter_Racks* selected, type **Countertop_Costs** and then click **OK**. **Close** the **Name Manager** dialog box and **Save** your workbook.

e. On the left side of your window, in the **row heading area**, point to the **row 15** heading and right-click to select the entire row and display a shortcut menu. Click **Insert** to insert a new blank row above. Click cell **A15**, type **Ribbons and Bows** and then press Tab. In cell **B15**, type **200** and press Tab. In cell **C15**, type **195** and press Tab. In cell **D15**, type **315** and press Tab. In cell **E15**, type **275** and press Enter.

f. On the **Formulas tab**, from the **Defined Names group**, display the **Name Manager** dialog box. In the

Name Manager dialog box, in the **Name** column, click **Wrapping_Costs**. At the bottom of the dialog box, click in the **Refers to** box and edit the reference, changing **$E$14** to **$15** to include the new row in the range. **Close** the **Name Manager** dialog box, and click **Yes** to save the changes you made to the name reference. **Save** your workbook.

g. On the **Formulas tab**, from the **Defined Names group**, display the **Name Manager** dialog box. Click **Wrapping_Costs**, and then click the **Edit** button. In the displayed **Edit Name** dialog box, with *Wrapping_Costs* highlighted, type **Packaging Costs** Click **OK**, and then **Close** the **Name Manager** dialog box. In the upper left corner of the window, click the **Name Box arrow** and notice the modified range name, *Packaging_Costs*. Click any cell to close the list, and then **Save** your workbook.

h. Select the range **A18:E18**. On the **Formulas tab**, in the **Defined Names group**, click **Create from Selection**. In the **Create Names from Selection** dialog box, click **OK**, and then click anywhere to cancel the selection. Click the **Name Box arrow**, and then click the name **Tags_and_Labels**. Notice that in the new range name, Excel inserted the underscore necessary to fill a blank space in the range name.

2 Display the **Annual Supply Costs** worksheet. In cell **B5**, type **=sum(S** Continue typing **howcase_Costs** and then press Enter. Your result is *41879*. In cell **B6**, type **=sum(P** and then on the displayed **Formula AutoComplete list**, double-click **Packaging_Costs** to insert the formula. Press Enter to display the result *10984*.

a. In cell **B7**, type **=sum(** and then on the **Formulas tab**, in the **Defined Names group**, click the **Use in Formula** button. From the displayed list, click **Countertop_Costs** and then press Enter to display the total *4475*.

b. In cell **B8**, use any of the techniques you just practiced to sum the cells containing the costs for **Tags and Labels Costs** and to display a result of *5768*. Click cell **B9**, hold down Alt and press = to insert the SUM function, and then press Enter to display a total of *63106*.

c. Select the nonadjacent cells **B5** and **B9**, and then from the **Home tab**, display the **Cell Styles** gallery. Under **Number Format**, apply the **Currency [0]** cell style. To the range **B6:B8**, apply the **Comma [0]** cell style. Click cell **B9** and apply the **Total** cell style.

(Project 4D Quarterly Cost Report and Lookup Form continues on the next page)

Content-Based Assessments

d. Select both worksheets so that *[Group]* displays in the title bar. With the two worksheets grouped, insert a footer in the left section that includes the file name. **Center** the worksheets horizontally on the page.

e. Display the **Document Information Panel** and in the **Author** box, type your **firstname** and **lastname** In the **Subject** box, type your course name and section number, and in the **Keywords** box, type **Retail Supply Category, Supply Costs** Return to **Normal** view and make cell **A1** active, display the grouped worksheets in **Print Preview**, **Close** the **Print Preview**, and then make any necessary corrections or adjustments.

f. **Save** your workbook. Print or submit the two worksheets in this workbook electronically as directed by your instructor. If required, print or create an electronic version of your worksheets with formulas displayed using the instructions in Activity 1.16 in Project 1A. **Close** this workbook, but leave Excel open.

3 From your student files, **Open** the file e04D_Packing_Slip, and then **Save** the file in your **Excel Chapter 4** folder as Lastname_Firstname_4D_Packing_Slip

a. Display the **Product Information** worksheet. Select the range **A4:C11**. On the **Data tab**, in the **Sort & Filter group**, click **Sort**. If necessary, drag the Sort dialog box to the right side of your screen so you can view columns A:C.

b. In the **Sort** dialog box, under **Column**, click the **Sort by arrow**. Notice that the selected range is now **A5:C11** and that the column titles in the range **A4:C4** display in the **Sort by** list. In the **Sort by** list, click **Style Code**, which is the first column heading and the column heading that Excel selects by default. Under **Sort On**, verify that *Values* displays, and under **Order**, verify that *A to Z* displays. Click **OK** to sort the data by *Style Code* in ascending order. **Save** your workbook.

c. Display the **Packing Slip** worksheet. In cell **A9**, type **B-TR** and press Tab. With cell **B9** as the active cell, on the **Formulas tab**, in the **Function Library group**, click **Lookup & Reference**, and then click **VLOOKUP**.

d. With the insertion point in the **Lookup_value** box, click cell **A9** to look up the description of Item B-TR. Click in the **Table_array** box, and then at the bottom of the workbook, click the **Product Information sheet tab**. On the displayed **Product Information** sheet,

select the range **A4:C11**, and then press F4. Click in the **Col_index_num** box, type **2** and then click **OK**.

e. With cell **B9** as the active cell and containing the VLOOKUP formula, point to the fill handle in the lower right corner of the cell, and then drag to fill the VLOOKUP formula down through cell **B18**. The *#N/A* error notation displays in the cells where you copied the formula because no values have been entered in Column A in those rows.

f. Click cell **C9**, type **12** as the quantity ordered, and then press Tab. In cell **D9**, type **Black** and press Tab. With cell **E9** as the active cell, on the **Formulas tab**, in the **Function Library group**, click **Lookup & Reference**, and then click **VLOOKUP**.

g. With the insertion point in the **Lookup_value** box, click cell **A9** to look up information for Item B-TR. Click in the **Table_array** box, display the **Product Information** sheet, and then select the range **A4:C11**. Press F4 to make the values in the range absolute.

h. In the **Col_index_num** box, type **3** to look up the price in the third column of the range, and then click **OK**. The Unit Price for the Travel bag displays in cell E9. Click cell **F9**, and notice that a formula to calculate the total for the item, Quantity times Unit Price, was already entered in the worksheet.

i. Click cell **E9**, and then copy the VLOOKUP formula down through cell **E18**. The *#N/A* error notation displays in the cells where you copied the formula, and also in cells F10:F18, because a value is not available to the formulas—values have not yet been entered in column A in those rows.

j. Click cell **A10**, type **B-BK** and press Tab two times. In cell **C10**, type **24** and press Tab. Notice that Excel calculates the total for this item in cell **F10**—*720.00*. In cell **D10**, type **Navy** and then press Enter. Notice that after data is entered in the row, the error notations no longer display. **Save** your workbook.

4 Display the Product Information sheet. Select the range **A4:A11**. On the **Formulas tab**, in the **Defined Names group**, click **Create from Selection**.

a. In the **Create Names from Selection** dialog box, be sure only the **Top row** check box is selected, and then click **OK**.

(Project 4D Quarterly Cost Report and Lookup Form continues on the next page)

Content-Based Assessments

Skills Review | Project **4D** Quarterly Cost
Report and Lookup Form (continued)

b. Display the **Packing Slip** worksheet, and then select the range **A9:A18**. On the **Data tab**, in the **Data Tools group**, click the **Data Validation** button. In the displayed **Data Validation** dialog box, be sure the **Settings tab** is selected.

c. Under **Validation criteria**, click the **Allow arrow**, and then click **List**. Click to position the insertion point in the **Source** box, type **=Style_Code** and then click **OK**.

d. Click cell **A11**, and notice that a list arrow displays at the right edge of the cell. In cell **A11**, click the list arrow to display the list. In the displayed list, click **L-T**. Press [Tab] two times, type **24** and press [Tab], type **Brown** and then press [Enter] to return to the beginning of the next row.

e. With cell **A12** active, click the **list arrow**, and then click **B-TK**. As the **Quantity**, type **18** and as the **Color**, type **Tan** Press [Enter]. In cell **A13**, type **B-W** and press [Tab]. An error message displays indicating that you entered a value that is not valid; that is, it is not on the validation list you created. In the displayed error message, click **Cancel** and then **Save** your workbook.

f. Select the unused **rows 13:18**, right-click over the selected rows, and then click **Delete**. In cell **F13**, **Sum** the order amounts and then apply the **Total** cell style.

5 Select both worksheets so that *[Group]* displays in the title bar. With the two worksheets grouped, insert a footer in the left section that includes the file name. **Center** the worksheets horizontally on the page.

a. Display the **Document Panel** and in the **Author** box, type your **firstname** and type your **lastname** In the **Subject** box, type your course name and section number, and in the **Keywords** box, type **luggage, bag, order, form** Return to **Normal** view and make cell **A1** active, display the grouped worksheets in **Print Preview**, **Close** the **Print Preview**, and then make any necessary corrections or adjustments. **Save** your workbook.

b. Print or submit the two worksheets in this workbook electronically as directed by your instructor. If required, print or create an electronic version of your worksheets with formulas displayed using the instructions in Activity 1.16 in Project 1A.

End You have completed Project 4D —————————

Apply **4A** skills from these Objectives:

▪ Use Financial Functions
▪ Use Goal Seek
▪ Create a Data Table

Mastering Excel | Project **4E** Condo Loan

In the following Mastering Excel project, you will create a worksheet for Jean Jacques Dupuis, President of Rubanne Specialties, that analyzes loan options for a condo in Montreal that the company is considering purchasing. Jean Jacques wants to provide a lodging facility for company visitors, but would like to keep the monthly loan payment below $6,000. The worksheets of your workbook will look similar to Figure 4.41.

Project Files

For Project 4E, you will need the following file:

e04E_Condo_Loan

You will save your workbook as:

Lastname_Firstname_4E_Condo_Loan

Project Results

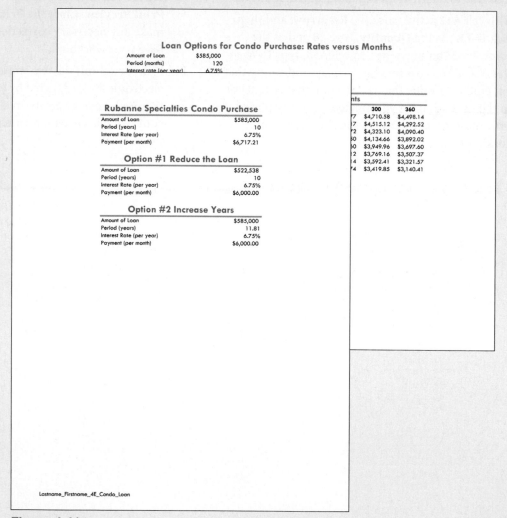

Figure 4.41

(Project 4E Condo Loan continues on the next page)

Content-Based Assessments

Mastering Excel | Project 4E Condo Loan (continued)

1 Start **Excel**. From your student files, locate and **Open** e04E_Condo_Loan. **Save** the file in your **Excel Chapter 4** folder as **Lastname_Firstname_4E_Condo_Loan**. In cell **B5**, insert the **PMT** function using the data from the range **B2:B5**—be sure to divide the interest rate by 12, multiply the years by 12, and display the payment as a positive number. The result, *$6,717.21*, is larger than the payment of $6,000.

2 Use **Goal Seek** so that the payment is under $6,000. Then, in **A7**, type **Option #1 Reduce the Loan** and then **Copy** the format from cell **A1** to cell **A7**. **Copy** the range **A2:B5**, and then **Paste** the **Values & Number Formatting** to cell **A8**. In cell **B2**, type **585000** to restore the original loan amount.

3 Use **Goal Seek** so that the payment does not exceed $6,000. In **A13**, type **Option #2 Increase Years**. Format the cell the same as cell **A7**. **Copy** the range **A2:B5**, and then **Paste** the **Values & Number Formatting** to cell **A14**. Display the value in **B15** with two decimal places, and then in cell **B3**, type **10** to restore the original value. Insert a footer with the **File Name** in the left section, and then **Center** the worksheet **Horizontally** on the page.

4 **Save** and return to **Normal** view. Set up a two-variable data table. Rename the **Sheet2 tab** to **Condo Payment Table** In the range **A2:B4**, enter the following row titles and data.

Amount of Loan	$585,000
Period (months)	120
Interest rate (per year)	6.75%

5 In cell **C8**, type **60**—the number of months in a 5-year loan. In **D8**, type **120**—the number of months in a 10-year loan. Fill the series through cell **H8**; apply **Bold** and **Center**.

6 Beginning in cell **B9**, enter varying interest rates in increments of .5% beginning with **8.5%** and ending with **5%**. Format all the interest rates with two decimal places, and then apply **Bold** and **Center**. In cell **B8**, enter a **PMT** function using the information in cells **B2:B4**. Be sure that you convert the interest rate to a monthly rate and that the result displays as a positive number.

7 Create a **Data Table** in the range **B8:H16** using the information in cells **B2:B4** in which the **Row input cell** is the **Period** and the **Column input cell** is the **Interest rate**. Copy the format from **B8** to the results in the data table. Format the range **E9:E10** with the **Note cell** style as two payment options that are close to but less than $6,000 per month. Change the **Orientation** to **Landscape**. Insert a footer with the **File Name** in the left section, and **Center** the worksheet **Horizontally** on the page. Return to **Normal** view and move to cell **A1**.

8 Display the **Document Panel** and in the **Author** box, type your **firstname** and type your **lastname** In the **Subject** box, type your course name and section number, and in the **Keywords** box, **condo, payment table**. **Print Preview**, make corrections, and **Save**. Print or submit electronically as directed.

End You have completed Project 4E ——————————————

Content-Based Assessments

Apply **4B** skills from these
Objectives:

4 Define Names

5 Use Defined Names in a Formula

6 Use Lookup Functions

7 Validate Data

Mastering Excel | Project **4F** Quarterly Cost Report and Lookup Form

In the following Mastering Excel project, you will assist Connor Fereday, the Vice President of Marketing at Rubanne Specialties, by defining names for ranges of cells in a workbook containing quarterly Advertising costs and by adding lookup functions to an Advertising Order form so that an order taker can complete the form quickly. Your completed workbooks will look similar to Figure 4.42.

Project Files

For Project 4F, you will need the following files:

> e04F_Advertising_Costs
> e04F_Advertising_Form

You will save your workbooks as:

> Lastname_Firstname_4F_Advertising_Costs
> Lastname_Firstname_4F_Advertising_Form

Project Results

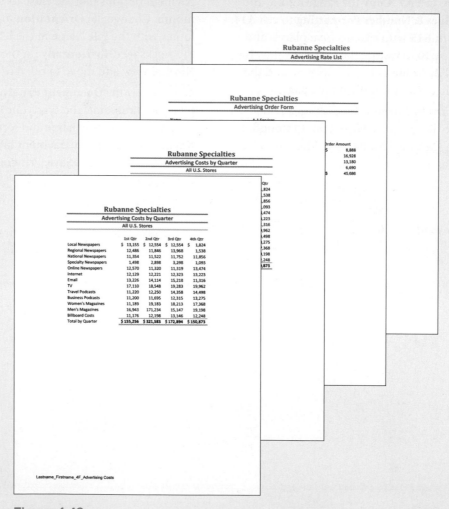

Figure 4.42

(Project 4F Quarterly Cost Report and Lookup Form continues on the next page)

Content-Based Assessments

1 From your student files, open **e04F_Advertising_
Costs. Save** it in your **Excel Chapter 4** folder as **Lastname_
Firstname_4F_Advertising_Costs** Display the **Advertising
Costs by Quarter** worksheet, and then apply appropriate
Currency [0], **Comma [0]**, and **Total** cell styles.

2 Name the following ranges: **B6:E9 Newspaper_
Costs B10:E14 Digital_Costs B15:B16 Magazine_Costs
B17:E17 Billboard_Costs Insert** a new row 15. In cell **A15**,
type **Business Podcasts** In cell **B15**, type **11200** In cell **C15**,
type **11695** In cell **D15**, type **12315** In cell **E15**, type **13275**.

3 Display **Name Manager**, click **Digital_Costs**, and then
include cell **E15**. Select the **Billboard_Costs**, and **Edit** the
name to **Outdoor_Costs**. Display the **Annual Advertising
Costs** sheet. In cell **B5**, type **=sum(N** and sum the values.
Do this for the other named ranges. Apply **Currency [0]**,
Comma [0], and **Total** cell styles. Sum all the costs. Group
the worksheets, insert a footer that includes the file name
and sheet tab name. **Center** the worksheets horizontally
on the page. Document properties should include the keywords **advertising costs. Save** your file and then print or
submit your worksheet electronically as directed by your
instructor. **Close** your file.

4 Open **e04F_Advertising_Form. Save** in **Excel Chapter 4**
folder as **Lastname_Firstname_4F_Advertising_Form**
Display the **Advertising Rate Information** sheet, select the
range **A4:C11**, and **Sort** by **Code**. Select the range **A4:A11**.
In the **Defined Names group**, click **Create from Selection**
with **Top row** selected, click **OK**. Display the **Advertising
Order Form** sheet; select range **A9:A18**. Display the **Data
Validation** button, select **List**, and then in the **Source** box,
type **=Code** Click **OK**.

5 Click cell **A9**, click the **list arrow**, click **D-PH**, and
then press Tab. With cell **B9** as the active cell, insert the
VLOOKUP function. As the **Lookup_value** box, click cell
A9. Click in the **Table_array** box, display the **Advertising
Rate Information** sheet, select the range **A4:C11**, and then
press F4 to make the cell reference absolute. In the
Col_index_num box, type **2** and then click **OK**.

6 With cell **B9** as the active cell, fill the VLOOKUP formula through cell **B18**. In cell **C9**, type **4** as the **Quantity
ordered** and press Tab. In cell **D9**, type **Regional** and
press Tab. With cell **E9** as the active cell, insert the
VLOOKUP function. As the **Lookup_value** box, click cell
A9, and then click in the **Table_array** box. Display the
Advertising Rate Information sheet, select the range
A4:C11, and then press F4. In the **Col_index_num** box,
type **3** and then click **OK. Copy** the VLOOKUP formula
through cell **E18**. Add the following orders:

Item	Quantity	Type
D-R	8	National
D-IN	10	Internet
B-BB	6	Billboard

7 Delete unused rows, sum the **Order Amount**, and
apply **Total** cell style. Group the worksheets, insert a footer
that includes the file name and sheet tab name. **Center** the
worksheets horizontally on the page. Document properties
should include the keywords **advertising costs** and **form
Save** your file and then print or submit your worksheet
electronically as directed by your instructor.

End **You have completed Project 4F**

Content-Based Assessments

1 Use Financial Functions

2 Use Goal Seek

3 Create a Data Table

4 Define Names

5 Use Defined Names in a Formula

6 Use Lookup Functions

7 Validate Data

Mastering Excel | Project **4G** Warehouse Loan and Lookup Form

In the following Mastering Excel project, you will create a worksheet for Jean Jacques Dupuis, President of Rubanne Specialties, that analyzes loan options for a warehouse that the company is considering purchasing. Jean Jacques wants to establish an additional storage facility in the United States, but would like to keep the monthly loan payment below $8,000. You will also assist Connor Fereday, the Vice President of Marketing at Rubanne Specialties by adding lookup functions to a Staff Planning form so that a manager can complete the form quickly. Your completed workbooks will look similar to Figure 4.43.

Project Files

For Project 4G, you will need the following files:

 e04G_Warehouse_Loan
 e04G_Staff_Form

You will save your workbooks as:

 Lastname_Firstname_4G_Warehouse_Loan
 Lastname_Firstname_4G_Staff_Form

Project Results

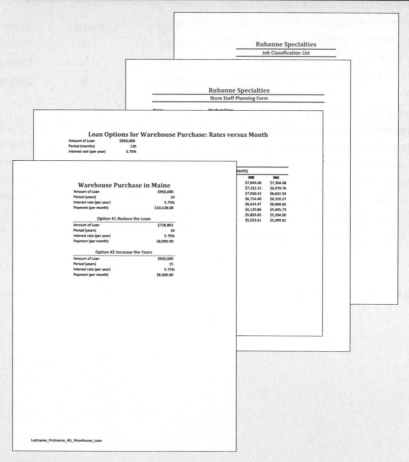

Figure 4.43

(Project 4G Warehouse Loan and Lookup Form continues on the next page)

Mastering Excel | Project 4G Warehouse Loan and Lookup Form (continued)

1 In your student files, locate and **Open** the file **e04G_Warehouse_Loan**, and **Save** it in your **Excel Chapter 4** folder as **Lastname_Firstname_4G_Warehouse_Loan** Display the **Warehouse Payment Table** sheet. In cell **B9**, enter rates in increments of .5% beginning with **8.5%** and ending with **5%** in cell B16. Format rates with two decimal places.

2 In cell **B8**, enter a **PMT** function using the information in cells **B2:B4**. Create a **Data Table** in the range **B8:H16** using the information in cells **B2:B4** in which the **Row input cell** is the **Period** and the **Column input cell** is the **Interest rate**. Apply the format from **B8** to the results in the data table. Select the two payment options closest to $8,000 per month and format the two options with the **Note** cell style.

3 Insert a footer that includes the file name, and document properties that include the keywords **warehouse loan** Change the **Orientation** to **Landscape**, **center** horizontally, and return to **Normal** view. **Print Preview**, **Save**, and then print or submit electronically as directed. **Close** this workbook.

4 Open the file **e04G_Staff_Form**, and **Save** it in your **Excel Chapter 4** folder as **Lastname_Firstname_4G_Staff_Form** On the **Job Information** sheet, select the range **A4:C11**, and then **Sort** the selection by **Job Code**. Name the range **A4:A11** by the name in the top row. Display the **Staffing Plan** sheet, and select the range **A9:A18**. Display the **Data Validation** dialog box, and validate from a **List** using the **Source =Job_Code**

5 Click cell **A9**, and then click **M-MG**. Click cell **B9**, and insert the **VLOOKUP** function. As the **Lookup_value**

box, click cell **A9**. Click in the **Table_array** box, display the **Job Information** sheet, select the range **A4:C11**, and then press F4 . In the **Col_index_num** box, type **2** and click **OK**.

6 With cell **B9** as the active cell, fill the VLOOKUP formula through cell **B18**. In cell **C9**, type **1** as the **# of Positions** and in cell **D9**, type **Management** as the **Type**. In cell **E9**, insert the **VLOOKUP** function. As the **Lookup_value** box, click cell **A9**, and then click in the **Table_array** box. Display the **Job Information** sheet, select the range **A4:C11**, and then press F4 . In the **Col_index_num** box, type **3** and then click **OK**. **Copy** the VLOOKUP formula down through cell **E18**.

7 Beginning in cell **A10**, add these staff positions:

Item	#of Positions	Type
C-CASH	4	Cashier
B-BYR	2	Buyer
M-AMG	2	Assistant Manager

8 Delete any unused rows between the last item and the Total row. Sum the **Budget Amount** column and apply the **Total** cell style. Group the worksheets, insert a footer in the left section with the file name, **center** horizontally, update the document properties with your name and course name and section, and add the **Keywords planning, staff Print Preview**, **Save**, and then submit it as directed. **Close** this workbook.

End You have completed Project 4G

Content-Based Assessments

GO! Fix It | Project **4H** Bag Costs by Quarter

Project Files

For Project 4H, you will need the following file:

> e04H_Bag_Costs

You will save your workbook as:

> Lastname_Firstname_4H_Bag_Costs

In this project, you will edit a worksheet to create range names, apply cell styles formatting, and check spelling on worksheets that display bag merchandise costs by quarter for Rubanne Specialties. From the student files that accompany this textbook, open the file e04H_Bag_Costs, and then save the file in your Excel Chapter 4 folder as **Lastname_Firstname_4H_Bag_Costs**

To complete the project, you must find and correct errors in formulas and formatting. In addition to errors that you find, you should know:

- There are two spelling errors.

- All data should be formatted with zero decimal places.

- There should be a named range for each of the following that should include appropriate data from correct ranges: *Handbag Costs*, *Travel Bag Costs*, *Tote Bag Costs*, and *Computer Bag Costs*. On the Annual Bag Costs worksheet, sum the quarterly costs of each named range.

- A footer should be inserted that includes the file name, and document properties should include the keywords **merchandise, bag category**

Save your file and then print or submit your worksheet electronically as directed by your instructor. To print formulas, refer to Activity 1.16. If you printed formulas, be sure to redisplay the worksheet by pressing Ctrl + `, and then exit Excel without saving.

End You have completed Project 4H ⎯⎯⎯⎯⎯⎯⎯⎯⎯⎯⎯⎯⎯⎯⎯⎯⎯⎯⎯

Content-Based Assessments

Apply a combination of the 4A and 4B skills.

GO! Make It | Project 4I Ohio Store Loan

Project Files

For Project 4I, you will need the following file:

New blank Excel workbook

You will save your workbook as:

Lastname_Firstname_4I_Ohio_Loan

Start a new blank Excel workbook and create the worksheet shown in Figure 4.44. In cell B7, insert the PMT function using the data in the range B2:B4. Then, create a data table in the range B7:H18 using periods of 6 months as shown, interest rates in .5% increments from 9.00% to 1.00%, and the information in cells B2:B4 in which the Row input cell is the Period and the Column input cell is the Interest rate. Apply the format from B8 to the results in the data table. Select the two payment options closest to $5,500 per month—one above and one below—and format the two options with the Note cell style. Rename Sheet 1 **Ohio Loan** Delete Sheet2 and Sheet3. Add your name, your course name and section number as the Subject, and include the Keywords **Cleveland, loan** Format the worksheet with a footer and centering, and Landscape, check in Print Preview, Save the file in your Excel Chapter 4 folder as **Lastname_Firstname_4I_Ohio_Loan** and then print or submit it electronically as directed.

Project Results

Figure 4.44

Loan Options for Cleveland: Rate versus Months

		24	30	36	42	48	54	60
Amount of Loan	$200,000							
Period (months)	36							
Interest rate (per year)	7.00%							
	$6,175.42							
9.00%	$9,136.95	$7,469.63	$6,359.95	$5,568.90	$4,977.01	$4,517.88	$4,151.67
8.50%	$9,091.13	$7,423.56	$6,313.51	$5,522.03	$4,929.66	$4,470.03	$4,103.31
8.00%	$9,045.46	$7,377.66	$6,267.27	$5,475.39	$4,882.58	$4,422.48	$4,055.28
7.50%	$8,999.92	$7,331.94	$6,221.24	$5,429.00	$4,835.78	$4,375.25	$4,007.59
7.00%	$8,954.52	$7,286.38	$6,175.42	$5,382.84	$4,789.25	$4,328.31	$3,960.24
6.50%	$8,909.25	$7,241.00	$6,129.80	$5,336.92	$4,742.99	$4,281.69	$3,913.23
6.00%	$8,864.12	$7,195.78	$6,084.39	$5,291.24	$4,697.01	$4,235.37	$3,866.56
5.50%	$8,819.13	$7,150.74	$6,039.18	$5,245.80	$4,651.30	$4,189.36	$3,820.23
5.00%	$8,774.28	$7,105.87	$5,994.18	$5,200.61	$4,605.86	$4,143.66	$3,774.25
4.50%	$8,729.56	$7,061.18	$5,949.38	$5,155.65	$4,560.70	$4,098.27	$3,728.60
4.00%	$8,684.98	$7,016.65	$5,904.80	$5,110.93	$4,515.81	$4,053.18	$3,683.30
3.50%	$8,640.54	$6,972.30	$5,860.42	$5,066.46	$4,471.20	$4,008.41	$3,638.35
3.00%	$8,596.24	$6,928.12	$5,816.24	$5,022.22	$4,426.87	$3,963.95	$3,593.74
2.50%	$8,552.08	$6,884.11	$5,772.28	$4,978.23	$4,382.81	$3,919.80	$3,549.47
2.00%	$8,508.05	$6,840.28	$5,728.52	$4,934.48	$4,339.02	$3,875.95	$3,505.53
1.50%	$8,464.17	$6,796.61	$5,684.96	$4,890.97	$4,295.52	$3,832.42	$3,461.98
1.00%	$8,420.42	$6,753.12	$5,641.62	$4,847.71	$4,252.29	$3,789.20	$3,418.75

Ohio Loan

End You have completed Project 4I

Content-Based Assessments

Apply a combination of the **4A** and **4B** skills.

GO! Solve It | Project **4J** Store Furnishings

Project Files

For Project 4J, you will need the following file:

e04J_Store_Furnishings

You will save your workbook as:

Lastname_Firstname_4J_Store_Furnishings

Open the file **e04J_Store_Furnishings** and save it as **Lastname_Firstname_4J_Store_Furnishings**

Complete the Store Furnishings Loan worksheet by using Goal Seek to explore two options for reducing the loan payment to approximately $7,500—either by reducing the loan or by increasing the number of years. Complete the Payment Table worksheet by creating a data table to calculate payments over 24–60 months with varying interest rates from 6.0% to 8.0% in .5% increments. Use Note cell style to indicate acceptable options. Include the file name in the footer, add appropriate properties, and submit it as directed.

		Performance Level	
		Exemplary: You consistently applied the relevant skills	**Proficient:** You sometimes, but not always, applied the relevant skills	**Developing:** You rarely or never applied the relevant skills
Performance Criteria	Use Financial Functions	The PMT Function is properly applied using supplied criteria.	The PMT Function is properly applied to some but not all supplied criteria.	The PMT Function is not properly applied and did not meet the supplied criteria.
	Use Goal Seek	Both Goal Seek outcomes were achieved using the supplied criteria.	One Goal Seek outcome was achieved using the supplied criteria.	No Goal Seek outcomes were achieved using the supplied criteria.
	Create a Data Table	All the criteria were met in the Data Table used to calculate the loan.	Some but not all the criteria were met in the Data Table used to calculate the loan.	The data table was not correctly calculated.

End You have completed Project 4J

Content-Based Assessments

Apply a combination of the 4A and 4B skills.

GO! Solve It | Project 4K Order Form

Project Files

For Project 4K, you will need the following file:

e04K_Order_Form

You will save your workbook as:

Lastname_Firstname_4K_Order_Form

Open the file e04K_Order_Form and save it as **Lastname_Firstname_4K_Order_Form**
Prepare the Product Information worksheet for a *VLOOKUP* function by sorting the items by
Style Code, and then create a named range for the Style Code information. On the Order Form
worksheet, using the named range, set data validation for the Item column. Insert the VLOOKUP
function in column B and column E, referencing the appropriate data in the Product Information
worksheet. Then enter the data below.

Item	Description	Quantity	Color
M-TF	Oversized Bags	12	Black
M-MC	Organizer Bags	24	Brown
C-S	Classic Bags	12	Black
C-T	Fabric Bags	36	Beige
C-R	Designer Bags	18	Black

Construct formulas to total the order, and then apply appropriate financial formatting. On both
sheets, include your name in the footer, add appropriate properties, and then submit them as directed.

	Performance Level		
	Exemplary: You consistently applied the relevant skills	Proficient: You sometimes, but not always, applied the relevant skills	Developing: You rarely or never applied the relevant skills
Use Lookup Functions	The VLOOKUP function correctly looks up data on the validation list.	The VLOOKUP function looks up some but not all the data on the validation list.	The VLOOKUP function does not display or does not look up any of the correct information.
Validate Data	The Validation List is sorted correctly.	Some of the Validation list was sorted.	The Validation List is not sorted.
Calculate and Format the Order Amount	The Order Amount and financial information is properly calculated and formatted.	Some, but not all, of the Order Amount and financial information is properly calculated and formatted.	Incorrect formulas and/or incorrect financial formatting were applied in most of the cells.

(Performance Criteria)

End You have completed Project 4K

Outcomes-Based Assessments

Rubric

The following outcomes-based assessments are *open-ended assessments*. That is, there is no specific correct result; your result will depend on your approach to the information provided. Make *Professional Quality* your goal. Use the following scoring rubric to guide you in *how* to approach the problem and then to evaluate *how well* your approach solves the problem.

The *criteria*—Software Mastery, Content, Format and Layout, and Process—represent the knowledge and skills you have gained that you can apply to solving the problem. The *levels of performance*—Professional Quality, Approaching Professional Quality, or Needs Quality Improvements—help you and your instructor evaluate your result.

	Your completed project is of Professional Quality if you:	Your completed project is Approaching Professional Quality if you:	Your completed project Needs Quality Improvements if you:
1-Software Mastery	Choose and apply the most appropriate skills, tools, and features and identify efficient methods to solve the problem.	Choose and apply some appropriate skills, tools, and features, but not in the most efficient manner.	Choose inappropriate skills, tools, or features, or are inefficient in solving the problem.
2-Content	Construct a solution that is clear and well organized, contains content that is accurate, appropriate to the audience and purpose, and is complete. Provide a solution that contains no errors in spelling, grammar, or style.	Construct a solution in which some components are unclear, poorly organized, inconsistent, or incomplete. Misjudge the needs of the audience. Have some errors in spelling, grammar, or style, but the errors do not detract from comprehension.	Construct a solution that is unclear, incomplete, or poorly organized; contains some inaccurate or inappropriate content; and contains many errors in spelling, grammar, or style. Do not solve the problem.
3-Format and Layout	Format and arrange all elements to communicate information and ideas, clarify function, illustrate relationships, and indicate relative importance.	Apply appropriate format and layout features to some elements, but not others. Overuse features, causing minor distraction.	Apply format and layout that does not communicate information or ideas clearly. Do not use format and layout features to clarify function, illustrate relationships, or indicate relative importance. Use available features excessively, causing distraction.
4-Process	Use an organized approach that integrates planning, development, self-assessment, revision, and reflection.	Demonstrate an organized approach in some areas, but not others; or, use an insufficient process of organization throughout.	Do not use an organized approach to solve the problem.

Outcomes-Based Assessments

GO! Think | Project **4L** Key Chains

Project Files

For Project 4L, you will need the following file:

e04L_Key_Chains

You will save your workbook as:

Lastname_Firstname_4L_Key_Chains

From your student files, open the file e04L_Key_Chains, and then save it in your chapter folder as **Lastname_Firstname_4L_Key_Chains** So that order takers do not have to type the Style Code, Description, and Unit Price in the Order Form worksheet, use the information on the Product Information sheet to create a validation list for the Item and then insert a VLOOKUP function in the Description and Unit Price columns. Then create an order for two of the Plush Animal Keychains (K-S) and two of the Classic Keychains (M-TF). Delete unused rows, create appropriate totals, apply financial formatting, and then save and submit it as directed.

 You have completed Project 4L ——————————

GO! Think | Project **4M** Delivery Van Purchase

Project Files

For Project 4M, you will need the following file:

New blank Excel document

You will save your document as:

Lastname_Firstname_4M_Van_Purchase

Etienne Alta, Chief Financial Officer for Rubanne Specialties, is exploring financing options for the purchase of four new delivery vans for the company, the cost of which totals $150,000. Using a format similar to the one you used in this chapter, create a worksheet that uses the PMT function to calculate the monthly payment for a loan of $150,000 for 36 months at a rate of 5.25%. Then, create a data table for varying interest rates from 7% to 3.5% in increments of 0.5% and for six periods—from 24 months to 60 months in 6-month increments. Use the Period as the row input and the interest rate as the column input. Apply the Note style to the two closest results to $3,500. Format the worksheet so that it is professional and easy to read and understand. Insert a footer with the file name and add appropriate document properties. Save the file as **Lastname_Firstname_4M_Van_Purchase**

You have completed Project 4M ——————————

Outcomes-Based Assessments

Apply a combination of the **4A** and **4B** skills.

You and GO! | Project **4N** Vehicle Loan

Project Files

For Project 4N, you will need the following file:

New blank Excel document

You will save your document as:

Lastname_Firstname_4N_Vehicle_Loan

In this chapter, you practiced using Excel to analyze the effect of interest rates and terms on loan payments. From a site such as Kelley Blue Book (www.kbb.com), research a vehicle that you would like to purchase and then begin a new blank workbook. Using a format similar to the one you practiced in this chapter, enter the price of the vehicle and the down payment if any. Subtract the down payment from the purchase price to determine the loan amount. Enter an interest rate of 5% and a loan term of 4 years. If you want to do so, use Goal Seek to determine options for a lower loan amount or a longer payment period, to match the monthly payment that you think you can afford. Insert a footer with the file name and center the worksheet horizontally on the page. Save your file as **Lastname_Firstname_4N_Vehicle_Loan** and submit it as directed.

 You have completed Project 4N —————————

Managing Large Workbooks and Using Advanced Sorting and Filtering

OUTCOMES

At the end of this chapter you will be able to:

OBJECTIVES

Mastering these objectives will enable you to:

PROJECT 5A

Manage large workbooks, create attractive workbooks, and save workbooks to share with others.

1. Navigate and Manage Large Worksheets (p. 301)
2. Enhance Worksheets with Themes and Styles (p. 307)
3. Format a Worksheet to Share with Others (p. 310)
4. Save Excel Data in Other File Formats (p. 316)

PROJECT 5B

Analyze information in a database format using advanced sort, filter, subtotaling, and outlining.

5. Use Advanced Sort Techniques (p. 323)
6. Use Custom and Advanced Filters (p. 328)
7. Subtotal, Outline, and Group a List of Data (p. 339)

Joy Brown/Shutterstock

In This Chapter

In this chapter, you will navigate within a large worksheet, insert a hyperlink in a worksheet, save a worksheet as a Web page, and save worksheets in other file formats to share with others. You will practice applying and modifying themes, styles, lines, and borders to enhance the format of your worksheets.

In this chapter, you will also use Excel's advanced table features and database capabilities to organize data in a useful manner. The skills in this chapter include advanced sorting, sorting on multiple columns, and custom filtering to compare subsets of data. You will also limit data to display records that meet one or more specific conditions, add subtotals, and outline data. These skills will help you visualize and analyze your data effectively.

The projects in this chapter relate to **Capital Cities Community College**, which provides high quality education and professional training to residents in the cities surrounding the nation's capital. Its five campuses serve over 50,000 students and offer more than 140 certificate programs and degrees. Over 2,100 faculty and staff make student success a top priority. CapCCC makes positive contributions to the community through cultural and athletic programs, health care, economic development activities, and partnerships with businesses and non-profit organizations.

Project 5A Large Worksheet for a Class Schedule

myitlab
Project 5A Training

Project Activities

In Activities 5.01 through 5.13, you will assist Charles Krasnov, Program Chair for Computer Information Systems, in formatting and navigating a large worksheet that lists the class schedule for the Business Office Systems and Computer Information Systems departments at Capital Cities Community College. You will also save Excel data in other file formats. The worksheets in your completed workbooks will look similar to Figure 5.1.

Project Files

For Project 5A, you will need the following files:

    e05A_Class_Schedule
    e05A_Faculty_Contacts
    e05A_Fall_Classes
    e05A_Teaching_Requests

You will save your workbooks as:

    Lastname_Firstname_5A_Class_Schedule (Excel Worksheet)
    Lastname_Firstname_5A_Faculty_Contacts (Excel Worksheet)
    Lastname_Firstname_5A_Fall_PDF (Adobe PDF Document)
    Lastname_Firstname_5A_Fall_XPS (XPS Document)
    Lastname_Firstname_5A_Schedule_CVS (Microsoft Office Excel Comma Separated
      Values File)
    Lastname_Firstname_5A_Schedule_Webpage (HTML Document)

Project Results

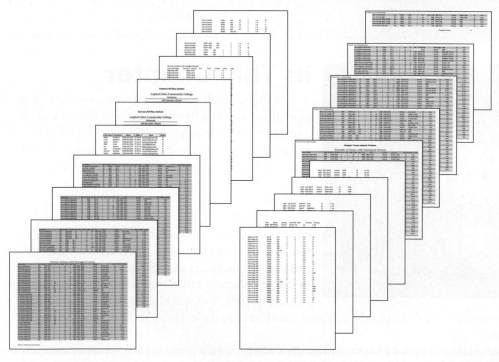

Figure 5.1
Project 5A Large Worksheet

Objective 1 | Navigate and Manage Large Worksheets

Because you cannot view all the columns and rows of a large worksheet on your screen at one time, Excel provides features that help you control the screen display and navigate the worksheet so you can locate information quickly. For example, you can hide columns and use the *Freeze Panes* command, which sets the column and row titles so that they remain on the screen while you scroll. The locked rows and columns become separate *panes*—portions of a worksheet window bounded by and separated from other portions by vertical or horizontal lines.

You can also use the *Find* command to find and select specific text, formatting, or a type of information within the workbook quickly.

Activity 5.01 | Using the Go To Special Command

Use the *Go To Special* command to move to cells that have special characteristics, for example, to cells that are blank or to cells that contain constants, as opposed to formulas.

1 **Start** Excel. From your student files, open **e05A_Class_Schedule**. In your storage location, create a new folder named **Excel Chapter 5** and then **Save** the file as **Lastname_Firstname_5A_Class_Schedule**

> **Another Way**
> Press Ctrl + G, and then in the lower left corner of the dialog box, click the Special button.

This worksheet lists the computer courses that are available for the upcoming semester in three college departments.

2 On the **Home tab**, in the **Editing group**, click the **Find & Select** button, and then click **Go To Special**. Compare your screen with Figure 5.2.

In the Go to Special dialog box, you can click an option button to move to cells that contain the special options listed.

Figure 5.2

Go To Special dialog box

Find & Select button

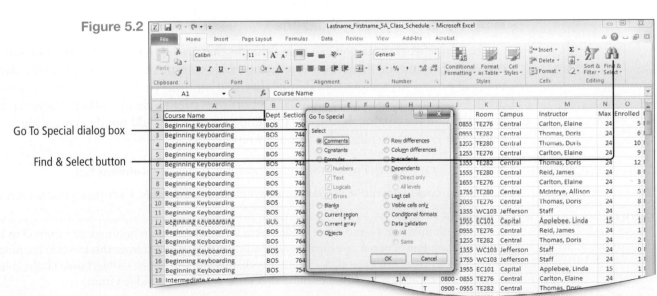

3 In the first column, click the **Blanks** option button, and then click **OK**.

All blank cells in the *active area* of the worksheet are located and selected, and the first blank cell—J124—is active. The active area is the area of the worksheet that contains data or has contained data—it does not include any empty cells that have not been used in this worksheet. Cell J124 is missing the time for a Linux/UNIX class held on Tuesday.

4 Point to cell **J124** and right-click. On the Mini toolbar, click the **Fill Color button arrow** 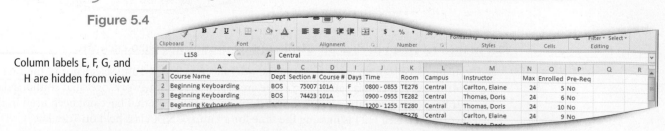 and then under **Standard Colors**, click the fourth color—**Yellow**—to highlight the blank cells.

This missing information must be researched before a time can be entered, and the yellow fill color will help locate this cell later, when the correct time for the class is determined.

5 Scroll down and locate the other two cells identified as blank—**J148** and **J160**—and compare your screen with Figure 5.3.

When you initiated the Go To Special command for Blank cells, Excel located and selected *all* blank cells in the active area. Thus, the formatting you applied to the first blank cell, yellow fill, was applied to all the selected cells.

Figure 5.3

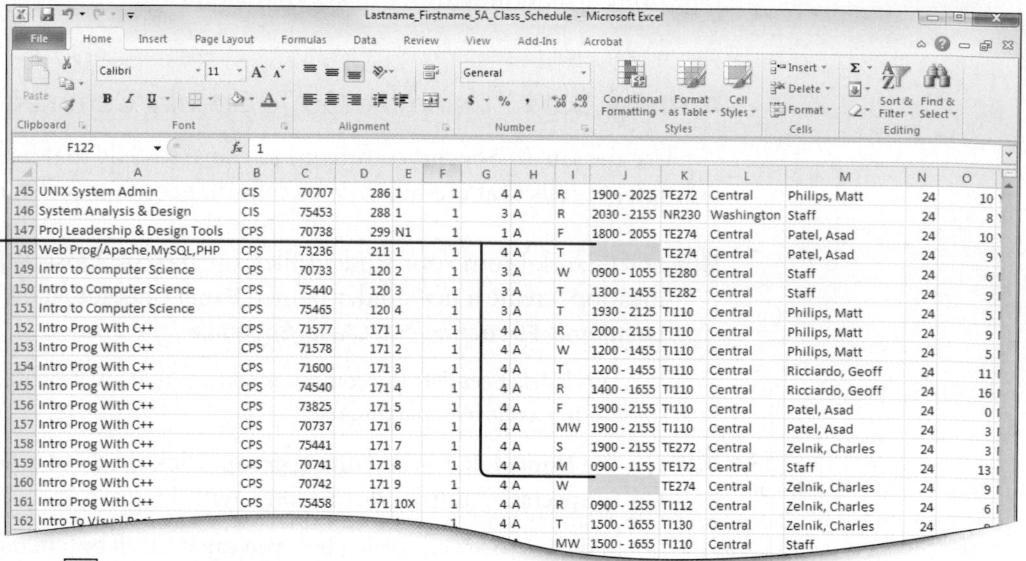

Blank cells with missing information highlighted

6 **Save** your workbook.

Activity 5.02 | Hiding Columns

In a large worksheet, you can hide columns that are not necessary for the immediate task, and then unhide them later. You can also hide columns or rows to control the data that will print or to remove confidential information from view—hidden data does not print. For example, to create a summary report, you could hide the columns between the row titles and the totals column, and the hidden columns would not display on the printed worksheet, resulting in a summary report.

Another Way

On the Home tab, in the Cells group, click the Format button. Under Visibility, point to Hide & Unhide, and then click Hide Columns.

1 Press Ctrl + Home. From the column heading area, select **columns E:H**.

2 Right-click over the selected columns, and then click **Hide**. Compare your screen with Figure 5.4.

Columns E, F, G, and H are hidden from view—the column headings skip from D to I. A black line between columns D and I indicates that columns from this location are hidden from view. After you click in another cell, this line will not be visible; however, the column letters provide a visual indication that some columns are hidden from view.

Figure 5.4

Column labels E, F, G, and H are hidden from view

3 Press `Ctrl` + `Home`, and then notice that the line between the **column D heading** and the **column I heading** is slightly darker, indicating hidden columns. **Save** 🖫 your workbook.

Activity 5.03 | Using the Go To Command

Use the *Go To* command to move to a specific cell or range of cells in a large worksheet.

1 On the **Home tab**, in the **Editing group**, click the **Find & Select** button, and then click **Go To**. In the **Go To** dialog box, with the insertion point blinking in the **Reference** box, type **m172** and then click **OK**.

2 With cell **M172** active, on the **Formulas tab**, in the **Functions Library group**, click the **More Functions** button, point to **Statistical**, and then click **COUNTIF**. As the **Range**, type **m2:m170** and as the **Criteria**, type **Staff** Click **OK**. Compare your screen with Figure 5.5.

> Your result is 47, indicating that 47 courses still indicate *Staff* and need an instructor assigned.

Figure 5.5

Your result is 47, indicating that 47 courses still indicate *Staff* and need an instructor assigned

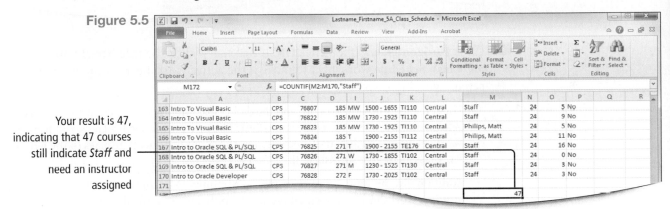

3 In cell **K172**, type **Unassigned classes** and press `Enter`.

4 Press `Ctrl` + `Home`, and then **Save** 🖫 your workbook.

Activity 5.04 | Arranging Multiple Workbooks and Splitting Worksheets

If you need to refer to information in one workbook while you have another workbook open, you can arrange the window to display sheets from more than one workbook—instead of jumping back and forth between the two workbooks from the taskbar. This is accomplished by using the *Arrange All* command, which tiles all open program windows on the screen. Additionally, you can view separate parts of the *same* worksheet on your screen by using the *Split* command, which splits the window into multiple resizable panes to view distant parts of your worksheet at once.

1 From **Backstage** view, display the **Open** dialog box, and then from your student files, open the file **e05A_Teaching_Requests**.

> The e05A_Teaching_Requests file opens, and your 5A_Class_Schedule file is no longer visible on your screen. This worksheet contains a list of instructors who submitted requests for classes they would like to teach. You need not save this file; it is for reference only.

2 On the **View tab**, in the **Window group**, click the **Switch Windows** button, and then at the bottom of the list, click your **5A_Class_Schedule** file to make it the active worksheet.

3 In the **Window group**, click the **Arrange All** button. Compare your screen with Figure 5.6.

Here, in the Arrange Windows dialog box, you can control how two or more worksheets from multiple open workbooks are arranged on the screen.

Figure 5.6

Arrange Windows dialog box

Options for viewing multiple worksheets on your screen

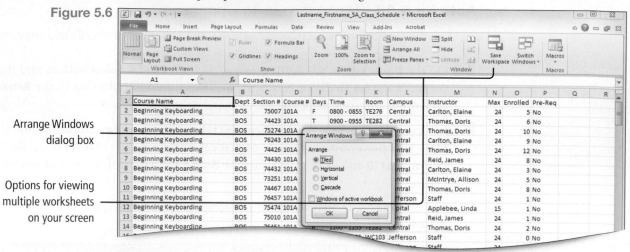

4 Click **Horizontal**, and then click **OK**. If necessary, click the title bar of your **5A_Class_Schedule** worksheet to make it the active worksheet. Compare your screen with Figure 5.7.

The screen is split horizontally, and the e05A_Teaching_Requests worksheet displays below your 5A_Class_Schedule worksheet. The active window displays scroll bars, its title bar displays in a slightly darker shade, and the green Excel icon displays to the left of your 5A_Class_Schedule worksheet title.

Additionally, the active window displays a Minimize, Maximize, and Close button. When multiple worksheets are open on the screen, only one is active at a time. To activate a worksheet, click anywhere on the worksheet or click the worksheet's title bar.

Figure 5.7

Title bar of active window is a slightly darker shade of grey

Excel icon displays in title bar of active sheet

Windows arranged horizontally

Minimize, Maximize, and Close buttons display for active window

Scroll bars display in active window

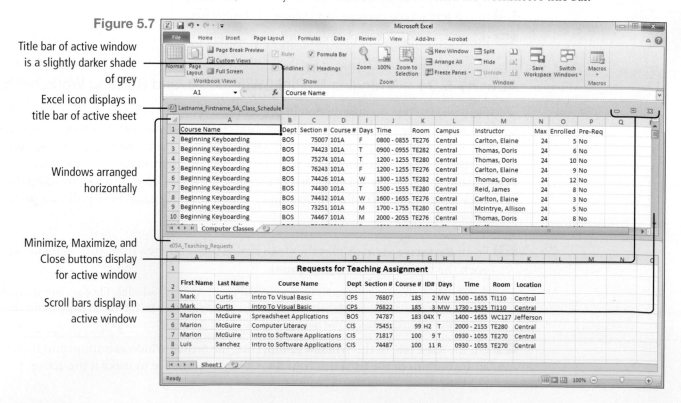

5 Press Ctrl + End to move to cell **P172**, which is now the end of the active area of the worksheet.

6 Click cell **A172**. In the **Window group**, click **Split** to split this upper window horizontally at row 172. Compare your screen with Figure 5.8.

> A light blue horizontal bar displays at the top of row 172, and two sets of vertical scroll bars display in the 5A_Class_Schedule worksheet—one in each of the two worksheet parts displayed in this window.

Figure 5.8

5A_Class_Schedule worksheet split into two panes

e05A_Teaching_Requests worksheet displays in lower window

Vertical scroll bars display in both panes of active worksheet

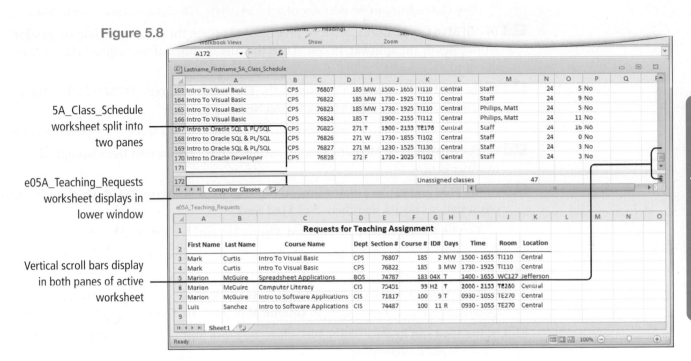

7 Above the **split bar**, click in any cell in **column C**. Press Ctrl + F to display the **Find tab** of the **Find and Replace** dialog box.

> Column C lists the Section # for each class. This is a unique number that identifies each class.

8 Drag the title bar of the dialog box into the upper right area of your screen. Then, in the lower half of your screen, look at the first request in the **e05A_Teaching_Requests** worksheet, which is from *Mark Curtis* to teach *Intro to Visual Basic Section # 76807*. In the **Find what** box, type **76807** so that you can locate the course in the **5A_Class_Schedule** worksheet.

9 Click **Find Next**, be sure that you can see the **Name Box**, and then compare your screen with Figure 5.9.

> Section # 76807 is located and selected in cell C163 of the Class Schedule worksheet.

Figure 5.9

Find and Replace dialog box

Name Box visible, indicates cell C163 found

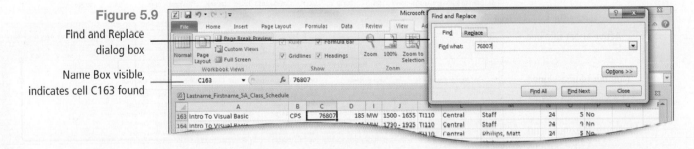

10 In your **5A_Class_Schedule** worksheet, click in cell **M163**, type **Curtis, Mark** to delete *Staff* and assign the class to Mr. Curtis. Press [Enter].

> The class is assigned to Mr. Curtis, and the number of unassigned classes, which you can view below the split bar, goes down by one, to 46. Use the Split command when you need to see two distant parts of the same worksheet simultaneously.

11 In the **e05A_Teaching_Requests** worksheet, look at **row 4** and notice that the next request, also from Mr. Curtis, is to teach *Section # 76822*.

> This class is listed in the next row of your 5A_Class_Schedule worksheet—row 164.

12 In cell **M164**, type **Curtis, Mark** or press [Enter] to accept the AutoComplete suggestion. Notice below the split bar, in cell **M172**, that the number of unassigned classes goes down to *45*.

13 In the **Find and Replace** dialog box, in the **Find what** box, type **74787** which is the next requested Section #, and then click **Find Next**.

> Section # 74787 in cell C66 is selected. Marion McGuire has requested to teach this class.

14 Click cell **M66**, type **McGuire, Marion** and press [Enter]; notice that the unassigned number is now *44*.

15 In the **Find and Replace** dialog box, in the **Find what** box, type **75451** which is the next requested Section #, and then click **Find Next**.

> Section # 75451 in cell C78 is selected. Marion McGuire has requested to teach this class also.

16 In cell **M78**, type **McGuire, Marion** and press [Enter]; *43* classes remain unassigned.

17 Continue to use the **Find and Replace** dialog box to locate the remaining two **Section #s** listed in the **e05A_Teaching_Requests** worksheet, and enter the appropriate instructor name for each class in **column M** of your **5A_Class_Schedule** worksheet.

18 In the **Find and Replace** dialog box, click the **Close** button. In cell **M172**, notice that *41* classes remain unassigned.

19 Click any cell in the **e05A_Teaching_Requests** worksheet to make it the active sheet, and then on this worksheet's title bar, at the far right end, notice that a **Minimize** [▬], **Maximize** [□], and **Close** button [✕] display. Compare your screen with Figure 5.10.

Figure 5.10

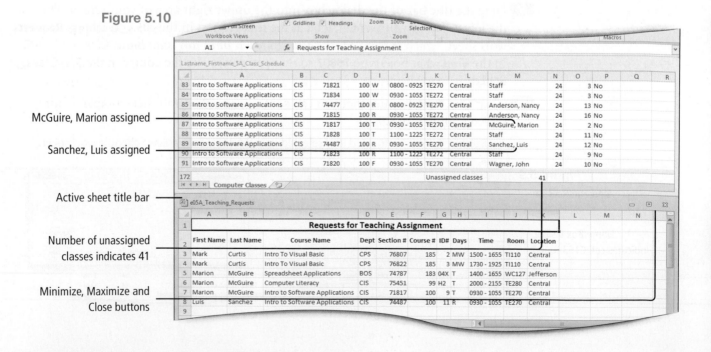

McGuire, Marion assigned

Sanchez, Luis assigned

Active sheet title bar

Number of unassigned classes indicates 41

Minimize, Maximize and Close buttons

20 On the title bar, click the **Close** button ⊠ to close this workbook. Then, on the title bar of your **5A_Class_Schedule** worksheet, click the **Maximize** button ▣ to restore the size of the worksheet to its full size.

21 On the **View tab**, in the **Window group**, click **Split** to remove the split.

22 Press Ctrl + Home. From the **column heading area**, select **columns D:I**—recall that columns E:H are still hidden. Right-click over the selected area, and then click **Unhide**.

> To redisplay hidden columns, first select the columns on either side of the hidden columns—columns D and I in this instance.

23 Press Ctrl + Home, and then **Save** 🔲 your workbook.

Objective 2 | Enhance Worksheets with Themes and Styles

Worksheets used to be uninteresting grids of columns and rows viewed primarily on paper by accountants and managers. Now individuals may commonly use worksheets to communicate information both within an organization and to the public. A worksheet might be seen by individuals in an e-mail, in a PowerPoint presentation, or in public blogs and publications. Thus, you will want to use some creative elements when preparing your worksheets.

Recall that a *theme* is a predesigned set of colors, fonts, lines, and fill effects that look good together and that can be applied to your entire Office 2010 file or to specific items. A theme combines two sets of fonts—one for text and one for headings. In the default Office theme, Cambria is the font for headings and Calibri is the font for body text.

In Excel, the applied theme has a set of complimentary *cell styles*—a defined set of formatting characteristics, such as fonts, font sizes, number formats, cell borders, and cell shading. The applied theme also has a set of complimentary table styles for data that you format as a table.

You can create your own themes, cells styles, and table styles.

Activity 5.05 | Changing and Customizing a Workbook Theme

1 Point to the **row 1 heading** to display the ➡ pointer, right-click, and then click **Insert** to insert a new blank row. In cell **A1**, type **Schedule of Classes with Unassigned Sections** and press Enter. On the **Home tab**, **Merge & Center** this title across the range **A1:P1**, and then apply the **Title** cell style.

2 On the **Page Layout tab**, in the **Themes group**, click the **Themes** button. Compare your screen with Figure 5.11.

The gallery of predesigned themes that come with Microsoft Office displays. Office—the default theme—is selected.

Figure 5.11

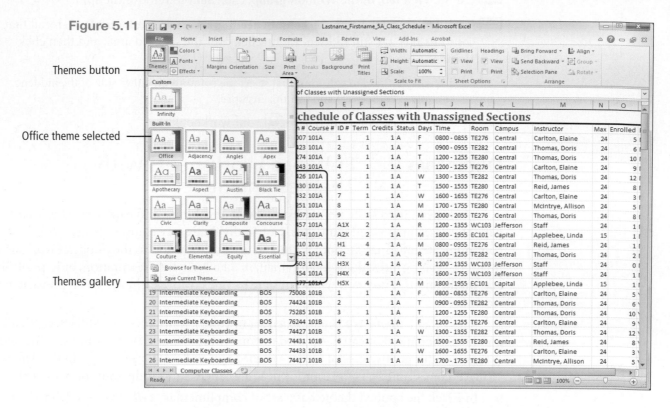

Themes button

Office theme selected

Themes gallery

3 Point to several of the themes and notice how Live Preview displays the colors and fonts associated with each theme. Then, click the **Flow** theme.

4 In the **Themes group**, click the **Fonts** button.

The fonts associated with the Flow theme are Calibri and Constantia, but you can customize a theme by mixing the Colors, Fonts, and Effects from any of the supplied themes.

5 Scroll to the top and click the **Office** fonts. **Save** 🔲 your workbook.

Activity 5.06 | Creating and Applying a Custom Table Style

Excel comes with many predefined table styles, also called quick styles, but if none of those meets your needs, you can also create and apply a custom table of your own design. Custom table styles that you create are stored only in the current workbook, so they are not available in other workbooks.

1 On the **Home tab**, in the **Styles group**, click the **Format as Table** button. At the bottom, click **New Table Style**.

2 In the **New Table Quick Style** dialog box, in the **Name** box, replace the existing text by typing **Class Schedule**

3 In the list under **Table Element**, click **First Row Stripe**, and then compare your screen with Figure 5.12.

Here you can select one or more elements of the table, and then customize the format for each element.

Figure 5.12

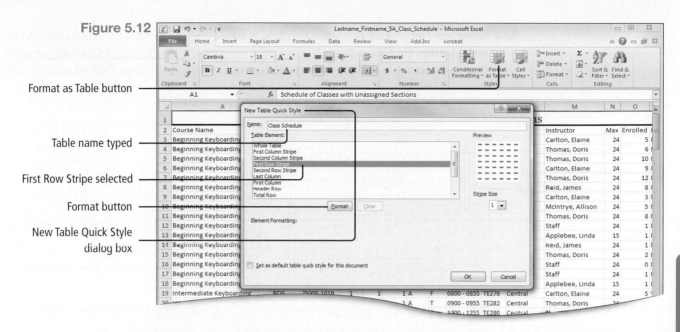

Format as Table button

Table name typed

First Row Stripe selected

Format button

New Table Quick Style
dialog box

4 Below the list of table elements, click the **Format** button. In the **Format Cells** dialog box, click the **Fill tab**. In the fourth column of colors, click the second color, and notice that the **Sample** area previews the color you selected.

5 In the lower right corner, click **OK**. In the list of table elements, click **Second Row Stripe**, click the **Format** button, and then in the fourth column of colors, click the third color. Click **OK**. Notice the **Preview** that shows the two colors.

6 In the list of table elements, click **Header Row**, click the **Format** button, and then in the third column of colors, click the fourth color.

7 Click **OK**, notice the **Preview**, and then compare your screen with Figure 5.13.

Figure 5.13

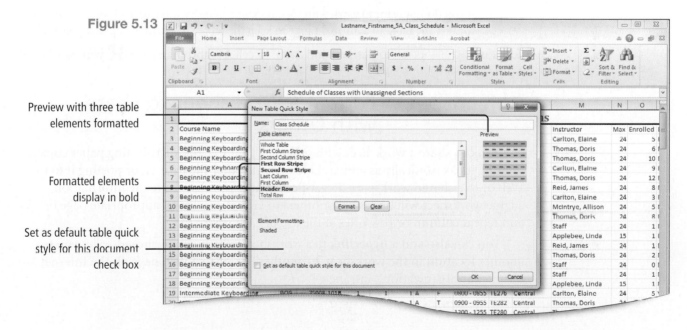

Preview with three table
elements formatted

Formatted elements
display in bold

Set as default table quick
style for this document
check box

8 In the lower left corner of the dialog box, click to select the check box **Set as default table quick style for this document**. Click **OK**.

You must select this check box to make your table style available in the gallery of table styles.

Excel | Chapter 5

9 Select the range **A2:P171**—do *not* include row 1 in your selection—and then in the **Styles group**, click **Format as Table**. At the top of the gallery, under **Custom**, point to your custom table style to display the ScreenTip *Class Schedule*. Compare your screen with Figure 5.14.

Figure 5.14

Format as Table button

Your custom style named
Class Schedule

Table Styles gallery

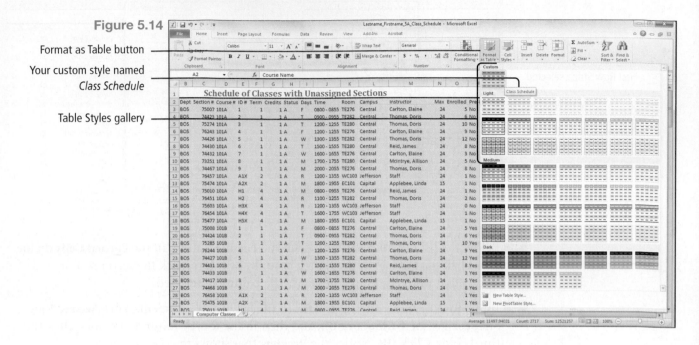

10 Click your **Class Schedule** table style, and then in the **Format As Table** dialog box, click **OK**. Then, because you do not need to filter the table, in the **Tools group**, click **Convert to Range**, and then click **Yes**.

If you do not want to work with your data in a table by filtering and sorting, you can convert the table to a normal range to keep the table style formatting that you applied.

11 Press Ctrl + Home to deselect and move to cell **A1**, and then **Save** 💾 your workbook.

Objective 3 | Format a Worksheet to Share with Others

You can share a worksheet with others by printing and distributing paper copies, sending it electronically as an Excel file or some other file format, or posting it to the Web or to a shared workspace. Regardless of how you distribute the information, a large worksheet will be easier for others to view if you insert appropriate page breaks and repeat column or row titles at the top of each page.

You can also add a *hyperlink* to a worksheet, which, when clicked, takes you to another location in the worksheet, to another file, or to a Web page on the Internet or on your organization's intranet.

Activity 5.07 | Previewing and Modifying Page Breaks

Before you print or electronically distribute a large worksheet, preview it to see where the pages will break across the columns and rows. You can move the page breaks to a column or row that groups the data logically, and you can change the orientation between portrait and landscape if you want to display more rows on the page (portrait) or more columns on the page (landscape). You can also apply *scaling* to the data to force the worksheet into a selected number of pages. Scaling reduces the horizontal and vertical size of the printed data by a percentage or by the number of pages that you specify.

Another Way

After selecting the columns, in the column heading area, point to any of the column borders and double-click.

1 From the column heading area, select **columns A:P**, in the **Cells group**, click the **Format** button, and then click **AutoFit Column Width**.

2 Click cell **A1**, and then press Ctrl + F2 to view the **Print Preview**. Notice that as currently formatted, the worksheet will print on 8 pages.

3 At the bottom of the **Print Preview**, click the **Next Page** button seven times to view the eight pages required to print this worksheet.

As you view each page, notice that pages 5 through 8 display the Time, Room, Campus, Instructor, Max, Enrolled, and Pre-Req columns that relate to the first four pages of the printout. You can see that the printed worksheet will be easier to read if all the information related to a class is on the same page.

4 On the Ribbon, click the **View tab** to return to the worksheet, and then in the **Workbook Views group**, click **Page Break Preview**. If the Welcome to Page Break Preview dialog box displays, click OK to close it. Compare your screen with Figure 5.15.

The Page Break Preview window displays blue dashed lines to show where the page breaks are in the current page layout for this worksheet.

Figure 5.15

Blue dotted lines show where pages are divided

Page number displays on the page

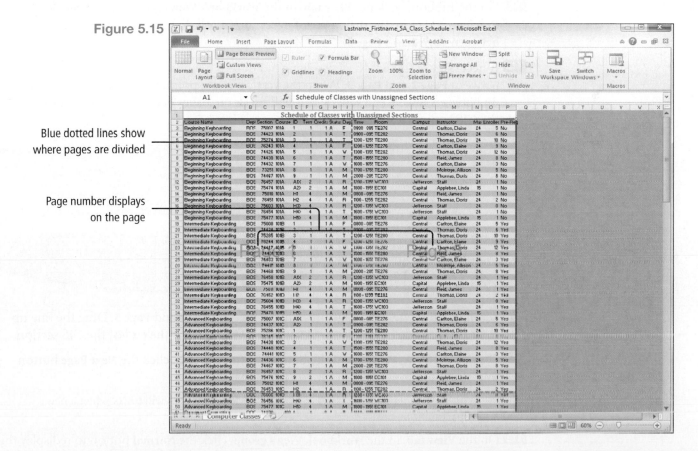

Note | Welcome to Page Break Preview

The Welcome to Page Break Preview dialog box may display with a message informing you that page breaks can be adjusted by clicking and dragging the breaks with your mouse. If this box displays, click OK to close it.

5 Scroll down to view the other pages and see where the page breaks are indicated. Then, in the **Workbook Views group**, click **Normal** to redisplay the worksheet in Normal view.

Dashed lines display at the page break locations on the worksheet.

Another Way

On the Page Layout tab, in the Page Setup group, click the Dialog Box Launcher button to display the Page Setup dialog box.

6 On the **Page Layout tab**, in the **Page Setup group**, set the **Orientation** to **Landscape**. Then, in the **Scale to Fit group**, click the **Width arrow**, and then click **1 page**. Click the **Height arrow** and click **4 pages**.

In the Scale to Fit group, there are two ways to override the default printout size. In the Scale box, you can specify a scaling factor from between 10 and 400 percent. Or, you can use the Width and Height arrows to fit the printout to a specified number of pages. To return to a full-size printout after scaling, in the Scale box, type 100 as the percentage.

7 From the **Insert tab**, insert a footer in the **left section** that includes the file name. Click in the **right section**, and then in the **Header & Footer Elements group**, click the **Page Number** button.

It is good practice to insert any headers or footers *before* making the final page break decisions on your worksheet.

8 Click any cell above the footer to exit the Footer area. Press Ctrl + F2 to display the Print Preview, and at the bottom, notice that the worksheet is now a total of four pages.

By applying the scaling, each complete row of data will fit on one page.

9 On the Ribbon, click the **View tab**, in the **Workbook Views group**, click **Page Break Preview**, and close the dialog box if necessary. Scroll down to view the page break between **Page 2** and **Page 3**.

10 If necessary, scroll left to view column A. Point to the horizontal page break line between **Page 2** and **Page 3**. When the vertical resize pointer ⟨↕⟩ displays, drag the line up between **row 77** and **row 78**; this will break the pages between the BOS courses and the CIS courses. Compare your screen with Figure 5.16.

Figure 5.16

Page break line moved between row 77 and 78

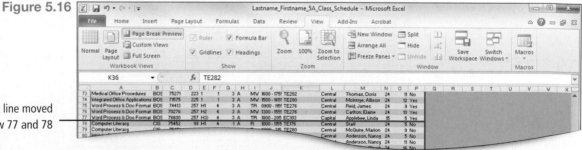

11 Scroll down to view the page break line between **Page 4** and **Page 5**. Drag the line up to break the page between **row 147** and **row 148**, which is the end of the CIS section.

12 Display the **Print Preview**. At the bottom of the window, click the **Next Page** button four times to scroll through the five pages that will print.

With the new page breaks that you have inserted, the pages will break when a new Department begins.

13 On the **View tab**, in the **Workbook Views group**, click the **Normal** button to redisplay the worksheet in Normal view. Press Ctrl + Home, and then click **Save** 💾.

Activity 5.08 | Repeating Column or Row Titles

Recall that when your worksheet layout spans multiple pages, you will typically want to repeat the column titles on each page. If your worksheet is wider than one page, you will also want to repeat the row titles on each page.

1 Display the **Print Preview**, scroll through the pages, and notice that the column titles display only on the first page.

> Repeating the column titles on each page will make it easier to understand and read the information on the pages.

2 On the **Page Layout tab**, in the **Page Setup group**, click the **Print Titles** button to display the **Sheet tab** of the **Page Setup** dialog box.

> Here you can select rows to repeat at the top of each page or columns to repeat at the left of each page.

3 Under **Print titles**, click in the **Rows to repeat at top** box, and then from the **row heading area**, select **row 2**. Compare your screen with Figure 5.17.

> A moving border surrounds row 2, and the mouse pointer displays as a black select row arrow. The absolute reference $2:$2 displays in the Rows to repeat at top box.

Figure 5.17

Absolute row reference

Row 2 selected to repeat at the top

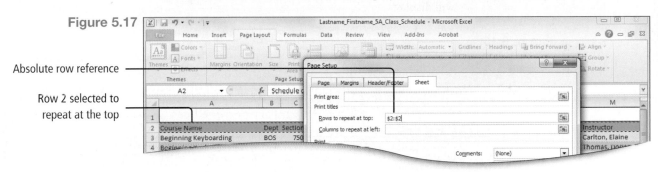

4 Click on **OK**. Display the **Print Preview**, scroll through the pages and notice that the column titles display at the top of each page. Verify that the page breaks are still located between each department. Display **Page 2**, and then compare your screen with Figure 5.18.

Figure 5.18

Column titles display at top of page

End of BOS section

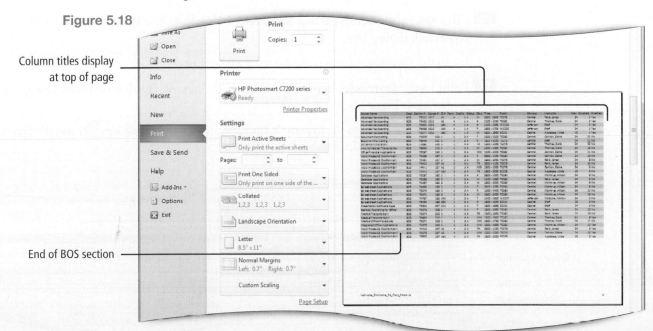

5 Click the **Home tab**, and then click **Save** 🔲.

Activity 5.09 | Inserting a Hyperlink in a Worksheet

Recall that a hyperlink is colored and underlined text that you can click to go to a file, a location in a file, a Web page on the Internet, or a Web page on your organization's intranet. Hyperlinks can be attached to text or to graphics. In this activity, you will add a hyperlink that will open a file that contains the contact information for instructors.

Another Way

Right-click the cell, and then click Hyperlink.

1 Click cell **M2**. On the **Insert tab**, in the **Links group**, click the **Hyperlink** button to display the **Insert Hyperlink** dialog box.

2 Under **Link to**, if necessary, click **Existing File or Web Page**. Click the **Look in arrow**, navigate to your student files, and then select the file **e05A_Faculty_Contacts**, which contains faculty contact information.

3 In the upper right corner of the **Insert Hyperlink** dialog box, click the **ScreenTip** button.

4 In the **Set Hyperlink ScreenTip** dialog box, in the **ScreenTip text** box, type **Click here for contact information** Compare your dialog box with Figure 5.19.

> When you point to the hyperlink on the worksheet, this is the text of the ScreenTip that will display.

Figure 5.19

Selected file

ScreenTip text

File location

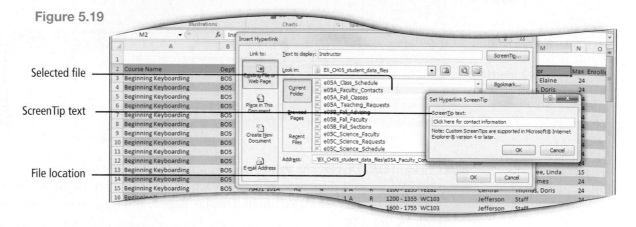

5 Click **OK** in the **Set Hyperlink ScreenTip** dialog box, and then click **OK** in the **Insert Hyperlink** dialog box.

> In the Flow theme, this is the color for a hyperlink.

6 Point to the **Instructor hyperlink** and read the ScreenTip that displays. Compare your screen with Figure 5.20.

> When you point to the hyperlink, the Link Select pointer displays 🖱 and the ScreenTip text you entered displays.

Figure 5.20

ScreenTip text

Link Select pointer

Text formatted as a hyperlink

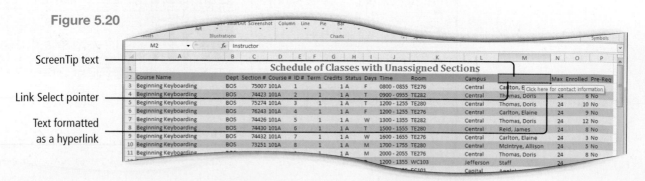

7 Click the **Instructor hyperlink**.

The e05A_Faculty_Contacts file opens and displays the contact information.

8 Click the **Close Window** button ⊠ to close the **e05A_Faculty_Contacts** file and redisplay your **5A_Class_Schedule** worksheet.

9 On the **Page Layout tab**, in the **Themes group**, click the **Colors arrow**. Notice that the **Flow** color scheme is selected, and then at the bottom of the page, click **Create New Theme Colors**. At the bottom of the dialog box, locate the colors for **Hyperlink** and **Followed Hyperlink**. Compare your screen with Figure 5.21.

Each color scheme uses a set of colors for a hyperlink and for a hyperlink that has been clicked (followed) one time. Now that you have followed your inserted hyperlink one time, the text displays in the Followed Hyperlink color. Here you can also change the colors for any of the colors associated with a theme.

Figure 5.21

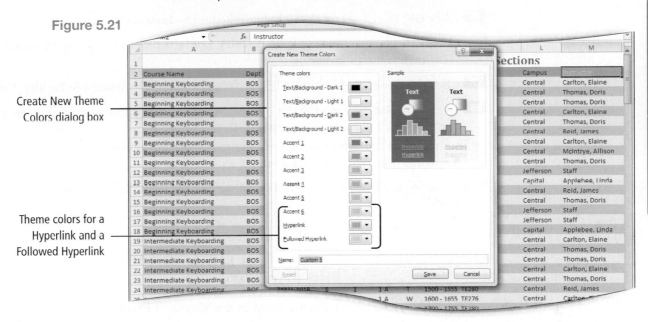

Create New Theme Colors dialog box

Theme colors for a Hyperlink and a Followed Hyperlink

10 In the lower corner of the dialog box, click **Cancel**, and then **Save** 🖫 your workbook.

Activity 5.10 | Modifying a Hyperlink

If the file to which the hyperlink refers is moved or renamed, or a Web page to which a hyperlink refers gets a new address, the hyperlink must be modified to reflect the change.

1 In cell **M2**, click the **Instructor hyperlink** to display the **e05A_Faculty_Contacts** worksheet.

2 From **Backstage** view, display the **Save As** dialog box, navigate to your **Excel Chapter 5** folder, name this file **Lastname_Firstname_5A_Faculty_Contacts**

3 Insert a footer in the **left section** with the file name, return to **Normal** view, click **Save** 🖫, and then click the **Close Window** button ⊠ to close your **5A_Faculty_Contacts** file and redisplay your **5A_Class_Schedule** file.

4 Right-click cell **M2**—the Instructor hyperlink—and then on the shortcut menu, click **Edit Hyperlink**.

5 In the **Edit Hyperlink** dialog box, click the **Look in arrow**, navigate to your **Excel Chapter 5** folder, and then select your **Lastname_Firstname_5A_Faculty_Contacts** file, as shown in Figure 5.22.

Figure 5.22

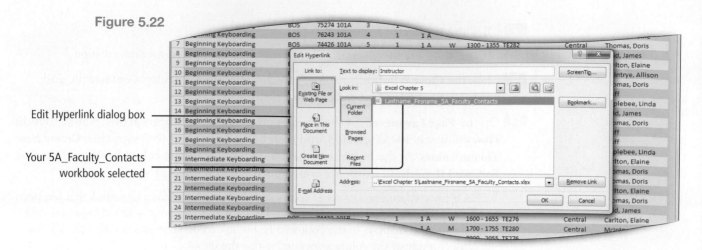

Edit Hyperlink dialog box

Your 5A_Faculty_Contacts
workbook selected

6 Click **OK**. In cell **M2**, click the hyperlinked text—**Instructor**.

> Your **Lastname_Firstname_5A_Faculty_Contacts** file displays on your screen, and your hyperlink is now up to date.

7 Click the **Close Window** button ⊠ to close **Lastname_Firstname_5A_Faculty_Contacts**.

8 Display **Backstage** view. On the right under the screen thumbnail, click **Properties**, and then click **Show Document Panel**. In the **Author** box, type your firstname and lastname, in the **Subject** box, type your course name and section number, and in the **Keywords** box, type **class schedule**

9 **Close** ☒ the **Document Properties**. Click **Save** 🔲; leave the **5A_Class_Schedule** workbook open.

Objective 4 | Save Excel Data in Other File Formats

By default, Excel 2010 files are saved in the Microsoft Excel Workbook file format with the *.xlsx file name extension*, which is a set of characters that helps your Windows operating system understand what kind of information is in a file and what program should open it.

Using the Save As command, you can choose to save an Excel file in another file format from the Save as type list. Some frequently used file formats are: Excel 97-2003 Workbook, Excel Template, Single File Web Page, Web Page, Excel Macro-Enabled Workbook, Text (Tab Delimited), or CSV (Comma Delimited).

For the purpose of posting Excel data to a Web site or transferring data to other applications, you can save your Excel file in a variety of other file formats. For example, saving an Excel worksheet as a *text file* separates the cells of each row with tab characters. Saving an Excel worksheet as a *CSV (comma separated values) file* separates the cells of each row with commas. This format is commonly used to import data into a database program.

You can also save an Excel file in an electronic format that is easy to read for the viewer of the workbook. Such files are not easily modified and are considered to be an electronic printed version of the worksheet.

Recall that you can also add a hyperlink to a worksheet, which, when clicked, takes you to another location in the worksheet, to another file, or to a Web page on the Internet or on your organization's intranet.

Activity 5.11 | Viewing and Saving a Workbook as a Web Page

Before you save a worksheet as a Web page, it is a good idea to view it as a Web page to see how it will display. When saving a multiple-page workbook as a Web page, all of the worksheets are available and can be accessed. You can also save a single worksheet as a Web page. Excel changes the contents of the worksheet into *HTML* (*Hypertext Markup Language*), which is a language Web browsers can interpret, when you save a worksheet as a Web page. In this activity, you will save and publish a worksheet as a Web page.

1 Be sure your **Lastname_Firstname_5A_Class_Schedule** workbook is open and displayed on your screen. Display the **Save As** dialog box, navigate to your **Excel Chapter 5** folder, in the lower portion of the dialog box, click the **Save as type arrow**, and then click **Web Page**.

> Your Excel files no longer display in the dialog box, because only files with the type Web Page are visible. The file type changes to Web Page and additional Web-based options display below.

2 In the lower portion of the dialog box, click the **Change Title** button.

> The text that you type here will become the title when the file displays as a Web page.

3 In the **Enter Text** dialog box, in the **Page title** box, using your own name, type **Computer Courses Lastname Firstname** Compare your screen with Figure 5.23.

Figure 5.23

Page title indicated —

Enter Text dialog box —

Save as type indicated as *Web Page* —

Additional options for saving as a Web Page —

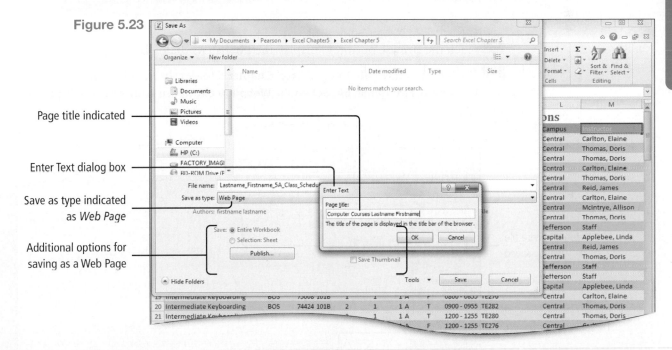

4 In the **Enter Text** dialog box, click **OK**, and notice that in the **Page title** box, your typed text displays.

5 In the **Save As** dialog box, click the **Publish** button.

6 In the **Publish as Web Page** dialog box, click the **Choose arrow**, and then click **Items on Computer Classes**—recall that the worksheet name is *Computer Classes*. In the lower left corner, if necessary, click to select (place a check mark in) the **Open published web page in browser** check box. Compare your screen with Figure 5.24.

> Under Item to publish, you can choose which elements to include as part of the Web page. You can select the entire workbook, a specific worksheet in the workbook, a range of cells, or previously published items that you are modifying. The *Open published Web page in browser* selection ensures that the Internet browser software, for example Internet Explorer, will automatically start and display the Web page.

Figure 5.24

Items on Computer Classes selected

Browse button

Web page title

File name and path

Open published web page in browser selected

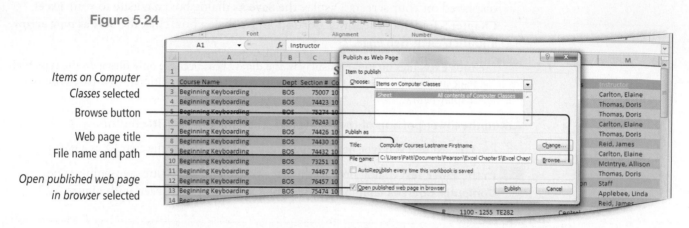

7 Click the **Browse** button to display the **Publish As** dialog box.

8 If necessary, navigate to your **Excel Chapter 5** folder. In the **File name** box, type **Lastname_Firstname_5A_Schedule_Webpage** Compare your screen with Figure 5.25.

Figure 5.25

Location where file will be saved

File name

Worksheet saved as Web Page

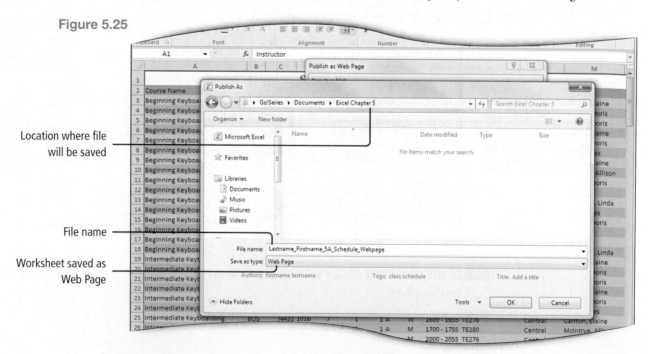

9 Click **OK**, and then on the displayed **Publish as Web Page** dialog box, click **Publish**. Compare your screen with Figure 5.26.

> The Web Page is saved in your selected folder, and the Class Schedule file opens in your Internet browser. The browser title bar displays the text you typed in the Enter Text dialog box.

Figure 5.26

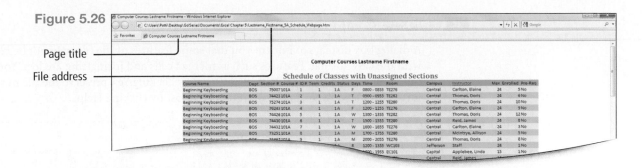

Page title

File address

10 If you are instructed to print your Web page on paper, consult the instructions to print from your specific browser software.

Your printed results will vary depending on which browser software you are using. Do not be concerned about the printout; Web pages are intended for viewing, not printing.

11 On the browser title bar, click the **Close** button [×]. Leave your **5A_Class_Schedule** Excel workbook open for the next activity.

Activity 5.12 | Saving Excel Data in CSV File Format

You can save an Excel worksheet as a comma separated values (CSV) file, which saves the contents of the cells by placing commas between them and an end-of-paragraph mark at the end of each row. This type of file can be readily exchanged with various database programs, and is also referred to as a *comma delimited file*.

1 Be sure your **Lastname_Firstname_5A_Class_Schedule** workbook is open and displayed on your screen. Display the **Save As** dialog box, click the **Save as type arrow**, and then click **CSV (Comma delimited)**. Be sure you are saving in your **Excel Chapter 5** folder. In the **File name** box, using your own name, type **Lastname_Firstname_5A_Schedule_CSV** Compare your dialog box with Figure 5.27.

Your Excel files no longer display, because only CSV files are displayed.

Figure 5.27

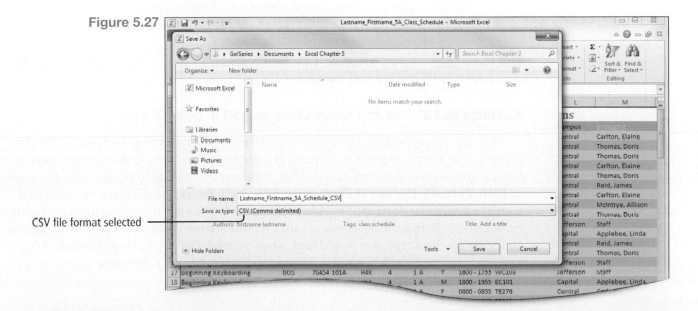

CSV file format selected

Excel | Chapter 5

2 Click **Save**. Compare your screen with Figure 5.28.

A dialog box displays to inform you that some features of the file may not be compatible with the CSV format. Features such as merged cells and formatting are lost. You can save the file and leave out incompatible features by clicking Yes, preserve the file in an Excel format by clicking No, or see what might be lost by clicking Help.

Figure 5.28

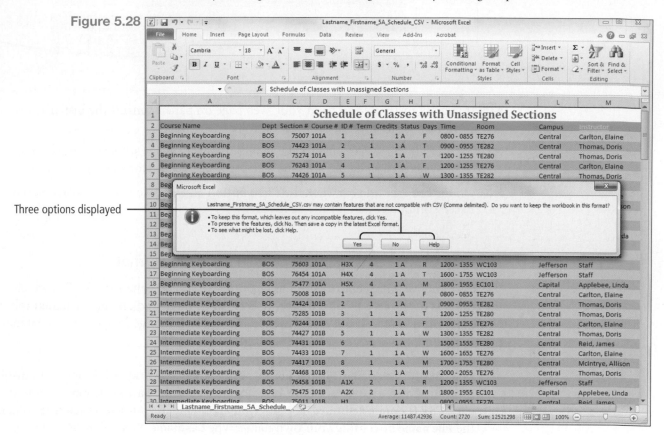

Three options displayed

3 Click **Yes** to keep the CSV format.

The file is saved in the new format. The new file name displays in the title bar. If file extensions—the three letters that identify the type of files—are displayed on your computer, you will also see *.csv* after the file name.

4 **Close** ☒ your **5A_Schedule_CSV** file. Click **Save** to save changes, and then click **Yes** to acknowledge the warning message.

Activity 5.13 | Saving Excel Data as a PDF or XPS File

You can create portable documents to share across applications and platforms with accurate visual representations. To publish a document and ensure that the appearance of the document is the same no matter what computer it is displayed on, save the document in *PDF (Portable Document Format)* or *XPS (XML Paper Specification)* format. PDF is a widely used format developed by Adobe Systems. XPS is a relatively new format developed by Microsoft. Both formats let you create a representation of *electronic paper* that displays your data on the screen as it would look when printed. Use one of these formats if you want someone to be able to view a document but not change it. In this activity, you will create PDF and XPS portable documents.

1 In Excel, from your student files, open the file **e05A_Fall_Classes**. Display the footer area, click in the **left section**, and then type **Lastname_Firstname_5A_Fall_PDF** Click in a cell just above the footer to exit the Footer.

2 Display the **Save As** dialog box and navigate to your **Excel Chapter 5** folder. Click the **Save as type arrow**, and then click **PDF**.

3 In the lower right section of the dialog box, if necessary, select the **Open file after publishing** check box. As the file name, type **Lastname_Firstname_5A_Fall_PDF** and then click **Save**.

> The file is saved in PDF format, and then opens as a PDF document.

4 **Close** ☒ the **Lastname_Firstname_5A_Fall_PDF** document.

5 With the **e05A_Fall_Classes** file open, edit the footer in the left section and type **Lastname_Firstname_5A_Fall_XPS** and then click any cell. In the lower right corner of your screen, on the status bar, click the **Normal** ⊞ button to return to **Normal** view.

6 Display the **Save As** dialog box, navigate to your **Excel Chapter 5** folder, and then in the **File name** box, type **Lastname_Firstname_5A_Fall_XPS**

7 At the bottom of the **Save As** dialog box, click the **Save as type arrow**, and then click **XPS Document**. In the lower right section of the **Save As** dialog box, if necessary, select the **Open file after publishing** check box, and then compare your screen with Figure 5.29.

Figure 5.29

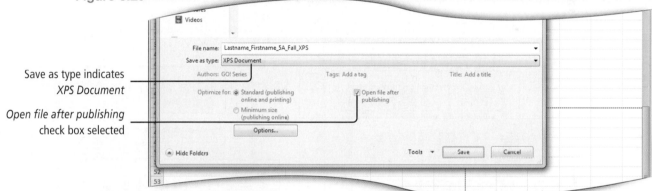

Save as type indicates *XPS Document*

Open file after publishing check box selected

8 Click the **Save** button.

> The file is saved in XPS format, and then opens as an XPS document in the XPS Viewer window.

9 **Close** ☒ the **XPS Viewer** window. **Close** the **e05A_Fall_Classes** file. **Don't Save** when the message displays—you do not need to save this file.

10 Submit your six files from this project as directed by your instructor, and then **Exit** Excel.

More Knowledge | Converting a Tab Delimited Text File to a Word Table

By choosing Text File as the file type, you can save an Excel worksheet as a text file, which saves the contents of the cells by placing a tab character, rather than commas, between the cells and an end-of-paragraph mark at the end of each row. This type of file can be readily exchanged with various database programs, in which it is referred to as a *tab delimited text file*. A text file can be converted from tab delimited text to a Word table. Word has a *Convert Text to Table* command that can easily convert a tabbed file into a table. A table displays in a row and column format, like an Excel spreadsheet.

End **You have completed Project 5A** ————————————————

Project 5B Sorted, Filtered, and Outlined Database

myitlab
Project 5B Training

Project Activities

In Activities 5.14 to 5.21 you will use advanced table features to provide Dr. John Mosier, the Dean of the Computer and Business Systems Division, information about the Fall course sections and assigned faculty in the Division. Your completed worksheets will look similar to Figure 5.30.

Project Files

For Project 5B, you will need the following files:

> e05B_Fall_Advising
> e05B_Fall_Faculty
> e05B_Fall_Sections

You will save your workbooks as:

> Lastname_Firstname_5B_Advising
> Lastname_Firstname_5B_Faculty
> Lastname_Firstname_5B_Sections

Project Results

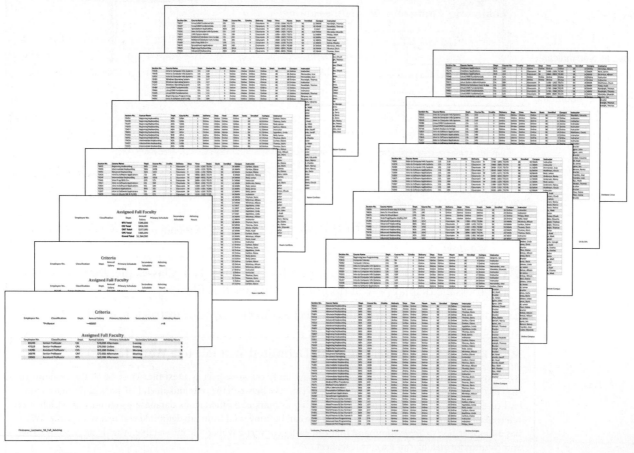

Figure 5.30
Project 5B Advising

Objective 5 | Use Advanced Sort Techniques

Sort means to organize data in a particular order; for example, alphabetizing a list of names. An *ascending* sort refers to text that is sorted alphabetically from A to Z, numbers sorted from lowest to highest, or dates and times sorted from earliest to latest. A *descending* sort refers to text that is sorted alphabetically from Z to A, numbers sorted from highest to lowest, or dates and times sorted from latest to earliest.

Sorting helps you to visualize your data. By sorting in various ways, you can find the data that you want, and then use your data to make good decisions. You can sort data in one column or in multiple columns. Most sort operations are column sorts, but you can also sort by rows.

Activity 5.14 | Sorting on Multiple Columns

To sort data based on several criteria at once, use the *Sort dialog box*, which enables you to sort by more than one column or row. For example, Dean Mosier wants to know, by department, how each course is delivered—either online or in a campus classroom. He also wants to examine the data to determine if there are any conflicts in room assignments. In this activity, you will convert the data into an Excel table, and then use the Sort dialog box to arrange the data to see the information the Dean needs.

1 **Start** Excel. From your student files, open **e05B_Fall_Sections**. Display the **Save As** dialog box, navigate to your **Excel Chapter 5** folder, and then save the workbook as **Lastname Firstname 5B Fall_Sections**

<table>
<tr><td>

Another Way

With cell A1 active, insert the table, and Excel will select all the contiguous data as the range.

</td></tr>
</table>

2 Be sure that the first worksheet, **Room Conflicts**, is the active sheet. In the **Name Box**, type **a1:m170** and press Enter to select this range. On the **Insert tab**, in the **Tables group**, click the **Table** button. In the **Create Table** dialog box, be sure that the **My table has headers** check box is selected, and then click **OK**.

3 On the **Design tab**, in the **Table Styles group**, click the **More** button ⬇, and then under **Light**, apply **Table Style Light 18**. Click any cell to deselect, and then compare your screen with Figure 5.31.

A table of data like this one forms a *database*—an organized collection of facts related to a specific topic. In this table, the topic relates to the Fall course sections for this division of the college.

Each table row forms a *record*—all of the categories of data pertaining to one person, place, thing, event, or idea. In this table, each course section is a record. Each table column forms a *field*—a single piece of information that is stored in every record.

When information is arranged as records in rows and fields in columns, then you can *query*—ask a question of—the data.

Figure 5.31

Sorting and filtering arrows in header row

Table Style Light 18 applied

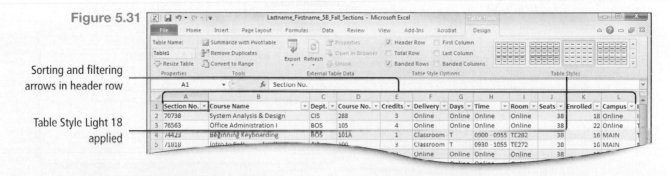

4 On the **Data tab**, in the **Sort & Filter group**, click the **Sort** button.

In the Sort dialog box, you can sort on up to 64 columns (levels) of data.

> **Note** | Defining data as a table prior to sort operations is optional.
>
> Defining your range of data as an Excel table is not required to perform sort operations. Doing so, however, is convenient if you plan to perform sorts on all of the data, because any sort commands will be performed on the entire table. Defining the data as a table also freezes the column titles automatically, so they will not move out of view as you scroll down a worksheet that contains many rows. If you want to sort only part of a list of data, do not convert the data to a table. Instead, select the range, and then click the Sort button.

5 In the **Sort** dialog box, under **Column**, click the **Sort by arrow**. Notice that the list displays in the order of the field names—the column titles. On the displayed list, click **Dept**.

6 Under **Sort On**, click the **arrow**, and then on the displayed list, click **Values**. Under **Order**, click the **arrow**, and then click **A to Z**. Compare your screen with Figure 5.32.

Values indicates that the sort will be based on the values in the cells of the Sort by column—the Dept. column. A to Z indicates that the values in the column will be sorted in ascending alphabetic order.

Figure 5.32

Sort dialog box

Worksheet will be sorted by Dept. name in alphabetic order

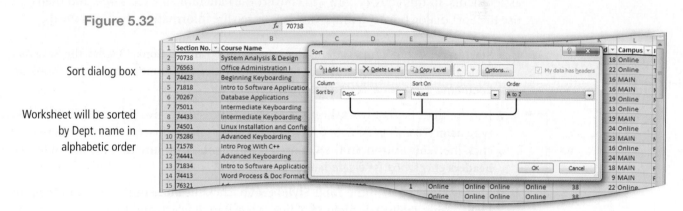

7 In the upper left corner of the **Sort** dialog box, click the **Add Level** button. In the second level row, click the **Then by arrow**, and then click **Course No**. Be sure that **Sort On** indicates *Values* and **Order** indicates *Smallest to Largest*.

When you initiate the sort operation, these numeric values will be sorted from the smallest number to the largest.

8 Click the **Add Level** button again. In the new row, under **Column**, click the **Then by arrow**, and then click **Section No**. Sort on **Values**, from **Smallest to Largest**. Compare your screen with Figure 5.33.

Figure 5.33

Dept. indicated in Sort by column (major sort)

Section No. indicated in Then by column (third level)

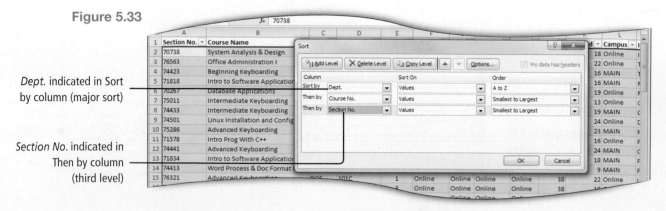

9 Click **OK**. Scroll down until **row 139** is at the top of the worksheet, take a moment to examine the arrangement of the data, and then compare your screen with Figure 5.34.

The first sort level, sometimes referred to as the *major sort*, is by the Dept. field in alphabetic order, so after the BOS department, the CIS department sections are listed, then the CNT department sections, then the CPS department sections, and so on.

The second sort level is by the Course No. field in ascending order, so within each department, the courses are sorted in ascending order by course number.

The third sort level is by the Section No. field in ascending order, so within each Course No. the section numbers display in ascending order.

Figure 5.34

Dept. field in alphabetic order

Within Course No. field, Section No. field in numerical order

Within Dept. field, Course No. field in numerical order

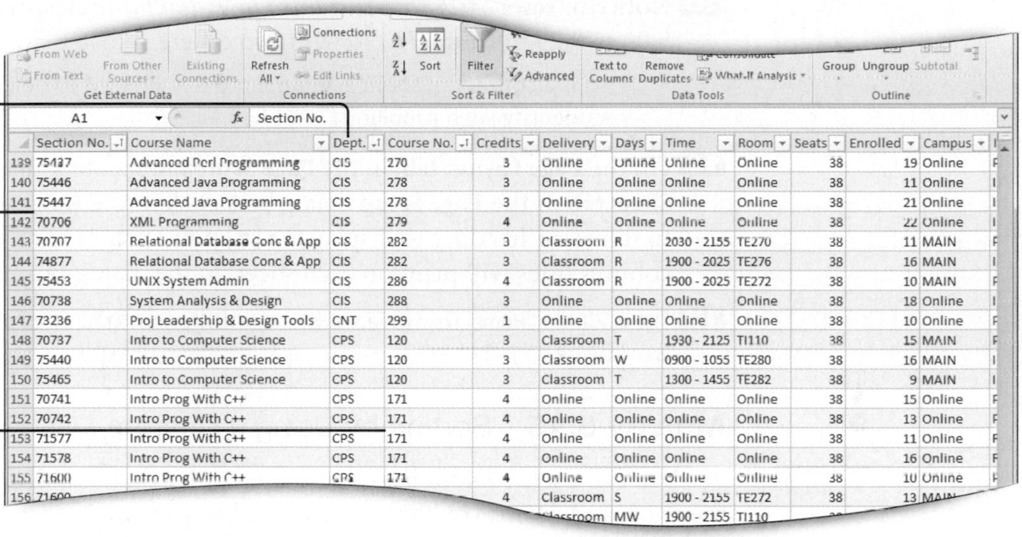

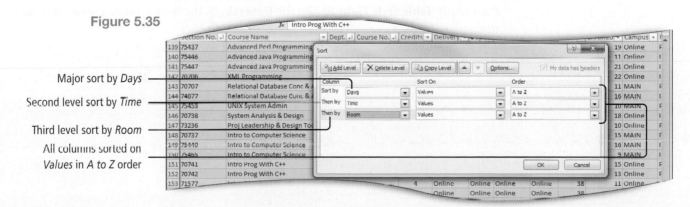

10 From the row heading area, select **rows 148:150**, and then notice that all three sections of the course *CPS 120 Intro to Computer Science* are offered in a campus classroom.

By studying the information in this arrangement, Dean Mosier can consider adding an additional section of this course in an online delivery.

Another Way

Click any row in the dialog box, click Delete Level, and then add new levels.

11 Click any cell to deselect. In the **Sort & Filter group**, click the **Sort** button to redisplay the **Sort** dialog box.

12 Under **Column**, in the first row, click the **Sort by** arrow, and then click **Days**, change the second sort level to **Time**, and change the third sort level to **Room**. For each sort level, sort on **Values** in **A to Z** order. Compare your screen with Figure 5.35.

Figure 5.35

Major sort by Days

Second level sort by Time

Third level sort by Room

All columns sorted on Values in A to Z order

13 Click **OK**, and then scroll to view the top of the worksheet.

Because the days are sorted alphabetically, F (for Friday) is listed first, and then the times for the Friday classes are sorted in ascending order. Within the Friday group, the classes are further sorted from the earliest to the latest. Within each time period, the data is further sorted by room.

14 Examine the sorted data. Notice that the first three classes listed are on *Friday*, at *12:00*, in room *TE276*, with *Elaine Carlton* as the instructor.

These are all keyboarding classes, and the instructor teaches the three levels of keyboarding at the same time, so this is not a room conflict.

15 Notice in **rows 24:25** that two *Intro to Visual Basic* classes are scheduled on *MW* from 8:00 to 9:25 in room *TE110* with two different instructors listed.

This is a conflict of room assignment that will need to be resolved. Sorting data can help you identify such problems.

16 On the **Page Layout tab**, in the **Page Setup group**, click the **Print Titles** button. On the **Sheet tab** of the **Page Setup** dialog box, click in the **Rows to repeat at top** box, point to the **row 1** heading to display the → pointer, and click to select **row 1** so that the column titles will print on each sheet. In the dialog box, click **OK**.

17 Press Ctrl + Home to move to the top of the worksheet, and then **Save** 🖫 your workbook.

Activity 5.15 | Sorting by Using a Custom List

You can use a **custom list** to sort in an order that you define. Excel includes a day-of-the-week and month-of-the-year custom list, so that you can sort chronologically by the days of the week or by the months of the year from January to December.

Optionally, you can create your own custom list by typing the values you want to sort by, in the order you want to sort them, from top to bottom; for example, *Fast*, *Medium*, *Slow*. A custom list that you define must be based on a value—text, number, date, or time.

In this activity, you will provide Dean Mosier with a list showing all the Fall sections sorted first by Delivery, with all online courses listed first. Within each delivery type—Online and Classroom—the data will be further sorted by Dept. and then by Course Name.

1 In the **sheet tab area**, click **Online-Campus** to display the *second* worksheet in the workbook.

2 In the **Name Box**, type **a1:m170** and press Enter to select the range, insert a table, and then apply **Table Style Light 20**. On the **Data tab**, in the **Sort & Filter group**, click **Sort** to display the **Sort** dialog box.

3 Set the first (major) level to sort by **Delivery**, and to sort on **Values**. Then, click the **Order arrow** for this sort level, and click **Custom List** to display the **Custom Lists** dialog box.

4 Under **Custom lists**, be sure **NEW LIST** is selected. Then, under **List entries**, click in the empty box and type **Online** Press Enter, and then type **Classroom** Compare your screen with Figure 5.36.

Figure 5.36

Custom Lists dialog box

NEW LIST selected

Major sort by Delivery, no additional levels

New entries typed for new custom list

Add button

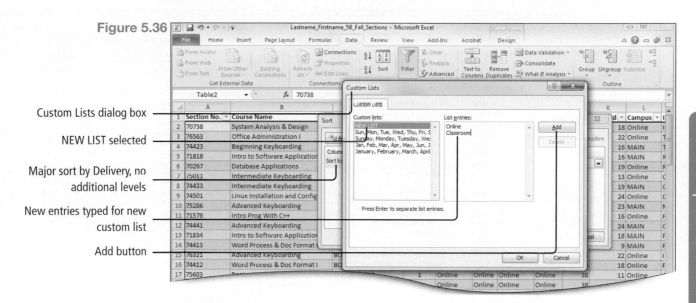

5 In the **Custom Lists** dialog box, click the **Add** button. On the left, under **Custom lists**, select **Online, Classroom**, and then click **OK** to redisplay the **Sort** dialog box.

6 In the **Sort** dialog box, click the **Add Level** button, and then as the second level sort, click **Dept**. Click the **Add Level** button again, and as the third level sort, click **Course Name**. Compare your screen with Figure 5.37.

Figure 5.37

Sort by *Delivery*, then by *Dept.*, then by *Course Name*

Sort Order is *Online, Classroom*

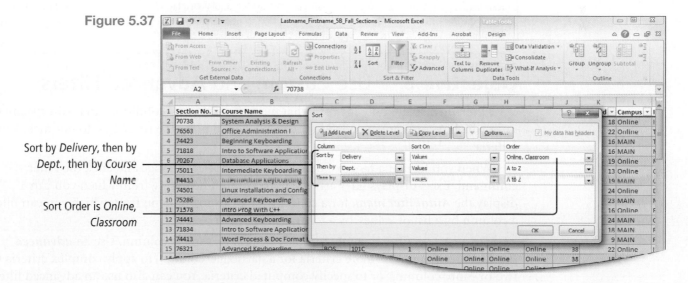

7 Click **OK** and then click any cell to deselect. Scroll down the worksheet, and notice that all of the online courses are listed first, and then scroll down to bring **row 92** into view, which is where the **Classroom** sections begin. Compare your screen with Figure 5.38.

Within each grouping, Online and Classroom, the sections are further sorted alphabetically by *Dept.* and then by *Course Name*.

Figure 5.38

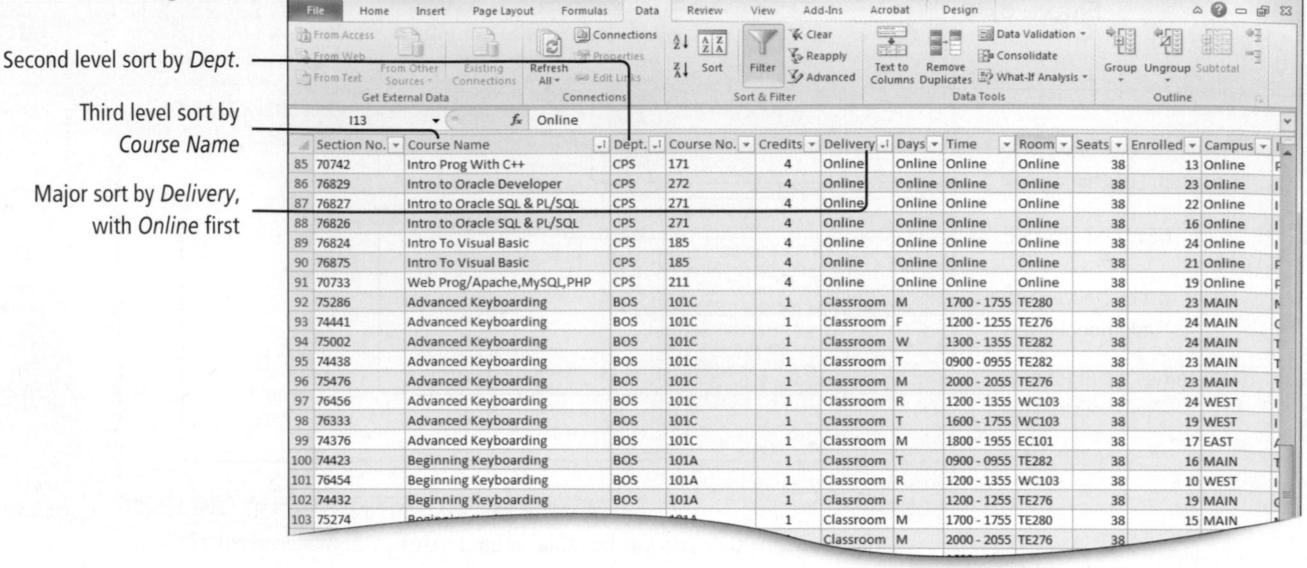

Second level sort by *Dept.*

Third level sort by *Course Name*

Major sort by *Delivery*, with *Online* first

	Section No.	Course Name	Dept.	Course No.	Credits	Delivery	Days	Time	Room	Seats	Enrolled	Campus
85	70742	Intro Prog With C++	CPS	171	4	Online	Online	Online	Online	38	13	Online
86	76829	Intro to Oracle Developer	CPS	272	4	Online	Online	Online	Online	38	23	Online
87	76827	Intro to Oracle SQL & PL/SQL	CPS	271	4	Online	Online	Online	Online	38	22	Online
88	76826	Intro to Oracle SQL & PL/SQL	CPS	271	4	Online	Online	Online	Online	38	16	Online
89	76824	Intro To Visual Basic	CPS	185	4	Online	Online	Online	Online	38	24	Online
90	76875	Intro To Visual Basic	CPS	185	4	Online	Online	Online	Online	38	21	Online
91	70733	Web Prog/Apache,MySQL,PHP	CPS	211	4	Online	Online	Online	Online	38	19	Online
92	75286	Advanced Keyboarding	BOS	101C	1	Classroom	M	1700 - 1755	TE280	38	23	MAIN
93	74441	Advanced Keyboarding	BOS	101C	1	Classroom	F	1200 - 1255	TE276	38	24	
94	75002	Advanced Keyboarding	BOS	101C	1	Classroom	W	1300 - 1355	TE282	38	24	
95	74438	Advanced Keyboarding	BOS	101C	1	Classroom	T	0900 - 0955	TE282	38	23	MAIN
96	75476	Advanced Keyboarding	BOS	101C	1	Classroom	T	2000 - 2055	TE276	38	23	MAIN
97	76456	Advanced Keyboarding	BOS	101C	1	Classroom	R	1200 - 1355	WC103	38	24	
98	76333	Advanced Keyboarding	BOS	101C	1	Classroom	T	1600 - 1755	TE282	38	19	WEST
99	74376	Advanced Keyboarding	BOS	101C	1	Classroom	M	1800 - 1955	EC101	38	17	EAST
100	74423	Beginning Keyboarding	BOS	101A	1	Classroom	T	0900 - 0955	TE282	38	16	MAIN
101	76454	Beginning Keyboarding	BOS	101A	1	Classroom	R	1200 - 1355	WC103	38	10	WEST
102	74432	Beginning Keyboarding	BOS	101A	1	Classroom	F	1200 - 1255	TE282	38	19	MAIN
103	75274	Beginning Keyboarding	BOS	101A	1	Classroom	M	1700 - 1755	TE280	38	15	MAIN
						Classroom	M	2000 - 2055	TE276	38		

8 Press [Ctrl] + [Home] to move to cell **A1**. On the **Page Layout tab**, click the **Print Titles** button, and then set **row 1** to repeat at the top of each page. **Save** your workbook.

More Knowledge | **A Custom List Remains Available for All Workbooks in Excel**

When you create a custom list, the list remains available for all workbooks that you use in Excel. To delete a custom list, display Excel Options, on the left click Advanced, under Display, click the Edit Custom Lists button, select the custom list, and then click the Delete button to permanently delete the custom list. Click OK to confirm the deletion. Click OK two more times to close both dialog boxes.

Objective 6 | Use Custom and Advanced Filters

Filtering displays only the rows that meet the *criteria*—conditions that you specify to limit which records are included in the results—and hides the rows that do not meet your criteria.

When you format a range of data as a table, or select a range and click the Filter command, Excel displays filter arrows in the column headings, from which you can display the *AutoFilter menu* for a column—a drop-down menu from which you can filter a column by a list of values, by a format, or by criteria.

Use a *custom filter* to apply complex criteria to a single column. Use an *advanced filter* to specify three or more criteria for a particular column, to apply complex criteria to two or more columns, or to specify computed criteria. You can also use an advanced filter for *extracting*—copying the selected rows to another part of the worksheet, instead of displaying the filtered list.

Activity 5.16 | Filtering by Format and Value Using AutoFilter

There are three types of filters that you can create with AutoFilter. You can filter by one or more values, for example *CIS* for the CIS department. You can filter by a format, such as cell color. Or, you can filter by criteria; for example, course sections that are greater than 2 credits, which would display courses that have 3 or more credits. Each of these filter types is mutually exclusive for the column; that is, you can use only one at a time.

1 From the **sheet tab area** at the lower edge of your screen, click **CIS & CPS** to display the *third* worksheet in the workbook.

2 Be sure that cell **A1** is the active cell, and then on the **Insert tab**, in the **Tables group**, click **Table**. In the **Create Table** dialog box, be sure that the data indicates the range *$A$1:$M$170*.

> The Table command causes Excel to suggest a table range based on the contiguous cells surrounding the active cell.

3 Click **OK** to accept the selection as the table range. Apply **Table Style Light 21** and click cell **A1** to deselect.

4 On the Ribbon, click the **Data tab**. In the **Sort & Filter group**, notice that the **Filter** button is active—it displays orange. In **row 1**, notice the **filter arrows** in each column title.

> Recall that when you format a range of data as an Excel table, filter arrows are automatically added in the header row of the table. A filter arrow, when clicked, displays the AutoFilter menu. On the Ribbon, the active Filter button indicates that the data is formatted to use filters.

5 In **column B**, notice that some courses are formatted with a yellow fill color, which indicates courses that have been designated as introductory courses recommended for high school seniors who want to take a college class.

6 In cell B1, click the **Course Name filter arrow**. On the **AutoFilter** menu, point to **Filter by Color**, point to the **yellow block**, and then click one time.

> Only courses with a yellow fill color in column B display; the status bar indicates that 79 of the 169 records display.

7 Point to the filter arrow in cell **B1**, and notice the ScreenTip *Course Name: Equals a Yellow cell color*. Notice also that a small funnel displays to the right of the arrow. Compare your screen with Figure 5.39.

> The funnel indicates that a filter is applied, and the ScreenTip indicates how the records are filtered.

Figure 5.39

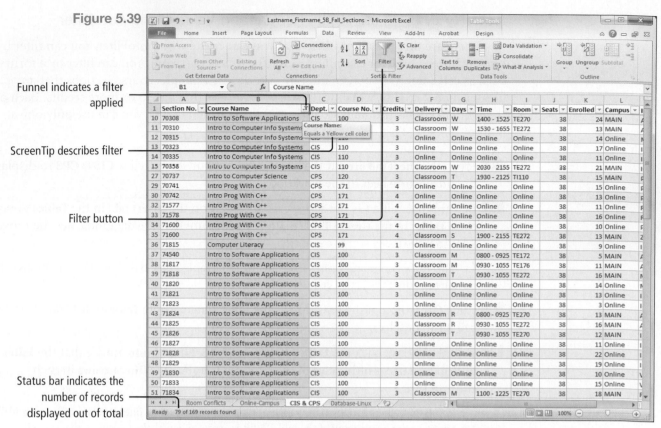

Funnel indicates a filter applied

ScreenTip describes filter

Filter button

Status bar indicates the number of records displayed out of total

8 In cell **B1**, click the **Course Name filter arrow**, and then click **Clear Filter From "Course Name"**. Then, in cell **B1**, point to the **Course Name filter arrow**, and notice that *(Showing All)* displays.

> The funnel no longer displays. The status bar no longer indicates that a filter is active. A filter arrow without a funnel means that filtering is enabled but not applied—if you point to the arrow, the ScreenTip will display *(Showing All)*.

9 Click cell **I5**, which contains the value *TE280*. Right-click over the selected cell, point to **Filter**, and then click **Filter by Selected Cell's Value**. Notice that only the courses that meet in Room TE280 display—all the other records are hidden.

> Excel filters the records by the selected value—TE280, and indicates in the status bar that 10 of the 169 records are displayed. This is a quick way to filter a set of records.

10 On the **Data tab**, in the **Sort & Filter group**, click the **Clear** button to clear all of the filters.

> Use this command to clear all filters from a group of records. This command also clears any sorts that were applied.

11 In cell **C1**, click the **Dept. filter arrow**. On the displayed list, click the **(Select All)** check box to clear all the check boxes, and then select the **CIS** and **CPS** check boxes. Click **OK**.

> The records are filtered so that only course sections in the CIS and CPS departments display. The status bar indicates that 93 of 169 records are found; that is, 93 course sections are either in the CIS or CPS departments.

12 In cell **E1**, click the **Credits filter arrow**, click the **(Select All)** check box to clear all the check boxes, and then select the **3** check box. Click **OK**.

> The status bar indicates that 61 of 169 records are found. That is, of the sections in either the CIS or CPS departments, 61 are 3-credit courses. Thus, you can see that filtering actions are *additive*—each additional filter that you apply is based on the current filter, which further reduces the number of records displayed.

13 In cell **F1**, click the **Delivery filter arrow**, and then using the technique you just practiced, filter the list further by **Online**.

> The status bar indicates 30 of 169 records found. That is, 30 course sections that are either in the CIS or CPS departments and that are 3-credit courses are offered online. The filter drop-down lists make it easy to apply filters that provide quick views of your data. For best results, be sure the data in the filtered column has the same data type; for example, in a column, be sure all the values are numbers or text.

14 Save 🖫 your workbook.

Activity 5.17 | Filtering by Custom Criteria Using AutoFilter

By using a custom filter, you can apply complex criteria to a single column. For example, you can use comparison criteria to compare two values by using the *comparison operators* such as Equals (=), Greater Than (>), or Less Than (<) singly or in combinations. When you compare two values by using these operators, your result is a logical value that is either true or false.

1 From the **sheet tabs area** at the lower edge of your screen, click **Database-Linux** to display the *fourth* worksheet in the workbook.

2 Be sure that cell **A1** is the active cell, and then on the **Insert tab**, in the **Tables group**, click **Table**. In the **Create Table** dialog box, be sure that the data indicates the range *$A$1:$M$170*. Click **OK**, and then apply **Table Style Light 19**. Click any cell to deselect.

> **Another Way**
>
> Click Custom Filter, click the first arrow in the first row, and then click is less than or equal to.

3 In cell **K1**, click the **Enrolled filter arrow**, point to **Number Filters**, and then click **Less Than Or Equal To**. In the first box, be sure that *is less than or equal to* displays, and then in the second box type **14** Compare your screen with Figure 5.40.

> In the displayed Custom AutoFilter dialog box, you can create a *compound filter*—a filter that uses more than one condition—and one that uses comparison operators.

Figure 5.40

Custom AutoFilter dialog box

Enrolled is less than or equal to 14

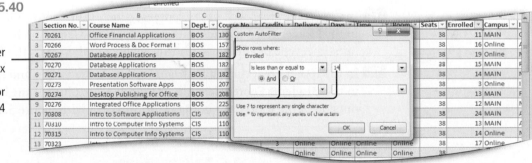

4 Click **OK** to display 69 records.

> This filter answers the question, *Which course sections have 14 or fewer students enrolled?*

5 On the **Data tab**, in the **Sort & Filter group**, **Clear** all filters.

6 In cell **B1**, click the **Course Name filter arrow**, point to **Text Filters**, and then click **Contains**.

7 In the **Custom AutoFilter** dialog box, under **Course Name**, in the first box, be sure that *contains* displays. In the box to the right, type **database**

8 Between the two rows of boxes, click the **Or** option button, and then for the second filter, in the first box, click the arrow, scroll down as necessary, and then click **contains**. In the second box, type **linux** and then compare your screen with Figure 5.41.

For the *Or comparison operator*, only one of the two comparison criteria that you specify must be true. Thus, by applying this filter, only courses that contain the words database or linux will display.

For the *And comparison operator,* each and every one of the comparison criteria that you specify must be true.

Figure 5.41

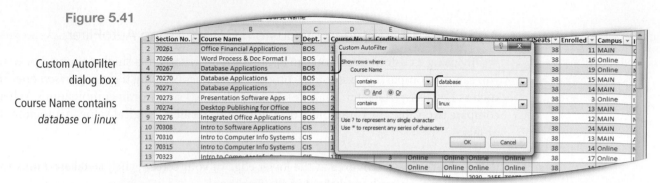

Custom AutoFilter dialog box

Course Name contains *database* or *linux*

9 Click **OK** to display 14 records.

This filter answers the question, *Which course sections relate to either databases or the Linux operating system?*

Activity 5.18 | Inserting the Sheet Name and Page Numbers in a Footer

You have practiced inserting the file name into the footer of a worksheet. In this activity, you will add the sheet name to the footer.

1 Point to any of the four sheet tabs, right-click, and then click **Select All Sheets**. With the sheets grouped, insert a footer in the left section that includes the file name.

2 In the footer area, click in the **center section** of the footer, and then on the **Design tab**, in the **Header & Footer Elements group**, click the **Page Number** button. Press Spacebar one time, type **of** and press Spacebar again, and then click the **Number of Pages** button.

3 In the footer area, click in the **right section** of the footer, and then on the **Design tab**, in the **Header & Footer Elements group**, click the **Sheet Name** button. Click a cell outside of the footer and compare your screen with Figure 5.42.

Figure 5.42

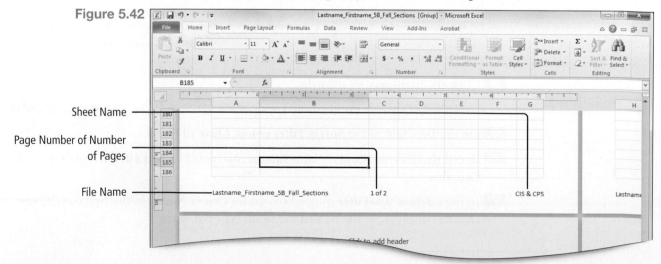

Sheet Name

Page Number of Number of Pages

File Name

4 On the **Page Layout tab**, set the orientation to **Landscape**, and set the **Width** to **1 page**. On the status bar, click the **Normal** button ▦. Press (Ctrl) + (Home) to move to cell **A1**.

> You may hear a double chime to alert you that the changes you made will apply to all the sheets in the Group.

5 Display the **Document Panel** and in the **Author** box, type your firstname and lastname, in the **Subject** box, type your course name and section number, and in the **Keywords** box, type **sort, filter, sections** Close ✕ the Document Properties. Display **Print Preview**.

> Ten pages display in Print Preview. The four worksheets in the workbook result in 10 pages—the first worksheet has four pages (green), the second worksheet has four pages (aqua), the third worksheet has one page (orange), and the fourth worksheet has one page (purple).

6 Redisplay the workbook, and then make any necessary corrections or adjustments.

7 **Save** 🖫 your workbook. Hold this workbook until the end of this project, and then print or submit the four worksheets—10 total pages—in this workbook electronically as directed by your instructor. There are no formulas in these worksheets. **Close** this workbook, but leave Excel open.

Activity 5.19 | Filtering by Using Advanced Criteria

Use an advanced filter when the data you want to filter requires complex criteria; for example, to specify three or more criteria for a particular column, to apply complex criteria to two or more columns, or to specify computed criteria. When you use the Advanced filter command, the Advanced dialog box displays, rather than the AutoFilter menu, and you type the criteria on the worksheet above the range you want to filter.

In this activity, you will create an advanced filter to determine which faculty members whose classification includes *Professor* and that have an annual salary of $60,000 or more, have 8 or more hours of assigned advising hours.

1 From your student files, open **e05B_Fall_Advising**. Display the **Save As** dialog box, navigate to your **Excel Chapter 5** folder, and then save the workbook as **Lastname_Firstname_5B_Fall_Advising**

2 Select the range **A6:G7**, right-click, and then click **Copy**.

> The first step in filtering by using advanced criteria is to create a *criteria range*—an area on your worksheet where you define the criteria for the filter. The criteria range indicates how the displayed records are filtered.

> Typically, the criteria range is placed *above* the data. The criteria range must have a row for the column headings and at least one row for the criteria—you will need additional rows if you have multiple criteria for a column. You can also add a title row. Separate the criteria range from the data by a blank row.

3 Point to cell **A1**, right-click, under **Paste Options**, click the first button, **Paste**, and then press (Esc) to cancel the moving border. Click cell **A1**, type **Criteria** and then press (Enter).

4 Select **rows 1:2**, on the **Home tab**, in the **Cells group**, click the **Format** button, and then click **AutoFit Row Height**. Compare your screen with Figure 5.43.

By copying the title and field names, you also copy the formatting that has been applied.

Figure 5.43

Cell A1 indicates *Criteria*

Criteria range created at the top of the worksheet

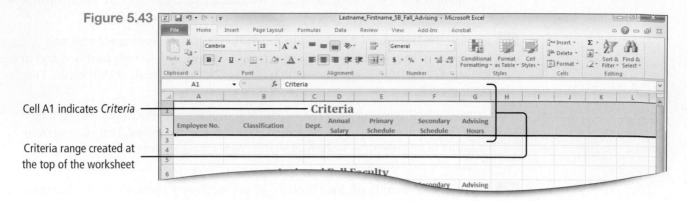

5 Select the range **A2:G3**—the column names and the blank row in the Criteria range. Click in the **Name Box**, and then type **Criteria** as shown in Figure 5.44.

Figure 5.44

Criteria typed in Name Box

A2:G3 selected

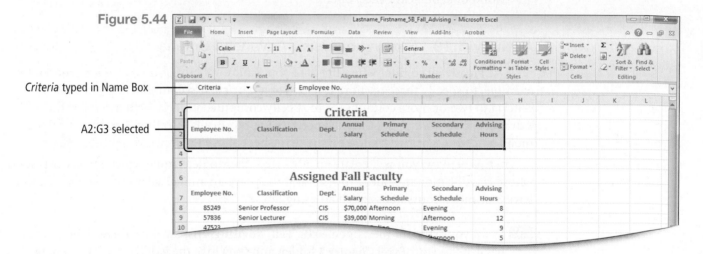

6 Press Enter to name the range.

By naming the range Criteria, which is a predefined name recognized by Excel, the reference to this range will automatically display as the Criteria range in the Advanced Filter dialog box. This defined criteria range includes the field names and one empty row, where the limiting criteria will be placed. It does not include the title *Criteria*.

7 Select the range **A7:G34**, insert a table, and then apply **Table Style Light 6**. Click anywhere in the table to deselect.

8 On the **Formulas tab**, in the **Defined Names** group, click the **Name Manager** button, and then compare your screen with Figure 5.45.

By defining the range as a table, Excel automatically assigns a name to the range. It is not required to format the range as a table—you could select the range and name it Table or Database—however doing so enables you to use the Table Tools, such as formatting and inserting a Total row into the filtered data.

The defined table range will automatically display as the List range in the Advanced Filter dialog box.

Figure 5.45

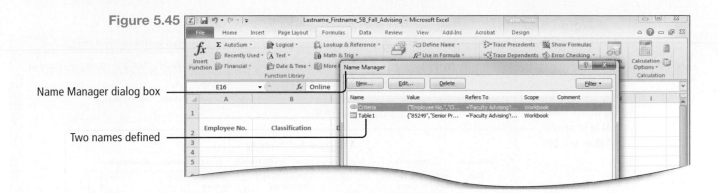

Name Manager dialog box ———

Two names defined ———

9 **Close** ✕ the **Name Manager** dialog box.

10 Scroll to view the top of the worksheet, click cell **D3**, type **>=60000** and then press Enter.

> This action creates a criteria using a comparison operator to look for salary values that are greater than or equal to $60,000. Do not include a comma when you type this value, because the comma is a cell format, not part of the value.

11 Click cell **A7**. On the **Data tab**, in the **Sort & Filter group**, click the **Advanced** button.

12 In the displayed **Advanced Filter** dialog box, locate the **List range**, and as necessary edit the range to indicate **$A$7:$G$34** which is your Excel table. Be sure the **Criteria range** is identified as cells **$A$2:$G$3** Compare your screen with Figure 5.46.

> Here you define the database area—the List range—and the Criteria range where the results will display. Both ranges use an absolute reference. Under Action, you can choose to display the results in the table—in-place—or copy the results to another location.

Figure 5.46

Filter the list, in-place option button selected

List range defined as the Excel table you inserted

Criteria range defined

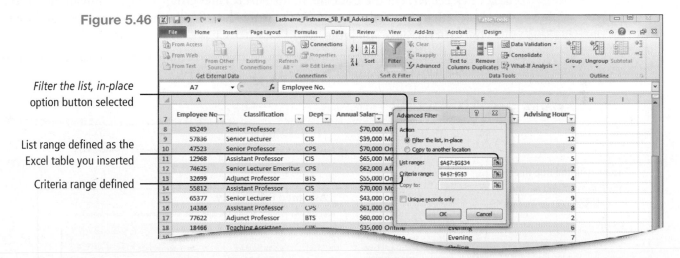

13 Click **OK** to have the filter results display in-place—in the table. At the top of your worksheet, click any blank cell; compare your screen with Figure 5.47.

> Only the records for faculty members whose salary is $60,000 or more display. The row numbers for the records that meet the criteria display in blue. The Advanced command disables the AutoFilter command and removes the AutoFilter arrows from the column headings.

Figure 5.47

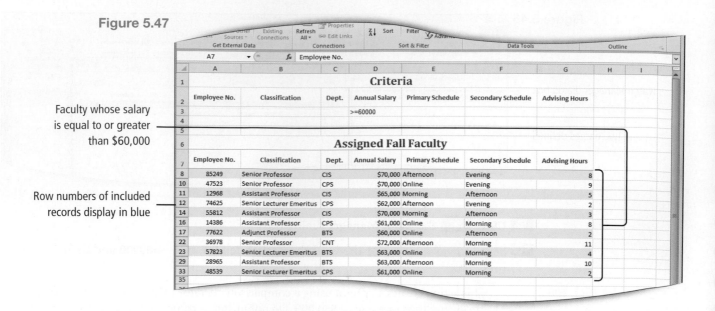

Faculty whose salary is equal to or greater than $60,000

Row numbers of included records display in blue

14 Click cell **B3**, type ***Professor** and then press Enter.

The asterisk (*) is a *wildcard*. Use a wildcard to search a field when you are uncertain of the exact value or you want to widen the search to include more records. The use of a wildcard enables you to include faculty whose classification ends with the word Professor. It directs Excel to find Professor and anything before it. The criterion in the Salary field still applies.

The use of two or more criteria on the same row is known as *compound criteria*—all conditions must be met for the records to be included in the results.

15 Click cell **A7**. On the **Data tab**, in the **Sort & Filter group**, click the **Advanced** button. Verify that the database range is correctly identified in the **List range** box and that the **Criteria range** still indicates *$A$2:$G$3*. Click **OK**. See Figure 5.48.

Only the eight faculty members with a classification containing *Professor* and a salary of $60,000 or more display.

Figure 5.48

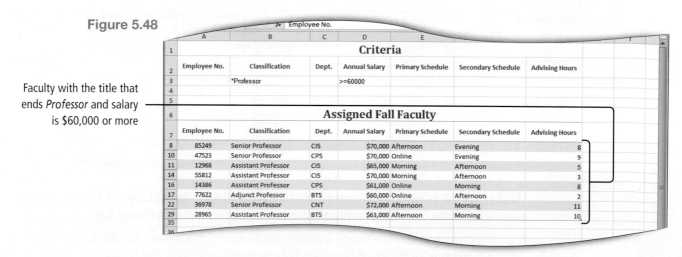

Faculty with the title that ends *Professor* and salary is $60,000 or more

16 Using the techniques you just practiced, filter the data further by adding an additional criteria—faculty who are assigned 8 hours or more of advising. Compare your result with Figure 5.49.

Five faculty members meet all three of the criteria in the Criteria range.

Figure 5.49

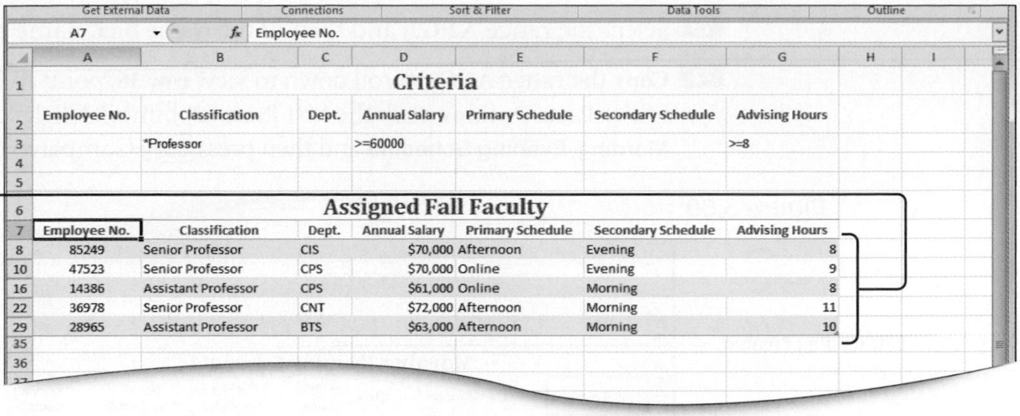

Faculty who have a title that ends *Professor*, a salary of $60,000 or more, and 8 or more advising hours

	A	B	C	D	E	F	G	H	I
1				**Criteria**					
2	Employee No.	Classification	Dept.	Annual Salary	Primary Schedule	Secondary Schedule	Advising Hours		
3		*Professor		>=60000			>=8		
4									
5									
6				**Assigned Fall Faculty**					
7	Employee No.	Classification	Dept.	Annual Salary	Primary Schedule	Secondary Schedule	Advising Hours		
8	85249	Senior Professor	CIS	$70,000	Afternoon	Evening	8		
10	47523	Senior Professor	CPS	$70,000	Online	Evening	9		
16	14386	Assistant Professor	CPS	$61,000	Online	Morning	8		
22	36978	Senior Professor	CNT	$72,000	Afternoon	Morning	11		
29	28965	Assistant Professor	BTS	$63,000	Afternoon	Morning	10		
35									
36									

17 Insert a footer in the **left section** that includes the file name, click outside the footer area, and then on the **Page Layout tab**, set the orientation to **Landscape**. On the status bar, click the **Normal** button. Press Ctrl + Home to move to cell **A1**.

18 Display the **Document Information Panel**, and in the **Author** box, type your firstname and lastname, in the **Subject** box, type your course name and section number, and in the **Keywords** box, type **advanced filter, advising**

19 Display the **Print Preview**. Near the bottom of the window, click **Page Setup** to display the **Page Setup** dialog box. Click the **Margins tab**, center the worksheet horizontally, and then click **OK**. Redisplay the worksheet and make any necessary corrections or adjustments.

20 **Save** your workbook. Hold this workbook until the end of this project, and then print or submit electronically as directed; there are no formulas in this worksheet. **Close** this workbook, but leave Excel open.

> **More Knowledge | Using Wildcards**
>
> A wildcard can help you locate information when you are uncertain how the information might be displayed in your records. The placement of the asterisk in relationship to the known value determines the result. If it is placed first, the variable will be in the beginning of the string of characters. For example, in a list of names if you used *son* as the criteria, it will look for any name that ends in *son*. The results might display *Peterson*, *Michelson*, and *Samuelson*. If the asterisk is at the end of the known value in the criteria, then the variable will be at the end. You can also include the asterisk wildcard at the beginning and at the end of a known value.
>
> A question mark (?) can also be used as part of your search criteria. Each question mark used in the criteria represents a single position or character that is unknown in a group of specified values. Searching for *m?n* would find, for example, *min*, *men*, and *man*; whereas searching for *m??d* would find, for example, *mind*, *mend*, *mold*.

Activity 5.20 | Extracting Filtered Rows

You can copy the results of a filter to another area of your worksheet, instead of displaying a filtered list as you did in the previous activity. The location to which you copy the records is the **Extract area**, and is commonly placed below the table of data. Using this technique you can **extract**—pull out—multiple sets of data for comparison purposes.

In this activity, you will extract data to compare how many faculty have a Morning-Evening schedule and how many have a Morning-Afternoon schedule.

1 From your student files, open **e05B_Fall_Faculty**. Display the **Save As** dialog box, navigate to your **Excel Chapter 5** folder, and then save the workbook as **Lastname_Firstname_5B_Fall_Faculty**

2 Be sure the first worksheet, **Schedule Comparison**, is the active sheet. **Copy** the range **A6:G7**, **Paste** it in cell **A1**, and then change the title in cell **A1** to **Criteria**

Excel | Chapter 5

3 Select the range **A2:G3**, and then in the **Name Box**, name this range **Criteria**

4 **Copy** the range **A1:G2**, scroll down to view **row 36**, point to cell **A36**, right-click, and then under **Paste Options**, click the first **Paste (P)** button. Click cell **A36**, change the title to **Morning-Evening Schedule** and then press [Enter]. Compare your screen with Figure 5.50.

Figure 5.50

Extract area created

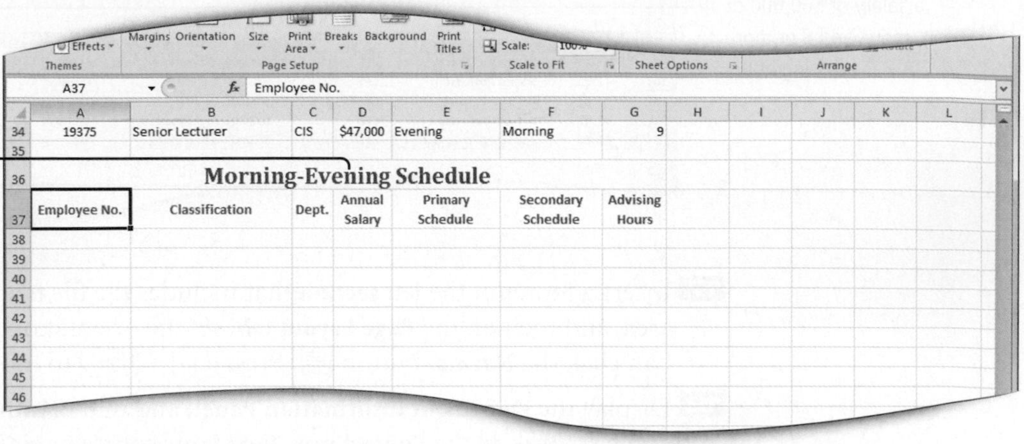

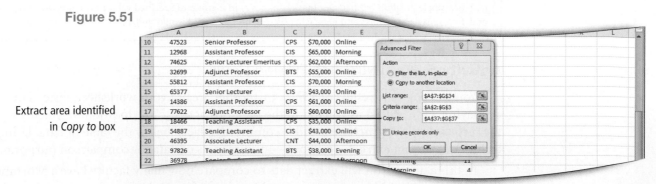

5 Select the range **A37:G37** and then in the **Name Box**, name this range **Extract**

This action defines the Extract area so that the range will display automatically in the Copy to box of the Advanced Filter dialog box. Excel recognizes *Extract* as the location in which to place the results of an advanced filter.

6 Select the range **A7:G34** and then in the **Name Box**, name this range **Database**

Excel recognizes the name *Criteria* as a criteria range, the name *Database* as the range to be filtered, and the name *Extract* for the area where you want to paste the result.

7 At the top of your worksheet, in cell **E3**, type **Morning** and in cell **F3**, type **Evening** and then press [Enter].

When applied, the filter will display only those records where the Primary Schedule is Morning and the Secondary Schedule is Evening.

8 On the **Data tab**, in the **Sort & Filter group**, click the **Advanced** button.

9 Under **Action**, click the **Copy to another location** option button. Verify that in the **Copy to** box, the absolute reference to the Extract area—*$A$37:$G$37*—displays. Compare your screen with Figure 5.51.

Figure 5.51

Extract area identified in *Copy to* box

10 Click **OK**, and then scroll to view the lower portion of your worksheet. Compare your screen with Figure 5.52.

Two records meet the criteria and are copied to the extract area on your worksheet. When you use an extract area in this manner, instead of reformatting the table to display the qualifying records, Excel places a copy of the qualifying records in the Extract area.

Figure 5.52

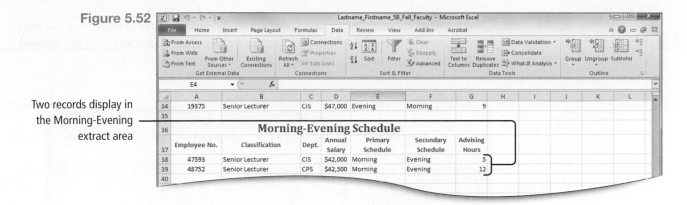

Two records display in
the Morning-Evening
extract area

11 **Copy** the range **A36:G37**, and then **Paste** it in cell **A41**. In cell **A41**, change the word *Evening* to **Afternoon**

12 At the top of your worksheet, in cell **F3**, change the criteria to **Afternoon** Display the **Advanced Filter** dialog box, and then click the **Copy to another location** option button.

13 In the **Copy to** box, click the **Collapse Dialog** button 📧, scroll down as necessary, and then select the range **A42:G42**. Click the **Expand Dialog** button 📧, and then click **OK**. Scroll to view the lower portion of the worksheet, and then compare your screen with Figure 5.53.

Three records meet the criteria and are copied to the extract area on your worksheet.

Figure 5.53

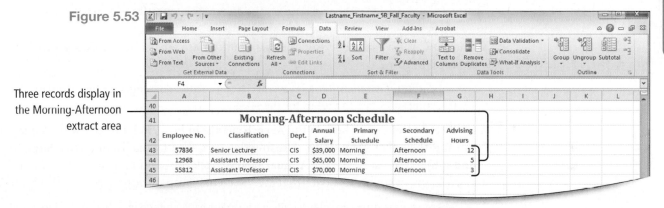

Three records display in
the Morning-Afternoon
extract area

14 **Save** 🖫 and then leave this workbook open for the next activity.

Objective 7 | Subtotal, Outline, and Group a List of Data

You can group and summarize a *list*—a series of rows that contains related data—by adding subtotals. The first step in adding subtotals is to sort the data by the field for which you want to create a subtotal.

Activity 5.21 | Subtotaling, Outlining, and Grouping a List of Data

In this activity, you will assist Dean Mosier in summarizing the faculty salaries by department.

1 In your **5B_Fall_Faculty** workbook, display the second worksheet—**Salaries by Department**.

2 Select the range **A2:G29**. On the **Data tab**, in the **Sort & Filter group**, click the **Sort** button. In the **Sort** dialog box, sort by the **Dept.** column, and then by the **Annual Salary** column. Compare your **Sort** dialog box with Figure 5.54.

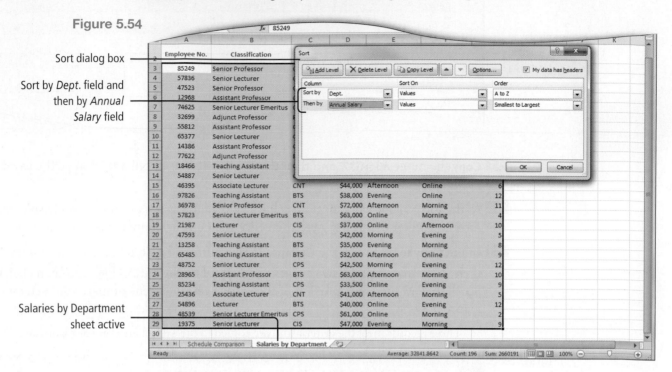

Figure 5.54

Sort dialog box

Sort by *Dept.* field and then by *Annual Salary* field

Salaries by Department sheet active

3 Click **OK**. With the range still selected, on the **Data tab**, in the **Outline group**, click the **Subtotal** button.

The *Subtotal command* totals several rows of related data together by automatically inserting subtotals and totals for the selected cells.

4 In the **Subtotal** dialog box, in the **At each change in** box, click the arrow to display the list, and then click **Dept.** In the **Use function** box, display the list and click **Sum**. In the **Add subtotal to** list, select the **Annual Salary** check box, and then scroll the list and *deselect* any other check boxes that are selected. Compare your screen with Figure 5.55.

These actions direct Excel to create a group for each change in value in the Dept. field. Excel will then use the Sum function to add a subtotal in the Annual Salary field. The check boxes at the bottom of the dialog box indicate how the subtotals will display.

Figure 5.55

Subtotal dialog box

Dept. indicated

Sum indicated

Add subtotal to *Annual Salary* field (no other boxes checked)

Place the subtotal below the data

5 Click **OK**, scroll to view the lower portion of the data, and then compare your screen with Figure 5.56.

At the end of each Dept. group, inserted rows containing the subtotals for the salaries within each department display.

Figure 5.56

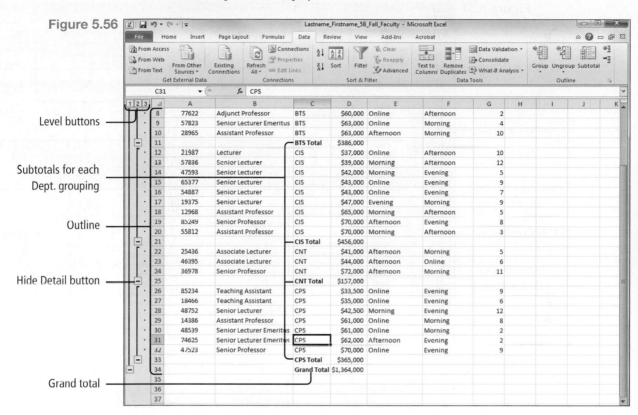

Level buttons

Subtotals for each
Dept. grouping

Outline

Hide Detail button

Grand total

6 Click any cell to deselect, and then along the left edge of your workbook, locate the outline.

When you add subtotals, Excel defines groups based on the rows used to calculate a subtotal. The groupings form an outline of your worksheet based on the criteria you indicated in the Subtotal dialog box, and the outline displays along the left side of your worksheet.

The outline bar along the left side of the worksheet enables you to show and hide levels of detail with a single mouse click. For example, you can show details with the totals, which is the default view. Or, you can show only the summary totals or only the grand total.

There are three types of controls in the outline. Hide Detail (−) collapses a group of cells, Show Detail (+) expands a collapsed group of cells, and the level buttons (1, 2, 3) can hide all levels of detail below the number clicked.

7 To the left of **row 25**, click the **Hide Detail** button (−) to collapse the detail for the **CNT** department.

Detail data refers to the subtotaled rows that are totaled and summarized. Detail data is typically adjacent to and either above or to the left of the summary data.

8 Select **rows 13:17**, and then on the **Data tab**, in the **Outline group**, click the **Group** button. Compare your screen with Figure 5.57.

A fourth group is created and a bar spans the group.

Figure 5.57

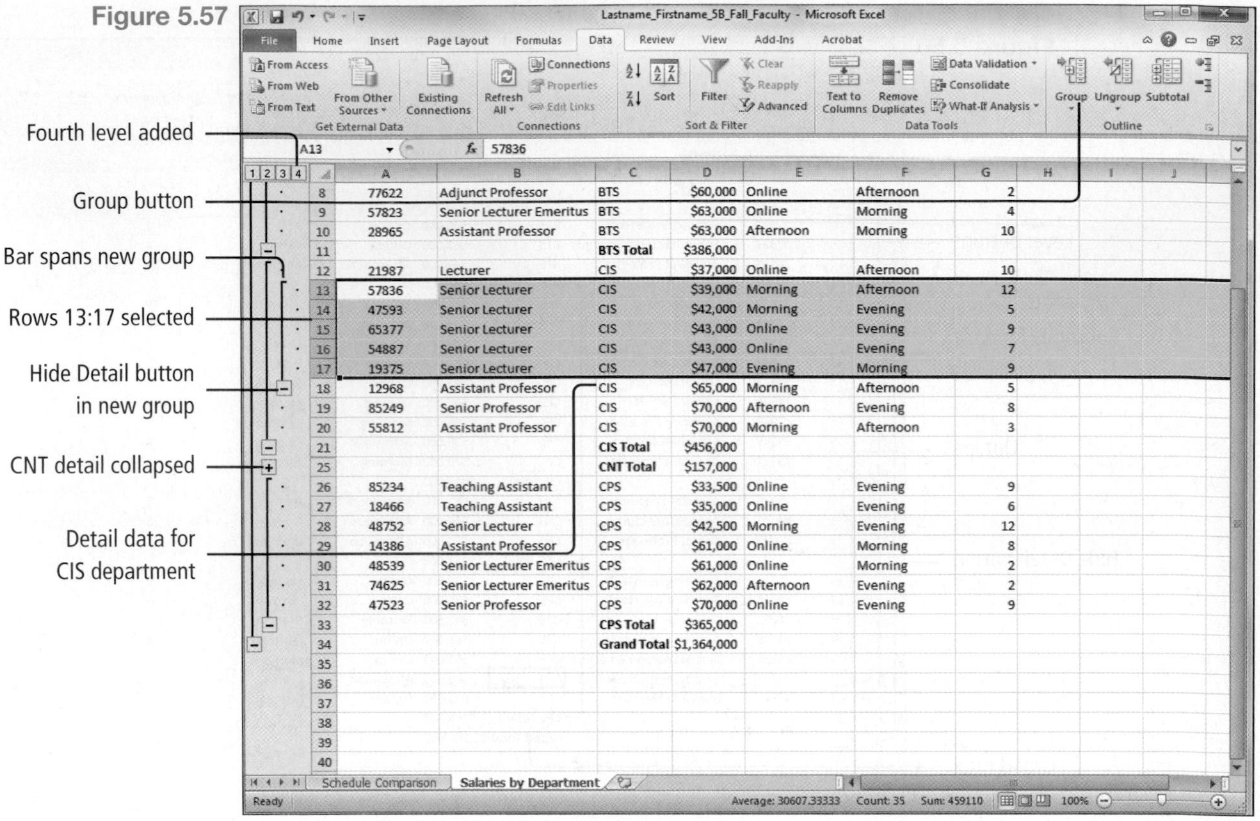

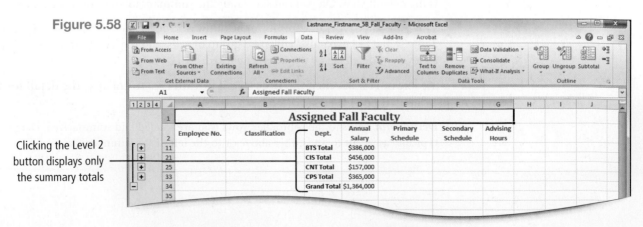

Fourth level added
Group button
Bar spans new group
Rows 13:17 selected
Hide Detail button in new group
CNT detail collapsed
Detail data for CIS department

9 To the left of **row 18**, click the **Hide Detail** button (−) for the new group, and notice that the group is collapsed and a break in the row numbers indicates that some rows are hidden from view.

Hiding the detail data in this manner does not change the subtotal for the CIS group—it remains $456,000.

10 At the top of the outline area, click the **Level 2** button to hide all Level 3 and 4 details and display only the Level 2 summary information and the Level 1 Grand Total. Press Ctrl + Home and compare your screen with Figure 5.58.

Figure 5.58

Clicking the Level 2 button displays only the summary totals

11 Group the two worksheets. Insert a footer in the **left section** that includes the file name, and in the **right section**, insert the **Sheet Name**. Click any cell to exit the footer area, and then on the status bar, click the **Normal** button. On the **Page Layout tab**, set the **Width** to **1 page** and set the **Height** to **1 page**—this will scale each worksheet to fit on a single page. You may hear a double chime. Press Ctrl + Home to move to cell **A1**.

12 Display the **Document Panel**, and in the **Author** box, type your firstname and lastname, in the **Subject** box, type your course name and section number, and in the **Keywords** box, type faculty, schedule, salaries **Close** X the **Document Properties**.

13 Display the **Print Preview**, redisplay the workbook, and then make any necessary corrections or adjustments.

14 **Save** 💾 your workbook. Along with your other two workbooks from this project, print or submit electronically as directed. If required, print or create an electronic version of your worksheets with formulas displayed, using the instructions in Activity 1.16 in Project 1A. **Close** Excel.

More Knowledge | Outlining a Worksheet

A horizontal outline bar can be created for data that is summarized by row, rather than summarized by column as it was in this activity. In addition, if the data is not organized so that Excel can outline it automatically, you can create an outline manually. To do so, on the Data tab, in the Outline group, click the Group button, and then click Auto Outline.

End **You have completed Project 5B** ————————————————————

Content-Based Assessments

Summary

In this chapter, you navigated and managed a large worksheet to locate, insert, and delete information. You also used two of Excel's formatting tools—Themes and Table Styles—to create custom enhanced results for an attractive worksheet. You saved Excel data in several file formats—Web page, CSV, PDF, and XPS. Finally, you used advanced sort and filter techniques along with subtotaling, outlining, and grouping for data analysis.

Key Terms

Matching

Match each term in the second column with its correct definition in the first column by writing the letter of the term on the blank line in front of the correct definition.

_____ 1. The command to set the column and row headings so that they remain on the screen while you scroll to other parts of the worksheet.

_____ 2. The command that tiles all open program windows on the screen.

_____ 3. A set of formatting characteristics that you can apply to a cell.

_____ 4. Colored and underlined text that, when clicked, takes you to another location in the worksheet, to another file, to a Web page on the Internet, or on your organization's intranet.

_____ 5. The file type that saves an Excel file so that there is a comma between each cell and a paragraph return at the end of each row.

_____ 6. The file type that saves an Excel file with tabs between each cell in a row and a paragraph return at the end of each row.

_____ 7. An organized collection of facts related to a specific topic.

_____ 8. All of the categories of data pertaining to one person, place, thing, event, or idea.

_____ 9. A single piece of information that is stored in every record.

A Arrange All

B AutoFilter menu

C Cell styles

D Comparison operators

E Criteria

F CSV file (comma separated values)

G Database

H Extract area

I Field

J Freeze Panes

K Hyperlink

L Query

M Record

N Tab delimited text file

O Wildcard

_____ 10. The term that refers to asking a question of the data in a database.

_____ 11. The term used for conditions that you specify that must be matched for the record to be included in the search results.

_____ 12. A menu of filtering commands that displays when you click one of the filter arrows in an Excel table.

_____ 13. The Equal sign (=), Greater Than sign (>), or Less Than sign (<) used singly or in combinations to compare two values.

_____ 14. A character such as the asterisk (*) used to search a field when you are uncertain of the exact value or when you want to widen the search to include more records.

_____ 15. The area where you place the results when copying the results of a filter to another location in the worksheet.

Multiple Choice

Circle the correct answer.

1. The command to find and select specific text, formatting, or type of information within a workbook quickly is:
   A. match   **B.** sort   **C.** find

2. A portion of a worksheet window bounded by and separated from other portions by vertical or horizontal bars is a:
   A. border   **B.** pane   **C.** window

3. A predesigned set of colors, fonts, lines, and fill effects that look good together is a:
   A. list   **B.** theme   **C.** text file

4. The page formatting that reduces the horizontal and vertical size of the printed data by a percentage or by the number of pages that you specify is:
   A. extracting   **B.** arranging   **C.** scaling

5. The file type developed by Adobe Systems that is a visual representation of a document is:
   A. PDF   **B.** XPS   **C.** CSV

6. The file type developed by Microsoft that is a visual representation of a document is:
   A. PDF   **B.** XPS   **C.** CSV

7. To organize data in a particular order is to:
   A. filter   **B.** sort   **C.** query

8. Numbers sorted from highest to lowest are sorted in:
   A. descending order   **B.** ascending order   **C.** major order

9. The term that describes filtering actions in which each additional filter that you apply is based on the current filter is:
   A. extracted   **B.** scaled   **C.** additive

10. The operator that requires each and every one of the comparison criteria that you specify must be true is the:
    A. Or operator   **B.** And operator   **C.** detail operator

Content-Based Assessments

Skills Review | Project **5C** Science Schedule

In the following Skills Review, you will assist Jack Littlefield, Program Chair for Science, in formatting and navigating a large worksheet that lists the class schedule for the Science departments at Capital Cities Community College. You will also save Excel data in other file formats. Your completed workbooks will look similar to Figure 5.59.

Project Files

For Project 5C, you will need the following files:

> e05C_Science_Faculty
> e05C_Science_Requests
> e05C_Science_Schedule

You will save your workbooks as:

> Lastname_Firstname_5C_Science_CSV
> Lastname_Firstname_5C_Science_Faculty
> Lastname_Firstname_5C_Science_Schedule
> Lastname_Firstname_5C_Science_Webpage

Project Results

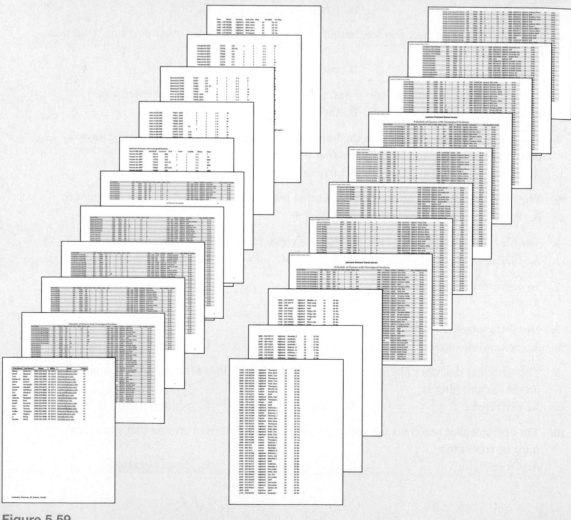

Figure 5.59

(Project 5C Science Schedule continues on the next page)

Content-Based Assessments

1 **Start** Excel. From your student files, open the file **e05C_Science_Schedule**. Display the **Save As** dialog box, navigate to your **Excel Chapter 5** folder, and then save the workbook as **Lastname_Firstname_5C_Science_Schedule**

a. On the **Home tab**, in the **Editing group**, click the **Find & Select** button, and then click **Go To Special**. In the first column, click the **Blanks** option button, and then click **OK** to select all blank cells in the worksheet's active area. Point to the selected cell **K31** and right-click. On the Mini toolbar, click the **Fill Color button arrow**, and then under **Standard Colors**, click the fourth color—**Yellow**—to fill all the selected blank cells. These cells still require Room assignments.

b. Press [Ctrl] + [Home]. From the column heading area, select **columns E:H**. Right-click over the selected area, and then click **Hide**.

c. On the **Home tab**, in the **Editing group**, click the **Find & Select** button, and then click **Go To**. In the **Go To** dialog box, in the **Reference** box, type **m172** and then click **OK**. With cell **M172** active, on the **Formulas tab**, click the **More Functions** button, point to **Statistical**, and then click **COUNTIF**. As the **Range**, type **m2:m170** and as the **Criteria**, type **Staff** Click **OK**. Your result is 27, indicating that 27 courses still indicate *Staff* and need an instructor assigned. In cell **I172**, type **Still need instructor assigned** and press [Enter]. Press [Ctrl] + [Home] and click **Save**.

2 From your student files, open **e05C_Science_Requests**. On the **View tab**, in the **Window group**, click the **Switch Windows** button, and then at the bottom of the list, click your **Lastname_Firstname_5C_Science_Schedule** file to make it the active worksheet. In the **Window group**, click the **Arrange All** button. Click **Horizontal**, and then click **OK**. If necessary, click the title bar of your **5C_Science_Schedule** worksheet to make it the active worksheet. Press [Ctrl] + [End] to move to cell **P172**.

a. Click cell **A172**. In the **Window group**, click **Split**. Above the split bar, click any cell in **column C**. Press [Ctrl] + [F] to display the **Find and Replace** dialog box. Locate the first request in the **e05C_Science_Requests** worksheet, which is from *Eric Marshall* to teach *Survey of Astronomy Section # 76822*. In the **Find**

what box, type **76822** so that you can locate the course in the worksheet.

b. Click **Find Next**. Drag the title bar of the dialog box into the upper right area of your screen so that you can see the **Name Box**, which indicates *C38*. In your **5C_Science_Schedule** worksheet, click in cell **M38**, type **Marshall, Eric** to delete *Staff* and assign the class to Mr. Marshall. Press [Enter].

c. Continue to use the **Find and Replace** dialog box to locate the remaining three **Section #s** listed in the **e05C_Science_Requests** worksheet, and enter the appropriate instructor name for each class in **column M** of your **5C_Science_Schedule** worksheet. **Close** the **Find and Replace** dialog box. In cell **M172**, notice that *23* classes remain unassigned.

d. Click any cell in the **e05C_Science_Requests** worksheet, and then on this worksheet's title bar, click the **Close** button. Then, on the title bar of your **5C_Science_Schedule** worksheet, click the **Maximize** button to restore the size of the worksheet to its full size. On the **View tab**, in the **Window group**, click **Split** to remove the split.

e. Press [Ctrl] + [Home]. From the **column heading area**, select **columns D:I**. Right-click over the selected area, and then click **Unhide**. Press [Ctrl] + [Home], and then **Save** your workbook.

3 Point to the **row 1 heading** to display the [→] pointer, right-click, and then click **Insert**. In cell **A1**, type **Schedule of Classes with Unassigned Sections Merge & Center** this title across the range **A1:P1**, and then apply the **Title** cell style.

a. On the **Page Layout tab**, in the **Themes group**, click the **Themes** button, and then, click the **Apex** theme. In the **Themes group**, click the **Fonts** button. Scroll to the top and click the **Office** fonts.

b. On the **Home tab**, in the **Styles group**, click the **Format as Table** button. At the bottom, click **New Table Style**. In the **New Table Quick Style** dialog box, in the **Name** box, replace the existing text by typing **Science Schedule** In the list under **Table Element**, click **First Row Stripe**, and then click the **Format** button. In the **Format Cells** dialog box, click the **Fill** tab. In the fifth column of colors, click the second color. In the lower right corner, click **OK**.

(Project 5C Science Schedule continues on the next page)

c. In the list of table elements, click **Second Row Stripe**, click the **Format** button, and then in the third row of colors, click the seventh color. Click **OK**. In the list of table elements, click **Header Row**, click the **Format** button, and then in the seventh column, click the fourth color. Click **OK**, in the lower left corner of the dialog box, click to select the check box **Set as default table quick style for this document**, and then click **OK**.

d. Select the range **A2:P171**, and then in the **Styles group**, click **Format as Table**. At the top of the gallery, under **Custom**, locate and click your custom **Science Schedule** table style. In the **Format As Table** dialog box, click **OK**. Then, because you do not need to filter the table, in the **Tools group**, click **Convert to Range**, and then click **Yes**. Press Ctrl + Home to deselect and move to cell **A1**. Click **Save**.

4 Select **columns A:P**, in the **Cells group**, click the **Format** button, and then click **AutoFit Column Width**. On the **Page Layout tab**, in the **Page Setup group**, set the **Orientation** to **Landscape**. Then, in the **Scale to Fit group**, click the **Width arrow**, and then click **1 page**. Click the **Height arrow** and click **4 pages**.

a. From the **Insert tab**, insert a footer in the **left section** that includes the file name. Click in the right section, and then in the **Header & Footer Elements group**, click the **Page Number** button. Click in a cell just above the footer to exit the Footer area.

b. On the **View tab**, in the **Workbook Views group**, click **Page Break Preview**, and close the dialog box if necessary. Point to the horizontal page break line between **Page 1** and **Page 2** to display the pointer, and then drag the line up between **row 42** and **row 43**. Position the break between **Page 2** and **Page 3** between **row 74** and **row 75**. Position the break between **Page 3** and **Page 4** between **row 116** and **row 117**. Position the break between **Page 4** and **Page 5** between **row 152** and **row 153**.

c. On the **View tab**, in the **Workbook Views group**, click the **Normal** button to redisplay the worksheet in **Normal** view, and then press Ctrl + Home.

d. Display the **Print Preview**, scroll through the pages, and notice that the column titles display only on the first page. Click the **Page Layout tab**, in the **Page Setup group**, click the **Print Titles** button to display the **Sheet tab** of the **Page Setup** dialog box.

e. Under **Print titles**, click in the **Rows to repeat at top** box, and then in the worksheet, select **row 2**. Click **OK**. Click **Save**.

5 From **Backstage** view, display the **Open** dialog box, and then from your student files, open the file **e05C_Science_Faculty**. Display the **Save As** dialog box, navigate to your **Excel Chapter 5** folder, and then save the file as **Lastname_Firstname_5C_Science_Faculty** Insert a footer in the **left section** with the file name, click outside the footer area, press Ctrl + Home and return to **Normal** view. Click **Save**, and then close this workbook to redisplay your **5C_Science_Schedule** workbook.

a. Click cell **M2**. On the **Insert tab**, in the **Links group**, click the **Hyperlink** button. Under **Link to**, click **Existing File or Web Page**. Click the **Look in arrow**, navigate to your **Excel Chapter 5** folder, and then select your **Lastname_Firstname_5C_Science_Faculty** workbook. Click **OK**.

b. Point to cell **M2** to display the pointer, and then click to confirm that the link opens the workbook containing the contact information. Close the workbook with the faculty contacts.

c. Point to cell **M2**, right-click, and then click **Edit Hyperlink**. In the upper right corner of the **Insert Hyperlink** dialog box, click the **ScreenTip** button. In the **ScreenTip text** box, type **Click here for contact information** Click **OK** two times. Point to cell **M2** and confirm that your ScreenTip displays.

d. Display the **Document Panel** and in the **Author** box, type your firstname and lastname, in the **Subject** box, type your course name and section number, and in the **Keywords** box, type **science schedule** **Close** the Document Panel and click **Save**. Leave the workbook open.

6 Display the **Save As** dialog box, in the lower portion, click the **Save as type arrow**, and then click **Web Page**.

a. Click the **Change Title** button. In the **Enter Text** dialog box, in the **Page title** box, using your own name, type **Lastname Firstname Science Courses** Click **OK**, and notice that in the **Page title** box, your typed text displays. In the **Save As** dialog box, click the **Publish** button.

b. In the **Publish as Web Page** dialog box, click the **Choose arrow**, and then click **Items on Science Classes**—recall that the worksheet name is *Science*

(Project 5C Science Schedule continues on the next page)

Classes. In the lower left corner, if necessary, click to select (place a check mark in) the **Open published web page in browser** check box.

c. Click the **Browse** button to display the **Publish As** dialog box. If necessary, navigate to your **Excel Chapter 5** folder. In the **File name** box, type **Lastname_Firstname_5C_Science_Webpage** Click **OK**, and then in the displayed **Publish as Web Page** dialog box, click **Publish**.

d. If you are instructed to print your Web page on paper, consult the instructions to print from your specific browser software. On the browser title bar, click the **Close** button. Leave your

Lastname_Firstname_5C_Science_Schedule workbook open for the next step.

e. Display the **Save As** dialog box, be sure you are saving in your **Excel Chapter 5** folder, set the **Save as type** to **CSV (Comma delimited)**, and as the **File name**, type **Lastname_Firstname_5C_Science_CSV** Click **Save**, and then click **Yes**.

f. **Close** your **5C_Science_CSV** file, click **Save**, and then click **Yes**. **Close** Excel. As directed by your instructor, submit the four files that comprise the results of this project.

End **You have completed Project 5C** ————————————————————

Content-Based Assessments

Skills Review | Project **5D** Spring Sections

In the following Skills Review, you will use advanced table features to provide Dr. Paula Marshall, the Dean of the Arts Division, information about the Spring course sections and assigned faculty in the Division. Your completed worksheets will look similar to Figure 5.60.

Project Files

For Project 5D, you will need the following files:

e05D_Spring_Faculty
e05D_Spring_Sections

You will save your workbooks as:

Lastname_Firstname_5D_Spring_Faculty
Lastname_Firstname_5D_Spring_Sections

Project Results

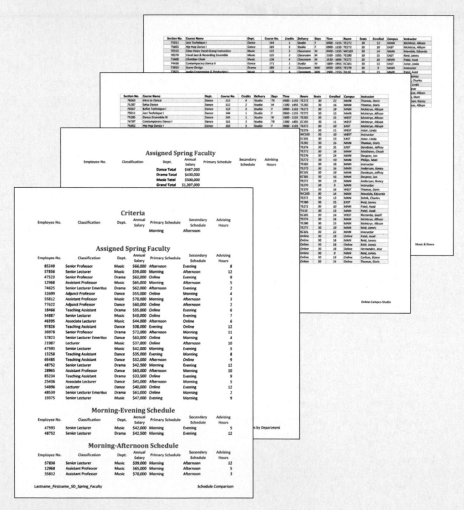

Figure 5.60

(Project 5D Spring Sections continues on the next page)

Skills Review | Project 5D Spring Sections (continued)

1 **Start** Excel. From your student files, open the file **e05D_Spring_Sections**, and then **Save** the file in your **Excel Chapter 5** folder as **Lastname_Firstname_5D_Spring_Sections** Be sure the first worksheet, **Online-Campus-Studio** displays.

a. On the **Data tab**, in the **Sort & Filter group**, click **Sort**. In the **Sort** dialog box, under **Column**, click the **Sort by arrow**, and then click **Delivery**. Under **Sort On**, click the **arrow**, and then click **Values**. Under **Order**, click the **Order arrow** for this sort level, and then click **Custom List**. In the dialog box, under **Custom lists**, be sure **NEW LIST** is selected. Then, under **List entries**, click in the empty box and type **Studio** Press [Enter], type **Classroom** Press [Enter], and then type **Online**

b. In the **Custom Lists** dialog box, click the **Add** button, and then click **OK**. If necessary, in the **Sort** dialog box, click the **Order arrow**, and then click your **Studio, Classroom, Online** custom list so that it displays in the **Order** box. Click the **Add Level** button, and then as the second level sort, click **Dept**. Click the **Add Level** button again, and as the third level sort, click **Course Name**. Click **OK**.

2 Click the **Music & Dance sheet tab** to display the *second* worksheet. In cell **C1**, click the **Dept. filter arrow**. On the displayed list, click the **(Select All)** check box to clear all the check boxes, and then select the **Music** and **Drama** check boxes. Click **OK**.

a. In cell **E1**, click the **Credits filter arrow**, and then filter the list further by **3**. In cell **F1**, click the **Delivery filter arrow**, and filter the list further by **Online**. The status bar information reveals that 4 of the 39 course sections that are either in the Music or Drama departments and that are 3-credit courses offered online.

b. On the **Data tab**, in the **Sort & Filter group**, **Clear all filters**. In cell **K1**, click the **Enrolled filter arrow**, point to **Number Filters**, and then click **Less Than Or Equal To**. In the first box, be sure that *is less than or equal to* displays, and then in the second box type **15** Click **OK** to display *16* records.

c. Right click over either of the two sheet tabs, and then click **Select All Sheets**. With the sheets grouped, insert a footer in the **left section** that includes the file name. Click in the **center section** of the footer, and then on the **Design tab**, in the **Header & Footer**

Elements group, click the **Page Number** button. Press [Spacebar] one time, type **of** and press [Spacebar] again, and then click the **Number of Pages** button. Click in the **right section** of the footer, and then on the **Design tab**, in the **Header & Footer Elements group**, click the **Sheet Name** button.

d. Click a cell outside of the footer, and then on the **Page Layout tab**, set the orientation to **Landscape**, and set the **Width** to **1 page**. Click the **Normal** button, and then press [Ctrl] + [Home] to move to cell **A1**.

e. Display the **Document Panel** and in the **Author** box, type your firstname and lastname, in the **Subject** box, type your course name and section number, and in the **Keywords** box, type **sort, filter, sections** **Close** the **Document Properties**, and then display **Print Preview**. Make any necessary corrections or adjustments.

f. **Save** your workbook. Hold this workbook until the end of this project, and then print or submit the two worksheets in this workbook electronically as directed by your instructor. **Close** this workbook, but leave Excel open.

3 From your student files, open **e05D_Spring_Faculty**. Display the **Save As** dialog box, navigate to your **Excel Chapter 5** folder, and then **Save** the workbook as **Lastname_Firstname_5D_Spring_Faculty** Be sure the **Schedule Comparison** worksheet is active. **Copy** the range **A6:G7**, **Paste** it in cell **A1**, and then change the title in cell **A1** to **Criteria**

a. Select the range **A2:G3**, and then in the **Name Box**, name this range **Criteria** Copy the range **A1:G2**, scroll down to view **row 34**, point to cell **A34**, right-click, and then click **Paste**. Click cell **A34**, and then change the title to **Morning-Evening Schedule** and then press [Enter]. Select the range **A35:G35** and then in the **Name Box**, name this range **Extract** Select the range **A7:G32** and then in the **Name Box**, name this range **Database**

b. At the top of your worksheet, in cell **E3**, type **Morning** and in cell **F3**, type **Evening** On the **Data tab**, in the **Sort & Filter group**, click the **Advanced** button. Under **Action**, click the **Copy to another location** option button. Verify that in the **Copy to** box—$A$35:$G$35—displays. Click **OK**, and then scroll to view the lower portion of your worksheet. Two records meet the criteria.

(Project 5D Spring Sections continues on the next page)

Excel | Chapter 5

c. Copy the range **A34:G35**, and then **Paste** it in cell **A39**. In cell **A39**, change the word *Evening* to **Afternoon** In cell **F3**, change the criteria to **Afternoon** Display the **Advanced Filter** dialog box, and then click the **Copy to another location** option button.

d. In the **Copy to** box, click the **Collapse Dialog** button, and then select the range **A40:G40**. Click the **Expand Dialog** button and then click **OK**. *Three* records meet the criteria and are copied to the extract area on your worksheet. **Save** the workbook.

4 Display the **Salaries by Department** worksheet. Select the range **A2:G30**. On the **Data tab**, in the **Sort & Filter group**, click the **Sort** button. In the **Sort** dialog box, sort by the **Dept.** column, and then by the **Annual Salary** column. Click **OK**.

a. With the range still selected, on the **Data tab**, in the **Outline group**, click the **Subtotal** button. In the **Subtotal** dialog box, in the **At each change in** box, display the list, and then click **Dept**. In the **Use function** box, display the list and click **Sum**. In the **Add subtotal to** list, select the **Annual Salary** check box, and then deselect any other check boxes. Click **OK**.

b. Click any cell to deselect, and then along the left edge of your workbook, locate the outline. To the left of **row 22**, click the **Hide Detail** button (-) to collapse the detail for the **Drama** department.

c. Select **rows 25:28**, and then on the **Data tab**, in the **Outline group**, click the **Group** button. To the left of

row 29, click the **Hide Detail** button. At the top of the outline area, click the **Level 2** button to hide all Level 3 and 4 details, and display only the Level 2 summary information, and the Level 1 Grand Total. Press Ctrl + Home.

d. Group the two worksheets. Insert a footer in the **left section** that includes the file name, and in the **right section**, insert the **Sheet Name**. Click any cell to exit the footer area. On the **Page Layout tab**, set the **Width** to **1 page** and set the **Height** to **1 page**—this will scale each worksheet to fit on a single page. On the status bar, click the **Normal** button. Press Ctrl + Home to move to cell **A1**.

e. Display the **Document Panel**, and in the **Author** box, type your firstname and lastname, in the **Subject** box, type your course name and section number, and in the **Keywords** box, type **faculty, schedule, salaries Close** the **Document Properties** and display the **Print Preview**. Make any necessary corrections or adjustments.

f. **Save** your workbook, and then close it. Along with your other workbook from this project, print or submit electronically as directed If required, print or create an electronic version of your worksheets with formulas displayed, using the instructions in Activity 1.16 in Project 1A. **Close** Excel.

End You have completed Project 5D

Content-Based Assessments

Apply **5A** skills from these Objectives:

1. Navigate and Manage Large Worksheets
2. Enhance Worksheets with Themes and Styles
3. Format a Worksheet to Share with Others
4. Save Excel Data in Other File Formats

Mastering Excel | Project **5E** Sports Schedule

In the following Mastering Excel project, you will assist Tom Bloomington, Athletic Director at Capital Cities Community College, in formatting and navigating a large worksheet that lists the sports events schedule for spring sports. You will also save Excel data in other file formats. Your completed workbooks will look similar to Figure 5.61.

Project Files

For Project 5E, you will need the following files:

e05E_Sports_Coaches
e05E_Referee_Requests
e05E_Sports_Schedule

You will save your workbooks as:

Lastname_Firstname_5E_Sports_Coaches
Lastname_Firstname_5E_Sports_PDF
Lastname_Firstname_5E_Sports_Schedule
Lastname_Firstname_5E_Sports_Webpage

Project Results

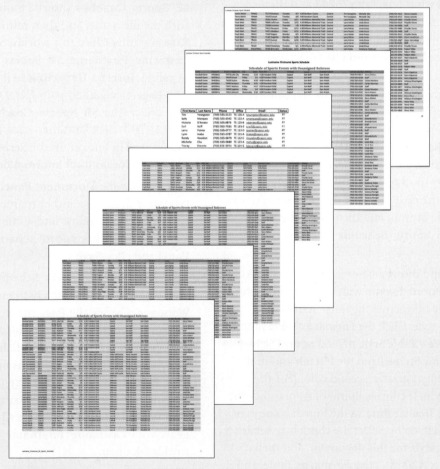

Figure 5.61

(Project 5E Sports Schedule continues on the next page)

Content-Based Assessments

1 Start **Excel**. Open the file **e05E_Sports_Schedule** and **Save** it in your **Excel Chapter 5** folder as **Lastname_Firstname_5E_Sports_Schedule Go To** cell **M82**, and then insert the **COUNTIF** function. Set the **Range** as **m2:m80** and the **Criteria** as **Staff** resulting in *23* sporting events that still require a Referee assigned. In cell **K82**, type **Events with Unassigned Referees** Press Ctrl + Home. Open the file **e05E_Referee_Requests**. Switch windows, and then click your **Lastname_Firstname_5E_Sports_Schedule** file. Click **Arrange All** so the files are **Horizontal** with your **Lastname_Firstname_5E_Sports_Schedule** as the active worksheet in the top window.

2 Go to cell **A82**, **Split** the window horizontally, and then above the split bar, click in any cell in **column C**. Display the **Find and Replace** dialog box. Locate the first request in the **e05E_Referee_Requests** worksheet, which is from *Danny Litowitz* to referee *Tennis Match Event # 76243*. In the **Find what** box, type **76243** and then click **Find Next**, which indicates cell *C48*. In the **Lastname_Firstname_5E_Sports_Schedule** worksheet, click in cell **M48**, and then type **Danny Litowitz** to assign him as the *Referee*.

3 Use the **Find** command to locate the remaining three **Event #s** listed in the **e05E_Referee_Requests** worksheet, and then enter the appropriate referee for each sports event in **column M** of your **5E_Sports_Schedule** worksheet. **Close** the **Find and Replace** dialog box. In cell **M82**, notice that *19* sports events still need a referee assigned. Click in the **e05E_Referee_Requests** worksheet to display the Close button, and then **Close** the workbook. **Maximize** your **5E_Sports_Schedule** worksheet, and then remove the **Split**.

4 Select **row 1** and **insert** a new blank row. In cell **A1**, type **Schedule of Sports Events with Unassigned Referees Merge & Center** the title across the range **A1:M1**, and then apply the **Title** cell style. Click the **Format as Table** button, and then create a **New Table Style** named **Sports Schedule** Format the **First Row Stripe** from the **Fill tab** and in the fifth column of colors, click the second color. For the **Second Row Stripe**, in the fifth column of colors, click the third color. For the **Header Row**, in the fourth column of colors click the fourth color. Select the check box **Set as default table quick style for this document**, and then click **OK**. Select the range **A2:M81**, click **Format as Table**, and

then select the **Custom** table style, *Sports Schedule*. In the **Tools group**, click **Convert to Range**, and then click **Yes**. Press Ctrl + Home to deselect and move to cell **A1**.

5 Select **columns A:M** and then apply **AutoFit Column Width**. Set the **Orientation** to **Landscape**, and then in the **Scale to Fit group**, set the **Width** to **1 page** and the **Height** to **4 pages**. Insert a footer in the **left section** that includes the file name, and in the **right section**, insert a page number. Apply **Page Break Preview**, and then drag the line to break **Page 1** after **row 49**—this will end the page with *TENNIS* and begin **Page 2** with *TRACK*. Return to **Normal** view. On the **Page Layout tab**, set **Print Titles** to repeat **row 2** at the top of each page. Display **Print Preview** and examine the pages. Redisplay the workbook, make any necessary adjustments, and then **Save**. Leave this workbook displayed.

6 Open the file **e05E_Sports_Coaches** and **Save** it in your **Excel Chapter 5** folder as **Lastname_Firstname_5E_Sports_Coaches** Insert a footer in the **left section** with the file name, and then return to **Normal** view. **Save** and then **Close** this workbook to redisplay your **Lastname_Firstname_5E_Sports_Schedule** workbook. In cell **J2**, **Insert** a **Hyperlink** to link to an **Existing File or Web Page,** navigate to your **Excel Chapter 5** folder, and then select your **5E_Sports_Coaches** workbook. Point to cell **J2**, right-click, and then click **Edit Hyperlink**. Click the **ScreenTip** button. In the **ScreenTip text** box, type **Click here for contact information** Click **OK** two times.

7 Display the **Document Panel** and in the **Author** box, type your firstname and lastname, in the **Subject** box, type your course name and section number, and in the **Keywords** box, type **sports schedule Close** the **Document Panel** and click **Save**.

8 **Save** your **5E_Sports_Schedule** workbook as a **Web Page** with the name **Lastname_Firstname_Sports_Webpage** Change the **Page title** to **Lastname Firstname Sports Schedule** and then **Publish**. If necessary, place a check mark in the **Open published web page in browser** check box, select **Items on Sporting Events**, and then **Publish**. If you are instructed to print your Web page on paper, consult the instructions to print from your specific browser software. **Close** your browser. Leave your **Lastname_Firstname_5E_Sports_Schedule** workbook open.

(Project 5E Sports Schedule continues on the next page)

Mastering Excel | Project **5E** Sports Schedule (continued)

9 Display the **Save As** dialog box, navigate to your **Excel Chapter 5** folder, set the **Save as type** to **PDF (Portable Document Format)**, and as the **File name** type **Lastname_Firstname_5E_Sports_PDF** Click **Save**. **Close** all files.

As directed by your instructor, print or submit electronically the four files that comprise the results of this project—two Excel files, a PDF file, and an HTML file.

End **You have completed Project 5E** ———————————

Content-Based Assessments

Apply **5B** skills from these Objectives:

5 Use Advanced Sort Techniques

6 Use Custom and Advanced Filters

7 Subtotal, Outline, and Group a List of Data

Mastering Excel | Project **5F** Vocational Programs

In the following Mastering Excel project, you will edit a worksheet for Ron Lattimer, Vice President of Instruction, with data that has been sorted, filtered, and grouped that analyzes vocational programs at Capital Cities Community College. The worksheets of your workbook will look similar to Figure 5.62.

Project Files

For Project 5F, you will need the following file:

> e05F_Vocational_Programs

You will save your workbook as:

> Lastname_Firstname_5F_Vocational_Programs

Project Results

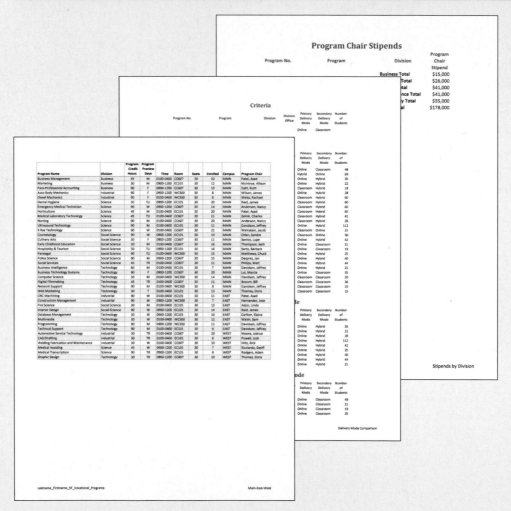

Figure 5.62

(Project 5F Vocational Programs continues on the next page)

Content-Based Assessments

Mastering Excel | Project **5F** Vocational Programs (continued)

1 **Start** Excel. **Open** the file **e05F_Vocational_ Programs**. **Save** the file in your **Excel Chapter 5** folder as **Lastname_Firstname_5F_Vocational_Programs** Display the *first* worksheet, **Main-East-West**. Select the range **A1:J40**, insert a table, and then apply **Table Style Light 18**. Click anywhere to deselect, on the **Data tab**, from the **Sort & Filter group**, display the **Sort** dialog box.

For the first sort level, sort by **Campus**, sort on **Values**, and then under **Order**, click the **arrow** and click **Custom List**. With **NEW LIST** selected, under **List entries**, type **Main** Press [Enter], type **East** Press [Enter], and then type **West** Click the **Add** button, and then click **OK**. In the **Order** box, click your **Main, East, West** custom list and click **OK**. Add a second level, sort by **Division** in alphabetical order on **Values**. Add a third level, sort by **Program Name** in alphabetical order on **Values**. Click **OK**.

2 On the **Design tab**, convert the data to a range. Display the *second* worksheet, **Delivery Mode Comparison**. **Copy** the range **A6:G7**. **Paste** it in cell **A1**, and then change the title in cell **A1** to **Criteria** Select the range **A2:G3**, and then in the **Name Box**, name this range **Criteria**

Copy the range **A1:G2**, scroll down to view **row 36**, point to cell **A36**, right-click, and then click **Paste**. Click cell **A36**, and then change the title to **Online-Hybrid Delivery Mode** and then press [Enter]. Select the range **A37:G37** and then in the **Name Box**, name this range **Extract** Select the range **A7:G34** and then in the **Name Box**, name this range **Database**

3 At the top of your worksheet, in cell **E3**, type **Online** and in cell **F3**, type **Hybrid** and then press [Enter]. On the **Data tab**, in the **Sort & Filter group**, click the **Advanced** button. Under **Action**, click the **Copy to another location** option button. Verify that in the **Copy to** box, the absolute reference to the Extract area—*$A$37:$G$37*—displays.

Click **OK**. **Copy** the range **A36:G37**, and then **Paste** it in cell **A48**. In cell **A48** change the word *Hybrid* to **Classroom** In cell **F3**, change the criteria to **Classroom** Display the **Advanced Filter** dialog box, and then click the **Copy to another location** option button. In the **Copy to** box, click the **Collapse Dialog** button, scroll down as necessary, and then select the range **A49:G49**. Click the **Expand Dialog** button, and then click **OK**.

4 Display the *third* worksheet—**Stipends by Division**. Select the range **A2:D41**. Display the **Sort** dialog box, **Sort** first by the **Division**, then by the **Program Chair Stipend**. Click **OK**. **Subtotal** at each change in **Division**, select the **Sum** function, add the subtotal to the **Program Chair Stipend**, and then click **OK**. **Group** the data so each **Division** is collapsed and a break in the row numbers indicates that some rows are hidden from view. Apply **AutoFit** to **column D** to display the **Grand Total**.

5 Select all three worksheets. Insert a footer in the **left section** that includes the file name, and in the **right section**, insert the **Sheet Name**. On the **Page Layout tab**, set the **Width** to **1 page** and set the **Height** to **1 page**. Click the **Margins** button, click **Custom Margins**, and then center horizontally. Return to **Normal** view, and then press [Ctrl] + [Home] to move to cell **A1**.

6 Display the **Document Panel**, and in the **Author** box, type your firstname and lastname, in the **Subject** box, type your course name and section number, and in the **Keywords** box, type **vocational programs** Examine the **Print Preview**, make any necessary corrections or adjustments, and then **Save** and **Close** the workbook. Print or submit your workbook electronically as directed. If required, print or create an electronic version of your worksheets with formulas displayed, using the instructions in Activity 1.16 in Project 1A. **Close** Excel.

End **You have completed Project 5F**

Content-Based Assessments

Apply **5A** and **5B** skills from these Objectives:

1. Navigate and Manage Large Worksheets
2. Enhance Worksheets with Themes and Styles
3. Format a Worksheet to Share with Others
4. Save Excel Data in Other File Formats
5. Use Advanced Sort Techniques
6. Use Custom and Advanced Filters
7. Subtotal, Outline, and Group a List of Data

Mastering Excel | Project **5G** Sports Programs

In the following Mastering Excel project, you will create a worksheet for Ron Latham, Assistant Director of Athletics, with data that has been sorted, filtered, and grouped and that analyzes sports programs at Capital Cities Community College. Assistant Director Latham will use this information to make decisions for these sports programs for the upcoming academic year. The worksheets of your workbook will look similar to Figure 5.63.

Project Files

For Project 5G, you will need the following files:

    e05G_Sports_Programs
    e05G_Coach_Information

You will save your workbook as:

    Lastname_Firstname_5G_Sports_Programs

Project Results

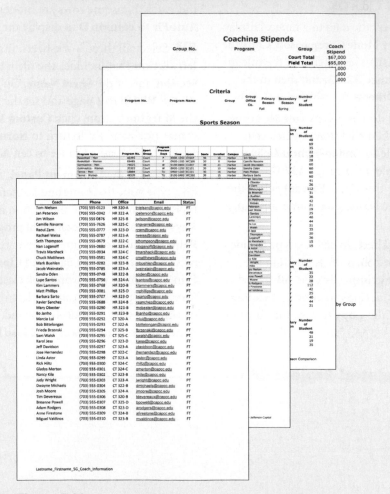

Figure 5.63

(Project 5G Sports Programs continues on the next page)

Content-Based Assessments

1 **Start** Excel. From your student files, locate and open **e05G_Sports_Programs**. **Save** the file in your **Excel Chapter 5** folder as **Lastname_Firstname_5G_Sports_Programs** Display the *first* worksheet, **Harbor-Jefferson-Capital**. Select the range **A1:J40**, insert a table, and then apply **Table Style Light 19**. In the **Sort** dialog box, **Sort** by **Campus**, sort on **Values**, and then click **Custom List**. With **NEW LIST** selected, under **List entries**, create entries for **Harbor** and **Jefferson** and **Capital** Click the **Add** button, and then click **OK**. If necessary, in the **Order** box, click your **Harbor, Jefferson, Capital** custom list so that it displays.

As the second level, sort the **Sport Group** column alphabetically on **Values**. As the third level, sort the **Program Name** column alphabetically on **Values**. Click **OK**, and then click anywhere to deselect. Convert the table to a range.

2 Display the *second* worksheet, **Sports Season Comparison**. **Copy** the range **A6:G7**, **Paste** it in cell **A1**, and then change the title in cell **A1** to **Criteria** Select the range **A2:G3**, and then in the **Name Box**, name this range **Criteria** Copy the range **A1:G2**, scroll down, right-click cell **A36**, and then **Paste** the copied range. Change the title in cell **A36** to **Fall-Summer Sports Season** Name the range **A37:G37** **Extract** and then name the range **A7:G34** **Database**

3 At the top of your worksheet, in cell **E3**, type **Fall** and in cell **F3**, type **Summer** On the **Data tab**, in the **Sort & Filter group**, click the **Advanced** button. Under **Action**, click the **Copy to another location** option button. Verify that in the **Copy to** box, the absolute reference to the Extract area—*$A$37:$G$37*—displays. Click **OK**.

4 Scroll to view the lower portion of your worksheet. Copy the range **A36:G37**, and then **Paste** it in cell **A48**. In cell **A48**, change the word *Summer* to **Spring** In cell **F3**, change the criteria to **Spring**

Display the **Advanced Filter** dialog box, and then click the **Copy to another location** option button. In the **Copy to** box, click the **Collapse Dialog** button, scroll down as necessary, and then select the range **A49:G49**. Click the **Expand Dialog** button, and then click **OK**. Scroll to view the lower portion of the worksheet.

5 Display the *third* worksheet—**Stipends by Group**. Select the range **A2:D41**. **Sort** by **Group**, then by the **Coach Stipend**. **Subtotal** at each change in **Group**, select the **Sum**

function, select the **Add subtotal to** the **Coach Stipend** check box, and then click **OK**. **Group** the data so each **Group** venue is collapsed and a break in the row numbers indicates that some rows are hidden from view. Display the **Level 2** summary information, and the **Level 1** Grand Total. AutoFit columns as necessary. Press [Ctrl] + [Home].

6 Select all three worksheets. Insert a footer in the **left section** that includes the file name, and in the **right section**, insert the **Sheet Name**. On the **Page Layout tab**, set the **Width** to **1 page** and set the **Height** to **1 page**. Display **Custom Margins** and **Center** the worksheets horizontally.

Return to **Normal** view, and then press [Ctrl] + [Home] to move to cell **A1**. Change the theme to **Solstice**, and then change the **Fonts** to **Aspect**. Display the **Document Panel**, and in the **Author** box, type your firstname and lastname, in the **Subject** box, type your course name and section number, and in the **Keywords** box, type **sports programs, campus, sports season, stipends** Display the worksheet in **Print Preview**, and then make any necessary corrections or adjustments.

7 Open the file **e05G_Coach_Information** and **Save** it in your **Excel Chapter 5** folder as **Lastname_Firstname_5G_Coach_Information** Insert a footer in the **left section** with the file name, and then return to **Normal** view. **Save** and then close this workbook to redisplay your **Lastname_Firstname_5G_Sports Programs** workbook.

8 On the **Harbor-Jefferson-Capital** worksheet, in cell **J1**, **Insert** a **Hyperlink** to link to an **Existing File or Web Page,** navigate to your **Excel Chapter 5** folder, and then select your **Lastname_Firstname_5G_Coach_Information** workbook. Point to cell **J1**, right-click, and then click **Edit Hyperlink**. Click the **ScreenTip** button. In the **ScreenTip text** box, type **Click here for contact information** Click **OK** two times. Change the **Font Color** in cell **J1** to **Indigo, Accent 6, Darker 50%**. **Save** the workbook.

9 Display the **Save As** dialog box, navigate to your **Excel Chapter 5** folder, set the **Save as type** to **XPS Document**, and as the **File name**, type **Lastname_Firstname_5G_Sports_XPS** Click **Save**. **Close** all files. As directed by your instructor, print or submit electronically the three files that comprise the results of this project—two Excel files and one XPS file. There are no formulas in this workbook. **Close** Excel.

End **You have completed Project 5G**

Content-Based Assessments

GO! Fix It | Project 5H Programs

Project Files

For Project 5H, you will need the following file:

e05H_Programs

You will save your workbook as:

Lastname_Firstname_5H_Programs

Open the file **e05H_Programs**, and then save the file in your Excel Chapter 5 folder as **Lastname_Firstname_5H_Programs** In row 36, notice that the extract area is supposed to show programs offered in both an Online mode and a Classroom mode. Edit this worksheet and use the Advanced Filter dialog box to filter and then display the correct data in the extract area. Add your name and course name, and section number to the document properties, and include **vocational programs** as the keywords.

Insert the file name in the footer, save your file, and then print or submit your worksheet electronically as directed by your instructor.

End You have completed Project 5H ———————————

Content-Based Assessments

Apply a combination of the **5A** and **5B** skills.

GO! Make It | Project **5I** Arts Faculty

Project Files

For Project 5I, you will need the following file:

e05I_Arts_Faculty

You will save your workbook as:

Lastname_Firstname_5I_Arts_Faculty

From your student files, open the file **e05I_Arts_Faculty**, and then save it in your chapter folder as **Lastname_Firstname_5I_Arts_Faculty** By using the skills you have practiced, format the worksheet as shown in Figure 5.64 by adding Subtotals using the Subtotal feature. Apply the Waveform theme. Insert the file name in the footer. Add your name, course name, and section number to the document properties, and include **arts faculty** as the keywords Submit as directed by your instructor.

Project Results

Arts Faculty

Employee No.	Classification	Department	Annual Salary	
254	Professor	Art	$	41,000
463	Professor	Art	$	44,000
369	Asst. Professor	Art	$	72,000
		Art Total	$	157,000
852	TA	Dance	$	33,500
487	Professor	Dance	$	42,500
		Dance Total	$	76,000
219	Lecturer	Music	$	37,000
578	Professor	Music	$	39,000
653	Asst. Professor	Music	$	43,000
		Music Total	$	119,000
654	TA	Theater	$	32,000
548	Professor	Theater	$	40,000
289	Asst. Professor	Theater	$	63,000
		Theater Total	$	135,000
		Grand Total	$	487,000

Lastname_Firstname_5I_Arts_Faculty

Figure 5.64

End You have completed Project 5I ————————————

Content-Based Assessments

Apply a combination of
the **5A** and **5B** skills.

GO! Solve It | Project **5J** Dept Tutors

Project Files

For Project 5J, you will need the following file:

e05J_Dept_Tutors

You will save your workbook as:

Lastname_Firstname_5J_Dept_Tutors

Open the file e05J_Dept_Tutors and save it in your chapter folder as **Lastname_Firstname_5J_Dept_Tutors**

The Director of the Tutoring Center wants to know which tutors who are classified as grad student tutors are available in the afternoons from the CNT and CPS departments. By using the table feature and filtering, filter the data to present the information requested. Include the file name in the footer, add appropriate properties, and then save your workbook. Submit as directed.

		Performance Level		
		Exemplary: You consistently applied the relevant skills	**Proficient:** You sometimes, but not always, applied the relevant skills	**Developing:** You rarely or never applied the relevant skills
Performance Criteria	**Convert Data to a Table**	The data is properly converted to a table.	Only part of the data is in the form of a table.	The data is not properly converted to a table.
	Filter on Multiple Columns	The Filter Function is properly applied using supplied criteria.	The Filter Function is properly applied to some but not all supplied criteria.	The Filter Function is not properly applied and did not meet the supplied criteria.

End You have completed Project 5J

Content-Based Assessments

Apply a combination of
the **5A** and **5B** skills.

GO! Solve It | Project **5K** Organizations

Project Files

For Project 5K, you will need the following file:

e05K_Organizations

You will save your workbook as:

Lastname_Firstname_5K_Organizations

Open the file e05K_Organizations and save it in your chapter file as **Lastname_Firstname_ 5K_Organizations**

To update the worksheet, sort the data by the organization name. Then, filter to display only those records that are missing a Contact Number. Format to print on one sheet in landscape. Include the file name in the footer, add appropriate properties, the keywords **student organizations**, save the file, and then submit as directed.

		Performance Level		
		Exemplary: You consistently applied the relevant skills	**Proficient:** You sometimes, but not always, applied the relevant skills	**Developing:** You rarely or never applied the relevant skills
Performance Criteria	**Use Sort Function**	The Sort function sorts the organization data in ascending order.	The organization data is sorted in the wrong order.	The organization data is not sorted.
	Filter for blank cells	Seven filtered records missing a contact number display.	The filter was applied incorrectly.	The list was not filtered.
	Page Layout	The page layout displays in landscape orientation on one page.	The page is missing either the landscape orientation or the scaling.	Neither landscape nor scaling applied to the page layout.

End You have completed Project 5K

Outcomes-Based Assessments

Rubric

The following outcomes-based assessments are *open-ended assessments*. That is, there is no specific correct result; your result will depend on your approach to the information provided. Make *Professional Quality* your goal. Use the following scoring rubric to guide you in *how* to approach the problem and then to evaluate *how well* your approach solves the problem.

The *criteria*—Software Mastery, Content, Format and Layout, and Process—represent the knowledge and skills you have gained that you can apply to solving the problem. The *levels of performance*—Professional Quality, Approaching Professional Quality, or Needs Quality Improvements—help you and your instructor evaluate your result.

	Your completed project is of Professional Quality if you:	Your completed project is Approaching Professional Quality if you:	Your completed project Needs Quality Improvements if you:
1-Software Mastery	Choose and apply the most appropriate skills, tools, and features and identify efficient methods to solve the problem.	Choose and apply some appropriate skills, tools, and features, but not in the most efficient manner.	Choose inappropriate skills, tools, or features, or are inefficient in solving the problem.
2-Content	Construct a solution that is clear and well organized, contains content that is accurate, appropriate to the audience and purpose, and is complete. Provide a solution that contains no errors in spelling, grammar, or style.	Construct a solution in which some components are unclear, poorly organized, inconsistent, or incomplete. Misjudge the needs of the audience. Have some errors in spelling, grammar, or style, but the errors do not detract from comprehension.	Construct a solution that is unclear, incomplete, or poorly organized; contains some inaccurate or inappropriate content; and contains many errors in spelling, grammar, or style. Do not solve the problem.
3-Format and Layout	Format and arrange all elements to communicate information and ideas, clarify function, illustrate relationships, and indicate relative importance.	Apply appropriate format and layout features to some elements, but not others. Overuse features, causing minor distraction.	Apply format and layout that does not communicate information or ideas clearly. Do not use format and layout features to clarify function, illustrate relationships, or indicate relative importance. Use available features excessively, causing distraction.
4-Process	Use an organized approach that integrates planning, development, self-assessment, revision, and reflection.	Demonstrate an organized approach in some areas, but not others; or, use an insufficient process of organization throughout.	Do not use an organized approach to solve the problem.

Outcomes-Based Assessments

GO! Think | Project **5L** Summer Sections

Project Files

For Project 5L, you will need the following file:

    e05L_Summer_Sections

You will save your workbook as:

    Lastname_Firstname_5L_Summer_Sections

From your student files, open the file e05L_Summer_Sections, and then save it in your chapter folder as **Lastname_Firstname_5L_Summer_Sections** Select the entire range and insert a table with headers. Create a custom table style, name it **Summer Sections**, and then apply it to the table. Create a custom sort, and then custom sort the Campus information in Online, Jefferson, Harbor, Capital order. Include the file name in the footer, add appropriate properties, the keywords **summer sections**, save the file as a PDF, and then submit as directed.

 You have completed Project 5L ————————————

GO! Think | Project **5M** Social Science

Project Files

For Project 5M, you will need the following file:

    e05M_Social_Science

You will save your workbook as:

    Lastname_Firstname_5M_Social_Science

From your student files, open the file e05M_Social_Science, and then save it in your chapter folder as **Lastname_Firstname_5M_Social_Science** Select the entire range and insert a table with headers. Create a custom sort, and then custom sort the Delivery information in Online, Classroom order. Within each delivery type—Online and Classroom—sort the data further by Dept. and then by Course Name. Hide column M, Status. Change the Theme to Opulent and the Font to Concourse. Include the file name in the footer, add appropriate properties, the keywords, **social science**, save the file, and then submit as directed.

End You have completed Project 5M ————————————

Excel | Chapter 5

Outcomes-Based Assessments

You and GO! | Project **5N** Personal Expenses

Project Files

For Project 5N, you will need the following file:

    e05N_Personal_Expenses

You will save your workbook as:

    Lastname_Firstname_5N_Personal_Expenses

In this chapter, you practiced using Excel to subtotal, outline, and group a list of data. You also practiced changing and customizing a workbook theme. From your student files, open **e05N_Personal_Expenses**, and then save it in your **Excel Chapter 5** folder as **Lastname_Firstname_5N_Personal_Expenses**

By using the skills you practiced in this chapter, modify the **Lastname_Firstname_5N_Personal_Expenses** worksheet by adding and deleting your personal expenses, as applicable. Sort the data by the Category column, and then by the Amount. Subtotal the data by Category, and Sum the Amount. Change and customize a table with your preferences and apply it to the worksheet. Title it **Personal Expenses**. Insert a footer with the file name. Add appropriate document properties and include the keywords **personal expenses**. Save your file as **Lastname_Firstname_5N_Personal_Expenses** and then print or submit electronically as directed.

End You have completed Project **5N**

Creating Charts, Diagrams, and Templates

OUTCOMES

At the end of this chapter you will be able to:

PROJECT 6A

Create 3-D column charts, line charts, process diagrams, and organization charts.

PROJECT 6B

Create and use an Excel template and protect worksheets to ensure consistency in formulas and data.

OBJECTIVES

Mastering these objectives will enable you to:

1. Create and Format Sparklines and a 3-D Column Chart (p. 369)
2. Create and Format a Line Chart (p. 378)
3. Create and Modify a SmartArt Graphic (p. 383)
4. Create and Modify an Organization Chart (p. 386)

5. Create an Excel Template (p. 390)
6. Protect a Worksheet (p. 397)
7. Create a Worksheet Based on a Template (p. 400)

ja'arman/Shutterstock

In This Chapter

In this chapter, you will create charts and diagrams to communicate data visually. Charts make a set of numbers easier to understand by displaying numerical data in a graphical format. Excel's SmartArt illustrations make diagrams, like an organizational chart or process cycle, easy to comprehend.

In this chapter, you will also use several predefined templates that can be used for common financial reports such as an expense report, sales invoice, or purchase order. Templates have built-in formulas for performing calculations based on the data that you enter. Templates are commonly used in organizations for standardization and protection of data. You will create and protect a template for an order form.

The **New York-New Jersey Job Fair** is a nonprofit organization that brings together employers and job seekers in the New York and New Jersey metropolitan areas. Each year the organization holds a number of targeted job fairs and the annual New York-New Jersey Job Fair draws over 900 employers in more than 75 industries and registers more than 30,000 candidates. Candidate registration is free; employers pay a nominal fee to display and present at the fairs. Candidate resumes and employer postings are managed by a state-of-the-art database system, allowing participants quick and accurate access to job data and candidate qualifications.

Project 6A Attendance Charts and Diagrams

myitlab
Project 6A Training

Project Activities

In Activities 6.01 through 6.17, you will create and format 3-D column and line charts for the New York-New Jersey Job Fair that display attendance patterns at the fairs over a five-year period. You will also create a process diagram and an organization chart. Your completed worksheets will look similar to Figure 6.1.

Project Files

For Project 6A, you will need the following file:

e06A_Attendance

You will save your workbook as:

Lastname_Firstname_6A_Attendance

Project Results

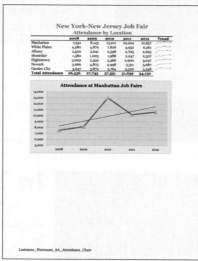

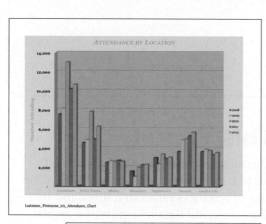

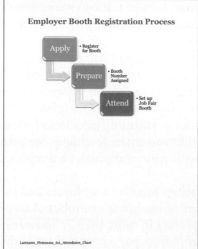

Figure 6.1
Project 6A Attendance Charts and Diagrams

Objective 1 | Create and Format Sparklines and a 3-D Column Chart

Recall that *sparklines* are tiny charts that fit within a cell and give a visual trend summary alongside your data. Recall also that a *column chart*, which presents data graphically in vertical columns, is useful to make comparisons among related data.

Activity 6.01 | Creating and Formatting Sparklines

To create sparklines, first select the data you want to plot—represent graphically—and then select the range of cells alongside each row of data where you want to display the sparklines.

1 **Start** Excel. From your student files, open the file **e06A_Attendance**. Display the **Save As** dialog box, navigate to the location where you will store your workbooks for this chapter, and then create a new folder named **Excel Chapter 6** Open your new folder, and then **Save** the workbook as **Lastname_Firstname_6A_Attendance**

> This data shows the number of applicants who have attended job fairs held over a five-year period at various locations in the greater New York-New Jersey area.

2 Select the range **A4:F10**. On the **Insert tab**, in the **Sparklines group**, click the **Line** button. Compare your screen with Figure 6.2.

> The Create Sparklines dialog box displays with the Data Range indicated as *A4:F10*.

Figure 6.2

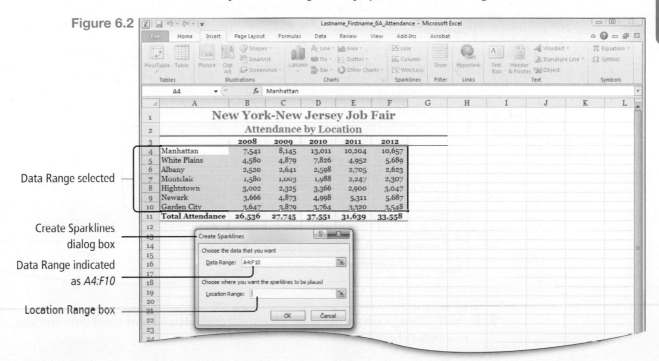

Data Range selected

Create Sparklines dialog box

Data Range indicated as *A4:F10*

Location Range box

Excel | Chapter 6

3 If necessary, drag the Create Sparklines dialog box so you can see column G. With the insertion point blinking in the **Location Range** box, select the range **G4:G10**. Compare your screen with Figure 6.3.

Figure 6.3

Location Range indicates *$G$4:$G$10*

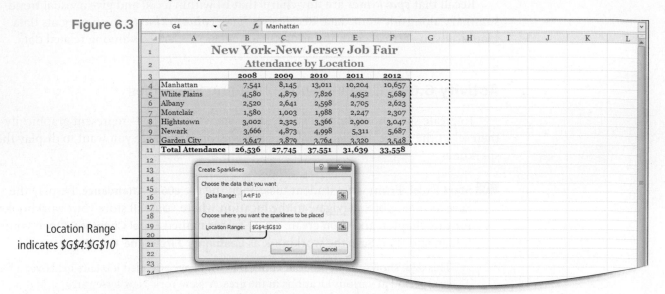

4 Click **OK**, and then compare your screen with Figure 6.4.

Sparklines display alongside each row of data and provide a quick visual trend summary for each city's job fair attendance. The sparklines provide a quick indication that for each location, attendance has had an overall upward trend over the five-year period.

Figure 6.4

Sparkline trends for each city

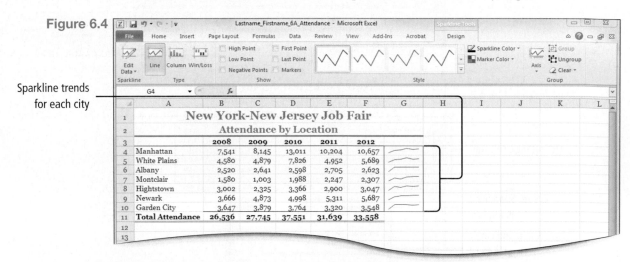

5 On the **Design tab**, in the **Show group**, select the **High Point** check box and the **Last Point** check box.

By adding the High Point and Last Point markers, you further emphasize the visual story that sparklines depict.

6 On the **Design tab**, in the **Style group**, click the **More** ⏷ button, and then in the third row, click the first style—**Sparkline Style Accent 1, (no dark or light)**.

7 In cell **G3**, type **Trend** and press Enter. Press Ctrl + Home, and then compare your screen with Figure 6.5.

Use styles in this manner to further enhance your sparklines.

Figure 6.5

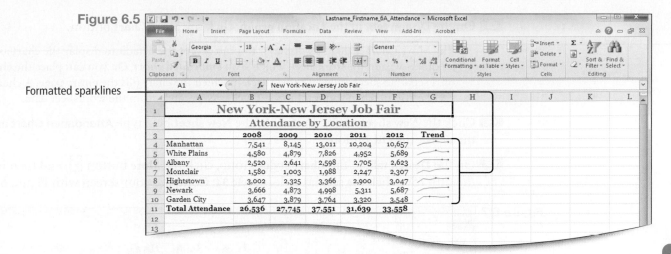

Formatted sparklines

8 Save 💾 your workbook.

Activity 6.02 │ Creating a 3-D Column Chart

A chart is a graphic representation of data. When you create a chart, first decide whether you are going to plot the values representing totals or the values representing details—you cannot plot both in the same chart. In this activity, you will select the details—the number of attendees at each location each year. To help the reader understand the chart, you will also select the *labels* for the data—the column and row headings that describe the values. Here, the labels are the location names and the years.

1 Take a moment to study the data elements shown in Figure 6.6.

Figure 6.6

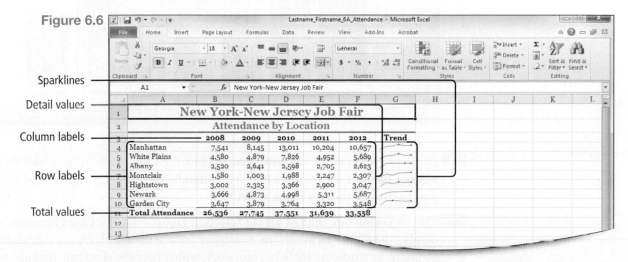

Sparklines

Detail values

Column labels

Row labels

Total values

2 Select the range **A3:F10**. On the **Insert tab**, in the **Charts group**, click the **Column** button. Under **3-D Column**, click the first chart—**3-D Clustered Column**.

The 3-D Clustered Column chart displays on the worksheet.

Excel │ Chapter 6

3 On the **Design tab**, in the **Location group**, click the **Move Chart** button.

The Move Chart dialog box displays. You can accept the default to display the chart as an object within the worksheet, which is an *embedded chart*. Or, you can place the chart on a separate sheet, called a *chart sheet*, in which the chart fills the entire page. A chart sheet is useful when you want to view a chart separately from the worksheet data.

4 Click the **New sheet** option button. In the **New sheet** box, type **Attendance Chart** and then click the **OK** button.

5 On the **Design tab**, in the **Chart Styles** group, click the **More** button ⏷, and then in the fifth row, click the second style—**Style 34**. Compare your screen with Figure 6.7.

Figure 6.7

3-D Clustered Column chart displays in the worksheet

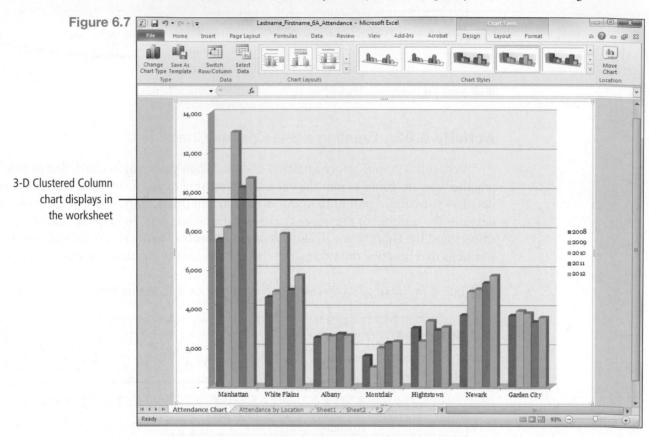

6 On the **Layout tab**, in the **Labels group**, click the **Chart Title** button, and then click **Above Chart**. In the **Formula Bar**, type **Attendance** as the chart title, and then press Enter to display the text in the chart.

7 On the **Layout tab**, in the **Current Selection group**, click the **Chart Elements arrow** to display the Chart Elements list. Compare your screen with Figure 6.8, and then take a moment to study the table in Figure 6.9, which lists the elements that are typically found in a chart.

The Chart Elements list displays. *Chart elements* are the objects that make up a chart. The entire chart and all of its elements comprise the *chart area*. From the Chart Elements list, you can select a chart element to format it.

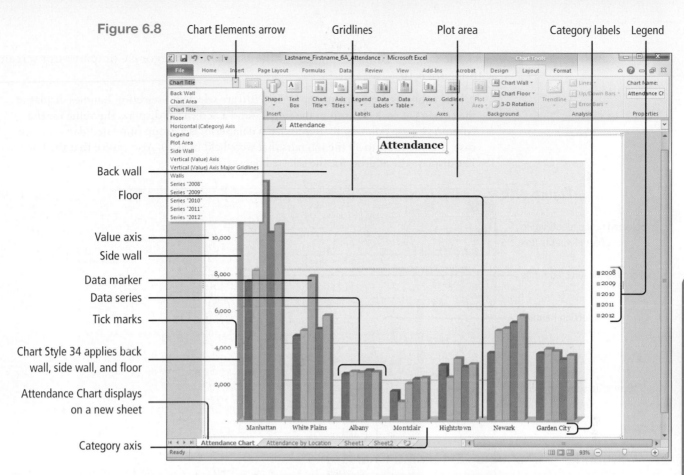

Figure 6.8

Chart Elements arrow · Gridlines · Plot area · Category labels · Legend

Back wall
Floor
Value axis
Side wall
Data marker
Data series
Tick marks
Chart Style 34 applies back wall, side wall, and floor
Attendance Chart displays on a new sheet
Category axis

Excel Chart Elements

Object	Description
Axis	A line that serves as a frame of reference for measurement and that borders the chart plot area.
Category labels	The labels that display along the bottom of the chart to identify the category of data.
Chart Area	The entire chart and all its elements.
Data labels	Labels that display the value, percentage, and/or category of each particular data point and can contain one or more of the choices listed—Series name, Category name, Value, or Percentage.
Data marker	A column, bar, area, dot, pie slice, or other symbol in a chart that represents a single data point.
Data points	The numeric values of the selected worksheet.
Data series	A group of related data points that are plotted in a chart.
Gridlines	Lines in the plot area that aid the eye in determining the plotted values.
Horizontal Category axis (x-axis)	The axis that displays along the bottom of the chart to identify the category of data. Excel uses the row titles as the category names.
Legend	A key that identifies patterns or colors that are assigned to the categories in the chart.
Major unit value	The value that determines the spacing between tick marks and between the gridlines in the plot area.
Plot area	The area bounded by the axes, including all the data series.
Tick mark labels	Identifying information for a tick mark generated from the cells on the worksheet used to create the chart.
Tick marks	The short lines that display on an axis at regular intervals.
Vertical Value axis (y-axis)	The axis that displays along the left side of the chart to identify the numerical scale on which the charted data is based.
Walls and floor	The areas surrounding a 3-D chart that give dimension and boundaries to the chart. Two walls and one floor display within the plot area.

Figure 6.0

8 Click the tallest column displayed for the Manhattan category. Compare your screen with Figure 6.10.

All the columns representing the Series *2010* are selected—selection handles display at the corners of each column in the series—and a ScreenTip displays the value for the column you are pointing to. Recall that a data series is a group of related data—in this case, the attendees to all the job fairs that were held in 2010. Also notice that the Formula Bar displays the address for the selected data series.

Figure 6.10

Selected range identified in Chart Elements Box

Formula for selected range

Selection handles

ScreenTip showing value

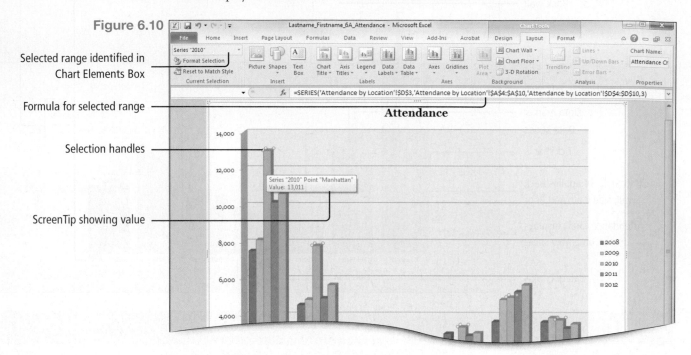

9 Locate the **Montclair** category, and then click the shortest column in that group.

The selected series changes to those columns that represent the attendees at the job fairs in 2009. The Formula Bar and Chart Elements box change and a new ScreenTip displays.

10 Click outside the chart area to deselect the series.

> **More Knowledge | Sizing Handles and Selection Handles**
>
> Sizing handles and selection handles look the same, and the terms are often used interchangeably. If a two-headed resize arrow—$\updownarrow$, $\leftrightarrow$, $\nwarrow$, $\nearrow$—displays when you point to boxes surrounding an object, it is a sizing handle; otherwise, it is a selection handle. Some objects in a chart cannot be resized, such as the category axis or the value axis, but they can be selected and then reformatted.

Activity 6.03 | Changing the Display of Chart Data

As you create a chart, you make choices about the data to include, the chart type, chart titles, and location. You can change the chart type, change the way the data displays, add or change titles, select different colors, and modify the background, scale, or chart location.

In the column chart you created, the attendance numbers are displayed along the value axis—the vertical axis—and the locations for each job fair are displayed along the category axis—the horizontal axis. The cells you select for a chart include the row and column labels from your worksheet. In a column or line chart, Excel selects whichever has *more* items—either the rows or the columns—and uses those labels to plot the data series, in this case, the locations.

After plotting the data series, Excel uses the remaining labels—in this example, the years identified in the row headings—to create the data series labels on the *legend*. The legend is the key that defines the colors used in the chart; here it identifies the data series for the years. A different color is used for each year in the data series. The chart, as currently displayed, compares the change in attendance year to year grouped by category location. You can change the chart to display the years on the category axis and the locations as the data series identified in the legend.

1 In the **Manhattan** category, click the second column.

> All columns with the same color are selected. The ScreenTip displays *Series "2009" Point "Manhattan" Value: 8,145.*

2 Point to each of the other gold columns that are selected and notice that the ScreenTip that displays identifies each gold column as being in the *Series "2009."*

3 On the **Design tab**, in the **Data group,** click the **Switch Row/Column** button, and then compare your screen with Figure 6.11.

> The chart changes to display the locations as the data series. The locations are the row headings in the worksheet and are now identified in the legend. The years display as the category labels.

Figure 6.11

Switch Row/Column button

Legend identifies location

Category (X) axis displays years

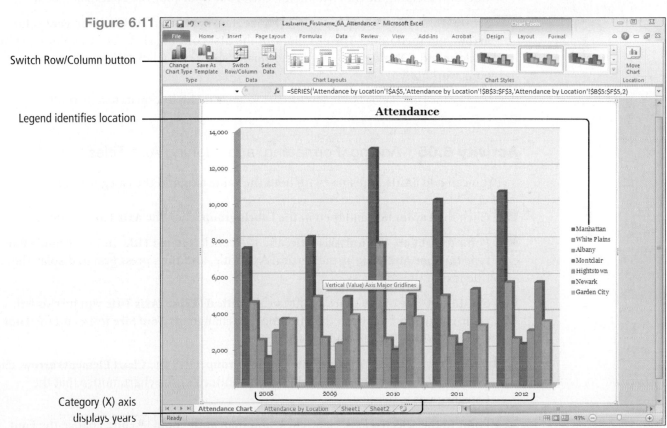

4 If necessary, click one of the gold columns. Point to each gold column and read the ScreenTip.

> The ScreenTips for the gold columns now identify this as the White Plains series.

5 On the **Design tab**, in the **Data group**, click the **Switch Row/Column** button again, and then **Save** 🖫 your workbook.

> The chart changes back to the more useful arrangement with the years identified in the legend and the locations displayed as the category labels.

> **More Knowledge** | Changing the Range of Data in a Chart
>
> After you have created a chart, you can adjust the range of data that is displayed in the chart. To do so, on the Design tab, in the Data group, click the Select Data button. Edit the source address displayed in the Chart data range box, or drag the data in the worksheet to adjust the range as needed.

Activity 6.04 | Editing and Formatting the Chart Title

The data displayed in the chart focuses on the *attendance by location*. It is good practice to create a chart title to reflect your charted data.

1 Click the **Chart Title**—*Attendance*—to select it, and then click to position the mouse pointer to the right of *Attendance*.

> To edit a title, click once to select the chart object, and then click a second time to position the insertion point in the title and change to editing mode.

2 Press [Spacebar] one time, and then type **by Location**

3 Point to the **Chart Title**—*Attendance by Location*—right-click the border of the chart title, and then on the shortcut menu, click **Font** to display the **Font** dialog box.

4 Set the **Font style** to **Bold Italic** and change the **Font Size** to **20**. Click the **Font color arrow**, and then under **Theme Colors**, in the first column, click the last color—**White, Background 1, Darker 50%**. Apply the **Small Caps** effect. Click **OK**, and then **Save** 🖫 your workbook.

> Use the Font dialog box in this manner to apply multiple formats to a chart title.

Activity 6.05 | Adding, Formatting, and Aligning Axis Titles

You can add a title to display with both the value axis and the category axis.

1 Click the **Layout tab**, and then in the **Labels group**, click the **Axis Titles** button.

2 Point to **Primary Vertical Axis Title**, and then click **Rotated Title**. In the **Formula Bar**, type **Number Attending** as the Vertical Axis Title, and then press [Enter] to display the title text in the chart.

3 On the left side of the chart, point to the **Vertical (Value) Axis Title** you just added, right-click, and then from the Mini toolbar, change the **Font Size** to **14** and the **Font Color** to **White, Background 1, Darker 50%**.

4 On the **Layout tab**, in the **Current Selection group**, click the **Chart Elements arrow**, click **Horizontal (Category) Axis**, and then at the bottom of the chart, notice that the **Category axis** is selected.

5 Point to the selected axis, right-click, and then apply **Bold** 🅱 and change the **Font Color** to **White, Background 1, Darker 50%**.

6 On the left side of the chart, point to any value in the **Value Axis**, and then right-click to select the **Vertical (Value) Axis**. On the Mini toolbar, change the **Font Size** to **12**.

7 **Save** 🖫 your workbook, and then compare your screen with Figure 6.12.

Figure 6.12

Vertical axis values changed to font size 12

Chart title changed to bold italic font style, 20 pt. font size, White, Background 1, Darker 50%, Small Caps effect

Vertical axis title changed to 14 pt. font size, font color to White, Background 1, Darker 50%

Horizontal axis changed to bold, font color to White, Background 1, Darker 50%

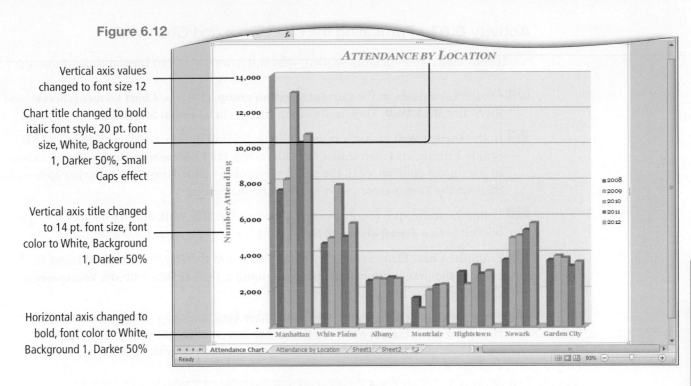

Activity 6.06 | Editing Source Data

One of the characteristics of an Excel chart is that it reflects changes made to the underlying data.

1 In the **White Plains** column cluster, point to the last column—**2012**. Notice that the *Value* for this column is *5,689*.

2 Display the **Attendance by Location** worksheet, and then in cell **F5**, type **6261** and press Enter.

3 Redisplay the **Attendance Chart** worksheet, and then point to the **White Plains** column for 2012. **Save** 💾 your workbook, and then compare your screen with Figure 6.13.

Figure 6.13

ScreenTip reflects the change in data

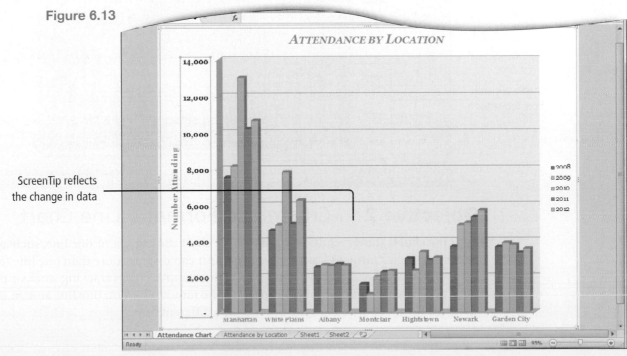

Activity 6.07 | Formatting the Chart Floor and Chart Walls

If your chart style includes shaded walls and a floor, you can format these elements.

1 On the **Layout tab**, in the **Current Selection group**, click the **Chart Elements arrow**, and then click **Back Wall**. Then in the same group, click **Format Selection**.

2 In the **Format Wall** dialog box, on the left, click **Fill**, on the right, click the **Solid fill** option button, and then under **Fill Color**, click the **Color arrow**. Under **Theme Colors**, in the fourth column, click the next to last color—**Blue-Gray, Text 2, Darker 25%**—and then set the **Transparency** to **75%**. **Close** the dialog box.

3 Using the technique you just practiced, select the **Side Wall**, and then apply the same fill, but with a **Transparency** of **60%**. In the lower right corner, click on **Close**.

4 From the **Chart Elements** list, select the **Floor**, and then apply a **Solid fill** using the last color in the first column—**White, Background 1, Darker 50%** with **0% Transparency**. **Close** the dialog box.

5 From the **Chart Elements** list, select the **Chart Area**, and then apply a **Solid fill** using **Green, Accent 5, Lighter 60%**—in the next to last column, the third color. **Close** the dialog box, click **Save**, and then compare your screen with Figure 6.14.

Figure 6.14

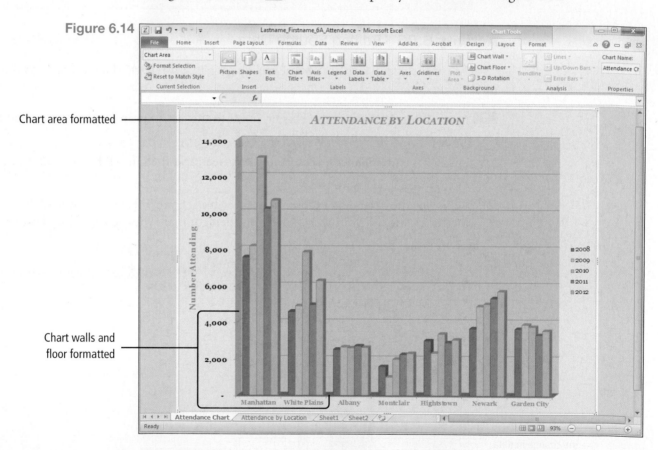

Chart area formatted

Chart walls and floor formatted

Objective 2 | Create and Format a Line Chart

Line charts show trends over time. A line chart can consist of one line, such as the price of a single company's stock over time, or it can display more than one line to show a comparison of related numbers over time. For example, charts tracking stock or mutual fund performance often display the price of the mutual fund on one line and an industry standard for that particular type of fund on a different line.

Activity 6.08 | Creating a Line Chart

In this activity, you will create a line chart showing the change in attendance at the New York-New Jersey Job Fair over a five-year period.

1 Display the **Attendance by Location** worksheet.

2 Select the range **A3:F4**, and then, on the **Insert tab**, in the **Charts group**, click the **Line** button. In the second row, click the first chart type—**Line with Markers**. Compare your screen with Figure 6.15.

Cell A3 must be included in the selection, despite being empty, because the same number of cells must be in each selected row. Excel identifies the first row as a category because of the empty first cell.

Figure 6.15

Line chart embedded in the worksheet

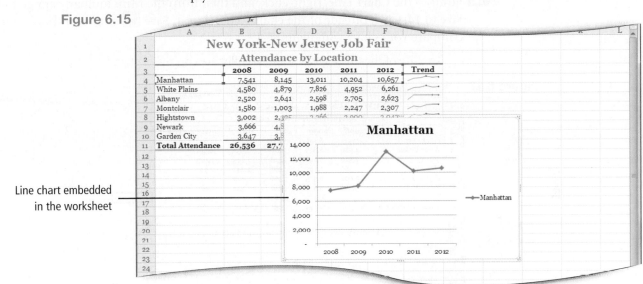

3 Point to the chart border to display the pointer, and then drag the upper left corner of the chart inside the upper left corner of cell **A13**.

4 Scroll down as necessary to view **row 30**. Point to the lower right corner of the chart to display the pointer, and then drag the lower right corner of the chart inside the lower right corner of cell **G29**. **Save** your workbook. Compare your screen with Figure 6.16.

When you use the corner sizing handles to resize an object, the proportional dimensions—the relative height and width—are retained.

Figure 6.16

Chart repositioned

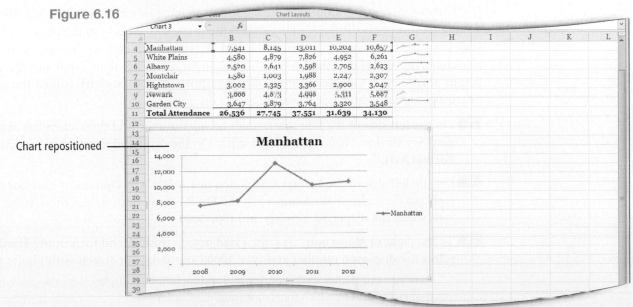

Excel | Chapter 6

Activity 6.09 | Deleting a Legend and Changing a Chart Title

When you select the chart type, the resulting chart might contain elements that you want to delete or change. In the line chart, the title is *Manhattan*, and there is a legend that also indicates *Manhattan*. Because there is only one line of data, a legend is unnecessary, and the chart title can be more specific.

1 In the embedded chart, click the **Legend**—*Manhattan*—to select it. Press Del.

> The legend is removed from the chart, and the chart plot area expands.

2 Click the **Chart Title**—*Manhattan*. In the **Formula Bar**, type **Attendance at Manhattan Job Fairs** as the chart title, and then press Enter to display the title text in the chart.

3 Point to the **Chart Title**, right-click, and then from the Mini toolbar, change the **Font Size** to **14**. Click outside of the chart to deselect it, **Save** 🔲 your workbook, and then compare your chart with Figure 6.17.

> The size of the title increases, and the plot area decreases slightly.

Figure 6.17

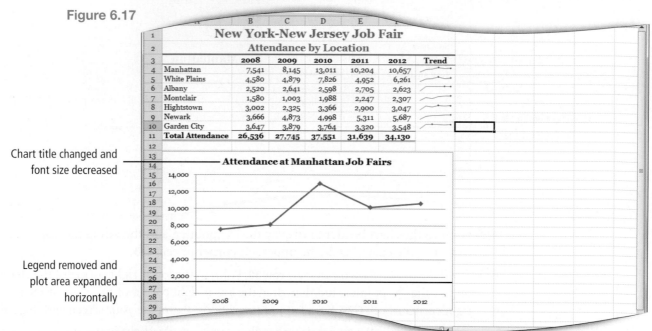

Chart title changed and font size decreased

Legend removed and plot area expanded horizontally

Activity 6.10 | Changing the Values on the Value Axis

You can change the values on the value axis to increase or decrease the variation among the numbers displayed. The *scale* is the range of numbers in the data series; the scale controls the minimum, maximum, and incremental values on the value axis. In the line chart, the attendance figures for Manhattan are all higher than 7,000, but the scale begins at zero, thus the line occupies only the upper area of the chart. Adjust the scale as necessary to make your charts meaningful to the reader.

1 On the left side of the line chart, point to any number, and then when the ScreenTip displays *Vertical (Value) Axis*, right-click. On the displayed shortcut menu, click **Format Axis**.

2 On the left side of the **Format Axis** dialog box, select **Axis Options**, if necessary. On the right, to the right of **Minimum**, click the **Fixed** option button, and then in the **Fixed** box, select the displayed number and type **5000**

3 To the right of **Major unit**, click the **Fixed** option button, and then in the **Fixed** box, select the displayed number and type **1000** Compare your screen with Figure 6.18.

> Here you can change the beginning and ending numbers displayed on the chart and also change the unit by which the major gridlines display.

Figure 6.18

Minimum changed to 5000

Major unit changed to 1000

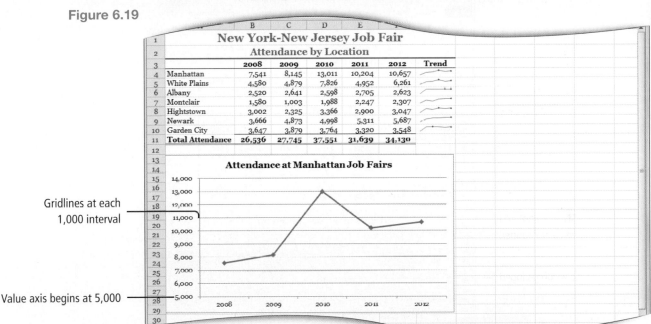

4 In the lower right corner, click **Close**. Click **Save** 🖫. Compare your screen with Figure 6.19.

> The Value Axis begins at 5000 with major gridlines at intervals of 1000. This will emphasize the change in attendance over the five years by starting the chart at a higher number and decreasing the interval for gridlines.

Figure 6.19

Gridlines at each 1,000 interval

Value axis begins at 5,000

Activity 6.11 | Formatting the Plot Area and the Data Series

1 Right-click anywhere within the gray lined **Plot Area**, and then from the displayed shortcut menu, click **Format Plot Area**.

> The Format Plot Area dialog box displays. Here you can change the border of the plot area or the background color.

2 On the left, select **Fill**, if necessary. On the right, click the **Solid fill** option button. Under **Fill Color**, click the **Color arrow**, and then under **Theme Colors**, in the first column, click the fourth color—**White, Background 1, Darker 25%**. **Close** the dialog box.

3 Point to the orange chart line, right-click, and then click **Format Data Series**.

> In the Format Data Series dialog box, you can change the *data markers*—the indicators for a data point value, which on the line chart is represented by a diamond shape. Here you can also change the line connecting the data markers.

4 On the left, click **Line Style**. On the right, use the spin box arrows to set the **Width** to **4 pt**.

5 On the left, click **Marker Options**. On the right, under **Marker Type**, click the **Built-in** option button, click the **Type arrow**, and then, from the displayed list, click the **triangle**—the third symbol in the list. Set the **Size** of the **Marker Type** to **12**.

6 On the left, click **Marker Fill**, click the **Solid fill** option button, and then click the **Color arrow**. Under **Theme Colors**, in the first column, click the last color—**White, Background 1, Darker 50%**.

7 On the left, click **Marker Line Color**, click the **No line** option button, and then click **Close**.

8 On the **Layout tab**, in the **Current Selection** group, click the **Chart Elements arrow**, and then click **Chart Area**. In the same group, click **Format Selection** to display the **Format Chart Area** dialog box, and then apply a **Solid fill** using **White, Background 1, Darker 15%**—in the first column, the third color. Click **Close**.

9 Click in any cell outside of the chart, Save 🔲 your workbook, and then compare your screen with Figure 6.20.

> The dialog box closes, and the data line and series markers change.

Figure 6.20

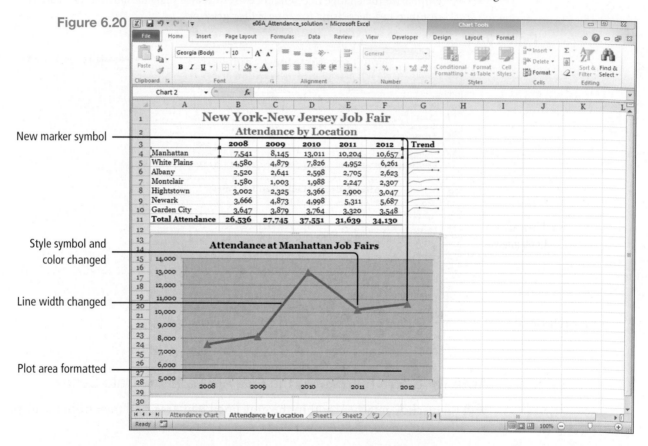

New marker symbol

Style symbol and color changed

Line width changed

Plot area formatted

Activity 6.12 | Inserting a Trendline

A *trendline* is a graphic representation of trends in a data series, such as a line sloping upward to represent increased sales over a period of months. A trendline is always associated with a data series, but it does not represent the data of that data series. Rather, a trendline depicts trends in the existing data.

1 Click slightly inside the chart border to select the entire chart. On the **Layout tab**, in the **Analysis group**, click the **Trendline** button, and then click **Linear Trendline**. **Save** 💾 your workbook, and then compare your screen with Figure 6.21.

A linear trendline displays in the chart. The chart shows a significant increase in attendance for 2010, a drop in attendance in 2011, but the trendline indicates an overall increasing trend in attendance over the past five years.

Figure 6.21

Linear trendline added

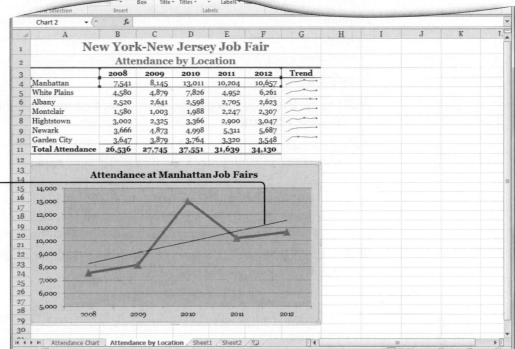

Objective 3 | Create and Modify a SmartArt Graphic

A *SmartArt graphic* is a visual representation of your information and ideas. You can create SmartArt graphics by choosing from among many different layouts to communicate complex messages and relationships easily and effectively.

Unlike charts, a SmartArt graphic does not depend on any underlying data in a worksheet; rather, it is a graphical tool that depicts ideas or associations. In the following activities, you will create a process diagram to illustrate how to register for an employer booth at the job fair.

Activity 6.13 | Creating a Process SmartArt Graphic

In this activity, you will use a Process SmartArt graphic, which shows steps in a process or timeline.

1 Click the **Sheet1 tab**, and rename the sheet tab **Process Chart** Click cell **A1** and type **Employer Booth Registration Process** and then press Enter.

2 Merge and center the text you just typed across **A1:H1**, apply the **Title** cell style, and change the **Font Size** to **24**.

3 On the **Insert tab**, in the **Illustrations group**, click the **SmartArt** button.

4 On the left, notice the types of SmartArt graphics that are available, and then take a moment to examine the table in Figure 6.22.

SmartArt

Use this SmartArt type:	To do this:
List	Show nonsequential information
Process	Show steps in a process or timeline
Cycle	Show a continual process
Hierarchy	Create an organization chart or show a decision tree
Relationship	Illustrate connections
Matrix	Show how parts relate to a whole
Pyramid	Use a series of pictures to show relationships
Picture	Use pictures in a diagram

Figure 6.22

5 On the left, click **Process**, and then in the first row, click the third option—**Step Down Process**. Click **OK**.

6 If necessary, in the Create Graphic group, click the Text Pane button. With your insertion point blinking in the first bullet, type **Apply**

> The text *Apply* displays in the ***Text Pane*** and in the first box in the diagram. Use the Text Pane, which displays to the left of the graphic, to build your graphic by entering and editing your text. The Text Pane is populated with placeholder text that you replace with your information. If you prefer, close the Text Pane and type directly into the graphic.

7 In the **Text Pane**, click the next bullet, which is indented, and then type **Register for Booth** Compare your screen with Figure 6.23.

Figure 6.23

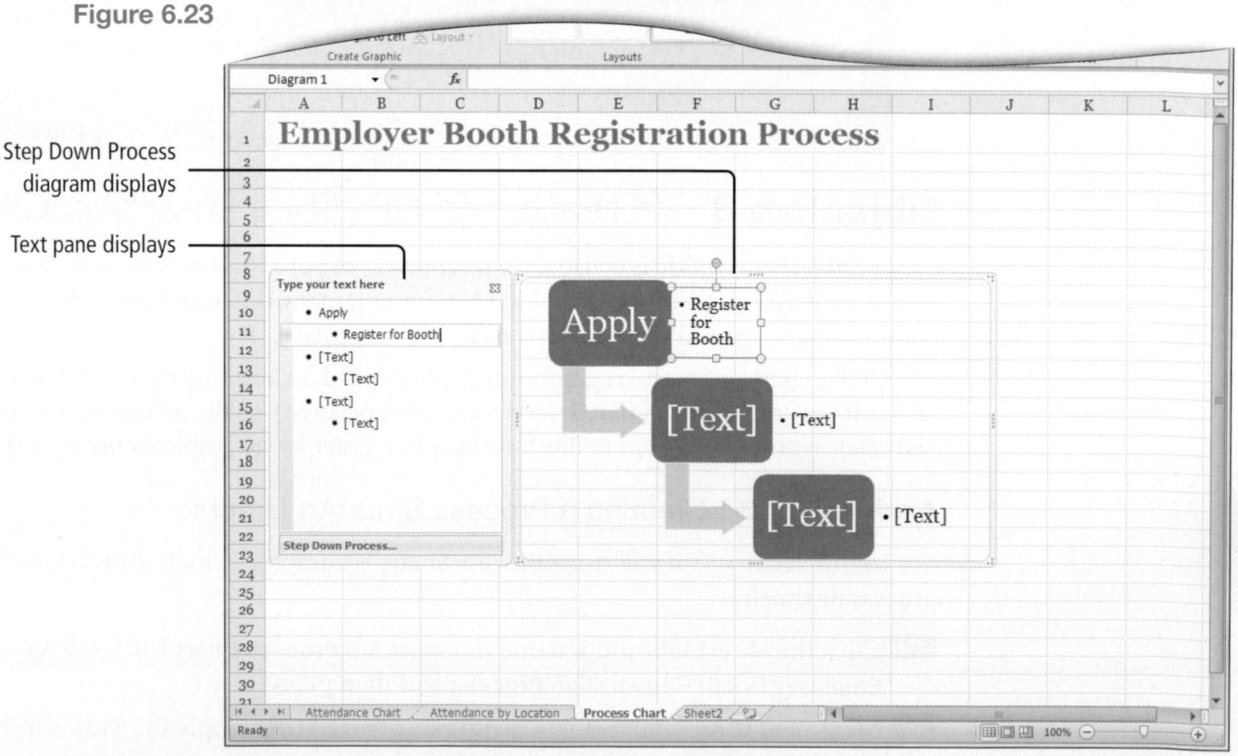

Step Down Process diagram displays

Text pane displays

8 In the **Text Pane**, click the next bullet, and then type **Prepare** Under *Prepare* click the indented bullet and type **Booth Number Assigned**

9 Click the next bullet and type **Attend** Click the next bullet, and then type **Set up Job Fair Booth** Compare your diagram with Figure 6.24.

> The Text Pane entries display on the left in the Text Pane, and the process diagram with entries displays on the right in the process diagram.

Figure 6.24

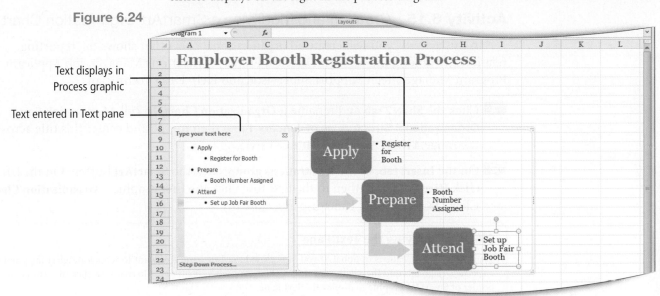

Text displays in Process graphic

Text entered in Text pane

10 **Close** ☒ the **Text Pane**, and then **Save** 💾 your workbook.

Activity 6.14 | Modifying the Diagram Style

Excel offers preformatted SmartArt styles that can be applied to a diagram.

1 With the SmartArt still selected, in the **SmartArt Styles group**, click the **More** ⊽ button. Under **3-D**, click the first style—**Polished**.

2 In the **SmartArt Styles group**, click the **Change Colors** button, and then under **Colorful**, click the third option—**Colorful Range – Accent Colors 3 to 4**.

3 By using the pointer, drag the upper left corner of the graphic border inside the upper left corner of cell **A4**. Point to the lower right corner of the graphic's border to display the pointer, and then drag to position the lower right corner inside the lower right corner of cell **H22**. **Save** 💾 your workbook, and then compare your screen with Figure 6.25.

Figure 6.25

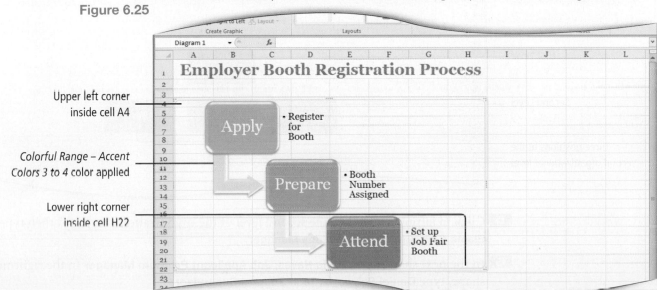

Upper left corner inside cell A4

Colorful Range – Accent Colors 3 to 4 color applied

Lower right corner inside cell H22

Objective 4 | Create and Modify an Organization Chart

An *organization chart* depicts reporting relationships within an organization.

Activity 6.15 | Creating and Modifying a SmartArt Organization Chart

In this activity, you will create an organizational chart that shows the reporting relationship among the Job Fair Director, Employer Relations Manager, Job Applicant Program Manager, Tech Support Supervisor, and Help Desk Technician.

1 Click the **Sheet2 tab** and rename it **Organization Chart**. In cell **A1**, type **Job Fair Organizational Structure as of January 1** and then merge and center this title across the range **A1:H1**. Apply the **Title** cell style.

2 On the **Insert tab**, in the **Illustrations group**, click the **SmartArt** button. On the left, click **Hierarchy**, and then in the first row, click the first graphic—**Organization Chart**. Click **OK**. If the Text Pane displays, close it.

> **Note** | Displaying the Text Pane
>
> Typing in the Text Pane is optional. If you have closed the Text Pane and want to reopen it, select the graphic, click the Design tab, and then in the Create Graphic group, click Text Pane. Alternatively, click the arrows on left border of SmartArt graphic to display the Text Pane.

3 In the graphic, click in the first [**Text**] box, and then type **Jennifer Patterson, Job Fair Director**

4 In the box below the *Job Fair Director*, click on the *edge* of the box to display a solid line border—if a dashed border displays, click the edge of the box again. With the box bordered with a solid line, press Del. Compare your screen with Figure 6.26.

Three shapes comprise the second level of the organization chart.

Figure 6.26

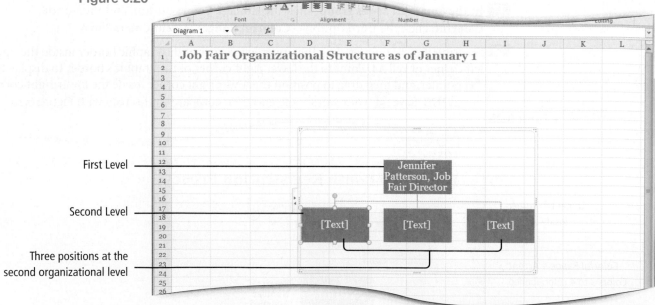

5 Click in leftmost shape on the second level of the organization chart, and then type **Elaine Chin, Employer Relations Manager**

6 In the next shape, type **Maria Naves, Job Applicant Program Manager** In the rightmost shape, type **Daniel Schwartz, Tech Support Supervisor**

Another Way

Alternatively, right-click the shape, click Add Shape, and then click Add Shape Below.

7 If necessary, click in the *Daniel Schwartz* shape. On the **Design tab**, in the **Create Graphic group**, click the **Add Shape arrow**, and then click **Add Shape Below**.

A new shape displays below the Tech Support Supervisor shape.

8 Type **Sergey Penvy, Help Desk Technician**

9 In the **SmartArt Styles group**, click the **More** button ⏷ , and then under **3-D**, click the first style—**Polished**. Click the **Change Colors** button, and then under **Colorful**, click the fifth color arrangement—**Colorful Range – Accent Colors 5 to 6**. Click **Save** 🔲 and then compare your screen with Figure 6.27.

Figure 6.27

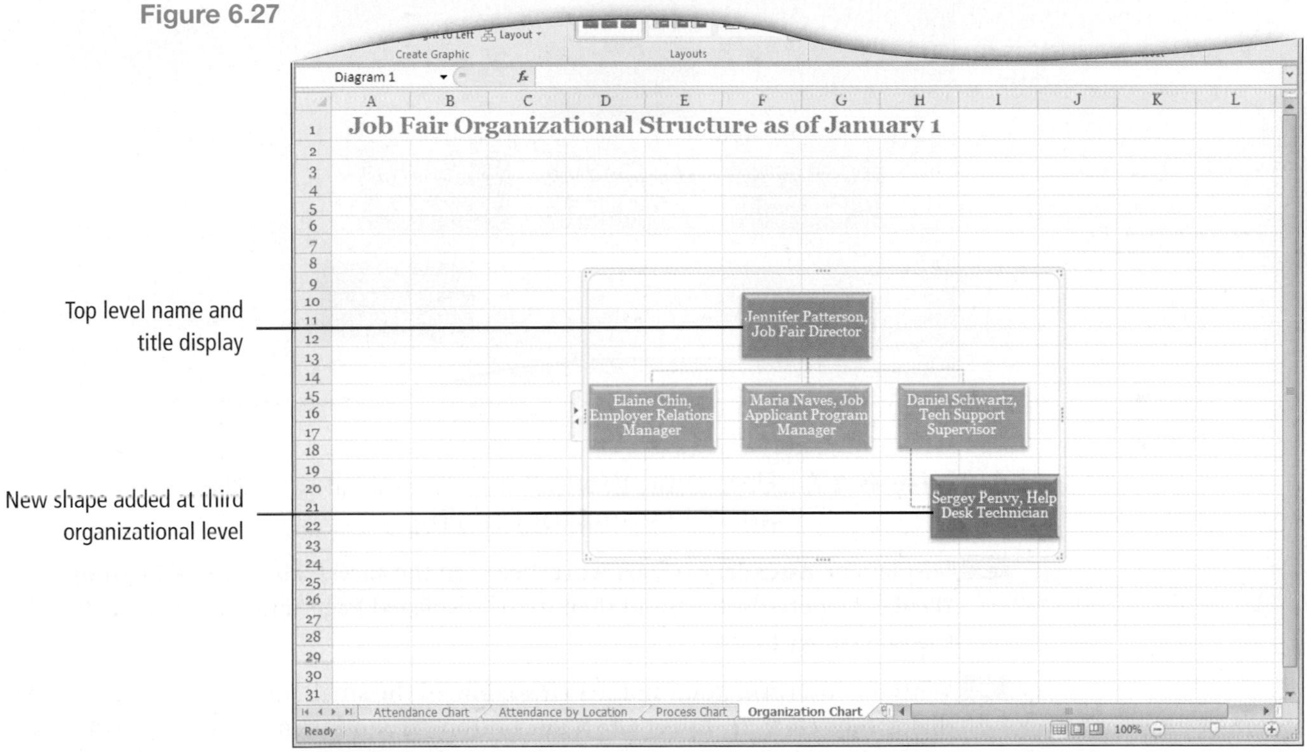

Top level name and title display

New shape added at third organizational level

Activity 6.16 | Adding Effects to a SmartArt Graphic

In this activity, you will change the formatting and layout of the graphic.

1 Click in the *Sergey Penvy* shape.

2 On the **Format tab**, in the **Shape Styles group**, click **Shape Fill**, and then under **Theme Colors**, in the next to last column, click the fifth color—**Green, Accent 5, Darker 25%**.

3 Click the edge of the *Sergey Penvy* shape so that it is surrounded by a solid line and sizing handles and the polished shape displays. Then, hold down Ctrl, and click each of the other shapes until all five are selected.

4 With all five shapes selected, in the **Shape Styles group**, click the **Shape Effects** button, point to **Bevel**, and then under **Bevel**, in the third row, click the second bevel shape—**Riblet**.

5 By using the 🖱 pointer, drag the upper left corner of the graphic inside the upper left corner of cell **A4**. By using the 🖱 pointer, drag the lower right corner of the chart inside the lower right corner of cell **H20**.

6 In the second level, in the shape for *Maria Naves*, click to position the insertion point after the comma, hold down Shift, and then press Enter to insert a line break. Press Del to delete the extra space.

7 Click cell **A1**, and then **Save** 💾 your workbook. Compare your screen with Figure 6.28.

Figure 6.28

Completed organization chart

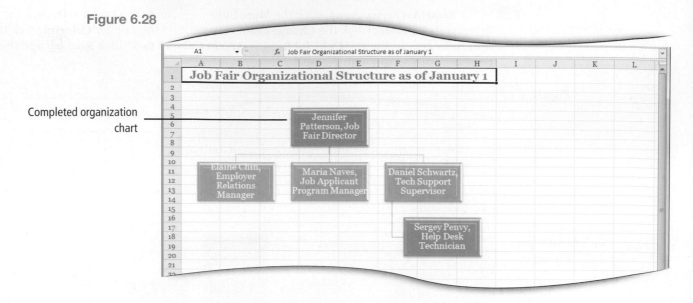

Activity 6.17 | Preparing Worksheets Containing Charts and Diagrams for Printing

1 Display the **Attendance Chart** worksheet. On the **Insert tab**, in the **Text group**, click the **Header & Footer** button, and then in the displayed **Page Setup** dialog box, click the **Custom Footer** button.

2 With the insertion point in the **Left section**, in the small toolbar in the center of the dialog box, click the **Insert File Name** button 📄, and then click **OK** two times.

3 Click the **Attendance by Location sheet tab**, hold down Ctrl, and then click the **Process Chart sheet tab** and the **Organization Chart sheet tab** to select the remaining three worksheets and group them.

4 With the three sheets grouped, insert a footer in the **left section** that includes the file name. Click outside the footer area, and then on the **Page Layout tab**, click the **Margins** button, click **Custom Margins**, and then center the sheets horizontally. Press Ctrl + Home and return to **Normal** ▦ view.

5 Right-click any of the four sheet tabs, and then click **Select All Sheets**. From **Backstage** view, display the **Document Panel**. In the **Author** box, delete any text, and then type your firstname and lastname. In the **Subject** box, type your course name and section number, and in the **Keywords** box, type **attendance statistics, organization charts** **Close** ✕ the **Document Panel**.

6 Press Ctrl + F2, examine the **Print Preview**, make any necessary adjustments, and then **Save** 💾 your workbook.

7 Print or submit your workbook electronically as directed by your instructor. **Close** Excel.

End **You have completed Project 6A**

Project 6B Order Form Template

Project 6B Training

Project Activities

In Activities 6.18 through 6.25, you will create, format, and edit a booth registration order form template for use by Job Fair staff to ensure that totals for items ordered are calculated accurately. You will also protect the template. Your completed worksheets will look similar to Figure 6.29.

Project Files

For Project 6B, you will need the following files:

New blank Excel workbook
c06B_Logo

You will save your workbooks as:

Lastname_Firstname_6B_Booth_Order
Lastname_Firstname_6B_Order_Template
Lastname_Firstname_6B_Topaz_Order

Project Results

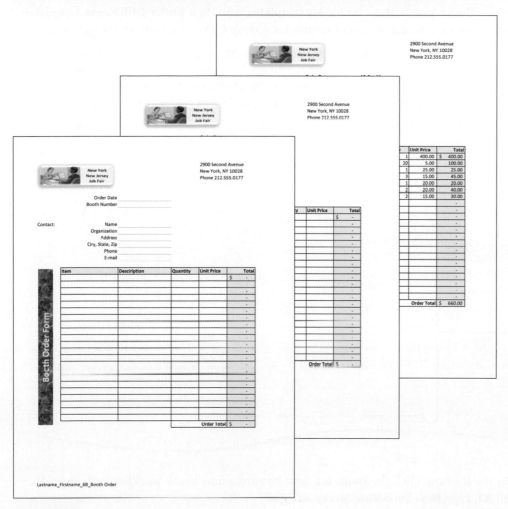

Figure 6.29
Project 6B Order Form Template

Objective 5 | Create an Excel Template

A *template* is a workbook that you create and use as the basis for other similar workbooks. Excel also has predesigned templates that include, among others, financial forms to record expenses, time worked, balance sheet items, and other common financial reports.

Standardization and *protection* are the two main reasons for creating templates for commonly used forms in an organization. Standardization means that all forms created within the organization will have a uniform appearance; the data will always be organized in the same manner. Protection means that individuals entering data cannot change areas of the worksheet that are protected, and thus, cannot alter important formulas and formats built in to the template.

Activity 6.18 | Entering Template Text

To create a template, start with a blank worksheet; enter the text, formatting, and formulas needed for the specific worksheet purpose, and then save the file as a template. Saving a workbook as a template adds the extension *.xltx* to the file name. In this activity, you will start a workbook for the purpose of creating a purchase order template.

1 **Start** Excel and display a new blank workbook. Click the **File tab**, and then in **Backstage** view, click the **New tab**.

2 Under **Home**, notice the icon for **My templates**, and then under **Office.com Templates**, notice the various categories of templates. Compare your screen with Figure 6.30.

When you create and save a template on your own computer by using the default save location, your template will be available to you for future use from *My templates*. From *Office.com Templates*, you can find and download many different predesigned templates from Microsoft's Office.com site. Microsoft updates this list frequently.

Figure 6.30
Available Office templates
Office.com templates (yours may vary)

3 On the Ribbon, click the **Home tab**, and be sure a new blank workbook displays. In cell **A1**, type **New York-New Jersey Job Fair**

4 Click in cell **E1**, type **2900 Second Avenue** and then press Enter. In cell **E2**, type **New York, NY 10028** and press Enter. In cell **E3** type **Phone 212.555.0177** and press Enter. Click cell **B6**, type **Order Date** and press Enter. In cell **B7**, type **Booth Number** press Enter.

5 Click cell **B10**. Type **Name** and press Enter. In cell **B11**, type **Organization** and press Enter. In cell **B12**, type **Address** and press Enter. In cell **B13**, type **City, State, Zip** and press Enter. In cell **B14**, type **Phone** and press Enter. In cell **B15**, type **E-mail** and press Enter. Click cell **A10**. Type **Contact:** and press Enter. Press Ctrl + Home.

These labels will comprise the form headings.

6 Click cell **B17**. Type **Item** and press Tab to move to cell **C17**. Continuing across **row 17**, in cell **C17**, type **Description** and press Tab, in cell **D17**, type **Quantity** and press Tab, in cell **E17**, type **Unit Price** and press Tab, and in cell **F17**, type **Total** and press Enter. Select the range **B17:F17**, and then in the **Font** group, click the **Bold** button **B**. Compare your screen with Figure 6.31, and then make any necessary corrections.

The column headings are added to the order form.

Figure 6.31

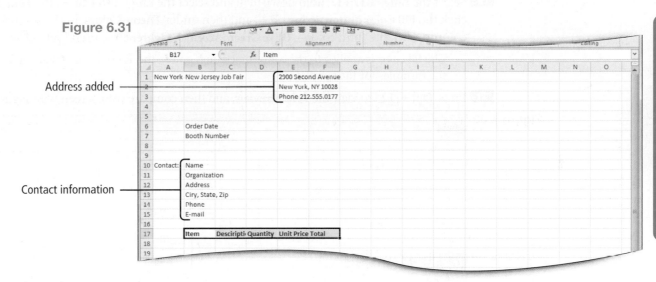

Address added

Contact information

7 Save the file in your **Excel Chapter 6** folder as **Lastname_Firstname_6B_Booth_Order**

Until the format and design of the order form is complete, you will save your work as a normal workbook.

Activity 6.19 | Formatting a Template

One of the goals in designing a template is to make it easy for others to complete. It should be obvious to the person completing the form what information is necessary and where to place the information.

1 Widen **column B** to **155 pixels**. Widen **column C** to **145 pixels**. Select **columns D:F** and widen to **75 pixels**.

2 Select the range **B6:B15**, hold down Ctrl and select the range **C10:C15**, and then on the **Home tab**, in the **Alignment group**, click the **Align Text Right** button.

3 Click cell **F17**, and then in the **Alignment group**, click the **Align Text Right** button.

4 Select the range **C6:C7**. In the **Alignment group**, click the **Dialog Box Launcher** button. In the **Format Cells** dialog box, click the **Border tab**. Under **Line**, in the **Style** list, click the first line in the first column—**the dotted line**.

5 Click the **Color arrow**, and then under **Theme Colors**, in the third column, click the fourth color—**Tan, Background 2, Darker 50%**. Under **Border**, click the **Middle Border** button, and the **Bottom Border** button. Click **OK**.

6 With the range **C6:C7** still selected, in the **Alignment group**, click the **Align Text Right** button 🔳. Then, with the range still selected, right-click, and on the Mini toolbar, click **Format Painter**, and then select the range **C10:C15** to copy the format.

> Inserting borders on cells in a template creates lines as a place to record information when the form is filled out. This provides a good visual cue to the person filling out the form as to where information should be placed.

7 Select the range **B17:F40**. Right-click the selected area and click **Format Cells**. From the displayed **Format Cells** dialog box, if necessary, click the **Border tab.** Under **Presets**, click the **Outline** button 🔲 and the **Inside** button 🔲, and then click **OK**.

> This action applies a grid of columns and rows, which is helpful to those individuals completing the form.

8 Select the range **B17:F17**, hold down ⌃Ctrl and select the range **F18:F40**. In the **Font group,** click the **Fill Color button arrow** 🎨▾, and then under **Theme Colors**, in the seventh column, click the third color—**Olive Green, Accent 3, Lighter 60%**. Press ⌃Ctrl + Home.

> The fill color is applied to the column headings and to the Total column that will contain the formulas for the template.

9 Press ⌃Ctrl + F2 to view the **Print Preview**, and then compare your screen with Figure 6.32.

Figure 6.32

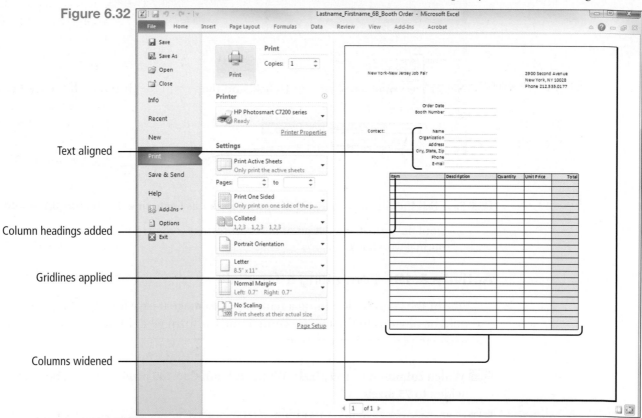

10 At the top of the navigation bar, click **Save** 💾 to save and return to your workbook.

> A dotted line on the worksheet indicates where the first page would end if the worksheet were printed as it is currently set up. As you develop your template, use the Print Preview to check your progress.

Activity 6.20 | Entering Template Formulas

After the text is entered and formatted in your template, add formulas to the cells where you want the result of the calculations to display. In this activity, you will create a formula in the Total column to determine the dollar value for the quantity of each item ordered, and then create another formula to sum the Total column.

1 In cell **F18**, type **=d18*e18** and press Enter.

> A value of 0 displays in cell F18. However, when the person entering information into the worksheet types the Quantity in cell D18 and the Unit Price in cell E18, the formula will multiply the two values to calculate a total for the item.

2 Use the fill handle to copy the formula in cell **F18** down through cell **F39**.

3 Click cell **F40**. On the **Home tab**, in the **Editing group**, click the **AutoSum** button Σ. Be sure the range displays as *F18:F39*, and then press Enter.

4 Select the range **E18:E39**. On the **Home tab**, in the **Number group**, click the **Comma Style** button ,.

> The Comma Style is applied; thus, when values are typed into the form, they will display with two decimals and commas in the appropriate locations.

5 Click cell **F18**, hold down Ctrl, and then click cell **F40**. In the **Number group**, click the **Accounting Number Format** button $ ▾. Select the range **F19:F39**, and then click the **Comma Style** button ,.

> Formats are applied to the Total column, and the zero in each cell displays as a hyphen.

6 Select the range **D40:E40**. In the **Alignment group**, click the **Merge and Center** button. Type **Order Total** and press Enter. Click cell **D40** again, and then in the **Alignment group**, click the **Align Text Right** button ▤. In the **Font** group, click the **Bold** button **B**.

> A label is added and formatted to identify the total for the entire order.

7 Select the range **B40:C40**, right-click, and then from the displayed list, click **Format Cells**. In the **Format Cells** dialog box, if necessary, click the **Border tab**, and then in the **Border preview** area, click the **Left Border** button ▥, the **Middle Border** button ▦ and the **Bottom Border** button ▧ to *remove* these borders from the preview—be sure the right and top lines remain in the preview area. Compare your dialog box with Figure 6.33.

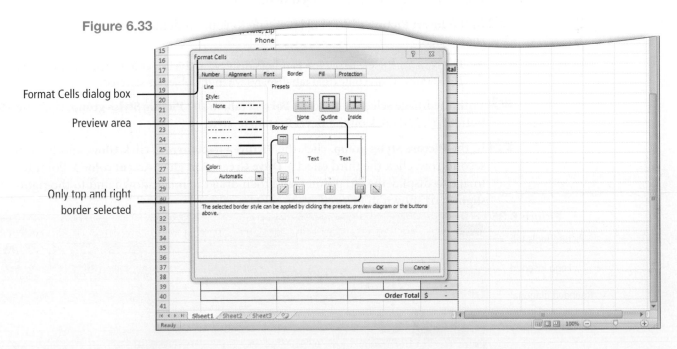

Figure 6.33

Format Cells dialog box

Preview area

Only top and right border selected

8 Click **OK**. Press Ctrl + F2 to view the **Print Preview**. Compare your screen with Figure 6.34.

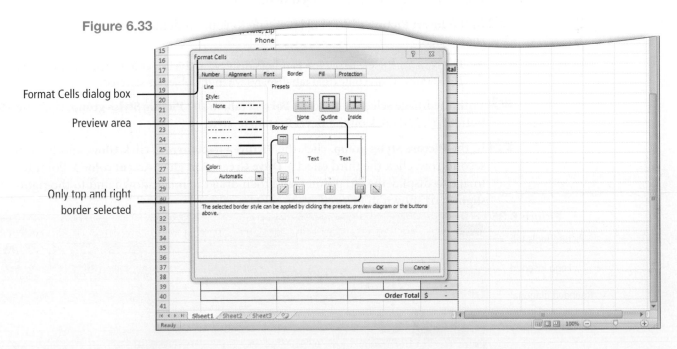

Excel | Chapter 6

Figure 6.34

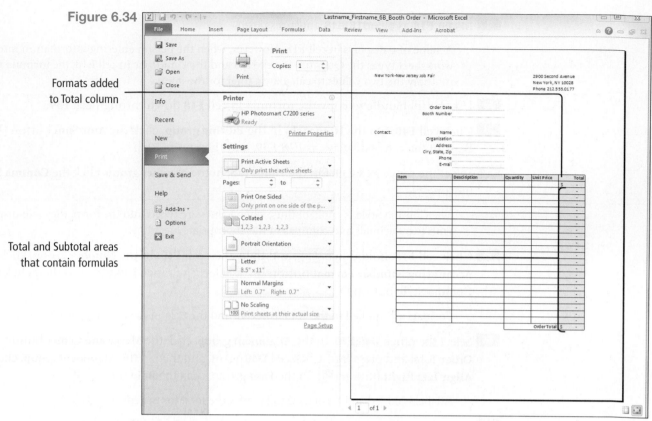

Formats added to Total column

Total and Subtotal areas that contain formulas

9 In the **Backstage** view, click **Save** to save and return to your workbook.

Activity 6.21 | Inserting and Modifying an Image

In the following activity, you will add a logo image to the form.

1 Click cell **A1** and press [Del] to remove the company name. On the **Insert tab**, in the **Illustrations group**, click the **Picture** button.

2 In the **Insert Picture** dialog box, navigate to your student files, and then insert the file **e06B_Logo**.

The New York-New Jersey Job Fair logo displays in the upper left corner of the worksheet. The Picture Tools contextual tab displays when the object is selected.

3 With the image selected, click the **Format tab**, in the **Picture Styles group**, click the **More** button, and click on the **Bevel Rectangle style**.

4 In the **Picture Styles group**, click the **Picture Effects arrow**, click **Glow**, and then in second row, click the third effect—**Olive Green**, **8 pt glow**, **Accent color 3**. Point to the image to display the pointer, and then drag the image down and to the right slightly, as shown in Figure 6.35.

Figure 6.35

Picture Tools tab

Logo inserted

Rounded diagonal corners and green glow effect display

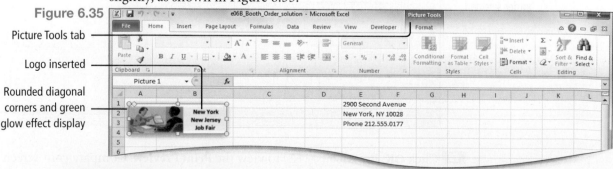

5 **Save** your workbook.

Activity 6.22 | Inserting and Modifying a WordArt Image

WordArt is a feature with which you can insert decorative text in your document, for example to create a stylized image for a heading or logo. Because WordArt is a graphical object, it can be moved and resized. In addition, you can change its shape and color. In this activity, you will create and modify a vertical WordArt heading and place it at the left side of the order form grid.

1 Scroll so that **row 16** is at the top of the Excel window. Then, click cell **A17**. On the **Insert tab**, in the **Text group**, click the **WordArt** button, and then in the fifth row, click the fourth WordArt—**Fill – Olive Green, Accent 3, Powder Bevel**. Type **Booth Order Form** and then compare your screen with Figure 6.36.

Figure 6.36

Row 16 at the top of the window

Rotation handle

Sizing handles

2 Select the text you just typed, right-click, and then from the Mini toolbar, set the **Font Size arrow** to **20**.

The WordArt image floats on your screen. Sizing handles display around the outside of the WordArt, and a green *rotation handle* displays on the top side of the image. Use the rotation handle to rotate an image to any angle.

3 Point to the green **rotation handle** until the 🔄 pointer displays, drag to the left until the WordArt is vertical, as shown in Figure 6.37, and then release the mouse button.

As you rotate the image, lines display to show the position where the image will be placed when you release the mouse button. You can use the rotation handle to revolve the image 360 degrees.

Figure 6.37

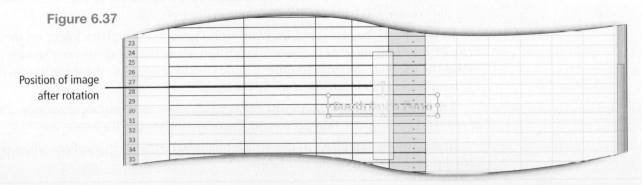

Position of image after rotation

4 Point to the edge of the **WordArt** image to display the ⊕ pointer. Drag the WordArt image to **column A** and align the top of the image with the top of cell **A17**—centered in the column.

5 At the lower edge of the WordArt image, point to the center resize handle and drag down so the end of the image aligns at the lower edge of cell **A39**.

6 With the WordArt still selected, on the **Format tab**, in the **Shape Styles group**, click the **Shape Fill arrow**, click **Texture**, and then in the third row, click the first texture— **Green Marble**. Compare your screen with Figure 6.38.

The WordArt text box fills with Green Marble texture and color.

Figure 6.38

WordArt image moved and aligned in cell A17

Fill changed to Green marble texture and color

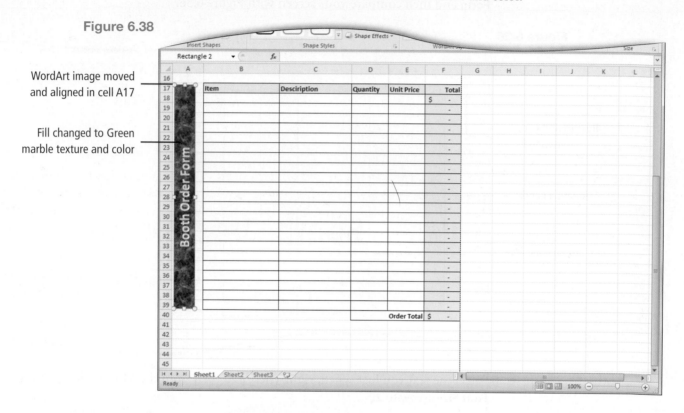

7 Delete any unused sheets. Press Ctrl + Home. Insert a footer in the **left section** that includes the file name. Click any cell outside the footer to deselect. On the status bar, click the **Normal** button ⊞. Press Ctrl + Home to move to the top of the worksheet. Click in any empty cell. **Save** 🖫 your workbook.

Activity 6.23 | Saving a File as a Template

After you complete the formatting and design of a worksheet that you would like to use over and over again, save it as a template file. When saved as a template file, the *.xltx* file extension is added to the file name instead of *.xlsx*.

By default, as the save location, Word will suggest the Templates folder on the hard drive of your computer, or the network location where the Excel software resides. This makes the template available to other people who have access to the same system from the My templates folder on the New tab in Backstage view.

Regardless of where the template file is saved, when the template is opened, a new *copy* of the workbook opens, thus preserving the original template for future use.

Instead of the Templates folder, which might be restricted in a college lab, you will save the template in your chapter folder.

1 From **Backstage** view, display the **Save As** dialog box, and then click the **Save as type arrow**. On the list, click **Excel Template**.

2 In the **address bar** at the top of the dialog box, notice that Excel suggests the **Templates** folder on your system as the default save location.

3 Navigate to your **Excel Chapter 6 folder**.

Alert! | Saving a Template

If you are working in a college computer lab, your college may have placed restrictions on saving files to the Templates folder. Saving to the Templates folder makes the template available to anyone at this computer when they click the File tab, and then click New. For this project, you will save the template in your chapter folder. The difference is that the template will be available to you only.

---

4 In the **File name** box, change the **File name** to **Lastname_Firstname_6B_Order_Template** and then click **Save**.

> A copy of the template is saved with your other files.

5 From **Backstage** view, click **Close** to close the file but leave Excel open.

6 From the **Start** menu, click **Computer**, navigate to your **Excel Chapter 6** folder, and then notice that the template file icon displays with a small gold bar at the top. This indicates that the file is a template, and not a workbook. Compare your screen with Figure 6.39.

Figure 6.39

File path (yours may vary) ———

Gold bar indicates the template format ———

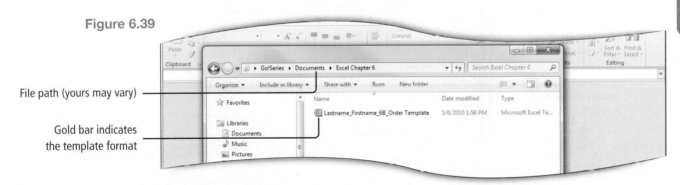

7 **Close** [X] the Windows Explorer window.

Objective 6 | Protect a Worksheet

When the template design is complete, you can enable the protection of the worksheet. Protection prevents anyone from changing the worksheet—they cannot insert, modify, delete, or format data in a locked cell.

For purposes of creating a form that you want someone to complete, you can protect the worksheet, and then unlock specific areas where you do want the person completing the form to enter data.

By default, all cells in Excel are *locked*—data cannot be typed into them. However, the locked feature is disabled until you protect the worksheet. After protection is enabled, the locked cells cannot be changed. Of course, you will want to designate some cells to be *unlocked*, so that individuals completing your form can type in their data.

Thus, the basic process is to determine the cells that you will allow people to change or unlock, and then protect the entire worksheet. Then, only the cells that you designated as unlocked will be available to any person using the worksheet. You may add an optional *password* to prevent someone from disabling the worksheet protection. The password can be any combination of numbers, letters, or symbols up to 15 characters long. The password should be shared only with people who have permission to change the template.

Activity 6.24 │ Protecting a Worksheet

1 From your **Excel Chapter 6** folder, open your template file **Lastname_Firstname_6B_ Order_Template**. Select the range **C6:C7**, hold down Ctrl, select the range **C10:C15** and the range **B18:E39**.

> The selected cells are the ones that you want individuals placing booth orders to be able to fill in—they should *not* be locked when protection is applied.

2 With the three ranges selected, on the **Home tab**, in the **Cells group**, click **Format**, and then click **Format Cells**. In the displayed **Format Cells** dialog box, click the **Protection tab**.

3 Click to *clear* the check mark from the **Locked** check box, and then compare your screen with Figure 6.40.

> Recall that all cells are locked by default, but the locking feature is only enabled when protection is applied. Therefore, you must *unlock* the cells you want to have available for use in this manner *before* you protect the worksheet.

Figure 6.40

For the selected cells, the Locked feature is cleared

Format Cells dialog box, Protection tab selected

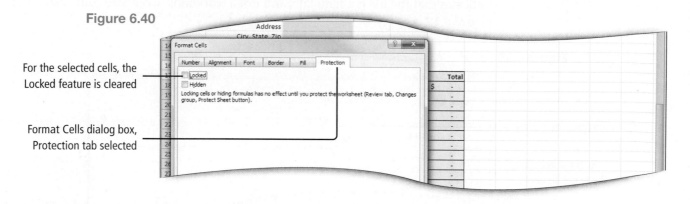

4 Click **OK** to close the **Format Cells** dialog box.

5 In the **Cells group**, click the **Format** button, and then under **Protection**, click **Protect Sheet**.

> The Protect Sheet dialog box displays. Under *Allow all users of this worksheet to*, the *Select locked cells* and *Select unlocked cells* check boxes are selected by default. The *Select locked cells* option allows the user to click the locked cells and *view* the formulas, but because the cells are locked, they cannot *change* the content or format of the locked cells. If you deselect this option, the user cannot view or even click in a locked cell.

> For the remaining check boxes, you can see that, because they are not selected, are restricted from performing all other actions on the worksheet.

6 Leave the first two check boxes selected. At the top of the dialog box, be sure the **Protect worksheet and contents of locked cells** check box is selected. In the **Password to unprotect sheet** box type **goseries** Compare your screen with Figure 6.41.

> The password does not display—rather bullets display as placeholders for each letter or character that is typed. Passwords are case sensitive, therefore, *GOSeries* is different from *goseries.*

Figure 6.41

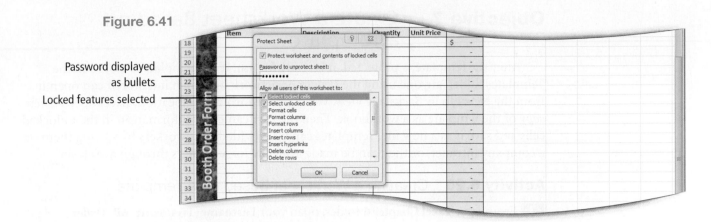

Password displayed
as bullets

Locked features selected

7 Click **OK**. In the displayed **Confirm Password** dialog box, type **goseries** to confirm the password, and then click **OK** to close both dialog boxes.

8 Click in any cell in the **Total** column, type **123** and observe what happens.

The number is not entered; instead a message informs you that the cell you are trying to change is protected and therefore, read-only.

9 Click **OK** to acknowledge the message. Click cell **D18**, type **2** and press Tab, type **150** and press Enter.

The numbers are recorded and the formulas in cell F18 and F40 calculate and display the results—$300.00.

10 On the **Quick Access Toolbar**, click the **Undo** button ↺ two times to remove the two numbers that you typed, and then click the **Save** button 🖫.

You have tested your template, and it is protected and saved.

Note | Footer Updates Automatically

The footer will update automatically when you save with a new name, so there is no need to change the footer.

---

11 Display the **Document Panel** and in the **Author** box, type your firstname and lastname, in the **Subject** box, type your course name and section number, and in the **Keywords** box, type **booth order form, template Close** ✕ the **Document Panel**.

12 Display the **Print Preview**, redisplay the workbook, and then make any necessary corrections or adjustments.

13 **Save** 🖫 your workbook, and then print or submit electronically as directed by your instructor. If required, print or create an electronic version of your worksheet with formulas displayed using the instructions in Activity 1.16 in Project 1A. **Close** the workbook, but leave Excel open.

More Knowledge | Modifying a Template

If you need to make changes to a template after it is protected, you must first remove the protection.

Objective 7 | Create a Worksheet Based on a Template

After the template is protected, it is ready for use. If the template is stored in the Templates folder, anyone using the system or network on which it is stored can open it from the New tab in Backstage view. When opened from this location, Excel opens a *new copy* of the template as a workbook. Then the user can enter information in the unlocked cells and save it as a new file. Templates can be provided to coworkers by storing them on a company intranet, or they can be made available to customers through a Web site.

Activity 6.25 | Creating a Worksheet Based on a Template

1 From your **Excel Chapter 6** folder, open your **Lastname_Firstname_6B_Order_Template** file.

2 From **Backstage** view, display the **Save As** dialog box, and then set the **Save as type** box to **Excel Workbook**—the first choice at the top of the list. Navigate to your **Excel Chapter 6** folder, and then in the **File name** box type **Lastname_Firstname_6B_Topaz_Order** Compare your screen with Figure 6.42.

> **Note | Creating a Workbook from a Template in the My Templates Folder in Backstage View**
>
> When you are able to open a template from the Templates folder in Backstage view, a new copy of the template opens as a workbook, not as a template, and displays a *1* at the end of the file name in the title bar. The *1* indicates a new workbook. Thus, if you are able to work from the Templates folder, the Save operation would automatically set the file type to Excel Workbook.

Figure 6.42

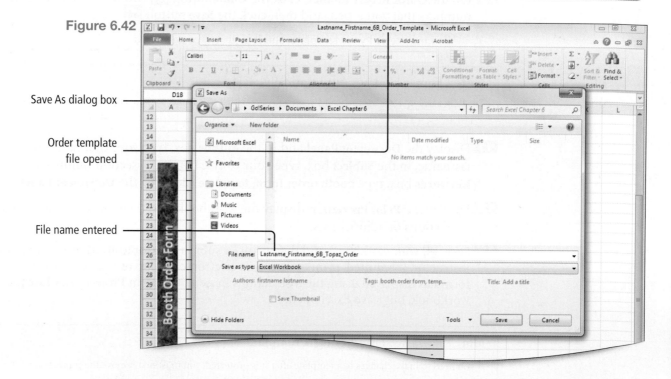

Save As dialog box

Order template file opened

File name entered

3 Press Enter. Click cell **C6**, type **October 13, 2016** press Enter, and notice that Excel applies the default date format. As the booth number, type **A-3421** and then press Enter three times to move to cell **C10**.

4 Starting in cell **C10**, enter the company information as follows:

Name	**McKenzie Peterson**
Company	**Topaz Business, Inc.**
Address	**653 Riverside Drive**
City, State, Postal code	**New York, NY 10025**
Phone	**212.555.0230**
E-mail	**mpeterson@topaz.net**

5 In cell **B18** type **Booth space** and press Tab, type **10 feet by 10 feet** and press Tab, type **1** and press Tab, type **400.00** and then press Tab.

6 Complete the order by entering the following items, pressing Tab to move from cell to cell. When you are finished, compare your screen with Figure 6.43.

Item	Description	Quantity	Unit Price
Booth Space	10 feet by 10 feet	1	400.00
Flooring	Carpet Squares	20	5.00
Table	6 feet, skirted	1	25.00
Chairs	Guest chair	3	15.00
Projector screen	Standard	1	20.00
Sign	Standard	2	20.00
Curtain	Back wall	2	15.00

Figure 6.43

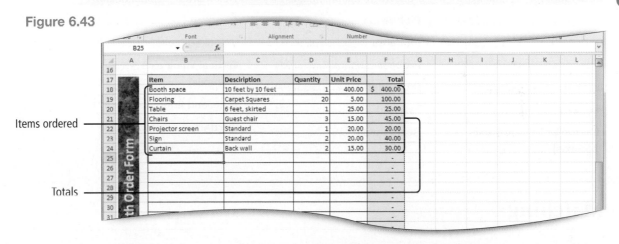

Items ordered

Totals

7 Display the **Document Panel**. Be sure your name displays in the **Author** box and your course name and section number displays in the **Subject** box. Change the **Keywords** box to **Topaz booth order** Be sure the file name displays in the left section of the footer and that the worksheet is horizontally centered.

8 Return to **Normal** view and make cell **A1** active, display the **Print Preview**, redisplay the workbook, and then make any necessary corrections or adjustments.

9 **Save** your workbook, and then print or submit electronically as directed by your instructor. If required, print or create an electronic version of your worksheet with formulas displayed using the instructions in Activity 1.16 in Project 1A. **Close** Excel.

End You have completed Project 6B

Content-Based Assessments

Summary

You created and modified a column chart to show a comparison among related numbers and a line chart to display a trend over time. Within each chart type, you identified and modified various chart objects and created and formatted titles and labels.

You created and modified a Process SmartArt graphic. You also created and modified a SmartArt organizational chart to practice building a hierarchy diagram.

You created and modified a template using text, formatting, formulas, locked and unlocked cells, and password protection for improved accuracy and record keeping.

Key Terms

Matching

Match each term in the second column with its correct definition in the first column by writing the letter of the term on the blank line in front of the correct definition.

_____ 1.   Tiny charts that fit within a cell and give a visual trend summary alongside your data.

_____ 2.   A type of chart that shows comparisons among related data.

_____ 3.   Lines in the plot area of a chart that aid the eye in determining plotted values.

_____ 4.   A chart that is inserted into the same worksheet that contains the data used to create the chart.

_____ 5.   A separate worksheet used to display an entire chart.

_____ 6.   A single value in a worksheet represented by a data marker in a chart.

_____ 7.   A group of related data points.

A Chart area

B Chart elements

C Chart sheet

D Column chart

E Data point

F Data series

G Embedded chart

H Gridlines

I Legend

J Line chart

K Scale

_____ 8. A chart element that identifies the patterns or colors that are assigned to the categories in the chart.

_____ 9. Objects that make up a chart.

_____ 10. The entire chart and all of its elements.

_____ 11. A type of chart that uses lines to show a trend over time.

_____ 12. The range of numbers in the data series that controls the minimum, maximum, and incremental values on the value axis.

_____ 13. A graphic representation of trends in a data series, such as a line sloping upward to represent increased sales over a period of months.

_____ 14. An Excel feature that provides a visual representation of your information and ideas.

_____ 15. An optional area in which you can type the text for a SmartArt graphic in a list format.

L SmartArt graphic

M Sparklines

N Text pane

O Trendline

Multiple Choice

Circle the correct answer.

1. A visual representation of numeric data in a worksheet is a:
   A. diagram
   B. graphic
   C. chart

2. The graphic element that represents a single data point is a:
   A. data marker
   B. data element
   C. data series

3. The data along the bottom of a chart displays on the:
   A. category axis
   B. value axis
   C. legend

4. The numbers along the left side of a chart display on the:
   A. category axis
   B. value axis
   C. legend

5. A diagram that shows hierarchical relationships is a:
   A. cycle chart
   B. list
   C. organization chart

6. When you create a template, Excel adds the file extension:
   A. .xlsx
   B. .xltx
   C. .xmlx

7. The process of locking cells in a workbook so that users cannot make any changes is:
   A. protection
   B. standardization
   C. passwording

8. Cells in a worksheet that cannot be edited are:
   A. merged cells
   B. blocked cells
   C. locked cells

9. A feature with which you can insert decorative text into your worksheet is:
   A. SmartArt
   B. WordArt
   C. GraphicArt

10. An optional element added to a template to prevent someone from disabling a worksheet's protection is:
    A. a password
    B. a security key
    C. a trendline

Content-Based Assessments

Apply **6A** skills from these Objectives:

1 Create and Format Sparklines and a 3-D Column Chart

2 Create and Format a Line Chart

3 Create and Modify a SmartArt Graphic

4 Create and Modify an Organization Chart

Skills Review | Project **6C** Employer Attendance

In the following Skills Review, you will assist Elaine Chin, Employer Relations Manager, in displaying the employer participation for the New York-New Jersey Job Fair in charts and diagrams. Your completed workbook will look similar to Figure 6.44.

Project Files

For Project 6C, you will need the following file:

e06C_Employer_Participation

You will save your workbook as:

Lastname_Firstname_6C_Employer_Participation

Project Results

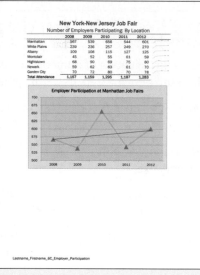

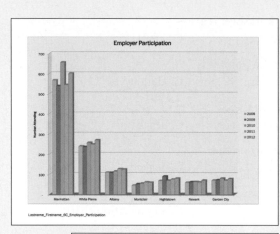

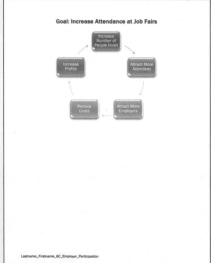

Figure 6.44

(Project 6C Employer Attendance continues on the next page)

1 **Start** Excel. From your student files, open **e06C_ Employer_Participation**. **Save** the file in your **Excel Chapter 6** folder as **Lastname_Firstname_6C_Employer_ Participation**

a. Select the range **A4:F10**. On the **Insert tab**, in the **Sparklines group**, click the **Line** button. With the insertion point in the **Location Range**, select the range **G4:G10**, and then click **OK**. On the **Design tab**, in the **Show group,** select the **High Point** check box and the **Last Point** check box. On the **Design tab**, in the **Style group**, click the **More** button, and then in the third row, click the first style—Sparkline Style Accent 1, (no dark or light). In cell **G3**, type **Trend**

b. Select the range **A3:F10**. On the **Insert tab**, in the **Charts group**, click the **Column** button. Under **3-D Column**, click the first chart—**3-D Clustered Column**. On the **Design tab**, in the **Location group**, click the **Move Chart** button. Click the **New sheet** option button, name the new sheet **Participation Chart** and then click **OK**. On the **Design tab**, in the **Chart Styles** group, click the **More** button, and then in the fifth row, click the second style—**Style 34**. On the **Layout tab**, in the **Labels group**, click the **Chart Title** button, and then click **Above Chart**. In the **Formula Bar**, type **Employer Participation** as the chart title, and then press Enter.

c. On the **Layout tab**, in the **Labels group**, click the **Axis Titles** button. Point to **Primary Vertical Axis Title**, and then click **Rotated Title**. In the **Formula Bar**, type **Number Attending** and then press Enter. **Save** your workbook.

d. In the **White Plains** column cluster, point to the last column—**2012**. Notice that the Value for this column is *255*. Display the **Participation by Location** worksheet, and then in cell **F5**, type **270** and press Enter.

e. Display the **Participation Chart**. On the **Layout tab**, in the **Current Selection group**, click the **Chart Elements arrow**, and then click **Back Wall**. Then in the same group, click **Format Selection**. In the **Format Wall** dialog box, on the left, click **Fill**, on the right, click the **Solid fill** option button, and then under **Fill Color**, click the **Color arrow**. Under **Theme Colors**, in the first column, click the third color—**White, Background 1, Darker 15%**—and then set the **Transparency** to 75%. **Close** the dialog box.

f. Using the same technique, select the **Side Wall**, and then apply the same fill, but with a **Transparency** of **60%**. To the **Floor**, apply a **Solid fill** using the last color in the first column—**White, Background 1, Darker 50%** with **0% Transparency**. To the **Chart Area**, apply a **Solid fill** using **Light Yellow, Background 2, Darker 10%**—in the third column, the second color. **Close** the dialog box.

2 Display the **Participation by Location** worksheet. Select the range **A3:F4**, and then on the **Insert tab**, in the **Charts group**, click the **Line** button. In the second row, click the first chart type—**Line with Markers**. Drag the upper left corner of the chart inside the upper left corner of cell **A13**. Drag the lower right corner of the chart inside the lower right corner of cell **G29**.

a. In the embedded chart, click the **Legend** *Manhattan* to select it. Press Del. Click the **Chart Title** *Manhattan*, type **Employer Participation at Manhattan Job Fairs** and press Enter. Point to the **Chart Title**, right-click, and then change the font size to **14**.

b. On the left side of the line chart, point to the **Vertical (Value) Axis**, right-click, and then click **Format Axis**. On the left, click **Axis Options**. Under **Axis Options**, to the right of **Minimum**, click the **Fixed** option button, and then in the **Fixed** box, select the displayed number and type **500** To the right of **Major unit**, click the **Fixed** option button, and then in the **Fixed** box, select the displayed number and type **25 Close** the dialog box.

c. Right-click anywhere within the **Plot Area**, click **Format Plot Area**, and then on the left, click **Fill**. Under **Fill**, click the **Solid fill** option button. Under **Fill Color**, click the **Color arrow**, and then under **Theme Colors**, in the first column, click the fourth color—**White, Background 1, Darker 25%**. **Close** the dialog box.

d. Point to the chart line, right-click, and then click **Format Data Series**. On the left, click **Line Style**. Set the **Width** to **4 pt**. On the left, click **Marker Options**. Under **Marker Type**, click the **Built-in** option button, click the **Type arrow**, and then click the **triangle**—the third symbol in the list. Set the **Size** to **14**.

e. On the left, click **Marker Fill**. Click the **Solid fill** option button, and then click the **Color arrow**. Under **Theme Colors**, in the first column, click the sixth color—**White, Background 1, Darker 50%**.

(Project 6C Employer Attendance continues on the next page)

f. On the left, select **Marker Line Color**, click the **No line** option button, and then click **Close**. Using any of the techniques you have practiced to select a chart element, select the **Chart Area**, display the **Format Chart Area** dialog box, and then apply a **Solid fill** using **White, Background 1, Darker 15%**—in the first column, the third color. Close the dialog box. Click in any cell outside of the chart.

g. Click the edge of the chart border to select the entire chart. On the **Layout tab**, in the **Analysis group**, click the **Trendline** button, and then click **Linear Trendline**. **Save** your workbook.

3 Click the **Sheet1 tab**, and then rename the sheet **Process Chart** In cell **A1**, type **Goal: Increase Attendance at Job Fairs** and then press **Enter**. Merge and center the text across the range **A1:H1** and apply the **Title** cell style. On the **Insert tab**, in the **Illustrations group**, click the **SmartArt** button. On the left, click **Cycle**, and then in the first row, click the third option—**Block Cycle**. Click **OK**.

a. On the **Design tab**, in the **Create Graphic group**, if necessary, click **Text Pane**. As the first bullet, type **Increase Number of People Hired** Click the next bullet, and then type **Attract More Attendees** As the third bullet, type **Attract More Employers** As the fourth bullet, type **Reduce Costs** As the last bullet, type **Increase Profits Close** the **Text Pane**.

b. Click the edge of the graphic to select it. On the **Design tab**, in the **SmartArt Styles group**, click the **More** button. Under **3-D**, click the first style—**Polished**. Click the **Change Colors** button, and then under **Colorful**, click the first option—**Colorful – Accent Colors**. Drag the upper left corner of the graphic into the left corner of cell **A3**. Drag the lower right corner inside the lower right corner of cell **H20**. Click cell **A1**, and then click **Save**.

4 Display **Sheet2** and rename the sheet tab **Organization Chart** In cell **A1**, type **Job Fair Employer Services Structure as of January 1** and then merge and center this title across the range **A1:H1**. Apply the **Title** cell style. On the **Insert tab**, in the **Illustrations group**, click the **SmartArt** button. On the left, click **Hierarchy**, and then in the first row, click the third graphic—**Name and Title Organization Chart**. Click **OK**.

a. If the Text Pane displays, close it. In the graphic, click in the first **[Text]** box, and then type **Janis Kile** Click

the edge of the small white box below *Janis Kile* to select it and type **Employer Manager** In the **[Text]** box below *Employer Manager*, click on the *edge* of the box to display a solid line border—if a dashed border displays, click the edge of the box again. With the box bordered with a solid line, press **Del**.

b. On the second level, click in the leftmost shape, and then using the technique you just practiced, type **Alex Tang** and **Operations Manager** In the next shape, type **Jo Peters** and **Marketing Specialist** In the rightmost shape, type **Rosa Tome** and **Finance Analyst** Hold down **Ctrl**, and then click the edge of each of the smaller title boxes to select all four. Then, right-click over any of the selected boxes, change the font size to **8**, and click **Center**.

c. Drag the upper left corner of the graphic into cell **A3** and the lower right corner into cell **H20**. On the **Design tab**, in the **SmartArt Styles group**, click the **More** button, and then apply **Intense Effect**. Change the colors to **Colorful – Accent Colors**.

d. Display the **Participation Chart** sheet. On the **Insert tab**, click **Header & Footer**, and then click **Custom Footer**. With the insertion point in the **left section**, from the small toolbar in the dialog box, click the **Insert File Name** button. Click **OK** two times.

e. Display the **Participation by Location** sheet. Hold down **Ctrl** and select the remaining two worksheets to group the three sheets. Insert a footer with the file name in the **left section**. Click outside the footer area to deselect. On the **Page Layout tab**, click the **Margins** button, click **Custom Margins**, and then center the sheets horizontally. Click **OK**. Return to **Normal** view and press **Ctrl** + **Home** to move to cell **A1**.

f. Right-click any of the sheet tabs and click **Select All Sheets** to select all four worksheets. From **Backstage** view, display the **Document Panel**, type your firstname and lastname as the author, type your course name and section in the **Subject** box, and as the **Keywords** type **employer participation, organization chart Close** the Document Information Panel.

g. Click **Save**. Display and examine the **Print Preview**, make any necessary corrections, **Save**, and then print or submit electronically as directed by your instructor. If you are directed to do so, print the formulas on the Participation by Location worksheet.

End You have completed Project 6C

Content-Based Assessments

Apply **6B** skills from these Objectives:

- **5** Create an Excel Template
- **6** Protect a Worksheet
- **7** Create a Worksheet Based on a Template

Skills Review | Project **6D** Purchase Order

In the following Skills Review, you will assist Job Fair Director, Jennifer Patterson, in creating a template for a Purchase Order, and then a Purchase Order for items with a logo and name imprint of the New York-New Jersey Job Fair. Your completed worksheets will look similar to Figure 6.45.

Project Files

For Project 6D, you will need the following file:

New blank Excel workbook

You will save your workbooks as:

Lastname_Firstname_6D_Purchase_Order
Lastname_Firstname_6D_PO_Template
Lastname_Firstname_6D_Hancock_PO

Project Results

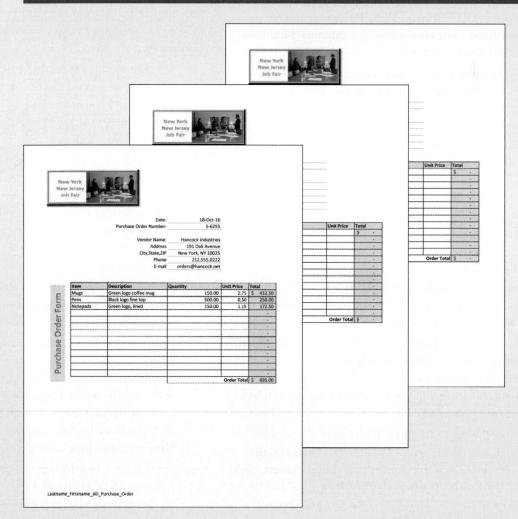

Figure 6.45

(Project 6D Purchase Order continues on the next page)

Content-Based Assessments

1 **Start** Excel and display a new blank workbook. Beginning in cell **E1**, type **2900 Second Avenue** and press [Enter]. In cell **E2**, type **New York, NY 10028** and in cell **E3**, type **Phone 212.555.0177** and press [Enter].

a. Click cell **C8**, type **Date:** and press [Enter]. In cell **C9**, type **Purchase Order Number:** Click cell **C11**. Type **Vendor Name:** and press [Enter]. In cell **C12**, type **Address** In cell **C13**, type **City, State, ZIP** In cell **C14**, type **Phone** In cell **C15**, type **E-mail**

b. Click cell **B18**. Type **Item** and press [Tab] to move to cell **C18**. Continuing across **row 18**, in cell **C18**, type **Description** and press [Tab], in cell **D18**, type **Quantity** and press [Tab], in cell **E18**, type **Unit Price** and press [Tab], and in cell **F18**, type **Total** and press [Enter]. Select the range **B18:F18** and apply **Bold**. **Save** the file in your **Excel Chapter 6** folder as **Lastname_Firstname_6D_Purchase_Order**

c. Widen **column B** to **100 pixels**, **column C** to **165 pixels** and **column D** to **145 pixels**. Select **columns E:F** and widen to **75 pixels**. Select the range **C8:C9**, hold down [Ctrl] and select the range **C11:C15**, and then on the **Home tab**, in the **Alignment group**, click the **Align Text Right** button.

d. Select the range **D8:D9**. In the **Alignment group**, click the **Dialog Box Launcher** button. In the **Format Cells** dialog box, click the **Border tab**. Under **Line**, in the **Style** list, click the first line in the first column—a dotted line. Click the **Color arrow**, and then under **Theme Colors**, in the last column, click the last color—**Orange, Accent 6, Darker 50%**. Under **Border**, click the **Middle Border** button and the **Bottom Border** button. Click **OK**.

e. With the range **D8:D9** still selected, in the **Alignment group**, click the **Align Text Right** button. Right-click over the selected range, on the Mini toolbar, click **Format Painter**, and then select the range **D11:D15** to copy the format.

f. Select the range **B18:F32**. Right-click the selected range and click **Format Cells**. In the **Format Cells** dialog box, click the **Border tab**. Under **Presets**, click the **Outline** button and the **Inside** button, and then click **OK**. Select the range **B18:F18**, hold down [Ctrl] and select the range **F19:F32**. In the **Font group**, click the **Fill Color button arrow**, and then under **Theme Colors**, in the last column, click the third color—**Orange, Accent 6, Lighter 60%**.

g. Press [Ctrl] + [Home]. Press [Ctrl] + [F2] to examine the **Print Preview**. In **Backstage** view, click **Save** to save and return to your workbook.

2 To construct a formula to multiply the Quantity times the Unit Price, in cell **F19**, type **=d19*e19** and press [Enter]. Use the fill handle to copy the formula in cell **F18** down through cell **F31**. Click cell **F32**. On the **Home tab**, in the **Editing group**, click the **AutoSum** button. Be sure the range displays as *F19:F31*, and then press [Enter]. Select the range **E19:E31**. In the **Number group**, click the **Comma Style** button. Click cell **F19**, hold down [Ctrl], and then click cell **F32**. In the **Number group**, click the **Accounting Number Format** button. Select the range **F20:F31**, and then click the **Comma Style** button. Select the range **D19:D31**, and then in the **Styles group**, click **Cell Styles**, and then under **Number Format**, click **Comma [0]**.

a. Select the range **D32:E32**. In the **Alignment group**, click the **Merge and Center** button. Type **Order Total** and press [Enter]. Click cell **D32** again, and then in the **Alignment group**, click the **Align Text Right** button. Apply **Bold**.

b. Select the range **B32:C32**, right-click, and then click **Format Cells**. On the **Border tab**, in the **Border** preview area, click the **Left Border** button, the **Middle Border** button and the **Bottom Border** button to *remove* these borders from the preview— be sure the right and top lines remain in the preview area. Click **OK**.

c. Press [Ctrl] + [F2] to view the **Print Preview**. In the **Backstage** view, click **Save** to save and return to your workbook.

d. Click cell **A1**. On the **Insert tab**, in the **Illustrations group**, click the **Picture** button. In the **Insert Picture** dialog box, navigate to your student files, and then insert the file **e06D_Logo**. With the image selected, click the **Format tab**, in the **Picture Styles group**, click the **More** button, and then locate and click the **Simple Frame, Black**. **Save** your workbook.

e. Scroll so that **row 16** is at the top of the Excel window. Then, click cell **A18**. On the **Insert tab**, in the **Text group**, click the **WordArt** button, and then in the fourth row, click the second WordArt— **Gradient Fill – Orange, Accent 6, Inner Shadow**. Type **Purchase Order Form** Select the text you just typed, right-click, and then from the Mini toolbar,

(Project 6D Purchase Order continues on the next page)

Skills Review | Project **6D** Purchase Order (continued)

set the **Font Size** to **20**. Drag the green rotation handle to the left until the WordArt is vertical. Then, drag the WordArt image to **column A** and align the top of the image with the top of cell **A18**—centered in the column. At the lower edge of the WordArt image, point to the center resize handle and drag down so the end of the image aligns at the lower edge of cell **A32**.

f. With the WordArt still selected, on the **Format tab**, in the **Shape Styles group**, click the **Shape Fill arrow**, click **Texture**, and then in the fourth row, click the second texture—**Recycled Paper**. Delete the unused sheets. Click to deselect the WordArt, and then press Ctrl + Home. Insert a footer in the **left section** that includes the file name. Click any cell outside the footer to deselect. On the status bar, click the **Normal** button. Press Ctrl + Home to move to the top of the worksheet. From **Backstage** view, display the **Document Panel**, type your firstname and lastname as the **Author**, your course name and section as the **Subject**, and purchase order as the **Keywords. Close** the Document Information Panel, and then **Save** your workbook.

g. From **Backstage** view, display the **Save As** dialog box, and then click the **Save as type arrow**. On the list, click **Excel Template**. In the **address bar** at the top of the dialog box, notice that Excel suggests the **Templates** folder on your system as the default save location. Navigate to your **Excel Chapter 6 folder**. In the **File name** box, change the **File name** to **Lastname_Firstname_6D_PO_Template** and then click **Save**.

3 Select the range **D8:D9**, hold down Ctrl, select the range **D11:D15** and the range **B19:E31**. With the three ranges selected, on the **Home tab**, in the **Cells group**, click **Format**, and then click **Format Cells**. In the displayed **Format Cells** dialog box, click the **Protection tab**. Click to *clear* the check mark from the **Locked** check box. Click **OK**.

a. In the **Cells group**, click the **Format** button, and then under **Protection**, click **Protect Sheet**. Under **Allow all users of this worksheet to:** leave the first two check boxes selected. At the top of the dialog box, be sure the **Protect worksheet and contents of locked cells** check box is selected. In the **Password to unprotect sheet** box, type **goseries** Click **OK**. In the displayed **Confirm Password** dialog box, type **goseries** to confirm the password, and then click **OK** to close both dialog boxes. Click **Save**.

b. Display the **Document Panel**. The **Author** and **Subject** boxes contain your previous information. As the **Keywords**, type **purchase order form, template Close** the Document Panel.

c. Check the **Print Preview**, and then **Save** your template.

4 To create a purchase order from your template, from **Backstage** view, display the **Save As** dialog box, and then set the **Save as type** box to **Excel Workbook**—the first choice at the top of the list. Navigate to your **Excel Chapter 6** folder, and then in the **File name** box, type **Lastname_Firstname_6D_Hancock_PO** Click **Save**.

a. Click cell **D8**, type **October 18, 2016** and press Enter— Excel applies the default date format. As the Purchase Order Number, type **S-6255** and then press Enter two times to move to cell **D11**. Beginning in cell **D11**, enter the vendor information as follows:

Vendor Name:	Hancock Industries
Address	191 Oak Avenue
City, State, ZIP	New York, NY 10025
Phone	212.555.0222
E-mail	orders@hancock.net

b. Click cell **B19**, and then complete the order by entering the following items as shown in Table 1, pressing Tab to move from cell to cell.

Table 1

Item	Description	Quantity	Unit Price
Mugs	Green logo coffee mug	150	2.75
Pens	Black logo fine tip	500	0.50
Notepads	Green logo, lined	150	1.15

- - - → (Return to Step 4b)

(Project 6D Purchase Order continues on the next page)

Content-Based Assessments

c. Display the **Document Panel**. Be sure your name displays in the **Author** box and your course name and section number displays in the **Subject** box. Change the **Keywords** to **Hancock, promotional items** Check the **Print Preview** to be sure the file name updated and displays in the left section of the footer.

d. **Save** your workbook. As directed by your instructor, print or submit electronically the three workbooks you created in this project. If required to do so, print or create an electronic version of your worksheets that contain formulas by following the instructions in Activity 1.16 in Project 1A. **Close** Excel.

 You have completed Project 6D ——————————————

Content-Based Assessments

Apply 6A skills from these Objectives:

■1 Create and Format Sparklines and a 3-D Column Chart

■2 Create and Format a Line Chart

■3 Create and Modify a SmartArt Graphic

■4 Create and Modify an Organization Chart

Mastering Excel | Project 6E Hires

In the following project, you will assist Elaine Chin, Employer Relations Manager, in tracking the number of people who get hired by an employer at each fair. You will create and modify a chart to display the number of people hired at the fairs in the past five years, create a diagram of the communities served, and create an organizational chart for staff at the Job Fair. Your completed worksheets will look similar to Figure 6.46.

Project Files

For Project 6E, you will need the following file:

e06E_Hires

You will save your workbook as:

Lastname_Firstname_6E_Hires

Project Results

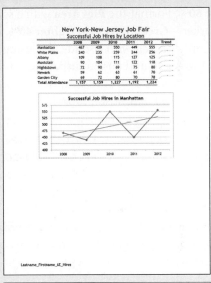

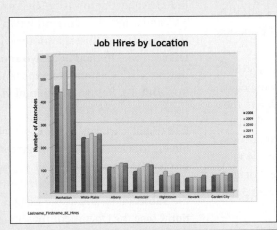

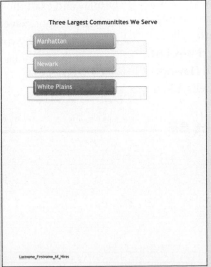

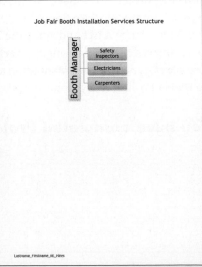

Figure 6.46

(Project 6E Hires continues on the next page)

Content-Based Assessments

Mastering Excel | Project 6E Hires (continued)

1 Start Excel. From your student files, open **e06E_Hires** and **Save** the file in your **Excel Chapter 6** folder as **Lastname_Firstname_6E_Hires** Using the data in the range **A4:F10**, insert **Sparklines** using the **Line** format. Place the sparklines in the range adjacent to the **2012** column, show the **High Point** and **Last Point**, and then apply Sparkline Style Accent 4- Darker 25%. Type **Trend** in the cell above the sparklines, and then use **Format Painter** to apply the format in cell **F3** to cell **G3**.

2 Using the data for the years and for each location (not the totals), create a 3-D Clustered Column chart on a separate chart sheet named **Hires by Location Chart** Apply **Style 18**, and add a **Chart Title** above the chart with the text **Job Hires by Location** Set the title's font size to **28**. Format the **Chart Area** with a solid fill using **Green, Accent 3, Lighter 80%**. Format the **Plot Area** with a solid fill two shades darker—**Green, Accent 3, Lighter 40%**. Format the floor and the side wall with a solid color using **Turquoise, Accent 2, Darker 50** and **80%** transparency. Add a rotated title to the vertical axis with the text **Number of Attendees Hired** and change the font size to **16**.

3 On the **Job Hires by Location** worksheet, using the data for Manhattan, insert a **Line with Markers** line chart. Position the chart between cells **A13** and **G26**. Delete the legend, change the chart title to **Successful Job Hires in Manhattan** and set the title's font size to **14**. Format the **Vertical (Value) Axis** so that the **Minimum** value is **400** and the **Major unit** is **25** Add a **Linear Trendline**. Format the **Line Color** of the trendline with **Orange, Accent 5** and set the **Line Style** to a width of **2 pt**.

4 Rename the **Sheet2** tab as **List Chart** In cell **A1**, type **Three Largest Communities We Serve** Merge and center this title across the range **A1:I1** and apply the **Title** cell style. Insert a **SmartArt** graphic using the **Vertical Box List**. In the three boxes, type, in order, **Manhattan** and **Newark** and **White Plains** Position the graphic between cells **A3** and

G16. Apply the **Inset** style and change the colors to **Colorful Range – Accent Colors 4 to 5**. Click cell **A1**.

5 Rename the **Sheet3 tab** as **Organization Chart** In cell **A1**, type **Job Fair Booth Installation Services Structure** Merge and center this title across the range **A1:H1** and apply the **Title** cell style. Insert a **SmartArt** graphic using **Horizontal Multi-Level Hierarchy**. In the vertical box, type **Booth Manager** and in the three remaining boxes, type **Safety Inspectors** and **Electricians** and **Carpenters** Position the graphic between cells **A4** and **H16**. Apply the **Subtle Effect** style and change the colors to **Colorful Range – Accent Colors 4 to 5**. Click cell **A1** to deselect.

6 Display the **Hires by Location Chart** sheet. On the **Insert tab**, click **Header & Footer**, and then click **Custom Footer**. With the insertion point in the **left section**, from the small toolbar in the dialog box, click the **Insert File Name** button. Click **OK** two times.

7 Display the **Job Hires by Location** sheet. Hold down Ctrl and select the remaining two worksheets to group the three sheets. Insert a footer with the file name in the **left section**. On the **Page Layout tab**, click the **Margins** button, click **Custom Margins**, and then center the sheets horizontally. Return to **Normal** view and press Ctrl + Home to move to cell **A1**.

8 Right-click any of the sheet tabs and click **Select All Sheets** to select all four worksheets. From **Backstage** view, display the **Document Panel**, type your firstname and lastname as the author, type your course name and section in the **Subject** box, and as the **Keywords**, type **hires by location** Close the Document Information Panel and **Save**. Display and examine the **Print Preview**, make any necessary corrections, **Save**, and then print or submit electronically as directed by your instructor. If you are directed to do so, print the formulas on the Job Hires by Location worksheet. **Close** Excel.

End You have completed Project 6E

Content-Based Assessments

Apply 6B skills from these Objectives:

5 Create an Excel Template

6 Protect a Worksheet

7 Create a Worksheet Based on a Template

Mastering Excel | Project **6F** Event Budget

In the following Mastering Excel project, you will create a budget template for the Manhattan location of the New York-New Jersey Job Fair. You will also create a worksheet based on the budget template for review by Louis Goldstein, Manhattan Job Fair Director. Your completed worksheets will look similar to Figure 6.47.

Project Files

For Project 6F, you will need the following files:

New blank Excel workbook
e06F_Logo

You will save your workbooks as:

Lastname_Firstname_6F_Budget_Template
Lastname_Firstname_6F_Manhattan_Budget

Project Results

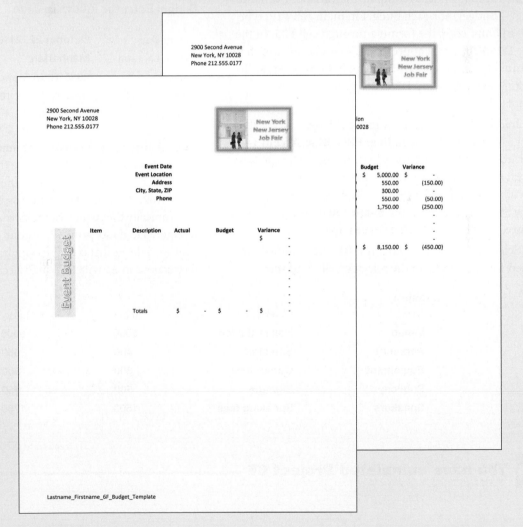

Figure 6.47

(Project 6F Event Budget continues on the next page)

Content-Based Assessments

Mastering Excel | Project 6F Event Budget (continued)

1 **Start** Excel and display a new blank workbook. In cell **A1**, type **2900 Second Avenue** In cell **A2**, type **New York, NY 10028** In cell **A3**, type **Phone 212.555.0177**

In cell **C8**, type **Event Date** In cell **C9**, type **Event Location** In cell **C10**, type **Address** In cell **C11**, type **City, State, ZIP** In cell **C12**, type **Phone**

In cell **B16**, type **Item** and press Tab. In cell **C16**, type **Description** In cell **D16**, type **Actual** In cell **E16**, type **Budget** In cell **F16**, type **Variance** Click cell **C26** and type **Totals**

2 To the ranges **C8:C12** and **B16:F16**, apply **Bold**. To the range **C8:C12**, apply **Align Text Right**. To the range **D8:D12**, apply **Align Text Left**. Widen **columns A:F** to **95 pixels**.

To construct a formula to compute the Variance (Variance = Actual – Budget) for each budget item, in cell **F17**, type **=d17-e17** and copy the formula through cell **F25**. In the range **D26:F26**, insert appropriate formulas to sum these columns. To the range **D18:F25**, apply **Comma Style**. To the ranges **D17:F17** and **D26:F26**, apply Accounting Number Format.

3 In cell **E1**, insert the picture **e06F_Logo**. Click cell **A16**, insert a **WordArt** using **Gradient Fill – Blue, Accent 1**—in the third row, the fourth WordArt. As the text, type **Event Budget** and set the **Font Size** to **24**. Rotate the WordArt vertically, and align it between cells **A16** and **A26**. In the **Shape Styles group**, click the **Shape Fill arrow**, click **Texture**, and then click **Blue tissue paper**.

4 Select the ranges **D8:D12** and **B17:E25**. Remove the **Locked** formatting from the selected cells, and then

protect the worksheet. Be sure the check box at the top and the first two check boxes in the list are selected, and as the password type **goseries** Complete the order by entering the following items as shown in **Table 1**.

Delete the unused worksheets. Insert a footer in the **left section** with the file name. Add your name, course information, and the keywords **budget template** to the **Document Information Panel**, and then check the **Print Preview**. **Save** your workbook as an **Excel Template** in your **Excel Chapter 6** folder as **Lastname_Firstname_6F_Budget_Template**

5 To create a new budget report using the template as your model, display the **Save As** dialog box again, and then **Save** the template as an **Excel Workbook** in your chapter folder as **Lastname_Firstname_6F_Manhattan_Budget** Enter the following data:

Event Date	**October 22, 2016**
Event Location	**Manhattan**
Address	**2885 Third Station**
City, State, ZIP	**New York, NY 10028**
Phone	**212.555.6575**

6 Change the **Keywords** to **Manhattan event budget** Examine the **Print Preview**; notice the file name is updated and displays in the left section of the footer. **Save** your workbook. As directed by your instructor, print or submit electronically the two workbooks you created in this project. If required to do so, print or create an electronic version of your worksheets that contain formulas by following the instructions in Activity 1.16 in Project 1A. **Close** Excel.

Table 1

Item	Description	Actual	Budget
Venue	Hall rental fee	5000	5000
Personnel	Site staff	400	550
Equipment	Computers	300	300
Publicity	Signage	500	550
Speakers	Speaking fees	1500	1750

(Return to Step 4)

 You have completed Project 6F

Content-Based Assessments

Apply 6A and 6B skills from these Objectives:

1. Create and Format Sparklines and a 3-D Column Chart
2. Create and Format a Line Chart
3. Create and Modify a SmartArt Graphic
4. Create and Modify an Organization Chart
5. Create an Excel Template
6. Protect a Worksheet
7. Create a Worksheet Based on a Template

Mastering Excel | Project 6G Internships and Travel Template

In the following project, you will assist Jan Stewart, Internship Coordinator, in tracking the number of internships by industry at each job fair and in creating a template to use for travel expenses. Your completed worksheets will look similar to Figure 6.48.

Project Files

For Project 6G, you will need the following files:

e06G_Internships
e06G_Travel_Expense

You will save your workbooks as:

Lastname_Firstname_6G_Internships
Lastname_Firstname_6G_Travel_Template
Lastname_Firstname_6G_Silverton_Report

Project Results

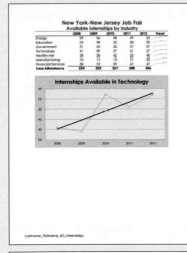

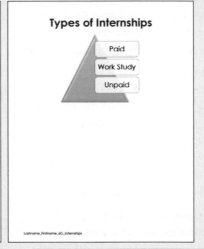

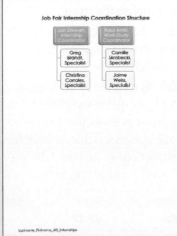

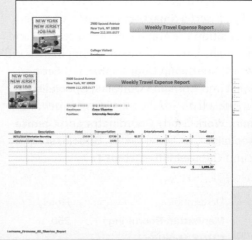

Figure 6.48

(Project 6G Internships and Travel Template continues on the next page)

Mastering Excel | Project **6G** Internships and Travel Template (continued)

1 Start **Excel**. From your student files, locate and open **e06G_Internships**. **Save** the file in your **Excel Chapter 6** folder as **Lastname_Firstname_6G_Internships** Using the range **A4:F10**, insert **Sparklines** in the **Line** format in the range adjacent to the last year of data. Show the **High Point** and **Last Point** and apply Sparkline Style Accent 4 - (no dark or light). In cell **G3**, type **Trend** and apply the format from cell **F3**.

2 Select the ranges representing the years (including the blank cell **A3**) and the data for **Technology** internships. Insert a line chart using the **Line with Markers** chart style. Reposition the chart between cells **A13** and **G29**. Delete the **Legend**. Change the **Chart Title** to **Internships Available in Technology** Edit the **Vertical (Value) Axis** to set the **Minimum** to **35** and the **Major unit** to **5**

3 Format the **Plot Area** with a solid fill using **Light Green, Background 2, Lighter 60%**. Format the **Chart Area** with a solid fill using **Olive Green, Accent 4, Lighter 60%**. Insert a **Linear Trendline** and change the width of the line to **2.5 pt**.

4 Rename **Sheet2** as **List Chart** In cell **A1**, type **Types of Internships** Merge and center the text across the range **A1:I1**, apply the **Title** cell style, and then set the **Font Size** to **36**. Insert a **SmartArt** graphic using the **Pyramid List**. Position the graphic between cells **A3** and **I18**. In the top text box, type **Paid** In the second text box, type **Work Study** and in the last box, type **Unpaid** Apply the **Inset** style and change the colors to **Colored Fill – Accent 1**.

5 Rename **Sheet3** as **Organization Chart** In cell **A1** type **Job Fair Internship Coordination Structure** and then merge and center this title across the range **A1:I1**. Apply the **Title** cell style. Insert a **SmartArt** graphic using the **Hierarchy List**. Position the graphic between cells **A3** and **I17**. On the left, create a list with the following names and titles: **Jan Stewart, Internship Coordinator** and **Greg Brandt, Specialist** and **Christina Corrales, Specialist** On the right, create a list with the following names and titles: **Rasa Amiri, Work-Study Coordinator** and **Camille Skrobecki, Specialist** and **Jaime Weiss, Specialist** Apply the **Inset** style and **Colored Fill – Accent 1**.

6 Group the three sheets, insert a footer with the file name in the **left section**, and then center the sheets horizontally. Display the **Document Panel**. Add your name, your course name and section, and the keywords **internship organization** Examine the **Print Preview**, **Save** and **Close** this workbook, but leave Excel open.

7 From your student files, open the file **e06G_Travel_Expense**. Display the **Save As** dialog box, and then **Save** the workbook as an **Excel Template** in your **Excel Chapter 6** folder with the name **Lastname_Firstname_6G_Travel_Template** In the range **H15:H21**, create formulas to sum the data in each row—do not include the *Date* or *Description* columns. In cell **H22**, create a formula to create a grand total of expenses for each date. Apply appropriate financial formatting to all the cells that will contain expenses, including the **Total** cell style in cell **H22**—refer to Figure 6.48.

8 Select the ranges **D8:D10**, hold down [Ctrl], and select **A15:G21**. Remove the **Locked** formatting from the selected cells and protect the worksheet. Be sure the top check box and the first two check boxes in the list are selected. As the password, type **goseries** Add your name, course information, and the **Keywords travel template** to the Document Information Panel. Insert a footer with the file name in the **left section**. Click **Save**.

9 To use the template for an employee's report, **Save** it as an **Excel Workbook** in your **Excel Chapter 6** folder with the file name **Lastname_Firstname_6G_Silverton_Report** As the **College Visited**, type **City University of New York** As the **Employee**, type **Gene Silverton** and as the **Position**, type **Internship Recruiter** Use the following data in Table 1 to complete the report:

10 Change the **Keywords** to **CUNY meeting** Examine the **Print Preview**; notice the file name is updated and displays in the left section of the footer. **Save** your workbook.

11 As directed by your instructor, print or submit electronically the two workbooks you created in this project. If required to do so, print or create an electronic version of your worksheets that contain formulas by following the instructions in Activity 1.16 in Project 1A. **Close** Excel.

Table 1

Date	Description	Hotel	Transport	Meals	Entertainment	Misc.
11-Oct-16	Manhattan Recruiting	250	127.50	62.37		
12-Oct-16	CUNY Meeting		23.50		595	37

(Return to Step 9)

 End **You have completed Project 6G**

Content-Based Assessments

GO! Fix It | Project 6H Operations Chart

Project Files

For Project 6H, you will need the following file:

e06H_Operations_Chart

You will save your workbook as:

Lastname_Firstname_6H_Operations_Chart

Open the file e06H_Operations_Chart, and then save the file in your Excel Chapter 6 folder as **Lastname_Firstname_6H_Operations_Chart** Edit the diagram so that employees whose job titles relate to College Recruiting and Internships fall under their respective areas. You might find it useful to open the Text Pane. Add your name and course information to the document properties, and include **recruiting operations, internship operations** as the keywords. Insert the file name in the footer, save your file, and then print or submit your worksheet electronically as directed by your instructor.

 You have completed Project 6H ——————————————

Excel | Chapter 6

Content-Based Assessments

GO! Make It | Project 6I Advertisers

Project Files

For Project 6I, you will need the following file:

e06I_Advertisers

You will save your workbook as:

Lastname_Firstname_6I_Advertisers

Each Job Fair event attracts numerous advertisers who place ads inside the event venue and on the various forms and handouts used by both the employers with booth space and the attendees. From your student files, open the file e06I_Advertisers, and then save it in your chapter folder as **Lastname_Firstname_6I_Advertisers** By using the skills you have practiced, create the worksheet shown in Figure 6.49. Include sparklines showing the high point, a line chart with a trendline to track the advertisers at the White Plains location, and format the chart as shown. Insert the file name in the footer, add appropriate information to the document properties including the keyword **advertisers** and submit as directed by your instructor.

Project Results

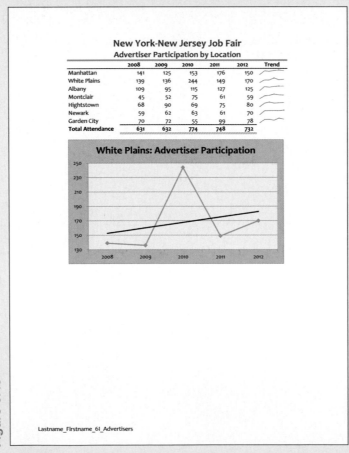

Figure 6.49

Lastname_Firstname_6I_Advertisers

End You have completed Project 6I

Content-Based Assessments

Apply a combination of the 6A and 6B skills.

GO! Solve It | Project **6J** Sponsors

Project Files

For Project 6J, you will need the following file:

e06J_Sponsors

You will save your workbook as:

Lastname_Firstname_6J_Sponsors

Open the file e06J_Sponsors and save it as **Lastname_Firstname_6J_Sponsors** Using the data for all locations, create a 3-D column chart to show sponsors by location. Format the chart attractively by applying varying colors of solid fill to the chart area, the plot area, and the floors and walls of the chart. Include a rotated vertical axis title and a chart title. Insert the file name in the footer of both sheets, add appropriate information to the document properties including the keyword **sponsors** and submit as directed by your instructor.

Performance Criteria	Performance Level		
	Exemplary: You consistently applied the relevant skills.	**Proficient:** You sometimes, but not always, applied the relevant skills.	**Developing:** You rarely or never applied the relevant skills.
Create a 3-D Column Chart	Location and year data is appropriately used to create a 3-D column chart.	Partial location and year data is used to create a 3-D column chart.	Location and year data is not used appropriately to create a 3-D column chart.
Format a 3-D Column Chart	The chart is attractively formatted with a variety of colors for the chart elements. The chart contains a chart title and a rotated vertical axis title.	The chart is attractively formatted with a variety of colors for some of the chart elements. The chart contains some but not all of the correct information for a chart title and a rotated vertical axis.	The chart is not attractively formatted with a variety of colors for the chart elements. The chart does not contain a chart title or a rotated vertical axis title.

End You have completed Project 6J

Content-Based Assessments

GO! Solve It | Project 6K Time Card

Project Files

For Project 6K, you will need the following file:

> e06K_Time_Card

You will save your workbook as:

> Lastname_Firstname_6K_Time_Template

Open the file e06K_Time_Card and save it as a template in your chapter file with the name **Lastname_Firstname_6K_Time_Template** Insert formulas to total the hours for the week, and a formula to calculate the total pay (Total Pay = Total Hours X Rate Per Hour). Apply appropriate number and financial formatting. Reposition the WordArt above the Time Card chart. Unlock the cells in which an individual would enter variable data, and then protect the sheet with the password **goseries** Insert the file name in the footer, add appropriate information to the document properties including the keywords **time card, payroll** and submit as directed by your instructor.

Performance Criteria	Performance Level		
	Exemplary: You consistently applied the relevant skills.	**Proficient:** You sometimes, but not always, applied the relevant skills.	**Developing:** You rarely or never applied the relevant skills.
Place WordArt Object and Apply Financial Formatting	Appropriate formulas, cell formatting, and WordArt placement are applied.	Appropriate formulas, cell formatting, and WordArt placement are partially applied.	Appropriate formulas, cell formatting, and WordArt placement are not applied.
Lock Formulas	Formula cells are locked and variable data cells are unlocked.	Only one of the formula cells or variable data cells has the locked or unlocked feature applied appropriately.	Formula cells are unlocked and variable data cells are locked.
Protect Worksheet	The worksheet is protected with the password **goseries**.	The worksheet is protected but not with the password **goseries**.	The worksheet is not protected with the password **goseries**.

End You have completed Project 6K —————

Outcomes-Based Assessments

Rubric

The following outcomes-based assessments are *open-ended assessments*. That is, there is no specific correct result; your result will depend on your approach to the information provided. Make *Professional Quality* your goal. Use the following scoring rubric to guide you in *how* to approach the problem and then to evaluate *how well* your approach solves the problem.

The *criteria*—Software Mastery, Content, Format and Layout, and Process—represent the knowledge and skills you have gained that you can apply to solving the problem. The *levels of performance*—Professional Quality, Approaching Professional Quality, or Needs Quality Improvements—help you and your instructor evaluate your result.

	Your completed project is of Professional Quality if you:	Your completed project is Approaching Professional Quality if you:	Your completed project Needs Quality Improvements if you:
1-Software Mastery	Choose and apply the most appropriate skills, tools, and features and identify efficient methods to solve the problem.	Choose and apply some appropriate skills, tools, and features, but not in the most efficient manner.	Choose inappropriate skills, tools, or features, or are inefficient in solving the problem.
2-Content	Construct a solution that is clear and well organized, contains content that is accurate, appropriate to the audience and purpose, and is complete. Provide a solution that contains no errors in spelling, grammar, or style.	Construct a solution in which some components are unclear, poorly organized, inconsistent, or incomplete. Misjudge the needs of the audience. Have some errors in spelling, grammar, or style, but the errors do not detract from comprehension.	Construct a solution that is unclear, incomplete, or poorly organized; contains some inaccurate or inappropriate content; and contains many errors in spelling, grammar, or style. Do not solve the problem.
3-Format and Layout	Format and arrange all elements to communicate information and ideas, clarify function, illustrate relationships, and indicate relative importance.	Apply appropriate format and layout features to some elements, but not others. Overuse features, causing minor distraction.	Apply format and layout that does not communicate information or ideas clearly. Do not use format and layout features to clarify function, illustrate relationships, or indicate relative importance. Use available features excessively, causing distraction.
4-Process	Use an organized approach that integrates planning, development, self-assessment, revision, and reflection.	Demonstrate an organized approach in some areas, but not others; or, use an insufficient process of organization throughout.	Do not use an organized approach to solve the problem.

Excel | Chapter 6

Outcomes-Based Assessments

Apply a combination of the **6A** and **6B** skills.

GO! Think | Project **6L** Tech Industry

Project Files

For Project 6L, you will need the following file:

　　e06L_Tech_Industry

You will save your workbook as:

　　Lastname_Firstname_6L_Tech_Industry

　　From your student files, open the file e06L_Tech_Industry, and then save it in your chapter folder as **Lastname_Firstname_6L_Tech_Industry** Format the data attractively, add appropriate formulas, add sparklines, and insert a line chart in the sheet that tracks the data for the White Plains location. Create a 3-D chart on a separate page based on the data in the worksheet, and format it attractively. Change the White Plains 2012 data point from 70 to 85. Insert the file name in the footer on each page, format each sheet for printing, add appropriate information to the document properties including the keywords **technology employers** and submit as directed by your instructor.

 You have completed Project 6L —————————

Apply a combination of the **6A** and **6B** skills.

GO! Think | Project **6M** Location List

Project Files

For Project 6M, you will need the following file:

　　e06M_Locations

You will save your workbook as:

　　Lastname_Firstname_6M_Locations

　　From your student files, open the file e06M_Locations, and then save it in your chapter folder as **Lastname_Firstname_6M_Locations** Select an appropriate SmartArt graphic to visually indicate the cities where Job Fairs will be held, which include Manhattan, White Plains, Albany, Montclair, Hightstown, Newark, Upper Saddle River, and Garden City. Arrange the cities in alphabetic order. Insert the file name in the footer, add appropriate information to the document properties including the keywords **fair locations** and submit as directed by your instructor.

 You have completed Project 6M —————————

Outcomes-Based Assessments

Apply a combination of the **6A** and **6B** skills.

You and GO! | Project **6N** Job Finding

Project Files

For Project 6N, you will need the following file:

New blank Excel workbook

You will save your workbook as:

Lastname_Firstname_6N_Job_Finding

In this chapter, you practiced using Excel to create SmartArt graphics. Think about the steps involved in searching for a job. If necessary, research some Internet sites for assistance. For example, go to *www.bls.gov* and type **Job Search Methods** in the search box. Then, create a visual guide to the job search steps or methods using one of the SmartArt graphics. Save the file in your chapter folder as **Lastname_Firstname_6N_Job_Finding** Format the worksheet attractively for printing, insert the file name in the footer, add appropriate information to the document properties including the keywords **job finding** and submit as directed by your instructor.

End You have completed Project 6N ———————————

Business Running Case

Razvan CHIRNOAGA/Shutterstock

In this project, you will apply the Excel skills you practiced in Chapters 4 through 6. This project relates to **Front Range Action Sports**, which is one of the country's largest retailers of sports gear and outdoor recreation merchandise. The company has large retail stores in Colorado, Washington, Oregon, Idaho, California, and New Mexico, in addition to a growing online business. Major merchandise categories include fishing, camping, rock climbing, winter sports, action sports, water sports, team sports, racquet sports, fitness, golf, apparel, and footwear.

In this project, you will apply skills you practiced from the Objectives in Excel Chapters 4 through 6. You will develop two workbooks for Frank Osei, the Vice President of Finance. You will create a loan payment table and an organization chart for the new Idaho store, develop a phone order form for the newest lines of apparel, create a chart displaying skier attendance, and standardize an expense report template to ensure accurate data entry for winter carnival expenses. Your completed worksheets will look similar to Figure 2.1.

Project Files

For Project BRC2, you will need the following files:

 eBRC2_Expense_Report
 eBRC2_Financial_Report
 eBRC2_Erica
 eBRC2_Kate
 eBRC2_Laura
 eBRC2_Sean
 eBRC2_Tyler

You will save your workbooks as:

 Lastname_Firstname_BRC2_Expense_Template
 Lastname_Firstname_BRC2_Financial_Report

Project Results

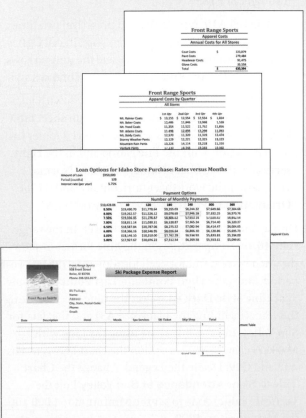

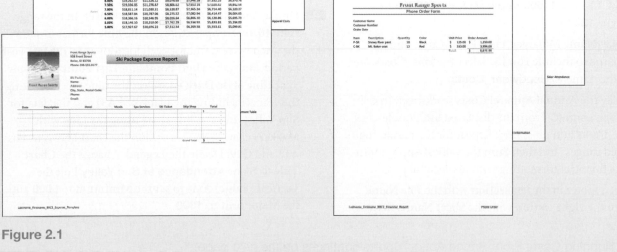

Figure 2.1

Business Running Case 2: Includes Objectives from Excel Chapters 4–6

Business Running Case   **425**

Business Running Case

Front Range Action Sports

1 **Start** Excel. From the student files that accompany this textbook, locate and open **eBRC2_Financial_Report**. In the location where you are storing your projects, create a new folder named **Front Range Action Sports** or navigate to this folder if you have already created it. **Save** the workbook as **Lastname_Firstname_BRC2_Financial_Report**

a. Display the **Idaho Store Payment Table** worksheet. In the range **B9:B16**, enter interest rates in increments of .5% beginning with **8.50%** and ending with **5.00%** Format rates with two decimal places, bold and centered. In cell **B8**, enter a **PMT** function using the information in the range **B2:B4**; be sure to divide the rate by 12 and insert a minus sign to enter the amount of the loan (Pv) as a negative number.

b. Create a **Data Table** in the range **B8:H16** using the information in cells **B2:B4** in which the **Row input cell** is the **Period** and the **Column input cell** is the **Interest rate**. Apply the format from **B8** to the results in the data table. Select the two payment options closest to and less than $8,000 per month and format the two options with the **Note** cell style.

c. Insert a footer in the **left section** with the **File Name** and in the **right section** with the **Sheet Name**. Return to **Normal** view, center the worksheet horizontally, and set the **Orientation** to **Landscape**. **Save** your workbook.

2 Display the **Quarterly Apparel Costs** worksheet, and then apply appropriate **Currency [0]**, **Comma [0]**, and **Total** cell styles. Name the following ranges: **B6:E10 Coat_Costs B11:E14 Pant_Costs B15:E16 Hat_Costs B17:E17 Glove_Costs** Insert a new row 15. In cell **A15**, type **Marmot Mountain Pants** In cell **B15**, type **11200** In cell **C15**, type **11695** In cell **D15**, type **12315** In cell **E15**, type **13275**

a. Display **Name Manager**, click **Pant_Costs** and edit the name to include **row15**. Select the **Hat_Costs**, and edit the name to **Headwear_Costs**

b. Display the **Annual Apparel Costs** worksheet. In cell **B5**, type **=sum(C** From the displayed list, double-click **Coat_Costs** and press Enter. Repeat for the remaining named ranges, and then **Sum** the values. Apply appropriate financial formatting with no decimal places.

c. Insert a footer in the **left section** with the **File Name** and in the **right section** with the **Sheet Name**. Return to **Normal** view, center the worksheet horizontally, and set the **Orientation** to **Portrait**. **Save** your workbook.

3 Display the **Product Information** worksheet. Select the range **A4:C11**, and then **Sort** by **Style Code**. Display the **Phone Order** worksheet. In cell **A9**, type **P-SR** and then press Tab. With cell **B9** as the active cell, insert the **VLOOKUP** function. As the **Lookup_value** box, click cell **A9**. Click in the **Table_array** box, display the **Product Information** worksheet, select the range **A4:C11**, and then press F4 to make the cell reference absolute. In the **Col_index_num** box, type **2** and then click **OK**.

a. With cell **B9** as the active cell, fill the VLOOKUP formula through cell **B18**. In cell **C9**, type **10** as the *Quantity ordered*. Press Tab. In cell **D9**, type **Black** and press Tab. With cell **E9** as the active cell, insert the **VLOOKUP** function. As the **Lookup_value** box, click cell **A9**, and then click in the **Table_array** box. Display the **Product Information** worksheet, select the range **A4:C11**. Press F4. In the **Col_index_num** box, type **3** Click **OK**. Copy the VLOOKUP formula through cell **E18**.

b. Click in cell **A10**, type **C-BK** and press Tab two times. In cell **C10**, type **12** and then press Tab. In cell **D10**, type **Red** and then press Enter. Delete the unused rows, sum the **Order Amount**, and apply the **Total** cell style.

c. Select the **Phone Order sheet tab**, hold down Ctrl, and then select the **Product Information sheet tab**. With the two worksheets selected, **Insert** a footer in the **left section** with the **File Name** and in the **right section** with the **Sheet Name**. Return to **Normal** view, center the worksheet horizontally, and set the **Orientation** to **Portrait**. **Save** your workbook.

4 Display the **Skier Attendance** worksheet. In the range **G4:G10**, insert **Sparklines** in the **Line** format to show the attendance trend for each location over the five-year period. Show the **High Point** and **Last Point** and apply **Sparkline Style Dark #4**. Select the ranges representing the years (including the blank cell **A3**) and the data for **Sun Valley**. Insert a line chart using the **Line with Markers** chart style. Reposition the chart between cells **A13** and **G29**. Delete the **Legend**. Change the **Chart Title** to **Skier Attendance at Sun Valley** Edit the **Vertical (Value) Axis** to set the **Minimum** to **5000** and the **Major unit** to **1000**

(Business Running Case: Front Range Action Sports continues on the next page)

Business Running Case

Front Range Action Sports (continued)

a. Format the **Plot Area** with a solid fill using **Blue, Accent 1, Lighter 80%**. Format the **Chart Area** with a solid fill using **Blue, Accent 1, Lighter 60%**. Change the width of the line to **4.0 pt.** and insert a **Linear Trendline**. Deselect the chart. Insert a footer in the **left section** with the **File Name** and in the **right section** with the **Sheet Name**. Return to **Normal** view, center the worksheet horizontally, and set the **Orientation** to **Portrait**. **Save** your workbook.

5 Display the **Sports Shop Team** worksheet. Insert a SmartArt graphic from the **Hierarchy** for a **Picture Organization Chart**. Position the graphic between cells **A3** and **O21**.

a. Delete the Assistant position box. Beginning at the top of the chart, insert a name, title, and picture for **Sean Thompson, Store Manager eBRC2_Sean**. Insert four staff members, all at the same level, from left to right as follows: **Kate Wallace, Customer Service eBRC2_Kate; Erica Wilson, Customer Service eBRC2_Erica; Tyler Weaver, Ski Technician eBRC2_Tyler;** and **Laura Anneton, Boot Specialist eBRC2_Laura**. Apply SmartArt style, **3-D Polished**.

b. Insert a footer in the **left section** with the **File Name** and in the **right section** with the **Sheet Name**. Return to **Normal** view, center the worksheet horizontally, scale the **Width** to **1 page**, and set the **Orientation** to **Landscape**. **Save** your workbook. Add your name, course information, and the **Keywords financial report** to the Document Panel. **Save** your workbook,

and then print or submit electronically as directed. If required, print or create an electronic version of your worksheets with formulas displayed using the instructions in Activity 1.16 in Project 1A. If you printed your formulas, be sure to redisplay the worksheet by pressing Ctrl + `. **Close** the workbook.

6 Open the file **eBRC2_Expense_Report**. Display the **Save As** dialog box, set **Save as type** to **Excel Template**, navigate to your **Front Range Action Sports** folder, and then **Save** the file as **Lastname_Firstname_BRC2_Expense_Template** In the range **H15:H21**, create formulas to sum the data in each row—do not include *Date* or *Description*. In cell **H22**, create a formula to create a grand total of expenses for each date. Apply appropriate financial formatting to cells that contain expenses. Apply the **Total** cell style to cell **H22**. Select the ranges **D7:F12** and **A15:G21**. Remove the Locked formatting from the selected cells and protect the worksheet. Be sure the top check box and the first two check boxes in the list are selected. As the password, type **goseries** Insert a footer with the **file name** in the **left section**, and then center horizontally. Add your name, course information, and the **Keywords expense report template Save** your template file, and then print or submit electronically as directed. If required, print or create an electronic version of your worksheets with formulas displayed using the instructions in Activity 1.16 in Project 1A. If you printed your formulas, be sure to redisplay the worksheet by pressing Ctrl + `.

End You have completed Business Running Case 2 ————————————

Creating PivotTable and PivotChart Reports and Auditing Worksheets

OUTCOMES

At the end of this chapter you will be able to:

OBJECTIVES

Mastering these objectives will enable you to:

PROJECT 7A

Query large amounts of data, subtotal and aggregate numeric data, and filter and group data to analyze for relationships and trends.

1. Create a PivotTable Report (p. 431)
2. Use Slicers and Search Filters (p. 437)
3. Modify a PivotTable Report (p. 444)
4. Create a PivotChart Report (p. 451)

PROJECT 7B

Audit workbook formulas to locate and correct errors.

5. Trace Precedents and Dependents to Audit Worksheet Formulas (p. 459)
6. Use Error Checking to Audit Worksheet Formulas (p. 466)
7. Use the Watch Window to Monitor Cell Values (p. 470)

haveseen/Shutterstock

In This Chapter

In this chapter, you will create a PivotTable report and a PivotChart report to organize and display data in useful arrangements. Organizations gather large amounts of numerical data, but the data is not useful until it is organized in a manner that reveals patterns or trends. You will subtotal and aggregate numeric data and summarize the data by categories and subcategories. You will extract information from data by organizing the data into groups from which trends, comparisons, patterns, and relationships can be determined, and you will create different views of the data so that more than one pattern or trend can be observed. In this chapter, you will also use Excel's auditing features to help you understand the construction of formulas in a worksheet, and locate and correct any errors.

The projects in this chapter relate to **The City of Orange Blossom Beach**, a coastal city located between Fort Lauderdale and Miami. The city's access to major transportation provides both residents and businesses an opportunity to compete in the global marketplace. Each year the city welcomes a large number of tourists who enjoy the warm climate and beautiful beaches, and who embark on cruises from this major cruise port. The city encourages best environmental practices and partners with cities in other countries to promote sound government at the local level.

Project 7A PivotTable and PivotChart

myitlab
Project 7A Training

Project Activities

In Activities 7.01 through 7.12, you will create a PivotTable report and a PivotChart report that summarize calls handled at Fire Department stations and Police Department precincts during the first quarter of the year for the City of Orange Blossom Beach. Your completed worksheets will look similar to Figure 7.1.

Project Files

For Project 7A, you will need the following file:

e07A_Fire_Police

You will save your workbook as:

Lastname_Firstname_7A_Fire_Police

Project Results

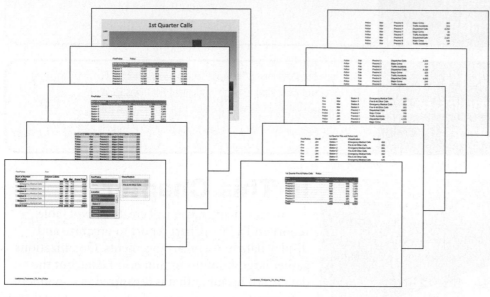

Figure 7.1
Project 7A Fire and Police Calls

Objective 1 | Create a PivotTable Report

A long list of numerical data is not useful until it is organized in a way that is meaningful to the reader. To combine and compare large amounts of data, use Excel's *PivotTable report*—also called simply a *PivotTable*—which is an interactive, cross-tabulated Excel report that summarizes and analyzes large amounts of data. By using a PivotTable report, you can show the same data in a table in more than one arrangement.

For example, you can manipulate the rows and columns of the table to view or summarize the data in different ways. In this manner, you *pivot*—turn—the information around to get varying views of the data. A PivotTable report is especially useful when you want to analyze related totals, such as when you have a long list of numbers to sum and you want to compare several facts about each total.

Activity 7.01 | Creating a PivotTable Report

The data you use to create your PivotTable report should be in the format of a list—a series of rows that contains related data—with column titles in the first row. Subsequent rows should contain data appropriate to its column title, and there should be no blank rows. Excel will use your column titles as the *field names*—the categories of data. The data in each column should be of the same type.

Sam Martinez, Director of Public Safety, prepares quarterly reports about Fire Department and Police Department calls. He tracks the total number of calls at each location grouped by the classifications used by the Fire Department and the Police Department.

To prepare for each City Council meeting, Mr. Martinez needs to know the average number of calls handled by each location during the quarter. He also needs a separate report regarding the number of major crimes reported by each Police Department precinct. Finally, he needs to know which Fire Department station has the lowest number of emergency medical calls during the quarter, in the event the City Council votes to close or combine facilities.

1 **Start** Excel. From your student files, open the file **e07A_Fire_Police**. Display the **Save As** dialog box, navigate to the location where you will store your workbooks for this chapter, and then create a new folder named **Excel Chapter 7** Open your new folder, and then **Save** the workbook as **Lastname_Firstname_7A_Fire_Police**

2 Take a moment to scroll through the worksheet and examine the data.

Recall that a PivotTable report combines and compares large amounts of data. This worksheet displays three months of calls. There are two classifications for Fire Department calls and three classifications for Police Department calls.

To place the information in proper locations on the PivotTable report, think about the questions Mr. Martinez wants to answer. For his internal tracking report, he needs to know the total number of calls handled at each Fire Department station or Police Department precinct during the first quarter—grouped according to the classifications used by the Fire Department and the Police Department.

Another Way

If your source data is already formatted as an Excel table, you can create a PivotTable easily by selecting a single cell within the source data, and then on the **Design tab**, in the **Tools group**, click **Summarize with PivotTable**.

3 Click cell **A2**. On the **Insert tab**, in the **Tables group**, click the **PivotTable button arrow**, and then click **PivotTable**. Compare your screen with Figure 7.2.

The Create PivotTable dialog box displays and a moving border surrounds the range of data—this is referred to as the *source data*. A cell in your data must be active before you create a PivotTable; in this manner you identify the source of your data. Notice that there are two possible sources of data: an Excel table or range in the current worksheet or an external data source, such as an Access database file. A moving border surrounds the data range in the current worksheet.

Figure 7.2

Selected data range surrounded by moving border

Select a table or range option button selected

New Worksheet option button selected

Create PivotTable dialog box

Table/Range indicated as *'Fire and Police Calls'!$A$2:$E$110*

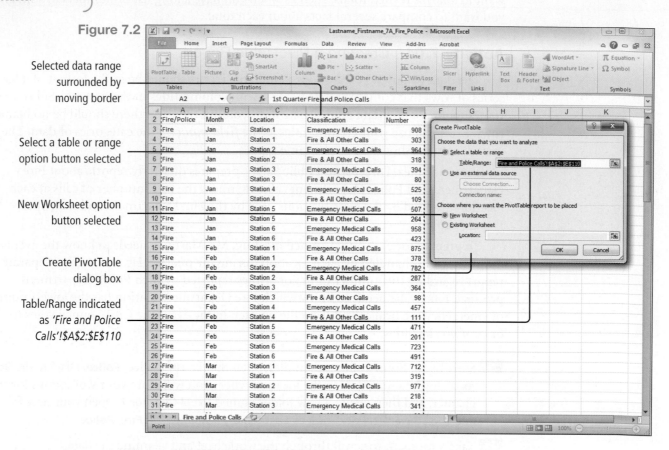

4 In the **Create PivotTable** dialog box, verify that the range of cells indicates '*Fire and Police Calls'!$A$2:$E$110*, and that the **New Worksheet** option button is selected.

The worksheet name *Fire and Police Calls*, indicated on the sheet tab, is included in the identified Table/Range. Because your table of data has no empty columns or rows, and a cell in the table is active, Excel is able to identify the range of data you want to use. You can choose to have the PivotTable report display on a separate sheet—the default setting—or on the same sheet as the data.

5 Click **OK**.

Excel adds a new sheet—Sheet1—to the workbook. On the *left* side of the new worksheet, Excel generates an empty PivotTable report.

On the *right* side of the worksheet, Excel displays the *PivotTable Field List*. The upper portion, referred to as the *field section*, lists the field names—the column titles from your source data. Use the field section to add fields to and remove fields from the PivotTable. The lower portion, referred to as the *layout section*, displays four areas where you can build the PivotTable by rearranging and repositioning fields. On the Ribbon, the PivotTable Tools add two tabs—Options and Design.

6 **Save** 🖫 your workbook, and then take a moment to study Figure 7.3 and the table in Figure 7.4.

Figure 7.3

Column Labels area: position fields to display as columns here

PivotTable Tools tab

PivotTable Field List

Empty PivotTable report

Field section

Values area: position Values fields to be summarized here

Report Filter area: position field by which to filter report here

Layout section

New sheet added

Row Labels area: position fields to display as rows here

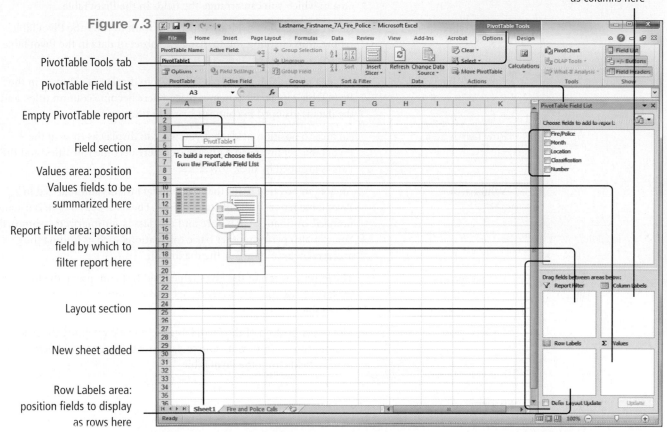

Excel | Chapter 7

Alert! | **Does the PivotTable Field List Not Display?**

If the PivotTable Field List is not visible, click any cell in the empty PivotTable report to display it. If you accidently click the Close button at the upper right corner of the PivotTable Field List, you can redisplay it by clicking any cell in the PivotTable report to display the PivotTable Tools tabs on the Ribbon. On the Options tab, in the Show group, click Field List.

PivotTable Screen Elements	
Screen Element	**Description**
PivotTable Field List	A window that lists, at the top, all of the fields—column titles—from the source data for use in the PivotTable report and at the bottom, an area in which you can arrange the fields in the PivotTable.
Report Filter area	An area to position fields by which you want to filter the PivotTable report, thus enabling you to display a subset of data in the PivotTable report.
Column Labels area	An area to position fields that you want to display as columns in the PivotTable report. Field names placed here become column titles, and the data is grouped in columns by these titles.
Row Labels area	An area to position fields that you want to display as rows in the PivotTable report. Field names placed here become row titles, and the data is grouped by these row titles.
Values area	An area to position fields that contain data that is summarized in a PivotTable report or PivotChart report. The data placed here is usually numeric or financial in nature and the data is summarized—summed. You can also perform other basic calculations such as finding the average, the minimum, or the maximum.
Layout section	The lower portion of the PivotTable Field List containing the four areas for layout; use this area to rearrange and reposition fields in the PivotTable.
Field section	The upper portion of the PivotTable Field List containing the fields—column titles—from your source data; use this area to add fields to and remove fields from the PivotTable.

Figure 7.4

Activity 7.02 | Adding Fields to a PivotTable Report

Recall that a PivotTable report can combine and compare large amounts of data for the purpose of analyzing related totals. By viewing the combined information in different ways, you can answer questions. Mr. Martinez, for example, wants to know how many calls of every classification were handled by each Fire Department station and Police Department precinct during the first quarter.

There are two ways to place the data from your list into the PivotTable report. From the PivotTable Field List, you can drag field names from the field section at the top and then drop them into one of the four areas in the layout section at the bottom. Or, you can select a field name in the field section at the top, and Excel will place the field in a default location based on the field's data type. If you want an arrangement other than the one you get by default, you can move fields from one location to another by simply dragging them between the various areas in the layout section.

1 On the right side of the worksheet, in the **PivotTable Field List**, in the **field section**, select the **Fire/Police** check box. Notice that Excel places the field in the **Row Labels area** of the **layout section**.

By default, non-numeric fields are added to the Row Labels area and numeric fields are added to the Values area, but you can move fields as desired.

Another Way

In the **Row Labels area**, click the **Fire/Police** arrow, and then click **Move to Report Filter**.

2 In the **layout section**, in the **Row Labels area**, point to **Fire/Police**, hold down the left mouse button, and then drag the field name upward into the **Report Filter area** above. Compare your screen with Figure 7.5.

Mr. Martinez wants to use the PivotTable report to analyze the call data by Department—either Fire Department calls or Police Department calls. To do so, filter the report based on the *Fire/Police* field by moving this field to the Report Filter area. The Report Filter filters the entire report based on this field.

As you drag, a small blue icon attaches to the mouse pointer to indicate you are moving a field. *Fire/Police* displays in the Report Filter area. On the left, the Fire/Police field is added at the top of the PivotTable report.

Figure 7.5

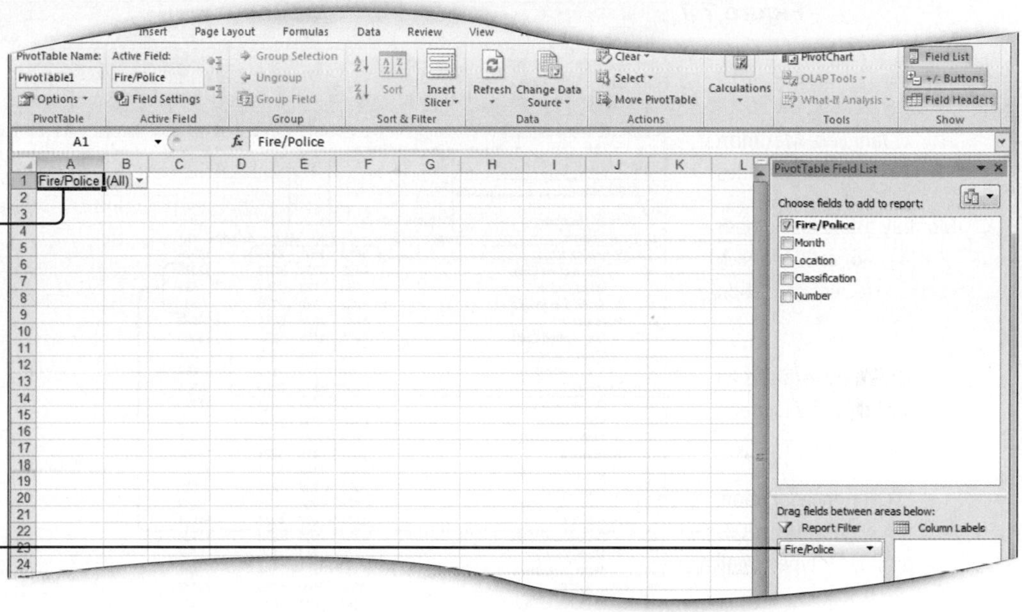

Fire/Police field added to the PivotTable report

Fire/Police field moved to Report Filter area

3 In the **PivotTable Field List**, in the **field section**, select the **Location** field check box.

In the layout section, the Location field displays in the Row Labels area. The Location names—Precincts and Stations—display as rows in the PivotTable report. There are eight Police Department precincts and six Fire Department stations. Recall that by default, non-numeric fields are added to the Row Labels area.

4 In the **PivotTable Field List**, in the **field section**, select the **Classification** field check box. Compare your screen with Figure 7.6.

In the layout section, the Classification field displays as the second field in the Row Labels area. The Classification names are added as indented row headings under each Police Department precinct location and under each Fire Department station location. In this manner, a row that is lower in position in the Row Labels area is *nested* within the row immediately above it. Notice that, under each precinct location, only the call classifications related to the Police Department display. Likewise, as you scroll down, under station locations, only the call classifications related to the Fire Department display.

Figure 7.6

For each Location row (Precinct or Station), Indented Classification rows display

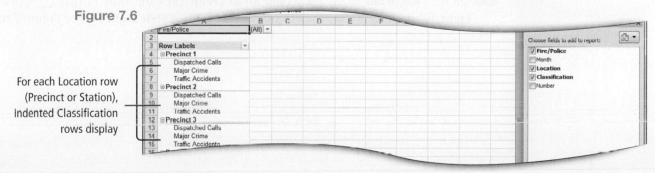

5 In the **PivotTable Field List**, from the **field section**, drag the **Month** field down to the **Column Labels area**. Then, in the **field section**, right-click the **Number** field, and then on the displayed list, click **Add to Values**. Compare your screen with Figure 7.7.

Use any of these techniques to place fields in the layout section. The arrangement of fields in the layout section reflects the arrangement of the data in the PivotTable report.

The PivotTable report is complete; the result is a group of related totals. The long list of figures from the Fire and Police Calls worksheet is summarized, and you can make comparisons among the data. *Sum of Number* displays in cell A3, which refers to the field name *Number*—the number of calls for each call classification has been summed.

Figure 7.7

Jan, Feb, Mar form Column titles

Monthly totals for number of calls for each Precinct or Station

Quarterly totals of all call types by location

For each location, quarterly totals display by type of call

Values area indicates the Number field is summed

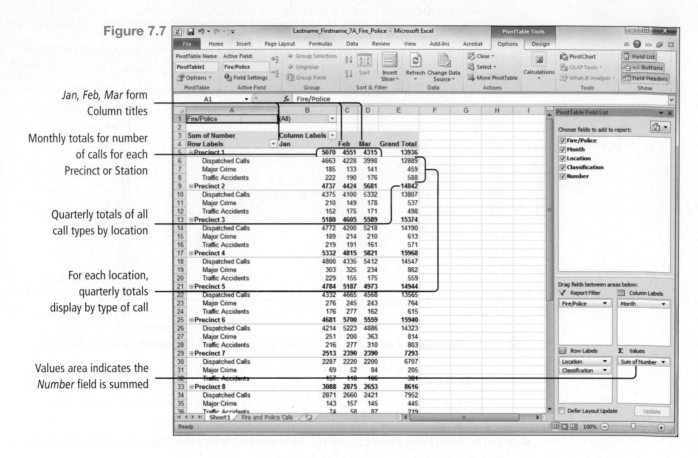

6 Click cell **B5**, point to the selected cell, and then notice the ScreenTip that displays.

Now that the data is organized and the number of calls calculated, you can view and compare various facts about the data. For example, you can see that in January, in Precinct 1, there was a total of 5,070 calls, compared with 4,551 calls in February. This summary information was not available in the original worksheet. By summarizing and pivoting (turning) data in various ways, you can see different information.

7 On the **Design tab**, in the **PivotTable Styles group**, click the **More** button ⊡. Under **Light**, in the second row, click the sixth style—**Pivot Style Light 12**. See Figure 7.8.

Figure 7.8

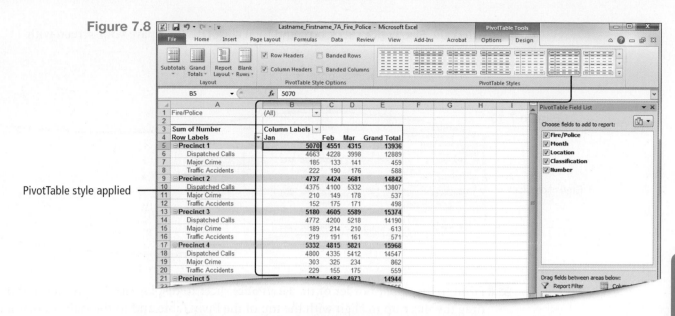

8 **Close** ⊠ the **PivotTable Field List**, and then **Save** 🖫 your workbook.

Objective 2 | Use Slicers and Search Filters

Activity 7.03 | Using a Slicer to Filter a PivotTable

You can *filter*—limit the display of data to only specific information—a PivotTable by using a search filter or by using *slicers*. Slicers are easy-to-use filtering controls with buttons that enable you to intuitively drill down through large amounts of data in an interactive way. Slicers display as movable floating objects on your worksheet in the same manner as charts and shapes.

Limiting the data displayed enables you to focus on parts of the data without the distraction of data you do not need to see. Mr. Martinez wants to limit the data to only the Fire Department information and then determine which Fire Department station had the lowest number of emergency medical calls. Then he wants to hide that station and look at the numbers for the remaining stations.

1 On the **Options tab**, in the **Sort & Filter group**, click the **Insert Slicer button arrow**, and then click **Insert Slicer**. Compare your screen with Figure 7.9.

The Insert Slicers dialog box displays all the field names from your PivotTable report.

Figure 7.9

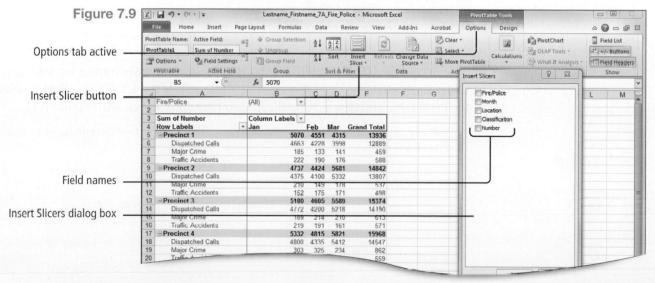

2 Select the **Fire/Police** check box, and then click **OK**. Compare your screen with Figure 7.10.

The Fire/Police slicer displays.

Figure 7.10

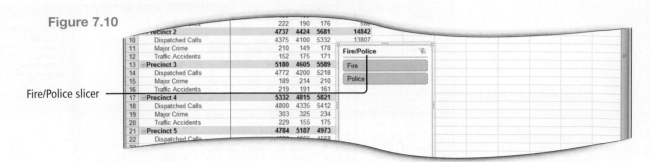

Fire/Police slicer

3 Point to the upper border of the **Fire/Police** slicer to display the ⬚ pointer, and then drag the slicer up to align with the top of the PivotTable and to the right so that it is not blocking your view of the PivotTable.

4 Point to the lower sizing handle on the **Fire/Police** slicer list until the ⬚ pointer displays, and then drag upward to shorten the length of the slicer to just below **Police**. Compare your screen with Figure 7.11.

A slicer includes a ***slicer header*** that indicates the category of the slicer items, ***filtering buttons*** to select the item by which to filter, and a ***Clear Filter*** button. When a filtering button is selected, the item is included in the filter. The Clear Filter button removes a filter. You can move a slicer to another location on the worksheet, and resize it as needed.

Figure 7.11

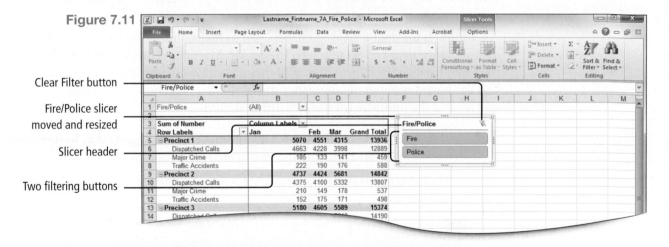

Clear Filter button

Fire/Police slicer moved and resized

Slicer header

Two filtering buttons

5 On the **Options tab**, in the **Slicer Styles group**, click the **More** button ⬚, and then under **Dark**, click the second slicer style—**Slicer Style Dark 2**. Click cell **A1** to select the PivotTable and deselect the slicer. Compare your screen with Figure 7.12.

You can apply various styles to slicers to make them easier to differentiate or to match the PivotTable report.

Figure 7.12

Cell A1 selected

Fire/Police field list slicer style changed

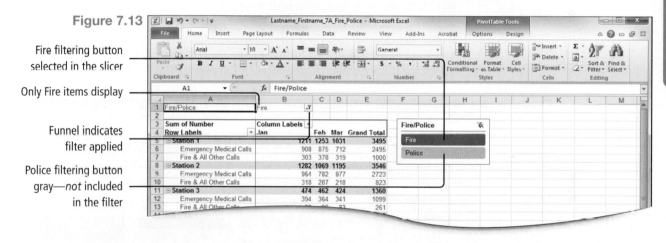

6 In the PivotTable report, notice that the Police Department precincts display first. Then, on the **Fire/Police slicer**, click the **Fire** filtering button, move your pointer out of the slicer, and then compare your screen with Figure 7.13.

> The records for the Police Department precincts are hidden and only the Fire Department station items display. Recall that filtering displays only the data that you want to see. A filtering button that is not selected—displays in gray—indicates that the item is *not* included in the filtered list. By looking at this slicer, you can see that only Fire items are included. Because slicers indicate the current filtering state, it is easy to see exactly what is shown in the PivotTable report—and also to see what is *not* shown.

Figure 7.13

Fire filtering button selected in the slicer

Only Fire items display

Funnel indicates filter applied

Police filtering button gray—*not* included in the filter

7 If necessary, click in cell A3 to select the PivotTable. On the **Options tab**, in the **Sort & Filter group**, click the **Insert Slicer button arrow**, and then click **Insert Slicer**. In the **Insert Slicers** dialog box, select the **Classification** check box, and then click **OK**.

8 Drag the **Classification slicer** to the right of the **Fire/Police slicer**, and then resize the field list to remove the blank area below **Traffic Accidents**. Notice that call classifications associated with the Police Department—*Dispatched Calls*, *Major Crime*, and *Traffic Accidents*—are dimmed.

> Because the PivotTable is currently filtered by Fire, no filters related to Police are available.

9 Display the **Slicer Styles** gallery, and then apply **Slicer Style Dark 3**. If necessary, widen the slicer to view the entire name of each filtering button, click cell **A1** to select the PivotTable, and then compare your screen with Figure 7.14.

Project 7A: PivotTable and PivotChart | **Excel** **439**

Excel | Chapter 7

Figure 7.14

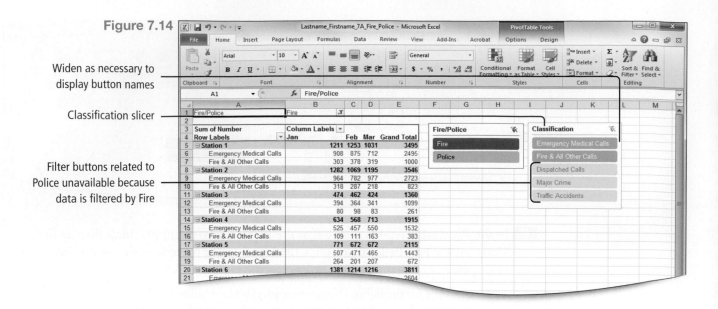

Widen as necessary to display button names

Classification slicer

Filter buttons related to Police unavailable because data is filtered by Fire

10 On the **Classification slicer**, click the **Emergency Medical Calls** filtering button, and then compare your screen with Figure 7.15.

> The data is further filtered by the call classification *Emergency Medical Calls*; that is, only Fire Department station items with *Emergency Medical Calls* as the call classification displays in the PivotTable report. Now, at a glance, Mr. Martinez can see which Fire Department station had the lowest number of emergency medical calls. Mr. Martinez may want to investigate this further to find the reason for the low number and to determine if the number is up or down from previous quarters.

Figure 7.15

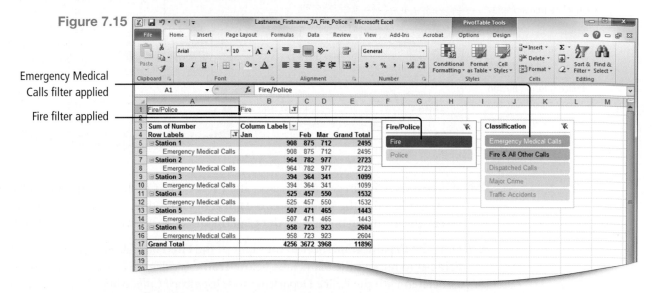

Emergency Medical Calls filter applied

Fire filter applied

11 With cell **A1** active, on the **Options tab**, in the **Sort & Filter group**, click the **Insert Slicer button arrow**, and then click **Insert Slicer**. In the **Insert Slicers** dialog box, select the **Location** check box, and then click **OK**.

12 Drag the **Location slicer** below the **Fire/Police slicer**, and notice that the **Precinct** filtering buttons are dimmed.

> Because the PivotTable is already filtered by Fire Department stations, and no Police Department precincts display in the PivotTable, the Precinct filtering buttons are dimmed—unavailable—for filtering in the current arrangement.

13 Shorten the **Location slicer** to display only the Stations, and then from the **Slicer Styles** gallery, apply **Slicer Style Dark 4**. Click cell **A1**, and then compare your screen with Figure 7.16.

> For each field of data in the PivotTable, you can display a slicer to enable ways to slice— display a thin piece of—the data in meaningful ways.

Figure 7.16

Location slicer with Slicer Style Dark 4 applied; resized to show only Fire Department stations

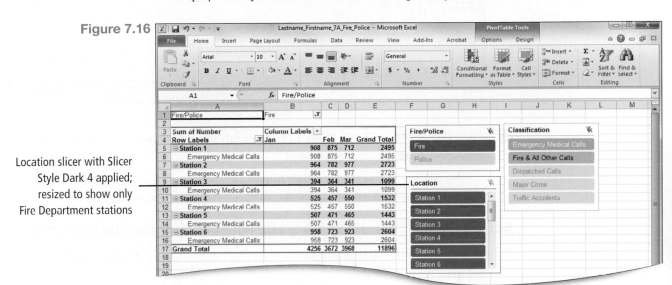

14 To display all the stations *except* Station 3, hold down Ctrl, and then in the **Location slicer**, click the **Station 3** filtering button. Release Ctrl, move the pointer away from the PivotTable, and then compare your screen with Figure 7.17.

> Use the Ctrl key in this manner to select all the filtering buttons *except* the one that you click. In the Location slicer, Stations 1, 2, 4, 5, and 6 are selected and Station 3 is not. In the PivotTable report, the Station 3 data is hidden, and only the data for Stations 1, 2, 4, 5, and 6 displays.

> The number of Emergency Medical Calls for the remaining Fire Department stations range from a low of 457 in February at Station 4 to a high of 977 in March at Station 2. The Grand Total recalculates to reflect only the five stations currently displayed.

Figure 7.17

Emergency Medical Calls filter applied

Station 3 data does *not* display

All Station filtering buttons selected *except* Station 3

Grand Total recalculated

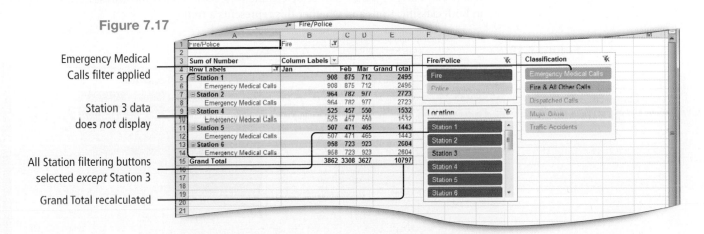

15 In the sheet tab area at the lower left of your screen, point to the **Sheet1** sheet tab, right-click, and then on the shortcut menu, click **Move or Copy**. In the **Move or Copy** dialog box, at the lower left, select the **Create a copy** check box. Compare your screen with Figure 7.18.

Excel | Chapter 7

Figure 7.18

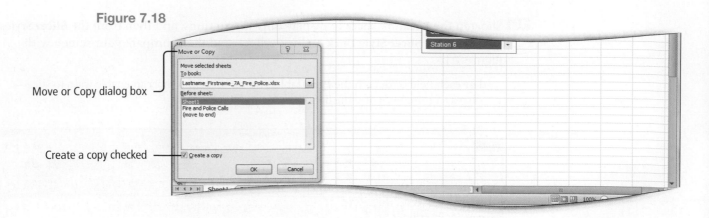

Move or Copy dialog box

Create a copy checked

16 Click **OK**. Right-click the **Sheet 1 (2)** sheet tab, click **Rename**, type **Slicers** and then press Enter. **Save** 🖫 your workbook.

> The sheet is copied and renamed. In this worksheet, your instructor will be able to verify that you have filtered the worksheet using slicers and the slicers are formatted.

Activity 7.04 | Clearing Filters and Filtering by Using the Search Box

Using the Search Filter is another way to filter data in a PivotTable report and find relevant information easily.

1 At the bottom of the Excel window, in the **sheet tabs area**, click the **Sheet1 sheet tab** to display this worksheet.

2 In the **Sheet1** worksheet, in the **Location slicer**, click the **Clear Filter** button 🔖.

> This action clears all the filters within a slicer; therefore, the data for all six Fire Department stations displays.

3 In the **Classification slicer**, click the **Fire & All Other Calls** filtering button, and then compare your screen with Figure 7.19.

> Clicking a filtering button cancels the selection of another filtering button, unless you hold down the Ctrl key to include multiple filters. By examining this data, Mr. Martinez can see that Station 3 also has the lowest number of *Fire & All Other Calls*. Mr. Martinez will need to investigate further to determine why Station 3 has the lowest number of calls in both classifications and whether this represents a trend.

Figure 7.19

Classification filtered by *Fire & All Other Calls*

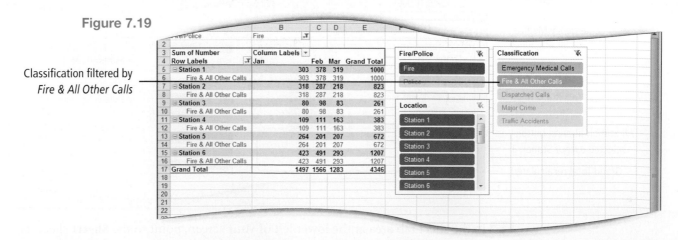

4 In the **Classification slicer**, click the **Clear Filter** button ☒. In the **Fire/Police** slicer, click the **Clear Filter** button ☒.

No filters are applied and data from both the Police Department and the Fire Department displays.

5 Point to the **Fire/Police slicer header** and right-click. On the shortcut menu, click **Remove "Fire/Police"**. By using the same technique, remove the **Location slicer** and the **Classification slicer**.

6 Click cell **A1** to select the PivotTable, and then on the **Options tab**, in the **Show group**, click the **Field List** button to display the **PivotTable Field List**. In the **field section**, point to **Location**, and then on the right, click the **Location arrow**. On the displayed list, click in the **Search** box, type **Station 3** and then click **OK**. Compare your screen with Figure 7.20.

The filter is applied and only Station 3 data displays.

Figure 7.20

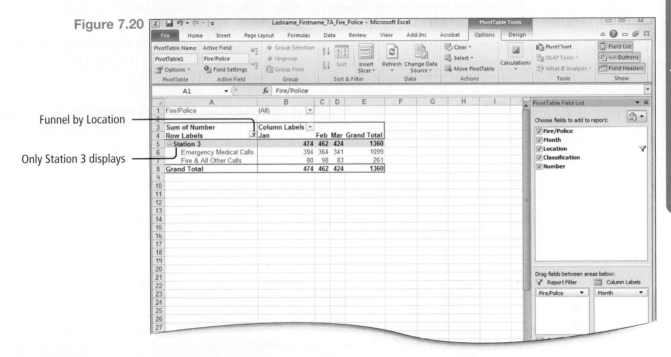

Funnel by Location

Only Station 3 displays

7 With cell **A1** still active, on the **Options tab**, in the **Actions group**, click the **Clear** button, and then click **Clear Filters**.

You can also clear filters by using this command.

8 **Save** 🖫 your workbook.

Objective 3 | Modify a PivotTable Report

You have seen how, after you have added fields to the PivotTable report, you can pivot (turn) the information in various ways; for example, by removing or rearranging the fields. With different views of your data, you can answer different questions. You can display a field as a column rather than a row. You can display parts of the data on separate pages; for example by creating separate pages for the Fire Department calls and Police Department calls. After data is displayed in a useful way, you can format it using any methods you have practiced.

Activity 7.05 | Rearranging a PivotTable Report

In the Fire/Police PivotTable report, a large amount of detail information displays. Although totals display for both the rows and the columns for each location and for each classification, it is still difficult for a reader to make comparisons across precincts and stations. Mr. Martinez needs to be able to respond to questions from City Council members representing different sections of the city. He must know the average number of service calls by department, by classification, and by precinct or station. For the City Council meeting, he does not need to see the monthly detail. In this activity, you will remove and rearrange fields to produce arrangements of this data that will be useful for answering questions at the City Council meeting.

> **Another Way**
>
> Click the **Month** arrow, and then click **Remove Field**.

1 In the **layout section** of the **Pivot Table Field List**, from the **Column Labels area**, drag the **Month** field name upward into the white **field section**—a black X attaches to the pointer as you drag—and then release the mouse button. Compare your screen with Figure 7.21.

The X indicates that the field is being removed from the PivotTable report. When you release the mouse button, the details for each month no longer display in the PivotTable report; only the quarterly totals for the various call classifications at each location display. In PivotTable Field List, *Month* is no longer selected or bold.

Figure 7.21

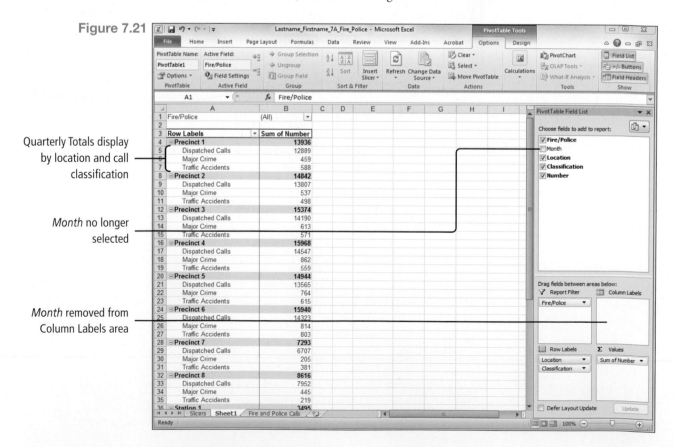

Quarterly Totals display by location and call classification

Month no longer selected

Month removed from Column Labels area

2 In the **layout section** of the **PivotTable Field List**, from the **Row Labels area**, drag the **Classification** field into the **Column Labels area**. Compare your screen with Figure 7.22.

By moving *Classification* from the Row Labels area to the Column Labels area, the various classifications become column titles instead of row titles. The classifications are arranged alphabetically across columns B:F. Now the police-related calls—Dispatched Calls, Major Crime, and Traffic Accidents—display as separate classifications.

Figure 7.22

Classifications display as column headings in B4:F4

Police-related calls (*Dispatched Calls, Major Crime,* and *Traffic Accidents*) as separate classifications

Only one level of row titles—the *Locations*

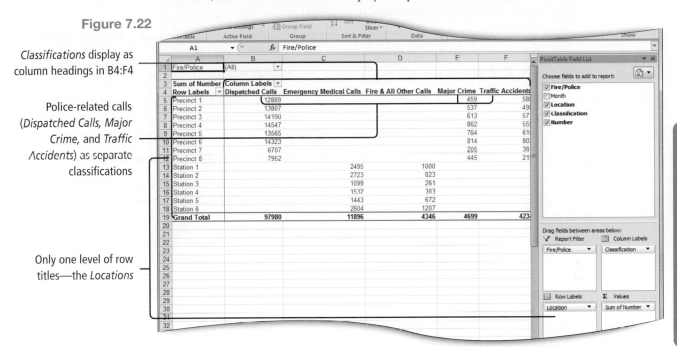

3 **Close** ⊠ the **PivotTable Field List**. Click cell **B4**—the column title *Dispatched Calls*. Right-click to display a shortcut menu, point to **Move**, and then click **Move "Dispatched Calls" Right**.

The Dispatched Calls column moves one column to the right.

4 Click cell **C4**, and then use the same technique to move the **Dispatched Calls** column to the right one column again. **Save** 🖫 your workbook, and then compare your screen with Figure 7.23.

By placing the three police-related call classifications adjacent to one another, you have a clearer view of the activity by location.

Figure 7.23

Police call classifications grouped together

Dispatched Calls column moved to Column D

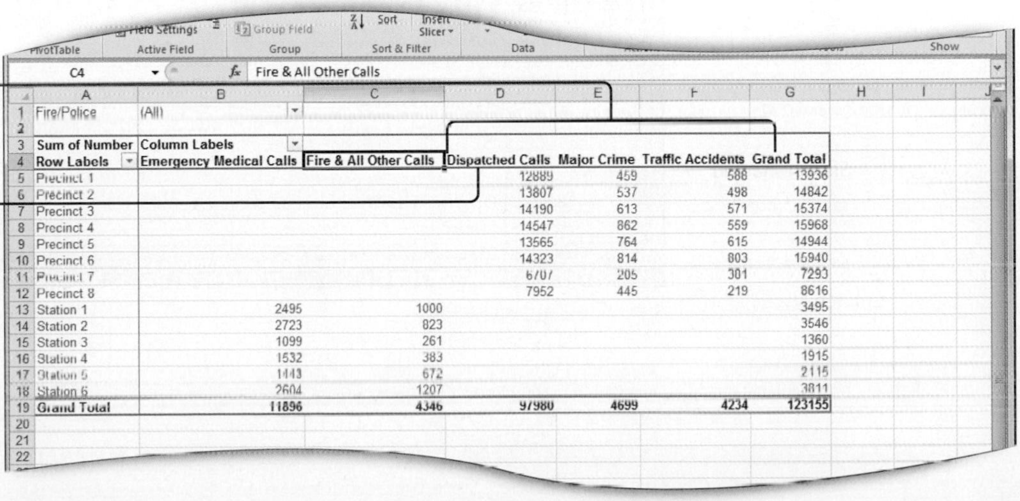

Activity 7.06 | Displaying PivotTable Report Details in a New Worksheet

From the PivotTable report, you can display details for a particular category of information in a separate worksheet. Mr. Martinez needs a separate report showing major crimes reported each month by precinct.

1 Click cell **E19**—the total for the *Major Crime* classification—and then point to the selected cell to view the ScreenTip.

To display the Major Crime field as a separate report, first select the total. Recall that the ScreenTips provide details about the cell's contents.

Another Way
Double-click a total to display the data on a new worksheet.

2 Right-click cell **E19**, and then click **Show Details**.

A new sheet—*Sheet3*—is added to your workbook, and the records for the Major Crime calls display, along with the other fields from the Excel source data. Notice that the *Month* field is included, even though that field is not used in the PivotTable report.

3 In cell **E1**, click the **filter arrow**, and then click **Sort Largest to Smallest**.

The data is sorted in descending order by the number of Major Crime calls that were handled by all precincts during the first quarter. A down arrow displays in the Number filter arrow to indicate a descending sort.

4 Rename the **Sheet3** tab **Major Crimes** Click cell **A1** to deselect the data, and then **Save** 💾 your workbook. Compare your screen with Figure 7.24.

Figure 7.24

Major Crime calls sorted from highest number to lowest number

Cell A1 active

Sheet renamed

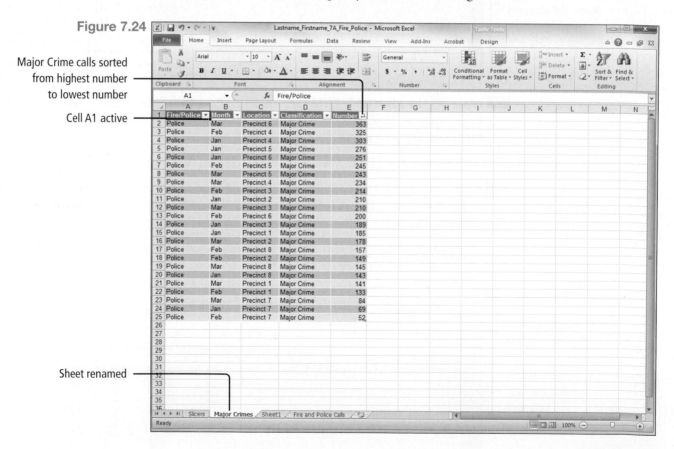

Activity 7.07 | Displaying PivotTable Data on Separate Pages

Recall that Mr. Martinez wanted to analyze the call data by Department—Police Department and Fire Department. To do so, you moved the Fire/Police field to the Report Filter area and filtered the entire report on this field.

Adding a field to the Report Filter area is optional; however, if the report is filtered in this manner, you can display multiple pages for your PivotTable data. For example, you can display the Fire Department calls on one page and the Police Department calls on another page. Doing so will make it easier to answer questions about the calls handled by each Department.

1 Click the **Sheet1 tab**, and then rename it **Combined Calls PivotTable**

2 Click cell **A1** to select the PivotTable report. On the **Options tab**, at the left end of the Ribbon in the **PivotTable group**, if necessary click the PivotTable button arrow, and then click the **Options button arrow**. (The button arrangement varies depending on your screen resolution.) Click **Show Report Filter Pages**. In the displayed dialog box, click **OK**.

> Because the Fire/Police field was placed in the Report Filter area, this action adds two new sheets to the workbook, one labeled *Fire* and another labeled *Police*.

3 Click the **Police sheet tab**.

> The data for the Police Department calls displays on a separate sheet. The data remains in the form of a PivotTable—you can move fields from a row position to a column position and vice versa.

4 Click the **Fire sheet tab**. **Save** 🖫 your workbook, and then compare your screen with Figure 7.25.

> The data for the Fire calls displays on a separate sheet.

Figure 7.25

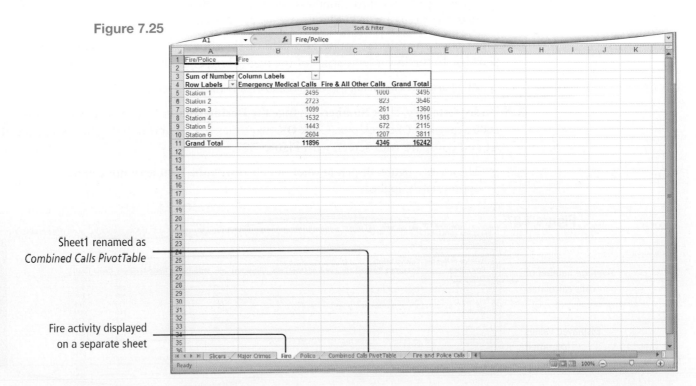

Sheet1 renamed as *Combined Calls PivotTable*

Fire activity displayed on a separate sheet

Activity 7.08 | Changing Calculations in a PivotTable Report

A PivotTable report combines and compares large amounts of data so that you can analyze related totals. The default calculation in a PivotTable report is to *sum* the numeric data. You can modify the calculation to display an average, minimum, maximum, or some other calculation. Here, Mr. Martinez needs to report the *average* number of calls for the first quarter.

Another Way

On the **Options tab**, in the **Active Field group**, click the **Field Settings** button.

1 Display the **Combined Calls PivotTable** worksheet. Point to any cell containing numerical data, right-click, and then click **Value Field Settings**.

The Value Field Settings dialog box displays. In the Custom Name box, *Sum of Number* displays; in the Summarize value field by list, *Sum* is selected.

2 Under **Summarize value field by**, click **Average**. Compare your screen with Figure 7.26.

The Custom Name box displays *Average of Number*.

Figure 7.26

Custom Name box indicates Average of Number

Summary calculation changed to Average

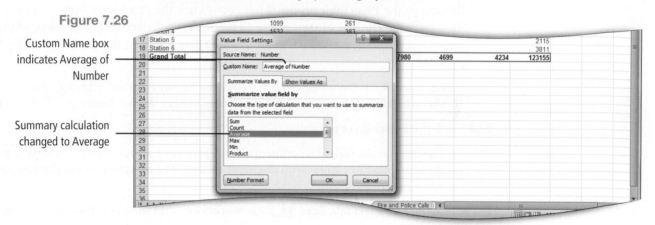

3 Click **OK**.

An average for the three months is calculated and displays with six or seven decimal places in the data cells. Cell A3 indicates *Average of Number*.

4 Right-click any numeric value, and then on the shortcut menu, click **Value Field Settings**. In the lower left corner of the dialog box, click the **Number Format** button.

The Format Cells dialog box displays, with only the Number tab included.

5 Under **Category**, click **Number**. Change the **Decimal places** box to **0**. Select the **Use 1000 Separator (,)** check box. Click **OK** two times to close both dialog boxes. Click cell **A1** and compare your screen with Figure 7.27.

The average figures display as whole numbers with the 1000 separator comma appropriately applied.

Figure 7.27

Average number of calls calculated

Displayed values formatted

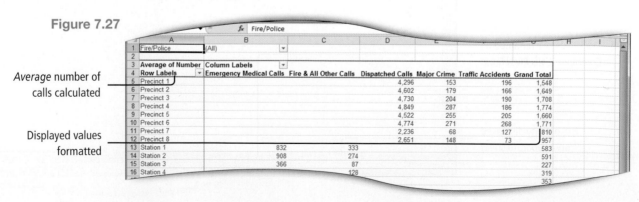

6 **Save** your workbook.

Activity 7.09 | Formatting a PivotTable Report

You can apply a PivotTable Style to the entire PivotTable report and change field names to make them easier to understand. For example, the field name *Average of Number* would be easier to understand as *Average Number of Calls*.

1 Click cell **A1**, type **1st Quarter Fire & Police Calls** and then press Enter.

2 Click cell **A3**, type **Average Number of Calls** and then press Enter. AutoFit **column A**.

3 On the **Design tab**, in the **PivotTable Styles group**, click the **More** button ⏷.

4 Under **Medium**, in the first row, click the second style—**Pivot Style Medium 2**. Click cell **G4** and type **Average** and then press Enter. Notice that cell **A19** changes to *Average*. Compare your screen with Figure 7.28.

Figure 7.28

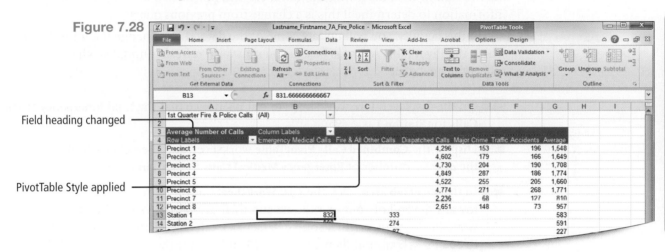

Field heading changed

PivotTable Style applied

5 Display the **Police** worksheet. On the **Design tab**, in the **PivotTable Styles group**, display the **PivotTable Styles** gallery, and then under **Medium**, in the first row apply the fourth style—**Pivot Style Medium 4**.

6 Point to any numerical value, right-click, and then click **Value Field Settings**. In the lower left corner, click the **Number Format** button. Under **Category**, click **Number**. Change the **Decimal places** box to **0**, and then select the **Use 1000 Separator (,)** check box. Click **OK** two times to close both dialog boxes. Click cell **A1**, and then compare your screen with Figure 7.29.

Figure 7.29

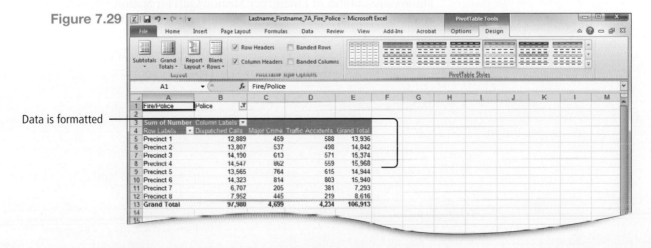

Data is formatted

7 Display the **Fire** worksheet. Using the techniques you just practiced, apply the **Pivot Style Medium 6** style to this PivotTable and format the numbers to display using the 1000 comma separator with no decimal places.

8 Save 🖫 your workbook.

Activity 7.10 | Updating PivotTable Report Data

In the previous activities, you created a combined PivotTable report to display the *average* number of calls by classification type for the Police Department precincts and the Fire Department stations. You created a separate PivotTable report for Fire and for Police to show the *total* number of calls for the quarter by Location and Classification. You also created a separate list of the major crimes by precinct. Finally, Station 3 was identified as the fire station with the lowest call numbers; Mr. Martinez plans to gather supporting information to determine if this is a change from previous quarters.

In this activity, you will update some of the data. If you change the underlying data on which the PivotTable report is based, you must also *refresh*—update—the PivotTable to reflect the new data.

1 On the displayed **Fire** worksheet, in cell **B5**, notice that the total **Emergency Medical Calls** for **Station 1** is *2,495*.

2 Display the **Combined Calls PivotTable** worksheet, and then click cell **B13**. Notice that the *average* number of **Emergency Medical Calls** for **Station 1** is *832*.

3 In the **sheet tab area**, click the **Last Worksheet** button ▶| to view the worksheets toward the end of your workbook, and then display the **Fire and Police Calls** worksheet—your original source data. Click cell **E3** and change the number from *908* to **808** Press [Enter], and then click cell **E15** and change the number from *875* to **775** and press [Enter].

> The calls for January and February were both mistakenly overstated by 100 calls and are reduced from 908 and 875 to 808 and 775, respectively.

4 Display the **Combined Calls PivotTable** worksheet. Although you adjusted the underlying data, notice that in cell **B13**, the average number of Emergency Medical Calls for Station 1 has not changed—it still indicates *832*.

5 On the **Options tab**, in the **Data group**, click the **Refresh All button arrow**, and then click **Refresh**. Compare your screen with Figure 7.30.

> The average number of Emergency Medical Calls for Station 1 updates to *765*, and the average for this type of call from all stations changes to *650*.

Figure 7.30

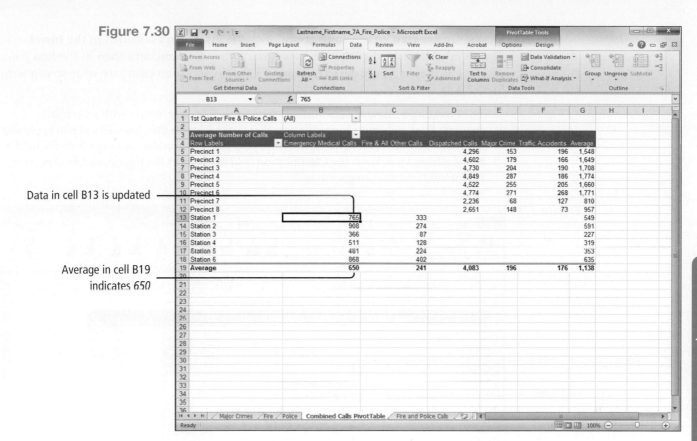

Data in cell B13 is updated

Average in cell B19 indicates *650*

6 Display the **Fire** worksheet, and then click cell **B5**. Notice that the total number of Emergency Medical Calls for Station 1 has been updated to *2,295*. **Save** 💾 your workbook.

Objective 4 | Create a PivotChart Report

A **PivotChart report** is a graphical representation of the data in a PivotTable report—referred to as the **associated PivotTable report**. A PivotChart report always has an associated PivotTable and the two are interactive; that is, if you change the field layout or data in the associated PivotTable report, the changes are immediately reflected in the PivotChart report. The reverse is also true. A PivotChart report and its associated PivotTable report must be in the same workbook.

Most of the operations you have practiced in standard charts work the same way in a PivotChart. A PivotChart report displays data series, categories, data markers, and axes in the same manner as a standard chart, and you can format them. There are some differences; for example, whereas standard charts are linked directly to a range of worksheet cells, PivotChart reports are based on the data source of the associated PivotTable report.

Activity 7.11 | Creating a PivotChart Report from a PivotTable Report

Mr. Martinez wants to analyze Police calls—specifically the calls related to Major Crime and Traffic Accidents—and he thinks that a chart would be useful to City Council members to convey this information.

1 Display the **Combined Calls PivotTable** worksheet, and then press `Ctrl` + `Home` to make cell **A1** the active cell and to select the PivotTable.

2 On the **Options tab**, in the **Tools group**, click the **PivotChart** button. On the **Insert Chart** dialog box, on the left side, if necessary, click **Column**, and then in the first row, click the first chart—**Clustered Column**. Click **OK**, and then compare your screen with Figure 7.31.

> The PivotChart displays *field buttons*. You can click on any button with an arrow to choose a filter and thus change the data that is displayed in the chart. Filters you apply will be reflected in the PivotTable report. After your chart is complete, you can hide the field buttons from view. Here, the Classification field items form the legend, and the Location field items form the category axis.

Figure 7.31

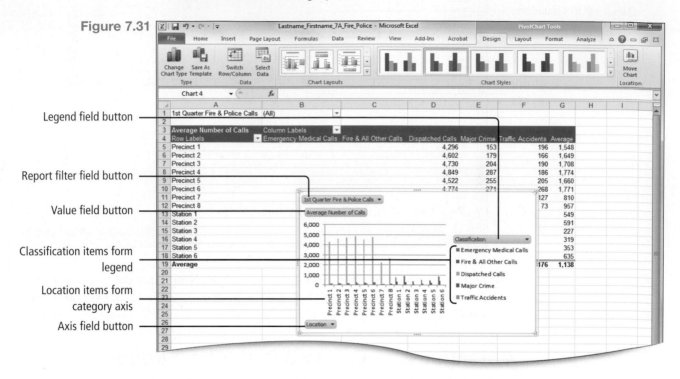

Legend field button

Report filter field button

Value field button

Classification items form legend

Location items form category axis

Axis field button

3 On the **Design tab**, in the **Location group**, click the **Move Chart** button. In the **Move Chart** dialog box, click the **New sheet** option button, replace the highlighted text *Chart1* by typing **1st Quarter Chart** and then click **OK**.

4 In the new chart sheet, on the **Design tab**, in the **Chart Layouts group**, click the **More** button, and then click the third chart layout—**Layout 3**—which includes a chart title and places the legend at the bottom of the chart. In the **Chart Styles group**, click the **More** button, and then apply **Style 26**.

5 Click the **Chart Title** and watch the **Formula Bar** as you type **1st Quarter Calls** and press Enter to display the title text in the chart. Compare your screen with Figure 7.32.

Figure 7.32

Chart Layout 3 applied

Chart Title

Legend at bottom

Chart displays on chart sheet

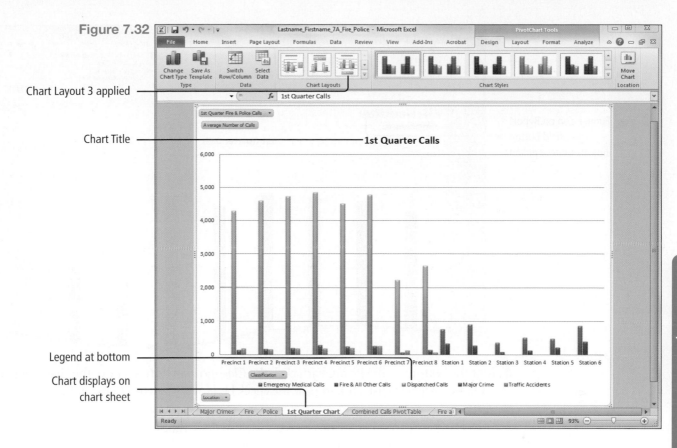

6 On the **Insert tab**, in the **Text group**, click the **Header & Footer** button. In the **Page Setup** dialog box, click the **Custom Footer** button. With the insertion point in the **left section**, from the small toolbar in the dialog box, click the **Insert File Name** button 🖼. Click **OK** two times. **Save** 🖫 your workbook.

Activity 7.12 | Modifying a PivotChart Report

You can filter and change the values of the data in the PivotChart report by using the gray field buttons that display on the chart. Recall that you can click on any button with an arrow to choose a filter, and that filters you apply will be reflected in the PivotTable report.

For example, most of the calls number in the hundreds, but the routine Dispatched Calls number in the thousands, resulting in a larger vertical scale. This disparity prevents Mr. Martinez from being able to easily compare the other two call classifications—Major Crime and Traffic Accidents. In this activity, you will filter the data to show only Police calls in the Major Crime and Traffic Accidents classifications. You will also change the summary data back to *total* number of calls rather than the average.

1 In the upper left corner of the chart, click the **Report Filter** field button, which indicates *1st Quarter Fire & Police Calls*. On the displayed list, in the lower left corner, select (place a check mark in) the **Select Multiple Items** check box. Then, click to *clear* the **(All)** check box, and select the **Police** check box. Click **OK**, and then compare your screen with Figure 7.33.

Only the Police precinct calls display.

Figure 7.33

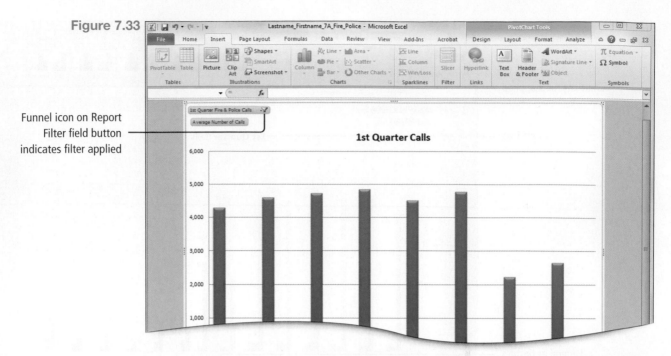

2 At the bottom of the PivotChart, click the *Classification* button above the chart **Legend**. On the displayed list, click to *clear* the check box for **Dispatched Calls**, and then click **OK**.

> This action removes the Dispatched Calls classification; only the two remaining call classifications for Police precincts display—Major Crime and Traffic Accidents. The Legend field button displays a funnel icon to indicate that a filter is applied. Because the number of dispatched calls is in the thousands, compared to hundreds for the other two call types, removing this classification allows for a clearer comparison.

3 On the **Design tab**, in the **Type group**, click the **Change Chart Type** button. In the **Change Chart Type** dialog box, in the first row, click the second chart type—**Stacked Column**—and then click **OK**. Compare your screen with Figure 7.34.

> Stacked columns display the two call classifications by location. Within each location, the stacked column shows the amount of activity as part of a whole.

Figure 7.34

Funnel icon on Report Filter field button indicates filter applied

Only precincts display on category axis

Applied filter causes legend to indicate only types of police-related calls

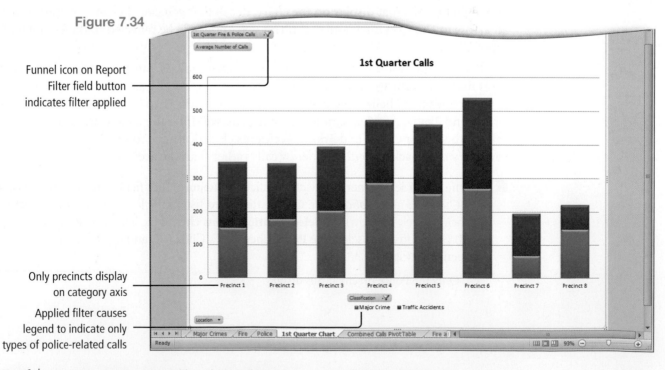

Funnel icon on Report Filter field button indicates filter applied

4 Display the **Combined Calls PivotTable** worksheet, and then compare your screen with Figure 7.35.

> The data is rearranged and only the precinct calls display. The fire station calls do not currently display on the Combined Calls PivotTable sheet. Each time you changed the PivotChart, the underlying PivotTable changed to reflect the new display of the data.

Figure 7.35

Only Police Precinct data displays because PivotChart is filtered

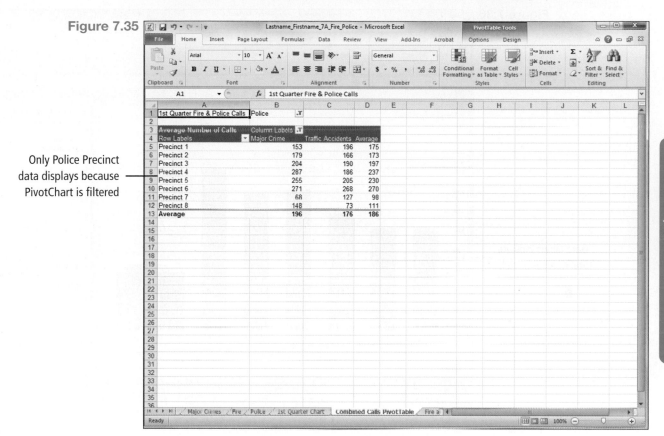

5 Click the **1st Quarter Chart sheet tab**, and then click in the chart title to make the chart active. On the **Layout tab**, in the **Labels group**, click the **Data Labels** button, and then click **Center**. Right-click any data label in the red data series, and then change the font size to **12** and apply **Bold B**; repeat this for the data labels in the blue data series.

> Labels display on each segment of the columns showing the value for that portion of the column. For the call classification at a particular station, the number represents the *average* number of calls per month in the three months that comprise the first quarter.

6 On the **Analyze tab**, in the **Show/Hide group**, click the **Field List** button.

> The PivotTable Field List displays. Here, you can change the way the data is summarized.

7 In the **Values area**, click **Average Number of Calls**, and then on the displayed list, click **Value Field Settings**. In the dialog box, click **Sum**, and then click **OK**. Compare your screen with Figure 7.36.

The chart changes to display the *total* number of calls rather than the average number of calls.

Figure 7.36

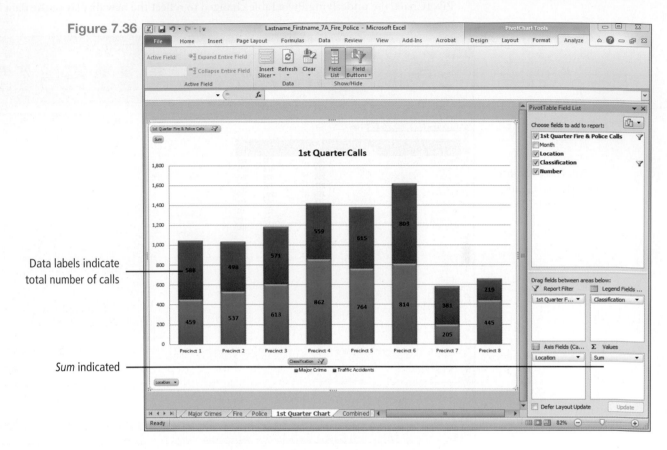

Data labels indicate total number of calls

Sum indicated

8 Display the **Combined Calls PivotTable** worksheet. **Close** the **PivotTable Field List**. In cells **D4** and **A13**, notice that *Average* is still indicated. Click cell **A13**, type **Total** and then press Enter.

Total displays in both cell D4 and cell A13.

9 Redisplay the chart sheet. On the **Layout tab**, in the **Current Selection group**, click the **Chart Elements arrow**, click **Chart Area**, and then click the **Format Selection** button. On the left, click **Fill**. On the right, click the **Solid fill** option button, click the **Color arrow**, and then in the fourth column, click the second color—**Dark Blue, Text 2, Lighter 80%**. Click **Close**.

10 Format the **Plot area** with a **Gradient fill**, using the **Preset color** named **Daybreak**. Right-click the **Chart Title**, change the font size to **32,** and then change the font color to **Dark Blue, Text 2**.

11 On the **Analyze tab**, in the **Show/Hide group**, click the **Field Buttons button arrow**, and then click **Hide All**. Click an outer edge of the chart to select the entire chart, and then compare your screen with Figure 7.37.

Figure 7.37

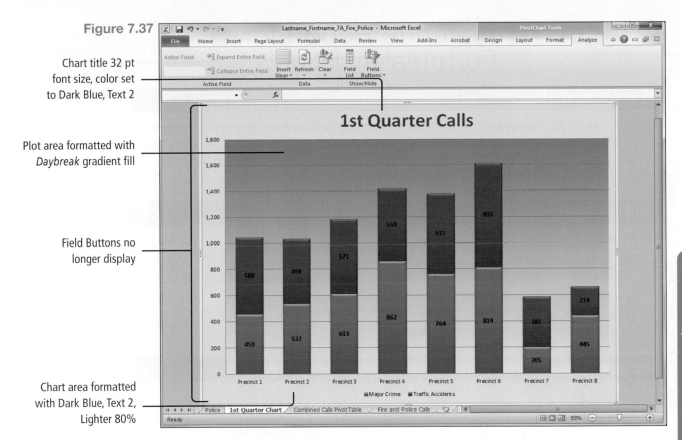

Chart title 32 pt font size, color set to Dark Blue, Text 2

Plot area formatted with *Daybreak* gradient fill

Field Buttons no longer display

Chart area formatted with Dark Blue, Text 2, Lighter 80%

12 Point to the **Combined Calls PivotTable sheet tab**, right-click, and then click **Select All Sheets**. Insert a footer in the **left section** that includes the **file name**. From the **Page Layout tab**, center the worksheets horizontally on the page, change the orientation to **Landscape**, and then in the **Scale to Fit group**, set the **Width** to **1 page**. On the status bar, click the **Normal** button ⊞. Press Ctrl + Home to move to the top of the worksheet.

13 Display the **Document Panel**. In the **Author** box, type your firstname and lastname, in the **Subject** box, type your course name and section number, and in the **Keywords** box, type **Fire, Police, call activity Close** the **Document Panel**.

14 With the sheets still grouped, display the **Print Preview**, and then examine the ten pages of your workbook. If necessary, make any needed corrections or adjustments.

15 Save 🖫 your workbook.

16 If you are required to print the workbook, print pages 1–6—the chart sheet and the worksheets that show your work. It is not necessary to print pages 7–10, which comprise your source data. Or, submit the workbook electronically as directed by your instructor. If required to do so, print your worksheets with formulas displayed using the instructions in Activity 1.16 in Project 1A.

More Knowledge | Creating the PivotChart Report First

You can create a PivotChart report from source data *before* creating a PivotTable report. To do so, click in the source data, on the Insert tab, in the Tables group, click the PivotTable arrow, and then click PivotChart. A dialog box named Create PivotTable with PivotChart displays. Click OK, and then, determine the chart layout by dragging fields from the displayed PivotTable Field List to specific areas on the chart sheet. As you select fields from the field section, Excel places report filters on the chart sheet, and simultaneously builds the associated PivotTable report in the same layout.

End **You have completed Project 7A** ――――――――

Project 7B Revenue Report for Formula Auditing

myitlab
Project 7B Training

Project Activities

In Activities 7.13 through 7.18 you will use the Formula Auditing features to review a fee revenue worksheet and to resolve the errors. You will also use the Watch Window to monitor changes in the cafeteria sales worksheets in the city's office complex. Your completed worksheets will look similar to Figure 7.38.

Project Files

For Project 7B, you will need the following files:

e07B_Fee_Revenue
e07B_Cafeteria_Sales

You will save your workbooks as:

Lastname_Firstname_7B_Fee_Revenue
Lastname_Firstname_7B_Cafeteria_Sales

Project Results

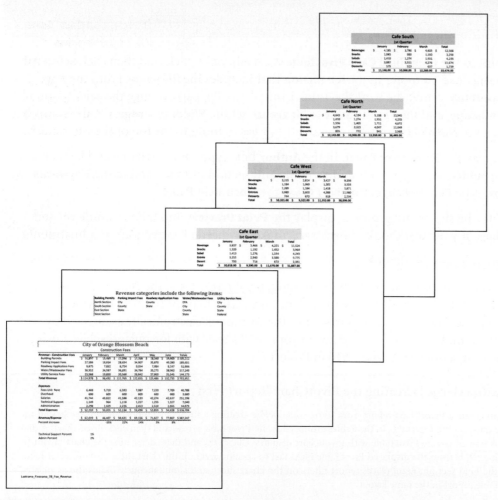

Figure 7.38
Project 7B Formula Auditing

Objective 5 | Trace Precedents and Dependents to Audit Worksheet Formulas

Auditing is the process of examining a worksheet for errors in *formulas*. Formulas are equations that perform calculations on values in your worksheet. A formula consists of a sequence of values, cell references, names, functions, or operators in a cell, which together produce a new value. Recall that a formula always begins with an equal sign.

Excel includes a group of *Formula Auditing* features, which consist of tools and commands accessible from the Formulas tab that help you check your worksheet for errors. In complex worksheets, use these Formula Auditing features to show relationships between cells and formulas, to ensure that formulas are logical and correct, and to resolve error messages. Although sometimes it is appropriate to hide the error message, at other times errors can indicate a problem that needs to be corrected.

Activity 7.13 | Using the Trace Precedents Command

Precedent cells are cells that are referred to by a formula in another cell. The *Trace Precedents command* displays arrows that indicate what cells affect the value of the cell that is selected. By using the Trace Precedents command, you can see the relationships between formulas and cells. As an auditing tool, the process of tracing a formula is a way to ensure that you constructed the formula correctly.

1 **Start** Excel. From your student files, open the file **e07B_Fee_Revenue**, and then **Save** the file in your **Excel Chapter 7** folder as **Lastname_Firstname_7B_Fee_Revenue** Compare your screen with Figure 7.39.

This worksheet details the revenue and expenses related to the construction fees collected by the City of Orange Blossom Beach over a six-month period. Several error notations are present (#VALUE!, #REF!, #DIV/0!), green triangles display in the top left corners of several cells indicating a potential error, and two columns are too narrow to fit the data, which Excel indicates by displaying pound signs—####.

Figure 7.39

Columns need to be widened

Green triangles

Error notations

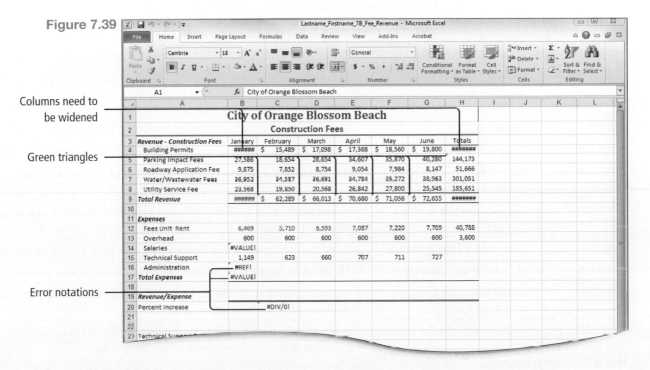

2 Display **Backstage** view, and then under the **Help tab**, click **Options**. In the **Excel Options** dialog box, click **Formulas**. Under **Error checking rules**, point to one of the small circles to display a ScreenTip. Compare your screen withFigure 7.40.

Here you can control which error checking rules you want to activate, and you can get information about each of the rules by clicking the small blue information icon at the end of each rule. By default, all but the next to last rule are selected, and it is recommended that you maintain the default settings. This textbook assumes the default settings.

Figure 7.40

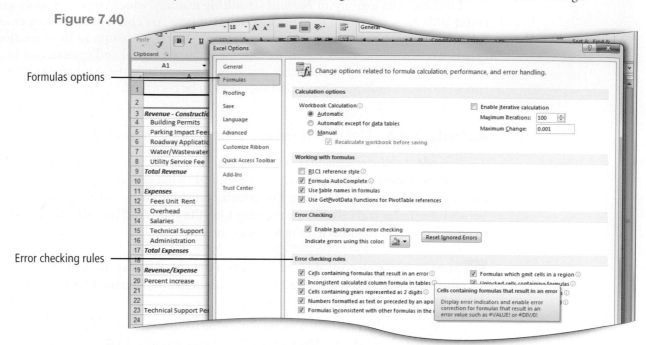

Formulas options

Error checking rules

3 In the lower right corner of the dialog box, click **Cancel** to close the dialog box.

4 Take a moment to study the table in Figure 7.41, which details some common error values that might display on your worksheets.

An *error value* is the result of a formula that Excel cannot evaluate correctly.

Excel Error Values

Error Value	Meaning	Possible Cause
#####	Cannot see data.	The column is not wide enough to display the entire value.
#DIV/0!	Cannot divide by zero.	The divisor in a formula refers to a blank cell or a cell that contains zero.
#NAME?	Does not recognize a name you used in a formula.	A function or a named range may be misspelled or does not exist.
#VALUE!	Cannot use a text field in a formula.	A formula refers to a cell that contains a text value rather than a numeric value or a formula.
#REF!	Cannot locate the reference.	A cell that is referenced in a formula may have been deleted or moved.
#N/A	No value is available.	No information is available for the calculation you want to perform.
#NUM!	Invalid argument in a worksheet function.	An unacceptable argument may have been used in a function. Or, a formula result could be too large or too small.
#NULL!	No common cells.	A space was entered between two ranges in a formula to indicate an intersection, but the ranges have no common cells.

Figure 7.41

Another Way

On the **Home tab**, in the **Cells group**, click the **Format** button, and then click **AutoFit Column Width**.

5 On your worksheet, in the **column heading area**, select **column B**, hold down Ctrl, and then select **column H**. Point to the *right* edge of either of the selected column headings to display the ⬌ pointer, and then double-click to apply AutoFit.

AutoFit widens the columns to accommodate the longest values in each column; the ##### errors no longer display.

6 In cell **C9**, notice the **green triangle** in the top left corner of the cell.

A green triangle in the upper left corner of a cell indicates that the formula in the cell is suspect for some reason. Typically, this is because the formula does not match the formulas in the cells next to it, or because it does not include all of the adjacent cells.

7 Click cell **C9**, to the left of the cell, point to the displayed **Error Checking** button ⬦, and then read the **ScreenTip** that displays. Compare your screen with Figure 7.42.

The ScreenTip indicates that adjacent cells containing numbers are not included in the formula. It is possible that the formula purposely consists of a group of cells that excludes some of the cells adjacent to it. However, because that is not as common as including *all* of the cells that are adjacent to one another, Excel flags this as a potential error.

Figure 7.42

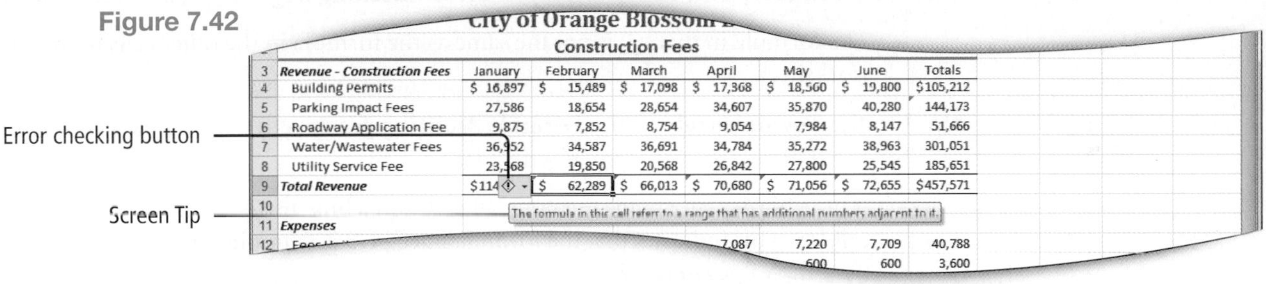

8 On the **Formulas tab**, in the **Formula Auditing group**, click the **Trace Precedents** button. Notice that the range **C6:C8** is bordered in blue and a blue arrow points to cell **C9**.

Recall that precedent cells are cells that are referred to by a formula in another cell. Here, the precedent cells are bordered in blue. A blue arrow, called a *tracer arrow*, displays from cells C6:C8, pointing to the selected cell C9. A tracer arrow shows the relationship between the active cell and its related cells. Tracer arrows are blue when pointing from a cell that provides data to another cell. Because this total should include *all* of the Construction Fees for February, this is an error in the formula—the formula should include the range C4:C8. By tracing the precedents, you can see that two cells were mistakenly left out of the formula.

9 To the left of cell **C9**, click the **Error Checking** button ⬦ to display a list of error checking options. Compare your screen with Figure 7.43.

Figure 7.43

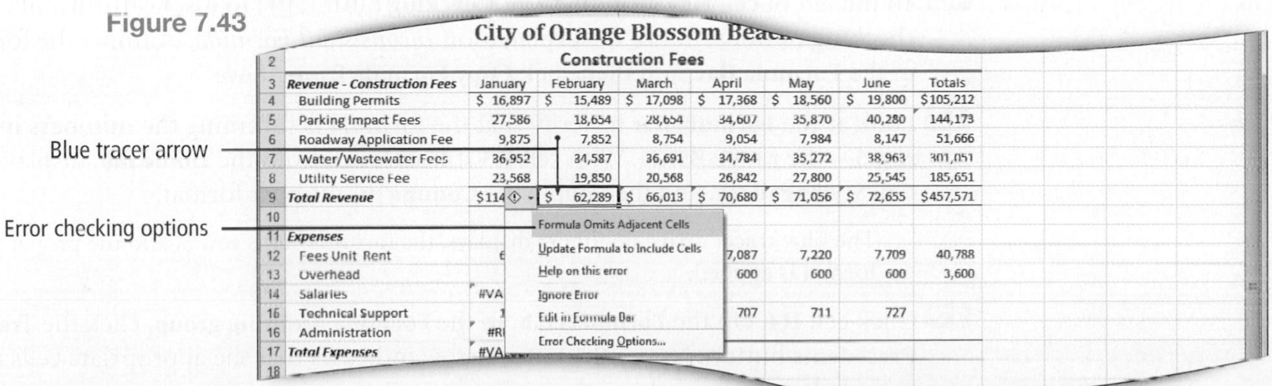

10 On the displayed list, notice that Excel indicates the potential error highlighted in blue—*Formula Omits Adjacent Cells*. Notice also that you can update the formula, seek help with the error, ignore the error, edit the formula in the Formula Bar, or display the Error Checking Options in the Excel Options dialog box. Click **Update Formula to Include Cells**, and then look at the formula in the **Formula Bar**.

> As shown in the Formula Bar, the formula is updated to include the range C4:C8; the green triangle no longer displays.

11 Click cell **D9**, which also displays a green triangle, and then point to the **Error Checking** button ![Error Checking button] to display the **ScreenTip**.

> The same error exists in cell D9—not all adjacent cells in the column were included in the formula. This error also exists in the range E9:G9. You can click in each cell and use the Error Checking button's options list to correct each formula; or, you can use the fill handle to copy the corrected formula in cell C9 to the remaining cells.

12 Click cell **C9**, drag the fill handle to copy the corrected formula to the range **D9:G9**, and then notice that all the green triangles are removed from the range.

13 Click cell **H5**, point to the displayed **Error Checking** button ![Error Checking button], and read the **ScreenTip**.

> The formula in this cell is not the same as the formula in the other cells in this area of the worksheet.

14 On the **Formulas tab**, in the **Formula Auditing group**, click the **Trace Precedents** button. Compare your screen with Figure 7.44.

> A blue border surrounds the range B8:G8, and a blue tracer arrow displays from cell B8 to cell H5. This indicates that the formula in cell H5 is summing the values in row 8 rather than the values in row 5.

Figure 7.44

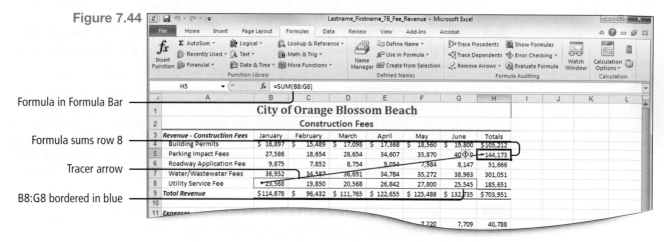

Formula in Formula Bar

Formula sums row 8

Tracer arrow

B8:G8 bordered in blue

15 To the left of cell **H5**, click the **Error Checking** button ![Error Checking button] to display the list of error checking options, notice the explanation *Inconsistent Formula*, examine the formula in the **Formula Bar**, and then click **Copy Formula from Above**.

16 Look at the **Formula Bar** to verify that the formula is summing the numbers in **row 5**—the range **B5:G5**. With cell **H5** still selected, from the **Home tab**, display the **Cell Styles gallery**, and then apply the **Comma [0]** number format.

> The blue tracer arrow no longer displays, the formula sums row 5, and the proper number format is applied.

17 Click cell **H4**. On the **Formulas tab**, in the **Formula Auditing group**, click the **Trace Precedents** button. Notice the tracer arrow indicates that the appropriate cells are included in the formula, as shown in Figure 7.45.

Figure 7.45

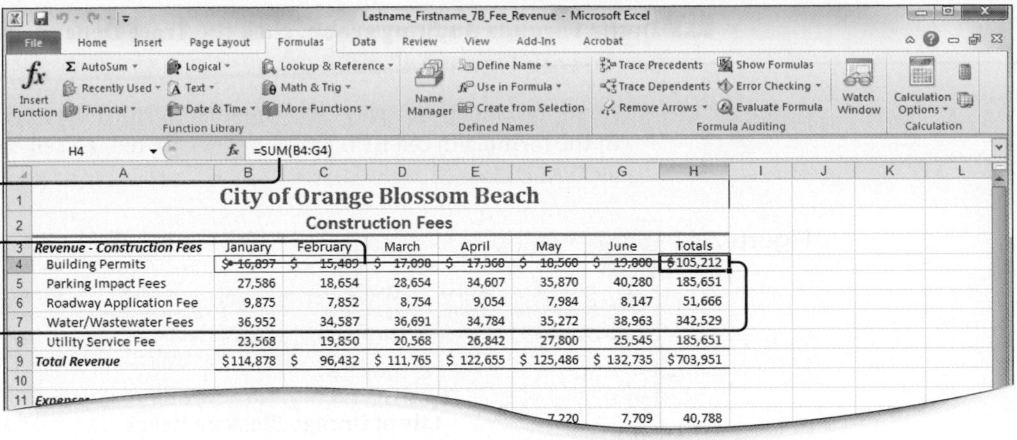

Formula in Formula Bar

Blue tracer arrow

Revenue - Construction Fees

Formula sums row 4

18 Click cell **H5**, click the **Trace Precedents** button, notice the **tracer arrow**, and then click cell **H6**. Click the **Trace Precedents** button, notice the tracer arrow, and verify that the correct cells are included in the formula.

19 Click cell **H7** and click the **Trace Precedents** button, and then click cell **H8** and click the **Trace Precedents** button. Compare your screen with Figure 7.46.

> Cells H7 and H8 display blue tracer arrows that are inconsistent with the other formulas in this column. However, green triangle indicators do not display in either of these cells. When auditing a worksheet, you cannot rely on the error values and green triangles alone. To ensure the accuracy of a worksheet you should use the Trace Precedents command to verify that all of the formulas are logical and correct.

Figure 7.46

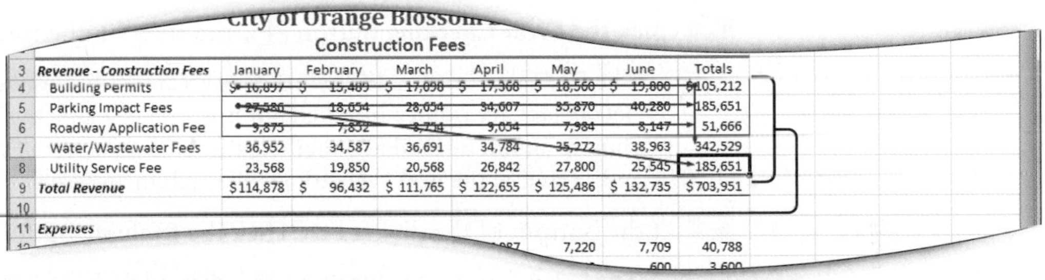

Blue tracer arrows

20 In the **Formula Auditing group**, click the **Remove Arrows** button. Click cell **H6**, and then use the fill handle to copy the correct formula down to cells **H7:H8**.

21 Save 💾 your workbook.

Activity 7.14 | Using the Trace Dependents Command

Dependent cells are cells that contain formulas that refer to other cells—they depend on the values of other cells to display a result. The *Trace Dependents command* displays arrows that indicate what cells are affected by the value of the currently selected cell.

1 Click cell **B14**, which displays the error *#VALUE!*. To the left of the cell, point to the **Error Checking** button 💠 and read the ScreenTip.

> This formula contains a reference to a cell that is of the wrong data type—a cell that does not contain a number.

2 In the **Formula Auditing group**, click the **Trace Precedents** button.

> A blue tracer arrow indicates that cell B3 is included in the formula. Because cell B3 contains text—*January*—and not a number, no mathematical calculation is possible. The salaries should be calculated as 5 percent of *Total Revenue*, plus the constant amount of 36,000.

Excel | Chapter 7

3 In the **Formula Auditing group**, click the **Trace Dependents** button. Compare your screen with Figure 7.47.

> A red tracer arrow displays showing that the formula in cell B17 depends on the result of the formula in cell B14. Tracer arrows are red if a cell contains an error value, such as #VALUE!.

Figure 7.47

Blue tracer arrow (pointing from a cell that provides data to another cell)

Red tracer arrow (cell contains an error value)

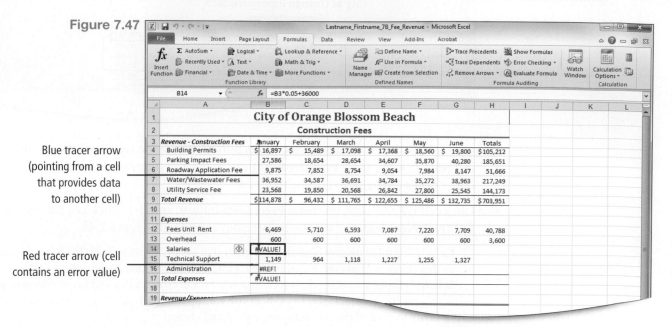

4 Click the **Error Checking** button 🖕, and then on the list, click **Show Calculation Steps**.

> The Evaluate Formula dialog box displays and indicates the formula as ="*January*"*0.05+ 36000*. January is not a number, nor is it a range name that refers to a group of numbers; thus, it cannot be used in a mathematical formula. At the bottom of the dialog box, Excel indicates that the next evaluation will result in an error.

5 At the bottom of the dialog box, click the **Evaluate** button.

> The formula in the **Evaluation** box indicates *#Value!+36000*. You can use this box to evaluate each step of the formula. With complex formulas, this can be helpful in examining each piece of a formula to see where the error has occurred.

6 **Close** the **Evaluate Formula** dialog box. With cell **B14** still the active cell, click in the **Formula Bar** and edit the formula to change cell **B3** to **B9** and then press [Enter].

> The error is removed and the result—*41,744*—displays in cell B14.

7 Click cell **B14**. Drag the fill handle to copy the corrected formula in cell **B14** across the row to cells **C14:G14**.

8 Click cell **B9**. In the **Formula Auditing group**, click the **Trace Dependents** button. Compare your screen with Figure 7.48.

> Each cell where an arrowhead displays indicates a dependent relationship.

Figure 7.48

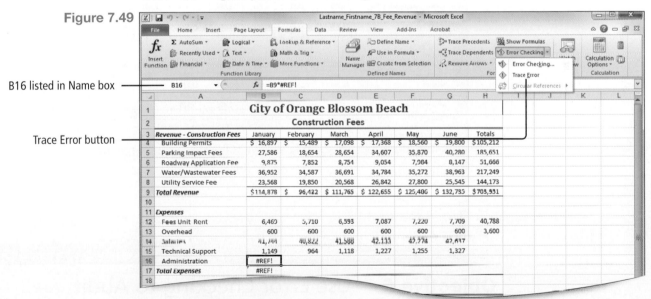

9 In the **Formula Auditing group**, click the **Remove Arrows button**.

10 Save your workbook.

Activity 7.15 | Using the Trace Error Command

Another tool you can use to help locate and resolve an error is the *Trace Error command*. Use this command to trace a selected error value such as #VALUE!, #REF!, #NAME?, or #DIV/0!.

1 Click cell **B16**, point to the displayed **Error Checking** button, and read the **ScreenTip**.

The error message indicates that a cell that was referenced in the formula has been moved or deleted, or the function is causing an invalid reference error. In other words, Excel does not know where to look to get the value that should be used in the formula.

2 In the **Formula Auditing group**, click the **Error Checking button arrow** to display a list, and then compare your screen with Figure 7.49.

Figure 7.49

B16 listed in Name box

Trace Error button

3 On the list, click the **Trace Error** button.

A precedent arrow is drawn from cell B9 to B16.

4 In the **Formula Auditing group**, click the **Error Checking button arrow**, and then click the **Trace Error** button again.

An arrow is drawn between cells B9 and B4 and the range B4:B8 is bordered in blue. The blue border indicates that this range is used in the formula in cell B9, which sums the values.

5 Click in cell **A24**. Type **Admin Percent** press ⟨Tab⟩, type **2** and then press ⟨Enter⟩.

> The percent used to calculate administrative expenses was moved or deleted from the worksheet, so you must re-enter the value. That way, it can be referenced in the formula in cell B16.

6 Click **B16**. Click the **Error Checking** button ⬧ to display the list of error checking options, and then click **Edit in Formula Bar**.

> The insertion point displays in the Formula Bar so that you can edit the formula.

7 Delete **#REF!** and type **b24** Press ⟨F4⟩ to make the cell reference absolute, and then press ⟨Enter⟩.

> The error notation in cell B16 is replaced with *2,298*. The corrected formula needs to be copied across row 16, and it needs to use an absolute reference. That way, the 2% Admin Percent will be applied to the construction fee figure for each month.

8 Click cell **B16**, and then drag the fill handle to copy the formula to the right to cells **C16:G16**.

9 **Save** 🖫 your workbook, press ⟨Ctrl⟩ + ⟨Home⟩, and then compare your screen with Figure 7.50.

Figure 7.50

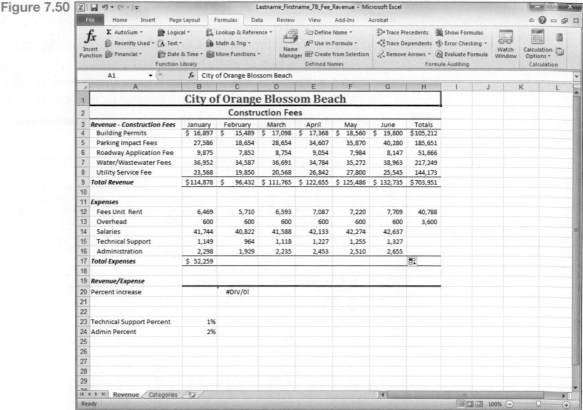

Objective 6 | Use Error Checking to Audit Worksheet Formulas

Activity 7.16 | Using Error Checking

The **Error Checking command** checks for common errors that occur in formulas. The behavior is similar to checking for spelling; that is, the command uses a set of rules to check for errors in formulas. The command opens the Error Checking dialog box, which provides an explanation about the error and enables you to move from one error to the next. Thus, you can review all of the errors on a worksheet.

1 Be sure that cell **A1** is the active cell. In the **Formula Auditing group**, click the **Error Checking button arrow**, and then click **Error Checking**.

The Error Checking dialog box displays, and indicates the first error—in cell C20. Here the error notation *#DIV/0!* displays. The Error Checking dialog box provides an explanation of this error—a formula or function is trying to divide by zero or by an empty cell.

2 In the **Error Checking** dialog box, click the **Show Calculation Steps** button.

The Evaluate Formula dialog box displays, and in the Evaluation box, *0/0* displays.

3 In the **Evaluate Formula** dialog box, click the **Evaluate** button.

The Evaluation box displays the error *#DIV/0!* and the Evaluate button changes to Restart.

4 Click the **Restart** button.

The formula *(C19-B19)/C19* displays; the first reference to cell C19 is underlined. The underline indicates that this is the part of the formula that is being evaluated. Each time you click the Evaluate button, it moves to the next cell reference or value in the formula.

5 In the **Evaluate Formula** dialog box, click the **Step In** button. Compare your screen with Figure 7.51.

A second box displays, which normally displays the value in the referenced cell. In this case, the cell that is referenced is empty, as indicated in the message in the lower part of the dialog box. In a complex formula, this dialog box can help you examine and understand each part of the formula and identify exactly where an error occurred.

Figure 7.51

The cell referenced, C19, is empty

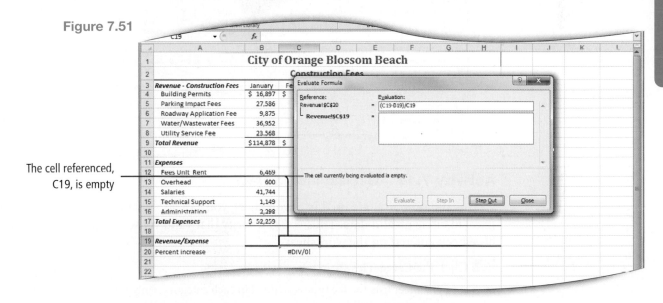

6 Click the **Step Out** button.

The cell evaluation box closes and the underline moves to the next cell in the formula—**B19**—which you can visually verify is empty by looking at the worksheet. To remove this error, you must complete the remainder of the worksheet.

7 **Close** the **Evaluate Formula** dialog box. In the **Error Checking** dialog box, click **Next**.

A message box indicates that the error checking is complete for the entire sheet.

8 Click **OK**.

Both the message box and the Error Checking dialog box close.

9 Click cell **H13** and then use the fill handle to copy this formula down to cells **H14:H16**. Click cell **B17** and use the fill handle to copy this formula to the right into cells **C17:H17**. Widen any columns, if necessary, to display all of the data.

The formulas in the rows and columns are completed.

10 Click cell **B19** and type **=b9-b17** Press [Enter], and then copy the formula to the right into cells **C19:H19**.

> The revenue/expense for each month is calculated. Notice that the #DIV/0! error in cell C20 is removed, but the formatting of the cell needs to be changed from dollars to percent.

11 Click cell **C20**, and on the **Home tab**, in the **Number group**, click the **Percent Style** button [%]. Copy the formula to the right into cells **D20:G20**.

> This formula calculates the percent change in revenue versus expenses, month to month.

12 Press [Ctrl] + [Home], **Save** [💾] your workbook. Compare your screen with Figure 7.52.

Figure 7.52

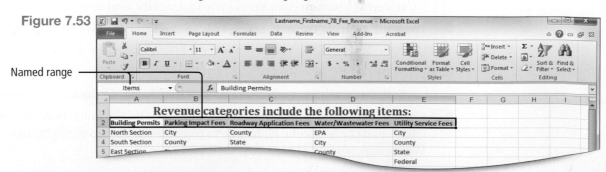

Activity 7.17 | Circling Invalid Data

If validation lists are used in a worksheet, you can apply data validation and instruct Excel to circle invalid data. Thus you can verify that valid values—values from the list—have been entered on the worksheet.

1 Click the **Categories sheet tab**.

> This sheet lists the fee types included in each category; only the fee types from these categories are valid.

2 Click the **Name Box arrow**, and then click **Items**, which is the only range name that shows in the list box. Compare your screen with Figure 7.53.

> The named range in row 2 is highlighted.

Figure 7.53

Named range

3 Display the **Revenue** worksheet. On the **Data tab**, in the **Data Tools group**, click the **Data Validation button arrow**, and then click **Circle Invalid Data**. Compare your screen with Figure 7.54.

Red circles display around Roadway Application Fee and Utility Service Fee.

Figure 7.54

Cells with invalid data circled

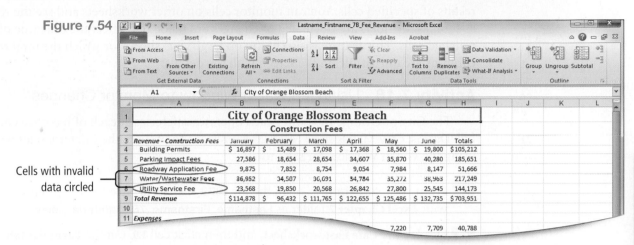

4 Click cell **A6**, and then click the arrow that displays at the right side of the cell.

The validation list displays.

5 From the displayed list, click **Roadway Application Fees**.

The item is corrected but the red circle is not removed.

6 Click cell **A8**, click the arrow, and then from the displayed list, click **Utility Service Fees**.

7 In the **Data Tools group**, click the **Data Validation button arrow**, and then click **Clear Validation Circles** to remove the circles.

8 In the **Data Tools group**, click the **Data Validation button arrow**, and then click the **Circle Invalid Data** button again.

No circles are applied, which confirms that the data is now valid against the validation list.

9 Save your workbook.

10 Select both worksheets so that *[Group]* displays in the title bar. With the two worksheets grouped, insert a footer in the left section that includes the file name. Center the worksheets horizontally on the page, and set the **Orientation** to **Landscape**. On the status bar, click the **Normal** button. Press Ctrl + Home.

11 Display the **Document Panel** and in the **Author** box, type your firstname and lastname, in the **Subject** box, type your course name and section number, and in the **Keywords** box, type construction fees Close the Document Panel. Display the grouped worksheets in **Print Preview**, **Close** the Print Preview, and then make any necessary corrections or adjustments.

12 Save your workbook.

13 Print or submit the two worksheets in this workbook electronically as directed by your instructor. If required, print or create an electronic version of your worksheets with formulas displayed using the instructions in Activity 1.16 in Project 1A.

Objective 7 | Use the Watch Window to Monitor Cell Values

You can monitor the values of cells in one part of a workbook while working on another part of the workbook by using the ***Watch Window***—a window that displays the results of specified cells. You can monitor cells on other worksheets and see the results as soon as formulas are calculated or changes are made that affect the outcome of the watched cells. This feature is also useful on large worksheets for which the total rows and columns are not visible on the screen with the details.

Activity 7.18 | Using the Watch Window to Monitor Changes

The City of Orange Blossom Beach operates cafeterias at each of its office complexes. Lila Darius, City Manager, has asked her assistant to prepare the cafeteria sales worksheets using the Watch Window for sales totals.

1 From your student files, open the file **e07B_Cafeteria_Sales** and then save the file in your **Excel Chapter 7** folder as **Lastname_Firstname_7B_Cafeteria_Sales**

2 Display the **Cafe East** worksheet, and then click cell **E9**. On the **Formulas tab**, in the **Formula Auditing group**, click the **Watch Window** button.

> The Watch Window displays. As you create totals for the columns and rows on each worksheet in this activity, you will be able to use the Watch Window to view the results for all the worksheets at once.

3 In the upper left corner of the **Watch Window**, click **Add Watch**. Drag the window below your data, and then compare your screen with Figure 7.55.

> The Add Watch dialog box displays the selected cell =*'Cafe East'!$E$9*.

Figure 7.55

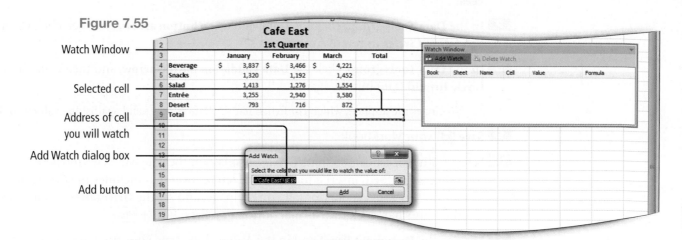

Watch Window
Selected cell
Address of cell you will watch
Add Watch dialog box
Add button

4 In the **Add Watch** dialog box, click **Add**.

> The workbook name, sheet name, and cell address display in the Watch Window. Because there is no value or formula in the cell at this time, the Name, Value, and Formula columns are empty.

5 Display the **Cafe West** worksheet, and then click cell **E9**. On the **Watch Window**, click **Add Watch**, and then in the **Add Watch** dialog box, click **Add**. Compare your screen with Figure 7.56.

A second cell is added to the Watch Window.

Figure 7.56

Two cells display in the Watch Window

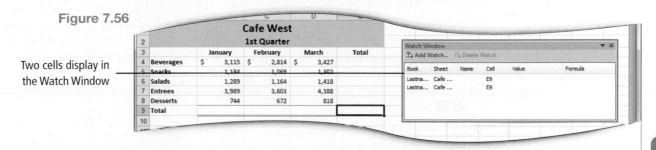

6 Following the same procedure, add cell **E9** from the **Cafe North** sheet and from the **Cafe South** sheet. Adjust the size of the Watch Window and columns as necessary to view all four sheets. Compare your screen with Figure 7.57, and verify that cell **E9** is listed for each of the four worksheets.

Figure 7.57

Four worksheet names

E9 from each worksheet

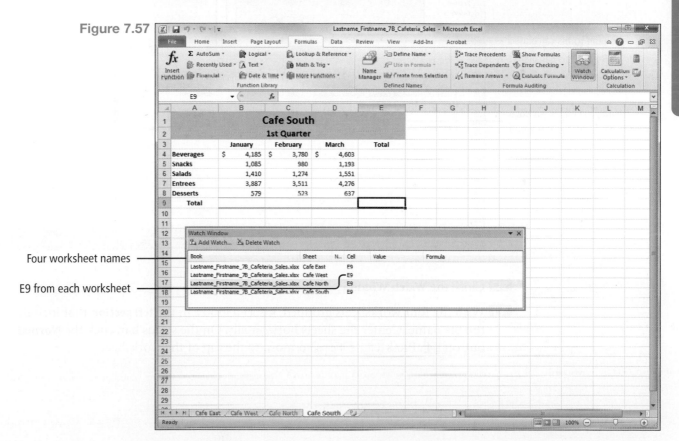

7 With the **Cafe South** sheet active, hold down Shift, and then click the **Cafe East** sheet.

The four Cafe worksheets are selected and *[Group]* displays in the title bar.

8 In the displayed **Cafe South** worksheet, select the range **B4:E9**.

This includes the data and the empty row and column immediately adjacent to the data. Because the sheets are grouped, this action is taking place on all four worksheets.

9 On the **Home tab**, in the **Editing group**, click the **Sum** button $\boxed{\Sigma}$. Compare your screen with Figure 7.58.

The totals for the rows and columns in this worksheet, as well as in the other three worksheets, are calculated. The results display immediately in the Watch Window, indicating that calculations took place on all four sheets simultaneously.

Figure 7.58

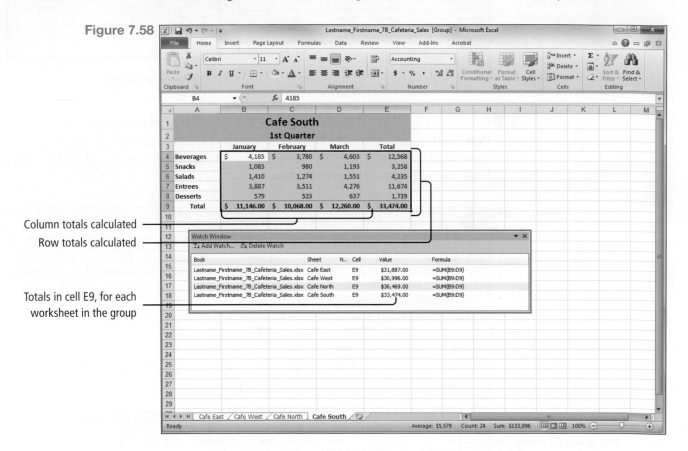

Column totals calculated

Row totals calculated

Totals in cell E9, for each worksheet in the group

10 Close the **Watch Window**.

11 With the four worksheets grouped, insert a footer in the **left section** that includes the file name. Center the sheets horizontally. On the status bar, click the **Normal** button $\boxed{\boxplus}$. Press $\boxed{\text{Ctrl}}$ + $\boxed{\text{Home}}$ to move to the top of the worksheet.

12 Display the **Document Panel**. In the **Author** box, type your firstname and lastname, in the **Subject** box, type your course name and section number, and in the **Keywords** box, type **cafeteria sales Close** the Document Panel. Display the grouped worksheets in **Print Preview**, and then view your worksheets. **Close** the print preview, and then make any necessary corrections or adjustments.

13 Right-click any sheet tab and from the displayed list click **Ungroup Sheets**. **Save** your workbook. Print or submit the four worksheets in this workbook electronically as directed by your instructor. If required, print your worksheets with formulas displayed using the instructions in Activity 1.16 in Project 1A.

End **You have completed Project 7B** ———————————————————

Content-Based Assessments

Summary

In this chapter, you created a PivotTable report and a PivotChart report to organize and display data. You practiced manipulating data in a PivotTable report and a PivotChart report to observe the different techniques that can be used to present and organize information into groups from which trends, comparisons, patterns, and relationships can be determined. You audited a worksheet to look for inconsistencies, to diagnose problems, or to correct errors. Finally, you used the Watch Window to view the results of consolidated data on all sheets at once.

Key Terms

Matching

Match each term in the second column with its correct definition in the first column by writing the letter of the term on the blank line in front of the correct definition.

_____ 1.   An interactive, cross-tabulated Excel report that summarizes and analyzes large amounts of data.

_____ 2.   The column titles from source data that form categories of data for a PivotTable report.

_____ 3.   Data in a worksheet or from an external source, arranged in rows and columns suitable for a PivotTable report.

_____ 4.   A window that lists the fields from the source data and an area in which you can arrange the fields in the PivotTable.

_____ 5.   The lower portion of the PivotTable Field List where you build the PivotTable report by rearranging and repositioning fields.

_____ 6.   A process by which you can limit the display of data to only specific information.

_____ 7.   Easy-to-use filtering controls with buttons that enable you to intuitively drill down through large amounts of data in an interactive way.

_____ 8.   The command to update a worksheet to reflect new data.

_____ 9.   A graphical representation of the data in a PivotTable report.

_____ 10.   The process of examining a worksheet for errors in formulas.

A Auditing

B Dependent cells

C Field names

D Filter

E Formulas

F Layout section

G PivotChart report

H PivotTable Field List

I PivotTable report

J Precedent cells

K Refresh

L Slicers

M Source data

N Tracer arrow

O Watch Window

_____ 11. Equations that perform calculations on values in a worksheet.

_____ 12. Cells that are referred to by a formula in another cell.

_____ 13. An indicator that shows the relationship between the active cell and its related cell.

_____ 14. Cells that contain formulas that refer to other cells.

_____ 15. A window that displays the results of specified cells.

Multiple Choice

Circle the correct answer.

1. The data for a PivotTable report should be in the format of a:
   A. chart　　　　　　　　　B. file　　　　　　　　　C. list

2. PivotTable field names are formed from the source data's:
   A. column titles　　　　　B. row titles　　　　　　C. sheet tab names

3. One possible source of data for a PivotTable report is:
   A. a Word template file　　B. a PowerPoint　　　　　C. an Access database file
   　　　　　　　　　　　　　　presentation file

4. The area in the layout section of the PivotTable Field List where data is summarized is the:
   A. Row Labels area　　　　B. Column Labels area　　C. Values areas

5. Slicers are used to:
   A. apply labels to data　　B. filter data　　　　　　C. sort data

6. The area in the layout section of the PivotTable Field List where you position fields by which you want to filter the PivotTable report is the:
   A. Row Labels area　　　　B. Report Filter area　　　C. Values areas

7. Tracer arrows are red if a cell contains:
   A. an Error Value　　　　　B. a green triangle　　　　C. a formula

8. Cells that are referred to by a formula in another cell are:
   A. Dependent cells　　　　B. Precedent cells　　　　C. Tracers

9. When pointing from a cell that provides data to another cell, the color of a tracer arrow is:
   A. Red　　　　　　　　　　B. White　　　　　　　　C. Blue

10. Cells that contain formulas that refer to other cells are:
    A. Dependent cells　　　　B. Precedent cells　　　　C. Tracers

Content-Based Assessments

Apply **7A** skills from these Objectives:

- **1** Create a PivotTable Report
- **2** Use Slicers and Search Filters
- **3** Modify a PivotTable Report
- **4** Create a PivotChart Report

Skills Review | Project **7C** Parks and Pools Calls

In the following Skills Review, you will assist Toby Harrison, Director of Parks and Recreation, in preparing a comparative report for phone calls received by the various park and pool facilities in the city. You will create and modify a PivotTable report and PivotChart report. The first six worksheets in your workbook will look similar to Figure 7.59.

Project Files

For Project 7C, you will need the following file:

e07C_Parks_Pools

You will save your workbook as:

Lastname_Firstname_7C_Parks_Pools

Project Results

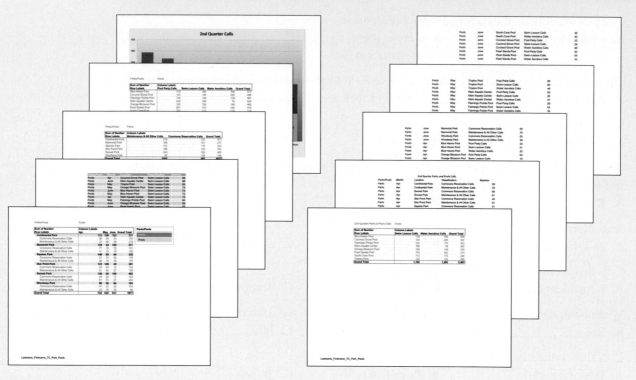

Figure 7.59

(Project 7C Parks and Pools Calls continues on the next page)

Content-Based Assessments

Skills Review | Project **7C** Parks and Pools Calls (continued)

1 **Start** Excel. From your student files, open **e07C_ Parks_Pools**. **Save** the file in your **Excel Chapter 7** folder as **Lastname_Firstname_Parks_Pools** Click cell **A2**. On the **Insert tab**, in the **Tables group**, click the **PivotTable button arrow**, and then click **PivotTable**.

  a. In the **Create PivotTable** dialog box, verify that the range of cells indicates '*Parks and Pools Calls*'!$A$2:$E$110 and that the **New Worksheet** option button is selected. Click **OK**. In the **PivotTable Field List**, in the **field section**, select the **Parks/Pools** check box. In the **layout section**, in the **Row Labels area**, point to **Parks/Pools**, and then drag the field name into the **Report Filter area** above.

  b. In the **PivotTable Field List**, in the **field section**, select the **Location** check box, and then select the **Classification** check box. In the **PivotTable Field List**, from the **field section**, drag the **Month** field down to the **Column Labels area**. In the **field section**, right-click the **Number** field, and click **Add to Values**. Any of these methods can be used to arrange the fields in the layout area.

  c. On the **Design tab**, in the **PivotTable Styles group**, click the **More** button, and then under **Light**, click **Pivot Style Light 13**.

2 On the **Options tab**, in the **Sort & Filter group**, click the **Insert Slicer button arrow**, and then click **Insert Slicer**. Select the **Parks/Pools** check box, and then click **OK**. Drag the **Parks/Pools** slicer to the right of the PivotTable. Shorten the slicer to just below **Pools**.

  a. On the **Options tab**, in the **Slicer Styles group**, click the **More** button, and then under **Dark**, click **Slicer Style Dark 5**. Click cell **A1**. On the **Parks/Pools slicer**, click the **Parks** filtering button. Point to the **Sheet1** sheet tab, right-click, and then click **Move or Copy**. In the **Move or Copy** dialog box, select the **Create a copy** check box. Click **OK**. Right-click the **Sheet 1 (2)** sheet tab, click **Rename**, and then type **Filtered by Parks**

  b. Display the **Sheet1** worksheet. In the **Parks/Pools slicer**, click the **Clear Filter** button. Point to the **Parks/Pools slicer header**, right-click, and then click **Remove "Parks/Pools"**.

3 In the **layout section** of the **PivotTable Field List**, from the **Column Labels area**, drag the **Month** field name upward into the white **field section** and then release the mouse button. In the **layout section**, from the **Row Labels**

area, drag the **Classification** field into the **Column Labels area**. **Close** the **PivotTable Field List**.

  a. Click cell **B4**. Right-click, point to **Move**, and then click **Move "Commons Reservations Calls" Right**. Point to cell **E19** and right-click; click **Show Details**. In cell **E1**, click the **filter arrow**, and then click **Sort Largest to Smallest**. Rename the **Sheet3** tab **Swim Lesson Calls** Apply **AutoFit** to columns **C:D**. Click cell **A1**.

  b. Click the **Sheet1 tab**, and then rename it **Combined Calls PivotTable**. Click cell **A1**. On the **Options tab**, in the **PivotTable group**, click the **Options button arrow**, and then click **Show Report Filter Pages**. In the displayed dialog box, click **OK** to create a worksheet for Parks and for Pools.

  c. Display the **Combined Calls PivotTable** worksheet. Point to any cell with numerical data, right-click, and then click **Value Field Settings**. Click the **Number Format** button, click **Number**, and then set the **Decimal places** to **0** and select the **Use 1000 Separator** check box. Click **OK** two times.

  d. Click cell **A1**. Type **2nd Quarter Parks & Pools Calls** press Enter, and then apply **AutoFit** to **column A**. By clicking the sheet tab navigation buttons as necessary, display the **Parks and Pools Calls** worksheet, which is your source data. Change the value in cell **E3** from *90* to **80** and then press Enter. Display the **Combined Calls PivotTable** worksheet. On the **Options tab**, in the **Data group**, click the **Refresh button arrow**, and then click **Refresh**.

4 Click cell **A1**. On the **Options tab**, in the **Tools group**, click the **PivotChart** button. On the **Insert Chart** dialog box, on the left click **Column**, click the first chart— **Clustered Column**, and then click **OK**. On the **Design tab**, in the **Location group**, click the **Move Chart** button. In the **Move Chart** dialog box, click the **New sheet** option button, replace the highlighted text *Chart1* by typing **2nd Quarter Chart** and then click **OK**. In the new chart sheet, on the **Design tab**, in the **Chart Layouts group**, click the **More** button, and then click **Layout 3**. In the **Chart Styles group**, click the **More** button, and then apply **Style 26**.

  a. Click the **Chart Title** and watch the **Formula Bar** as you type **2nd Quarter Calls** and press Enter. On the **Insert tab**, in the **Text group**, click the **Header & Footer** button. In the **Page Setup** dialog box, click the **Custom Footer** button. With the insertion point

(Project 7C Parks and Pools Calls continues on the next page)

Excel | Chapter 7

Excel | Chapter 7

in the **left section**, from the small toolbar in the dialog box, click the **Insert File Name** button, and then click **OK** two times.

b. In the upper left corner of the chart, click the **Report Filter** field button, which indicates *2nd Quarter Parks & Pools Calls*. On the displayed list, in the lower left corner, select (place a check mark in) the **Select Multiple Items** check box. Then, click to *clear* the **(All)** check box, select the **Pools** check box, and then click **OK**. At the bottom of the PivotChart, click the **Legend** field button, which indicates *Classification*. Click to *clear* the check box for **Pool Party Calls**, and then click **OK**.

c. On the **Design tab**, in the **Type group**, click the **Change Chart Type** button. In the **Change Chart Type** dialog box, click **Stacked Column,** and then click **OK**. On the **Layout tab**, in the **Labels group**, click the **Data Labels** button, and then click **Center**. Right-click any data label in the pink data series, and then change the font size to **12** and apply **Bold**. Repeat for the data labels in the green data series.

d. On the **Layout tab**, in the **Current Selection group**, click the **Chart Elements arrow**, click **Chart Area**, and then click the **Format Selection** button. On the left, click **Fill**. On the right, click the **Solid fill** option button, click the **Color arrow**, and then in the fifth column, click the second color—**Green, Accent 1, Lighter 80%**. Click **Close**. Format the **Plot area** with

a **Gradient fill**, using the **Preset color** named **Moss**, and then click **Close**.

e. On the **Analyze tab**, in the **Show/Hide group**, click the **Field Buttons button arrow**, and then click **Hide All**.

f. Point to the **Combined Calls PivotTable sheet tab**, right-click, and then click **Select All Sheets**. Insert a footer in the **left section** that includes the **file name**. From the **Page Layout tab**, center the worksheets horizontally on the page, change the orientation to **Landscape**, and then in the **Scale to Fit group**, set the **Width** to **1 page**. On the status bar, click the **Normal** button. Press Ctrl + Home to move to the top of the worksheet. Display the **Document Panel**. In the **Author** box, type your firstname and lastname, in the **Subject** box, type your course name and section number, and in the **Keywords** box, type **Parks, Pools, call activity Close** the **Document Panel**. **Save** your workbook. With the sheets still grouped, display the **Print Preview**, and then examine the ten pages of your workbook. If necessary, make any necessary corrections or adjustments. If you are required to print the workbook, print pages 1–6—the chart sheet and the worksheets that show your work. It is not necessary to print pages 7–10, which comprise your source data. Or, submit the workbook electronically as directed by your instructor. If required to do so, print your worksheets with formulas displayed using the instructions in Activity 1.16 in Project 1A.

End You have completed Project 7C ————————————

Content-Based Assessments

Apply 7B skills from these Objectives:

5 Trace Precedents and Dependents to Audit Worksheet Formulas

6 Use Error Checking to Audit Worksheet Formulas

7 Use the Watch Window to Monitor Cell Values

Skills Review | Project 7D License Fees

In the following Skills Review, you will use the Formula Auditing tools to review a fee revenue worksheet for Amanda Ramos, Director of Finance for the City of Orange Blossom Beach. You will also use the Watch Window to edit the city's utility cost worksheets. Your completed workbooks will look similar to Figure 7.60.

Project Files

For Project 7D, you will need the following files:

    e07D_License_Fees
    e07D_Utilities

You will save your workbooks as:

    Lastname_Firstname_7D_License_Fees
    Lastname_Firstname_7D_Utilities

Project Results

Figure 7.60

(Project 7D License Fees continues on the next page)

1 **Start** Excel. From your student files, open the file **e07D_License_Fees**. In your **Excel Chapter 7** folder, **Save** the file as **Lastname_Firstname_7D_License_Fees**

a. In the **column heading area**, select **column B**, hold down Ctrl, and then select **column H**. Point to the *right* edge of either of the selected column headings to display the ⬌ pointer, and then double-click to AutoFit the columns.

b. Click cell **C9**. On the **Formulas tab**, in the **Formula Auditing group**, click the **Trace Precedents** button. To the left of the cell, click the displayed **Error Checking** button, and then click **Update Formula to Include Cells**. Drag the fill handle to copy the corrected formula in cell **C9** to the range **D9:G9**.

c. Click cell **H5**, and then point to the displayed **Error Checking** button to read the ScreenTip. On the **Formulas tab**, in the **Formula Auditing group**, click the **Trace Precedents** button. To the left of cell **H5**, click the **Error Checking** button to display the list of error checking options, click **Copy Formula from Above**, and then look at the **Formula Bar** to verify that the formula is summing the numbers in **row 5**. With cell **H5** still selected, from the **Home tab**, display the **Cell Styles gallery**, and then apply the **Comma [0]** number format.

d. Click cell **H6**, on the **Formulas tab**, click the **Trace Precedents** button; verify that the row is correctly summed. Click cell **H7**, click the **Trace Precedents** button; notice that the formula is not correct. Click cell **H8**, click the **Trace Precedents** button; notice that the formula is not correct. In the **Formula Auditing group**, click the **Remove Arrows** button. Click cell **H6**, and then use the fill handle to copy the correct formula down to cells **H7:H8**.

2 Click cell **B14**, which displays the error *#VALUE!*. To the left of the cell, point to the **Error Checking** button and read the ScreenTip. In the **Formula Auditing group**, click the **Trace Precedents** button.

a. Click the displayed **Error Checking** button, and then on the list, click **Show Calculation Steps**; notice that the formula is trying to multiply by a text value.

b. **Close** the **Evaluate Formula** dialog box. With cell **B14** still the active cell, click in the **Formula Bar**, and then edit the formula to change the reference to cell **B3** to **B9** and press Enter. Click cell **B14**, and then drag

the fill handle to copy the corrected formula across the row to cells **C14:G14**.

3 Click cell **B16**, point to the displayed **Error Checking** button, and read the ScreenTip. In the **Formula Auditing group**, click the **Error Checking button arrow** to display a list. On the list, click the **Trace Error** button. In the **Formula Auditing group**, click the **Error Checking button arrow**, and then click the **Trace Error** button again to view the precedent cells. Click in cell **A24**. Type **Admin Percent** and press Tab, and then type **2** to fill in the missing data.

a. Click **B16**. Remove the arrows. Click the **Error Checking** button to display the list of error checking options, and then click **Edit in Formula Bar**. Delete *#REF!*. Type **b24** and press F4 to make the cell reference absolute. Press Enter. Click cell **B16**, and then use the fill handle to copy the formula to the right to cells **C16:G16**.

4 Click cell **A1**. In the **Formula Auditing group**, click the **Error Checking button arrow**, and then click **Error Checking**—cell **C20** is selected. In the **Error Checking** dialog box, click the **Show Calculation Steps** button; notice that the divisor is an empty cell. In the **Evaluate Formula** dialog box, click the **Evaluate** button. Click the **Restart** button.

a. In the **Evaluate Formula** dialog box, click the **Step In** button to examine the formula. Click the **Step Out** button. **Close** the **Evaluate Formula** dialog box.

b. In the **Error Checking** dialog box, click **Next**. Click **OK**. Click cell **H13**, and then use the fill handle to copy this formula down to cells **H14:H16**. Click cell **B17** and drag the fill handle to copy this formula to the right into cells **C17:H17**.

c. Click cell **B19** and type **=b9-b17** Press Enter, and then copy the formula to the right into cells **C19:H19**. Click cell **C20**, and then on the **Home tab**, in the **Number group**, click the **Percent Style** button. Copy the formula to the right into cells **D20:G20**.

5 Display the **Categories** worksheet. To the left of the **Formula Bar**, click the **Name Box arrow**, and then click **Items**—the only range name in the worksheet. Examine the selected range.

a. Redisplay the **Revenue** worksheet. On the **Data tab**, in the **Data Tools group**, click the **Data Validation button arrow**, and then click **Circle Invalid Data**.

(Project 7D License Fees continues on the next page)

Skills Review | Project **7D** License Fees (continued)

b. Click cell **A6**, and then click the arrow at the right side of the cell. From the displayed list, click **Realtor License Fees**. In the **Data Tools group**, click the **Data Validation button arrow**, and then click **Clear Validation Circles**.

c. Select both worksheets so that *[Group]* displays in the title bar. With the two worksheets grouped, insert a footer in the **left section** that includes the file name. Center the worksheets horizontally. Set the **Orientation** to **Landscape** and the **Width** to **1** page. On the status bar, click the **Normal** button. Press Ctrl + Home.

d. Display the **Document Panel** and in the **Author** box, type your firstname and lastname, in the **Subject** box, type your course name and section number, and in the **Keywords** box, type **license fees** Close the Document Information Panel. Display the grouped worksheets in **Print Preview**, close the print preview, and then make any necessary corrections or adjustments. **Save** your workbook. Print or submit the two worksheets in this workbook electronically as directed by your instructor. If required, print or create an electronic version of your worksheets with formulas displayed using the instructions in Activity 1.16 in Project 1A. **Close** the workbook; leave Excel open.

6 From your student files, open the file **e07D_Utilities**, and then **Save** the file in your **Excel Chapter 7** folder as **Lastname_Firstname_7D_Utilities** Display the **Region 1** worksheet, and then click cell **E8**. On the **Formulas tab**, in the **Formula Auditing group**, click the **Watch Window** button. In the upper left corner of the **Watch Window**, click **Add Watch**. In the **Add Watch** dialog box, click **Add**.

a. Display the **Region 2** worksheet, and then by using the same technique, add cell **E8** from the **Region 2** worksheet. Repeat for the **Region 3** worksheet and

for the **Region 4** worksheet. Adjust the size of the **Watch Window** and columns as necessary to view all four sheets, and verify that cell **E8** is listed for each of the four worksheets.

b. With the **Region 4** worksheet active, hold down Shift and click the **Region 1** sheet tab to select all four worksheets. In the displayed **Region 4** worksheet, select the range **B4:E8**. On the **Home tab**, in the **Editing group**, click the **Sum** button. **Close** the **Watch Window**. Select the range **E5:E7**, and then apply **Comma Style** with zero decimal places.

c. With the four worksheets grouped, insert a footer in the **left section** that includes the file name. Center the sheets horizontally. On the status bar, click the **Normal** button. Press Ctrl + Home to move to the top of the worksheet.

d. Display the **Document Panel**. In the **Author** box, type your firstname and lastname, in the **Subject** box, type your course name and section number, and in the **Keywords** box, type **utilities, regional offices Close** the Document Information Panel. Display the grouped worksheets in **Print Preview**. Redisplay the worksheets.

e. Right-click any sheet tab and from the displayed list click **Ungroup Sheets**. Make any necessary corrections or adjustments. **Save** your workbook. Print or submit the four worksheets in this workbook electronically as directed by your instructor. If required, print or create an electronic version of your worksheets with formulas displayed using the instructions in Activity 1.16 in Project 1A. **Close** Excel.

End You have completed Project 7D ———————————

Content-Based Assessments

Apply **7A** skills from these Objectives:

1️⃣ Create a PivotTable Report

2️⃣ Use Slicers and Search Filters

3️⃣ Modify a PivotTable Report

4️⃣ Create a PivotChart Report

Mastering Excel | Project **7E** Concessions Revenue

In the following Mastering Excel project, you will help Toby Harrison, the Director of Parks and Recreation, create and modify a PivotTable report and PivotChart report to analyze revenue from park concessions such as food, boat rentals, and golf fees. Your completed workbooks will look similar to Figure 7.61.

Project Files

For Project 7E, you will need the following file:

e07E_Concessions_Revenue

You will save your workbook as:

Lastname_Firstname_7E_Concessions_Revenue

Project Results

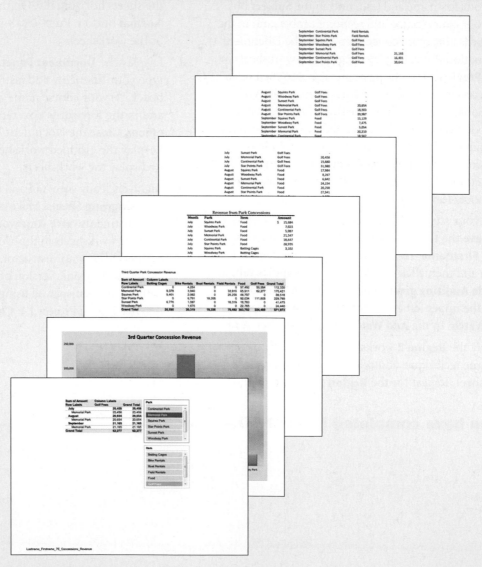

Figure 7.61

(Project 7E Concessions Revenue continues on the next page)

Mastering Excel | Project **7E** Concessions Revenue (continued)

1 **Start** Excel. From your student files, open **e07E_Concessions_Revenue** and **Save** the file in your **Excel Chapter 7** folder as **Lastname_Firstname_7E_Concessions_Revenue**

2 Click cell **A2**. On the **Insert tab**, in the **Tables group**, click the **PivotTable button arrow**, click **PivotTable**, and then click **OK**. Place the **Month** and **Park** fields in the **Row Labels area**. Place the **Item** field in the **Column Labels area**. Place the **Amount** field in the **Values area**. **Close** the **PivotTable Field List**.

3 Click any cell in the PivotTable to make it active. Insert a slicer for the **Park** field and for the **Item** field. Resize and move the slicers so that they are to the right of the PivotTable, with the Park slicer above the Item slicer. Apply **Slicer Style Dark 2** and **Slicer Style Dark 3** to the slicers respectively.

4 Filter first by **Memorial Park**, and then by **Golf Fees**. Right-click any value in the PivotTable report, display the **Value Field Settings** dialog box, and then format the **Number** category to display zero decimal places and the **1000 Separator**. Move the two slicers to the immediate right of the filtered PivotTable, and then make a copy of this worksheet. Name the copied worksheet **Memorial-3Q Golf Fees**

5 Rename **Sheet1 Concessions Revenue** Clear the filters and remove the slicers. In cell **A1**, type **Third**

Quarter Park Concession Revenue Click anywhere in the PivotTable to select it, on the **Options tab**, in the **Show group**, click the **Field List** button, and then *remove* the **Month** field from the **Row Labels** area in the layout section to display only the Grand Totals for each park and for each item. **Close** the **PivotTable Field List**.

6 Insert a **PivotChart** using the **Stacked Bar** chart type. Move the chart to a new worksheet named **3rd Quarter Concessions Chart** Apply the **Layout 3** chart layout and **Chart Style 26**. As the **Chart Title**, type **3rd Quarter Concession Revenue** Format the **Plot Area** with the **Gradient** fill **Gold**. Format the **Chart Area** with a solid fill using **Olive Green, Accent 3, Lighter 60%** in the seventh column, the third color. From the **Analyze tab**, hide all of the field buttons on the chart. Insert a custom footer with the file name in the left section.

7 Select all worksheets. Insert a footer with the file name in the **left section**. Change the **Orientation** to **Landscape**, set the **Width** to **1 page**, and center the sheets horizontally. To the **Document Panel**, add your firstname and lastname as the **Author**, add your course name and section number as the **Subject**, and add **concession revenue** as the **Keywords**. Display **Print Preview**, make corrections or adjustments. **Save** and **Close** the workbook. Print or submit electronically as directed. Pages 1–3 contain your new data; pages 4–7 contain the original source data. There are no formulas in this workbook. **Close** Excel.

End **You have completed Project 7E** ——————————

Content-Based Assessments

Mastering Excel | Project **7F** Beverage Revenue

In the following Mastering Excel project, you will assist Amanda Ramos, Director of Finance, by using the Formula Auditing features and visual inspection to find and correct several types of errors. Your completed workbook will look similar to Figure 7.62.

Project Files

For Project 7F, you will need the following file:

e07F_Beverage_Revenue

You will save your workbook as:

Lastname_Firstname_7F_Beverage_Revenue

Project Results

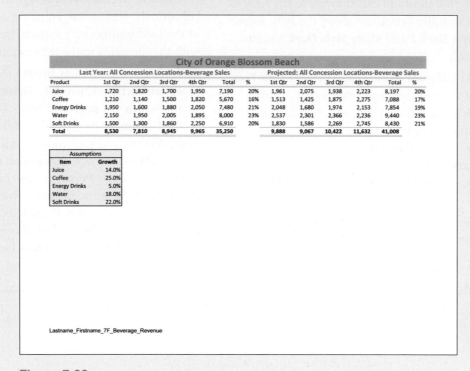

Figure 7.62

(Project 7F Beverage Revenue continues on the next page)

Mastering Excel | Project **7F** Beverage Revenue (continued)

1 **Start** Excel. From your student files, open the file **e07F_Beverage_Revenue**, and then **Save** the file in your **Excel Chapter 7** folder as **Lastname_Firstname_7F_Beverage_Revenue**

2 Click cell **I5**, which displays a green triangle indicating a potential error, and then on the **Formulas tab**, click the **Trace Precedents** button. Click the displayed **Error Checking** button, and then click **Edit in Formula Bar**. Change $B$14 to **$B$15** and press Enter so that the formula is using the Growth Assumption for *Coffee*, not for Juice.

3 On the **Formulas tab**, in the **Formula Auditing group**, click the **Error Checking** button to begin checking for errors from this point in the worksheet. In cell **M6**, the flagged error, notice the formula is trying to divide by cell **L10**, which is empty. Click the **Edit in Formula Bar** button, change **10** to **9** and then in the **Error Checking** dialog box, click **Resume**.

4 In cell **F7**, examine the error information, and then click **Copy Formula from Above**. Examine the error in cell **J8**, and then click **Copy Formula from Left**. Click **OK**. Use **Format Painter** to copy the format in cell **M5** to cell **M6**.

5 Insert a footer with the file name in the **left section**, center the worksheet horizontally, and then set the Orientation to **Landscape**. Display the Document Properties, add your name as the **Author**, type your course name and section in the **Subject** box, and as the **Keywords**, type **concessions, beverage sales Close** the Document Information Panel and **Save** your workbook. Display and examine the **Print Preview**, make any necessary corrections, **Save**, and then print or submit electronically as directed by your instructor. If you are directed to do so, print the formulas. **Close** Excel.

End **You have completed Project 7F** ——————————————————————

Excel | Chapter 7

Content-Based Assessments

Apply **7A** and **7B** skills
from these Objectives:

1. Create a PivotTable Report
2. Use Slicers and Search Filters
3. Modify a PivotTable Report
4. Create a PivotChart Report
5. Trace Precedents and Dependents to Audit Worksheet Formulas
6. Use Error Checking to Audit Worksheet Formulas
7. Use the Watch Window to Monitor Cell Values

Mastering Excel | Project **7G** Aquatics Revenue

In the following Mastering Excel project, you will assist Toby Harrison, the Director of Pools and Recreation, in creating and modifying a PivotTable report and a PivotChart report to analyze revenue from the Aquatics Program. Your completed workbooks will look similar to Figure 7.63.

Project Files

For Project 7G, you will need the following files:

e07G_Aquatics_Revenue
e07G_Food_Revenue

You will save your workbooks as:

Lastname_Firstname_7G_Aquatics_Revenue
Lastname_Firstname_7G_Food_Revenue

Project Results

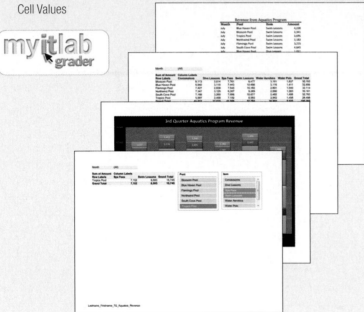
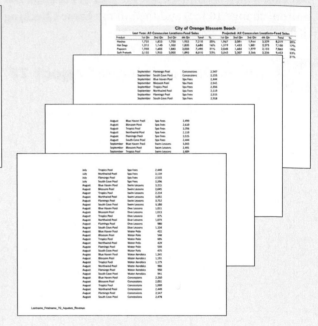

Figure 7.63

(Project 7G Aquatics Revenue continues on the next page)

Content-Based Assessments

Mastering Excel | Project **7G** Aquatics Revenue (continued)

1 From your student files, open the file **e07G_Aquatics_Revenue**. **Save** the file as **Lastname_Firstname_7G_Aquatics_Revenue** in your **Excel Chapter 7** folder.

2 Click cell **A2**, and then insert a **PivotTable**. Use the **Month** field as the **Report Filter**. Use the **Pool** field as the row labels and the **Item** field as the column labels. Place the **Amount** field in the **Values area**. **Close** the **PivotTable Field List**.

3 Click any cell in the PivotTable to make it active. Right-click any value in the PivotTable report, display the **Value Field Settings** dialog box, and then format the **Number** category to display zero decimal places and the **1000 Separator**. Insert a slicer for the **Pool** field and for the **Item** field. Apply **Slicer Style Dark 5** and **Slicer Style Dark 6** to the slicers respectively.

4 By using the two slicers, filter the data to show, for the **Tropics Pool**, the total revenue for **Spa Fees** and **Swim Lessons**. Resize and move the two slicers to the right of the filtered PivotTable, and then make a copy of this worksheet. Name the copied worksheet **Tropics Pool-3Q Swim and Spa**

5 Rename **Sheet1 3Q Revenue** In each slicer, click the **Clear Filter** button to the right of the slicer header, and then remove the slicers from the worksheet. Insert a **PivotChart** using the **Stacked Column** chart type. Move the chart to a new worksheet named **3Q Revenue Chart** Apply the **Layout 3** chart layout and **Chart Style 42**. As the **Chart Title** type **3rd Quarter Aquatics Program Revenue** Add centered data labels, and then hide all of the field buttons on the chart. Insert a custom footer with the file name in the **left section**.

6 Display the **3Q Revenue** worksheet, select all the worksheets, and then insert a footer with the file name in the **left section**. Change the **Orientation** to **Landscape**, set the **Width** to **1 page**, and center the sheets horizontally. To the **Document Panel**, add your firstname and lastname as the **Author**, add your course name and section number

as the **Subject**, and add **aquatics program, revenue** as the **Keywords**. Display **Print Preview**, make any corrections or adjustments, and then **Save** the workbook. Print or submit electronically as directed. Pages 1–3 contain your new data; pages 4–7 contain the original source data. There are no formulas in this workbook. **Close** this workbook, but leave Excel open.

7 From your student files, open **e07G_Food_Revenue**, and then **Save** the file in your **Excel Chapter 7** folder as **Lastname_Firstname_7G_Food_Revenue**

8 Click cell **I5**, and then on the **Formulas tab**, click the **Trace Precedents** button. Click the displayed **Error Checking** button, and then click **Edit in Formula Bar**. Change *$B$14* to **$B$15** and press (Enter) so that the formula is using the Growth Assumption for *Hot Dogs*, not for *Nachos*.

9 On the **Formulas tab**, in the **Formula Auditing group**, click the **Error Checking** button. In cell **M6**, notice the formula is trying to divide by cell **L10**, which is empty. Click the **Edit in Formula Bar** button, change **10** to **9** and then in the **Error Checking** dialog box, click **Resume**.

10 In cell **F7**, examine the error information, and then click **Copy Formula from Above**. Examine the error in cell **J8**, and then click **Copy Formula from Left**. Click **OK**. Use **Format Painter** to copy the format in cell **M5** to cell **M6**.

11 Insert a footer with the file name in the **left section**, center the worksheet horizontally, and then set the Orientation to **Landscape**. To the **Document Panel**, add your firstname and lastname as the **Author**, add your course name and section number as the **Subject**, and add **concessions, food sales** as the **Keywords**. Display and examine the **Print Preview**, make any necessary corrections, **Save**, and then print or submit electronically as directed by your instructor. If required, print or create an electronic version of your worksheets with formulas displayed using the instructions in Activity 1.16 in Project 1A. **Close** Excel.

End **You have completed Project 7G**

Content-Based Assessments

Apply a combination of
the **7A** and **7B** skills.

GO! Fix It | Project **7H** Snack Concessions Revenue

Project Files

For Project 7H, you will need the following file:

> e07H_Snacks_Revenue

You will save your workbook as:

> Lastname_Firstname_7H_Snacks_Revenue

Open the file e07H_Snacks_Revenue, and then save the file in your Excel Chapter 7 folder as **Lastname_Firstname_7H_Snacks_Revenue** Examine the workbook visually for errors, look at the cells with formulas (it is useful to click cells with formulas and then click Trace Precedents), and use the Formula Auditing tools as necessary to resolve all errors in the worksheet. Add your name and course information to the document properties, and include **concessions, snacks revenue** as the keywords. Insert the file name in the footer, use landscape orientation, center the worksheet horizontally, save your file, and then print or submit your workbook electronically as directed by your instructor.

End **You have completed Project 7H** ⎯⎯⎯⎯⎯⎯⎯⎯⎯⎯

Excel | Chapter 7: Creating PivotTable and PivotChart Reports and Auditing Worksheets

Content-Based Assessments

Apply a combination of the **7A** and **7B** skills.

GO! Make It | Project 7I City Services Revenue

Project Files

For Project 7I, you will need the following file:

> e07I_City_Services

You will save your workbook as:

> Lastname_Firstname_7I_City_Services

Open the file e07I_City_Services; save it in your Excel Chapter 7 folder as **Lastname_ Firstname_7I_City_Services** From the PivotTable, create the PivotChart shown in Figure 7.64. Format the plot area and the chart area with a light aqua color. Hide all field buttons. Add a custom footer in the left section of the chart. Select the remaining sheets, insert the file name in the footer, and center horizontally. Add your name, your course name and section, and the keywords **water, electric** to the document properties. Save the file, and then print or submit electronically as directed by your instructor.

Project Results

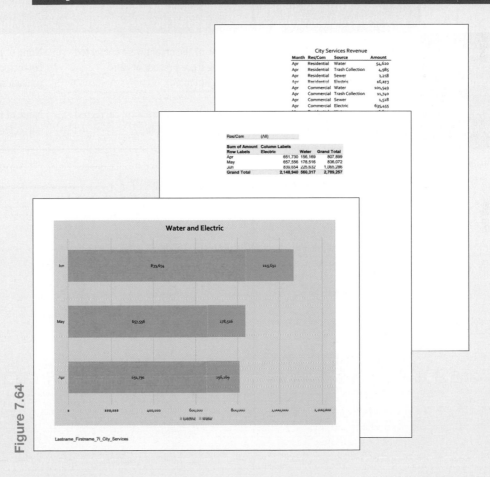

Figure 7.64

End You have completed Project 7I

Content-Based Assessments

GO! Solve It | Project **7J** Fixed Assets

Project Files

For Project 7J, you will need the following file:

    e07J_Fixed_Assets

You will save your workbook as:

    Lastname_Firstname_7J_Fixed_Assets

Open the file **e07J_Fixed_Assets** and save it as **Lastname_Firstname_7J_Fixed_Assets**
Using Excel's Formula Auditing tools, check for errors and make corrections to the worksheet.
Insert the file name in the footer in the left section. Center horizontally, add appropriate
information to the document properties including the keywords **fixed assets** and submit as
directed by your instructor.

		Performance Level	
	Exemplary: You consistently applied the relevant skills.	**Proficient:** You sometimes, but not always, applied the relevant skills.	**Developing:** You rarely or never applied the relevant skills.
Trace Formula Precedents and Dependents	Trace precedents and dependents were used to identify and correct errors.	Some of the errors were corrected using trace precedents and dependents.	None of the errors were corrected using trace precedents and dependents.
Use Error Checking	Error Checking was used to identify and correct errors.	Some of the errors were corrected using Error Checking.	None of the errors were corrected using Error Checking.

(Performance Criteria)

End **You have completed Project 7J** ⎯⎯⎯⎯⎯⎯⎯⎯⎯⎯⎯⎯

GO! Solve It | Project 7K Park Expenses

Project Files

For Project 7K, you will need the following file:

e07K_Park_Expenses

You will save your workbook as:

Lastname_Firstname_7K_Park_Expenses

Open the file **e07K_Park_Expenses** and save it as **Lastname_Firstname_7K_Park_Expenses** From the source data, create a PivotTable. Use the Month and Park fields as Row Labels. Use the Expense Item field as a Column Label. Place the Amount field in the Values area. Format the numbers to display zero decimal places and the 1000 separator. Format the PivotTable with an attractive style. Create a PivotChart on a separate sheet using the column chart style, and then use the report filters on the chart to show only the data for June, only the data for Squires, Star Point, and Sunset Parks, and only the expenses for Equipment, Grounds & Maintenance, and Utilities. Format the chart attractively. On all sheets, insert the file name in the footer in the left section. Set the orientation to landscape and center horizontally. Add appropriate information to the document properties including the keyword **parks grounds expenses** and submit as directed by your instructor.

	Performance Level		
	Exemplary: You consistently applied the relevant skills.	**Proficient:** You sometimes, but not always, applied the relevant skills.	**Developing:** You rarely or never applied the relevant skills.
Create a PivotTable Report	The PivotTable Report displays Month and Park in Row labels, Expense Item in Column Labels area, and amount field in the Values area.	The PivotTable Report displays some of the items from the field list, but not all according to the directions.	The PivotTable was not created.
Format a PivotTable Report	The PivotTable is formatted with the numbers displaying zero decimal places, the 1000 separator, and an attractive style.	The PivotTable is formatted with some but not all of the formatting, numbers displaying zero decimal places, 1000 separator, and some attractive formatting.	The PivotTable was not formatted.
Create and Format a PivotChart	A PivotChart displays on a separate sheet using the column chart style. The chart is filtered showing the data for June, only for Squires, Star Point, and Sunset Parks, and only the expenses for Equipment, Grounds & Maintenance, and Utilities. The chart is formatted attractively.	A PivotChart displays on a separate sheet using the column chart style. The chart is filtered showing some but not all of the data for June, only for Squires, Star Point, and Sunset Parks, and only the expenses for Equipment, Grounds & Maintenance, and Utilities. Some of the chart is formatted attractively.	The PivotChart was not created.

End You have completed Project 7K

Outcomes-Based Assessments

Rubric

The following outcomes-based assessments are *open-ended assessments*. That is, there is no specific correct result; your result will depend on your approach to the information provided. Make *Professional Quality* your goal. Use the following scoring rubric to guide you in *how* to approach the problem and then to evaluate *how well* your approach solves the problem.

The *criteria*—Software Mastery, Content, Format and Layout, and Process—represent the knowledge and skills you have gained that you can apply to solving the problem. The *levels of performance*—Professional Quality, Approaching Professional Quality, or Needs Quality Improvements—help you and your instructor evaluate your result.

	Your completed project is of Professional Quality if you:	Your completed project is Approaching Professional Quality if you:	Your completed project Needs Quality Improvements if you:
1-Software Mastery	Choose and apply the most appropriate skills, tools, and features and identify efficient methods to solve the problem.	Choose and apply some appropriate skills, tools, and features, but not in the most efficient manner.	Choose inappropriate skills, tools, or features, or are inefficient in solving the problem.
2-Content	Construct a solution that is clear and well organized, contains content that is accurate, appropriate to the audience and purpose, and is complete. Provide a solution that contains no errors in spelling, grammar, or style.	Construct a solution in which some components are unclear, poorly organized, inconsistent, or incomplete. Misjudge the needs of the audience. Have some errors in spelling, grammar, or style, but the errors do not detract from comprehension.	Construct a solution that is unclear, incomplete, or poorly organized; contains some inaccurate or inappropriate content; and contains many errors in spelling, grammar, or style. Do not solve the problem.
3-Format and Layout	Format and arrange all elements to communicate information and ideas, clarify function, illustrate relationships, and indicate relative importance.	Apply appropriate format and layout features to some elements, but not others. Overuse features, causing minor distraction.	Apply format and layout that does not communicate information or ideas clearly. Do not use format and layout features to clarify function, illustrate relationships, or indicate relative importance. Use available features excessively, causing distraction.
4-Process	Use an organized approach that integrates planning, development, self-assessment, revision, and reflection.	Demonstrate an organized approach in some areas, but not others; or, use an insufficient process of organization throughout.	Do not use an organized approach to solve the problem.

Outcomes-Based Assessments

Apply a combination of the **7A** and **7B** skills.

GO! Think | Project **7L** Golf Course Revenue

Project Files

For Project 7L, you will need the following file:

e07L_Golf_Courses

You will save your workbook as:

Lastname_Firstname_7L_Golf_Courses

Open the file e07L_Golf_Courses, and then save it in your chapter folder as **Lastname_Firstname_7L_Golf_Courses** From the source data, create a PivotTable report and filter the report on Month. Use Course as row labels and Item as column labels. Sum the amounts. Create an attractive PivotChart report for the 3rd Quarter Revenue. Exclude Logo Shirts and Golf Balls from the PivotChart. Insert the file name in the left section of the footer on each page, center horizontally, set the orientation to landscape, add appropriate information to the document properties, including the keywords **golf courses revenue** and submit as directed by your instructor.

 You have completed Project 7L ———————————

Apply a combination of the **7A** and **7B** skills.

GO! Think | Project **7M** Pool Expenses

Project Files

For Project 7M, you will need the following file:

e07M_Pool_Expenses

You will save your workbook as:

Lastname_Firstname_7M_Pool_Expenses

From your student files, open the file e07M_Pool_Expenses, and then save it in your chapter folder as **Lastname_Firstname_7M_Pool_Expenses** From the source data, create a PivotTable filtered on Month, and with the pool names as rows and the expense items as columns. Format the values appropriately. Create a PivotChart on a separate sheet using the stacked column, and format it attractively. Filter the chart to include only the Blue Haven, Grove, Pearl Sands, and South Cove pools. Add data labels. Insert appropriate footers on all sheets, add appropriate information to the document properties including the keywords **pool expenses** and submit as directed by your instructor.

 You have completed Project 7M ———————————

Outcomes-Based Assessments

Apply a combination of the **7A** and **7B** skills.

You and GO! | Project **7N** Inventory

Project Files

For Project 7N, you will need the following file:

New blank worksheet

You will save your workbook as:

Lastname_Firstname_7N_Inventory

In this activity, you will make a list of something that you own and use a PivotTable to evaluate the data. Prepare a list of something that you own—CDs, DVDs, books, sporting equipment—along with other information such as author or artist. In that list, include the name of the item, the purchase price—you can approximate the purchase price—and the approximate date of the last time you used the item. Provide a rating for the item from 1 to 5 to indicate how much you use the item and include the rating scale in the form. (Use 1 for the lowest and 5 for the highest.) Using the skills you have practiced, provide summary data for the list. Then prepare a PivotTable to display the frequency with which you used the item and to identify your favorite items.

Save the workbook as **Lastname_Firstname_7N_Inventory**. Format the worksheet attractively for printing, insert the file name in the footer, add appropriate information to the document properties including the keyword **inventory** and submit as directed by your instructor.

 End **You have completed Project 7N** ————————————————

Using the Data Analysis, Solver, and Scenario Features

OUTCOMES

At the end of this chapter you will be able to:

OBJECTIVES

Mastering these objectives will enable you to:

PROJECT 8A
Analyze sales data to evaluate business solutions and compare data with a line chart.

1. Calculate a Moving Average (p. 497)
2. Project Income and Expenses (p. 503)
3. Determine a Break-Even Point (p. 505)

PROJECT 8B
Use Solver and Scenario Tools to evaluate complex formulas.

4. Use Solver (p. 510)
5. Evaluate Complex Formulas (p. 516)
6. Create Scenarios (p. 518)

olly/shutterstock

In This Chapter

Because organizations forecast future results based on current trends, in this chapter, you will use Excel tools to analyze data, project values, determine and chart the moving average of sales, project sales based on an expected growth rate, and determine and chart a break-even point.

You will also use the Solver and Scenario tools to evaluate complex formulas and to search for possible solutions to business problems. Solver can analyze financial planning problems that involve a quantity that changes over time. By using a scenario, you can look at a set of values and project forward to focus on possible results.

The projects in this chapter relate to **Oceana Palm Grill**, which is a chain of 25 casual, full-service restaurants based in Austin, Texas. The Oceana Palm Grill owners plan an aggressive expansion program. To expand by 15 additional restaurants in North Carolina and Florida by 2018, the company must attract new investors, develop new menus, and recruit new employees, all while adhering to the company's quality guidelines and maintaining its reputation for excellent service. To succeed, the company plans to build on its past success and maintain its quality elements.

Project 8A Sales Analysis

myitlab
Project 8A Training

Project Activities

In Activities 8.01 through 8.06, you will use Excel's data analysis tools to determine the moving average of sales for the first six weeks at the new Oceana Palm Grill restaurant in Charlotte, North Carolina. Then you will project sales based on an expected growth rate and determine the break-even point for the restaurant. Your completed worksheets will look similar to Figure 8.1.

Project Files

For Project 8A, you will need the following file:

e08A_Charlotte_Sales

You will save your workbook as:

Lastname_Firstname_8A_Charlotte_Sales

Project Results

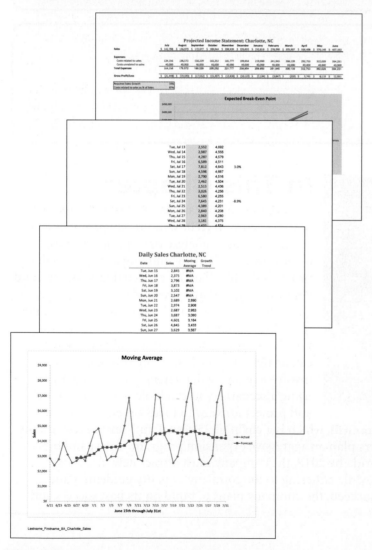

Figure 8.1
Project 8A Charlotte Sales

Objective 1 | Calculate a Moving Average

Start-up businesses usually operate at a loss while the business grows, with an expectation that at some future point, the business will become profitable. Owners and investors want to know if the business is on track to become profitable and when the point of profitability is likely to occur.

Excel offers Data Analysis tools, which range from basic to very sophisticated, to help you project future results based on past performance. One of the basic tools is a *moving average*. A moving average is a sequence of averages computed from parts of a data series. In a chart, a moving average smoothes the fluctuations in data, thus showing a pattern or trend more clearly. When you use a moving average, you choose how many preceding intervals to include in the average. A series of averages is calculated by moving—or changing—the range of cells used to calculate each average.

Activity 8.01 | Creating a Custom Number Format

Joseph Mabry, the Chief Financial Officer of Oceana Palm Grill, wants to see how sales have grown in the first six weeks at the new restaurant in Charlotte, North Carolina. Because there is a wide variation in sales at restaurants between weekday and weekend sales, Mr. Mabry first needs to add the day of the week to the Charlotte sales report. To accomplish this, you will customize the format applied to the date. You can customize numbers or dates when the available options do not match your needs.

1 **Start** Excel. From your student files, open the file **e08A_Charlotte_Sales**. Display the **Save As** dialog box, navigate to the location where you will store your workbooks for this chapter, and then create a new folder named **Excel Chapter 8** In your new folder, **Save** the workbook as **Lastname_Firstname_8A_Charlotte_Sales**

This Sales worksheet displays dates in column A and the sales for each date in column B. July sales are highlighted in aqua.

2 Click cell **A3**. On the **Home tab**, in the **Number group**, click the **Dialog Box Launcher**. In the **Format Cells** dialog box, be sure the **Number tab** is selected. Compare your screen with Figure 8.2.

Figure 8.2

Format Cells dialog box

Number tab selected

Excel | Chapter 8

3 Under **Category**, click **Custom**. Examine the table in Figure 8.3 to familiarize yourself with the codes used to create a custom date format.

Custom codes display under Type, and the code for the selected date in cell A3 displays in the Type box. You can use this format as a starting point and then modify it or you can type a new code in the Type box.

Date Codes

To display	Use this code
Months as 1–12	m
Months as 01–12	mm
Months as Jan–Dec	mmm
Months as January–December	mmmm
Months as the first letter of the month	mmmmm
Days as 1–31	d
Days as 01–31	dd
Days as Sun–Sat	ddd
Days as Sunday–Saturday	dddd
Years as 00–99	yy
Years as 1900–9999	yyyy

Figure 8.3

4 Select the code in the **Type** box and type **ddd, mmm dd** to replace it. Compare your screen with Figure 8.4.

As you type, you can see the date displayed in the new format in the Sample box. This code creates a date that displays as *Tue, Jun 15*. The comma displays as a comma.

Figure 8.4

New format in the Sample box

Code for new date format

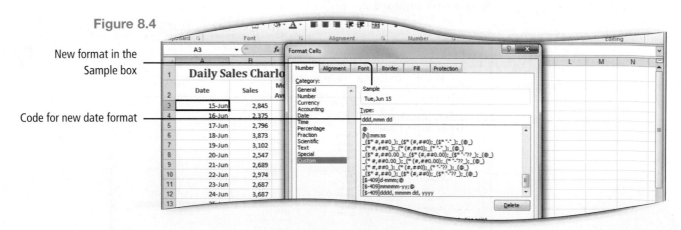

5 Click **OK** and notice the new date format in cell **A3**. Drag the fill handle to copy the new format down through cell **A49**. Press Ctrl + Home, click **Save** 🖫, and then compare your screen with Figure 8.5.

Figure 8.5

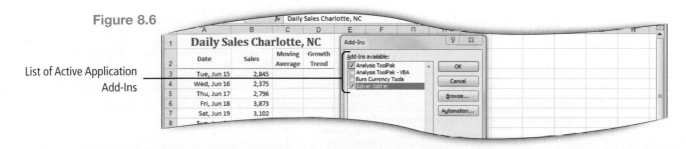

Customized date format applied

Activity 8.02 | Calculating a Moving Average

Recall that a moving average calculates an average for a group of numbers over a specified interval. The number range that is averaged is constantly changing, dropping off the first number in the range and adding on the most recent number. In this manner, you can see a trend for widely fluctuating numbers. The sales activity for the new Charlotte restaurant has been strong on the weekends and slower during the week. You need to determine if, overall, the sales activity is trending upward or downward. The moving average tool is one of several Data Analysis tools.

1 From **Backstage** view, click **Options**. In the **Excel Options** dialog box, on the left, click **Add-Ins**. At the bottom of the dialog box, verify that the **Manage** box displays *Excel Add-ins*, and then click the **Go** button. In the **Add-Ins** dialog box, if necessary, select the **Analysis ToolPak** check box. Compare your screen with Figure 8.6.

Add-ins are optional commands and features that are not immediately available; you must first install and/or activate an add-in to use it.

Figure 8.6

List of Active Application Add-Ins

2 Click **OK**, and then click cell **A2** to make it the active cell. On the **Data tab**, in the **Analysis group**, click the **Data Analysis** button. Scroll the list as necessary, and then click **Moving Average**. Click **OK**.

The Moving Average dialog box displays. Here you define the input range, the *interval*—the number of cells to include in the average—and the output range.

Another Way

Click the **Collapse Dialog Box** button, select the range B2:B49, and then click the **Expand Dialog Box** button.

3 With the insertion point blinking in the **Input Range** box, type **b2:b49** and then select the **Labels in First Row** checkbox.

> The input range consists of the sales figures for the first six weeks, from Jun 15 through Jul 31. The first cell in the range, B2, contains the label *Sales*.

4 Click in the **Interval** box, and then type **7**

> The moving average will be a weekly (7-day) average of sales. The first average will be from Tue, Jun 15 through Mon, Jun 21. The next average will be from Wed, Jun 16 through Tue, Jun 22. This pattern—dropping the oldest date and adding in the next date—will continue for the entire range.

5 Click in the **Output Range** box, type **c3** and then select the **Chart Output** check box. Compare your **Moving Average** dialog box with Figure 8.7.

Figure 8.7

Input range defined

Label in the first row

7-day interval used for average

Output range starts here

Results will be charted

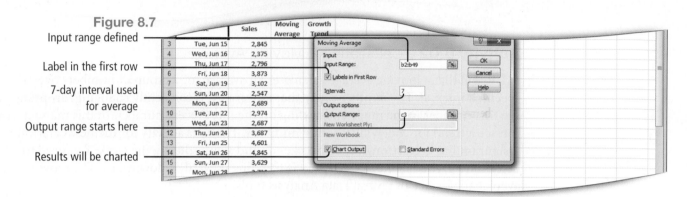

6 Click **OK**. Save your workbook, and then compare your screen with Figure 8.8.

> The moving averages display in column C and a chart is added to the worksheet. The first six cells in column C display the error code *#N/A* because there were not seven numbers available to use in the average. Green triangles display because the formulas in these cells refer to a range that has additional numbers adjacent. The first average—for Tue, Jun 15 through Mon, Jun 21—is *2,890*.

Figure 8.8

Chart comparing actual to moving average

Moving averages

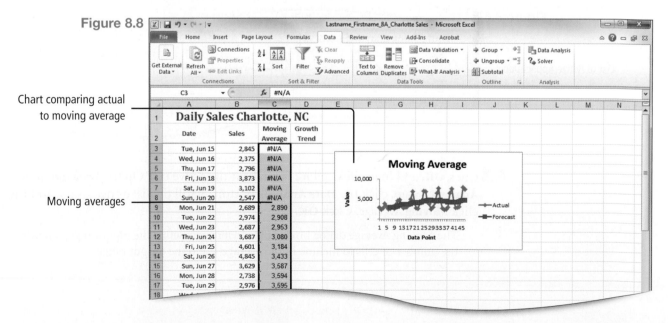

Activity 8.03 | Modifying the Moving Average Chart

To gain a clearer image of a trend, you can modify the moving average chart.

1 Click the outer edge of the chart to select it, and then on the **Design tab**, in the **Location group**, click the **Move Chart** button.

2 Click the **New sheet** option button, type **Sales Trend Chart** and then click **OK**.

> By displaying this chart on a separate chart sheet, you can more easily see the actual data points—in dark blue—versus the moving average—in red—which is labeled *Forecast*. The horizontal category axis—the X-axis—is titled *Data Point*. This represents the dates for each sales figure. You can see by the red line that, overall, the sales activity for the first six weeks is trending slightly upward.

Another Way

Right-click the axis, and then on the short-cut menu, click **Select Data**.

3 At the bottom of the chart, point to any of the data points to display the ScreenTip *Horizontal (Category) Axis*, and then click to select the axis. On the **Design tab**, in the **Data group**, click the **Select Data** button.

> In the Select Data Source dialog box, you can change the category axis labels to display the range of dates that correspond to the sales figures.

4 In the **Select Data Source** dialog box, under **Horizontal (Category) Axis Labels**, click the **Edit** button. Click the **Sales sheet tab** to display the second worksheet, and then select the range **A9:A49**.Compare your screen with Figure 8.9.

> The selected range displays in the dialog box. You can select the range of cells to use as labels for the category axis. Start with cell A9 because that is the first row for which there is a moving average calculation.

Figure 8.9

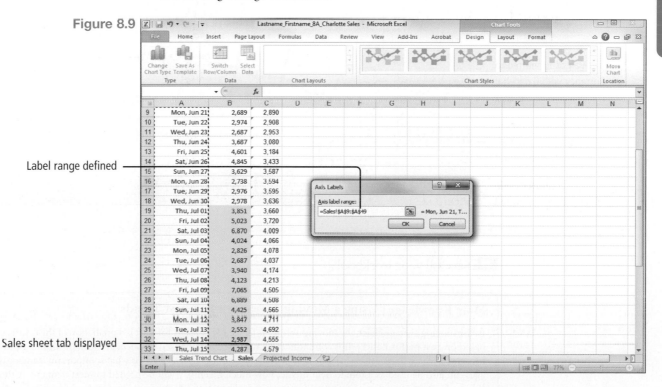

Label range defined

Sales sheet tab displayed

5 In the **Axis Labels** dialog box, click **OK**. In the **Select Data Source** dialog box, click **OK**.

> Dates display along the category axis at the bottom of the chart.

6 Right-click the **Category Axis**, and then on the shortcut menu, click **Format Axis**. In the **Format Axis** dialog box, on the left, click **Number**, and then under **Category**, click **Date**. Under **Type**, click the **3/14** format, and then click **Close**.

> This action shortens the date format.

7 Click the **Horizontal Axis Title**—Data Point—to select it. On the **Formula** type **June 15th through July 31st** and then press ⌷Enter⌷. Point to the **Horizontal Axis Title**, right-click, and then on the Mini toolbar, change the font size to **12**. Click the **Vertical Axis Title**—Value—to select it. On the **Formula Bar** type **Sales** and then press ⌷Enter⌷. Point to the **Vertical Axis Title**, right-click, and then on the Mini toolbar, change the font size to **12**.

The Horizontal Axis and Vertical Axis titles are changed and formatted.

8 Right-click the **Vertical Axis**, and then on the shortcut menu, click **Format Axis**. In the **Format Axis** dialog box, on the left, click **Number**, and then under **Category**, click **Currency**. To the right of **Decimal places**, click **0**, and then click **Close**. Compare your chart with Figure 8.10.

This action changes the values to Currency with 0 decimal places.

Figure 8.10

Vertical Axis title changed and formatted

Values formatted to Currency with 0 decimal places

Dates display along the category axis with shortened format

Horizontal Axis title changed and formatted

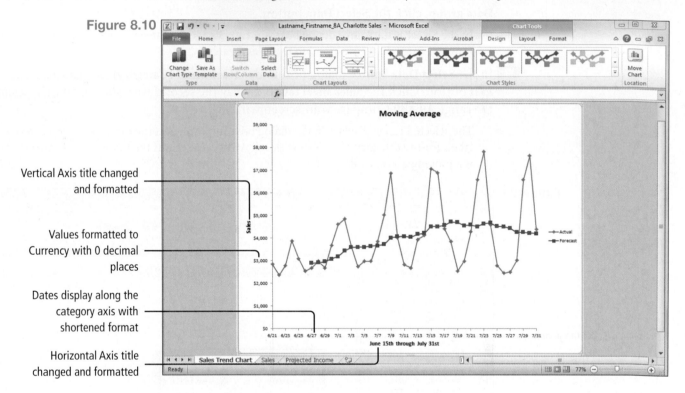

9 **Save** 💾 your workbook.

More Knowledge | Using a Moving Average to Forecast Trends

In the moving average chart, the moving average is labeled *Forecast*. A forecast is a prediction of the future, often based on past performances. It is common to see moving averages used to calculate stock or mutual fund performance, where fluctuations in value may be frequent, but the overall trend is what is important. Moving averages can also be used as a tool to help predict how much inventory will be needed to meet demand. Although this is a forecasting tool, it is important to recognize its limitations. A moving average is based on historical data, and it is not necessarily a good prediction of what will occur in the future. Changes in the economy, competition, or other factors can affect sales dramatically, causing the moving average trend to change.

Activity 8.04 | Calculating Growth Based on a Moving Average

You can also use a moving average to calculate a growth rate at different intervals.

1 Display the **Sales** worksheet. Click cell **D21**, type **=(c21-c14)/c14** and then press ⏎Enter.

> This formula calculates a weekly sales growth percentage from one Saturday to the next, based on the moving average.

2 Scroll to position **row 21** near the top of your screen. Point to cell **D21**, right-click, and then on the Mini toolbar, click the **Percent Style** button ⏺%⏺. Click the **Increase Decimal** button ⏺.0→.00⏺ one time to display one decimal place—your result is *16.8%*.

3 With cell **D21** still selected, point to the cell and right-click, and then click **Copy**. Point to cell **D28**, right-click, and then under Paste Options, click the **Paste** button ⏺.

> The formula is copied to the next date that is a Saturday.

4 Point to cell **D35**, right-click, and then click the **Paste** button ⏺. Continue in the same manner to paste the formula in cells **D42** and **D49** for the next two Saturday dates. Click the **Save** ⏺ button, and then compare your screen with Figure 8.11.

> The formula results show that the trend has moved up and down over five weeks of business.

Figure 8.11

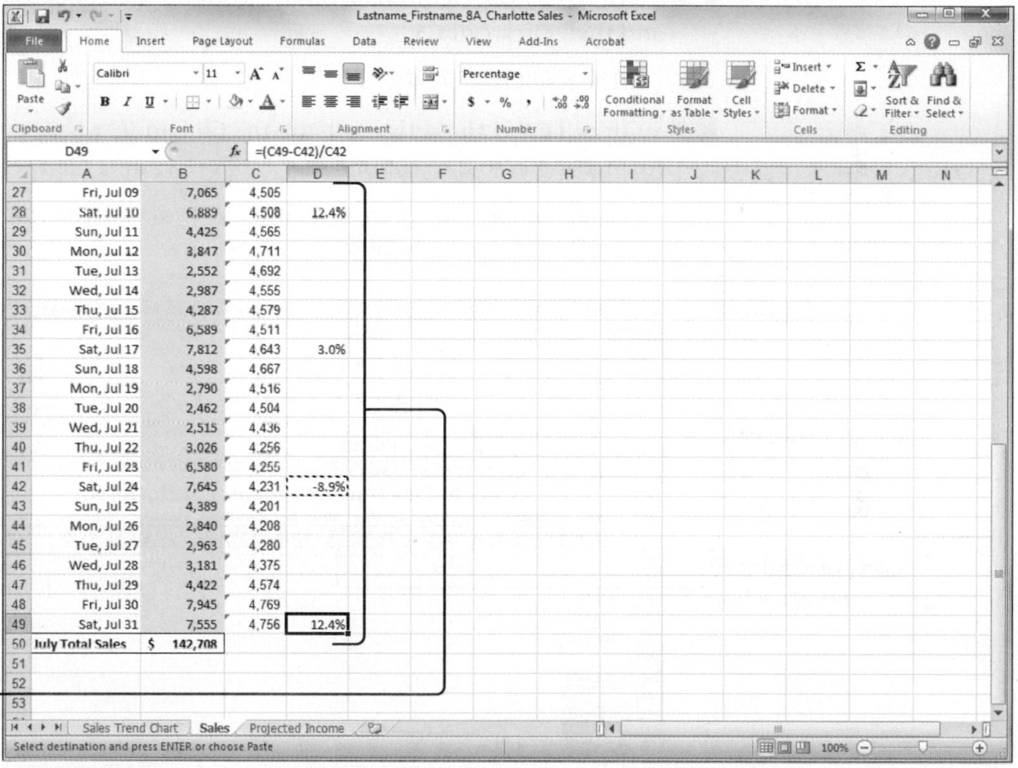

Week-to-week change based on moving average

Objective 2 | Project Income and Expenses

Income generally consists of sales for products and services. In a restaurant, this includes the sale of food and beverages. Expenses can be classified according to two broad categories: fixed expenses and variable expenses. *Fixed expenses* remain the same each month regardless of the amount of activity. They include items such as rent, utilities, insurance, and general overhead. *Variable expenses* vary depending on the amount of sales. In a restaurant, the cost of the food—otherwise known as cost of goods sold—and wages are the two most common variable expenses. In this activity, you will work with a worksheet that uses these two broad categories of expenses.

Activity 8.05 | Projecting Income and Expenses

1 In your **8A_Charlotte_Sales** workbook, display the **Projected Income** worksheet.

This sheet contains the first portion of an income statement for the Charlotte restaurant. You will project sales and expenses through June of next year.

2 Click cell **B2**, and then use the fill handle to fill the months for a year—from July to June—across to **column M**. With the range **B2:M2** selected, apply **Center** ☰. Select **columns B:M** and set the column width to **75 pixels**.

3 Click cell **B3** and examine the formula in the **Formula Bar**.

This cell references the sales for July, found in cell B50 on the Sales worksheet.

4 Click cell **C3**, type **=b3*(1+b12)** and then press Enter.

This formula takes the previous month's sales in cell B3 and multiplies it by 110% to determine a growth rate of 10 percent over the previous month—*156978.8*. Cell B12 indicates the Required Sales Growth rate of 10%, and the absolute cell reference is used so this formula can be copied across the row.

5 Point to cell **B3**, right-click, on the Mini toolbar, click the **Format Painter** button ✍, and then click cell **C3**.

The result is *$156,979*.

6 With cell **C3** as the active cell, use the fill handle to copy the formula and the formatting across to **column M**. Compare your screen with Figure 8.12.

Based on this projection, by June of next year, the Charlotte restaurant should have *$407,163* in monthly sales.

Figure 8.12

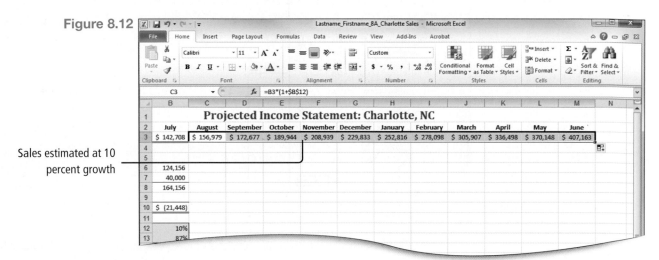

Sales estimated at 10 percent growth

7 Click cell **B6** and examine the formula.

This formula multiplies the sales for July by the value in cell B13—*87%*. It is estimated that variable expenses for the first year will be 87 percent of sales. An absolute reference is used so this formula can be copied across the worksheet.

8 Use the fill handle to copy the formula from cell **B6** across the row to **column M**.

The variable expenses, which are based on sales, are projected for the next year. Variable expenses for June are calculated to be *$354,231*.

9 Click cell **B7**.

These are fixed costs—costs such as rent and insurance that are not directly tied to sales—which total 40,000.

10 Use the fill handle to copy the formula from cell **B7** across the row to **column M**.

11 Select the range **C8:M8**, and then on the **Home tab**, in the **Editing group**, click the **Sum** button Σ. Compare your screen with Figure 8.13.

For each month, the total expenses are calculated.

Figure 8.13

Total expenses

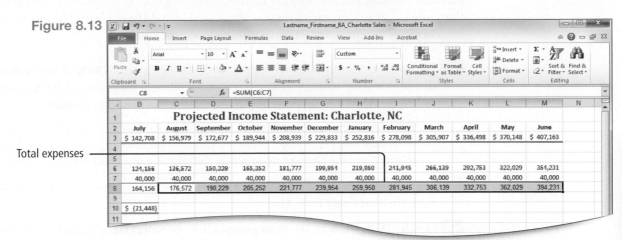

12 Click cell **B10**.

This formula calculates the gross profit or loss for a month—sales minus expenses.

13 Use the fill handle to copy the formula from cell **B10** across to **column M**. **Save** 💾 your workbook, and then compare your screen with Figure 8.14.

In April, if the sales growth estimates are met, the restaurant will break even—income will equal expenses—and actually show a profit of $3,745.

Figure 8.14

Profit or loss

Break-even occurs in April

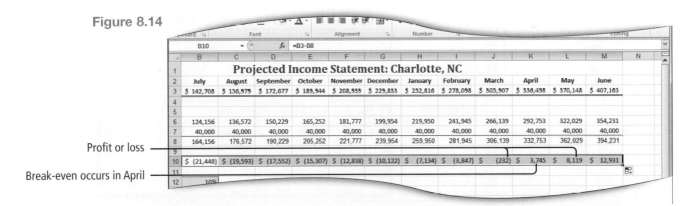

Objective 3 | Determine a Break-Even Point

The goal of a business is to make a profit. However, a new business often operates at a loss for a period of time before becoming profitable. The point at which a company starts to make a profit is known as the **break-even** point. A break-even point can be calculated for a product, a branch office, a division, or an entire company. The Oceana Palm Grill restaurants use a model for new restaurants that projects 10 percent growth, month-to-month, in the first year, with the expectation that sometime during the first year the restaurant will start to make a profit. Mr. Mabry wants to estimate when the new Charlotte restaurant will become profitable, based on sales for its first full month of business.

Excel | Chapter 8

Activity 8.06 | Charting the Break-Even Point With a Line Chart

You can chart the results of the estimated income statement to create a visual image of the income and expenses and the projected break-even point.

Recall that a *line chart* displays trends over time. Time is displayed along the bottom axis and the data point values are connected with a line. If you want to compare more than one set of values, each group is connected by a different line. The curves and directions of the lines make trends noticeable to the reader.

1 In the lower right corner of your screen, set the Zoom to **80%** so that **columns A:M** display on your screen—if you have a wide screen, this may not be necessary. Select the range **A2:M3**. Hold down Ctrl, and then select the range **A8:M8**.

By selecting the income totals and the expense totals, you will be able to see where they cross each other on a graph when you chart the break-even point. By including the months in row 2 and the labels in column A in the selection, the chart will be properly labeled.

2 On the **Insert tab**, in the **Charts group**, click the **Line** button, and then under **2-D Line**, click the first chart type, **Line**.

3 On the **Design tab**, in the **Data group**, click the **Select Data** button. In the **Select Data Source** dialog box, verify that the **Chart data range** is *A2:M3* and *A8:M8*. Compare your screen with Figure 8.15.

The Chart data range box displays the selected range—including the sheet name—using absolute references.

Figure 8.15

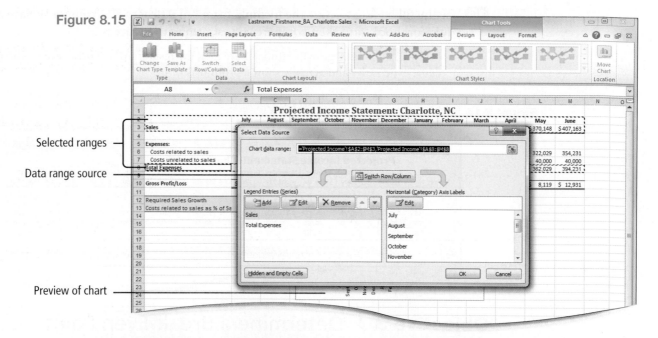

Selected ranges

Data range source

Preview of chart

4 Click **OK**. On **Layout tab**, in the **Labels group**, click the **Chart Title** button, click **Above Chart**, and then watch the **Formula Bar** as you type **Expected Break-Even Point** Press Enter.

5 By using the pointer, drag to position the upper left corner of the chart inside the upper left corner of cell **B15**.

6 Scroll to position **row 13** near the top of your screen. Drag the lower right sizing handle of the chart inside the lower right corner of cell **M36**. Compare your chart with the one shown in Figure 8.16.

Figure 8.16

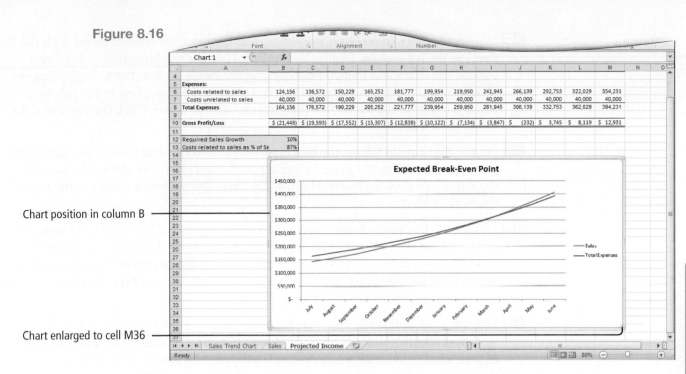

Chart position in column B

Chart enlarged to cell M36

7 On the left side of the chart, right-click the **Value Axis**, and then on the shortcut menu, click **Format Axis**.

8 In the **Format Axis** dialog box, on the left, verify that **Axis Options** is selected. Under **Axis Options**, click the **Minimum Fixed** option button. To the immediate right, delete the text in the **Fixed** box, and then type **100000** Press Enter.

9 On the **Design tab**, apply **Chart Style 18**. Format the **Chart Area** and the **Plot Area** with a **Solid fill** using the Theme Color **Tan, Background 2, Darker 10%**. Compare your screen with Figure 8.17.

Because there are no figures less than $100,000, changing the scale in this manner provides more vertical space on the chart and results in a more dramatic slope on the line.

Figure 8.17

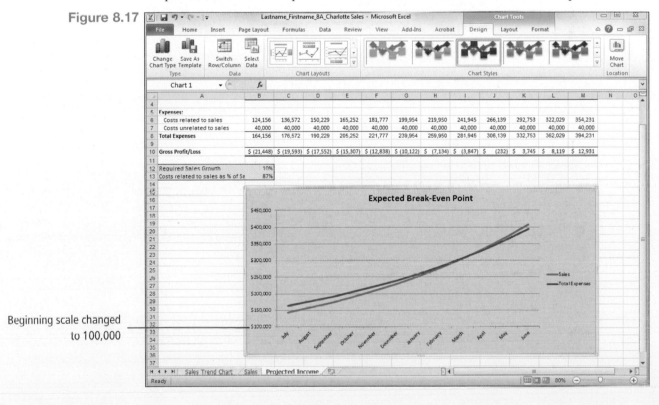

Beginning scale changed to 100,000

10 Display the **Sales Trend Chart** worksheet, and then insert a custom footer with the file name in the **left section**. Display the **Projected Income** worksheet, click anywhere outside the chart, and then, if necessary, set the **Zoom** back to **100%**. Right-click the sheet tab, and then click **Select All Sheets** so that *[Group]* displays in the title bar. Insert a footer in the **left section** that includes the file name. Click the cell above the footer to deselect it.

11 On the **Page Layout tab**, set the **Orientation** to **Landscape**, and then in the **Scale to Fit group**, set the **Width** to **1 page**. Center the worksheets horizontally on the page. On the status bar, click the **Normal** button ⊞. Press Ctrl + Home to move to the top of the worksheet.

12 Display the **Document Panel**. **Close** the Document Information Panel and **Save** your workbook. In the **Author** box, type your firstname and lastname, in the **Subject** box, type your course name and section number, and in the **Keywords** box, type **moving average, break-even point** Display the grouped worksheets in **Print Preview**. Make any necessary corrections or adjustments.

13 Save 🖫 your workbook, and then **Print** the three worksheets or submit your workbook electronically as directed. If required, print or create an electronic version of your worksheets with formulas displayed using the instructions in Activity 1.16 in Project 1A.

14 If you printed your formulas, be sure to redisplay the worksheet by pressing Ctrl + `. **Close** the workbook. If you are prompted to save changes, click **No** so that you do not save the changes to the Print layout that you used for printing formulas. **Exit** Excel.

End **You have completed Project 8A** ———————————————

Project 8B Staffing Analysis

Project Activities

In Activities 8.07 through 8.13, you will assist Laura Mabry Hernandez, manager of the Austin East restaurant, in determining the most efficient work schedule for the server staff. Your completed worksheet will look similar to Figure 8.18.

Project Files

For Project 8B, you will need the following file:

    e08B_Staffing_Analysis

You will save your workbook as:

    Lastname_Firstname_8B_Staffing_Analysis

Project Results

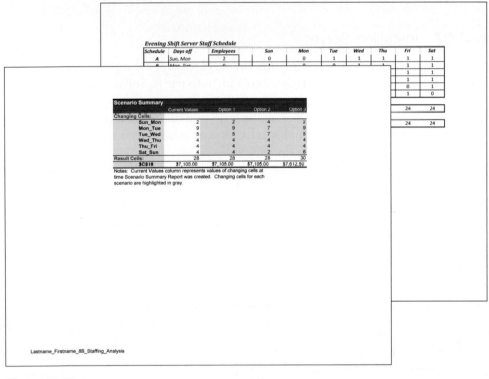

Figure 8.18
Project 8B Staffing Analysis

Objective 4 | Use Solver

Solver is an Excel's what-if analysis tool with which you can find an optimal (maximum or minimum) value for a formula in one cell—referred to as the *objective cell*—subject to constraints, or limits, on the values of other formula cells on a worksheet.

Use Solver when you need to make a decision that involves more than one variable. For example, the manager of the Austin East restaurant needs to determine the number of servers to assign to each evening shift so there are enough servers to handle customer demand, but not too many servers for the work required. Additionally, the schedule must allow each server to have two consecutive days off. Solver can help determine values like these—values that result in minimums, maximums, or specific results.

When you use Solver, the focus is on the objective cell—the cell that contains a formula for the results you are trying to determine, such as minimum weekly payroll expense. Your worksheet will have *decision variables*—also referred to as *variable cells*—that are cells in which the values will change to achieve the desired results. Your worksheet will also have *constraint cells*—cells that contain values that limit or restrict the outcome. As an example of a constraint, in determining a work schedule, you cannot schedule more than the total number of employees on the payroll.

Activity 8.07 | Installing Solver

Recall that add-ins are optional commands and features that are not immediately available; you must first install and/or activate an add-in to use it. Solver is an add-in.

1 **Start** Excel. Click the **Data tab**, and then at the right end of the **Data tab**, check to see if the **Analysis group** and **Solver** button display. Compare your screen with Figure 8.19.

Figure 8.19

Data tab

Solver button

Analysis group

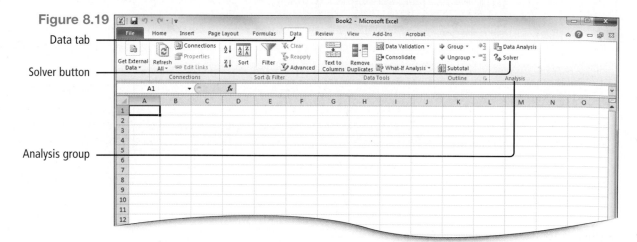

2 If the **Solver** button displays, Solver has been installed on your computer and you can move to Activity 8.08. If the Solver button does *not* display, complete the remaining steps in this activity to install it.

3 From **Backstage** view, display **Options**. On the left, click **Add-Ins**, and then at the bottom of the screen, in the **Manage** box, if necessary, select **Excel Add-ins**. Compare your screen with Figure 8.20.

Figure 8.20

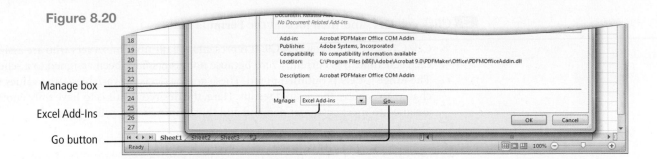

Manage box
Excel Add-Ins
Go button

4 Click **Go**.

The Add-Ins dialog box displays.

5 Select the **Solver Add-in** check box, and then click **OK**.

The Solver Add-in is installed. On the Data tab, in the Analysis group, the Solver button displays.

Activity 8.08 | Understanding a Solver Worksheet

The manager of the Austin East restaurant wants to minimize the weekly payroll expense by scheduling only enough servers to handle established customer activity. She has reviewed customer activity for the past three months and determined how many servers are needed for the evening schedule on each day of the week. For example, more servers are needed on Friday and Saturday evenings than on Tuesday and Wednesday evenings. You will use Solver to determine the number of servers to schedule for each evening shift to meet the demand while minimizing the payroll expense. Before you can solve the problem of minimizing payroll expenses, familiarize yourself with the components of the worksheet.

1 From your student files, open the file **e08B_Staffing_Analysis**. Display the **Save As** dialog box, navigate to your **Excel Chapter 8** folder, and then **Save** the workbook as **Lastname_Firstname_8B_Staffing_Analysis**

2 Examine the range **A3:K9**, and then compare your screen with Figure 8.21.

Six possible schedules are labeled—A through F. On the right, column B lists the two consecutive days off for each schedule. For example, servers who work Schedule B have Monday and Tuesday off. Servers who work Schedule C have Tuesday and Wednesday off.

For each schedule, the cells in columns E through K indicate a 0 for days off and a 1 for days worked. For example, Schedule B indicates 0 under Mon and Tue—the days off—and 1 under Sun, Wed, Thu, Fri, and Sat—the days worked.

Figure 8.21

Days off indicated by 0
Days off for each schedule
Schedule label
Days worked indicated by 1

Schedule	Days off	Employees	Sun	Mon	Tue	Wed	Thu	Fri	Sat
Evening Shift Server Staff Schedule									
A	Sun, Mon		0	0	1	1	1	1	1
B	Mon, Tue		1	0	0	1	1	1	1
C	Tue, Wed		1	1	0	0	1	1	1
D	Wed, Thu		1	1	1	0	0	1	1
E	Thu, Fri		1	1	1	1	0	0	1
F	Sat, Sun		0	1	1	1	1	1	0
	Schedule Totals:	0	0	0	0	0	0	0	0
	Total Demand:		22	17	14	15	20	24	24
Weekly Wage Per Server:	$ 253.75								
Weekly Payroll Expense:	$0.00								

Excel | Chapter 8

Project 8B: Staffing Analysis | **Excel** **511**

3 Click cell **C11**, and then look at the **Formula Bar**.

Cell C11 sums the range C4:C9. It represents the number of servers who are assigned to each schedule. It is currently zero because no servers have been assigned to a schedule. The range C4:C9 is outlined in red. These are the decision variables—the values that will change to achieve the desired results. Here, the desired result is to have only enough staff assigned to meet customer demand and thus minimize payroll expense.

4 Click cell **C15** and examine the formula.

This formula calculates the weekly wage, based on $7.25 per hour, multiplied by seven hours worked each day, multiplied by five days worked per week. The proposed schedule shows all servers working five days each week.

5 Click cell **C16**, which is outlined in brown.

This cell calculates the total weekly payroll expense by multiplying the number of servers scheduled to work—cell C11—by the Weekly Wage Per Server—cell C15. Cell C16 is the objective cell. Recall that the objective cell contains the result that you are trying to achieve. In this instance, you are trying to achieve the minimum payroll expense that must be paid while maintaining enough servers on duty to meet established customer demand.

6 Select the range **E13:K13**.

These cells represent the minimum number of servers required to serve the number of customers expected each day of the week. The cells in this row will be one of the *constraints* used to determine the minimum weekly payroll expense. Recall that constraints are conditions or restrictions that must be met. In this case, the number of servers scheduled must be equal to or greater than the number required for each day.

7 Click cell **E11**.

The formulas in this row multiply the number of people assigned to work each schedule, arriving at a total number available each day of the week. This formula will be examined in greater detail in the next objective.

8 Click cell **C4**, and then click the **Name Box arrow**. Notice that cell **C4** has been named *Sun_Mon*. Compare your screen with Figure 8.22 and take a moment to review each of the cells you will work with in this project.

The cells in the range C4:C9, the decision variables, have been named with their corresponding schedule name.

Figure 8.22

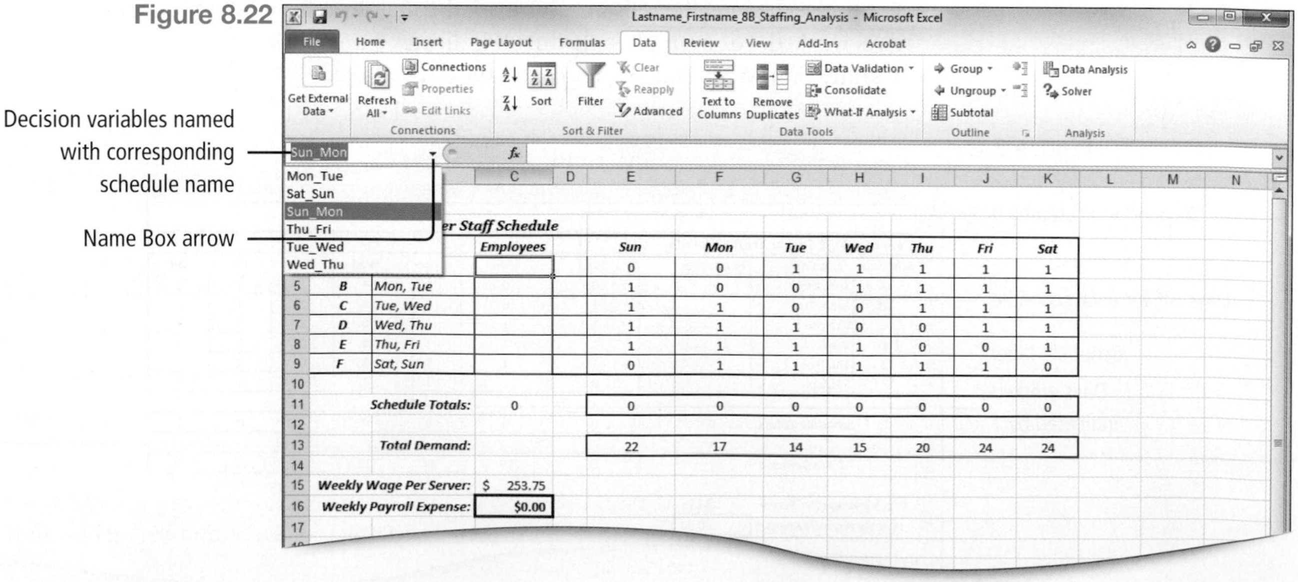

Decision variables named with corresponding schedule name

Name Box arrow

Activity 8.09 | Using Solver

In this activity, you will use Solver to determine the minimum payroll expense; that is, the minimum number of servers who can be on duty and still meet expected customer demand. This process involves identifying the objective cell, the decision variable cells, and the constraint cells.

1 Click cell **C16**—the objective cell. On the **Data tab**, in the **Analysis group**, click the **Solver** button. If necessary, drag the displayed **Solver Parameters** dialog box to the right side of your worksheet. Compare your screen with Figure 8.23.

> The Solver Parameters dialog box displays and cell C16 displays as an absolute reference in the Set Objective box. A moving border surrounds cell C16.

Figure 8.23

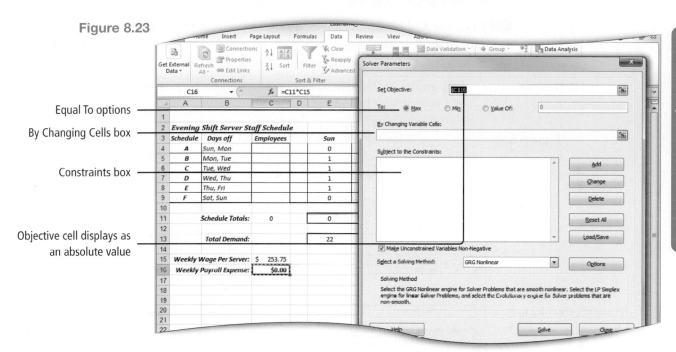

Equal To options
By Changing Cells box
Constraints box
Objective cell displays as an absolute value

2 To the right of **To**, click the **Min** option button.

> The three option buttons here enable you to use the Solver tool to maximize, minimize, or solve for a specific value.

3 Click in the **By Changing Variable Cells** box, and then select the range **C4:C9**.

> The range displays as an absolute reference. In this cell range, Solver will place the optimum number of servers who must be assigned to each schedule to minimize payroll and meet the constraints that are set.

4 To the right of the **Subject to the Constraints** area, click the **Add** button.

> In the Add Constraint dialog box, you enter constraints—limitations caused by various circumstances.

5 With the insertion point blinking in the **Cell Reference** box, select the range **C4:C9**.

6 In the middle box, click the arrow, and then click **int**. Compare your screen with Figure 8.24.

> This constraint requires that only an *integer*—a whole number—can be used, because you cannot assign part of a person as a server. In the Add Constraint dialog box, in the Constraint box, *integer* displays.

Figure 8.24

Constraint requires
an integer
Absolute reference to
the changing cells

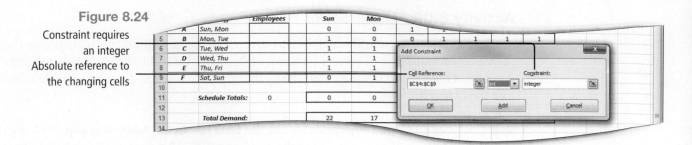

		Employees	Sun	Mon				
A	Sun, Mon		0	0	1			
5 B	Mon, Tue		1	0	0	1	1	1	1
6 C	Tue, Wed		1	1				
7 D	Wed, Thu		1	1				
8 E	Thu, Fri		1	1				
9 F	Sat, Sun		0	1				
10								
11	Schedule Totals:	0	0	0				
12								
13	Total Demand:		22	17				
14								

Add Constraint dialog box shown:
Cell Reference: $C$4:$C$9 int Constraint: integer
OK   Add   Cancel

7 Click **OK**.

The Add Constraint dialog box closes and the first constraint is added to the Solver Parameters dialog box.

8 Click the **Add** button. With the insertion point in the **Cell Reference** box, select the range **C4:C9**. In the middle box, click the **arrow**, and then click >=. In the **Constraint** box, type **0** Compare your dialog box with Figure 8.25.

This constraint (limitation) requires that the number of servers assigned to each schedule be a positive number—a negative number of servers cannot be assigned.

Figure 8.25

Changing cells must be
greater than or equal to 0

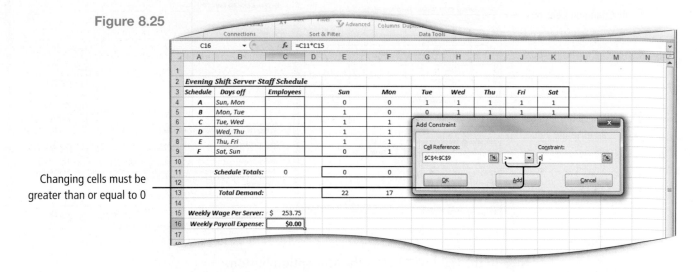

C16   fx =C11*C15

	A	B	C	D	E	F	G	H	I	J	K	L	M	N
1														
2	Evening Shift Server Staff Schedule													
3	Schedule	Days off	Employees		Sun	Mon	Tue	Wed	Thu	Fri	Sat			
4	A	Sun, Mon			0	0	1	1	1	1	1			
5	B	Mon, Tue			1	0	0	1	1	1	1			
6	C	Tue, Wed			1	1								
7	D	Wed, Thu			1	1								
8	E	Thu, Fri			1	1								
9	F	Sat, Sun			0	1								
10														
11		Schedule Totals:	0		0	0								
12														
13		Total Demand:			22	17								
14														
15	Weekly Wage Per Server:	$	253.75											
16	Weekly Payroll Expense:	$0.00											
17														

Add Constraint dialog box shown:
Cell Reference: $C$4:$C$9 >= Constraint: 0
OK   Add   Cancel

9 Click **OK**.

The second constraint is added to the Solver Parameters dialog box.

10 Click the **Add** button. In the **Cell Reference** box, select the range **E11:K11**. In the middle box, click the **arrow**, and then click >=. In the **Constraint** box, select the range **E13:K13**.

This constraint requires that the number of servers assigned to each shift be greater than or equal to the number of servers required each day to meet the projected demand. For example, on Saturday, the number of servers assigned must be at least 24.

11 Click **OK**. Compare your dialog box with Figure 8.26.

Three constraints display in the Solver Parameters dialog box. First, the number of servers assigned to any given Schedule—C4:C9—must be a whole number. Second, the number of servers—C4:C9—assigned to any given Schedule must be a positive number greater than zero. Third, the number of servers—E11:K11—assigned to each day's shift must be equal to or greater than the number of servers needed to meet the established demand in cells E13:K13. With the constraints established, you can solve for (calculate) the minimum payroll expense.

Figure 8.26

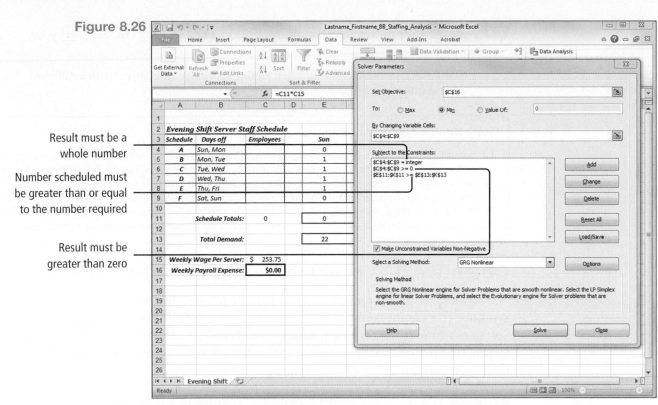

Result must be a whole number

Number scheduled must be greater than or equal to the number required

Result must be greater than zero

12 At the bottom of the **Solver Parameters** dialog box, click the **Solve** button, and then compare your screen with Figure 8.27.

> The Solver Results dialog box displays. The decision variables—the cell range C4:C9—displays the number of servers who should be assigned to each Schedule to meet the demand while minimizing payroll. Cell C16—the objective cell—shows the Weekly Payroll Expense as *$7,105.00*, and the number of servers who will work each schedule displays in cells E11:K11. Thus, to adequately staff the evening shifts and to give servers two consecutive days off requires a total of 28 servers each working 5 days a week and 7 hours each day—cell C11. The minimum payroll expense for 28 servers is $7,105—28 servers times $253.75

Figure 8.27

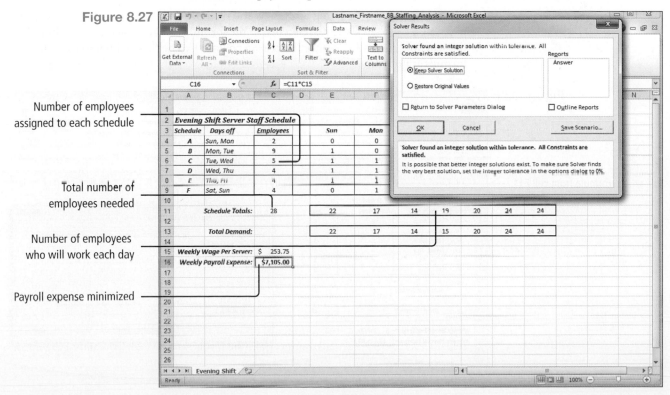

Number of employees assigned to each schedule

Total number of employees needed

Number of employees who will work each day

Payroll expense minimized

13 With the **Keep Solver Solution** option button selected, click **OK**. **Save** your workbook.

> This is one possible solution. Later, you will consider alternatives with a different distribution of staff over the week.

More Knowledge | **Solver Reports**

The Solver Results dialog box offers three reports—Answer, Sensitivity, and Limits—that can be created to help you understand the results. The Answer Report displays the original and final values for the objective cell and the decision variables. It also shows the impact of the constraints on determining values for the decision variables and whether the result for each cell is binding or nonbinding. It helps you understand where there may be some flexibility in the results if you want to do further analysis or consider other alternatives. The Sensitivity and Limits reports are not meaningful in the current example because of the integer constraints that have been applied.

Objective 5 | Evaluate Complex Formulas

You have seen that formulas can contain many cell references and mathematical symbols. To examine complex formulas, use **Evaluate Formula**, a command that enables you to examine and if necessary, **debug**—locate and correct errors—a formula step by step so that you can see the value for each cell used in the formula and watch the calculations as the formula is constructed.

Activity 8.10 | Evaluating Complex Formulas

The formulas in row 11 of your Staffing Analysis workbook calculate the number of employees who are scheduled to work each day. In these formulas, the number in column C is multiplied by the number found under each day of the week—a 1 or 0. Recall that a *1* indicates a workday and a *0* indicates a day off. For example, the formula in F11 is the sum of C4*F4+C5*F5+C6*F6+C7*F7+C8*F8+C9*F9.

1 Click cell **E11**. On the **Formulas tab**, in the **Formula Auditing group**, click the **Evaluate Formula** button. Compare your screen with Figure 8.28.

> The Evaluate Formula dialog box opens and the formula from cell E11 displays. The cells in column C use an absolute reference so the formula can be copied to the other cells in the schedule and still reference the cells in column C. The first cell reference in the formula is underlined.

Figure 8.28

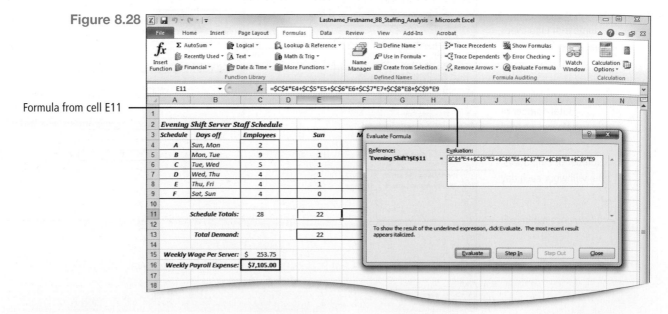

2 At the bottom of the **Evaluate Formula** dialog box, click **Evaluate**.

The cell reference—$C$4—is replaced by *2*, the value in that cell; the next cell reference is underlined.

3 Click **Step In**. Compare your screen with Figure 8.29.

In the Evaluate Formula dialog box, a box displays below the formula and displays *0*—the value of cell E4. Notice that *E4* displays in blue in the formula and displays as the active cell in the worksheet. If necessary, move the dialog box out of the way.

Figure 8.29

Cell E4 shows as the active cell on the worksheet

Value of highlighted cell reference displays in a second box

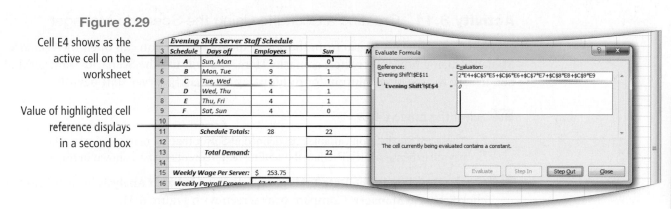

4 Click **Step Out**.

The first part of the formula—*2*0*—displays.

5 Click **Evaluate**.

The first part of the formula is calculated and displays *0*; the next cell reference—$C$5—is underlined.

6 Click **Evaluate** again.

The value of cell C5 is *9* and the next cell reference—E5—is underlined.

7 Click **Evaluate** again.

The value of cell E5 displays *1*, and values in the formula now show *0+9*1*. In the next step, after you click Evaluate two more times, this part of the formula will be calculated and only *9* will display.

8 Click **Evaluate** two times and notice that *9* displays for the total of the first two parts of the formula. Continue to click **Evaluate** until only *22* displays, and watch the remainder of the calculation as it is created. Compare your screen with Figure 8.30.

The result at the end of the calculation is *22* and the Evaluate button indicates *Restart*.

Figure 8.30

Evaluate button indicates Restart

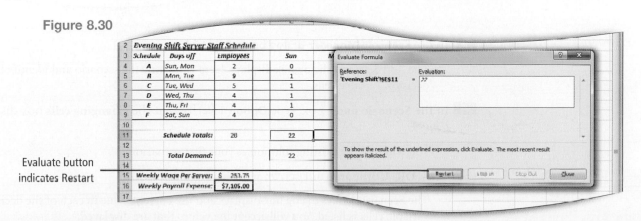

9 Click **Close** to close the **Evaluate Formula** dialog box.

Objective 6 | Create Scenarios

The current solution indicates nine servers assigned to *Schedule B, Mon and Tue off*, and only two servers assigned to *Schedule A, Sun and Mon off*. Ms. Hernandez wants to see what would happen if she assigned more servers to Schedule A. You can create several possible solutions to a problem and then use Excel's ***Scenario Manager*** tool to compare the alternatives. A ***scenario*** is a set of values that Excel saves and can substitute automatically in your worksheet.

Activity 8.11 | Creating a Scenario Using the Scenario Manager

You can create a scenario from the Solver dialog box, or you can open the Scenario Manager dialog box and create a scenario. Here, you will use the Scenario Manager dialog box to save the existing solution for minimizing the weekly server staff payroll.

1 Select the range **C4:C9**.

> These are the decision variable cells defined in Solver that are used to calculate the minimum payroll expense while matching the staffing requirements that are shown in row 11.

2 On the **Data tab**, in the **Data Tools group**, click the **What-If Analysis** button, and then click **Scenario Manager**. Compare your screen with Figure 8.31.

> The Scenario Manager dialog box displays. It shows that no scenarios have been defined.

Figure 8.31

Scenario Manager dialog box

No scenarios defined

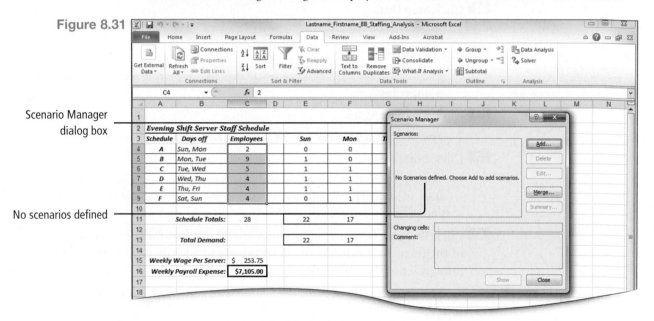

3 In the **Scenario Manager** dialog box, click **Add**.

> The Add Scenario dialog box displays. Here you name the scenario and identify the decision variable cells.

4 In the **Scenario name** box, type **Option 1** Verify that the **Changing cells** box displays *C4:C9*.

> You will save the existing solution as your first scenario.

5 Click **OK**. Compare your screen with Figure 8.32.

> The Scenario Values dialog box displays and the current value in each of the decision variable cells is listed. You will accept the values that are displayed.

Figure 8.32

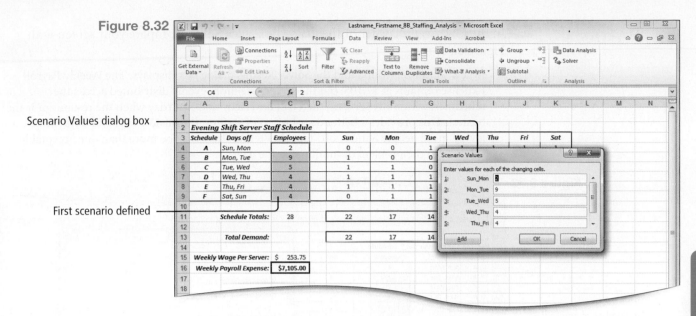

Scenario Values dialog box

First scenario defined

6 In the **Scenario Values** dialog box, click **OK**.

> The Scenario Manager dialog box redisplays, and the first scenario is listed in the Scenarios box as *Option 1*.

7 In the **Scenario Manager** dialog box, click **Close**. **Save** 🖫 your workbook.

Activity 8.12 | Creating a Scenario Using Solver

You can also create a scenario using the Solver Parameters dialog box. Ms. Hernandez wants to add another schedule option that would assign more servers to Schedule A so more people could be off on Sunday, a more traditional day off, and to help balance the numbers of shifts among employees.

1 Click cell **C16**—the objective cell. On the **Data tab**, in the **Analysis group**, click the **Solver** button. In the **Solver Parameters** dialog box, verify that the **Set Objective** box displays *$C$16* and the **By Changing Variable Cells** box displays *$C$4:$C$9*.

> The values from the first solution display in the Solver Parameters dialog box.

2 To the right of **Subject to the Constraints** box, click the **Add** button.

3 In the **Add Constraint** dialog box, click the **Cell Reference** box, and then click cell **C4**. In the middle box, click the **arrow**, and then click =. In the **Constraint** box, type **4**

> This constraint will assign four servers to *Schedule A—Sun and Mon off*.

4 Click **OK**.

> A fourth constraint is added to the Solver Parameters dialog box. Recall that because each of the cells in the range C4:C9 were named, the constraint displays as *Sun_Mon =4*. The range name displays when you summarize the alternatives you are creating.

Excel | Chapter 8

5 In the lower right corner of the dialog box, click **Solve**. Compare your screen with Figure 8.33.

A new solution is found and the Solver Results dialog box displays. The Weekly Payroll Expense remains at $7,105, but the servers are more evenly distributed across the schedules, with more servers scheduled on Friday and Saturday when the restaurant is the busiest. This provides a better distribution of staff on the busiest weekend days, while giving more people Sunday off. This shows that there may be more than one acceptable solution to the problem of minimizing the payroll.

Figure 8.33

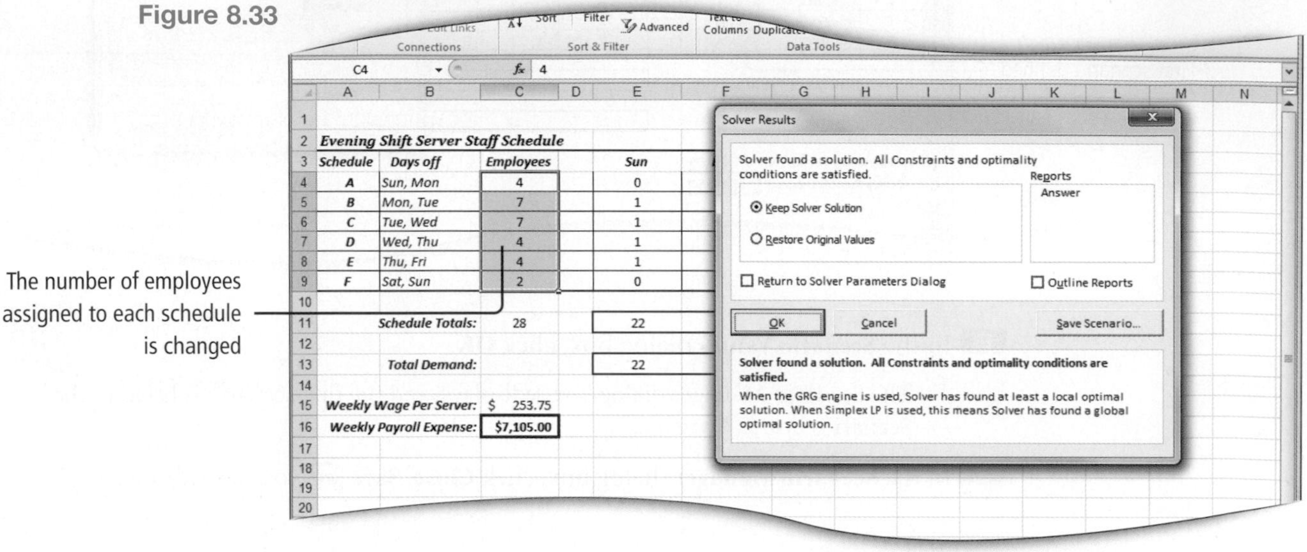

The number of employees assigned to each schedule is changed

6 Click **Save Scenario** to display the **Save Scenario** dialog box.

7 In the **Scenario Name** box, type **Option 2** and then click **OK**.

A second scenario is saved and the Solver Results dialog box displays.

8 In the **Solver Results** dialog box, click the **Restore Original Values** option button, and then click **OK**. **Save** 🖫 your workbook.

The dialog box closes and the previous solution is redisplayed on the worksheet.

Activity 8.13 | Creating a Scenario Summary

Ms. Hernandez wants to see what would happen if she schedules six servers to have Saturday off. Schedule F includes both Saturday and Sunday off, which would give more employees a traditional weekend off. After the third scenario is created, you will view a summary of the results of all three alternatives.

1 Verify that cell **C16** is still the active cell. On the **Data tab**, in the **Analysis group**, click the **Solver** button.

In the Solver Parameters dialog box, all four constraints (from Option 2) display, even though the currently displayed solution—Option 1—does not use the constraint that requires four servers be assigned to schedule A—*Sun_Mon = 4*.

2 In the **Subject to the Constraints** box, select the fourth constraint—**Sun_Mon = 4**—and then click **Delete**.

3 Click **Add**.

4 In the **Add Constraint** dialog box, click in the **Cell Reference** box, and then select cell **C9**. Change the middle box to =. In the **Constraint** box, type **6** and then click **OK**. Compare your screen with Figure 8.34.

Four constraints are listed in the Solver Parameters dialog box.

Figure 8.34

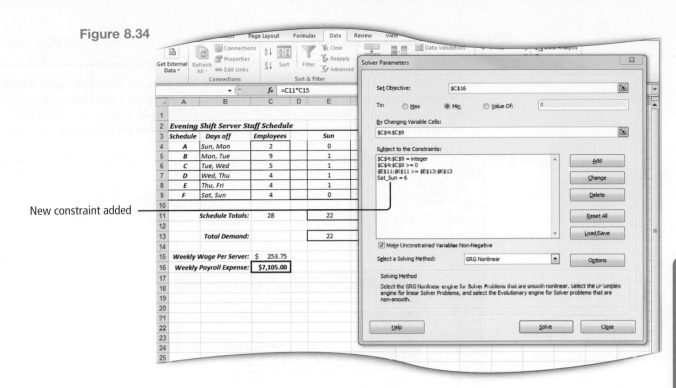

New constraint added

5 Click **Solve**.

A new solution is found; however, the Weekly Payroll Expense in cell C16 increases to $7,612.50, and the number of servers required to meet this scenario in cell C11 increases to 30.

6 Click **Save Scenario**. In the **Save Scenario** dialog box, type **Option 3** and then click **OK**.

The third scenario is saved and the Solver Results dialog box displays.

7 Click the **Restore Original Values** option button, and then click **OK**.

The previous solution is restored to the worksheet.

8 On the **Data tab**, in the **Data Tools group**, click the **What-If Analysis** button, and then click **Scenario Manager**. Compare your screen with Figure 8.35.

The Scenario Manager dialog box displays the three scenario names that you have created.

Figure 8.35

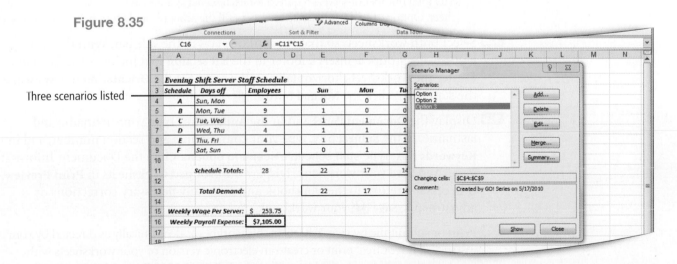

Three scenarios listed

9 In the **Scenario Manager** dialog box, click **Summary**.

The Scenario Summary dialog box displays. Here you can choose between a Scenario summary, which displays the data in a table, or a Scenario PivotTable report.

10 Be sure the **Scenario summary** option button is selected, and then click **OK**. Compare your screen with Figure 8.36.

> Excel inserts a new worksheet in your workbook—the *Scenario Summary* sheet, which compares the three options side by side. The results for Option 1 and Option 2 indicate the same amount in the results cell—$7,105.00—and Option 3 indicates $7,612.50 in payroll expenses. The outline pane displays along the top and left side of the worksheet.

Figure 8.36

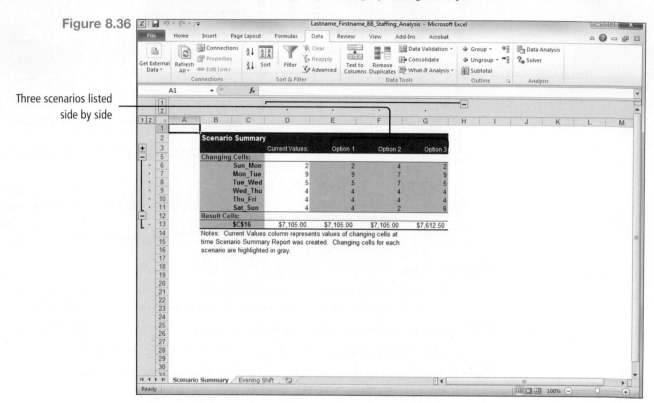

Three scenarios listed side by side

11 Select the range **D12:G12** and then, on the **Home tab**, in the **Editing group**, click the **Sum** button Σ. **Save** 🖫 your workbook.

> The total number of servers required for each scenario is added to the Scenario Summary sheet. Options 1 and 2 require 28 servers to fill the schedule and Option 3 requires 30 servers.

12 Select both worksheets so that *[Group]* displays in the title bar. With the two worksheets grouped, insert a footer in the **left section** that includes the file name. Center the worksheets horizontally on the page. Set the **Orientation** to **Landscape**. On the status bar, click the **Normal** button 🖼. Press Ctrl + Home.

13 Display the **Document Panel** and in the **Author** box, type your firstname and lastname, in the **Subject** box, type your course name and section number, and in the **Keywords** box, type **staff schedule scenario options Close** the Document Information Panel and **Save** your workbook. Display the grouped worksheets in **Print Preview**. If necessary, return to the workbook and make any necessary corrections or adjustments. **Save** 🖫 your workbook.

14 **Print** or submit the two worksheets in this workbook electronically as directed by your instructor. If required, print or create an electronic version of your worksheets with formulas displayed using the instructions in Activity 1.16 in Project 1A. **Close** and exit Excel.

End **You have completed Project 8B**

Content-Based Assessments

Summary

In this chapter, you created a custom number format and computed a moving average. You projected future growth based on assumptions and then charted the break-even point. You worked with Solver and Scenario Manager. Solver uses an objective cell to maximize, minimize, or solve for a specific value. You used constraints to restrict the outcome to an acceptable result. The solution that Solver helped you determine was saved as a scenario—a possible answer for the problem. You created several scenarios and then compared them side by side in a table. You used an auditing tool to examine a complex formula.

Key Terms

Add-ins 499	**Evaluate Formula** 516	**Objective cell** 510
Break-even 505	**Fixed expenses**...............503	**Scenario** 518
Constraint cells 510	**Integer** 513	**Scenario Manager** 518
Constraints 512	**Interval**............................499	**Solver**...............................510
Debug 516	**Line chart** 506	**Variable cells**..................510
Decision variables 510	**Moving average** 497	**Variable expenses** 503

Matching

Match each term in the second column with its correct definition in the first column by writing the letter of the term on the blank line in front of the correct definition.

_____ 1. A sequence of averages computed from parts of a data series that smoothes fluctuations in data to show a trend more clearly.

_____ 2. In a moving average, the number of cells to include in the average.

_____ 3. Expenses that remain the same each month.

_____ 4. A point at which an entity covers its costs and starts to make a profit.

_____ 5. A what-if analysis tool that can help you find an optimal value for a formula in one cell—subject to constraints on the values of other formula cells on a worksheet.

_____ 6. In Solver, a cell that contains a formula for the results you are trying to determine, usually defined as a minimum, a maximum, or a specified value.

_____ 7. In Solver, cells that will change to achieve a desired result.

_____ 8. Expenses that vary depending upon the amount of sales.

_____ 9. Optional commands and features that are not immediately available and must be installed or activated to use.

_____ 10. An auditing tool that helps you examine complex formulas.

_____ 11. A process by which you try to locate and correct errors step by step.

A Add-ins

B Break-even

C Debug

D Decision variables

E Evaluate Formula

F Fixed expenses

G Forecast

H Interval

I Moving average

J Objective cell

K Scenario

L Scenario Manager

M Solver

N Variable expenses

O What-if analysis

_____ 12. A what-if analysis tool that compares alternatives.

_____ 13. A set of values that Excel saves and can substitute automatically in your worksheet.

_____ 14. In a chart of a moving average, the label that is given to the moving average line.

_____ 15. The general process of changing values in cells to see the effect on formulas in other cells.

Multiple Choice

Circle the correct answer.

Excel | Chapter 8

1. To create a custom number format to display the full name of each month, use:
   A. mm   B. mmm   C. mmmm

2. To determine a trend from a widely fluctuating set of numbers, you could calculate a:
   A. break-even point   B. moving average   C. moving target

3. A moving average calculates an average for a group of numbers over a specified:
   A. interval   B. target   C. variable

4. A forecast is a prediction of the future, often based on:
   A. current performances   B. past performances   C. future performances

5. Examples of variable expenses in a restaurant are:
   A. food and wages   B. rent   C. general overhead

6. The amount of money that is made in excess of expenses, and which managers often seek to maximize, is:
   A. break-even point   B. total expenses   C. profit

7. Solver is a command in Excel's:
   A. Analysis group   B. Formulas group   C. Auditing group

8. Restrictions that are used in Solver to limit the results are called:
   A. variables   B. constraints   C. filters

9. The tool that enables you to compare alternatives is:
   A. Scenario Manager   B. Solver   C. Formula Auditing

10. Features that are Add-ins are activated through the:
    A. Excel Options dialog box   B. Data Analysis tools   C. Formula Auditing group

Content-Based Assessments

1. Calculate a Moving Average
2. Project Income and Expenses
3. Determine a Break-Even Point

Skills Review | Project **8C** Orlando Sales

In the following Skills Review, you will create a worksheet for Joseph Mabry, the Chief Financial Officer of Oceana Palm Grill, who wants to see how sales have grown in the first six weeks at the new restaurant in Orlando, Florida. Your completed worksheets will look similar to Figure 8.37.

For Project 8C, you will need the following file:

e08C_Orlando_Sales

You will save your workbook as:

Lastname_Firstname_8C_Orlando_Sales

Project Results

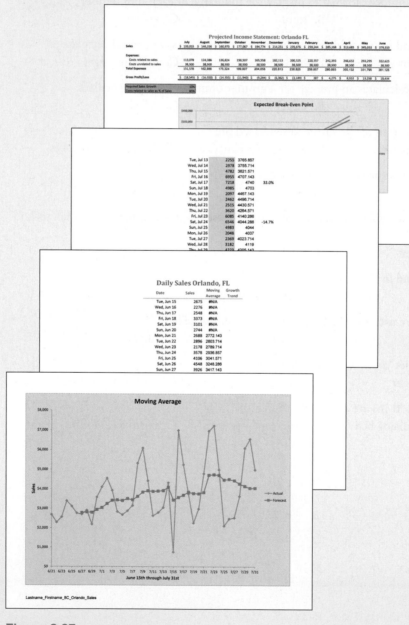

Figure 8.37

(Project 8C Orlando Sales continues on the next page)

Skills Review | Project **8C** Orlando Sales (continued)

1 **Start** Excel. From your student files, open the file **e08C_Orlando Sales**, and then in your **Excel Chapter 8** folder, **Save** the file as **Lastname_Firstname_8C_Orlando_Sales**

a. Make the Sales worksheet active, and then click cell **A3**. On the **Home tab**, in the **Number group**, click the **Dialog Box Launcher** button. In the **Format Cells** dialog box, be sure the **Number tab** is selected. Under **Category**, click **Custom**. Select the code in the **Type** box and type **ddd, mmm dd** to replace it. Click **OK**, and then drag the fill handle to copy the new format down through cell **A49**. Press **Ctrl** + **Home**.

b. From **Backstage** view, click **Options**. In the **Excel Options** dialog box, on the left, click **Add-Ins**. At the bottom of the dialog box, verify that the **Manage** box displays *Excel Add-ins*, and then click the **Go** button. In the **Add-Ins** dialog box, if necessary, select the **Analysis ToolPak** check box. Click **OK**.

c. Click cell **A2**. On the **Data tab**, in the **Analysis group**, click the **Data Analysis** button. Scroll the list as necessary, and then click **Moving Average**. Click **OK**. Click in the **Input Range** box, type **b2:b49** and then select the **Labels in First Row** check box. Click in the **Interval** box, and then type **7** Click in the **Output Range** box, type **c3** and then select the **Chart Output** check box. Click **OK**.

d. Click the outer edge of the chart to select it and then, on the **Design tab**, in the **Location group**, click the **Move Chart** button. Click the **New sheet** option button, type **Sales Trend Chart** and then click **OK**. At the bottom of the chart, point to any of the data points to display the ScreenTip *Horizontal (Category) Axis*, and then click to select the axis. On the **Design tab**, in the **Data group**, click the **Select Data** button. In the **Select Data Source** dialog box, under **Horizontal (Category) Axis Labels**, click the **Edit** button. Display the **Sales** worksheet, and then select the range **A9:A49**. In the **Axis Labels** dialog box, click **OK**. In the **Select Data Source** dialog box, click **OK**.

e. Right-click the **Category Axis**, and then on the shortcut menu, click **Format Axis**. In the **Format Axis** dialog box, on the left, click **Number**, and then under **Category**, click **Date**. Under **Type**, click the **3/14** format, and then click **Close**. Click the **Horizontal Axis Title** to select it. On the **Formula bar** type **June 15th through July 01st** and then press **Enter**. Point to the **Horizontal Axis Title**, right-click,

and then on the Mini toolbar, change the font size to **12**. Click the **Vertical Axis Title** to select it. On the **Formula Bar** type **Sales** and then press **Enter**. Point to the **Vertical Axis Title**, right-click, and then on the Mini toolbar, change the font size to **12**. Right-click the **Vertical Axis**, and then on the shortcut menu, click **Format Axis**. In the **Format Axis** dialog box, on the left, click **Number**, and then under **Category**, click **Currency**. To the right of **Decimal places**, type **0** and then click **Close**.

f. Display the **Sales** worksheet. Click cell **D21**, and then type **=(c21-c14)/c14** Press **Enter**. Scroll to position **row 21** near the top of your screen. Point to cell **D21**, right-click, and then on the Mini toolbar, click the **Percent Style** button. Click the **Increase Decimal** button one time to display one decimal. With cell **D21** still selected, point to the cell and right-click, and then click **Copy**. Point to cell **D28**, right-click, and then click the **Paste** button. **Copy** the result in cell **D28**, and paste it in cell **D35**. **Copy** the result in cell **D35**, and paste it in cell **D42**. **Copy** the result in cell **D42**, and paste it in cell **D49**.

2 Display the **Projected Income** worksheet. Click cell **B2**, and then use the fill handle to fill the months for a year—from July to June—across to **column M**. With the range **B2:M2** selected, apply **Center**. Select **columns B:M** and set the column width to **75 pixels**.

a. Click cell **B3**; in the **Formula Bar**, notice the cell reference. Click cell **C3**, type **=b3*(1+b12)** and then press **Enter**. Point to cell **B3**, right-click, on the Mini toolbar, click the **Format Painter** button, and then click cell **C3**. Use the fill handle to copy the formula in cell **C3** across the row to cell **M3**.

b. Click cell **B6** and examine the formula. Use the fill handle to copy the formula from cell **B6** across the row to cell **M6**. **Copy** the formula in cell **B7** across the row to cell **M7**. Select the range **C8:M8**, and then on the **Home tab**, in the **Editing group**, click the **Sum** button. **Copy** the formula in cell **B10** across the row to cell **M10**.

3 In the lower right corner of your screen, if necessary, set the Zoom to **80%** so that **columns A:M** display on your screen. Select the range **A2:M3**. Hold down **Ctrl** and select the range **A8:M8**. On the **Insert tab**, in the **Charts group**, click the **Line** button, and then under **2-D Line**, click the first chart type, **Line**.

(Project 8C Orlando Sales continues on the next page)

Content-Based Assessments

a. On the **Design tab**, in the **Data group**, click the **Select Data** button. In the **Select Data Source** dialog box, verify that the **Chart data range** is *A2:M3* and *A8:M8*. Click **OK**. On the **Layout tab**, in the **Labels group**, click the **Chart Title** button, click **Above Chart**, and then type **Expected Break-Even Point** Press Enter.

b. Drag to position the upper left corner of the chart inside the upper left corner of cell **B15**. Scroll to position **row 13** near the top of your screen. Drag the lower right corner of the chart inside the lower right corner of cell **M36**.

c. On the left side of the chart, right-click the **Value Axis**, and then on the shortcut menu, click **Format Axis**. In the **Format Axis** dialog box, on the left, verify that **Axis Options** is selected. Under **Axis Options**, click the **Minimum Fixed** option button. To the immediate right, delete the text in the **Fixed** box, and then type **100000** Press Enter.

d. On the **Design tab**, apply **Chart Style 18**. Format both the **Plot Area** and the **Chart Area** with a **Solid fill** using the color **Brown, Accent 2, Lighter 80%**.

e. Display the **Sales Trend Chart** worksheet. Format both the **Chart Area** and the **Plot Area** with a **Solid fill** using the color **Blue-Gray, Accent 4, Lighter 80%**. On this chart sheet, insert a custom footer with the file name in the **left section**.

4 Display the **Projected Income** worksheet, click anywhere outside the chart, and then, if necessary, set the

Zoom back to **100%**. Right-click the sheet tab, and then click **Select All Sheets** so that *[Group]* displays in the title bar. With the worksheets grouped, insert a footer in the **left section** that includes the file name. Click the cell above the footer to deselect it.

a. On the **Page Layout tab**, set the **Orientation** to **Landscape**, and then in the **Scale to Fit group**, set the **Width** to **1 page**. Center the worksheets horizontally on the page. On the status bar, click the **Normal** button. Press Ctrl + Home to move to the top of the worksheet.

b. Display the **Document Panel**. In the **Author** box, type your firstname and lastname, in the **Subject** box, type your course name and section number, and in the **Keywords** box, type **Orlando, break-even** **Close** the Document Information Panel and **Save** your workbook. Display the grouped worksheets in **Print Preview**; if necessary return to the workbook and make any necessary corrections or adjustments.

c. **Save** your workbook, and then print the three worksheets or submit your workbook electronically as directed. If required, print or create an electronic version of your worksheets with formulas displayed using the instructions in Activity 1.16 in Project 1A.

d. If you printed your formulas, be sure to redisplay the worksheet by pressing Ctrl + `. **Close** the workbook. If you are prompted to save changes, click **No** so that you do not save the changes to the Print layout that you used for printing formulas. **Exit** Excel.

End **You have completed Project 8C** ————————————————

Content-Based Assessments

Apply 8B skills from these Objectives:

- ◆ Use Solver
- ◆ Evaluate Complex Formulas
- ◆ Create Scenarios

Skills Review | Project **8D** Charlotte Staffing

In the following Skills Review, you will assist Gloria Stewart, manager of the Charlotte restaurant, in determining the most efficient work schedule for the evening server staff. Your completed worksheets will look similar to Figure 8.38.

Project Files

For Project 8D, you will need the following file:

e08D_Charlotte_Staffing

You will save your workbook as:

Lastname_Firstname_8D_Charlotte_Staffing

Project Results

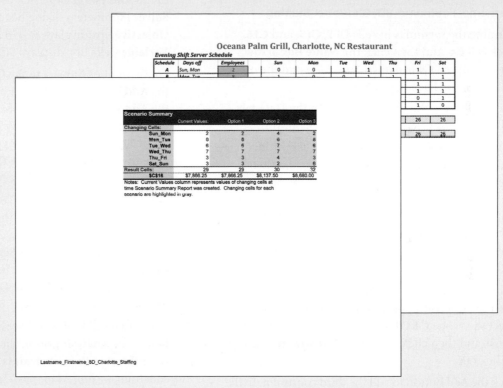

Figure 8.38

(Project 8D Charlotte Staffing continues on the next page)

1 **Start** Excel. Click the **Data tab**, and then at the right end of the **Data tab**, check to see if the **Analysis group** and **Solver** button display. If the **Solver** button displays, Solver is installed; move to step a. If the Solver button does *not* display, from **Backstage** view, click **Options**. On the left, click **Add-Ins**, and then at the bottom of the screen, in the **Manage** box, if necessary, select **Excel Add-ins**. Click **Go**. Select the **Solver Add-in** check box, and then click **OK**.

a.   From your student files, open the file **e08D_Charlotte_Staffing**. Display the **Save As** dialog box, navigate to your **Excel Chapter 8** folder, and then **Save** the workbook as **Lastname_Firstname_8D_Charlotte_Staffing**

b.   Examine the formulas in cells **C11**, **C15**, and **C16**. Click cell **C4**, and then click the **Name Box arrow**; notice that cell **C4** is named *Sun_Mon* and the other schedules also have been named.

c.   Click cell **C16**—the objective cell. On the **Data tab**, in the **Analysis group**, click the **Solver** button.

d.   To the right of **To**, click the **Min** option button. Click in the **By Changing Variable Cells** box, and then select the range **C4:C9**. To the right of the **Subject to the Constraints** area, click the **Add** button to add the first constraint. With the insertion point blinking in the **Cell Reference** box, select the range **C4:C9**. In the middle box, click the arrow, and then click **int**. Click **OK**—the result must be a whole number.

e.   Click the **Add** button to add the second constraint. With the insertion point in the **Cell Reference** box, select the range **C4:C9**. In the middle box, click the arrow, and then click **>=**. In the **Constraint** box, type **0** Click **OK**.

f.   Click the **Add** button to add the third constraint. In the **Cell Reference** box, select the range **E11:K11**. In the middle box, click the arrow, and then click **>=**. In the **Constraint** box, select the range **E13:K13**. Click **OK**; the result must be equal to or greater than the demand for each day. At the bottom of the **Solver Parameters** dialog box, click the **Solve** button. With the **Keep Solver Solution** option button selected, click **OK**. Cell **C16** indicates *$7,866.25*.

2 Click cell **E11**. On the **Formulas tab**, in the **Formula Auditing group**, click the **Evaluate Formula** button. At the bottom of the **Evaluate Formula** dialog box, click **Evaluate**.

a.   Click **Step In**. Click **Step Out**. To watch how the calculation is created, click **Evaluate** until only *24* displays. Click **Close** to close the **Evaluate Formula** dialog box.

3 Select the range **C4:C9**. On the **Data tab**, in the **Data Tools group**, click the **What-If Analysis** button, and then click **Scenario Manager**. In the **Scenario Manager** dialog box, click **Add**. In the **Scenario name** box, type **Option 1** Verify that the **Changing cells** box displays *C4:C9*. Click **OK**. In the **Scenario Values** dialog box, click **OK**. In the **Scenario Manager** dialog box, click **Close**.

a.   Click cell **C16**—the objective cell. On the **Data tab**, in the **Analysis group**, click the **Solver** button. In the **Solver Parameters** dialog box, verify that the **Set Objective** box displays *$C$16* and the **By Changing Variable Cells** box displays *$C$4:$C$9*.

b.   To the right of **Subject to the Constraints** box, click the **Add** button to add an additional constraint. In the **Add Constraint** dialog box, click the **Cell Reference** box, and then click cell **C4**. In the middle box, click the arrow, and then click **=**. In the **Constraint** box, type **4** Click **OK**; this constraint will raise the number of employees who have Sunday and Monday off to 4.

c.   In the lower right corner of the dialog box, click **Solve**. Click **Save Scenario** to display the **Save Scenario** dialog box. In the **Scenario Name** box, type **Option 2** and then click **OK**. In the **Solver Results** dialog box, click the **Restore Original Values** option button, and then click **OK**.

d.   Verify that cell **C16** is still the active cell. On the **Data tab**, in the **Analysis group**, click the **Solver** button. In the **Subject to the Constraints** box, select the fourth constraint—*Sun_Mon = 4*—and then click **Delete** to delete this constraint.

e.   Click **Add**. In the **Add Constraint** dialog box, click in the **Cell Reference** box, and then select cell **C9**. Change the middle box to **=**. In the **Constraint** box, type **6** and then click **OK**; this constraint will raise the number of employees who have Saturday and Sunday off to 6.

f.   Click **Solve**. Click **Save Scenario**. In the **Save Scenario** dialog box, type **Option 3** and then click **OK**. Click the **Restore Original Values** option button, and then click **OK**.

(Project 8D Charlotte Staffing continues on the next page)

Skills Review | Project **8D** Charlotte Staffing (continued)

g. On the **Data tab**, in the **Data Tools group**, click the **What-If Analysis** button, and then click **Scenario Manager**. In the **Scenario Manager** dialog box, click **Summary**. Be sure the **Scenario summary** option button is selected, and then click **OK** to summarize the three Options on a new worksheet. Select the range **D12:G12** and then, on the **Home tab**, in the **Editing group**, click the **Sum** button.

4 Select both worksheets so that *[Group]* displays in the title bar. With the two worksheets grouped, insert a footer in the **left section** that includes the file name. Center the worksheets horizontally on the page. Set the **Orientation** to **Landscape**. On the status bar, click the **Normal** button. Press Ctrl + Home.

a. Display the **Document Panel** and in the **Author** box, type your firstname and lastname, in the **Subject** box, type your course name and section number, and in the **Keywords** box, type **Charlotte, server schedule Close** the Document Information Panel and **Save** your workbook. Display the grouped worksheets in **Print Preview**. If necessary, return to the workbook and make any necessary corrections or adjustments. **Save** your workbook.

b. Print or submit the two worksheets in this workbook electronically as directed by your instructor. If required, print or create an electronic version of your worksheets with formulas displayed using the instructions in Activity 1.16 in Project 1A. **Close** and exit Excel.

End **You have completed Project 8D** ——————————————

Content-Based Assessments

Apply **8A** skills from these Objectives:

1. Calculate a Moving Average
2. Project Income and Expenses
3. Determine a Break-Even Point

Mastering Excel | Project **8E** Seafood Inventory

In this Mastering Excel project, you will create a worksheet for Joe Flores, manager of the Dallas region, who wants to analyze the fluctuation in the quantity of shrimp that is used at the four Dallas restaurants. In this project, you will use the moving average tool to help identify the variation in shrimp usage in recipes over a four-week period. Your completed worksheets will look similar to Figure 8.39.

Project Files

For Project 8E, you will need the following file:

   e08E_Seafood_Inventory

You will save your workbook as:

   Lastname_Firstname_8E_Seafood_Inventory

Project Results

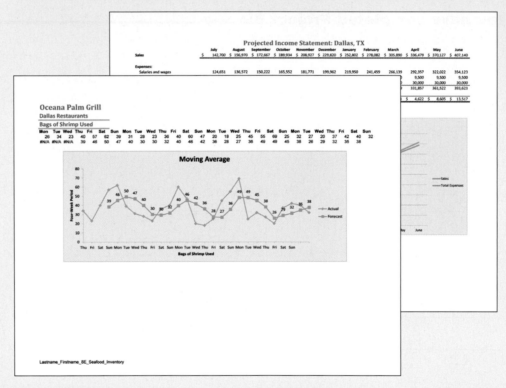

Figure 8.39

(Project 8E Seafood Inventory continues on the next page)

Content-Based Assessments

1 **Start** Excel. From your student files, open the file **e08E_Seafood Inventory**, and then **Save** it in your **Excel Chapter 8** folder as **Lastname_Firstname_8E_Seafood_ Inventory** Be sure the **Analysis ToolPak** is enabled.

2 On the **Data tab**, in the **Analysis group**, click the **Data Analysis** button, click **Moving Average**, and then click **OK**. Type **a5:ab5** as the **Input Range**, **4** as the **Interval**, and **a6** as the **Output Range**. Select the **Labels in First Row** and **Chart Output** check boxes. Click **OK**. Position the chart between cells **C8** and **Z29**. Edit the **Vertical Axis Title** to **Bags of Shrimp Used** Edit the **Horizontal Axis Title** to **Four-Week Period**

3 Click the **Category Axis** to select it. On the **Design tab**, in the **Data group**, click **Select Data**. In the **Select Data Source** dialog box, click the **Horizontal (Category) Axis Labels Edit** button. In the **Axis Labels** dialog box, select the range **D4:AB4**, and then click **OK** two times. Select the range **D6:AB6**, right-click, and then click **Format Cells**. Click the **Number tab**. Under **Category**, click **Number**, change the **Decimal places** box to **0**, and then click **OK**.

4 Click any data point in the **Forecast line** to select the **Forecast Data Markers**. On the **Layout tab**, in the **Labels group**, click the **Data Labels** button, and then from the displayed list, click **Above**. Format both the **Chart Area** and the **Plot Area** with a **Solid fill** using the color **Green, Accent 4, Lighter 80%**. Click any cell to deselect the chart, and then press Ctrl + Home.

5 Display the **Projected Income** worksheet. Click cell **C3**, type =b3*(1+b13) and then press Enter. **Copy** the formula in cell **C3** across to cell **M3**. **Copy** the formula in cell **B9** across to cell **M9**. Hold down Ctrl and select the nonadjacent ranges **A2:M3** and **A9:M9**, and then insert a **2-D Line** chart. On **Layout tab**, in the **Labels group**, click the **Chart Title** button, click **Above Chart**, and then type **Expected Break-Even Point**

Position the chart between cell **B15** and cell **M36**. On the **Design tab**, apply **Chart Style 18**. Format both the **Plot Area** and the **Chart Area** with a **Solid fill** using the color **Gold, Accent 1, Lighter 80%**.

6 Click any cell to deselect the chart, and then press Ctrl + Home. Select all the sheets and insert a footer in the **left section** that includes the file name. Set the **Orientation** to **Landscape**, and set the **Width** to **1 page**. Center the worksheets horizontally. Click the **Normal** button. Press Ctrl + Home to move to the top of the worksheet.

7 Display the **Document Panel** and in the **Author** box, type your firstname and your lastname. In the **Subject** box, type your course name and section number, and in the **Keywords** box, type **Dallas, seafood inventory** Display the grouped worksheets in the **Print Preview**, make any necessary corrections, **close** the Document Information Panel and **Save** your workbook. Print or submit your workbook electronically. If required, print or create an electronic version of your worksheets with formulas displayed using the instructions in Activity 1.16 in Project 1A. **Close** and exit Excel.

End **You have completed Project 8E**

Content-Based Assessments

Apply **8B** skills from these Objectives:

- **4** Use Solver
- **5** Evaluate Complex Formulas
- **6** Create Scenarios

Mastering Excel | Project **8F** Seafood Chowder

In this Mastering Excel project, you will assist Laura Mabry Hernandez, manager of the Austin East restaurant, by using Solver to create several scenarios for how much of each of the three seafood ingredients—scallops, shrimp, and fish—to include in the chowder at the new seasonal prices to maintain a profit margin of 35 percent on a serving of chowder at the current wholesale seafood costs. Your completed worksheet will look similar to Figure 8.40.

Project Files

For Project 8F, you will need the following file:

e08F_Seafood_Chowder

You will save your workbook as:

Lastname_Firstname_8F_Seafood_Chowder

Project Results

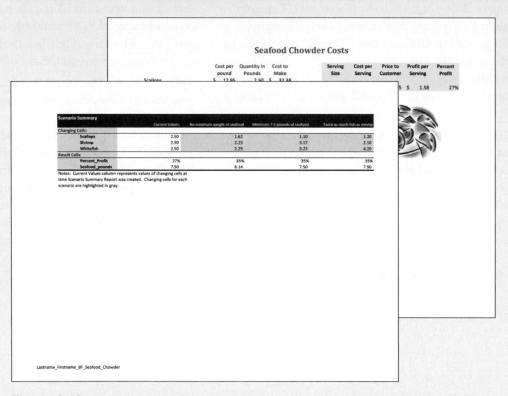

Figure 8.40

(Project 8F Seafood Chowder continues on the next page)

Content-Based Assessments

1 **Start** Excel. From your student files, open the file **e08F_Seafood_Chowder**, and then **Save** the file in your **Excel Chapter 8** folder as **Lastname_Firstname_8F_ Seafood_Chowder** Be sure that **Solver** is installed.

2 On the **Data tab**, in the **Analysis group**, click the **Solver** button. In the **Solver Parameters** dialog box, in the **Set Objective** box, type **$J$5** To the right of **To**, click the **Value of** option button. In the box to the right, select the existing value, and then type **35%**

3 Click in the **By Changing Variable Cells** box, and then select the range **C4:C6**. Click **Solve**. Click the **Save Scenario** button. In the **Scenario Name** box, type **No minimum weight of seafood** and click **OK**. In the **Solver Results** dialog box, click the **Restore Original Values** option button, and then click **OK**.

4 On the **Data tab**, in the **Analysis group**, click the **Solver** button. In the displayed **Solver Parameters** dialog box, click the **Add** button. In the **Add Constraint** dialog box, click in the **Cell Reference** box, and then click cell **C7**. Change the middle box to >= and in the **Constraint** box, type **7.5** Click **OK**. Click **Solve**. Click the **Save Scenario** button. In the **Scenario Name** box, type **Minimum 7.5 pounds of seafood** and click **OK**. In the **Solver Results** dialog box, click the **Restore Original Values** option button, and then click **OK**.

5 In the **Analysis group**, click **Solver** to display the **Solver Parameters** dialog box. Click the **Add** button. In

the **Add Constraint** dialog box, click in the **Cell Reference** box, and then click cell **C6**. Change the middle box to = In the **Constraint** box, click cell **C5**, and then type ***2** Click **OK**. Click **Solve**. Click the **Save Scenario** button. In the **Scenario Name** box, type **Twice as much fish as shrimp** and click **OK**. In the **Solver Results** dialog box, click the **Restore Original Values** option button, and then click **OK**.

6 On the **Data tab**, in the **Data Tools group**, click the **What-If Analysis** button, click **Scenario Manager**. In the **Scenario Manager** dialog box, click **Summary**. In the **Result cells** box, click cell **J5**, hold down Ctrl, and then click cell **C7**. Click **OK**.

7 **Select All Sheets** and insert a footer with the file name in the **left section**, center the worksheets horizontally, set the orientation to **Landscape**, and then set the **Width** to **1 page**. Return to **Normal** view and press Ctrl + Home to make cell **A1** active. Display the **Document Panel**, add your name as the author, type your course name and section in the **Subject** box, and as the **Keywords**, type **seafood chowder, recipe costs** Close the Document Information Panel and **Save** your workbook. Display and examine the **Print Preview**, make any necessary corrections, **Save**, and then print or submit electronically as directed by your instructor. **Exit** Excel. If required, print or create an electronic version of your worksheets with formulas displayed using the instructions in Activity 1.16 in Project 1A.

End **You have completed Project 8F**

Content-Based Assessments

Apply **8A** and **8B** skills
from these Objectives:

1. Calculate a Moving Average
2. Project Income and Expenses
3. Determine a Break-Even Point
4. Use Solver
5. Evaluate Complex Formulas
6. Create Scenarios

Mastering Excel | Project 8G Income Model

In this Mastering Excel project, you will assist Joseph Mabry, CFO of Oceana Palm Grill, and use a worksheet model and use Solver to create several scenarios that would result in breaking even six months after opening. Your completed worksheets will look similar to Figure 8.41.

Project Files

For Project 8G, you will need the following file:

e08G_Income_Model

You will save your workbooks as:

Lastname_Firstname_8G_Income_Model

Project Results

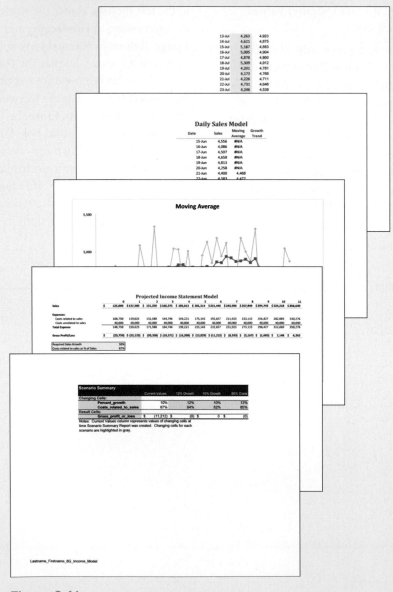

Figure 8.41

(Project 8G Income Model continues on the next page)

1 From your student files, open **e08G_Income_Model**. **Save** the file as **Lastname_Firstname_8G_Income_Model** in your **Excel Chapter 8** folder. Take a moment to examine the **Projected Income** worksheet. In this model for projecting the income, a new restaurant is expected to break even ten months after opening. Management wants to examine the assumptions and see what changes are needed to shorten the time it takes to break even. Month 0 is the first month of operation and it assumes that a new restaurant will gross $125,000 in sales in the opening month. The costs related to sales are assumed to be 87%; fixed costs are $40,000; and the anticipated growth rate in the first year, month-to-month, is 10%. The worksheet extends these assumptions out to month 11, which is the end of the first year of operation.

2 Click cell **B20**. On the **Formulas tab**, in **Formula Auditing group**, click **Evaluate Formula**. In the displayed dialog box, click **Evaluate**. Click **Step In**. Click **Step Out**. Continue to click **Evaluate** to see the calculation of the value in cell **B20**. Click **Close**. This formula refers to a cell that uses the FV (Future Value) function; recall that this function returns the future value of an investment based on periodic, constant payments and a constant interest rate.

3 Click cell **B15**, type **6** and then press Enter. Notice in the green shaded area that *Sales* changes to *$221,445* and the *Gross Profit/Loss* changes to *($11,212)*. Note that these match the figures under Month 6 in cells H3 and H10, respectively. Management wants to create several scenarios that would result in breaking even six months after opening.

4 On the **Data tab**, in the **Analysis group**, click **Solver**. In the **Solver Parameters** dialog box, in the **Set Objective** box, click the **Collapse Dialog Box** button, and then click cell **$B$20**. Be sure *$B$20* displays. Click the **Expand Dialog Box** button. Change the **To** option to a **Value Of 0** Click in the **By Changing Variable Cells** box, click the **Collapse Dialog Box** button, and then click cell **B16**. Hold down Ctrl, and then click cell **B18** so that *$B$16,$B$18* is indicated. In this manner, you will be able to change both the growth rate (in cell B16) and the costs related to sales percent (in cell B18). Click the **Expand Dialog Box** button.

5 Click the **Solve** button. A solution is found that would increase growth to *12%* and reduce costs related to sales to *84%*. Click the **Save Scenario** button and name

this scenario **12% Growth** Click the **Restore Original Values** option button, and then click **OK**.

6 Display the **Solver Parameters** dialog box again. Click the **Add** button, and then add a constraint that requires **Percent growth** to be less than or equal to **10%** Click **OK**, click **Solve**, and then **Save** this scenario as **10% Growth** Restore the original values and click **OK**.

7 Display the **Solver Parameters** dialog box. **Delete** the existing constraint. **Add** a constraint for the **Costs related to sales** to equal **85%** Click **OK**, click **Solve**, **Save** the scenario as **85% Costs** and then restore the original values and click **OK** to close the dialog box.

8 On the **Data tab**, in the **Data Tools group**, click the **What-If Analysis** button, and then display the **Scenario Manager** dialog box. Click **Summary**. Be sure the **Scenario summary** option button is selected, and then click **OK** to create the new worksheet with a summary of the scenarios.

9 Display the **Projected Income** worksheet. Hold down Ctrl and select the nonadjacent ranges **A2:M3** and **A8:M8**. Insert a **2-D Line** chart. On the **Layout tab**, in the **Labels group**, click the **Chart Title** button, click **Above Chart**, and then type **Expected Break-Even Point** Position the chart between cell **B22** and cell **L40**. Format both the **Plot Area** and the **Chart Area** with a **Solid fill** using the color **Olive Green, Accent 4, Lighter 80%**. Add a horizontal axis title with the text **Month Number** Click any cell to deselect the chart.

10 Display the **Sales** worksheet. On the **Data tab**, in the **Analysis group**, click the **Data Analysis** button, and then create a **Moving Average**. As the **Input Range**, type **b2:b49** as the **Interval** type **7** and as the **Output Range** type **c3** Select the **Labels in First Row** and **Chart Output** check boxes. Click **OK**. Click the outer edge of the chart to select it, and then move the chart to a new sheet named **Sales Trend Chart**.

11 At the bottom of the chart, right-click any value on the category axis, and then click **Select Data**. In the **Select Data Source** dialog box, under **Horizontal (Category) Axis Labels**, click the **Edit** button. Display the **Sales** worksheet, and then select the range **A9:A49**. Click **OK** two times. Right-click the **Category Axis**, and then on the shortcut menu, click **Format Axis**. In the **Format Axis** dialog box, on the left, click **Number**, and then under **Category**, click **Date**. Under **Type**, click the **3/14** format, and then click **Close**.

(Project 8G Income Model continues on the next page)

Mastering Excel | Project **8G** Income Model (continued)

12 On the category axis, change *Data Point* to **Date** On the value axis, set the *Minimum* to **3500** and set the **Major unit** to **500** On this chart sheet, insert a custom footer with the file name in the **left section**.

13 Right-click any of the other sheet tabs, and then select all the sheets. Insert a footer with the file name in the **left section**, center the worksheets horizontally, and then set the orientation to **Landscape** and the **Width** to **1 page**. Return to **Normal** view and make cell **A1** active. To the **Document Panel**, add your firstname and lastname as the **Author**, add your course name and section number as the **Subject**, and add **income, sales model** as the **Keywords**. **Close** the Document Information Panel and **Save** your workbook. Display and examine the **Print Preview**, make any necessary corrections, **Save**, and then print or submit electronically as directed by your instructor. If required, print or create an electronic version of your worksheets with formulas displayed using the instructions in Activity 1.16 in Project 1A. **Exit** Excel.

End **You have completed Project 8G** ─────────────────────

Content-Based Assessments

GO! Fix It | Project **8H** Maintenance Expenses

Project Files

For Project 8H, you will need the following file:

    e08H_Maintenance_Expenses

You will save your workbook as:

    Lastname_Firstname_8H_Maintenance_Expenses

Open the file e08H_Maintenance_Expenses, and then save the file in your Excel Chapter 8 folder as **Lastname_Firstname_8H_Maintenance Expenses** A moving average was created for monthly expenses over a three-year period using an interval of 2. Instead, management wants to view the moving average with an interval of 12. Delete the chart, and then on the Expenses Data worksheet, delete the output data in row 4. Create a new moving average using an interval of 12. Move the chart to a separate sheet named Moving Average, and apply appropriate axes titles. Add your name and course information to the document properties, and include **maintenance expenses** as the keywords. On the chart sheet, insert a custom footer with the file name in the left section. On the Expenses Data worksheet, insert the file name in the left section of the footer. For both sheets, use Landscape orientation, set the width to 1 page, and center the worksheets horizontally. Save your file, and then print or submit your worksheet electronically as directed by your instructor.

End **You have completed Project 8H** _____

Content-Based Assessments

Apply a combination of the **8A** and **8B** skills.

GO! Make It | Project **8I** Oyster Usage

Project Files

For Project 8I, you will need the following file:

> e08I_Oyster_Usage

You will save your workbook as:

> Lastname_Firstname_8I_Oyster_Usage

Open the file e08I_Oyster_Usage and then save it in your Excel Chapter 8 folder as **Lastname_Firstname_8I_Oyster_Usage** From the data, using an interval of 7 days, a fixed minimum of 10, and a major unit of 10, compute and create the Moving Average Chart shown in Figure 8.42. Position and format the chart and format the data labels as shown in Figure 8.42. Insert a footer, add your name, your course name and section, and the keywords **oyster usage** to the document properties. Save the file, and then print or submit electronically as directed by your instructor.

Project Results

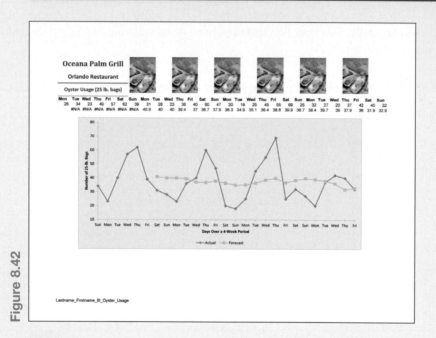

Figure 8.42

End You have completed Project 8I

Content-Based Assessments

Apply a combination of the **8A** and **8B** skills.

GO! Solve It | Project **8J** Tampa Income

Project Files

For Project 8J, you will need the following file:

e08J_Tampa_Income

You will save your workbook as:

Lastname_Firstname_8J_Tampa_Income

Open the file e08J_Tampa_Income and save it in your chapter folder as **Lastname_Firstname_8J_Tampa_Income** On the Projected Income worksheet, insert a 2-D line chart below the data to display the projected break-even point over 12 months for the Tampa, Florida, restaurant. Use the Sales and Total Expenses data to create the chart. Format the chart attractively with an appropriate chart title. Insert the file name in the footer in the left section. Set the orientation to Landscape and the Width to 1 page. Center horizontally, add appropriate information to the document properties including the keywords **break-even point** and submit as directed by your instructor.

		Performance Level		
		Exemplary: You consistently applied the relevant skills	**Proficient:** You sometimes, but not always, applied the relevant skills	**Developing:** You rarely or never applied the relevant skills
Performance Criteria	Charting the Break-Even Point With a Line Chart	A 2-D line chart is inserted displaying the break-even point using correct data.	A 2-D line chart is inserted displaying the break-even point using some but not all of the correct data.	A 2-D break-even point line chart is not inserted.
	Charting the Break-Even Point With a Line Chart	The chart is formatted with attractive colors and appropriate chart title.	The chart is formatted with attractive colors and/or has an appropriate chart title, but not both.	The chart is not formatted and does not have a title.

End You have completed Project 8J

Content-Based Assessments

Apply a combination of
the 8A and 8B skills.

GO! Solve It | Project **8K** Oceana Salad

Project Files

For Project 8K, you will need the following file:

  e08K_Oceana_Salad

You will save your workbook as:

  Lastname_Firstname_8K_Oceana_Salad

Open the file e08K_Oceana_Salad and save it as **Lastname_Firstname_8K_Oceana_Salad**
Be sure that Solver is installed. Create three scenarios and a summary. Set the objective cell to J5,
value of 60%. Solve for **No minimum weight of vegetables** by changing variable cells to the range
C4:C6. Solve for **Minimum 5 pounds of vegetables** by using the constraints cell C5, >=, and 5.
Solve for **Twice as many vegetables as greens** by using the constraints cell C6, =, C5*2. Create
a Scenario Summary. On all sheets, insert the file name in the footer in the left section. Set the
orientation to Landscape, width to 1 page, and center horizontally. Add appropriate information
to the document properties including the keywords **oceana salad** and submit as directed by your
instructor.

		Performance Level		
		Exemplary: You consistently applied the relevant skills	**Proficient:** You sometimes, but not always, applied the relevant skills	**Developing:** You rarely or never applied the relevant skills
Performance Criteria	**Use Solver to Create Scenarios**	Three scenarios were created using Solver based on the instructions.	Two scenarios were created using Solver based on the instructions.	None or one scenario was created using Solver based on the instructions.
	Create a Scenario Summary	A Scenario Summary listing three scenarios was created.	A Scenario Summary listing two scenarios was created.	A Scenario Summary was not created.

End You have completed Project 8K

Outcomes-Based Assessments

Rubric

The following outcomes-based assessments are *open-ended assessments*. That is, there is no specific correct result; your result will depend on your approach to the information provided. Make *Professional Quality* your goal. Use the following scoring rubric to guide you in *how to* approach the problem, and then to evaluate *how well* your approach solves the problem.

The *criteria*—Software Mastery, Content, Format and Layout, and Process—represent the knowledge and skills you have gained that you can apply to solving the problem. The *levels of performance*—Professional Quality, Approaching Professional Quality, or Needs Quality Improvements—help you and your instructor evaluate your result.

	Your completed project is of Professional Quality if you:	Your completed project is Approaching Professional Quality if you:	Your completed project Needs Quality Improvements if you:
1-Software Mastery	Choose and apply the most appropriate skills, tools, and features and identify efficient methods to solve the problem.	Choose and apply some appropriate skills, tools, and features, but not in the most efficient manner.	Choose inappropriate skills, tools, or features, or are inefficient in solving the problem.
2-Content	Construct a solution that is clear and well organized, contains content that is accurate, appropriate to the audience and purpose, and is complete. Provide a solution that contains no errors in spelling, grammar, or style.	Construct a solution in which some components are unclear, poorly organized, inconsistent, or incomplete. Misjudge the needs of the audience. Have some errors in spelling, grammar, or style, but the errors do not detract from comprehension.	Construct a solution that is unclear, incomplete, or poorly organized; contains some inaccurate or inappropriate content; and contains many errors in spelling, grammar, or style. Do not solve the problem.
3-Format and Layout	Format and arrange all elements to communicate information and ideas, clarify function, illustrate relationships, and indicate relative importance.	Apply appropriate format and layout features to some elements, but not others. Overuse features, causing minor distraction.	Apply format and layout that does not communicate information or ideas clearly. Do not use format and layout features to clarify function, illustrate relationships, or indicate relative importance. Use available features excessively, causing distraction.
4-Process	Use an organized approach that integrates planning, development, self-assessment, revision, and reflection.	Demonstrate an organized approach in some areas, but not others; or, use an insufficient process of organization throughout.	Do not use an organized approach to solve the problem.

Outcomes-Based Assessments

GO! Think | Project **8L** Seasonings Inventory

Project Files

For Project 8L, you will need the following file:

    e08L_Seasonings_Inventory

You will save your workbook as:

    Lastname_Firstname_8L_Seasonings_Inventory

Open the file e08L_Seasonings_Inventory, and then save it in your chapter folder as **Lastname_Firstname_8L_Seasonings_Inventory** From the source data, create a Moving Average chart to help identify the variation in seafood seasoning used over a four-week period. Begin the output range in cell A6. Move the chart to a new sheet. Format the chart attractively. Insert the file name in the left section of the footer on each page, center horizontally, set the orientation to Landscape, add appropriate information to the document properties, including the keywords **seasonings inventory** and submit as directed by your instructor.

 End You have completed Project 8L ———————————————

GO! Think | Project **8M** PT Staff

Project Files

For Project 8M, you will need the following file:

    e08M_PT_Staff

You will save your workbook as:

    Lastname_Firstname_8M_PT_Staff

Open the file e08M_PT_Staff and save it as **Lastname_Firstname_8M_PT_Staff** Be sure that Solver is installed. Use Solver to determine the optimum schedule for part-time servers for the weekday schedule at the Charlotte, North Carolina, restaurant.

Solve for Option 1, in which you want the objective (cell D16) to have the minimum (Min) number of employees scheduled by changing the number of employees (D4:D9). The first constraint is to be sure that you have enough (>=) employees (E11:Q11) to meet expected demand (E13:Q13) and the second constraint is to be sure that only whole numbers are used (because you cannot schedule part of a person to work). This solution uses 97.00 hours and has 9 employees scheduled at 10:30 in the morning, which are 7 more than needed.

Keep this solution, and solve for Option 2 by adding an additional constraint that allows no more than two employees to be scheduled for the first shift. (Hint: D4 <=2.) This solution sets Total Hours to 100.50 with 8 employees scheduled for the second shift (11:00-3:00). In this scenario, the greatest surplus of staff (7 employees) occurs between 2:00 and 3:00. Keep this solution by clicking OK.

Create a Scenario Summary for the two options. Select all sheets and insert the file name in the footer in the left section. Set the orientation to Landscape, set the width to 1 page, and center the sheets horizontally. Add appropriate information to the document properties including the keywords **weekday work schedule, part-time staff** and submit as directed by your instructor.

End You have completed Project 8M ———————————————

Outcomes-Based Assessments

Apply a combination of the **8A** and **8B** skills.

You and GO! | Project **8N** Entertainment

Project Files

For Project 8N, you will need the following file:

New blank workbook

You will save your workbook as:

Lastname_Firstname_8N_Entertainment

Review the amounts you spend on personal entertainment such as restaurants, movies, music CDs, or other types of expenses. Use a moving average to determine if there is a trend to your spending for entertainment. To do this project, you need records such as receipts or checkbook records; or you can estimate figures based on how much you think you spend for these items. If the records are kept monthly, you need at least 12 months' worth of records. If you have individual receipts, you need at least 12, which you can organize by equal time intervals, such as weeks.

Open a blank workbook and save the file as **Lastname_Firstname_8N_Entertainment** Enter a title for your worksheet in cell A1. Starting in cell A3, enter field names across row 3 for the intervals of time you decide to use, such as weeks or months. You need at least 12 of these intervals. It is acceptable to have zero values that represent periods in which you did not spend any money on entertainment. Use the moving average data analysis tool to chart the values. Choose at least a three-month interval. Display the chart on its own worksheet. Display the values on each data point in the forecast line. Select one of the data label numbers on the forecast line and apply a custom number format. Use the $#,##0 option. Change the title on the chart to Money Spent on Entertainment. Change the Category Axis to display the time intervals in row 3. Change the alignment of the data labels on the forecast line to display above the line.

Format the worksheet attractively for printing, insert the file name in the footer, add appropriate information to the document properties including the keyword **entertainment** and submit as directed by your instructor.

End **You have completed Project 8N** ————————————————

Using Macros and
Visual Basic for Applications

OUTCOMES
At the end of this chapter you will be able to:

OBJECTIVES
Mastering these objectives will enable you to:

PROJECT 9A
Record a macro to automate complex and repetitive tasks.

1. Record a Macro (p. 549)
2. Assign a Macro to a Button on the Quick Access Toolbar (p. 555)
3. Modify a Macro (p. 557)

PROJECT 9B
Ensure accuracy and automate instructions using VBA commands and ActiveX Controls.

4. Write a VBA Procedure to Use an ActiveX Control (p. 562)
5. Restore Initial Settings (p. 575)

In This Chapter

In this chapter, you will automate Excel worksheets to make it easier to perform complex tasks and faster to perform repetitive actions. You can program Excel to perform tasks that are not represented by existing commands or you can program Excel to validate data against complex criteria that require more than a simple comparison.

Because individuals who do the same type of work each day may use a specific sequence of Excel commands repeatedly, Excel enables you to record a sequence of commands and then activate the sequence with a single button or keystroke. If Excel does not have a command that you need, you can write a set of commands using a programming language to accomplish the task. Then, you can attach the program to a button that is placed on the worksheet.

The projects in this chapter relate to **Pine Valley Human Resources Consulting**, which provides its customers with services such as Employee Benefits Administration, Recruitment Services, Payroll Processing, Computer Technology Training, and Corporate Health and Wellness Programs. Customers are typically small and mid-size companies who, for cost savings and efficiency, use an outside source for such services. The company has recently added services related to Employee Assistance Programs, which benefit employees by achieving better work, life, and family balance.

Project 9A Travel Expenses

myitlab
Project 9A Training

In Activities 9.01 through 9.07, you will set a macro security level, remove file protection, record a macro, and assign a macro to the Quick Access Toolbar. You will test and modify a macro to fill in employee information for a Travel Expense Report. Your completed worksheet will look similar to Figure 9.1.

Project Files

For Project 9A, you will need the following file:

   e09A_Travel_Macro

You will save your workbook as:

   Lastname_Firstname_9A_Travel_Macro

Project Results

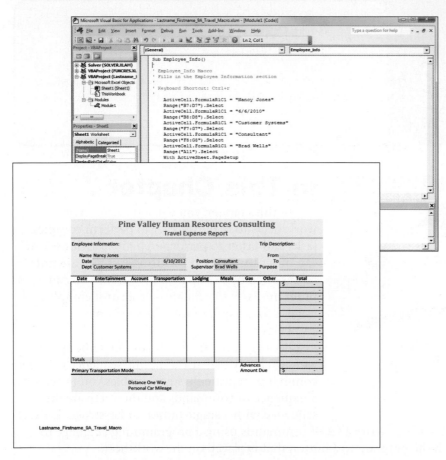

Figure 9.1
Project 9A Travel Expenses

Objective 1 | Record a Macro

A *macro* is an action or a set of actions with which you can automate tasks by grouping a series of commands into a single command. You can perform the command with a single mouse click, a keyboard shortcut, or when a workbook opens.

For example, you could record a macro that automatically enters employee names in the first column, alphabetizes the names, and then applies a fill color to the cells containing the names. When you have a sequence of actions that you perform frequently, record the actions as a macro to automate the task.

Macros are recorded in the *Visual Basic for Applications* programming language—also referred to as *VBA*—which is the language used to write computer programs within the Microsoft Windows environment.

To work with macros, you must:

- Add the Developer tab to the Ribbon, which displays the commands you will need to work with macros.
- Select a macro security setting to enable macros when using Excel.
- Save the workbook that includes macros as an Excel Macro-Enabled Workbook file type.

Activity 9.01 | Adding the Developer Tab to the Ribbon

The macro commands are located on the Developer tab, which, by default, does not display in Excel. You must enable the Developer tab from the Excel Options dialog box. In this activity, you will add the Developer tab to the Ribbon.

1 **Start** Excel and display a new blank workbook. In **Backstage** view, click **Options**.

2 In the **Excel Options** dialog box, on the left, click **Customize Ribbon**. On the right, under **Main Tabs**, select the **Developer** check box, and then compare your screen with Figure 9.2.

Figure 9.2

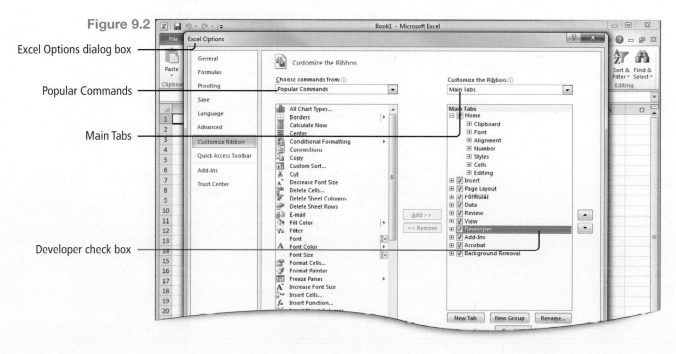

Excel Options dialog box

Popular Commands

Main Tabs

Developer check box

3 In the lower right corner, click **OK**. On the Ribbon, click the **Developer tab**, and then compare your screen with Figure 9.3.

> The *Developer tab* displays on the Ribbon. The *Code group* contains the commands you will need to work with macros.

Figure 9.3

Developer tab

Code group

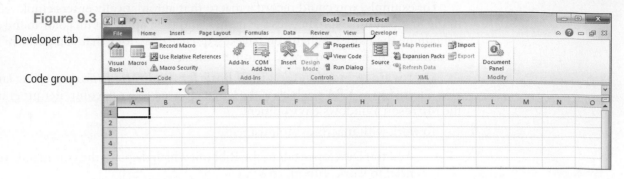

Activity 9.02 | Changing the Macro Security Settings in Excel

Opening an Excel workbook that has a macro attached to it might cause a message to display, indicating that macros are disabled. To enable the macro in the workbook, you must set the security level on your computer to allow the option of enabling the macros. In this activity, you will change the security setting so that you can choose to enable macros when you open a workbook that contains a macro.

1 On the **Developer tab**, in the **Code group**, click the **Macro Security** button. Compare your screen with Figure 9.4, and then take a moment to study the table in Figure 9.5.

> The Trust Center dialog box displays. On the left, Macro Settings is selected. The Macro Settings enable you to decide, each time you open a workbook, how or whether to run the macros that are contained in the workbook. The table in Figure 9.5 summarizes how macro virus protection works under each setting. Regardless of which option you choose, any installed antivirus software that works with your Microsoft Office software will scan the workbook for known viruses before it is opened. In an organization, you may not be permitted to change these settings without permission from your System Administrator. Any macro setting changes that you make in Excel in the Macro Settings category apply only to Excel and do not affect any other Office program.

Figure 9.4

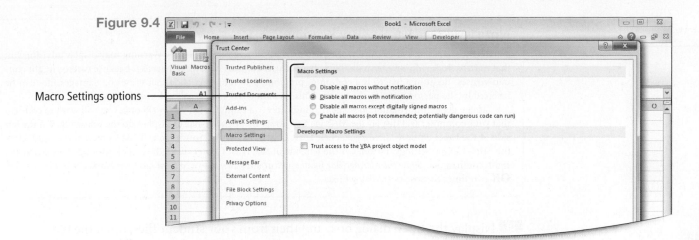

Macro Settings options

Macro Settings and Their Effects

Macro Setting	Description
Disable all macros without notification	This setting disables all macros and security alerts unless the Excel document is in a trusted location.
Disable all macros with notification	This setting is enabled by default. You are alerted if macros are present in the workbook. This setting enables you to choose each time you open a workbook whether or not to run the macros that are contained in the workbook.
Disable all macros except digitally signed macros	This setting enables macros from trusted publishers to run; otherwise, this setting is the same as the disable all macros with notification setting.
Enable all macros (not recommended; potentially dangerous code can run)	Use this setting when you want to enable all macros to run on a temporary basis. It is not recommended as a permanent setting because it makes your computer vulnerable to potential malicious code.

Figure 9.5

2 Under **Macro Settings**, verify that the default option button —**Disable all macros with notification**—is selected, and then click **OK**.

By choosing this option, you decide each time you open a workbook whether or not to run the macros that are contained in the workbook. Thus, when you attempt to open a workbook that contains a macro, Excel prompts you with a Security Warning. By selecting the security level *Disable all macros with notification*, you have the option of enabling macros on a file-by-file basis. Doing so allows you to use macros if the file is from a trusted source. This security level causes a Security Warning to display, indicating that macros have been disabled, and gives you the option to enable or disable macros.

Excel | Chapter 9

Note | Message Bar Security Warnings

When you open a macro-enabled workbook, on the Message Bar, a Security Warning may display advising you that macros in the file have been disabled. The security concern regarding macros is because macros might contain viruses. Because a macro is a computer program, programming code that erases or damages files can be inserted by the person creating the macro. This unauthorized code is called a *macro virus*.

If you get an information message that indicates you cannot open the workbook, you will want to confirm that your computer will display the Message Bar. To set the Message Bar to display, do the following: On the left side of the Excel Options dialog box, click Trust Center. Under Microsoft Excel Trust Center, at the right, click the Trust Center Settings button. On the left side of the Trust Center dialog box, click Message Bar and at the right, confirm that *Show the Message Bar in all applications when active content has been blocked* is selected. Click **OK** two times to close both dialog boxes.

3 Display the **Open** dialog box, and then from your student files, open the file **e09A_Travel_Macro**. Display the **Save As** dialog box, navigate to the location where you will save your projects for this chapter, and then create a new folder for **Excel Chapter 9**

4 Click the **Save as type arrow**, and then click **Excel Macro-Enabled Workbook**. In the **File name** box, type **Lastname_Firstname_9A_Travel_Macro** and then compare your screen with Figure 9.6. Click **Save**.

Selecting *Excel Macro-Enabled Workbook* saves the Excel file in the XML-based format, allowing macros to be saved to the workbook.

Figure 9.6

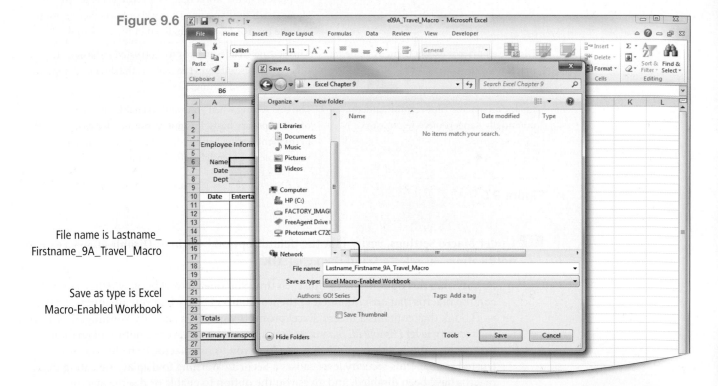

File name is Lastname_Firstname_9A_Travel_Macro

Save as type is Excel Macro-Enabled Workbook

5 Insert a footer in the **left section** that includes the file name. Return to **Normal** view and scroll to view the top of the worksheet. Display the **Document Panel**, in the **Author** box, type your firstname and lastname, in the **Subject** box, type your course name and section number, and then in the **Keywords** box, type **travel expense form, macro**

6 **Close** ☒ the **Document Panel**, and then **Save** 🔲 your workbook.

> **More Knowledge** | Sharing Files that Contain Macros
>
> Excel provides safeguards that help protect against viruses that can be transmitted by macros. If you share macros with others, you can certify them with a digital signature so that other users can verify that they are from a trustworthy source. A **digital signature** is an electronic, encryption-based, secure stamp of authentication on a macro or document. The digital signature confirms that the macro or document originated from the signer and has not been altered. If a file has been digitally signed, a certificate that identifies the source displays; then you can decide whether this is a trusted source before you activate the macros.

Activity 9.03 | Unprotecting a Workbook

This workbook is a form that employees of Pine Valley Human Resources Consulting use to report travel expenses. The worksheet is protected so that employees can fill in their travel expense information only in the unlocked cells. A worksheet must be *unprotected* to record a macro.

1 On the **Review tab**, in the **Changes group**, click the **Protect Workbook** button.

2 In the **Unprotect Workbook** dialog box, type **travel** which is the password applied to this form, and then click **OK**.

Activity 9.04 | Recording a Macro

The macro recorder records all the steps (keystrokes and mouse clicks) that you require to complete the actions you want your macro to perform—*except* for navigation on the Ribbon, which is not included in the recorded steps. When you record a macro, assign it a name so that you can refer to the macro name later. In this activity, you will record a macro that will fill in employee information for a specific employee on a Travel Expense form.

> **Another Way**
>
> On the View tab, in the Macros group, click the Macros button arrow, and then click Record Macro.

1 Be sure that cell **B6** is the active cell. On the **Developer tab**, in the **Code group**, click the **Record Macro** button.

The Record Macro dialog box displays. Here, you name the macro, assign a shortcut key, and start the recording. The **Record Macro** command records your actions in the Visual Basic for Applications programming language.

2 In the **Macro name** box, delete the existing text, and then type **Employee_Info**

The first character of the macro name must be a letter. Following characters can be letters, numbers, or underscore characters. Spaces are not permitted in a macro name; an underscore character works well as a word separator. Do not use a macro name that could be a cell reference—you will get an error message that the macro name is not valid.

3 In the **Shortcut key** box, type **r**

You can create a shortcut key to execute the macro, in this instance *Ctrl + r*. If you do not specify a shortcut key at the time you create the macro, you can add it later. Shortcut keys are case sensitive.

> **Note** | Assigning Shortcut Keys to a Macro
>
> The Excel program uses shortcut keys for common commands, such as Ctrl + S for saving a file or Ctrl + P for printing a file. When you assign a shortcut key to a macro, it takes precedence over the shortcut keys that are built into Excel. For this reason, use caution when you assign a shortcut key so that you do not override an existing shortcut. To see a list of Excel shortcut keys, in the Excel Help files, in the Search window box, type *keyboard shortcuts*, and then examine the topic *Keyboard shortcuts in Excel 2010*.

4 Click the **Store macro in arrow** to see the available options.

> You can store a macro in *This Workbook*—the default setting—in *New Workbook*, or in a *Personal Macro Workbook*. The *New Workbook* option opens a new workbook and adds the macro to that workbook. The *Personal Macro Workbook* is a workbook where you can store macros that you want to be able to use in other workbooks.

5 Be sure **This Workbook** is selected, and then click the **Store macro in arrow** to close the list. Click in the **Description** box. Type **Fills in the Employee Information section** Compare your screen with Figure 9.7.

Figure 9.7

Macro name

Shortcut key added

Macro stored in This Workbook

Macro description

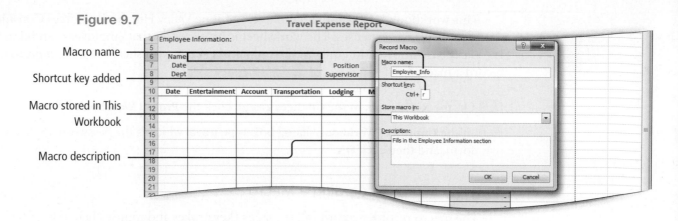

6 Click **OK**, and in the lower left corner of your screen, notice the square blue button indicating that a macro is recording.

> The macro recorder is turned on. From this point forward, every action you take will be recorded as part of the macro. Be assured that the amount of time you take between actions is not being recorded, so there is no need to rush. Take your time; recall that your actions are being recorded by the macro recorder. If you make an error, take the appropriate steps to correct it; the corrective steps will simply become part of the macro, and you can edit the mistakes out of the macro later.

7 In cell **B6**, type **Nancy Jones** and then press Enter. With cell **B7** active, hold down Ctrl and press ; (semicolon), which will insert the current date. Press Enter.

8 With cell **B8** active, type **Customer Systems** Click in cell **F7** and type **Consultant** and then press Enter. In cell **F8**, type **Brad Wells** and then click cell **A11**, so that when the macro completes, the first cell in the data area is active to begin filling in the travel information.

9 On the **Developer tab**, in the **Code group**, click the **Stop Recording** button. Compare your screen with Figure 9.8.

> The macro stops recording and cell A11 is selected. The Stop Recording button returns to a Record Macro button on the Ribbon. In the status bar, if you point to the button to the right of *Ready*, the ScreenTip indicates *No macros are currently recording. Click to begin recording a new macro.*

Figure 9.8

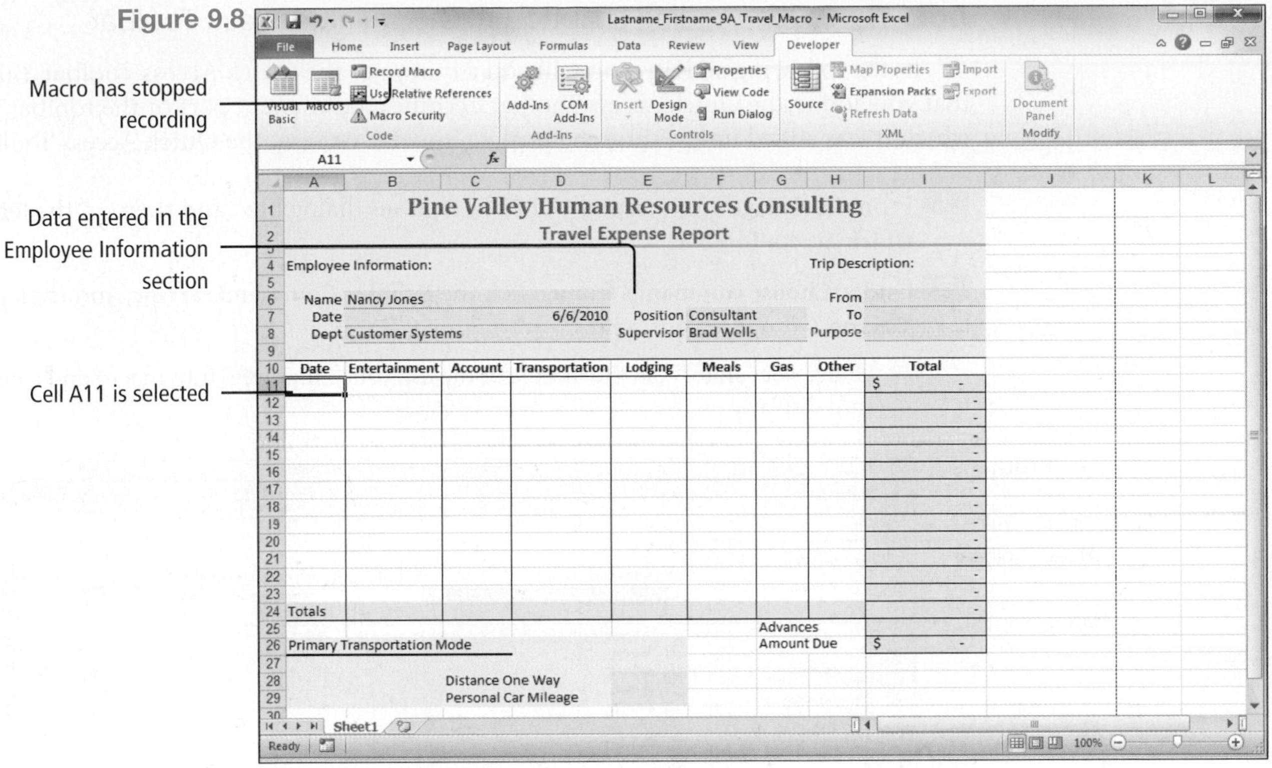
Macro has stopped recording
Data entered in the Employee Information section
Cell A11 is selected
Lastname_Firstname_9A_Travel_Macro - Microsoft Excel
Pine Valley Human Resources Consulting
Travel Expense Report
Employee Information:
Trip Description:
Name Nancy Jones
Date 6/6/2010
Dept Customer Systems
Position Consultant
Supervisor Brad Wells
From
To
Purpose
Date
Entertainment
Account
Transportation
Lodging
Meals
Gas
Other
Total
Totals
Advances
Amount Due
Primary Transportation Mode
Distance One Way
Personal Car Mileage
Sheet1

10 Delete the text you just typed in the five cells—**B6**, **B7**, **B8**, **F7**, **F8**—and then click cell **B6**. Then, to test that your macro will fill in the employee information and the date, run the macro by pressing the shortcut key Ctrl + R.

The shortcut key activates the macro, the employee information is filled in, and cell A11 is selected.

11 **Save** your workbook.

Objective 2 | Assign a Macro to a Button on the Quick Access Toolbar

You have practiced activating a macro with a keyboard shortcut, but another option is to activate a macro by clicking a button on the Quick Access Toolbar. To do so, you must create a new toolbar button. Then, anyone who uses the workbook can click the button on the Quick Access Toolbar to activate the macro.

Activity 9.05 | Adding a Button to the Quick Access Toolbar

In the following activity, you will add a button to the Quick Access Toolbar. Buttons that you add to the Quick Access Toolbar become a permanent part of the toolbar to which it was added unless you specifically remove it or reset the Quick Access Toolbar.

1 From **Backstage** view, display the **Excel Options** dialog box, and then on the left, click **Quick Access Toolbar**.

2 Under **Choose commands from:**, click the **Popular Commands arrow**, and then click **Macros**. Compare your screen with Figure 9.9.

> Under <Separator>, in the middle of the list, your Employee_Info macro and a default icon display.

Figure 9.9

Customize the Quick Access Toolbar

Macros selected

Employee_Info macro and default icon display

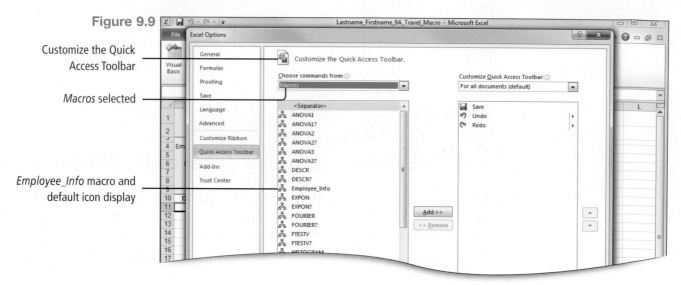

3 Click your **Employee_Info** macro, and then, in the center of the dialog box, click the **Add** button. Compare your screen with Figure 9.10.

> The Employee_Info macro displays on the right in the panel that contains buttons that currently display on the Quick Access Toolbar.

Figure 9.10

Employee_Info added to the Customize the Quick Access Toolbar pane

Employee_Info

Add button

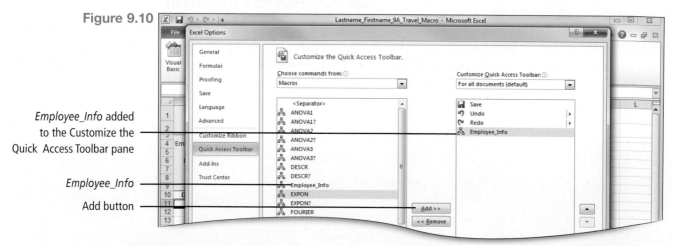

4 On the right, click your newly added **Employee_Info** command, and then at the bottom of the panel, on the left, click the **Modify** button. Compare your screen with Figure 9.11.

> The Modify Button dialog box displays. The first symbol is selected and at the bottom of the dialog box, Display name indicates *Employee_Info*.

Figure 9.11

Modify Button dialog box

Display name:
Employee_Info

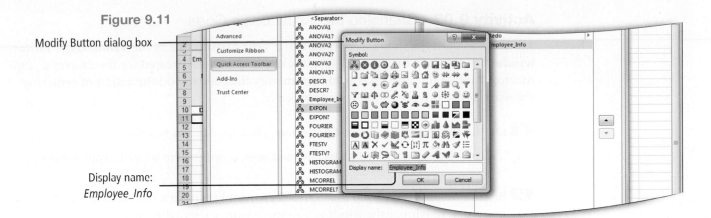

5 Under **Symbol**, in the fourth row, click the last icon—the **Smiley Face** button—and then click **OK** two times. **Save** 🖫 your workbook, and then compare your screen with Figure 9.12.

> TheSmileyFace icon displays on the Quick Access Toolbar.

Figure 9.12

The *Smiley Face* icon
displays on the Quick
Access Toolbar

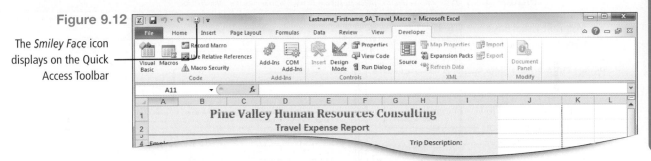

Activity 9.06 | Testing the Macro Button

After you add the button, test it to verify that the button performs as you intended. When you point to the button, the ScreenTip describes the name of the button. The action that causes your macro to run is called an ***event*** and might be a combination of keystrokes or the click of a button on the Quick Access Toolbar.

1 Select the nonadjacent ranges **B6:B8** and **F7:F8** and press Del so that these cells are empty again.

2 Click cell **B6**, and then on the **Quick Access Toolbar**, click your new **Employee_Info** button—the Smiley Face.

> The employee information is filled in, and cell A11 is selected.

Objective 3 | Modify a Macro

When you record a macro, the Record Macro command stores the macro in a module using the Visual Basic for Applications programming language—also called VBA. A ***module*** is the programming code written in VBA when you record a new macro, the place where the VBA code is stored. A module consists of ***procedures***, which is a unit of computer code that performs an action. Procedures are commonly referred to as *sub procedures*, or simply *subs*. A module can contain several sub procedures. VBA is used to write computer programs within the Microsoft Windows environment. As your actions are recorded, VBA code is created. If you want to modify the way your macro performs, you can modify the actual code that was created by the macro.

Activity 9.07 | Changing the Visual Basic Code

You can view the module containing the Visual Basic code in the **Visual Basic Editor window**. In this activity, you will open the module that was created for the *Employee_Info* macro, examine the VBA code, and then modify the code to add the action of centering the worksheet both horizontally and vertically.

1 On the **Developer tab,** in the **Code group**, click the **Macros** button.

The Macro dialog box displays and the *Employee_Info* macro is listed. From this dialog box, you can also run the macro.

2 Be sure the **Employee_Info** macro is selected, and then click the **Edit** button. If necessary, maximize the window. Compare your screen with Figure 9.13.

The Project pane displays on the left. The Microsoft Visual Basic Code window displays. If necessary, maximize the code window. Your Code window may be configured differently than the one shown in Figure 9.13. This window has several panes that can be displayed, and some of the available panes may be opened or closed.

Figure 9.13

Microsoft Visual Basic Editor Code window

Project - VBA Project pane

VBA code created to preview page 1 of the report

Beginning and ending statements

Comments that describe the macro

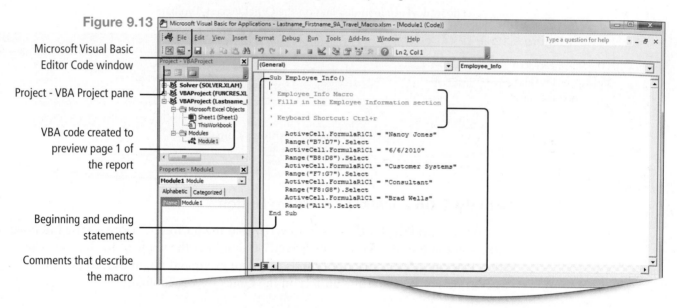

3 In the **Code window,** locate the green and black lines of text that comprise the comments and code for the Employee_Info macro.

The first section, displayed in green and in lines preceded by an apostrophe ('), consists of comments that describe the macro. These comments do not affect the function of the macro. Here, the comments include the data you entered when you created the macro—the macro name and description and the shortcut key that was assigned.

The VBA code that follows, in black type, includes the instructions to select the cell ranges and enter data. A set of instructions that accomplishes a specific task is called a **sub procedure**, which is abbreviated as **sub**. *Sub* indicates the beginning of the sub procedure. *End Sub* indicates the end of the sub procedure.

4 At the end of the *last* line of code—*Range("A11").Select*—click to place the insertion point after *Select*, and then press Enter.

In this manner, you can insert a blank line to type new code.

5 On the new, empty line type **With ActiveSheet.PageSetup** and then press Enter.

The word *With* notes the beginning of a **VBA construct**—an instruction that enables the macro to perform multiple operations on a single object.

6 Press [Tab] to indent and type **.CenterHorizontally = True** Press [Enter] and type **.CenterVertically = True** and then press [Enter].

The two centering commands are indented to make it easier to read the code. Verify that you typed the period preceding each line of code. The period identifies the command that follows. Instructions that have a beginning and ending statement, such as *With* and *End With* should be indented at the same level. You can indent code by using the [Tab] key. After you have indented to a certain level, when you press [Enter] the text will continue to wrap to that same level of indentation. To decrease the level of indentation, press [Shift] + [Tab], which will move the indentation toward the left margin.

7 Press [Shift] + [Tab], and then type **End With** Compare your screen with Figure 9.14.

End With is the closing statement for this construct—the *With—End With* construct is ended, and both the beginning and ending statements are indented at the same level. The spaces before and after the equals signs were added automatically.

Figure 9.14

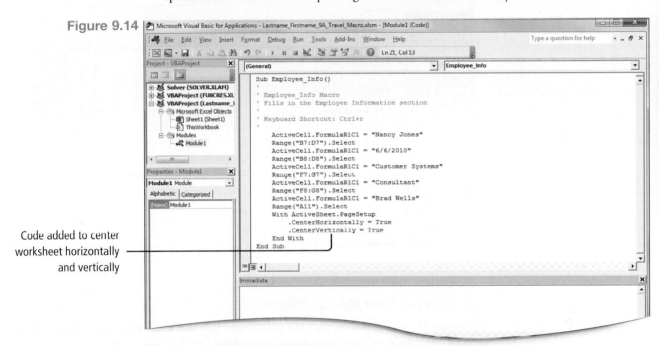

Code added to center worksheet horizontally and vertically

8 To print your module on paper, at the top of the window, in the menu bar, click **File** to display a menu, and then click **Print**. In the **Print - VBAProject** dialog box, under **Print What**, verify that **Code** is selected, and then click **OK**.

The macro VBA code prints; this provides printed documentation for your module.

Note | To Create an Electronic Printout of Your VBA Code Window

You can create an electronic version of your code window as follows: On your keyboard, press your [PrtScr] key to place a copy of the screen on the Office Clipboard. Then, open Word, and then press [Ctrl] + [V] to paste the contents of the Clipboard into the Word document. Save the Word document as Lastname_Firstname_9A_VBA_Code and submit it as directed.

---

9 In the upper left corner, click **File**, and then click **Close and Return to Microsoft Excel**.

The Visual Basic window closes and the worksheet displays on the screen.

10 Select the nonadjacent ranges **B6:B8** and **F7:F8** and press ⟨Del⟩ so that these cells are empty again. Select cell **B6**. On the **Quick Access Toolbar**, click the **Employee_Info** button that you created, and then display the **Print Preview**. Notice that the worksheet is now centered both horizontally and vertically. Compare your screen with Figure 9.15.

Figure 9.15

Worksheet centered horizontally and vertically

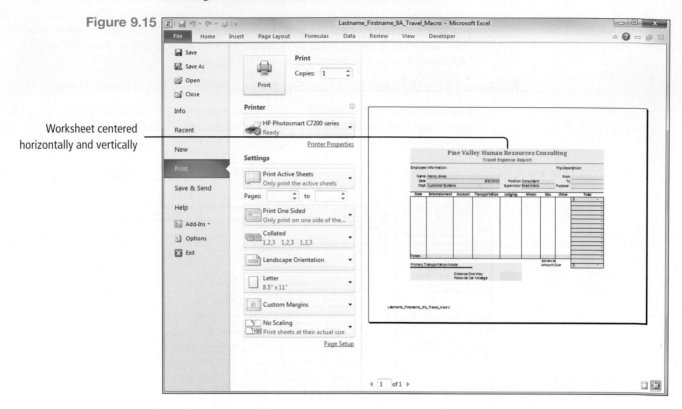

Alert | Does an Error Message Display?

If you made a mistake in entering the code, you will see a Microsoft Visual Basic dialog box informing you of the error. The message will vary, depending on the error that you have made. If this happens, in the dialog box, click the Debug button. This action will return you to the Microsoft Visual Basic Editor window and the line of code with the error will be highlighted in yellow. Examine the code and compare it with the instructions. Look for a typing error, a missing dot, or a missing line of code. Correct the error and then, on the File menu, click Close and Return to Microsoft Excel. In the message box, click OK to stop the debugger. Test the button again. If you are unable to resolve the error, seek assistance from your instructor or lab assistant.

---

11 **Save** your workbook, and then print or submit it electronically as directed.

12 If required by your instructor, print or create an electronic version of your worksheets with formulas displayed by using the instructions in Activity 1.16, and then **Exit** Excel without saving so that you do not save the changes you made to print formulas.

End **You have completed Project 9A** ——————————————————

Project 9B VBA Procedure

myitlab
Project 9B Training

Project Activities

In Activities 9.08 through 9.13, you will assist Brendon Eubanks, Controller at Pine Valley Human Resources Consulting, by writing a set of commands in the VBA programming language using ActiveX Control buttons to automate the travel policy guidelines for expense reports. Your completed workbook will look similar to Figure 9.16.

Project Files

For Project 9B, you will need the following file:

e09B_Travel_VBA

You will save your workbook as:

Lastname_Firstname_9B_Travel_VBA

Project Results

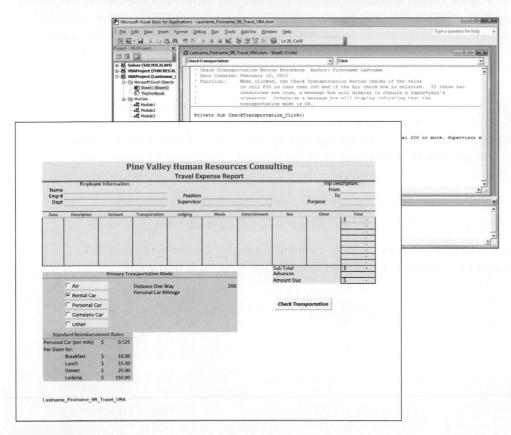

Figure 9.16
Project 9B Travel VBA

Objective 4 | Write a VBA Procedure to Use an ActiveX Control

Within VBA, you can write a procedure that will insert an **ActiveX control** into your form. A procedure is a named sequence of statements in a computer program that performs a task. An ActiveX control is a graphic object, such as a check box or a button, that you place on a form to display or enter data, to perform an action, or to make the form easier to read. When the person filling in the form clicks the ActiveX control, a macro runs that automates a task or offers options.

Activity 9.08 | Inserting ActiveX Controls

ActiveX controls are especially useful for forms that individuals complete online, because you can control different events that occur when the control is used. In the following activity, you will insert **check boxes**. A check box is a type of ActiveX control that the person filling in the form can select to indicate a choice.

Pine Valley Human Resources Consulting has a policy that requires employees to use ground transportation—company car, company van, rental car, or personal car—for trips under 200 miles. Unless absolutely necessary, employees should not use air transportation for such short trips. In this project, you will design a travel expense form that will verify that any time an employee submits an expense report that lists *air* as the mode of travel, the form will automatically check to verify that the one-way distance is over 200 miles, and if it is not, a message will display indicating that a supervisor signature is required.

1 **Start** Excel. From your student files, locate the file **e09B_Travel_VBA**, and notice the file icon that displays for a macro-enabled workbook—a small exclamation point displays on the file icon. Open and **Save** the file in your **Excel Chapter 9** folder as an **Excel Macro-Enabled Workbook** with the file name **Lastname_Firstname_9B_Travel_VBA** If necessary, on the Security Warning bar, click Enable Content.

2 On the **Developer tab**, in the **Controls group**, click the **Insert** button.

A gallery of Form Controls and ActiveX Controls displays.

3 Under **ActiveX Controls**, point to each button to display the ScreenTip. Take a moment to study the description of the ActiveX controls in the table in Figure 9.17.

ActiveX Controls

Button	ScreenTip	Description
	Command Button	Inserts a Command Button control to which code can be attached, initiating an action when clicked.
	Combo Box	Inserts a combo box control, which displays a list of choices from another source; the user can either select a choice from the list or type his or her own entry in the box.
	Check Box	Inserts a check box control that can be turned on (selected) or turned off (cleared).
	Image	Inserts an image control to embed a picture.
	Label	Inserts a text label to provide information about a control.
	List Box	Inserts a list box control, which displays a list of choices.
	More Controls	Displays a list of additional controls.
	Option Button	Inserts an option button control to indicate an on/off choice.
	Scroll Bar	Inserts a scroll bar control, which scrolls through a range of values.
	Spin Button	Inserts a spin button control, which displays a range of numbers from which the user can increase or decrease a value.
	Text Box	Inserts a text box control in which the user can type text.
	Toggle Button	Inserts a toggle button control, which remains pressed in when clicked, and then releases when clicked again.

Figure 9.17

4 Under **ActiveX Controls**, click the **Check Box** button ☑ and notice that the mouse pointer changes to the ⊞ shape.

5 Point to the upper left corner of cell **B20** and drag to insert a check box object that is approximately the height of the cell and the width of columns **B:C** as shown in Figure 9.18. The size and placement need not be exact—you will adjust the size and placement later. If you are not satisfied with your result, click **Undo** and begin again, or use the sizing handles to adjust the size.

> The object name—*CheckBox1*—displays in the check box and also displays in the Name Box. An EMBED formula displays on the Formula Bar.

> The formula defines the object as an embedded object and includes the name of the object source. Recall that to *embed* means to insert something created in one program into another program. ActiveX controls are not part of Excel but may be added to it. This provides other software vendors and individuals the opportunity to write ActiveX controls to handle a wide variety of desired actions. The More Controls button at the end of the ActiveX Controls gallery lists many additional ActiveX controls, and there are more available for download from Internet sites.

Figure 9.18

EMBED formula

CheckBox1 ActiveX control

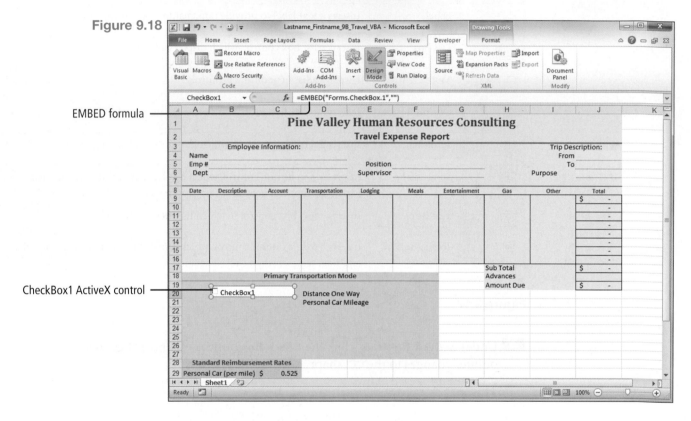

6 Repeat this process to add four more check boxes of the same approximate size under **CheckBox1**. Verify that the boxes do not overlap—leave a slight space between each box. Try to keep the check boxes within the tan shaded area, but the exact size and placement need not be precise—you will adjust them later. Use any technique for moving and sizing objects that you have practiced, and then compare your screen with Figure 9.19.

> ActiveX controls are not attached to cells—rather, they float on the worksheet like inserted Shapes or SmartArt. When you are adding ActiveX controls to your worksheet, you are working in *Design Mode*. This mode or view enables you to work with the controls. When you want to return to the worksheet, click the Design Mode button to toggle it off. In the worksheet, you could use the Go To command to go to the cell where an ActiveX control sits and select the cell, but not select the ActiveX control that floats on top of the cell.

Figure 9.19

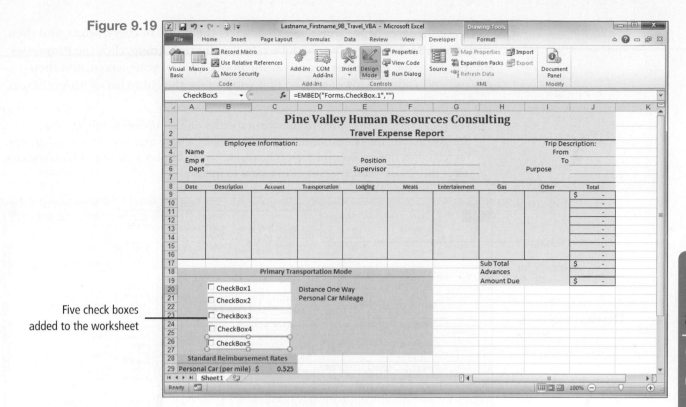

Five check boxes
added to the worksheet

7 Click **CheckBox1**, and then on the **Developer tab**, in the **Controls group**, notice that the **Design Mode** button is active.

> When you add controls, the Design Mode is activated. Use the Design Mode button to move in and out of Design Mode.

8 With **CheckBox1** selected, hold down Ctrl, and click on each of the remaining check boxes so that all five check boxes are selected.

9 On the **Page Layout tab**, in the **Arrange group**, click the **Align** button, and then click **Align Left** to align the check boxes on the left. **Save** your workbook.

Activity 9.09 | Changing the Properties of an ActiveX Control

Each ActiveX control has a set of *properties*—characteristics—that you can change. This is similar to formatting a shape by changing its color, font, or some other property. There are many properties associated with ActiveX controls, and the properties vary depending on the type of control. In this activity, you will change the name of each of the five check boxes, change the caption that displays in each check box, and change the height and width of each check box.

1 Click the **Developer tab**. In the **Controls group**, verify that the **Design Mode** button is active.

Excel | Chapter 9

2 Click another area of the worksheet to deselect the group of check boxes, and then click **CheckBox1** to select the check box. In the **Controls group**, click the **Properties** button. Drag the **Properties** pane near the upper right of your screen, and then expand and widen its lower edge so that you can see the entire list of properties, as shown in Figure 9.20.

> The properties are organized in alphabetical order on the *Alphabetic* tab. On the *Categorized* tab, the same properties are listed, but they are organized by logical groups. You can click the arrow at the top of the dialog box to display a list from which you can select the object whose properties you want to modify.

Figure 9.20

Properties dialog box

Alphabetic list

CheckBox1 displayed in list box

CheckBox1 selected

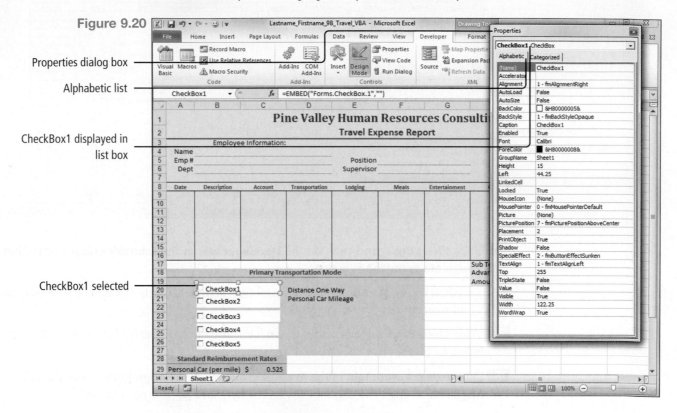

3 At the top of the **Alphabetic** list, in the first column, click **(Name)**, and then type **Air** Notice that your typing displays in the column to the right. Press Enter, and notice that *Air* displays in the **Name Box**.

> Use the (Name) field when you need to refer to an object in a program. The naming convention is the same for naming cells in Excel; that is, the name cannot include spaces or punctuation marks.

4 In the first column, click the **Caption** property, type **Air** and then press Enter.

> The text in the check box changes to *Air*.

5 Under **Alphabetic**, click **Height** and type **15.75** click **Width** and type **84.75** and then press Enter. Compare your screen with Figure 9.21.

> The check box resizes to a height of 15.75 pixels and a width of 84.75 pixels.

Figure 9.21

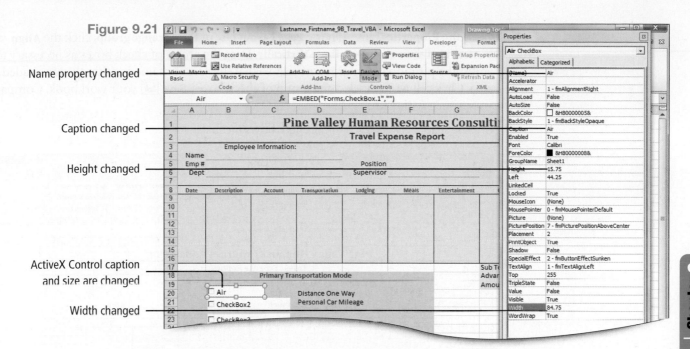

Name property changed

Caption changed

Height changed

ActiveX Control caption
and size are changed

Width changed

6 Click **CheckBox2** to select the check box, and notice that the **Properties** pane displays the properties for *CheckBox2*.

7 In the **Properties** pane, click (**Name**), type without any spaces **RentalCar** and then press Enter. Click the **Caption** property, and then type, *with* a space, **Rental Car** Click **Height** and type **15.75** Click **Width** and type **84.75** and press Enter.

8 Using the technique you just practiced, change the properties for the remaining three check boxes as follows. (Hint: You can hold down Ctrl, select the remaining check boxes, and then change the Height and Width properties in all three simultaneously. You must change the Name and Caption of each check box individually.)

ActiveX Control	Name	Caption	Height	Width
CheckBox3	**PersonalCar**	**Personal Car**	**15.75**	**84.75**
CheckBox4	**CompanyCar**	**Company Car**	**15.75**	**84.75**
CheckBox5	**Other**	**Other**	**15.75**	**84.75**

9 In the tan shaded area of the worksheet, select the **Air** check box, hold down Ctrl, and then click each of the other check boxes to select all five check boxes.

If you want to change the same property for a group of objects, you can select all of them and then change the property.

10 In the **Properties** pane, click **BackColor**, click the **BackColor arrow**, click the **System tab**, scroll down and click **Button Light Shadow**.

Excel | Chapter 9

11 **Close** the **Properties** pane. On the **Page Layout tab**, in the **Arrange group**, click the **Align** button, and then click **Distribute Vertically**. Drag the group of check boxes as necessary to adjust the position of the group of cells so that they are contained within the tan shaded area. Click cell **A1** to deselect the group of check boxes. **Save** 🖫 your workbook. Compare your screen with Figure 9.22.

The space between each of the check boxes is equal.

Figure 9.22

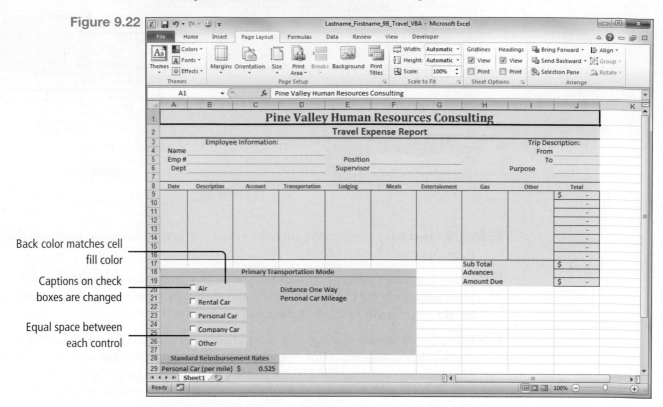

Back color matches cell fill color

Captions on check boxes are changed

Equal space between each control

Activity 9.10 | Writing a VBA Procedure for a Command Button

Because the use of ground transportation for trips that are less than 200 miles one way is recommended, if the value in the *Distance One Way* cell is less than 200 and the employee checks *Air*, then the expense report requires a supervisor's signature. In this activity, you will add a Command Button control and then write a VBA procedure to test whether both of these conditions are true; that is, *Air* transportation was used, and the distance one way was less than 200 miles. If both conditions are true, a warning message will display indicating that a supervisor's signature is required in the Supervisor box. First, you will write a procedure that tests whether the *Air* check box is selected, and then you will modify the procedure that will test whether the distance one way is less than 200 miles.

1 Click cell **H22** to identify the location where you will place a Command Button. On the **Developer tab**, in the **Controls group**, click the **Insert** button, and then under **ActiveX Controls**, click the **Command Button** 🔳 . Point to cell **H22**, and then click one time to insert a Command Button. Compare your screen with Figure 9.23.

The Command Button is added and a portion of the text *CommandButton1* displays as the caption on the button. By selecting cell H22, you have a visual cue as to where to place the Command Button. Recall, however, that ActiveX objects are not actually attached to a cell— the cell address is only a guide to direct you to the location where the control will be placed.

Figure 9.23

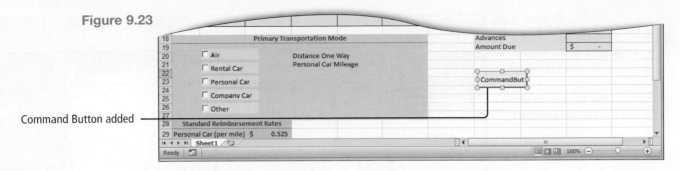

Command Button added

2 In the **Controls group**, click the **Properties** button. In the **Properties** pane, click **(Name)**, and then type **CheckTransportation** Click the **Caption** property, and then type **Check Transportation** Click **AutoSize**, click the **AutoSize arrow**, and then click **True**.

> The button is resizes to accommodate the new caption.

3 In the **Properties** pane, click **Font**, and then click the **Font build** button [...] to display the **Font** dialog box. Under **Font style**, click **Bold Italic**, and then click **OK**. Compare your screen with Figure 9.24.

Figure 9.24

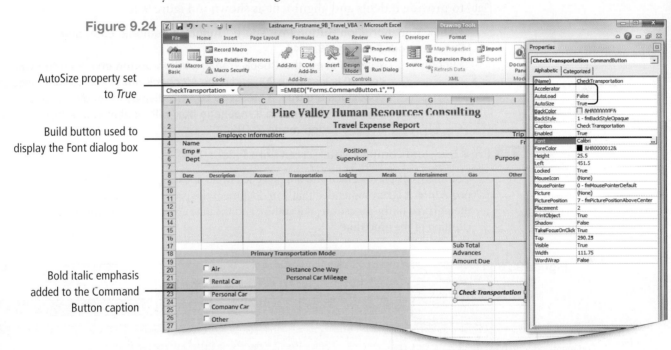

AutoSize property set to *True*

Build button used to display the Font dialog box

Bold italic emphasis added to the Command Button caption

Another Way

In Design Mode, right-click the command button, and then click View Code, or in Design Mode, double-click the command button.

4 **Close** ☒ the **Properties** pane. Be sure the **Check Transportation** control is selected. On the **Developer tab**, in the **Controls group**, click the **View Code** button. In the **Object** box, click the **arrow**, and then on the displayed list, click **CheckTransportation**. Compare your screen with Figure 9.25.

> The Microsoft Visual Basic Code window displays and *CheckTransportation* displays in the Object box at the top of the window. This is the name of the selected ActiveX control. The beginning of this VBA procedure is indicated by *Private Sub CheckTransportation_Click()*. *Private* indicates that this procedure can be used only in this workbook. *End Sub* indicates the end of the procedure. The event that will activate the Check Transportation Command Button is one click of the button.

Figure 9.25

Name of selected
ActiveX control displays
in Object box

Indicates the end of a
VBA sub procedure

Indicates the beginning of
a VBA sub procedure

Event (action) that will
start the procedure is *Click*

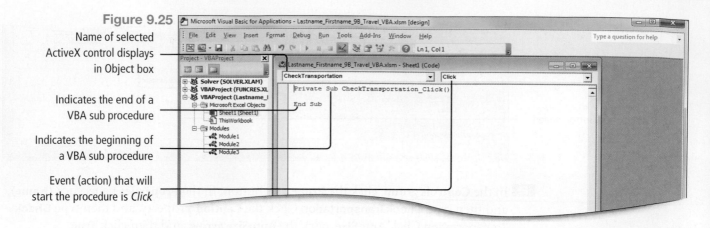

5 Click to the left of *Private Sub CheckTransportation_Click()* to place the insertion point there, and then press Enter to insert an blank line. Press ↑ to move to the blank line, and then type the following comments spaced as shown. Enter your first name and last name as the author. At the end of each line, press Enter, and as necessary, press Tab to provide indents and alignment as shown in Figure 9.26.

```
' Check Transportation Button Procedure   Author: Firstname Lastname
' Date Created:  February 18, 2012
' Function:      When clicked, the Check Transportation button checks if the value in
'                cell F20 is less than 200 and if the Air check box is selected. If these two
'                conditions are true, a message box will display to require a supervisor's
'                signature. Otherwise a message box will display indicating that the
'                transportation mode is OK.
```

6 Press Enter, and compare your screen with Figure 9.26.

Comments display in green and are preceded by an apostrophe ('). When writing a VBA procedure, it is recommended that you document the procedure with comments to indicate the purpose of the procedure, the author, and the date created. Comments do not affect the running of the procedure.

Figure 9.26

Comments added

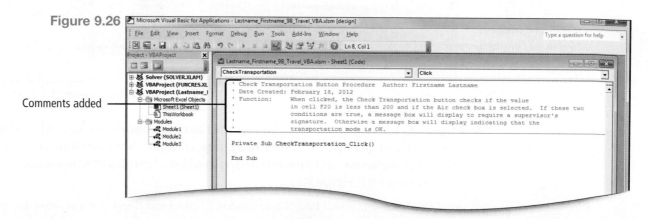

Another Way

There are several techniques you can use when writing VBA code. The code to create the message box could also be written as:
MsgBox "To travel by air, miles one way should be 200 or more.", , "Air"
MsgBox
The VBA code that you typed defined each component of the message box and then used a line to identify the parts that were used.

7 Click to position the insertion point on the blank line under *Private Sub CheckTransportation_Click()*. Press Enter, and then press Tab. Type the lines of VBA code spaced as shown below. Use the Tab key to indent the middle three lines and Shift + Tab to reduce the indent by one tab for the last line. As you type, a prompt box will display to assist you with the VBA syntax. Ignore the prompts and type the code as shown. When you are finished, compare your screen with Figure 9.27.

```
If Air = True Then
        TitleBarText = "Air"
        MessageText = "To use air transportation, miles one way should equal
        200 or more."
        MsgBox MessageText, , TitleBarText
End If
```

Figure 9.27

Message

Title on message box

Tests whether the Air
check box is selected

End of *If* statement

Defines the parts of the
message box statement

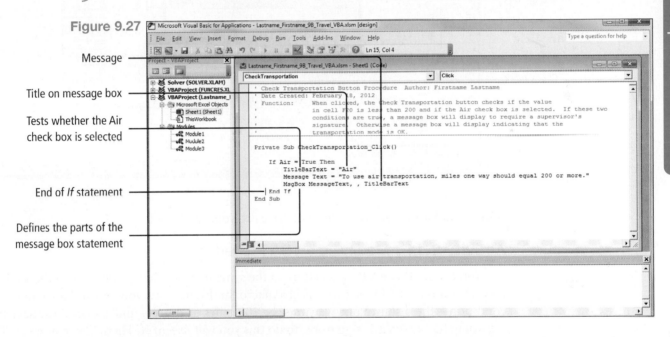

8 In the upper left corner, click **File** to display a menu, and then click **Close and Return to Microsoft Excel**.

9 In the **Controls group**, click the **Design Mode** button to exit Design Mode.

10 In the tan shaded section, select the **Air** check box, and then click the **Check Transportation** Command Button. If an error message displays, see the Alert box that follows for instructions on how to resolve the error. Compare your screen with Figure 9.28.

A check mark displays in the Air check box, and the Air message box displays.

Figure 9.28

Air message box

Check mark

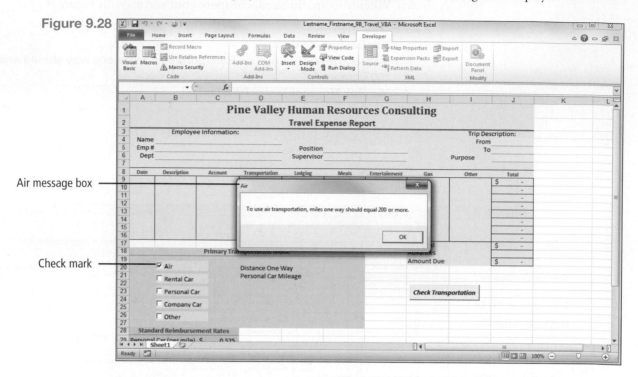

11 In the **Air** message box, click **OK. Save** 🖫 your workbook.

Activity 9.11 | Modifying a VBA Procedure

You can modify a VBA procedure in the same manner that you modified the VBA code that was created when you used a macro. In this activity, you will add a second condition—the distance one way must be 200 miles or more—and a second message box regarding the supervisor signature. To do this you will use an If, Then, Else statement. This is similar to the Conditional If statement, which does one thing if the condition is true and another thing if the condition is false.

Alert | If an Error Message Displays

If you made a mistake in entering the code, you will see a Microsoft Visual Basic dialog box informing you of the error. The message varies depending on the error that you have made. If this happens, in the dialog box, click the Debug button. This action returns you to the Microsoft Visual Basic Editor window, and the line of code with the error will be highlighted in yellow. Examine the code and compare it with the instructions. Look for a typing error, a missing dot, or a missing line of code. Correct the error, and then on the File menu, click Close and Return to Microsoft Excel. In the message box, click OK to stop the debugger. Test the button again. If you are unable to resolve the error, seek assistance from your instructor or lab assistant.

---

1 In the **Controls group**, click the **Design Mode** button, and then click the **View Code** button.

2 At the end of the first line of code, click to place the insertion point to the *left* of the word *Then*. Type the following line of code, pressing (Spacebar) one time at the end:

And Range("F20").Value < 200

3 Be sure the first line of code now reads: *If Air = True And Range("F20").Value < 200 Then*

4 In the *MessageText* line, click to the left of the closing quotation mark, press (Spacebar), and then type a second sentence as follows: **Supervisor must sign submitted Expense Form.**

The message text is modified to read: *"To use air transportation miles one way should equal 200 or more. Supervisor must sign submitted Expense Form."* The line of text extends across the Visual Basic Editor window, and the screen scrolls to the right.

5 Scroll to the left. At the end of the fourth line of code, place the insertion point after *TitleBarText* and press (Enter), and then press (Shift) + (Tab). Type the following code spaced as shown below:

Else
    TitleBarText = "Travel Method Checked"
    MessageText = "Travel method OK."
    MsgBox MessageText, , TitleBarText

This code will cause a second message box to display if the Air check box is selected and the mileage is 200 or more. This message box will also display if the Air check box is not selected. Compare your VBA code with Figure 9.29.

Figure 9.29

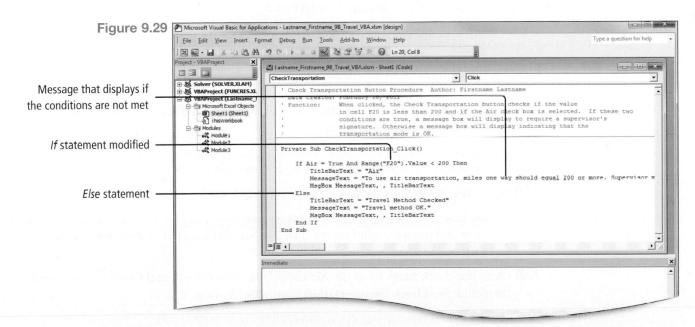

Message that displays if the conditions are not met

If statement modified

Else statement

6 Click **File**, and then click **Close and Return to Microsoft Excel**. On the **Developer tab**, in the **Controls group**, click the **Design Mode** button to exit Design Mode. **Save** your workbook.

Activity 9.12 | Testing the VBA Procedure and the ActiveX Control

After you create a VBA procedure, you must test it to verify that it works as you intended.

1 Be sure the **Air** check box is still selected—it displays a check mark—and that the **Design Mode** button is not selected. In cell **F20**, type **150** and then press Enter. Click the **Check Transportation** button. Compare your screen with Figure 9.30.

The first message box displays and informs you that a supervisor's signature is required.

Figure 9.30

Message advising that a supervisor's signature is required

Air travel selected

Mileage less than 200 miles

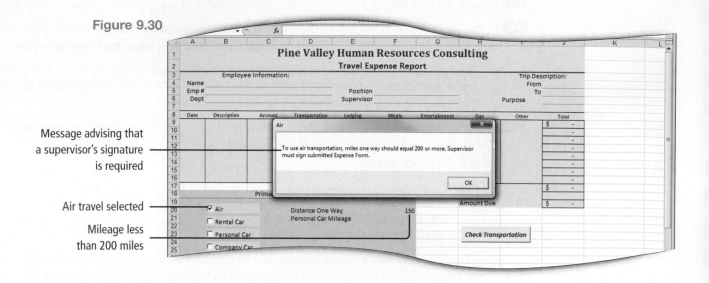

> **Alert | Does an Error Message Display?**
>
> If an error message displays, in the message box, click Debug to return to the Visual Basic Editor window and correct the error that is highlighted in yellow. After correcting the highlighted error, on the File menu, click Close and Return to Microsoft Excel. Repeat Step 1 to continue.

2 In the **Air** message box, click **OK**. Click cell **F20**, type **200** and then press Enter. Click the **Check Transportation** button.

The second message box displays indicating *Travel method OK*. If you get the first message box, return to the code and correct the cell reference to F20.

3 In the **Travel Method Checked** message box, click **OK**.

You have tested both conditions for using air transportation—when the miles are 200 or more, and when the miles are less than 200. You also need to test the Command Button when other modes of transportation are used.

4 Clear the check mark from the **Air** check box. Select the **Rental Car** check box, and then click the **Check Transportation** Command Button.

The second message box displays indicating *Travel method OK*.

5 Click **OK** to acknowledge the message.

6 In the **Controls group**, click the **Design Mode** button, and then click the **View Code** button.

7 If you are directed to submit your file electronically, skip to Step 8. On the **File** tab, click **Print**, and then in the **Print – VBA Project** dialog box, click **OK** to print a copy of your VBA code.

8 Click **File** and then click **Close and Return to Microsoft Excel**. In the **Controls group**, click the **Design Mode** button to exit Design Mode.

9 Insert a footer in the **left section** that includes the file name. On the status bar, click the **Normal** button , and then press [Ctrl] + [Home] to move to the top of the worksheet. Display the **Document Panel** and in the **Author** box, type your Firstname and Lastname, in the **Subject** box, type your course name and section number, and in the **Keywords** box, type **expense report VBA Close** [×] the Document Panel. Display the worksheet in **Print Preview**, and then make any necessary corrections or adjustments.

10 Save [💾] your workbook, and then submit as directed by your instructor. **Close** the workbook.

Objective 5 | Restore Initial Settings

When you use a computer in a public location such as a college computer lab, or when you use someone else's computer, it is proper computer etiquette to return it to the condition in which you found it. In this chapter, you created a macro and then placed a button on the Quick Access Toolbar.

Activity 9.13 | Removing the Quick Access Toolbar Button and the Macro

1 Right-click the **Smiley Face** icon on the **Quick Access Toolbar,** and then click **Remove from Quick Access Toolbar**.

2 On the **Developer tab**, in the **Code group**, click the **Macros** button.

3 Verify that the Macro dialog box is empty. If the Employee_Info macro you created is displayed, select the macro name, and then click the **Delete** button.

> The Employee_Info button is removed from the Quick Access Toolbar.
>
> The Employee_Info macro is part of the workbooks Lastname_Firstname_9A_Travel_ Macro and Lastname_Firstname_9B_Travel_VBA and will not be deleted from those files. Because the workbooks are closed, the macro name should not display in this list of macros. If you accidentally saved the macro in another place and it displays in this list, it should now be deleted.

4 Click the **Cancel** button. **Close** Excel.

End **You have completed Project 9B** ————————————————————

Content-Based Assessments

Summary

In this chapter, you automated an Excel worksheet to perform complex tasks faster and to perform repetitive actions using macros and the programming language called Visual Basic for Applications (VBA). You attached a macro to the Quick Access Toolbar and assigned a keyboard shortcut. You modified VBA code. Finally, you created an ActiveX control.

Key Terms

ActiveX controls 562

Check boxes 562

Design Mode..................564

Digital signature 553

Embed 564

Event 557

Macro............................549

Macro virus 552

Module...........................557

Procedure 557

Properties 565

Record Macro.................553

Sub................................558

Sub procedure 558

VBA 549

VBA construct................558

Visual Basic Editor
  window 558

Visual Basic for
  Applications 549

Matching

Match each term in the second column with its correct definition in the first column by writing the letter of the term on the blank line in front of the correct definition.

_____ 1.   A series of commands that are grouped together as a single command.

_____ 2.   The programming language used to write computer programs within the Microsoft Windows environment.

_____ 3.   The abbreviation for Visual Basic for Applications programming language.

_____ 4.   Malicious lines of code in a macro program that are written with the intent of erasing or damaging files on another computer.

_____ 5.   An electronic, encryption-based, secure stamp of authentication on a macro or document.

_____ 6.   A command that records your actions in Visual Basic for Applications programming language.

_____ 7.   The action, such as a combination of keystrokes, or the click of a button, that causes a program or macro to run.

_____ 8.   When you record a macro, the place where the VBA code is stored.

_____ 9.   A named sequence of statements in a computer program that performs a task.

_____ 10.   An area where you can view the module containing Visual Basic code.

_____ 11.   In computer programming, the name given to a set of instructions that accomplishes a specific task.

_____ 12.   An instruction that enables the macro to perform multiple operations on a single object.

A ActiveX controls

B Digital signature

C Embed

D Event

E Macro

F Macro virus

G Module

H Procedure

I Properties

J Record Macro

K Sub procedure

L VBA

M VBA construct

N Visual Basic Editor window

O Visual Basic for Applications

Content-Based Assessments

_____ 13. Graphic objects that can run macros or scripts to automate a task or offer options.

_____ 14. To insert something created in one computer program into another computer program.

_____ 15. Characteristics of ActiveX controls that can be changed.

Multiple Choice

Circle the correct answer.

1. When developing ActiveX controls, you work in:
   A. Test Mode   **B.** Code Mode   **C.** Design Mode

2. To make a letter a shortcut key, precede the letter with:
   A. Ctrl   **B.** Alt   **C.** Home

3. In VBA code, each line that contains a comment is preceded by:
   A. an exclamation point   **B.** an apostrophe— single quote   **C.** a double quote

4. To examine VBA code, in the Controls group, click:
   A. Properties   **B.** View Code   **C.** Run Dialog

5. To make code easier to read in the Code window, beginning and ending statements are formatted to the same level by:
   A. aligning left   **B.** aligning center   **C.** aligning right

6. Comments added to VBA code display in:
   A. red text   **B.** blue text   **C.** green text

7. To give you the option of approving or blocking files that contain macros, you should set your macro security level to:
   A. Disable all macros without notification   **B.** Disable all macros with notification   **C.** Enable all macros

8. To modify the Quick Access Toolbar, go to the following tab in the Excel Options dialog box:
   A. Customize Ribbon   **B.** Quick Access Toolbar   **C.** Add-Ins

9. After you create a macro and assign it to a button or menu item, to ensure that it works as expected, it needs to be:
   A. tested   **B.** protected   **C.** viewed

10. A combination of keys to execute a macro or program is known as a:
    A. procedure   **B.** sub   **C.** shortcut key

Content-Based Assessments

Apply **9A** skills from these Objectives:

1. Record a Macro
2. Assign a Macro to a Button on the Quick Access Toolbar
3. Modify a Macro

Skills Review | Project **9C** Summary Reports

In the following Skills Review, you will assist Tiffany Shin, Training Director, in creating a macro that will make it easier for staff members to include the required information in their training department expense reports. You will assign the macro to a button on the Quick Access Toolbar, and then modify the macro by changing the Visual Basic Code. Your completed worksheets will look similar to Figure 9.31.

Project Files

For Project 9C, you will need the following file:

e09C_Training_Macro

You will save your workbook as:

Lastname_Firstname_9C_Training_Macro

Project Results

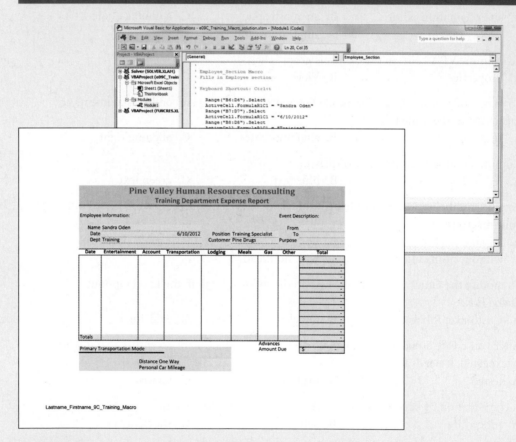

Figure 9.31

(Project 9C Summary Reports continues on the next page)

1 **Start** Excel and display a new blank workbook. In **Backstage** view, click **Options**. If necessary, in the **Excel Options** dialog box, on the left, click **Customize Ribbon**. On the right, under **Main Tabs**, select the **Developer** check box. In the lower right corner, click **OK**. On the Ribbon, click the **Developer tab**.

a. On the **Developer tab**, in the **Code group**, click the **Macro Security** button. Under **Macro Settings**, verify that the default option button—**Disable all macros with notification**—is selected, and then click **OK**. Display the **Open** dialog box, and then from your student files, open the file **c09C_Training_ Macro**. Display the **Save As** dialog box, navigate to your **Excel Chapter 9** folder, click the **Save as type arrow**, and then click **Excel Macro-Enabled Workbook**. In the **File name** box, type **Lastname_ Firstname_9C_Training_Macro**

b. Insert a footer in the **left section** that includes the file name. Return to **Normal** view and scroll to view the top of the worksheet. Display the **Document Panel**, in the **Author** box, type your first name and last name, in the **Subject** box, type your course name and section number, and then in the **Keywords** box, type **training expense form, macro Close** the **Document Panel**, and then **Save** your workbook.

c. On the **Review tab**, in the **Changes group**, click the **Protect Workbook** button. In the **Unprotect Workbook** dialog box, type **training** which is the password applied to this form, and then click **OK**.

d. Be sure that cell **B6** is the active cell. On the **Developer tab**, in the **Code group**, click the **Record Macro** button. In the **Macro name** box, delete the existing text, and then type **Employee_Section** In the **Shortcut key** box, type **t** Click the **Store macro in arrow**, then click **This Workbook**. Click in the **Description** box. Type **Fills in the Employee section** Click **OK**.

e. In cell **B6**, type **Sandra Oden** and then press Enter. With cell **B7** active, hold down Ctrl and press ; (semicolon), which will insert the current date. Press Enter. With cell **B8** active, type **Training** Click in cell **F7** and type **Training Specialist** and then press Enter. In cell **F8**, type **Pine Drugs** and then click cell **A11**, so that when the macro completes, the first cell in the data area is active to begin filling in the travel information. On the **Developer tab**, in the **Code**

group, click the **Stop Recording** button. Delete the text you just typed in the five cells—**B6**, **B7**, **B8**, **F7**, **F8**—and then click cell **B6**. Then, to test that your macro will fill in the employee information and the date, run the macro by pressing the shortcut key Ctrl + T. **Save** your workbook.

2 From **Backstage** view, display the **Excel Options** dialog box, and then on the left, click **Quick Access Toolbar**. Under **Choose commands from:**, click the **Popular Commands arrow**, and then click **Macros**. Click your **Employee_Section** macro, and then, in the center of the dialog box, click the **Add** button. On the right, click your newly added **Employee_Section** command, and then in the lower right corner, click the **Modify** button. Under **Symbol**, in the seventh row, click the seventh icon—the **Checkered Square** button—and then click **OK** two times. **Save** your workbook.

a. Select the nonadjacent ranges **B6:B8** and **F7:F8** and press Del so that these cells are empty again. Click cell **B6**, and then on the Quick Access Toolbar, click your new **Employee_Section** button—the Checkered Square.

3 On the **Developer tab,** in the **Code group**, click the **Macros** button. Be sure the **Employee_Section** macro is selected, and then click the **Edit** button. In the **Code window**, locate the green and black lines of text that comprise the comments and code for the Employee_ Section macro. At the end of the *last* line of code— *Range("A11") .Select*—click to place the insertion point after *Select,* and then press Enter.

a. On the new, empty line, type **With ActiveSheet .PageSetup** and then press Enter. Press Tab to indent and type **.CenterHorizontally = True** Press Enter and type **.CenterVertically = True** and then press Enter. Press Shift + Tab, and then type **End With**

b. To print your module on paper, at the top of the window, in the menu bar, click **File** to display a menu, and then click **Print**. In the **Print - VBA Project** dialog box, under **Print What**, verify that **Code** is selected, and then click **OK**.

c. Display the **File** menu, click **Close and Return to Microsoft Excel**. Delete the text in **B6:B8, F7:F8**, click cell **B6**, and then on the **Quick Access Toolbar**, click the **Employee_Section** button that you created, so that the macro is re-run and includes the centering you added to the macro. Display and check the **Print**

(Project 9C Summary Reports continues on the next page)

Excel | Chapter 9

Content-Based Assessments

Skills Review | Project **9C** Summary Reports (continued)

Preview. Right-click the **Checkered Square** icon on the **Quick Access Toolbar,** and then click **Remove from Quick Access Toolbar**.

d. **Save** your workbook, and then print or submit electronically as directed. If required by your instructor, print or create an electronic version of your worksheets with formulas displayed by using the instructions in Activity 1.16, and then **Exit** Excel without saving so that you do not save the changes you made to print formulas.

 You have completed Project 9C ⎯⎯⎯⎯⎯⎯⎯⎯⎯⎯⎯⎯⎯⎯⎯⎯⎯⎯⎯

Apply **9B** skills from these Objectives:

4 Write a VBA Procedure to Use an ActiveX Control

5 Restore Initial Settings

Skills Review | Project **9D** Recruitment Report

In the following Skills Review, you will assist Tiffany Shin, Training Director at Pine Valley Human Resources Consulting, by writing a set of commands in the VBA programming language, using ActiveX Control buttons to automate the Recruitment Department policy guidelines for expense reports. Your completed workbook will look similar to Figure 9.32.

Project Files

For Project 9D, you will need the following file:

e09D_Recruitment_VBA

You will save your workbook as:

Lastname_Firstname_9D_Recruitment_VBA

Project Results

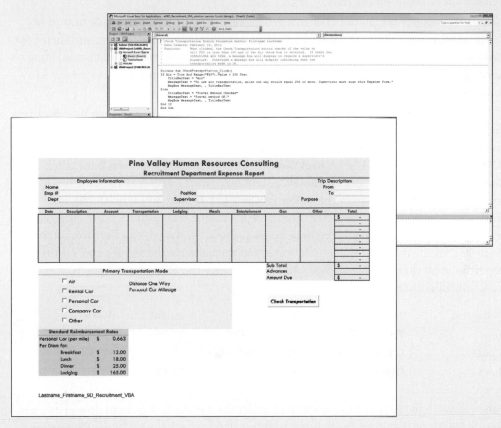

Figure 9.32

(Project 9D Recruitment Report continues on the next page)

Content-Based Assessments

1 **Start** Excel. From your student files, locate and open the file **e09D_Recruitment_VBA**, and then **Save** the file in your **Excel Chapter 9** folder as an **Excel Macro-Enabled Workbook** with the file name **Lastname_Firstname_9D_Recruitment_VBA** If necessary, on the Security Warning bar, click Enable Content.

a. On the **Developer tab**, in the **Controls group**, click the **Insert** button. Under **ActiveX Controls**, click the **Check Box** button. Point to the upper left corner of cell **B20** and drag to insert a check box object that is approximately the height of the cell and the width of columns **B:C**. Repeat this process to add four more check boxes of the same approximate size under **CheckBox1**.

b. Click **CheckBox1**, and then on the **Developer tab**, in the **Controls group**, notice that the **Design Mode** button is active. With **CheckBox1** selected, hold down Ctrl and click on each of the remaining check boxes so that all five check boxes are selected. On the **Page Layout tab**, in the **Arrange group**, click the **Align** button, and then click **Align Left** to align the check boxes on the left.

2 Click the **Developer tab**. In the **Controls group**, verify that the **Design Mode** button is active. Click another area of the worksheet to deselect the group of check boxes, and then click **CheckBox1** to select the check box. In the **Controls group**, click the **Properties** button. Drag the **Properties** pane near the upper right of your screen, and then expand its lower edge so that you can see the entire list of properties.

a. At the top of the **Alphabetic** list, in the first column, click **(Name)**, and then type **Air** Press Enter, and notice that *Air* displays in the **Name Box**. In the first column, click the **Caption** property, type **Air** and then press Enter. Click **Height** and type **15.75** click **Width** and type **84.75** and then press Enter. Click **CheckBox2** to select it. In the **Properties** pane, click **(Name)**, type without any spaces **RentalCar** and then press Enter. Click the **Caption** property, and then type, *with* a space, **Rental Car** Click **Height** and type **15.75** Click **Width** and type **84.75** and press Enter. Using the technique you just practiced, change the properties for the remaining three check boxes as shown in the table. (Hint: You can hold down Ctrl, select the remaining check boxes, and then change the Height and Width properties in all three simultaneously. You must change the Name and Caption of each check box individually.)

ActiveX Control	Name	Caption	Height	Width
CheckBox3	**PersonalCar**	**Personal Car**	**15.75**	**84.75**
CheckBox4	**CompanyCar**	**Company Car**	**15.75**	**84.75**
CheckBox5	**Other**	**Other**	**15.75**	**84.75**

b. In the yellow shaded area of the worksheet, select the **Air** check box, hold down Ctrl, and then click each of the other check boxes to select all five check boxes. In the **Properties** pane, click **BackColor**, click the **BackColor arrow**, click the **System tab**, scroll down and click **Button Light Shadow**. **Close** the **Properties** pane. On the **Page Layout tab**, in the **Arrange group**, click the **Align** button, and then click **Distribute Vertically**. Drag the group of check boxes as necessary to adjust the position of the group so that they are contained within the yellow shaded area. Click cell **A1** to deselect the group of check boxes. Click **Save**.

3 Click cell **H22** to identify the location where you will place a Command Button. On the **Developer tab**, in the **Controls group**, click the **Insert** button, and then under **ActiveX**

(Project 9D Recruitment Report continues on the next page)

Controls, click the **Command Button**. Point to cell **H22**, and then click one time to insert the button.

a. In the **Controls group**, click the **Properties** button. In the **Properties** pane, click **(Name)**, and then type **CheckTransportation** Click the **Caption** property, and then type **Check Transportation** Click **AutoSize**, click the **AutoSize arrow**, and then click **True**. In the **Properties** pane, click **Font**, and then click the **Font build** button to display the **Font** dialog box. Under **Font style**, click **Bold Italic**, and then click **OK**. **Close** the **Properties** pane. Be sure the **Check Transportation** control is selected. On the **Developer tab**, in the **Controls group**, click the **View Code** button. In the **Object** box, click the **first arrow**, and then on the displayed list, click **CheckTransportation**.

b. Click to the left of *Private Sub CheckTransportation_Click()* to place the insertion point there, and then press Enter to insert a blank line. Press ↑ to move to the blank line, and then type the following comments spaced as shown. Use your own name as the author. At the end of each line, press Enter, and as necessary, press Tab to provide indents and alignment.

```
' Check Transportation Button Procedure    Author: Firstname Lastname
' Date Created:    February 18, 2013
' Function:        When clicked, the Check Transportation button checks if the value in
'                  cell F20 is less than 200 and if the Air check box is selected. If these two
'                  conditions are true, a message box will display to require a supervisor's
'                  signature. Otherwise a message box will display indicating that the
'                  transportation mode is OK.
```

c. Press Enter. Click to position the insertion point on the blank line under *Private Sub CheckTransportation_Click()*. Press Enter, and then press Tab. Type the lines of VBA code spaced as shown below. Use the Tab key to indent the middle three lines and Shift + Tab to reduce the indent by one tab for the last line. As you type, a prompt box will display to assist you with the VBA syntax. Ignore the prompts and type the code as shown.

```
If Air = True Then
    TitleBarText = "Air"
    MessageText = "To use air transportation, miles one way should equal 200 or more."
    MsgBox MessageText, , TitleBarText
End If
```

d. In the upper left corner, click **File** to display a menu, and then click **Close and Return to Microsoft Excel**. In the **Controls group**, click the **Design Mode** button to exit Design Mode. In the yellow shaded section, select the **Air** check box, and then click the **Check Transportation** Command Button. Click **OK** to acknowledge the message.

4 In the **Controls group**, click the **Design Mode** button, and then click the **View Code** button. At the end of the first line of code, click to place the insertion point to the left of the word *Then*. Type the following line of code, pressing Spacebar at the end:

And Range("F20").Value < 200

a. Be sure the first line of code now reads: *If Air = True And Range("F20").Value < 200 Then* In the *MessageText* line, click to the left of the closing quotation mark, press Spacebar, and then type a second sentence as follows:

Supervisor must sign this Expense Form.

(Project 9D Recruitment Report continues on the next page)

Content-Based Assessments

b. Scroll to the left. At the end of the fourth line of code, place the insertion point after TitleBarText and press ⏎Enter⏎. Then press ⏎Shift⏎ + ⏎Tab⏎. Type the following code spaced as shown in the following:

```
Else
    TitleBarText = "Travel Method Checked"
    MessageText = "Travel method OK."
    MsgBox MessageText, , TitleBarText
```

This code will cause a second message box to display if the Air check box is selected and the mileage is 200 or more. This message box will also display if the Air check box is not selected.

c. On the **File tab**, click **Close and Return to Microsoft Excel**. In the **Controls group**, click the **Design Mode** button to return to the active worksheet. Be sure the **Air** check box is still selected—it displays a check mark. In cell **F20**, type **150** and then press ⏎Enter⏎. Click the **Check Transportation** button. In the **Air** message box, click **OK**. Click cell **F20**, type **200** and then press ⏎Enter⏎. Click the **Check Transportation** button.

d. In the **Travel Method Checked** message box, click **OK**. Clear the check mark from the **Air** check box. Select the **Rental Car** check box, and then click the **Check Transportation** Command Button. Click **OK** to acknowledge the message.

e. In the **Controls group**, click the **View Code** button. If you are directed to submit your file electronically, skip to Step f. On the **File tab**, click **Print**, and then on the **Print–VBAProject** dialog box, click **OK** to print a copy of your VBA code.

f. On the **File tab**, click **Close and Return to Microsoft Excel**. In the **Controls group**, click the **Design Mode** button to exit Design Mode. Clear all the check boxes and clear cell **F20**. Insert a footer in the **left section** that includes the file name. On the status bar, click the **Normal** button, and then press ⏎Ctrl⏎ + ⏎Home⏎ to move to the top of the worksheet. Display the **Document Panel** and in the **Author** box, type your firstname and lastname, in the **Subject** box, type your course name and section number, and in the **Keywords** box, type **recruitment department expense report VBA Close** the Document Information Panel. Display the worksheet in **Print Preview**, and then make any necessary corrections or adjustments. **Save** your workbook, and then submit it as directed by your instructor. **Close** the workbook.

End **You have completed Project 9D** ————————————————

Content-Based Assessments

Apply **9A** skills from these Objectives:

1. Record a Macro
2. Assign a Macro to a Button on the Quick Access Toolbar
3. Modify a Macro

Mastering Excel | Project **9E** Operations Report

In the following Mastering Excel project, you will assist Larry Poirier, Project Director, in creating a macro that will assign an operations department heading required on all reports. You will assign the macro to the Quick Access Toolbar, and then modify the macro by changing the Visual Basic Code. Your completed worksheet will look similar to Figure 9.33.

Project Files

For Project 9E, you will need the following file:

e09E_Operations_Macro

You will save your workbook as:

Lastname_Firstname_9E_Operations_Macro

Project Results

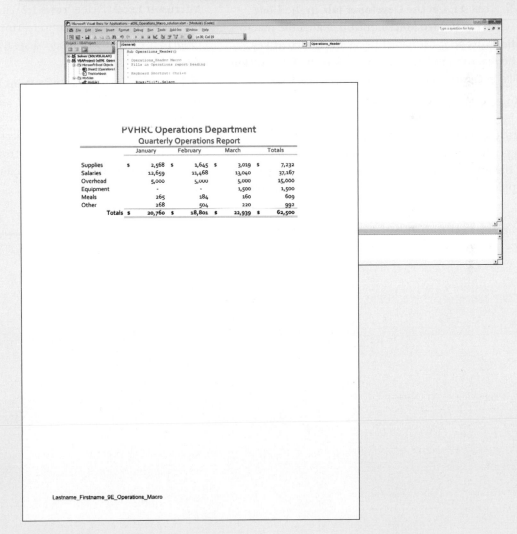

Figure 9.33

(Project 9E Operations Report continues on the next page)

Content-Based Assessments

Mastering Excel | Project **9E** Operations Report (continued)

1 **Start** Excel. Be sure the **Developer tab** is enabled and that the **Macro Settings** are set to **Disable all macros with notification**. From your student files, open the file **e09E_Operations_Macro**. Display the **Save As** dialog box, navigate to your **Excel Chapter 9** folder, set the **Save as type** to **Excel Macro-Enabled Workbook**, and as the file name, type **Lastname_Firstname_9E_Operations_Macro**

2 Insert a footer in the **left section** that includes the file name. Display the **Document Panel**. In the **Author** box, type your firstname and lastname, in the **Subject** box, type your course name and section number, and then in the **Keywords** box, type **operations department header, macro Close** the Document Information Panel.

3 Click cell **A1**. On the **Developer tab**, in the **Code group**, click the **Record Macro** button. Name the macro **Operations_Header** use Ctrl + O as the **Shortcut key**, store the macro in this workbook, and as the **Description**, type **Fills in Operations report heading** Click **OK**.

4 Right-click the **row 1** header, click **Insert**, and then press F4 to repeat the action—two blank rows are inserted at the top of the worksheet. Click cell **A1**, and then type **PVHRC Operations Department** Merge and center the text you just typed across the range **A1:E1**, and then apply the **Title** cell style. In cell **A2**, type **Quarterly**

Report and then Merge and Center the text you just typed across the range **A2:E2**, and then apply the **Heading 1** cell style. Center the worksheet horizontally, click cell **A1**, and then stop recording the macro. Delete **rows 1:2**, click cell **A1**, and then test the macro by pressing Ctrl + O.

5 On the **Developer tab**, in the **Code group**, click the **Macros** button. Verify that the **Operations_Header** macro is selected, and then click the **Edit** button. Scroll down and locate the first instance of *End With*, and then in the fourth line following End With, edit *"Quarterly Report"* to indicate **"Quarterly Operations Report"** If required by your instructor, print the code.

6 Click **File**, and then click **Close and Return to Microsoft Excel**. Delete **rows 1:2**, click cell **A1**, and then use the keyboard shortcut to re-run the macro to test that *Quarterly Operations Report* displays as the subtitle of the report.

7 Display the worksheet in **Print Preview**. If necessary, return to the workbook and make any necessary corrections or adjustments. **Save** your workbook. Print the worksheet or submit your workbook electronically as directed. If required, print or create an electronic version of your worksheets with formulas displayed using the instructions in Activity 1.16 in Project 1A.

End **You have completed Project 9E** ────────────────

Content-Based Assessments

Apply 9B skills from these Objectives:

- **4** Write a VBA Procedure to Use an ActiveX Control
- **5** Restore Initial Settings

Mastering Excel | Project **9F** Evaluation Form

In the following Mastering Excel project, you will assist Tiffany Shin, Training Director, by adding ActiveX controls to an evaluation form to gather feedback about training seminars. You will write VBA code to create input boxes that the respondent will use to enter information about the seminar. Your completed worksheet will look similar to Figure 9.34.

Project Files

For Project 9F, you will need the following file:

e09F_Evaluation_VBA

You will save your workbook as:

Lastname_Firstname_9F_Evaluation_VBA

Project Results

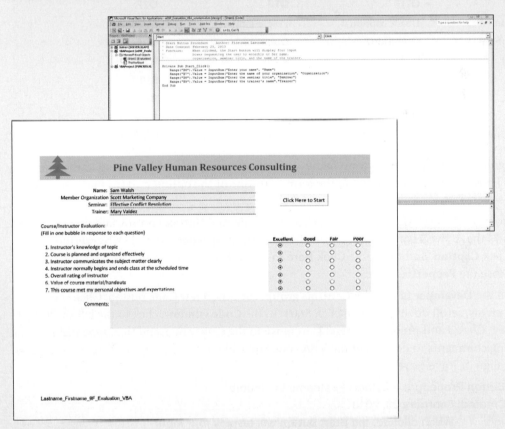

Figure 9.34

(Project 9F Evaluation Form continues on the next page)

Content-Based Assessments

Mastering Excel | Project **9F** Evaluation Form (continued)

1 **Start** Excel. From your student files, locate the file **e09F_Evaluation_VBA**. **Save** the file in your **Excel Chapter 9** folder as an **Excel Macro-Enabled Workbook** with the file name **Lastname_ Firstname_9F_Evaluation_VBA** If necessary, on the Security Warning bar, click Enable Content.

2 Display the **ActiveX Controls** gallery. Click the **Option Button** control, and then click cell **G20**. On the **Developer tab**, in the **Controls group**, click the **Properties** button. In the **Properties** pane, click (**Name**) and type **Q7E** Click the **Caption** property, and then delete the caption, **OptionButton1** Click **GroupName**, and then type **Question7** Change the **Height** property to **9.75** Change the **Left** property to **465** Change **Top** to **279** and **Width** to **9.75** Click the **SpecialEffect arrow**, and then click **0 – fmButtonEffectFlat**.

3 Using the same technique, add three more option buttons in **row 20** and set the following properties:

Location/Property	Cell H20	Cell I20	Cell J20
Name	**Q7G**	**Q7F**	**Q7P**
Caption	Delete caption	Delete caption	Delete caption
GroupName	**Question7**	**Question7**	**Question7**
Height	**9.75**	**9.75**	**9.75**
Left	**519.75**	**567**	**618**
Top	**279**	**279**	**279**
Width	**9.75**	**9.75**	**9.75**
SpecialEffect	0 fmButtonEffectFlat	0 fmButtonEffectFlat	0 fmButtonEffectFlat

By assigning *Question7* as the group name, you define each button as belonging to the same group. Thus, for the person filling in the form, only one of the option buttons in that group can be selected.

4 From the **ActiveX Controls** gallery, click the **Command Button** control, and then click cell **G7** to add the ActiveX control to the worksheet. In the **Properties** pane, click **Name** and type **Start** Click **Caption**, and then type **Click Here to Start** Double-click **AutoSize** to change it to *True*. **Close** the **Properties** pane.

5 On the **Developer tab**, in the **Controls group**, click the **View Code** button. Click the **Object arrow**, scroll down and then click **Start**. In the **Code window**, click to the left of *Private Sub Start_Click()* and press [Enter]. Press [↑] to move to the empty line, and then type the following comments to document the VBA code you will write. Use your own name, and press [Tab] to align or leave extra space.

' Start Button Procedure   Author: Firstname Lastname
' Date Created: February 23, 2013
' Function: When clicked, the Start button will display four input
'   boxes requesting the user to enter his or her name,
'   organization, seminar title, and the name of the trainer.

6 Press [Enter]. Click in the empty line following *Private Sub Start_Click()*, press [Tab], and then type the following VBA code:

Range("B6").Value = InputBox("Enter your name", "Name")

Range("B7").Value = InputBox("Enter the name of your organization", "Organization")

Range("B8").Value = InputBox("Enter the seminar title", "Seminar")

Range("B9").Value = InputBox("Enter the trainer's name", "Trainer")

(Project 9F Evaluation Form continues on the next page)

Content-Based Assessments

7 Click **File** and then click **Print** to print the code, or submit the code electronically as directed. Click **File**, and then click **Close and Return to Microsoft Excel**. On the **Developer tab**, in the **Controls group**, click the **Design Mode** button to exit Design Mode.

8 Click your new Command Button to test it, and type the following in each of the input boxes that display; click **OK** to close each box:

Name	**Sam Walsh**
Organization	**Scott Marketing Company**
Seminar	**Effective Conflict Resolution**
Trainer	**Mary Valdez**

9 Click an option button, for example *Excellent*, for each of the seven questions. Now, test to see what happens when you change your mind and select a different rating for the one of the questions—the original button is cleared, and only the new button is selected. By identifying the options for each question as a *group*, the person filling in the form can select only one option.

10 Insert a footer in the **left section** that includes the file name. On the status bar, click the **Normal** button, and then press Ctrl + Home to move to the top of the worksheet. Display the **Document Panel** and in the **Author** box, type your firstname and lastname, in the **Subject** box, type your course name and section number, and in the **Keywords** box, type **evaluation report VBA Close** the Document Panel. Display the worksheet in **Print Preview**, and then make any necessary corrections or adjustments. **Save** your workbook, and then submit as directed by your instructor. **Close** the workbook.

End You have completed Project 9F ————————————

Content-Based Assessments

Apply **9A** and **9B** skills
from these Objectives:

1 Record a Macro

2 Assign a Macro to a
Button on the Quick
Access Toolbar

3 Modify a Macro

4 Write a VBA
Procedure to Use an
ActiveX Control

5 Restore Initial
Settings

Mastering Excel | Project **9G** Name Tags

In this project, you will assist Tiffany Shin, Training Director, by creating a macro to print name tags with a tree graphic. Two different styles of attendee name tags are used by Pine Valley Human Resources Consulting for its training seminars. You will examine the code generated by the macro and use it as a model for creating an ActiveX control—a Command Button—and writing the necessary VBA code to print the name tag with a leaf graphic. Your completed worksheets will look similar to Figure 9.35.

Project Files

For Project 9G, you will need the following file:

e09G_Name_Tags

You will save your workbook as:

Lastname_Firstname_9G_Name_Tags

Project Results

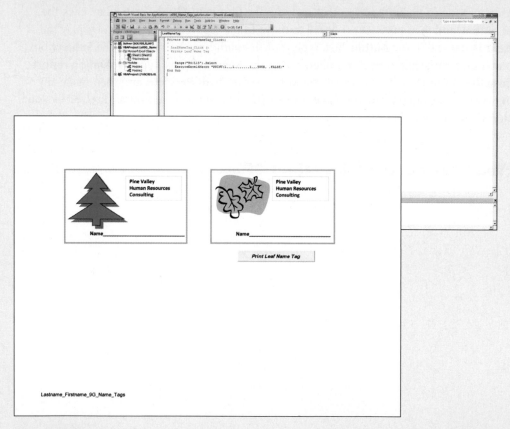

Figure 9.35

(Project 9G Name Tags continues on the next page)

Content-Based Assessments

1 **Start** Excel. Be sure the **Developer tab** is enabled and that the **Macro Settings** are set to **Disable all macros with notification**. From your student files, open the file e09G_Name_Tags. Click **Enable Content**. Display the **Save As** dialog box, **Save** the file in your **Excel Chapter 9** folder as an **Excel Macro-Enabled Workbook** with the name Lastname_Firstname_9G_Name_Tags

2 Insert a footer in the **left section** that includes the file name. Display the **Document Panel**, in the **Author** box, type your firstname and lastname, in the **Subject** box, type your course name and section number, and then in the **Keywords** box, type **name tags** Close the Document Panel.

3 Verify that cell **A1** is the active cell. On the **Developer tab**, in the **Code group**, click the **Record Macro** button. Name the macro **TreeNameTag** and assign **n** as the **Shortcut key**. Store the macro in this workbook, and as the description, type **Macro for name tags** Click **OK**.

4 Select the range **B4:F15**. Click the **File tab**, and then click **Print**. In the **Print Preview**, under **Settings**, click the first button arrow, click **Print Selection,** and then click the **Print** button. On the **Developer tab**, in the **Code group**, click the **Stop Recording** button. Click cell **A1** to deselect, and then test the macro by pressing [Ctrl] + [N].

5 On the **Developer tab**, in the **Controls group**, click the **Insert** button, and then under **ActiveX Controls**, click the **Command Button**. Drag to insert a Command Button object for the range **I17:K18**.

6 With the button selected, display the **Properties** pane. As the **(Name)**, type **LeafNameTag** and as the **Caption** type **Print Leaf Name Tag** Change the **Height** to

23.25 and the **Width** to **150** Set the **BackColor** to **Button Light Shadow**, and change the **Font style** to **Bold Italic**. **Close** the **Properties** pane.

7 On the **Developer tab**, in the **Code group**, click the **Macros** button and be sure **TreeNameTag** is selected. Click the **Edit** button. On the displayed **Microsoft Visual Basic for Applications** window, select all of the code between *Sub TreeNameTag ()* and *End Sub*. Right-click over the selection, and then click **Copy**. Click the **File tab**, and then click **Close and Return to Microsoft Excel.**

8 Select the **Print Leaf Name Tag** command button. On the **Developer tab**, in the **Controls group**, click the **View Code** button. At the top of the **Microsoft Visual Basic for Applications** window, click the **(General) arrow**, and then click **LeafNameTag**. In the **Microsoft Visual Basic for Applications** window, be sure the insertion point is at the beginning of the line below *Private Sub LeafNameTag_Click ()*. Right-click, and then click **Paste**. In the green comment code, replace *TreeNameTag Macro* with **LeafNameTag Command Button** Replace *Macro for name tags* with **Prints Leaf Name Tag** Delete Keyboard Shortcut: Ctrl + n. Edit the range to **("H4:L15")** Click the **File tab**, and **then Close and Return to Microsoft Excel**.

9 On the **Developer tab** in the **Controls group**, click the **Design Mode button** to turn off Design Mode. Test the button by clicking the **Print Leaf Name Tag Command Button**. The name tag will print. Click cell **A1** to deselect. Display the worksheet in **Print Preview**, change the setting to **Print Active Sheets**, and then make any necessary corrections or adjustments. **Save** your workbook, and then submit as directed by your instructor. **Close** the workbook.

End **You have completed Project 9G**

Content-Based Assessments

GO! Fix It | Project **9H** Finance Report

Project Files

For Project 9H, you will need the following file:

    e09H_Finance_Macro

You will save your workbook as:

    Lastname_Firstname_9H_Finance_Macro

Open the file e09H_Finance_Macro, and then save the file in your Excel Chapter 9 folder as **Lastname_Firstname_9H_Finance_Macro** A macro was created by the Finance Department to add documentation to the Quarterly Finance Expense Summary reports. Re-record the macro so that the red fill color is replaced by a more visually pleasing fill color—Blue, Accent 1 in the range A12:B13. In cell A12, type **Created by** In cell A13, type **Audited by** In cell B12, type **Susan Lammers** In cell B13, type **Tony Alvarez** In cell A14, type **Pine Valley Human Resources Consulting** and select Calibri font, size 11, bold for a more readable font style. Add your name and course information to the document properties, and include **finance macro** as the keywords. Insert the file name in the left section of the footer, center the worksheet horizontally. Save your file, and then print or submit your worksheet electronically as directed by your instructor.

End **You have completed Project 9H** ————————————————

Content-Based Assessments

Apply a combination of the **9A** and **9B** skills.

GO! Make It | Project **9I** Timecard

Project Files

For Project 9I, you will need the following file:

e09I_Timecard_Macro

You will save your workbook as:

Lastname_Firstname_9I_Timecard_Macro

Open the file e09I_Timecard_Macro; save it in your Excel Chapter 9 folder as **Lastname_Firstname_9I_Timecard_Macro**

Create a macro to automatically fill in the employee information shown in Figure 9.36. Use Ctrl + t as the shortcut key and type **Fills in employee information** as the macro description. The file is protected; **timecard** is the password.

Name	Kelley McKown			Employee ID	EE-071154
Street Address	55 Starr Street	Position	Consultant	Phone	315-555-0055
City, State, ZIP Code	Pine Valley, NY 13210	Supervisor	Karl Jess	Email	kelley@pvhrc.biz

Insert a footer, add your name, your course name and section, and the keywords **timecard macro** to the document properties. Save the file, and then print the worksheet and the macro code or submit electronically as directed by your instructor.

Project Results

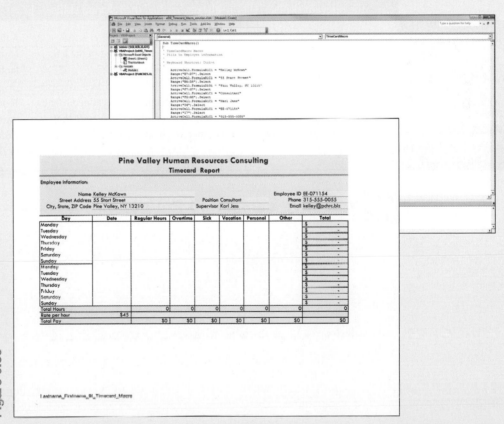

Figure 9.36

End **You have completed Project 9I** —————————————

Excel | Chapter 9

Content-Based Assessments

GO! Solve It | Project **9J** Filename Macro

Project Files

For Project 9J, you will need the following file:

New blank Excel workbook

You will save your workbook as:

Lastname_Firstname_9J_Filename_Macro

Open a blank workbook and save it as an Excel Macro-Enabled Workbook **Lastname_Firstname_9J_Filename_Macro** In all the Excel projects you have completed in this textbook, you created a custom footer with the file name in the left section of the footer. In this project, you will create a macro to place the file name in the footer and then assign it to a macro button. Enter a title for your worksheet in cell A1. Using the techniques you have practiced in this chapter, start the Macro Recorder and name the new macro **InsertFooter** Create a macro that will place the file name in the left section of the footer. Click Sheet 2, and type a title for the worksheet in cell A1. Test your InsertFooter macro button. Preview Sheet 2 to see whether the macro executed correctly—the file name displays in the left section of the footer. View the VBA code that was generated by your macro. Add your name to the comment, and then print the code. Close the file and save the changes. Add appropriate name and course information to the document properties including the keywords **filename macro** and then submit as directed by your instructor.

	Performance Level		
	Exemplary: You consistently applied the relevant skills.	**Proficient:** You sometimes, but not always, applied the relevant skills.	**Developing:** You rarely or never applied the relevant skills.
Create a Macro	A macro was created that inserts the file name in the left section of the footer.	A macro was created that inserts the file name but was not placed in the left section of the footer.	A macro that inserts the file name in the left section of the footer was not created.
Change the Visual Basic Code	Your name was added to the comment section of the VBA code that was generated by the macro.	Only part of your name was added to the comment section of the VBA code that was generated by the macro.	Your name was not added to the comment section of the VBA code that was generated by the macro.

Performance Criteria

End You have completed Project 9J ———————————

GO! Solve It | Project **9K** Book Evaluation

Project Files

For Project 9K, you will need the following file:

e09K_Book_VBA

You will save your workbook as:

Lastname_Firstname_9K_Book_VBA

Open the file e09K_Book_VBA and save it as an Excel Macro-Enabled Workbook **Lastname_Firstname_9K_Book_VBA** In the following Mastering Excel project, you will assist Tiffany Shin, Training Director, by adding an ActiveX control Command Button to an evaluation form to gather feedback from the consultants about a new book that will be used at customer seminars. In cell H7, add an ActiveX control Command Button to the worksheet. In the properties, change the name to **Start** caption to **Click Here to Start** and AutoSize to *True*. Add the following comments to the VBA code:

' Start Button Procedure Author: Firstname Lastname

' Date Created: March 16, 2013

' Function: When clicked, the Start button will display four input

'   boxes requesting the user to enter his or her name,

'   position, department, and email.

Add the following VBA code:

Range("B6").Value = InputBox("Enter your name", "Name")

Range("B7").Value = InputBox("Enter the name of your position", "Position")

Range("B8").Value = InputBox("Enter the name of your department", "Department")

Range("B9").Value = InputBox("Enter your email", "Email")

Add appropriate name and course information to the document properties including the keywords **book evaluation VBA** and then submit as directed by your instructor.

	Performance Level		
	Exemplary: You consistently applied the relevant skills.	**Proficient:** You sometimes, but not always, applied the relevant skills.	**Developing:** You rarely or never applied the relevant skills.
Insert an ActiveX Control Command Button and Change Properties	An ActiveX Control Command Button was inserted and appropriate, and name, caption, and AutoSize properties were assigned.	An ActiveX Control Command Button was inserted and but was not at all appropriate, and name, caption, and AutoSize properties were assigned.	An ActiveX Control Command Button was not inserted.
Write a VBA Procedure for a Command Button	A VBA Procedure for a Start Command Button was correctly written.	A VBA Procedure for a Start Command Button was only partially written.	A VBA Procedure for a Start Command Button was not written.

Performance Criteria

End You have completed Project 9K

Outcomes-Based Assessments

Rubric

The following outcomes-based assessments are *open-ended assessments*. That is, there is no specific correct result; your result will depend on your approach to the information provided. Make *Professional Quality* your goal. Use the following scoring rubric to guide you in *how* to approach the problem, and then to evaluate *how well* your approach solves the problem.

The *criteria*—Software Mastery, Content, Format and Layout, and Process—represent the knowledge and skills you have gained that you can apply to solving the problem. The *levels of performance*—Professional Quality, Approaching Professional Quality, or Needs Quality Improvements—help you and your instructor evaluate your result.

	Your completed project is of Professional Quality if you:	Your completed project is Approaching Professional Quality if you:	Your completed project Needs Quality Improvements if you:
1-Software Mastery	Choose and apply the most appropriate skills, tools, and features and identify efficient methods to solve the problem.	Choose and apply some appropriate skills, tools, and features, but not in the most efficient manner.	Choose inappropriate skills, tools, or features, or are inefficient in solving the problem.
2-Content	Construct a solution that is clear and well organized, contains content that is accurate, appropriate to the audience and purpose, and is complete. Provide a solution that contains no errors in spelling, grammar, or style.	Construct a solution in which some components are unclear, poorly organized, inconsistent, or incomplete. Misjudge the needs of the audience. Have some errors in spelling, grammar, or style, but the errors do not detract from comprehension.	Construct a solution that is unclear, incomplete, or poorly organized; contains some inaccurate or inappropriate content; and contains many errors in spelling, grammar, or style. Do not solve the problem.
3-Format and Layout	Format and arrange all elements to communicate information and ideas, clarify function, illustrate relationships, and indicate relative importance.	Apply appropriate format and layout features to some elements, but not others. Overuse features, causing minor distraction.	Apply format and layout that does not communicate information or ideas clearly. Do not use format and layout features to clarify function, illustrate relationships, or indicate relative importance. Use available features excessively, causing distraction.
4-Process	Use an organized approach that integrates planning, development, self-assessment, revision, and reflection.	Demonstrate an organized approach in some areas, but not others; or, use an insufficient process of organization throughout.	Do not use an organized approach to solve the problem.

Outcomes-Based Assessments

Apply a combination of the **9A** and **9B** skills.

GO! Think | Project **9L** Accounting Department

Project Files

For Project 9L, you will need the following file:

> e09L_Accounting_Macro

You will save your workbook as:

> Lastname_Firstname_9L_Accounting_Macro

Open the file e09L_Accounting_Macro, and then save it in your chapter folder as **Lastname_Firstname_9L_Accounting_Macro**

Record a macro that will assign a header that is required on all reports—Pine Valley Human Resources Consulting in the left section and Accounting Department in the right section. Assign the macro to the Quick Access Toolbar. Re-record the macro to change the font on the header to Britannic Bold, Regular, 14, and then stop recording the macro. Insert the file name in the left section of the footer, center horizontally, add appropriate information to the document properties including the keywords **accounting macro** and submit as directed by your instructor.

End You have completed Project 9L

Outcomes-Based Assessments

GO! Think | Project **9M** Sign In Sheet

Project Files

For Project 9M, you will need the following file:

e09M_Sign_In

You will save your workbook as:

Lastname_Firstname_9M_Sign_In

Open the file e09M_Sign_In, and then save it in your chapter folder as **Lastname_Firstname_9M_Sign_In** You will edit a computerized seminar sign-in form so that prompts will display to assist the seminar leader in filling in the form. In cell B2, insert an ActiveX Command Button. In the Properties pane, for (Name) type **Information** for Caption, type **Seminar Information** and for AutoSize, click *True*. Change the font to Comic Sans MS; 12. In the Code window, click to the left of *Private Sub Information_Click()*, and then press Enter to insert an empty line. Press ↑ to move to the empty line, and then type the following comments spaced as shown, using your name as the author.

```
' Seminar Information Booth Procedure
' Date Created: June 20, 2015    Author: Firstname Lastname
' Purpose:    When clicked, the Seminar Information button will display
'             user boxes that request information about the seminar,
'             including the seminar title, date, and trainer's name.
```

Press Enter.

Click to position the insertion point on the empty line under *Private Sub Information_Click()*. Press Enter, and then press Tab. Type the following lines of code spaced as shown.

```
Range("C9:E9").Value = InputBox("Seminar Title", "Enter")
Range("C10:E10").Value = InputBox("Date of Seminar", "Enter")
Range("C11:E11").Value = InputBox("Trainer's Name", "Enter")
Range("B14:C14").Select
```

Close and Return to Microsoft Excel. Exit Design Mode. On the View tab, in the Show group, click the Headings check box to clear the Heading. To test your inserted ActiveX control, click the Seminar Information Command Button and type the following information in each of the three dialog boxes that display, clicking OK to close each one:

Enter Seminar Title	Planning for Change
Date of Seminar	July 31, 2015
Trainer's Name	Susan Thompson

Insert the file name in the left section of the footer, center horizontally, add appropriate information to the document properties including the keywords **Sign in VBA** and submit the file and a copy of the VBA code as directed by your instructor.

End You have completed Project 9M

Outcomes-Based Assessments

You and GO! | Project **9N** Personal Footer

Project Files

For Project 9N, you will need the following file:

New blank Excel workbook

You will save your workbook as:

Lastname_Firstname_9N_Personal_Footer

Open a blank workbook and save the file as **Lastname_Firstname_9N_Personal_Footer** Create a personal budget. Create a macro that adds a footer with your preferred information in the three footer sections. Select a button for the macro, and then assign it to the Quick Access Toolbar. Add appropriate information to the document properties including the keywords **personal footer** and submit as directed by your instructor.

 You have completed Project 9N —————————————————

Business Running Case

Razvan CHIRNOAGA/Shutterstock

This project relates to **Front Range Action Sports**, which is one of the country's largest retailers of sports gear and outdoor recreation merchandise. The company has large retail stores in Colorado, Washington, Oregon, Idaho, California, and New Mexico, in addition to a growing online business. Major merchandise categories include fishing, camping, rock climbing, winter sports, action sports, water sports, team sports, racquet sports, fitness, golf, apparel, and footwear.

In this project, you will apply skills you practiced from the Objectives in Excel Chapters 7 through 9 You will develop a workbook for Frank Osei, the Vice President of Finance. You will create a PivotTable and a PivotChart to display revenue for several winter programs. Next, you will assist Mr. Osei in examining assumptions to see what changes are needed to shorten the time it takes to break even on opening a new store. Finally, you will create a macro that will assign an operations department heading that is required on all reports. Your completed worksheets will look similar to the ones shown in Figure 3.1.

Project Files

For Project BRC 3, you will need the following file:

eBRC3_Annual_Report

You will save your workbook as:

Lastname_Firstname_BRC3_
Annual_Report

Project Results

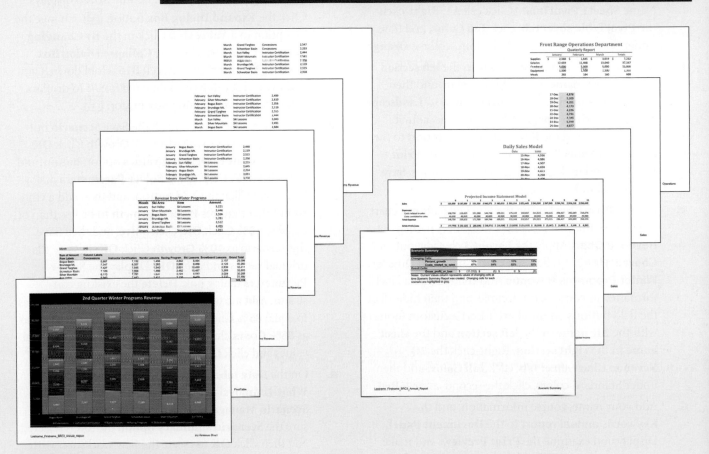

Figure 3.1

Front Range Action Sports

1 **Start** Excel. From the student data files that accompany this textbook, locate and open **eBRC3_Annual_Report**. In the location where you are storing your projects, navigate to your folder **Front Range Action Sports** or create this folder if you have not already done so. **Save** the workbook as **Lastname_Firstname_BRC3_Annual_Report**

a. On the **Winter Programs Revenue** worksheet, click cell **A2**, and then insert a **PivotTable**. Use the **Month** field as the **Report Filter**. Use the **Ski Area** field as the row labels and the **Item** field as the column labels. Place the **Amount** field in the **Values area**. **Close** the **PivotTable Field List**. Right-click any value in the PivotTable report, display the **Value Field Settings** dialog box, and then format the **Number** category to display zero decimal places and the **1000 Separator**. Name **Sheet1 PivotTable**. Click cell **A1**. Right-click the **PivotTable sheet tab**, click **Tab Color**, and then under Standard colors, click the third color—**Orange**.

b. Insert a footer with the **file name** in the **left section** and the **sheet name** in the **right section**, and then center **Horizontally**. Set the **orientation** to **Landscape** and the **Width** to **1 page**. Add your name, course information, and the **Keywords annual report** to the **Document Panel**. Display and examine the **Print Preview**, and make any necessary corrections. **Save** your workbook.

c. Insert a **PivotChart** using the **Stacked Column** chart type. Move the chart to a new worksheet named **2Q Revenue Chart** Apply the **Layout 3** chart layout and **Chart Style 42**. As the **Chart Title**, type **2nd Quarter Winter Programs Revenue** Add centered data labels, formatted as comma, no decimal, and then hide all of the field buttons on the chart. Insert a custom footer with the **file name** in the **left section** and the **sheet name** in the **right section**. Right-click the **2Q Revenue Chart sheet tab**, click **Tab Color**, and then under Standard colors, click the second color—**Red**.

d. Add your name, course information, and the **Keywords annual report** to the **Document Panel**. Display and examine the **Print Preview**, and make any necessary corrections. **Save** your workbook.

2 Display the **Projected Income** worksheet. Month 0 is the first month of operation and it assumes that a new store will gross $125,000 in sales in the opening month. The costs related to sales are assumed to be 87%, fixed

costs are $40,000, and the anticipated growth rate in the first year—month-to-month—is 10%. The worksheet extends these assumptions out to Month 11, which is the end of the first year of operation.

a. Click cell **B20**. On the **Formulas tab**, in **Formula Auditing group**, click **Evaluate Formula**. In the displayed dialog box, click **Evaluate**. Click **Step In**. Click **Step Out**. Continue to click **Evaluate** to see the calculation of the value in cell **B20**. Click **Close**. Click cell **B15**, type **6** and then press Enter to create scenarios that would result in breaking even six months after opening the store.

b. On the **Data tab**, in the **Analysis group**, click **Solver**. In the **Solver Parameters** dialog box, in the **Set Objective** box, click the **Collapse Dialog Box** button, and then click cell **B20**. Be sure *$B$20* displays. Click the **Expand Dialog Box** button. Change the **To** option to a **Value Of 0** Click in the **By Changing Variable Cells** box, click the **Collapse Dialog Box** button, and then click cell **B16**. Hold down Ctrl, and then click cell **B18** so that *$B$16,$B$18* displays. Click the **Expand Dialog Box** button.

c. Click the **Solve** button. Click the **Save Scenario** button and name this scenario **12% Growth** Click **OK**. Click the **Restore Original Values** option button, and then click **OK**. Display the **Solver Parameters** dialog box again. Click the **Add** button, and then add a constraint that requires **Percent growth** to be less than or equal to **10%** Click **OK**, click **Solve**, and then **Save** this scenario as **10% Growth** Click **OK**. Restore the original values and click **OK**. Display the **Solver Parameters** dialog box. **Delete** the existing constraint. **Add** a constraint for the **Costs related to sales** to equal **85%** Click **OK**, click **Solve**, **Save** the scenario as **85% Costs** click **OK**, and then restore the original values and click **OK**.

d. On the **Data tab**, in the **Data Tools group**, click the **What-If Analysis** button, and then display the **Scenario Manager** dialog box. Click **Summary**. Be sure the **Scenario summary** option button is selected, and then click **OK** to create the new worksheet with a summary of the scenarios. Right-click the **Scenario Summary sheet tab**, click **Tab Color**, and then under Standard colors, click the sixth color—**Green**.

e. Insert a footer with the **file name** in the **left section** and the **sheet name** in the **right section**, and then

(Business Running Case: Front Range Action Sports continues on the next page)

Business Running Case

Front Range Action Sports (continued)

center **Horizontally**. Set the **orientation** to **Landscape** and the **Width** to **1 page**. Add your name, course information, and the **Keywords annual report** to the **Document Panel**. Display and examine the **Print Preview**, and make any necessary corrections. **Save** your workbook.

f. Display the **Projected Income** worksheet. Hold down Ctrl and select the nonadjacent ranges **A2:M3** and **A8:M8**. Insert a **2-D Line** chart. On the **Layout tab**, in the **Labels group**, click the **Chart Title** button, click **Above Chart**, and then type **Expected Break-Even Point** Position the chart between cell **B22** and cell **L42**. Format both the **Plot Area** and the **Chart Area** with a **Solid fill** using the color **Dark Green, Accent 4, Lighter 80%**. Add a horizontal axis title with the text **Month Number** Click any cell to deselect the chart.

g. Insert a footer with the **file name** in the **left section** and the **sheet name** in the **right section**, and then center **Horizontally**. Set the **orientation** to **Landscape** and the **Width** to **1 page**. Add your name, course information, and the **Keywords annual report** to the **Document Panel**. Display and examine the **Print Preview**, and make any necessary corrections. **Save** your workbook.

3 Display the **Operations** worksheet. Click cell **A1**. On the **Developer tab**, in the **Code group**, click the **Record Macro** button. Name the macro **Operations_Header** and use Ctrl + **o** as the **Shortcut key**. Store the macro in this workbook, and as the **Description**, type **Fills in Operations report heading** Click **OK**.

a. Right-click the **row 1** header, click **Insert**, and then press F4 to repeat the action. Click cell **A1**, and then type **Front Range Operations Department** Merge and center the text across the range **A1:E1**, and then apply the **Title** cell style. In cell **A2**, type **Quarterly Report Merge and Center** the text across the range **A2:E2**, and then apply the **Heading 1** cell style. Click cell **A1**, and then stop recording the macro. Delete **rows 1:2**; test the macro. Click cell **A1** to return to the top of the worksheet.

4 Group the worksheets and insert a footer with the file name in the left section and the sheet name in the right section, and then center Horizontally. Examine the workbook in **Print Preview**, and make any necessary corrections. **Save** your workbook, and then print or submit electronically as directed. **Close** the workbook and **Exit** Excel.

End You have completed Business Running Case 3

Business Running Case 3: Includes Objectives from Excel Chapters 7-9

External Data, Database Functions, and Side-by-Side Tables

OUTCOMES

At the end of this chapter you will be able to:

OBJECTIVES

Mastering these objectives will enable you to:

PROJECT 10A

Use database functions in Excel by importing external data and querying a database.

1. Get External Data into Excel (p. 607)
2. Create a Query and Use the Query Wizard to Sort and Filter (p. 615)
3. Use DAVERAGE and DSUM Database Functions (p. 621)
4. Use DCOUNT and DGET Database Functions (p. 625)

PROJECT 10B

Create and use a side-by-side table.

5. Insert a Second Table into a Worksheet (p. 631)
6. Apply Conditional Formatting to Side-by-Side Tables (p. 634)
7. Insert a Screenshot (p. 636)
8. Create Custom Headers and Footers (p. 638)

In This Chapter

In this chapter, you will use Excel's database capabilities to organize data. The skills you will practice include importing data into Excel from other sources and querying data in the database. You will also practice limiting data to display records that meet one or more specific conditions. You will add subtotals, and you will group and outline data. You will use database functions to summarize information and analyze data. You will insert a second table in a worksheet and sort data in side-by-side tables, apply conditional formatting to data using icon sets, and insert a screen shot from the Internet into a worksheet. Finally, you will create custom headers and footers.

The projects in this chapter relate to **University Medical Center,** which is the premier patient care and research institution serving the metropolitan area of Miami, Florida. Because of its outstanding reputation in the medical community and around the world, University Medical Center is able to attract top physicians, scientists, and researchers in all fields of medicine and achieve a level of funding that allows it to build and operate state-of-the-art facilities. Individuals throughout the area travel to University Medical Center for diagnosis and care.

Lorelyn Medina/Shutterstock

Project 10A Medical Center Information

myitlab
Project 10A Training

Project Activities

In Activities 10.01 through 10.10, you will import data about medical center nurses, doctors, patients, and supplies into Excel, and query the database to locate information. Your completed worksheet will look similar to Figure 10.1.

Project Files

For Project 10A, you will need the following files:

e10A_Contacts (Access database)
e10A_Health_Seminars (HTML Document)
e10A_Medical_Center (Excel Workbook)
e10A_Nurse_Information (Access database)
e10A_Orthopedic_Supplies (XML Document)
e10A_Physician_Information (Text Document)

You will save your workbook as:

Lastname_Firstname_10A_Medical_Center

Project Results

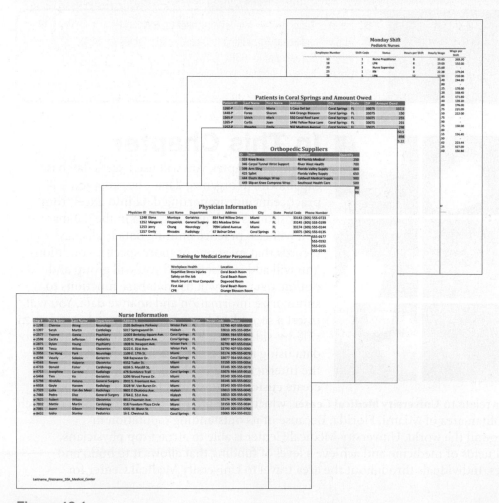

Figure 10.1
Project 10A Medical Center Information

Objective 1 | Get External Data into Excel

You have used many of Excel's powerful tools for analyzing data, but what if the data you want to analyze is not in Excel? You can get data that resides outside of Excel *into* Excel by using the commands located on the Data tab in the ***Get External Data group***. This group of commands enables you to bring data from an Access database, from the Web, from a text file, from an XML file—among others—into Excel without repeatedly copying the data. Then, you can apply Excel's data analysis tools to the data. You can also establish connections to the external data so that you can automatically update your Excel workbook from the original data whenever the original data source gets new information.

> **Note** | To Maintain Connections to External Data
>
> To connect to data when you open a workbook, you must enable data connections by using the Trust Center bar or by putting the workbook in a trusted location. For information, display the Excel Options dialog box, on the left, click Trust Center, click the Trust Center Settings button, and then on the left, click External Content. Here you can make decisions about enabling connections.

Activity 10.01 | Importing Information into Excel from an Access Database

Information in an Access database is organized in a format of horizontal rows and vertical columns—just like an Excel worksheet. Each horizontal row stores all of the data about one database item and is referred to as a ***record***. Each vertical column stores information that describes the record and is referred to as a ***field***. Information stored in a format of rows and columns is referred to as a ***table***.

In this activity, you will import information into Excel from an Access database.

1 **Start** Excel. From your student files, open the file **e10A_Medical_Center**. In your storage location, create a new folder named **Excel Chapter 10** and then **Save** the file as **Lastname_Firstname_10A_Medical_Center**

2 At the bottom of the Excel window, in the row of sheet tabs, locate the horizontal scroll bar. At the left end of the scroll bar, point to the Expand button to display the ⟨+⟩ pointer, and then drag to the right to decrease the width of the scroll bar to display all six worksheets in this workbook as shown in Figure 10.2.

Figure 10.2

Horizontal scroll bar —

Six worksheet tabs display —

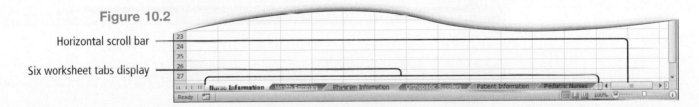

3 Be sure the first worksheet, **Nurse Information**, is the active sheet. Click in cell **A2**. On the **Data tab**, in the **Get External Data group**, if necessary, click the **Get External Data button arrow**, and then click the **From Access** button.

4 In the **Select Data Source** dialog box, navigate to your student files, click the Access file **e10A_Nurse_Information**, and then in the lower right corner of the dialog box, click **Open**.

The Import Data dialog box displays. The option buttons that are selected indicate that the information will be imported as a table and into the existing worksheet in cell A2—the active cell.

Microsoft Access is a database program used to manage database files. In this manner, you can import data from Access or from other database programs.

5 In the **Import Data** dialog box, be sure that the **Table** option button is selected, and then click **OK**. Compare your screen with Figure 10.3.

Excel imports the table of nurse information. Beside each column title, an arrow displays for easy sorting and filtering. The field names display in row 2 and the records display in rows 3 to 22.

Figure 10.3

Arrows at top of each column

Field names in row 2

Records display in rows 3 to 22

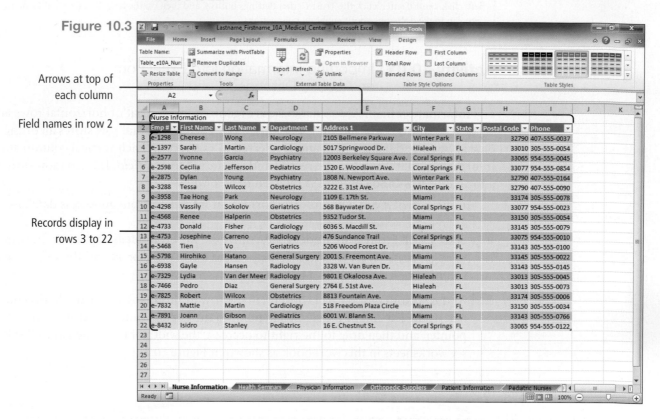

6 **Merge & Center** the text in cell **A1** across the range **A1:I1**, and then apply the **Title** cell style.

7 **Save** 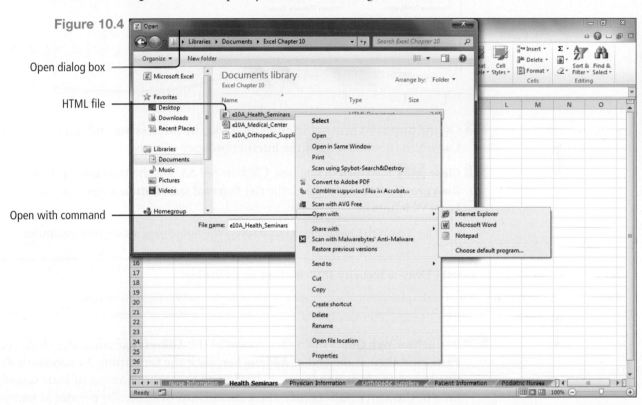 your workbook.

Activity 10.02 | Importing Information into Excel from a Web Page

In this activity, you will import information into Excel from a Web page.

1 Make the next worksheet—**Health Seminars**—the active sheet.

2 Press ⌗Ctrl⌗ + ⌗F12⌗ to display the **Open** dialog box. Navigate to your student files, right-click the HTML file **e10A_Health_Seminars**, and then on the shortcut menu, point to **Open with**. Compare your screen with Figure 10.4.

Figure 10.4

Open dialog box

HTML file

Open with command

3 Click **Internet Explorer** (or your Internet browser). Compare your screen with Figure 10.5.

The Internet browser opens and displays a University Medical Center Web page containing two tables of data with health seminar titles and locations.

Figure 10.5

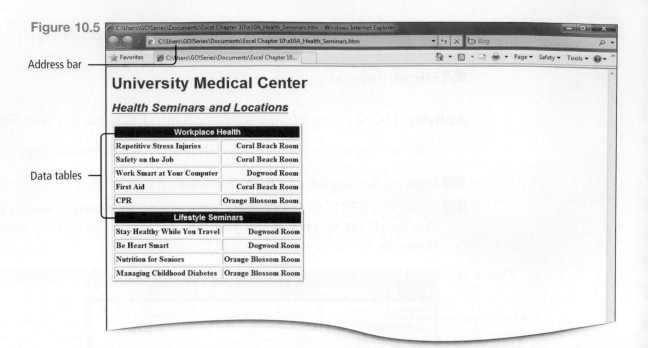

Address bar

Data tables

4 On the displayed browser window, point to the **Address bar** and right-click, click **Copy**, and then **Close** ⊠ the Internet browser window.

5 **Close** ⊠ the **Open** dialog box. Click in cell **A3**. On the **Data tab**, in the **Get External Data group**, if necessary, click the **Get External Data button arrow**, and then click the **From Web** button.

The New Web Query dialog box displays the home page set on your computer.

> **Alert! | Does a Security Information Box Display?**
>
> If your home page contains secure data, click Yes to display the Web page information.

6 In the **New Web Query** dialog box, point to the **Address bar** and right-click, click **Paste**, and then at the end of **Address bar**, click the **Go** button. As necessary, drag the title bar of the **New Web Query** dialog box to the upper portion of your screen, and then in the lower right corner of the dialog box, drag the ⬚ pointer as necessary to resize the dialog box and display the two tables on the Web page. Compare your screen with Figure 10.6.

Yellow arrows mark the beginning of each table in the Web page. You import tables by selecting the yellow arrow.

Figure 10.6

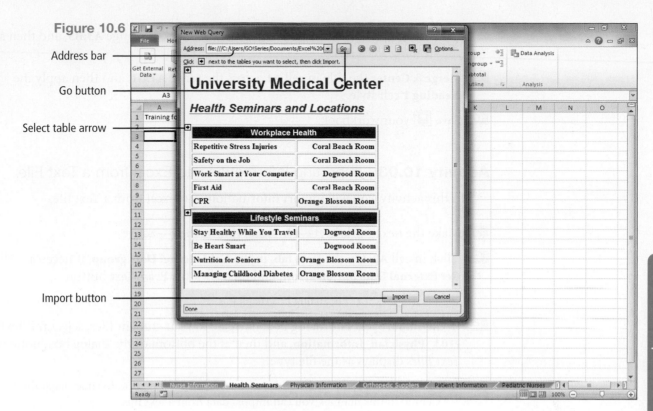

Address bar

Go button

Select table arrow

Import button

7 On the left side of the **Workplace Health** table, click the **yellow arrow** to select the table. In the lower right corner of the dialog box, click the **Import** button, and then on the displayed **Import Data** dialog box, verify that the **Existing worksheet** option button and cell **A3** are selected. Click **OK**, and then compare your screen with Figure 10.7.

The Workplace Health table data is imported and displays on the Health Seminars worksheet.

Figure 10.7

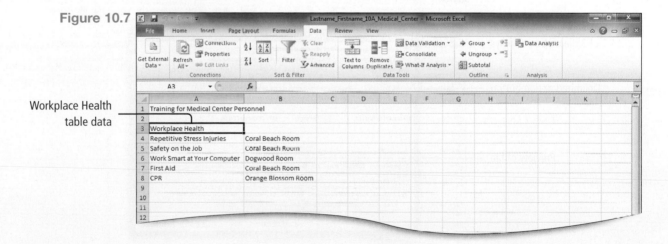

Workplace Health table data

Excel | Chapter 10

8 In cell **B3**, type **Location** and then press `Enter`. Select the range **A3:B3**, and then apply the **Heading 3** cell style.

9 **Merge & Center** the title in cell **A1** across the range **A1:B1**, and then apply the **Heading 1** cell style.

10 **Save** 💾 your workbook.

Activity 10.03 │ Importing Information into Excel from a Text File

In this activity, you will import information into Excel from a Text file.

1 Make the next worksheet—**Physician Information**—active.

2 Click in cell **A2**. On the **Data tab**, in the **Get External Data group**, if necessary click the **Get External Data button arrow**, and then click the **From Text** button.

> The Import Text File dialog box displays.

3 In the **Import Text File** dialog box, navigate to your student files, select the Text file **e10A_Physician_Information**, and then at the bottom of the dialog box, notice that *Text Files* displays as the file type.

> The Physician Information file contains contact information for doctors at the Medical Center. In this manner, you can import data from a text file.

4 With the **e10A_Physician_Information** file selected, click the **Import** button. Compare your screen with Figure 10.8.

> The Text Import Wizard – Step 1 of 3 dialog box displays. The Text Import Wizard determines that the Physician Information file is delimited—separated by commas or tabs—and selects the Delimited option button. At the bottom of the dialog box, a preview of the data displays.

Figure 10.8

Text Import Wizard – Step 1 of 3 dialog box displays

Delimited option button

Preview of file

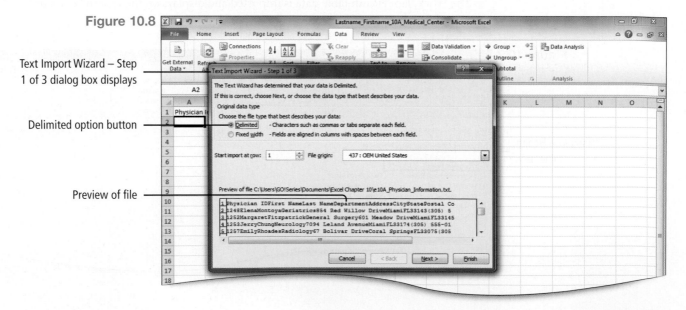

5 Click **Next**, and then compare your screen with Figure 10.9.

The Text Import Wizard – Step 2 of 3 dialog box displays. Here you can set the delimiters your data contains. Under Delimiters, the Tab check box is selected. At the bottom of the dialog box, the Data preview displays.

Figure 10.9

Tab box selected

Data preview

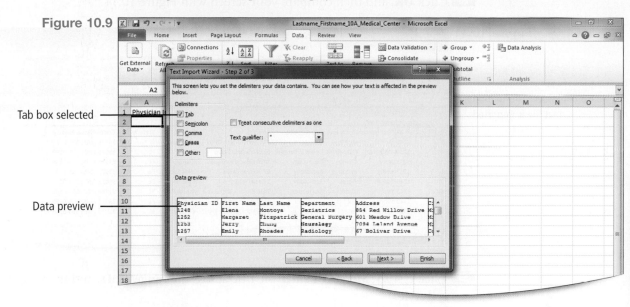

6 Click **Next**, and then compare your screen with Figure 10.10.

The Text Import Wizard – Step 3 of 3 dialog box displays. Here you can select each column and see the data format. Under Column data format, the General option button is selected. At the bottom of the dialog box, the Data preview displays.

Figure 10.10

General option selected

Data preview

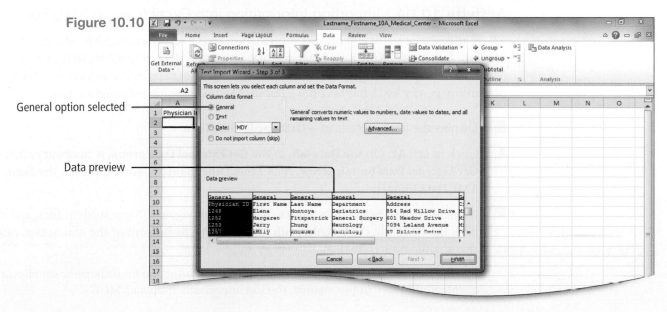

7 Click **Finish**.

The Import Data dialog box displays, indicating that the table will be imported into the existing worksheet in cell A2—the active cell.

8 Click **OK**, and then compare your screen with Figure 10.11.

Figure 10.11

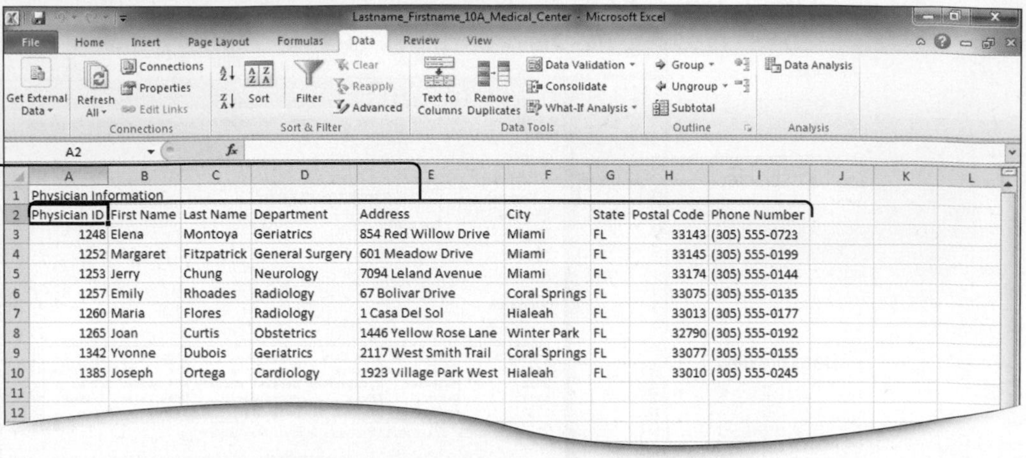

Physician Information text file is imported

	A	B	C	D	E	F	G	H	I	J	K	L
1	Physician Information											
2	Physician ID	First Name	Last Name	Department	Address	City	State	Postal Code	Phone Number			
3	1248	Elena	Montoya	Geriatrics	854 Red Willow Drive	Miami	FL	33143	(305) 555-0723			
4	1252	Margaret	Fitzpatrick	General Surgery	601 Meadow Drive	Miami	FL	33145	(305) 555-0199			
5	1253	Jerry	Chung	Neurology	7094 Leland Avenue	Miami	FL	33174	(305) 555-0144			
6	1257	Emily	Rhoades	Radiology	67 Bolivar Drive	Coral Springs	FL	33075	(305) 555-0135			
7	1260	Maria	Flores	Radiology	1 Casa Del Sol	Hialeah	FL	33013	(305) 555-0177			
8	1265	Joan	Curtis	Obstetrics	1446 Yellow Rose Lane	Winter Park	FL	32790	(305) 555-0192			
9	1342	Yvonne	Dubois	Geriatrics	2117 West Smith Trail	Coral Springs	FL	33077	(305) 555-0155			
10	1385	Joseph	Ortega	Cardiology	1923 Village Park West	Hialeah	FL	33010	(305) 555-0245			
11												
12												

9 Click cell **A1**, **Merge & Center** the title across the range **A1:I1**, and then apply the **Title** cell style.

10 Select the range **A2:I2**, apply **Center** alignment, and then apply the **Heading 3** cell style.

11 **Save** your workbook.

Activity 10.04 | Importing Information into Excel from an XML File

In this activity, you will import information into Excel from an XML file. *Extensible Markup Language (XML)* is a language that structures data in text files so that it can be read by other systems, regardless of the hardware platform or operating system. Such portability is why XML has become a popular technology for exchanging data.

1 Display the next worksheet—**Orthopedic Suppliers**.

2 Click in cell **A2**. On the **Data tab**, in the **Get External Data group**, if necessary click the **Get External Data button arrow**, click **From Other Sources**, and then click the **From XML Data Import**.

3 In the displayed **Select Data Source** dialog box, navigate to your student files, and then click the XML file **e10A_Orthopedic_Supplies**. At the bottom of the dialog box, notice that the file type is *XML Files*.

The Orthopedic Supplies file contains supplier information for orthopedic supplies at the Medical Center. In this manner, you can import data from an XML file.

4 With the **e10A_Orthopedic_Supplies** file selected, click the **Open** button.

A Microsoft Excel information message displays. The specified XML source does not refer to a schema. A *schema* is an XML file that contains the rules for what can and cannot reside in an XML data file. Schemas are not required in XML, but they can be useful in ensuring that any data inserted into an XML document follows predefined rules for both content and structure.

5 Click **OK** to display the **Import Data** dialog box. Notice that the data will be imported as an XML table into the existing worksheet in cell **A2**—the active cell.

6 Click **OK**, and then compare your screen with Figure 10.12.

The table of orthopedic suppliers is imported as an Excel table with filter arrows in the column titles. The field names display in row 2 and the records display in rows 3 to 10.

Figure 10.12

Arrows at top of each column header

Field names in row 2

Records display in rows 3 to 10

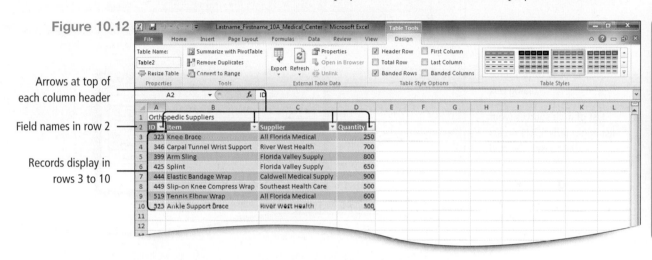

7 Click cell **A1**, **Merge & Center** the title across the range **A1:D1**, and then apply the **Title** cell style.

8 Save your workbook.

Objective 2 | Create a Query and Use the Query Wizard to Sort and Filter

A *query* is a means of finding the records that answer a particular question about the data. Because the word *query* means *to ask a question*, you can think of a query as a question formed in a manner that Excel can interpret.

Activity 10.05 | Creating a Query and Filtering and Sorting Data by Using the Query Wizard

In the following activity, you will create a query and then filter and sort data using a wizard. A wizard is a feature in Microsoft Office programs that walks you step by step through a process. The process involves choosing the data source, and then indicating the fields you want to include in the query result. The query—the question that you want to ask—is *What is the name, complete mailing address, and Patient ID of every patient in the database who lives in Coral Springs, and how much do they owe?*

1 Display the next worksheet—**Patient Information**.

2 Click in cell **A2**. On the **Data tab**, in the **Get External Data group**, if necessary click the **Get External Data button arrow**, and then click the **From Other Sources** button. Click **From Microsoft Query**.

3 In the displayed **Choose Data Source** dialog box, verify that the **Databases tab** is active and, at the bottom, be sure the **Use the Query Wizard to create/edit queries** check box is selected. Then, click **MS Access Database***. Compare your screen with Figure 10.13.

Figure 10.13

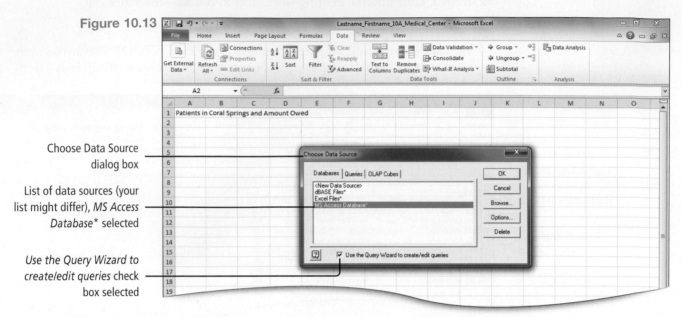

Choose Data Source dialog box

List of data sources (your list might differ), *MS Access Database** selected

Use the Query Wizard to create/edit queries check box selected

4 Click **OK** to display the **Select Database** dialog box.

5 Under **Directories**, be sure the folder containing your student files is selected—if necessary, scroll down to view and select the folder. Then, under **Database Name**, click **e10A_Contacts.accdb**. Compare your screen with Figure 10.14.

Connecting to data source displays with red dots moving between the icons.

Figure 10.14

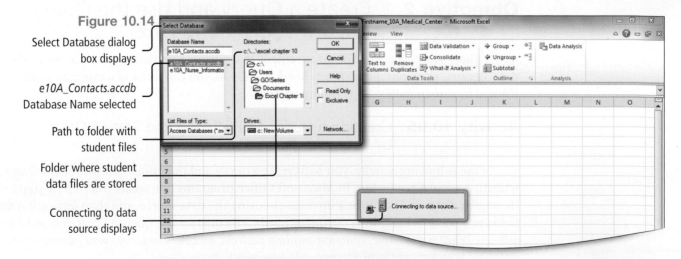

Select Database dialog box displays

e10A_Contacts.accdb Database Name selected

Path to folder with student files

Folder where student data files are stored

Connecting to data source displays

6 Click **OK**, and then compare your screen with Figure 10.15.

The Query Wizard – Choose Columns dialog box displays. Here you choose what columns of data you want to include in your query.

Figure 10.15

Query Wizard – Choose
Columns dialog box displays

Tables in the
Contacts database

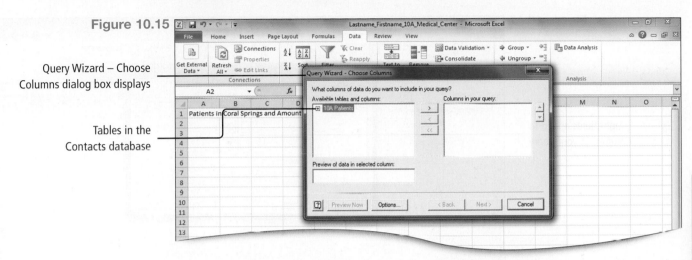

7 Under **Available tables and columns**, to the left of **10A Patients**, click + to expand the table and view the column names.

The column names display. To create a query, first choose the data source—the table from which you will select the data you want. To find the name and complete mailing address of every patient and how much he or she owes, you will need the 10A Patients table.

> **Another Way**
>
> Alternatively, double-click the field name to move it to the Columns in your query list.

8 Under **Available tables and columns**, click **Patient ID**, and then click the **Add Field** button > to move the field to the **Columns in your query** list on the right. Using the same technique, add the **Last Name** field to the list. Compare your screen with Figure 10.16.

Recall that you choose the fields that you want to include in your resulting query.

Figure 10.16

Two fields added to
Columns in your query

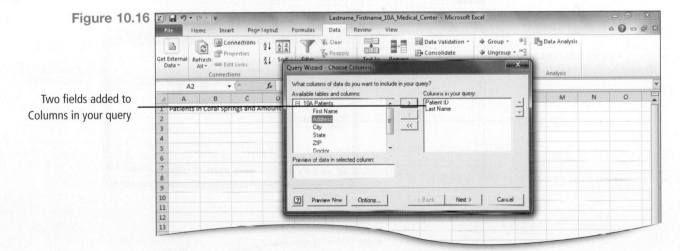

9 Using either the **Add Field** button **>** or by double-clicking, add the following fields to the **Columns in your query** list: **First Name, Address, City, State, ZIP, Amount Owed**. Compare your screen with Figure 10.17.

Figure 10.17

Eight fields added to Columns in your query

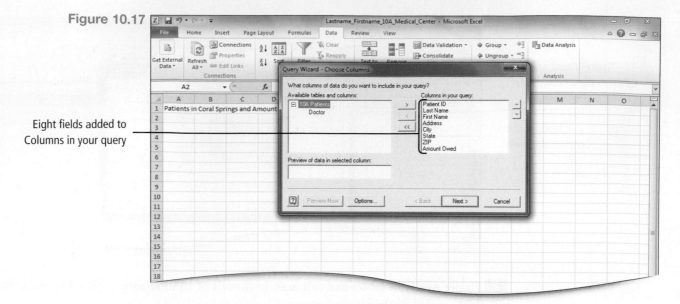

10 In the lower right corner, click the **Next** button.

> The Query Wizard – Filter Data dialog box displays. Here you filter the data to specify which *rows* to include in your query.

11 Under **Column to filter**, click **ZIP**. Under **Only include rows where**, click in the **ZIP box** to display a list, and then click **equals**. In the box to the right, click the **arrow**, and then click **33075**. Compare your screen with Figure 10.18.

Figure 10.18

Only include rows where ZIP equals 33075

ZIP selected

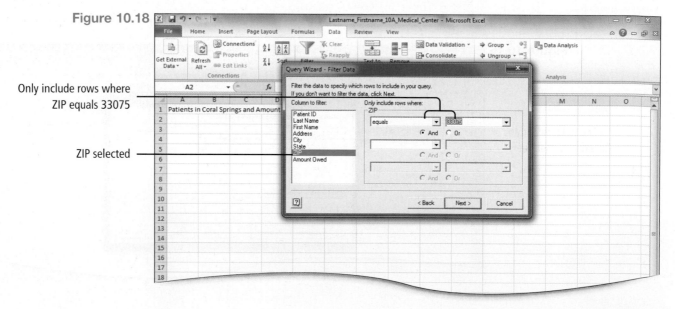

12 Click the **Next** button. In the displayed **Query Wizard – Sort Order** dialog box, under **Sort by**, click the **arrow**, and then click **Amount Owed**. Verify that the **Ascending** option button is selected. Compare your screen with Figure 10.19.

In the Query Wizard – Sort Order dialog box, you specify how you want your data sorted—in this instance, in Ascending order by Amount Owed.

Figure 10.19

Ascending option button selected

Amount Owed selected

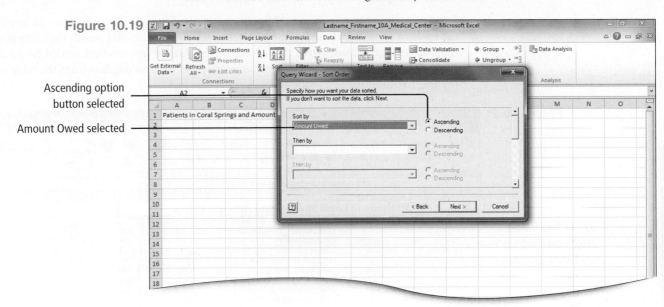

13 In the lower right corner, click the **Next** button. Compare your screen with Figure 10.20.

The Query Wizard – Finish dialog box displays. Here you specify what you would like to do next with the query information.

Figure 10.20

Return Data to Microsoft Excel is selected

Finish button

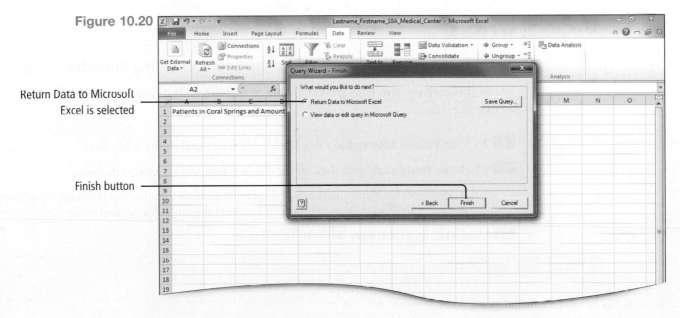

14 Be sure the **Return Data to Microsoft Excel** option button is selected, and then click **Finish**.

15 In the displayed **Import Data** dialog box, verify that the **Table** option button is selected, that the **Existing worksheet** option button is selected, and that cell **$A$2** is indicated. Click **OK**.

16 In cell **A1**, **Merge & Center** the title across the range **A1:H1**, and then apply the **Title** cell style. Compare your screen with Figure 10.21.

> Excel runs the query—performs the actions indicated in your query design—by searching the table of records included in the query, finding the records that match the criteria, and then importing and displaying the records on the Patient Information worksheet so that you can see the results. In this manner, a query pulls out and displays from the table only the information that you requested.

Figure 10.21

Query data filtered, sorted, and imported into Excel worksheet

Amount Owed sorted in ascending order

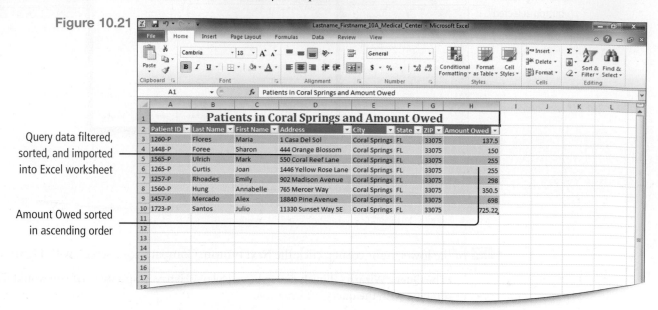

17 **Save** your workbook.

Activity 10.06 | Converting a Range and Formatting Imported Data

In this activity, you will convert a table of imported data into a range, and then format the data.

1 In your **Patient Information** worksheet, click any cell in the table data.

2 Click the **Design tab**, and then in the **Tools group**, click **Convert to Range**.

> A Microsoft Excel information box displays indicating that this will permanently remove the query definition from the sheet and convert the table to a normal range.

3 Click **OK**, and then **Save** your workbook.

Objective 3 | Use DAVERAGE and DSUM Database Functions

In Excel, you can not only track and manage financial and numerical data, but you can also create simple databases. A *database* is a collection of data related to a particular topic or purpose. *Data* refers to facts about people, events, things, or ideas. Data that is organized in a useful manner is referred to as *information*. An example of information at the University Medical Center is the list of nurses who work in various departments or who work various shifts.

Recall that *functions* are predefined formulas that perform calculations by using specific values, called *arguments*. Database functions are identified by the letter *D*—each function starts with a D, for example, DSUM and DAVERAGE. The initial letter *D* identifies to Excel that a database range will be used in the formula, rather than a single column or row of numbers.

Activity 10.07 | Using the DAVERAGE Database Function

The *syntax*—arrangement of elements—for the majority of database functions is: DFunction Name(database, field, criteria), where *database* identifies the range of cells where the data is displayed, *field* is the field name to be considered, and *criteria* is the range of cells where the search criteria has been defined. The criteria is defined in a separate area on the worksheet. In this activity, you will use the *DAVERAGE function* to determine the average hourly wage for LPNs (Licensed Practical Nurses) in the pediatric wing of the hospital.

1 In your workbook, display the next worksheet—**Pediatric Nurses**.

This worksheet lists the Employee Number, Shift Code, Status, Hours per Shift, Hourly Wage, and Wage per Shift for pediatric nurses who work on Mondays. The Wage per Shift field contains a formula that multiplies the Hours per Shift in column D times the Hourly Wage in column E. The number in the Shift Code field is a code for the shift. Not all nurses work on Mondays; thus, some rows indicate 0 hours per shift.

The Shift Codes represent the following hours:

Shift	Code
Day (6a–2p)	1
Evening (7p-3a)	2
Afternoon (12p–8p)	3
Night (10p-6a)	4
Day 12-hr (6a-6p)	5
Night 12-hr (6p-6a)	6

2 Widen **column A** to **210 pixels**. In cell **A28**, type **Average Hourly Wage for LPNs** and press Tab.

Average Hourly Wage for LPNs will form the label for the function you will enter.

3 Point to cell **C3**, right-click, and then click **Copy**. Scroll down, point to cell **C28**, right-click, and then click **Paste** 📋.

> Cell C28 will form the first cell in the criteria range for the DAVERAGE function, which must consist of at least two vertical cells. The top cell is the field name that is to be searched, and the cell immediately below it is the criteria used in the function search.

4 In cell **C29**, type **LPN** and press `Tab`.

> The value—LPN—is the search criteria.

Another Way

Alternatively, on the Formulas tab, in the Function Library group, click Insert Function.

5 Click cell **B28**, and then to the left of the **Formula Bar**, click the **Insert Function** button 𝑓𝑥.

> You can use the Insert Function dialog box to locate any function in Excel.

6 In the **Insert Function** dialog box, click the **Or select a category arrow**, and then from the displayed list, click **Database**. In the **Select a function** box, click **DAVERAGE**, and then click **OK**. Compare your screen with Figure 10.22.

> The Function Arguments dialog box for DAVERAGE displays.

Figure 10.22

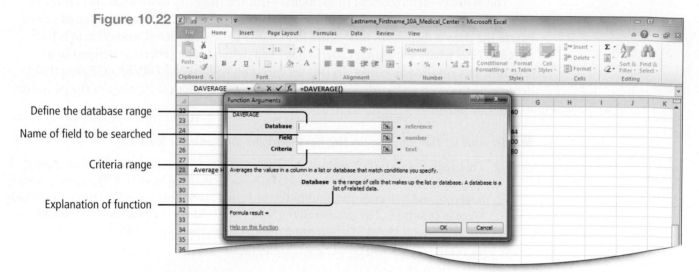

Define the database range
Name of field to be searched
Criteria range
Explanation of function

7 In the **Database** box, click the **Collapse Dialog Box** button 📷, and then select the range **A3:F26**. Then, in the collapsed dialog box, click the **Expand Dialog Box** button 📷.

> This action defines the database range in the first argument box.

8 In the **Field** box, type **Hourly Wage** and press `Tab`.

> This action identifies the field or column in the database that you want to average; the insertion point moves to the Criteria box. Excel adds quotation marks around the Field name, which identifies it as a string of characters to use in the search.

9 With the insertion point in the **Criteria** box, select the range **C28:C29**—the criteria range that was previously defined. Compare your screen with Figure 10.23.

> The two cells in the criteria range will limit the DAVERAGE calculation to only those records where *Status* is equal to *LPN*—RNs and Nurse Supervisors will not be included.

Figure 10.23

Database range identified

Hourly Wage field will be used in the calculation

Criteria range defined

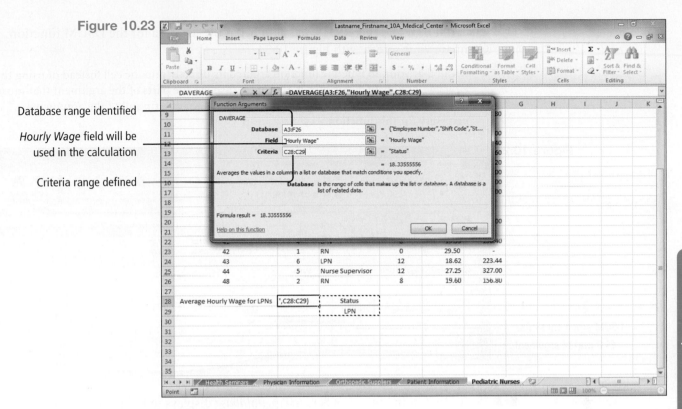

10 Click **OK**. Right click cell **B28**, and then on the Mini toolbar, apply **Accounting Number Format** $.

> The result, *$18.34*, displays in cell B28. This is the average hourly wage for LPNs who work in the pediatric wing of the hospital on Mondays.

11 Save your workbook.

Activity 10.08 | Using the DSUM Database Function

The ***DSUM function*** will sum a column of values in a database that is limited by criteria set for one or more cells. In this activity, you will sum the *Wage per Shift* for RNs who work in the Pediatric wing on Mondays.

1 In cell **A31**, type **Wage per Shift for RNs** and press Tab.

2 Select and then copy the range **C3:D3**. Point to cell **C31** and right-click, and then click **Paste**.

3 In cell **C32**, type **RN** and press Tab. In cell **D32**, type **>0** and then press Enter.

> The *Status* will be limited to RN, and the *Hours Worked* will be limited to those RNs who worked a number of hours greater than zero. This is a ***compound criteria***—both conditions must be met for the record to be included in the calculation.

Excel | Chapter 10

4 Click cell **B31**, and then type **=dsum(** to begin the formula for the DSUM function. Compare your screen with Figure 10.24.

> Recall that you can type the function arguments directly into the cell instead of using the *Function Argument* dialog box. A ScreenTip displays the parts of the argument that must be included, which guides you through the process of entering all of the arguments necessary for this function.

Figure 10.24

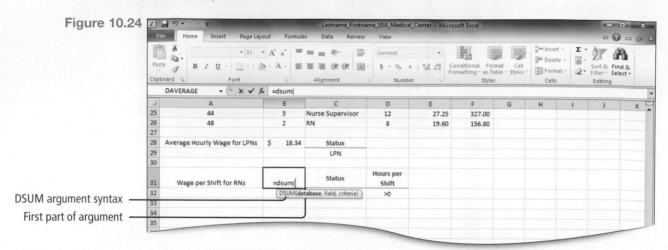

DSUM argument syntax

First part of argument

5 Notice that in the function ScreenTip, *database* displays in bold, indicating that you must select a range that is the database. Select the range **A3:F26**, and then type **,** (a comma). Compare your screen with Figure 10.25.

> The database range is defined, and the *field* argument displays in bold.

Figure 10.25

Formula Bar displays the formula as you create it

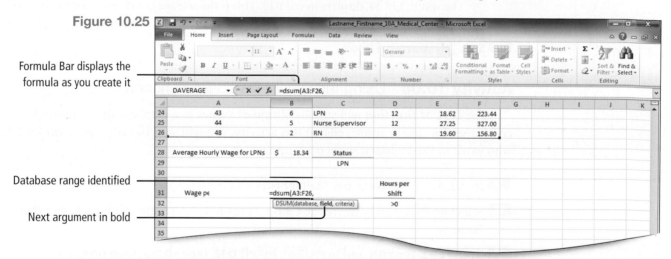

Database range identified

Next argument in bold

6 Notice that in the function ScreenTip, *field* displays in bold, indicating that you must type the name of the field. Being sure to include the comma, type **"Wage per Shift",** to enter the second part of the argument; you can look at the Formula Bar to see your typing and correct as necessary.

> The field that you want to sum is the *Wage per Shift* field, so the field name is entered as the second argument. The quotation marks define this as a string of characters; it must match the field name exactly. The comma separates this argument from the next argument.

7 As indicated by *criteria* in the ScreenTip, type the criteria as **C31:D32** and then press Enter.

> After you type the criteria range, Excel automatically adds a closing parenthesis. The final result of the formula—1323.24—displays in cell B31. The total cost to pay all the RNs who work in the Pediatric wing on Mondays is $1,323.24.

8 Right-click cell **B31** and apply the **Accounting Number Format** $ ▾ .

9 With cell **B31** active, examine the parts of the DSUM function on the **Formula Bar**, and then compare your screen with Figure 10.26.

Figure 10.26

Database range defined

Field used in calculation identified

Criteria area defined

Result of DSUM function

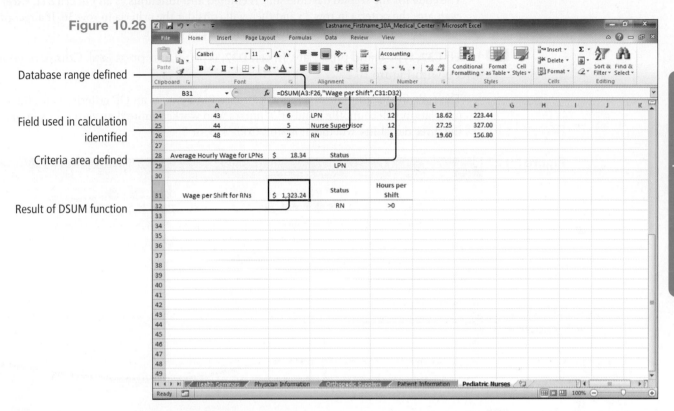

10 **Save** 🖫 your workbook.

Objective 4 | Use DCOUNT and DGET Database Functions

The *DCOUNT function* is similar to the COUNT function. Within a database list, it counts the number of occurrences of a specified condition—criterion. The *DGET function* extracts from your data table a single record that matches the conditions you specify.

Activity 10.09 | Using DCOUNT

In this activity, you will count the number of nurses who work the Day shift.

1 In cell **A34**, type **Count Day Shift (Code 1, 3, 5)** and press Tab.

> This forms the label for the function. Three shifts include daytime hours—Shift Codes 1, 3, and 5—so include all three in the criteria range.

2 Click cell **B3**, hold down ⌃Ctrl and click cell **D3**. Right-click either of selected cells, and then click **Copy**. Scroll down, point to cell **C34**, right-click, and then click **Paste** 📋.

3 In cell **C35**, type **1** and press Tab. In cell **D35**, type **>0** and press Enter.

> The Shift Code value for the first daytime shift, which is *1*, is entered. To meet the conditions of this compound criteria, a nurse must be assigned to Shift 1 and work greater than zero hours.

4 In cell **C36**, type **3** and press Tab. In cell **D36**, type **>0** and press Enter.

> The code for the second daytime shift is entered and functions as an *OR* criteria. Excel evaluates the criteria in row 35 and then will consider the criteria in row 36. If a record meets either condition it will be included in the calculation.

5 In cell **C37**, type **5** and press Tab. In cell **D37**, type **>0** and press Enter. Compare your screen with Figure 10.27.

> The code for the third daytime shift—5—also functions as an *OR* criteria. Thus, the calculation will count the number of nurses who worked more than zero hours in one of the three day shifts, whether it is Shift Code 1, 3, or 5.

Figure 10.27

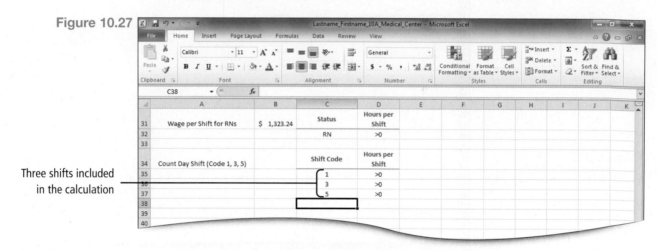

Three shifts included in the calculation

6 Click cell **B34**. To the left of the **Formula Bar**, click the **Insert Function** button *fx*.

7 Click the **Or select a category arrow**, and then click **Database**. In the **Select a function** box, click **DCOUNT**, and then click **OK**.

> The Function Arguments dialog box for DCOUNT displays.

8 In the **Database** box, click the **Collapse Dialog Box** button 📝. Move the collapsed box to the upper right corner of your screen. Scroll as necessary, and then select the range **A3:F26**.

9 In the collapsed dialog box, click the **Expand Dialog Box** button 🔲.

> The database range is defined and displays in the first argument box.

10 In the **Field** box, type **Employee Number** and then press Tab.

The *Employee Number* field will be counted.

11 With the insertion point in the **Criteria** box, click the **Collapse Dialog Box** button 📷, scroll as necessary, and then select the range **C34:D37**—the criteria area that was previously defined. In the collapsed dialog box, click the **Expand Dialog Box** button 📷. Compare your **Function Arguments** dialog box with Figure 10.28.

Figure 10.28

Database range identified

Employee Number field will be counted

Criteria range identified, limiting count to daytime shifts

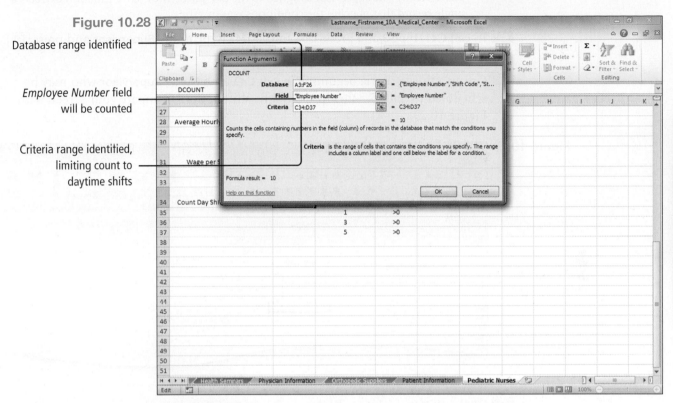

12 Click **OK**.

The result, *10*, displays in cell B34. This is the total number of nurses assigned to work the day shift in the pediatric wing of the hospital on Mondays.

13 **Save** 💾 your workbook.

Activity 10.10 | Using DGET

The DGET function extracts a *single* record that matches the conditions you specify. If more than one record matches the conditions, DGET returns the #NUM! error code. If no record matches the conditions, DGET returns the #VALUE! error code.

1 In cell **A39**, type **Day-Nurse Supervisor ID** and press Tab.

This forms the label for the function, which will determine the employee number for the day shift nurse supervisor.

2 Copy the range **B3:D3**, and then paste it in cell **C39**.

3 In cell **C40**, type **1** and press [Tab]. In cell **D40**, type **Nurse Supervisor** and press [Tab]. Widen **column D** to **115 pixels**.

4 In cell **E40**, type **>0** and then press [Enter].

> This criteria searches for an employee working Shift 1 with the status of *Nurse Supervisor*. There is only one supervisor assigned to the day shift—the DGET function extracts a single record that matches the conditions you specify.

5 In cell **C41**, type **3** and press [Tab]. In cell **D41**, type **Nurse Supervisor** and press [Tab]. In cell **E41**, type **>0** and press [Enter].

6 Create a third criteria beginning in cell **C42** for a **Nurse Supervisor** who may be scheduled to Shift 5—the third daytime shift option. Compare your screen with Figure 10.29.

Figure 10.29

Shift Codes for shifts 1, 3, and 5

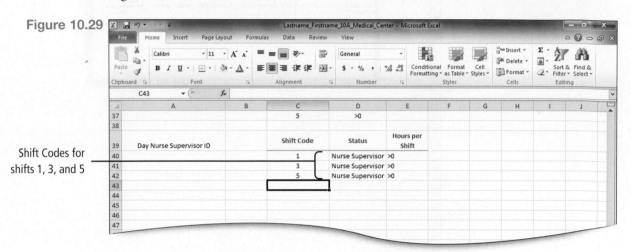

7 Click cell **B39**, and then display the **Insert Function** dialog box.

8 Be sure the **Or select a category** box displays **Database**. Under **Select a function**, click **DGET**, and then click **OK**.

> The Function Arguments dialog box for DGET displays.

Another Way
Alternatively, select the range with your mouse.

9 In the **Database** box, type the range **a3:f26**

> The database range is defined and displays in the first argument box.

10 In the **Field** box, type **Employee Number** and then press [Tab].

> Excel will *get*—locate—the *Employee Number* of the nurse who meets the criteria.

11 In the **Criteria** box, type the range **c39:e42** Compare your dialog box with Figure 10.30.

> The criteria range is defined.

Figure 10.30

Database range identified ——

Employee Number field found ——

Criteria area identified ——

Criteria definition ——

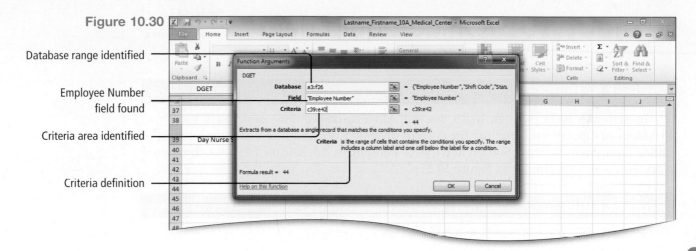

12 Click **OK**.

The result, *44*, displays in cell B39. This is the *Employee Number* of the Nurse Supervisor assigned to work the day shift on Monday in the pediatric wing of the hospital.

13 Select the range **A28:A39**, and then on the **Home tab**, in the **Alignment group**, click **Align Text Left**. Apply the **Heading 4** cell style.

14 Group the worksheets. Insert a footer in the **left section** with the **File Name**, click above the footer area to deselect, and then return to **Normal** view. Make cell **A1** the active cell. With the worksheets still grouped, display the **Document Panel**. In the **Author** box, type your firstname and lastname, in the **Subject** box, type your course name and section number, and in the **Keywords** box, type **medical center information** **Close** the **Document Panel**.

15 **Save** your workbook. Print or submit your workbook electronically. If required, print or create an electronic version of your worksheets with formulas displayed using the instructions in Activity 1.16 in Project 1A. If you printed your formulas, be sure to redisplay the worksheet by pressing Ctrl + `. **Close** the workbook and **Exit** Excel.

> **Note** | To Print a Multi-Sheet Workbook
>
> If you are printing this workbook, to print all the pages, either group the sheets, or under Settings, select Print Entire Workbook.

End **You have completed Project 10A**

Project 10B Office Equipment Inventory

myitlab
Project 10B Training

Project Activities

In Activities 10.11 through 10.15, you will edit a worksheet for Gerald Neff, Vice President of Operations, detailing the current inventory of two office equipment types—Office Equipment Nursing Station and Office Equipment Administrative. Your completed worksheet will look similar to Figure 10.31.

Project Files

For Project 10B, you will need the following files:

    e10B_Equipment_Inventory
    e10B_logo

You will save your workbook as:

    Lastname_Firstname_10B_Equipment_Inventory

Project Results

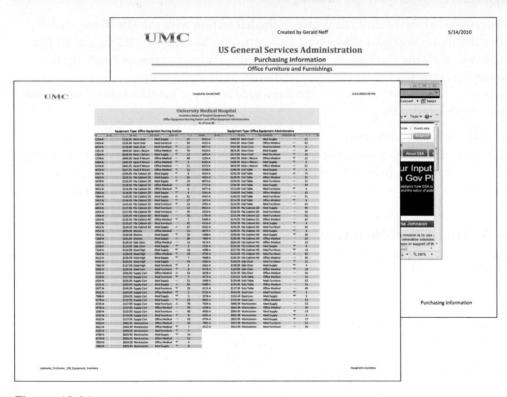

Figure 10.31
Project 10B Equipment Inventory

Objective 5 | Insert a Second Table into a Worksheet

In Excel, you can insert a table beside another table in the *same* worksheet, and then work with the data in each table separately. This enables you to view and compare similar sets of data.

Activity 10.11 | Inserting a Second Table into a Worksheet

1 **Start** Excel. From your student files, open the file **e10B_Equipment_Inventory**. In your **Excel Chapter 10** folder, **Save** the file as **Lastname_Firstname_10B_Equipment_Inventory**

2 On the **Equipment Inventory** worksheet, select the range **A7:E62**, and then on the **Insert tab**, in the **Tables group**, click the **Table** button. In the **Create Table** dialog box, verify that =$A$7:$E$62 displays as the data range and that the **My table has headers** check box is selected. Click **OK**.

> The Office Equipment Nursing Station data converts to a table, a table style is applied, and the headings display filter arrows.

3 From the sheet tab area at the bottom of the Excel window, click the **Administrative** sheet tab, select the range **A1:E52**, right-click over the selection, and then on the shortcut menu, click **Copy**.

4 Display the **Equipment Inventory** sheet tab, scroll up as necessary, point to cell **F6** and right-click, and then on the shortcut menu, under **Paste Options**, click the **Paste** button. Click any cell to deselect. Compare your screen with Figure 10.32.

> The data regarding Office Equipment Administrative is added to the right of the Office Equipment Nursing Station table.

Figure 10.32

Office Equipment Administrative data displays

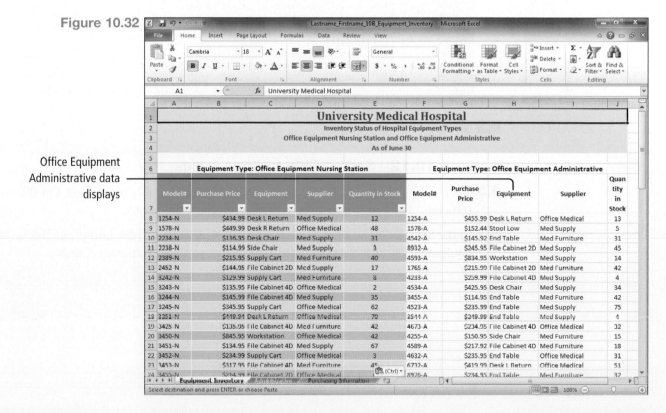

Excel | Chapter 10

5 Select the range **F7:J57**. On the **Insert tab**, in the **Tables group**, click the **Table** button, and then in the **Create Table** dialog box, verify that the data range is *=$F$7:$J$57* and that the **My table has headers** check box is selected.

Side-by-side tables do *not* have to contain the same number of rows or columns.

6 Click **OK**. On the **Design tab**, in the **Table Styles group**, click the **More** button ⌄, and then under **Medium**, click **Table Style Medium 11**. Click any cell to deselect. Compare your screen with Figure 10.33.

The data for Office Equipment Administrative is converted to a table, a style is applied, and the headings display filter arrows.

Figure 10.33

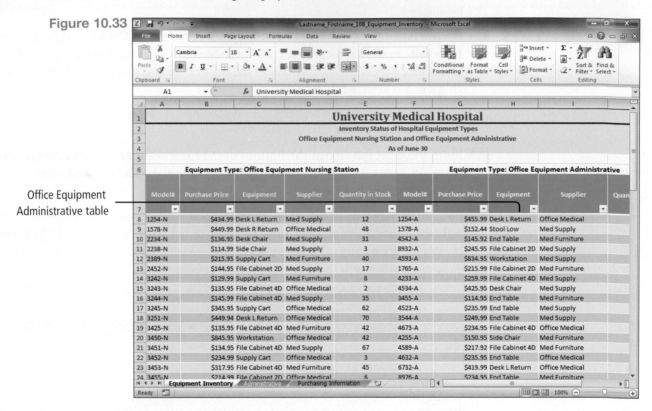

Office Equipment Administrative table

7 **Save** 🖫 your workbook.

Activity 10.12 | Sorting Side-by-Side Tables

1 Click any cell in the **Office Equipment Nursing Station** table on the left. On the **Data tab**, click the **Sort** button to display the **Sort** dialog box.

2 In the **Sort** dialog box, under **Column**, click the **Sort by** arrow, and then click **Equipment**. Be sure **Sort On** indicates *Values* and **Order** indicates *A to Z*.

3 In the upper left corner, click **Add Level**. Under **Column**, click the **Then by** arrow, and then click **Purchase Price**. Click the **Order arrow**, and set the sort order to **Largest to Smallest**. Compare your screen with Figure 10.34.

Figure 10.34

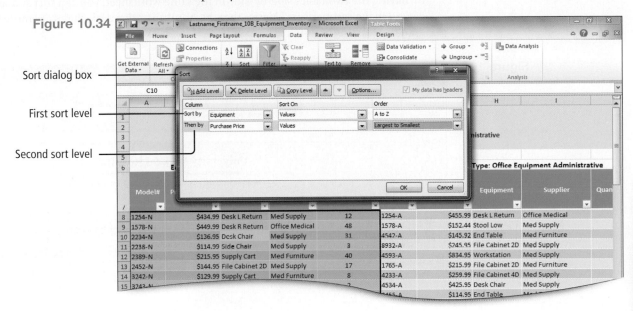

Sort dialog box

First sort level

Second sort level

4 Click **OK**, and then compare your screen with Figure 10.35.

The Equipment column is sorted alphabetically, and within each equipment type, the items are sorted by Purchase Price from the highest to lowest.

Figure 10.35

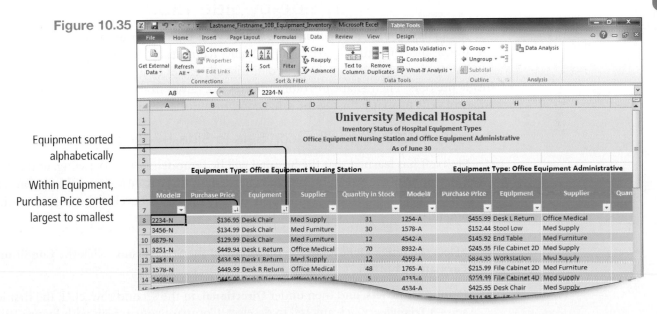

Equipment sorted alphabetically

Within Equipment, Purchase Price sorted largest to smallest

5 Using the same technique and sort orders, sort the **Office Equipment Administrative** table. Compare your screen with Figure 10.36.

By having the two tables side-by-side in the same worksheet, you can sort similar sets of data to make comparisons. Notice that the Administrative desk chairs are more expensive than the Nursing Station desk chairs.

Figure 10.36

Both tables sorted first by Equipment and then by Purchase Price

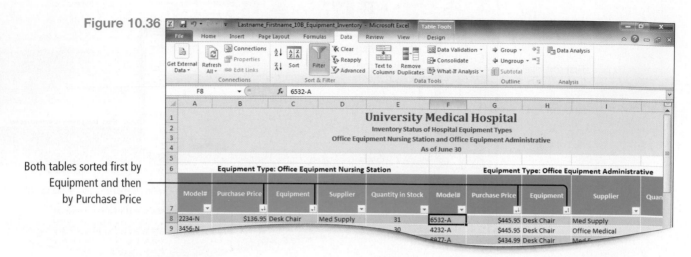

6 Save 💾 your workbook.

Objective 6 | Apply Conditional Formatting to Side-by-Side Tables

Recall that *conditional formatting* makes your data easier to interpret by changing the appearance of your data based on its value. *Icon sets* are sets of three, four, or five small graphic images that make your data visually easier to interpret. The icons are placed inside the cells. Their shape or color indicates the values in the cells relative to all other adjacent cells formatted using the same condition.

Activity 10.13 | Applying Icon Sets to Side-by-Side Tables

Mr. Neff has learned that the hospital will be remodeling the East wing, and that an inventory of hospital office equipment is needed. In this activity, you will use icon sets as the conditional formatting to distinguish visually the Stock Level of the hospital office equipment.

1 Select the range **E8:E62**. On the **Home tab**, in the **Styles group**, click the **Conditional Formatting** button.

2 Point to **Icon Sets**, and then under **Directional**, in the second row, click the first icon set—**3 Triangles**. Click any cell to deselect. Compare your screen with Figure 10.37.

In this icon set, a colored triangle provides the visual cue about the value of a cell relative to other cells. A green upward pointing triangle represents a higher value, a yellow bar represents a mid-level value, and a red downward pointing triangle represents a lower value. Icon sets are useful to quickly identify higher and lower numbers within a large group of data, such as very high or very low levels of inventory.

Figure 10.37

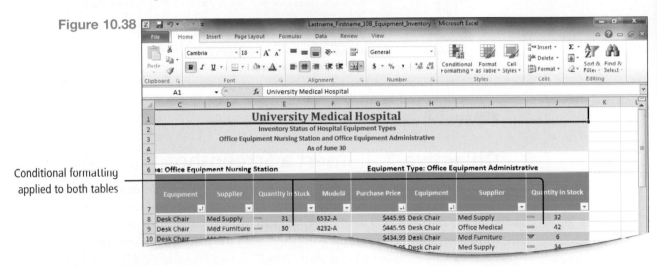

Colored triangles and bars
indicate inventory level

3 Using the technique you just practiced, apply the same icon set to indicate the *Quantity in Stock* in for the **Office Equipment Administrative** equipment type. Press Ctrl + Home to make cell **A1** the active cell, and then compare your screen with Figure 10.38.

Figure 10.38

Conditional formatting
applied to both tables

4 Click anywhere in the **Office Equipment Administrative** table to activate the table. Click the **Design tab** and then in the **Tools group**, click the **Convert to Range** button. In the displayed message box, click **Yes** to convert the table to a normal range.

The list arrows are removed from the column titles; the color and shading formats applied from the table style remain.

Excel | Chapter 10

5 Using the same technique, convert the **Office Equipment Nursing Station** table to a range, and then compare your screen with Figure 10.39.

Figure 10.39

Colored triangles and bars displayed

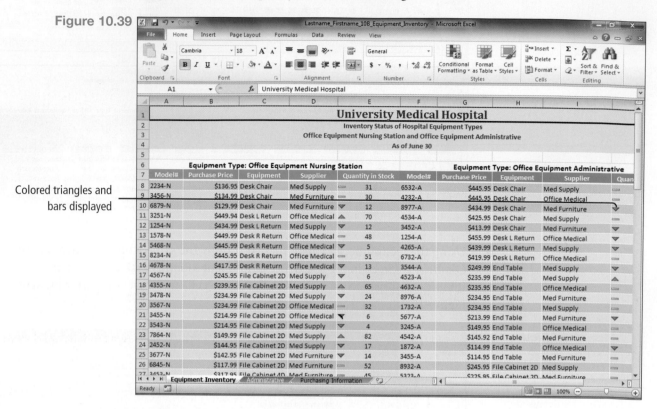

6 Save 💾 your workbook.

Objective 7 | Insert a Screenshot

A *screenshot* is an image of an active window on your computer that you can insert into a worksheet. Screenshots are especially useful when you want to insert an image of a Web site into an Excel worksheet. You can insert a screenshot of any open window on your computer, and then print the worksheet with the inserted screenshot.

Activity 10.14 | Inserting a ScreenShot

The University Medical Center is enrolled in the government purchasing program for acquiring office furniture. In this activity, you will go to the U.S. General Services Administration Web site, search for information about furniture, and then insert the information into an Excel worksheet.

1 Display the third worksheet in the workbook—**Purchasing Information**.

2 In the **Purchasing Information** worksheet, click cell **A5**. **Start** your Internet browser. In the **address bar**, type **www.gsa.gov** and press Enter to navigate to the site.

The U.S. General Services Administration Web page displays.

3 From the taskbar, redisplay your **10B_Purchasing_Information** workbook. On the **Insert tab**, in the **Illustrations group**, click **Screenshot**. In the displayed gallery, point to the GSA screen to display the ScreenTip, and then compare your screen with Figure 10.40.

All of your open windows display in the Available Windows gallery and are available to insert into your worksheet.

Figure 10.40

Insert tab, Illustrations group

Screenshot button

Available Windows gallery (your screen may vary)

GSA ScreenTip

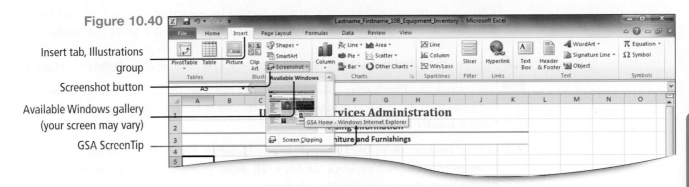

4 Click the **GSA** screenshot, and notice that the screen image displays in your worksheet and is selected.

5 On the **Format tab**, in the **Size group**, change the **Shape Height** to **5.25"** and then compare your screen with Figure 10.41.

Figure 10.41

Height changed to 5.25"

Screenshot inserted (yours may vary)

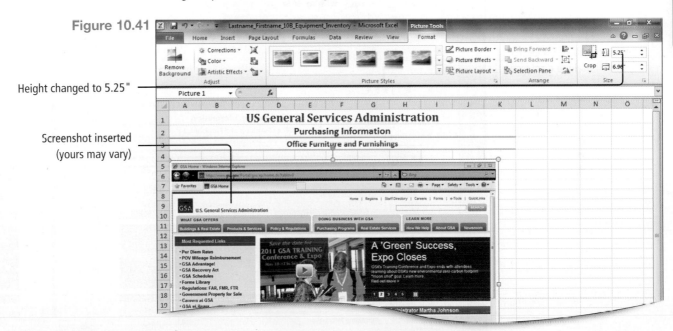

6 **Save** 💾 your workbook.

Objective 8 | Create Custom Headers and Footers

You can create custom headers and footers to provide useful information about your worksheet. You can type your own text or insert header and footer elements such as pictures, page numbers, and the date and time.

Activity 10.15 | Creating Custom Headers and Footers

In this activity, you will create a custom header by inserting a logo, text, and the date and time. You will create a custom footer by inserting Header & Footer Elements.

1 Point to the **Administrative** sheet tab, right-click, and then click **Delete** two times.

2 Right-click the **Purchasing Information** sheet tab, and then click **Select All Sheets**. On the **Insert tab**, in the **Text group**, click the **Header & Footer** button, and then click in the **left header** section of the header.

3 On the **Design tab**, in the **Header & Footer Elements group**, click the **Picture** button. From your student files, click the file **e10B_logo**, and then click **Insert**. Click above the header. Compare your screen with Figure 10.42.

A logo of the University Medical Center displays in the left section of the header.

Figure 10.42

University Medical Center logo displayed

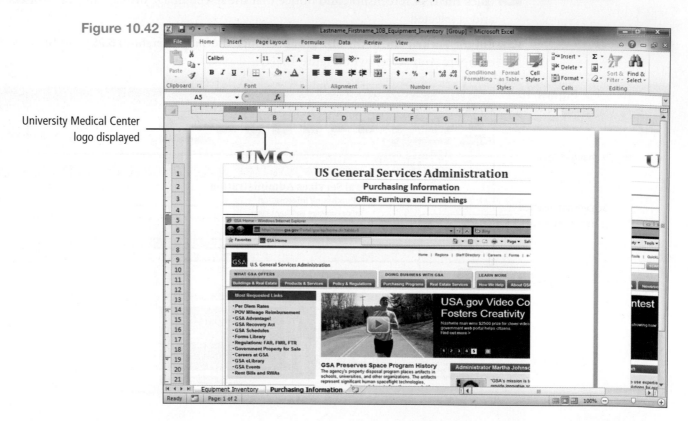

4 Click in the **middle header section**, type **Created by Gerald Neff** and then press Tab to move to the **right header section**. On the **Design tab**, in the **Header & Footer Elements group**, click the **Current Date** button, press Spacebar, and then click the **Current Time** button. Click above the header. Compare your screen with Figure 10.43.

> In the header, the logo displays in the left section, text displays in the middle section, and the date and time display in the right section.

Figure 10.43

The logo, text, date and time display (your date and time will differ)

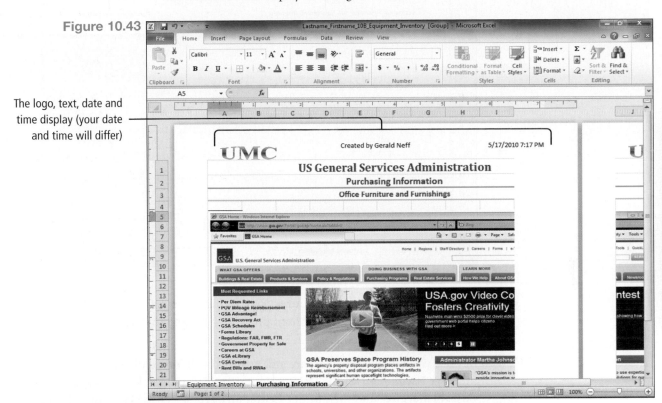

5 On the **Insert tab**, in the **Text group**, click **Header & Footer**, and then click **Go to Footer**.

6 Click in the **left section**, and then insert the **File Name**. Click in the **right section**, and then click the **Sheet Name** button. Click a cell just above the footer area to deselect, and then compare your screen with Figure 10.44.

> In the footer, the file name displays in the left section and the sheet name displays in the right section.

Figure 10.44

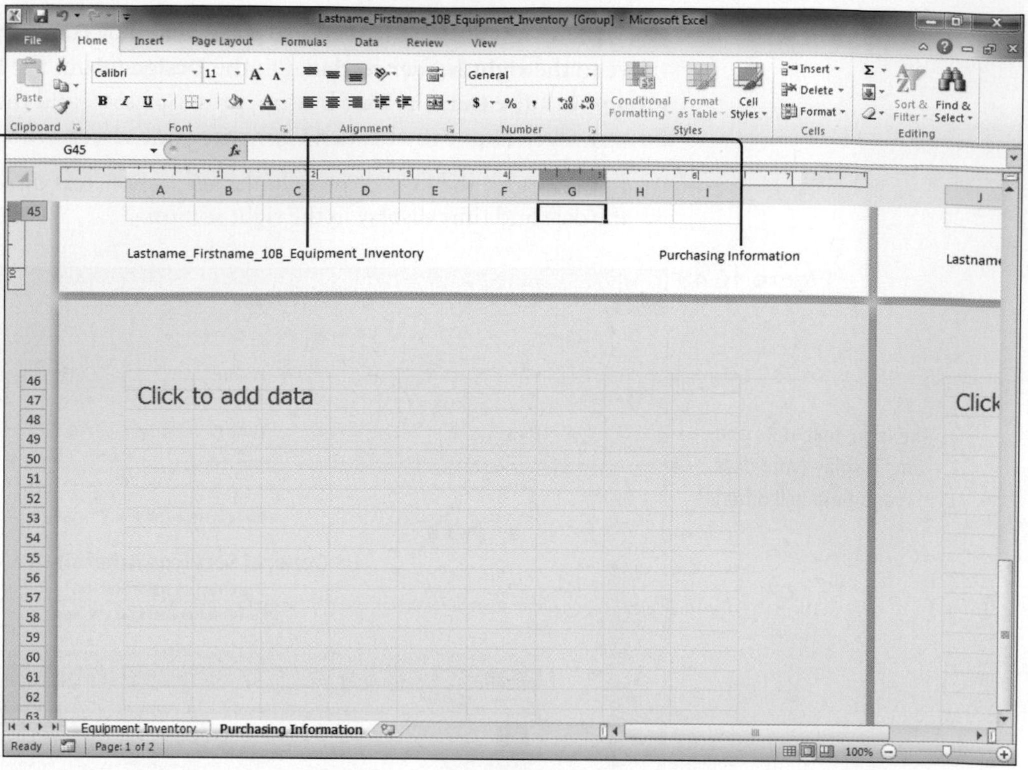

The file name and sheet name inserted in footer

7 In the lower right corner of your screen, in the status bar, click the **Normal** button ⊞ to return to **Normal** view, and then press [Ctrl] + [Home] to display the top of your worksheet.

8 Be sure your two worksheets are still grouped—*[Group]* displays in the title bar. On the **Page Layout tab**, set the **Orientation** to **Landscape**. Click the **Margins** button, click **Custom Margins**, and then under **Center on page**, select the **Horizontally** check box. Click **OK**.

9 In the **Scale to Fit group**, set the **Width** to **1 page** and the **Height** to **1 page**. Press [Ctrl] + [F2] to check the **Print Preview**, and then return to the workbook.

The first worksheet is slightly wider and taller than the normal margins, so scaling in this manner will keep all the information on one page.

10 With the worksheets still grouped, display the **Document Panel**. In the **Author** box, type your firstname and lastname, in the **Subject** box type, your course name and section number, and in the **Keywords** box type **office equipment, inventory Close** the **Document Panel**.

11 Save 🖫 your workbook. Print or submit your workbook electronically. If required, print or create an electronic version of your worksheets with formulas displayed using the instructions in Activity 1.16 in Project 1A. **Close** the workbook and **Exit** Excel.

Note | To Print a Multi-Sheet Workbook

If you are printing this workbook, to print all the pages, either group the sheets, or under Settings, select Print Entire Workbook.

End **You have completed Project 10B** ───────────────

Content-Based Assessments

Summary

In this chapter, you used Excel's database capabilities to organize data. The skills you practiced included importing data into Excel from other sources and querying data in the database. You used database functions to summarize information and analyze data. You inserted a second table in a worksheet and sorted data in side-by-side tables, applied conditional formatting to data using icon sets, and inserted a screenshot from the Internet onto a worksheet. Finally, you created custom headers and footers.

Key Terms

Matching

Match each term in the second column with its correct definition in the first column by writing the letter of the term on the blank line in front of the correct definition.

_____ 1. A group of commands that enables you to bring data from an Access database, from the Web, from a text file, or from an XML file into Excel without repeatedly copying the data.

_____ 2. This is stored in rows and contains all the data about one item in a database.

_____ 3. This is stored in columns and contains a specific type of data such as name, employee number, or social security number.

_____ 4. Information that is stored in a format of rows and columns.

_____ 5. A language that structures data in text files so that it can be read by other systems, regardless of the hardware platform or operating system.

_____ 6. An XML file that contains the rules for what can and cannot reside in an XML data file.

_____ 7. A process of restricting records through the use of criteria conditions that displays records that answer a question for you about the data.

_____ 8. A collection of data related to a particular topic or purpose.

_____ 9. Facts about people, events, things, or ideas.

_____ 10. Data that has been organized in a useful manner.

_____ 11. Predefined formulas that perform calculations by using specific values, called arguments, in a particular order or structure.

_____ 12. The arrangement of the arguments in a function.

A Data

B Database

C DGET function

D Extensible Markup Language (XML)

E Field

F Functions

G Get External Data group

H Icon sets

I Information

J Query

K Record

L Schema

M Screenshot

N Syntax

O Table

_____ 13. A function that extracts from your data table a single record that matches the conditions you specify.

_____ 14. A group of three, four, or five small graphic images that make your data visually easier to interpret and are used to add emphasis to the conditional format of a list.

_____ 15. An image of an active window on your computer that you can insert into a worksheet.

Multiple Choice

Circle the correct answer.

1. Icon sets are grouped in sets of this many icons:
   A. 1, 2, 3   B. 2, 3, 4   C. 3, 4, 5

2. A database program developed by Microsoft and used to manage database files is called:
   A. XML   B. Access   C. Visual Basic

3. To print an entire multi-sheet workbook, you can:
   A. Group the Sheets   B. Print the Selection   C. Enable Active Sheets

4. A database function that determines the arithmetic mean in a database:
   A. DCOUNT   B. DAVERAGE   C. DSUM

5. A database function that determines how many records match one or more conditions:
   A. DCOUNT   B. DGET   C. DSUM

6. The database function that finds a total of values in one column based on criteria that are applied to other fields in a database:
   A. DCOUNT   B. DGET   C. DSUM

7. Bringing data in from an external data source is known as:
   A. Importing   B. Exporting   C. Enabling

8. Formatting characteristics that are applied to cells when the value in the cell meets a specified condition are called:
   A. Cell styles   B. Conditional formats   C. Table styles

9. Conditional formatting icon sets are placed:
   A. Inside a cell   B. Outside a cell   C. Below a cell

10. In Excel, you can insert a screenshot of:
    A. Only the active window   B. Exclusively screen clippings   C. Any open window

Content-Based Assessments

Apply **10A** skills from these Objectives:

■1 Get External Data into Excel

■2 Create a Query and Use the Query Wizard to Sort and Filter

■3 Use DAVERAGE and DSUM Database Functions

■4 Use DCOUNT and DGET Database Functions

Skills Review | Project **10C** Lab Information

In the following Skills Review, you will import data about lab department technicians, hematologists, blood bank services, and lab suppliers into Excel, and query the database to locate information. Your completed worksheets will look similar to Figure 10.45.

Project Files

For Project 10C, you will need the following files:

> e10C_Blood_Banks (Access database)
> e10C_Hematologist_Information (Text Document)
> e10C_Lab_Dept (Excel Workbook)
> e10C_Lab_Seminars (HTML Document)
> e10C_Lab_Supplies (XML Document)
> e10C_Technician_Information (Access Database)

You will save your workbook as:

> Lastname_Firstname_10C_Lab_Dept

Project Results

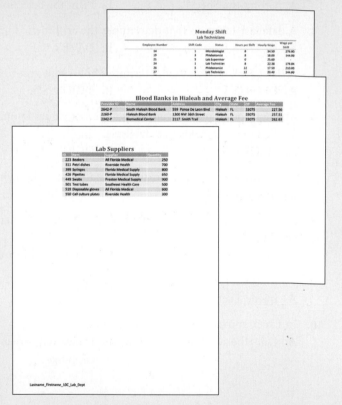

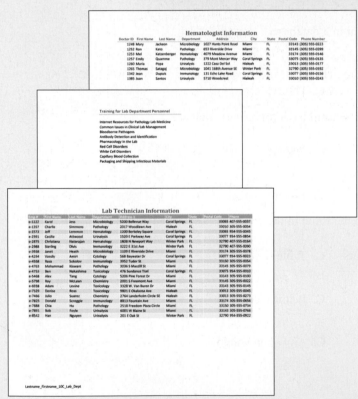

Figure 10.45

(Project 10C Lab Information continues on the next page)

Skills Review | Project **10C** Lab Information (continued)

1 **Start** Excel. From your student files, open the Excel file **e10C_Lab_Dept**. **Save** the file in your **Excel Chapter 10** folder as **Lastname_Firstname_10C_Lab_Dept**

a. Display the first worksheet—**Lab Tech Information**. Click in cell **A2**. On the **Data tab**, in the **Get External Data group**, if necessary click the **Get External Data button arrow**, and then click the **From Access** button. In the **Select Data Source** dialog box, navigate to your student files, click the Access file **e10C_Technician_ Information**, and then click **Open**.

b. In the **Import Data** dialog box, be sure that the **Table** option button is selected, and then click **OK**. **Merge & Center** the text in cell **A1** across the range **A1:I1**, and then apply the **Title** cell style.

2 Display the **Lab Seminars** worksheet. Press Ctrl + F12 to display the **Open** dialog box. Navigate to your student files, right-click the HTML file **e10C_Lab_Seminars**, and then on the shortcut menu, point to **Open with**, and then click **Internet Explorer** (or your Internet browser).

a. On your browser screen, point to the **Address bar** and right-click, click **Copy**, and then **Close** the Internet browser window. **Close** the **Open** dialog box. Click in cell **A3**. On the **Data tab**, in the **Get External Data group**, if necessary, click the **Get External Data button arrow**, and then click the **From Web** button.

b. In the **New Web Query** dialog box, point to the **Address bar** and right-click, click **Paste**, and then at the end of **Address bar**, click the **Go** button. As necessary, drag the title bar of the **New Web Query** dialog box to the upper portion of your screen, and then in the lower right corner of the dialog box, drag the pointer as necessary to resize the dialog box and display the table on the Web page.

c. On the left side of the **Continuing Education Lab Seminars** table, click the **yellow arrow** to select the table. In the lower right corner of the dialog box, click the **Import** button, and then on the displayed **Import Data** dialog box, verify that the **Existing worksheet** option button and cell **A3** are selected. Click **OK**. Select cell **A1**, and then apply the **Heading 2** cell style.

3 Display the **Hematologist Information** worksheet. Click in cell **A2**. On the **Data tab**, in the **Get External Data group**, click the **From Text** button. In the **Import Text File**

dialog box, navigate to your student files, select the Text file **e10C_Hematologist_Information** and then click the **Import** button. Click **Next**, click **Next** again, click **Finish**, and then click **OK**.

a. Click cell **A1**, **Merge & Center** the title across the range **A1:I1**, and then apply the **Title** cell style. Select the range **A2:I2**, apply **Center** alignment, and then apply the **Heading 3** cell style.

4 Display the **Lab Suppliers** worksheet. Click in cell **A2**. On the **Data tab**, in the **Get External Data group**, click **From Other Sources**, and then click **From XML Data Import**.

a. In the displayed **Select Data Source** dialog box, navigate to your student files, click to select the XML file **e10C_Lab_Supplies**, and then click the **Open** button. Click **OK** to display the **Import Data** dialog box, and then click **OK**. Click cell **A1**, **Merge & Center** the title across the range **A1:D1**, and then apply the **Title** cell style.

5 Display the **Blood Bank Info** worksheet. Click in cell **A2**. On the **Data tab**, in the **Get External Data group**, if necessary click the **Get External Data button arrow**, and then click the **From Other Sources** button. Click **From Microsoft Query**.

a. In the displayed **Choose Data Source** dialog box, verify that the **Databases tab** is active and, at the bottom, the **Use the Query Wizard to create/edit queries** check box is selected. Then, click **MS Access Database***. Click **OK** to display the **Select Database** dialog box. Under **Directories**, be sure the folder containing your student files is selected—if necessary, scroll down to view and select the folder. Then, under **Database Name**, click **e10C_Blood_ Banks.accdb**. Click **OK**.

b. Under **Available tables and columns**, to the left of **10C Blood Bank Services**, click + to expand the table and view the column names. Under **Available tables and columns**, click **Provider ID**, and then click the **Add Field** button to move the field to the **Columns in your query** list on the right. Using the same technique, add the **Name** field to the list.

c. Using either the **Add Field** button or double-click, add the following fields to the **Columns in your query** list: **Address, City, State, ZIP, Average Fee**. In the lower right corner, click the **Next** button. Under

(Project 10C Lab Information continues on the next page)

Content-Based Assessments

Skills Review | Project **10C** Lab Information (continued)

Column to filter, click **ZIP**. Under **Only include rows where**, click in the **ZIP** box to display a list, and then click **equals**. In the box to the right, click the **arrow**, and then click **33075**.

d. Click the **Next** button. In the displayed **Query Wizard – Sort Order** dialog box, under **Sort by**, click the **arrow**, and then click **Average Fee**. Verify that the **Ascending** option button is selected. In the lower right corner, click the **Next** button.

e. Be sure the **Return Data to Microsoft Excel** option button is selected, and then click **Finish**. In the displayed **Import Data** dialog box, verify that the **Table** option button is selected, that the **Existing worksheet** option button is selected, and that cell **$A$2** is indicated. Click **OK**. In cell **A1**, **Merge & Center** the title across the range **A1:G1**, and then apply the **Title** cell style.

6 In your **Blood Bank Info** worksheet, click any cell in the table data. Click the **Design tab**, and then in the **Tools group**, click **Convert to Range**. Click **OK**.

7 Display the **Lab Technicians** worksheet. Widen **column A** to **260 pixels**. In cell **A28**, type **Average Hourly Wage for Phlebotomists** and press Tab. Scroll up, point to cell **C3**, right-click, and then click **Copy**. Scroll down, point to cell **C28**, right-click, and then click **Paste**.

a. In cell **C29**, type **Phlebotomist** and press Tab. Click cell **B28**, and then to the left of the **Formula Bar**, click the **Insert Function** button. In the **Insert Function** dialog box, click the **Or select a category arrow**, and then from the displayed list, click **Database**. In the **Select a function** box, click **DAVERAGE**, and then click **OK**.

b. In the **Database** box, click the **Collapse Dialog Box** button, and then select the range **A3:F26**. Then, in the collapsed dialog box, click the **Expand Dialog Box** button. In the **Field** box, type **Hourly Wage** and press Tab. With the insertion point in the **Criteria** box, select the range **C28:C29**. Click **OK**. Right-click cell **B28**, and then from the Mini toolbar, apply **Accounting Number Format**.

8 In cell **A31**, type **Wage per Shift for Lab Technicians** and press Tab. Select and then copy the range **C3:D3**. Point to cell **C31** and right-click, and then click **Paste**. In cell **C32**, type **Lab Technician** and press Tab. In cell **D32**, type **>0** and then press Enter.

a. Click cell **B31**, and then type **=dsum(** to begin the formula for the DSUM function. Select the range **A3:F26**, and then type **,** (a comma). Being sure to include the comma, type **"Wage per Shift",** to enter the second part of the argument. As indicated by *criteria* in the ScreenTip, type the criteria as **c31:d32** and then press Enter. Right-click cell **B31** and apply **Accounting Number Format**.

9 In cell **A34**, type **Count Day Shift (Code 1, 3, 5)** and press Tab. Click cell **B3**, hold down Ctrl and click cell **D3**. Right-click either of the selected cells, and then click **Copy**. Scroll down, point to cell **C34**, right-click, and then click **Paste**.

a. In cell **C35**, type **1** and press Tab. In cell **D35**, type **>0** and press Enter. In cell **C36**, type **3** and press Tab. In cell **D36**, type **>0** and press Enter. In cell **C37**, type **5** and press Tab. In cell **D37**, type **>0** and press Enter.

b. Click cell **B34**. To the left of the **Formula Bar**, click the **Insert Function** button. Click the **Or select a category arrow**, and then click **Database**. In the **Select a function** box, click **DCOUNT**, and then click **OK**.

c. In the **Database** box, click the **Collapse Dialog Box** button. Move the collapsed box to the upper right corner of your screen. Scroll as necessary, and then select the range **A3:F26**. In the collapsed dialog box, click the **Expand Dialog Box** button.

d. In the **Field** box, type **Employee Number** and then press Tab. With the insertion point in the **Criteria** box, click the **Collapse Dialog Box** button, scroll as necessary, and then select the range **C34:D37**. In the collapsed dialog box, click the **Expand Dialog** button. Click **OK**.

10 In cell **A39**, type **Day-Lab Supervisor ID** and press Tab. Copy the range **B3:D3**, and then paste it in cell **C39**. In cell **C40**, type **1** and press Tab. In cell **D40**, type **Lab Supervisor** and press Tab. Widen **column D** to **100 pixels**. In cell **E40**, type **>0** and then press Enter. In cell **C41**, type **3** and press Tab. In cell **D41**, type **Lab Supervisor** and press Tab. In cell **E41**, type **>0** and press Enter. Create a third criteria beginning in cell **C42** for a **Lab Supervisor** who may be scheduled to Shift 5—the third daytime shift option.

a. Click cell **B39**, and then display the **Insert Function** dialog box. Be sure the **Or select a category** box displays **Database**. Under **Select a function**, click **DGET**, and then click **OK**.

(Project 10C Lab Information continues on the next page)

Content-Based Assessments

Skills Review | Project **10C** Lab Information (continued)

b. In the **Database** box, type the range **a3:f26** In the **Field** box, type **Employee Number** and then press Tab. In the **Criteria** box, type the range **c39:e42** Click **OK**.

c. Select the range **A28:A39**, and then on the **Home tab**, in the **Alignment group**, click **Align Text Left**. Apply the **Heading 4** cell style.

11 Display the first worksheet—**Lab Tech Information**. In the sheet tab area, point to any sheet tab, right-click, and then click **Select All Sheets**.

a. On the **Insert tab**, in the **Text group**, click the **Header & Footer** button. In the **Navigation group**, click **Go to Footer**. Click in the **left section**, insert the **File Name**, click above the footer area to deselect, and then return to **Normal** view. Make cell **A1** the active cell. In the **Scale to Fit group**, set the **Width** to **1 page** and the **Height** to **1 page**.

b. With the worksheets still grouped, display the **Document Panel**. In the **Author** box type your firstname and lastname, in the **Subject** box, type your course name and section number, and in the **Keywords** box, type **lab department information** **Close** the **Document Panel**. **Save** your workbook. Print or submit your workbook electronically. If required, print or create an electronic version of your worksheets with formulas displayed using the instructions in Activity 1.16 in Project 1A. If you printed your formulas, be sure to redisplay the worksheet. **Close** the workbook and **Exit** Excel.

End **You have completed Project 10C** ————————

Excel | Chapter 10

Content-Based Assessments

Apply **10B** skills from these Objectives:

5 Insert a Second Table into a Worksheet

6 Apply Conditional Formatting to Side-by-Side Tables

7 Insert a Screenshot

8 Create Custom Headers and Footers

Skills Review | Project **10D** Medical Supplies

In the following Skills Review, you will edit a worksheet for Gerald Neff, Vice President of Operations, detailing the current inventory of two medical supply types—Medical Supplies, Hospital and Medical Supplies, Physician's Clinic. Your completed worksheets will look similar to Figure 10.46.

Project Files

For Project 10D, you will need the following files:

> e10D_Medical_Supplies
> e10D_logo

You will save your workbook as:

> Lastname_Firstname_10D_Medical_Supplies

Project Results

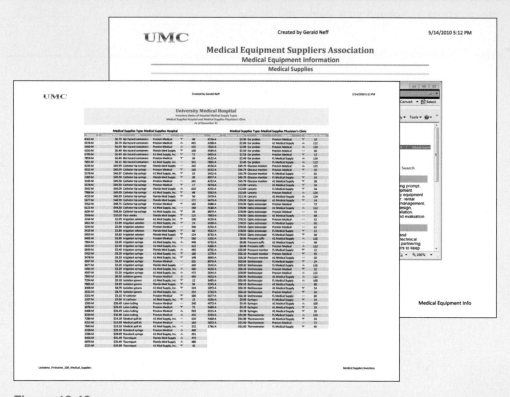

Figure 10.46

(Project 10D Medical Supplies continues on the next page)

Content-Based Assessments

1 **Start** Excel. From your student files, open the file e10D_Medical_Supplies. In your **Excel Chapter 10** folder, **Save** the file as **Lastname_Firstname_10D_Medical_Supplies**

a. Display the **Medical Supplies Inventory** worksheet. Select the range **A7:F62**, and then on the **Insert tab**, in the **Tables group**, click the **Table** button. In the **Create Table** dialog box, verify that =$A$7:$E$62 displays as the data range and that the **My table has headers** check box is selected. Click **OK**.

b. Display the **Physician's Clinic** worksheet, select the range **A1:E52**, right-click over the selection, and then on the shortcut menu, click **Copy**. Display the **Medical Supplies Inventory** worksheet, scroll up as necessary, point to cell **F6** and right-click, and then on the shortcut menu, under **Paste Options**, click the **Paste** button. Click any cell to deselect.

c. Select the range **F7:J57**. On the **Insert tab**, in the **Tables group**, click the **Table** button, and then in the **Create Table** dialog box, verify that the data range is =$F$7:$J$57 and that the **My table has headers** check box is selected. Click **OK**. On the **Design tab**, in the **Table Styles group**, click the **More** button and then under **Medium**, click **Table Style Medium 11**.

2 Click any cell in the **Medical Supplies Hospital** table on the left. On the **Data tab**, click the **Sort** button to display the **Sort** dialog box.

a. In the **Sort** dialog box, under **Column**, click the **Sort by arrow**, and then click **Item**. Be sure **Sort On** indicates *Values* and **Order** indicates *A to Z*. In the upper left corner, click **Add Level**. Under **Column**, click the **Then by arrow**, and then click **Purchase Price**. Click the **Order arrow** and set the sort order to **Largest to Smallest**. Click **OK**. Using the same technique and sort orders, sort the **Medical Supplies Physician's Clinic** table. Widen **column H** to **115 pixels**.

3 Select the range **E8:E62**. On the **Home tab**, in the **Styles group**, click the **Conditional Formatting** button. Point to **Icon Sets**, and then under **Directional**, in the second row, click the first icon set—**3 Triangles**. Click any cell to deselect.

a. Apply the same icon set to indicate the *Quantity in Stock* in for the **Medical Supplies Physician's Clinic** supply type. Press **Ctrl** + **Home** to make cell **A1** the active cell.

b. Click anywhere in the **Medical Supplies Physician's Clinic** table to activate the table. Click the **Design tab**, and then in the **Tools group**, click the **Convert to Range** button. In the displayed message box, click **Yes** to convert the table to a normal range. Convert the **Medical Supplies Hospital** table to a range.

4 Display the third worksheet in the workbook— **Medical Equipment Info**. In the **Medical Equipment Info** worksheet, click cell **A5**. **Start** your Internet browser. In the **address bar**, type http://dseis.od.nih.gov and press **Enter** to navigate to the site.

a. From the taskbar, redisplay your **10D_Medical_Supplies** workbook. On the **Insert tab**, in the **Illustrations group**, click **Screenshot**. In the displayed gallery, point to the *Division of Scientific Equipment and Instrumentation Services* screen to display the ScreenTip.

b. Click the screenshot, and notice that the screen image displays in your worksheet and is selected. Click the **Format tab**, in the **Size group**, change the **Shape Height** to **4"** and then drag the image as necessary so that it is centered just below the heading.

5 Point to the **Physician's Clinic** sheet tab, right-click, and then click **Delete**. Click **Delete** a second time to confirm the deletion. Right-click the **Medical Equipment Info** sheet tab, and then click **Select All Sheets**. On the **Insert tab**, in the **Text group**, click the **Header & Footer** button, and then in the **Header**, click in the **left section**.

a. On the **Design tab**, in the **Header & Footer Elements group**, click the **Picture** button. From your student files, click the file e10D_logo, and then click **Insert**. Click above the header to deselect the header area.

b. Click in the **middle header section**, type **Created by Gerald Neff** and then press **Tab** to move to the **right header section**. On the **Design tab**, in the **Header & Footer Elements group**, click the **Current Date** button, press **Spacebar**, and then click the **Current Time** button. Click above the header.

c. On the **Insert tab**, in the **Text group**, click **Header & Footer**, and then click **Go to Footer**. Click in the **left section**, and then insert the **File Name**. Click in the **right section**, and then click the **Sheet Name** button. Click a cell just above the footer area to deselect. In the lower right corner of your screen, in the status bar, click the **Normal** button to return to **Normal** view, and then press **Ctrl** + **Home** to display the top of your worksheet.

(Project 10D Medical Supplies continues on the next page)

Content-Based Assessments

Skills Review | Project **10D** Medical Supplies (continued)

 Be sure your two worksheets are still grouped—*[Group]* displays in the title bar. On the **Page Layout tab**, set the **Orientation** to **Landscape**. Click the **Margins** button, click **Custom Margins**, and then under **Center on page**, select the **Horizontally** check box. Click **OK**.

a. In the **Scale to Fit group**, set the **Width** to **1 page** and the **Height** to **1 page**. Press [Ctrl] + [F2] to check the **Print Preview**, and then return to the workbook.

b. With the worksheets still grouped, show the **Document Panel**. In the **Author** box, type your firstname and lastname, in the **Subject** box, type your course name and section number, and in the **Keywords** box, type **medical supplies, inventory** **Close** the **Document Panel**.

c. **Save** your workbook. Print or submit your workbook electronically. If required, print or create an electronic version of your worksheets with formulas displayed using the instructions in Activity 1.16 in Project 1A. **Close** the workbook and **Exit** Excel.

End **You have completed Project 10D**

Content-Based Assessments

Apply 10A skills from these Objectives:

1 Get External Data into Excel

2 Create a Query and Use the Query Wizard to Sort and Filter

3 Use DAVERAGE and DSUM Database Functions

4 Use DCOUNT and DGET Database Functions

Mastering Excel | Project 10E ER Department

In the following Mastering Excel project, you will import data about Emergency department technicians, ER doctors, paramedic services, and emergency suppliers into Excel, and query the database to locate information. Your completed worksheet will look similar to Figure 10.47.

Project Files

For Project 10E, you will need the following files:

e10E_Emergency_Training (HTML Document)
e10E_ER_Dept (Excel workbook)
e10E_ER_Doctors (Text Document)
e10E_ER_Staff (Access database)
e10E_Paramedic_Contacts (Access database)

You will save your workbook as:

Lastname_Firstname_10E_ER_Dept

Project Results

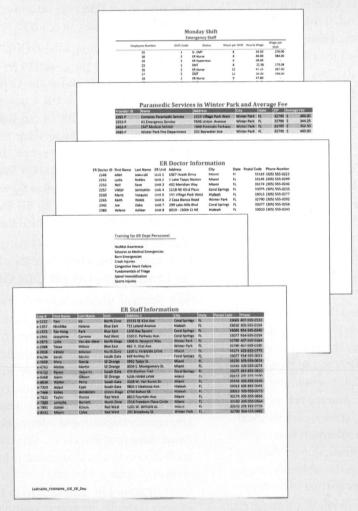

Figure 10.47

(Project 10E ER Department continues on the next page)

1 **Start** Excel. From your student files, open the Excel workbook **e10E_ER_Dept**. **Save** the file in your **Excel Chapter 10** folder as **Lastname_Firstname_10E_ER_Dept** Display the **ER Staff Information** worksheet. Click cell **A2**. On the **Data tab**, in the **Get External Data group**, click the **From Access** button. From your student files, select the Access file **e10E_ER_Staff** as the data source, and then click **Open**. Import the data as a table in the existing worksheet.

2 Display the **Emergency Training** worksheet. Display the **Open** dialog box, and then in your student files, right-click the HTML file **e10E_Emergency_Training**. Open the file with your Internet browser. In the browser, point to the **Address bar**, right-click, click **Copy**, and then **Close** the browser window and **Close** the **Open** dialog box. Click in cell **A3**, and then get external data **From Web**. In the **New Web Query** dialog box, point to the **Address bar** and right-click, click **Paste**, and then at the end of **Address bar**, click the **Go** button. On the left side of the **Emergency Training** table, click the **yellow arrow** to select the table, and then click **Import**. Click **OK** to import the data.

3 Display the **ER Doctors** worksheet; click cell **A2**. Get external data **From Text**, and then from your student files import **e10E_ER_Doctors**. In the wizard, click **Next**, click **Next** again, click **Finish**, and then click **OK**. Select the range **A2:I2**, and apply **Center** alignment.

4 Display the **Paramedic Services** worksheet; click cell **A2**. Get external data from a **Microsoft Query**. As the data source, click **MS Access Database***, and then be sure the check box to use the Query Wizard is selected. Click **OK**. If necessary, navigate to your student files for this chapter, and then under **Database Name**, click **e10E_Paramedic_Contacts.accdb**. Click **OK**.

5 Click + to expand the table, and then add *all* the fields to the **Columns in your query** list on the right, and then click **Next**. Under **Column to filter**, click **ZIP**. Under **Only include rows where**, click in the **ZIP** box, and then click **equals**. In the box to the right, click the **arrow**, and then click **32790**. Click **Next**. **Sort by** the **Average Fee** in **Ascending** order. In the lower right corner, click the **Next** button. Be sure the **Return Data to Microsoft Excel** option button is selected, and then click **Finish**. Import the table into the existing workbook. Convert the table to a range, and then apply **Accounting Number Format** to the fees.

6 Display the **Emergency Staff** worksheet. Copy cell **C3**, and then paste it to cell **C28**. In cell **C29**, type **ER Nurse** and

press Tab. Click cell **B28**, and then insert the **DAVERAGE** function. As the **Database**, the range **a3:f26** As the **Field**, type **Hourly Wage** and as the **Criteria**, use the range **c28:c29** Click **OK**. Apply **Accounting Number Format** to the result.

7 Copy the range **C3:D3**, and then paste it to cell **C31**. In cell **C32**, type **EMT** and press Tab. In cell **D32**, type **>0** In cell **B31**, type **=dsum(** select the range **A3:F26**, type **,** (a comma), and then being sure to include the comma, type **"Wage per Shift",** to enter the second part of the argument. Then type **c31:d32)** as the criteria and press Enter. Apply **Accounting Number Format** to the result.

8 To count the number of ER nurses who work the Day shift, click cell **B3**, hold down Ctrl and click cell **D3**. Right-click either of selected cells, click **Copy**, and then paste the selection to cell **C34**. In cell **C35**, type **1** and press Tab. In cell **D35**, type **>0** and press Enter. In cell **C36**, type **3** press Tab, and then in cell **D36**, type **>0** and press Enter. In cell **C37**, type **5** and press Tab. In cell **D37**, type **>0** and press Enter.

9 In cell **B34**, insert the **DCOUNT** function. As the **Database**, use the range **a3:f26** As the **Field**, type **Employee Number** and as the **Criteria**, use the range **c34:d37** and then click **OK**. Copy the range **B3:D3**, and then paste it in cell **C39**. In cell **C40**, type **1** and press Tab. In cell **D40**, type **ER Supervisor** and press Tab. In cell **E40**, type **>0** and then press Enter. In cell **C41**, type **3** and press Tab. In cell **D41**, type **ER Supervisor** and press Tab. In cell **E41**, type **>0** and press Enter. Create a third criteria beginning in cell **C42** for an **ER Supervisor** who may be scheduled to Shift 5—the third daytime shift option.

10 In **B39**, insert the **DGET** function. As the database, type **a3:f26** as the **Field**, type **Employee Number** and as the **Criteria**, type **c39:e42** Click **OK**. Your result is *47*.

11 Select all the sheets, insert a footer in the **left section** with the **File Name**, click above the footer area to deselect. Return to **Normal** view, and then make cell **A1** the active cell. With the worksheets still grouped, display the **Document Panel**. In the **Author** box, type your firstname and lastname, in the **Subject** box, type your course name and section number, and in the **Keywords** box, type **emergency department information Close** the **Document Panel**. **Save** your workbook. Print or submit your workbook electronically. If required, print or create an electronic version of your worksheets with formulas displayed using the instructions in Activity 1.16 in Project 1A. If you printed your formulas, be sure to redisplay the worksheet by pressing Ctrl + `. **Close** the workbook and **Exit** Excel.

End **You have completed Project 10E**

Content-Based Assessments

Apply **10B** skills from these Objectives:

5 Insert a Second Table into a Worksheet

6 Apply Conditional Formatting to Side-by-Side Tables

7 Insert a Screenshot

8 Create Custom Headers and Footers

Mastering Excel | Project **10F** Beverage Supplies

In the following Mastering Excel project, you will edit a worksheet for Gerald Neff, Vice President of Operations, detailing the current inventory of two beverage supply types—Beverage Supplies Staff and Beverage Supplies Guests. Your completed worksheet will look similar to Figure 10.48.

Project Files

For Project 10F, you will need the following files:

e10F_Beverage_Supplies
e10F_logo

You will save your workbook as:

Lastname_Firstname_10F_Beverage_Supplies

Project Results

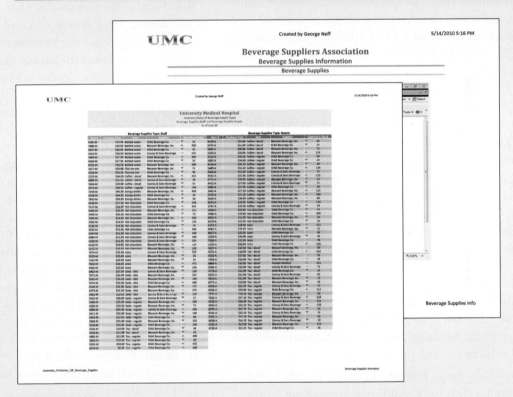

Figure 10.48

(Project 10F Beverage Supplies continues on the next page)

Excel | Chapter 10

1 **Start** Excel. From your student files, open the file **e10F_Beverage_Supplies**, and then **Save** the file in your **Excel Chapter 10** folder as **Lastname_Firstname_10F_ Beverage_Supplies** Display the **Beverage Supplies Inventory** sheet tab. Select the range **A7:E62**, and then on the **Insert tab**, in the **Tables group**, click the **Table** button. In the **Create Table** dialog box, verify that =$A$7:$E$62 displays as the data range and that the **My table has headers** check box is selected. Click **OK**. From the sheet tab area at the bottom of the Excel window, click the **Guests** sheet tab, select the range **A1:E52**, right-click over the selection, and then on the shortcut menu, click **Copy**. Display the **Beverage Supplies Inventory** sheet tab, point to cell **F6** and right-click, and then on the shortcut menu, under **Paste Options**, click the **Paste** button. Click any cell to deselect. Select the range **F7:J57**. On the **Insert tab**, in the **Tables group**, click the **Table** button, and then in the **Create Table** dialog box, verify that the data range is =$F$7:$J$57 and that the **My table has headers** check box is selected. Click **OK**. On the **Design tab**, in the **Table Styles group**, click the **More** button and then under **Medium**, click **Table Style Medium 11**.

2 Click any cell in the **Beverage Supplies Type: Staff** table on the left. On the **Data tab**, click the **Sort** button to display the **Sort** dialog box. In the **Sort** dialog box, under **Column**, click the **Sort by arrow**, and then click **Item**. Be sure **Sort On** indicates *Values* and **Order** indicates *A to Z*. In the upper left corner, click **Add Level**. Under **Column**, click the **Then by arrow**, and then click **Purchase Price**. Click the **Order arrow**, and set the sort order to **Largest to Smallest**. Click **OK**. Using the same technique and sort orders, sort the **Beverage Supplies Type: Guests** table. Widen **column I** to **160** pixels.

3 Select the range **E8:E62**. On the **Home tab**, in the **Styles group**, click the **Conditional Formatting** button. Point to **Icon Sets**, and then under **Directional**, in the second row, click the first icon set—**3 Triangles**. Click any cell to deselect. Using the technique you just practiced, apply the same icon set to indicate the *Quantity in Stock* for the **Beverage Supplies Type: Guests** table. Press **Ctrl** + **Home** to make cell **A1** the active cell. Click anywhere in the **Beverage Supplies Type: Guests** table to activate the table. Click the **Design tab** and then in the **Tools group**, click the **Convert to Range** button, and then click **Yes**. Using the same technique, convert the **Beverage Supplies Type: Staff** table to a range.

4 Display the third worksheet in the workbook— **Beverage Supplies Info**, and then click cell **A5**. **Start** your Internet browser. In the **address bar**, type **www.beverageserviceassociation.com** and press **Enter** to navigate to the site. From the taskbar, redisplay your **10F_Beverage_Supplies** workbook. On the **Insert tab**, in the **Illustrations group**, click **Screenshot**. In the displayed gallery, point to the **Beverage Service Association** screen to display the ScreenTip. Click the **Beverage Service Association** screenshot, and notice that the screen image displays in your worksheet and is selected. Click the **Format tab**, in the **Size group**, change the **Shape Height** to **5.25"**

5 Point to the **Guests** sheet tab, right-click, and then click **Delete**. Click **Delete** a second time to confirm the deletion. Right-click the **Beverage Supplies Info** sheet tab, and then click **Select All Sheets**. On the **Insert tab**, in the **Text group**, click the **Header & Footer** button, and then click in the **left header** section of the header. On the **Design tab**, in the **Header & Footer Elements group**, click the **Picture** button. From your student files, click the file **e10F_logo**, and then click **Insert**. Click above the header. Click in the **middle header section**, type **Created by Gerald Neff** and then press **Tab** to move to the **right header section**. On the **Design tab**, in the **Header & Footer Elements group**, click the **Current Date** button, press **Spacebar**, and then click the **Current Time** button. Click above the header. On the **Insert tab**, in the **Text group**, click **Header & Footer**, and then click **Go to Footer**. Click in the **left section**, and then insert the **File Name**. Click in the **right section**, and then click the **Sheet Name** button. Click a cell just above the footer area to deselect. In the lower right corner of your screen, in the status bar, click the **Normal** button to return to **Normal** view, and then press **Ctrl** + **Home** to display the top of your worksheet.

6 Be sure your two worksheets are still grouped— *[Group]* displays in the title bar. On the **Page Layout tab**, set the **Orientation** to **Landscape**. Click the **Margins** button, click **Custom Margins**, and then under **Center on page**, select the **Horizontally** check box. Click **OK**. In the **Scale to Fit group**, set the **Width** to **1 page** and the **Height** to **1 page**. Press **Ctrl** + **F2** to check the **Print Preview**, and then return to the workbook. With the worksheets still grouped, display the **Document Panel**. In the **Author** box, type your firstname and lastname, in the **Subject** box, type your course name and section number, and in the

(Project 10F Beverage Supplies continues on the next page)

Mastering Excel | Project **10F** Beverage Supplies (continued)

Keywords box, type **beverage supplies, inventory Close** the **Document Panel**. **Save** your workbook. Print or submit your workbook electronically. If required, print or create an electronic version of your worksheets with formulas displayed using the instructions in Activity 1.16 in Project 1A. **Close** the workbook and **Exit** Excel.

 You have completed Project 10F ───────────────

Content-Based Assessments

Apply **10A** and **10B** skills from these Objectives:

1 Get External Data into Excel

2 Create a Query and Use the Query Wizard to Sort and Filter

3 Use DAVERAGE and DSUM Database Functions

4 Use DCOUNT and DGET Database Functions

5 Insert a Second Table into a Worksheet

6 Apply Conditional Formatting to Side-by-Side Tables

7 Insert a Screenshot

8 Create Custom Headers and Footers

Mastering Excel | Project **10G** Pharmacy Department

In the following Mastering Excel project, you will import data about Pharmacy suppliers. You will edit a worksheet for Gerald Neff, Vice President of Operations, detailing the current inventory of two pharmacy supply types—Hospital and Physician's Clinic. Your completed worksheet will look similar to Figure 10.49.

Project Files

For Project 10G, you will need the following files:

e10G_Pharmacy_Suppliers (Access database)
e10G_Pharmacy_Supplies (Excel Workbook)

You will save your workbook as:

Lastname_Firstname_10G_Pharmacy_Supplies

Project Results

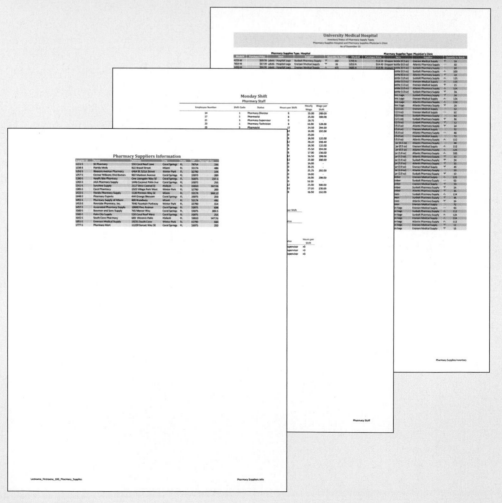

Figure 10.49

(Project 10G Pharmacy Department continues on the next page)

Content-Based Assessments

1 **Start** Excel. From your student files, open the file **e10G_Pharmacy_Supplies**. **Save** the file in your **Excel Chapter 10** folder as **Lastname_Firstname_10G_Pharmacy_Supplies** Display the **Pharmacy Suppliers Info** worksheet. Click in cell **A2**. On the **Data tab**, in the **Get External Data group**, click the **From Access** button. From your student files, select the Access file **e10G_Pharmacy_Suppliers** as the data source, and then click **Open**. Import the data as a table in the existing worksheet.

2 Display the **Pharmacy Staff** worksheet. Copy cell **C3**, and then paste it to cell **C28**. In cell **C29**, type **Pharmacist** and press Tab . Click cell **B28**, and then insert the **DAVERAGE** function. As the **Database**, use the range **a3:f26** as the **Field**, type **Hourly Wage** and as the **Criteria**, use the range **c28:c29**. Click **OK**. Apply **Accounting Number Format** to the result. In **B39**, insert the **DGET** function. As the **Database**, type **a3:f26** as the **Field**, type **Employee Number** and as the **Criteria**, type **c39:e42** Your result is **44**.

3 Display the **Pharmacy Supplies Inventory** sheet tab. Select the range **A7:E62**, and then on the **Insert tab**, in the **Tables group**, click the **Table** button. In the **Create Table** dialog box, verify that =$A$7:$E$62 displays as the data range and that the **My table has headers** check box is selected. Click **OK**. From the sheet tab area at the bottom of the Excel window, click the **Physician's Clinic** sheet tab, select the range **A1:E52**, right-click over the selection, and then on the shortcut menu, click **Copy**. Display the **Pharmacy Supplies Inventory** sheet tab, point to cell **F6** and right-click, and then on the shortcut menu, under **Paste Options**, click the **Paste** button. Click any cell to deselect. Select the range **F7:J57**. On the **Insert tab**, in the **Tables group**, click the **Table** button, and then in the **Create Table** dialog box, verify that the data range is =$F$7:$J$57 and that the **My table has headers** check box is selected. Click **OK**. On the **Design tab**, in the

Table Styles group, click the **More** button and then under **Medium**, click **Table Style Medium 11**. **Autofit** columns **H** and **I**.

4 Select the range **E8:E62**. On the **Home tab**, in the **Styles group**, click the **Conditional Formatting** button. Point to **Icon Sets**, and then under **Directional**, in the second row, click the first icon set—**3 Triangles**. Click any cell to deselect. Using the technique you just practiced, apply the same icon set to indicate the *Quantity in Stock* for the **Pharmacy Supplies Type: Physician's Clinic**. Press Ctrl + Home to make cell **A1** the active cell. Click anywhere in the **Pharmacy Supplies Type: Physician's Clinic** table to activate the table. Click the **Design tab** and then in the **Tools group**, click the **Convert to Range** button, and then click **Yes**. Using the same technique, convert the **Pharmacy Supplies Type: Hospital** table to a range. **Delete** the **Physician's Clinic** worksheet.

5 Select all the sheets, insert a footer in the **left section**, insert the **File Name**, and in the **right section**, insert the **Sheet Name**. Click above the footer area to deselect. Return to **Normal** view, and then make cell **A1** the active cell. Be sure your three worksheets are grouped—*[Group]* displays in the title bar. Click the **Margins** button, click **Custom Margins**, and then under **Center on page**, select the **Horizontally** check box. Click **OK**. In the **Scale to Fit group**, set the **Width** to **1 page** and the **Height** to **1 page**. Press Ctrl + F2 to check the **Print Preview**, and then return to the workbook. With the worksheets still grouped, display the **Document Panel**. In the **Author** box, type your firstname and lastname, in the **Subject** box, type your course name and section number, and in the **Keywords** box, type **pharmacy supplies, inventory** Close the **Document Panel**. **Save** your workbook. Print or submit your workbook electronically. If required, print or create an electronic version of your worksheets with formulas displayed using the instructions in Activity 1.16 in Project 1A. **Close** the workbook and **Exit** Excel.

End **You have completed Project 10G**

GO! Fix It | Project **10H** Imaging Technicians

Project Files

For Project 10H, you will need the following file:

e10H_Imaging_Technicians

You will save your workbook as:

Lastname_Firstname_10H_Imaging_Technicians

Open the file e10H_Imaging_Technicians, and then save the file in your Excel Chapter 10 folder as **Lastname_Firstname_10H_Imaging_Technicians** Examine the workbook. Correct any database functions that display errors. In the left section of the footer, insert the file name. Add your name and course information to the document properties, and include **imaging technicians** as the keywords. Save your file, and then print or submit your worksheet electronically as directed by your instructor.

 You have completed Project 10H

Content-Based Assessments

Apply a combination of the 10A and 10B skills.

GO! Make It | Project 10I Snack Supplies

Project Files

For Project 10I, you will need the following file:

e10I_Snack_Supplies

You will save your workbook as:

Lastname_Firstname_10I_Snack_Supplies

Open the file e10I_Snack_Supplies; save it in your Excel Chapter 10 folder as **Lastname_ Firstname_10I_Snack_Supplies** Apply conditional formatting to the Quantity in Stock columns and convert the tables to a range as shown in Figure 10.50. Insert a footer in the left section with the File Name, add your name, your course name and section, and the keywords **snack supplies, inventory** to the document properties. Save the file, and then print the worksheet or submit your worksheet electronically as directed by your instructor.

Project Results

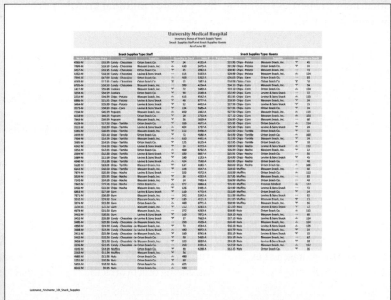

Figure 10.50

End You have completed Project 10I

Content-Based Assessments

Apply a combination of
the 10A and 10B skills.

GO! Solve It | Project 10J Medical Imaging Suppliers

Project Files

For Project 10J, you will need the following files:

    e10J_Medical_Imaging
    e10J_Imaging_Contacts

You will save your workbook as:

    Lastname_Firstname_10J_Medical_Imaging

Open the file **e10J_Medical_Imaging** and save it in your chapter folder as **Lastname_Firstname_10J_Medical_Imaging** On the Medical Imaging Providers worksheet, click in cell **A2**, and then click Get External Data into Excel from Other Sources—From Microsoft Query. Import the MS Access Database* file **e10J_Imaging_Contacts.accdb**. Add all fields to the query. Filter on ZIP 33075 and sort Average Fee in Ascending order. Change to Convert table to a range. In cell A1, format the title attractively. Insert the file name in the footer in the left section. Set the orientation to Landscape and the Width to 1 page. Center horizontally, add appropriate information to the document properties including the keywords **medical imaging providers** and submit as directed by your instructor.

	Performance Level		
	Exemplary: You consistently applied the relevant skills.	**Proficient:** You sometimes, but not always, applied the relevant skills.	**Developing:** You rarely or never applied the relevant skills.
Import Information into Excel from an Access Database	The Imaging Contacts Access database was imported into an Excel workbook correctly.	Not applicable.	The Imaging Contacts Access database was not imported into an Excel workbook.
Create a Query and Use the Query Wizard to Sort and Filter	A query was created that included all fields, filtered on ZIP 33075, and sorted the Average Fee in Ascending order correctly.	A query was created that included some fields, filtered on ZIP 33075, and sorted the Average Fee in Ascending order correctly.	A query was created that included some fields and did not filter on ZIP 33075 or sort the Average Fee in Ascending order.
Apply Convert to Range to a table	The Convert to Range function was applied correctly to a table.	Not applicable.	The Convert to Range function was not applied to a table.

End You have completed Project 10J

Content-Based Assessments

Apply a combination of the **10A** and **10B** skills.

GO! Solve It | Project **10K** Gift Shop Supplies

Project Files

For Project 10K, you will need the following file:

> e10K_Gift_Shop

You will save your workbook as:

> Lastname_Firstname_10K_Gift_Shop

Open the file **e10K_Gift_Shop** and save it as **Lastname_Firstname_10K_Gift_Shop** Insert a table to the Gift Shop Supplies Type: Hospital for the range A7:E62. On the Clinic sheet tab, select and copy the range A1:E52, and then on the Gift Shop Inventory sheet, paste it in the range F6:J57. Insert a Table, and then apply Table Style Medium 11. Delete the Clinic sheet. In each table's *Quantity in Stock* column, apply the Conditional Formatting Icon Sets, Directional, 3 Triangles. Convert each table to a Range. Insert the file name in the footer in the left section. Set the orientation to landscape and center horizontally. Add appropriate information to the document properties including the keywords **gift shop supplies, inventory** and submit as directed by your instructor.

Performance Criteria	Performance Level		
	Exemplary: You consistently applied the relevant skills.	**Proficient:** You sometimes, but not always, applied the relevant skills.	**Developing:** You rarely or never applied the relevant skills.
Insert a Second Table in a Worksheet	A second table is inserted in a worksheet, and tables display side-by-side.	A second table is inserted in a worksheet, but tables do not display side-by-side.	A second table was not inserted in a worksheet.
Apply Conditional Formatting to Side-by-Side Tables	Conditional Formatting Icon Sets, Directional, 3 Triangles is applied to the Quantity in Stock columns.	Conditional Formatting Icon Sets, Directional, 3 Triangles is applied to one but not the other Quantity in Stock column.	Conditional Formatting was not applied to the Quantity in Stock columns.
Convert a Table to a Range	The tables are converted to a range.	One but not the other table is converted to a range.	The tables are not converted to a range.

End You have completed Project 10K

Outcomes-Based Assessments

Rubric

The following outcomes-based assessments are *open-ended assessments*. That is, there is no specific correct result; your result will depend on your approach to the information provided. Make *Professional Quality* your goal. Use the following scoring rubric to guide you in *how* to approach the problem, and then to evaluate *how well* your approach solves the problem.

The *criteria*—Software Mastery, Content, Format and Layout, and Process—represent the knowledge and skills you have gained that you can apply to solving the problem. The *levels of performance*—Professional Quality, Approaching Professional Quality, or Needs Quality Improvements—help you and your instructor evaluate your result.

	Your completed project is of Professional Quality if you:	Your completed project is Approaching Professional Quality if you:	Your completed project Needs Quality Improvements if you:
1-Software Mastery	Choose and apply the most appropriate skills, tools, and features and identify efficient methods to solve the problem.	Choose and apply some appropriate skills, tools, and features, but not in the most efficient manner.	Choose inappropriate skills, tools, or features, or are inefficient in solving the problem.
2-Content	Construct a solution that is clear and well organized, contains content that is accurate, appropriate to the audience and purpose, and is complete. Provide a solution that contains no errors in spelling, grammar, or style.	Construct a solution in which some components are unclear, poorly organized, inconsistent, or incomplete. Misjudge the needs of the audience. Have some errors in spelling, grammar, or style, but the errors do not detract from comprehension.	Construct a solution that is unclear, incomplete, or poorly organized; contains some inaccurate or inappropriate content; and contains many errors in spelling, grammar, or style. Do not solve the problem.
3-Format and Layout	Format and arrange all elements to communicate information and ideas, clarify function, illustrate relationships, and indicate relative importance.	Apply appropriate format and layout features to some elements, but not others. Overuse features, causing minor distraction.	Apply format and layout that does not communicate information or ideas clearly. Do not use format and layout features to clarify function, illustrate relationships, or indicate relative importance. Use available features excessively, causing distraction.
4-Process	Use an organized approach that integrates planning, development, self-assessment, revision, and reflection.	Demonstrate an organized approach in some areas, but not others; or, use an insufficient process of organization throughout.	Do not use an organized approach to solve the problem.

Outcomes-Based Assessments

Apply a combination of the **10A** and **10B** skills.

GO! Think | Project **10L** Facilities Pay

Project Files

For Project 10L, you will need the following file:

> e10L_Facilities_Pay

You will save your workbook as:

> Lastname_Firstname_10L_Facilities_Pay

Open the file **e10L_Facilities_Pay**, and then save it in your chapter folder as **Lastname_Firstname_10L_Facilities_Pay** In this project, you will use a worksheet that contains payroll information for the facilities staff. You will calculate the average pay and count how many employees have worked for the hospital for over five years.

In cell A26, type **Average hourly wage for Housekeeping** In cell E26, type **Classification** and in cell E27, type **Housekeeping** Click cell C27, and insert the DAVERAGE function. In the Database box, select the range A3:F24. In the Field box, type **Hourly Rate** With the Criteria box active, select the range E26:E27, and then click OK. Apply Currency Style to cell C27. In cell A29, type **Number of employees hired prior to 1/1/00** In cell E29, type **Hire Date** and then in cell E30, type **<1/1/00** Click cell C30 and insert the DCOUNT function. In the Database box, select the range A3:F24. In the Field box, type **Emp #** With the Criteria box active, select the range E29:E30, and then click OK.

Insert the file name in the left section of the footer and center horizontally. Add appropriate information to the document properties, including the keywords **facilities pay** and submit as directed by your instructor.

 You have completed Project 10L ————————

Apply a combination of the **10A** and **10B** skills.

GO! Think | Project **10M** Institutes of Health

Project Files

For Project 10M, you will need the following file:

> e10M_Health_Institutes

You will save your workbook as:

> Lastname_Firstname_10M_Health_Institutes

Open the file **e10M_Health_Institutes** and save it as **Lastname_Firstname_10M_Health_Institutes** Insert a table in the Name and Date Established data, and then sort by date, smallest to largest. Convert the table to a range. Merge and center the title across the data, and apply the Title style. Insert a screen shot of the National Institutes of Health website, *www.nih.gov*, below the data and change the height size to 5.25". Insert a custom header with NIH in the right section. Insert a custom footer with the file name in the left section and the date in the right section. Set the width to 1 page. Add appropriate information to the document properties including the keywords **national institutes of health** and submit as directed by your instructor.

 You have completed Project 10M ————————

Outcomes-Based Assessments

Apply a combination of the 10A and 10B skills.

You and GO! | Project **10N** Budget

Project Files

For Project 10N, you will need the following file:

New blank workbook

You will save your workbook as:

Lastname_Firstname_10N_Budget

Open a blank workbook and save the file as **Lastname_Firstname_10N_Budget** Create a personal budget that displays your Budget versus Actual expenses. In the Actual column, apply Conditional Formatting Icon Sets. Create a custom footer with the file name in the left section and the Date and Time in the right section. Set the orientation to landscape and center horizontally. Add appropriate information to the document properties including the keywords **budget, conditional formatting** and submit as directed by your instructor.

 You have completed Project 10N ⎯⎯⎯⎯⎯⎯⎯⎯⎯⎯⎯⎯

Collaborating with Others and Preparing a Workbook for Distribution

OUTCOMES

At the end of this chapter you will be able to:

PROJECT 11A
Assemble changes from multiple sources to collaborate with others.

OBJECTIVES

Mastering these objectives will enable you to:

1. Create a Shared Workbook (p. 667)
2. Track Changes Made to a Workbook (p. 670)
3. Merge Workbooks and Accept Changes (p. 673)

PROJECT 11B
Inspect a document, prepare a workbook for distribution, and store a document in the cloud.

4. Prepare a Final Workbook for Distribution (p. 682)
5. Upload a Workbook to SkyDrive (p. 688)

Joe Brown/Shutterstock

In This Chapter

In this chapter, you will assemble changes from multiple sources to collaborate with others. The process of collaborating typically involves sending a worksheet to others and asking each person to review the worksheet and make changes or add comments. Changes made by different individuals can be tracked and then accepted or rejected. Additionally, you will compare two different versions of a workbook and merge them together.

You will also prepare a final workbook for distribution, inspect the workbook for hidden information, add security by encrypting the workbook with a password, digitally sign the workbook to assure that the signer is who they claim to be, and upload the workbook to a network location.

The projects in this chapter relate to **Laurel College**. The college offers this diverse geographic area a wide range of academic and career programs, including associate degrees, certificate programs, and non-credit continuing education and personal development courses. The college makes positive contributions to the community through cultural and athletic programs and partnerships with businesses and nonprofit organizations. The college also provides industry-specific training programs for local businesses through its growing Economic Development Center.

Project 11A Summer Schedule

Project Activities

In Activities 11.01 through 11.09, you will create a shared workbook so that it can be reviewed by the different department chairpersons in the college's Business Division. Various individuals in the Business Division will be able to edit and comment on the information in the workbook. Your completed workbook will look similar to Figure 11.1.

Project Files

For Project 11A, you will need the following file:

e11A_Summer_Schedule

You will save your workbook as:

Lastname_Firstname_11A_Summer_Schedule

Project Results

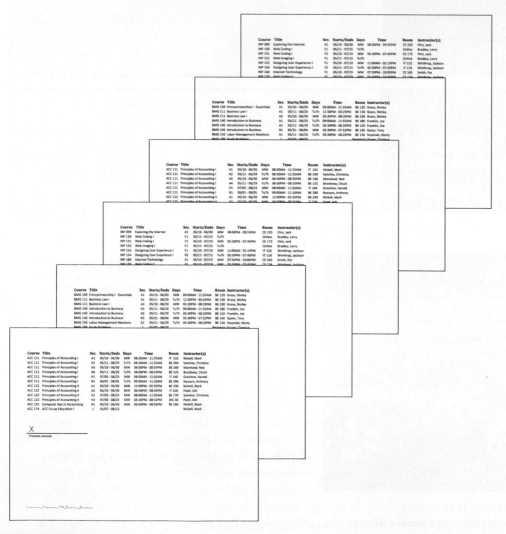

Figure 11.1
Project 11A Summer Schedule

Objective 1 | Create a Shared Workbook

In Excel, *collaboration* refers to the process of working jointly with others to review, comment on, and make necessary changes to a *shared workbook*. A shared workbook is a workbook set up to allow multiple users on a network to view and make changes to the workbook at the same time. Typically the users are on an *intranet*, which is a network within an organization and that uses Internet technologies. When the collaboration process is complete, as the owner of the shared workbook, you can accept or reject the input suggested by others.

Activity 11.01 | Locating and Modifying Workbook Properties

Every Excel workbook file has *properties*, which are details about a file that describe or identify the file, including the title, author name, subject, and keywords that identify the file's topic or contents—also known as *metadata*. Properties also include the size and location of the file. You can change file properties before the file is distributed so that the recipients will know who distributed the file. Some property information displays when you point to a file in a displayed list of files, such as in My Computer or in the Open dialog box.

1 **Start** Excel. From your student files, open the file **e11A_Summer_Schedule**. Display the **Save As** dialog box, navigate to the location where you are storing your files for this chapter, and then create a new folder named **Excel Chapter 11** Open the new folder, and then **Save** the file in your **Excel Chapter 11** folder as **Lastname_Firstname_11A_Summer_Schedule**

> This workbook contains three worksheets listing the proposed summer classes for three departments in the Business Division.

2 Select all three worksheets so that *[Group]* displays in the title bar. On the **Insert tab**, in the **Text group**, click **Header & Footer**, and then in the **Navigation group**, click **Go to Footer**.

3 Click in the **left section** just above the word *Footer*, and then add the **File Name**. Click in a cell above the footer to close the footer area, return to **Normal** ⊞ view, and then press [Ctrl] + [Home] to move to the top of the sheet.

4 In **Backstage** view, on the **Info tab**, at the top of the screen, notice that the location of this file on your computer displays. On the right, notice that some of the more common properties for this file display, for example, the file *Size* and *Author*.

5 Under **Properties**, point to the text *Add a title*, and then click one time. Type **Proposed Summer Schedule** and then compare your screen with Figure 11.2.

> Some of the properties displayed on the Info tab can be changed. For example, you can add a *Title*, add *Tags*, and add *Categories*.

Figure 11.2

Path indicates location of file (yours may vary)

Properties related to this file

Title *Proposed Summer Schedule* added

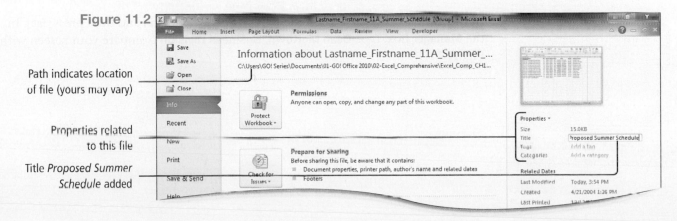

6 Under **Related People**, point to the text *Jason Klein,* who is the author. In the lower right corner of the displayed **Contact Card**, click the **Expand Contact Card arrow** ∨, and then compare your screen with Figure 11.3.

> In a networked environment, from this Contact Card you could send an e-mail to this individual, initiate an IM (Instant Messaging) session, schedule a meeting in Outlook, or look up contact information such as a phone number.

Figure 11.3

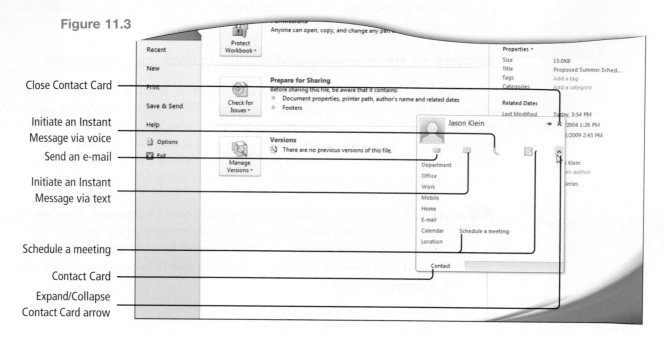

Close Contact Card

Initiate an Instant Message via voice

Send an e-mail

Initiate an Instant Message via text

Schedule a meeting

Contact Card

Expand/Collapse Contact Card arrow

7 **Close** ⊠ the **Contact Card**, and then click **Properties**. On the list, click **Advanced Properties**, and then in the dialog box, if necessary click the **General tab**.

> In the Properties dialog box for a file, there are additional properties that you can view and change. Here, on the General tab, you can see the date the file was last accessed. The Attributes area is dimmed because these properties cannot be changed while the file is open.

8 Click the **Summary tab**.

> The Author name *Jason Klein* was generated from the computer on which the file was originally created. If you receive a file from someone else, which you then modify and use, the original author's name remains with the file, even when you save the file with a new name. If you want your name, division, or company to be associated with the file, change the information located here. Information entered here can also be used by search engines to help locate files.

9 In the **Author** box, delete *Jason Klein,* type **Sean Thompson** and then press [Tab]. In the **Manager** box, type **Dean McKown, Business Division** Compare your screen with Figure 11.4.

Figure 11.4

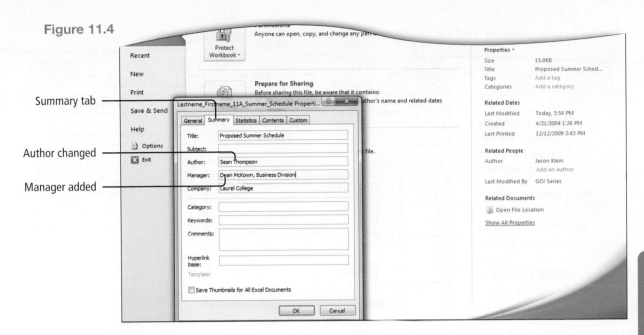

Summary tab

Author changed

Manager added

10 Click **OK**. In the upper right corner of **Backstage** view, click the screen thumbnail to return to the worksheet. Point to the **Accounting sheet tab**, right-click, and then click **Ungroup Sheets**.

11 Save 🖫 your workbook.

> **More Knowledge | Changing Attributes**
>
> One of the attributes that displays in the Properties dialog box is the *Read-only* property. If this property is selected, the file can be read or copied, but it cannot be changed or saved. This property cannot be set while the file is open. To change a file to Read-only, display the file list in Windows Explorer, right-click the file name, and then click Properties. In the Properties dialog box, select the Read-only attribute, and then click OK. When the file is opened, *[Read-only]* will display in the title bar, which indicates that the file cannot be changed or saved. If you need to use a Read-only file, save it with a *new* file name, which preserves the original file.

Activity 11.02 | Activating Track Changes to Create a Shared Workbook

When you share a workbook with others, you control the collaboration process by using Excel's *Track Changes* feature, which logs details about workbook changes including insertions and deletions. When you activate the Track Changes feature, the workbook automatically becomes a shared workbook.

1 On the **Review tab**, in the **Changes group**, click the **Track Changes** button, and then click **Highlight Changes**.

2 Click to select the **Track Changes while editing** check box, which activates the Track Changes feature and saves the file as a shared workbook.

3 Verify that the **When** check box is selected and indicates *All*. Select the **Who** check box and be sure *Everyone* is indicated. Verify that the **Highlight changes on screen** check box is selected, and then compare your screen with Figure 11.5.

> Use onscreen highlighting when there are minimal changes in the workbook or when you want to see, at a glance, what has changed.

Excel | Chapter 11

Figure 11.5

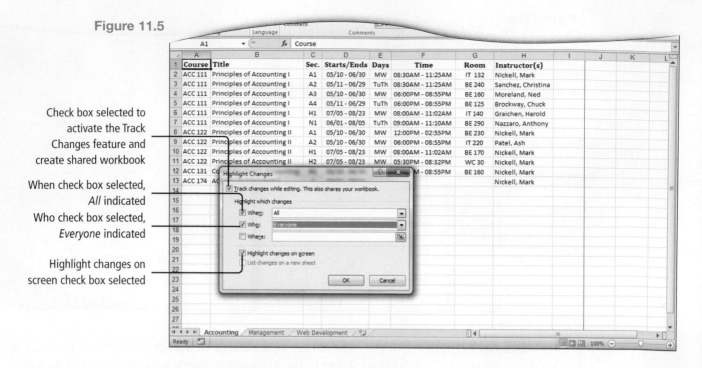

Check box selected to
activate the Track
Changes feature and
create shared workbook

When check box selected,
All indicated

Who check box selected,
Everyone indicated

Highlight changes on
screen check box selected

4 Click **OK**.

A message box displays, informing you that this action will save the workbook.

5 Click **OK** to continue.

The workbook is saved, and *[Shared]* displays on the title bar. The file is ready to be shared by others who will make changes to the proposed summer schedule.

6 Display **Backstage** view, and then click **Close** to close the file and leave Excel open.

Objective 2 | Track Changes Made to a Workbook

As others make changes to a shared workbook, you can view and track the changes they make by viewing the details in the ***change history***—information that is maintained about changes made in past editing sessions. The information includes the name of the person who made each change, when the change was made, and what data was changed. After the changes are recorded, you can review the shared file and accept or reject the changes.

Activity 11.03 | Making a Copy of a Shared Workbook

For individuals who do not have access to the network, make a copy of the shared workbook and send it to them by e-mail. After changes are made to this copy of the shared workbook, it can be returned and merged with the original shared workbook. In this manner, you can view all the changes made by reviewers—even from reviewers who did not have access to the shared workbook. In the following activity, you will make a copy of the shared workbook for Janet Bowman, Chair of the Management Department, because she will not have access to the college's network during the review period.

1 Press Ctrl + F12 to display the **Open** dialog box. Navigate to your **Excel Chapter 11** folder, point to your **Lastname_Firstname_11A_Summer_Schedule** file, right-click, and then on the shortcut menu, click **Copy**.

2 Right-click in an empty space below or to the right of the list of files, and then on the shortcut menu click **Paste**. Compare your screen with Figure 11.6.

> A copy of the shared file is created and is named *Lastname_Firstname_11A_Summer_Schedule - Copy*.

Figure 11.6

Your Excel Chapter 11 folder

Original file

Copy of file indicates - *Copy*

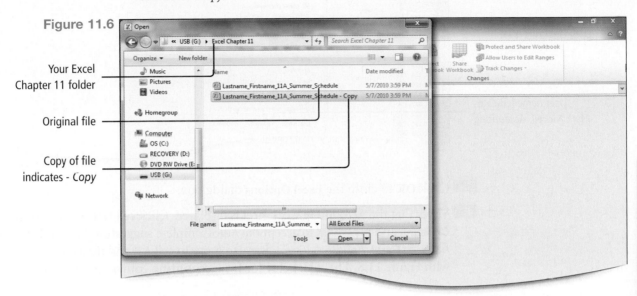

3 **Close** the **Open** dialog box.

Activity 11.04 | Making Changes to a Shared Workbook

Recall that each department's chairperson needs to review the summer schedule and make any necessary changes. In the following activity, you will open the file and make the changes for Mark Nickell, Chair of the Accounting Department, and for Jackson Winthrop, Chair of the Web Development Department.

1 Display the **Open** dialog box, navigate to your chapter folder, and then open your **Lastname_Firstname_11A_Summer_Schedule** file—open the original, *not* the copy that you made.

> Notice that the title bar displays *[Shared]* at the end of the file name.

2 Display **Backstage** view, and then near the bottom of the **Backstage tabs**, click **Options**. In the **Excel Options** dialog box, on the left, verify **General** is selected.

3 Under **Personalize your copy of Microsoft Office**, click in the **User name** box.

> The Excel Options dialog box displays, and the *User name* assigned to your computer displays.

4 On a piece of paper, write down the User name that displays so that you can restore it later. Select the User name text, type **Mark Nickell, Accounting** to replace the selected User name text. Compare your screen with Figure 11.7.

> From this point forward, any changes made to the file will display this user name until you change the User name again.

> **Note** | Changing the User Name
>
> Under normal circumstances, you would not change the user name. The person making changes would be using his or her own computer, which would already display their name in the User name box. In this project, you are changing the user name for instructional purposes.

Excel | Chapter 11

Figure 11.7

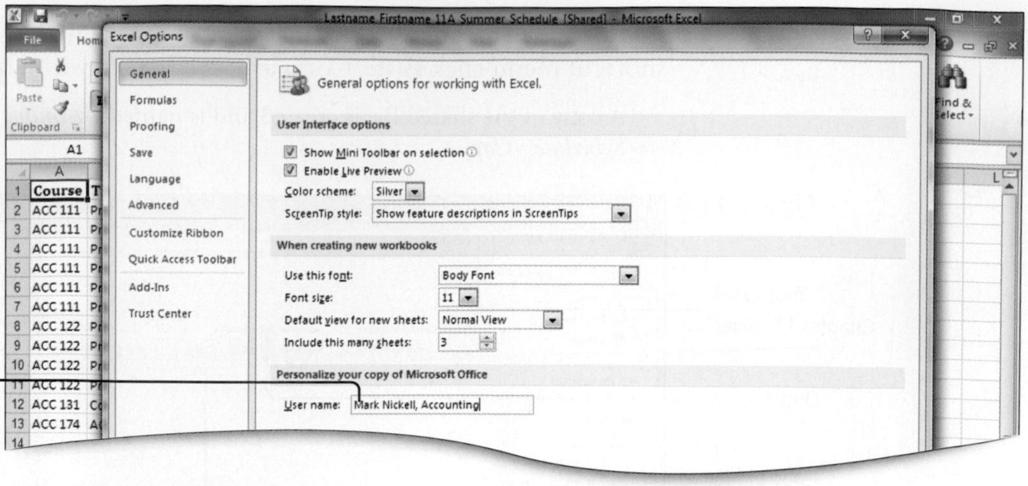

User name indicates
Mark Nickell, Accounting

5 Click **OK** to close the **Excel Options** dialog box.

6 Verify that the **Accounting** worksheet is displayed. Click cell **H10**, begin to type **Sanchez, Christina** and press [Enter] to accept the AutoComplete suggestion. In cell **H11**, change the name to **Patel, Ash** Press [Ctrl] + [Home] to move to cell **A1**, and then compare your screen with Figure 11.8. The instructor for two accounting courses is changed.

Figure 11.8

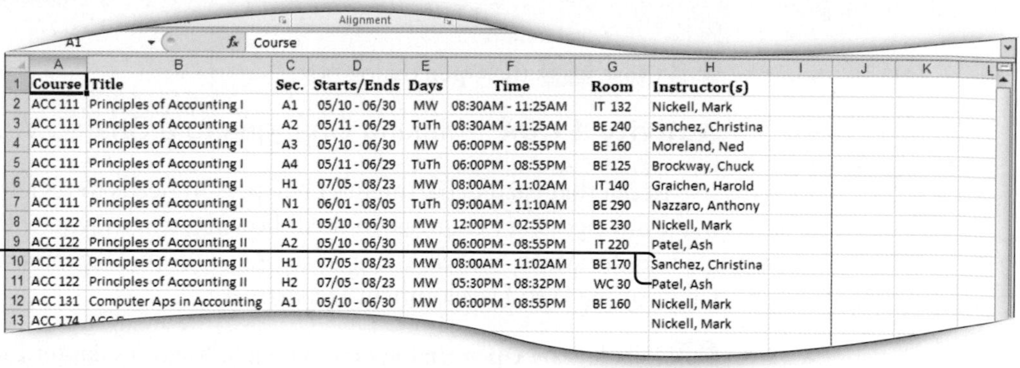

Two instructor names
changed in cells
H10 and H11

7 On the **Review tab**, in the **Changes group**, click the **Track Changes** button, and then click **Highlight Changes**. In the **Highlight Changes** dialog box, click the **When arrow**, and then click **All**. If necessary, select the **Who** check box, and be sure that it indicates *Everyone*. Click **OK**.

By activating Highlight Changes, the two cells changed by Mark Nickell are outlined in blue with a Track Changes indicator shown in the upper left corner of each cell.

8 Point to each of the changed cells to view the ScreenTip, which indicates the change that was made and the date and time the change was made. See Figure 11.9.

Figure 11.9

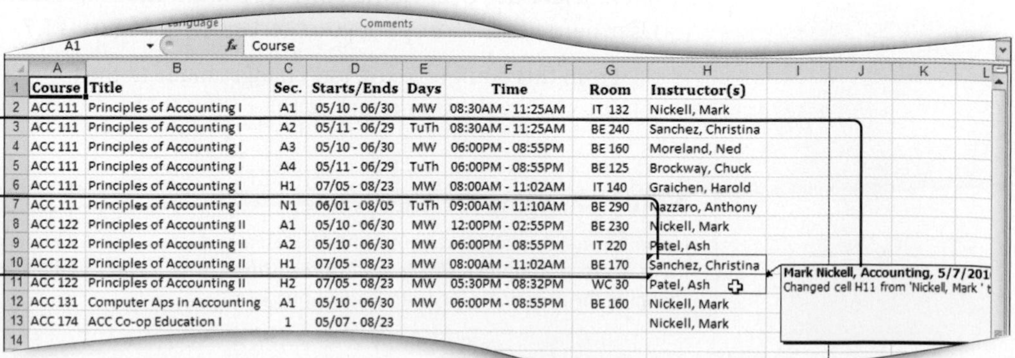

ScreenTip (your
date will differ)

Track Changes
indicator in cell

Changed cells
outlined in blue

9 Save 🖫 your workbook, and then in the upper right corner of your screen, click the lower **Close Window** button ⊠ to close the file and leave Excel open.

10 Press [Ctrl] + [F12] to display the **Open** dialog box. Navigate to and then reopen your **Lastname_Firstname_11A_Summer_Schedule** file—*not* the copy.

11 From **Backstage** view, display the **Excel Options** dialog box, and then using the technique you practiced, change the **User name** to **Jackson Winthrop, Web Development** and then click **OK**.

To change the user name for the next set of changes, you must close and then reopen the file.

12 Display the **Web Development** worksheet. Click cell **F3** and type **Online** Click cell **F5**, type **Online** and then press [Enter].

This completes the changes made by Mr. Winthrop, Chair of the Web Development Department.

13 Press [Ctrl] + [Home] to make cell **A1** the active cell. **Save** 🖫 your workbook. **Close** ⊠ the file and leave Excel open.

Activity 11.05 | Making Changes to a Copy of the Shared Workbook

Recall that a copy of the shared workbook was prepared for Janet Bowman, Chair of the Management Department. In this activity, you will make Ms. Bowman's changes on her copy of the shared workbook.

1 Open the **Lastname_Firstname_11A_Summer_Schedule - Copy** file that you created earlier.

Notice that the title bar displays *Copy [Shared]* at the end of the file name.

2 From **Backstage** view, display the **Excel Options** dialog box, and then change the **User name** to **Janet Bowman, Management** and then click **OK**.

3 Display the **Management** worksheet. Click cell **G9** and type **Permission** Click cell **H12** and type **Bandino, Michael** Select **column G** and apply **AutoFit**.

4 Save 🖫 your workbook, and then **Close** ⊠ Excel.

Objective 3 | Merge Workbooks and Accept Changes

After others make changes to the shared workbook, you can view and then accept or reject their changes. When more than one copy of the shared workbook contains marked changes, first merge the workbooks so that you can view everyone's changes in a single workbook.

Activity 11.06 | Merging Revisions

Recall that because she was not connected to the network, the Chair of the Management Department made her changes on a separate copy of the shared workbook. In this activity, you will merge the two workbooks so that you can view everyone's changes in a single workbook.

1 **Start** Excel. From **Backstage** view, display the **Excel Options** dialog box, and then change the **User name** to **Dean McKown** Click **OK** to close the dialog box, and then open your **Lastname_Firstname_11A_Summer_Schedule** file.

The Dean of the Business Division must review the changes before the file is submitted to the Vice President for final schedule preparation.

2 Display the **Accounting** worksheet. On the **Review tab**, in the **Changes group**, click the **Track Changes** button, and then click **Highlight Changes**.

3 In the displayed **Highlight Changes** dialog box, click the **When arrow**, and then click **All**. Click the **Who arrow**, and then click **Everyone but Me**. Click **OK**. Compare your screen with Figure 11.10.

> By selecting *Everyone but Me*, you can accept or reject changes without your own actions being recorded as a change. A Track Changes indicator displays in the upper left corner of the cells that were changed on this worksheet, and the cells display a colored border.

Figure 11.10

Two changed cells identified

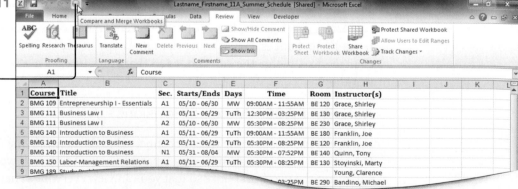

4 Display the **Web Development** worksheet and notice the borders around cells **F3** and **F5** indicating that changes have been made.

Another Way

Right-click the **Quick Access Toolbar**, click **Customize Quick Access Toolbar**, click the **Choose commands from arrow**, click **Commands Not in the Ribbon**, scroll as necessary, and then click **Compare and Merge Workbooks**. Click **Add** and then click **OK**.

5 Display the **Management** worksheet, and notice that no changes are indicated because changes for this department were made on another copy of the shared workbook.

6 From **Backstage** view, display the **Excel Options** dialog box, and then on the left, click **Quick Access Toolbar**.

7 At the top of the dialog box, under **Customize the Quick Access Toolbar**, click the **Choose commands from arrow**, and then click **Commands Not in the Ribbon**. In the list below, scroll as necessary, click **Compare and Merge Workbooks**, in the center click the **Add** button, and then click **OK**. Compare your screen with Figure 11.11.

> The Compare and Merge Workbooks command is added to the Quick Access Toolbar.

Figure 11.11

Compare and Merge Workbooks command on the Quick Access Toolbar

8 On the Quick Access Toolbar, click the **Compare and Merge Workbooks** button. In the **Select Files to Merge Into Current Workbook** dialog box, navigate to your **Excel Chapter 11** folder. Compare your screen with Figure 11.12.

> Here you select the workbook to be merged into the open workbook.

Figure 11.12

Select Files to Merge Into Current Workbook dialog box

Path to your chapter folder displayed in address bar

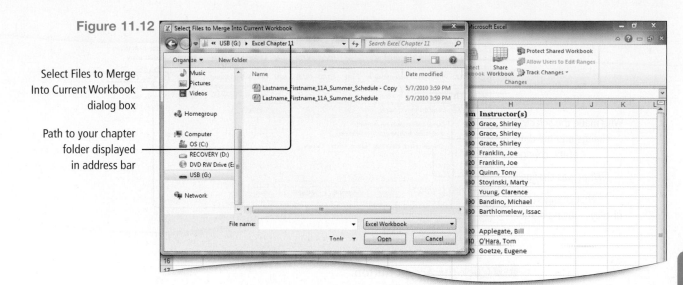

9 Locate your **Lastname_Firstname_11A_Summer_Schedule - Copy** file—if necessary, point to the file names to display the complete file name in the ScreenTip—and then click to select it. Click **OK**, and then compare your screen with Figure 11.13.

> After a moment, a colored border displays around cells G9 and H12 on the Management sheet, and the changes from the file Lastname_Firstname_11A_Summer_Schedule - Copy are merged into the original file.

Figure 11.13

Changes from the merged file bordered

	A	B	C	D	E	F	G	H	I	J	K
1	Course	Title	Sec.	Starts/Ends	Days	Time	Room	Instructor(s)			
2	BMG 109	Entrepreneurship I - Essentials	A1	05/10 - 06/30	MW	09:00AM - 11:55AM	BE 120	Grace, Shirley			
3	BMG 111	Business Law I	A1	05/11 - 06/29	TuTh	12:30PM - 03:25PM	BE 130	Grace, Shirley			
4	BMG 111	Business Law I	A2	05/11 - 06/30	MW	05:30PM - 08:25PM	BE 230	Grace, Shirley			
5	BMG 140	Introduction to Business	A1	05/11 - 06/29	TuTh	09:00AM - 11:55AM	BE 180	Franklin, Joe			
6	BMG 140	Introduction to Business	A2	05/11 - 06/29	TuTh	05:30PM - 08:25PM	BE 120	Franklin, Joe			
7	BMG 140	Introduction to Business	N1	05/31 - 08/04	MW	05:30PM - 07:52PM	BE 140	Quinn, Tony			
8	BMG 150	Labor-Management Relations	A1	05/11 - 06/29	TuTh	05:30PM - 08:25PM	BE 130	Stoyinski, Marty			
9	BMG 189	Study Problems	1	05/07 - 08/23			Permission	Young, Clarence			
10	BMG 200	Human Relations in Business	A1	05/10 - 06/30	MW	12:30PM - 03:25PM	BE 290	Bandino, Michael			
11	BMG 207	Business Communication	A1	05/11 - 06/29	TuTh	05:30PM - 08:25PM	BE 180	Barthlomelew, Issac			
12	BMG 207	Business Communication	N1	05/31 - 08/04	MW	08:00AM - 10:22AM		Bandino, Michael			
13	BMG 208	Principles of Management	A1	05/10 - 06/30	MW	05:30PM - 08:25PM	WC 20	Applegate, Bill			
14	BMG 265	Business Statistics	N1	05/31 - 08/04	MW	11:00AM - 01:22PM	BE140	O'Hara, Tom			
15	BMG 279	Performance Management	A2	05/10 - 06/30	MW	05:30PM - 08:25PM	BE 270	Goetze, Eugene			
16											
17											

Activity 11.07 | Accepting or Rejecting Tracked Changes

Now that each person's changes have been incorporated into one copy of the workbook, you can review each change and decide whether to accept the change and keep the new value or to reject the change and keep the cell's original value. After a proposed change is accepted or rejected, the tracking notation is removed from the cell.

1 Display the **Accounting** worksheet. On the **Review tab**, in the **Changes group**, click the **Track Changes** button, and then click **Accept/Reject Changes**.

> The Select Changes to Accept or Reject dialog box displays. Here you set the parameters for reviewing changes.

2 Verify that the **When** box indicates *Not yet reviewed*. Change the **Who** box to indicate **Everyone**, and then click **OK**. Compare your screen with Figure 11.14.

> The Accept or Reject Changes dialog box displays, and the first changed cell is surrounded by a moving border. If necessary, drag the dialog box so you can view the changed cell.

Figure 11.14

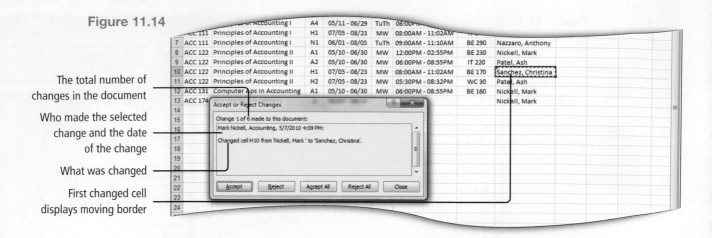

The total number of changes in the document

Who made the selected change and the date of the change

What was changed

First changed cell displays moving border

3 Click the **Accept** button.

The change is accepted and the next changed cell displays a moving border. The Accept or Reject Changes dialog box displays the information for the change in cell H11—from *Nickell, Mark* to *Patel, Ash*.

4 Click the **Accept** button. Compare your screen with Figure 11.15.

The change is accepted and the next change, which is on the Web Development worksheet, is selected. This is the third of six changes that were made to the shared workbook.

Figure 11.15

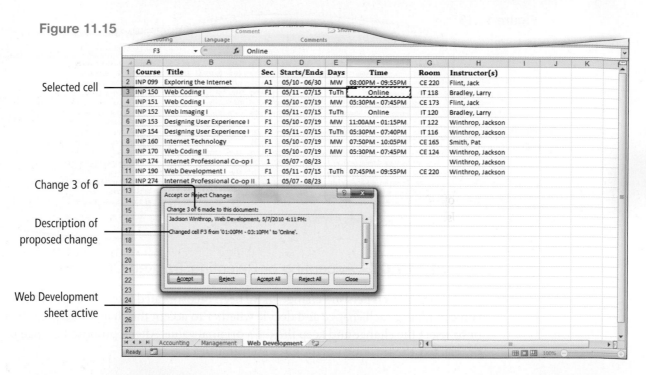

Selected cell

Change 3 of 6

Description of proposed change

Web Development sheet active

5 Click the **Reject** button.

The change is rejected, and the cell returns to its former value—a specific time range. Online classes must be indicated in the Room column rather than the Time column, and the Time column must be left blank. You will adjust this later. The next change is selected.

6 **Reject** the next change—change 4 of 6.

The change is rejected. The next change, in cell G9, which was changed from blank to *Permission*, is selected on the Management worksheet.

7 Click **Accept**, and then **Accept** the last change—a change in instructor to *Michael Bandino*.

The cells that were changed to *Online* were returned to a specific time range. All the changes have been reviewed, and the Accept or Reject Changes dialog box closes. The Accounting sheet redisplays on the screen, and the changes that were reviewed and accepted are still indicated on the sheet.

8 Display the **Web Development** worksheet, click cell **F3**, and then press Del. Press Tab and in cell **G3**, type **Online**. Click cell **F5** and press Del. Press Tab and in cell **G5**, type **Online** and press Enter. Compare your screen with Figure 11.16.

The classes taught by Larry Bradley are online classes, so the Time column is left blank and *Online* is entered in the Room column.

Figure 11.16

Room indicates *Online*

Times removed

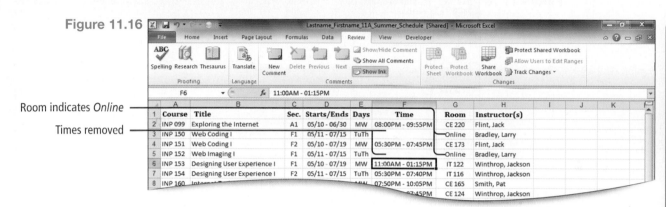

9 **Save** 📁 your workbook.

Activity 11.08 | Removing the Shared Designation, Resetting the User Name, and Removing a Command from the Quick Access Toolbar

After the changes have been reviewed and before the workbook is published, the Shared designation must be removed from the workbook. Removing the Shared designation will also turn off the Track Changes feature and remove the tracking indicators. Because you changed the User name for this project, you will also restore your computer's original User name.

1 On the **Review tab**, in the **Changes group**, click the **Share Workbook** button. Compare your screen with Figure 11.17.

The Share Workbook dialog box displays and indicates the name of the person who is currently using the file—*Dean McKown*.

Figure 11.17

Share Workbook dialog box

Changes are allowed by more than one user at a time

Person currently using the workbook

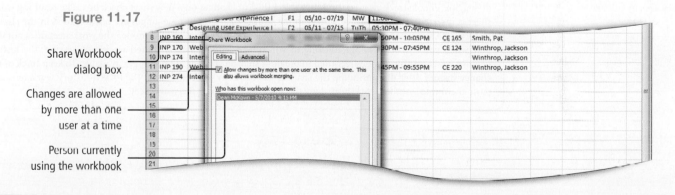

2 Clear the **Allow changes by more than one user at the same time** check box, and then click **OK**. On the displayed **Microsoft Excel** information box, click **Yes**.

> The dialog box closes, *[Shared]* no longer displays on the title bar, and the tracking indicators are removed from the changed cells.

3 Display **Backstage** view, and then at the bottom of the **Backstage tabs**, click **Options**. In the **Excel Options** dialog box, on the left, click **General**.

4 Under **Personalize your copy of Microsoft Office**, click in the **User name** box. Compare your screen with Figure 11.18.

> The Excel Options dialog box displays, and *Dean McKown* displays as the *User name*.

Figure 11.18

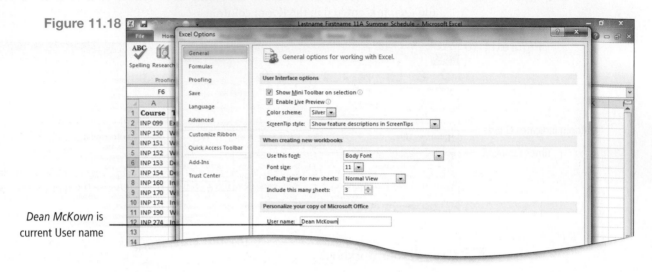

Dean McKown is current User name

5 Select the text *Dean McKown*, and then type the name that you wrote down in Activity 11.04 to replace the selected User name text, and then click **OK**.

> The original User name is restored.

6 On the **Quick Access Toolbar**, right-click the **Compare and Merge Workbooks** button ⬡, and then click **Remove from Quick Access Toolbar**. Click **OK** to close the **Excel Options** dialog box.

More Knowledge | Change History

Recall that in a shared workbook, information that is maintained about changes made in past editing sessions is called the change history. The change history includes the name of the person who made each change, when the change was made, and what data was changed. When this feature is enabled, Excel creates a history worksheet detailing the changes made to the shared workbook. To enable change history, in the Highlight Changes dialog box, enable track changes, and then select the List changes on a new sheet check box. The resulting worksheet is inserted after the last worksheet in the workbook. Formatting changes are not recorded in the change history. The history worksheet displays only when a worksheet is in shared mode. The worksheet does not display when you turn off change tracking. If you subsequently restart a shared workbook session, the history begins anew, and any changes recorded in previous sharing sessions are no longer available. To keep track of the change history after discontinuing the sharing session, copy the contents of the locked history worksheet and paste them into another worksheet, copy the worksheet, or print the worksheet.

Activity 11.09 | Adding a Signature Line

A *digital signature*, also called a *digital ID* or a *digital certificate*, is a digital means of proving identity and authenticity. Digital certificates are issued by a certification authority, and like a driver's license, can expire or be revoked.

You must have a current digital certificate to digitally sign an Office document. You can obtain a digital certificate from a *certificate authority*, which is a commercial organization that issues digital certificates, keeps track of who is assigned to a certificate, signs certificates to verify their validity, and tracks which certificates are revoked or expired. Institutions, governments, and corporations can also issue their own digital certificates. A digital certificate works by providing a cryptographic key pair that is associated with a digital signature.

A digital certificate authenticates—verifies that people and products are who and what they claim to be—the digital signature. A digital signature helps to assure that the signer is who they claim to be, helps to assure that the document content has not been changed or tampered with since it was digitally signed, and helps to prove to all parties the origin of the signed content. It cannot be repudiated—the signer cannot deny association with the signed content.

A digital signature may be visible or invisible. In either case, the digital signature references a digital certificate, which authenticates the *source* of the signature. When you create your own certificate, it is referred to as a *self-signed* project. Certificates you create yourself are considered unauthenticated; however, self-signed projects are considered safer to open than those with no certificates at all. In this activity, you will create a digital signature line for the Summer Schedule workbook.

1 Display the **Accounting** worksheet, and then click cell **A15**. On the **Insert tab**, in the **Text group**, click the **Signature Line button arrow**, and then click **Microsoft Office Signature Line**. In the displayed **Microsoft Excel** dialog box, click **OK**. Compare your screen with Figure 11.19.

> The Signature Setup dialog box displays. A *signature line* specifies the individual who must sign the document. Inserting an actual digital signature requires that you obtain a digital ID.

Figure 11.19

Signature Setup dialog box

Excel | Chapter 11

2 In the **Signature Setup** dialog box, with the insertion point blinking in the **Suggested signer** box and *using your own name*, type **Firstname Lastname** and then click **OK**. Compare your screen with Figure 11.20.

> The signature line with a large X displays on the worksheet. *Firstname Lastname* displays below the signature line.

Figure 11.20

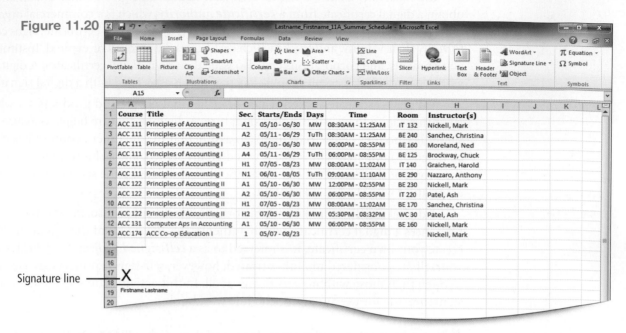

Signature line

3 Display the **Document Panel** and in the **Author** box, delete the contents, and then type your Firstname and Lastname. In the **Subject** box, type your course name and section number, and in the **Keywords** box, type **summer courses Close** ✕ the Document Panel.

4 Display and check the **Print Preview**, make any necessary corrections. **Save** 🖫 and then print or submit your workbook electronically as directed. **Close** ✕ and **Exit** Excel.

End **You have completed Project 11A** ─────────

Project 11B Distributed Workbook

Project Activities

In Activities 11.10 through 11.14, you will assist Michael Schaeffler, Vice President of Academic Affairs, in distributing a workbook to the instructional deans at the college. Your completed workbook will look similar to Figure 11.21.

Project Files

For Project 11B, you will need the following file:

e11B_Courses

You will save your workbooks as:

Lastname_Firstname_11B_Courses
Lastname_Firstname_11B_Courses_Compatibility
Lastname_Firstname_11B_Courses_Encrypted

Project Results

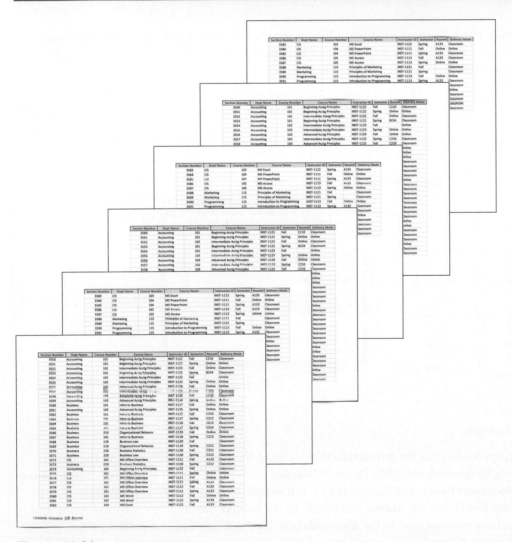

Figure 11.21
Project 11B Distributed Workbook

Objective 4 | Prepare a Final Workbook for Distribution

Before distributing Excel workbooks to others, review the contents of the workbook to ensure that it does not contain sensitive or personal information that you do not want to share with other people. Such information might be stored in the document itself or in the document properties.

Activity 11.10 | Ensuring Backward-Compatibility in a Workbook

To ensure that an Excel 2010 workbook does not have compatibility issues that cause a significant loss of functionality or a minor loss of fidelity in an earlier version of Excel, you can run the *Compatibility Checker*. The Compatibility Checker finds any potential compatibility issues and creates a report so that you can resolve the issues. When you work on a workbook in Compatibility Mode, where the workbook is in Excel 97-2003 file format (.xls) instead of the newer XML-based file format (.xlsx), the Compatibility Checker runs automatically when you save a workbook. In this activity, you will run the Compatibility Checker to identify features in the workbook that cannot be transferred to earlier versions of Excel.

1 **Start** Excel. From your student files, open the file **e11B_Courses**. Display **Backstage** view, in the center panel, click the **Check for Issues** button, and then click **Check Compatibility**. Compare your screen with Figure 11.22.

> The Microsoft Excel - Compatibility Checker dialog box displays. The Compatibility Checker displays one minor loss of fidelity issue with formatting styles. The formats—cell title fill and font Theme Colors—will be converted to the closest format available when the worksheet is saved in an earlier version of Excel.

Figure 11.22

Compatibility Checker dialog box

Minor loss of fidelity

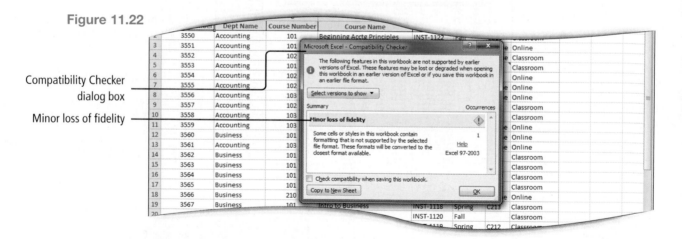

2 Click **OK**.

3 Insert a footer in the **left section** that includes the **File Name**. Click above the footer area to deselect, and then return to **Normal** view. Make cell **A1** the active cell. Show the **Document Panel**. The Author field is not supported in Excel 97-2003 Workbook type; therefore, leave the **Author** box blank. In the **Subject** box, type your course name and section number, and in the **Keywords** box, type **courses list, compatibility** Close ⊠ the **Document Panel**.

4 Press F12 to display the **Save As** dialog box. At the bottom of the dialog box, click the **Save as type arrow**, and then near the top of the list, click **Excel 97-2003 Workbook**. **Save** the file in your **Excel Chapter 11** folder as **Lastname_Firstname_11B_Courses_ Compatibility**

> The Microsoft Excel - Compatibility Checker dialog box displays.

5 In the **Microsoft Excel - Compatibility Checker** dialog box, click the **Continue** button.

> The file is saved in an earlier version of Excel—Excel 97-2003.

6 In **Backstage** view, click **Close** to close the workbook. Leave Excel open for the next activity.

Activity 11.11 | Inspecting a Document

In this activity, you will use the *Document Inspector*, which is an Excel feature that can find and remove hidden properties and personal information in a workbook. In this activity, you will inspect the workbook and review the results that the Document Inspector finds to determine what information, if any, should be removed. Because some information is not needed by the distribution recipients of the Courses document, Michael Schaeffler, Vice President of Academic Affairs, has asked you to remove some information.

1 From your student files, open the file **e11B_Courses** and then **Save** the file in your **Excel Chapter 11** folder as **Lastname_Firstname_11B_Courses** Insert a footer in the **left section** that includes the **File Name**. Click above the footer area to deselect, and then return to **Normal** view. Make cell **A1** the active cell. Show the **Document Panel**. In the **Author** box, type your firstname and lastname, in the **Subject** box, type your course name and section number, and in the **Keywords** box, type **courses list** Close ⊠ the **Document Panel**. **Save** 🖬 the worksheet.

2 Display **Backstage** view, be sure the **Info tab** is active, and then in the **Prepare for Sharing group**, click the **Check for Issues** button. On the displayed list, click **Inspect Document**. Compare your screen with Figure 11.23.

> The Document Inspector dialog box displays and lists the various types of content that will be checked. By default, all the check boxes are selected.

Figure 11.23

Info tab active

Document Inspector dialog box

All check boxes are selected

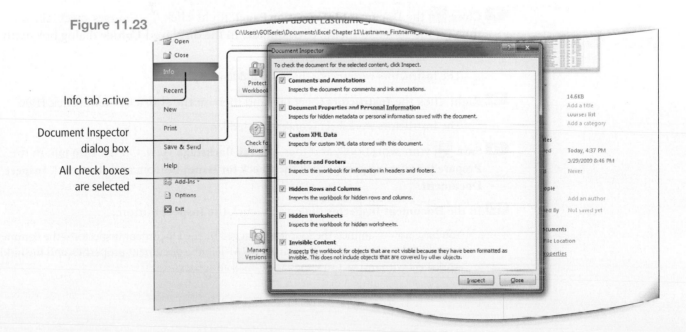

3 In the lower right corner of the dialog box, click the **Inspect** button. Compare your screen with Figure 11.24.

The Document Inspector indicates four categories that contain sensitive or personal information. A red exclamation point and a Remove All button display in the inspection results for these four categories. In this workbook, the Document Inspector found comments, document properties, footer, and a hidden worksheet.

Figure 11.24

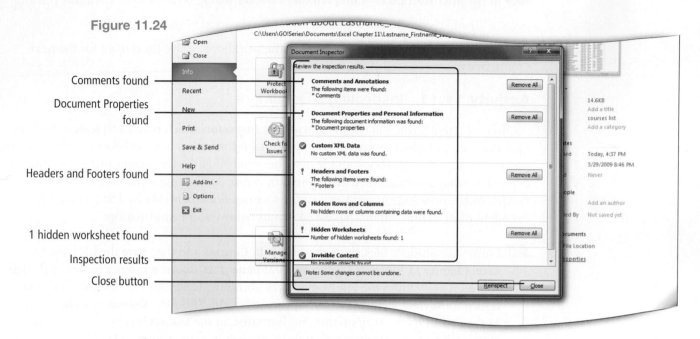

Comments found

Document Properties found

Headers and Footers found

1 hidden worksheet found

Inspection results

Close button

4 Click the **Close** button to close the **Document Inspector** dialog box, and then in the upper right corner of **Backstage** view, click the screen thumbnail to return to the worksheet.

5 Click cell **G5**, and notice the comment that displays.

6 Display **Backstage** view, click the **Properties** button, and then click **Show Document Panel**. Notice that in the **Status** box, *DRAFT* displays.

7 Close ☒ the **Document Information Panel**. Right-click the **Courses** sheet tab, and then on the shortcut menu, click **Unhide**. In the displayed **Unhide** dialog box, with *Instructors* selected, click **OK**.

The Instructors worksheet, which was hidden, displays.

8 Right-click the **Instructors** sheet tab, and then on the shortcut menu, click **Hide**.

The Instructors worksheet is once again hidden.

9 Save 🖫 your workbook, and then display **Backstage** view. On the **Info tab**, in the **Prepare for Sharing group**, click the **Check for Issues** button, and then click **Inspect Document**.

10 In the **Document Inspector** dialog box, click the **Inspect** button.

You have now examined the four items flagged by the Document Inspector—the comment regarding the new podium, the subject DRAFT in the document properties, and the hidden worksheet with instructor names and e-mail addresses.

11 To the right of **Comments and Annotations**, click the **Remove All** button. To the right of **Document Properties and Personal Information**, click the **Remove All** button. To the right of **Headers and Footers**, click the **Remove All** button. To the right of **Hidden Worksheets**, click the **Remove All** button. Compare your screen with Figure 11.25.

The comments, document properties, footer, and hidden worksheet are removed from the file. This information is not needed by the distribution recipients of the Courses document. If you remove the hidden worksheet, you are losing this data, so if you want to keep it, make a copy elsewhere.

Figure 11.25

Comments successfully removed

Document Properties and personal information successfully removed

Headers and footers were removed

Hidden worksheet removed

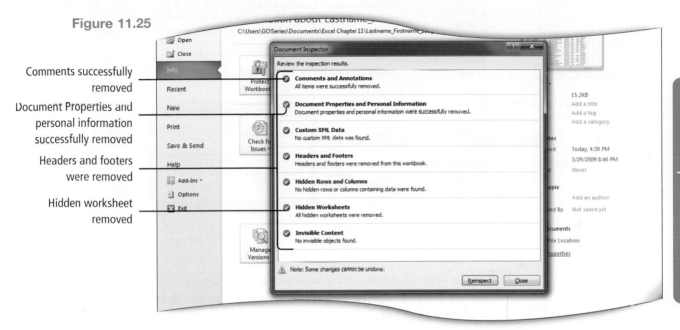

12 In the lower right corner of the **Document Inspector** dialog box, click the **Close** button.

13 In the upper right corner of **Backstage** view, click the screen thumbnail to return to the worksheet. Insert a footer in the **left section** that includes the **File Name**, and then click **Save**.

Activity 11.12 | Encrypting a Workbook

You can provide another level of security for your workbook by adding encryption. *Encryption* is the process by which a file is encoded so that it cannot be *opened* without the proper password. Encryption is more than simple password protection—the process digitally obscures information to make it unreadable without a proper key to decode it. Passwords prevent users from *editing* a worksheet or the entire workbook. Encryption is different—it prevents users from *opening* the file. In this activity, you will apply encryption to your Courses workbook.

1 With your **Lastname_Firstname_11B_Courses** workbook open, press [F12] to display the **Save As** dialog box, and then **Save** the file in your **Excel Chapter 11** folder as **Lastname_Firstname_11B_Courses_Encrypted** Add a footer in the **left section** that includes the **File Name**. Click above the footer area to deselect, and then return to **Normal** view. Make cell **A1** the active cell. Show the **Document Panel**. In the **Author** box, type your firstname and lastname, in the **Subject** box, type your course name and section number, and in the **Keywords** box, type **courses list, encrypted Close** the **Document Panel**.

2 Display **Backstage** view, and be sure the **Info tab** is active. In the **Permissions group**, click the **Protect Workbook** button, and then on the displayed list, click **Encrypt with Password**. Compare your screen with Figure 11.26.

The Encrypt Document dialog box displays. A box in which to type the password and a note of caution about entering passwords displays.

Figure 11.26

Protect Workbook button in the Permissions group in Backstage view

Encrypt Document dialog box

Password box

Caution note

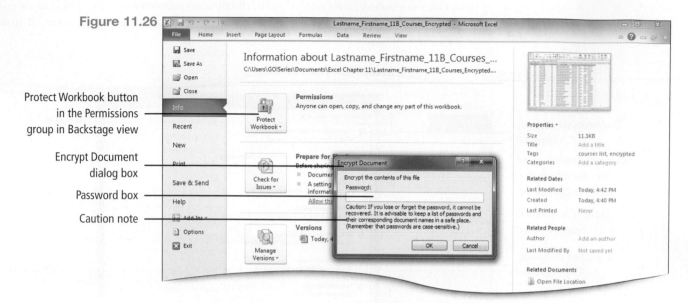

3 In the displayed **Encrypt Document** dialog box, with the insertion point blinking in the **Password** box, type **go** and then click **OK**. In the **Reenter password** box, type **go** and then click **OK**.

More Knowledge | Making Passwords More Secure

The Windows Help system has the following suggestions for secure passwords: "A more secure or strong password is one that's difficult for others to determine by guessing or by using automated programs. Strong passwords contain 7-16 characters, do not include common words˙or names, and combine uppercase letters, lowercase letters, numbers, and symbols."

---

4 Click **Save** and **Close** the workbook. Leave Excel open.

5 Press `Ctrl` + `F12` to display the **Open** dialog box. Navigate to your **Excel Chapter 11** folder, and then open your **Lastname_Firstname_11B_Courses_Encrypted** file.

The Password dialog box displays. The workbook cannot be opened without the password.

6 Type **go** and then click **OK**.

Your Lastname_Firstname_11B_Courses_Encrypted workbook opens.

Alert! | Does the Workbook Not Open?

If the workbook does not open, you may have mistyped the password; try typing the password again. If the workbook still does not open, you may have mistyped the password and the reenter password when you encrypted the workbook. There is no simple way to recover a mistyped password from an encrypted document. Open the Lastname_Firstname_11B_Courses file, and repeat Steps 1 through 6.

Activity 11.13 | Marking a Workbook as Final

Before you share a workbook, you can apply the *Mark as Final command*, which makes the document read-only. The Mark as Final command prevents additional changes to the document and disables typing, editing comments, and proofing marks. When the document is opened by others, the user will be notified by Microsoft Excel that the document has been *Marked as Final*. In this activity, you will mark the workbook as final.

1 With your **Lastname_Firstname_11B_Courses_Encrypted** workbook open, display **Backstage** view. With the **Info tab** active, in the **Permissions group**, click the **Protect Workbook** button, and then click **Mark as Final**.

> The Microsoft Excel dialog box displays and indicates that the workbook will be marked as final and then saved.

2 Click **OK**. Read the displayed message box, and then click **OK**. Click the **Home tab** to return to the worksheet, and then compare your screen to Figure 11.27.

> The workbook is marked as final. The title bar displays *[Read-Only]* to indicate the file can be read but not edited. A yellow bar displays below the Ribbon tabs, indicating that *An author has marked this workbook as final to discourage editing.* The Marked as Final icon [Marked as Final] displays on the status bar. If someone opening the file clicks the Edit Anyway button, the workbook will no longer be *Marked as Final* and will not be a Read-Only file.

Figure 11.27

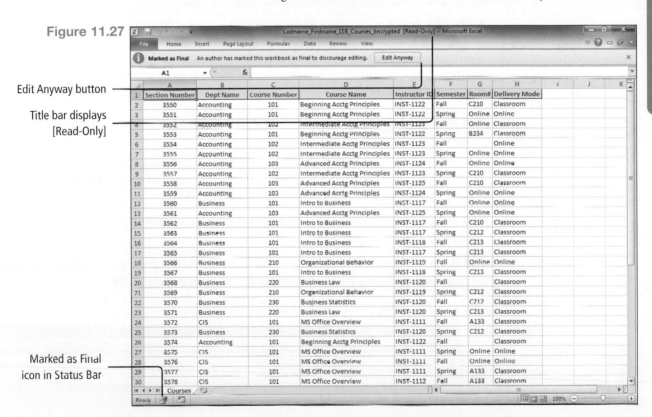

Edit Anyway button

Title bar displays [Read-Only]

Marked as Final icon in Status Bar

3 Click any cell and type a number or text to confirm the workbook cannot be edited. **Close** Excel.

> **More Knowledge | Mark as Final Feature**
>
> The Mark as Final command is not a security feature. Anyone can edit a document that has been marked as final by removing the Mark as Final status from the document, editing the file, and then reapplying the Mark as Final status. To ensure that a workbook cannot be edited, you must password protect the workbook. Mark as Final signifies the intent of the author that the document is final in content.

Objective 5 | Upload a Workbook to SkyDrive

Microsoft offers a free online service, ***Windows Live SkyDrive***, which provides file storage and file sharing services on a Windows Live Internet site. You can upload files and then access them from any computer with Internet access and Web browsing software such as Internet Explorer.

SkyDrive uses ***Windows Live ID*** for security to control access to your files. Online file storage is helpful for keeping files in one location rather than on multiple devices or in several locations. It is also useful for sharing files with others who can access your information with an Internet browser. In SkyDrive, you can share files or keep them private.

Windows Live Essentials, of which SkyDrive is a part, enables you to engage in a form of ***cloud computing***, which means using the Web servers of a third party provider—Microsoft in this instance—on the Internet—the cloud—to store files and run applications.

> **More Knowledge | The Windows Live Essentials Suite of Products Is Fast Changing**
>
> Windows Live Essentials is a free collection of applications and services for Windows 7, and includes instant messaging, e-mail, Photo Gallery, and blogging, among other services. The number of applications and their features are growing and expanding, so you will want to stay informed about this valuable and free set of tools. Because these tools are growing rapidly as individuals move more and more to cloud computing, the steps and screens in Activity 11.14 may work differently than described here.

Activity 11.14 | Uploading a Workbook to SkyDrive

In this activity, you will navigate to the Windows Live site, create a Windows Live account if you do not already have one, and then sign in to access the SkyDrive file storage and file sharing services.

1 **Start** your Internet browser. Click in the **address bar**, and then replace the existing text by typing **http://skydrive.live.com** Press [Enter].

> The Windows Live SkyDrive page displays. If you have a Windows Live account, the Windows Live ID sign in option displays. If you do not have a Windows Live account, the Windows Live SkyDrive home page displays.

2 If you have a Windows Live account, sign in to display the Windows SkyDrive page and move to Step 5.

3 If you do not have a Windows Live account, at the center of the displayed page, click the **Sign up** button. Compare your screen with Figure 11.28.

> The Create your Windows Live ID page displays.

Figure 11.28

Windows Live ———

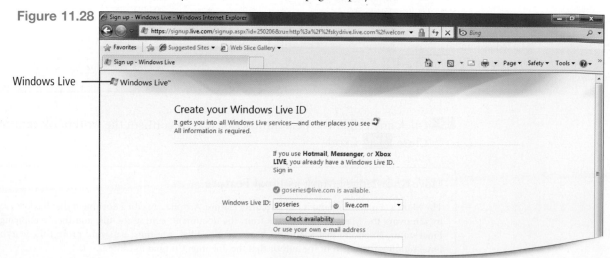

4 Complete the Sign up questions on the first page, and then continue on to the next page to complete all questions. Compare your screen with Figure 11.29.

The SkyDrive page displays options for document storage.

Figure 11.29

SkyDrive ———

Create folder ———

Folders ———

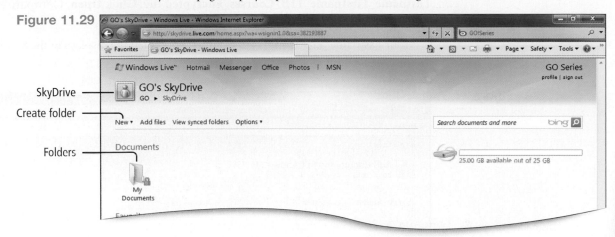

5 Click the **New arrow**, and then click **Folder**. As the **Name,** type **Chapter 11** To the right of **Share with: Just me**, click **Change**, and then on the **Share with**: slide bar, click and drag the marker to **Everyone (public).** Click the **Next** button. Compare your screen with Figure 11.30.

Figure 11.30

Storage location path ———

Add files to
Chapter 11 folder here ———

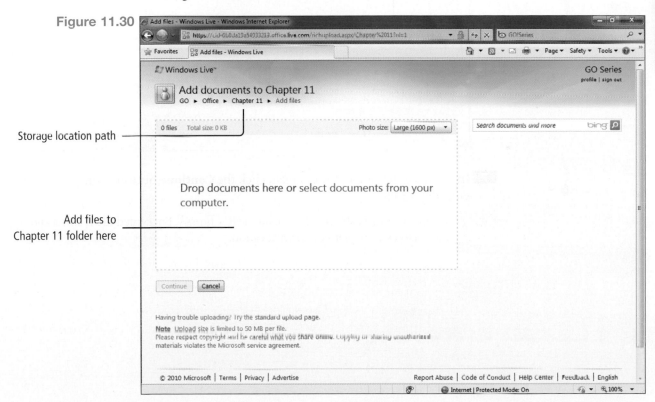

6 In the **Drop documents here or select documents from your computer** area, click the **select documents from your computer** link, to display the **Open** dialog box. In the **Open** dialog box, navigate to your **Excel Chapter 11** folder, and then select your **Lastname_Firstname_11B_Courses_Encrypted** file. Click **Open**. Compare your screen with Figure 11.31.

> Your Lastname_Firstname_11B_Courses_Encrypted file displays in the temporary drop files area.

Figure 11.31

Lastname_Firstname_
11B_Courses file

Drop files area

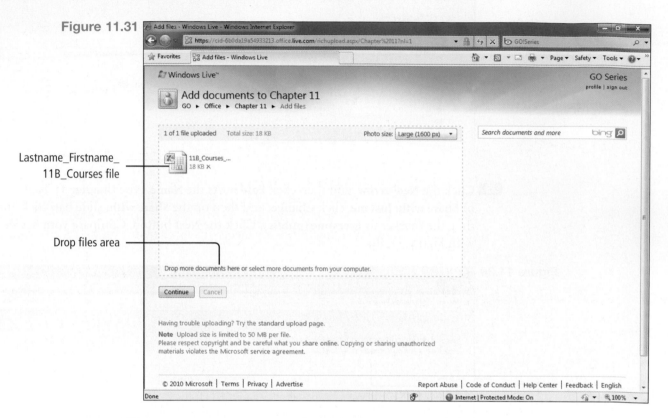

7 In the lower left area of the screen, click the **Continue** button. Compare your screen with Figure 11.32.

> A copy of your Lastname_Firstname_11B_Courses_Encrypted file is saved and displays in the Chapter 11 SkyDrive storage location.

Figure 11.32

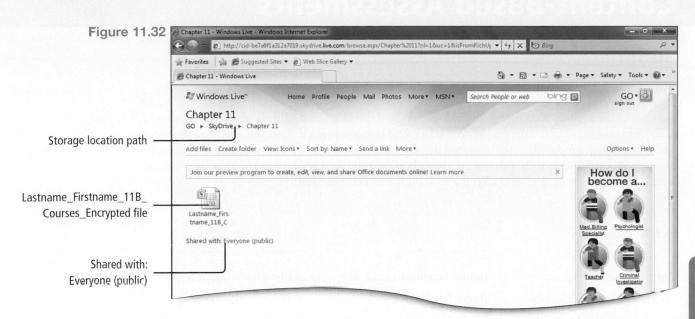

Storage location path

Lastname_Firstname_11B_
Courses_Encrypted file

Shared with:
Everyone (public)

8 In the upper right corner of the screen, click **Sign out** to exit Windows Live SkyDrive. If directed by your instructor, use the Windows Snipping Tool to create a snip of your screen showing your uploaded file to your new SkyDrive account. **Close** the Internet browser. **Print** the three worksheets or submit your workbooks electronically as directed.

End **You have completed Project 11B**

Content-Based Assessments

Summary

In this chapter, you assembled changes from multiple sources to collaborate with others. You made changes to documents by different individuals, tracked the changes, and then accepted or rejected them. You compared two different versions of a workbook and merged them together. You prepared a final workbook for distribution, inspected the workbook for hidden information, added security by encrypting a workbook with a password, digitally signed the workbook to assure that the signer is whom they claim to be, and uploaded the workbook to a network location.

Key Terms

Certificate authority 679

Change history 670

Cloud computing 688

Collaboration 667

Compatibility
   Checker 682

Digital certificate 679

Digital ID 679

Digital signature 679

Document Inspector 683

Encryption 685

Intranet 667

Mark as Final
   command 687

Metadata 667

Properties 667

Self-signed 679

Shared workbook 667

Signature line 679

Track Changes 669

Windows Live ID............688

Windows Live
   SkyDrive 688

Matching

Match each term in the second column with its correct definition in the first column by writing the letter of the term on the blank line in front of the correct definition.

_____ 1. The process of working jointly with others.

_____ 2. A workbook set up to allow multiple users on a network to view and make changes at the same time.

_____ 3. A network within an organization that uses Internet technologies.

_____ 4. Characteristics of an object that can be changed; details about a file that help identify it, such as the author, date created, and file name.

_____ 5. An Excel feature with which you can record and view changes made by others to a shared workbook.

_____ 6. Information that is maintained about changes made in past editing sessions.

_____ 7. An electronic encryption-based, secure stamp of authentication on a document.

_____ 8. A commercial organization that issues digital certificates, keeps track of who is assigned to a certificate, signs certificates to verify their validity, and tracks which certificates are revoked or expired.

_____ 9. An unauthenticated certificate created by the signer of a document.

_____ 10. A line in a document that specifies the individual who must sign the document.

_____ 11. The process of restricting access to files by scrambling the contents with a program.

_____ 12. A command that makes the document read-only and prevents additional changes to the document and disables typing, editing comments, and proofing marks.

A Certificate authority

B Change history

C Cloud computing

D Collaboration

E Digital ID

F Document Inspector

G Encryption

H Intranet

I Mark as Final

J Properties

K Self-signed

L Shared workbook

M Signature line

N Track Changes

O Windows Live SkyDrive

_____ 13. A feature that can find and remove hidden properties and personal information in a workbook.

_____ 14. A free online service that provides file storage and file sharing services on a Windows Live Internet site.

_____ 15. Use of Web servers of a third party provider on the Internet to store files and run applications.

Multiple Choice

Circle the correct answer.

1. Details about file properties are called:
   A. Data
   B. Metadata
   C. Megadata

2. If the _Read-only_ property is selected, the file can be:
   A. Read or copied, but it cannot be changed or saved
   B. Changed or saved, but cannot be read or copied
   C. Read or copied, but it cannot be changed or shared

3. When you turn on Track Changes and save the workbook, this term displays in the title bar:
   A. Created
   B. Tracked
   C. Shared

4. To ensure that an Excel 2010 workbook does not have issues that cause a significant loss of functionality or a minor loss of fidelity in an earlier version of Excel, you can run the:
   A. Compatibility Checker
   B. Document Inspector
   C. Password Protector

5. The Document Inspector finds:
   A. Hidden properties and personal information
   B. Tracked changes information
   C. Encrypted file information

6. Encrypting a file:
   A. Password protects information
   B. Digitally obscures information
   C. Inspects information

7. An encrypted file:
   A. Can be opened without a password
   B. Is top secret
   C. Cannot be opened without a password

8. The Mark as Final command changes a file to:
   A. Read-only
   B. Encrypted
   C. Password protected

9. The Mark as Final command is:
   A. A security feature
   B. Not a security feature
   C. Password protection

10. A security feature of Windows Live SkyDrive to control access to files is:
    A. Windows Live Endorsement
    B. Windows Live Certificate Authority
    C. Windows Live ID

Content-Based Assessments

Apply 11A skills from these Objectives:

1. Create a Shared Workbook
2. Track Changes Made to a Workbook
3. Merge Workbooks and Accept Changes

Skills Review | Project 11C Fall Schedule

In the following Skills Review, you will create a shared workbook so that it can be reviewed by the different department chairpersons in the college's Business Division. Various individuals in the Business Division will be able to edit and comment on the information in the workbook. Your completed worksheets will look similar to Figure 11.33.

Project Files

For Project 11C, you will need the following file:

e11C_Fall_Schedule

You will save your workbook as:

Lastname_Firstname_11C_Fall_Schedule

Project Results

Figure 11.33

(Project 11C Fall Schedule continues on the next page)

Content-Based Assessments

1 **Start** Excel. From your student files, open the file **e11C_Fall_Schedule**. Display the **Save As** dialog box, navigate to the location where you are storing your files for this chapter, and then **Save** the file in your **Excel Chapter 11** folder as **Lastname_Firstname_11C_Fall_Schedule**

a. Select all three worksheets so that *[Group]* displays in the title bar. On the **Insert tab**, in the **Text group**, click **Header & Footer**, and then in the **Navigation group**, click **Go to Footer**. Click in the **left section**, and then add the **File Name**. Click in a cell above the footer to close the footer area, return to **Normal** view, and then press Ctrl + Home to move to the top of the sheet.

b. In **Backstage** view, on the **Info tab**, at the top of the screen, notice that the location of this file on your computer displays. On the right, notice that some of the more common properties for this file display; for example the file *Size* and *Author*.

c. Under **Properties**, point to the text *Add a title*, and then click one time. Type **Proposed Fall Schedule** Under **Related People**, point to the text *Molly Morton*, who is the author. In the lower right corner of the displayed **Contact Card**, click the **Expand Contact Card arrow** ∨.

d. **Close** the **Contact Card**, and then click **Properties.** On the list, click **Advanced Properties**, and then in the dialog box, if necessary click the **General tab**. Click the **Summary tab**. In the **Author** box, delete *Molly Morton*, type **Kate Jones** and then press Tab. In the **Manager** box, type **Dean McKown, Business Division.**

e. Click **OK**. In the upper right corner of **Backstage** view, click the screen thumbnail to return to the worksheet. Point to the **Business Technology sheet tab**, right-click, and then click **Ungroup Sheets**. **Save** your workbook.

2 On the **Review tab**, in the **Changes group**, click the **Track Changes** button, and then click **Highlight Changes**. Click to select the **Track Changes while editing** check box, which activates the Track Changes feature and saves the file as a shared workbook. Verify that the **When** check box is selected and indicates *All*. Select the **Who** check box and be sure *Everyone* is indicated. Verify that the **Highlight changes on screen** check box is selected. Click **OK**.

Click **OK** to continue. Display **Backstage** view, and then click **Close** to close the file and leave Excel open.

a. Press Ctrl + F12 to display the **Open** dialog box. Navigate to your **Excel Chapter 11** folder, point to your **Lastname_Firstname_11C_Fall_Schedule** file, right-click, and then on the shortcut menu, click **Copy**. Right-click in an empty space below or to the right of the list of files, and then on the shortcut menu click **Paste**. **Close** the **Open** dialog box.

3 Display the **Open** dialog box, navigate to your chapter folder, and then open your **Lastname_Firstname_11C_Fall_Schedule** file—open the original, *not* the copy that you made. Display **Backstage** view, and then near the bottom of the **Backstage tabs**, click **Options**. In the **Excel Options** dialog box, on the left, verify that **General** is selected. On a piece of paper, write down the User name that displays so that you can restore it later. Select the **User name** text, type **Donna Bell, Business Technology** to replace the selected User name text.

a. Click **OK** to close the **Excel Options** dialog box. Verify that the **Business Technology** worksheet is displayed. Click cell **H10**, begin to type **Taylor, Jared** and press Enter to accept the AutoComplete suggestion. In cell **H11**, change the name to **Kim, Grace**. Press Ctrl + Home to move to cell **A1**.

b. On the **Review tab**, in the **Changes group**, click the **Track Changes** button, and then click **Highlight Changes**. In the **Highlight Changes** dialog box, click the **When arrow**, and then click **All**. If necessary, select the **Who** check box, and be sure that it indicates **Everyone**. Click **OK**. Point to each of the changed cells to view the **ScreenTip**, which indicates the change that was made and the date and time the change was made. **Save** your workbook, and then in the upper right corner of your screen, click the lower **Close Window** button to close the file and leave Excel open.

c. Press Ctrl + F12 to display the **Open** dialog box. Navigate to and then reopen your **Lastname_Firstname_11A_Fall_Schedule** file—*not* the copy. From **Backstage** view, display the **Excel Options** dialog box, and then using the technique you practiced, change the **User name** to **Doug Mallard, Marketing** and then click **OK**.

(Project 11C Fall Schedule continues on the next page)

d. Display the **Marketing** worksheet. Click cell **F3** and type **Online** Click cell **F5**, type **Online** and then press Enter. Press Ctrl + Home to make cell **A1** the active cell. **Save** your workbook. **Close** the file and leave Excel open.

e. Open the **Lastname_Firstname_11A_Fall_Schedule - Copy** file that you created earlier. From **Backstage** view, display the **Excel Options** dialog box, and then change the **User name** to Rick Mazzitelli, Business Management and then click **OK**. Display the **Business Management** worksheet. Click cell **G9** and type **Permission** Click cell **H12** and type **Liu, Leo** Select **column G** and apply **AutoFit**. **Save** your workbook, and then **Close** Excel.

4 **Start** Excel. From **Backstage** view, display the **Excel Options** dialog box, and then change the **User name** to Dean McKown Click **OK** to close the dialog box, and then open your **Lastname_Firstname_11C_Fall_Schedule** file.

a. Display the **Business Technology** worksheet. On the **Review tab**, in the **Changes group**, click the **Track Changes** button, and then click **Highlight Changes**. In the displayed **Highlight Changes** dialog box, click the **When arrow**, and then click **All**. Click the **Who arrow**, and then click **Everyone but Me**. Click **OK**.

b. Display the **Marketing** worksheet and notice the borders around cells **F3** and **F5** indicating that changes have been made. Display the **Business Management** worksheet, and notice that no changes are indicated because changes for this department were made on another copy of the shared workbook.

c. From **Backstage** view, display the **Excel Options** dialog box, and then on the left, click **Quick Access Toolbar**. At the top of the dialog box, under **Customize the Quick Access Toolbar**, click the **Choose commands from arrow**, and then click **Commands Not in the Ribbon**. In the list below, scroll as necessary, click **Compare and Merge Workbooks**, in the center click the **Add** button, and then click **OK**. On the **Quick Access Toolbar**, click the **Compare and Merge Workbooks** button. In the **Select Files to Merge Into Current Workbook** dialog box, navigate to your **Excel Chapter 11** folder. Locate your **Lastname_Firstname_ 11A_Fall_Schedule - Copy** file—if necessary point to the file names to display the complete file name in the ScreenTip—and then click to select it. Click **OK**.

5 Display the **Business Technology** worksheet. On the **Review tab**, in the **Changes group**, click the **Track Changes** button, and then click **Accept/Reject Changes**. Verify that the **When** box indicates *Not yet reviewed*. Change the **Who** box to indicate **Everyone**, and then click **OK**.

a. Click the **Accept** button. Click the **Accept** button one more time. Click the **Reject** button. **Reject** the next change—change 4 of 6. Click **Accept**, and then **Accept** the last change—a change in instructor to *Liu, Leo*.

b. Display the **Marketing** worksheet, click cell **F3**, and then press Del. Press Tab and in cell **G3**, type **Online** Click cell **F5** and press Del. Press Tab and in cell **G5**, type **Online** and press Enter. **Save** your workbook.

6 On the **Review tab**, in the **Changes group**, click the **Share Workbook** button. Clear the **Allow changes by more than one user at the same time** check box, and then click **OK**. On the displayed **Microsoft Excel** information box, click **Yes**.

a. Display **Backstage** view, and then at the bottom of the **Backstage tabs**, click **Options**. In the **Excel Options** dialog box, on the left, click **General**. Under **Personalize your copy of Microsoft Office**, click in the **User name** box.

b. Select the text *Dean McKown*, and then type the name that you wrote down in Step 3 to replace the selected User name text, and then click **OK**. On the **Quick Access Toolbar**, right-click the **Compare and Merge Workbooks** button, and then click **Remove from Quick Access Toolbar**. Click **OK** to Close the **Excel Options** dialog box.

7 Display the **Business Technology** worksheet, and then click cell **A15**. On the **Insert tab**, in the **Text group**, click the **Signature Line button arrow**, and then click **Microsoft Office Signature Line**. In the displayed **Microsoft Excel** dialog box, click **OK**. In the **Signature Setup** dialog box, with the insertion point blinking in the **Suggested signer** box and *using your own name*, type **Firstname Lastname** and then click **OK**.

a. Display the **Document Panel** and in the **Author** box, delete the contents and then type your firstname and lastname. In the **Subject** box, type your course name and section number, and in the **Keywords** box, type **fall courses Close** the **Document Panel**. Select all the sheets and check the **Print Preview**, make any necessary corrections. **Save** and then print or submit your workbook electronically as directed.

 You have completed Project 11C ——————————

Content-Based Assessments

Apply 11B skills from these Objectives:

4 Prepare a Final Workbook for Distribution

5 Upload a Workbook to SkyDrive

Skills Review | Project **11D** Distributed Class Workbook

In the following Skills Review, you will assist Michael Schaeffler, Vice President of Academic Affairs, in distributing a workbook for social science classes to the instructional deans at the college. Your completed worksheets will look similar to Figure 11.34.

Project Files

For Project 11D, you will need the following file:

e11D_Classes

You will save your workbooks as:

Lastname_Firstname_11D_Classes
Lastname_Firstname_11D_Classes_Compatibility
Lastname_Firstname_11D_Classes_Encrypted

Project Results

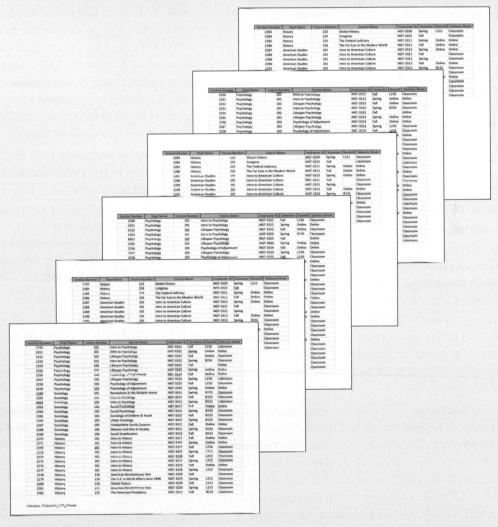

Figure 11.34

(Project 11D Distributed Class Workbook continues on the next page)

1 **Start** Excel. From your student files, open the file **e11D_ Classes** and then **Save** the file in your **Excel Chapter 11** folder as **Lastname_Firstname_11D_Classes_Compatibility**

  a. Display **Backstage** view, in the center panel, click the **Check for Issues** button, and then click **Check Compatibility**. Click **OK**.

  b. Insert a footer in the **left section** that includes the **File Name**. Click above the footer area to deselect, and then return to **Normal** view. Make cell **A1** the active cell. Display the **Document Panel**. In the **Author** box, type your firstname and lastname, in the **Subject** box, type your course name and section number, and in the **Keywords** box, type **classes list, compatibility Close** the **Document Panel**.

  c. Press **F12** to display the **Save As** dialog box. In the lower portion of the dialog box, click the **Save as type arrow**, click **Excel 97-2003 Workbook**, and then click **Save**. Click the **Continue** button. **Close** your workbook. Leave Excel open for the next activity.

2 From your student files, open the file **e11D_Classes** and then **Save** the file in your **Excel Chapter 11** folder as **Lastname_Firstname_11D_Classes** Insert a footer in the **left section** that includes the **File Name**. Return to **Normal** view. Make cell **A1** the active cell. Show the **Document Panel**. In the **Author** box, type your firstname and lastname, in the **Subject** box, type your course name and section number, and in the **Keywords** box, type **classes list Close** the **Document Panel**. Click **Save**.

  a. Display **Backstage** view, be sure the **Info tab** is active, and then in the **Prepare for Sharing group**, click the **Check for Issues** button. On the displayed list, click **Inspect Document**. In the lower right corner of the dialog box, click the **Inspect** button. Click the **Close** button to close the **Document Inspector** dialog box, and then in the upper right corner of **Backstage** view, click the screen thumbnail to return to the worksheet. Click cell **G5**, and notice the comment that displays.

  b. Display **Backstage** view, click the **Properties** button, and then click **Show Document Panel**. Notice that in the **Status** box, *DRAFT* displays. **Close** the **Document Properties** panel. Right-click the **Classes** sheet tab, and then on the shortcut menu, click **Unhide**. In the displayed **Unhide** dialog box, with *Instructors* selected, click **OK**. Right-click the **Instructors** sheet tab, and then on the shortcut menu, click **Hide**.

  c. **Save** your workbook, and then display **Backstage** view. On the **Info tab**, in the **Prepare for Sharing group**, click the **Check for Issues** button, and then click **Inspect Document**. In the **Document Inspector** dialog box, click the **Inspect** button. To the right of **Comments and Annotations**, click the **Remove All** button. To the right of **Document Properties and Personal Information**, click the **Remove All** button. To the right of **Headers and Footers**, click the **Remove All** button. To the right of **Hidden Worksheets**, click the **Remove All** button.

  d. In the lower right corner of the **Document Inspector** dialog box, click the **Close** button. In the upper right corner of **Backstage** view, click the screen thumbnail to return to the worksheet. Insert a footer in the **left section** that includes the **File Name**, and then click **Save**.

3 With your **Lastname_Firstname_11D_Classes** file open, press **F12** to display the **Save As** dialog box, and then **Save** the file in your **Excel Chapter 11** folder as **Lastname_Firstname_11D_Classes_Encrypted** Show the **Document Panel**. In the **Author** box, type your firstname and lastname, in the **Subject** box, type your course name and section number, and in the **Keywords** box, type **classes list, encrypted Close** the **Document Panel**.

  a. Display **Backstage** view and be sure the **Info tab** is active. In the **Permissions group**, click the **Protect Workbook** button, and then on the displayed list, click **Encrypt with Password**. In the displayed **Encrypt Document** dialog box, with the insertion point blinking in the **Password** box, type **go** and then click **OK**. In the **Reenter password** box, type **go** and then click **OK**.

  b. Click thumbnail or **File** tab to return to the workbook, then **Save** and **Close** the workbook, but leave Excel open. Press **Ctrl** + **F12** to display the **Open** dialog box. Navigate to your Excel **Chapter 11** folder, and then open your **Lastname_Firstname_11D_Classes_ Encrypted** file. Type **go** and then click **OK**.

4 With the **Lastname_Firstname_11D_Classes_ Encrypted** file open, display **Backstage** view. With the **Info tab** active, in the **Permissions group**, click the **Protect Workbook** button, and then click **Mark as Final**. Click **OK**. Read the displayed message box, and then click **OK**. Click the thumbnail or **File** tab to return to the workbook, then click any cell in the worksheet and type a number or text to confirm that you cannot edit the workbook. **Close** the workbook and **Exit** Excel.

(Project 11D Distributed Class Workbook continues on the next page)

Skills Review | Project **11D** Distributed Class Workbook (continued)

5 **Start** your Internet browser. Click in the **address bar**, and then replace the existing text by typing **http://skydrive.live.com** Press Enter.

   a. If you have a Windows Live account, sign in to display the **Windows SkyDrive** page. If you do not have a Windows Live account, at the center of the displayed page, click the **Sign up** button and complete the Sign up questions.

   b. If necessary, click the **New arrow**, click **Folder**, and as the **Name** type **Chapter 11** Click the **Share with arrow**, and then click **Everyone (public).** Click the **Next** button. In the **Drop files here** area, click the

Select documents from your computer link to display the **Open** dialog box. In the **Open** dialog box, navigate to your **Excel Chapter 11** folder, and then select your **Lastname_Firstname_11D_ Classes_Encrypted** file. Click **Open**. In the lower left area of the screen, click the **Continue** button. In the upper right corner of the screen, click **Sign out**.

6 If directed by your instructor, use the Windows Snipping Tool to create a snip of your screen showing your uploaded file to Windows Live SkyDrive. **Close** the Internet browser. **Print** the three worksheets or submit your workbooks electronically as directed.

End **You have completed Project 11D** ───────────────

Excel | Chapter 11

Content-Based Assessments

Apply **11A** skills from these Objectives:

1 Create a Shared Workbook

2 Track Changes Made to a Workbook

3 Merge Workbooks and Accept Changes

Mastering Excel | Project **11E** Scholarship Classes

In the following Mastering Excel project, you will create a shared workbook, change the user name, and then make changes to the workbook for the Continuing Education Division of Laurel College. Laurel College offers a selection of free (scholarship) classes to nonprofit agencies. The class list from the previous semester must be updated for the upcoming semester. Then you will review the changes that were made and accept or reject the changes. Your completed worksheet will look similar to Figure 11.35.

Project Files

For Project 11E, you will need the following file:

e11E_Scholarship_Classes

You will save your workbook as:

Lastname_Firstname_11E_Scholarship_Classes

Project Results

Scholarship Classes for Nonprofit Agencies

Fall

Title	Dates	Time	Class Number
Introduction to Access	Sept 17 & 24	8 AM-12 PM	OS 325
Intermediate Access	Oct 1 & 8	8 AM-12 PM	OS 326
Introduction to Excel	Oct 15 & 22	1-5 PM	OS 322
Intermediate Excel	Oct 29 & Nov 5	8 AM-12 PM	OS 310
Introduction to PowerPoint	Oct 15 & 22	8 AM-12 PM	OS 328
Introduction to Word	Nov 12 & 19	1-5 PM	OS 319
Intermediate Word	Dec 3 & 10	1-5 PM	OS 320
MS Publisher	Nov 12 & 19	8 AM-12 PM	OS 345

Lastname_Firstname_11E_Scholarship_Classes

Figure 11.35

(Project 11E Scholarship Classes continues on the next page)

Mastering Excel | Project **11E** Scholarship Classes (continued)

1 **Start** Excel. From your student files, open the Excel workbook **e11E_Scholarship_Classes**. **Save** the file in your **Excel Chapter 11** folder as **Lastname_Firstname_ 11E_Scholarship_Classes** Insert a footer in the **left section** with the **File Name**, and then click above the footer area to deselect. Return to **Normal** view, and then make cell **A1** the active cell. Display the **Document Panel**. In the **Subject** box, type your course name and section number, and in the **Keywords** box, type **scholarship classes Close** the **Document Panel**.

2 In **Backstage** view, under **Properties**, point to the text *Add a Title* box, and then click one time. Type **Fall Nonprofit Classes** Under **Related People**, notice that the author's name is *Mary Tuttle* and thus she is the originator of this file, which will be used for making changes to the class offerings.

3 Return to the **NonProfits** worksheet. Click cell **A3**, type **Fall** and press Enter. On the **Review tab**, in the **Changes group**, click the **Track Changes arrow**, and then click **Highlight Changes**. In the **Highlight Changes** dialog box, select the **Track changes while editing** check box. Be sure the **When** check box is selected and indicates *All* and that the **Who** check box is selected and indicates *Everyone*. Click **OK**. In the message box, click **OK** to save the workbook. *[Shared]* is displayed in the title bar. Recall that when you activate the Track Changes feature, Excel saves the workbook as a shared file.

4 **Close** the file and then reopen it. Display **Backstage** view and click **Options**. In the **Excel Options** dialog box, verify **General** is selected. Under **Personalize your copy of Microsoft Office**, write down the name that displays in the **User name** box so that you can restore it later, and then in the **User name** box, type **Nancy Hamilton** and click **OK**. From this point forward, changes made to the workbook will be recorded as being made by the user *Nancy Hamilton*.

5 Select the range **B6:B13** and press Del. In **column B**, starting in cell **B6** enter the following dates:

Sept 17 & 24
Oct 1 & 8
Oct 15 & 22
Oct 29 & Nov 5
Oct 15 & 22
Nov 12 & 19
Dec 3 & 10
Nov 12 & 19

6 Press Ctrl + Home to return to cell **A1**. **Save** the file, and then **Close** it. Open your **Lastname_Firstname_11E_ Scholarship_Classes** file again, and verify that **A1** is the active cell. Display **Backstage** view, click **Options**, and change the **User name** to **Pat Hanna** Click **OK**. Now you will review the changes that have been made.

7 On the **Review tab**, in the **Changes group**, click the **Track Changes arrow**, and then click **Accept/Reject Changes**. In the **Select Changes to Accept or Reject** dialog box, be sure the **When** check box is selected and that it indicates *Not yet reviewed*. Be sure the **Who** check box is selected, click its arrow, and then click **Everyone but Me**. Click **OK**. The first date that was changed is surrounded by a border. Click **Accept**. The first change is accepted, and the second change is indicated. Click **Accept**, and then click **Accept All**. All the changes are accepted, and the dialog box closes.

8 **Save** your workbook. Print or submit your workbook electronically. **Close** the workbook. Display **Backstage** view, click **Options**, and verify that the **General tab** is selected. In the **User name** box, type the name that you wrote down in Step 4 to restore the original setting, and then click **OK**. **Exit** Excel.

End **You have completed Project 11E** ——————————————

Content-Based Assessments

Apply 11B skills from these Objectives:

◄ Prepare a Final Workbook for Distribution

5 Upload a Workbook to SkyDrive

Mastering Excel | Project 11F Instruments Distributed Workbook

In the following Mastering Excel project, you will assist Leon McKinney, Associate Dean of Music, in distributing a workbook of musical instruments inventory to the music faculty at the college. Your completed worksheets will look similar to Figure 11.36.

Project Files

For Project 11F, you will need the following file:

e11F_Music

You will save your workbooks as:

Lastname_Firstname_11F_Music
Lastname_Firstname_11F_Music_ Compatibility
Lastname_Firstname_11F_Music_Encrypted

Project Results

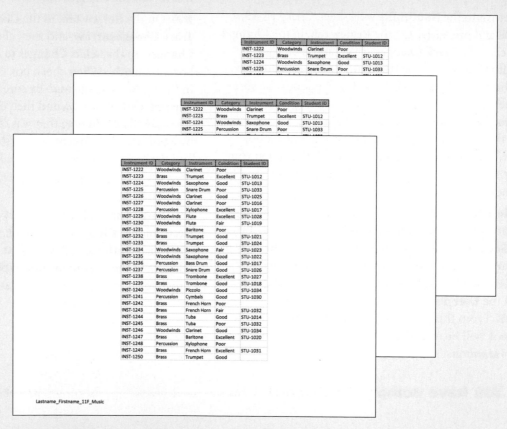

Figure 11.36

(Project 11F Instruments Distributed Workbook continues on the next page)

1 **Start** Excel. From your student files, open the file **e11F_Music**. Display **Backstage** view, click the **Check for Issues** button, and then click **Check Compatibility**. Click **OK**. Insert a footer in the **left section** that includes the **File Name**. Return to **Normal** view. Make cell **A1** the active cell. Display the **Document Panel**. In the **Subject** box, type your course name and section number, and in the **Keywords** box, type **musical instruments, compatibility Close** the **Document Panel**. Press F12 to display the **Save As** dialog box. Save the file in your **Excel Chapter 11** folder as **Lastname_Firstname_11F_Music_Compatibility** Click the **Save as type arrow**, click **Excel 97-2003 Workbook**, and then click **Save**. Click the **Continue** button. **Close** your workbook. Leave Excel open for the next activity.

2 Open the file **e11F_Music** and then **Save** the file in your **Excel Chapter 11** folder as **Lastname_Firstname_ 11F_Music** Insert a footer in the **left section** that includes the **File Name**. Return to **Normal** view. Make cell **A1** the active cell. Display the **Document Panel**. In the **Author** box, type your firstname and lastname, in the **Subject** box, type your course name and section number, and in the **Keywords** box, type **musical instruments Close** the **Document Panel**. **Save** your workbook. Display **Backstage** view, click the **Check for Issues** button, click **Inspect Document**, and then click the **Inspect** button. Click the **Close** button, and then return to the worksheet. Click cell **D5**, and notice the comment that displays. Display **Backstage** view, click the **Properties** button, and then click **Show Document Panel**. Notice that in the **Status** box, *DRAFT* displays. **Close** the **Document Properties** panel. Right-click the **Musical Instruments Inventory sheet tab**, and then click **Unhide**. In the displayed **Unhide** dialog box, with *Music Instructors* selected, click **OK**. Right-click the **Music Instructors sheet tab**, and click **Hide**.

3 **Save** your workbook, and then display **Backstage** view. Click the **Check for Issues** button, and then click **Inspect Document**. In the **Document Inspector** dialog box, click the **Inspect** button. To the right of **Comments and Annotations**, click the **Remove All** button. To the right of **Document Properties and Personal Information**, click the **Remove All** button. To the right of **Hidden Worksheets**, click the **Remove All** button. In the **Document Inspector** dialog box, click the **Close** button. In **Backstage** view, return to the document, and then click **Save**.

4 With your **Lastname_Firstname_11F_Music** file open, press F12 to display the **Save As** dialog box, and then

Save the file in your **Excel Chapter 11** folder as **Lastname_Firstname_11F_Music_Encrypted**. Be sure a footer is inserted in the **left section** that includes the **File Name**. Return to **Normal** view. Make cell **A1** the active cell. Display the **Document Panel**. In the **Author** box, type your firstname and lastname, in the **Subject** box, type your course name and section number, and in the **Keywords** box, type **musical instruments, encrypted Close** the **Document Panel**. Display **Backstage** view and click the **Protect Workbook** button, and then click **Encrypt with Password**. In the displayed **Encrypt Document** dialog box, in the **Password** box, type **go** and then click **OK**. In the **Reenter password** box, type **go** and then click **OK**. Click the **File tab**, **Close** the workbook, **Save**, but leave Excel open. Press Ctrl + F12 to display the **Open** dialog box. Navigate to your **Excel Chapter 11** folder, and then open your **Lastname_Firstname_11F_Music_Encrypted** file. Type **go** and then click **OK**.

5 With the **Lastname_Firstname_11F_Music_Encrypted** file open, display **Backstage** view. With the **Info tab** active, click the **Protect Workbook** button, and then click **Mark as Final**. Click **OK** two times. Return to the worksheet. Confirm that you cannot edit the workbook. **Close** the workbook and **Exit** Excel.

6 **Start** your Internet browser. Click in the **address bar**, and then replace the existing text by typing **http://skydrive.live.com** Press Enter. If you have a Windows Live account, sign in to display the **Windows SkyDrive** page. If you do not have a Windows Live account, at the center of the displayed page, click the **Sign up** button and complete the Sign up questions. If necessary, click the **New arrow**, click **Folder**, and as the **Name** type **Chapter 11** Click the **Share with arrow**, and then click **Everyone (public)**. Click the **Next** button. If a Chapter 11 folder already exists, click the **Chapter 11** folder, and then click **Add** files. Click the **Select documents from your computer** link, to display the **Open** dialog box. In the **Open** dialog box, navigate to your **Excel Chapter 11** folder, and then select your **Lastname_Firstname_11B_Courses_ Encrypted** file. Click **Open**. In the lower left area of the screen, click the **Continue** button. In the upper right corner of the screen, click **Sign out** to exit Windows Live SkyDrive.

7 If directed by your instructor, use the Windows Snipping Tool to create a snip of your screen showing your uploaded file to your new SkyDrive. **Close** the Internet browser. **Print** the three worksheets or submit your workbooks electronically as directed.

End **You have completed Project 11F**

Apply **11A** and **11B**
skills from these
Objectives:

1. Create a Shared Workbook
2. Track Changes Made to a Workbook
3. Merge Workbooks and Accept Changes
4. Prepare a Final Workbook for Distribution
5. Upload a Workbook to SkyDrive

Mastering Excel | Project **11G** Sports Distributed Workbook

In the following Mastering Excel project, you will assist Scott Tewel, Athletic Director, in distributing a workbook of sports equipment inventory to the sports coaches at the college. You will also create a shared workbook that the Athletics Department will use to review proposed salary changes. Your completed worksheet will look similar to Figure 11.37.

Project Files

For Project 11G, you will need the following files:

> e11G_Sports
> e11G_Salary

You will save your workbooks as:

> Lastname_Firstname_11G_Sports
> Lastname_Firstname_11G_Sports_Compatibility
> Lastname_Firstname_11G_Sports_Encrypted
> Lastname_Firstname_11G_Salary

Project Results

Figure 11.37

(Project 11G Sports Distributed Workbook continues on the next page)

Content-Based Assessments

Mastering Excel | Project 11G Sports Distributed
Workbook (continued)

1 **Start** Excel. From your student files, open the file **e11G_Sports**. Display **Backstage** view, click the **Check for Issues** button, and then click **Check Compatibility**. Click **OK**. Insert a footer in the **left section** that includes the **File Name**. Return to **Normal** view. Make cell **A1** the active cell. Display the **Document Panel**. In the **Author** box, type your firstname and lastname, in the **Subject** box, type your course name and section number, and in the **Keywords** box, type **sports equipment, compatibility** Close the **Document Panel**. Press F12 to display the **Save As** dialog box. **Save** the file in your **Excel Chapter 11** folder as **Lastname_Firstname_11G_Sports_Compatibility** Click the **Save as type arrow**, click **Excel 97-2003 Workbook**, and then click **Save**. Click the **Continue** button. **Close** your workbook. Leave Excel open for the next activity.

2 From your student files, open the file **e11G_Sports** and then **Save** the file in your **Excel Chapter 11** folder as **Lastname_Firstname_11G_Sports** Insert a footer in the **left section** that includes the **File Name**. Return to **Normal** view. Make cell **A1** the active cell. Display the **Document Panel**. In the **Author** box, type your firstname and lastname, in the **Subject** box, type your course name and section number, and in the **Keywords** box, type **sports equipment** Close the **Document Panel**. **Save** your workbook. Display **Backstage** view, be sure the **Info tab** is active, and then click the **Check for Issues** button. Click **Inspect Document**. Click the **Inspect** button. Click the **Close** button, and then return to the worksheet. Click cell **D5**, and notice the comment that displays. Display **Backstage** view, click the **Properties** button, and then click **Show Document Panel**. Notice that in the **Status** box, *DRAFT* displays. **Close** the **Document Properties** panel. Right-click the **Sports Equipment Inventory** sheet tab, and then click **Unhide**. In the displayed **Unhide** dialog box, with *Coaches* selected, click **OK**. Right-click the **Coaches** sheet tab, and click **Hide**. **Save** your workbook, and then display **Backstage** view. On the **Info tab**, click the **Check for Issues** button, and then click **Inspect Document**. In the **Document Inspector** dialog box, click the **Inspect** button. To the right of **Comments and Annotations**, click the **Remove All** button. To the right of **Document Properties and Personal Information**, click the **Remove All** button. To the right of **Hidden Worksheets**, click the **Remove All** button. In the **Document Inspector** dialog box, click the **Close** button. In **Backstage** view, return to the worksheet, and then click **Save**.

3 With your **Lastname_Firstname_11G_Sports** file open, press F12 to display the **Save As** dialog box, and then **Save** the file in your **Excel Chapter 11** folder as **Lastname_Firstname_11G_Sports_Encrypted** Be sure a footer is inserted in the **left section** that includes the **File Name**. Return to **Normal** view. Make cell **A1** the active cell. Display the **Document Panel**. In the **Author** box, type your firstname and lastname, in the **Subject** box, type your course name and section number, and in the **Keywords** box, type **sports equipment, encrypted** Close the **Document Panel**. Display **Backstage** view, click the **Protect Workbook** button, and then click **Encrypt with Password**. In the displayed **Encrypt Document** dialog box, in the **Password** box, type **go** and then click **OK**. In the **Reenter password** box, type **go** and then click **OK**. **Save** and **Close** the workbook, but leave Excel open. Press Ctrl + F12 to display the **Open** dialog box. Navigate to your **Excel Chapter 11** folder, and then open your **Lastname_Firstname_11G_Sports_Encrypted** file. Type **go** and then click **OK**.

4 With the **Lastname_Firstname_11G_Sports_Encrypted** file open, display **Backstage** view. With the **Info tab** active, click the **Protect Workbook** button, and then click **Mark as Final**. Click **OK** two times. Return to the worksheet. Confirm that you cannot edit the workbook. **Close** the workbook and **Exit** Excel.

5 **Start** your Internet browser. Click in the **address bar**, and then replace the existing text by typing **http://skydrive.live.com** Press Enter. If you have a Windows Live account, sign in to display the **Windows SkyDrive** page. If you do not have a Windows Live account, at the center of the displayed page, click the **Sign up** button and complete the Sign up questions. If necessary, click the **New arrow**, click **Folder**, and as the **Name** type **Chapter 11** Click the **Share with arrow**, and then click **Everyone (public)**. Click the **Next** button. If a Chapter 11 folder already exists, click the **Chapter 11** folder, and then click **Add files**.

Click the **Select documents from your computer** link, to display the **Open** dialog box. In the **Open** dialog box, navigate to your **Excel Chapter 11** folder, and then select your **Lastname_Firstname_11G_Sports_Encrypted** file. Click **Open**. In the lower left area of the screen, click the **Continue** button. In the upper right corner of the screen, click **Sign out** to exit Windows Live SkyDrive.

6 If directed by your instructor, use the Windows Snipping Tool to create a snip of your screen showing

(Project 11G Sports Distributed Workbook continues on the next page)

your uploaded file to your new SkyDrive. **Close** the Internet browser. **Print** the three worksheets or submit your workbooks electronically as directed.

7 From your student files, open the file **e11G_Salary**. **Save** the file in your **Excel Chapter 11** folder as **Lastname_Firstname_11G_Salary** Group the sheets and insert a footer in the **left section** that includes the **File Name**. Return to **Normal** view. Make cell **A1** the active cell. Display the **Document Panel**. In the **Author** box, type your firstname and lastname, in the **Subject** box, type your course name and section number, and in the **Keywords** box, type **salary** **Close** the **Document Panel**. Ungroup the sheets.

8 Take a moment to examine the worksheet. The **Salary Ranges** sheet shows selected salary grades at the college. Examine the other two sheets. Each sheet contains a list of employees, their current grade and salary, and their proposed grade and salary based on a 2 percent increase. Within the Athletics Department, this information will be sent to the Chairs of the Aquatics and Sports Departments to review and adjust. Overall, the pay increases for the next fiscal year must be 2 percent on average, unless a promotion requires an increase in grade. Moving to a higher grade automatically includes a salary increase.

9 Display the **Highlight Changes** dialog box. Select the **Track changes while editing** check box, and be sure **When** indicates *All*, and **Who** is selected and indicates *Everyone*. Click **OK** to save the workbook. **Close** the file, and then open it again. Display **Backstage** view and click **Options** to open the **Excel Options** dialog box. Write down the current **User name**, and then change the **User name** to **Dan McMurray** and then click **OK**.

10 From this point forward, changes made to the workbook will be recorded as being made by Dan McMurray, Chair of the Aquatics Department. Click the **Aquatics sheet tab** and change the following proposed salaries and anticipated grade for Desprez:

Last Name	Anticipated Grade	Proposed Salary
Anderson		48000
Desprez	17	46800
Wagner		53000

11 **Save** the file and **Close** it. Reopen the file and change the **User name** to **Henry Totenberg** From this

point forward, any changes made to the workbook will be recorded as being made by Henry Totenberg, Chair of the Sports Department. Click the **Sports sheet** and change the following proposed salaries and anticipated grade for Reid:

Last Name	Anticipated Grade	Proposed Salary
Matthews		57000
Patel		50100
Reid	17	45500
Zelnik		49900

12 **Save** the file and **Close** it. Reopen the file and change the **User name** to **Dean Atchison** the Dean of Business, who will accept or reject the changes. Display the **Highlight Changes** dialog box, change **When** to **All**, and be sure **Who** is selected and displays **Everyone**. Click **OK**. Click each new salary in **column F**. Notice that salary changes were a change from a simple 2 percent increase to a specified amount. Now that some salaries have been changed by Department Chairs, you will calculate the overall salary increase.

13 On the **Aquatics sheet**, in cell **G11**, enter a formula to calculate the percentage increase that the proposed salary total is over the present salary total. *Hint: = (Proposed Salary-Present Salary)/Present Salary*. Format the result as a percentage with two decimals. Your result should be 2.14%. Similarly, on the **Sports sheet**, in cell **G12**, calculate the percentage increase in total salary. Your result is 2.27%.

14 Display the **Select Changes to Accept or Reject** dialog box and save if prompted. Review changes for **Everyone but Me**. Accept all changes except the change for *Matthews* in the Sports Department. After reviewing the changes, change Matthews's **Anticipated Grade** to **20** The higher grade is necessary to give him a full 2 percent increase in salary. The percentage for the Sports sheet changes to 2.40%.

15 **Save** your workbook. **Print** or submit your workbook electronically. If required, print or create an electronic version of your worksheets with formulas displayed using the instructions in Activity 1.16 in Project 1A. If you printed your formulas, be sure to redisplay the worksheet by pressing [Ctrl] + [']. Open a blank **Excel** workbook and in the **Excel Options** dialog box, change the **User name** back to the user name that you wrote down in Step 9. **Close** the workbook and **Exit** Excel.

End You have completed Project 11G

Content-Based Assessments

Apply a combination of the 11A and 11B skills.

GO! Fix It | Project 11H Fall Schedule

Project Files

For Project 11H, you will need the following file:

    e11H_Fall_Schedule

You will save your workbook as:

    Lastname_Firstname_11H_Fall_Compatibility

Open the file **e11H_Fall_Schedule** and examine the properties of the workbook. Fix the author name and company using Advanced Properties to your Firstname Lastname and change the name of the company to the name of your college. Inspect the Document and Remove all Hidden worksheets. In the left section of the footer, insert the file name. In Document Properties, be sure your name displays, add your course information to the document properties, and include **fall schedule** as the keywords. Save your file as **Lastname_Firstname_11H_Fall_ Compatibility** as an Excel 97-2003 workbook, and then print or submit your worksheet electronically as directed by your instructor.

End You have completed Project 11H ————————————

Content-Based Assessments

Apply a combination of the **11A** and **11B** skills.

GO! Make It | Project 11I Fall Sports

Project Files

For Project 11I, you will need the following file:

e11I_Fall_Sports

You will save your workbook as:

Lastname_Firstname_11I_Fall_Encrypted

Open the file **e11I_Fall_Sports**; save it in your Excel Chapter 11 folder as **Lastname_Firstname_11I_Fall_Encrypted** Hide the Coaches worksheet as shown in Figure 11.38. Encrypt the file with the password *go*. Insert a footer in the left section, add your name, your course name and section, and the keywords **fall sports equipment, inventory** to the document properties. Apply Mark as Final to the workbook. Save the file, and then print the worksheet and submit electronically as directed by your instructor.

Project Results

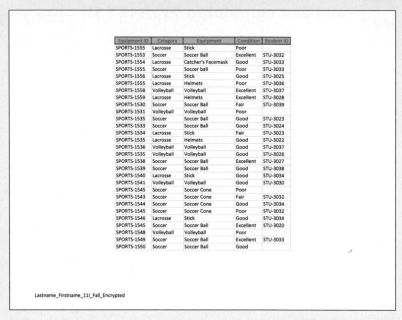

Figure 11.38

End You have completed Project 11I

Content-Based Assessments

Apply a combination of the 11A and 11B skills.

GO! Solve It | Project **11J** Weekend Classes

Project Files

For Project 11J, you will need the following file:

> e11J_Weekend_Classes

You will save your workbook as:

> Lastname_Firstname_11J_Weekend_Classes

Open the file e11J_Weekend_Classes and save it in your chapter folder as **Lastname_Firstname_11J_Weekend_Classes** Insert the file name in the footer in the left section and add appropriate information to the document properties including the keywords **weekend classes** In Properties, in the *Title* box, type **Weekend Classes** Notice that the author's name is *Maureen Thorp* and thus she is the originator of this file, which will be used for making changes to the class offerings. Click cell A3, and type **Weekend** Using Track Changes, highlight the changes. Be sure the Track changes while editing check box is selected, the When check box is selected and indicates *All*, and the Who check box is selected and indicates *Everyone*. Save the workbook. Be sure *[Shared]* is displayed in the title bar. Recall that when you activate the Track Changes feature, Excel saves the workbook as a shared file. Close the file and then reopen it. In the Excel Options dialog box, display the User name box. Write down the name that displays so that you can restore it later, and then change the name to **John Diaz** From this point forward, changes made to the workbook will be recorded as being made by the user *John Diaz*. Select the range B6:B8 and press [Del]. In column B, starting in cell B6 enter the following dates:

> **Nov 1 & 24**
> **Oct 1 & 8**
> **Oct 5 & 21**

Save the file, and then Close it. Open your Lastname_Firstname_11J_Weekend_Classes file again, and change the User name to **Aaron Stern** and review the changes that have been made. Using Track Changes, Accept/Reject Changes. In the Select Changes to Accept or Reject dialog box, be sure the When check box is selected and that it indicates *Not yet reviewed*. Be sure the Who check box is selected, click its arrow, and then click Everyone but Me. For the first date that was changed, click Accept. The first change is accepted, and the second change is indicated. Click Accept, and then click Accept one more time. All the changes are accepted, and the dialog box closes. Save your workbook. Print or submit your workbook electronically. Close the workbook. Display Backstage view, click Options, and verify that the General tab is selected. In the User name box, type the name that you wrote down earlier to restore the original setting, and then click OK. Exit Excel.

	Performance Level		
	Exemplary: You consistently applied the relevant skills.	**Proficient:** You sometimes, but not always, applied the relevant skills.	**Developing:** You rarely or never applied the relevant skills.
Performance Criteria — Create a Shared Workbook	A shared workbook is created.	Not applicable.	A shared workbook is not created.
Track Changes Made to a Workbook	All Track changes are made to the workbook.	Only some of the Track changes are made to the workbook.	None of the Track changes are made to the workbook.

End You have completed Project 11J

Content-Based Assessments

GO! Solve It | Project **11K** Scholarships

Project Files

For Project 11K, you will need the following file:

e11K_Scholarships

You will save your workbook as:

Lastname_Firstname_11K_Scholarships

Open the file e11K_Scholarships and save it as **Lastname_Firstname_11K_Scholarships**
Inspect the document and remove the hidden worksheet. Encrypt the workbook with the password
go. Insert the file name in the footer in the left section. Add appropriate information to the document
properties including the keyword **scholarships** Mark the workbook as Final. Submit as directed by
your instructor.

<table>
<tr><td rowspan="2"></td><th colspan="3">Performance Level</th></tr>
<tr>
<th>Exemplary:
You consistently applied
the relevant skills.</th>
<th>Proficient:
You sometimes, but not always,
applied the relevant skills.</th>
<th>Developing:
You rarely or never applied
the relevant skills.</th>
</tr>
<tr>
<td>**Inspect a Document**</td>
<td>The document has been inspected for a hidden worksheet.</td>
<td>Not applicable</td>
<td>The document has not been inspected for a hidden worksheet.</td>
</tr>
<tr>
<td>**Encrypt a Workbook**</td>
<td>The document has been encrypted with *go* as the password.</td>
<td>Not applicable</td>
<td>The document has not been encrypted with a password.</td>
</tr>
<tr>
<td>**Mark a Workbook as Final**</td>
<td>The document has been Marked as Final.</td>
<td>Not applicable</td>
<td>The document has not been Marked as Final.</td>
</tr>
</table>

Performance Criteria

End **You have completed Project 11K** ⎯⎯⎯⎯⎯⎯⎯⎯⎯⎯⎯⎯

Outcomes-Based Assessments

Rubric

The following outcomes-based assessments are *open-ended assessments*. That is, there is no specific correct result; your result will depend on your approach to the information provided. Make *Professional Quality* your goal. Use the following scoring rubric to guide you in *how* to approach the problem, and then to evaluate *how well* your approach solves the problem.

The *criteria*—Software Mastery, Content, Format and Layout, and Process—represent the knowledge and skills you have gained that you can apply to solving the problem. The *levels of performance*—Professional Quality, Approaching Professional Quality, or Needs Quality Improvements—help you and your instructor evaluate your result.

	Your completed project is of Professional Quality if you:	Your completed project is Approaching Professional Quality if you:	Your completed project Needs Quality Improvements if you:
1-Software Mastery	Choose and apply the most appropriate skills, tools, and features and identify efficient methods to solve the problem.	Choose and apply some appropriate skills, tools, and features, but not in the most efficient manner.	Choose inappropriate skills, tools, or features, or are inefficient in solving the problem.
2-Content	Construct a solution that is clear and well organized, contains content that is accurate, appropriate to the audience and purpose, and is complete. Provide a solution that contains no errors in spelling, grammar, or style.	Construct a solution in which some components are unclear, poorly organized, inconsistent, or incomplete. Misjudge the needs of the audience. Have some errors in spelling, grammar, or style, but the errors do not detract from comprehension.	Construct a solution that is unclear, incomplete, or poorly organized; contains some inaccurate or inappropriate content; and contains many errors in spelling, grammar, or style. Do not solve the problem.
3-Format and Layout	Format and arrange all elements to communicate information and ideas, clarify function, illustrate relationships, and indicate relative importance.	Apply appropriate format and layout features to some elements, but not others. Overuse features, causing minor distraction.	Apply format and layout that does not communicate information or ideas clearly. Do not use format and layout features to clarify function, illustrate relationships, or indicate relative importance. Use available features excessively, causing distraction.
4-Process	Use an organized approach that integrates planning, development, self-assessment, revision, and reflection.	Demonstrate an organized approach in some areas, but not others; or, use an insufficient process of organization throughout.	Do not use an organized approach to solve the problem.

Outcomes-Based Assessments

GO! Think | Project **11L** Budget

Project Files

For Project 11L, you will need the following file:

e11L_Budget

You will save your workbook as:

Lastname_Firstname_11L_Budget

Open the file e11L_Budget, and then save it in your chapter folder as **Lastname_Firstname_ 11L_Budget** You will create a shared file and a copy of the workbook so that it can be completed by the various department chairs who need to do so. Then you will enter the proposed budget figures for each department. Finally, you will merge the workbooks and review and accept or reject the changes. Take a moment to examine the workbook. There are three worksheets for the three department names shown on the sheet tabs. The previous year's budget and actual figures are shown, as well as the current year's budget and actual year-to-date figures as of March 31. The college is on a fiscal year budget that begins July 1 and ends June 30. The figures indicated for the current year represent nine months of expenses (July 1 through March 31); this is the time period during which most of the funds are usually spent.

Turn on the Track changes while editing, Make a copy of the the Lastname_Firstname_11L_ Budget file and then open the original file. Write down the User name that displays in Excel Options to restore it later. Change the user name to **Mary Markley, Nursing** Be sure the Nursing sheet tab is displayed. In column F, starting in cell F6, enter the following budget figures:

1800
3500
2600
5000
1000
1800

Save the file and then Close it. Reopen your Lastname_Firstname_11L_Budget file. Change the User name to **Pat Andrews, Dental Assisting** Click the Dental Assisting sheet tab, and then enter the following budget figures in column F:

1500
15000
2600
5000
1000
2000

Save the file and then Close it. Open your Lastname_Firstname_11L_Budget - Copy file. Change the User name to **Samuel Manchester, Radiology** Click the Radiology sheet tab. In column F enter the following budget figures, and then Save and Close the file.

1200
10000
2200
3200
1000
1400

Open your Lastname_Firstname_11L_Budget file. Change the User name to **Dean Meyers** so that you can review all the various changes for the Division Dean. Add the Compare and Merge Workbooks command to the Quick Access Toolbar. Click Compare and Merge Workbooks. Select your Lastname_Firstname_11L_Budget - Copy file, and then click OK. Display the Highlight Changes

(Project 11L Budget continues on the next page)

Outcomes-Based Assessments

GO! Think | Project **11L** Budget (continued)

dialog box. Be sure the When check box is selected and that *All* is displayed. Select the Who check box, and then display *Everyone*. First you will view the changes and make any necessary adjustments. Click the Nursing sheet tab. Because the total budget and individual items seem reasonable, no changes are needed for the Nursing budget. Click the Dental Assisting sheet tab. Change cell F7 to **9,000** The total budget needs to be reduced, and the equipment expense seems excessive. Click the Radiology sheet tab. Because the total budget and individual items seem reasonable, no changes are needed for the Radiology budget.

Next, using Track Changes, click Accept/Reject Changes. Save the workbook. In the Select Changes to Accept or Reject dialog box, if necessary select the When check box, and then be sure *Not yet reviewed* is displayed and the Who check box, and then select Everyone but Me. Click OK. In the Accept or Reject Changes dialog box, click Accept All. Clear the check mark from Allow changes by more than one user at the same time check box, and then click OK. Click Yes to confirm. Select all three worksheets, and then display the Page Setup dialog box. Create a Custom footer, and in the Left section, add the File name. Add appropriate information to the document properties including the keyword **budget** Save and Close the file. Submit as directed by your instructor. Display a blank worksheet, and then display the Excel Options dialog box. On the General tab, restore the original User name to the name that you wrote down earlier, and then click OK. Remove the Compare and Merge Workbooks button from the Quick Access Toolbar.

End You have completed Project 11L ———————————

Apply a combination of the **11A** and **11B** skills.

GO! Think | Project **11M** Purchase Orders

Project Files

For Project 11M, you will need the following file:

e11M_Purchase_Orders

You will save your workbook as:

Lastname_Firstname_11M_Purchase_Orders

Open the file e11M_Purchase_Orders and save it as **Lastname_Firstname_11M_Purchase_Orders** Inspect the document and remove the hidden worksheet and all comments and annotations. Encrypt the workbook with the password *go*. Insert a footer with the file name in the left section. Add appropriate information to the document properties including the keywords **purchase orders** Mark the workbook as Final. Submit as directed by your instructor.

 End You have completed Project 11M ———————————

Apply a combination of the **11A** and **11B** skills.

You and GO! | Project **11N** Digital Signature

Project Files

For Project 11N, you will need the following file:

New blank workbook

You will save your workbook as:

Lastname_Firstname_11N_Digital_Signature

Open a blank workbook and save the file as **Lastname_Firstname_11N_Digital_Signature** Create a digital signature with your name to use on your personal documents. Add appropriate information to the document properties including the keywords **digital signature** and submit as directed by your instructor.

End **You have completed Project 11N** ———————————————

Business Running Case

Razvan CHIRNOAGA/Shutterstock

This project relates to **Front Range Action Sports**, which is one of the country's largest retailers of sports gear and outdoor recreation merchandise. The company has large retail stores in Colorado, Washington, Oregon, Idaho, California, and New Mexico, in addition to a growing online business. Major merchandise categories include fishing, camping, rock climbing, winter sports, action sports, water sports, team sports, racquet sports, fitness, golf, apparel, and footwear.

In this project, you will apply skills you practiced from the Objectives in Excel Chapters 10 and 11. You will develop a workbook for Frank Osei, the Vice President of Finance. You will import data about Sports suppliers and query the database to locate information. You will assist Mr. Osei in distributing a workbook of equipment and clothing inventory to the department managers. You will also create a shared workbook that the Store Manager will use to review proposed salary changes. Your completed worksheets will look similar to the ones shown in Figure 4.1.

Project Files

For Project BRC 4, you will need the following files:

  eBRC4_Company_Report
  eBRC4_Sports_Suppliers
  (Access file)

You will save your workbook as:

  Lastname_Firstname_BRC4_Company_
  Report

Project Results

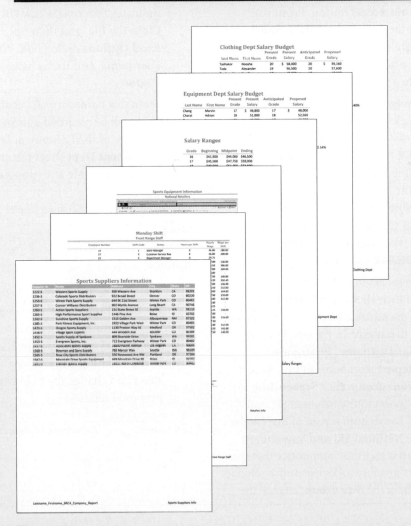

Figure 4.1

Business Running Case

Front Range Action Sports

1 **Start** Excel. From the student files that accompany this textbook, locate and open **eBRC4_Company_Report**. In the location where you are storing your projects, create a new folder named **Front_Range_Action_Sports** or navigate to this folder if you have already created it. **Save** the workbook as **Lastname_Firstname_BRC4_Company_Report** Group the worksheets, and insert a footer in the **left section** that includes the **File Name** and in the **right section**, includes the **Sheet Name**. Return to **Normal** view. Make cell **A1** the active cell. Display the **Document Panel**. In the **Author** box, type your firstname and lastname, in the **Subject** box, type your course name and section number, and in the **Keywords** box, type **company report Close** the **Document Panel**. Ungroup the worksheets.

a. Display the **Sports Suppliers Info** worksheet. Click in cell **A2**. On the **Data tab**, in the **Get External Data group**, click the **From Access** button. From your student files, select the Access file **eBRC4_Sports_Suppliers** as the data source, and then click **Open**. Import the data as a table in the existing worksheet. Convert the table to a range.

2 Display the **Front Range Staff** worksheet. Copy cell **C3**, and then paste it to cell **C28**. In cell **C29**, type **Customer Service Rep** and press `Tab`. Click cell **B28**, and then insert the **DAVERAGE** function. As the **Database**, use the range **A3:F26** as the **Field**, type **Hourly Wage** and as the **Criteria**, use the range **C28:C29** Click **OK**. Apply **Accounting Number Format** to the result. In **B39**, insert the **DGET** function. As the **Database**, type **A3:F26** as the **Field**, type **Employee Number** and as the **Criteria**, type **C39:E42** Your result is *44*.

3 Display the third worksheet in the workbook—**Retailers Info**—and then click cell **A5**. **Start** your Internet browser. In the **address bar**, type **www.nssra.com** and press `Enter` to navigate to the site. From the taskbar, redisplay your **Lastname_Firstname_BRC4_Company_Report** workbook. On the **Insert tab**, in the **Illustrations group**, click **Screenshot**. In the displayed gallery, point to the National Ski and Snowboard Retailers Association screen to display the **ScreenTip**. Click the **National Ski and Snowboard Retailers Association** screenshot, and notice that the screen image displays in your worksheet and is selected. Click the **Format tab**, in the **Size group**, change the **Shape Height** to **4.1"**

4 Display the **Salary Ranges** worksheet. Take a moment to examine the worksheet. The Salary Ranges sheet shows selected salary grades at Front Range Sports. Examine the other two sheets, **Equipment Department** and **Clothing Dept**. Each sheet contains a list of employees, their current grade and salary, and their proposed grade and salary based on a 2 percent increase. This information will be sent to the Department Managers of the Equipment and Clothing departments to review and adjust. Overall, the pay increases for the next fiscal year must be 2 percent on average, unless a promotion requires an increase in grade. Moving to a higher grade automatically includes a salary increase.

a. Display the **Highlight Changes** dialog box. Select the **Track changes while editing** check box, and be sure **When** indicates *All*, and **Who** is selected and indicates *Everyone*. Click **OK** to save the workbook. **Close** the file, and then open it again. Display the **Excel Options** dialog box. Write down the current **User name**, and then change the **User name** to **Tony Paxton**

b. From this point forward, changes made to the workbook will be recorded as being made by Tony Paxton, Manager of the Equipment Department. Click the **Equipment Dept sheet tab** and change the following anticipated grade and proposed salaries:

Last Name	Anticipated Grade	Proposed Salary
Chang		48000
Desprez	17	46800
Natarajan		53000

c. **Save** the file and **Close** it. Reopen the file and change the **User name** to **Randy Houston** From this point forward, any changes made to the workbook will be recorded as being made by Randy Houston, Manager of the Clothing Department. Click the **Clothing Dept sheet** and change the following anticipated grade and proposed salaries:

Last Name	Anticipated Grade	Proposed Salary
Tada		57000
Nicholson		50100
Chu	17	45500
Andersen		49900

(Business Running Case: Front Range Action Sports continues on the next page)

Business Running Case

Front Range Action Sports (continued)

d. **Save** the file and **Close** it. Reopen the file and change the **User name** to **Chris Jackson** the Store Director, who will accept or reject the changes. Display the **Highlight Changes** dialog box, change **When** to *All*, and be sure **Who** is selected and displays *Everyone*. Click each new salary in **column F**. Notice that salary changes were a change from a simple 2 percent increase to a specified amount. Now that some salaries have been changed by Department Managers, you will calculate the overall salary increase.

e. On the **Equipment Dept sheet**, in cell **G11**, enter a formula to calculate the percentage increase that the proposed salary total is over the present salary total. *Hint: = (Proposed Salary-Present Salary)/Present Salary.* Format the result as a percentage with two decimals. Your result should be 2.14%. Similarly, on the **Clothing Dept sheet**, in cell **G12**, calculate the percentage increase in total salary and format the results. Your result is 2.27%.

f. Display the **Select Changes to Accept or Reject** dialog box and save if prompted. Review changes for **Everyone but Me**. Accept all changes except the change for *Tada* in the Clothing department. After reviewing the changes, change Tada **Anticipated Grade** to **20** The higher grade is necessary to give him a full 2 percent increase in salary. The percentage for the Clothing Dept sheet changes to 2.40%.

5 **Save** the workbook. In the **Excel Options** dialog box, change the **User name** back to the user name that you wrote down earlier. **Print** or submit your workbook electronically. If required, print or create an electronic version of your worksheets with formulas displayed using the instructions in Activity 1.16 in Project 1A. If you printed your formulas, be sure to redisplay the worksheet by pressing Ctrl + `. **Close** the workbook and **Exit** Excel.

End **You have completed Business Running Case 4**

Glossary

.xlsx file name extension The default file format used by Excel 2010 to save an Excel workbook.

3-D The shortened term for *three-dimensional*, which refers to an image that appears to have all three spatial dimensions—length, width, and depth.

Absolute cell reference A cell reference that refers to cells by their fixed position in a worksheet; an absolute cell reference remains the same when the formula is copied.

Accounting Number Format The Excel number format that applies a thousand comma separator where appropriate, inserts a fixed U.S. Dollar sign aligned at the left edge of the cell, applies two decimal places, and leaves a small amount of space at the right edge of the cell to accommodate a parenthesis for negative numbers.

Active area The area of the worksheet that contains data or has contained data—it does not include any empty cells that have not been used in the worksheet.

Active cell The cell, surrounded by a black border, ready to receive data or be affected by the next Excel command.

ActiveX controls Graphic objects, such as check boxes or buttons, that you place on a form to display or enter data, perform an action, or make the form easier to read. When the person filling in the form clicks the ActiveX control, a macro or script runs that automates a task or offers options.

Add-ins Optional commands and features that are not immediately available and must be installed or activated to use.

Additive The term that describes the behavior of a filter when each additional filter that you apply is based on the current filter, and which further reduces the number of records displayed.

Address bar The bar at the top of a folder window with which you can navigate to a different folder or library, or go back to a previous one.

Advanced Filter A filter that can specify three or more criteria for a particular column, apply complex criteria to two or more columns, or specify computed criteria.

Alignment The placement of paragraph text relative to the left and right margins.

All Programs An area of the Start menu that displays all the available programs on your computer system.

And comparison operator The comparison operator that requires each and every one of the comparison criteria to be true.

Application Another term for a program.

Arguments The values that an Excel function uses to perform calculations or operations.

Arithmetic operators The symbols +, −, *, /, %, and ∧ used to denote addition, subtraction (or negation), multiplication, division, percentage, and exponentiation in an Excel formula.

Arrange All The command that tiles all open program windows on the screen.

Ascending The term that refers to the arrangement of text that is sorted alphabetically from A to Z, numbers sorted from lowest to highest, or dates and times sorted from earliest to latest.

Associated PivotTable report The PivotTable report in a workbook that is interactive with its PivotTable chart.

Auditing The process of examining a worksheet for errors in formulas.

Auto Fill An Excel feature that generates and extends values into adjacent cells based on the values of selected cells.

AutoComplete (Excel) A feature that speeds your typing and lessens the likelihood of errors; if the first few characters you type in a cell match an existing entry in the column, Excel fills in the remaining characters for you.

AutoFilter menu A drop-down menu from which you can filter a column by a list of values, by a format, or by criteria.

AutoFit An Excel feature that adjusts the width of a column to fit the cell content of the widest cell in the column.

AutoPlay A Windows feature that displays when you insert a CD, a DVD, or other removable device, and which lets you choose which program to use to start different kinds of media, such as music CDs, or CDs and DVDs containing photos.

AutoSum Another name for the *SUM* function.

AVERAGE function An Excel function that adds a group of values, and then divides the result by the number of values in the group.

Axis A line that serves as a frame of reference for measurement and which borders the chart plot area.

Back and Forward buttons Buttons at the top of a folder window that work in conjunction with the address bar to change folders by going backward or forward one folder at a time.

Backstage tabs The area along the left side of Backstage view with tabs to display various pages of commands.

Backstage view A centralized space for file management tasks; for example, opening, saving, printing, publishing, or sharing a file. A navigation pane displays along the left side with tabs that group file-related tasks together.

Base The starting point; used in calculating the rate of increase, which is the amount of increase divided by the base.

Bevel A shape effect that uses shading and shadows to make the edges of a shape appear to be curved or angled.

Break-even A point at which an entity covers its costs and starts to make a profit.

Category axis The area along the bottom of a chart that identifies the categories of data; also referred to as the *x-axis*.

Category labels The labels that display along the bottom of a chart to identify the categories of data; Excel uses the row titles as the category names.

Cell The intersection of a column and a row.

Cell address Another name for a *cell reference*.

Cell content Anything typed into a cell.

Cell reference The identification of a specific cell by its intersecting column letter and row number.

Cell style A defined set of formatting characteristics, such as font, font size, font color, cell borders, and cell shading.

Center alignment The alignment of text or objects that is centered horizontally between the left and right margin.

Certificate authority The certificate associated with a digital signature that is issued to the reputable signer. A commercial organization that issues digital certificates, keeps track of who is assigned to a certificate,

G-1

signs certificates to verify their validity, and tracks which certificates are revoked or expired.

Change history Information that is maintained about changes made in past editing sessions.

Chart (Excel) The graphic representation of data in a worksheet; data presented as a chart is usually easier to understand than a table of numbers.

Chart area The entire chart and all of its elements.

Chart elements Objects that make up a chart.

Chart Elements box The box in the Chart Tools tabs from which you can select a chart element so that you can format it.

Chart layout The combination of chart elements that can be displayed in a chart such as a title, legend, labels for the columns, and the table of charted cells.

Chart Layouts gallery A group of predesigned chart layouts that you can apply to an Excel chart.

Chart sheet A workbook sheet that contains only a chart.

Chart style The overall visual look of a chart in terms of its graphic effects, colors, and backgrounds; for example, you can have flat or beveled columns, colors that solid or transparent, and backgrounds that are dark or light.

Chart Styles gallery A group of predesigned chart styles that you can apply to an Excel chart.

Chart types Various chart formats used in a way that is meaningful to the reader; common examples are column charts, pie charts, and line charts.

Check boxes A type of ActiveX control that the person filling in the form can select to indicate a choice.

Clear Filter A command that removes a filter.

Click The action of pressing the left button on your mouse pointing device one time.

Cloud computing Use of Web servers of a third-party provider on the Internet to store files and run applications.

Collaboration The process of working jointly with others.

Column A vertical group of cells in a worksheet.

Column chart A chart in which the data is arranged in columns and which is useful for showing data changes over a period of time or for illustrating comparisons among items.

Column heading The letter that displays at the top of a vertical group of cells in a worksheet; beginning with the first letter of the alphabet, a unique letter or combination of letters identifies each column.

Column Labels area An area in the layout section of the PivotTable Field List in which you can position fields that you want to display as columns in the PivotTable report; field names placed here become column titles, and the data is grouped in columns by these titles.

Comma delimited file A file type that saves the contents of the cells by placing commas between them and an end-of-paragraph mark at the end of each row; also referred to as a *CSV (comma separated values) file*.

Comma Style The Excel number format that inserts thousand comma separators where appropriate and applies two decimal places; Comma Style also leaves space at the right to accommodate a parenthesis when negative numbers are present.

Command An instruction to a computer program that causes an action to be carried out.

Common dialog boxes The set of dialog boxes that includes Open, Save, and Save As, which are provided by the Windows programming

interface, and which display and operate in all of the Office programs in the same manner.

Comparison operator Symbols that evaluate each value to determine if it is the same (=), greater than (>), less than (<), or in between a range of values as specified by the criteria.

Compatibility Checker A feature that finds any potential compatibility issues and creates a report so that you can resolve the issues.

Compound criteria The use of two or more criteria on the same row—all conditions must be met for the records to be included in the results.

Compound filter A filter that uses more than one condition—and one that uses comparison operators.

Compressed file A file that has been reduced in size and thus takes up less storage space and can be transferred to other computers quickly.

Conditional format A format that changes the appearance of a cell—for example, by adding cell shading or font color—based on a condition; if the condition is true, the cell is formatted based on that condition, and if the condition is false, the cell is *not* formatted.

Constant value Numbers, text, dates, or times of day that you type into a cell.

Constraint cells Cells that contain values that limit or restrict the outcome.

Constraints In Solver, values that limit or restrict the outcome.

Context sensitive A command associated with activities in which you are engaged; often activated by right-clicking a screen item.

Context sensitive command A command associated with activities in which you are engaged.

Contextual tabs Tabs that are added to the Ribbon automatically when a specific object, such as a picture, is selected, and that contain commands relevant to the selected object.

Copy A command that duplicates a selection and places it on the Clipboard.

COUNTIF function A statistical function that counts the number of cells within a range that meet the given condition and that has two arguments—the range of cells to check and the criteria.

Criteria (Excel) Conditions that you specify in a logical function.

Criteria range An area on your worksheet where you define the criteria for the filter, and which indicates how the displayed records are filtered.

CSV (comma separated values) file A file type in which the cells in each row are separated by commas; also referred to as a *comma delimited file*.

Custom Filter A filter with which you can apply complex criteria to a single column.

Custom list A sort order that you can define.

Cut A command that removes a selection and places it on the Clipboard.

Cycle A continual process diagram.

Data Facts about people, events, things, or ideas.

Data (Excel) Text or numbers in a cell.

Data bar A cell format consisting of a shaded bar that provides a visual cue to the reader about the value of a cell relative to other cells; the length of the bar represents the value in the cell—a longer bar represents a higher value and a shorter bar represents s lower value.

Data labels Labels that display the value, percentage, and/or category of each particular data point and can contain one or more of the choices listed—Series name, Category name, Value, or Percentage.

Data marker A column, bar, area, dot, pie slice, or other symbol in a chart that represents a single data point; related data points form a data series.

Data point A value that originates in a worksheet cell and that is represented in a chart by a data marker.

Data series Related data points represented by data markers; each data series has a unique color or pattern represented in the chart legend.

Data table (Excel) A range of cells that shows how changing certain values in your formulas affect the results of those formulas and that makes it easy to calculate multiple versions in one operation.

Data validation (Excel) A technique by which you can control the type of data or the values that are entered into a cell by limiting the acceptable values to a defined list.

Database An organized collection of facts related to a specific topic.

DAVERAGE function A function that determines an average in a database that is limited by criteria set for one or more cells.

DCOUNT function A function that counts the number of occurrences of a specified condition in a database.

Debug A method to locate and correct errors step by step.

Decision variables In Solver, cells that will change to achieve a desired result; also called Variable cells.

Default The term that refers to the current selection or setting that is automatically used by a computer program unless you specify otherwise.

Defined name A word or string of characters in Excel that represents a cell, a range of cells, a formula, or a constant value; also referred to as simply a *name*.

Dependent cells Cells that contain formulas that refer to other cells.

Descending The term that refers to the arrangement of text that is sorted alphabetically from Z to A, numbers sorted from highest to lowest, or dates and times sorted from latest to earliest.

Deselect The action of canceling the selection of an object or block of text by clicking outside of the selection.

Design mode An Excel view in which you can work with ActiveX controls.

Desktop In Windows, the opening screen that simulates your work area.

Detail data The subtotaled rows that are totaled and summarized; typically adjacent to and either above or to the left of the summary data.

Detail sheets The worksheets that contain the details of the information summarized on a summary sheet.

Details pane The area at the bottom of a folder window that displays the most common file properties.

DGET function A function that extracts from your data table a single record that matches the conditions you specify.

Dialog box A small window that contains options for completing a task.

Dialog Box Launcher A small icon that displays to the right of some group names on the Ribbon, and which opens a related dialog box or task pane providing additional options and commands related to that group.

Digital certificate A digital means of proving identity and authenticity.

Digital ID Another name for digital signature—an electronic encryption-based, secure stamp of authentication on a document.

Digital signature An electronic, encryption-based, secure stamp of authentication on a macro or document.

Displayed value The data that displays in a cell.

Document Inspector A feature that can find and remove hidden properties and personal information in a workbook.

Document properties Details about a file that describe or identify it, including the title, author name, subject, and keywords that identify the document's topic or contents; also known as *metadata*.

Double-click The action of clicking the left mouse button two times in rapid succession.

Drag The action of holding down the left mouse button while moving your mouse.

Drag and drop The action of moving a selection by dragging it to a new location.

DSUM function A function that sums a column of values in a database that is limited by criteria set for one or more cells.

Edit The actions of making changes to text or graphics in an Office file.

Ellipsis A set of three dots indicating incompleteness; when following a command name, indicates that a dialog box will display.

Embed The action of inserting something created in one program into another program.

Embedded chart A chart that is inserted into the same worksheet that contains the data used to create the chart.

Encryption The process of restricting access to files by scrambling the contents with a program.

Enhanced ScreenTip A ScreenTip that displays more descriptive text than a normal ScreenTip.

Error Checking command A command that checks for common errors that occur in formulas.

Error value The result of a formula that Excel cannot evaluate correctly.

Evaluate Formula An auditing tool that helps you examine complex formulas.

Event The action that causes a program or macro to run, such as clicking a button or a command or pressing a combination of keys.

Excel table A series of rows and columns that contains related data that is managed independently from the data in other rows and columns in the worksheet.

Expand Formula Bar button An Excel window element with which you can increase the height of the Formula Bar to display lengthy cell content.

Expand horizontal scroll bar button An Excel window element with which you can increase the width of the horizontal scroll bar.

Explode The action of pulling out one or more pie slices from a pie chart for emphasis.

Extensible Markup Language (XML) A language that structures data in text files so that it can be read by other systems, regardless of the hardware platform or operating system.

Extract 1. To decompress, or pull out, files from a compressed form. 2. The location to which you copy the records is the Extract area, and is commonly placed below the table of data. Using this technique you can extract—pull out—multiple sets of data for comparison purposes.

Extract area The location to which you copy records when extracting filtered rows.

Extracting The process of pulling out multiple sets of data for comparison purposes.

Field A specific type of data such as name, employee number, or social security number that is stored in columns.

Field buttons Buttons on a PivotChart with an arrow to choose a filter, and thus change the data that is displayed in the chart.

Field names The column titles from source data that form categories of data for a PivotTable report.

Field section The upper portion of the PivotTable Field List that contains the names of all the field names—the column titles in the source data.

File A collection of information stored on a computer under a single name, for example a Word document or a PowerPoint presentation.

File list In a folder window, the area on the right that displays the contents of the current folder or library.

Fill The inside color of an object.

Fill handle The small black square in the lower right corner of a selected cell.

Filter The process of displaying only a portion of the data based on matching a specific value to show only the data that meets the criteria that you specify.

Filtering A process in which only the rows that meet the criteria display; rows that do not meet the criteria are hidden.

Filtering buttons The buttons on a slicer which you use to select the item by which to filter.

Financial functions Pre-built formulas that perform common business calculations such as calculating a loan payment on a vehicle or calculating how much to save each month to buy something; financial functions commonly involve a period of time such as months or years.

Find A command that finds and selects specific text or formatting.

Find and replace (Excel) A command that searches the cells in a worksheet—or in a selected range—for matches and then replaces each match with a replacement value of your choice.

Fixed expenses Expenses that remain the same each month.

Folder A container in which you store files.

Folder window In Windows, a window that displays the contents of the current folder, library, or device, and contains helpful parts so that you can navigate.

Font A set of characters with the same design and shape.

Font styles Formatting emphasis such as bold, italic, and underline.

Footer A reserved area for text or graphics that displays at the bottom of each page in a document.

Format (Excel) Changing the appearance of cells and worksheet elements to make a worksheet attractive and easy to read.

Format as you type The Excel feature by which a cell takes on the formatting of the number typed into the cell.

Format Painter An Office feature that copies formatting from one selection of text to another.

Formatting The process of establishing the overall appearance of text, graphics, and pages in an Office file—for example, in a Word document.

Formatting marks Characters that display on the screen, but do not print, indicating where the Enter key, the Spacebar, and the Tab key were pressed; also called *nonprinting characters*.

Formula An equation that performs mathematical calculations on values in a worksheet.

Formula Auditing Tools and commands accessible from the Formulas tab that help you check your worksheet for errors.

Formula AutoComplete An Excel feature which, after typing an = (equal sign) and the beginning letter or letters of a function name, displays a list of function names that match the typed letter(s).

Formula Bar An element in the Excel window that displays the value or formula contained in the active cell; here you can also enter or edit values or formulas.

Freeze Panes A command that enables you to select one or more rows or columns and freeze (lock) them into place; the locked rows and columns become separate panes.

Function A predefined formula—a formula that Excel has already built for you—that performs calculations by using specific values in a particular order or structure.

Functions Predefined formulas that perform calculations by using specific values, called arguments, in a particular order or structure.

Fund A sum of money set aside for a specific purpose.

Future value (Fv) The value at the end of the time periods in an Excel function; the cash balance you want to attain after the last payment is made—usually zero for loans.

Gallery An Office feature that displays a list of potential results instead of just the command name.

General format The default format that Excel applies to numbers; this format has no specific characteristics—whatever you type in the cell will display, with the exception that trailing zeros to the right of a decimal point will not display.

General fund The term used to describe money set aside for the normal operating activities of a government entity such as a city.

Get External Data group A group of commands that enables you to bring data from an Access database, from the Web, from a text file, or from an XML file into Excel without repeatedly copying the data.

Go To A command that moves to a specific cell or range of cells that you specify.

Go To Special A command that moves to cells that have special characteristics, for example, to cells that are blank or to cells that contain constants, as opposed to formulas.

Goal Seek One of Excel's What-If Analysis tools that provides a method to find a specific value for a cell by adjusting the value of one other cell—find the right input when you know the result you want.

Gridlines Lines in the plot area that aid the eye in determining the plotted values.

Groups On the Office Ribbon, the sets of related commands that you might need for a specific type of task.

Header A reserved area for text or graphics that displays at the top of each page in a document.

Hierarchy A category of SmartArt graphics used to create an organization chart or show a decision tree.

HLOOKUP An Excel function that looks up values that are displayed horizontally in a row.

Horizontal Category axis (x-axis) This displays along the bottom of the chart to identify the category of data.

Horizontal window split box (Excel) An Excel window element with which you can split the worksheet into two horizontal views of the same worksheet.

HTML (Hypertext Markup Language) A language Web browsers can interpret when you save a worksheet as a Web page.

Hyperlink Text or graphics that, when clicked, take you to another location in the worksheet, to another file, or to a Web page on the Internet or on your organization's intranet.

Icons Pictures that represent a program, a file, a folder, or some other object.

Icon sets A group of three, four, or five small graphic images that make your data visually easier to interpret and are used to add emphasis to the conditional format of a list.

IF function A function that uses a logical test to check whether a condition is met, and then returns one value if true, and another value if false.

Info tab The tab in Backstage view that displays information about the current file.

Information Data that has been organized in a useful manner.

Insert Worksheet button Located on the row of sheet tabs, a sheet tab that, when clicked, inserts an additional worksheet into the workbook.

Insertion point A blinking vertical line that indicates where text or graphics will be inserted.

Integer A whole number used in mathematical computations.

Interest The amount charged for the use of borrowed money.

Interval In a moving average, the number of cells to include in the average.

Intranet A network within an organization that uses Internet technologies.

Keyboard shortcut A combination of two or more keyboard keys, used to perform a task that would otherwise require a mouse.

KeyTips The letter that displays on a command in the Ribbon and that indicates the key you can press to activate the command when keyboard control of the Ribbon is activated.

Labels Column and row headings that describe the values and help the reader understand the chart.

Landscape orientation A page orientation in which the paper is wider than it is tall.

Layout section The lower portion of the PivotTable field list that has four areas where you can build the PivotTable report by rearranging and repositioning fields.

Left alignment (Excel) The cell format in which characters align at the left edge of the cell; this is the default for text entries and is an example of formatting information stored in a cell.

Legend A chart element that identifies the patterns or colors that are assigned to the categories in the chart.

Lettered column headings The area along the top edge of a worksheet that identifies each column with a unique letter or combination of letters.

Library In Windows, a collection of items, such as files and folders, assembled from various locations that might be on your computer, an external hard drive, removable media, or someone else's computer.

Line chart A chart type that is useful to display trends over time; time displays along the bottom axis and the data point values are connected with a line.

List 1. A series of rows that contains related data that you can group by adding subtotals. 2. A category of SmartArt graphics used to show non-sequential information.

Live Preview A technology that shows the result of applying an editing or formatting change as you point to possible results—*before* you actually apply it.

Location Any disk drive, folder, or other place in which you can store files and folders.

Locked [cells] Formula cells that prevent others from changing the formulas in the template.

Logical functions A group of functions that test for specific conditions and that typically use conditional tests to determine whether specified conditions are true or false.

Logical test Any value or expression that can be evaluated as being true or false.

Lookup functions A group of Excel functions that look up a value in a defined range of cells located in another part of the workbook to find a corresponding value.

Macro A series of commands and functions that are grouped together as a single command.

Macro virus A malicious macro that is written with the intent to erase or damage files on another computer.

Major sort A term sometimes used to refer to the first sort level in the Sort dialog box.

Major unit value A number that determines the spacing between tick marks and between the gridlines in the plot area.

Mark As Final command A command which makes the document read-only and prevents additional changes to the document and disables typing, editing comments, and proofing marks.

Matrix A category of SmartArt graphics used to show how parts relate to a whole.

MAX function An Excel function that determines the largest value in a selected range of values.

MEDIAN function An Excel function that finds the middle value that has as many values above it in the group as are below it; it differs from AVERAGE in that the result is not affected as much by a single value that is greatly different from the others.

Merge & Center A command that joins selected cells in an Excel worksheet into one larger cell and centers the contents in the new cell.

Metadata Details about a file that describe or identify it, including the title, author name, subject, and keywords that identify the document's topic or contents; also known as *document properties*.

Microsoft Access A database program, with which you can collect, track, and report data.

Microsoft Communicator An Office program that brings together multiple modes of communication, including instant messaging, video conferencing, telephony, application sharing, and file transfer.

Microsoft Excel A spreadsheet program, with which you calculate and analyze numbers and create charts.

Microsoft InfoPath An Office program that enables you to create forms and gather data.

Microsoft Office 2010 A Microsoft suite of products that includes programs, servers, and services for individuals, small organizations, and large enterprises to perform specific tasks.

Microsoft OneNote An Office program with which you can manage notes that you make at meetings or in classes.

Microsoft Outlook An Office program with which you can manage e-mail and organizational activities.

Microsoft PowerPoint A presentation program, with which you can communicate information with high-impact graphics.

Microsoft Publisher An Office program with which you can create desktop publishing documents such as brochures.

Microsoft SharePoint Workspace An Office program that enables you to share information with others in a team environment.

Microsoft Word A word processing program, also referred to as an authoring program, with which you create and share documents by using its writing tools.

MIN function An Excel function that determines the smallest value in a selected range of values.

Mini toolbar A small toolbar containing frequently used formatting commands that displays as a result of selecting text or objects.

Module The programming code written in VBA when you record a new macro; the place where the VBA code is stored.

Moving average A sequence of averages computed from parts of a data series; it is used to smooth out fluctuations in data to show a pattern or trend more clearly.

Name A word or string of characters in Excel that represents a cell, a range of cells, a formula, or a constant value; also referred to as a *defined name*.

Name Box An element of the Excel window that displays the name of the selected cell, table, chart, or object.

Navigate The process of exploring within the organizing structure of Windows.

Navigate (Excel) The process of moving within a worksheet or workbook.

Navigation pane (Windows) In a folder window, the area on the left in which you can navigate to, open, and display favorites, libraries, folders, saved searches, and an expandable list of drives.

Nonprinting characters Characters that display on the screen, but do not print, indicating where the Enter key, the Spacebar, and the Tab key were pressed; also called *formatting marks*.

Normal view (Excel) A screen view that maximizes the number of cells visible on your screen and keeps the column letters and row numbers close to the columns and rows.

NOW function An Excel function that retrieves the date and time from your computer's calendar and clock and inserts the information into the selected cell.

Nper The abbreviation for *number of time periods* in various Excel functions.

Number format A specific way in which Excel displays numbers in a cell.

Number values Constant values consisting of only numbers.

Numbered row headings The area along the left edge of a worksheet that identifies each row with a unique number.

Objective cell In Solver, a cell that contains a formula for the results you are trying to determine, usually defined as a minimum, a maximum, or a specified value.

Office Clipboard A temporary storage area that holds text or graphics that you select and then cut or copy.

One-variable data table A data table that changes the value in only one cell.

Operators The symbols with which you can specify the type of calculation you want to perform in an Excel formula.

Option button A round button that allows you to make one choice among two or more options.

Options dialog box A dialog box within each Office application where you can select program settings and other options and preferences.

Or comparison operator The comparison operator that requires only one of the two comparison criteria that you specify to be true.

Order of operations The mathematical rules for performing multiple calculations within a formula.

Organization chart A type of graphic that is useful to depict reporting relationships within an organization.

Page Layout view A screen view in which you can use the rulers to measure the width and height of data, set margins for printing, hide or display the numbered row headings and the lettered column headings, and change the page orientation; this view is useful for preparing your worksheet for printing.

Pane (Excel) A portion of a worksheet window bounded by and separated from other portions by vertical and horizontal bars.

Paragraph symbol The symbol ¶ that represents a paragraph.

Password An optional element of a template added to prevent someone from disabling a worksheet's protection.

Paste The action of placing text or objects that have been copied or moved from one location to another location.

Paste area The target destination for data that has been cut or copied using the Office Clipboard.

Paste Options gallery (Excel) A gallery of buttons that provides a Live Preview of all the Paste options available in the current context.

PDF (Portable Document Format) file A file format that creates an image that preserves the look of your file, but that cannot be easily changed; a popular format for sending documents electronically, because the document will display on most computers.

Percent for new value = base percent + percent of increase The formula for calculating a percentage by which a value increases by adding the base percentage—usually 100%—to the percent increase.

Percentage rate of increase The percent by which one number increases over another number.

Picture A type of graphic that is useful to display pictures in a diagram.

Picture element A point of light measured in dots per square inch on a screen; 64 pixels equals 8.43 characters, which is the average number of digits that will fit in a cell in an Excel worksheet using the default font.

Pie chart A chart that shows the relationship of each part to a whole.

PivotChart report A graphical representation of the data in a PivotTable report.

PivotTable Another name for Excel's PivotTable report.

PivotTable Field List A window that lists, at the top, all of the fields—column titles—from the source data for use in the PivotTable report and at the bottom, an area in which you can arrange the fields in the PivotTable.

PivotTable report An interactive, cross-tabulated Excel report that summarizes and analyzes large amounts of data.

Pixel The abbreviated name for a *picture element*.

Plot area The area bounded by the axes of a chart, including all the data series.

PMT function An Excel function that calculates the payment for a loan based on constant payments and at a constant interest rate.

Point The action of moving your mouse pointer over something on your screen.

Point and click method The technique of constructing a formula by pointing to and then clicking cells; this method is convenient when the referenced cells are not adjacent to one another.

Pointer Any symbol that displays on your screen in response to moving your mouse.

Points A measurement of the size of a font; there are 72 points in an inch, with 10-12 points being the most commonly used font size.

Portrait orientation A page orientation in which the paper is taller than it is wide.

Precedent cells Cells that are referred to by a formula in another cell.

Present value (Pv) The total amount that a series of future payments is worth now; also known as the *principal*.

Preview pane button In a folder window, the button on the toolbar with which you can display a preview of the contents of a file without opening it in a program.

Principal Another term for present value.

Print Preview A view of a document as it will appear when you print it.

Print Titles An Excel command that enables you to specify rows and columns to repeat on each printed page.

Procedure A named sequence of statements in a computer program that performs a task.

Process A category of SmartArt graphics that is used to show steps in a process or timeline.

Program A set of instructions that a computer uses to perform a specific task, such as word processing, accounting, or data management; also called an *application*.

Program-level control buttons In an Office program, the buttons on the right edge of the title bar that minimize, restore, or close the program.

Properties Characteristics of an object that can be changed; details about a file that help identify it, such as the author, date created, and file name.

Protected view A security feature in Office 2010 that protects your computer from malicious files by opening them in a restricted environment until you enable them; you might encounter this feature if you open a file from an e-mail or download files from the Internet.

Protection This prevents anyone from altering the formulas or changing other template components.

Pt. The abbreviation for *point*; for example when referring to a font size.

Pyramid A category of SmartArt graphics that uses a series of pictures to show relationships.

Query A process of restricting records through the use of criteria conditions that will display records that will answer a question about the data.

Quick Access Toolbar In an Office program, the small row of buttons in the upper left corner of the screen from which you can perform frequently used commands.

Quick Commands The commands Save, Save As, Open, and Close that display at the top of the navigation pane in Backstage view.

Range Two or more selected cells on a worksheet that are adjacent or nonadjacent; because the range is treated as a single unit, you can make the same changes or combination of changes to more than one cell at a time.

Range finder An Excel feature that outlines cells in color to indicate which cells are used in a formula; useful for verifying which cells are referenced in a formula.

Rate In the Excel PMT function, the term used to indicate the interest rate for a loan.

Rate = amount of increase/base The mathematical formula to calculate a rate of increase.

Read-Only A property assigned to a file that prevents the file from being modified or deleted; it indicates that you cannot save any changes to the displayed document unless you first save it with a new name.

Record All the categories of data pertaining to one person, place, thing, event, or idea.

Record Macro A command that records your actions in Visual Basic for Applications (VBA).

Refresh The command to update a worksheet to reflect the new data.

Relationship A category of SmartArt graphics that is used to illustrate connections.

Relative cell reference In a formula, the address of a cell based on the relative position of the cell that contains the formula and the cell referred to.

Report Filter area An area in the layout section of the PivotTable Field List in which you can position fields by which you want to filter the PivotTable report, thus enabling you to display a subset of data in the PivotTable report.

Ribbon The user interface in Office 2010 that groups the commands for performing related tasks on tabs across the upper portion of the program window.

Ribbon tabs The tabs on the Office Ribbon that display the names of the task-oriented groups of commands.

Right-click The action of clicking the right mouse button one time.

Rotation handle A green circle that displays on the top side of a selected object.

Rounding A procedure in which you determine which digit at the right of the number will be the last digit displayed and then increase it by one if the next digit to its right is 5, 6, 7, 8, or 9.

Row A horizontal group of cells in a worksheet.

Row heading The numbers along the left side of an Excel worksheet that designate the row numbers.

Row Labels area An area in the layout section of the PivotTable Field List in which you can position fields that you want to display as rows in the PivotTable report; field names placed here become row titles, and the data is grouped by these row titles.

Sans serif A font design with no lines or extensions on the ends of characters.

Scale The range of numbers in the data series that controls the minimum, maximum, and incremental values on the value axis.

Scale to Fit Excel commands that enable you to stretch or shrink the width, height, or both, of printed output to fit a maximum number of pages.

Scaling (Excel) The group of commands by which you can reduce the horizontal and vertical size of the printed data by a percentage or by the number of pages that you specify.

Scenario A set of values that Excel saves and can substitute automatically in your worksheet.

Scenario Manager A what-if analysis tool that compares alternatives.

Schema An XML file that contains the rules for what can and cannot reside in an XML data file.

Scope The location within which a defined name is recognized without qualification—usually either to a specific worksheet or to the entire workbook.

Screenshot An image of an active window on your computer that you can insert into a worksheet.

ScreenTip A small box that that displays useful information when you perform various mouse actions such as pointing to screen elements or dragging.

Scroll bar A vertical or horizontal bar in a window or a pane to assist in bringing an area into view, and which contains a scroll box and scroll arrows.

Scroll box The box in the vertical and horizontal scroll bars that can be dragged to reposition the contents of a window or pane on the screen.

Search box In a folder window, the box in which you can type a word or a phrase to look for an item in the current folder or library.

Select To highlight, by dragging with your mouse, areas of text or data or graphics, so that the selection can be edited, formatted, copied, or moved.

Select All box A box in the upper left corner of the worksheet grid that, when clicked, selects all the cells in a worksheet.

Self-signed An unauthenticated certificate created by the signer of a document.

Series A group of things that come one after another in succession; for example, January, February, March, and so on.

Serif font A font design that includes small line extensions on the ends of the letters to guide the eye in reading from left to right.

Shared workbook A workbook set up to allow multiple users on a network to view and make changes at the same time.

Sheet tab scrolling buttons Buttons to the left of the sheet tabs used to display Excel sheet tabs that are not in view; used when there are more sheet tabs than will display in the space provided.

Sheet tabs The labels along the lower border of the Excel window that identify each worksheet.

Shortcut menu A menu that displays commands and options relevant to the selected text or object.

Signature line A line in a document that specifies the individual who must sign the document.

Slicer header This indicates the name at the top of a slicer that indicates the category of the slicer items.

Slicers Easy-to-use filtering controls with buttons that enable you to intuitively drill down through large amounts of data in an interactive way.

SmartArt graphic A visual representation of your information and ideas.

Solver A what-if analysis tool that can help you find an optimal value for a formula in one cell—subject to constraints on the values of other formula cells on a worksheet.

Sort The process of arranging data in a specific order based on the value in each field.

Sort dialog box A dialog box in which you can sort data based on several criteria at once, and which enables a sort by more than one column or row.

Source data Data in an Excel worksheet, or from an external source, arranged in columns and rows in a format suitable to be used for a PivotTable report table or range in the current worksheet.

Sparkline A tiny chart in the background of a cell that gives a visual trend summary alongside your data; makes a pattern more obvious.

Sparklines Tiny charts that fit within a cell and give a visual trend summary alongside your data.

Split The command that enables you to view separate parts of the same worksheet on your screen; splits the window into multiple resizable panes to view distant parts of the worksheet at one time.

Split button A button divided into two parts and in which clicking the main part of the button performs a command and clicking the arrow opens a menu with choices.

Spreadsheet Another name for a *worksheet*.

Standardization All forms created within the organization will have a uniform appearance; the data will always be organized in the same manner.

Start button The button on the Windows taskbar that displays the Start menu.

Start menu The Windows menu that provides a list of choices and is the main gateway to your computer's programs, folders, and settings.

Statistical functions Excel functions, including the AVERAGE, MEDIAN, MIN, and MAX functions, which are useful to analyze a group of measurements.

Status bar The area along the lower edge of an Office program window that displays file information on the left and buttons to control how the window looks on the right.

Status bar (Excel) The area along the lower edge of the Excel window that displays, on the left side, the current cell mode, page number, and worksheet information; on the right side, when numerical data is selected, common calculations such as Sum and Average display.

Sub The abbreviation for a sub procedure.

Sub procedure A set of instructions that accomplishes a specific task.

Subfolder A folder within a folder.

Subtotal command The command that totals several rows of related data together by automatically inserting subtotals and totals for the selected cells.

SUM function A predefined formula that adds all the numbers in a selected range of cells.

Summary sheet A worksheet where totals from other worksheets are displayed and summarized.

Syntax The arrangement of the arguments in a function.

Tab delimited text file A file type in which cells are separated by tabs; this type of file can be readily exchanged with various database programs.

Table Information stored in a format of rows and columns.

Table array A defined range of cells, arranged in a column or a row, used in a VLOOKUP or HLOOKUP function.

Tabs On the Office Ribbon, the name of each activity area in the Office Ribbon.

Tags Custom file properties that you create to help find and organize your own files.

Task pane A window within a Microsoft Office application in which you can enter options for completing a command.

Template A workbook used as a pattern for creating other workbooks.

Text box A movable resizable container for text or graphics.

Text file A file type that separates the cells of each row with tab characters.

Text pane This always displays to the left of the graphic, is populated with placeholder text, and is used to build a graphic by entering and editing text.

Text values Constant values consisting of only text, and which usually provides information about number values; also referred to as *labels*.

Theme A predesigned set of colors, fonts, lines, and fill effects that look good together and that can be applied to your entire document or to specific items.

Tick mark labels Identifying information for a tick mark generated from the cells on the worksheet used to create the chart.

Tick marks The short lines that display on an axis at regular intervals.

Title bar The bar at the top edge of the program window that indicates the name of the current file and the program name.

Toggle button A button that can be turned on by clicking it once, and then turned off by clicking it again.

Toolbar In a folder window, a row of buttons with which you can perform common tasks, such as changing the view of your files and folders or burning files to a CD.

Trace Dependents command A command that displays arrows that indicate what cells are affected by the value of the currently selected cell.

Trace Error command A tool that helps locate and resolve an error by tracing the selected error value.

Trace Precedents command A command that displays arrows to indicate what cells affect the value of the cell that is selected.

Tracer arrow An indicator that shows the relationship between the active cell and its related cell.

Track Changes A feature in which you can make changes that can be viewed by others and also in which the changes can be accepted or rejected.

Trendline A graphic representation of trends in a data series, such as a line sloping upward to represent increased sales over a period of months.

Triple-click The action of clicking the left mouse button three times in rapid succession.

Trusted Documents A security feature in Office 2010 that remembers which files you have already enabled; you might encounter this feature if you open a file from an e-mail or download files from the Internet.

Two-variable data table A data table that changes the values in two cells.

Type argument An optional argument in the PMT function that assumes that the payment will be made at the end of each time period.

Underlying formula The formula entered in a cell and visible only on the Formula Bar.

Underlying value The data that displays in the Formula Bar.

Unlocked [cells] Cells in a template that may be filled in.

USB flash drive A small data storage device that plugs into a computer USB port.

Validation list (Excel) A list of values that are acceptable for a group of cells; only values on the list are valid and any value *not* on the list is considered invalid.

Value Another name for a *constant value*.

Value after increase = base x percent for new value The formula for calculating the value after an increase by multiplying the original value—the base—by the percent for new value (see the *Percent for new value* formula).

Value axis A numerical scale on the left side of a chart that shows the range of numbers for the data points; also referred to as the *y-axis*.

Values area An area in the layout section of the PivotTable Field List in which you can position fields that contain data that is summarized in a PivotTable report or PivotChart report; the data placed here is usually numeric or financial in nature and the data is summarized—summed.

Variable cells In Solver, cells that will change to achieve a desired result; also called *Decision variables*.

Variable expenses Expenses that vary depending on the amount of sales.

VBA The abbreviation for the Visual Basic for Applications programming language.

VBA construct An instruction that enables a macro to perform multiple operations on a single object.

Vertical Value axis (y-axis) This displays along the left side of the chart to identify the numerical scale on which the charted data is based.

Vertical window split box (Excel) A small box on the vertical scroll bar with which you can split the window into two vertical views of the same worksheet.

Views button In a folder window, a toolbar button with which you can choose how to view the contents of the current location.

Visual Basic Editor window The window in which you can view Visual Basic modules written for Windows-based applications.

Visual Basic for Applications The programming language used to write computer programs in the Microsoft Windows environment.

VLOOKUP An Excel function that looks up values that are displayed vertically in a column.

Volatile A term used to describe an Excel function that is subject to change each time the workbook is reopened; for example the NOW function updates itself to the current date and time each time the workbook is opened.

Walls and floor The areas surrounding a 3-D chart that give dimension and boundaries to the chart.

Watch Window A window that displays the results of specified cells.

What-if analysis The process of changing the values in cells to see how those changes affect the outcome of formulas in a worksheet.

Wildcard A character, for example the asterisk or question mark, used to search a field when you are uncertain of the exact value or when you want to widen the search to include more records.

Window A rectangular area on a computer screen in which programs and content appear, and which can be moved, resized, minimized, or closed.

Windows Explorer The program that displays the files and folders on your computer, and which is at work anytime you are viewing the contents of files and folders in a window.

Windows Live ID A security feature of Windows Live SkyDrive that controls access to files.

Windows Live SkyDrive A free online service that provides file storage and file sharing services on a Windows Live Internet site.

Windows taskbar The area along the lower edge of the Windows desktop that contains the Start button and an area to display buttons for open programs.

WordArt A feature that transforms text into a stylized image that you can use to create a distinctive logo or heading.

Workbook An Excel file that contains one or more worksheets.

Workbook-level buttons Buttons at the far right of the Ribbon tabs that minimize or restore a displayed workbook.

Worksheet The primary document that you use in Excel to work with and store data, and which is formatted as a pattern of uniformly spaced horizontal and vertical lines.

x-axis Another name for the horizontal *(category) axis*.

XPS (XML Paper Specification) A file type, developed by Microsoft, that provides an accurate visual representation of a document across applications and platforms.

y-axis Another name for the vertical *(value) axis*.

Zoom The action of increasing or decreasing the viewing area on the screen.

Index

Manage box, Excel Add-ins, 499, 510
margins
    alignment, 34
    center alignment, 34
    rulers, 27
Margins button, Custom Margins, 639
Margins tab, 255, 337
Marker Line Color, 382
Marker Options, Solid fill, 382
matrix, SmartArt type, 384
MAX function, 120
Maximize button, 304, 306
MEDIAN function, 119–120
menus. *See also specific menus*
    shortcut, 11
    shortcuts, 501
    Start, All Programs, 7
Merge & Center button, 64–65, 247, 250, 609, 611, 614, 620
    Alignment group, 393
    Home tab, 251, 307
    Title cell style, 307
Message tab, 276
metadata, 14, 667
Microsoft. *See specific programs*
Middle Align Button, 251
Middle Border button, 391, 393
MIN function, 120
Minimize button, 304, 306
minimizing, Ribbon, 31–32
Minimum Fixed option button, Axis Options, 507
Mini toolbar, 10, 36, 255
    Accounting Number Format button, 623
    Fill Color button arrow, 302
    Font Size, 376
    Format Painter, 254
    Percent Style button, 502
Modify Button dialog box, macros, 556
modules
    procedures, 557
    VBA, 557
Month field, Column Labels area, 436
More button
    Chart Layouts group, 452
    Design tab, 323, 437, 631
    Options tab, 438
More Commands dialog box, 28
More Controls, ActiveX controls, 562
More Functions button, 303
mouse pointer, 9
Move Chart button, Design tab, 372, 452, 501
Move or Copy dialog box, Sheet tab, 441
moving
    cell data, 121–122
    in documents, keyboard shortcuts, 38
    worksheets, 154–155
moving average
    calculations, 497–503
      growth, 502–503
    forecasts, 502
    modifying, 501–502
Moving Average dialog box, intervals, 500
multiple columns, sorting, 323–326
multiple workbooks, 303–307
multiplication, order of operations, 197
multi-sheet workbooks, printing, 629

My data has headers, 269
My table has headers, Create Table dialog box, 631
My Templates, 390, 400

N

#N/A error value, 270, 272, 460, 500
names, 257–261. *See also* **defined names**
    _ (underscore), 260
    cells, 258
    Create from Selection command, 273
    definition, 259
    files, footers, 332–333
    formatting, 264
    groups, 8
    saving files, 22–25
    workbooks, 51–52
    worksheets, 138–139
Name Box, 52, 258, 260, 261, 262, 264
    criteria range, 334
    Find Next, 305
    Formula Bar, 259
    Items, 468
    New Table Quick Style, 308
    PMT function, 252
Name column, Name Manager dialog box, 262
#NAME? error value, 265, 460
Name Manager button
    Defined Names group, 261, 274
    Formulas tab, 334
Name Manager dialog box
    Defined Names group, 262, 263
    Name column, 262
    New button, 261
    Refers to box, 262
navigation
    definition, 3
    documents, keyboard shortcuts, 38
    large worksheets, 301
    worksheets, 53–54, 138–139
      keyboard shortcuts, 57
Navigation group, Go to Footer, 667
Navigation pane, 5
nesting, Row Labels area, 435
New button, Name Manager dialog box, 261
NEW LIST, Custom Lists dialog box, 327
New Name dialog box, 258, 259
New sheet box, New sheet option button, 372
New sheet option button, New sheet box, 372
New tab, Backstage view, 390
New Table Quick Style, Name box, 308
New Web Query dialog box, Address bar, 610
New York-New Jersey Job Fair, 367–423
Next, Error Checking button, 467
Next Page, Print Preview, 311, 312
nonprinting characters, definition, 25
Normal, 73, 276
    status bar, 255, 574
    Workbook Views group, 312
Note cell, Data and Model, 254
NOW function, 128–129
nper. *See* **number of payments**
Nper box, 252
#NULL! error value, 460

T

SINGLE PC LICENSE AGREEMENT AND LIMITED WARRANTY

READ THIS LICENSE CAREFULLY BEFORE OPENING THIS PACKAGE. BY OPENING THIS PACKAGE, YOU ARE AGREEING TO THE TERMS AND CONDITIONS OF THIS LICENSE. IF YOU DO NOT AGREE, DO NOT OPEN THE PACKAGE. PROMPTLY RETURN THE UNOPENED PACKAGE AND ALL ACCOMPANYING ITEMS TO THE PLACE YOU OBTAINED THEM. *THESE TERMS APPLY TO ALL LICENSED SOFTWARE ON THE DISK EXCEPT THAT THE TERMS FOR USE OF ANY SHAREWARE OR FREEWARE ON THE DISKETTES ARE AS SET FORTH IN THE ELECTRONIC LICENSE LOCATED ON THE DISK:*

1. GRANT OF LICENSE and OWNERSHIP: The enclosed computer programs ("Software") are licensed, not sold, to you by Prentice-Hall, Inc. ("We" or the "Company") and in consideration of your purchase or adoption of the accompanying Company textbooks and/or other materials, and your agreement to these terms. We reserve any rights not granted to you. You own only the disk(s) but we and/or our licensors own the Software itself. This license allows you to use and display your copy of the Software on a single computer (i.e., with a single CPU) at a single location for academic use only, so long as you comply with the terms of this Agreement. You may make one copy for back up, or transfer your copy to another CPU, provided that the Software is usable on only one computer.

2. RESTRICTIONS: You may not transfer or distribute the Software or documentation to anyone else. Except for backup, you may not copy the documentation or the Software. You may not network the Software or otherwise use it on more than one computer or computer terminal at the same time. You may not reverse engineer, disassemble, decompile, modify, adapt, translate, or create derivative works based on the Software or the Documentation. You may be held legally responsible for any copying or copyright infringement which is caused by your failure to abide by the terms of these restrictions.

3. TERMINATION: This license is effective until terminated. This license will terminate automatically without notice from the Company if you fail to comply with any provisions or limitations of this license. Upon termination, you shall destroy the Documentation and all copies of the Software. All provisions of this Agreement as to limitation and disclaimer of warranties, limitation of liability, remedies or damages, and our ownership rights shall survive termination.

4.DISCLAIMER OF WARRANTY: THE COMPANY AND ITS LICENSORS MAKE NO WARRANTIES ABOUT THE SOFTWARE, WHICH IS PROVIDED "AS-IS." IF THE DISK IS DEFECTIVE IN MATERIALS OR WORKMANSHIP, YOUR ONLY REMEDY IS TO RETURN IT TO THE COMPANY WITHIN 30 DAYS FOR REPLACEMENT UNLESS THE COMPANY DETERMINES IN GOOD FAITH THAT THE DISK HAS BEEN MISUSED OR IMPROPERLY INSTALLED, REPAIRED, ALTERED OR DAMAGED. THE COMPANY DISCLAIMS ALL WARRANTIES, EXPRESS OR IMPLIED, INCLUDING WITHOUT LIMITATION, THE IMPLIED WARRANTIES OF MERCHANTABILITY AND FITNESS FOR A PARTICULAR PURPOSE. THE COMPANY DOES NOT WARRANT, GUARANTEE OR MAKE ANY REPRESENTATION REGARDING THE ACCURACY, RELIABILITY, CURRENTNESS, USE, OR RESULTS OF USE, OF THE SOFTWARE.

5. LIMITATION OF REMEDIES AND DAMAGES: IN NO EVENT, SHALL THE COMPANY OR ITS EMPLOYEES, AGENTS, LICENSORS OR CONTRACTORS BE LIABLE FOR ANY INCIDENTAL, INDIRECT, SPECIAL OR CONSEQUENTIAL DAMAGES ARISING OUT OF OR IN CONNECTION WITH THIS LICENSE OR THE SOFTWARE, INCLUDING, WITHOUT LIMITATION, LOSS OF USE, LOSS OF DATA, LOSS OF INCOME OR PROFIT, OR OTHER LOSSES SUSTAINED AS A RESULT OF INJURY TO ANY PERSON, OR LOSS OF OR DAMAGE TO PROPERTY, OR CLAIMS OF THIRD PARTIES, EVEN IF THE COMPANY OR AN AUTHORIZED REPRESENTATIVE OF THE COMPANY HAS BEEN ADVISED OF THE POSSIBILITY OF SUCH DAMAGES. SOME JURISDICTIONS DO NOT ALLOW THE LIMITATION OF DAMAGES IN CERTAIN CIRCUMSTANCES, SO THE ABOVE LIMITATIONS MAY NOT ALWAYS APPLY.

6. GENERAL: THIS AGREEMENT SHALL BE CONSTRUED IN ACCORDANCE WITH THE LAWS OF THE UNITED STATES OF AMERICA AND THE STATE OF NEW YORK, APPLICABLE TO CONTRACTS MADE IN NEW YORK, AND SHALL BENEFIT THE COMPANY, ITS AFFILIATES AND ASSIGNEES. This Agreement is the complete and exclusive statement of the agreement between you and the Company and supersedes all proposals, prior agreements, oral or written, and any other communications between you and the company or any of its representatives relating to the subject matter. If you are a U.S. Government user, this Software is licensed with "restricted rights" as set forth in subparagraphs (a)-(d) of the Commercial Computer-Restricted Rights clause at FAR 52.227-19 or in subparagraphs (c)(1)(ii) of the Rights in Technical Data and Computer Software clause at DFARS 252.227-7013, and similar clauses, as applicable.

Should you have any questions concerning this agreement or if you wish to contact the Company for any reason, please contact in writing:

Multimedia Production,
Higher Education Division,
Prentice-Hall, Inc.,
1 Lake Street,
Upper Saddle River NJ 07458.